LAST TRAIN TO MEMPHIS

THE RISE OF ELVIS PRESLEY

September 1958

PETER GURALNICK

BACK BAY BOOKS

LITTLE, BROWN AND COMPANY

BOSTON · NEW YORK · LONDON

FIRST PAPERBACK EDITION

FRONTISPIECE:
KATZ DRUG STORE OPENING, SEPTEMBER 8, 1954. (OPAL WALKER)

Permissions to quote from copyrighted material appear on page 561.

Library of Congress Cataloging-in-Publication Data

Guralnick, Peter.
    Last train to Memphis: the rise of Elvis Presley / Peter
Guralnick. — 1st ed.
        p.   cm.
    Includes bibliographical references and index.
    ISBN 0-316-33220-8 (HC) 0-316-33225-9 (pb)
    1. Presley, Elvis, 1935–1977 — Childhood and youth. 2. Rock
musicians — United States — Biography. I. Title.
ML420.P96G87   1994
782.42166′092—dc20
[B]   94-10763

10 9 8 7 6 5
MV-NY

DESIGNED BY SUSAN MARSH

Printed in the United States of America

24-1-04

LAST TRAIN TO MEMPHIS

"Peter Guralnick has done the impossible: He has brought a freshness, an innocence, and a seriousness to the life of Elvis Presley. . . . To accomplish this, he interviewed scores of people, plowed through the mini-industry of Presley publishing, and then wiped the slate clean: Guralnick gives us a life of Elvis as if it had never been told before, and in a sense, it hasn't, not this way."
— *Entertainment Weekly*

∾

"Unrivaled account of Elvis as he walks the path between heaven and nature in an America that was wide open, when anything was possible, not the whitewashed golden calf but the incendiary musical firebrand loner who conquered the western world, he steps from the pages, you can feel him breathe, this book cancels out all others."
— Bob Dylan

∾

"*Last Train* is a story that crackles and breathes, that brings to life the people, neighborhoods, schools, homes, churches, picnics, recording studios, and clubs that were part of Presley's life. It has the depth of a good history and the richness of literature."
— *Detroit Free Press*

∾

"Guralnick has written a new standard biography. . . . Like an incarnation of Whitman's philosophy, the Elvis Presley Peter Guralnick has given us contains multitudes. . . . Extraordinary."
— Dave Marsh

∾

"Bound to be the definitive biography . . . an American epic that belongs on every bookshelf."   — *Kirkus Reviews*

∾

"As with his other writings on American music, Peter Guralnick sends you rushing back to the recordings with fresh ears. This is the finest compliment that I can pay someone writing about music."
— Elvis Costello

1. LAUDERDALE COURTS
2. 698 SAFFARANS
3. HUMES HIGH SCHOOL
4. SUZORE NO. 2 & CHARLIE'S RECORD SHOP
5. UNITED PAINT
6. ST. JOSEPH'S HOSPITAL
7. ELLIS AUDITORIUM
8. 462 ALABAMA
9. POPLAR TUNES
10. CROWN ELECTRIC
11. 572 POPLAR
12. GAYOSO HOTEL
13. LOEW'S STATE
14. HOTEL PEABODY
15. HOTEL CHISCA
16. SUN RECORDS
17. K'S DRIVE-IN
18. ASSEMBLY OF GOD CHURCH
19. LEONARD'S DRIVE-IN
20. EAST TRIGG BAPTIST CHURCH
21. KATZ DRUG STORE
22. 2414 LAMAR

MUD ISLAND

SAFFARANS

WINCHESTER
MARKET
EXCHANGE
ALABAMA

FRONT
MAIN
SECOND
THIRD

MADISON

MANASSAS

UNION
GAYOSO
BEALE

MARSHALL

VANCE

CALHOUN

LAUDERDALE

MISSISSIPPI RIVER

MEMPHIS & ARKANSAS BRIDGE

CRUMP

MISSISSIPPI

McLEMORE

LUCY

TRIGG

McKELLAR LAKE

RIVERSIDE PARK

THIRD / HIGHWAY 61

*For my mother and father
and for Alexandra*

Contents

Author's Note

"Biography" meant a book about someone's life. Only, for me, it was to become a kind of pursuit, a tracking of the physical trail of someone's path through the past, a following of footsteps. You would never catch them; no, you would never quite catch them. But maybe, if you were lucky, you might write about the pursuit of that fleeting figure in such a way as to bring it alive in the present.

— Richard Holmes, *Footsteps: Adventures of a Romantic Biographer*

I FIRST WROTE about Elvis Presley in 1967. I did so because I loved his music and I felt that it had been unjustly ridiculed and neglected. I was not writing about movies, image, or popularity. I was writing about someone whom I thought of as a great blues singer (I might today amend the term to "heart" singer, in the sense that he sang all the songs he really cared about — blues and gospel and even otherwise inexplicably sentimental numbers — without barrier or affectation) and who I imagined must conceive of himself in the same way. In that same spirit of barrierlessness I sent Elvis a copy of the review at his address, 3764 Highway 51 South (later renamed Elvis Presley Boulevard) in Memphis, and I got a printed Christmas card in reply.

I wrote about him a number of times over the years, seeking in one way or another to rescue him from both his detractors and admirers. What I wrote was based on passionate listen ig, research, and interviewing, and, of course, the kind of speculation that we inevitably apply to anything, or anyone, whom we admire from a distant shore. I wouldn't altogether disown anything that I wrote, though in retrospect I might correct a good deal of its perspective. But I don't know if I ever thought about the real Elvis Presley until I was driving down McLemore Avenue in South Memphis one day in 1983, past the old Stax studio, with a friend named Rose Clayton. Rose, a native Memphian, pointed out a drugstore where Elvis' cousin used to work. Elvis used to hang out there, she said; he would sit at the soda fountain, drumming his fingers on the counter-top. "Poor baby," said Rose, and something went off in my head. This wasn't *"Elvis Presley"*; this was a kid hanging out at a soda fountain in South Memphis, someone who could be observed, just like you or me, daydreaming, listening to the jukebox, drinking a milk shake, waiting for his cousin to get off work. "Poor baby."

I didn't come to the book itself for several years after that, but this was the vision that sustained it. When I finally decided to write the book, I had one simple aim in mind — at least it seemed simple to me at the start: to keep the story within "real" time, to allow the characters to freely breathe their own air, to avoid imposing the judgment of another age, or even the alarums that hindsight inevitably lends. That was what I wanted to do, both because I wanted to remain true to my "characters" — real-life figures whom I had come to know and like in the course of both my travels and research — and because I wanted to suggest the dimensions of a world, the world in which Elvis Presley had grown up, the world which had shaped him and which he in turn had unwittingly shaped, with all the homeliness and beauty that everyday life entails.

Discovering the reality of that world was something like stepping off the edge of my own. The British historian Richard Holmes describes the biographer as "a sort of tramp permanently knocking at the kitchen window and secretly hoping he might be invited in for supper." Holmes is presumably alluding to the researcher's attempt to penetrate the recesses of history, but he might as well be describing the literal truth. If one cannot recognize one's status as an outsider, if I were not able to laugh at the comic contretemps in which I have often found myself over the years, then I would be lacking in the humility necessary for the task. But if one were not vain enough, on the other hand, to think it possible to make sense of the mass of random detail that makes up a life, if one did not imagine oneself capable somehow of the most diverse explorations, divagations, and transcendental leaps, then one would never seek to tell the story. "The moment one begins to investigate the truth of the simplest facts which one has accepted as true," wrote Leonard Woolf in his autobiography, "it is as though one had stepped off a firm narrow path into a bog or a quicksand — every step one takes one steps deeper into the bog of uncertainty." And it is that uncertainty which must be taken as both an unavoidable given and the only real starting point.

For this book I interviewed hundreds of firsthand participants. To my great joy, and not incidental distraction, I discovered worlds within worlds: the world of quartet singing; the pioneering spirit of post–World War II radio; the many worlds of Memphis (which I might have thought I already knew); the carnival world of self-invention and self-promotion out of which Colonel Thomas A. Parker emerged; the small-time dreams of a music industry that had not yet defined itself; the larger dreams of an art form that had not yet been explored. I have tried to suggest these worlds, and the men and women who peopled them, with a respect for the intricacy, complexity, and integrity of their makeup, but, of course, one can only suggest. As for the central figure, I have tried to convey his complexity and irreducibility as well. This is an heroic story, I believe, and ultimately perhaps a tragic one, but — like any of our lives and characters — it is not all of one piece, it does not lend itself to one interpretation exclusively, nor do all its parts reflect anything that resembles an undifferentiated whole. To say this, I hope, is not to throw up one's hands at the impossibility of the task; it is, simply, to embrace the variousness, and uniqueness, of human experience.

I wanted to tell a true story. I wanted to rescue Elvis Presley from the dreary bondage of myth, from the oppressive aftershock of cultural significance. To the extent that I have succeeded, I suppose, I have merely opened up the subject to new aftershocks, new forms of encapsulation. Like any biographer, I am sure, I have worried over scenes, imagined and reimagined the way that things must have been, all too keenly aware of my own limitations of perspective and the distorting lens of history. I have sought to reconcile accounts that cannot be reconciled, and I have engaged in the kind of dialogue with my subject that Richard Holmes describes as leading to "a relationship of *trust*" between biographer and subject. As Holmes points out, trust is what one seeks, implicitly, to achieve, and yet there is always the possibility that trust is misplaced: "The possibility of error," he insists, "is constant in all biography."

That is why I would like to suggest that this work, like any other, is a beginning, not an end, an invitation to inquiry, not an attempt at foreclosure upon it. So much of what becomes a story, whether formally or merely in the relation of a dinner-table anecdote, is based upon verbal shorthand, metaphorical leaps of faith, *interpretation* of the facts at hand. It should be clearly understood: facts can change, and new interpretations can, at any moment, alter our interpretation of them. This is *my* story of Elvis Presley: it cannot be *the* story of Elvis Presley. There is no such thing; even autobiography, or perhaps autobiography most of all, represents an editing of the facts, a selection of detail, an attempt to make sense of the various, arbitrary developments of real life. In the end, there should be nothing shocking about human existence, because, in the end, whatever has occurred is simply human. If I have succeeded in my aim, I have given the reader the tools to create his or her own portrait of a young Elvis Presley, the opportunity to reinvent and reinterpret, within the broad context of a particular time and place, the early life of a remarkable American original.

LAST TRAIN TO MEMPHIS

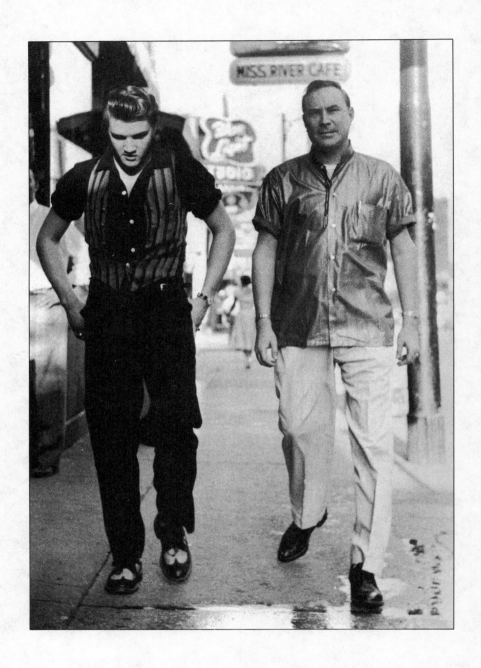

WITH DEWEY PHILLIPS, BEALE STREET, 1956. (ROBERT WILLIAMS)

PROLOGUE: MEMPHIS, 1950

I T IS LATE MAY or early June, hot, steamy; a fetid breeze comes in off the river and wafts its way through the elegant lobby of the Hotel Peabody, where, it is said, the Mississippi Delta begins. There is a steady hum of conversation in the room — polite, understated, well bred, but never letting up: the room is redolent with the suggestion of business dealings transacted in grandiloquent style, amid curlicues of cigar smoke rising toward the high Florentine ceiling, with the anticipation of a social evening to come. When the novelist William Faulkner is in town, he always stays at the Peabody; perhaps he is observing this very scene.

Out on the street men pass by, walking with deliberate speed. They are wearing Panama hats and straw boaters; some are in shirtsleeves and suspenders, wearing their pants high up on their waist; most are more formally dressed in summer-weight seersucker suits. The women generally look cool and elegant in broad, shadowing hats and light summer dresses. The Negroes whom you see all fulfill a function: they are maids, bootblacks, barbers, bellboys, each playing a familiar, muted role. But if you wanted to get another sense of the life of these accommodating, uncomplaining, almost invisible handmaidens and impersonal valets to white wealth and power, you would only have to go around the corner, to Beale Street, a lively, thriving, brightly colored metropolis of quite another sort.

In the Peabody Drugstore, on the corner of Union and Second, a well-dressed, elegant-looking young man of twenty-seven sits, nervously drumming his fingers on the countertop. His tie is carefully knotted, his luxuriant chestnut-brown hair is carefully sculpted in such a fashion that you know that this might be the feature of which he is most proud; he is smoking a Chesterfield in a slender cigarette holder and wearing a gold pocket chain. He is an arresting-looking young man in every way, but it is his eyes which truly compel attention. Set low under fairly prominent brows, they are neither small nor especially close together, but they give

3

the impression in a photograph that they are squinting, in real life that their possessor is gazing into your very soul. Right now they are looking about, distracted, not focusing on anything in particular, until at last they catch sight of the very person they are looking for, as a tall, redheaded, loose-limbed, and rawboned young man, clearly from the country and not ashamed of it, bursts through the door. His mouth curls in a little smile that suggests neither the need for, nor the hint of, any apology; his brightly patterned shirt stands at odds with the elegance of the earlier arrival, whom he evidently does not know but greets with an expansive wave, an infectious bonhomie, and then a clap on the back and a loudly brayed "Dee-gaw!"

The newcomer, Dewey Phillips, is twenty-four years old and already a radio celebrity, with his own show on WHBQ broadcasting from the Gayoso Hotel just up the street. He is on the air from 10:00 P.M. to midnight every weekday, and until 1:00 A.M. on Saturday nights, while keeping his job in the record department at W. T. Grant's, on South Main. The music that he plays is some of the finest American vernacular music ever recorded: in the course of one fifteen-minute segment, you might hear Muddy Waters' latest hit, a gospel number by the Soul Stirrers (with their great singer, R. H. Harris), Larry Darnell's "For You, My Love," and Wynonie Harris' "Good Rockin' Tonight" — "boogies, blues, and spirituals," as the *Memphis Commercial Appeal* reports in a full-length feature. He mangles the names of his advertisers, plays 78s at the wrong speed, and appends to every commercial message the grace note "I don't care where you go or how you go, just tell 'em Phillips sent you." Only recently one of his listeners was taken to the hospital emergency ward and announced to a startled medical staff that Phillips had sent him. He has perhaps the most popular show on Memphis radio, with talk of Mutual broadcast syndication. Tastes being what they are, and the postwar world being as unpredictable and unconventionally wide open as it has become, there is only one thing that is truly startling about his success: the music that he plays, and the listeners that he reaches, are almost exclusively black.

That is why Sam Phillips has wanted so badly to meet him. Aside from the coincidence of their names, there is a coincidence of purpose which links these two very disparate-seeming young men. Just six months ago, Sam Phillips, with the assistance of Marion Keisker, a prominent Memphis radio personality best known for her *Kitty Kelly* show on WREC, launched his own studio, the Memphis Recording Service, at 706 Union Avenue, with the avowed purpose of recording "Negro artists in the South who wanted to make a record [and] just had no place to go. . . . I set up a studio just to make records with some of those great Negro artists." Phillips, an engineer and sometime disc jockey on WREC, the CBS affiliate whose offices were in the Peabody, had come to town in 1945. He had started in radio as a teenager in his native region of Muscle Shoals, Alabama, and at twenty-two was engineering the network broadcasts every night from the Peabody Skyway. And yet despite his abiding love for big band music — for the Dorsey brothers and Glenn Miller, Freddy Martin and Ted Weems — he had come to feel that it was all just too programmed, that "the girl singer just sat up there and looked pretty, the musicians might have played the damn song four thousand times, but they were *still* turning the pages!"

At the same time Sam believed wholeheartedly in the music that he had grown up with as a child, in the glorious spiritual offerings of the Negro church, in the tales and songs of Uncle Silas Payne, who had worked on his father's farm and told the little boy stories of Memphis' Beale Street, trips to the Molasses River, and the battercake trees which grew up next to the sausage trees in Africa. "I listened to that beautiful a cappella singing — the windows of the black Methodist church just half a block down from Highland Baptist would all be open, and I was just fascinated by the rhythms. Even when they hoed, they'd get a rhythm going, maybe more than one, and there was that beautiful rhythmic silence of the cotton fields, with a hoe hitting a rock every now and then just as it spaded through the dirt, and then the singing, especially if the wind happened to be from the right direction — believe me, all that said a lot to me."

Many children have been entranced by just such encounters, but they grow up, they put aside childish things, in Sam Phillips' words, they *conform.* Sam Phillips believed in something else. He believed — entirely and without reservation — in differentness, in independence, in individuation, he believed in himself, and he believed — even to the point of articulating it in public and private utterances from earliest adulthood on — in the scope and beauty of African-American culture. He wanted, he said, "genuine, untutored negro" music; he was looking for "Negroes with field mud on their boots and patches in their overalls . . . battered instruments and unfettered techniques." The music that he was attempting to record was the very music that Dewey Phillips was playing on the air.

The ostensible reason for his meeting with Dewey was that his uncle-in-law, Jimmy Connolly, who was general manager of the 250-watt station WJLD in Bessemer, Alabama, where he had gone after first hiring Sam in Muscle Shoals, had launched a program called *The Atomic Boogie Hour*. This was an afternoon program similar to the kind of show that Dewey had started in Memphis and that was springing up in one form or another all across the South: black music on a white radio station with a strong Negro audience and a growing, if for the most part unacknowledged, core of young white listeners with a growing, if for the most part unexamined, buying power. The owner of the station, a Mr. Johnson, didn't want Connolly doing the show anymore, because it was "lowbrow," and Sam had told his uncle-in-law about "this cat that's on the air here that you wouldn't believe." Jimmy suggested that he talk to Dewey about coming to Bessemer, and Sam agreed, but his heart wasn't in it. "I just didn't want Dewey leaving Memphis. I even backed off a little on my recommendation afterwards: I told Jimmy, 'Well, your *Atomic Boogie Hour* is fantastic, but I'm just not sure if Dewey would fit in. This is a guy that somehow or another generates a night atmosphere. . . . What we need in Memphis is exactly what Dewey Phillips is doing.' I could have gotten Dewey a job just like that, but I told him, I said, 'Dewey, I'm going to try to get something going, in the way of making records.' "

Who knows what they did in the immediate aftermath of that initial meeting? Perhaps they wandered over to Beale Street, where Dewey, who has been described as "transracial" by more than one admirer, could go wherever he liked, where Dewey, Sam came to see with some ambivalence, was "a hero, everyone loved him." Perhaps they walked by the Hippodrome, where Roy Brown or Larry Darnell or Wynonie Harris could have been playing that very evening. They might have run into club owner–entrepreneur Andrew "Sunbeam" Mitchell or the Beale Street Blues Boy himself, B. B. King, whom Sam would start to record for the California-based RPM (Modern) label just around this time. One-man band Joe Hill Louis was probably playing in Handy Park. Or they might have just decided to go down to Johnny Mills' Barbecue at Fourth and Beale for a fish sandwich.

Wherever they went, Dewey would have been greeted with cries of delighted recognition, and he returned those greetings with unfeigned goodwill, unfettered enthusiasm, a delighted exclamation of his own. Sam, meanwhile, quieter, more reserved, more formal somehow, hung back, soaking up a scene that held long-standing reverberations for him as well. He had dreamt of Beale Street long before he ever saw it, from the stories that Uncle Silas had spun, and his first view of it, at sixteen, had not failed to live up to his expectations. He was on his way to Dallas with his older brother Jud and some friends to hear the Reverend George W. Truett preach, but he was drawn, it seemed, almost inexorably to Beale, because "to me Beale Street was the most famous place in the South. We got in at five or six o'clock in the morning and it was pouring down rain, but we just drove up and down, and it was so much more than I had even envisioned. I don't know if I can explain it to this day — my eyes had to be very big, because I saw everything, from winos to people dressed up fit to kill, young, old, city slickers and people straight out of the cotton fields, somehow or another you could tell: *every damn one of them was glad to be there.* Beale Street represented for me something that I hoped to see one day for all people, something that they could say, I'm a part of this somehow." This was Sam Phillips' vision, and he kept it with him when he moved to Memphis with his wife and infant son some six years later. Memphis had drawn him like a magnet, but not for the elegant appointments of the Hotel Peabody or the big band broadcasts from the Skyway. It was Beale Street that lured him in a way he would never be able to fully explain and Beale Street with which, as it was, he could never be fully comfortable.

Sam and Dewey Phillips went on to become closer than brothers; they propped each other up in times of trouble and undoubtedly dragged each other down on some occasions as well. They became business partners for the briefest of moments, within just a month or two of that initial meeting, when Sam launched a label called The Phillips, which put out one official release ("Boogie in the Park," by Joe Hill Louis, with three hundred copies pressed), and then dissolved it for reasons never fully specified. For all of their shared values, however, for all of their shared dreams and schemes and the fact that they were laboring in the same field (Sam continued to record blues singers like Howlin' Wolf and B. B. King for some time for various labels and then started up a label of his own; Daddy-O-Dewey just got bigger and bigger on the radio), they were not destined to come together in business or in the history books for another four years, one year after the unheralded and altogether unanticipated arrival of an eighteen-year-old Elvis Presley in Sam Phillips' Sun recording studio.

THE PRESLEYS were themselves relatively recent arrivals in Memphis in 1950, having picked up stakes in their native Tupelo, Mississippi, in the fall of 1948, when their only child was thirteen years old. Their adjustment to city life was difficult at first. Although the husband, Vernon, had worked in a munitions plant in Memphis for much of the war, good, steady peacetime work was not easy to come by, and the three of them were crammed into a single room in one boardinghouse or another for the first few months after their arrival. Wary, watchful, shy almost to the point of reclusiveness, the boy was obviously frightened by his new surroundings, and on his first day of school at sixteen-hundred-student Humes High (which went from seventh to twelfth grade) he was back at the rooming house almost before his father had finished dropping him off. Vernon found him "so nervous he was bug-eyed. When I asked what was the matter, he said he didn't know where the office was and classes had started and there were so many kids. He was afraid they'd laugh at him." His father, a taciturn, suspicious man, understood: in some ways the Presleys gave the impression to both relatives and neighbors that they lived in their own private world. "I thought about it a minute," said Vernon, "and I knew what he meant. So I said, 'Son, that's all right for today, but tomorrow you be there, nine o'clock, and no foolin'!' "

In February 1949, Vernon finally landed a regular job, at United Paint Company, just a few blocks away from the rooming house on Poplar they had moved into, and on June 17 he applied for admission to Lauderdale Courts, a neat public assistance housing project administered by the Memphis Housing Authority. In September their application was finally approved, and they moved to 185 Winchester, Apartment 328, just around the corner from where they were presently living. The rent was thirty-five dollars a month for a two-bedroom ground-floor apartment in a well-maintained neighborly complex. Everyone in Lauderdale Courts felt as if they were on their way somewhere. If only in terms of aspirations, for the Presley family it was a big step up.

TUPELO CIRCA 1942. (COURTESY OF THE ESTATE OF ELVIS PRESLEY)

TUPELO: ABOVE THE HIGHWAY

VERNON PRESLEY was never particularly well regarded in Tupelo. He was a man of few words and little evident ambition, and even in the separate municipality of East Tupelo, where he lived with his family "above the highway," a tiny warren of houses clustered together on five unpaved streets running off the Old Saltillo Road, he was seen as something of a vacant if hardworking soul, good-looking, handsome even, but unlikely ever to go anywhere. East Tupelo itself was separated by more than just the geographical barrier of two small creeks, corn and cotton fields, and the Mobile & Ohio and St. Louis & San Francisco railroad tracks from the life of a parent city which was hailed in the 1938 WPA Guide as "perhaps Mississippi's best example of what contemporary commentators call the 'New South.' " East Tupelo, on the other hand, was a part of the New South that tended to get glossed over, the home of many of the "poor white" factory workers and sharecroppers who could fuel a vision of "industry rising in the midst of agriculture and agricultural customs" so long as the social particulars of that vision were not scrutinized too closely. "Over the years of its existence and even after its merger with Tupelo [in 1946]," wrote a local historian, "East Tupelo had the reputation of being an extremely rough town. Some citizens doubt that it was worse than other small towns, but others declare it to have been the roughest town in North Mississippi. The town had its red light district called 'Goosehollow.' . . . By 1940 the tiny community of East Tupelo was known to have at least nine bootleggers."

In 1936 the mayor of East Tupelo was Vernon Presley's uncle, Noah, who lived on Kelly Street above the highway, owned a small grocery store, and drove the school bus. Noah's brother, Jessie, Vernon's father, was relatively comfortable as well, if not as upstanding a member of the community. He owned his own home on Old Saltillo Road, just above Kelly Street, and he worked fairly steadily, even if he had a reputation as a hard drinker and a "rogue." Vernon, by way of contrast, showed little drive or direction.

Though he worked hard to maintain a succession of Depression-limited jobs (milkman, sharecropper, handyman, WPA laborer), he never really seemed to make a go of it, and he never seemed to particularly care about making a go of it either. Closemouthed, recessive, almost brooding at times, "dry" in the description of his friends, Vernon did appear to care deeply about his little family: his wife, Gladys Smith, whom he married in 1933; his son, Elvis Aron Presley, who was born on January 8, 1935; the twin, Jesse Garon, whom they had lost. He built a home in preparation for the birth, a two-room shotgun shack next to his parents' four-room "big house," with the help of his father and his older brother, Vester (who in September 1935 would marry Gladys' sister Clettes). He took out what amounted to a mortgage of $180 from Orville Bean, on whose dairy farm he and his father occasionally worked, with the property remaining Bean's until the loan was paid off. There was a pump and an outhouse in the back, and although East Tupelo was one of the first beneficiaries of the TVA rural electrification program, the new home was lit with oil lamps when he and Gladys moved in in December 1934.

Gladys Presley, everyone agreed, was the spark of that marriage. Where Vernon was taciturn to the point of sullenness, she was voluble, lively, full of spunk. They had both dropped out of school at an early age, but Gladys — who had grown up on a succession of farms in the area with seven brothers and sisters — took a backseat to no one. When she was twenty, her father died, and she heard of a job at the Tupelo Garment Plant that paid two dollars a day for a twelve-hour workday. There was a bus to pick up the girls who lived out in the country, but not long after starting work she decided to move to town, and she settled herself and her family on Kelly Street in the little community above the highway, in East Tupelo, where her uncles Sims and Gains Mansell already lived and Gains co-pastored the tiny new First Assembly of God Church that had sprung up in a tent on a vacant lot. That was where she met Vernon Presley. She saw him on the street, and then she met him at a typically charismatic, "Holy Roller"–type church service. In June 1933 they ran off with another couple and got married in Pontotoc, Mississippi, where Vernon, still a minor, added five years to his age and claimed to be twenty-two, while Gladys reduced hers by two, to nineteen. They borrowed the three dollars for the license from their friends Marshall and Vona Mae Brown, with whom they moved in for a short time after the marriage.

Gladys had a difficult pregnancy and toward the end had to quit her job at the Garment Plant. When she came to term, Vernon's mother, Minnie, a midwife named Edna Martin, and one other woman attended her until the midwife called the doctor, sixty-eight-year-old William Robert Hunt. At about four in the morning of January 8, he delivered a baby, stillborn, then thirty-five minutes later another boy. The twins were named Jesse Garon and Elvis Aron, with the rhyming middle names intended to match. Aron (pronounced with a long *a* and the emphasis on the first syllable) was for Vernon's friend Aaron Kennedy, Elvis was Vernon's middle name, and Jesse, of course, was for his father. The dead twin was buried in an unmarked grave in Priceville Cemetery, just below Old Saltillo Road, and was never forgotten either in the legend that accompanied his celebrated younger brother or in family memory. As a child Elvis was said to have frequently visited his brother's grave; as an adult he referred to his twin again and again, reinforced by Gladys' belief that "when one twin died, the one that lived got all the strength of both." Shortly after the birth both mother and child were taken to the hospital, and Gladys was never able to have another baby. The physician's fifteen-dollar fee was paid by welfare.

Elvis grew up a loved and precious child. He was, everyone agreed, unusually close to his mother. Vernon spoke of it after his son became famous, almost as if it were a source of wonder that anyone could be that close. Throughout her life the son would call her by pet names, they would communicate by baby talk, "she worshiped him," said a neighbor, "from the day he was born." He was attached to his father as well. "When we went swimming, Elvis would have fits if he saw me dive," Vernon recalled. "He was so afraid something would happen to me." And Gladys told of a house fire in East Tupelo, when Vernon ran in and out of the burning building trying to salvage a neighbor's belongings. "Elvis was so sure that his daddy was going to get hurt that he screamed and cried. I had to hold him to keep him from running in after Vernon. I said right sharp, 'Elvis, you just stop that. Your daddy knows what he's doing.' " Elvis' own view of his growing up was more prosaic. "My mama never let me out of her sight. I couldn't go down to the creek with the other kids. Sometimes when I was little, I used to run off. Mama would whip me, and I thought she didn't love me."

In that respect, and in every other, there was not much out of the ordinary about the young Presley family. They were a little peculiar, perhaps, in their insularity, but they were active in church and community, and they had realistic hopes and expectations for their only child. Vernon was, in his own view, a "common laborer," but Gladys was determined that her son would graduate from high school.

In 1937 Gladys' uncle Gains became sole preacher at the Assembly of God Church, which was now housed in a modest wood-framed structure on Adams Street built primarily by Gains. Many in the tiny congregation later recalled a very young Elvis Presley throwing himself into the hymn singing with abandon, and Gladys liked to tell how "when Elvis was just a little fellow, not more than two years old, he would slide down off my lap, run into the aisle and scramble up to the platform. There he would stand looking at the choir and trying to sing with them. He was too little to know the words . . . but he could carry the tune and he would watch their faces and try to do as they did."

It was shortly thereafter that the life of the Presley family was forever changed, or at least diverted from what might have been a more pre-dictable course. Vernon, Gladys' brother Travis, and a man named Lether Gable were charged on November 16, 1937, with "uttering a forged instru-ment" — altering, and then cashing, a four-dollar check of Orville Bean's made out to Vernon to pay for a hog. On May 25, 1938, Vernon and his two companions were sentenced to three years in Parchman Farm.

In fact, he remained in prison for only eight months, but this was a shaping event in the young family's life. In later years Elvis would often say of his father, "My daddy may seem hard, but you don't know what he's been through," and though it was never a secret, it was always a source of shame. "It was no big disgrace," said Corene Randle Smith, a childhood neighbor. "Everyone realized that Mr. Bean just made an example of him, and that he was on the up-and-up, except maybe that one little time." But it seemed to mark, in a more permanent way, Vernon's view of himself; it reinforced his mistrust of the world and, while he remained dedicated to his little family, led him to show less and less of himself to others.

During the brief time that he was in prison, Gladys lost the house and moved in briefly with her in-laws next door. There was no love lost between Gladys and Jessie, though, and soon mother and child moved to Tupelo, where Gladys lived with her cousins Frank and Leona Richards on Maple Street and got a job at the Mid-South Laundry. The Richards' daugh-ter, Corinne, retained vivid memories of the forlorn mother and son. When Elvis played ball with the other children out in the street, Corinne said, Gladys was "afraid that he would get run over. She didn't want him out of her sight. She had always been lively, but after [Vernon] went to prison she was awful nervous." To writer Elaine Dundy, Leona recalled Elvis sitting on the porch "crying his eyes out because his daddy was away." On weekends Gladys and her son frequently rode the Greyhound five hours each way to visit Vernon at Parchman.

Vernon, Travis, and Lether Gable were released from jail on February 6, 1939, in response to a community petition, and a letter from Orville Bean requesting sentence suspension. The Presleys continued to live with Gladys' cousins for a brief time, and all three experienced what Leona Richards called "action nightmares," sleepwalking episodes that none could recall in the morning. They soon moved back to East Tupelo, going from one small rented house to another.

In 1940 Vernon purchased a six-horsepower 1930 Chevrolet truck for $50, and in the fall of 1941 Elvis started school at the seven-hundred-pupil East Tupelo Consolidated (grades 1 through 12), on Lake Street, across Highway 78, about half a mile away from the little village off Old Saltillo Road. Every day Gladys walked Elvis proudly to school, a small towheaded youngster accompanied by his dark-haired, flashing-eyed mother, the two of them clasping hands tightly when they got to the highway, a picture of apprehensive devotion.

"Though we had friends and relatives, including my parents," Vernon recalled, "the three of us formed our own private world." The little boy was as insular in his way as his parents. Apart from family, his few friends from that period have painted him as separate from any crowd — there are no recollections of a "gang," just isolated memories of making cars out of apple crates, playing out behind someone's house, going fishing once in a while with James Ausborn, who lived over by the school. "Mrs. Presley would say to be back at two, and he'd get worried, keep looking at the sun, say, 'I believe it's about two o'clock. We better go.' " He was a gentle boy, his father said; "[one time] I asked him to go hunting with me, but when he answered, 'Daddy, I don't want to kill birds,' I didn't try to persuade him to go against his feelings." Once he learned to read he loved comic books; they captured his imagination — he loved the brightly colored pages and the forceful images of power and success. "Elvis would hear us worrying about our debts, being out of work and sickness," his mother recollected proudly, "and he'd say, 'Don't you worry none, Baby. When I grow up, I'm going to buy you a fine house and pay everything you owe at the grocery store and get two Cadillacs — one for you and Daddy, and one for me.' " "I [just] didn't want him to have to steal one," said Vernon.

For the most part he failed to distinguish himself in any way. At school he was "an average student," "sweet and average," according to his teach-ers, and he himself rarely spoke of his childhood years, except to note that they had not been easy and, occasionally, to recall moments of rejection. With his father, toward the end of his life, he reminisced about the time Vernon had taken him to see his first movie, "and we couldn't let the church know anything about it." The picture that you see of him with his third-grade class shows a little boy standing apart, arms folded, hair neatly combed, his mouth inverted in that familiar pout. Everyone else — the Farrars, the Harrises, Odell Clark — seems connected somehow, grouped together, smiling, arms around each other's shoulders. Elvis stands apart — not shunned, just apart. That is not the way any of his classmates ever remembered it, but it is how the picture looks.

There are a multitude of semiapocryphal stories from these years, most based on the kind of homely memories of childhood that any of us is likely to possess: who focuses upon the classmate who is out of the picture, why should anyone have noticed Elvis Presley in particular or committed to memory his every utterance, noted his views on issues of the day, or even imagined that he would ever come to anything? The war was going on, but it seems never to have impinged upon memories of growing up in East Tupelo, except, perhaps, to have provided opportunities for employment. In late 1942, after working for a short period of time in Ozark, Alabama, some three hundred miles from home, Vernon got a job on the construc-tion of a POW camp in Como, Mississippi. Shortly thereafter he went to work for the Dunn Construction Company in Millington, Tennessee, just outside of Memphis, living in company barracks and returning home on weekends because he was unable to find lodgings for his family. "I'd tramp all over town looking for so much as a single room. I'd find one, and first thing they would ask is, 'You got any children?' And I'd say I had a little boy. Then they'd shut . . . the door."

In May of 1943 the whole family moved briefly to Pascagoula, Missis-sippi, near Biloxi on the Gulf Coast, with Vernon's cousin Sales and his wife, Annie, and their children. Vernon and Sales had found work on a WPA project to expand the Pascagoula shipyards, but the two families stayed little more than a month, until Sales and Annie announced that they were heading home. Vernon bravely declared that he thought he and his family would stay, but he caught up with Sales on the road before Sales and Annie had gotten very far, and both families headed back to Tupelo together. Upon his return Vernon found regular employment as a driver for

L. P. McCarty and Sons, a wholesale grocer, and the Presley family entered into a period of relative prosperity, with the First Assembly Church serving as their social as well as moral focus. On August 18, 1945, with the war barely over, Vernon used the savings that he had accumulated to make a down payment of two hundred dollars on a new home on Berry Street, once again owned by Orville Bean, and around the same time, with his cousin Sales' sponsorship, became a deacon in the church. This was undoubtedly the high point of the Presleys' life in East Tupelo.

Obviously this is not the whole picture, but in the absence of time travel, what collection of random snapshots could provide one? One of the most common stories to have made its way down through the years is that the Presleys formed a popular gospel trio who sang in church, traveled about to various revival meetings in the area, and generally stood out in people's memories as a foreshadowing of what was just over the horizon. It is not difficult to understand where the story would come from: the Presleys, like every other member of the small congregation, did sing in church; they did go to revival meetings; Vernon and Gladys most likely sang "quartet-style" with Sales and Annie in church and at home. But the story that they formed any kind of traveling trio is most likely not true. As Elvis himself said in a 1965 interview, "I sang some with my folks in the Assembly of God church choir [but] it was a small church, so you couldn't sing too loud," and he told Hollywood reporter Army Archerd that he "trioed" with his mother and father — but only as part of that same congregation. There is no mention on his part of anything resembling "professional" experience and no credible contemporary witness in the face of relatives (Corinne Richards), childhood friends and neighbors (Corene Randle Smith, whose mother was Elvis' Sunday school teacher), and the minister who taught him to play guitar (Frank Smith, Corene's husband) who recalled otherwise or found the suggestion highly implausible.

What is not only plausible but clearly the case is that Elvis himself, on his own and without reference to anyone else's dreams, plans, or imaginings, was drawn to music in a way that he couldn't fully express, found a kind of peace in the music, was able to imagine something that he could express only to his mother. Still, it must have come as a surprise even to Gladys when Elvis Presley, her shy, dreamy, oddly playful child, got up and sang in front of an audience of several hundred at the age of ten at the annual Mississippi-Alabama Fair and Dairy Show at the Fairgrounds in the middle of downtown Tupelo.

It came about, evidently (though here, too, the story is unavoidably muddled), after he sang "Old Shep," the Red Foley "weeper" about a boy and his dog, at the morning prayer program at school. His teacher, Mrs. Oleta Grimes, who had moved in two doors down from the Presleys on Old Saltillo Road in 1936 and was, not entirely coincidentally, the daughter of Orville Bean, was so impressed by his singing that she brought him to the principal, Mr. Cole, who in turn entered the fifth-grader in the radio talent contest sponsored by local station WELO on Children's Day (Wednesday, October 3, 1945) at the fair. All the local schools were let out, teachers and children were transported to town by school bus and then marched from the courthouse lawn down the hill to the Fairgrounds, where they were guests of the fair. A prize was given to the school with the greatest proportional representation, and there were individual prizes in the talent contest, from a $25 war bond down to $2.50 for rides. The five-day-long fair included a livestock show, cattle auctions, mule- and horse-pulling contests, and poultry competition, but the Duke of Paducah and a Grand Ole Opry Company which included Minnie Pearl and Pee Wee King were advertised as well. Annie Presley, Sales' wife, recalled the fair as the highlight of both Presley families' social year, when the two couples would share a baby-sitter and go out together for the fair's last night.

The newspaper did not cover the children's contest or even list the winner of the competition. Over the years there have been a number of claimants to the throne, but to Elvis Presley it mattered little who actually won. "They entered me in a talent show," he said in a 1972 interview. "I wore glasses, no music, and I won, I think it was fifth place in this state talent contest. I got a whipping the same day, my mother whipped me for something — I don't know, [going on] one of the rides. Destroyed my ego completely." Gladys gave a more vivid account in 1956, minus the whipping. "I'll never forget, the man at the gate just took it for granted I was Elvis' big sister and sold me a schoolkid's ticket same as him. Elvis had no way to make music, and the other kids wouldn't accompany him. He just climbed up on a chair so he could reach the microphone and he sang 'Old Shep.' " He probably had his picture taken in the western booth, too, just as he would two years later, complete with cowboy hat, chaps, and western backdrop. Although, somewhat surprisingly, there seems to have been little awareness of his triumph among friends and classmates, and he evidently did not sing at the fair again, Elvis always spoke of the event, without embroidery, as the first time he sang in public, and the whipping is a more convincing detail than the conventional story, which has Vernon listening in on the contest on his delivery-truck radio.

It was not long after the contest that he got his first guitar. The chronology can be argued any way you like (and has been), but it appears likely that he got the guitar for his eleventh birthday, since in all of Elvis' own accounts — and in most of the early publicity accounts as well — he sang unaccompanied at the fair simply because he did not have a guitar. In many of those same accounts he was supposed to have gotten the guitar as a birthday present, and the 1956 *TV Radio Mirror* biography has him getting his first guitar the day after a storm which frightened Gladys and him (the tornado of 1936 had been a traumatic event that literally flattened Tupelo, killing 201 people and injuring more than 1,000). In fact there was a small tornado on January 7, 1946, the day before his eleventh birthday. In any case Elvis wanted a bicycle, he said, and the only reason he ended up with the guitar was because his mother was worried that he might get run over, not to mention the fact that the guitar was considerably less expensive (he got the bicycle not long afterward anyway). "Son, wouldn't you rather have the guitar?" Gladys concluded. "It would help you with your singing, and everyone does enjoy hearing you sing."

His uncle Vester, who played frequently in honky-tonks and at country dances and had a great appreciation for country music, and Gladys' brother Johnny Smith taught him a few chords, but it was the new pastor, twenty-one-year-old Frank Smith, who provided the greatest influence. Smith, who had come to Tupelo from Meridian, Mississippi, for a revival in early 1944 and then returned to stay when he married the Presleys' fifteen-year-old neighbor Corene Randle later that year, distinctly recalled the little boy coming to him with the guitar he had just acquired. "I always played the guitar, and I guess he picked up some from that, because a couple of years [after Smith's arrival] he got a guitar and really applied himself. He bought a book that showed how to place your fingers in position, and I went over to his house a time or two, or he would come to where I was, and I would show him some runs and different chords from what he was learning out of his book. That was all: not enough to say I taught him how to play, but I helped him." From his newfound knowledge Elvis started playing for the "special singing" portion of the service, although Smith had to call him up to get him to perform. "I would have to insist on him [getting up there], he didn't push himself. At the special

singings we might have someone do a Blackwood Brothers type of quartet number, different ones in the church would get up or maybe somebody visiting would sing, but there were no other kids to sing with him at
that time. He sang quite a few times, and he was liked."

Smith put no particular stock in music other than to glorify the Lord
and never found it anything but painful to have to dredge up the memory
of teaching an eleven-year-old how to play the guitar when this was
scarcely relevant to his life's work. Yet even to him Elvis' commitment to
music was clear-cut, not just from his singing in church but from the trips
that he, the Smiths, and many other East Tupeloans would make to town
on Saturday afternoon to attend the WELO Jamboree, a kind of amateur
hour which was broadcast from the courthouse. "A whole crowd went
down, grown-ups and kids. You got in line to perform, it was just something to do on Saturday. And he would go to the radio station to play and
sing — there was nothing to highlight him, really, he was just one of the
kids."

WELO HAD BEGUN BROADCASTING on South Spring Street,
above the Black and White dry goods store, on May 15, 1941. There
were a number of local talents involved in starting up the station, including Charlie Boren, its colorful announcer, and Archie Mackey, a local
bandleader and radio technician who had been instrumental in establishing Tupelo's first radio station, WDIX, some years earlier, but the hillbilly
star of the station in 1946 was a twenty-three-year-old native of Smithville,
some twenty miles to the southeast, Carvel Lee Ausborn, who went by
the name of Mississippi Slim. Ausborn, who had taken up guitar at the age
of thirteen to pursue a career in music, was inspired by Jimmie Rodgers,
though Hank Williams and Ernest Tubb became almost equal influences
in the forties. Probably his greatest influence, however, was his cousin
Rod Brasfield, a prominent country comedian, also from Smithville, who
joined the Opry in 1944 and toured with Hank Williams, while his
brother, Uncle Cyp Brasfield, became a regular on the Ozark Jubilee and
wrote material for Rod and his comedy partner, Minnie Pearl. Though
Mississippi Slim never attained such heights, he traveled all over the country with Goober and His Kentuckians and the Bisbee's Comedians tent
show and even played the Opry once or twice, largely on the strength of
his cousin's connections. Just about every prominent musician who

passed through Tupelo played with Slim at one time or another, from Merle "Red" Taylor (who furnished the fiddle melody for Bill Monroe's "Uncle Pen") to college-bound youths like Bill Mitchell (who in later life, after a career in politics, would win many national old-time fiddle contests), to weekend pickers like Slim's uncle Clinton. "He was a good entertainer," recalled Bill Mitchell, "put on a pretty good show, love songs with comedy (he came from a family of comedians) — it was a pretty lively show. The people really enjoyed it." In addition to a regular early-morning program on weekdays, Slim had a noontime show every Saturday called *Singin' and Pickin' Hillbilly* that served as a lead-in to the Jamboree, on which he also appeared. This was where Elvis first encountered the world of entertainment.

Archie Mackey's memory was of a young boy accompanied by his father. "Vernon said that his boy didn't know but two songs," said Mackey, another Jamboree regular, who claimed that he had Elvis sing both, with Slim accompanying him on guitar. Some have suggested that Slim was reluctant to play behind an "amateur" and that announcer Charlie Boren practically had to force him to do so, while others have sought credit for first carrying Elvis to the station. It's all somewhat academic. Like everyone else, he was drawn by the music and by the show. He was not the only child to perform, though according to Bill Mitchell most of the others were girls. And, it seemed, none of the others felt it like he did.

"He was crazy about music," said James Ausborn, Slim's kid brother and Elvis' schoolmate at East Tupelo Consolidated. "That's all he talked about. A lot of people didn't like my brother, they thought he was sort of corny, but, you know, they had to get a mail truck to bring all his cards and letters. Elvis would always say, 'Let's go to your brother's program today. Can you go up there with me? I want him to show me some more chords on the guitar.' We'd walk into town on Saturday, go down to the station on Spring Street [this was the broadcast before the Jamboree], a lot of times the studio would be full but my brother would always show him some chords. Sometimes he would say, 'I ain't got time to fool with you today,' but he'd always sit down and show him. Then maybe he'd sing him a couple of songs, and Elvis would try to sing them himself. I think gospel sort of inspired him to be in music, but then my brother helped carry it on."

Music had become his consuming passion. With the exception of a couple of playmates who shared his interest, like James, or who might have looked up to him for it, no one really noticed. His uncle Vester, who said that his mother's people, the Hoods, were "musicians out of this world," never noticed the transformation. Frank Smith saw him as one of the crowd, not really "eager" for music — "he just liked it." Even his parents might have missed this development in their closely watched son: "He always knew," said Vernon, as if he and Gladys had ever doubted, "he was going to do something. When we didn't have a dime, he used to sit on the doorstep and say, 'One of these days it'll be different.' "

If you picture him, picture someone you might have missed: a wide-eyed, silent child scuffling his feet, wearing overalls. He stands in line in the courtroom, waiting his turn to tiptoe up to the mike. His small child's voice carries a quavering note of yearning — other children get up and do letter-perfect recitals, big burly men frail on their beat-up guitars, but Elvis cradles his like a bird. After the broadcast is over, as the crowd slowly dissipates, the little boy hangs around on the outskirts of the group, watching Mississippi Slim and the other musicians pack up. He walks out behind them onto the courthouse square, with the statue of the Confederate soldier facing the Lyric Theater, the movie house that he and his friends never go to because it costs fifteen cents, a nickel more than the Strand. He hangs around on the edge of the crowd, nervously shifting from one foot to the other, desperately sidestepping every offer of a ride back to East Tupelo. He is waiting for an invitation, and in his determination to wait he shows the kind of watchful perseverance that is the hallmark of his solitary style. Maybe his friend James will say something to his brother, will suggest that they go off and have a Nehi together. Meanwhile he hangs on every word that is spoken, every glance exchanged: talk of the music, talk of the Opry, what cousin Rod Brasfield had to say the last time he was in town.

He soaks it all in. While others allow themselves to be distracted, his nervous attention never wanders; his fingers are constantly drumming against his pants leg, but his gaze bores in on the singer and the scene. Does he hang around with Slim? It's hard to imagine where. He dreams of *being* Slim. He dreams of wearing a western shirt with fancy pockets and sparkles and a scarf around his neck. Slim knows all the Opry stars. He knows Tex Ritter — the boy has heard the story a dozen times, but he doesn't mind if he hears it one more time from James: how Tex Ritter was making a personal appearance over in Nettleton with one of his movies, and Slim said to his little brother, "You want to go? You talking all the time about Tex Ritter, I'll show you that me and him is friends." So they went over to Nettleton, where Tex played a few songs before they showed his film, and then he signed some autographs. He had his six-guns on. Then all of a sudden he looked out and said, "I'll be damned, there's old Mississippi Slim sitting out there in the front row," and he stopped everything he was doing and went out and shook his hand. Then he said, "You come on right up here, and why don't you do a song for us." When he shook James' hand, James thought his hand was going to break, that was the kind of grip old Tex Ritter had. That was exactly the way it happened.

"I took the guitar, and I watched people," Elvis recalled, "and I learned to play a little bit. But I would never sing in public. I was very shy about it, you know." Every Saturday night he would listen to the Opry. He and Gladys and Vernon, his cousin Harold (whose mother, Rhetha, has died and who lives with them part of the time), maybe Grandma Minnie, too, now that Grandpa has lit out and she is living with them mostly — you had just better not run down the battery before the Saturday-night broadcast. The adults laugh and exchange glances at some of the jokes and tell half-remembered stories about the performers: Roy Acuff and Ernest Tubb, the Willis Brothers and Bill Monroe, here's that Red Foley to do "Old Shep" that Elvis sung at the fair. The music can carry you off to faraway places. But no one really knows. Daddy loves him. Mama will take care of him. There is nothing in his life that they do not know except for this. It is his secret passion.

I N THE SUMMER of 1946 the Presleys moved from East Tupelo to town. Vernon was not able to keep up payments on the Berry Street house and sold it — or transferred the payments — to his friend Aaron Kennedy. They moved first to Commerce Street, and then to Mulberry Alley, virtually next to the Fairgrounds and opposite Tupelo's teeming black quarter, Shake Rag, which abutted the Leake and Goodlett Lumberyard on East Main Street. The house was just a shack, one of three in the little alley, but it was moving into town that was the real comedown. In East Tupelo the Presleys had risen to a level of respectability that they might never have expected to attain. They were at ease among family and friends who shared the same background and experience. In Tupelo they were scorned, like virtually anyone from above the highway, as poor white trash. To Ernest Bowen, whose father's woodworking shop was just across the alley and who had only recently gone to work as city salesman for L. P. McCarty and Sons, Vernon's principal employer, the Presleys looked like the kind of family who moved every time the rent came due. In Bowen's opinion, "Vernon had no ambition whatsoever. It didn't bother him if they threw him out of his little house — he's going to get another one. Many times the salespeople would get together and would give samples, canned food, to Vernon. He was a sorry sort, what we call a real ne'er-do-well." Bill Mitchell, on the other hand, who got his first real job around this time, also driving for L. P. McCarty, and who, like Bowen, had tangential musical connections with Elvis (Bowen became the long-time general manager at WELO within a few years of the Presleys' departure for Memphis, while Mitchell recalled playing fiddle behind the boy in Mississippi Slim's band on the Jamboree), remembered Vernon's kindness and taciturn nature as well as his evident lack of ambition.

It's doubtful if either ever really knew Vernon or his family: certainly they would have had no way of imagining their hopes and dreams, and for all the pictures that we get of Vernon as an improvident loafer, there appears never to have been a time that he was not working or actively in pursuit of work. He supported his mother, after all, and he had taken in Gladys' sister's boy. When Elvis went to visit his cousin Willie Wileman (Willie's grandmother was Minnie's sister, and he was later to become a versatile and well-known musician in the Tupelo area), he was the sophisticated city cousin. From Willie's point of view: "All of us were country kids. We wore overalls, and he wore pants and a shirt. We would ride bicycles together — he would always get out and mix and mingle. But he was a city dude!"

In the fall of 1946 Elvis started a new school, Milam, which went from grades 5 through 9 and was about half a mile from Mulberry Alley. He failed to make much of an impression on any of his sixth-grade classmates, but that would hardly have been surprising, irrespective of social status, given Elvis' own cautious, watchful nature. Despite Willie Wileman's testimony, in the sixth-grade-class picture he is the only child in overalls, the only one visibly struggling to put on a happy postwar face, the only one whose expression gives any harbinger of a different kind of future. He looks curious, optimistic, at ease with himself — but no more a part of the group picture than he was in the earlier school snapshot. His seventh-grade classmate Roland Tindall moved to town himself from Dorsey, Mississippi, the year before and had encountered the same sort of dislocation. "It was unbelievable, the change, from leaving all my friends, the people I had grown up with and known from — well, you just knew everyone. Then, to come to Tupelo and have three classes of one grade, I mean in this time you can't really comprehend it. I wanted to go back to the country." To Elvis it was altogether bewildering and, at the same time, no more bewildering than anything else that was happening in his life. He was watching, he was waiting — but he didn't know for what.

The Presleys moved around some in the next year, and Gladys went back to work at the Mid-South Laundry. By the time Elvis started the seventh grade, they were living on North Green Street, closer to school and in a respectable enough neighborhood, but in a respectable *colored* neighborhood. Unlike Shake Rag, which had a Catfish Row kind of appearance and was destined to be obliterated in the first urban renewal project to be carried out in the state of Mississippi, in 1968, North Green Street ran right up against one of the "better," more exclusive, white sections of town and consisted, for the most part, of neatly kept one- and two-family homes. Although the house that they rented was designated as one of two or three "white" houses in the area, they were surrounded by black families, black churches, black social clubs, and black schools (the Lee County Training School, where Ben Branch taught music for years before moving to Memphis and joining the Stax horn section, was just down the hill). To friends and relatives this was a matter of some note — this was not South Tupelo, for example, where all the mill workers and factory hands lived — and not all of their old friends came to visit the Presleys in their new home, but it was nothing so shocking or out-of-the-way that it would prevent Gladys' sister Lillian and her family from occupying the same rental when Gladys and Vernon left.

It was in his seventh-grade year that Elvis started taking his guitar to school every day. Although teachers in later years would recall the early manifestations of a child prodigy, many students viewed his playing more dubiously, dismissing it with the same faint wrinkle of distaste with which they would greet déclassé fare of any sort ("hillbilly" music and "race" music probably fell into the same category in this regard). Others, like Roland Tindall, admired him for what they saw almost as a declaration of faith. "Elvis would bring his guitar to school, as far as I know, from the very beginning of the school year. At that time the basement of Milam was like a recess area, you went there during lunch hour — it was all open down there for the children to stay out of the wet and cold. Many times Elvis and a boy named Billy Welch would play and sing down there, and we would stay inside just to hear them. Once in a while Elvis might perform for an activity period in the classroom, but only occasionally, because those type of children didn't believe in country music and that was what he sang. He told us he was going to the Grand Ole Opry. Not bragging: he just made the statement." "He brought his guitar to school when it wasn't raining," said James Ausborn, Mississippi Slim's brother, who had recently moved to town himself. "He'd bring his guitar swung over his back and put it in his locker till lunchtime. Then everybody would set around, and he would sing and strum on that guitar. All he talked about was music — not the Opry so much as gospel music. That was what he sung mostly."

A classmate, Shirley Lumpkin, told Elaine Dundy, author of *Elvis and Gladys,* "The nicest thing I can say about him was that he was a loner," and another classmate, Kenneth Holditch, recalled him to Dundy as "a sad, shy, not especially attractive boy" whose guitar playing was not likely to win any prizes. Many of the other children made fun of him as a "trashy" kind of boy playing trashy "hillbilly" music, but Elvis stuck to his guns. Without ever confronting his denigrators or his critics, he continued to do the one thing that was important to him: he continued to make music.

Neither Roland nor James ever visited Elvis at his home on North Green Street, although James continued to go to the radio station with him and, occasionally, to the movies. Roland, by his own account, was not a social person. "All the socializing I did was at school, but we were very close friends there. At Christmastime in the seventh grade he gave me a little truck, and he gave Billy something of a similar sort — it was one of his own toys. I remember that impressed me, that he wanted to do something so badly that he would give us one of his toys when he couldn't afford anything else."

Frank and Corene Smith visited shortly before the Presleys left Tupelo for good, but by then they, too, had fallen somewhat out of touch with their old parishioners, and Vernon and Gladys were not attending church as regularly either. Because the house that they were renting was clearly reserved for white people, to the Smiths the Presleys "were not living in the black community," a distinction that Vernon and Gladys would certainly have made themselves, but a distinction that might have been lost in a real sense on their twelve-year-old son. Living across Main Street from the jumble of crooked alleyways and tumbledown shacks that made up Shake Rag, he would have to have sensed something of the life, he could not have missed the tumultuous bursts of song, the colorful street vendors' cries, he would have observed it all with intense curiosity, and he might have envied the sharp flashes of emotion, the bright splashes of color, the feelings so boldly on display. But he was forever sitting at the gate; there was no entry point for a stranger, there was no way in.

On North Green Street, "Elvis aron Presley" (as he signed his library card that year) was like the "Invisible Man" — he was the boy who lived in Dr. Green's house, he *belonged,* he had business there. For the first time he was truly in the midst of another world, a world so different that he might as well have stepped right onto the movie screen, and yet he was an unseen, and unsuspected, presence — like Superman or Captain Marvel, unprepossessing in their workaday disguises, but capable of more than anyone could ever imagine, he was just waiting for the opportunity to fulfill his destiny.

You walked by the Elks Club just off Green, where a small combo that patterned itself on Louis Jordan might be playing "Ain't Nobody Here But Us Chickens," or Jimmy Lunceford or Earl "Fatha" Hines might stop in after playing a dance at the Armory on the Fairgrounds downtown. You walked by a bar and barely heard the wailing of the jukebox over the noise of men and women drinking and gambling and signifying the sounds of love. On weekends the churches would be jumping, in a fashion not dissimilar to an Assembly of God congregation when it started speaking in tongues, but with a joyfulness and a sense of celebration, an expelling of emotion that was embarrassing for a closeted young boy to see at close hand — it seemed sometimes as if they were in the throes of a kind of passion that was not meant to be revealed in public.

Several times a year, in warm weather, a slightly moth-eaten, crudely patched tent would be erected on a vacant lot on the east side of Green for a revival: Friday night, Saturday night, all day Sunday, people would come from all over, dressed up in their finest regalia, the women in pink and yellow and hot fuchsia, wearing fantastic feathered boa hats and carrying their weight without apology, the preachers preaching without anything to hold them back, getting lost in their Bible, chanting, breathing, snorting rhythmically, gutturally, breathlessly, until their voices soared off into song. You didn't have to go inside to get the feeling — the sound, the sense, the allure, were all around you. You only had to walk up the street and the street was *rocking*. Well-to-do white college boys and their dates would come out for the show on Saturday night — there was really nothing like it, you had to hand it to the colored people, they really knew how to live. The college boys were strictly tourists, though. If you lived on North Green Street, you breathed it in, as natural as air — after a while you got used to it, it became yours, too, *it was almost like being in church.*

In the fall of 1948 Elvis started school again. Sometime in the first month or two, a few of the "rougher-type" boys took his guitar and cut the strings, but some of his eighth-grade classmates chipped in and bought him another set. When he announced in the first week of November that he and his family were leaving for Memphis, the other children were surprised but not shocked. People like the Presleys moved all the time. On his last day of school, Friday, November 5, a classmate named Leroy Green recalled to writer Vince Staten, he gave a little concert. The last song he sang was "A Leaf on a Tree" and, according to Green, "most people wouldn't believe this, but I went up to him and I told him, 'Elvis, one of these days you're gonna be famous.' And he smiled at me and said, 'I sure hope so.' "

They moved on a Saturday, Vernon explained, so that Elvis wouldn't miss a day of school. "We were broke, man, broke," Elvis declared in later years, "and we left Tupelo overnight. Dad packed all our belongings in boxes and put them in the trunk and on top of a 1939 Plymouth [actually a '37]. We just headed for Memphis. Things had to be better." According to Gladys: "We'd been talking about moving to Memphis. One day we just made up our minds. We sold off our furniture, loaded our clothes and things into this old car we had, and just set out." Elaine Dundy posited in *Elvis and Gladys* that Vernon Presley was fired by L. P. McCarty for using the company truck to deliver bootleg whiskey, but Gladys' cousin Corinne Richards recalled prior discussion of the move and saw it as part of a family migration, soon to be joined by other Presleys and other Smiths. In any event, Tupelo was a dead end. What they were looking for in Memphis might have been difficult to articulate, but what they were seeking to escape was perfectly clear. "I told Elvis," said Vernon, "that I'd work for him and buy him everything I could afford. If he had problems, he could come to me and I'd try to understand. I also said, 'But, son, if you see anything wrong going on, promise me you'll have no part of it. Just don't let anything happen so that I'd have to talk to you between bars. That's the only thing that would break my heart.' "

"There were times we had nothing to eat but corn bread and water," recalled Vernon not long before he died, "but we always had compassion for people. Poor we were, I'll never deny that. But trash we weren't. . . . We never had any prejudice. We never put anybody down. Neither did Elvis."

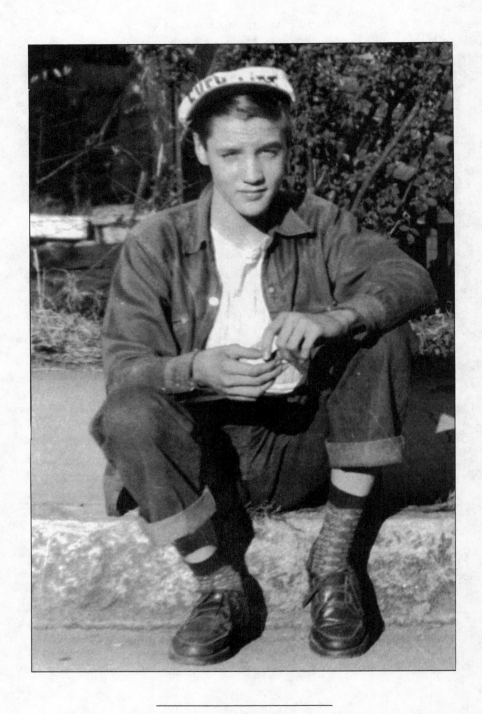

MEMPHIS CIRCA 1950. (COURTESY OF JIMMY DENSON)

MEMPHIS: THE COURTS

A SMALL, FAIR-HAIRED BOY, fourteen years old, sits on the front steps of the three-story brick building. It is twilight, and you would never notice him if you didn't know he was there. There is scarcely a word of greeting to any of the frequent passersby: men coming home from work, boys playing corkball, little girls dressed up in their Sunday best visiting a neighbor's apartment with their mama. A sailor from the nearby Millington base passes by on Third, while a jaunty teenager, wearing a neat Eisenhower jacket and wide, billowing pants, turns the corner from Market Mall, the tree-lined, grassy way that divides Lauderdale Courts, a trim collection of public-assisted garden apartments in the heart of downtown Memphis. Two blocks away is Ellis Auditorium, where they have boxing and musical events and the high schools all graduate in the spring. Ellis sits on the corner of Main, which, of course, in 1949 is the hub of Memphis city life. Movie theaters line Main Street: the Malco, Loew's State, the Strand, all on South Main "downtown," the Suzore No. 2, a second-run house on North Main just up the street, where you can gain admission for a dime. There are buses that run up and down Main, but if you don't have the money, all you have to do is walk. The Hotel Peabody is no more than three quarters of a mile away. Goldsmith's giant department store, which offers the latest in fashions and furnishings and can serve as readily for dreams as for purchases, sits on the west side of Main, with the corner of Beale, and the beginning of the colored section, just beyond. There is a world within a stone's throw of the Courts, but there is a world within it, too.

The young boy silently watches and observes: the black children playing in front of the two little ramshackle shacks just across the street from the well-maintained redbrick apartment buildings; the nurses changing shifts at St. Joseph's; the trolley cars on Jackson; the bigger boys coming back from playing football at the Triangle on the northeast end of the Courts. Finally he spots his father coming home from work just two blocks away. Vernon Presley is carrying his lunch pail. He turns in from Third and comes down the path, not hurrying but not lingering either. The towheaded little boy rises from the stoop, as if it were coincidence that he should be sitting out there. The two of them flash each other a quick half smile, the boy and the man; then they turn in, enter the door of 185 Winchester, go up the steps to the first-floor landing and in the door of Apartment 328, where dinner is waiting. Gladys looks at them both. Maybe she says "I was just beginning to worry." Does she give the man a quick kiss? Perhaps. The picture is blurred. But she hugs the boy as if he might have been gone for years.

WHEN THE PRESLEYS arrived in Memphis on November 6, 1948, they moved into a downtown rooming house at 370 Washington Street, then some six months later into another one nearby, at 572 Poplar, just around the corner from the Courts. They may have found the latter through a neighbor from Tupelo, Mrs. Tressie Miller, who lived upstairs; maybe Vernon had even stayed in one of the boardinghouses during the war. The house on Poplar, like many others in the area, was a big old Victorian-style edifice that had been cut up into sixteen single-room apartments, three or four to a floor, with a shared bathroom at the end of the hall. The Presleys paid $9.50 a week rent and cooked their meals on a hot plate. In the evening the whole family might cross the street to attend services at the Reverend J. J. Denson's Poplar Street Mission. The Reverend Denson had a fine voice. He played the guitar, and there was always lots of singing and shouting and carrying on as well as a communal supper to be shared. Some nights the family would have dinner with Mrs. Miller and reminisce about Tupelo. Gladys got a job as a sewing machine operator at Fashion Curtains, and then, after her brother Travis and his wife, Lorraine, had moved up within a few weeks of the Presleys' arrival, Vernon and Travis found work at Precision Tool, a munitions manufacturer — perhaps he had worked there during the war. It was over at Kansas and McLemore, about two miles away; in good weather Vernon and Travis could walk, in bad weather they might drive or take the bus up Third. Poplar Avenue was a busy commercial thoroughfare, but it was an isolating one as well. It was hard to get to know people in the city, and Gladys tried to persuade her other brothers and sisters and in-laws to join them. "The places that they moved in up there didn't seem much better than what they had down here," sniffed her cousin Corinne Richards Tate, but eventually most of the family moved up, forming a little enclave in the vicinity of Third and Poplar.

The new address was within easy walking distance of United Paint, where Vernon had gotten a job as a loader in February, but they lived there for less than a month before putting in an application for public housing in June. Vernon was making 85 cents an hour, $40.38 a week with overtime, when Jane Richardson, a home service adviser for the Memphis Housing Authority, interviewed Gladys Presley in the Poplar Avenue rooming house on June 17, 1949. She noted the poor conditions under which they were living, a prerequisite for consideration. Miss Richardson wrote: "Cook, eat, and sleep in one room. Share bath. No privacy. . . . Need housing. Persons interviewed are Mrs. Presley and son. Nice boy. They seem very nice and deserving. Lauderdale if possible, near husband's work."

They finally gained admission to the Courts on September 20, at the start of Elvis' freshman year at Humes. The rent was $35 a month, about what they had been paying on Poplar, but instead of a single room they got two bedrooms, a living room, a kitchen, and a bathroom of their own. There was a $2,500 ceiling on annual family income as a qualification for continued tenancy, and it was noted that the Presleys possessed no telephone and a car that barely ran, and that Vernon sent $10 every month to his mother in West Point, Mississippi. The repairs that the apartment needed were detailed on a Housing Authority form on the day they moved in: "Wall around bath tub needs repair . . . apartment in need of paint job . . . 1 shade will not roll in bedroom . . . light in front hall will not stay on . . . oven door will not shut tight . . . one leg broke off cabinet . . . bathroom sink stopped up . . . faucet in kitchen sink needs repairs." But this marked the real beginning of the Presleys' arrival in Memphis.

I don't think anyone visiting the latter-day Courts could get a sense of what the Courts were like at that time: a humming, bustling little village, full of kids and ambition. Forty years later graduates of the Courts would include doctors, lawyers, judges, and successful businessmen, and many would have achieved the Housing Authority goal ("From slums to public housing to private ownership") in a single generation. The homes, 433 units in all, were inspected at frequent but unspecified intervals ("We always found Mrs. Presley to be an excellent housekeeper," Jane Richardson told Elvis biographer Jerry Hopkins, "and a very nice person. . . . She kept [the oak floors] waxed all the time"), and the grounds were immaculate. For many of the residents it was "like we'd come into the money." For some it was the first time they had ever had indoor plumbing or taken a real bath.

It would be easy to romanticize the sense of hope and striving that dominated the Courts, because this was still a hard, tough world in which many of the kids came from broken homes, the quickest way to resolve a problem was with your fists, and you would rather die (if you were male, anyway) than articulate your innermost hopes and dreams. But it would be wrong to ignore the sense of social aspiration, and of pride, too, because that was the dominant tone of the Courts. The prevailing attitude was that you didn't talk about it, you just did it. Yet it was an idyllic world, too. For a kid growing up there was a degree of comfort, a sense of place, and a reassuring sense that everyone was heading in the same direction, everyone was looking toward a bright new day. In many ways it mirrored the comfortable small-town environment of Tupelo. It was just the kind of thing that a wide-eyed boy from the country, too doubtful to know what he really felt, too fearful to express it even if he did, needed. It was home.

T HE PRESLEYS themselves were not atypical Lauderdale residents: Mr. Presley dour and grave on the outside, a decent man, a good provider, a man whose taciturnity not infrequently conveyed a sense of suspiciousness, of mild disapproval; Mrs. Presley working part-time at Fashion Curtains, attending Stanley Products (Tupperware-like) parties with the other ladies, laughing, sociable, exchanging recipes and small confidences, but sometimes bringing her adolescent son along, too — he never said anything, just sat silently by her side — which caused some of the women to talk. Mrs. Presley was much more popular than Mr. Presley. Everyone spoke of her warmth and liveliness and spontaneous expressions of emotion, but there was also a sense of a family set apart, a sealed-off world that few outsiders ever penetrated. They didn't attend any one church regularly, for the most part they were not joiners, but as much as anything else the sense that others got of their separateness seemed to center on their son. "They treated him like he was two years old," said Mrs. Ruby Black, most of whose ten children had grown up in the Courts. But even to Gladys' sister Lillian, who, once she and her family had moved to Memphis, too, could look out her back door and practically see Gladys' living room window, there was something about Vernon and Gladys' focus on their only child that turned even family into outsiders. "He was particular about his funny books, Elvis — he wouldn't even let anyone look at them. Grandma Presley would tell my little boys, 'No, you can't look at them. Elvis will get mad at me.' He had his own dishes that he'd eat out of. A knife and fork and spoon. Mrs. Presley would say, 'I'm gonna set the table,' and she always washed his things and set them over there by their selves: his plate and his spoon and his bowl, whatever. She says, 'Don't you eat out of that.' I said, 'Why?' She said, 'That's Elvis'. He wouldn't eat a bite if he knowed anybody had eat out of them.' " "He never spent a night away from home until he was seventeen," Vernon told an interviewer, with only slight exaggeration, in 1978.

He went to school each day, walking the ten blocks down Jackson to Manassas, where Humes stood imposing and monolithic and the halls reverberated with the clatter of voices, locker doors slamming, students seemingly confident of their destination, whatever it might be. At first he was frightened — this was a school where the principal was not reluctant to enunciate or act upon his philosophy and could write as his message in the graduation yearbook, "If one has no scruples about embarrassing this institution, he would do well to withdraw because hereafter we shall oppose the readmittance of one who has knowingly and willingly defamed the school's good name." That was something to think about — probably every day — but after the first day he got used to it, it was a whole new world to study, and gradually he even came to feel at home.

At first Gladys walked him to the corner, until he made friends in the neighborhood. Outside of the Courts there was no one who really noticed much about him his first two years at Humes. "He was a gentle, obedient boy, and he always went out of his way to try to do what you asked him to do," said Susie Johnson, his ninth-grade homeroom teacher. "His English was atrocious . . . but he had a warm and sunny quality about him which made people respond." "He was during his first years in our school a shy boy. . . . At times he seemed to feel more at ease with [the teachers] than with his fellow students," wrote Mildred Scrivener, his twelfth-grade homeroom and history teacher, in 1957. "Thinking back now, I wonder if he wasn't overly conscious that he and his parents had just moved from Tupelo, that the other students were familiar with the place and knew each other. If so, it was a typical bit of teenaged near-sightedness."

His grades were decent. In the eighth grade he got an A in language
and a C in music. In a rare moment of self-assertion, he challenged the
contention of his music teacher, Miss Marmann, that he couldn't sing.
Yes, he could, he said, she just didn't appreciate his type of singing, and he
brought his guitar to class the next day and sang Fairley Holden and His
Six Ice Cold Papas' 1947 hit, "Keep Them Cold Icy Fingers Off of Me."
According to a classmate, Katie Mae Shook, Miss Marmann "agreed that
Elvis was right when he said that she didn't appreciate his kind of singing." In the ninth grade he got Bs in English, science, and math. "My
older brother went to school with him," recalled singer Barbara Pittman,
"and he and some of the other boys used to hide behind buildings and
throw things at him — rotten fruit and stuff — because he was different,
because he was quiet and he stuttered and he was a mama's boy." Sophomore year he joined ROTC, became a library volunteer worker, and took
wood shop, where he made projects for his mother. His grandmother was
living with them part of the time, and Gladys was working at the coffee
urn at Britling's Cafeteria downtown.

In pictures he does not look any different from his fellow students,
neither humbler nor poorer nor more flamboyant. The only difference
that one might detect is that he appears more diffident than his classmates. No one else appears to have any reservation about buying in — the
pictured students are models of comportment and posture. But surely
that is not fair either. What is so touching about this portrait of the American dream, circa 1950, is the conscious striving on everyone's face, not
least that of the young cadet, Elvis Aron Presley, who wore his ROTC
uniform proudly everywhere, his face stern, his posture erect, his demeanor, one senses, boundlessly optimistic. In retrospect he clearly felt
the same pride in Humes that most of his classmates did: that it was
tough, tough but fair, and that one of the proudest achievements of his
life would be simply getting through.

In the Courts, meanwhile, his world was rapidly expanding. There
were three other boys in his building — Buzzy Forbess, Paul Dougher,
and Farley Guy — and Buzzy ran into him one day on his way to visit
Paul. "Paul lived on the third floor (Farley lived on the second, right over
Elvis), and Elvis was standing out on one of the little stairways out in
front of the building, talking to some other people. And I went by and had
some funny books in my hand rolled up. First time I ever saw him, I said,
'Hi, how ya doing?' and slapped him on the back of the head with the

funny books, and he slapped me upside the head as I went by. We like to got in a scrape. But as soon as I looked at him, and he looked at me, we both grinned and shook hands and I went upstairs to see Paul. That was how we become friends." Soon the four of them were virtually inseparable. Together they formed a football team to play other neighborhoods, they rode their bikes, went to the movies, when it was warm enough they hung out at Malone Pool just a few blocks away, where they eyed the girls and made awkward stabs at actually swimming. It was nothing to brag about, said Buzzy, "just kids growing up together. If somebody moved into the Courts, they was going to get involved with *everybody*, one way or another. If you was going to have a party, everybody was going to get invited. We did all the things that you do. We lived two or three blocks from Main Street. We was right in the middle of everything. What we didn't do was crack the books and study a lot. We were close enough. We were good friends."

One time Buzzy got hurt in one of their football games against another neighborhood team. "I was bleeding and pretty bruised, and Mrs. Presley started crying. She was a softhearted lady. But Mr. Presley was a fine person, too. I was around him enough to know that a lot of Elvis' wit and abilities came from his dad. I loved Mrs. Presley to death, but as far as the humor, the dry humor — that's Mr. Presley. Most people smile with their lips, but he laughed with his eyes. Dry wit, dry smile — Elvis got an awful lot of that from him."

Elvis and Buzzy and Farley and Paul roamed all around the downtown area; they walked everywhere together in a jaunty group, passing kosher butcher shops and Italian fruit stands, exploring the dock area below Front Street, observing the bustling prosperity of the downtown shoppers, checking out the blues guitarist and washtub bass player who stood out in front of the Green Owl, on the corner of Market, when the weather was good. Sometimes they might travel as far as the corner of Beale and Main, or they might even venture a block down Beale to get their pictures taken at the Blue Light Studio, four for a quarter, but there was no need to wander very far, there was so much going on all around them, a riot of sounds, colors, hustle, and excitement, even for a kid who'd grown up in the city. The summer after his freshman year Vernon bought Elvis a push lawn mower, and the four of them would go around with the mower and a couple of hand sickles soliciting yard work at four dollars per yard. "The first evening he came in," said Vernon, "and sat there with a frown on his face and laid fifty cents out. Then all at once he broke out laughing and pulled a handful of change out of his pocket . . . and he had about seven dollars."

Elvis' musical interests remained something of a secret his first couple of years at Humes. He didn't bring his guitar to school, and he rarely carried it around the Courts with him. "With the three of us he played," said Buzzy. "He wasn't shy about it, but he wasn't the kind of kid you just turn him around and put him onstage, either. He got used to it right there with us." One time Farley's mother complained that he was making too much racket, and the Housing Authority got several other complaints from older tenants, but Miss Richardson would just "ask him to tune down a little bit," and he always would. He shared a tenth-grade biology class with Buzzy and was going to bring his guitar to school for the class's Christmas party. "He even practiced two or three songs," said Buzzy, "Christmas-type songs, but he chickened out — didn't even bring it." He doesn't seem to have told any of his friends about the Mississippi-Alabama Fair; he never spoke of Mississippi Slim.

And yet, one feels, he never lost sight of music for a moment. In fact, if he had never left the apartment, just listening to the radio would have been a big step toward completing his musical education. Memphis radio in 1950 was an Aladdin's lamp of musical vistas and styles. Late at night Elvis could have listened — along with most of the other kids in the Courts and half of Memphis, it seemed — to Daddy-O-Dewey, Dewey Phillips, broadcasting from the Gayoso on WHBQ. In one typical 1951 segment he would have heard Rosco Gordon's "Booted" (which had been recorded in Memphis, at Sam Phillips' studio), Muddy Waters' "She Moves Me," "Lonesome Christmas" by Lowell Fulson, and Elmore James' brand-new "Dust My Broom," all current hits, and all collector's classics some forty years later. "Rocket 88," which has frequently been tagged the first rock 'n' roll record, came out of Sam Phillips' studio in 1951, too, and merited a write-up in the paper that led with the somewhat arch suggestion, "If you have a song you can't get published, you might ask Sam Phillips for help." "Come on, good people," exhorted Dewey, telling his public to buy their threads at Lansky Brothers on Beale. "Do like me and pay for 'em while you wearing 'em out, or when they catch up with you, *dee-gawwwww!* And be sure and tell 'em Phillips sent you!" In the morning there was Bob Neal's wake-up show on WMPS, hillbilly music and cornpone humor in a relaxed Arthur Godfrey style of presentation, and at 12:30 P.M. Neal offered thirty minutes of gospel with the Blackwood Brothers, who had recently moved to Memphis and joined the First Assembly of God Church on McLemore Avenue. The first half of the *High Noon Round-Up* featured country singer Eddie Hill, who along with the Louvin Brothers, Gladys Presley's favorite country group (the Blackwoods were her favorite quartet, though Vernon and Elvis preferred the somewhat livelier Statesmen), was among Memphis' biggest hillbilly stars.

If you changed the dial to WDIA, which since its switchover in 1949 to an all-black programming policy had billed itself as "The Mother Station of the Negroes," you could hear not only local blues star B. B. King, deejaying and playing his own music live on the air, but also such genuine personalities as Professor Nat D. Williams, history teacher at Booker T. Washington High School, columnist for Memphis' Negro newspaper, the *World*, and longtime master of ceremonies at the Palace Theatre's Amateur Night; comedic genius A. C. "Moohah" Williams; and the cosmopolitan Maurice "Hot Rod" Hulbert, not to mention the Spirit of Memphis Quartet, who had their own fifteen-minute program and made even the Carnation Milk jingle reverberate with feeling. On Sunday night on WHBQ the sermons of the Reverend W. Herbert Brewster, author of such Negro spiritual classics as Mahalia Jackson's "Move On Up a Little Higher" and Clara Ward's "How I Got Over," were broadcast live from the East Trigg Baptist Church, with his famed soloist, Queen C. Anderson, leading the musical interludes.

There would have been no way for any but the most avid student to keep up with it all — and this doesn't even begin to take into account Howlin' Wolf and Sonny Boy Williamson's broadcasts from West Memphis, Arkansas, just across the river, Sleepy Eyed John's hillbilly parade on WHHM, all the regular showcases for popular tunes of the day, the big band broadcasts from the Peabody Skyway, and, of course, the Opry broadcasts on Saturday night. Here was an education of a sort, and of a quality, virtually unimaginable today and, in an age and a place that were strictly segregated in every respect, an education that was color-blind. "In one aspect of America's cultural life," wrote *Billboard*'s pioneering music editor Paul Ackerman, looking back in 1958 on the impact of the music that had first arrived in such profusion after the war, "integration has already taken place." This was as true in 1950 as it was in 1958 — but only in the privacy of the home, and only where music was truly in the air.

P ERHAPS IT WAS at one of the ladies' Stanley Products parties that Gladys first asked Mrs. Mattie Denson, wife of the Reverend J. J. Denson, if her husband could possibly give her son guitar lessons. Mrs. Denson said her husband would be glad to help ("He has such a nice voice," said Mrs. Presley), but it was her son Jesse Lee who was the real talent in the family. Jesse Lee was not thrilled when she told him about the idea. At eighteen he was two and a half years older than Mrs. Presley's son in 1950 and possessed a well-deserved reputation as a school truant and something of a delinquent. He had run away from home for the first time at the age of nine, had started playing professionally when he was not much older, and had been in and out of one juvenile correctional facility or another for much of his young life. A superb athlete, he fought one of the most memorable Golden Gloves matches in Memphis history in 1952, when he lost the bantamweight championship to fellow Courts resident George Blancet and made the papers for performing Hank Snow's "Golden Rocket" and the semiclassical "Blue Prelude" in between bouts as well.

He didn't want to teach Elvis, he told his mother, because the other boy "was very shy, and kind of timid. 'He's scared of the other kids that I pal around with,' I said. 'They're tough kids, and I'm afraid they're going to tease me, and then I'll get my hands all broken up from having to defend myself . . . and I don't think I should do it!' Well, she turned around and walked away and said, 'Jesse Lee, remember: "Whatsoever you do for these the least of my brothers, that you would do unto me." ' I said, 'Send him over, Mama.'

"He showed up, he had a little itty-bitty, Gene Autry–type guitar that he really couldn't play. He couldn't press the strings down on it they was set so high, so I let him practice on mine — I had a little Martin. I just tried to show him basic chords. I would take his fingers and place them, say, 'You're pressing the wrong strings with the wrong fingers,' trying to straighten him out. He couldn't really complete a song for a long time, couldn't move his fingers and go with the flow of the music, but once I straightened him out he started to learn to do it right."

Every Saturday and Sunday, Elvis would show up with his guitar. Although Mrs. Denson was a champion of Christian fellowship, it didn't extend so far as to let the boys practice in her home, so they went down to the laundry room underneath the Presleys' apartment. Lee's friends Dorsey Burnette and his younger brother, Johnny, whose family had lived across from the Densons for thirteen years on Pontotoc Street, were frequently present and, as Lee had predicted, did give Elvis a hard time. Dorsey was another prominent Golden Gloves boxer, but as many of their friends remarked, he and Johnny just liked to fight, and the more pacific Elvis referred to them somewhat ruefully as the Daltons, after the famous outlaw gang.

Lee dazzled the other boys with his virtuosic execution of "Wildwood Flower" and "Under the Double Eagle," not to mention the tremolo yodel that he had developed for his vocal showpieces. With still another resident of the Courts, Johnny Black, whose older brother Bill was a sometime professional musician, the five boys became well known for their concerts on Market Mall, the cool, leafy path that ran down the middle of the Courts. Often in the evening the boys would sing, harmonizing on "Cool Water" and "Riders in the Sky," showcasing Lee's guitar and his vocals, too, on numbers like "I'm Movin' On," "Tennessee Waltz," or just about any Eddy Arnold song you could name. In the summertime there were informal dances on the lawn, while older residents sat on their porches and patted their hands and the sound carried all over the Courts. Lee Denson's older brother, Jimmy, recalled them as a group centering around his younger brother. "They walked single file, Indian-fashion, four or five teenage boys holding their guitars wherever they went." To Johnny Black it was more of a loose-knit association: "We would play under the trees, underneath those big magnolia trees — I've got pictures of us all. It was just whoever would come, whoever showed up. We'd have a mandolin maybe, three or four guitars, and the people would gather. We weren't trying to impress the world, we were just playing to have a good time."

No one has ever remembered Elvis Presley in the foreground of any of these pictures, but he clearly showed up in the back, hovering on the edges of the frame, tentatively forming his chords, joining in occasionally on the background vocals. When he missed a note, he threw up his hands in the air and then shrugged with a shy, self-deprecating grin that caused his audience to laugh. To the older boys he was a mush-mouthed little country boy, a mama's boy who deserved a certain amount of respect just for not letting himself be run off. To Buzzy and Farley and Paul he was something of a hero — their memories centered on their friend. Like younger boys of every generation they don't think much of the older boys, they see them as bullies and boors, if they ever get in that position themselves, they tell each other, they will never act that way.

Everyone reacts in predictable enough fashion, except for the dreamy boy at the edge of the picture. For Elvis it is as if he has been set down in a foreign land. Music both thrills and holds him in its hypnotic sway. With music he is transported to another place, he experiences a soft dreamy feeling, a sense of almost cushiony release, but at the same time it is as hard and concrete as desire. The older boys might be surprised that he knows the words to every song that they have sung (Lee Denson, for one, has no idea that he has not taught "Old Shep" to his bumbling pupil); he may well know the lyrics to every song that they might ever want to sing — the words imprint themselves on his memory, he has only to hear them once or twice, the chords, too, it is just his fingers which stubbornly resist. In his mind he hears the song differently; it is less florid at times, less like the Irish tenor John McCormack on the sentimental songs, more dramatic on the hillbilly ones. The only songs he would not change are the gospel numbers — those he would do just as they have been done, by the Statesmen, the Blackwood Brothers, the Sunshine Boys. It would seem like sacrilege almost to alter those songs.

He sits alone on the steps of the apartment house at night, fingering the chords softly in the dark. His voice barely rises above a murmur, but he is looking for attention, mostly from the girls, from Betty McMahan, his "first love," and from Billie Wardlaw, who lives next door to Betty on the third floor and took Betty's place when Betty started going with a boy from Arkansas. Betty had met Gladys before she met her son. "She used to come out and we had lawn chairs, or we'd sit on the steps. My mother and his mother started a conversation. Finally one night I guess she just forced him to come outside and sit with us and talk." Billie Wardlaw moved in with her mother at fourteen in 1950 — even before Betty broke up with him, he started courting Billie. "Elvis was a great kisser, and since we were always playing spin the bottle in the dark, he didn't let his shyness get in the way. . . . Lots of times when my mother and I would walk home, Elvis would be outside picking his guitar in the dark. His mother and dad would be sitting out there on quilts, listening. Elvis would do anything in the dark. . . . Once my mother told him, 'Elvis, you sing so good you ought to be singing on the radio.' He blushed and told my mother, 'Mrs. Rooker, I can't sing.' "

He likes the company of women, he loves to be around women, women of all ages, he feels more comfortable with them — it isn't something he would want to admit to his friends, or even perhaps to himself. His aunt Lillian notices it: "He'd get out there at night with the girls and he just sang his head off. He was different with the girls — I'm embarrassed to tell, but he'd rather have a whole bunch of girls around him than the boys — he didn't care a thing about the boys." The women seem to sense something coming out of him, something he himself may not even know he possesses: it is an aching kind of vulnerability, an unspecified yearning; when Sam Phillips meets him just two or three years later, in 1953, he senses much the same quality but calls it insecurity. "He tried not to show it, but he felt so *inferior*. He reminded me of a black man in that way; his insecurity was so *markedly* like that of a black person." Bathed in the soft glow of the streetlight, he appears almost handsome — the acne that embarrasses him doesn't show up so badly, and the adolescent features, which can appear coarse in the cold light of day, take on a kind of delicacy that is almost beautiful. He sings Eddy Arnold's "Molly Darling," a Kay Starr number, "Harbor Lights," Bing and Gary Crosby's "Moonlight Bay," all soft, sweet songs, in a soft, slightly quavering voice, and then, satisfied, takes his comb out of his back pocket and runs it through his hair in a practiced gesture clearly at odds with his hesitancy of manner. With the women, though, he can do no wrong: young girls or old ladies, they seem drawn to his quiet, hesitant approach, his decorous humility, his respectful scrutiny. The men may have their doubts, but to the women he is a nice boy, a kind boy, someone both thoughtful and attentive, someone who truly cares.

THE SUMMER BEFORE his junior year in high school Elvis went to work at Precision Tool, where his father had started when they first moved to Memphis and where his uncles Johnny and Travis Smith and Vester Presley all continued to work. He was making twenty-seven dollars a week, but it didn't last long, because an insurance inspector found out that he was underage, so he went back to his yard business with Buzzy, Farley, and Paul. Sophomore year he had worked as an usher at

Loew's State for much of the fall, giving the Presleys three breadwinners for a while and enabling them to purchase a television set and have Vernon's mother, Minnie, move in with them full-time.

Junior year was something of a watershed; even his teachers remarked upon the change. His hair was different — he was using more Rose Oil hair tonic and Vaseline to keep it down, and he had grown sideburns both to look older and to emulate the appearance of the kind of cross-country truck driver that he sometimes said he wanted to be ("Wild-looking guys, they had scars, I used to lay on the side of the road and watch [them] drive their big diesel trucks"). He seemed to have gained in self-confidence, and his appearance was more distinctive; without calling attention to himself in words he demanded it by his dress and demeanor ("It was just something I wanted to do, I wasn't trying to be better than anybody else"). He even went out for football, an ambition that he had harbored for some time but that proved to be the single, dramatic misstep in an otherwise carefully navigated high school career. By trying out for the team he made himself vulnerable to the very forces which most scorned him, and in perhaps the best-known story of his growing-up years some of the other players ganged up on him in the locker room and threatened to cut his hair, and the coach eventually kicked him off the team when he refused. Whether it happened exactly that way or not, there is little question that he had his pride hurt, and he frequently referred to the incident in later life with some ruefulness and anger.

He went back to work at Loew's State, on South Main, but that didn't last long either, after he got into a fight with another usher who he thought had been a stool pigeon and was fired by the manager. In November 1951, Gladys got a job at St. Joseph's Hospital as a nurse's aide at $4 a day, six days a week. St. Joseph's was just a couple of blocks from their home, and she was very proud of the job, but she had to quit the following February after the Memphis Housing Authority threatened to evict them because their combined family income exceeded the maximum allowed. "Illness in the family," Vernon wrote to the Housing Authority by way of explanation. He had hurt his back and been out of work for a while. "Wife is not working [now]. Trying to pay ourselves out of debt. Bills are pressing and don't want to be sued." In February they got a new lease at a reduced rent of $43 a month and a $3,000 ceiling on income. By June they had recovered enough financially to purchase a 1941 Lincoln coupe, which Elvis was encouraged to consider "his" car. "My daddy was something wonderful to me," said Elvis to a 1956 interviewer. One time, Vernon recalled, Elvis brought the car home and "came running up yelling, 'Hi, Dad, I put fifteen cents' worth of gasoline into the car.' Everyone laughed, and he like to have died of embarrassment."

He didn't need the car, though, for the majority of his common pursuits. He had seen the lights of Main Street, and as Bob Johnson of the *Memphis Press-Scimitar* wrote in 1956 in the first official fan biography: "Elvis saw the street late, with the signs glowing, and to this day it holds a spell over him. . . . Sometimes with his friends, sometimes alone, Elvis would head for Main Street, where the windows, the bustle of moving traffic, the hurrying crowd gave him something to watch and wonder about."

He started hanging out at Charlie's, a little record store, which was at first situated next to the Suzore No. 2 on North Main across the alley from the firehouse, then directly across the street. It had a jukebox and a little soda fountain and even sold "dirty" Redd Foxx comedy records under the counter — and within a short time Elvis became a regular there, sometimes alone, as Bob Johnson suggested, sometimes with friends. He might go to the movies, where you could still see a double feature for a dime, stop by the firehouse, where the firemen, who welcomed any diversion, were always happy to hear him sing a song, then sidle into Charlie's, not to buy anything, necessarily, just to listen, to handle the precious 78s, to put a nickel in the jukebox every once in a while. The proprietor, Charlie Hazelgrove, never kicked anyone out; the store was a hangout for teenagers who were passionate about music, which was why Buzzy Forbess, for example, never went in there at all. For while he and Elvis were the best of friends, that part of Elvis' life did not impinge on his own. "One time we were hanging around Charlie's," recalled Johnny Black, a more casual acquaintance but a *musician,* "and Elvis said to me, 'Johnny, someday I'm going to be driving Cadillacs.' It's so weird to think about — we're talking about an era when we probably couldn't have gotten the money together for a Coke between us."

He wandered down the street, past Loew's to the corner of Beale and Main, then headed down Beale to Lansky's clothing store. A lot of kids liked to go on Beale just to watch the colored acting up. One store a few doors down from Lansky's had its customers lie down on the floor to be measured, with the salesman drawing a chalk outline for a new suit with the gravest of faces; another displayed the tuxedo that local mobster Ma-

chine Gun Kelly was said to have been mowed down in, bullet holes intact. The political machine of Boss E. H. Crump took a benevolent attitude toward its Negro population — anything went on Beale Street, up to
the point that it threatened the safety of whites — but city censor Lloyd
Binford consistently bowdlerized Lena Horne's movies and banned the
Hollywood comedy *Brewster's Millions,* because costar Eddie "Rochester"
Anderson had "too familiar a way about him, and the picture presents too
much racial mixture." In the late 1940s he banned the stage musical *Annie
Get Your Gun,* because it had a Negro railroad conductor and "we don't
have any Negro conductors in the South. Of course it can't show here. It's
social equality in action."

For Elvis, though, it was the clothing, it was the styles, the bold fashions, that drew him in, as he gazed hungrily into Lansky's windows. He
made a definite impression on Guy and Bernard Lansky, the brothers who
owned and operated the store. "He came down and looked through the
windows before he had any money — we knew him strictly by face," recalled Guy. "He was working at the theater at that time, holes in his shoes
and socks, real shabbily dressed, but he stood out, his hair, sure, but it was
his . . . what I'm trying to say, it was his, you know, manners. He was just
a very nice person."

At noon — if it was a Saturday or a vacation day or maybe just a day
when he cut school — he headed down to the WMPS studio on the corner of Union and Main for the *High Noon Round-Up,* where the Blackwood
Brothers appeared live with WMPS DJ Bob Neal emceeing. "I suppose
that was where I saw him for the first time," said Bob Neal, who would
become his first manager several years later and who, like Guy Lansky,
was struck more by his manner than his appearance. Even James Blackwood, leader of the Blackwood Brothers Quartet, who had a national
hit on RCA in 1951 with "The Man Upstairs," remembered the hungry-
looking young boy, as did his counterpart in the Statesmen, lead singer
Jake Hess, who recalled meeting Elvis at this time not in Memphis but in
Tupelo, when the Presleys were presumably back for a visit. How, Jake
Hess was asked, could he remember the boy? Weren't there other fans
equally ardent in their enthusiasm? To Hess, a spectacular singer with the
kind of soaring tenor voice and controlled vibrato that Elvis would explicitly aspire to, it was not prescience that caused him to notice but, rather,
something about the young man's fierce, burning desire. "I mean, we
didn't know Elvis Presley from a sack of sand. He was just nice, a nice kid,

this bright-eyed boy asking all kinds of questions, and asking in a way that you would really want to tell him. He wanted to know about the spiritual aspects of it — did you have to do this or that? He wanted to know if he would be handicapped because he couldn't read music. He was such a bright-eyed boy, you know, he just looked important, even as a kid."

He became a regular at the All-Night Gospel Singings, which had started at Ellis Auditorium up the street and all through the South in the previous two or three years, not with his friends from the Courts or even with musician friends like Lee Denson and the Burnette brothers, who had started playing the roadhouses by now, but by himself, with his mother and father, maybe with his cousin Junior or Gene, with whoever would go — but he rarely missed a show. Once a month Ellis was filled for what amounted to a marathon sing-off, into the early hours of the morning, among the top white gospel quartets of the day. He sat there mesmerized by what he later described as "the big heavy rhythm beats" of some of the spiritual numbers and the delicate beauty of others. There was probably no type of music that he didn't love, but quartet music was the center of his musical universe. Gospel music combined the spiritual force that he felt in all music with the sense of physical release and exaltation for which, it seemed, he was casting about. And the shows — the shows themselves were the broadest of panoplies, running the full spectrum of gospel styles, from the dignified "shape note"-influenced singing of older groups like the Speer Family and the Chuck Wagon Gang, to the flashy showmanship of the Sunshine Boys, to the stately harmonies of the Blackwoods, who adapted many of their hits from the new spiritual style of such Negro quartets as the Soul Stirrers and the Original Gospel Harmonettes of Birmingham. There were hints of the Ink Spots and the Golden Gate Quartet, and even of contemporary rhythm and blues singers like Clyde McPhatter and Roy Hamilton, in their beautifully arranged, precisely articulated stylings, but for all of his admiration for the Blackwoods' work, it was the Statesmen who really captured Elvis' imagination.

The Statesmen were an electric combination, anchored by the disarmingly conventional and unremittingly cheerful manner of their accompanist, leader, and founder, Hovie Lister, and featuring some of the most thrillingly emotive singing and daringly unconventional showmanship in the entertainment world. Sharply dressed in suits that might have come out of the window of Lansky's, they piled tenor on top of countertenor, and then falsetto on top of that, building to Jake Hess' virtuosic lead. Meanwhile bass singer Jim Wetherington, known universally as the Big Chief, maintained a steady bottom, ceaselessly jiggling first his left leg, then his right, with the material of the pants leg ballooning out and shimmering. "He went about as far as you could go in gospel music," said Jake Hess. "The women would jump up, just like they do for the pop shows." Preachers frequently objected to the lewd movements, racial fundamentalists decried the debt to Negro spirituals (particularly in the overt emotionalism of the delivery), but audiences reacted with screams and swoons. It was a different kind of spirituality, but spirituality nonetheless, as the group ran, not walked, out onto the stage, singers tossed the microphone back and forth, and Jake Hess at the audience's coaxing repeated the thrilling climax of his last song over and over again, as Chief maintained his tireless act.

Music, more and more, became the focus of his life. At parties in the Courts Elvis would always sing, sometimes to the point that his friends would groan, "Oh, no, not again!" He was still extremely shy, didn't know how to dance, and sometimes would play only with the lights out, even in as intimate a setting as his cousin Bobbie's birthday party, said his aunt Lillian. "I moved everything out of the living room, and Elvis come in, brought his guitar, but we had to put the lights out before he'd sing. We had a fire in the fireplace, but it wasn't enough light to show his face. He got way over yonder in the corner — that's just how shy he was." He sang quite a few of Kay Starr's songs, he was partial to Teresa Brewer, Joni James, Bing Crosby, Eddie Fisher, and Perry Como as well as Hank Williams and Eddy Arnold. Some evenings Vernon and Gladys would go to the movies so that he, Buzzy, Paul, and Farley could have a party in the apartment. Elvis would never play a slow song, Buzzy said, when Buzzy was dancing with Elvis' girlfriend, Billie Wardlaw, though Billie broke up with him not long afterward when she started going with a sailor she had met at the USO on Third Street. Elvis' reaction when he saw another boy's picture in her wallet surprised her. "He grabbed it out of my purse and began stomping and grinding it into the ground with the heel of his shoe." When she actually broke up with him, "he started crying. Until that night I had never seen a man, or a boy, cry."

Occasionally Buzzy and the other boys would arrange with Miss Richmond, the Lauderdale Courts supervisor, to use the basement under the main office on Lauderdale. She would give them the key, and they would set up tables and issue invitations, charging twenty-five cents per couple. They'd have Cokes and popcorn and a record player, and in the course of the evening Elvis would never fail to sing. One time he accompanied Buzzy and Paul, who had joined the Junior Order of the Oddfellows and made monthly trips to area hospitals as a kind of civic project, when they went to the Home for Incurables out on McLemore in South Memphis. Ordinarily they just passed out ice cream and cookies and spoke to the patients, but this time, to Buzzy's surprise, Elvis had brought his guitar with him and got up and sang, making it in Buzzy's view the first time he ever entertained in Memphis outside of the Courts.

Senior year he went to work for MARL Metal Products, a furniture-assembling plant on Georgia near the Memphis and Arkansas Bridge, where he worked from 3:00 to 11:30 P.M. each day, but the work took its toll. According to a teacher, Mildred Scrivener: "Elvis was working too hard. He was in my homeroom, and he also was in one of my history classes. One thing I have always been very strict about is the matter of sleeping in class. Nothing can spread yawns and boredom so fast from row to row. But the day came when Elvis fell asleep in class. . . . That day when the class bell shrilled, Elvis, like a little boy, raised his head, got to his feet, and wandered out like a sleepwalker." "It got so hard on him," said Gladys, "he was so beat all the time, we made him quit, and I went [back] to work at St. Joseph's Hospital."

That evidently got them thrown out of the Courts. Despite Vernon's back troubles, in November 1952 it was determined that the Presleys' projected annual income had risen to $4,133, well over Housing Authority limits, and on November 17 the Presley family got an eviction notice, requiring them to move out by February 28. In a sense their eviction could be seen as evidence of upward mobility, though it seems unlikely Vernon would have taken it that way at the time.

Elvis meanwhile was making a greater claim on his schoolmates' attention. It seemed as if he was determined to make a statement, he was intent upon setting himself apart, without ever raising his voice or changing from the polite, well-mannered boy that he knew he would always be. By his dress, his hair, his demeanor, though, he was making a ringing declaration of independence. More and more to his fellow schoolmates he was a "squirrel," a misfit, a freak, as he would later describe himself, but not a freak to himself. Photographs show an increasing self-confidence, an increasingly studied self-image, even as he was being increasingly rejected by others. He entered a citywide automobile-safety contest sponsored by the Junior Chamber of Commerce and was pictured in the paper changing a tire, expression pensive, dress immaculate: where others wore short-sleeved shirts and work pants and boots, Elvis is spectacularly attired in what could be a pink and black drape jacket, dress pants and loafers, and black shirt.

Red West, the All-Memphis football player who was reputed to have rescued Elvis in the football-team incident and thus laid the groundwork for a lifelong friendship, admired that he had the guts to be different, but "I really felt sorry for him. He seemed very lonely and had no real friends. He just didn't seem to be able to fit in." To Ronny Trout, who shared a workbench with him in wood shop though they were a couple of years apart in school, it was as if he were newly creating himself. "He would wear dress pants to school every day — everybody else wore jeans, but he wore dress pants. And he would wear a coat and fashion a scarf like an ascot tie, as if he were a movie star. Of course he got a lot of flak for this, because he stood out like a sore thumb. People thought, 'That's really weird.' It was like he was already portraying something that he wanted to be. One thing I noticed, and I never really knew what to make of this: when he walked, the way he carried himself, it almost looked as if he was getting ready to draw a gun, he would kind of spin around like a gunfighter. It was weird.

"The way I found out he could play the guitar — I never remember seeing him have it in school, but one of the projects we had in wood shop was to bring an article from home that needed to be repaired, and our wood shop instructor, Mr. Widdop, would look at it and evaluate what had to be done, and that would be our project for a six-week time period. Anyway, I brought something from home, and Elvis brought a guitar. And he fooled around with it, sanded it, used some rosin glue and fixed a crack in it, stained it, varnished it, then he took this real fine steel wool to get all the bubbles out of the lacquer and bring it down to a satin finish so it looked really good. Then he put the strings back on it and was tuning it just before the period ended. So, naturally, somebody came up and said, 'Hey, man, can you play that thing?' And he said, 'No, not really. I just know a few chords. My uncle's taught me a few chords.' So they said, 'Why don't you play something for us?' He said, 'Naw, I can't do that,' and he kept tuning it. Well, somebody grabbed him from behind and locked his arms behind him, and another guy got his car keys out of his pocket, and they said, 'If you play something, you'll get your car keys back.' He said, 'Well, okay, I'll try, but I really don't know that much.' And he started picking out the melody to a song that most people today probably wouldn't even know called 'Under the Double Eagle,' and he did it very expertly. And it just blew me away. I didn't even know he could play that guitar — I just thought he was fixing it for somebody else.''

More and more, it seemed, his determination to be himself — his determination to be a *different* self — grew. He started wearing a black bolero jacket that he had bought at Lansky's and a pair of dress pants with a stripe down the side that made him look, some said, like a carhop. He was constantly fooling with his hair — combing it, mussing it up, training it, brushing the sides back, seemingly oblivious to the attention he was getting from teachers and fellow students alike ("We had grown accustomed to those sideburns," wrote Miss Scrivener in the nostalgic afterglow of success). One time he got a home permanent and came into school the next day asking if he didn't look like Tony Curtis.

He put a couple of gallons of gas in the Lincoln and cruised around town by himself or with his cousin Gene or Bobbie — to Leonard's Barbecue, to the drugstore where Gene worked as a soda jerk; every afternoon he stopped by St. Joseph's to visit his mother at work, and once or twice he and Gene drove down to Tupelo to visit old friends. Perhaps he attended the Midnight Rambles at the Handy Theater, on Park and Airways. Everyone else did. A whole gang would get together on Sunday night and go out to the colored district in Orange Mound for the late show, which was whites-only. There you could catch Eddie "Cleanhead" Vinson, Ivory Joe Hunter, Wynonie Harris, even Dizzy Gillespie, and local acts like Bobby "Blue" Bland, Little Junior Parker, and the comedy team of Rufus (Thomas) and Bones. Was Elvis there — or was he just at home, lying on his bed and listening to Dewey Phillips and dreaming of a world that the music alone could transport him to? By himself he would venture out east to Overton Park, the 330-acre expanse that housed the zoo he had first visited as a child (his uncle Noah had driven the East Tupelo schoolchildren in his school bus), "the same place," he later recalled, "that I did my first concert. I used to go there and listen to the concerts they had with big orchestras. I watched the conductor, listened to the music for hours by myself — I was fascinated by the fact that these guys could play for hours, you know, and most of the time the conductor wouldn't even look at his sheet. . . . I had records by Mario Lanza when I was seventeen, eighteen years old, I would listen to the Metropolitan Opera. I just loved music. Music period.''

THE PRESLEYS moved out of the Courts on January 7, 1953. At first they moved to a rooming house at 698 Saffarans, just a couple of blocks from Humes, but then at the beginning of April they moved back to their old neighborhood at 462 Alabama, opposite the Blacks' house on the northeast end of the Courts. Johnny, like his older brother Bill, had by now taken up the bass, married, and moved out of his mother's home, but like all of his grown brothers and sisters he visited frequently and came back to play music with his friends from the Courts from time to time. "We just thought he was pretty," Bill's wife, Evelyn, said of the women's reaction to Elvis. "We'd sit out there under the tree in front of Mrs. Black's with him playing guitar: Bill's mama said he was her boy-friend! We knew he could play, but we didn't think it was any big deal.''

The house on Alabama was a big Victorian set on a rise and divided up into two good-size apartments. The rent was fifty dollars a month, payable to a Mrs. Dubrovner, whose husband had been a kosher butcher and who lived down the street herself, and both Mrs. Dubrovner and the Presleys' upstairs neighbors, Rabbi Alfred Fruchter and his wife, Jeanette, showed a considerable amount of kindness, and financial consideration, toward the new tenants. Mrs. Presley visited with Mrs. Fruchter almost every afternoon after work, and the Fruchters were particularly fond of the boy, who would turn on the electricity or light the gas for them on the Sabbath when it was forbidden for Orthodox Jews to do so for them-selves. "They never had much," said Mrs. Fruchter, but every Saturday morning Vernon and Elvis "would stand outside and polish that old Lin-coln like it was a Cadillac.''

On April 9, 1953, the Humes High Band presented its "Annual Min-strel" show in the Humes Auditorium at 8:00 P.M. It was a Thursday night, and much of the school had turned out to see the dancers, twirlers, xylophone trio, male quartets, band performances, and comic turns. On a printed program that listed twenty-two acts, the sixteenth entry captured a number of people's attention. "Guitarist. . . . Elvis Prestly," it read. He had told only one or two of his friends beforehand, and even they were not fully convinced he would go through with it. For the minstrel show he wore a red flannel shirt that he had borrowed from Buzzy, and he appeared neither visibly nervous nor particularly at ease either. Unlike some of the kids, who were practiced showmen (Gloria Trout, Ronny's sister, starred in virtually every show that was ever put on at Humes and was renowned for her dance technique), he didn't appear to know what to do when he stumbled out onstage, stood there for what seemed like a full minute, looked at the audience sidelong from under hooded eyes, and finally, as if an internal switch had somehow clicked on, began to sing.

"I wasn't popular in school, I wasn't dating anybody [there]. I failed music — only thing I ever failed. And then they entered me in this talent show, and I came out and did my [first number,] 'Till I Waltz Again with You' by Teresa Brewer, and when I came onstage I heard people kind of rumbling and whispering and so forth, 'cause nobody knew I even sang. It was amazing how popular I became after that. Then I went on through high school and I graduated."

He sang at the homeroom picnic at Overton Park. "While other students were dashing around . . . playing games," wrote Miss Scrivener, "Elvis sat by himself plunking softly at that guitar. The other students began gathering around. There was something about his quiet, plaintive singing which drew them like a magnet. It wasn't the rock 'n' roll for which he later became famous . . . more like [the ballad] 'Love Me Tender.' . . . He went on and on singing his young heart out."

Toward the end of the school year he took Regis Vaughan, a fourteen-year-old freshman at Holy Name School, to the senior prom, which was held at the Continental Ballroom in the Hotel Peabody. He had started going with Regis, whom he had met while she was living with her mother in the Courts the previous year, in February, and they went together all spring. Generally they would double-date with Elvis' cousin Gene and go to a movie or out to the "Teen Canteen" overlooking McKellar Lake at Riverside Park, a recreation spot in South Memphis that was very popular. He sang one song to her, "My Happiness," over and over, and when they went to the gospel All-Night Singings at Ellis, he embarrassed her by singing along with each of the groups, trying to hit the low notes with the bass singer, the high ones with the lead tenor. For the prom he borrowed a car and wore a shiny new blue suit, but they never danced once the whole evening because Elvis said he didn't know how. Afterward they were supposed to meet some friends of Elvis' at Leonard's Barbecue and go to a party, but the friends didn't show up. He never told Regis about the talent show at school, he never talked about becoming a singer, "he talked about finding a job so that he could afford to buy a house for his mama."

He graduated on June 3, 1953, in a program that took place at 8:00 P.M. in Ellis Auditorium's South Hall. The Senior Glee Club sang a selection by Rachmaninoff and "Nocturne" by the Czech composer Zdenko Fibich. Elvis was visibly proud that he had made it through, and Vernon and Gladys were no less elated. They had the diploma framed, and it was placed in an honored spot in their home. The 1953 yearbook, the *Herald,* announced in its "Class Prophecy" that "we are reminded at this time to not forget to invite you all out to the 'Silver Horse' on Onion [Union] Avenue to hear the singing hillbillies of the road. Elvis Presley, Albert Teague, Doris Wilburn, and Mary Ann Propst are doing a bit of picking and singing out that-away." Meanwhile, Elvis had been visiting the Tennessee Employment Security Office regularly since March, looking for a job, preferably as a machinist, to "help work off [his family's] financial obligation." Finally, on July 1 he was sent to M. B. Parker Machinists, which had a temporary position open that paid thirty-six dollars a week. He was out in the world.

SAM PHILLIPS AT 706 UNION AVENUE. (COURTESY OF GARY HARDY, SUN STUDIO)

"MY HAPPINESS"

ON JULY 15, 1953, an article appeared in the *Memphis Press-Scimitar* about a new group, which was making records for a label that had just started up locally. The Prisonaires were the group. They had begun their career inside the walls of the Tennessee State Penitentiary, in Nashville, where they had come to the attention of Red Wortham, a small-time Nashville song publisher. Wortham contacted Jim Bulleit, only recently the proprietor of his own self-named record company in Nashville (the Bullet label had had a number-one pop hit with Francis Craig's "Near You" in 1947 and had released B. B. King's first sides, in 1949) and a recent investor in the new Memphis label. Bulleit called his partner, Sam Phillips, reported the *Press-Scimitar* story, "and said he had something sensational. . . . Phillips, who has been operating [his studio, the Memphis Recording Service] since [January] 1950, and has established a reputation as an expert in recording negro talent, was skeptical — until he heard the tape. Then came the problem of how to get the prisoners for a record-cutting session." The newly appointed warden, James Edwards, however, was fully committed to the principle of prisoner rehabilitation, as was Governor Frank Clement, a close friend and fellow townsman of Edwards'. And so on June 1, "Bulleit drove the five singing prisoners to Memphis, the composer having to stay in prison. An armed guard and a trusty came along, the record company paying the expenses."

The Prisonaires arrived at 706 Union Avenue to make their first record for the fledgling Sun label, which, despite Sam Phillips' considerable experience in the record business (he had been leasing sides to the r&b labels Chess and RPM for three years now and had made an abortive start at his own label a year before), had put out fewer than a dozen releases to date. "They worked from 10:30 A.M. to 8:30 P.M.," the article noted, "until the records were cut just right to suit painstaking Mr. Phillips."

"Just Walkin' in the Rain" came out about the same time that the local story did. It went on to become a hit, as the reporter, Clark Porteous, had predicted it would, if nowhere near as big a hit as it would become when Johnnie Ray recorded it three years later, in 1956. It was the song that put Sun Records on the map, though, and, very likely, the item that captured the attention of Elvis Presley as he read about the studio, the label, and "painstaking" Sam Phillips, who had staked his reputation on a recording by an unknown singing group and a song whose plaintive notes Elvis heard reverberating over and over again in his mind and in his memory and on the air.

Why didn't everyone else come running to 706 Union Avenue at this point? Why didn't Lee Denson and Johnny Black and Johnny and Dorsey Burnette and the dozens of other aspiring young singers and players in and around the city flock to the doors of the Memphis Recording Service, just up the street from the newspaper and less than a mile away from the teeming downtown area? I don't know. It may have had something to do with the fact that Sun started out as a blues and "race" label, it may simply have been that none of the others was as innocent, or as open, as a young Elvis Presley, who could dream of success beyond the scope of his knowledge or experience. It's a question that I put to nearly every Memphis musician that I interviewed in the course of doing this book, but the closest that I got to an answer was that they simply didn't think of it — they were too caught up in other things, boxing or girls, playing the honky-tonks, some of them made recordings of their own voice in a booth at the five-and-dime for twenty-five cents, they may even have harbored the ambition to get on the radio and become a star, like Slim Rhodes or Eddie Hill — but it never seems to have occurred to any of them that there was even a possibility of making records, at least not here in Memphis. Did it occur to Elvis Presley? Perhaps. Perhaps, like so many things in his life, it was no more than inchoate desire, a vision he could scarcely make out, words that remained unformed. But it was a vision that he pursued.

He showed up at the office of the Memphis Recording Service sometime in mid to late summer 1953, two or three months after graduation. Sun Records, and the Memphis Recording Service, were a two-person operation set in a storefront next to Mrs. Dell Taylor's restaurant and renting for $75 or $80 a month. Venetian blinds made it impossible to see through the plate glass window from the outside, but when you walked in the door into a shallow reception area that had been partitioned off from the studio

directly behind it, you saw a blond woman of thirty-five or thirty-six behind a desk wedged into the far left corner of the room. Marion Keisker
would have been a familiar voice to virtually anyone who listened to
Memphis radio over the past twenty-five years. A native Memphian, she
had made her radio debut on the weekly children's hour *Wynken, Blynken,
and Nod* on WREC in 1929 at the age of twelve and had been appearing on
one show or another ever since. A 1938 graduate of Memphis' Southwestern College, where she had majored in English and medieval French, she
had been the host of the very popular *Meet Kitty Kelly* since 1946, a talk
show on which as the eponymous hostess she interviewed visiting celebrities or simply discoursed on subjects of her own choosing if a guest didn't
happen to be on hand. In addition to *Kitty Kelly,* which was on the air five
days a week, as well as the nightly broadcasts of *Treasury Bandstand* from
the Peabody Skyway, she wrote, produced, and directed as many as fourteen other programs at a time on WREC and was an industrious on- and
off-air personality. It was at WREC, located in basement offices at the
Hotel Peabody, that she first met Sam Phillips.

Phillips, a native of Florence, Alabama, had arrived in town at the age
of twenty-two with four years of broadcast experience under his belt. The
youngest of eight children, he had originally intended to become a crimi-
nal defense lawyer and help the downtrodden, like Clarence Darrow, but
he had been forced to give up that ambition when his father died and he
dropped out of high school in his senior year to help take care of his
mother and deaf-mute aunt. As the captain, occasional drummer, and
sousaphonist of Coffee High's seventy-two-piece marching band, perhaps
it was only natural that he should think about entering into a career involving music, but he saw himself as possessing no appreciable musical
talent and nothing like the personality of his flamboyant older brother
Jud. "I was the greenest persimmon on the tree. If you took a bite of me,
you didn't like me too much." Jud was the guy "with the overwhelming
personality, it was impossible not to like Jud Phillips," but Sam valued
himself for his ability to perceive, and bring out, the best in others; he believed in *communication.* And he believed unwaveringly in the communications possibilities that radio had to offer.

His first job was at Muscle Shoals' WLAY, where Jud managed, and
occasionally sang in, various gospel quartets and where Jake Hess (later to
join the Statesmen) got his start. He moved from there to Decatur, Alabama, then, very briefly, to Nashville's WLAC, finally arriving at WREC

in the summer of 1945 with his wife and infant son. He went to work as an announcer and maintenance and broadcast engineer, supervising the big band broadcasts from "high atop the Hotel Peabody Skyway" every night with Marion Keisker. He was inspired equally by the well-bred elegance and "fanaticism for sound" of station owner Hoyt Wooten, who had started the station in his hometown of Coldwater, Mississippi, in 1920, and Phillips himself cut a handsome, almost matinee idol–like figure, though he remained quiet and reserved, a strict teetotaler who continued to be overshadowed by his more gregarious older brother (Jud was now broadcasting on WREC with the Jolly Boys Quartet).

Much as he loved music, though, and, more important, much as he continued to prize radio as an instrument of communication, Phillips was dissatisfied. He found the big band performances drearily predictable — as lofty as the inspiration for the music might be, the musicians, he felt, were mostly just going through the motions. Phillips, a man of fiercely independent spirit, wanted to do something different — "I was shooting for that damn row that hadn't been plowed." He also had a vision that no one else at WREC, evidently, shared: Sam Phillips possessed an almost Whitmanesque belief not just in the nobility of the American dream but in the nobility of that dream as it filtered down to its most downtrodden citizen, the Negro. "I saw — I don't remember when, but I saw as a child — I thought to myself: suppose that I would have been born *black*. Suppose that I would have been born a little bit more down on the economic ladder. I think I felt from the beginning the total inequity of man's inhumanity to his brother. And it didn't take its place with me of getting up in the pulpit and preaching. It took on the aspect with me that *someday I would act on my feelings, I would show them on an individual, one-to-one basis.*"

That was how he came to open his studio in January 1950, with the idea of providing a service, and an opportunity, for "some of [the] great Negro artists" of the mid South that had simply not been available before. "As word got around," wrote the *Press-Scimitar*'s Bob Johnson in 1955, "Sam's studio became host to strange visitors," and Sam insisted on plumbing that strangeness, no matter how sophisticated a veneer they might present to him at first. He recorded cotton-patch blues and slightly more sophisticated rhythm and blues, leasing the sides to the Chess label in Chicago and RPM Records out on the West Coast and doing everything from recording bar mitzvahs and political speeches to getting the concession for the PA system at the Peabody and at Russwood Park, the baseball stadium on Madison. He ordinarily worked no less than an eighteen-hour day, putting in a full schedule at the station, getting to the studio late in the afternoon, returning to the Peabody in the evening for the Skyway broadcasts, then back to the studio, where he might have left the Howlin' Wolf or "Doctor" Isaiah Ross, the discoverer of a cure for the "Boogie Disease," in the middle of a session. It was not uncommon when he came in to work to be greeted with remarks like "Well, you smell okay. I guess you haven't been hanging around those niggers today." The strain of sustaining this kind of schedule eventually led to a nervous breakdown, and he was hospitalized twice at Gartly-Ramsay Hospital, where he received electroshock therapy. It was, he said, the only time in his life that he was ever scared — twenty-eight years old, with a wife and two little boys, no money, no real prospects, nothing but his own faith in himself, and his vision, to sustain him. He quit the radio station unhesitantly, though, when Hoyt Wooten made a sarcastic remark about his absences. "Mr. Wooten," he said, "you are a cruel man," and, in June 1951, left the employ of WREC forever. He had business cards printed that stated: "We record anything — anywhere — anytime. A complete service to fill every recording need." His partner in this venture from the beginning was Marion Keisker, six years older than Sam, well regarded in Memphis even beyond her radio celebrity, a cultured divorcée with a nine-year-old son, who fell hopelessly in love with Sam.

"He was a beautiful young man. Beautiful beyond belief, but still that country touch, that country rawness. He was slim and had those incredible eyes; despite some of the images that have been given of him, he was very, very particular about his appearance with touches of real elegance, beautifully groomed, terrible about his hair. He would talk about this idea that he had, this dream, I suppose, to have a facility where black people could come and play their own music, a place where they would feel free and relaxed to do it. One day we were riding along, and he saw that spot on Union, and he said, 'That's the spot I want.' With many difficulties we got the place, and we raised the money, and between us we did everything. We laid all the tile, we painted the acoustic boards, I put in the bathroom, Sam put in the control room — what little equipment he had always had to be the best. I knew *nothing* about the music, and I didn't care a bit. My association, my contribution, my participation was based totally on my personal relationship with Sam in a way that is totally unbelievable to me now. All I wanted to do was to make it possible for him to fulfill his vision — all I wanted to do was to do what would make him happy."

By the summer of 1953 the fledgling record label had already had one big hit (Rufus Thomas' "Bear Cat") and was well on its way to two others (both "Feelin' Good" by Little Junior Parker and "Just Walkin' in the Rain" by the Prisonaires made the charts in the fall), but the partnership with Jim Bulleit, which had seemed essential to Sam both for Bulleit's financial investment and his expertise when they were starting up the label just six months earlier, was already falling apart. Sam Phillips was never really one for partnerships anyway ("I'm a competitive bastard. My one big mistake was my inability to delegate authority"), and with Jim Bulleit on the road spending money in a manner that Sam considered profligate and responding to Sam's concerns with telegrams that declared "Cold words on paper cannot fully explain this," Sam was in the midst of trying to extricate himself from the arrangement. He had brought in his brother Jud to go on the road with Bulleit, but Jud and Bulleit didn't get along any better than Sam and Jim, so things were at a frustrating impasse in August 1953.

At least that was how Marion always remembered it when she painfully tried to reconstruct the moment when an eighteen-year-old Elvis Presley, shy, a little woebegone, cradling his battered, beat-up child's guitar, first walked into the recording studio. Marion remembered that there had been an argument — she recalled that she was herself in tears because Sam had spoken harshly to her. Sometimes in her memory of that moment Jud was in the back room arguing with Sam over money, sometimes Sam and Jim Bulleit were at Miss Taylor's restaurant next door ("third booth by the window" was the Sun Records office in the absence of any extra space in the crammed storefront headquarters), sometimes the reception area was jammed with people waiting to make a record, sometimes not — but always the young boy with the long, greasy, dirty-blond hair poked his head in the door shyly, tentatively, looking as if he were ready to withdraw at a moment's notice if you just said boo to him, using that look to gain entrance, determined somehow to make himself known.

Elvis had passed 706 Union often, walking, driving — perhaps he had hesitated once or twice outside the door, simply wanting to make sure of the location. When he finally entered, there is little question that he stepped through the doorway with the idea, if not of stardom — because who could imagine stardom? what could it mean? — at the very least of being discovered. In later years he would always say that he wanted to make a personal record "to surprise my mother." Or "I just wanted to hear what I sounded like." But, of course, if he had simply wanted to record his voice, he could have paid twenty-five cents at W. T. Grant's on Main Street, where Lee Denson had made dozens of records, which he kept at home and played for his friends. Instead, Elvis went to a professional facility, where a man who had been written up in the papers would hear him sing.

It was a Saturday. Elvis was working five days a week at M. B. Parker Machinists' Shop, though he would switch soon to Precision Tool, where he and his cousin Gene would work on a shell assembly line. It was hot, and there was no air-conditioning in the waiting room, but the woman behind the desk looked cool in her cotton dress, her blond hair set in a permanent wave, her face a picture of genteel composure and kind respectability. Marion looked up from her typewriter to see the boy approach her almost sideways, figurative hat in hand. Can I help you? she said. She could barely hear his stammered reply — but, of course, she knew what he was there for, what else could he be there for with his guitar and that desperate look of *need* in his eyes? She told him how much it would cost to make a two-sided acetate — $3.98 plus tax, for another dollar you could have a tape copy as well, but he chose the less expensive option. While he sat there waiting, Marion told Jerry Hopkins in a 1970 interview, "we had a conversation, which I had reason to remember for many, many years afterwards, having gone through it with every editor that I tried to talk to during the time that I was promoting him for Sun.

> He said, "If you know anyone that needs a singer. . . ."
> And I said, "What kind of a singer are you?"
> He said, "I sing all kinds."
> I said, "Who do you sound like?"
> "I don't sound like nobody."
> I thought, Oh yeah, one of those. . . . "What do you sing, hillbilly?"
> "I sing hillbilly."
> "Well, who do you sound like in hillbilly?"
> "I don't sound like nobody."

The truth, Marion discovered, was not that far removed from the boy's improbable self-description. From the first quavering notes of the first song that he sang, it was obvious that there was something different about him, something unique — you could detect his influences, but he *didn't* sound like anyone else. There is a quality of unutterable plaintiveness as Elvis sings "My Happiness," a 1948 pop hit for Jon and Sandra Steele that he had performed over and over in the Courts, a sentimental ballad that couldn't have been further from anyone's imagining of rock 'n' roll, past or present, without a hint of foreshadowing or any black influence other than the clear tenor of Bill Kenny of the Ink Spots — it is just a pure, yearning, almost desperately pleading solo voice reaching for effect, a crying note alternating with a crooning fullness of tone that in turn yields to a sharp nasality betraying its possessor's intentions. The guitar, Elvis said, "sounded like somebody beating on a bucket lid," and the record represents almost exactly what the boys and girls in the Courts must have heard over the last several years, with an added factor of nervousness that Elvis must surely have felt. But even that is not particularly detectable — there is a strange sense of calm, an almost unsettling stillness in the midst of great drama, the kind of poise that comes as both a surprise and a revelation. When he finished the one song, he embarked upon "That's When Your Heartaches Begin," a smooth pop ballad that the Ink Spots had originally cut in 1941, with a deep spoken part for their baritone singer, Hoppy Jones. Here he was not so successful in his rendition, running out of time, or inspiration, and simply declaring "That's the end" at the conclusion of the song. The boy looked up expectantly at the man in the control booth. Mr. Phillips nodded and said politely that he was an "interesting" singer. "We might give you a call sometime." He even had Miss Keisker make a note of the boy's name, which she misspelled and then editorialized beside it: "Good ballad singer. Hold."

When it was all over, he sat in the outer lobby while Miss Keisker typed out the label copy on the blank sides of a Prisonaires label ("Softly and Tenderly," Sun 189). The singer's name was typed underneath the title on each side. Mr. Phillips never came out front, though the boy hung around for a while talking with the woman. He was disappointed that he didn't have a chance to say good-bye. But he walked out of the studio with his acetate and with the conviction that something was going to happen.

Nothing did. Nothing happened for the longest time. All through the fall he would stop by the studio, park the old Lincoln precisely by the curb, turn his collar up, pat down his hair, and manfully stride in the door. Miss Keisker was always very nice, Miss Keisker never failed to recognize him. He would try to make small talk, he would ask if, possibly, she had run into a band that was looking for a singer — he conveyed an impression of longing, of neediness, that always stayed with her. Sometimes Mr. Phillips might be present, but he didn't have time for small talk, he was always busy, he was *making records*. That was what Elvis wanted to do — that was what he wanted to do more than anything else in the world, but he didn't know how to go about it, other than to put himself in the way of it at the only place he knew to do so. Each time he entered the waiting room it was with a somewhat heavier step and somewhat lowered expectations, but he forced himself, he didn't know anything else to do. Gradually he began to doubt that anything would ever happen, and his visits became less frequent. He tried to appear indifferent, but his need showed through. In January 1954 he went in again and cut another little record — Joni James' "I'll Never Stand in Your Way" and an old Jimmy Wakely tune, "It Wouldn't Be the Same Without You," but his lack of confidence betrayed him, and he sounds more abrupt, more insecure, this time than he did the first. He was at an impasse — unlike the hero in comic books and fairy tales, he had not yet been discovered in his true guise, underneath his outer rags. And yet, Marion felt, almost maternally, he was a child who was clearly marked for success of some kind. "He was," she said, "so ingenuous there was no way he could go wrong."

WITH DIXIE LOCKE, SOUTH SIDE JUNIOR PROM, 1955. (MICHAEL OCHS ARCHIVES)

"WITHOUT YOU"

IN JANUARY 1954 he started attending church regularly for the first time since the family had left Tupelo. Vernon and Gladys occasionally went to a service at one of the nearby churches or missions, but for the most part they were content to remain at home, secure in their belief if not in their observance. Vernon was out of work more and more with a bad back; at forty-two — though she admitted to only thirty-eight — Gladys had put on a considerable amount of weight, and Elvis told employers and fellow workers alike that all he wanted to do was to make enough money to buy his mama and daddy a house. For her part, Gladys simply wanted to see her son married, she wanted grandkids, she wanted to know he was happy and settled before she died.

She was pleased, then, when he started going to the Assembly of God Church at 1084 McLemore in South Memphis. The Assembly of God in Memphis had started out in a tent and later moved to a storefront location on South Third and finally into a church on McLemore in 1948. In 1954 Pastor James Hamill, a well-educated, fire-and-brimstone preacher who denounced movies and dancing from the pulpit and encouraged ecstatic demonstrations of faith (such as speaking in tongues) in his church, had been minister for ten years. Over that time membership had grown to close to two thousand, three buses were dispatched each Sunday to pick up congregants without automobiles (one of the stops was at Winchester and Third, just outside the Presleys' door), and since 1950 the famous Blackwood Brothers Quartet and their families had been prominent members of the congregation. When they were in town, the Blackwoods performed frequently at a church service that was renowned for its music (the hundred-voice church choir was well known throughout Memphis), and only recently Cecil Blackwood, a newly married resident of Lauderdale Courts and a nephew of founding member and leader James Blackwood, had started a kind of junior quartet, the Songfellows, with Pastor Hamill's son, Jimmy, a student at Memphis State. They were also members of the Bible study class that met each Sunday at 9:30 A.M. as broader members of a Young Men's Christian group called the Christ Ambassadors.

That was where Dixie Locke first saw Elvis Presley. She had not seen him before, though she and her family were faithful members of the church since its days on South Third, not far from where they lived. Dixie was fifteen and a sophomore at South Side High. Her father worked for Railway Express, and she and her three sisters shared a single bedroom, while her parents slept in the living room. If her father went to bed at 8:00 because he had to go to work early, that was when everyone went to bed.

She had a boyfriend at the time, but it wasn't anything really special. She was bright, attractive, and with two older sisters — one of whom had eloped at fourteen and was now back home — was alert to a world whose existence she could barely have glimpsed. In the half hour before the boys and girls split off into their respective classes, she noticed the new boy, dressed so oddly in pink and black, with his long greasy hair and fidgety manner, as he sought so desperately to become a part of the group. The other kids all laughed at him a little, they made fun of him, but strictly for his appearance — he appeared to be serious about his Bible studies. The other girls thought he was *peculiar:* "He was just so different, all the other guys were like replicas of their dads." And yet to Dixie he was different in another way. "To watch him you would think, even then, he was really shy. What was so strange was that he would do anything to call attention to himself, but I really think he was doing it to prove something to himself more than to the people around him. Inside, even then, I think he knew that he was different. I knew the first time I met him that he was not like other people."

Dixie and her girlfriends went out nearly every weekend to the Rainbow Rollerdrome, east on Lamar (Highway 78 to Tupelo), just beyond the city limits. They rode the bus in their skating skirts; Dixie had one of black corduroy with white satin lining, and she wore white tights underneath. The Rainbow was a big teenage hangout, with a snack bar and a jukebox, an organist who played the "Grand March" for the skaters, and a swimming pool next door. There were dance contests on the floor and generally, on a weekend night, up to six or seven hundred kids, who could gather without any fear of trouble or any concern that they might be getting in with a bad crowd. One Sunday at church, at the end of January, Dixie started talking with some girlfriends about her plans for the upcoming weekend. She spoke loudly enough so that the boys in the groups next to them might overhear, and particularly so that the new boy, who was pretending not to be paying any attention, would know. She wasn't sure that he would come, she thought it almost brazen of herself to be doing this, but she wanted very badly to see him. When she arrived at the rink on Saturday night with her girlfriends, she noticed with a little start that he was there, but she ignored him, pretending to herself that she hadn't seen him until one of her friends said, "Did you know that boy, Elvis Presley, was here?" She said, "Yeah, I saw him," kind of casually, and then watched for a while to see what he was going to do. He was standing by the rail with his skates on, wearing a kind of bolero outfit, short black bullfighter's jacket, ruffled shirt, black pegged pants with a pale pink stripe down the legs. He was leaning up against the rail all by himself, trying to look detached, nonchalantly surveying the floor aswirl with activity, and after a while Dixie realized *he couldn't skate.* She took pity on him at last, went up and introduced herself. He said, "Yeah, I know," and hung his head down, then tossed back his hair. Finally he asked Dixie if she wanted to go get a Coke, "and I said yes, and we went to the snack area, and I don't think we ever went back out to the skating floor the whole night." They talked and talked and talked; it was almost as if he had been waiting to unburden himself all his life. He talked about how he wanted to join the Songfellows, how he had spoken with Cecil and Jimmy Hamill about it and maybe they were going to give him a try-out. It was as if "he had a plan, he knew that he had a talent, there was something for his life that he was supposed to do. It was like from that moment on there was nobody else there."

The first session was over at 10:00 P.M., and Dixie was supposed to go home with her friends, but she told them to leave without her. Elvis asked if she could stay for the second session, and while he was standing there, she pretended to call her mother from the pay phone, but she dialed a number at random (she wouldn't have wanted to admit that she didn't have a phone but had to call her uncle and aunt next door anyway) and gabbled on at length about the nice boy from church that she happened to have run into and how they were going to stay for the second session but she would be home right after midnight. She had never done anything like this before, but she didn't think twice about it. In the end they didn't even stay. After she made the call, he suggested that they go to a drive-in; why didn't they go to K's on Crump Boulevard, where they could get a hamburger and a milk shake? They kept talking as they finally unlaced their skates. He opened the door of the Lincoln for her and was careful to explain that it wasn't his (he wanted to see if she would still go out with him, he explained afterward, if he didn't have a car), and they drove west into town on Lamar until it ran into Crump, talking the whole way.

She sat close to him on the front seat, closer than you ever would on a normal first date, and at K's she kissed him sitting in the parking lot. It was a chaste kiss, a loving kiss — Dixie wasn't planning to keep this a secret for long, even from her mother. She was so swept up in it, he was, too, it was like nothing that had ever happened to either one of them before. When he dropped her off at her door, he whispered that he would call her next week, Wednesday or Thursday probably, about going out on the weekend — there was never any question that they would see each other again, and again. She tiptoed in the door, knowing she was late, even for the late session — she was bound to wake up her parents, her father was going to kill her, but she didn't care, not really, she was truly in love.

H E CALLED THE NEXT DAY. Her aunt called over to her from next door, just as the family was sitting down to a Sunday dinner of fried chicken. When she hadn't seen him at church that morning, her heart sank a little, but she never doubted that she would hear from him. And now he couldn't even wait a day.

They went out that night to the movies, and then again on Wednesday night. She still hadn't let him meet her parents, inventing one excuse or another, for him and for them, but then on Saturday, just a week from the night they had truly met, he came to pick her up at the house and she brought him inside to meet her family, as much because he wanted to as because she knew she had to. She had tried to prepare everyone, but she found when she met him at the door that she was scarcely prepared herself: she had forgotten how *different* he looked, she had forgotten about his hair and his dress, she hadn't thought about the effect it might have on others. At night in bed she had whispered to her sisters about him, and she had confided to her diary that she had at last found her one true love. She had even told her mother what she had done when she called from the skating rink, but she had emphasized that he came from a good family (which she didn't really know — he acted like she was some kind of royalty because she was from South Memphis, though they were as poor as

Job's turkey) and that she had met him in *church*. Now as her father addressed him gravely, and Elvis mumbled his replies, tossing his head back whenever he said, "Yes, sir," and "No, sir," and presenting the gravest, most respectful mien, she wasn't so sure, she knew that she loved him, but she saw him for the first time as her father must see him. There was no way of telling what her father was thinking, he never gave any clue — he gave his full attention without ever saying much of anything. All the boys she and her sisters had ever brought to the house were scared of Mr. Locke, big (six foot two), impassive, but if he ever made up his mind about something he didn't hesitate to let you, or anyone else, know about it, and you just did it, regardless. Her mother was calling her — she didn't want to leave Elvis alone with her father, but she felt she had no choice. In the kitchen, "my mother read me the riot act: 'How can you go out with a boy like that?' — that kind of thing. I was saying, 'Mother, you can't go by the way . . . Just because his hair is long, or he's not dressed like everybody else. . . .' I was really defending him, telling her what a nice boy he was — I had met him at church, after all. And meanwhile I was afraid they would say something that would hurt his feelings and he would just leave."

Eventually they escaped — her sister met him briefly, she was perfectly nice to him to his face, but behind his back she raised her eyebrows so Dixie could see what she really thought. The next day her uncle offered Dixie $2 for the boy if he would just get a haircut. It didn't matter, none of it mattered; that night he gave her his ring, that meant they were going steady, neither of them would see anybody else — ever.

Two weeks later she met his parents. It was a weekday night, cool for February, when he picked her up and drove her back to Alabama Street. She was amazed to discover that even though neither parent was working (Mr. Presley was out of work at the moment with a bad back, and Mrs. Presley's employment at St. Joseph's had evidently stopped) and Elvis' salary at Precision could scarcely have amounted to more than $50 a week, they had a piano, a piano *and* a television set, and he was calling *her* "high class"! She wanted so badly to like his mother, but Mrs. Presley seemed suspicious at first, she seemed nervous and apprehensive, she had a hundred questions for Dixie — where her father worked, how big a family she came from, where she and Elvis had met, how long they had been going out, what school she attended. Mr. Presley was polite, attentive, but he had nothing much to say, "it was almost like he was an outsider, not part of the group." Eventually Mrs. Presley shooed Elvis and his dad to one side to pursue the questioning on her own. Elvis was pacing back and forth, he would come in and out of the room and touch her on the shoulder, as if to say it was all right, then disappear again. He was clearly beside himself, just waiting to get out of there, but it went on and on. And after an hour or two a number of relatives came over — his cousin Gene, whom she had already met, a bunch of other cousins (it seemed like his only friends were his family), and they all sat around and played Monopoly. She was embarrassed and self-conscious, and aware that Elvis would be mad at her if she acted all "prim and proper," if she wasn't just herself. Finally they were able to leave: "He was so relieved, I think he couldn't wait to take me home, so he could come back and say, 'What do you think?' to his mom. You know, they had such a strong love and respect for each other, she was just totally devoted to him, it was like this mutual admiration. A day or two later, I said something like 'I wonder what your mother thinks . . .' or 'I hope . . . ,' something like that, and he said, 'Oh, you don't have to worry about that, she thinks you're neat.' I knew I had her stamp of approval then."

They went out almost every night, even weeknights. If they didn't, they spoke on the phone, long heartfelt conversations, until her uncle and aunt got mad about her monopolizing the line. At one point her dad put a halt to their seeing each other for a few days, but her family soon came "to love him almost as much as I did. They saw that I was serious, and he was always so polite, and they knew it was a very honest relationship, they trusted us together as far as our conduct was concerned. Within a very short time he was just part of the family."

Mrs. Presley, to Dixie, was almost like a second mother, and the Presley house on Alabama became like a second home to her. Some days Mr. Presley would come and pick her up at her house on Lucy after school so she could meet Elvis the moment he got home from work. Sometimes, if Mr. Presley didn't feel like driving, she would ride the bus. "Which was very unusual for those days — that was another one of those things that my mom and dad were not at all in favor of — but I didn't think there was anything wrong with it for me." Not infrequently she visited Mrs. Presley on her own — one time they went to a Stanley Products party together, often they just sat and talked. There was one subject they had in common about which each had an inexhaustible curiosity, but they shared a number of other interests as well. Mrs. Presley showed Dixie her recipes, and occasionally they would go shopping together, maybe even pick out a surprise for Elvis. Dixie found Mrs. Presley to be one of the warmest, most wonderful, and genuine people she had ever met. "In no time we were just great friends. We could call and talk to each other and enjoy each other — whether Elvis was there or not. We could just laugh and have a good time together." But even at fifteen Dixie soon realized that the Presleys were different from her own family in at least two significant respects. One was the role that Vernon played. Perhaps because it was in such sharp contrast to her own father's role and behavior ("I had seen my dad go to work with a brace on his back for years, and he had a very physically demanding job"), his passivity struck her particularly forcefully. "I never saw him be unkind. I never saw him drink or be unruly, I'm sure he was a very loving husband and devoted to his family, and it probably had to do with his self-esteem — but it was like he was an outsider, really, he wasn't really part of Elvis and Mrs. Presley's group. I mean, it sounds weird, but they had such a strong love and respect for each other, and I don't think there was a lot of respect for him during that time. It was almost like Elvis was the father and his dad was just the little boy."

The other striking difference was their view of the outside world. The Lockes regarded the world at large comfortably, as a friendly, for the most part unthreatening sort of place. Coming from a big family herself, having an even larger extended family through the church and all the church activities in which she took part, Dixie was accustomed to a large circle of acquaintances, a constant whirl of social activity, and an open-door policy at home, where friends and family were likely to drop in without notice (they had to — there was no telephone!). The Presleys, by contrast, she felt, regarded the world with suspicion. They had few close friends outside of family; apart from his cousins, Dixie never met any of Elvis' friends. In fact "he just came into our crowd completely, there was nobody he went to school with, nobody from the neighborhood that he palled around with at that point particularly.

"Mrs. Presley was a very humble person, and it was almost like she felt inferior around people where she didn't feel like she quite fit in — maybe she didn't have the right hairdo or the right dress to wear. She had a couple of lady friends from Lauderdale Courts, and one of them had a daughter who really thought Elvis was for her. One night we were all sitting on the porch, and this girl came over — as I remember it she was a very attractive girl — and when she came in, it was as if she belonged there, it was like she was so comfortable with being in the house and being with Elvis that she made me feel uncomfortable. So I just set back and was just kind of reserved and quiet, and Mrs. Presley said, 'Let's have a glass of iced tea' or something. Normally I just would have gotten up and gotten it, but before I could say anything, the other girl said, 'Oh, I'll go fix it.' When she left, I'll never forget, Mrs. Presley got onto me good. She said, 'I could just pinch you. Why did you just set there and let her take over?' She said, 'Don't you ever do that again. You know you're just as at home here as Elvis is. You get up and do something next time, just like you would if you were in your own home.'

"She and I were just so close, sometimes Elvis would talk to me and say things that normally he would reserve for his mother, little pet names and gestures, put his face almost in your face and talk like they talked, how sweet you looked today, that kind of thing, just the way he always talked with his mother. And I would think, 'Oh, don't do that in front of her.' 'Cause that was just for her.''

They saw each other all the time. When the weather turned warm, they sat out on the front porch, either at Dixie's house or on the long brick-pillared porch on Alabama — they would sit on the swing and Elvis would sing to her sometimes: ''Tomorrow Night,'' ''My Happiness,'' sweet, tender little ballads. He was slightly inhibited and didn't sing very loud if he thought her family was around. Often they would walk down to the corner and get a purple cow or a milk shake at the Dairy Queen, then go and sit on a bench in Gaston Park, just a few blocks from Dixie's house. A big date was going to the movies at the Suzore No. 2 on North Main, fifty cents' worth of gas, fifty cents for the movies, and a dollar for something to eat at K's or Leonard's afterward. They loved each other, they were committed to remaining ''pure'' until marriage, they shared everything with each other, there were no secrets. One time there was a crisis at work; Elvis was told if he didn't get a haircut he would be fired. He was so embarrassed by the haircut he got that he didn't want anyone to see him, and it didn't help when Dixie's uncle, who had been telling him to get a haircut all along, kidded him about it. He was so sensitive — Dixie had never met anyone as sensitive as him. One time early in their relationship he got upset with her at a drive-in, about something that she had said in front of his cousin, and he got out of the car and was going to hitchhike home. Another time he got into a fight with his mother and was going to leave — forever. He came over to Dixie's house to say good-bye.

They cried in each other's arms; then she watched him drive off, and promptly drive back again, as she stood on her front porch. They couldn't be separated — ever. They talked about marriage, but they were going to wait. When they got married they wanted their families to share in it.

T HEY WENT TO CHURCH together, though not as often as Dixie would have liked. Elvis was good about attending his Bible class, but he didn't always go to the service and sometimes he would just pick her up afterward. Sometimes when they did attend, they would arrive with a group of young people just before the service and sit in the back, making sure that parents and elders knew they were present. Then when the service was well under way and all eyes were on Reverend Hamill, they would sneak out the door and drive down to the colored church at East Trigg, less than a mile away, where the Reverend Brewster delivered his stirring sermons and Queen C. Anderson and the Brewsteraires were the featured soloists. They reveled in the exotic atmosphere, the music was out of this world — but they could only stay a few minutes, they had to get back to First Assembly before they were missed. Sometimes at night they would come back for the WHBQ broadcast of *Camp Meeting of the Air*. Often James Blackwood would be present, and Pastor Hamill's son, Jimmy, and the other Songfellows frequently attended; there was in fact a whole contingent of whites who came to be uplifted by the music and by Dr. Brewster's eloquence and probity of character. Dr. Brewster constantly preached on the theme that a better day was coming, one in which all men could walk as brothers, while across Memphis Sam Phillips listened on his radio every Sunday without fail, and future Sun producer Jack Clement often attended with his father, a Baptist deacon and choir director, "because it was a happening place, it was heartfelt, that's what was happening in Memphis."

They went to the movies — double features — at least twice a week. A couple of times Elvis took Dixie to Humes. Once he sang a song on the talent show in which he told her he had performed the previous year. He paraded proudly in front of his old schoolmates, put his arm around her, talked with some of the guys that he knew from the Courts, while all the while turning her hand over in his — he didn't so much want to introduce her into his world as show her off to it. It was a little bit the same when they visited Tupelo. Once they went with Mr. and Mrs. Presley and visited relatives; another time they went down with Elvis' aunt Clettes and uncle Vester, and once again Elvis showed every respect to his uncles and aunts and cousins down there, but it was definitely a "look at me" kind of thing. He was proud of himself, proud of his clothes, proud of his girl, proud of what he had learned in the city — and why not? In Dixie's view he had every reason to feel that way about himself.

Mostly, though, they stayed close to home, didn't do anything that exotic — it was almost like playing house. Sometimes they would baby-sit for Dixie's cousins and just sit there and watch TV. Sometimes Mr. and Mrs. Presley would go out, leaving them the house to themselves. Much of the time they stayed in the same North Memphis neighborhood where the Presleys had lived for the past five and a half years. The Suzore No. 2 was just around the corner and was cheaper than any of the movie palaces uptown — even if you did run the risk of finding rats underfoot when the lights came up. Charlie's Record Shop moved across the street that spring; the bus stopped right in front of it, and sometimes Dixie met Elvis there. Evidently the proprietor and his wife, Helen, had known Elvis for some time, because after a few visits he introduced her to them, and after that they always greeted her in a friendly way, even if Elvis hadn't arrived yet. There was a jukebox playing all the time and a little soda fountain where you could get a Coke or a NuGrape soda — and then there were the hundreds of 78s, not just the latest hits but r&b hits from years before, too. There were two or three listening booths, and if it wasn't crowded you could hang around for hours sometimes just listening to the music. That was where Elvis first played her the original of one of the songs he sang all the time, Lonnie Johnson's "Tomorrow Night." It was good, but it wasn't as good as Elvis'. That was where she first heard the original versions of a lot of the songs that he sang, and sometimes if he wanted to try a new one he would ask her for the words, because she always had a good memory for music.

He seemed to know quite a few of the kids who hung out there, but he never introduced her. He told her about a record *he* had made a few months before at some little record company out on Union, but he never played it for her, and he never told her that Charlie had put it on the jukebox for a while right in the store, with his name written out in script on the jukebox selection list. Once in a very rare while one or the other of them would actually buy a record — they both had record players at home, and Elvis had a small, treasured collection. Sometimes he would bring some of his favorite records over to her house, and they would just sit there and listen.

More and more she realized how much he loved music. As spring turned to summer, he would sing to her for hours sometimes, free of the self-consciousness that had plagued him initially, particularly around her family. She didn't know whether he was singing to her or just singing for the sake of singing, but his face took on a luminous quality, there was a special expression that he had when he was momentarily at rest. At the Presleys' he was always fooling around on the piano, picking out a tune that they might have heard on the radio — he could play anything after hearing it once or twice, nothing fancy, simply sticking to the melody. Sometimes he would sit at the piano and just sing hymns. Occasionally Gladys might join in, though never Vernon, and Dixie was very self-conscious about her own voice, but they would all gather around the piano in a tight little group, participating if only by their presence and by their approval. "We shared everything, we talked about *everything* — he would talk to me about things that I'm confident he never would have revealed to anyone else. But nothing was ever said about what he wanted to do. Maybe he had deep ambitions that we didn't talk about, because in his mind it was so completely alien, but he wasn't trying to be a musician at night or anything like that. I just thought he was a guy who played the guitar and loved music."

He did talk to her about his ambition to join the Songfellows, but that was just a little amateur quartet out of church. At some point that spring he confessed to her that he had auditioned for the group and been turned down — he was deeply disappointed, and even though he told Dixie that the reason they hadn't taken him was that the guy they thought was going to leave had decided to stay, it seemed obvious that he didn't believe it. "They told me I couldn't sing," he told his father. Jimmy Hamill, the minister's son, said, "Elvis, why don't you give it up?" He was hurt, Dixie said, "but it was like, 'Well, that didn't work out, let's go on to the rest of it.' "

Without fail they attended the monthly All-Night Singings at Ellis that the Blackwood Brothers sponsored. They had each gone on their own before they ever met and happily discovered that this was yet another thing they had in common. They loved the Speer Family and the Le-Fevres out of Atlanta, Wally Fowler never failed to shake the audience up with "Gospel Boogie," and they thrilled to the Sunshine Boys, featuring the zoom bass of J. D. Sumner, formerly of the Stamps' Sunny South Quartet. The Statesmen and the Blackwoods both had RCA Victor contracts, and in the spring of 1954 the Blackwood Brothers went up to New York and won the *Arthur Godfrey's Talent Scouts* contest, which it seemed everyone in Memphis must have watched. Elvis and Dixie never went backstage at Ellis — they would never have dared, and they had no reason to — but during the intermissions they joined the other fans who clustered around the tables that each group set up to sell their records and songbooks and hung on their every word. They knew James Blackwood, of course; they saw him at church all the time and had great respect for the dignified appearance and professionalism of the group, with their dark suits, precise diction, and carefully worked out harmonies. But it was the Statesmen who remained their favorites — listen to Jake, Elvis would say to Dixie as he hit yet another thrilling high note with that controlled vibrato and the crowd went wild and called for him to do it again. As for Big Chief, he went about as far as you could go, it seemed: the crowd just loved him, they were with him from the moment he first walked out onstage, and when he started in to shaking his leg and dancing around, they just about tore the rafters off. Pastor Hamill wouldn't approve, he didn't think much of quartet singing in any form, despite his son's participation and the celebrity the Blackwood Brothers lent his church. Good Christian people didn't seek out that sort of adulation, good Christian people didn't need to shake their leg and dance the hootchy-koo up onstage, good Christian people were saved by faith, not stardom — but Elvis and Dixie didn't care. "We were just so impressed with them, we practically worshiped Jake Hess, we were like groupies, I guess, the quartets were like part of our family."

They would even go down to WMPS sometimes just to catch the noontime broadcasts that Bob Neal hosted. Dixie had never been to a radio station before, but Elvis was right at home, finding them a seat in the front row, nodding curtly at James Blackwood while looking away from him as if it was accidental — there was never any more contact than that. Elvis couldn't be still, he was fidgeting constantly, drumming his fingers on the side of the chair, his leg going all the time. It drove Dixie's mother crazy, she'd ask her if there was something the matter with him, even bring it to Elvis' attention, and Dixie would defend him without fail, but it embarrassed her, too. She wondered if there *was* something the matter; she supposed he would grow out of it, she just wished he

JANUARY–JULY 1954 ∿ 79

wouldn't do it in public. They enjoyed the broadcasts. Sometimes while Bob was doing the commercials James or one of the other Blackwoods would sneak up behind him and comb his hair down over his eyes and the audience would bust out laughing.

Starting in April they began to go out to Riverside Park every week, two or three times a week, whenever it was warm enough. Sometimes on the weekends they would eat fried chicken on the bluff; McKellar Lake was full of boaters and water-skiers and young couples just having a good time. More often than not, they would double-date with Elvis' cousin Gene, who was going out off and on with Dixie's sister Juanita. Elvis and Gene were goofy together — they acted as if they had some kind of joke going on between them all the time, speaking in a kind of private language that no one else could understand, laughing at things that weren't funny to anyone else. It made Dixie momentarily uncomfortable, as if somehow she were being excluded, as if — despite all the intimacies that they had shared and the ease with which she could have embarrassed *him* (she thought that Elvis must be the most easily embarrassed boy she had ever met) — as if she were somehow the outsider. But then she remembered the innate sweetness of his nature, the dreams and confidences they shared: "He was not a phony, he was not a put-on, he was not a show-off, and once you were around him long enough to see him be himself, not just act the clown, anyone could see his real self, you could see his sweetness, you could see the humility, you could see the desire to please." It was just that he and Gene acted funny together sometimes.

So many nights they ended up at the park, with or without Gene, in a group or by themselves, but whether they came alone or with others it seemed like they always connected with their crowd. They hung out at the pavilion area overlooking the lake, where you could get a Coke or listen to the jukebox and dance at Rocky's Lakeside refreshment stand, a screened-in area especially for teens. Usually there would be at least ten or twelve couples in the parking lot, and, without too much coaxing, Elvis could always be induced to get his guitar out of the backseat and, leaning up against the car, start to play. "He wasn't shy, he just had to be asked — I think he just didn't want to impose. No one else ever did it, no one else had the nerve. He sang songs that were popular and a lot of the old blues-type songs; he did some of the old spirituals, too. You know, it was funny. Right from the start it was as if he had a power over people, it was like they were transformed. It wasn't that he demanded anybody's attention, but they certainly reacted that way — it didn't matter how rough they were or whether they even acted like they were going to be interested or not, they *were,* once he started singing. Like when Pastor Hamill walked up in the pulpit he commanded everyone's attention, it was the same thing with Elvis, it was always that way." Sometimes he would command their attention with a beautiful love song, then change the lyrics to parody the song, but he always kept their attention. "People were just mesmerized, and he loved being the center of attention. I think he could have sung to everybody in the entire city of Memphis and not cared at all."

Sometimes they would just park in the lot overlooking the lake and listen to the radio, looking down at the water. They listened to Dewey Phillips playing the rhythm and blues hits on *Red Hot and Blue,* never country music. They got a big kick out of Dewey's Dizzy Dean impressions, his constant pitch to his audience to go out and buy a "fur-lined mousetrap," and his ads for locally brewed Falstaff beer ("If you can't drink it, freeze it and eat it. If you can't do that, open up a cotton-picking rib and POUR it in"). "Call Sam!" Dewey repeated at frequent intervals, almost as punctuation for his show — but, for his part, Elvis never spoke to Dixie about Sam; she had practically forgotten about the record that he said he had made, and as far as she was concerned they could just keep coming out to Riverside Park forever, Elvis would go on singing to her and their friends, they would get married someday, and life would go on, just as it was meant to be. Every so often a police car would pass by, sweeping the parking lot with the big beam of its spotlight, making sure no boy was taking unwanted advantage, no girl was going to get in trouble. But there was nothing like that to worry about here. You had two level-headed teenagers listening to Dewey Phillips on the radio who knew when it was time to go home.

Toward the end of April, Elvis got a new job. He hadn't been happy with the old one since they made him get a haircut, and the new one on Poplar was just around the corner from the Courts. It involved working for an electrical contractor, Crown Electric, and he was going to be driving a truck, bringing supplies out to the industrial building sites. If he wanted he would have a chance to train as an electrician; it was a long apprenticeship and required going to night school, but the opportunity was there. The owners, Mr. and Mrs. Tipler, seemed very nice — they were warm and considerate and seemed to accept their new employee for who he was.

In fact, Gladys Tipler had been warned by the lady at the employment office that she might find the new applicant's appearance a bit off-putting. But, the woman said, he was a good boy, despite his appearance, and the Tiplers were won over by his polite manner and by his clear devotion to his mother. He just wanted to help her, he told them at his job interview on a Monday, and they hired him on the spot, never regretting the decision, although Mrs. Tipler was bemused that he spent so much time on his hair when he arrived in the morning and every time he came back in from a run. She finally sent him to her hairdresser, Blake Johnson, of Blake's Coiffures at Poplar and Lauderdale, but he would go only after closing time because he was embarrassed. Once in a while at work he might see Paul Burlison, who was well on his way to becoming a master electrician and whom he knew from playing around the Courts and from playing with Dorsey Burnette, yet another employee of Crown. Paul and Dorsey told him about some of the places they played out near the naval base in Millington, and Dorsey told him about one night he had played at Shadow Lawn in Oakland with Johnny Black's brother Bill, and a guitarist named Scotty Moore, from Gadsden, Tennessee, who had only recently gotten out of the navy himself and was now living in Memphis. There had been a big brawl that night, and Dorsey had gotten stabbed in the tailbone. He and his father and his brother, Johnny, had gone out looking for the guys who had done it, but they never found them. Dorsey and Paul invited Elvis to come out and play with them some night if he felt like it, but he told them he didn't think so, he was kind of tied up with other things right now, he might be playing out at the Home for Incurables again, and he had a little thing coming up at the Girls' Club over on Alabama — his voice trailed off in a mumble.

His paycheck came to forty dollars a week, and every Friday he came home and presented it to his father. It was, Dixie noted with some amazement, almost as if it were Elvis' responsibility to take care of his dad. "He just took out enough to last us for the week, fifty cents for gas, a dollar-fifty to get us into the Suzore three times maybe, a little bit extra for food, the rest was for his mom and dad." There was no reluctance about it whatsoever, it was just the way things were; his parents were getting older, he told Dixie, and he wanted to take care of them. And they were just so proud of him, too — Mrs. Presley bragged on him every chance she got, and it seemed like he was equally proud of the strides he had made, for himself and his family. One time he came to pick Dixie up at her house after work, and they must have been doing a dirty job, because he was a mess, wearing greasy overalls with a hole in them. Dixie's mother wanted to take a picture of them both, but he hid behind a clothesline so you couldn't see the clothes he had on.

One Saturday in mid May Elvis floored Dixie. He had run into a mutual friend, Ronnie Smith, at the Cotton Carnival. Dixie knew Ronald from the neighborhood and from South Side High, but Elvis had met him at a birthday party and discovered a mutual passion for music, as well as for cars and girls. With Ronnie he had played a couple of little gigs (the highlight was a Lodge banquet at the Columbia Mutual Towers on Main), but at sixteen Ronald was also a member of a full-fledged professional band led by Eddie Bond, and, he said, Eddie was looking for a singer. Why didn't Elvis stop by? He had a tryout that night, Elvis told Dixie excitedly, at a club called the Hi-Hat on South Third, not far from her house. He wondered if she would go with him — he *needed* her to go with him, they would just stay a little while, then they could go to a movie or McKellar Lake or something.

Dixie didn't know what to say; of course she would go, but it was so completely out of the blue. If he had asked her to come see him sing with a professional quartet, now that would have been a shock, but at least it would have been in line with something she might have anticipated, something in keeping with what she and he both saw as a kind of *spiritual* gift. And what if someone saw them, what if one of her parents' friends saw her going into the club or there was a Railway Express co-worker of her father's sitting inside? It didn't stop her, of course. Nor did she ever question Elvis' judgment. "He was just so nervous, I was nervous, too. When we got there, there weren't a lot of people, but there was a dance floor and there were drinks being served, because the man said something to us when we came in about our being too young to even be in there. I had a Coke. We sat at a table and drank Cokes."

The featured performer, Eddie Bond, was a seasoned veteran of twenty-one who had been playing around town since he was fifteen and had just gotten out of the navy. A confident entertainer and self-styled entrepreneur who twenty years later would run for sheriff of Memphis (in 1969 he composed "The Ballad of Buford Pusser," around which the popular movie *Walking Tall* was constructed), Bond came over to the table to say hello. He asked Elvis what he did for a living, and Elvis said he drove a truck for Crown Electric, but Dixie was embarrassed for him because he couldn't stop drumming his fingers on the table. He had gotten a haircut especially for this performance, and he was wearing his bullfighter's outfit with a pink shirt. In no time it was his turn to go onstage. He did two songs by himself, just strumming his guitar and singing; Dixie thought he was wonderful, but before she knew it, it was over. "It was almost like ohh-let's-hurry-and-get-out-of-here, glad-it-was-over type of thing." Before leaving he conferred briefly with Eddie Bond, but Dixie was at a distance and he never told her what was said. In later years Bond would boast jocularly that he was "the only person who ever fired [Elvis Presley] from the bandstand" and explain that it was the club owners who forced him to turn down the fledgling performer. Ronnie Smith was under the impression that Eddie wanted to book him into another, rougher joint across the street so that Eddie could have two bands working at the same time. Elvis for his part took it as a bitter rejection. Bond told him, he confided to his friend George Klein in 1957, that he had better stick with driving a truck " 'because you're never going to make it as a singer.' We were on a train going to Hollywood to make *Jailhouse Rock,* and Elvis said, 'I wonder what Eddie Bond thinks now. Man, that sonofabitch broke my heart.' "

The days went by. More and more, Dixie said, there was talk of marriage. "We came very close one day to getting in the car and driving to Hernando, Mississippi — *anyone* could get married in Hernando. We talked about it several times very seriously, about what we would do after we got married and where we would live. We were seriously talking about it, but I don't know how, one of us always had the good sense to say, 'But what if — ?' I was still in school, and it would have just broken my mom and dad's heart." Dixie was going to start her summer job at Goldsmith's in the cosmetics department soon, but before she did, she and her family were going away on vacation, to visit relatives in Florida for the first two weeks of July. She was worried about that — it would be their first separation, and Elvis got so jealous, he hated for her just to be with other people, let alone other boys. Dixie enjoyed being with people, "but he couldn't stand it if I was doing something that didn't involve him, he was kind of possessive in that respect." Sometimes Dixie thought the whole family was just too wrapped up in themselves, or maybe it was just in their dreams for Elvis; it was so hard to get inside that tight little circle. But then again, she knew that was just the way country people were sometimes.

They picnicked in Overton Park, they went fishing together one time, though Elvis wasn't much of a "nature boy"; he drove her around in the Crown Electric truck and got reprimanded by Mr. Tipler for getting off his route and running late. He always had his guitar in the truck with him, and he would play for his fellow workers at the drop of a hat. Mrs. Tipler told him to "put down that damn guitar, it's going to be the ruination of you," but she said it with an indulgent smile. He was no longer so sure himself that he had the makings of a good electrician, because, as he said in a 1956 interview, he didn't know if he had the requisite attention span. "I was in doubt as to whether I would ever make it, because you had to keep your mind right on what you're doing, you can't be the least bit absentminded or you're liable to blow somebody's house up. I didn't think I was the type for it, but I was going to give it a try."

He was also going to continue to give recording a try. Marion Keisker saw his truck pass by the studio often, and once in a while he would stop in at 706 Union in his work clothes and cast about for a conversational subject, shifting nervously from one foot to the other. He was always asking her if she knew of a band, trying to assume an ease and a familiarity which he obviously did not feel, and her heart went out to him. Dixie, too, sensed that the tryout with Eddie Bond was not simply an isolated incident, though in this one area, evidently, he did not confide his innermost feelings to her. She had no doubt that if he wanted to make a record he would make a record, but she had no idea what making a record really meant — unless it meant getting on the radio. She knew he could never stand to make his living from playing dives and honky-tonks like the Hi Hat, she just wasn't sure what the alternatives were, or how you got to be on Bob Neal's *High Noon Round-Up* with the Blackwood Brothers and Eddie Hill.

On Saturday, June 26, just a week before Dixie was scheduled to leave for Florida, Elvis finally got his chance. Miss Keisker called around noon. "She said, 'Can you be here by three?' " he said in later years, whenever he recounted the story. "I was there by the time she hung up the phone."

What had happened was that, on his last trip to Nashville, in May, to record the Prisonaires, Sam had picked up an acetate from Red Wortham, the song publisher who had originally steered the Prisonaires to Sun. Phillips had listened to the song over and over, a plaintive lament called "Without You," sung in a quavering voice that sounded like a cross between the Ink Spots and a sentimental Irish tenor. It was undeniably amateurish, but there was *something* about it, it had a quality of yearning to it, and Phillips felt with the right voice maybe it could be something. Its purity, its simplicity, above all the very amateurishness of the performance, put him in mind of the kid who had been stopping by — he was not a pest, exactly, but he kept turning up — for the last nine or ten months. What was his name? he asked Marion, who seemed somewhat taken with the boy, a shy, insecure kid ("He was *beyond* shy," Sam thought) who had obviously never sung anywhere in his life. "Elvis Presley," Marion said and made the call.

They worked on the number all afternoon. When it became obvious that for whatever reason the boy was not going to get it right — maybe "Without You" wasn't the right song for him, maybe he was just intimidated by the damn studio — Phillips had him run down just about every song he knew. He wasn't much of a guitar player, but the world didn't need any more damn virtuosos; what the world needed, Sam Phillips was convinced, was *communication,* and that was what he sensed in there somewhere, underlying everything, in this boy's voice. "I guess I must have sat there at least three hours," Elvis told *Memphis Press-Scimitar* reporter Bob Johnson in 1956. "I sang everything I knew — pop stuff, spirituals, just a few words of [anything] I remembered." Sam watched him intently through the glass of the control room window — he was no longer taping him, and in almost every respect this session had to be accounted a dismal failure, but still there was *something.* . . . Every so often the boy looked up at him, as if for approval: was he doing all right? Sam just nodded and spoke in that smooth, reassuring voice. "You're doing just fine. Now just relax. Let me hear something that really means something to you now." Soothing, crooning, his eyes locked into the boy's through the plate glass window that he had built so that his eyes would be level with the performer's when he was sitting at the control room console, he didn't really know if they were getting anywhere or not, it was just so damned hard to tell when you were dealing with a bunch of damn amateurs, but it was only from amateurs, he firmly believed, that you ever got any real freshness of feeling.

When it was over, Elvis was exhausted, he felt limp but strangely elated, too. "I was an overnight sensation," he always told interviewers in later years. "A year after they heard me the first time, they called me back!" Everyone caught the boyish modesty, but they may have overlooked the understandable pride. Mr. Phillips *had* called him back — his perseverance had paid off. And while nothing was said about what would happen next, there was little doubt in Elvis' mind that something would. He had finally gotten his break. He drove over to Dixie's in a strange state of detachment — they went to the movies that night, and he mentioned in passing that he had made a record.

ON THE EVENING of Wednesday, June 30, tragedy struck. Dixie came home the next day to find her mother waiting for her at the door with the gravest expression. She sat Dixie down in the kitchen and told her there had been a terrible accident — the Blackwood Brothers' plane had crashed the night before somewhere in Alabama, it wasn't all of them, it was just R.W. and the bass singer, Bill Lyles, but they had both been killed. Dixie stared at her mother, she couldn't believe it at first, then her eyes filled up with tears. Bill? R.W.? Bill's wife, Ruth, was her Sunday school teacher. She was inconsolable. She called some of her friends. Nobody could believe it. The Blackwood Brothers were their own; the most progressive and businesslike of all gospel groups, they had had their own plane since the fall of 1952. According to the news accounts they had performed at noon with the Statesmen at the Chilton County Peach Festival in Clanton, Alabama. Evidently, the sponsors had asked them to stick around for the afternoon festivities, and when it came time to leave, there was still a big crowd, with automobiles parked all around the field. R.W. wanted to take the plane up before it got dark, to see how much clearance they had for takeoff. When he made his landing approach, everybody thought he was just showing off, but then the plane didn't straighten up, it just bounced and burst into flames, and you could see the charred figures in the plane. James Blackwood, a slight, slender man, screamed that he was going in and started for the plane, but Jake Hess wrapped him in a bear hug and didn't let go until James finally subsided. On the ride back to Memphis that night James said to Jake that he would never sing again, but Jake said he owed it to the people to go on.

Elvis came straight from work to Dixie's house — he didn't even bother to change. It was obvious from his tear-streaked face that he knew what had happened. They didn't say anything, just threw themselves into each other's arms, even with her mother there. They went to Gaston Park that night and sipped on milk shakes and cried and cried. What would happen to the Blackwood Brothers? they wondered. The quartet would just fall apart. Their poor families. It seemed like the world was coming to an end.

The funeral the next day was one of the biggest in Memphis history — it was the first time that a funeral service had ever been conducted at Ellis Auditorium. The Statesmen sang, and so did the Speers and five other quartets. Governor Frank Clement, who had been present at the Blackwoods' last Memphis appearance, on June 18, delivered a sincere and emotional eulogy; Clement, after all, was not only a friend to the quartets, he had presided over the growth of the Nashville recording industry and was one of the key factors in the Prisonaires getting their recording break. There were close to five thousand people present — they opened up the North Hall when the South Hall was filled, and so beloved were the Blackwoods, reported the papers, that "a number of negroes called the Auditorium asking if they could attend the funeral, and the galleries were reserved for negroes, Chauncey Barbour, Auditorium manager, said." The Reverend Hamill preached the sermon, and Dr. Robert G. Lee of Bellevue Baptist Church delivered the prayer. Elvis and Dixie sat with Mr. and Mrs. Presley and held hands. Dixie couldn't believe she was leaving for Florida the next day. She couldn't leave — she didn't want to leave — she wasn't going to leave him, not now. They clung to each other through most of the night, and in the morning Elvis came over as the Lockes packed up for their trip. He left around noon, after an exchange of promises to be true. They would both write, they said, he would try to call — he took down all the numbers and places she would be staying. They could barely let go of each other. Her parents discreetly left them alone. It had been a highly emotional time. When she came back, Dixie reassured him, reassured herself through swollen, tearstained eyes, nothing would have changed, everything would still be the same, they would still have the summer, they would still have their whole lives in front of them.

JULY 28, 1954. (MEMPHIS BROOKS MUSEUM / MICHAEL OCHS ARCHIVES)

"THAT'S ALL RIGHT"

THAT AFTERNOON a young guitarist named Scotty Moore stopped by 706 Union, ostensibly to find out how his record was doing. He had been coming by the studio for several months now, trying to get somewhere with his group, the Starlite Wranglers, trying to get a leg up in the business. The group, which had existed in various configurations since Scotty's discharge from the navy in early 1952, consisted of fellow guitarist Clyde Rush, steel guitarist Millard Yow, and bass player Bill Black, all of whom worked at Firestone, and a variety of interchangeable vocalists. Scotty, who worked as a hatter at his brothers' dry cleaning establishment at 613 North McClean, had recently brought in Doug Poindexter, a baker with a penchant for Hank Williams tunes, as permanent lead singer, and he had had a big star made up with Christmas lights that flashed on and off to advertise the band's name on the bandstand. They had a few regular bookings through the spring — they continued to play the same rough club out toward Somerville where Scotty and Bill had backed up Dorsey Burnette — and they played a couple of clubs around town. They landed a radio spot on West Memphis station KWEM, and Scotty got them a regular booking at the Bon Air, which had previously featured nothing but pop. The next step, clearly, was to make a record.

That was what led the Starlite Wranglers to the Memphis Recording Service. Doug Poindexter asked Bill Fitzgerald at Music Sales, the local independent record distributor, how they "could get on MGM like Hank Williams," and Fitzgerald, who distributed the Sun label among others, suggested that they try Sam Phillips. It was Scotty, as manager of the band and prime instigator of their upward professional mobility, who did this, with some trepidation, one afternoon after he got off work.

He and Sam hit it off almost instantly. Sam saw in Scotty an ambitious young man of twenty-two, not content with the limited vistas that lay before him — he didn't know what he wanted exactly, but he wanted something more than a lifetime of blocking hats or playing clubs and eventually giving it up to go into some little retail business. Scotty was looking for something *different,* Sam sensed, and he was a good listener besides. Soon the two of them got into the habit of meeting several days a week at 2:00 in the afternoon when Scotty got off work — Scotty would just stop by, and they would go next door to Miss Taylor's restaurant for a cup of coffee and talk about the future. To Sam, who at thirty-one had seen more than his share of ups and downs, it was an opportunity to expound upon his ideas to an audience that was not only sympathetic: Scotty clearly *enjoyed* plotting and scheming and dreaming about the changes that were just around the corner. To Scotty, who had grown up on a farm in Gadsden with the feeling that the world had passed him by (his father and his three older brothers had had a band, but by the time Scotty came along, fifteen years after the next-youngest brother, they had given it up) and who had joined the navy at sixteen, this was heaven. He was married for the second time, had two kids living out in Washington with his first wife, and aspired to playing jazz, like Barney Kessel, Tal Farlow, or country virtuosos Merle Travis and Chet Atkins. He was serious but self-taught, he had quit in the middle of his second year of high school, and here was somebody in Memphis telling him, with a conviction that defied gainsaying, that there was a chance that something could happen, that change was on the way. "Sam had an uncanny knack for pulling things out of people that they didn't even know they had. He knew there was a crossover coming. He foresaw it. I think that recording all those black artists had to give him an insight; he just didn't know where that insight would lead. Sam came from pretty much the same background as the rest of us, basically. We were just looking for something, we didn't know quite what it was, we would just sit there over coffee and say to each other, 'What is it? What should we do? How can we do it?' "

Eventually Scotty persuaded Sam to record the Wranglers, and on May 25, 1954, they recorded two sides, which Scotty wrote (he gave half of the credit for one song to Doug Poindexter because he was the vocalist and a third of the other to his brother for writing the lead sheet). The record was released at the beginning of June and never went anywhere — by the end of summer it had sold approximately three hundred copies — but Scotty continued to stop by the studio, knowing that the record wasn't his ticket to the future, the Starlite Wranglers were just a hillbilly band, but feeling somehow that if he stuck close to Sam Phillips he would find out what the future was.

Sometime around the middle of May he started hearing about a young ballad singer with possibilities. There was something different about his voice, Sam said; Sam was interested in trying him out on this new song he had picked up on his latest trip to Nashville to record the Prisonaires. At some point Marion mentioned his name, Elvis Presley — to Scotty it sounded like "a name out of science fiction" — but since Sam kept talking about him, he asked Sam to dig up a telephone number and address, maybe they could get together, maybe this kid really had something. Somehow Sam never seemed to have the information on hand, he always said he'd have Marion look it up the next day, and Scotty was keenly disappointed on this Saturday afternoon to find out that the boy had actually been in the studio just a week before and that they had worked unsuccessfully on the Nashville song. "This particular day," Scotty said, "it was about five in the afternoon — Marion was having coffee with us, and Sam said, 'Get his name and phone number out of the file.' Then he turned to me and said, 'Why don't you give him a call and get him to come over to your house and see what you think of him?' Bill Black lived just three doors down from me on Belz that ran into Firestone — I had actually moved just to be near Bill — and Sam said, 'You and Bill can just give him a listen, kind of feel him out.'"

Scotty called Elvis that evening, right after supper. His mother answered and said that Elvis was at the movies, at the Suzore No. 2. Scotty said that he "represented Sun Records," and Mrs. Presley said that she would get him out of the movies. There was a call back within an hour; Scotty explained who he was and what he wanted to do. The boy seemed to take it all in stride — his voice sounded confident enough, but wary. "I told him I was working with Sam Phillips and possibly would like to audition him if he was interested, and he said he guessed so. So we made an appointment for the next day at my house."

On Sunday, July 4, Elvis showed up at Scotty's house on Belz in his old Lincoln. He was wearing a black shirt, pink pants with a black stripe, white shoes, and a greasy ducktail, and asked "Is this the right place?" when Scotty's wife, Bobbie, answered the door. Bobbie asked him to have a seat and went to get Scotty. "I said, 'That boy is here.' He said, 'What boy?' I said, 'I can't remember his name, it's the one you're supposed to see today.' Scotty asked me to go down to Bill's house and see if Bill would come practice with them — Bill's bass was already in our apartment, because Bill and Evelyn had two kids, and there was more room there."

After a few minutes of awkward small talk, Bill showed up and they got down to business. Elvis hunched over his guitar and mumbled something about not really knowing what to play, then launched into disconnected fragments, seemingly, of every song he knew. Scotty and Bill fell in behind him on numbers like Billy Eckstine's "I Apologize"; the Ink Spots' "If I Didn't Care"; "Tomorrow Night"; Eddy Arnold's latest hit, "I Really Don't Want to Know"; Hank Snow's "I Don't Hurt Anymore"; and a Dean Martin–styled version of Jo Stafford's "You Belong to Me." They were all ballads, all sung in a yearning, quavery tenor that didn't seem ready to settle anywhere soon and accompanied by the most rudimentary strummed guitar. At some point Bill flopped down on the sofa, and there was some talk about how Elvis lived on Alabama, just across from Bill's mother, and how Elvis knew Bill's brother Johnny. Bill, the most affable man in the world and the clown of the Starlite Wranglers ("He never met a stranger," Scotty has said in seeking to describe him), said he had heard from Johnny just the other day, Johnny had been in Corpus Christi since he got laid off from Firestone. They talked a little about the football games down at the Triangle, and Bill said it was funny they had never formally met before, but, of course, he had left home before the Presleys moved into the Courts, he had gone into the army at eighteen, and when he got out in 1946 he was already married. There were a lot of musicians in Memphis, and you couldn't know them all — Elvis didn't happen to know a guitar player named Luther Perkins who lived just around the corner, did he? Elvis met all of Bill's attempts at conversation with perfunctory nods and stammered little asides of agreement that you could barely make out — he was polite enough, but it was almost as if he was filled with a need to say something that couldn't find proper expression, and he couldn't stop fidgeting. "He was as green as a gourd," Scotty would recall, with amusement, as his reaction at the time.

When Bobbie came back with Evelyn and Bill's sister, Mary Ann, they were still playing, but "all of a sudden there was a crowd, we probably scared Elvis," said Bobbie. "It was almost all slow ballads. 'I Love You Because' is the one that I remember." Eventually Elvis left, trailing clouds of oily smoke behind him in the humpbacked old Lincoln. "What'd you think?" Scotty asked, hoping that Bill might have seen something in the boy that he didn't. "Well, he didn't impress me too damn much," said Bill. "Snotty-nosed kid coming in here with those wild clothes and everything." But what about his singing? Scotty asked, almost desperately — he *wanted* the kid to be good for reasons that he didn't even care to examine. "Well, it was all right, nothing out of the ordinary — I mean, the cat can sing. . . ."

That was Scotty's opinion, too. It was all right, nothing special — he couldn't see where the boy had added all that much to the songs that he had sung; Scotty didn't think he was going to make the world forget about Eddy Arnold or Hank Snow. But he called Sam anyway, what else was he going to do after making such a fuss about meeting the kid? What did you think? Sam asked.

"I said, 'He didn't really knock me out.' I said, 'The boy's got a good voice.' I told him a lot of the songs he sang. Sam said, 'Well, I think I'll call him, get him to come down to the studio tomorrow, we'll just set up an audition and see what he sounds like coming back off of tape.' I said, 'Shall we bring in the whole band?' And he said, 'Naw, just you and Bill come over, just something for a little rhythm. No use making a big deal about it.' "

The next night everybody showed up around 7:00. There was some desultory small talk, Bill and Scotty joked nervously among themselves, and Sam tried to make the boy feel at ease, carefully observing the way in which he both withheld himself and tried to thrust himself into the conversation at the same time. He reminded Sam so much of some of the blues singers he had recorded, simultaneously proud and needy. At last, after a few minutes of aimless chatter and letting them all get a little bit used to being in the studio, Sam turned to the boy and said, "Well, what do you want to sing?" This occasioned even more self-conscious confusion as the three musicians tried to come up with something that they all knew and could play — *all the way through* — but after a number of false starts, they finally settled on "Harbor Lights," which had been a big hit for Bing Crosby in 1950, and worked it through to the end, then tried Leon Payne's "I Love You Because," a beautiful country ballad that had been a number-one country hit for its author in 1949 and a number-two hit for Ernest Tubb on the hillbilly charts the same year. They tried up to a dozen takes, running through the song again and again — sometimes the boy led off with several bars of whistling, sometimes he simply launched into the verse. The recitation altered slightly each time that he repeated it, but each time he flung himself into it, seemingly trying to make it new. Sometimes he simply blurted out the words, sometimes his singing voice shifted to a thin, pinched, almost nasal tone before returning to the high, keening tenor in which he sang the rest of the song — it was as if, Sam thought, he wanted to put everything he had ever known or heard into one song. And Scotty's guitar part was too damn complicated, he was trying too damn hard to sound like Chet Atkins, but there was that strange sense of inconsolable desire in the voice, there was *emotion* being communicated.

Sam sat in the control room, tapping his fingers absentmindedly on the console. All his attention was focused on the studio, on the interaction of the musicians, the sound they were getting, the feeling that was behind the sound. Every so often he would come out and change a mike placement slightly, talk with the boy a little, not just to bullshit with him but to make him feel at home, to try to make him feel really at home. It was always a question of how long you could go on like this, you wanted the artist to get familiar with the studio, but being in the studio could take on a kind of mind-numbing quality of its own, it could smooth over the rough edges, you could take refuge in the little space that you had created for yourself and banish the very element of spontaneity you were seeking to achieve.

For Elvis it seemed like it had been going on for hours, and he began to get the feeling that nothing was ever going to happen. When Mr. Phillips had called, he had taken the news calmly to begin with, he had tried to banish all thoughts of results or consequences, but now it seemed as if he could think of nothing else. He was getting more and more frustrated, he flung himself desperately into each new version of "I Love You Because," trying to make it live, trying to make it new, but he saw his chances slipping away as they returned to the beginning of the song over and over again with numbing familiarity. . . .

Finally they decided to take a break — it was late, and everybody had to work the next day. Maybe they ought to just give it up for the night, come back on Tuesday and try it again. Scotty and Bill were sipping Cokes, not saying much of anything, Mr. Phillips was doing something in the control room, and, as Elvis explained it afterward, "this song popped into my mind that I had heard years ago, and I started kidding around with [it]." It was a song that he told Johnny Black he had written when he sang it in the Courts, and Johnny believed him. The song was "That's All Right [Mama]," an old blues number by Arthur "Big Boy" Crudup.

"All of a sudden," said Scotty, "Elvis just started singing this song, jumping around and acting the fool, and then Bill picked up his bass, and he started acting the fool, too, and I started playing with them. Sam, I think, had the door to the control booth open — I don't know, he was either editing some tape, or doing something — and he stuck his head out and said, 'What are you doing?' And we said, 'We don't know.' 'Well, back up,' he said, 'try to find a place to start, and do it again.' "

SAM RECOGNIZED IT right away. He was amazed that the boy even knew Arthur "Big Boy" Crudup — nothing in any of the songs he had tried so far gave any indication that he was drawn to this kind of music at all. But this was the sort of music that Sam had long ago wholeheartedly embraced, this was the sort of music of which he said, "This is where the soul of man never dies." And the way the boy performed it, it came across with a freshness and an exuberance, it came across with the kind of clear-eyed, unabashed *originality* that Sam sought in all the music that he recorded — it was "different," it was itself.

They worked on it. They worked hard on it, but without any of the laboriousness that had gone into the efforts to cut "I Love You Because." Sam tried to get Scotty to cut down on the instrumental flourishes — "Simplify, simplify!" was the watchword. "If we wanted Chet Atkins," said Sam good-humoredly, "we would have brought him up from Nashville and gotten him in the damn studio!" He was delighted with the rhythmic propulsion Bill Black brought to the sound. It was a slap beat and a tonal beat at the same time. He may not have been as good a bass player as his brother Johnny; in fact, Sam said, "Bill was one of the worst bass players in the world, *technically,* but, man, could he slap that thing!" And yet that wasn't it either — it was the *chemistry.* There was Scotty, and there was Bill, and there was Elvis scared to death in the middle, "but sounding so fresh, because it *was* fresh to him."

They worked on it over and over, refining the song, but the center never changed. It always opened with the ringing sound of Elvis' rhythm guitar, up till this moment almost a handicap to be gotten over. Then there was Elvis' vocal, loose and free and full of confidence, holding it together. And Scotty and Bill just fell in with an easy, swinging gait that was the very epitome of what Sam had dreamt of but never fully imagined. The first time Sam played it back for them, "we couldn't believe it was us," said Bill. "It just sounded sort of raw and ragged," said Scotty. "We thought it was exciting, but what was it? It was just so completely different. But it just really flipped Sam — he felt it really had something. We just sort of shook our heads and said, 'Well, that's fine, but good God, they'll run us out of town!' " And Elvis? Elvis flung himself into the recording process. You only have to listen to the tape to hear the confidence grow. By the last take (only two false starts and one complete alternate take remain), there is a different singer in the studio than the one who started out the evening — nothing had been said, nothing had been articulated, but everything had changed.

Sam Phillips sat in the studio after the session was over and everyone had gone home. It was not unusual for him to hang around until two or three in the morning, sometimes recording, sometimes just thinking about what was going to become of his business and his family in these perilous times, sometimes mulling over his vision of the future. He knew that something was in the wind. He knew from his experience recording blues, and from his fascination with black culture, that there was something intrinsic to the music that could translate, that *did* translate. "It got so you could sell a half million copies of a rhythm and blues record," Sam told a Memphis reporter in 1959, reminiscing about his overnight success. "These records appealed to white youngsters just as Uncle Silas [Payne's] songs and stories used to appeal to me. . . . But there was something in many of those youngsters that resisted buying this music. The Southern ones especially felt a resistance that even they probably didn't quite understand. They liked the music, but they weren't sure whether they ought to like it or not. So I got to thinking how many records you could sell if you could find white performers who could play and sing in this same exciting, alive way."

The next night everyone came to the studio, but nothing much happened. They tried a number of different songs — they even gave the Rodgers and Hart standard "Blue Moon" (a 1949 hit for Billy Eckstine) a passing try — but nothing really clicked, and both that evening and the next were spent in more or less getting to know one another musically. Nonetheless, Sam had little doubt of what had transpired in the studio that first night. There was always the question of whether or not it was a fluke; as far as that went, only time would tell. But Sam Phillips was never one to hold back, when he believed in something he just plunged ahead. And so, on Wednesday night, after calling an early halt to the proceedings, he telephoned Dewey Phillips down at the new WHBQ studio in the Hotel Chisca. "Get yourself a wheelbarrow full of goober dust," Dewey was very likely announcing when Sam made the call, "and roll it in the door [of whatever sponsor Dewey happened to be representing], and tell 'em Phillips sent you. *And call Sam!*"

DEWEY PHILLIPS in 1954 was very nearly at the apogee of his renown and glory. From a fifteen-minute unpaid spot that he had talked his way into while managing the record department at W. T. Grant's, he had graduated to a 9:00-to-midnight slot six nights a week. According to the Memphis papers he would get as many as three thousand letters a week and forty to fifty telegrams a night, a measure not just of his audience but of the *fervor* of that audience. When, a year or two later, he asked his listeners to blow their horns at 10:00 in the evening, the whole city, it was said, erupted with a single sound, and when the police chief, who was also listening, called to remind Dewey of Memphis' antinoise ordinance and begged him not to do it again, Dewey announced on the air, "Well, good people, Chief MacDonald just called me, and he said we can't do that anymore. Now I was going to have you do it at eleven o'clock, but the chief told me we couldn't do it, so whatever you do at eleven o'clock, don't blow your horns." The results were predictable.

One night an assistant started a fire in the wastebasket and convinced Dewey that the hotel was on fire, but Dewey, a hero of the Battle of Hurtgen Forest, kept right on broadcasting, directing the fire department down to the station and staying on the air until the hoax was discovered. He broadcast in stereo before stereo was invented, playing the same record on two turntables which never started or ended together, creating a phased effect that pleased Dewey unless it got so far out of line that he took the needle off both records with a scrawk and announced that he was just going to have to start all over and try it again.

WDIA DJ and r&b singer Rufus Thomas referred to Dewey as "a man who just happened to be white," and he never lost his Negro audience, even after the white teenage audience that Sam sensed out there made itself known. He went everywhere in Memphis, paraded proudly down Beale Street, greeted the same people who, the *Commercial Appeal* reported in 1950, had flocked to Grant's "just to see the man 'what gets himself so messed up.' " He had several chances to go national but passed them up — or allowed them to pass *him* up — by remaining himself. There were two kinds of people in Memphis, the *Press-Scimitar* declared in 1956, "those who are amused and fascinated by Dewey, and those who, when they accidentally tune in, jump as tho stung by a wasp and hurriedly switch to something nice and cultural, like Guy Lombardo." "He was a genius," said Sam Phillips, "and I don't call many people geniuses."

DEWEY STOPPED BY the recording studio after his show. It was well after midnight, but that was as good a time as any for Dewey. "Dewey [was] completely unpredictable," wrote *Press-Scimitar* reporter Bob Johnson, his (and Sam's) friend, in various celebrations of his spirit over the years. "He would call at three or four A.M. and insist I listen to something over the phone. I tried to tell him it was no time to be phoning anyone, but Dewey had no sense of time. Sometimes I wonder if there is a real Dewey, or if he's just something that happens as he goes along." If he was a personality that just unfolded, though, it was because he cared so much about what he was doing. Whatever Dewey did, everyone agreed, was from the heart. Ordinarily, when he stopped by the studio, all he could talk about at first was the show. "Oh God, he loved his show," Sam Phillips said. "He wasn't just playing records and cutting the monitor down. He was enjoying everything he said, every record that he played, every response that he got from his listeners. Dewey could get more excited than anyone you ever saw." And he loved to argue with Sam. To Marion Keisker, Sam and Dewey were so close that she couldn't stand to be in the same room with the two of them — and it wasn't just that she saw Dewey as a bad influence (though she did). She was also, she admitted, jealous; she saw Dewey as a threat. "Dewey loved to argue with Sam, just for the sake of arguing," recalled the singer Dickey Lee. "Talking about how Sam can intimidate people, one night Sam was off on one of his tirades, and right in the middle Dewey had a rubber band and snapped it at Sam and hit him in the head. He thought it was the funniest thing. Sam would get so mad at Dewey, but he loved him. Dewey always referred to Sam as his half brother, even though they weren't related at all."

This particular night, though, there wasn't any arguing. Sam had something he wanted to play for Dewey, he said right off, and he was uncharacteristically nervous about it. Sam Phillips didn't like to ask a favor of anyone — and he didn't really consider that he was asking a favor now — but he was asking Dewey to *listen* to something, he was asking him to consider something that had never previously existed on this earth; this wasn't just a matter of sitting around and bullshitting and letting Dewey absorb whatever happened to come his way. "But, you know it was a funny thing," said Sam. "There was an element of Dewey that was conservative, too. When he picked a damn record, he didn't want to be wrong. 'Cause he had that thing going, 'How much bullshit have you got in you, man, and when are you gonna deliver?' It so happened, by God, that people believed Dewey, and he delivered. 'Cause when he went on the air [he didn't have any scientific method], he just blabbed it right out, 'It's gonna be a hit, it's gonna be a hit, it's the biggest thing you ever heard. I'll tell you what, man, it's gonna knock you out.' And, you know, as much as he respected me and loved me, Dewey had some real hang-ups about what could be done locally — it was like if somebody was five hundred or a thousand miles away there was more intrigue about them. So it was an elongated education process, really, he wanted to make you prove it to him unequivocally. And he was so into the finished product he didn't care how it came about, it was just, what did you deliver for him to make his show great? I think he was just beginning to feel that by God, there was a legitimate record crusader in this town."

Dewey opened a Falstaff and sprinkled some salt in it, then sat back and listened intently as Sam played the tape of the single song over and over. Dewey knew the song, of course; he had played the Arthur "Big Boy" Crudup version many times on his own show. It was the sound that puzzled him. For once there was not much conversation as the two men listened, each wondering what exactly the other thought. "He was reticent, and I was glad that he was," said Sam. "If he hadn't been reticent, it would have scared me to death, if he had said, 'Hey, man, this is a hit, it's a hit,' I would have thought Dewey was just trying to make me feel good. What I was thinking was, where you going to go with this, it's not black, it's not white, it's not pop, it's not country, and I think Dewey was the same way. He was fascinated by it — there was no question about that — I mean, he loved the damn record, but it was a question of where do we go from here?"

They stayed up listening and talking in comparatively muted tones until 2:00 or 3:00 in the morning, when both men finally returned home to their respective families and beds. Then, what to Sam's surprise, the phone rang early the next morning, and it was Dewey. "I didn't sleep well last night, man," Dewey announced. Sam said, "Man, you should have slept pretty good, with all that Jack Daniel's and beer in you." No, Dewey said, he hadn't been able to sleep, because he kept thinking about that record, he wanted it for his show tonight, in fact he wanted two copies, and he said, "We ain't letting anybody know." His reticence, Sam said, was over on that day.

Sam cut the acetates that afternoon and brought them down to the station. He called Elvis after work to tell him that Dewey would most likely be playing the record on his show that night. Elvis' response was not uncharacteristic. "He fixed the radio and told us to leave it on that station," said Gladys, "and then he went to the movies. I guess he was just too nervous to listen." "I thought people would laugh at me," Elvis told C. Robert Jennings of the *Saturday Evening Post* in 1965. "Some did, and some are still laughing, I guess."

Vernon and Gladys did listen. They sat glued to the radio with Vernon's mother, Minnie, and the rest of the relatives listening in their nearby homes, until at last, at 9:30 or 10:00, Dewey announced that he had a new record, it wasn't even a record, actually, it was a dub of a new record that Sam was going to be putting out next week, and it was going to be a *hit*, dee-gaw, ain't that right, Myrtle ("Moo," went the cow), and he slapped the acetate — the acetates — on the turntables.

The response was instantaneous. Forty-seven phone calls, it was said, came in right away, along with fourteen telegrams — or was it 114 phone calls and forty-seven telegrams? — he played the record seven times in a row, eleven times, seven times over the course of the rest of the program. In retrospect it doesn't really matter; it seemed as if all of Memphis was listening as Dewey kept up his nonstop patter, egging his radio audience on, encouraging them to join him in the discovery of a new voice, proclaiming to the world that Daddy-O-Dewey played the hits, that we way uptown, about as far uptown as you can get, did anybody want to buy a fur-lined duck? And if that one didn't flat git it for you, you can go to. . . . And tell 'em Phillips sent you!

For Gladys the biggest shock was "hearing them say his name over the radio just before they put on that record. That shook me so it stayed with me right through the whole song — Elvis Presley — just my son's name. I couldn't rightly hear the record the first time round." She didn't have time to think about it for long anyway, because almost immediately the phone rang. It was Dewey for Elvis. When she told him Elvis was at the movies, he said, "Mrs. Presley, you just get that cotton-picking son of yours down here to the station. I played that record of his, and them bird-brain phones haven't stopped ringing since." Gladys went down one aisle of the Suzore No. 2, and Vernon went down the other — or at least so the story goes — and within minutes Elvis was at the station.

"I was scared to death," Elvis said. "I was shaking all over, I just couldn't believe it, but Dewey kept telling me to cool it, [this] was really happening."

"Sit down, I'm gone interview you" were his first words to the frightened nineteen-year-old, Dewey told writer Stanley Booth in 1967. "He said, 'Mr. Phillips, I don't know nothing about being interviewed.' 'Just don't say nothing dirty,' I told him. He sat down, and I said I'd let him know when we were ready to start. I had a couple of records cued up, and while they played we talked. I asked him where he went to high school, and he said, 'Humes.' I wanted to get that out, because a lot of people listening had thought he was colored. Finally I said, 'All right, Elvis, thank you very much.' 'Aren't you gone interview me?' he asked. 'I already have,' I said. 'The mike's been open the whole time.' He broke out in a cold sweat."

It was Thursday, July 8. Elvis escaped out in the hot night air. He walked back up Main to Third Street and then over to Alabama. Dewey wound up his show and called his wife, Dot. How'd she like it? he asked. "I told him I loved it," Dot told the *Trenton* (Tennessee) *Herald Gazette* in 1978, ten years after Dewey's death. "He went on to say that he believed Elvis had a hit. . . . Dewey cherished that moment with Elvis. He would tell it time and time again."

Sam Phillips was at the studio that night. He didn't see Elvis, and he didn't see Dewey until after the show, but he knew what had happened, he knew that the reaction had come, the phone lines had lit up without anyone thinking about what the singer looked like, "they didn't give a fuck about classifying him, in Memphis, Tennessee, *they liked what they heard.*" He knew, too, that now the real work would begin.

* * *

T HE NEWS TRAVELED like wildfire. Billie Chiles, a classmate of Elvis' at Humes who had never been exactly entranced by his music, was at a sock hop at the Holy Rosary Catholic Church. "Sometime during the evening a couple went outside to the parking lot," Billie told former *Press-Scimitar* reporter Bill Burk thirty-five years later, "and turned their [car] radio on. . . . They came running downstairs yelling, 'Come up here quick! You ain't going to believe what Dewey Phillips is playing on the radio!' " Another classmate, George Klein, who had been president of the class of 1953, stopped by Dewey's radio show that Saturday night. He had just completed his freshman year at Memphis State, where he was majoring in communications, and had served as a gofer for Dewey, "kind of a baby-sitter," the previous summer, and in fact for much of the past school year. For this summer he had gotten a job working at KOSE, in Osceola, Arkansas, hitchhiking the fifty miles home after his Saturday shift to spend Sunday with his mother and his Memphis friends. This particular Saturday night he stopped by the station, as he generally did, just as Dewey was about to go on the air, and Dewey greeted him, as he generally did, with, " 'Hey mother, when'd you get in?'

"Then he said, 'Guess what? Come here.' And he took a record and put his hand over the label and put it on the turntable. He played the record and said, 'Guess who that is.' I said, 'Shit, Dewey, I don't know. Who is it?' He said, 'You know this guy, you went to school with the boy,' and I knew then it had to be Elvis. 'Sam brought the record by the other night,' he said, 'and I played the sonofabitch fourteen times, and we got about five hundred phone calls. It's gonna be a hit!' "

With all the excitement, Sam Phillips realized, now they were really going to have to come up with something else in a hurry; they *needed* a second side just to be able to put a record out. He felt that nothing they had recorded to date was suitable, so they went back into the studio on Friday night, and sometime in the next couple of days they came up with something equally improbable, equally "different," and equally exciting.

"Blue Moon of Kentucky" had been a hit for Bill Monroe in 1946, well before the term "bluegrass" came into popular usage. In Monroe's version it was a beautiful waltz familiar to anyone who listened to the Grand Ole Opry and revered by every hillbilly musician who had ever picked up a stringed instrument. "We spent three or four nights trying to get a back side," Scotty said, "something that would be in the same kind of vein. We'd gone through this song and that song, just running through them —

I don't think any of them were ever put on tape — and then Bill jumped up and started clowning, beating on his bass and singing 'Blue Moon of Kentucky,' in a high falsetto voice, more or less mimicking Bill Monroe. And Elvis started banging on the guitar, playing rhythm and singing, and I joined in and it just gelled.

"It's funny how they both come about by accident. There was nothing like a direction, there was just a certain . . . feel. You know, Elvis wasn't considered a real good rhythm player on guitar, but you listen to 'That's All Right, Mama,' he starts with the rhythm, just the open rhythm, and then the slap [bass] starts — he had a feel for rhythm on the stuff that we did that's very hard for anybody to do the same way."

"Blue Moon of Kentucky" evolved from a slow, bluesy version in 4/4 time with tentative instrumentation and a rather ornate vocal into a high-spirited declaration of exuberant self-discovery, driven by Elvis' ringing rhythm guitar and a propulsive mix of Scotty's chording riffs and single-string filigree. For the first time Sam made extensive use of what he had come to call slapback, a kind of homemade echo device that was created by running the original recording signal through a second Ampex machine and thereby achieving an almost sibilant phased effect. This undoubtedly added not only to the presence but to the excitement of the recording, and, of course, echo had the capacity of covering up a multitude of sins, but what held it all together most of all was Sam's belief in the uniqueness of what they were doing. What kept the musicians from ever giving up was Sam's lulling faith: "All right, boys, we just about on it now," you can almost hear him saying. "Do it again. Just do it one more time for me." When he felt like he had reached the limit of his creativity, Carl Perkins said of recording for Sam just a year or two later, Sam would coax him to "walk out on a limb, I'd try things I knew I couldn't do, and I'd get in a corner trying to do it and then have to work my way out of it. I'd say, 'Mr. Phillips, that's terrible.' He said, 'That's original.' I said, 'But it's just a big original mistake.' And he said, 'That's what Sun Records is. That's what we are.'"

"That's fine now" you can actually hear Sam say, at the end of one early take of "Blue Moon of Kentucky." He speaks in a soothing, almost crooning voice, the voice of reason, the voice of confident imperturbability. "Hell, that's different," he says to the three musicians awaiting his verdict. "That's a pop song now, nearly about." And Elvis, Scotty, and Bill all burst out in nervous, self-reassuring laughter.

Almost as soon as the song was cut, Sam got two-sided dubs not just to Dewey, who had had an exclusive now for a couple of days, but to Bob Neal, the early-morning DJ and host of the *High Noon Round-Up* at WMPS, Dick Stuart at the West Memphis station, KWEM, and Sleepy Eyed John, a country jock at WHHM, who also led a big western-style swing band and booked the Eagle's Nest out at the Clearpool complex on Lamar. All three got on the record right away, playing the second side mainly, but Sleepy Eyed John evidently showed some business interest in the young singer, which disturbed Sam. "Sleepy Eyed John hated what we were doing at 706, he made no bones about it. I continued to carry records to him because he played them, but I think he played them because he thought by picking them apart he could make people see that this was not really music." Sleepy Eyed John was a "businessman," not the lowest form of life in Sam's eyes, because Sam considered himself a businessman, but if you were a businessman exclusively, solely interested in making money, you were worth little more than a bucketful of warm spit. To forestall Sleepy Eye, Sam suggested to Scotty that he become the manager of record, just as he was already manager of the Starlite Wranglers. "He was exactly what we needed. Scotty had the demeanor and the manner — he wasn't going to give Elvis any unnecessary problems about 'You do this' and 'You do that,' and you could trust him all the way. We didn't need some hotshot manager — hell, Scotty just wanted to help keep the vehicle together."

On Monday, July 12, just a week after they had first met, Scotty became the official manager. "Whereas, W.S. Moore, III, is a band leader and a booking agent," the agreement read, "and Elvis Presley, a minor, age 19 years, is a singer of reputation and renown, and possesses bright promises of large success. . . ." Scotty got 10 percent off the top, and then at Sam's suggestion the group would divide any income with a 50–25–25 split. The original idea was that Elvis would become part of the Wranglers show, a kind of added attraction, which would make "two acts in one," Scotty said, and in fact that was the way it was set up for the following Saturday at the Bon Air, the Wranglers' regular weekend gig. The record was manufactured that week at Buster Williams' Plastic Products on Chelsea Avenue, in Memphis, and by the time that it was officially released as Sun record number 209 on Monday, July 19, six thousand local orders had already come in. Ed Leek, a Humes classmate who was pre-med at Memphis State, described going down to the plant and watching the first records come off the press with Elvis, who was "like a little kid at Christmas." Others were hearing the record for the first time. Jack Clement, who was singing with Sleepy Eyed John's band occasionally and studying English and journalism at Memphis State, turned on the radio one morning and heard "Blue Moon of Kentucky" — "it was just what I'd been wanting to hear. It was real. I loved the simplicity of it, and so did everybody I know that heard it. There were some people I know that quarreled with the look, but *everybody* loved the way that it sounded. All it took was one play."

Meanwhile, Dixie was still down in Florida with no idea what was going on. There was only the mysterious telegram that she got at her cousin's house ("We were on the move all the time, so we didn't talk to each other on the phone") — "HURRY HOME. MY RECORD IS DOING GREAT," it read. "I thought, 'What!' And I thought, this can't be for real. But I knew it was."

O N SATURDAY, JULY 17, Sam Phillips carried Elvis out to the Bon Air Club, at Summer and Mendenhall, to execute the first part of the plan that he and Scotty had devised. Dewey mentioned on the air that night that he might stop by after his show, and perhaps that added to the crowd, but it was a normal Saturday-night crowd, "pure redneck," according to Sam, loud, hard-drinking, a little rowdy, in love with their hillbilly music, out for a good time. Elvis and Sam sat at a little table while the band finished its set, and Elvis got more and more nervous. "This was Elvis' first appearance, period, and he was absolutely mortified. Now look, this was a small club, and it was all rednecks — and I don't mean any bad connotation by that — but you had better be careful looking like Elvis did in a redneck joint and not singing hillbilly songs and you want to live. You got a bunch of people drinking, and then you try to come on with some music, untried, unproved, you're unknown. I swear, he just came off real good."

He sang his two songs — they were the only songs the trio really *knew* — and Scotty and Bill hung around for a few minutes, but then it was time for the Wranglers to go back up on the bandstand, and Elvis and Sam left. At that point all of the confidence that he had generated onstage seemed to deflate. "He said, 'Mr. Phillips, I just feel like . . . I failed.' I said, 'Elvis, are you kidding? You were really good.' I didn't say *great*, I said,

'The only thing that could have been better would have been if you had enjoyed it onstage.' You see, I was honest with him, I didn't feed him a line of bullshit, and he couldn't shoot any holes in that."

As for the Wranglers, there was friction, Scotty said, right from the start. To begin with, they hadn't realized they wouldn't all be backing Elvis up, though, of course, that wouldn't have worked, Scotty knew, because they hadn't backed him on the record. Then, too, there seemed to be a resentment based not just on the reception that the kid got, which was nothing out of the ordinary, but on the way he looked, the way he dressed, his whole demeanor — which was. To Sam it was a revelation. He hadn't looked at Elvis Presley as a "physical specimen. I wasn't thinking, 'Is he going to look good onstage, is he going to be a great performer?' I was just looking for something that nobody could categorize." That was what Sam saw at the club that night, and it was what the Wranglers saw, too — but their reactions were entirely different.

Sam called Bob Neal right after the Bon Air appearance. Neal, the WMPS DJ, was putting on a "hillbilly hoedown featur[ing] favorite folk ballads in a sylvan folk setting" and starring, "in person, the sensational radio-recording star" Slim Whitman, of the Louisiana Hayride, who would sing his hits, "Rosemarie," "Secret Love," and, undoubtedly, "Indian Love Call." The show was at the outdoor amphitheater in Overton Park, and Sam asked Neal if he could add this new Memphis act to the bill. Bob, the most affable of entrepreneurs, said sure, as long as Sam got the boy into the musicians' union, which Sam had Marion immediately set about to do. He didn't say anything about it to Elvis at first, because he didn't want to get him too worked up — but he thought he would try to place an ad in the paper with the Poplar Tunes record shop the following week, assuming that it all worked out.

Dixie came home on Sunday, too late to see Elvis that night. The first song that the family heard on the radio when they got back into town was "Blue Moon of Kentucky." On Monday, Dixie called Elvis at Crown Electric first thing in the morning, and he told her to meet him at home after work, he didn't want to have to go home and change and clean up and drive over to her house before seeing her. "I had on a pale blue fitted skirt and a red blouse, and his mom and dad and I were sitting on the porch. They were just so excited they couldn't believe it, they told me about the studio and the record and the people calling and saying, 'Is this your son?' Then I saw him walking down Alabama Street, I could see him a block away, and I couldn't wait for him to get there, and he couldn't wait to get there. And when he came in we had to go over the whole thing all over again. And we had to say, Hi, how you doing? Good vacation? Did you get my telegram? Yeah, I did. And he said something about my outfit, and we were just very polite for a minute, and then he walked in the door like, 'I'm going for a drink or something.' And he said, 'Come here just a minute, Dixie.' So I got up and went in the door so we could get our kiss, because we hadn't seen each other in so long — it had been two weeks! — but we were so polite about it, because we were right there in front of his mother and daddy. It was a sweet day, I can still visualize it, I kept thinking, 'Please don't let him change,' but, you know, after that things were never the same."

They seemed the same for quite some time, though. Dixie rode with him on his route in the Crown Electric truck. They continued to see each other almost every night. They stopped by Dewey's radio show once or twice and sat with Dewey while he screamed and shouted and carried on. One night Elvis put in a plug for Crown Electric, and the switchboard was so jammed with calls the next day that the Tiplers took Elvis off his route and had him answer the phone. The Tiplers were almost as excited about his success as Mr. and Mrs. Presley. They went out to see him the first night he played the club, bringing friends and employees, and were only disappointed that he was not allowed to sing more songs.

Some nights there would be rehearsals over at Scotty's, and Dixie would sit with the wives, Bobbie and Evelyn, older married women in their twenties (Dixie was still not quite sixteen), while they rehearsed. Once they stopped by the Sun studio, but Dixie found Sam a little frightening, not like Dewey, who put you right at your ease, even if he was a little vulgar. Sam was kind of off-putting, though — the force of his gaze, the way it locked in on Elvis, made it seem as if he didn't have much use for, or interest in, Dixie, and as a result she was even quieter than normal in his presence. On the Saturday night after she got home they played again out at the Bon Air, but Dixie, of course, couldn't go because they served alcoholic drinks, so she waited at home for it to be over. When he finally came by to pick her up, he had forgotten his coat, and she rode out to the club with him, but "it was like another world. The people recognized him, and he had to go back onstage and sing again. It was like I was sitting there, thinking, 'I'm not really in this, I'm watching it somewhere.'"

The following week, ads for the July 30 Overton Park show started to appear. One spelled his name "Ellis Presley," one left it out altogether, and the day of the performance there was an ad with Slim Whitman's picture at the top that announced "ELVIS PRESLEY, New Memphis Star Who Sings 'Blue Moon of Kentucky' and 'That's All Right, Mama,' " along with a small Poplar Tunes ad urging patrons to "buy all of Slim Whitman's Imperial Records — Elvis Presley's Sun records" at the record store at 305 Poplar. On Tuesday at lunchtime Marion Keisker took Elvis just down the street to the Press-Scimitar Building at 495 Union. She had hoped to have her old college friend Bob Johnson do the story, but Johnson advised her that they had "a new kid who was handling a lot of that" — Edwin Howard, the editor's son — and maybe it would be more politic to let him write it up. Marion arrived with Elvis in tow, Howard recalled. "I'll never forget. . . . He look[ed] like the wrath of God. Pimples all over his face. Ducktail hair. Had a funny-looking thin bow tie on. . . . He was very hard to interview. About all I could get out of him was yes and no."

The article was headed "In a Spin" and led off with:

Elvis Presley can be forgiven for going round and round in more ways than one these days. A 19-year-old Humes High graduate, he has just signed a recording contract with Sun Record Co. of Memphis, and already has a disk out that promises to be the biggest hit that Sun has ever pressed. . . . "The odd thing about it," says Marion Keisker of the Sun office, "is that both sides seem to be equally popular on popular, folk, and race record programs. This boy has something that seems to appeal to everybody. We've just gotten the sample records out to the disk jockeys and distributors in other cities, but we got big orders yesterday from Dallas and Atlanta."

True to Howard's recollection, there is not a single direct quote from the subject of the article, and the photograph that accompanies it shows an unsmiling three-quarter view with clip-on bow tie and hair to which grease has been liberally applied in a vain attempt to make it behave — it is standing up a little wildly in front, and two strands have escaped, pointing outward like antennae. He is wearing a western-style shirt-jacket with white-stitched, button-down breast pockets and wide lapels, he appears to be wearing eye shadow, and all in all he looks like a combination of something from outer space and the polite, well-mannered, sober, and sensitive boy that he really was. He looked, Dixie thought, very handsome, and was. He looked, Elvis Presley thought, not quite right, but close to the way he wanted to look.

F RIDAY, JULY 30, was hot and sticky. Dixie and Elvis must have spoken to each other at least half a dozen times during the day. Although he never liked to talk about it, she knew how nervous he must be, and driving up Poplar as they approached the park, she noticed that his fingers drummed an even steadier tattoo than usual on the metal dashboard. Mr. and Mrs. Presley were there — they came with a bunch of other relatives. Some of the boys and girls Dixie knew from church, the ones you would see at the roller rink, and some of their other friends were present, too — but mostly it was an undifferentiated mass who were there to see not "Ellis Presley" but Slim Whitman, the handsome, mustachioed star, or Billy Walker, the Tall Texan, who had just had his first big hit with "Thank You for Calling." These were hillbilly singers, this was a hillbilly crowd — Dixie was scared to death, not for herself but for how Elvis would feel if they just sat there and went, 'Huh?' What if they made fun of him, what if this was the end of his dream?

Sam Phillips was late getting to the show. "I had to park a long ways away, and when I got there he was standing on the steps at the back of the shell looking kind of pitiful — well, maybe *pitiful* is the wrong word, I knew it was the way he was going to look: *unsure*. And he just grabbed me and said, 'Man, I'm so glad to see you, Mr. Phillips. I-I-I-I — ' You know, that was just the way Elvis did. 'I-I-I-I just didn't know what I was going to do.' Well, you know, it's like when somebody's mother is real sick and you tell them everything is going to be all right, and yet you know there's the possibility that his mother might die. I said, 'Look, Elvis, we'll find out whether they like you or not.' And then I said, *'They're gonna love you.'* Now I didn't *know* that, and if you want to call me a liar or a fake for saying something that I didn't know to be the truth — but I believed that once he started to sing and they saw him, I don't mean the stage act, once they heard that voice and the beautiful simplicity of what those three musicians were putting down. . . . You see, Elvis had confidence in me, he saw that when I walked up I always had some kind of assured look, and yet he knew I wasn't going to throw him to the lions either. So I gave him my best clubhouse pitch, not too many curves, 'cause I knew even if he

struck out four times and left three people on base each time, after the
ball game was over that could be overcome, too."

When Elvis went onstage, Scotty said, his knees were knocking so
loud you could almost hear them. Bob Neal made the introduction, and
then the three musicians, none of whom had ever appeared in a setting
even remotely resembling this one, were on their own. The singer fiddled
with the mike, twisting it so hard his knuckles turned white, but when he
struck the opening chord of "That's All Right," Scotty and Bill fell in
loosely behind him, and he raised up on the balls of his feet, leaning forward into the mike, his lips twisted involuntarily into a kind of sneer, as
his legs began to quiver. "I was scared stiff," he explained afterward. "It
was my first big appearance in front of an audience, and I came out and I
was doing [my first number], and everybody was hollering and I didn't
know what they were hollering at."

"We were all scared to death," said Scotty. "Here we come with two
little funky instruments and a whole park full of people, and Elvis, instead
of just standing flat-footed and tapping his foot, well, he was kind of jiggling. That was just his way of tapping his foot. Plus I think with those old
loose britches that we wore — they weren't pegged, they had lots of material and pleated fronts — you shook your leg, and it made it look like all
hell was going on under there. During the instrumental parts he would
back off from the mike and be playing and shaking, and the crowd would
just go wild, but he thought they were actually making fun of him."

He sang his second song, "Blue Moon of Kentucky," which pretty
much exhausted the group's repertoire at this point, and the crowd went
even wilder. Bill clowned and rode his bass, gave ever more confident
whoops in the background, and hit his instrument a double lick. "It was
really a wild sound, like a jungle drum or something," Elvis recalled with
some wonder. "I came offstage, and my manager told me that they was
hollering because I was wiggling my legs. I went back out for an encore,
and I did a little more, and the more I did, the wilder they went."

Sam Phillips and Bob Neal stood watching from the wings. This was
something beyond either of their wildest expectations. As Elvis sang
"Blue Moon of Kentucky" again, for his encore, he showed even greater
confidence and more untrammeled movement. "It was a real eye-
opener," said Neal, who had had no reason to expect anything whatsoever of this untried, unproven nineteen-year-old. "He just automatically
did things right." "They still wanted Slim," said Sam, "but they wanted

Elvis, too. When they got done cheering for Elvis, they were cheering for Slim. And when Slim came out onstage — and this shows you what a great gentleman Slim Whitman was — he said, 'You know, I can understand your reaction, 'cause I was standing backstage and I was enjoying it just as much as you.' How're you going to do better than that?"

Meanwhile, for Dixie there were sharply mixed emotions. She wasn't shocked by his movements, she had seen him do similar things many times just singing for their friends at Riverside Park, "it was his natural way of performing." And it wasn't that different from what Chief did at the All-Night Singings either — even the reaction and the size of the crowd were comparable too. Even so, she said, "I don't think he was prepared for what was about to happen. He knew this was what he wanted to do and that it was breaking for him, but I don't think he [ever] thought everybody would just go crazy. I wanted to tell [some of the girls who were screaming], 'Shut up and leave him alone. What do you think you're doing here?' And I felt like all of a sudden I was not a part of what he was doing. He was doing something so totally *him* that I was not a part of it. . . . And he loved it."

IN THE WEEKS that followed the Overton Park show, Sam Phillips was on the road almost constantly. Ever since starting up Sun Records again the previous year, he had traveled between sixty-five thousand and seventy-five thousand miles, visiting each of his forty-two distributors, meeting jukebox operators, disc jockeys, record-store owners, buyers and sellers. For all the pointedness with which Sam eschewed convention (and conventions), there were very few people in the business that he did not know and who did not in turn recognize and respect the unswerving commitment that drove this slim, elegant, intense young man with the preacher's faith and the piercing gaze. For each of his trips Sam loaded up the trunk of his car with records and set off on a road that ended in a fitful few hours of sleep, more often than not at the local YMCA, before he moved on to meet the next early-morning jock. Meanwhile, Marion kept things going at home, paying bills, fending off creditors, meeting orders, ordering up labels, dealing with the pressing plant, and fulfilling all the other responsibilities that being half of a cash-poor two-person operation entailed. In the six and a half months before "That's All Right" came out, Sun Records had released twelve records, none of them as substantial a hit as Rufus Thomas' "Bear Cat," which had occasioned a bitter lawsuit from Duke Records' Don Robey (he claimed that "Bear Cat" infringed his copyright on Big Mama Thornton's "Hound Dog") and the eventual forfeiture of a considerable amount of money. In the five months following the release of Sun number 209, the company released only three additional records, one of them (the only one to come out before November) the follow-up disc by Elvis Presley. Clearly Sam Phillips' attention was focused on his new artist, and just as clearly it was not simply because of the economic opportunities that he foresaw. For Sam Phillips saw a revolution on the way.

It was not an easy vision to fulfill. When he came around looking for jocks to play Little Junior Parker or Rufus Thomas, trying to sell distributors on their sales potential, the task was easy by comparison: he was dealing with a defined market, and if he happened to believe in the undefined potential of that market, the *crossover* potential, that is, more than his listener, that was merely a matter of degree. Here, though, all the rules were out the window. "I remember talking to T. Tommy Cutrer [the top country jock] at KCIJ in Shreveport, who's one of the greatest guys in the world — and one thing I never did do is try to overpower somebody with my convictions of what I had in my little black bag. 'If you can give me some play on it, I'd appreciate it. If you can't, I understand.' T. Tommy told me, 'Sam, they'll run me out of town.'" Fats Washington, on the other hand, was a paraplegic black man with a rhythm and blues show who had been crippled in the war. "He played my r&b records, all of them. But when I wanted him to play 'That's All Right,' he played it for me, but he said on the air, 'I just want to tell all my listeners I got Sam Phillips in the studio with me here, and he thinks this is gonna be a hit record, and I'm telling him that this man should not be played after the sun comes up in the morning, it's so country.' I'll never forget that statement, but he was honest about it.

"Paul Berlin was the hottest disc jockey in Houston at the time, and I taught him how to run the board. When he was a little chap on Lowenstein's Junior Theater on Saturdays on WREC, I put him on the air and he'd come in after the show and want me to show him the control boards and everything. Then he became the number-one disc jockey in Houston, and he was playing Tennessee Ernie Ford and Patti Page, all the big pop artists of the time, and he told me, 'Sam, your music is just so ragged, I just can't handle it right now. Maybe later on.'

"I never forced myself in any door or left where they felt I didn't at least intend to. I never said, 'Well, you wait and see,' 'cause, hell, I didn't know myself. I worked with the counter people in the distributorships. I talked to unbelievable numbers of jukebox operators and retail [merchants]. On Mondays you would usually see your jukebox operators and give them a whole week to change their program — Wednesday was usually the last day they could come in and get the newest stuff. Retail was usually Wednesday and Thursday, Tuesday if they were out in the country. I'd come in, say, to Atlanta or Dallas, and if there was something the counter person was on the fence about, they would buy in very limited quantity just so they wouldn't get stuck. The thing I would never do was go in and not tell the distributor what reaction I had from other distributors across the country. I told them the truth. Many times I believed so much in what I had that I wanted to tell them things that really wasn't true. But I knew I had to face them again, so I just told them what I felt — and a lot of times I felt real discouraged.

"One night I left Houston going into Dallas on a Sunday night, and I [ran into] a dust storm sixty miles out of there. I'd already checked out of the Sam Houston Hotel, and I'd had bad reports in Houston, they just didn't understand 'That's All Right, Mama.' I turned around and went back [to Houston] to keep from smothering to death. The next morning I got up and drove on into Dallas, and when I got there — Alta Hayes was the counter girl, and she looked at me and said, 'Sam, you look like hell.' I said, 'Well, thank you, you look nice, too, Alta.' She was a good-looking woman and a great person, and she had a great ear, too. She said, 'Well, let's go up to the corner and have a cup of coffee.' We went up there, and I really didn't want a damn thing, and she sat there and told me, 'Sam, look, don't worry about this thing, you look worn out. This guy is going to be a hit, I don't give a damn what they say.' And I said, 'Well, Alta, I hope you're right.'"

It was a lonely path, and one that Sam trod without regard to personal gain or popularity ("I could be a mean motherfucker. Now this may sound like a contradiction, because I needed everybody's help, but I didn't need myself kissing anyone's ass"). He was a man swept up by a belief, in a sound and in an idea. And as discouraged as he might sometimes get, as harsh as the reality of selling this new music might be, he never strayed from his belief, he never allowed himself to be distracted from his main goal. Which was to get them to *listen*.

In Tupelo, Elvis' hometown, Ernest Bowen, who had worked with Vernon Presley for L. P. McCarty and Sons and whose father had employed Vernon briefly after the war, was now sales manager at WELO. Bowen had met Sam Phillips while Sam was still working at WREC and playing the big band music that Bowen loved, and he liked the man — but he didn't like the new music one bit. As a result WELO was not playing this new record by a hometown boy, despite countless requests from local teenagers. "They were just worrying us to death. Sam called and said, 'I understand you're getting requests for Elvis Presley's music.' I said, 'Yeah.' He said, 'You're not going to play it?' I told him it was a bunch of crap." Rather than take offense, Sam patiently explained that he could understand Ernest's feelings but that this was not a question of personal taste: the world had changed, communications had changed, and while Sam himself was still a country boy at heart, it was no longer the days of the horse and buggy and the courthouse square, as great as those days had been. " 'So you might as well start playing it,' he said. So we did, and from there on," Bowen concluded, "the music began to change, and changed rapidly after that. Younger people started listening to radio instead of putting a nickel in the jukebox. I look back on it, and that was where it began to turn."

THERE WAS NO QUESTION that the record was a hit in Memphis. As one of the first national magazine articles announced nearly a year later: "The current greeting among [Memphis] teenagers is still a rhythmical line from the song: 'Ta dee da dee dee da.' " On August 7, 1954, *Billboard*, which under the editorial direction of Paul Ackerman had long championed the cause of Sun ("Paul Ackerman had a great dedication," said Sam Phillips, "to all the talented people who never had a chance"), reviewed the new single in its "Spotlight" section under the heading "Talent." "Presley is a potent new chanter," read the review, "who can sock over a tune for either the country or the r&b markets. . . . A strong new talent." Which was precisely the point Sam was trying to get across. Meanwhile, there was practically no one in town who hadn't heard the record and didn't have an opinion about it. Ronny Trout, who had been Elvis' shop partner at Humes during Elvis' senior year, saw it on a jukebox at the hamburger stand across from the Dairy Delight where he worked and stared in disbelief. "I thought, Surely, no, that's not, it couldn't be. But heck, with a name like that . . . So I invested a nickel and played the first one, 'That's All Right, Mama,' and I said, That's him! Then I had to play the other."

Red West, the star of the Humes football team, who, along with Ronny, still had another year of high school to go, heard Dewey play it on the radio when he was putting in time at bivouac camp at the Memphis Air Force Base. He was flabbergasted to hear someone that he had considered a nonentity, really, on the radio — it was like going into a movie theater and seeing an acquaintance on the screen. "It was bigger than life," he said. "That's the way it was to me. I was happy for him, but it was kind of unbelievable."

Johnny Black was in Texas. "I was in Corpus Christi, and I picked up a Houston station, and they were playing 'That's All Right, Mama.' " He recognized the song and the singer right away, he heard Bill's slapping bass, and he announced to his wife, " 'We're going back to Memphis, 'cause something is happening there, and I want to be a part of it.' "

In the aftermath of the Overton Park show, "That's All Right" was probably the best-selling record in town. Every DJ in Memphis was on it now, and it seemed like everybody was jumping on the bandwagon. Ronnie Smith called up for Eddie Bond to see if Elvis might like to sing with them now, but Elvis said he had been working hard with Scotty and Bill, he couldn't just quit, though he appreciated the invitation. For Elvis and Dixie it was an idyllic time, a momentary lull in the action when everyone knew that it was all bound to explode but they went about their business as if it wasn't. For Dixie, looking back, it was easy to say that this was the point at which it all began to end, this was the point at which she lost him and the world claimed him, but at the time she was just so proud of him; all through that summer she rode around feeling that all eyes were on her, because he was her boyfriend and she was going to be Mrs. Elvis Presley.

They continued to go to Riverside Park, they continued to drink their milk shakes in the little park near Dixie's house and go out to Leonard's for hamburgers and go to the drive-in movies and sit on the front porch and spoon. Elvis asked Charlie Hazelgrove if he would put the record on the jukebox at the Blues Shop, and he brought the record out to the Rainbow skating rink, too, where, the owner, Joe Pieraccini, said, Elvis listened to it on the jukebox over and over again. Some afternoons they would rehearse at Scotty's brothers' dry cleaning plant, and Dixie would sit there, her mind caught up in other things. The Songfellows, Elvis told her, were looking for a new singer now that Cecil had replaced R.W. in the Blackwood Brothers, but he didn't think he would join even if he was asked, he thought he would just see where this new business might lead. Dixie, who had never imagined any calling higher than quartet singer, just nodded. Whatever he wanted to do — things were going along so nicely.

One Sunday evening a week or so after the Overton Park show, she went over to KWEM, in West Memphis, with the band for a brief radio appearance. Several nights they rehearsed in Scotty's living room, with Scotty calling the rehearsal and Bobbie serving sandwiches but Elvis indicating what he wanted to sing. Sometimes he would know no more than two or three lines from a song, and everyone would be ransacking their memory for the lyrics. Sometimes, if it was a song that she and Elvis had listened to at Charlie's, Dixie might help supply the lyrics herself, or Elvis would just ad-lib something and they would move on to the next number. Scotty and Bill took an active role in Elvis' education. "They taught him how to stand," said Bill's wife, Evelyn. "They coached him on how to hold his guitar and to do all this stuff in front of the mike. He had to learn all that." "It was kind of like we adopted him," said Bobbie Moore. "We had to make sure that he got to the dates, we had to make sure that he got home, we had to make sure that he didn't get into trouble. He was just a kid — he was nice, but he could be kind of a brat, too!"

With Elvis everything always had to be funny, Bobbie said, he was always acting up, whereas Scotty, who enjoyed a good joke, too, believed there was a time and a place for everything. One time Scotty and Bill were loading up after their second or third Saturday at the Bon Air while Elvis and Bobbie stood by the car. "Scotty came out, and he put his amplifier in the trunk, and Elvis said, 'I'm trying to get a date with your wife.' Scotty didn't say a word, but I thought, 'Oh-oh, you shouldn't have said that' — because he wasn't, really. Scotty didn't say a word. He went ahead and got in the driver's seat. I said, 'We better get in the car before he leaves.' I knew he didn't take that as a joke."

One night Elvis stayed over after the show. Bobbie wasn't expecting him to, "but then Scotty said, 'You got some linen for the couch?' so I made up a bed. Elvis was never tired, he could stay up all night after a show, and he was always pacing. He wasn't shy! He wouldn't think anything of walking around, poking his head in the bedroom, every time he'd come over he'd look in the refrigerator, walk around, go look out the door. He just couldn't be still. The time he stayed over, the next morning Scotty says, 'Elvis likes his eggs cooked hard as a rock.' So I fried his eggs as hard as I could, 'cause I like mine done, too. He sat there, and he said, 'Can you cook it a little more?' Well, I cooked it until you couldn't get that egg any harder, and he ate a bunch of toast and bacon but only a couple of bites of that egg. That was the first time I ever remember him spending the night away from home. His mother always waited up for him — she said she couldn't go to sleep until Elvis got home — so maybe he called her to tell her he was spending the night."

Scotty took his duties as manager seriously. He and Sam agreed that it made no sense to put Elvis into some of the rough joints that Scotty and Bill had been playing, so he went looking for schoolhouses to book and local Elks Club and Lions Club events within a seventy-five-mile radius of Memphis that might be looking for a singer. He tried his hometown of Gadsden and got turned down by his old principal, who didn't think they'd make enough money to pay the light bill, but he got some dates over in Mississippi and Arkansas starting in September. In the meantime they played out at the Kennedy Veterans Hospital one Saturday afternoon and in the basement rec room of St. Mary's, across from the Courts, where they gained additional exposure if not pay. At Kennedy they played for the paraplegic and quadriplegic ward under the auspices of the B'nai B'rith, and even there they made quite an impact, according to Monte Weiner, a classmate of Elvis' at Humes, whose mother booked the shows. "My mother brought a group out once a month, and she knew of Elvis through me, though I didn't really know him in school. He did it for several months in a row, the first time was right after the record came out, and they'd bring people on stretchers and wheelchairs down to the little room where he was going to perform. I remember they rolled the beds out into the middle of the floor, and I watched their faces while he and his group were performing, doing something completely different from anything I had ever heard before. The patients couldn't move at all, but their facial expressions — it was like they were trying to clap by their facial expressions. It was a really remarkable thing, that's all I can tell you."

J UST ONE WEEK after Overton Park they started playing as the intermission act out at the Eagle's Nest on their own — without the Starlite Wranglers, who had not taken the success of Scotty's new discovery very well at all. In fact the Overton Park appearance seems to have marked the end of the group, although they did not formally break up for another couple of months. Dixie sometimes baby-sat for Evelyn so that she could go out to the show, and the five of them — the Blacks, the Moores, and Elvis — would go out to eat afterward at Earl's Drive-in downtown. Elvis never had any money in his pocket, Bobbie said; since they had joined the union, they no longer got paid on the job but had to go down to the union hall on Monday to collect, so the "girls" generally ended up paying. "Elvis would ask Scotty, 'Can I have another hamburger or a milk shake?' And Scotty would say, 'You'll have to ask her,' " said Bobbie. " 'She's got the money.' " "I found out he didn't like ketchup," said Evelyn. " 'Cause if I put ketchup on my french fries, he wouldn't eat them. It got to where I put ketchup on them every time — otherwise he'd eat every one!"

It wasn't too long before the intermission shows at the Eagle's Nest became a kind of underground sensation. It was Sleepy Eyed John who booked the club, and Sleepy Eyed John whose band continued to play the main dance sets, but from the start Elvis was clearly an attraction. "Elvis Presley Tonight," the little newspaper squib announced. "See and hear Elvis singing 'That's All Right' and 'Blue Moon of Kentucky,' Admission $1.20 (Including Tax)." Sometimes it was "Ladies' Nite, Too (Ladies .50)," and many of the ads cheerfully admonished, "Don't Wear a Tie Unless Your Wife Makes You," but as the momentum built over the course of the month, with perhaps half a dozen different appearances, in addition to one or two at other clubs around town, you didn't need any gimmicks to build attendance. At first Vernon had wanted to take a sock at Sleepy Eyed John because of some of the sarcastic things Sleepy Eye had said about his son's record on the air. He was going to go up to the station, he told Sam Phillips, and take care of him. "I said, 'Now wait a minute, Mr. Presley, that's not the way it works. The worst thing you can do is go over there. All he wants to do is to create some noise. Let's kill the sonofabitch with kindness.' " Vernon was dubious, but he allowed himself to be dissuaded, and when he and Gladys went out to the club, he was glad that he had. Other members of the family came out on occasion: Gladys' sister Lillian and her husband, who remained pessimistic about the boy's prospects; Vernon's brother, Vester, and his wife, Clettes, another of Gladys' sisters, who took a couple of snapshots of a very young, very blond, and somewhat uncomfortable-looking Elvis Presley standing in front of the Eagle's Nest sign.

James and Gladys Tipler came out to the Eagle's Nest, too. They continued to feel great pride in their employee and even brought some of their big construction clients. "He wanted us to come out and see him so he would feel he had some friends in the audience," Mrs. Tipler said. "He had quite a bit of trouble with stage fright." Sometimes he wore his bolero jacket, sometimes he wore a striped sports jacket with a velvet collar that he had recently bought at Lansky's, occasionally he favored western clothes. His favorite colors were pink and black. "I remember the first check he gave me," said Guy Lansky, who had known him from the time he first pressed his face to the Beale Street clothing store window. "It was hard to take. I think it was five hundred dollars from Sam Phillips, and he asked me to cash it for him, and he bought some clothes and some jewelry — I had a little jewelry store on the side. And I was still skeptical of him because of his appearance, I remember running to the bank to see if it was good. Years later, after he got Graceland, I used to take my kids out there, and I remember he showed me that sports coat that he had bought years before — boy, he loved that coat, it was still in his closet."

He seemed to gain more and more of a sense of himself, greater and greater self-assurance onstage and off. "His movement was a natural thing," said Scotty, "but he was also very conscious of what got a reaction. He'd do something one time and then he would expand on it real quick." According to Reggie Young, who was seventeen at the time and would join Eddie Bond's band, the Stompers, the following year, all the teenagers who were out at the swimming pool that gave the Clearpool complex its name (the Eagle's Nest was over the changing room) would rush in as soon as they heard Elvis, Scotty, and Bill start to play. Then all the kids went back outside when Sleepy Eyed John's band took the stage again, fifteen minutes later. "Sleepy Eyed John was all into Ray Price's big western swing band at that time," said his sometime lead vocalist and MC, Jack Clement, who went on to become Sam Phillips' right-hand man at Sun and one of the most brilliantly idiosyncratic producers and confabulators that Nashville ever produced. "Eight or nine pieces, three fiddles, all that kind of stuff — that's where Sleepy Eye thought music was going. Of course nobody agreed with him, and Elvis would come on and do the floor show, just the three of them. He seemed to be handling it all very well, you know, in a young-gentleman fashion, he was kind of reserved but not really shy — that was his demeanor. I was going with my fiancée, Doris, we got married in December, and Doris would come to the dance and sit at a table and when I was up there singing Elvis would be over there trying to get Doris to go out with him. Doris was a very pretty girl — I didn't mind if he flirted with Doris, I liked him. I would get up there and do my set, and then I'd bring him on and he would really cut up.''

Marion Keisker saw Elvis frequently all through August. He would stop by the studio from time to time to find out how his record was doing or just to hang around and chat. He remained grateful to Marion, as he would be all his life, for helping him ''get his first break,'' and she in turn saw in him an almost magical quality that both protected him and in turn brought out the best in others. ''My total image of Elvis was as a child. His attitude towards people was the equivalent of tipping your hat as you walk down the street — 'Good evening, ma'am, good evening, sir' — but not showing off. He never said a wrong thing from the very first night he appeared on the Dewey Phillips show — he was like a mirror in a way: whatever you were looking for, you were going to find in him. It was not in him to lie or say anything malicious. He had all the intricacy of the very simple.''

As for Sam, increasingly he saw in the boy something to mirror his own self-image, the kind of person whose ''insecurity drove him, and yet he was an extremely patient person for achieving a kind of success [that his contemporaries could only dream of], he was absolutely, unequivocally going to sing. He was not an eloquent person, but many times without a direct statement he was eloquent in starting something that told you exactly what he was thinking.'' A person still subject to mood swings (''Sam was a driven man,'' said Marion) yet one who always maintained the appearance of calm and self-assurance, Sam saw in Elvis the very person that he was but rarely showed. Where Elvis appeared unsure, tongue-tied, incapable of expressing himself, Sam saw in him the same sort of burning ambition, he was only lacking the ability to *verbalize* it.

Sam had always seen it as his mission to ''open up an area of freedom within the artist himself, to help him to express what *he* believed his message to be,'' and here he had found his perfect Trilby. To Sam the person who presented himself had never played anywhere before he entered the Sun studio, ''he didn't play with bands, he didn't go to this little club and pick and grin. All he did was set with the guitar on the side of his bed at home. I don't think he even played on the front porch.'' This was what Elvis conveyed, without words, and in a way it was true. When Elvis was with Scotty, when Elvis was in the Sun studio, it was as if he were reborn.

To Sam, as much as to Marion, he was the personification of an ideal, the embodiment of a vision that Sam had carried with him from the farm in Florence — he represented the *innocence* that had made the country great in combination with "the elements of the soil, the sky, the water, even the wind, the quiet nights, people living on plantations, never out of debt, hoping to eat, lights up the river — that's what they used to call Memphis. That was where it all came together. And Elvis Presley may not have been able to verbalize all that — but he damn sure wasn't dumb, and he damn sure was intuitive, and he damn sure had an appreciation for the total spirituality of the human existence, even if he would never have thought of the term. That was what he cared about."

That was Elvis' mark — he conveyed his spirituality without being able, or needing, to express it. And all these adults with their more complicated lives and dreams and passions and hopes looked for themselves in his simplicity.

ON AUGUST 28 the record entered the *Billboard* regional charts. It showed up at number three on the C&W Territorial Best Sellers for the week of August 18, behind Hank Snow's "I Don't Hurt Anymore" and a Kitty Wells–Red Foley duet, but it was "Blue Moon of Kentucky" that was the hit. On the strength of these credentials, and on the basis of the record's striking local success, Sam Phillips approached Jim Denny, manager of the Grand Ole Opry, with the idea that the Opry could at least offer the boy a little exposure. After all, Sam adjured Denny, whom he knew from the year he had spent in Nashville, it was no longer the old mule-and-wagon days, wasn't it time to allow something new to breathe? Sam wasn't saying the boy was necessarily going to set the world on fire, but give youth a chance, damnit. Jim Denny listened; he was a hard man, Sam knew — he was not about to win any popularity contests — but he was a fair man, too. He had heard the record, he told Sam, it wasn't really to his taste, but if Sam could give him a little time, well, maybe if the band was in the area at some point he could fit them in. Sam hung up the phone — he was well enough pleased. He could wait as long as he had to. At least Denny hadn't said no.

Others were noticing the waves the new record was making. In Nashville, Bill Monroe, far from being offended at the "sacrilege" which had

been committed on his song, approached Carter Stanley, another prominent bluegrass musician, after the Opry one Saturday night. "He said, 'I
want you to hear something,' and he had never said anything like that to
me before." He played Stanley the "new" version of "Blue Moon of Kentucky." "I laughed a little bit and looked around, and everybody else was
laughing except Bill. He said, 'You better do that record [at Stanley's scheduled recording session] tomorrow if you want to sell some records.' . . . He
said, 'I'm going to do it [at his own recording session] next Sunday.'" And
Monroe helped supervise Stanley's session on Sunday, August 29, then
recut "Blue Moon of Kentucky" himself in 4/4 time, as he had said he
would, the following week.

The major record labels, too, couldn't help but notice what was going
on. Jim Denny, in addition to his duties as general manager of the Opry,
was also proprietor of Cedarwood Publishing, which in turn was tied in
with Decca Records, and Decca's Paul Cohen pricked up his ears at this
new phenomenon. Sam's friend Randy Wood, who operated a big one-step
and mail-order record business in Gallatin, Tennessee, and had enjoyed a
good deal of success with his own Dot Record Company, expressed mild
interest as well. Meanwhile, RCA Records in New York had come to be
aware of this rising new star, and this upstart new label, not simply because
of the write-ups in *Billboard* and *Cash Box* but because of the reports they
were getting from their own agents in the field. "All of our distributors
were aware of Sam Phillips," said Chick Crumpacker, who had become
national country and western promotion manager working under a&r
(artist and repertoire) director Steve Sholes in April. "There was all this talk
about what this insurgent Sun Records was doing, quite a bit of it pejorative. Also, we would get these reports from the field, from Sam Esgro, who
was based in Memphis, and Brad McCuen, who had the RCA field from the
middle of Tennessee into Virginia and the Carolinas."

McCuen, a thirty-three-year-old transplanted New Yorker, who filed a
report to Steve Sholes that summer, vividly recalled his first encounter with
Elvis Presley. "My bell-cow area was East Tennessee. If a record made it in
the tri-city area of Kingsport, Johnson City, and Bristol on down through to
Knoxville, it would go national, so I was just very conscious of that area.
One of our best record dealers was Sam Morrison in Knoxville, right on
Market Square. He was one of the first southern record dealers that I knew
to do the New York City trick of putting a loudspeaker out over his doorsill

and playing the music for the market crowd, who had come in to sell their produce. This one particular time Sam grabbed me and said, 'There's something very interesting happening here, it's really weird,' and he went and got Elvis' record, which was just out, and put 'That's All Right' on the player. 'What do you think?' he said. 'I can't get enough of it. I'm selling at least a box a day.' I was amazed, but I said, 'It's just a normal rhythm and blues record, isn't it?' He said, 'No, it isn't, it's selling to a country audience.'

"Well, at just that point an old country man in his fifties came in, I say jokingly he had more hair growing out of his ears and nose than he did on his head, and he said in an easy Tennessee drawl, "By granny, I want that record.' I couldn't figure it out, because here was an obvious country fan. Then Sam turned the record over and played 'Blue Moon of Kentucky,' and I figured, 'Well, he probably wants it for that.' But that wasn't it — it was really 'That's All Right.' So I bought two copies of the record and sent one to Steve Sholes, and Steve said, 'You've got to be kidding!' But I told him that Sam Morrison must have gone through about five thousand, and it was selling in Kingsport and the tri-cities area. And Sam Esgro and I kept sending him reports."

ON SEPTEMBER 8 the *Memphis Press-Scimitar* announced "Fun on a Grand Scale" at the opening of the new Lamar-Airways Shopping Center. The festivities over the next few days would include Indian ceremonies, "Scottish, hillbilly and Indian music groups, radio, television and recording personalities," a twenty-eight-foot "robot" Indian, lavish prizes, and the presence of "a number of celebrities . . . including Mayor Tobey." Also included was the "newest Memphis hit in the recording business . . . Elvis Presley of 'That's All Right, Mama' and 'Blue Moon of Kentucky' fame," who would be appearing along with Sleepy Eyed John's Eagle's Nest band on a flatbed truck in front of Katz Drug Store on opening night, Thursday, between 9:00 and 10:00. "Blue Moon of Kentucky" was number one on the Memphis c&w chart at this point, with "That's All Right" showing up at number seven.

The parking lot was jammed when Elvis arrived with Dixie, and George Klein, who was back at Memphis State for the fall semester, was broadcasting from inside the giant wooden Indian. Scotty and Bill were already present, and Sleepy Eye was all set up onstage, but the crowd seemed restive. It was made up almost exclusively of teenagers — there were lots of them, more than could ever have fit into the Eagle's Nest — and if they didn't equal the size of the Overton Park audience, this time it was obvious who they were there for.

George emerged from the Indian to come up and introduce the band, and Elvis lit up to see his old Humes classmate, the president of the senior class and editor of the yearbook, especially when George said he had been playing the record over the air in Osceola all summer. They caught up with each other very briefly — Elvis hadn't seen George to talk to since graduation, fifteen months before — but it was perfectly evident how their situations had changed. They spoke of friends in common, and then it was time to go onstage. George gave them the big buildup, he mentioned that he had gone to school with this rising young star, he conveyed a sense of significance and respect in his trained announcer's voice that Sleepy Eye would never have suggested, but there was no preparation for the sound that greeted them, for the whoosh of anticipation, the screams, and the mass intake of breath as Elvis Presley bounded to the microphone. Dixie hadn't really seen him perform since Overton Park — and here they were not far from the Rainbow skating rink, where she had first met her "secret love."

Scotty knew that day. "This was the first we could see what was happening. 'Cause it was a whole parking lot full of kids, and they just went crazy." They liked Bill's clowning, and Elvis' gyrations had advanced way beyond Overton even at this point, but it was the beat that really got to them, and it was the kids' response that drove the music to another level. It was so out of control it was almost frightening.

After the show Elvis hung around a little — there were a bunch of people that he knew in the crowd, and they all wanted to talk to him, some of them even wanted his autograph. Looking at him, watching him open up to people in the way she had always known he could, Dixie thought maybe this was as far as he would go, this was success on the highest level that a normal person could ever hope for. George was genuinely excited. He had to go back to making announcements and deejaying inside the Indian, but they really ought to get together sometime, he said. There were some guys in the audience, too, who were muttering under their breath that they didn't see what the big fuss was all about, this guy was weird in his black pants with the pink stripe, his greasy hair and pimply face — it looked almost like he was wearing makeup. In Florida, Lee

Denson heard from his brothers and sisters about the splash that Elvis was making around town, and he couldn't believe it. Here was a kid barely able to form a chord when Lee tried to teach him in the Courts just a couple of years earlier — of all of them he was the *least* likely to succeed. Lee was playing a regular gig while also working as a bellhop in Key West. Ernest Hemingway, the writer, had declared him to be his favorite singer one night at Sloppy Joe's, and here Elvis Presley was stirring up all this fuss. "The difference between me and him," said Lee, "was I went for it. I drove for it. New York, Hollywood — I went everywhere for it. And he fell into the shithole and came up with the gold watch and chain."

TOP: ELVIS, BILL, SCOTTY, AND SAM PHILLIPS, 1954.
(COURTESY OF GARY HARDY, SUN STUDIO)
BOTTOM: WITH BOB NEAL, 1955. (COURTESY OF GER RIJFF)

GOOD ROCKIN' TONIGHT

I T WAS A TWO-HUNDRED-MILE RIDE to Nashville, but the four of them were comfortable enough in Sam Phillips' four-door black 1951 Cadillac, with Bill's bass strapped to the roof. It was Saturday, October 2. Elvis, Scotty, and Bill had played their regular Friday-night gig at the Eagle's Nest; their record "Blue Moon of Kentucky" was near the top of the charts in Memphis and just beginning to break in Nashville and New Orleans; and they had every reason to feel that they had reached the pinnacle of their musical career — because tonight *they were going to play the Opry.*

Jim Denny had finally succumbed to Sam's argument that there was no need to think about putting the boy on as a regular, he didn't have to think of this as a normal "tryout," *just give the boy a chance.* Denny seemed no more convinced than he had been in the first place — perhaps he was just worn down by Sam's persistence — but he agreed to give the young man a one-time spot on Hank Snow's segment of the show. He could perform a single song with his band, the country number "Blue Moon of Kentucky." If it was worth it to Sam and the boys to drive over just for that, well, then, Denny was willing to give them the shot.

In the meantime Sam had also heard from the Louisiana Hayride, the Opry's more innovative rival in Shreveport, which, unlike the Opry, actually *wanted* this new act. The Hayride, which Denny referred to derisively as the Opry's farm club because so many of its big acts eventually defected to Nashville, had discovered Hank Williams in 1948 and broken such stars as Slim Whitman, Webb Pierce, and, most recently, Jim Reeves and Faron Young. But Sam put them off because, he explained to Hayride booking agent Pappy Covington, he wanted to play the Opry first. As soon as the boys had fulfilled this prior commitment, he told Pappy, stretching the truth a little, Elvis could appear on the Hayride. There was no doubt in his mind, he said, that Elvis could make a hit with the Hayride audience, and they could set it up for just a week or two after the

Opry appearance, but he had committed himself to Jim Denny that the boy would appear on the Opry first. He was walking a thin line, he knew. He didn't for a minute want to lose the Hayride, but he wasn't going to give up the opportunity to see a new, untried artist get his national debut on the hallowed Grand Ole Opry.

Ryman Auditorium was like a tattered shrine to the three musicians, none of whom had ever attended, let alone played, a show at the Opry before. They wandered around the dilapidated old building, erected as a tabernacle in 1886 and still retaining the old wooden pews for seats, in something of a daze. They were both overwhelmed at the sense of history contained in the room — the music they had been listening to all their lives emanated from this cramped little stage — and somewhat disillusioned, too, that the Grand Ole Opry was not, well, grander. Backstage the other musicians mingled freely, exchanging small talk and greetings, tuning up, donning makeup and costumes, without any of the formality or protocol that you might have expected from stars but with all of the remoteness, whether real or perceived, of big leaguers sniffing at bushers just up from the minors. Twenty-one-year-old bass player Buddy Killen, who had just started as chief and only song plugger for Tree Music, the publishing house that WSM program director Jack Stapp had set up in 1951, came up to the obviously out-of-place young singer and introduced himself. "[Elvis] said, 'They're going to hate me.' I said, 'They're not going to hate you. You're going to be fine.' He said, 'If they'd just let me leave, I'd go right now.' " Marty Robbins saw evidence of the same insecurity, but when Elvis spotted Chet Atkins backstage, he introduced himself and then, knowing Scotty's admiration for Atkins' playing, pulled Scotty over, too, saying, "My guitar player wants to meet you." Atkins noted with asperity that the kid appeared to be wearing eye makeup.

Probably of all the Opry legends the one they were most leery of running into was Bill Monroe. Many in the country field continued to view the Sun version of "Blue Moon of Kentucky" as a desecration, and even Sam had heard that Monroe was going to take their head off for their untrammeled interpretation of his stately lament ("I'd heard he was going to break my jaw!"). But when they met Monroe, conservatively dressed in dark suit and tie and trademark white hat and at forty-three already an elder statesman possessed of a dignity that permitted neither bullshit nor informality, he came right out and complimented them. As a matter of fact, he told them, he had cut a new version of the song for Decca, due out next week, that followed their pattern.

There were two additional surprises. Marion Keisker, left behind in Memphis to keep the studio doors open, abandoned her post and caught a bus to Nashville, where she thought at first she would just stay out in the audience so as not to spook them but before long found her way backstage and joined the little group. Then Bill peeked out at the audience and, much to his surprise, discovered his wife, Evelyn, and Scotty's wife, Bobbie, in the front row. "I think he was kind of glad to see us," said Bobbie, " 'cause they were wanting to come back to Memphis that night, and Sam was going to stay over in Nashville. You see, they had told Evelyn and me, 'Y'all can't go. We're all going in one car, and there's no room for you.' Well, I accepted that, but then around noon, a couple of hours after they left, Evelyn came over to the house and said, 'Let's go to Nashville.' I said, 'Oh, I don't know about that, we might get in trouble,' but, you know, we really were like Lucy and Ethel, so then I said, 'What the heck!' and we drove over. Bill stuck his head out the stage door and saw us, but when Scotty saw me backstage, it was like he'd seen a ghost!"

At 10:15 Grant Turner announced the Hank Snow segment of the show, sponsored by Royal Crown Cola, and Snow, whose son, Jimmie Rodgers Snow, had just approached Elvis admiringly, got lost in his introduction of a young man from Memphis who has just made a hit record, let's give him a nice round of applause, to the point that he forgot the young singer's name. Elvis bounced out the same way that he always did, as if he had just fallen off a fast-moving train, and did his one number. Scotty and Bill were more nervous than he was — to them, it seemed, there was nowhere to go but down from here, and they could sense from the polite, but somewhat tepid, reception that this was exactly where they were going. Afterward they were like a boxing management team trying to rationalize defeat. Everyone was *nice* to them as they gawked and huddled — they'd gotten a *good* reception, Bobbie and Evelyn insisted, and Bill introduced himself to everyone, laughing and cracking jokes, while Scotty stood off to one side a little stiffly, waiting to be introduced. Before leaving, Sam conferred briefly with Mr. Denny, who confirmed that Elvis Presley just did not fit the Opry mold, but, he told Sam, " 'This boy is not bad.' He didn't give me any great accolades, he just grabbed me by my skinny arm and said, 'This boy is not bad.' Well, people put down Jim

Denny, nobody much liked Jim, he was a damn tough man, but *he did me a favor."*

They left not long afterward and wandered down the hill to 417 Broadway, the location of the Ernest Tubb Record Shop, where they were scheduled to play the famous Midnight Jamboree (the Jamboree went on the air live from the record store at the conclusion of the Opry broadcast). Their first impression of the shop was how small it was, but maybe that was just because of how crammed it was with record bins and all the people who had already arrived for the start of the broadcast. Someone introduced Elvis to Ernest Tubb, and Tubb, the most gracious and courteous of entertainers, listened patiently as the nineteen-year-old poured out his love for Tubb's music and told him that it was his real ambition to sing country music. "He said, 'They tell me if I'm going to make any money, though, I've got to sing [this other kind of music]. What should I do?' I said, 'Elvis, you ever have any money?' He said, 'No, sir.' I said, 'Well, you just go ahead and do what they tell you to do. Make your money. Then you can do what *you* want to do.' "

Scotty and Bill headed back to Memphis with their errant wives after the broadcast. They felt simultaneously elated and depressed (they had made it to the big time, even if they were now in all likelihood on the road to oblivion), but for Sam Phillips the evening was an unmitigated triumph. To play the Opry — and *then* to get approval, however grudging, from Jim Denny and Bill Monroe! Even the criticism would not hurt. It could be used, Sam was firmly convinced, to further the boy's appeal — if he could just turn around some of this damn rejection he was getting, if he could just straighten out some of the wrongheaded thinking he was encountering, the blind could be made to see, the lame could be made to walk. "I *needed* the attention that I got from the people that hated what I was doing, that acted like: 'Here is somebody trying to thrust junk on us and classify it as our music.' Well, fuck them, *let them do the classifying*. I just had to peak that damn pyramid, or else the damn sonofabitch would have fallen down." And with Elvis Presley, Sam Phillips was sure he had the means to peak the pyramid.

ELVIS PRESLEY'S second Sun single was released on the Monday before his Opry appearance. It was, if anything, an even bolder declaration of intent than the first, especially the strident blues number "Good

Rockin' Tonight," which rocked more confidently than anything they could have imagined in those first, uncertain days in the studio. Maybe Sam still couldn't diagram the path, but, he felt, they were finally beginning to find their way to "that damn row that hadn't been plowed."

They had seized every opportunity they could to get into the studio all through August, but Sam was on the road so much, and the band was working so many weekends (while still holding down full-time jobs), that this was easier said than accomplished. On August 19 they spent hours doing take after take of "Blue Moon," in an eerie, clippity-clop version that resembled a cross between Slim Whitman's "Indian Love Call" and some of the falsetto flights of the r&b "bird" groups (the Orioles, the Ravens, the Larks). After it was all over, Sam wasn't satisfied that they had anything worth releasing, but he never uttered a word of demurral for fear of discouraging the unfettered freshness and enthusiasm of the singer. "The sessions would go on and on," said Marion Keisker, "each record was sweated out. Sam showed patience beyond belief — in a personality that's not really given to patience."

The problem did not appear to have so much to do with time, in any case, as with confidence and direction. They had captured the ring once, seemingly by accident, but now no one appeared to have a clear vision of how to capture it again, and Sam was reluctant to impose his own. "I had a mental picture, as sure as God is on His throne I had a mental picture of what I wanted to hear, certainly not note for note, but I knew the essence of what we were trying to do. But I also knew that the worst thing I could do was to be impatient, to try to force the issue — sometimes you can make a suggestion just [to change] one bar and you kill the whole song. And sometimes you can be too cocky around people who are insecure and just intimidate them. I mean, as far as actually saying, 'Hey, man, don't be scared,' I've never told anybody in my life not to be scared of the microphone — don't go calling attention to the thing you know they are already scared of. I was never a real forward person, because I didn't give a damn about jumping out in front to be seen, but I tried to envelop them in my feelings of security."

Over the course of the next few weeks they made several attempts at "Satisfied," Martha Carson's rousing spiritual hit from 1951, and "Tomorrow Night," the Lonnie Johnson blues ballad which Elvis had crooned so often to Dixie. They made any number of false starts on other tunes, all of them erased because tape was expensive, after all, and they just weren't going anywhere. The slow numbers, Sam said, "would hang you out to dry," but he was determined to give Elvis' creative imagination free play. He was equally determined, said Marion, not to release anything even a jot below the standard they had already set; he wanted to be sure he had done all that he could to make every record as good as it was "humanly possible to make it." From Sam's point of view: "I wanted simplicity, where we could look at what we were hearing mentally and say, 'Man, this guy has just got it.' But I wanted some biting bullshit, too. Everything had to be a stinger. To me every one of those sessions was like I was filming *Gone With the Wind.*"

Finally, starting on September 10, they hit a streak — once again it seemed almost as if they had stumbled onto it by accident, but when they did it was, as Sam Phillips said, as if it had been waiting for them all along. They cut "Just Because," a rollicking, honky-tonk blues which the Shelton Brothers had originally recorded as the Lone Star Cowboys in 1933. The great good humor and burbling effervescence of the new trio version can be traced in equal parts to the singer's confident exploitation of his gospel-learned technique (here for the first time we hear the characteristic Presley drop to a slurred lower register), Bill Black's almost comically thumping bass, and Scotty's increasingly rhythm-driven guitar. "It was almost a total rhythm thing," Scotty said. "With only the three of us we had to make every note count." Although Sam never released this cut or the next one either, a weepy version of Jimmy Wakely's 1941 "I'll Never Let You Go (Little Darlin')" with a tagged-on, double-time ending, both are characterized by the kind of playfulness and adventurousness of spirit that Sam was looking for, the fresh, almost "impudent" attitude that he was seeking to unlock.

With "I Don't Care If the Sun Don't Shine," an even more unlikely transformation took place. Originally written for the Disney animated feature *Cinderella* by Mack David, brother of the celebrated pop composer Hal David (Mack himself wrote such well-known songs as "Bippidi Bobbidi Boo" and "La Vie en Rose"), the song didn't make the film score's final cut, but it was popularized in 1950 by Patti Page and by Dean Martin in conjunction with Paul Weston and His Dixie Eight. The rhythmic approach couldn't have been more different, but it was Martin's version on which Elvis' is clearly based; for all the energy that Elvis, Scotty, and Bill impart to the song, and for all the high spirits of Elvis' vocalizing, it is Martin's lazily insouciant spirit that comes through. It's as if Dennis the Menace met the drawling English character actor George Sanders. "That's what he heard in Dean," said Sam, who was well aware of Martin's influence, "that little bit of mischievousness that he had in his soul when he cut up a little bit — [that's why] he loved Dean Martin's singing."

With the last song of the session, Wynonie Harris' r&b classic "Good Rockin' Tonight," everything finally fell into place. By this time everyone may have been getting a little testy, and no one was really sure whether they had anything or not, but as Scotty said, "Sam had an uncanny knack for pulling stuff out of you. Once you got a direction, he'd work you so hard you'd work your butt off, he'd make you so mad you'd want to kill him, but he wouldn't let go until he got that little something extra sometimes you didn't even know you had." He would insist that they play nothing but rhythm, he would have them change keys just when they finally got used to the one they were in, and he called for tempos so slow sometimes that everyone was ready to scream. "A lot of times it was a tempo that I absolutely knew they weren't going to like, but we were in a situation where we just weren't getting anywhere, and when they came back [to the original tempo], it was like they'd hit a home run."

To Marion Keisker it was like a puzzle to which only Sam had the key. "I still remember the times when everyone would be so tired, and then some little funny thing would set us off — I'd see Elvis literally rolling around on the floor, and Bill Black just stretched out with his old broken-down bass fiddle, just laughing and goofing off. It was a great spirit of — I don't know, everyone was trying very hard, but everyone was trying to hang very loose through the whole thing. [Sometimes] if Elvis would do something absolutely extraordinary and somebody would hit a clinker or something would go wrong before the tape was completed, Sam would say, 'Well, let's go back, and you hold on to what you did there. I want that.' And Elvis would say, 'What did I do? What did I do?' Because it was all so instinctive that he simply didn't know."

Sam's one organizing principle was that it had to be fun. "I could tolerate anything, we could have tensions as long as I knew that we all had confidence in what we were trying to do, and I could get everybody relaxed to the point where they could hear and react to something without that threshold of apprehension where you almost get to a point where you can't do anything right. Every time we did a number I wanted to make sure to the best of my ability that everybody *enjoyed* it."

In the case of this final number, that sense of enjoyment comes through from the very first note, as Elvis' voice takes on a burr of aggression that is missing from the previous recordings, the band for the first time becomes the fused rhythm instrument that Sam had been seeking all along, and there is a sense of driving, high-flying good times almost in defiance of societal norms. "Have you heard the news?" is the opening declaration, drawn out and dramatic. "There's good rocking tonight."

The other dramatic element to declare itself was the quality that Sam thought he had sensed in Elvis from the start, that strange, unexpected impulse that had led the boy to launch himself into "That's All Right, Mama" in the first place — it seemed to come out of nowhere, and yet, Sam felt, he heard something of the same feeling in the sentimental ballads, too. He equated the insecurity that came through so unmistakably in the boy's stance and demeanor with the sense of inferiority — social, psychological, perceptual — that was projected by the great Negro talents he had sought out and recorded. Sam couldn't be sure, he *thought* he sensed in Elvis a kindred spirit, someone who shared with him a secret, almost subversive attraction not just to black music but to black culture, to an inchoate striving, a belief in the equality of man. This was something that Sam felt could never be articulated; each man was doomed to stumble in his own darkness, if only because the stakes were so high.

"I had to keep my nose clean. They could have said, 'This goddam rebel down here is gonna turn his back on us. Why should we give this nigger-loving sonofabitch a break?' It took some subtle thinking on my part — I'm telling you [some] resolute facts here. But I had the ability to be patient. I was able to hold on almost with a religious fervor, but definitely subdued — I wasn't looking for no tall stumps to preach from. And I sensed in him the same kind of empathy. I don't think he was aware of my motivation for doing what I was trying to do — not consciously anyway — but *intuitively* he felt it. I never discussed it — I don't think it would have been very wise to talk about it, for me to say, 'Hey, man, we're going against —.' Or, 'We're trying to put pop music down and bring in black —.' The lack of prejudice on the part of Elvis Presley had to be one of the biggest things that ever could have happened to us, though. It was almost subversive, sneaking around through the music — but we hit things a little bit, don't you think? I went out into this no-man's-land, and I knocked the shit out of the color line."

Sam knew that he had found a kindred spirit in other ways as well. Over the course of the next month, as he worked at trying to set up the

Opry appearance, as he took around an acetate of the new single and encountered the same resistance in Nashville from old friends like WLAC
DJ Gene Nobles and one-stop record distributors Randy Wood and Ernie
Young, all strictly rhythm and blues men, he nevertheless knew that his
instincts had not been wrong. Getting to know the boy a little better, getting him to open up a little more, having the chance to talk to him not just
about music but about life and love and women, he sensed a potential
that even he had not fully anticipated. "I was amazed. Here I am twelve
years older than him, I'm thirty-one and he's nineteen, and I've been exposed to all kinds of music and lived through the damn Depression, and
yet he had the most intuitive ability to hear songs without ever having to
classify them, or *himself,* of anyone I've ever known outside of Jerry Lee
Lewis and myself. It seemed like he had a photographic memory for every
damn song he ever heard — and he was one of the most introspective
human beings that I've ever met. You see, Elvis Presley knew what it was
like to be poor, but that damn sure didn't make him prejudiced. *He didn't
draw any lines.* And like [*Billboard* editor] Paul Ackerman said, you have to
be an awful smart person or dumb as hell (and you *know* he wasn't dumb)
to put out that kind of thinking."

Elvis Presley, our homegrown hillbilly singer, is continuing his
swift, steady stride toward national prominence in the rural rhythm
field. Latest honor to come his way is as guest performer with the
Louisiana Hayride, to be broadcast Saturday night over KWKH,
Shreveport. Louisiana Hayride is about the second or third most popular hillbilly program on the air. The tops is Nashville's Grand Ole
Opry, which never takes anyone but long-established stars in the
country music field. But Presley has already appeared on the Grand
Ole Opry — on October 2 — and neither customers nor fellow performers wanted him to quit. It is unprecedented for Grand Ole Opry
to take a performer on the basis of a single record, which is what Presley had until two weeks ago.

— *Memphis Commercial Appeal,* October 14, 1954

S AM CALLED PAPPY COVINGTON, the talent booker for the Hayride,
on the Monday after the Opry appearance. They settled on a date less

than two weeks away, both because that suited Sam's purposes and because Tillman Franks, who had made the contact for Pappy in the first place, had a chance to book his act, Jimmy and Johnny, into the Eddy County Barn Dance in Carlsbad, New Mexico, if he could find a replacement for them on the Hayride. Jimmy and Johnny had the number-three hillbilly hit in the country on Chicago's Chess Records, and Tillman had been offered $500 by Carlsbad promoter Ray Schaffer (as opposed to $24 apiece, Hayride scale). As a result Tillman approached Hayride director Horace Logan about this singer he had heard on T. Tommy Cutrer's program on KCIJ. Tillman had thought the singer was black, and so had Horace, the flamboyant, pistol-toting MC of the Hayride, when Tillman played the record for him. But T. Tommy, who was playing the record only as a favor to Sam Phillips after Sam came through town a couple of months before (the two men knew each other from T.'s brief stint with WREC just after the war), quickly disabused Horace and Tillman of the notion: after all, hadn't Slim Whitman and Billy Walker shared the same stage with the boy in Memphis? And Tillman, a pepper pot of a man possessed of the greatest enthusiasm and love for the music (he had already managed, and lost, Webb Pierce and Bill Carlisle, helped guide Slim Whitman's career, and would go on to manage Johnny Horton while continuing to play bass on the Hayride), got Pappy Covington to take it from there.

The Hayride was a little over six years old at this point. It had been predated by a similar program, the KWKH Saturday Night Roundup, before the war and, as the *Commercial Appeal* stated, was probably the second most popular hillbilly program on the air, with a 50,000-watt clear-channel signal that rivaled the Opry's, reaching up to twenty-eight states, and a CBS hookup that enabled it to reach 198 stations for an hour the third Saturday of every month. The hallmark of the Hayride was innovation, and it was as the Opry's brash younger cousin that the Hayride really made its mark. Hank Williams, Kitty Wells, Webb Pierce, Faron Young, the Carlisles, David Houston, Jim Reeves, all debuted on the Hayride before eventually lighting out for Nashville, and under the leadership of Horace Logan it continued to be a haven for new talent, fast-paced variety, and new directions. The Hayride audiences in the thirty-eight-hundred-seat Municipal Auditorium showed the same kind of enthusiasm as the performers, and Logan placed microphones out among the crowd to register their reaction, whether to something that was going out over the air or to longtime announcer Ray Bartlett (who broadcast during the day as rhythm and blues DJ Groovey Boy) doing unrestrained somersaults and back flips onstage. Shreveport was a lively music town, just on the cusp of oil affluence and with the kind of unassuming racial mix (nothing like desegregation, of course, but with two populations living cheek by jowl, locked in an inescapable cultural alliance) that gave Memphis its own musical flavor. The Hayride had everything, in fact, except an aggressive booking agency to support its acts (Pappy Covington had the job only because he had a lease on the building) and record companies to sign them. This was the principal reason for the one-way migration to Nashville, but in the fall of 1954 it looked as if the supply of new talent might be inexhaustible, and the Hayride had grown accustomed to thumbing its nose at the Opry, which Horace Logan referred to frequently on the air as "the Tennessee branch of the Hayride."

Sam, Elvis, Scotty, and Bill set out for Shreveport, a good seven- or eight-hour ride from Memphis, not long after the boys got off work at their regular Friday-night gig at the Eagle's Nest. They missed the turnoff at Greenville, Mississippi, because Bill had everybody laughing so hard at one of his jokes, and then Scotty almost hit a team of mules as they struggled to make up the time. When they finally got to Shreveport, they checked into the Captain Shreve Hotel downtown — they got a big double room and a smaller adjoining room — and then they had to wait forever while Elvis combed his hair. Sam took the boys around to meet Pappy, who made them feel "like four hundred million dollars, just this kindly, fatherly old man who made you feel like you were the greatest thing that could ever walk into his office. I thought that was the best thing that could happen for these young men and even myself." From there he and Elvis went and paid their respects to T. Tommy, who had until recently been laid up from an automobile accident in which he had lost a leg, though he continued to broadcast from his bed at home. Elvis was wearing a typical black and pink outfit and, according to T. Tommy, "his hair was long and greasy and he didn't look clean. My wife commented afterwards, she said, 'That boy needs to wash his neck.' " T. Tommy, a highly astute, charming, and capable man who kept up a little band of his own at the time and went on to become a Tennessee state senator and a top Teamster official, still had doubts about how far this boy was going to go, and Elvis scarcely opened his mouth the whole time, but Sam was such a believer, and T. Tommy was nothing if not a pragmatist, so he figured, Well, let's just see where it goes.

From there Sam made the rest of his rounds. He stopped by Stan's Record Shop at 728 Texas Street, just around the corner from the auditorium, where they chatted with Stan Lewis, a prematurely white-haired twenty-seven-year-old veteran of the music business who had started out supplying five jukeboxes from the back of his parents' Italian grocery store, then purchased the little record shop that had been his supplier as a full-time business for his wife and himself. Stan's older brother, Ace, was the drummer in T. Tommy's band, alternating with their first cousin, D. J. Fontana, who played with Hoot and Curley on the Hayride as well, and Stan had known Sam Phillips ever since Sam first went into the business. As the principal one-stop and independent distributor in the area, he was without question interested in this new artist — but not *too* interested, because not only was the artist unknown, the genre was untried. Still, Stan had been instrumental in placing Jimmy and Johnny with Chess, previously a blues label almost exclusively, and he was now reaping the benefits of their success. He was *always* open to new talent, he told Sam; what was good for one was good for all.

Elvis meanwhile drifted over to the auditorium. It was bigger than the Opry, with spacious dressing rooms for the stars and a large common dressing room on the second floor. The folding chairs on the floor could be taken up for dances or basketball exhibitions, and the balcony curved around on either side of the stage, giving the room a natural echo. He walked out on the stage with his eyes fixed on the floor, looked up once briefly as if measuring the crowd, and then walked back to the hotel. The Negro shacks in the Bottoms, just a few blocks from the grand auditorium entrance, were not much different than the ramshackle structures of Shake Rag, in Tupelo, or the primitive shotguns of South Memphis; Shreveport's bustling downtown just a couple of blocks away was busy and full of life, and when he ran into Scotty and Bill in the hotel coffee shop, Bill already had his eye on a pretty waitress. . . .

When he arrived back at the auditorium that night, it was completely different, transformed by the presence not just of an audience and musicians in colorful western outfits but by the almost palpable anticipation that something was going to happen. He was wearing a pink jacket, white pants, a black shirt, a brightly colored clip-on bow tie, and the kind of two-tone shoes that were known as corespondent shoes, because they were the kind that a snappy salesman or a corespondent in a divorce case might be expected to wear. Scotty and Bill were wearing matching western shirts with decorative bibs and dark ties. Bill's battered bass looked as if it were held together with baling wire, Elvis cradled his child-size guitar, and only Scotty's handsome Gibson ES 295 lent a touch of professional class to the trio. But everyone was taken with the boy. Tillman Franks, who had dispatched Jimmy and Johnny to Carlsbad but remained behind to play bass in the house band, was almost bouncing with anticipation. Pappy Covington greeted Sam and the boys warmly, as if he hadn't seen them in months. Even Horace Logan, renowned not just for his impresario's instincts but for his frosty air of self-congratulation, seemed to take to the boy — there was something about him that brought out almost a protective quality, even in seasoned professionals.

Sam left to take his seat in the audience. Although he had put up a brave front all day, he really didn't know how it was going to come out, and he felt like he should do his best to at least *try* to cue up a sympathetic response from the crowd. He had to admit that he was worried; the boy looked as if he was scared to death, and even though you could rationalize that they were all experienced veterans by now — all those nights at the Eagle's Nest, the triumph at Overton Park, and of course their Opry appearance — in another way everyone knew that this could be the end of the line.

Horace Logan was out onstage. "Is there anyone from Mississippi? Anyone from Arkansas? Let's hear it from the folks from Oklahoma. Now who here's from Louisiana? Now how many of y'all are from the great state of Texas?" A mighty roar went up as the Western Union clock on the wall registered 8:00 P.M. precisely and the band struck up the familiar Hayride theme, based on the old Negro "minstrel" song, "Raise a Ruckus Tonight." "Come along, everybody come along," the audience all joined in, "while the moon is shining bright / We're going to have a wonderful time / At the Louisiana Hayride tonight."

A tall, skinny singer from Shreveport with a television show in Monroe sidled up to the new sensation — he was barely twenty himself and had been knocked out by Elvis Presley ever since hearing the first record at Jiffy Fowler's Twin City Amusements, a jukebox operation in West Monroe. "I said, 'Hello, Elvis, my name is Merle Kilgore.' He turned around and said, 'Oh, you worked with Hank Williams.' I said, 'Yeah.' He said, 'You wrote "More and More" [a number-one hit for Webb Pierce in the fall of 1954]!' I said, 'Yeah.' He said, 'I want to meet Tibby Edwards.' It was the first thing he said to me. Tibby recorded for Mercury, and he was a star. I said, 'He's my buddy, we room together here in Shreveport.' And I went and got Tibby and introduced him to Elvis. That's how we got to be friends."

JUST A FEW WEEKS AGO," intoned announcer Frank Page's impressively measured radio voice, "a young man from Memphis, Tennessee, recorded a song on the Sun label, and in just a matter of a few weeks that record has skyrocketed right up the charts. It's really doing good all over the country. He's only nineteen years old. He has a new, distinctive style. Elvis Presley. Let's give him a nice hand . . . Elvis, how are you this evening?"

"Just fine, how are you, sir?"

"You all geared up with your band —"

"I'm all geared up!"

"To let us hear your songs?"

"Well, I'd like to say how happy we are to be out here. It's a real honor for us to hav — get a chance to appear on the Louisiana Hayride. And we're going to do a song for you — You got anything else to say, sir?"

"No, I'm ready."

"We're gonna do a song for you we got on the Sun record, it goes something like this . . ." And with that he launched into the first side of his first Sun single.

The cheers that went up from the audience were encouraged by Frank Page and Horace Logan as they stood to the side of the Lucky Strike backdrop. The microphones hanging out over the floor were turned up when Scotty took a somewhat uncertain solo, and the audience politely responded. Elvis was visibly nervous, his knees were practically knocking together, and the jackknife action of his legs was about all, Sam Phillips was convinced, that was preventing him from blowing his brains out. The reaction was not all that different from the one he had gotten on the Opry — he was so ill at ease it was hard for the audience to really like him, even though it was clear to Sam that they might want to do just that,

that they were ready, like Memphis audiences, to respond to the boy's *charm.*

In between shows he went backstage to talk to Elvis. Merle Kilgore noticed them off in a corner huddled together as Sam exhorted Elvis to just relax: the people were there to see him, just let them see what you got, put on your kind of show, if it didn't work, well, the hell with it, at least we can say we tried. Elvis, Merle noted, looked like he was scared stiff, but then Sam Phillips went to take his seat among the audience, after a little while the trio came out to do their two numbers, and this time it was entirely different. Much of the younger audience from the first show had stayed for the second, Tillman Franks observed, and now they were ready for what the new singer had to offer. For Sam it was a moment never to be forgotten.

"There was a college up in Texarkana where Elvis' records had gotten hot, and some of the young people from that college had turned up. Well, when he got through that first number, they were on their feet — and not just them either. Some big fat lady — I mean, it took an effort for her to get up, and she got up and didn't stop talking, right in the middle of the next number, she didn't know who I was, she just said, 'Man, have you ever heard anything that good?' And, honestly, the tonal impact couldn't have competed with the Maddox Brothers and Rose, or the Carlisles, who had been on the week before — I mean, they were *pros.* But Elvis had this factor of communication, I think the audience saw in him the desire to please, he had that little innocence about him, and yet he had something about him that was almost impudent in a way, that was his crutch. He certainly didn't mean to be impudent, but he had enough of that along with what he could convey that was just beautiful and lovely — and I'm not talking about his physical beauty, because he didn't look that pretty then or that good-looking, by conventional standards he should have been thrown off that stage. But I calculated that stuff in my mind: are they going to resent him with his long sideburns — that could be a plus or a minus. But when he came through like he did, it was neither. *He stood on his own.*"

He did the same two numbers that he had for the first show — there were no encores, because Mr. Logan was very strict about encores, you didn't take one unless there was a genuine eruption of the sort that overwhelmed Hank Williams when he sang "Lovesick Blues" seven times in a row and could have kept going all night. For Elvis and Scotty and Bill it wasn't anything like that, but all three grew visibly more confident, and Elvis, for all the terror that had just engulfed him, responded warmly to the crowd's enthusiasm for him. Some of the Hayride veterans, like twenty-seven-year-old Jimmy "C" Newman, who had just had his first big hit on Randy Wood's Dot label with "Cry, Cry Darling," regarded the proceedings with a certain amount of suspicion. "I'd never seen anything like it before. Here comes this guy, I guess you could almost call him an amateur, rings of dirt on his neck, but he had it all right from the start. He didn't work into it, he just knew what he was going to do. We'd just stand in the wings and shake our heads. 'It can't be, it can't last, it's got to be a fad.' "

"I think he scared them a little [in the first show]," said Merle Kilgore. "He was really on the toes of his feet singing. I think they thought he was going to jump off the stage. But when he came back out, he destroyed them — by now they knew he wasn't going to jump off the stage and beat them, and they absolutely exploded."

"What he did," said Jimmy "C" Newman, "was he changed it all around. After that we had to go to Texas to work, there wasn't any work anywhere else, because all they wanted was someone to imitate Elvis, to jump up and down on the stage and make a fool of themselves. It was embarrassing to me to see it — Elvis could do it, but few others could."

I N THE OCTOBER 16 issue of *Billboard,* the same date as the first Hayride appearance, there was a small item in Bill Sachs' "Folk Talent and Tunes" announcing that "Bob Neal of WMPS, Memphis, is planning fall tours with Elvis Presley, the Louvin Brothers, and J.E. and Maxine Brown." Neal, who had not had a great deal of personal contact with Elvis since the Overton Park show, in July, had been out to see the trio several times at the Eagle's Nest and was impressed with their potential. Though he had never been involved in management, he had been booking shows in and around Memphis for the last five years, doing local promotion for Opry and Hayride packages and promoting little shows of his own in Arkansas and Mississippi, anywhere, in fact, within the two-hundred-mile radius of the WMPS broadcast signal. He publicized the shows, of course, on his own popular early-morning program, which was on from 5:00 to 8:00, as well as the *High Noon Round-Up,* featuring the

Blackwood Brothers, Eddie Hill, and other hillbilly entertainment, which Elvis had frequently attended. Neal called Sam Phillips and asked if the group had any representation. Sam said not really — Scotty was handling management for the time being, just taking care of things more or less on an interim basis — and the two men agreed that maybe it would be worth having Bob try some bookings, seeing how it worked out. Bob spoke to Elvis, and the boy seemed agreeable, though he certainly didn't have much to say. And Scotty didn't appear to have any objections; from all that Neal could see, he simply wanted to go back to being a musician. So Bob went ahead and set up some civic club and schoolhouse bookings for November and early December — in towns like Bruce and Iuka, Mississippi; Helena and Leechville, Arkansas — places to which he had brought his shows many times in the past, where folks knew him and enjoyed his ukelele playing and laughed in recognition of his comfortable, carefully honed cornpone humor.

On October 20 the *Press-Scimitar* proudly announced under the headline "Elvis Presley Clicks": "Elvis Presley, Memphis' swift-rising young hillbilly singing star, is now a regular member of the Louisiana Hayride Show. . . . The Hayride specializes in picking promising young rural rhythm talent — and it took just one guest appearance last Saturday for the young Memphian to become a regular." The announcement was somewhat premature (Sam was still working out an arrangement with Pappy Covington and Horace Logan), but Elvis promptly quit his job, and Scotty and Bill quit theirs, too. They did so with the bravest of intentions, but with not a little trepidation, either. "I hated to let him go," said Mr. Tipler, who with his wife continued to go out to the Eagle's Nest, "[but] I could see that he was going places. I just told him, 'I understand that you can't work and stay out all night, too.' I've always been one that if somebody can benefit their self, make more of themselves, I don't never ask them to stay." Vernon, according to Elvis, took a somewhat less sanguine view. "My daddy had seen a lot of people who played guitars and stuff and didn't work, so he said: 'You should make up your mind either about being an electrician or playing a guitar. I never saw a guitar player that was worth a damn.' "

He missed the Hayride for the next two weeks. There had been nothing finalized by the twenty-third, and they were booked at the Eagle's Nest the following weekend, so they hung around Memphis, practiced at Scotty's house, and basked in all the attention that was coming their way.

They felt like great things were about to happen, if they could just get back to Shreveport. Tillman Franks had promised them work, Pappy Covington had assured them that he could get them gigs through the little booking agency that he operated out of the Hayride offices — they were just itching to get on with their new life. But in the meantime the kids would all be out at Clearpool the weekend of October 29–30 — they were playing both Friday and Saturday nights — and it would serve as something of a Memphis send-off.

That Friday night Bob Neal brought a visitor out to the club. Oscar Davis, known as the Baron of the Box Office, was a flamboyant fifty-year-old veteran of the vaudeville, carnival, and country circuits. With his jaunty boutonniere and elegant cigarette holder, his drawling Boston accent and his habit of fixing his listener in his gaze and focusing all of his considerable charm upon him or her, he could boast truthfully that he had spent more money than many millionaires had ever made, which was one reason that he was perennially broke. A true bon vivant, he lived up to the advertising slogan he used for every show that he promoted: DON'T YOU DARE MISS IT!

That was how he happened to be in Memphis at this particular juncture. Oscar had worked promotions on his own for years, he had managed and been associated with stars from Hank Williams to Roy Acuff to Ernest Tubb and Minnie Pearl, and he had established a model for the modern country music promoter, but because of his impecunious ways, he occasionally found himself in the employ of one or another of his protégés. On this trip to Memphis he had been doing advance work for "Colonel" Tom Parker, whom Bob Neal had originally met some years before in connection with an Eddy Arnold show at Russwood Park that Neal had emceed. The Colonel had since split with Arnold, whom he had guided to unsurpassed heights in the country music field, over "personal differences" and a question of artistic direction. Parker had put Eddy Arnold in pictures; he had hooked him up with Abe Lastfogel, president of the William Morris Agency, and booked him into Las Vegas; he had carefully supervised every last detail of Arnold's career. But Arnold wanted to go into television, and he wanted to spend his own, and the Colonel's, money. The result was that in August 1953 Arnold fired his manager out of the blue, a bitter blow to Tom Parker's pride but one that he was well on his way to overcoming with his recent signing of country's new number-one star, Hank Snow, to a limited partnership agreement. Part of the terms of his severance with Arnold were that he would continue to book Arnold on a regional basis, and to that end he had set up a ten-day tour of the mid South in the fall of 1954. Memphis was the fifth date on that tour.

In the course of his Memphis travels, Oscar stopped by the WMPS studio to cut some spots for the show that afternoon and, as was his wont, asked Bob Neal what was going on around town. Neal, who had his finger in a number of pies, gave him a rapid rundown and then happened to mention this young singer, Elvis Presley, with whom he had an upcoming tour. Oscar had heard of Elvis, there was quite a stir about the boy, and he wondered if there might not be a chance to see the kid — maybe he or Tom could do something for him. As a matter of fact, said Neal, the boy happened to be playing out at the Eagle's Nest that night: why didn't they just drive out together and catch the show?

Elvis, Scotty, and Bill were thrilled to meet this larger-than-life character with his stories of the big time, the glamorous world that they could only read about in fan magazines like *Country Song Roundup* and *Country & Western Jamboree*. Davis cut quite a figure in the rough-and-tumble atmosphere of the club, and when he invited Elvis to stop by the show at Ellis Auditorium on Sunday — he would be back in town by then after traveling to Nashville the next day and advancing the upcoming Monday and Tuesday shows there — Elvis jumped at the chance. Maybe, Mr. Davis suggested, he would even be able to introduce Elvis to Eddy Arnold, who was always interested in new talent.

That Sunday at 6:00 P.M. Elvis walked up the familiar steps of the entrance to Ellis Auditorium. The show included Minnie Pearl, guitar virtuoso Hank Garland, local hillbilly star Eddie Hill, and the singing group the Jordanaires, not to mention Robert Powers, the World's Smallest Hillbilly Singer. The man at the box office recognized him immediately and gave him the tickets that had been left in his name, and he attracted a good deal of attention himself sitting up front in his pink shirt and black pants and sharp white shoes. Eddy sang "Don't Rob Another Man's Castle," "I'll Hold You in My Heart," "Any Time," and "I Really Don't Want to Know" (his latest number-one hit), all in that effortlessly flowing voice, with the smooth quartet backing of the Jordanaires.

After the show was over, Bob Neal found Elvis and took him backstage, where he wandered around the unfamiliar setting in a kind of daze. Oscar Davis came over and seemed genuinely pleased to see him; he introduced him to Eddy and to Hoyt Hawkins of the Jordanaires. He had really enjoyed the group's singing, Elvis mumbled with his eyes on the floor. Well, they had enjoyed *his* singing, too, Hoyt said. They had heard his record on the radio when they were out in California with Eddy. He sounded like a quartet singer to them. Elvis blushed and fidgeted with his hands. If he ever got to the point where he had the kind of success that Eddy Arnold had, he said, he would like to get a group like the Jordanaires to sing with him; if he ever achieved that kind of success he would like them to sing behind him on record — did Hoyt think that was possible? Hoyt said he was sure that it was; they did lots of background work in Nashville, it was more and more popular nowadays — they'd love to work with him someday. Oscar seemed anxious for them to go. There was a little coffee shop across the street, maybe he and Elvis and Bob Neal could go over there and have a Coke or a cup of coffee. A heavyset man in a rumpled, ready-made suit with a cigar stuck in his mouth eyed them briefly from across the room, then turned his attention elsewhere. Who was that? Elvis asked Oscar as they exited the backstage area. That, said Oscar, with a respectful but somewhat impatient gesture, was Colonel Parker.

THE FOLLOWING SATURDAY NIGHT he signed a standard union contract with the Hayride for a period of one year. He would receive $18 per appearance as leader; Scotty and Bill would get $12 apiece. And they were permitted to miss five dates a year for outside bookings, though Mr. Logan assured him that informal arrangements could be made if other circumstances arose. Vernon and Gladys accompanied him to Shreveport to sign the contract, and they all stayed at the Captain Shreve Hotel.

That same week, with "Good Rockin' Tonight" number three on the Memphis charts and the first single still showing up on territorial charts throughout the South, *Billboard* ran a review of the new single, once again in the "Spotlight" section. "Elvis Presley," it said, "proves again that he is a sock new singer with his performances on these two oldies. His style is both country and r.&b. and he can appeal to pop." Sam Phillips was delighted. It wasn't simply that this gave him further ammunition in his crusade — it was becoming increasingly clear that there was a groundswell building which distributors and jukebox operators and one-stops could ignore only at their peril. Bill Haley had a couple of records out there that proved the same damn point, and every day Sam was seeing new evidence of it in the country boys who were showing up on his doorstep because they were hearing something in the music that, without being able to put a tag on it, they had recognized all along. And Sam *knew* that a day was coming, he knew as sure as he was born that a day was coming when this music would prevail, he didn't need any damn industry backslapping to convince him of it — but this was *Billboard*, after all, this was Paul Ackerman, a man whom he had yet to meet but for whom he had the deepest respect, and he was hearing the same thing in the music that Sam Phillips was.

Gladys dutifully pasted the review in the scrapbook she was keeping — she couldn't believe how rapidly it was filling up. She and Dixie talked excitedly about his new "career." They chewed over every scrap of information that either of them could come up with, it didn't seem possible somehow that all of this could be happening, and happening so fast — you should have seen the young people in Shreveport, she told Dixie excitedly, they practically went crazy over him, he had to come back and do an encore both shows. And the hotel was so nice, too. . . .

D IXIE WAS WORRIED about Elvis. When he was gone, she worried about him, she prayed for his success and she prayed that the success wouldn't change him. When he was at home, she worried that things were in fact changing, that where just three months ago the main thing on both their minds was marriage and whether they would have the strength to wait, now it seemed his mind was always somewhere else. She wondered if it was on *someone else,* but she didn't think so, she was sure not, it was just that he was always so distracted, and everywhere he went he was recognized, some of the girls were almost shameless the way they called attention to themselves, and he really didn't seem to mind. They stopped by the Chisca to visit with Dewey while he did his radio show, and Elvis went down there sometimes by himself. She didn't know what exactly they did afterward: sometimes they played pool, sometimes they just watched movies in Dewey's garage, and she knew that they went down on Beale, because he told her about meeting B. B. King and about some of the colorful clubs and club owners that he had run into. He seemed really excited about it — he had seen a nattily dressed Lowell Fulson at the Club Handy, and he sang her some of Fulson's brand-new number, "Reconsider Baby," which she might have heard if there was still time to listen to records at Charlie's; he described how Calvin Newborn did the splits while he was playing the guitar at the Flamingo Lounge. The pure enthusiasm, the wide-eyed fascination, the hunger for new experience, were all very much part of the boy she knew, but there was something different about him, too, she knew it and Mrs. Presley did also, but neither one of them wanted to confess it to the other, so they skirted the issue and merely expressed their concern that the boys would drive carefully.

Toward the end of football season Elvis drove by Humes just as the football team was heading out to Bartlett to play a game. One of the star players, Red West, who had been on the team as a freshman when Elvis had tried out junior year, spotted him just as the team was getting on the bus and called out to him. "Congratulations," he said when Elvis got out of his old Lincoln coupe and ambled over. He invited Elvis to come watch the game, so Elvis followed the bus out to Bartlett and, when the game was over, asked Red if he wouldn't like to come out to a show he was doing that weekend, and for the rest of the school year Red accompanied him off and on to shows that were booked on the weekends.

He liked having Red around, it made him feel more comfortable, and Red got along okay with Scotty and Bill, but still he felt strange in Memphis, he felt almost as if people were making more of him than he deserved, as if he were onstage all the time and never quite at ease, never able to be entirely himself. He was becoming a hometown celebrity of sorts and didn't know how to act. On November 8 they played out at Memphis State for a blood drive, and he had his picture taken with Mayor Tobey. "He would look in the papers," said Guy Lansky, "he was worried about what they said about him." Ronnie Smith recalled running into Elvis at WHHM one day, "and he said, 'Come on, Ron, I'll show you my new Cadillac.' We got in the elevator and came back down and went around the parking lot and kept walking until we was in front of the telephone company. That was where his old Lincoln was parked!" Sometimes old friends passed him on the street — he didn't know if they were laughing at him, or if it was because they disapproved, or if they thought he felt somehow that he was above them now.

In Shreveport it was different. It was as if he were a different person; he could create a whole new image for himself and never have anyone bring up the old one. In Shreveport the girls were falling all over themselves to get to him. When he and Scotty and Bill returned to Shreveport the week after Gladys and Vernon came down, they holed up at the Al-Ida Motel in Bossier City, across the river, and the girls started showing up almost as soon as they arrived, as if they sensed his presence. For a kid who had spent scarcely a night away from home in his nineteen years, it was like being away at summer camp: he had always loved flirting with the girls, he loved playing with them and teasing them, but now there was no one around to see that it didn't go too far. And they didn't seem too concerned about it either. In between shows at the auditorium he would peek out from behind the curtain, then, when he spotted someone that he liked, swagger over to the concession stand, place his arm over her shoulder, and drape his other arm around someone else, acting almost like he was drunk, even though everyone knew he didn't drink.

"He was a typical teenager," said Scotty. "Kind of wild, but more like in a mischievous kind of way. He loved pranks and practical jokes. We had to practically beat him with a stick to get him out of bed. His parents were very protective. His mama would corner me and say, 'Take care of my boy. Make sure he eats. Make sure he —' You know, whatever. Typical mother stuff. But it always came down to me. He didn't seem to mind; there was nothing phony about it, he truly loved his mother. He was just a typical coddled son, that's about all you can say, very shy — he was more comfortable just sitting there with a guitar than trying to talk to you. Bill and I would usually be the ones to do most of the talking, and yet he could be very extroverted, too. You know, I'd been all over and he'd never been outside the city limits. He watched and he learned, I never said anything to him because we communicated pretty much without talking anyway — but most of what he didn't know, it was just that nobody had ever told him. When he got to Shreveport, he was just running around, I think, sowing his wild oats."

With Merle Kilgore he would hang out at Murrell's Cafe, on Market Street, opposite the Hayride offices. They would sit for hours sometimes, eating hamburgers and talking about music and eyeing the girls. "He reminded me of Hank Williams," said Merle, who as a fourteen-year-old had met Williams and whose admiration for his idol continued to know no bounds. "Something in his eyes. He'd ask you a question, and his eyes would be asking you another question. It was that look. He'd wait for the answer, but his eyes would be asking the question. I'd only seen that in Hank and Elvis." Sometimes they would go down to the bus station to play pinball with Tibby Edwards or stop by Stan's Record Shop to thumb through the rhythm and blues racks. You ate when you wanted, you slept when you wanted, the girls came running after you — it was a teenager's dream. Every night he called home and spoke to his mother; frequently he called Dixie to express his undying love. But then he was free to do whatever he wanted.

They worked one night at the Lake Cliff Club, where Hoot and Curley played ordinarily. Elvis was attracted to Hoot's pretty daughter, Mary Alice, but he was kind of nervous about asking Hoot, the steel player on Slim Whitman's "Indian Love Call," for permission to take her out. The gig at the Lake Cliff turned into something of a joke. Hoot and Curley had been playing there for six years, and they had their following, but unfortunately their following hadn't been alerted to the fact that they wouldn't be playing at the Lake Cliff that night, and if they didn't throw things, they did practically everything but. By the end of the first set the club had just about emptied out, and it was, in Scotty's assessment, "a complete bust."

On the basis of Tillman Franks' enthusiasm, and his promise of work, they settled in at the Al-Ida for what was intended to be a two-week period in the middle of November, only to discover that Tillman, who had suddenly become persona non grata at the Hayride, couldn't deliver. Just how panicked they must have felt can be deduced from Scotty's vivid memories of being "marooned" in Shreveport, stranded without even the money to pay their hotel bill or buy enough gas to get back to Memphis. In fact they were not stranded for long, and they may simply have spent all their money in expectation of making more. In any case, within days Pappy Covington had work for them in Gladewater, Texas, some sixty miles west of Shreveport.

Pappy called Tom Perryman, a young go-getter who had made his mark in Gladewater at radio station KSIJ, where he had been working since 1949. In addition to deejaying, he had served as engineer, newsman, sports announcer, sales manager, program director, and general manager at various times and also started a local talent show, which he broadcast first from the studio, then, as it grew, from the local community center and the three-hundred-seat movie theater in town. Eventually he put the show on the road, where it played schoolhouses and high school gymnasiums in towns throughout the outlying area. Perryman also booked Hayride shows and occasionally put recording artists with his traveling talent

show as a kind of extra draw, which was how he met Jim Reeves, then a
DJ in Henderson, Texas, whom he later came to manage and partner in
various enterprises. He began to book some of these single artists into
clubs and honky-tonks like the Reo Palm Isle in Longview and in general
was one of the busiest promoters in Northeast Texas, a territory that appeared to be as music-mad as Memphis or any other region in the country. He had been playing "Blue Moon of Kentucky" since it first came out,
"because of the unique arrangement. That sound was just something you
never heard." So he was not completely at a loss when Pappy Covington,
with whom he had already booked quite a number of shows, called on a
Monday morning and wondered "if I had a place where I could put an act
right quick.

"He said, 'There are some boys down here that are broke, they don't
have the money to get back to Memphis.' Well, I had a friend that had a
honky-tonk right out on the Tyler Highway. So I said, 'Yeah, I guess so,'
and I called this buddy of mine, and he said, 'Yeah, I'm not doing anything, come on out. Who are they?' I said it was this new act out of Memphis called Elvis Presley. So sure enough, I played that record a lot the
next two or three days and come Friday night, here they come. Just Elvis
and Scotty and Bill in a Chevrolet with that big old bass on top of the car.

"The way it would work, I would book the show, the club owner
would take the bar, and I would take the money off the door. My wife,
Billie, would usually work the door. Then we would pay the expenses of
the gig, if you had to pay a sponsor or what little advertising there might
be. Most of the advertising was done on my [radio] show, and we'd do a
live show from the studio, too, promoting that night's performance. Then
I would take fifteen percent of the gross, and what was left would go to
the act. I never will forget: that first night we took in a total of ninety dollars. That was all we had. Of course I didn't take any of it. I knew those
boys needed the money, so I gave them all of it.

"You know, he was really a natural. When Elvis was performing, everyone had the same basic reaction. It was almost spontaneous. It reminded me of the early days, of where I was raised in East Texas and
going to these 'Holy Roller' Brush Arbor meetings: seeing these people
get religion. I said, 'Man, that's something.' You'd see it in the later years
with the big sound systems and the lights, but Elvis could do it if there
wasn't but ten people [in the room]. He never realized what he had till

later years. He said, 'Man, this sure is a good crowd in this part of the country. Are they always that way?' I said, 'No, man. They never seen anything like you.' Nobody had.

"It won't happen again in this generation or the next, I don't believe. He just came along at the right time with the right thing. Because it was after the war. People my age grew up with the big band music in the forties. But those kids, the generation that were children during the war, they had no music to identify with, they were looking for something they could identify with, and this new sound was a combination of it all."

On Thursday, November 25, Elvis was booked into Houston for the first time, at the Houston Hoedown, where he was listed way down on the bill but made a considerable impression on the MC for the popular live broadcast, KNUZ's Biff Collie, who also happened to have a partnership in the club. Collie, a native of San Antonio and a ten-year broadcast veteran at the age of twenty-eight, was a highly influential figure in radio and in fact the person who had originally gotten T. Tommy Cutrer his job in Shreveport. It was through T. Tommy and Tillman Franks, with whom Biff also went way back, that Biff first heard of Elvis Presley. In fact, he had stopped off in Memphis with Tillman just the week before to see him perform, after first picking up Tillman in Shreveport on the way to the third annual Country Music Disc Jockey convention in Nashville, which Biff had had a considerable hand in organizing. Tillman's act, Jimmy and Johnny, was booked into the Eagle's Nest on Wednesday night with this new Memphis "phenom" that Biff had been hearing so much about, so he and Tillman stopped by the club.

Biff was not that impressed. The boy was "different" enough but not really "sensational"; if anything, Jimmy and Johnny took the show. At the same time he was intrigued by a combination of elements that he saw coming together in one package for the first time — the boy seemed like "a Mississippi gospel singer singing black music, that's about as real as I could figure." On the basis of that observation, not to mention Tillman's unflagging enthusiasm and the recommendation of Bob Neal, whom he saw out at the club that night and with whom he spent time at the convention, he was happy to book him on the Hoedown for $150, and he started playing Elvis Presley records as soon as he got back to Houston.

The reaction to Elvis' Hoedown appearance was good, and he was held over "by popular demand" for two additional nights, but to Biff the nature of his act was about the same as what he had observed in Memphis. The repertoire was extremely limited, and the boy was obviously just learning the ropes, though by now Biff Collie was beginning to see the light, even if he wasn't sure exactly why. "I said, 'Don't you do any slow songs?' He said, 'I don't . . . I don't . . . I like to do these things because they make me feel good, you know.' I said, 'Yeah, they like this stuff that you are doing pretty good, it seems like, but this rhythm and blues stuff is not going to stay forever. You really need to sing some slow songs.' His reaction was, 'I don't like . . . I don't . . . I just like to sing . . . You know, they make me feel good.'

"That night after we were through we went across the street to Stuart's Drive Inn restaurant, and we sat down at a booth and ordered something, and I saw Sonny Stuart come through. His dad was the boss, and he was learning the business at the time. And I winked at him and said, 'Just for fun, get the girl upstairs on the PA to page Elvis Presley.' He said, 'How do you spell that?' And they did it three or four times over a period of fifteen minutes, and, obviously, nothing happened. Nothing at all. And I remember telling Elvis that night, 'One of these days you'll have to have somebody to keep you from getting run over.' And that was — again, it was not because of what he had done there. I just felt like something was going to happen."

The next day Elvis sent a telegram home from Houston. "HI BABIES," it read. "HERE'S THE MONEY TO PAY THE BILLS. DON'T TELL NO ONE HOW MUCH I SENT I WILL SEND MORE NEXT WEEK. THERE IS A CARD IN THE MAIL. LOVE ELVIS."

MEANWHILE, Bob Neal was looking on his new project with increasing enthusiasm; the idea of becoming Elvis Presley's full-fledged manager was beginning to appeal to him more and more. The few dates that they had done together only confirmed his view of the boy's potential. So did the reports that kept coming in from Louisiana and East Texas. And while they had not yet signed any official papers, there was no question in his mind that this was an experiment that could fail only if he chose to walk away from it. Here at last was an opportunity to get in on the ground floor of something instead of just signing on to another Nashville package promotion; it could be a chance of going all the way to the top.

Because that was where Bob Neal quickly judged this kid was heading.

Not much older than Bob's oldest boy, Sonny, and, seemingly, without the ability to articulate what it was he was really looking for, the kid seemed to possess as unerring an instinct for how to connect with an audience — as well as the fierce drive and determination to accomplish it — as Neal had seen in his dozen years in radio and four or five years of serious promotion. In the parts of Mississippi and Arkansas where the Hayride signal came in strongest, he seemed to practically explode, coming out onstage like a sprinter out of the starting blocks, with an energy and a crackling enthusiasm that could barely be contained. In places where he was less well known, on the other hand, "they didn't know exactly how to take him, they just didn't know what to do. Sometimes they were a very quiet audience. A lot of them would come out to the shows because they had been followers of my radio show, and it was a little frustrating to Elvis sometimes. They would gather around to ask me about my family and my kids and so forth, and they would more or less ignore Elvis. [But] the more they sat on their hands, the harder he worked to break them up. His show developed in that sometimes if he was onstage and just through some accidental movement there would be a big scream or reaction, he would automatically remember. On the other hand, if he devised something and got a dead reaction, he would never worry about it, he would drop it and go on to something else. It was just as automatic as breathing to him."

Nearly as important as this natural gift, though, were the two men who made up the remaining two thirds of the trio. They may not have been the best musicians in the world, but Elvis felt perfectly at ease with them, and in those rare instances when his own instincts failed, Bill's always took over. These were *country* audiences they were playing for, and Bill's rough-hewn humor and memory for old Opry routines, in addition to a thoroughly ingratiating personality, always stood him in good stead. Sometimes Bill would come out of the audience dressed like a hobo and yelling, "Wait a minute, I want to play with y'all. I can play just as good as you can!" Other times he might brandish an oversize pair of bloomers that Bobbie and Evelyn had bought for the act or black out his front teeth or tell one of the old jokes about Rotterdam ("Rotterdam socks off!" was the punch line), and the audience always went crazy when he rode that bass, egging Elvis on with both arms uplifted and the bass between his legs like a Brahma bull. He could save Elvis, too, if the boy got too far out on a limb or misjudged the audience for its tolerance of his novelty, vulgarity, or simply his bad jokes. "On some of the early shows," said Scotty, whose unassailable calm and ability to deal with any crisis that came up were just as integral a part of the whole experience, "if it hadn't been for Bill, we would have fallen flat on our face. Because Elvis was such an oddity, if you will, when people first saw him, they were practically in shock. But Bill's antics loosened them up."

Admission, generally, was $1 for adults, 50 cents for children, with 10 percent retained for expenses and 15 percent taken off the top, after the local sponsor or Kiwanis Club had been paid. Sometimes there might be as much as $300 to divide, with $45 going to Bob and the rest split 50–25–25 between Elvis, Scotty, and Bill. Just as often there was less, but one or two commissions of $25 to $45 a week were a nice supplement to a comfortable DJ's salary, and if you added up all the little side benefits that a popular radio personality was heir to, it didn't make for a bad living.

There were any number of other signs that business was likely to pick up in the near future. *Billboard* magazine noted that the records were still ping-ponging around on the charts (the week of November 17, "Blue Moon of Kentucky" was number five in Memphis and "Good Rockin' Tonight" number eight), while in a DJ poll Elvis Presley was named eighth Most Promising C&W Artist behind Tommy Collins, Justin Tubb, Jimmy and Johnny, the Browns, and Jimmy Newman, among others. Meanwhile Bob Neal announced his own third annual listeners' poll, which had Elvis in tenth position behind such country stalwarts as Webb Pierce, Faron Young, Ray Price, Hank Snow, and Kitty Wells. The December 11 issue of *Billboard* reported in its "Folk Talent and Tunes" column that "the hottest piece of merchandise on the . . . Louisiana Hayride at the moment is Elvis Presley, the youngster with the hillbilly blues beat," while Marty Robbins recorded a creditable country version of "That's All Right" for Columbia on December 7.

What struck Neal most of all, though, was the boy's ambition, something he might have missed altogether if it hadn't been for his wife. Sometimes coming back from the shows, on the drive home to Memphis, Elvis would ride with Bob and Helen, so that Bob, who had his 5:00 A.M. show coming up practically as soon as they got into town, could catch some sleep. Elvis would talk to Helen then in a way that he didn't seem able to talk to Bob, or even to Scotty and Bill — he would reveal himself in fragments that Neal would catch in moments between wakefulness and sleep or as Helen would describe it to him afterward. "He would talk about his aspirations and plans," Neal told Elvis biographer Jerry Hopkins. "Helen said he talked not in terms of being a moderate success; his ambition was to be big in movies and so forth. He'd ask her, did she think he could make it, and her response — well, she was a believer, too — she felt that he could go as far as he wanted to. From the very first he had great ambitions to be nothing in the ordinary, but just to go all the way with it."

D IXIE HOPED, with Christmas coming, that Elvis would be able to spend a little more time at home. This would be their first Christmas together, and she really wanted to make it special. When he got back from Texas, he had brought her something in anticipation of Christmas, a pair of shorts and a sleeveless blouse in pale pink. He wanted her to try it on right away, and she was excited, too, because she loved the outfit, but she loved his enthusiasm about it even more. They had never been much for gift giving — they just didn't have the money. But she knew that Christmas this year was going to be different.

Elvis had already given himself a present some months before, a 1942 Martin guitar that he had bought for $175 from the O. K. Houck Company on Union. He was a little self-conscious about it; it seemed kind of extravagant to pay so much money, but this was the way he now made his living, he told himself, and he never hesitated, except when the man threw his old guitar in the trash. "The man gave me eight dollars on the trade-in," he told anyone who would listen afterward, still a little openmouthed with disbelief. "Shucks, it still played good." He had his first name spelled out in black metallic letters across the blond wood of the D-18, so that it came out smartly on a diagonal below the fret board, and the guitar looked a lot more professional than his old one, but, Elvis joked, he frailed away at it just the same.

They went by Humes for the Christmas show, and all the teachers and kids flocked around, but some of them acted stuck-up, like they thought he was going to act stuck-up first, which didn't seem right at all. They went by Scotty's to rehearse for a session that they managed to get in not long before Christmas. First they did an old blues number that had become a western swing standard in different versions by Bob Wills and his brothers, Billy Jack and Johnnie Lee, over the years. The new version opened up in a beautiful, slow, lilting blues tempo that almost seemed to tease the listener, until Elvis announced, with just a trace of amusement in his voice, "Hold it, fellas, that don't move me. Let's get real, real gone for a change." And plunged into what became known as "Milkcow Blues Boogie." The other side was a new song by a Covington, Tennessee, theater manager named Jack Sallee, whom Sam had met when he came into the Memphis Recording Service to make some promos for his Friday-night hillbilly jamboree. Sam said he was looking for original material for his new artist, and Sallee went home and wrote a song. "You're a Heart-breaker" was the first of Elvis' songs on which Sam Phillips owned the publishing, and it was also the closest that they had come to date to an explicitly country number.

They played the Hayride on the eighteenth, then Bobbie waited for Scotty to come home with her Chevrolet. "Scotty was supposed to be home in time for me to go Christmas shopping. They were using the car, and I was riding the bus. They were supposed to come home Thursday night after a show (Christmas was on a Saturday). I said, 'Well, I'll just wait until you get here and go finish my Christmas shopping.' When they hadn't gotten home by the middle of the afternoon on Friday, I decided that they had stayed over, but I still didn't go out. I said, 'I'm not going to go riding the bus. Scotty just won't get anything for Christmas.' They came in about five-thirty, and I said, 'Why didn't you come home last night?' And they said, 'Elvis wanted to stay in Shreveport and do his Christmas shopping this morning.' I said, 'Okay, Elvis gets what Elvis wants, and you don't get a Christmas present!' But Scotty wasn't too much on that anyway."

Elvis and Dixie spent all day Christmas together, first at Dixie's house, then at the Presleys'. Elvis gave her a suit that he must have bought in Shreveport — she loved it, everything he got her was something she liked, but it wasn't like she thought it was going to be, somehow. Here he had just breezed into town the night before, and now he told her he was going to have to be off again before she even knew it. He was scheduled to play in Houston for Biff Collie at the Cook's Hoedown Yuletide Jamboree on the twenty-eighth, and then at a special New Year's Night broadcast from Eagle's Hall, which Biff had also set up.

She waved good-bye as they drove off and then went over to the Presleys', where she and Gladys alternately shared their pride in the course his life had taken and consoled each other over what they both had lost.

LOUISIANA HAYRIDE. (LANGSTON McEACHERN)

FORBIDDEN FRUIT

LVIS SIGNED WITH BOB NEAL formally at the start of the year. The official picture, which ran in the trades and in the March issue of *Country & Western Jamboree,* shows him sitting at a desk with a fireplace behind him, pen poised, grin crooked, hair perfectly coiffed. Sam Phillips and Bob Neal stand beside him on either side. Sam has his hand companionably on Elvis' right shoulder, Bob is wearing a broad smile and an elaborately bowed western tie, while all three stare straight into the camera. Because he was still technically a minor, Mr. and Mrs. Vernon Presley signed the contract as parents and legal guardians, with every expectation that this would mark a dramatic upturn in their son's fortunes.

It did, almost from the start. Bob had bookings that would keep Elvis on the road for much of January, with a hometown debut at Ellis Auditorium scheduled for February 6, 1955. He was also in the process of making a solid connection with Colonel Tom Parker, who through his new management and booking-agency partnership with Hank Snow was in a position to put Elvis in front of a greatly expanded audience. Although the Colonel at first appeared somewhat reluctant to get involved, he was now talking about trying Elvis out on a Hank Snow package tour that started in New Mexico in mid February. For the present Elvis was booked into West Texas the week of January 2 on a Hayride package; then, after returning to Shreveport, he played nearby New Boston, Texas, and on the twelfth he was scheduled to play Clarksdale, Mississippi, with the brother-sister duo of Jim Ed and Maxine Brown and "Tater" Bob Neal as MC, going to Helena, Arkansas, the next night with the same bill. The following week there was a solid block of bookings in the area around Corinth, Mississippi, with a side excursion to Sikeston, Missouri, then a return to the Gladewater area for a five-day tour the week after that.

He didn't always take the show. Jim Ed and Maxine Brown were a highly polished act. They had had a number-eight national hit the previ-

ous summer with "Looking Back to See," were comparative veterans of
the Hayride, and had an audience that turned out for them every time.
Jim Ed was a big, good-looking guy, just a year older than Elvis and not
above preening himself for the girls; his sister, Maxine, was attractive and
outgoing, and they never failed to reach a good portion of the crowd.
Tom Perryman remembered one show he put on in Gilmer, Texas, near
Gladewater, when the Browns actually came out on top. "They did a lot
of their harmony gospel songs, and they had their big record, and there
was a lot of older family people there. That was the only time I ever saw
anybody steal the show from Elvis. Of course it was a big thrill for the
Browns." Most of the time, though, they didn't seem to know what had
hit them. It wasn't that they were any less popular or that the fans didn't
flock around them when they came out after the performance to sign
autographs and sell their records; it was just that when that boy was onstage, it was like nothing that had ever been before. Whether people liked
it or not, they didn't seem able to think of anything else, and it prevented
them from focusing on just about anything that followed.

In Corinth, Mississippi, the show was sponsored by the local Jaycees
Club and scheduled to take place at the courthouse, and local DJ/singer
Buddy Bain was on the bill. Buddy, who was thirty-one and had had his
chance in Nashville, where he had deejayed on WSM after a five-year stint
in Knoxville with Chet Atkins, didn't particularly like the new style. He
was a traditional country singer himself, who had grown up admiring
Gene Autry and Jimmie Rodgers, but he had met Sam Phillips at WLAY
in Muscle Shoals, and he knew the Presleys from the Tupelo area, where
he had grown up and where his sisters Mary and Marie had worked with
Gladys in the sewing room at Reed Manufacturing Company. So when
Sam brought not only the first record but the boy himself down to radio
station WCMA in Corinth one sweltering day the previous summer,
Buddy played it ("Well, I played 'Blue Moon of Kentucky'; 'That's All
Right' was a little too much for me") and interviewed Elvis himself for
about ten minutes on the air.

By the time he returned to Corinth, in January, Elvis was something
of a local phenomenon, and Buddy was featured on the bill, along with his
singing partner, fifteen-year-old Kay Crotts from Michie, Tennessee,
whom he would marry three years later. Buddy had been plugging the
Browns' appearance all week because he had kind of a crush on Maxine
("We had hit it off real good. She wrote to me, and I wrote to her, and I

thought something might really come of it until I found out later that she had actually done so many disc jockeys that way, you know, to get them to play her record"), and he was skeptical of the new performer's attraction because he had heard that Bob Neal had paid half a dozen local girls fifty cents apiece to scream, but he was quickly won over.

"You know, they came to make fun of him, but they ended up backstage practically trying to tear him apart. He *was* the show, even then — it wasn't like anything you ever heard. But there was one little thing that happened before the show I'll never forget. They got in in the middle of the afternoon, and we had a little two-story house in Corinth, my mother and I, and we had a girl that would come in and cook for us because my mother was in a wheelchair. Well, I invited Elvis and Maxine and Jim Ed over to the house. And before we had supper, we gave Jim Ed and Maxine my bedroom to lie down in and take a nap. And Elvis said, 'I'd like to lie down, too. The living room sofa's fine for me.' So he lay down on this long red plastic sofa that we had, with his feet over the end, he just went right out. And when I woke him up for supper, the little girl that worked for us, Martha Morris, had filled that table full of food, but all he would eat was some corn bread, and he asked if we didn't have any buttermilk. Well, I chased down to the store for it, and he just crumbled up that corn bread in the buttermilk and ate a whole lot of it and said, 'This is delicious. Just what I want.' After supper was over, my mother was sitting by the window, looking out like she always did, and Elvis went over and said, 'Mrs. Bain, I really enjoyed the meal.' And he kissed her on the cheek, which my mama wasn't used to because *I* didn't even kiss her, I just said, 'Thank you, Mama.' She was a stern woman. When he went out of the room for a minute, she said, 'Who was that slobbering all over me?' I said, 'Mama, that was Elvis Presley.' She said, 'I wondered who that was.'

"Then we all sat down and looked at my scrapbooks. I had lots of pictures from my early career, in Nashville and Raleigh, North Carolina, and the famous Renfro Valley Barn Dance, and he said to me, 'I hope someday I can be as famous as you are. I sure would like to get to Nashville someday.' And you know what I said to him? I remember it as well as if it were yesterday. I said, 'Elvis, if you'll learn you some good country songs, you just might get on the Grand Ole Opry.' Of course he was very polite and thanked me, and then we went to the show."

Backstage at the show Elvis took advantage of his newfound friendship to harmonize with Buddy's singing partner on a Blackwood Brothers song. "We were going to sing a gospel song on our show entitled 'I'm Feeling Mighty Fine.' We all had little practice sessions before going out onstage, and Kay and I were singing over in a corner, and Elvis walked over and said, 'Buddy, scoot on over, you can't sing that song. Let me sing it with Kay.' So he and Kay sang it, and he did his version much different from the way I did mine. 'Cause I did mine just plain, and he did his, 'Well-uh, uh-uh' — you know, like he did. Well, Kay didn't really like it, at least she said she didn't, but I was real jealous of the way they sung it, and he just kept singing it over and over again, there's no telling how many times they sung that chorus, he just didn't know when to stop. But once he got onstage, it was all over." And after the show was done, the mild-mannered boy asked Buddy to point him toward the best-looking girl in the crowd and joked that he would find out if she was wearing falsies or not.

I T WAS ALL LIKE A DREAM from which he was afraid he might one day awaken. It seemed sometimes like it was happening to someone else, and when he spoke of it, it was often with a quality of wonderment likely to strike doubt not so much in his listener's mind as in his own. When he returned home for the show at Ellis, there was a full, four-column spread in the *Memphis Press-Scimitar* by Miss Keisker's friend Mr. Johnson, an affable, easygoing fellow in a battered newspaperman's hat, who spent as much time with Mr. Phillips as he did with the somewhat tongue-tied subject of his story. "Suddenly Singing Elvis Presley Zooms into Recording Stardom," read the headline, with the explanatory introductory phrase, "Thru the Patience of Sam Phillips," running above. The article was accompanied by a photograph of Elvis, Scotty, and Bill in the studio, and underneath the photograph it said, "A white man's voice singing negro rhythms with a rural flavor [has] changed life overnight for Elvis Presley." The body of the text mapped out in plain, accurate, and generally admiring terms the story of his meteoric rise: growing up in Tupelo, moving to Memphis, lugging his guitar every day to Humes. It described how Sam Phillips had discovered his talent, how Dewey Phillips had revealed it to the world, how Elvis had been invited to appear on the Grand Ole Opry, "hillbilly heaven," within a month of the debut of his first record and was today a star of the Louisiana Hayride. The article made note, too, of the phenomenon that had helped give rise to the young man's success and of Sam Phillips' contribution to it. "That's All Right," Johnson noted, was "in the R&B idiom of negro field jazz, 'Blue Moon' more in the country field, but there was a curious blending of the two different musics in both." The last section of the story, headlined "In a Class Alone," stressed the unclassifiability of Elvis' talent and the likelihood of a glowing future for this good-looking young star with the "slumbrous" eyes who, with his new manager, Bob Neal, had recently opened up an office downtown under the title of Elvis Presley Enterprises. "Spin 'em again, boys," wrote Bob Johnson, announcing in bold type everything that Elvis himself had been afraid to even whisper to his friends: the celebrity, the dramatic impact of his success, its scale, the almost unmentionable thrill that went with it.

There were two shows, at 3:00 and 8:00 P.M. The ad in the paper placed him fourth on a "Five Star" bill, with Faron Young and Ferlin Huskey headlining and "Beautiful Gospel Singer" Martha Carson making her Memphis debut, but it was clear from all the attention he was getting that a good deal was expected of him. The first show went fine. He sang his new songs, "Milkcow Blues Boogie" and "You're a Heartbreaker," as well as "That's All Right" and "Good Rockin' Tonight," and he told Ronnie Smith backstage how much fun he was having on the road. He was fascinated, too, with the performance of Martha Carson, a spectacular redhead who looked like a movie star and sang and moved like Sister Rosetta Tharpe when she performed her trademark hit, "Satisfied," and a host of traditional "colored" spirituals. She broke several strings, danced ecstatically at the end of a long guitar cord, and in general created the kind of smoldering intensity and infectious enthusiasm that he sought to achieve in his own performance. He asked Miss Carson afterward if she knew a particular Statesmen number, and he made it clear that "he knew the words to every song that I had ever had out." He told her that he would like to record her song, "Satisfied," someday and that he hoped that they would be billed together again sometime soon. "He was very complimentary and very interested in what I did. I could feel this was sincere, it was from the heart — it wasn't just someone saying this, he just really idolized me, and I could feel it."

In between shows he and Scotty went across the street to a meeting Bob had set up with Colonel Parker. The Colonel had finally added him to Hank Snow's upcoming southwestern tour, which was to start a week from Monday, and Bob said he thought it would be a good idea if they all got together and talked a little bit about the future. In addition to Bob and Colonel Parker, Sam Phillips would also be attending, along with the Colonel's front man, Oscar Davis (whom Elvis had met in connection with the Eddy Arnold show three months before), and Tom Diskin, Parker's associate in Jamboree Attractions, the booking agency in which he and Snow were partners. Ironically, Scotty had contacted Diskin in December, at the Chicago office listed in *Billboard,* to see if the agency might be interested in booking Elvis. He had gotten his reply only three weeks earlier, a stock letter of rejection which apparently failed to make any connection between the blind inquiry and the new act in whom the Colonel was already taking an interest on the basis of a very encouraging report from Texarkana DJ Uncle Dudley about the New Boston date. In fact, Diskin joined the Colonel on a quick visit to Shreveport to watch the boy on the Hayride on January 15, just two days after the letter was mailed. Scotty had heard that the Colonel was in the audience and even thought he might have spotted him standing toward the back of the auditorium. But Parker hadn't come around to see them afterward, and though he spent much of January in touch with Neal about the tour, he had had no direct contact with the musicians until now.

The meeting at Palumbo's did not get off to an auspicious start. The tension in the air was already marked when Elvis and Scotty walked in. Colonel Parker was sitting there with a big cigar, his jaw thrust out, and a pugnacious expression on his face, as Diskin, his young lieutenant, tried to explain to Mr. Phillips that the Colonel didn't really mean anything against the Sun label in particular, that he was just trying to point out the shortcomings that would attach to any small record label, which necessarily lacked the kind of distribution that a major company like RCA, with which the Colonel had been associated for many years through both Eddy Arnold and Hank Snow, could offer. Oscar Davis, sharp as ever with a fresh flower in his buttonhole and his cigarette holder cocked elegantly, just so, was plainly unhappy with his crude associate. And Sam was seething. What did Tom Parker mean — he wasn't going to call that damn mountebank by some phony title — by saying that Elvis was going to get nowhere on Sun? This was a helluva way to start a business conference. His own deep-set eyes bored in on the Colonel, but Parker's gaze never wavered, and both men sat locked in silent combat until finally Bob Neal broke the tension and suggested they discuss some of the specifics of the upcoming tour.

This could be a very fine opportunity for them all, Oscar Davis said with genuine feeling: it would give Sam a chance to get his records into new territories, it would offer young Elvis here an opportunity to expand his audience, and if things worked out it could cement a long-standing relationship — Davis undoubtedly hesitated on the word *partnership* — between Colonel Parker and our good friend Bob Neal and allow it to develop in exciting new directions. The Colonel only glowered, and Oscar was confounded as to just what he could be up to. As for Elvis, Bob had explained to him the Colonel's far-flung connections, not just in the world of country music, but in Hollywood as well. Mr. Phillips had only reinforced what Bob had said. From what he understood, Sam declared before actually meeting him, there wasn't a better *promoter* in the business than Tom Parker, and right now they could certainly use all the help they could get. But what, Elvis might well have been led to wonder at this point, was Colonel Parker's compelling attraction?

T HOMAS A. PARKER on first impression was a heavyset, crude, and blustering man with a brilliant mind and a guttural accent, which he claimed to have acquired in West Virginia, where, he said, he had been born forty-five years before. Orphaned as a child (the exact age varied from one telling to the next), he had run away and joined the circus, in this case the Great Parker Pony Circus, which he said was owned by an uncle. From there he had drifted into the carny life, eventually ending up in Tampa, where the Royal American show wintered and where, after half a dozen years "in the life," he had married an older divorcée named Marie Mott in 1935 and settled down. He pursued a number of civilian ventures, eventually becoming field agent (this could be translated as "Chief Dogcatcher," and often was in later years by the Colonel) for the Tampa Humane Society, a privately endowed animal shelter, where he and his family were given a free apartment above the pound. On his own he enterprisingly founded a pet cemetery that offered "Perpetual Care for Deceased Pets" while also promoting and working closely with country singers Gene Austin and Roy Acuff and film star Tom Mix on their Florida tours. Acuff, then known as the King of the Hillbillies, tried to persuade him to move to Nashville, and Parker seemed ready to entertain the idea if Acuff would consider leaving the Opry and giving Parker a free managerial hand. Acuff declined, and perhaps because Tom Parker was not quite ready to give up all his carny ties, this was the point at which they reached a parting of the ways. It wasn't until a few years later, in 1944, when he met twenty-six-year-old Eddy Arnold headlining an Opry tent show tour, that he finally made his move.

Arnold, who had just left Pee Wee King's Golden West Cowboys and signed with RCA Records, was a big, handsome, square-jawed baritone with a full-throated melodic style altogether different from the conventional Nashville approach. Parker must have sensed in him the potential that he was looking for, because he went into show business now with the same creative, full-bore intensity that had always marked him in the carny world. According to Oscar Davis, who first met Parker in Florida while Davis was managing Ernest Tubb, there had never been another manager of this sort before. In his attention to every aspect of his client's career, in his devotion to mapping out a program and to carrying it out in the most meticulous detail, in his use of radio for "exploitation" and his belief that his word was his bond, that a contract, once agreed upon, was a sacred commitment *on both sides,* Tom Parker "as a manager was tops, the greatest in the world. He was an uncanny businessman, very astute, he adjusted the cost so there was never a time when a promoter made more money than he did. If I were to select anyone in the amusement field — and I've been through it from 1912 on up — I would select him; I don't think anyone has beaten him on a deal. He'll read you very quickly. Working with the carnivals taught him that everything wasn't the way that it looks on the surface, that everyone has their weaknesses. Tom was a strong man. He'd lay the law down, and you went that way or you didn't play."

To Biff Collie, the Houston DJ, the difference between the Colonel and Oscar — Davis' chronic impecuniousness aside — was that the Colonel "always thought far beyond where he was," while to Gabe Tucker, who met Parker when Gabe was playing bass for Eddy Arnold and who worked with him on and off for almost thirty years, "his operation was completely different" because of his attention to detail. "Most managers back then would just call up [the local promoter] and say, 'Okay, can you book a tour down there?' And the manager would never leave his office. But he didn't work that way. He'd go out before, check out the place, he'd ask how many seats in the auditorium — not to be smart, but because we knowed percentagewise, if we had a five-thousand-seat auditorium, we knew how many [Eddy Arnold] songbooks to take in and how many we was going to sell. His theory was altogether different than most of them that come to Nashville. He was a carny."

Once he got together with Eddy Arnold he concentrated his focus exclusively on his single client. He moved up to Nashville and virtually moved in with Arnold and his wife, Sally. "When Tom's your manager, he's all you," wrote Arnold in his 1969 autobiography, *It's a Long Way from Chester County.* "He lives and breathes his artist. I once said to him . . . 'Tom, why don't you get yourself a hobby — play golf, go boating, or something?' He looked me straight in the eye and said, 'You're my hobby.' " One of the keys to Parker's success, as Arnold saw it, was his apparent crudity. "Earthy, I guess a lot of people might describe him; uneducated maybe. A lot of times people think they're dealing with a rube. 'Oh, I can take him,' they decide. They don't take him. He's ahead of 'em before they even sit down across a table . . . he fools 'em. They think, because his English might be faulty (he might say a word wrong here and there), 'Oh, I'll handle him.' They walk right into his web!"

Arnold had three number-one hits in 1947 and the following year was persuaded by Parker to reluctantly quit the Opry: there were just too many other opportunities. In October 1948 Parker used his carnival connections to get himself an honorary colonel's commission from Louisiana governor and noted country singer Jimmie Davis, the listed composer of "You Are My Sunshine." From now on, he told Gabe Tucker, who accompanied him to the investiture, "see to it . . . that everyone addresses me as the Colonel." Within a year or two after that he had gotten Arnold into the movies, hooked Eddy up with William Morris, the leading Hollywood talent agency, gotten him on Milton Berle's top-rated television show, and even booked him into Las Vegas. It was a far cry from what any previous country music manager had envisioned for his talent (though a few might have dreamt of it, none achieved it), but eventually the exclusivity of his focus got him into trouble.

In 1953, in an episode that has been widely reported but never fully explained, Eddy Arnold fired him. According to Elvis biographer Jerry Hopkins, who got the story from Oscar Davis, "It was an argument in Las Vegas that made the relationship collapse. Parker had been laying out a two-page newspaper advertisement as a surprise to Eddy . . . and when Eddy walked into the Colonel's room unexpectedly, Parker quickly hid the lay-out, Eddy accused him of doing something behind his back, one thing led to another, and pretty soon Eddy was without a manager, Parker was without a star." It may have had something to do with a weekly television show, too, in which Arnold was persuaded, against the

Colonel's always sober fiscal advice, to invest a great deal of his own money, and it was undoubtedly true, as Gabe noted, that Arnold and Parker "were dissipating much of their energy ironing out the difference in their personalities and private lives." They went on working together in a booking arrangement that was part of an amicable separation agreement, and they never ceased to be personally cordial, but it must have come as a terrible blow to Parker to be abandoned so abruptly by his protégé, in a manner that left him unavoidably exposed in the glare of the show biz spotlight.

Within a year he had rebounded, after initially making his office in the lobby of Nashville radio station WSM, where with Oscar Davis and other independent operators he used the lobby phone to book his acts. "When the phone rang," according to *Billboard* editor Bill Williams, "by agreement whoever was closest answered it by the number . . . and between them they lined up more clients and did more business than the Opry's Service Bureau, which was directly across the hall, while WSM blithely picked up the tab — for years!" By the spring of 1954, though, he was working extensively with Hank Snow, whose "I Don't Hurt Anymore" was the sensation of the first six months of the year. In its November 6 issue *Billboard* announced that Colonel Tom Parker of Jamboree Attractions had "inked a pact with Hank Snow to handle the latter exclusively on personals. After the first of the year . . . he'll take over management of Hank Snow Enterprises, which includes radio, TV, film and recording commitments." He was back in the big time.

And yet, oddly enough, he remained something of an enigma, an unpredictable quantity, certainly, for someone in so visible a position who did not exactly eschew the public eye. Something about his background simply didn't make sense. "No one knows very much about his boyhood," said Oscar Davis, who doubted the story about the Great Parker Pony Circus when he spoke to Jerry Hopkins in 1970. "I never knew if he had brothers or sisters; he's a bit of a mystery." From time to time he would explode in a fit of temper, or perhaps just an outburst of exuberant good humor, in a language that none of his associates recognized or understood. They wondered if he was speaking German, but he always stipulated that it was Dutch, with a twinkle in his eye that left them in little doubt that he was pulling their leg.

He kept nearly everyone, even his closest associates, at arm's length. "You have one fault," he told his brother-in-law, Bitsy Mott. "You make too many friends." His cold eyes belied his occasional warmheartedness; his absolute honesty in business affairs conflicted with the opportunism that always drove him to come out on top not just in formal dealings but in day-to-day affairs as well (he would spend a hundred dollars, it was said, to beat you out of a dollar). "He got a helluva kick," Chet Atkins declared, "out of getting someone to pick up the check. Or out of just beating you in a deal — any kind of a deal." He was capable of real generosity, but more than anything else he loved the game. As Gabe Tucker observed, he lived in a world of mirrors — he never really left the carnival world, in which "they speak a different language. All of them is just like the Colonel; they'll cut your throat just to watch you bleed. But they've got their own laws, it's a game with them, to outsmart you, you're always the pigeon to them." In Gabe's view, and in Oscar Davis', too, everyone else in the Colonel's estimation was a little bit of a fool.

IT WAS LITTLE WONDER, then, that Sam Phillips should take so instant, and visceral, a dislike to the man sitting opposite him in the little restaurant on Poplar. On the other hand, Tom Parker was one of the few people in the business able to provide a match for Sam. These were two very strong, independent men with two very different visions of life. Sam's embraced the sweep of history; it very consciously conjured up the agrarian hero as the focus of the democratic dream. The Colonel's vision, on the other hand, denied history; it centered on the here and now, focusing on survival by wit and instinct in a universe that was indifferent at best. There was room enough for sentiment in the Colonel's view but little for philosophy; Sam was perhaps less inclined to the sentimental gesture but more to the humanitarian impulse. They didn't like each other, clearly, but their needs suited each other, at least for the time being.

And Sam's need for Parker and Jamboree Attractions was, if anything, greater than Parker's need for any untested twenty-year-old. Parker was right in terms of the blunt challenge he had thrown out: Elvis Presley could get only so far with Sun Records. Sun Records could get only so far without a considerable infusion of cash to cover the signing and promotion of new talent, increased pressing costs, expanded distribution, and the wherewithal to provide some kind of breathing space. Bob Neal had been just the thing, Sam was convinced, but in the short time he had been working with Elvis he had taken the boy about as far as he could go on his own — he had brought Elvis to his audience, booked him all through Mississippi and Arkansas, and tied in with other local promoters like Tom Perryman, Biff Collie, and Jim LeFan, so that Elvis Presley was now an authentic regional sensation. The new record had been well reviewed just the previous week in *Billboard* ("Presley continues to impress with each release as one of the slickest talents to come up in the country field in a long, long time"), records were selling like crazy in Memphis, New Orleans, Dallas, Little Rock, Houston, and all over West Texas, and after only three months Elvis Presley was becoming an attraction the likes of which the Louisiana Hayride had never seen. *But he needed a national stage.*

Elvis excused himself to go back to the auditorium with Scotty, and the five men sat around for a little while longer. They talked about details of the tour: money and bookings, the towns and auditoriums (some of them already familiar) that Elvis would be playing during this brief ten-day tour. It was just a start, but if it worked . . . Neal dreamt about television and movies. He didn't say anything, but they were saving out money from their appearances, building up a little fund for a trip to New York to audition for Arthur Godfrey — he hadn't even mentioned it to Sam. They were working almost every night now, he told the Colonel, busting out everywhere they played, creating some kind of sensation or another, just like Colonel Parker had heard about in New Boston. The Colonel grunted. As far as the Colonel was concerned, if this music was going to be made popular it might as well be made popular by Tommy Sands, a young protégé of his in Shreveport — and that was just what he thought he would write to Steve Sholes after his encounter with Phillips today. Wait'll you see the evening show, Bob Neal persisted. Simply on the basis of his own experience, there was little doubt in Neal's mind that Tom Parker was the best in the business. In his heart of hearts he envisioned a kind of partnership of interests. He couldn't wait to begin. Once this tour was over, Neal *knew* there would be more — more tours, more appearances, with or without the Colonel. He couldn't wait to break out of the mid-South territory.

T HE TOUR — WITH HANK SNOW HEADLINING, the Carter Sisters and Mother Maybelle, and celebrated comedian Whitey Ford (better known as the Duke of Paducah) — opened in Roswell, New Mexico, eight days later. Elvis was booked into Lubbock, Texas, the night before, where he played the Fair Park auditorium for the second time in little more than a month. Also on the bill was Jimmie Rodgers Snow, Hank's son, who was scheduled to join the tour the next night as well. Just a few months younger than Elvis, Snow was bowled over by his first exposure to this kid in "a chartreuse jacket and black pants with a white stripe down the side, and the kids were just going wild. I'd never seen anyone quite like him — even as a kid he had that something about him, he just *had* it. I had never heard of Elvis Presley when I went out there, I had no idea who he was, the Colonel just called me in — him and Tom Diskin — and said, 'I got you booked with this guy, Elvis Presley, out in Lubbock, Texas.' But we talked that night, we ran around that night, as a matter of fact Buddy Holly was hanging around the show [actually Holly opened the show with his friend Bob Montgomery]. And we just became friends immediately."

They joined up with the others in Roswell and two nights later played Odessa, where Elvis was already something of a local legend from his one previous area appearance, in early January. Typical was the enthusiasm of a nineteen-year-old Odessa musician named Roy Orbison, who had had Elvis on his local TV show the first time he had come to town after seeing him on Dallas' Big "D" Jamboree. Orbison later said of that first encounter: "His energy was incredible, his instinct was just amazing. . . . Actually it affected me exactly the same way as when I first saw that David Lynch film [*Blue Velvet*]. I just didn't know what to make of it. There was just no reference point in the culture to compare it."

Hank Snow might well have agreed, though he would have been looking at the subject from a slightly different point of view. Snow, a proud, aloof Canadian of diminutive stature and iron will, kept his distance from the "young punk," with little evident recollection of the fact that he had introduced him on the Opry just four months earlier and little apparent affinity for the figure he was cutting. Elvis for his part made it clear to Jimmy that he idolized his dad — he knew every one of Hank Snow's songs and persisted in singing snatches of even the most obscure of them ("Brand on My Heart," "Just a Faded Petal from a Beautiful Bouquet," "I'm Gonna Bid My Blues Goodbye"), as if to prove that somehow he belonged.

To Jimmie Rodgers Snow, named for the "Father of Country Music" and with a firsthand view of the cost of success — from sudden uprootings in the middle of the school year to broken promises, bitter disappointment, and the sound of his father's typewriter pecking away as he personally answered every last item of fan correspondence — it was almost as if a vision had entered his world, a vision of peculiar purity and innocence that seemed free of all the frustrating struggle and harsh ugliness of the performer's reality. "He didn't drink, he'd carry a cigarette around in his mouth, one of those filter types, never light it because he didn't smoke, but he'd play with it. I remember how cool he was in my mind. I wanted to sing like him. I wanted to dress like him and do things that I never cared about till I met him. He was the change that was coming to America. With Jimmy Dean and all that. I don't think anybody saw it. Dad had no idea what Elvis Presley would become. Colonel probably saw it more than anybody, but I don't think he saw Elvis Presley for more than an entertainer at that time. I used to ride in the car with him and Scotty and Bill — oh, he was the worst guy in the world to ride with, 'cause he was talking to you the whole time, speeding up and his feet moving all the time, he'd work the stations on the radio dial like crazy, listen to different things, country, spirituals, he loved gospel music. I was just fascinated with him. Watching him comb his hair of a morning using three different hair oils, butch wax for the front like you'd use for a crew cut, one kind of hair oil for the top, another for the back. I asked him why he used that butch wax, and he said that was so when he performed his hair would fall down a certain way. He thought that was cool. I also remember that when he would wear a pair of socks, rather than get them washed he'd roll them up and throw them in the suitcase, and if you opened it up it would knock you down. He'd have that thing full of dirty stuff, and a lot of times he would just throw it away and you'd wonder how this clean-cut-looking kid could be so disorganized, but he always took care of his hair. He would take his socks off sometimes and you could be on the bed next to him, and he'd smell up the whole room, but the women could care less. He was Elvis."

That was the way the crowd reacted, too. Almost immediately the Hank Snow show had a problem. "Dad was in his heyday, he was drawing the crowds, and in many of the places that we performed at the beginning they didn't know Elvis, but it didn't matter if they knew him or not — nobody followed Elvis." It was the oddest thing. This nice, polite, well-mannered boy became transformed onstage in a manner that seemed to contradict everything that you might discern about his private personality. "He was this punk kid," Roy Orbison recalled from his original vantage point in the audience. "Just a real raw cat singing like a bird.

. . . First thing, he came out and spat on the stage. In fact he spat out a piece of gum. . . . Plus he told some real bad, crude jokes — you know, this dumb off-color humor — which weren't funny. And his diction was real coarse, like a truck driver's. . . . I can't overemphasize how shocking he looked and seemed to me that night."

His energy was fierce; his sense of competitive fire seemed to overwhelm the shy, deferential kid within; every minute he was onstage was like an incendiary explosion. "There never was a country act that could follow him," said Bob Neal. "With this type of show he would have a big crowd, and then when he appeared, he just tore them up completely." The trouble was, according to Neal, his competitive spirit got the best of him. He didn't want anyone to dislike him, he especially didn't want any of the other performers to think that he had the *big head*, "but he was up against the tops and he always tried to outdo them."

You have only to listen to the few live recordings from that period that have survived. The repertoire is distinctly limited, and Scotty occasionally gets lost in his solos, but Elvis and the boys just *tear* into each song, whether it's "That's All Right" or "Tweedle Dee" or Ray Charles' brand-new hit, "I Got a Woman." The intensity that you get in each performance bears no relation even to the classic recordings on Sun, and while it may not surpass them, in nearly every case it leaves them sounding dry. If Hank Snow felt angry and humiliated in front of his own audience, though, he knew a commercial trend when he spotted one. Jimmie Rodgers Snow was entranced. Before he left the tour in Bastrop, Louisiana, he invited Elvis to come motorcycle riding with him in Nashville sometime soon. Even the Colonel, who still professed profound disinterest, showed a different side to Elvis than Jimmy had ever seen him show before. "He wouldn't go out of his way for nobody. He was always jumping on my case about being on time, carrying a little bit more, giving me this advice, that advice." He was "a hard-nosed man," said Jimmy, much like his own father, and yet even Parker seemed to have fallen under the spell of this irrepressible youth, he seemed as taken as everyone else by the unfeigned enthusiasm, the undisguised eagerness for experience — only the boyfriends of some of his more uninhibited female fans seemed to take exception. Jimmy had no idea where it was going to end, he was more and more confused about the muddle that his own life was falling into under the growing influence of alcohol and pills, but he *knew* that Elvis Presley had a future in the business.

Elvis himself was increasingly coming to believe it, although he continued to discount the idea to family and friends. Every night he called Dixie as well as his mother from each stop on the tour. He told them how it had gone, he told them with almost wide-eyed wonder how the audience had reacted, he told them who he had met and what they had said. "He was always excited about what happened," said Dixie. "He'd say, 'Guess who I saw.' Or: 'Hank Snow was there.' " It was almost as if he were suspended between two worlds. He studied each performer — he watched carefully from backstage with much the same appreciation as the audience, but with a keen sense of what they were doing, what really knocked the fans out, and how each performer achieved it. Between shows he would seek out opportunities to sing with other members of the troupe, and they were all captivated, much as the audience was, by the young man's ingenuous charm.

He could read every audience; it was, evidently, an innate skill. "I see people all different ages and things," he said years later, trying to explain it. "If I do something good, they let me know it. If I don't, they let me know that, too. It's a give-and-take proposition in that they give me back the inspiration. I work absolutely to them. . . . They bring it out of me: the inspiration. The ham." Even if they didn't respond at first he could always get to them. "He would study a crowd," said Tillman Franks of the Hayride tours. "He would look at them, see that he'd gotten through to them, then give them a little bit more. He had electricity between him and that audience, same as Hank Williams did. Hank just give everything he had — he didn't worry about it, he just did it. But Elvis masterminded the situation. He was a genius at it."

"He knew, of course, that his main thrust was to the women," said Jimmie Rodgers Snow. "I saw grandmas dancing in the aisles. I saw a mother and daughter actually bidding for his attention and jealous of each other. It was uncanny: they would just get totally captivated by this guy." "He was always unhappy about the reaction from the boys," said Bob Neal, "because he very much wanted to be one of the boys and a favorite of theirs, but the boys reacted very violently in many areas because, I suppose, of the way the girls acted. It hurt him. You know, we'd talk about it sometimes for hours at a time, driving; he really couldn't understand it. But there was just no way, apparently, that a lot of these young teenaged fellows would change their minds. They just resented him because of the way the girls reacted to him."

But if that was a cloud on the horizon, it was only the casing for the silver lining. There was no aspect of Elvis' new life with which he was not entranced. When the Carter Sisters and Mother Maybelle joined the tour, he and Scotty both were a little taken with Anita, the youngest sister, and they considered it a great triumph when they could get her to ride with them, away from the watchful eye of Mother Maybelle. On one of the last dates of the tour, near Hope, Arkansas, they got stuck on a back road looking for a shortcut to town, and Scotty tried to make time with Anita in the backseat while the others did what they could to persuade a farmer to help pull them out of the mud. "All of us were in the back of this pickup truck," recalled Jimmy Snow, "just laughing — on our way to Hope to do a show."

Two days later the tour ended in Bastrop. Hank Snow was long since departed (his last show had been in Monroe, Louisiana, the previous Friday), and there was no definite commitment from Jamboree for the future, but there was a sure sense that they had accomplished what they set out to do: they had expanded their audience and had a good time doing it.

THAT SATURDAY, February 26, they made their first trip north, to Cleveland, to play the Circle Theater Jamboree. Bob Neal accompanied the boys in hopes that this might lead to even further exposure, that through the contacts he made at radio stations along the way, or just by being on the scene, *something might happen*. Other than that, he had no firm expectations — they didn't even have a definite place to stay. Tommy Edwards, "the City Slicker Turned Country Boy" and host of the Hillbilly Jamboree, had been playing Elvis' records on WERE since the previous fall and was an unqualified fan; there was a big market for this music in Cleveland, he assured Neal. With all of the southerners who had flocked to town looking for work after the war, in addition to the large black population that occupied the Hough district and a diverse ethnic population, Cleveland was a real music town. Every Friday night there was a rhythm and blues show at the Circle, and the Jamboree had unearthed so many hillbillies that Edwards had invited them to educate him as to what they wanted to hear.

But probably the biggest indicator of the change that was coming in music was the startling success of Alan Freed, who, both on the air and as a concert promoter, had discovered the same young white audience for rhythm and blues that Dewey Phillips had found in Memphis. Freed, as flamboyant as Dewey and as opportunistic in business as Dewey was lacking in business sense, had left Cleveland just months earlier for the even more lucrative New York market, where he continued to crusade for the same kind of music, introduced the all-star rhythm and blues revue (the Drifters, the Clovers, Fats Domino, Big Joe Turner, and half a dozen more premier acts all on the same bill), and claimed to have coined, and even copyrighted, the term "rock & roll." And how about Bill Haley, who was very popular here in town; had Bob Neal ever seen him perform? He had done a rhythm and blues show with his western-style band, the Comets, some eighteen months earlier with Billy Ward and His Dominoes and former heavyweight champion Joe Louis and his orchestra. It seemed like right here in Cleveland all the dividing lines and musical barriers were coming down.

The show that night went fine. Elvis remained largely unheralded in Cleveland (his records were little more than "turntable hits" there, since Sun's distribution did not extend effectively that far), but if Bob Neal had been apprehensive about a northern audience's receptivity to this new music, his fears were quickly put to rest. Elvis went over the same as he had throughout the South: the young people went wild, and the older folks covered their mouths. Bill's souvenir photo sales were brisk, as he mixed easily with the fans and made change from his money belt, and Tommy Edwards sold a fair number of their records (which they had carried up from Memphis in the trunk of Bob's car) in the lobby. After the show Edwards said there was someone he wanted Neal to meet. In fact it was the very person who had put on the Billy Ward–Bill Haley show, just returned from his four-hour Saturday-afternoon shift on WCBS in New York. Maybe Elvis could do another interview, even though they had already done an on-the-air promotion for the Jamboree on Edwards' show that afternoon. They went down to the station, and there they met Bill Randle.

Bill Randle was a legend in radio at that time. Tall, scholarly-looking with black horn-rimmed glasses, he had just been written up in *Time* two weeks before in a story that announced, "For the past year the top U.S. deejay has been Cleveland's Bill Randle, 31, a confident, prepossessing fellow who spins his tunes six afternoons a week (from 2 to 7 P.M. on station WERE)." According to the article, Randle had predicted all but one of the top five best-sellers of 1954, discovered Johnnie Ray, changed the name of the Crew-Cuts (from the Canadaires) as well as finding them their first hit, drove a Jaguar, and made $100,000 a year, with his Saturday-afternoon CBS network show in New York the latest in his series of unprecedented accomplishments. "Randle's explanation of his success: 'I'm constantly getting a mass of records. I weed out those that are obviously bad and play the rest on my program to get listener reaction. Then I feed the results into a machine. I'm the machine. I'm a Univac [computer]. It's so accurate that I can tell my listeners, "This tune will be No. 1 in four weeks."'" When asked if he liked the music that he played, Randle, whose personal taste ran to jazz and classical music and who had been fired from a Detroit radio station several years earlier for refusing to play pop ("It was a tremendous emotional problem switching to popular music. . . . It was almost a physical thing bringing myself to play the records"), Randle declared, cheerfully, in *Time*'s estimation: "I'm a complete schizophrenic about this. I'm in the business of giving the public what it wants. This stuff is simply merchandise, and I understand it."

It was through Tommy Edwards that Randle had first heard Elvis Presley's music, but while Edwards played "Blue Moon of Kentucky" for his country audience, Randle heard something in the blues. It wasn't until he started going to New York in January, though, that he actually started playing Presley, and then he aired "Good Rockin' Tonight" on his CBS show, which according to Randle made him persona non grata at the station for a while.

They did the interview down at the WERE studio that night, as Randle played all three of Presley's Sun records and was altogether won over. "He was extremely shy, talked about Pat Boone and Bill Haley as idols, and called me Mr. Randle. Very gentlemanly, very interesting, he knew a lot about the music and the people and the personalities in Memphis, and it was very exciting." He was almost equally impressed with Bob Neal. "Bob Neal to my mind was a really interesting person. He was very bright. He was a country disc jockey, but he was also a businessman-entrepreneur-hustler — but with a lot of class." Randle invited Neal to stay over at his place, and they stayed up much of the night talking. By the end of the evening Randle was convinced that Neal "had a big artist on his way," and he gave Neal the name of a contact in song publishing who he thought could help get Presley a tryout on *Arthur Godfrey's Talent Scouts*. When they parted in the morning, Randle wished Neal luck with his boy and said he hoped he'd get a chance to see him perform when they returned to Cleveland and the Circle Theater the following month. Then Randle had his Sunday-afternoon radio show to do, and Neal and the boys had a long drive back to Memphis.

Memphis seemed almost tame upon their return. It had been more than three weeks since Elvis had last seen Dixie, their longest separation, and he felt like he had all kinds of things to tell her, but when it came down to it, it seemed like he didn't have all that much to tell. They went to the monthly All-Night Singing at Ellis, where James Blackwood left Elvis' name at the door, then announced that he was in the audience and invited him backstage after the show. They went to the movies — *The Blackboard Jungle* opened that month, with Bill Haley's "Rock Around the Clock" blasting out over the opening credits. For the first time they didn't have to worry about money, they could buy all the new records they wanted at Charlie's and Poplar Tunes and Reuben Cherry's Home of the Blues, where Elvis bought every red and black Atlantic and silver and blue Chess record that he could find. They dropped in to see Dewey Phillips, and Dewey always made a big fuss, announcing in his superexcited pitchman's voice that Elvis was in the studio, firing a few questions at him that Elvis answered with surprising ease on the air. He played football down at the Triangle a few times, but he felt increasingly uncomfortable with the old gang. They stopped by the new office on Union, whose recurrent motif was pink and black: fan club membership cards, stationery, and envelopes all matched Elvis' preferred personal decor, and Bob's wife, Helen, said they had several hundred fan club members enrolled already. On March 15, Elvis signed an amended one-year agreement with Neal, giving Neal a 15 percent commission and subject to renewal in March 1956, when, if necessary, it could be revised again.

Meanwhile, the group had its second recording session in little more than a month. They had gone into the studio at the beginning of February, just before the start of the Jamboree tour, with the idea of recording their next single, but like every other session, this one had come hard. They tried Ray Charles' current hit, "I Got a Woman," already a staple of their live act, as well as "Trying to Get to You," an unusual gospel-based ballad by an obscure rhythm and blues group from Washington, D.C., called the Eagles, but neither one worked out. The one number they did come up with, though, was probably the best they had gotten in the studio to date. Taken from a fairly pallid original by Arthur Gunter that hit the rhythm and blues charts at the end of January, "Baby, Let's Play

House" virtually exploded with energy and high spirits and the sheer bubbling irrepressibility that Sam Phillips had first sensed in Elvis' voice.
"Whoa, baby, baby, baby, baby, baby," Elvis opened in an ascending, hic-
coughing stutter that knocked everybody out with its utterly unpredictable, uninhibited, and gloriously playful ridiculousness, and when he
changed Gunter's original lyric from "You may have religion" to "You
may drive a pink Cadillac" ("But don't you be nobody's fool"), he defined
something of his own, not to mention his generation's, aspirations. This
looked like it could become their biggest record yet, everyone agreed. All
they needed was a B side.

    While they were out on tour, Stan Kesler wrote it. Kesler, the steel
guitarist in Clyde Leoppard's Snearly Ranch Boys, had been hanging
around the studio since the fall, when he had been drawn in by the
strange new sounds he had heard on the radio ("I never heard anything
like it before"). The Snearly Ranch Boys were looking to make a record,
which they eventually did, but Sam Phillips picked out Kesler, along with
Muscle Shoals–area musicians Quinton Claunch (guitar) and Bill Cantrell
(fiddle), to form a kind of rhythm section for a bunch of little country
demo sessions he put together in the fall and winter of 1954–55 on artists as
diverse as fourteen-year-old Maggie Sue Wimberley, the Miller Sisters,
Charlie Feathers, and a new rocking hillbilly artist out of Jackson, Tennessee, a kind of hopped-up Hank Williams named Carl Perkins. He put out
limited-release singles on each of these, mostly on a nonunion subsidiary
label he formed just for that purpose, called Flip, but with almost all of
Sam's energies still focused on Elvis none of the records did anything
much.

    It was clear, though, that Sam was thinking of the future and seeking
ways to expand upon Sun's newfound success. Times were still tough,
money remained tight, and Sam was still feeling the pinch from buying
out his partner, Jim Bulleit, the year before, but there was no question of
his settling for being known as a one-artist producer. Sam Phillips' ambitions were much grander than that: he had great hopes for this new boy
Perkins, "one of the great plowhands in the world," as he later described
him, and he was "so impressed with the pain and feeling in his country
singing" that he felt this might be "someone who could revolutionize the
country end of the business." He was equally impressed with yet another
young man who had shown up on the Sun doorstep in the wake of Presley's success and continued to hang around until Sam gave him an audi-

tion. There was something about the quality of this young appliance salesman's voice — it was in a way akin to Ernest Tubb's in its homespun *honesty* (he kept telling the boy not to try to sound like anyone else, not to worry if his sound and his style were untutored, not even to rehearse too much, "because I was interested in spontaneity, too"). He didn't release a record on Johnny Cash until the following summer, but he was working with him and Perkins and Charlie Feathers and a host of others all through the winter and spring.

That was why Stan Kesler kept hanging around. He sensed that something new was about to happen, and he wanted to be a part of it when it did. When he heard that Sam was looking for material for the next Presley session, he immediately went home and wrote a number called "I'm Left, You're Right, She's Gone" with fellow band member Bill Taylor (trumpet player with the Snearly Ranch Boys) based on the melody of the Campbell's Soup commercial. He borrowed Clyde Leoppard's tape recorder, had Taylor demo the song, and sat around the studio chatting with Marion until Sam came in and listened to it. As it turned out, Sam liked the song, and Elvis must have a little bit, too, because it was the one number that they concentrated on at the session the following week.

What was different about this session was that for the first time they used a drummer. Sam had always said that he wanted to take the trio format as far as he could — and in fact they started out this session as a trio — but Sam felt like there was something missing, and he called up a young musician who had come in with his high school band the previous year to make an acetate of a couple of big band jazz numbers. Jimmie Lott was a junior in high school at the time but unfazed by the action. "I had bronchitis, but I loaded up my drums into my mom's car. Elvis was standing in the doorway of the studio. He had long greasy ducktails, which was not too cool with my [crowd]." They jumped into a Jimmie Rodgers Snow number that Elvis wanted to cut, "How Do You Think I Feel," to which Lott contributed a Latin beat, but they couldn't get it right and soon went back to the Kesler-Taylor composition that Elvis, Scotty, and Bill had been fooling around with all evening. They had run up more than a dozen takes already, trying to transform a simple country tune into a wrenchingly slow blues number patterned on the Delmore Brothers' "Blues Stay Away from Me." Elvis was uncomfortable with the idea of doing a straight-out country tune, and Sam could understand that, but even as they came closer to what they were aiming for, Sam knew they were just getting further apart: hell, they *all* knew it in some part of their souls. The Campbell's Soup melody just wasn't altogether suited to a blues treatment.

Once the drums were added, providing a solid, jangling background, there wasn't so much weight on Elvis' vocals, and he got the pretty, almost delicate tone that Sam had envisioned for the tune all along, breaking his voice in a manner halfway between traditional country style and his newly patented hiccough, with Scotty supplying his smoothest Chet Atkins licks on top of the blues variations that still lingered from earlier versions It didn't really match some of the other stuff they'd gotten, but it was just the kind of thing Sam felt they needed ("We didn't need that Nashville country, but I wanted the simplicity of the melody line — you know, we had to do a little bit of crawling around just to see where we were before we got into the race"). At the end of the session, as Jimmie Lott was packing up his drums, Sam asked him if he would be interested in working some more with the group, but Jimmie, who would later play in Warren Smith's band and record again in the Sun studio, demurred without much hesitation. "I told him I had another year of school and couldn't."

Some two weeks later, on March 23, they went up to New York with Bob Neal. They flew because their booking schedule was so tight that they didn't have time to drive or take the train (*Billboard* of April 2 reported that the group was "set solid through April"). It was the first time that Elvis or Bill had flown, and the first time any of the boys had visited New York. They gawked at the skyscrapers and took a subway ride. Bob, who had been to the city before, pointed out the sights to them while Bill kidded around, crossed his eyes, and acted like a cheerful hick. When they got to the studio, though, the response was decidedly cool, the lady conducting the audition conveyed a "don't call us we'll call you" kind of attitude, and they never even got to see Arthur Godfrey. It was very disappointing to them all, not least to Bob Neal, who had been building this up as an opportunity to break into the big time — television was a *national* market, and Arthur Godfrey was the vehicle by which the Blackwood Brothers had become nationally known. They had been saving up for months for this trip, and now they might just as well have flushed the money down the toilet. Bill Randle's friend Max Kendrick reported back to Randle somewhat indignantly that this new kid just wasn't ready for the big time — he showed up for the audition badly dressed and seemed nervous and ill prepared — and Randle felt that Kendrick was a little distant as a result for some months thereafter.

Elvis and Scotty and Bill had no time for reflection, however. They hit the road again almost immediately. They were driving a 1954 pink-and-white Cadillac by now. Elvis had gotten a 1951 Cosmopolitan Lincoln with only ten thousand miles on it at the beginning of the year, the first "new" car he had ever owned. He had had a rack put on top for the bass, painted "Elvis Presley — Sun Records" on the side, and was so proud of it that he wouldn't allow anyone even to smoke inside the car. Bill had wrecked it in March, driving it under a hay truck late one night in Arkansas, but Elvis had been able to assuage his disappointment, with Bob Neal's help, by purchasing the Cadillac.

They were constantly on the go. Sometimes it seemed as if they didn't even have time to sleep. Houston, Dallas, Lubbock and all through West Texas. Hayride shows in Galveston, Waco, and Baton Rouge. Hawkins, Gilmer, and Tyler, Texas, all within calling distance of Tom Perryman's Gladewater radio signal. All the little towns scattered throughout the Mississippi and Arkansas Delta. Back to Cleveland for another date at the Circle Theater. El Dorado. Texarkana. The Hayride. "It was always exciting," in Elvis' view. "We slept in the back of the car, and we'd do a show and get offstage and get in the car and drive to the next town and sometimes just get there in time to wash up [and] do the show." Scotty and Bill were chasing the girls, and the girls were chasing Elvis — and frequently catching up with him. Everywhere he went he created a sensation. "He's the new rage," said a Louisiana radio executive in an interview with the British musical press. "Sings hillbilly in r&b time. Can you figure that out. He wears pink pants and a black coat . . . [and] he's going terrific. If he doesn't suffer too much popularity, he'll be all right."

"This cat came out," said future country singer Bob Luman, still an eighteen-year-old high school student in Kilgore, Texas, "in red pants and a green coat and a pink shirt and socks, and he had this sneer on his face and he stood behind the mike for five minutes, I'll bet, before he made a move. Then he hit his guitar a lick, and he broke two strings. Hell, I'd been playing ten years, and I hadn't broken a *total* of two strings. So there he was, these two strings dangling, and he hadn't done anything except break the strings yet, and these high school girls were screaming and fainting and running up to the stage, and then he started to move his hips real slow like he had a thing for his guitar. . . . For the next nine days he played one-nighters around Kilgore, and after school every day me and my girl would get in the car and go wherever he was playing that night. That's the last time I tried to sing like Webb Pierce or Lefty Frizzell."

Not surprisingly, he was not entirely unaffected by all this adulation. While everyone agreed that he continued to maintain a remarkably polite and deferential manner and never failed to show his elders an uncommon degree of respect, those meeting him for the first time encountered a somewhat different figure than they would have met six months, or even three months, before — more confident perhaps, understandably more suspicious, but overall simply more *himself*. Sometimes this could lead to sudden displays of temper, as at the Hayride, when in a famous local incident he punched the doorkeeper, a teenager named Shorty, in the nose, because Shorty either opened or closed the door on his fans. Everyone was surprised by the incident, no one more so than Elvis himself, who immediately apologized profusely and offered to pay all of the doctor's bills. The Miller Sisters, the performing duo that Sam had been working with, who met Elvis at a show in Saltillo, Mississippi, just down the road from where he was born, found him stuck-up and conceited. "He was really cocky," said one. "I remember Elvis asked me to hold his guitar, and I said, 'Hold it yourself. I'm not your flunky!' " But, of course, that may have just been his way with one woman.

"Elvis Presley continues to gather speed over the South," wrote Cecil Holifield, operator of the Record Shops in Midland and Odessa, Texas, in the June 4 edition of *Billboard*.

West Texas is his hottest territory to date, and he is the teenagers' favorite wherever he appears. His original appearance in the area was in January with Billy Walker . . . to more than 1600 paid admissions. In February, with Hank Snow at Odessa . . . paid attendance hit over 4000. On April 1 we booked only Elvis and his boys, Bill and Scotty, plus Floyd Cramer on piano and a local boy on drums for a rockin' and rollin' dance for teenagers, and pulled 850 paid admissions. . . . Incidentally, our sales of Presley's four records have beat any individual artist in our eight years in the record business.

With a new Jamboree tour coming up in May, headlined by Hank Snow and covering the entire mid South, Elvis and Scotty and Bill were not about to start looking back. They didn't have the time. Bob Neal was excited and optimistic about all the connections Tom Parker was helping them to make. He felt as if they were finally about to move up to another league.

THE TOUR BEGAN on May 1 in New Orleans, the day after Elvis' fourth Sun single, "Baby, Let's Play House," was released. It was billed as a three-week, twenty-city tour that would employ thirty-one different artists, some of whom would pick up and leave the tour at various points. Headliners were Hank Snow, Slim Whitman, and the Carter Sisters with Mother Maybelle, and Martha Carson and Faron Young would join the show in Florida. In a solution the Colonel devised to prevent the kind of thing that had happened on the last tour, there would be a first half of "younger talent" that included Jimmie Rodgers Snow, the Davis Sisters, and the Wilburn Brothers, with "one of the newest though most exciting personalities in the Hillbilly field . . . [whose] singing style is completely different from any other singer in the field," Elvis Presley, appearing just before the intermission.

There were near-riots almost everywhere they played. Johnny Rivers saw the show in Baton Rouge and decided, "I wanna be like *that* guy," while in Mobile, Jimmie Rodgers Snow remembered Elvis being chased across a football field. There were girls in every city, and after the show Elvis never lacked for company, cruising around town in the pink and white Cadillac he had just acquired to replace the Lincoln (once again he had his name painted in black on the door). Jimmy Snow roomed with him on this tour, "and he would run the women, he'd run two or three of them in one night — whether or not he was actually making love to all three, I don't know, because he was kind of private in that sense and if I thought he was going to run some women in the room with him, I didn't stay. But I just think he wanted them around, it was a sense of insecurity, I guess, because I don't think he was a user. He just loved women, and I think they knew that."

Every night he called his parents at their new home on Lamar just to let them know how he was doing, how the show had gone, to find out how they were. Many nights Dixie was there, and he liked that, both because it saved him a call and because he knew that they were keeping an eye on her. "He didn't want to relinquish that control, regardless of how long he was gone or what he was doing; [he wanted to know] that I was still going to be sitting there. If I wasn't there, he would ask his parents, 'Was Dixie there?' Or: 'Have you heard from her? Has she been over? Did she spend the night?' I think he expected his parents to kind of keep me there while he was gone so I wouldn't do anything else — but it just got to be harder and harder after a while." He wanted to know how they liked the new house — they were still renting, of course, but it was the first time since they had moved to Memphis that they had had a real home of their own. How was Daddy feeling? Was his back any better? No, he reassured Gladys, she didn't have to worry, he was doing just fine — he knew it both-ered her the way the audiences did sometimes, but they weren't going to hurt him any. Yes, they were taking good care of the new Caddy, wasn't it the prettiest thing? No, they were being careful. He didn't know if he'd even let Bill drive this one! And how was the pretty little pink and white Crown Victoria he had bought for them? It was the first new car they had ever owned. He tried to reassure her: he was safe, he was happy, he was still hers. But Gladys was not to be reassured. Some part of her feared what was about to happen. Some part of her feared what she saw was happening already. "I know she worshiped him, and he did her," said Dixie, "to the point where she would almost be jealous of anything else that took his time. I think she really had trouble accepting him as his popularity grew. It grew hard for her to let everybody have him. I had the same feelings. He did not belong to [us] anymore."

H E MET MAE BOREN AXTON, publicist for the Florida leg of the tour, at the first Florida date, in Daytona Beach. A forty-year-old English teacher at Paxon High School in Jacksonville, where her husband was the football coach, Axton had gotten into country music through the back door when she was asked by *Life Today,* a magazine for which she did occasional freelance work, to write an article on "hillbilly" music. Though she had been born in Fort Worth, Texas, and grew up in Okla-homa (her brother, David, later became a prominent U.S. senator from Oklahoma), she claimed to have no idea what hillbilly music was. "We listened to the opera, and my teacher taught me classical, and folk songs I knew, but the term 'hillbilly' was foreign to me." Her research took her to Nashville, where she met Minnie Pearl, who introduced her as a coun-try songwriter to powerful song publishing executive Fred Rose. Taking

Mae for what Minnie Pearl said she was, Rose told her he needed a novelty song for a Dub Dickerson recording session that afternoon, and she
wrote one, if only to prove her newfound friend correct.

Soon she had gotten a number of her songs cut (Dub Dickerson recorded more of their collaborations, as did Tommy Durden) while continuing to write stories for fan club magazines. She hooked up with the
Colonel in 1953 on a Hank Snow tour and began doing advance press
work for him in the Jacksonville-Orlando-Daytona area. As a woman
who was both attractive and feisty, Mae claimed to be the only person
that she knew ever to get an apology out of the Colonel. Ordinarily, his
one response to any form of criticism was "The Colonel is the boss."
"You be the boss," she said angrily when he tried this line on her. "Be
the big wheel. But don't ever ask me to do another thing for you."
Which led to the apology. Despite this incident, or perhaps because of it,
she always got along well with the Colonel and for a time even served as
Hank Snow's personal publicist. She was energetic and resourceful and
proved an excellent local PR woman on a management team that left
nothing to chance.

They were scheduled to play Daytona Beach on May 7, and Mae met
them at the motel. "I had gotten up real early and gone and done an interview about the show that night and about Elvis, and I came back
around eleven, and, you know, the back of the motel was facing the
ocean, the little rails were up there, the little iron rails. And I walked out
of my door — my room was right near Elvis' — and Elvis was leaning
over looking at the ocean. Of course there were a lot of people on the
beach, and I said, 'Hi, honey, how are you doing?' And he looked up and
said, 'Fine.' He said, 'Miz Axton, look at that ocean.' Of course I had
seen it a million times. He said, 'I can't believe that it's so big.' It just
overwhelmed him. He said, 'I'd give anything in the world to find
enough money to bring my mother and daddy down here to see it.'
That just went through my heart. 'Cause I looked down here, and here
were all these other kids, different show members for that night, all the
guys looking for cute little girls. But his priority was doing something for
his mother and daddy."

In the interview he persisted in calling her Miz Axton, and she suggested that he "just make it Mae. That makes it better. . . . Elvis," she said,
"you are sort of a bebop artist more than anything else, aren't you? Is that
what they call you?"

Elvis: Well, I never have given myself a name, but a lot of the disc jockeys call me — bopping hillbilly and bebop, I don't know what else. . . .

Mae: I think that's very fine. And you've started touring the country, and you've covered a lot of territory in the last two months, I believe.

Elvis: Yes, ma'am, I've covered a lot — mostly in West Texas is where, that's where my records are hottest. Around in San Angelo and Lubbock and Midland and Amarillo —

Mae: They tell me they almost mobbed you there, the teenagers, they like you so much. But I happen to know you have toured all down in the eastern part of the country, too. Down through Florida and around and that the people went for you there about as well as out in West Texas, isn't that right?

Elvis: Well, I wasn't very well known down here — you know, I'm with a small company, and my records don't have the distribution that they should have, but —

Mae: . . . You know, I watched you perform one time down in Florida, and I noticed that the older people got as big a kick out of you as the teenagers, I think that was an amazing thing.

Elvis: Well, I imagine it's just the way we, all three of us move on the stage, you know, we act like we —

Mae: Yes, and we mustn't leave out Scotty and Bill. They really do a terrific job of backing you up.

Elvis: They sure do. I really am lucky to have those two boys, 'cause they really are good. Each one of them have an individual style of their own.

Mae: You know, what I can't understand is how you keep that leg shaking just at the right [general laughter] tempo all the time you're singing.

Elvis: Well, it gets hard sometimes. I have to stop and rest it — but it just automatically wiggles like that.

Mae: Is that it? Just automatically does it? You started back in high school, didn't you?

Elvis: Ah —

Mae: Singing around, public performances with school and things of that sort?

Elvis: Well, no, I never did sing anywhere in public in my life till I made this first record.

Mae: Is that right?

Elvis: Yes, ma'am.

Mae: And then you just went right on into their hearts, and you're doing a wonderful job, and I want to congratulate you on that, and I want to say, too, Elvis, it's been very nice having you in the studio —

Elvis: Well, thank you very much, Mae, and I'd like to personally thank you for really promoting my records down here because you really have done a wonderful job, and I really do appreciate it, because if you don't have people backing you, people pushing you, well, you might as well quit.

Later that night at the show Mae ran into one of her former students, now a student nurse. Elvis was onstage, "and she was just right into it, didn't know who he was, none of them did. But she was just ahhhh — all of them were, even some of the old ones were doing like that. I looked at the faces — they were loving it. And I said, 'Hey, honey, what is it about this kid?' And she said, 'Awww, Miz Axton, he's just a great big beautiful hunk of forbidden fruit.' "

They played Orlando that week, and local reporter Jean Yothers, still evidently in somewhat of a daze several days later, wrote it up in the *Orlando Sentinel* of May 16.

What hillbilly music does to the hillbilly music fan is absolutely phenomenal. It transports him into a wild, emotional and audible state of ecstasy. He never sits back sedately patting his palms politely and uttering bravos of music appreciation as his long-hair counterpart. He thunders his appreciation for the country-style music and nasal-twanged singing he loves by whistling shrilly through teeth, pounding the palms together with the whirling momentum of a souped-up paddle wheel, stomping the floor and ejecting yip-yip

noises like the barks of a hound dog when it finally runs down a particularly elusive coon.

That's the way it was, friends, at the big Hank Snow show and
all-star Grand Ole Opry Jamboree staged last week in municipal auditorium to jam-packed houses both performances. It was as hot as blue
blazes within the tired sanctums of the barnish auditorium, but the
hillbilly fans turned out in droves and seemed oblivious to the heat.
. . . The whole shebang seemed like a cross between the enthusiasm
displayed at a wrestling match and old-fashioned camp meeting. . . .

This was my first tangle with a hillbilly jamboree, a poignant contrast to Metropolitan Opera in Atlanta, I must say. I was awed and
with all due respect to opera in Atlanta, I got a tremendous boot out
of this loud, uninhibited music that's sending the country crazy. . . .

Ferron [Faron] Young was real sharp singing that ditty about living fast, loving hard, dying young and leaving a beautiful memory,
but what really stole the show was this 20-year-old sensation, Elvis
Presley, a real sex box as far as the teenage girls are concerned. They
squealed themselves silly over this fellow in orange coat and sideburns who "sent" them with his unique arrangement of Shake, Rattle
and Roll. And following the program, Elvis was surrounded by girlies
asking for autographs. He would give each a long, slow look with
drooped eyelids and comply. They ate it up. The crowd also ate up a
peppy and perspiring Miss Martha Carson calling the parquet-sitting
spectators "you folks a-sitten over there on the shelves" and the same
Miss Carson breaking two guitar strings and a pick with her strong
strumming of This Old House and Count Your Blessings. Fans were
forever rushing up near the stage snapping flashbulb pictures during
the program, and they all instinctively recognized a tune with recognizable roars before the second plunk of the guitar had been sounded.
It was amazing! Hillbilly music is here to stay, yo'all!

On the thirteenth they played Jacksonville. Before the show Mae took
Elvis and some of the other musicians out to dinner, and she tried to
wheedle him out of the frilly pink shirt he was wearing. "Skeeter Davis
was there, and June and Anita [Carter], and some of the boys with Elvis,
and I said, 'Elvis, that's vulgar. And it would make me such a pretty
blouse.' And Skeeter said, 'I want it,' and June said, 'I want it.' And he just
kind of grinned. And I said, 'Elvis, you ought to give it to us, one of us

anyway, because they are just going to tear it off you tonight.' Not really thinking about it — knowing the people liked him but not really thinking about it."

That night at the show, in front of fourteen thousand people, he announced at the conclusion of his act: "Girls, I'll see you all backstage." Almost immediately they were after him. The police got him into the Gator Bowl's dugout locker room, where Mae and the Colonel were totaling up the night's receipts. Most of the other acts were backstage, too, Mae recalled, when the fans started pouring in through an overhead window that had been inadvertently left open. "I heard feet like a thundering herd, and the next thing I knew I heard this voice from the shower area. I started running, and three or four policemen started running, too, and by the time we got there several hundred must have crawled in — well, maybe not that many, but a lot — and Elvis was on top of one of the showers looking sheepish and scared, like 'What'd I do?' and his shirt was shredded and his coat was torn to pieces. Somebody had even gotten his belt and his socks and these cute little boots — they were not cowboy boots, he was up there with nothing but his pants on and they were trying to pull at *them* up on the shower. Of course the police started getting them out, and I never will forget Faron Young — this one little girl had kind of a little hump at the back, and he kicked at her, and these little boots fell out."

The Colonel, said Mae, "and I don't mean it derogatorily, got dollar marks in his eyes." It was Jacksonville, said Oscar Davis, that marked the turning point — that was the real eye-opener, the Colonel said to him. By the time the show got to Richmond three days later, it was as if Elvis had never been anything but the Colonel's boy. The whole troupe was staying at the old Jefferson Hotel, and by happenstance RCA c&w promotion manager Chick Crumpacker was in Richmond on one of his three-or-four-times-a-year southern swings to meet DJs, distributors, and field reps. Regional representative Brad McCuen, who had heard Elvis' first record in Knoxville the previous year and, witnessing the reaction to it, sent it on to New York with a glowing report, persuaded Crumpacker to go to the show, and Crumpacker, a sophisticated, serious, and witty Northwestern School of Music graduate who continued to write classical compositions but had a healthy respect for "America's folk music," enthusiastically accepted. Both Crumpacker and McCuen knew the Colonel not only from his present association with Hank Snow and his former management of

Eddy Arnold, RCA's two leading country artists, but because each had briefly accompanied the RCA Country Caravan, which the Colonel had managed the previous year. Both had had interesting experiences with the Colonel. In Jacksonville the previous April, in Chick's presence, Parker had accused publicist Anne Fulchino of "deliberately steering *Life* and *Look* magazine people, whom she had gotten to cover the show, away from him and his wife Marie, who he bragged were responsible for the Caravan's success. When I attempted to explain that this wasn't so, he turned nearly physical and said he would have both our jobs over it." Brad, who had worked extensively with Snow and Eddy Arnold for a number of years, had enjoyed a more congenial relationship overall, but from the opportunity he had had to watch the Colonel in action, he, too, was fully aware of Parker's mania for control, his need to maintain the upper hand, and his predilection for unpredictable acts in order to keep even close friends and associates on their toes. Neither man was entirely certain of the reception they would get, but, true to form, the Colonel surprised them by acting as if he couldn't have been more pleased to see two such old and dear friends.

They were even more surprised by the show they saw that night. Although Chick had been prepared to some extent by McCuen's description of the music, and he might have heard one or two of the records himself in passing, neither one of them had seen the boy perform, and neither was prepared for either the ferocity of his performance or the reaction to it. "We were astounded by the reaction," said Chick, "both among the Richmonders and in ourselves. There were kids in the audience — it was definitely a noisier audience than I remembered from the Caravan the year before. And lo and behold, out comes this guy whose picture we had seen in the trade papers, and he was something else. All the mannerisms were more or less in place. The body language — I don't remember exactly what he sang, but there were frequent belches into the mike, and the clincher came when he took his chewing gum out and tossed it into the audience. This, of course, was shocking, it was wild — but what really got the listeners was his energy and *the way he sang the songs*. The effect was galvanic. It was also somewhat embarrassing, because as friends and promoters of Jimmie Rodgers Snow, we had to watch him be totally eclipsed."

The next morning they had breakfast with the Colonel and Hank Snow. Then to Chick's surprise: "In walks the young star. And the first impression I had is the one that will always stick: that he was so unassuming, he seemed somewhat withdrawn at first, looked nervously around the room, but he had this quality — he was very, very smart behind it all, and he knew how to flatter people. We talked about the show, exchanged views about the crowd, the turnout, the other artists — he was very affable, he would say to Brad and me how much he enjoyed being with us; 'I like you, Chick,' he said. And while this may well have been a ploy, it worked. We liked him, immensely, from the start."

Chick finished up his trip in Louisville, but not before purchasing all four of Elvis' Sun records, two copies of each, one to present to RCA's country and western division head, Steve Sholes. "Throughout that spring and the early part of that summer I did a lot of wishful thinking with Sholes — maybe we could sign this guy. But as far as I know, there were no rumors at this point that his contract was for sale. There was no question that the Colonel had his eye on him, though, the Colonel was *definitely* taking a proprietary attitude, even if nothing was explicitly said or voiced."

TAMPA, JULY 1955. (POPSIE. COURTESY OF GER RIJFF)

MYSTERY TRAIN

BOB NEAL, manager of Elvis Presley," declared the July 9 issue of *Billboard*, "reports that his charge this week begins a fortnight's vacation before embarking on a busy summer and fall schedule being arranged by Col. Tom Parker, Jamboree Attractions, Madison, Tenn."

He had been working steadily, virtually every night, since the show at Ellis Auditorium on February 6, and in that short time he had come further than either he or his manager had ever dared hope. He had opened up new territory, more than held his own with some of the biggest Opry stars, and attracted the favor of a man who had it in his power, Neal insisted, to do even more for him than he had already done.

On balance Bob Neal was well satisfied: he had seen bookings pick up, watched his own and Elvis' material situations dramatically improve, and redrafted their agreement to last until March 1956, with an option to renew. He had also witnessed the kind of growth he would never have taken on faith, an almost exponential progression that had taken place in the boy himself, not just in his stage manner (which would alone have been remarkable enough) but in an appetite for change and self-improvement that seemed to know no experiential bounds. Not that the boy would ever be mistaken for an intellectual — and he was far too jittery to be called introspective. But he soaked up influences like litmus paper; he was open to new people and new ideas and new experiences in a way that defied social stereotype. He was *serious* about his work. Whenever Neal went by the house, he found him with a stack of records — Ray Charles and Big Joe Turner and Big Mama Thornton and Arthur "Big Boy" Crudup — that he studied with all the avidity that other kids focused on their college exams. He listened over and over, seeming to hear something that no one else could hear, while able to carry on a perfectly coherent conversation at the same time on the subject of bookings or the upcoming Florida tour (what were they going to do in Jacksonville for an encore?) or something that Helen needed to know for the fan club, with Dixie all the while sitting by his side.

Vernon was around most of the time — he didn't seem terribly ambitious about going out and looking for a job. Bob was a little worried about that; you could never tell what went on inside a family, and Bob wondered if there might not be "a little rift" between father and son over the father's disinclination to work. "But Gladys kept the family together, she was very down-to-earth, always concerned about his health and well-being, and was always concerned about those of us around him. He was very aware of the fact that she did everything she possibly could to help give him a chance, and he wanted so much to do big things and nice things particularly for his mother. I remember coming back from a show one night, he was commenting to Helen, 'Oh, I just want to be big, because I want to do something for my folks.' He said, 'They're getting old.' I looked at Elvis, and I said, 'Elvis, how old do you think I am?' And he said, 'Well, I don't know.' . . . I was, I think, a year or two older than Vernon."

Elvis was glad to be home while at the same time anxious to be on to the next step. It had all started to get to him a little toward the end of the tour. Just one month before, on June 5, on the road between Hope and Texarkana a wheel bearing caught fire, and he had watched his pretty pink Cadillac burn up. He had had it for little more than two months, and he was as proud of it as anything he had ever owned. For a moment, as Scotty and Bill gave him a hard time and the instruments and clothing sat forlornly by the side of the road, it was like watching all his dreams go up in flames — but then there was business to be taken care of, they had to charter a plane to get to the next show, call Bob, get someone to drive the Crown Victoria down to meet them in Dallas, move *on*. Then on July 4 he found himself playing a picnic with the Blackwood Brothers and the Statesmen Quartet at gospel promoter W. B. Nowlin's All-Day Singing and dinner on the ground in De Leon, Texas. He showed up in his pink suit, according to James Blackwood, but whether or not he knew anything in advance about Nowlin's annual picnic event (it had started seven years earlier with Eddy Arnold and the Stamps Quartet; in 1950 Hank Williams had been booked with the Blackwoods), there was something about the scene that brought him up short: all those families gathered with their kids, eating fried chicken in the afternoon sunlight under the pecan trees in Hodges Park.

"I ain't gonna sing nothing but gospel music today," he told James in the

Blackwood Brothers' new bus as they swapped stories and songs, and nothing that James could say would dissuade him. Onstage it was almost as if he were spellbound; he didn't respond when people called out for his songs, "he fell flat on his face," said J. D. Sumner, the bass singer with the group. The spell — if that was what it was — was broken later that afternoon when he played a second show with the whole troupe at an indoor jamboree in nearby Stephenville that also featured Slim Willett ("Don't Let the Stars Get in Your Eyes") and then a third in Brownwood that evening. "It was mighty warm in our rec. hall," reported Stephenville DJ/promoter Bill Bentley, "but next year it will be cool, as we have decided to air condition it."

Even coming home was not like coming home exactly. For one thing, he was coming home to a new house, the first single-family structure the Presleys had lived in since moving to Memphis, and even though he had slept there before, it was never for more than a night or two, he had been on the road so steadily since they had moved in some two months before. It was a modest two-bedroom brick bungalow at 2414 Lamar, partway between Katz Drug Store, where Elvis and Scotty and Bill had created such a sensation not ten months previously, and the Rainbow skating rink, where Elvis and Dixie had first met. If you continued east on Lamar, it took you past the Eagle's Nest and, as Highway 78, all the way to Tupelo. It was the road on which the Presleys had first arrived in Memphis, and he didn't know how many times he had traveled it, going in and out of town as a small child and as a young man, but somehow it seemed different now, he felt almost like a stranger. For the first couple of days after he got home he mostly slept.

The next-door neighbors, the Bakers, with three teenagers in the family, two boys and a girl, waited eagerly for their first real glimpse of the young scion of the house. The Presleys didn't have a phone of their own for quite some time — it was difficult to get a new phone installed in those days — so Mr. and Mrs. Presley were frequent visitors to the Bakers' house to make calls, and Mrs. Baker had had a memorable encounter with Mrs. Presley on the night they had moved in. Mr. Presley must still have been moving things from their old house, because he wasn't there when one of her cousins burst in on the Bakers and announced that Mrs. Presley had passed out on the bed. The cousin didn't know if the Presleys had a regular doctor of their own, so Mrs. Baker called her own doctor, who came out and pronounced Mrs. Presley a sick woman — Mrs. Baker understood it was diabetes or a bad heart, something along those lines. Which was a shame in such a young woman. Since then, while they never became exactly friends, Mrs. Baker had felt sorry for Mrs. Presley, the nicest-mannered person but a "nervous creature" who seemed to carry such a burden of sadness that she couldn't stand to even be in the house alone.

The night that Elvis' Cadillac burned up, as the Bakers remembered it, they got the call, but Mrs. Presley seemed to know what was the matter even before she picked up the phone. After that she could scarcely bear to even contemplate the dangers that her son faced out on the road. As much as she wanted success for him, it was almost as if any satisfaction she might take in it was gone. One time she invited Mrs. Baker and her daughter, Sarah, over to the house. "Come here, come here," she said, and showed them his closet, full of clothes in black and pink. She was so proud of all his shoes and the suits hanging up, and she talked about her son in a manner that she talked about nothing else. She convinced Mrs. Baker that he didn't deserve all the criticism that was being directed at him, that he wasn't vulgar in his movements, that he didn't mean anything by it, he just put his whole self into what he did.

Mr. Presley was another story altogether. He was what you might call a very "dry" man, never offering much in the way of amenities or even response. Mr. Baker had even started latching the screen door for a while, because Mr. Presley would walk in without so much as a knock, to use the phone or borrow something, day or night — he didn't mean anything by it, he just didn't know any better, they supposed, but Mr. Baker didn't like it so he put a hook on the door. They watched Vernon in the yard, working with a brother or brother-in-law occasionally, installing air conditioners in new cars whenever, it seemed, he felt like it, and they felt even sorrier for poor Mrs. Presley, but they knew the family was very dedicated to one another — they were even talking about buying the little house someday and adding on a room for Mr. Presley's mother, who stayed with them much of the time.

When he finally got used to being home, Elvis started popping in on the Bakers to make some calls, and to take some, too, showing a gracious-ness and a natural ease that they could never forget. The first time the two younger kids, Jack and Sarah, saw him, he was on the phone, and he turned to them and introduced himself, as if they would have no idea who he was. It was as if, fourteen-year-old Sarah thought, "he was looking up to you, whoever you were, he certainly didn't want any of us to treat him like he was more important than any of us were."

"We'll have to double-date sometime," he said to eighteen-year-old Don Baker, and though they never did, no one in the family suspected him of hypocrisy; it was all just part of the "mannerliness" that announced in a contradictory way (because it denoted such self-assurance) "I am really someone." When they saw him on the phone, they imagined that he was speaking to Hollywood, to far-off, distant lands, even though he was probably just talking to Scotty, his guitarist, or Colonel Parker in Nashville, who called more and more frequently, it seemed, with details of his upcoming tour. As the days passed they could hear him playing his records, the rhythm and blues music that Dewey Phillips played on the air, through the open windows of the little house on the busy city street on a still, hot summer's day.

T HERE WAS SO MUCH TO DO in the little time that he had left. Now that he had a real place of his own, Scotty and Bill came by a few times to rehearse. They played out on the little screened-in porch, and the kids next door and their friends sat out on the grass and listened. "What do you want to hear?" Bill said to them, clowning around, and Elvis favored them with his dazzling smile, asking if they liked the music. With Bob Neal's help once again (the title and financing were still in Bob's name) he purchased another Cadillac, brand-new this time, and at Helen Neal's suggestion had it painted in his customized colors of pink and black. When he drove it down to Lansky's, he showed it off proudly to everyone on Beale and then walked up to Guy Lansky in the store dangling the keys. "He told me to drive it around the block. He said, 'Mr. Lansky, I want you to tell me what you think of it.' He loved it, and this was the biggest mistake I ever made: here I am heavily in debt with all this merchandise, and I think, 'If I drive it around the block, if I wreck this automobile, it's gonna cost me a ton of money.' So I refused him. And he was really disappointed. He felt bad that I wouldn't drive it: he couldn't get over it. He loved that automobile, and here I dropped him. I've felt bad about it ever since." He got a new Martin D-28 guitar, too, bigger than the D-18, with a hand-tooled leather case that muffled the sound a little but looked almost as sharp as the pink-and-black Cadillac.

Dixie came by the house just as often as she ever had. Young Jack Baker and his sister spied on them sometimes holding hands in the backyard, playing with the little white dog that Sarah took care of when the

Presleys were away. Elvis had just taken Dixie to her junior prom, borrowing Bob Neal's brand-new Lincoln for the occasion and double-dating with Dixie's best friend, Bessie Wolverton, and his cousin Gene. He looked handsome in his white tuxedo jacket; she was really proud of him and proud to be able to show him off to all her friends. She tried to make friends with some of his new acquaintances, but she found it harder and harder to fit into his life. She knew Red West, of course — Red had been with him off and on all winter and spring, and since school had gotten out he had started accompanying Elvis regularly on tour. When he went off to college in the fall, she knew, Elvis wanted to get him a car. Red was nice enough, he was always courteous to her, anyway, but some of the new guys who had started hanging around just weren't the kind of people that she and Elvis had ever been drawn to. "They used horrible language, they all smoked, everybody had a drink — it was a group of people I was totally uncomfortable with." More and more, it seemed, he wanted to be with the crowd, they rarely were alone together even in the brief time that they had; "a lot of times he had to go with the guys and party around, that sort of thing." She could understand when he went off to play football with Red at Guthrie Park or down at the Triangle with his old friends, but sometimes it seemed as if he had been swept up in the turmoil himself — he came alive only when other people were around and seemed to crave their attention in a way that neither of them had imagined he ever would.

They had broken up more than once already. Usually the argument was about what *she* was doing while he was away, though really, she suspected, the shoe should have been on the other foot. He couldn't stand for her to have any kind of independent existence, even as he was escaping the very world they had constructed for themselves. What was she doing? Who was she seeing? Where had she been when he called? She wasn't going to lie about it. "Of course I had other friends, the same circle of girlfriends I had always had. I wasn't dating anybody, but we would go out to a canteen called the Busy Betty on Lamar. They had a jukebox, and we'd dance. It got to the point where, Look, you're gone three weeks, and I'm supposed to just sit here every weekend and watch TV? That was the basis of every argument we ever had. He was very possessive and very jealous. I think he knew that what he was asking was unreasonable, but there was nothing he could do about it. It was very dramatic. Several times I gave him back his class ring, or he took it back. And that would last maybe a day, maybe just that night, sometimes before I would get in the house he would drive around the block and come back and say, 'Wait,' and we would sit out on the porch and cry about it. Sometimes my mother would come to the door two or three times and peck on the glass and say, 'Come in,' and I'd say, 'Just a minute.' I thought, you know, 'I can't leave,' because we were both so upset and we were going to break up and we didn't want to break up, because we were still friends. You know, I probably spent more time with his mom and dad than he did with them. When he was out of town, I would go over and stay with them, I spent the night lots of times and slept in his bed while he was gone. Mrs. Presley and I cooked together and ate, and we'd walk. We'd come up-town and just browse around. We'd just kind of console each other."

HIS MIND WAS INCREASINGLY on things that hadn't happened yet — things that Bob Neal and Mr. Phillips had told him would come about, things that Colonel Parker had promised would come to pass before too long in ways that he couldn't altogether imagine. He told Dixie about the Colonel, though she wasn't sure she understood; he talked with Bob about all the ways in which the Colonel would be able to help them out; he talked to his parents all the time about this Colonel Parker, who had done such a great job promoting the last Florida tour. He kept telling them about Colonel Parker, said Vernon, "talking about [what] a great man he had met, how smart he was and all of that. . . . Gladys and I warned him that we really didn't know anything about this man, and anyway, he had an agreement with Bob Neal." Bob would be a part of any arrangement that was made, Elvis assured them. This was something that Bob couldn't really handle on his own. Bob knew that as well as anyone. Bob didn't have the connections that Colonel Parker had. The Colonel had friends in high places. The Colonel had been to Hollywood.

He wanted it as badly as anything he had ever wanted in his life, and he went about getting it in exactly the same single-minded way, even though — it was kind of funny — he could no more name what it was than he could have predicted what was going to happen when he first walked in the door of the Sun studio. Gladys didn't want to hear any more about what the Colonel could do for them; she was simply fearful for her son, while Vernon reacted after a fashion of his own. He was proud of his boy, to the casual acquaintance he showed all the slow-witted pride of a man who'd won the lottery, but to those who knew this handsome, soft-spoken man, withdrawn at times almost to the point of sullenness, he seemed increasingly unsure of himself, increasingly adrift. To Dixie both parents were equally affected. "I think a lot of it had to do with Mr. and Mrs. Presley's resistance to the lifestyle that he was getting into — they had no control over him anymore. It was a very frustrating feeling." And yet the father knew what the boy was saying probably made sense. He liked Bob, he was comfortable with Bob, you could *talk* to Bob — and like he told the boy, he didn't know a thing about this Colonel Parker. But he supposed he was going to have to learn, because the man never stopped calling and sending telegrams; he obviously didn't worry about his long-distance bills. And he was beginning to see that what this Colonel fellow was saying to Elvis was probably true: Memphis wasn't big enough, Sun Records didn't have the kind of national distribution or pay the kind of money that the big companies did, he could see *that*. Marion Keisker detected what she felt was a very noticeable change in manner toward Sam. "I got the feeling that Mr. Presley felt that Sun Records depended on Elvis Presley rather than vice versa. One day he said within my earshot, 'Well, you know, the studio wouldn't be nothing without my boy.' I don't think Sam was even there, but I thought, 'Well, that does it.' The whole picture was changing."

Meanwhile Bob Neal was fielding offers, or at least inquiries, on an almost weekly basis from nearly every major and independent label with whom he had any contact. According to Neal, "Sam had let it be known that he would be interested in talking to them if the money was right," and while Neal made it clear that he did not represent the record company in any way, that he was only an intermediary, most of the offers came through him. Sam always turned them down or upped the ante in such a way that he could be confident that *he* would be turned down. One time Columbia head Mitch Miller, who had been hyped by Bill Randle, the Cleveland DJ (Randle had recently handed Miller "The Yellow Rose of Texas," Columbia's, and Miller's, latest hit), reached Neal on the phone in a West Texas motel. "He said, 'What do you want?' I said, 'I'll find out,' and I called Sam. As I recall, it was around eighteen thousand dollars that Sam was asking that day, so I called Mitch back, and he said, 'Oh, forget it, nobody's worth that much.' " Frank Walker, president of MGM, telegrammed Sam on June 8 after having heard from Sam's brother Jud that Elvis' contract was available, and Sam turned down Decca when they made an offer that met Jud's price. Capitol, Mercury, Chess, Atlantic, Randy Wood's Dot label (currently enjoying great success with Wood's latest discovery, Pat Boone), and RCA all exhibited active interest — there were rumblings throughout the entire industry.

And while Sam liked to act as if selling Elvis' contract were the furthest thing from his mind, as though all this was happening solely at the instigation of strangers, or that Bob Neal was going around without authorization just shooting off his mouth, Bob knew that Sam was strapped for cash, that the little record company was stretched to the limit by its very success, and that Jud was pressing Sam for money (he either wanted some return on his investment or cash to buy out the minority interest he had acquired when he helped Sam buy out Jim Bulleit the previous year). As Marion said, Sam was not a "partner-type person in any form or fashion," but Bob knew that if Sam wanted to preserve his vaunted independence, if he wanted to keep his label and move forward in the new directions he was eager to explore, he was going to have to make a hard decision soon.

Bob reported some of the offers to Elvis; others he kept to himself. He didn't want to overwhelm the boy with *possibilities,* and after some years in the business himself he knew that most of them would come to nothing. But it was clear that something was going on — you didn't have so many important people talking about you, looking to jump on the bandwagon, if the bandwagon wasn't getting ready to move out. He thought they were positioned just about perfectly. The July 16 issue of *Billboard* showed "Baby, Let's Play House" at number fifteen on the national country and western charts, and the summer issue of *Country Song Roundup,* with a picture of Hank Snow on the cover, featured the story "Elvis Presley — Folk Music Fireball," following national features in *Cowboy Songs* and *Country & Western Jamboree.* Bob liked the boy — he couldn't say anything bad about him, he was almost like another member of the family. They all went waterskiing on McKellar Lake together and picnicked out at Riverside Park; when Bob's son Sonny ran for student council in the spring, Elvis and Scotty and Bill appeared at the Messick High chapel program in support of his campaign, and Elvis regarded Helen almost like a second mother. Bob couldn't imagine ever losing him, and when he talked to Colonel Parker about all their far-flung plans, it was never with anything less than a sense of partnership in a glowing future. There were certain unpleasant realities to be faced, to be sure: the financial arrangements with Scotty and Bill were going to have to be changed, and they would have to be satisfied with a salaried status rather than the original agreement, which gave 50 percent to Elvis and 25 percent to each of them. But Elvis understood that, and they would have to understand it, too. The kids were coming out to see Elvis now — it wasn't the Blue Moon Boys who were drawing the crowds. With a little luck, and with the Colonel's invaluable assistance, Bob Neal was firmly convinced, from here on in it was going to be nothing but smooth sailing.

ON JULY 11, Elvis went back into the Sun studio. In about a week he would be out on the road again, and it seemed like he had scarcely been home at all. Everywhere he went around town — on Beale Street, at the movies, at a drive-in for a hamburger, just waiting at a stoplight — it seemed as if he was known, it seemed as if something was *expected* of him, and he was always prepared to oblige, with a wink, with a wave, with a knowing but deferential nod of his head. Only in the studio were things still the same: Marion in the outer room, with the venetian blinds slanted to fight the heat, Sam in the control room, waiting, watching, always ready for something to happen, Scotty and Bill reassuringly constant — they would never change. For this session Mr. Phillips had brought in another original number and another drummer. The song was, once again, a country composition by Stan Kesler, the steel guitar player who had written "I'm Left, You're Right, She's Gone," and the drummer was Johnny Bernero, who played regularly with a number of different country bands and worked at the Memphis Light, Gas and Water Company across the street.

The song, Sam knew, was not to Elvis' taste — "he just didn't dig it at first. Maybe it was a little too country, the chord progression, and it was a slow song, too. But I loved the hook line, and I thought it was something we needed at that point to show a little more diversification. So I called Johnny — he was either in there that day, or I called him, 'cause he had played on some other things for me. And we got it going, and he was doing four-four on the beat, and I said, 'That don't help us worth a shit, Johnny.' I told him, 'What I want you to do is do your rim shot snare on the offbeat, but keep it four-four until we go into the chorus. Then you go in and go with the bass beat at two-four.' And by doing that, it sounds like

'I Forgot to Remember to Forget' is twice as fast as it really is. And Elvis really loved it then."

With the next cut there was no need for any such trickery. They were just fooling around without the drummer when they hit on a lick from "Mystery Train," the song Sam had originally cut on Little Junior Parker and the Blue Flames just two years before, and they went from there. It was the driving rhythm-based kind of blues that Sam had been feeding Scotty ever since they started recording, and the three of them fell in with the same natural exuberance that they had first applied to "That's All Right," but with a degree of knowledge — of themselves as much as of any musical technique — that they had not possessed a year earlier. "There was an extra bar of rhythm thrown in at one point," said Scotty, "that if I sat down to play it myself right now, I couldn't, but with him singing it felt natural." "It was the greatest thing I ever did on Elvis," said Sam. "It was a feeling song that so many people had experienced — I mean, it was a big thing, to put a loved one on a train: are they leaving you forever? Maybe they'll never be back. 'Train I ride, sixteen coaches long' — you can take it from the inside of the coach, or you can take it from the outside, standing looking in. Junior was going to make it fifty coaches, but I said, no, sixteen coaches is a helluva lot, that sounds like it's coming out of a small town. It was pure rhythm. And at the end, Elvis was laughing, because he didn't think it was a take, but I'm sorry, it was a fucking masterpiece!"

The last cut they did was a rhythm and blues number, "Trying to Get to You," that they had tried without success earlier in the year. This time it was as free and unfettered as anything they had ever done, even with the addition of Johnny Bernero on drums and Elvis chording on piano, and like "Mystery Train" it aspired to a higher kind of — mystery, for want of a better word. There was a floating sense of inner harmony mixed with a ferocious hunger, a desperate striving linked to a pure out-pouring of joy, that seemed to just tumble out of the music. It was the very attainment of art and passion, the natural beauty of the instinctive soul that Sam Phillips had been searching for ever since he first started in music, and there was no question that Elvis knew that he had achieved it.

For the few remaining days of his holiday he cruised around town — with Dixie, with Red and his cousin Gene, he stopped in to see Dewey at the radio station. With Dewey he visited the clubs on Beale, where

Dewey was still hailed as a conquering hero and this white boy who sang the blues was readily accepted as yet another of Dewey's crazy ideas. "Elvis had the feel of Beale Street," said Sam Phillips. "He was probably more at home there than he was on Main. You know, Elvis didn't walk into Lansky Brothers because someone suggested, 'Why don't you buy a chartreuse fucking shirt?' " "We had a lot of fun with him," said WDIA's Professor Nat D. Williams, the unofficial ambassador of Beale. "Elvis Presley on Beale Street when he first started was a favorite man. . . . Always he had that certain humanness about him that Negroes like to put in their songs." That was what he was aiming for, that common human element, and that was what he achieved — there was nowhere he couldn't go that in one sense or another he didn't feel at home, but if that was so, why was it that he felt increasingly like a stranger, as if he alone sensed not only the breadth of possibilities but the dangers lurking in the great world that existed outside of his hometown?

Then he was back on the road, in Texas first, next in a return to Florida that was marked by mounting expectations and increased attention from the press. Few doubted that the Colonel fueled either those expectations or that attention. The show was headlined by philosopher/comic Andy Griffith ("You saw him in U.S. Steel Hour TV production No Time for Sergeants NOW SEE HIM IN PERSON") and also included Ferlin Huskey with His Hush Puppies, Marty Robbins, Jimmie Rodgers Snow, "newcomers" Tommy Collins and Glenn Reeves, and "EXTRA EXTRA By Popular Demand ELVIS PRESLEY with Scotty & Bill." At the bottom of each newspaper ad came Oscar Davis' tag line, *"Don't You Dare Miss It,"* and few Florida country music fans did.

In Jacksonville, the scene of the first riot, in May, there was another near-riot, and "before he could be rescued from his swooning admirers," *Cash Box* reported in an account that could have been written by the Colonel himself, "they had relieved him of his tie, handkerchiefs, belt, and the greater part of his coat and shirt. Col. Tom Parker presented him with a new sports coat to replace the one snatched by souvenir collectors."

The Florida tour ended in Tampa on July 31, and he immediately began another, a five-day package set up by Bob Neal, this time with Webb Pierce, Wanda Jackson, and new Sun recording artist Johnny Cash. They played Sheffield, Alabama, on August 2, then on the third they were booked into Little Rock, which Mr. and Mrs. Presley, who had yet to assent to the new agreement naming the Colonel "special adviser" to both Elvis and Bob Neal, were scheduled to attend. Vernon seemed pretty much ready to sign, but Gladys continued to balk. She was frightened by the riots in Florida, she said, she didn't know why there was such a rush to do anything at this point, she was afraid of what might happen to her boy. Well, that was certainly understandable, said the Colonel — he, too, felt like maybe her boy was being overworked. But if the money was right, why, then, Bob wouldn't have to book him into so many of these little dates, he could even think about taking some time off, maybe going to Florida with Mr. and Mrs. Presley or spending a few days with Colonel and Mrs. Parker over in Madison. The Colonel would never want to see any repetition of what had happened in Jacksonville, and there was certainly no need to sign anything now. Once they got things straightened out, though, he could guarantee Mrs. Presley that nothing like the Jacksonville incident would ever happen again.

Although he himself had to be in Hollywood to attend to some movie business for Hank Snow, the Colonel arranged for country comedian Whitey Ford, the Duke of Paducah ("I'm goin' back to the wagon, these shoes are killing me"), to meet the senior Presleys in Little Rock. Ford, a Little Rock native, had worked the original Hank Snow tour in February and was a longtime friend and associate of the Colonel's as well as a neighbor. He was also known for his work with church and youth groups, and though he was not on the bill, he was playing the White River Carnival in Batesville with Elvis two days later and was glad to help the Colonel make his case. "Mrs. Presley was reluctant," Ford told writer Vince Staten, "very reluctant at first. She didn't want Elvis to make any changes, because he was under all these contracts. But I told her these could all be bought up. . . . I told her I had known the Colonel for years and that he really knew all the angles for producing successful shows." Elvis' friend Jimmie Rodgers Snow had done his best to convey pretty much the same message. "They were country people, and Colonel was very slick — I'm sure they picked up on that. I think they were more concerned with sticking with Bob Neal. The idea was to explain to them that they had to progress and go forward. I probably talked more to Mrs. Presley than to Vernon, because she was really the one who made the decisions."

For the time being Gladys was still not fully convinced. "He seemed like a smart man," said Vernon of the Colonel, "but we still didn't know too much about him, so we didn't sign." Elvis was frustrated, angry, and bitterly disappointed with his parents. He felt like they just didn't understand, but he had no choice other than to accept the Colonel's assurances that they would come around. There was nothing to worry about, the Colonel intoned without the slightest hint of doubt, they had made a fine beginning. It would all work out in the end.

He played Camden, Arkansas, the following night and then on August 5 returned to Memphis in a triumphant homecoming concert at the Overton Park Shell, the site of his initial unpremeditated triumph as the misspelled bottom of a bill starring Slim Whitman and Billy Walker. This time he was second headliner (beneath Webb Pierce and the Wondering Boys) of a twenty-two-act bill that marked the finale of "the eighth annual Bob Neal Country jamboree series," and the story in the *Press-Scimitar* the next day had images of hometown heroes Elvis Presley and Johnny Cash superimposed on a shirtsleeved crowd of four thousand that jammed the shell while "several hundred had to be turned away." Marion Keisker attended the show, the first time she had seen Elvis perform since the Opry appearince nearly a year before, and described how she "heard someone screaming, and I'm really a very restrained person publicly, but all of a sudden I realized, 'It's me!' This staid mother of a young son — I'd lost my total stupid mind." It didn't altogether surprise her in a way. She adored Elvis, and she was experiencing the most bittersweet feelings of dread, regret, and a measure of anticipation as she watched the drama play itself out.

For the first time since she had known him, Sam simply didn't seem to know what to do. It would clearly be to their advantage for Parker to peddle the contract, and it would probably be to Elvis' advantage at this point, too. Somehow, though, it was as if Sam simply could not commit himself to the bargain he knew he had to make. "Of course I never actually met the Colonel until the [RCA] contract signing, but I felt that Sam had a great deal of contempt for him. I don't know if I ever heard Sam actually say anything pejorative, but I felt that other than Sam's self-interest, he didn't feel it was in Elvis' best interest to go with Colonel Parker even at that point. I think it was the only thing Elvis ever did against Sam's advice, though Sam might deny it. He didn't think it would be a wise thing, but since it seemed inevitable, he didn't fight it. And Elvis was so innately ingenuous. It's when you lie and digress that you get into trouble, but I don't think he ever said a wrong thing into a microphone or camera his whole life."

The day after the concert the new single came out, to be greeted with a

Billboard "Spotlight" review that declared it "a splendid coupling" and a "Best Buy" write-up three weeks later that said, "With each release Presley has been coming more and more to the forefront. His current record has wasted no time in establishing itself. Already it appears on the Memphis and Houston territorial charts. It is also reported selling well in Richmond, Atlanta, Durham, Nashville and Dallas."

Meanwhile, the Colonel pulled out all the stops. In the immediate aftermath of the Little Rock meeting, he bypassed Bob Neal altogether, making direct contact with Vernon and Gladys and conveying some of his impatience with what he considered to be Neal's "inefficient" method of doing business. Knowing the Presleys' high regard for Hank Snow, he had Snow, too, make a number of telephone calls. "I think Colonel would have used anybody to influence them," said Jimmie Rodgers Snow, "because they were slow and he was smart enough to realize that he could not directly influence them himself. But I'll tell you what, I think they probably signed not so much because of Parker and what he'd do, but because they liked my dad."

On August 15 they all met once again, in Memphis, and Elvis proudly affixed his signature at the top of a document that named "Col. Thomas A. Parker" as "special adviser to Elvis Presley ['artist'] and Bob Neal ['manager'] for the period of one year and two one-year options for the sum of two thousand, five hundred dollars per year, payable in five payments of five hundred dollars each, to negotiate and assist in any way possible the build-up of Elvis Presley as an artist. Col. Parker will be reimbursed for any out-of-pocket expenses for travelling, promotion, advertising as approved by Elvis Presley and his manager."

The Colonel retained exclusive rights to one hundred appearances over the course of the next year, for which the artist would be paid $200 each, "including his musicians." In addition, in the event that "negotiations come to a complete standstill and Elvis Presley and his manager and associates decide to freelance," the Colonel would be reimbursed for his expenses and, "at the special rate of one hundred seventy five dollars per day for the first appearance and two hundred fifty dollars for the second appearance and three hundred fifty dollars [for the third]," the Colonel retained exclusive territorial rights to "San Antonio, El Paso, Phoenix, Tucson, Albuquerque, Oklahoma City, Denver, Wichita Falls, Wichita, New Orleans, Mobile, Jacksonville, Pensacola, Tampa, Miami, Orlando,

Charleston, Greenville, Spartanburg, Asheville, Knoxville, Roanoke, Richmond, Norfolk, Washington, D.C., Philadelphia, Newark, New York, Pittsburgh, Chicago, Omaha, Milwaukee, Minneapolis, St. Paul, Des Moines, Los Angeles, Amarillo, Houston, Galveston, Corpus Christi, Las Vegas, Reno, Cleveland, Dayton, Akron, and Columbus.

"Colonel Parker," the agreement concluded, "is to negotiate all renewals on existing contracts."

With that Elvis was back on tour, only now as an official member of Hank Snow's Jamboree Attractions. On the surface nothing had really changed, unless it was to embolden the trio to add a permanent fourth member. Going back into Texarkana at the end of the month for the fourth or fifth time in less than a year, Bob and Elvis, Scotty, and Bill made a promotional spot in so casual and disarming a manner that it might have been taking place in someone's living room. "We want to invite everybody out to the show," said Scotty. "And they've all been asking about the drummer who we had up there last time [four months earlier], D. J. Fontana. He's going to be with us. He's a regular member of our band now . . ." "Tell you what," says Bob, "before we call over some other folks here to talk, Elvis Presley, how you doin'?"

"Fine, Bobert," says a relaxed young voice. "How you gettin' along?"

"Oh, doin' grand," says Bob without so much as a blink. "I know all the folks down at Texarkana been raising such a whoop and a holler for you to come down and whoop and holler at 'em that they got this great big double show scheduled for Friday night at the auditorium down there. What do you think about it?" And they engage in an extended colloquy on the subject before Bob introduces "one of the noisiest guys in all this outfit . . . Bill Black, who pumps on the bass and occasionally tells a story or two, and just in general messes things up. Bill, come over and say howdy to your fans in Texarkana."

For a moment we hear the warm molasses drawl of the man that Scotty said "never met a stranger." "Bob, I just wanted to say one thing," he says. "Friday night we'll be down there, and I'll have a brand spanking new pose of Elvis for a picture, and they'll be selling at the same old price of only a quarter. And I'll have about four or five million of them. If anybody would like to have just one, why, I'll have plenty of 'em, before the show, during intermission, after the show — the fact is, I may sell them out there all night long. That's all I got to say."

It is all so relaxed and homespun, it's hard to believe that Elvis Presley is poised on the brink of something — stardom, success, a precipice so steep that it must be at least as fearsome as it is inviting. "I would like to invite everybody out Friday night to see our big show," he declares, at Bob Neal's urging, to promote a crowd. "Because I don't know when we'll be coming back that way. . . . It'll probably be a pretty long while before we can come back to Texarkana," he concludes, with no way of knowing, and not really caring, when that might be.

COLONEL PARKER, GLADYS, ELVIS, AND VERNON PRESLEY:
RCA SIGNING CEREMONY, SUN STUDIO, NOVEMBER 21, 1955.
(COURTESY OF GARY HARDY, SUN STUDIO)

THE PIED PIPERS

THE COLONEL QUICKLY consolidated his position. When Arnold Shaw, the newly named general professional manager of the E. B. Marks publishing company, visited him in Madison in August, the Colonel could talk of nothing but Presley. "What's your interest, Colonel?" Shaw asked him. With something less than full disclosure of the facts but utter candor nonetheless, the Colonel said, "This kid is now managed by Bob Neal of Memphis. But I'll have him when Neal's contract finishes in less than a year." Even Bob seemed to recognize the inevitability of the conclusion and ceded most of his authority to the Colonel while still terming it "a partnership deal." He did renegotiate the Hayride contract with Horace Logan, at the beginning of September, so that when the first year came to an end on November 12, 1955, the Hayride would pick up its option at $200 an appearance, a considerable increase from the $18 union scale that Elvis had been getting up till then. The pretext, according to Logan, was for Elvis to be able to carry a drummer on a regular basis, but the reality was that he was "the hottest thing in show business." The contract stipulated that "artist is given the right to miss 1 Saturday's performance during each 60 [day] period," but Logan added a side agreement penalizing him $400 for every additional show that he missed. Unbeknownst to Neal, evidently, the Colonel urged Vernon not to sign the agreement. He wanted the elder Presleys to withhold their signatures as guardians until he had a better idea of where things stood with a new record deal — but Vernon went ahead and signed anyway.

Neal also had the unpleasant task of telling Scotty and Bill that they were about to go on a fixed salary. What made it even worse was that it was Scotty and Bill who had finally persuaded Elvis to add D.J. on drums by agreeing to share the cost of his $100-a-week salary among them — Elvis wanted a drummer, but he kept saying he couldn't afford it until the other musicians indicated their willingness to pitch in. According to Neal:

"The eventual basic decision [to put the band on salary] went back to Elvis. We talked about it quite a few times, talked about it with his parents, and finally decided that it had to be done. I had to handle that, and I remember that there was quite a bit of unhappiness at that time plus threats that maybe they would quit, but as it worked out they went ahead in that particular situation." Scotty and Bill were inclined to put it down to the Colonel's interference, though Bob was certainly prepared to take the heat. He knew that the worst thing in the world would have been for them to blame Elvis, and he did everything he could to insulate the boy, but it turned out he didn't have to do much. Elvis had a habit of sliding out from under things on his own, and in this case he seemed to do it without any outside help.

For the first time, though, Bob Neal was beginning to wonder about his own role: what exactly was he supposed to *do?* Despite the smoothing over of tempers and the affable addition of D.J., there remained an undercurrent of ill feeling and suspiciousness that had never been present before. There was a sense of uncertainty about what was going to happen next — at one point the Colonel had even suggested that Elvis leave Scotty and Bill and D.J. behind and use Hank Snow's band on an upcoming tour. Bob squelched that before it even got to Elvis, but you could never tell how far that kind of thinking permeated the general atmosphere. Snow's band knew of the rumor, and if they did, how much further did it have to go to get to Scotty and Bill?

It was as if the Colonel were trying to throw everyone into some degree of turmoil — and doing a pretty good job of it, too. Even Sam was edgy about just what was going on. He seemed nervous about business in general: his lawsuit with Duke Records owner Don Robey over Robey's alleged theft of his artist Little Junior Parker was rapidly coming to a boil; he had a radio station that he was about to open up in the brand-new Holiday Inn downtown (the third in a brand-new chain owned by Sam's friend Kemmons Wilson); he had a number of new artists in whom he had faith but whom he had not yet been able to break; and he was obviously feeling the pinch of various unnamed financial pressures. But most of all he seemed thrown into uncharacteristic confusion by the Colonel — he clearly wanted what the Colonel had to offer, which was the promise of some sort of financial security, and he just as clearly feared it, too.

There was a single abortive Sun session that fall to try to get a B side for "Trying to Get to You." Sam once again had Johnny Bernero on drums, and they worked on the Billy Emerson blues "When It Rains, It Really Pours," which had been a favorite of Elvis' since it first came out in January. The mood was edgy, though, the playing tentative, and the session quickly broke up without any of the good feeling or unflagging optimism that had characterized every other recording date. At one point they took a break, Bernero recalled to Sun historian Colin Escott, "when Elvis went up into the control room with Sam. They were up there about thirty minutes. We were just sitting around on the studio floor chewing the fat. Then Elvis came back down and came over to me and said, 'John, we're not going to finish this session, but I really appreciate you coming over.' He gave me fifty dollars. The next thing I knew, Sam had sold his contract."

Meanwhile the Colonel systematically went about his business, which seemed for the most part to consist of playing one potential bidder off against another. There was no question of where the Colonel wanted to end up: he had been doing business with RCA, the label of both Eddy Arnold and Hank Snow, for more than ten years now, and he had been working with the same man for most of that time. Steve Sholes had handled artist and repertoire duties for both Arnold and Snow, and Colonel Parker had extensive connections within the company, all the way up to Singles Division Manager Bill Bullock. At the same time he wasn't going to let RCA take *anything* for granted, nor was he even sure how committed they were to his artist, or to advancing the kind of money that it was going to take to get the boy out of his Sun Records contract. So he continued to actively encourage the other companies in their interest, up to the point where he and Bob Neal were fielding almost daily offers.

Other events were conspiring — or being actively solicited as coconspirators — to move things rapidly along. Hill and Range, one of the most prominent of the BMI family of upstart young song publishers who had taken advantage of the boom in "race" and "hillbilly" recording after the war, was well on its way toward bringing out an Elvis Presley song folio, an event which had its genesis at the Jimmie Rodgers Festival in May. That was where Hill and Range representative Grelun Landon, in company with his friend RCA promo man Chick Crumpacker, had seen Elvis perform for the first time. Knocked out by the show, he had contacted his bosses, Jean and Julian Aberbach. The Aberbachs, Viennese refugees with a long history in European music publishing, had set up Hill and Range in 1945 to celebrate "America's native folk music" (the first part of their title

stood for "hillbilly," the second for "the wide-open range") and specialized in "partnership publishing" almost from the start. This was a way of
drawing in stars like Ernest Tubb, Bob Wills, Bill Monroe, and Hank
Snow, by allowing them for the first time to participate on a 50–50 basis in
the publishing end of the business (up till now, almost without exception,
the writer had been forced to surrender all of his publishing interests,
which represented half of the performance royalties earned by a song, to
the music publisher who did him the favor of representing his songs).
Landon urged the Aberbachs to contact Sam Phillips right away so that
they could get in on the ground floor of this remarkable new phenomenon, and by early summer 1955 they had done so, working out a deal with
Phillips and Bob Neal.

Meanwhile, Cleveland DJ Bill Randle, who had had extensive dealings
with Hill and Range over the years (everyone stood to gain by this network of informal associations, not excluding the artist, though his songs
were likely to come from a source to which his a&r director or an influential DJ like Randle might be tied), approached the Aberbachs on his own.
At the same time Freddy Bienstock, the Aberbachs' young chief lieutenant and cousin, who had already heard about Presley from Randle, got a
phone call from Hank Snow touting the twenty-year-old performer. The
Colonel was not altogether happy about the contract Bob Neal had
agreed to on the folio deal, nor was he unaware of Randle's belief, fostered by the Aberbachs' desire to recruit Randle to start a talent management company for Hill and Range, that he would end up as the boy's
manager. But Tom Parker had sufficient confidence in his own business
acumen, and in his ability to write his own contract somewhere down the
line, that he turned a blind eye toward the Aberbachs' maneuverings and
Randle's ambitions and simply permitted everyone to think whatever
they wanted to think. As he told Arnold Shaw, the first time he had sold
an act to a promoter, he had been "taken to the cleaner's. . . . So I went
home, found the clause that did me in, cut it out, and pasted it on a piece
of paper. The next time . . . I got taken by another clause. . . . One day I
put all those smart-assed clauses together — and that's the contract you're
holding!"

Randle, in the meantime, was about to shoot a movie short, a self-
promotion called *The Pied Piper of Cleveland,* in which he was planning to
use the boy, and that might come in handy in the marketing of his contract. Or it might not. It didn't really matter. There was nothing that

couldn't be set right so long as you kept your eye on the ball — everyone else, he knew from experience, was likely to take their eye off it. In the Colonel's master plan, if he *had* a master plan, the main thing was to get all the parties working toward the same end without realizing, or even suspecting, that they were not the only ones in the game. In this, in a peculiar way, he and the boy were alike. It did not escape the Colonel's notice that everyone who met the boy, even for an instant, felt that they were the favored one — almost as a result of the boy's innocence and lack of guile. It was a rare gift, something which could not be taught, something which the Colonel particularly appreciated and of which he could wholeheartedly approve. It gave them something in common.

Otherwise it was business as usual: tours, bookings, keeping the publicity machine greased. "[Washington, D.C.–based promoter] Connie B. Gay says that a 19-year-old boy named Elvis Presley will be the next sensation of the country and Western (hillbilly) music field," it was announced in the "TV and Radio People" column of a Tidewater newspaper on September 4. "Presley has crossed bebop with country music and, according to Gay, 'is the hottest thing in the hillbilly field.' " All the DJ polls and fan magazines showed Elvis Presley rising to the top of "the folk music world — not through picking, yodeling, or balladeering — but by belting out his numbers in a rock 'em sock 'em rhythm style." And finally, in an October issue of *Billboard,* under the headline "New Policy Combines Pops-C&W," it was announced, "Col. Tom Parker of Jamboree Attractions, one of the nation's major bookers and promoters of country & western talent, instituted a new policy when he presented a combination of popular and country & western music on a recent one-nighter tour. Parker teamed Bill Haley & His Comets with Hank Snow for an extended tour, which opened in Omaha, Oct. 10. . . . Elvis Presley joined the Snow-Haley tour in Oklahoma City." Even the poster bore out the separate-but-equal angle. "'IN PERSON,'' read the top half. "The Nation's No. 1 Rhythm & Blues Artist Bill Haley and his Comets. Of 'Rock Around the Clock' and 'Shake, Rattle and Roll' fame PLUS Elvis Presley with Scotty and Bill." While at the bottom Hank Snow, the "Singing Ranger," with an "All Star Cast," was showcased with his picture headlining his half of the bill.

The idea was pretty much as the *Billboard* article stated. The Colonel had approached Haley's manager, the almost equally colorful Lord Jim Ferguson, with the pitch that he had this kid: "I can take him over, but I want him to get some experience." To which Ferguson, who was managing one of the hottest acts in the country at a time when it was not clear in what direction the country was likely to go next, had readily assented, given the kid's chart success and the drawing power that Snow could bring to the bill. But for the Colonel the point was something more. RCA was certainly interested — but they weren't *that* interested yet. If they were going to put up the money needed to purchase Presley's contract from Sun, they were going to have to believe not just in the artist but in the movement. This was simply one more way of showing them that there really was something happening out there, that Presley was not just another hillbilly sensation. Once the big-city boys got that point, Colonel Thomas A. Parker was convinced, the rest would be easy.

Elvis himself was thrilled to be on the bill. Bill Haley, out of Chester, Pennsylvania, had had a string of western-flavored records, some more successful than others, since 1946, when he was twenty-one years old. In 1951 he had recorded a cover of "Rocket 88," the Sam Phillips production that has frequently been cited as marking the birth of rock 'n' roll, and since then he had put out a steady stream of releases combining an r&b sensibility with a hillbilly boogie feel and big band, western swing (accordion, steel, and saxophone) instrumentation. It was a mix that defied categorization and made considerable impact on the charts in 1953 and 1954, but it failed to achieve any kind of breakthrough success for Haley until the movie *The Blackboard Jungle* came out in March 1955. Haley's 1954 recording, "Rock Around the Clock," which had sold about seventy-five thousand copies its first time around, was selected to play over the opening credits, and the song went to number one, bestowing upon Haley instant star status (though he would never have another hit that came close to matching it, he continued to work off it profitably until the day he died). His version of Big Joe Turner's "Shake, Rattle and Roll," long a staple of Elvis' show, was a credible act of rhythm and blues homage, and he was poised on the edge of a brief movie career (*Rock Around the Clock,* the lightly fictionalized "Bill Haley Story," with Alan Freed playing a strong supporting role, came out at the beginning of the following year). His music may have lacked the purity and edge that Elvis had achieved in the studio, and certainly his live performances missed out on the smoldering sexuality of Elvis' appearances, but Haley at this point was a *star,* and Elvis was clearly drawn to that stardom, as if it might just rub off on him. Haley for his part was perfectly glad to help a kid who, for all he knew, had never been outside the Memphis city limits before.

"Now this was a long time before he was a big hit, you know," Haley recalled to interviewer Ken Terry. "He was a big tall young kid. He didn't have too much personality at that time. . . . The first time I remember talking to Elvis was in, I think, Oklahoma City. He was standing backstage, and we were getting ready to go on. And he came over and told me he was a fan of mine and we talked — an awful nice kid. . . . He wanted to learn, which was the important thing. I remember one night he went out and did a show and asked me what I thought. I had watched the show, and I told him, 'Elvis, you're leaning too much on ballads and what have you. You've got a natural rhythm feeling, so do your rhythm tunes.' . . . He had the attitude which most young kids do that he was really going to go out there and stop the show and knock Bill Haley off the stage, which at that time was an impossibility because we were number one. And he went out and he was facing Bill Haley fans. . . . When I came back after doing my show he was kind of half crying in the dressing room, very downhearted, and I sat down with him and I told him, 'Look, you got a lot of talent,' and I explained to him a lot of things. He and I buddied together for about a week and a half after that."

In other respects life on the road was just the usual form of insanity: shows increasingly marked by sheer, unrestrained pandemonium; crazy girls who would do anything just about anywhere and, not infrequently, the complications of jealous boyfriends; desperate drives to make the next show after staying up all night in the town where they had played their last one; two or three calls a day home, no matter what else was going on, or who else was around; firecrackers. "Elvis was one of those guys that had a lot of nervous energy," said D. J. Fontana, the newest member of the band. "A superhyper guy — superhyper. Always jumping around or doing something. He never got tired, but when he did, he'd just crash eleven or twelve hours straight in those days. He was always doing something. We'd be driving down the road, we'd never get to a show date on time, because we'd stop every thirty miles to buy firecrackers. He'd make us stop at every other stand, that sucker would. I'd say, 'We've got a bagful.' And he'd say, 'Well, you know, man, we might need some more.' We'd stop and buy some more firecrackers just for something to do."

He was headlining his own show now almost everywhere. In West Texas it was the Elvis Presley Jamboree, with a supporting cast of up to a dozen that included Johnny Cash, Porter Wagoner, and Wanda Jackson. In Lubbock the young singer Buddy Holly, now actively looking for a recording contract of his own, opened the bill for him once again and sought his advice. In Houston he went to see Bob Wills with Tillman Franks on an off night and was amused when Wills told the promoter, Biff Collie, "Bring the young punk back."

He was finally getting used to it, up to a point. He no longer believed it was all just going to go away — even though in interviews he was still inclined, with becoming modesty, to say that he did. Part of him still didn't believe that it was all really happening: the records, the shows, the success, the Colonel, the sex. But part of him — most of him — did. It was all over with Dixie, he realized. He didn't want it to be, but that was the way it had to be. They had talked it over — over and over again. He never really told her that he had been unfaithful, but he knew that she knew. And he knew that she forgave him. It wasn't a life for a decent Christian girl — sometimes when things got quiet or he was alone for a moment and had time to contemplate, he wasn't so sure it was a life for a decent Christian of any sort — but, he thought, he could handle it. And if he couldn't, if it got too much for him, he could always go back, couldn't he? Dixie had told Gladys that it was over, and the two women had cried about it together, but they had agreed they would always be friends because they both loved him so. When she told her own mother, her mother was almost equally upset. "It was hard for my family to accept. They loved him dearly, too. Mother would say, 'Well, what are you going to do if you meet somebody else and get married, and after you get married, Elvis comes back and says, 'Hey, I made a mistake, and I want you to come and be my wife'? And I said, 'Well, I'll just divorce whoever I'm married to and go live with him.' It was so simple in my mind. I thought: 'That's what I'll do.' "

The Presleys, meanwhile, had moved again, just around the corner this time, to 1414 Getwell, which got them off a busy thoroughfare, and they were angry at their former landlord anyway for trying to hold them up, Vernon felt, when they had expressed an interest in purchasing the Lamar Avenue house. Once again they were forced to move in Elvis' absence, and once again Gladys wished that he could simply stop right now, buy a little business with the money he had made, marry Dixie, have three children. But she knew it wasn't to be. And she clung to his telephone calls, they spoke to each other in a language all their own, as she proudly kept track of his growing fame. She kept up her scrapbook religiously. Just as she once saved all of his baby pictures and school reports and memorabilia, now she saved every story she came across that was written about him; she and Vernon looked at them again and again. "When Elvis was a youngster down in Tupelo, Mississippi, folks used to stop him on the street and say, 'Sing for us, Elvis,' " read the latest, in *Country Song Roundup*. "And he would . . . standing on the street corners, in the hot Mississippi sun . . . or in church . . . or at school . . . anywhere someone wanted to hear him, he'd sing." And in the Saturday, October 22, 1955, edition of the *Cleveland Press*, in Bill Randle's column, next to Amy Vanderbilt's and just above a review of a spoken-word recording of T. S. Eliot's *Old Possum's Book of Practical Cats*, was an item called "Turntable Topics," which read: "Turning my life into a frenzy this week was a shooting company from Universal International Pictures. I'm not a Gable at acting, so I'm fortunate to be supported in this film short by Pat Boone, the Four Lads, Bill Haley and his Comets, and the phenomenal Elvis Presley. Called 'Top Jock,' the film will run about 15 minutes when it hits your movie house."

ELVIS PLAYED Cleveland's Circle Theater once again, on Wednesday night, October 19, in an all-star country music jamboree headlined by Roy Acuff and Kitty Wells. The next day Randle's film was scheduled to be shot at 1:00 in the afternoon at the Brooklyn High School auditorium in front of the school's three thousand students, and then at 8:00 that night at St. Michael's Hall, at East 100th and Union. Randle had filmed a number of shorts before — with Peggy Lee and Benny Goodman and Stan Kenton — and in fact the idea was for this one to end up in New York with performances by Patti Page, Tony Bennett, Nat King Cole, and other "legitimate" pop stars. But Cleveland was the jumping-off point and proved hospitable enough until Universal director Arthur Cohen balked at the idea of putting on Presley, after watching his Circle Theater performance and going through initial run-throughs at the high school auditorium the next day. According to Randle: "He thought he was 'pitiful,' completely unacceptable, not worth the time and effort to set up the numbers. I told him about the phenomenal response Presley was getting . . . but Cohen was adamant and proceeded to film the established stars as they went on." Randle then consulted with cameraman Jack Barnett, who agreed to film Presley if Randle would pay for the overtime shooting himself. This proved to be an effective solution, and the show went on.

Pat Boone never forgot the occasion of his first meeting with Elvis Presley. Boone, just twenty-one years old and a student at North Texas State Teachers College (he would transfer to Columbia University the following year), had grown up in Nashville and was married to Red Foley's daughter, Shirley. He had already won Ted Mack's *Original Amateur Hour,* made frequent appearances on the Arthur Godfrey show, and had enjoyed success on two Nashville labels, achieving a national hit on Dot with a cover of the Charms' "Two Hearts" earlier in the year. At the moment his new single, the El Dorados' "At My Front Door (Crazy Little Mama)," was just beginning to climb the pop charts. Randle picked him up at the airport, "and on the way into town he told me about a kid on the show who was going to be a big star, I asked him who it was, and he said, 'Elvis Presley, from Memphis, Tennessee.' I said, 'Oh yeah?' I had lived in Texas, and I had seen his name on some country jukeboxes, and I wondered how in the world a hillbilly could be the next big thing, especially with a name like Elvis Presley. So I was curious, and sure enough, at the high school auditorium where we did this thing, he came backstage, and already he had a little entourage [probably Red and his cousin Gene]. Now, nobody in Cleveland had ever heard of him, so the fact that he had an entourage struck me as funny. I went over dressed in my button-down collar and thin tie and white buck shoes and introduced myself. He mumbled something I couldn't understand, leaned back against the wall with his head down, and never looked me in the eye. So, I said, 'Boy, Bill Randle thinks you're really going to be big,' and he said, "Mmm . . . mrrrbbllee . . . ,' sort of a country twang mumble. I just couldn't tell what he was saying. He had his shirt collar turned up, and his hair was real greasy, and it was, well, he was always looking down, you know, like he couldn't look up. I thought to myself, what's the matter with this guy? I thought his performance would be a catastrophe, that he'd pass out onstage or something."

Elvis was glad to see Bill Haley, whom he had left in Texas just the previous week. DJ Tommy Edwards wanted to take a picture of the two of them together, and while they were backstage in the dressing room, Elvis remarked that he hoped these Yankees liked his music, giving Haley no indication that he had ever played Cleveland before. Randle introduced him to Mike Stewart, a big bear of a man who had been very successful in managing the Four Lads and would one day take over the United Artists label. Stewart was so impressed by both the boy's talent and charm that he called Mitch Miller at Columbia Records the following day, only adding to the chorus of praise that Randle had started and that Miller clearly wished would go away.

The show itself was a great success. Each act did four or five numbers, with Elvis, Scotty, and Bill (D.J. doesn't seem to have made the trip) performing "That's All Right," "Blue Moon of Kentucky," "Good Rockin' Tonight," and his latest coupling, "Mystery Train" and "I Forgot to Remember to Forget," which had entered the national country charts the month before. Pat Boone's fears were not realized. When Elvis hit the stage in his tweedy brown jacket, red socks, white bucks, and white pleated shirt with boldly embroidered front, he looked to Boone "like he had just gotten off a motorcycle. He had his shirt open, and he looked like he was laughing at something, like he had some private joke, you know? He didn't say anything, just went into some rockabilly type song, and the kids loved it. I was really surprised. Then he opened his mouth and said something, and it was so hillbilly that he lost the crowd. Then he sang another song and won them over again. As long as he didn't talk, he was okay. It took me a long time to win that crowd."

It went pretty much the same at St. Michael's, only with greater intensity. Unlike the scene at the high school, where the kids were restrained by the looming presence of their teachers (the athletic director, Mr. Joy, held the doors to keep the students away from Pat Boone), here the girls screamed without restraint and fought to get to Elvis and Boone as they performed. When Presley broke the strings on his guitar, Randle said, and then smashed the guitar on the floor, "it was mass hysteria. We needed police to get him out of the hall, clothes torn, a sleeve ripped from his jacket. Boone also got the same response. He said after the show that he had never believed what had happened could have happened to him. He said for the first time he felt he was going to make it all the way — like Pat Boone."

There was no question that Bill Randle had spotted a winner, and for the entire length of time that he was in negotiations for an executive position with Hill and Range (which ended in November, when he turned down the song publisher's deal and decided to go with a more lucrative stock-option arrangement with the Cleveland radio station WERE), he had no doubt that he was still in the picture. The Aberbach brothers were clearly anxious for him to stay involved with Presley (or was that a ploy to get Randle to sign with them?), the film was just waiting on the New York shoot, and if they could successfully negotiate union problems there, it would emerge as the first movie short devoted to the new music, with the focus on what its subtitle suggested: *A Day in the Life of a Famous Disc Jockey.* Randle maintained good television and Las Vegas connections, which was where he thought the boy's career should be headed. But reality now came jarringly face-to-face with Bill Randle. For Colonel Parker at almost exactly this time took fate into his own hands, went to New York and ensconced himself at the Warwick Hotel, where, armed with an impressively sweeping document from Vernon and Gladys Presley authorizing him to represent their boy (he had dictated its legalistic language to them in an October 20 telegram of his own), he for the first time formally entertained offers for an artist whose contract he did not, strictly speaking, formally possess. Four days later, on October 24, he contacted Sam Phillips, informing him of his new managerial status and demanding that he name his "best flat price for complete dissolution free and clear of the talent and recording services of Elvis Presley."

This was, finally, too much for Phillips. Up till then it had all been something of a dance whose consummation, if preordained, had not yet had to be squarely faced. Now with a hit record on his hands and new expenses cropping up seemingly every day on every front, Phillips felt as if not only his relationship with Elvis but the credibility of his record company was being undermined by this continuing atmosphere of uncertainty that he had himself allowed to be set in motion. "I was pissed off. I got so goddam mad, I called up Bob Neal and I said, 'Bob, you know what the hell you doing to me?' He said, 'Aw, Sam, I ain't doing nothing,' and I said, 'Goddammit, you're associated with Tom Parker and he's putting out this bullshit, after all of what I've been through to get this guy going, he's putting the word out to my distributors that I'm gonna sell Elvis' contract.' I said, 'Man, this is killing me, you're not just messing with an artist contract here, you messing with my life, man. You just don't deal with these people [the distributors] unfairly. They're in this damn thing, too.' I had worked my ass off — driven sixty-five to seventy-five thousand miles a year to gain their confidence, not only on Elvis but going back to the first damn releases on Sun. I said, 'This could cost me the company.' I said, 'This has got to stop.'

"So I called Tom Parker at the Warwick Hotel in New York, and he said, 'Sa-a-am, how you doin'?' And I said, 'Well, I ain't doing worth a damn.' I said, 'Look, Tom, this has been going on now basically for three or four months, but I thought nothing of it, 'cause I couldn't get confirmation from Bob Neal that you good friends of mine would be trying to do me in — advertently or inadvertently.' He said, 'Oh, noooo, Sam, no, I don't understand thaaaat.' And then he said, 'But *would* you be interested in selling Elvis' contract?' And I said, 'Well, I just might could be.' 'How much you think you want for him?' He didn't say how much he was thinking — just how much would I take. So I said, 'I hadn't really thought about it, Tom. But I'll let you know.' So he said, 'Well, look, think about it, and let me know.' And I thought about it about thirty seconds and called him back."

The price that he named was $35,000, plus $5,000 he owed Elvis in back royalties, more than anyone had ever paid for a popular recording artist (by comparison, Columbia had paid $25,000 for the contract of Frankie Laine, an established star, in 1951). Thus formally empowered, the Colonel really got down to business with RCA and Hill and Range.

To understand why Sam Phillips would want to sell Elvis' contract in the first place one must understand a complex web of circumstances. To begin with, despite all the success that he had enjoyed in the last year, he was in somewhat desperate financial straits. The demands of manufacturing a hit record (out-of-control manufacturing costs primarily, which had to be paid up front with no guarantee that a great number of the records would not come back as returns from distributors with thirty or sixty days to pay) had stretched his limited resources to the breaking point. In January he had written to his brother Jud: "I have told you repeatedly that Sun liabilities are three times the assets and I have been making every effort possible to keep out of bankruptcy. . . . Anyone less interested in saving face would have given it up long ago, but I intend to pay every dollar the company owes — including you — even while I know there is no possible way to ever get out with a dollar."

In October he finally managed to pay Jud off. He had also completed arrangements to open his first radio station, WHER, with a big band format and an "all-girl" lineup that featured both his assistant, Marion Keisker, and his wife, Becky, among the on-the-air talent. He was working around the clock and beside himself with worry over how he was going to keep his various enterprises afloat. Presley's royalties were already overdue, and he didn't doubt that Tom Parker, as his position became more entrenched, was unlikely to be as forbearing as Bob Neal about contractual niceties. More than anything else Sam Phillips was not about to be beholden to any man. He was *not* going to be known as the proprietor of a one-artist company — he had other artists to develop, he had a number that Carl Perkins had sung to him the other night on the telephone that he believed was going to be a bigger hit than anything he had put out to date, he had no hesitation about selling the damn contract. The only hesitation he had was turning the boy over to that damn barker who called himself Colonel, but, he reasoned, "any time you think you know what the public is going to want, that's when you know you're looking at a damn fool when you're looking in the mirror. I thought, Well, if I can just get some money. . . . But I wanted Elvis to succeed so bad — and this is kind of a selfish thing, but I've got to say it — because I didn't want them to be able to say, 'Well, this was just a fluke.' "

On Friday, October 28, back home in Madison, Tom Parker got a telegram from W. W. Bullock, RCA's singles division manager, that $25,000 was as high as RCA was willing to go. On Saturday he and his assistant Tom Diskin went over to Memphis to meet with Sam Phillips and Bob Neal at the offices of WHER, which had finally gone on the air that morning after several days of what the newspaper called "ladylike tardiness," equipment delays and problems with the transmitter. Sam had been up three days straight at this point installing the ground system and running all the checks. By apparent coincidence Hill and Range attorney Ben Starr arrived on this very day to work out a deal tied in with the forthcoming Elvis Presley song folio, whereby Hill and Range was licensed to represent the Sun publishing catalogue in Europe as well as to actively promote domestic cover versions of Sun catalogue songs. After listening to Hill and Range's offer, Sam left Starr in the studio and joined the others in the Holiday Inn restaurant next door, squeezing into a booth with Neal opposite Parker and Diskin. Parker brought up the money situation once again, as if to make sure he had heard correctly over what might have been a bad telephone line. Thirty-five thousand? he said. Well, you know that's a lot of money. I don't know if I can raise that kind of money on an unproven talent. He went over great in Jacksonville, but you talking about $35,000. That's right, chimed in Tom Diskin. That's a helluva lot of money. How much money you made on that boy, anyway? According to Sam Phillips: "I said, 'It's none of your goddam business. In addition to that, I didn't invite you down here. I invited Tom Parker.' Tom elbowed Diskin on the outside seat of this booth and said, 'Shut your mouth.' 'Cause, man, I was ready to get up and whip his ass. Or get whipped. Parker said, 'Look, I don't know where we can go.' He said, 'Sam, there's not a lot of people believe in this thing. But how can we work this deal?' I said, 'Well, first thing, you just keep Tom Diskin's mouth shut.' "

They finally worked out an option deal. The option would take effect on Monday, October 31, and allow Parker two weeks to raise $5,000 (until midnight, November 15). The deal was predicated on a $35,000 purchase price — not surprisingly, Sam Phillips did not budge, and undoubtedly part of him was hoping that the price would not be met — and the full amount had to be raised, and the contract executed, within one month, by December 1, 1955. The $5,000 was not refundable, and the deadline would not be extended. It was a gamble on Tom Parker's part. He was committed at this point. If he didn't come through, he was unlikely to get another chance. Mr. and Mrs. Presley believed in him, at least for the time being; Bob Neal had simply caved in; and the boy — the boy, he thought, would follow him to the ends of the earth. The boy simply didn't care. And only the Colonel knew that the money wasn't there.

Sam Phillips, for his part, was also struck by an uncharacteristic moment of doubt. Upon his return to the radio studio, and after having taken care of the Hill and Range business, Sam ran into Kemmons Wilson, the visionary founder of Holiday Inn and the man who was temporarily providing Sam with free office space. If there was anyone whom Sam Phillips looked up to in the realm of business, it was Kemmons Wilson, and suddenly fearful of what he had done, he asked Wilson his opinion. "He said, 'Jesus Christ, thirty-five thousand dollars? Hell, he can't even sing, man. Take the money!' I said, 'Well, I just done it, and I don't know if they will come through or not.' He said, 'You better hope they do.' So I felt better about it — but I was torn."

F OR BOTH TOM PARKER and Sam Phillips the next two weeks were a period of intense, and sometimes frenetic, activity. On Sunday, October 30, Sam set off for Houston with Marion Keisker for a preliminary injunction hearing in federal court on his lawsuit against Duke Records. It was his son Knox's tenth birthday, and he was so worn out by all of his conflicting obligations that he had to pull over in a cow pasture by the side of the road outside of Shreveport to catch some sleep. When he returned to Memphis, he made a conscious point of talking to Elvis about the deal, but after reassuring Elvis that he would speak to Steve Sholes personally, that he would never abandon him, there was not much else to say, and Elvis, never the most verbally expressive of individuals in any case, pretty much conveyed the same attitude that he had already articulated to Bob Neal. "Elvis did ask me once or twice, did I think they

[RCA] could record him as good as they did at Sun," Neal said, "and I said, 'No reason why not.' He didn't really seem too terribly excited, except he was excited by the idea that he was increasing in value all the time. . . . He was not the type that would just get completely broke up over something, it was sort of like, 'I knew this was going to happen. It's great, let's keep it rolling.' "

Tom Parker, on the other hand, spent almost all of his time trying to maneuver RCA into raising their offer, either by indicating the interest of other companies, which by now were in all practical terms out of the picture, or by attempting to tie in the Hill and Range folio deal in some manner beneficial to the purchase price of the contract. By the time of the DJ convention in Nashville, on November 10, the Colonel was sure enough of his deal that everyone knew there was something in the air, but whether RCA was aware that Sam Phillips would not move off his original price or Phillips knew of the RCA shortfall is doubtful. It may well be that the Colonel was simply counting on RCA's increasing commitment to the *idea* of the deal to carry them through the unpleasant financial details.

RCA head of specialty singles Steve Sholes (he oversaw not just the country and western but the gospel and r&b divisions as well) was at the convention as a matter of course, and the Colonel spent as much time as possible with him and publicity director Anne Fulchino, not one of his biggest fans after the scene he had made in Florida the previous year, mapping out variations on his vision of the future. He did not neglect to point out that both *Cash Box* and *Billboard* had selected his boy as most promising new c&w artist in disc jockey polls, and in fact each presented him with a scroll at the convention to go with the plaque he received from *Country & Western Jamboree* for topping their readers' poll with 250, 000 votes for "New Star of the Year." Probably the elephant that the Colonel had tethered outside of the Hickory Room of the Andrew Jackson Hotel did not fail to make its implicit point either, while at the same time proclaiming, 'Like an elephant Hank Snow never forgets. Thanks Dee Jays."

As for Elvis, he scarcely had time to breeze in and breeze out, flying out of Nashville late Friday night for a few hours at home before taking off again early the next morning for a mill opening in Carthage, Texas, and a Hayride performance that night, then flying back to Memphis for an all-star "Western Swing Jamboree" at Ellis Auditorium Sunday afternoon and evening. The convention itself went by like a blur — the Colonel introducing him to many old friends (not to mention Mr. Sholes), Hank

Snow taking him under his wing, Bob Neal reining in old friends and colleagues, everyone having fun and doing business. There were girls all over
the hotel and parties to introduce you to the girls (if you needed an introduction). Hill and Range representative Grelun Landon brought him
proofs of the song folio and showed them to him and Bob Neal: the cover
was printed in pink and black, and the back had a studio photograph of Vernon and Gladys Presley, looking youthful and happy (Gladys' mouth was
open, her hair had been done by Mr. Tommy at Goldsmith's, she looked as
pretty as a doll).

He had never realized before how many friends he had in the business. Biff Collie was here and T. Tommy Cutrer, with his deep booming
voice, who had just moved up from Shreveport; all the local DJs and promoters were there, and they were all treating him, he noticed, as if he
were somehow . . . *different.* He didn't feel any different, though, he was
still just like a kid bouncing on his toes itching to get on with it. When he
ran into RCA head of country and western promotion Chick Crumpacker, whom he had met first in Richmond and then in Meridian, Mississippi, the previous spring, he announced proudly, "Hey, I'm with you
guys now." And to Buddy Bain, the Corinth DJ who had hosted him at
the outset of the year and showed him a scrapbook filled with Opry pictures, he announced proudly, with a big grin, "Buddy, I believe I'm gonna
make it. The Colonel just sold my contract to RCA." To which Buddy
replied, "I believe you are."

So many people wanted one thing or another from him — he didn't
have time to sit still for all that. He didn't mind signing autographs, and
he was glad to shoot the breeze about music or any other subject with
anyone who came up to him, but he didn't want to talk business with anyone, heck, he didn't know anything *about* business, that's what Bob and
Colonel were there for. Mae Boren Axton, the lady from Jacksonville who
worked for Colonel in Florida, had been trying to get him to listen to this
song ever since he got in — she kept saying it would be his first million-
seller, he could have it if he would just make it his first single release on
RCA, she was so pleased that he had gotten this wonderful deal. He didn't
feel like listening to any songs now, there was so much to do, but Bob
finally got him to go up to the room with him and Mae, and he really
liked it, he said, "Hot dog, Mae, play it again," and she played it over and
over — it was really different, a little like Roy Brown's "Hard Luck
Blues," only this was about a hotel, a heartbreak hotel, where the bell-

hop's tears kept flowing and the desk clerk was dressed in black. He knew the whole song before he left the room. "That's gonna be my next record," he said, nodding at Bob Neal so Mae would know he was serious and maybe leave him alone about it now.

On Sunday he played Ellis in what was billed by the *Press-Scimitar* as a rare local appearance. He was the headliner, with his name above Hank Thompson and Carl Smith, and that new boy from Jackson, Carl Perkins, was at the bottom of the bill. Both his parents were present — Colonel made sure of that, and that they were well treated. Both Colonel and Hank Snow had been calling Mr. and Mrs. Presley regularly to reassure them that everything was all right, that this new RCA deal was really going to come about, and they had even stopped by to visit once or twice at the little house on Getwell. Gladys still didn't like the Colonel, he knew that, but she was finally getting more used to his ways, and while Vernon didn't ever say much, he seemed to know which side his bread was buttered on. At the show that night Elvis wore his oversize red suit and climbed up on top of Bill's bass fiddle with him after popping three or four strings on his guitar. "Scotty's onstage to keep order," said someone in the audience, and after the show was over all the performers signed autographs while still onstage, with Elvis prowling around on the balls of his feet, like a caged tiger, one observer noted, unable to find a release for all that energy.

On November 15, the day the option had to be picked up, the Colonel was still feverishly working out the deal. Bill Bullock continued to balk over the price to the very end, with Parker telegramming him one last time to remind him that time was running out and that if they didn't pick up the option now, he believed the price would simply go up again. Personally, said the Colonel, he believed the price was too high, and, he emphasized, he had nothing to gain from the deal, other than to protect everyone's interests, but he believed that they should go ahead because *the talent was there*. He had managed to stop Sam Phillips from releasing a new Sun single, he said, but the clear implication was that he couldn't stop him for long. He reminded Bullock of the price once again and of the condition that he had inserted, no doubt as one last way of accentuating the difference between himself and Bob Neal, that there would be three national television appearances guaranteed in the contract. Then he pointed out that the banks closed in Madison at 2:00.

Bullock was finally convinced. With his go-ahead, Parker called Phillips to ask if he wanted the money wired to conform strictly to the dead-line. No, Sam said, he could just mail it if he wanted, and sent a telegram to that effect. They would have to get together in the next week or so to finalize the deal, and that would, naturally, take place in Memphis. The Colonel went to his bank in Madison and sent the money air mail, special delivery, then wrote to H. Coleman Tily III, RCA's legal representative, and thanked him for all the help he and Bullock had been. The Colonel hoped he had done all right on the deal; he had done the best he could in the absence of their guiding hand. He reminded Tily of the three guest appearances that had to be part of the deal, or else he would lose his credi-bility with the Presleys, and then he gave instructions as to how his reim-bursement check should be made out, with a clear notation that it was a refund, not a commission; as an RCA shareholder he was simply proud to have advanced the money.

In Memphis Sam Phillips felt momentarily bereft. Part of him had never fully believed that the deal would actually go through; part of him knew that it had to. But he plunged back into his recording activity, spent long hours at the new radio studio, started gearing up his new release schedule (he was determined to have "Blue Suede Shoes," the new Carl Perkins record, out by the first of the year), and continued to pursue his claim against Duke Records, which was due for resolution by the end of the month.

Six days later, on November 21, Steve Sholes, Ben Starr, Coleman Tily, the Colonel, Tom Diskin, Hank Snow, local RCA distributor Jim Crudgington, and regional rep Sam Esgro all converged on the little Sun studio for the signing of the papers. Colonel Parker came accompanied by a document dated the same day stipulating that out of the 40 percent in combined commissions due the Colonel and Bob Neal (25 percent to the Colonel, 15 percent to Neal), there would be an even split for the duration of Neal's agreement, until March 15, 1956. The buyout agreement itself was a simple two-page document in which Sun Records agreed to turn over all tapes and cease all distribution and sales of previously released re-cordings as of December 31, 1955, while the managers "do hereby sell, as-sign and transfer unto RCA all of their right, title and interest in and to" the previously exercised option agreement. The purchase price was $35,000; RCA undertook responsibility for the payment of all back royal-ties and held Sun Records harmless from any subsequent claims. Out of all this Elvis Presley would get a royalty of 5 percent as opposed to the 3 percent that he was currently receiving from Sun — this amounted to almost two cents more per record sold, which over the course of a million sales would come to about $18,000.

In addition, as the result of a co-publishing arrangement that the Colonel had entered into with Hill and Range (who probably contributed substantially themselves toward the purchase price), Elvis would now receive half of the two-cent statutory mechanical fee and half of the two-cent broadcast fee on all new Hill and Range compositions that he recorded, which would be registered through his own publishing company. If at this point he were to start writing songs as well, or, perhaps more pertinently, if he were to start claiming songwriting credit for songs he recorded, a practice going back to time immemorial in the recording industry, he could increase his income by up to another two cents per side. Hill and Range, meanwhile, stood to gain an almost incalculable advantage over their competitors in the field by securing not just an inside track, but what amounted to virtually a right of first refusal from the hottest new singing sensation in the country.

After the contract was signed, there was a picture-taking ceremony, with different configurations of the various parties involved. In one Elvis is flanked by the Colonel and Hank Snow, proud partners in Jamboree Attractions, while Bob Neal, to Snow's left, jovially approves; in another Gladys plants a kiss upon her son's cheek and clutches her black handbag as the Colonel pats her on the shoulder and Vernon looks stiffly on. In yet another Sam and Elvis shake hands across RCA attorney Coleman Tily. In all the pictures all the men are beaming — everyone has seemingly gotten exactly what he wanted. After the picture taking a number of the participants dropped by for a brief on-air appearance on Marion Keisker's show in the brand-new WHER studios. "They thought it would be great fun," said Marion, "if they all came over and we announced it. So they all crowded into the little control room, and we did a little four- or five-way interview, well, not really an interview, just a little chat. And in the course of it, I remember, Hank Snow said, 'I'm very proud this boy made his first appearance on the national scene on my section of the Grand Ole Opry.' And he was being such a pompous ass about it, I couldn't help it, but I said, 'Yes, and I remember, you had to ask him what his name was.' That was a rather tactless thing for me to do."

Bob Johnson's story in the *Press-Scimitar* the following day was headlined "Memphis Singer Presley Signed by RCA-Victor for Recording Work."

> Elvis Presley, 20, Memphis recording star and entertainer who zoomed into bigtime and the big money almost overnight, has been released from his contract with Sun Record Co. of Memphis. . . . Phillips and RCA officials did not reveal terms but said the money involved is probably the highest ever paid for a contract release for a country-western recording artist. "I feel Elvis is one of the most talented youngsters today," Phillips said, "and by releasing his contract to RCA-Victor we will give him the opportunity of entering the largest organization of its kind in the world, so his talents can be given the fullest opportunity."

To further capitalize on that opportunity Elvis and the Colonel flew into New York on November 30 for a whirlwind visit to RCA's New York headquarters the next day. On December 2 Elvis was back on the road, playing to a decidedly modest crowd in Atlanta and joining an Opry package headlined by Roy Acuff and Kitty Wells the following night in Montgomery, Alabama, for which he was paid $400. That same day's issue of *Billboard* magazine ran a banner headline announcing, "Double Deals Hurl Presley into Stardom," and speculating shrewdly about the bright future that might well lie ahead.

> Elvis Presley, one of the most sought-after warblers this year, signed two big-time contracts as a recording artist, writer and publisher. RCA Victor beat out the diskery competition and signed the 19-year-old to a three years–plus options contract. Besides which, Hill & Range inked him to a long-time exclusive writing pact and at the same time set up a separate publishing firm, Elvis Presley Music, Inc., which will operate within the H&R fold. . . . Altho Sun has sold Presley primarily as a c.&w. artist, Victor plans to push his platters in all three fields — pop, r.&b., and c.&w. However, RCA Victor's specialty singles chief, Steve Sholes (who will record Presley), plans to cut the warbler with the same backing — electric guitar, bass fiddle, drums and Presley himself on rhythm guitar — featured on his previous Sun waxings.

THE DORSEY SHOW, MARCH 17, 1956. (ALFRED WERTHEIMER)

STAGE SHOW

No matter what people say about you, son, you know who you are and that's all that matters.

> — Gladys Presley to her son as quoted by Harold Loyd
> in *Elvis Presley's Graceland Gates*

The last admonishment I had to Elvis was, "Look, you know how to do it now, you go over there and don't let anybody tell you — they believe enough in you that they've laid some cold cash down, so you let them know what you feel and what you want to do."

> — Sam Phillips on his advice to Elvis Presley, late fall
> 1955

O N TUESDAY, JANUARY 10, 1956, two days after his twenty-first birthday, Elvis Presley entered the RCA studio in Nashville for the first time. Just before Christmas Steve Sholes had sent him a brief note proposing ten titles for his consideration, along with acetate demos and lead sheets for each of the songs. The selection included ballads, novelty numbers, country weepers, blues, and "beat" songs, which Sholes urged him to learn and then let the RCA a&r man know which of them he liked best. About a week before the session, at the Variety Club in Memphis, an after-hours "members only" club for entertainment people and businessmen, Elvis sat down at the beat-up old upright and picked out "Heartbreak Hotel" for Dewey, announcing he was going to cut it in Nashville the following week.

Sholes meanwhile got in touch with Chet Atkins, his Nashville coordinator and one of Scotty's principal inspirations on guitar, about booking the studio and putting together a band for the session. The band was no problem — they would use Elvis' regular group with Chet on rhythm. In addition, Atkins contacted Floyd Cramer, who had just moved to Nashville and had played piano behind Elvis on the Hayride and on tour over the past year, as well as Gordon Stoker of the Jordanaires, the popular quartet who had toured with Eddy Arnold and were singing background on an increasing number of Nashville sessions. He would not be able to employ the full group, Atkins explained to Stoker; RCA had just signed the renowned Speer Family gospel quartet, and he wanted to use Ben and Brock Speer to augment the sound on any ballads they might cut at the session.

Steve Sholes was becoming increasingly nervous. At the DJ convention the previous November, wrote *Billboard* editor Paul Ackerman, the prevailing attitude was, "Anyone who buys [Elvis Presley] will get stuck," and the prevailing attitude at the New York home office was no more comforting. Sholes, ordinarily the most cautious of men, was not unaware that with this signing he had put his neck on the line. He had little doubt that there was enough corporate jealousy to bury him, and it didn't help his state of mind any when Sam Phillips put out his latest release, an upbeat, rambunctious rocker called "Blue Suede Shoes" by twenty-three-year-old Carl Perkins, just before the new year. "Steve was afraid he'd bought the wrong one," Chet Atkins observed, and there is little question that many at RCA would have been exceedingly quick to agree.

In the weeks following the signing, however, RCA as a corporate entity did everything they could to capitalize on their investment. On December 2 they put out their own version of Elvis' last Sun single, "I Forgot to Remember to Forget," still riding high on the country charts after eleven weeks and destined now to reach number one and stay on the charts for another twenty-eight. In addition they rereleased each of the four other Sun singles on December 20, while, in related developments, Hill and Range finally came out with the Elvis Presley songbook and the Colonel announced on December 17 that his boy had been contracted for four appearances on CBS' *Stage Show*, hosted by Jimmy and Tommy Dorsey, which comedian Jackie Gleason produced as a lead-in to his own highly successful Saturday-night show. NBC had also been in the running, the Colonel declared, with fellow RCA artist Perry Como, whose show ran opposite Gleason's, making an unsuccessful bid for Mr. Presley's services. "The most talked-about new personality in the last 10 years of recorded music," declared RCA's full-page ad in *Billboard* on December 3, featuring a dynamic picture of Elvis Presley, legs astraddle, eyes closed, shouting out his blues, and a small italicized notice below: "Bob Neal, manager/under direction of Hank Snow Jamboree Attractions/Col. Tom Parker, general manager."

R CA HAD ITS STUDIO in a building that it shared with the Methodist TV, Radio and Film Commission. The room was big, high-ceilinged, with an arched roof that created a tendency, according to Atkins, for bass notes to "roll around for a long time." The first session was booked for 2:00 in the afternoon, an unlikely hour, but neither Sholes nor Chet was much for night sessions. D. J. Fontana sat attentively behind his drums; it was his first recording date with the group, and he knew that there must be lots of equally good drummers in Nashville. Floyd Cramer, with a young wife to support, was wondering if he had made the right decision leaving Shreveport and whether there would be a living for him in studio work, while Steve Sholes, sitting behind the control room glass with his lead sheets and his song lists and little insight into how the boy was going to react to the new studio and the new situation, couldn't help but feel that this was not a very auspicious beginning from any point of view. To be working with such a ragtag group, especially under such trying circumstances; to feel himself under the jealous scrutiny not just of his own record company but of an entire industry; to be seeking to duplicate the "slapback" sound that was so integral a part of the singer's appeal while his own engineers professed ignorance as to just how Sam Phillips had achieved it — this was not a position he was happy to find himself in. Bill kept chewing gum and cracking jokes, but it was evident that even he felt the tension in the air, and it didn't make Scotty feel any better when, after making small talk with Atkins about the unique qualities of their Echosonic amps, a custom-made item which Scotty had gotten six months earlier after hearing Chet employ it to particular effect on "Mister Sandman," he asked Chet what he wanted them to do. "Just go on doing what you been doing" was his musical idol's characteristically phlegmatic reply. "He was just old Cool Hand Luke himself," said Scotty. "He wasn't there to disturb or anything. [The whole thing] was a drastic change for us at first — at first I think it seemed a little cold. The engineer called take numbers instead of, 'Hey, do it again.' My feeling was not necessarily we're in the big time, just now we had a little more professional atmosphere. . . . We were fresh meat!"

Elvis alone failed to show any sign of strain. He was wearing pink pants with a blue stripe and was clearly excited about the occasion. He flung himself into the first number, Ray Charles' "I Got a Woman," which had been a staple of their stage act for nearly a year, and sang it again and again, zeroing in on the half-time, bluesy finish that had always been a climax of the live performance. There appeared to be no doubt or hesitation. It didn't seem to bother him that for the first time they were hearing the echo effect in the studio (Sam Phillips' slapback was in essence an electronic adjustment after the fact; the only way to get a similar effect in the McGavock Street studio — and then it was only a crude approximation — was by placing a mike and an amp at opposite ends of the long hallway at the front of the building and feeding that back into the main room). He was just biding his time, as he had learned to do from Sam Phillips, until they got it *right*. A couple of times Steve Sholes might have called it a master take, but the boy was insistent, in a nice way, that he could do better, that it wasn't there yet. Atkins, ordinarily unemotional and undemonstrative, was so struck by the performance that he called his wife and told her to come down to the studio right away. "I told her she'd never see anything like this again, it was just so damn exciting."

The next song was "Heartbreak Hotel," the number Mae Axton had brought to the convention, which he had told Dewey he was going to record. It was an odd, almost morbid composition, which Axton had written with Tommy Durden after Tommy showed her a Miami newspaper story about a man who had committed suicide and left a note saying, "I walk a lonely street." "It stunned me," said Mae. "I said to Tommy, 'Everybody in the world has somebody who cares. Let's put a Heartbreak Hotel at the end of this lonely street.' And he said, 'Let's do.' So we wrote it." Mae promised the song to Buddy Killen at Tree Publishing, and she gave a third of the writer's credit to Elvis. "I don't know why," said Buddy, "she said she wanted to buy him a car." Hill and Range tried to get the publishing, but Mae held firm, which must have frustrated Steve Sholes even more.

It was a strange choice by any kind of conventional wisdom: gloomy, world-weary, definitely at odds with the irrepressibly vibrant image that Elvis had projected from the start, both in performance and on all his records to date. In theory it may not have been an altogether comfortable fit, and Sam Phillips pronounced the finished product a "morbid mess," but Elvis clearly believed in it and put everything he had into it, and whatever Sholes' or Chet's personal reservations, the heavy overlay of echo and D.J.'s rim shots created a powerful, emotion-laden atmosphere of upbeat despair.

The entire three-hour evening session was spent putting down "Money Honey," yet another r&b staple of the live act, and the single session that was held the following afternoon was consumed recording the two ballads that Steve Sholes had brought in, with the makeshift three-man vocal group providing only adequate background harmonies. Gordon Stoker in particular was dissatisfied. Stoker, who had met the boy on the Eddy Arnold bill that played Memphis fourteen months before, was upset that his own group had not been used and felt that the sound was unprofessional, with a "quartet" made up of a low bass and two natural tenors. The songs came out all right ("I Was the One" was always Elvis' favorite from the session), but Stoker was not very impressed with Presley's ballad-singing abilities and left the session angry at both Chet and Steve Sholes for showing him so little consideration.

All in all it was a somewhat desultory beginning, and Steve Sholes could not have been happy going back to New York with two r&b covers, a singularly odd original on which Hill and Range didn't even own the publishing, and two ballads unlike anything Elvis Presley had ever recorded before. He couldn't have felt any better when, upon his return, his superiors were so put off by what they heard, Sholes said, that they wanted him to turn around and head straight back to Nashville. "They all told me it didn't sound like anything, it didn't sound like his other record[s], and I'd better not release it, better go back and record it again." Sholes argued that it had taken him two days to get this, if he went back it would just be throwing good money after bad; besides, they had an opportunity for another session in New York at the end of the month and they needed to put something out right away.

Elvis meanwhile remained unfazed by anyone else's doubts. Back in Memphis he appeared on a father's night show at Humes, just as he had appeared the previous month in a Christmas show produced by Miss Scrivener to raise money to help out needy students. He bought a brand-new 1956 Plymouth station wagon for his parents, too, and he stopped by the Chisca to fill in Dewey's radio audience on what he'd been up to lately, talking with Dewey off-air as the records played and Dewey got more and more excited about the world he was entering and the future that stretched out before him.

At the Memphis Recording Service at 706, all attention was focused on the two new Sun releases, Carl Perkins' "Blue Suede Shoes" and Johnny Cash's stark "Folsom Prison Blues." Elvis told Marion and Mr. Phillips all about the Nashville session and the upcoming Dorsey broadcasts; Sam was a big swing band fan and had always pointed to Tommy Dorsey's "Boogie Woogie" as the start of it all. Sam didn't really press him much about the session — he considered Steve Sholes a man of integrity and didn't want to get in the middle of anything. They sat for a few minutes in the little outer office, not really saying much, but secure in the knowledge that things were moving along pretty much according to plan. Elvis felt comfortable with Sam and Marion, he felt at home in the little studio — "there was no place he'd rather be," said Sam, "that's just a fact. If you ever befriended him, he never forgot it. He had difficulty building true friendships, and I had that difficulty, too. I have a lot of friends, but I am just not a person who builds relationships easily. Elvis was the same way. He was just, innately, a loner."

He heard from Steve Sholes again around January 20, just a week before his scheduled departure for New York. Sholes suggested six songs this time, including "Pins and Needles in My Heart," a 1945 Roy Acuff number that Sholes thought he might be able to "get with." A carbon copy of the letter, of course, went to the Colonel, who was busy making plans based on a future that nobody else could see.

The Colonel's vision of the future centered on mass exposure, something he had tried with Eddy Arnold with a good deal of success. With Elvis, though, it was different. "I think there was a big difference in the time. . . . The Eddy Arnold era and the Elvis era were entirely different," said country comedian Minnie Pearl, who worked with the Colonel in both eras. They were different because, according to Pearl, as big a star as Arnold became, Elvis was the Colonel's dream, the perfect vehicle for all the Colonel's elaborately worked out and ingenious promotional schemes. Elvis was the purest of postwar products, the commodity that had been missing from the shelves in an expanding marketplace of leisure time and disposable cash. The Colonel "slept, ate, and breathed Elvis," just as he had Eddy Arnold — but the times had changed, and the personalities of the performers were dissimilar as well: Elvis was fresh-faced and eager to please, pure plasticity in an informational age that required a protean hero.

Television was the key to the deal. The Colonel realized it — hell, Bob Neal had realized it, that was what he had been aiming for when he took Elvis to New York to try out for *Arthur Godfrey's Talent Scouts*. How many people could you reach with one national appearance as opposed to all the one-night stands, the endless promotions and exploitations, that you did before picking up stakes and moving on to the next town? There was no comparison, even for an old carnival hand like Tom Parker. The trick was in controlling the game. You had a boy who could be ruined by any number of variables: sex, scandal, familiarity, loss of self-belief. The idea was to remove him from those variables. The trick was to expose him, but expose him only so much, to define, and control, the level of acceptable danger. The Colonel had a number of powerful allies, a carefully assembled team that included Abe Lastfogel, head of the William Morris Agency, and his second in command, Harry Kalcheim, who had set up the Dorsey contact; Jean and Julian Aberbach of Hill and Range, who along with Lastfogel went back to the days of Eddy Arnold; he had all of his contacts from all of the years with RCA, and he had peripheral players like Bill Randle, with his vast radio audience, working for the Colonel's interests without necessarily even knowing it. All he had to do was to get them working for themselves without working against each other, the key was to put together a team where all the players functioned smoothly but only the team manager knew everyone's function and position. It was a neat trick, but one that he was sure he could pull off — if only the boy came through. And he had little doubt that he would.

THE WEEK BEFORE the first Dorsey appearance Elvis was off on yet another Texas tour. On Saturday night he told the Hayride performers about his upcoming television appearances, and they all wished him luck — he was off for a month now on a Jamboree Attractions tour of the Southeast that was booked around the four consecutive Saturday-night television appearances. According to Maylon Humphries, a Shreveport buddy and occasional performer who was on college break, "He was sitting around in Hoot and Curley's dressing room, and Curley says, 'Elvis, you're going to make a fortune off this,' and he looked down and took a deep breath and says, 'Not really.' And he named what he was getting. 'But, you know, Curley,' he said, 'Mr. Parker says more people will be seeing me on these four shows' — and he didn't say Colonel, he said Mr. Parker — 'than I would be exposed to for the rest of my life on the Hayride.'" Which left everyone with something to think about.

He flew into New York on Wednesday, January 25, with the Colonel and on Thursday met with various top RCA executives. Steve Sholes took him in to see Larry Kanaga, the head of the record division, and Sholes almost sank through the floor when Elvis buzzed Kanaga with the electric buzzer concealed in his hand. Then Sholes took him over to the publicity department, where he met Anne Fulchino, the attractive young Bostonian who had modernized pop and c&w publicity practices at RCA but had been pleading with Sholes to bring her the right new artist to work with so that she could really break pop in a big way. "Steve brought Elvis in and introduced him to me. He shook my hand, and he had that electric buzzer. I said, 'Honey, that may be big in Memphis, but it's never going to work in New York.' Fortunately, he had a sense of humor, so we just laughed about it, but he never used that stupid buzzer again.

"He was a very quick study, a cornball kid who was a quick study. We took him to lunch that day, and he didn't know which end of the fork to use, but, you know, he never made the same mistake twice. This was a kid who knew where he wanted to go, and he was very single-minded about it. We had a little discussion that day about what he wanted to do, what the long-range goals were and what the steps would be in the publicity campaign. I explained to him that this should be done very methodically, this should be a long-range plan, I had to know what he wanted to do, and we both had to agree that he was capable of getting there. I was drawing little pyramids in my notebook to show him, and we discussed things like concert tours, I knew there was an acting possibility from the very beginning. He understood all this. He wanted it, and he had the talent. After lunch I asked him to wait in my office, and I went to see Steve. I said to Steve, 'We got him!' The guy that we'd been looking for."

There was a rehearsal late Saturday morning at the Nola Studios, on Broadway between Fifty-first and Fifty-second, just a couple of blocks from the Warwick Hotel, where the Colonel and Elvis and the band were all staying. The Colonel and a William Morris agent introduced Elvis to the Dorseys and their mother, "and Elvis exhibited a kind of deference and courtesy," observed Arnold Shaw, who had brought Presley to Bill

Randle's attention early on, "that patently puzzled" the Dorseys, not normally known for either their deference or courtesy. Scotty, who was interested in sound engineering, checked out the control booth, while D.J., who had never been to New York before ("We didn't know what to expect. We didn't know what kind of people they were — we figured they'd just gobble us up"), met his boyhood idol, drummer Louie Bellson; Bellson invited him out for coffee and turned out to be a really "nice guy." Elvis hung around at the back of the hall, playing with Hill and Range representative Grelun Landon's five-year-old son and talking to Grelun and Chick Crumpacker, among others, about the time that his car had burned up on the highway. He had seen his whole career "going up in smoke," he said. They had clambered up on a hillside to watch the car burn when all of a sudden the horn went off and died in a crescendo, he told them, like a dying cow. He talked about some of his favorite performers, Bill Kenny and the Ink Spots in particular, and named his favorite movie actor as James Dean, whose "Rebel Without a Pebble," he said, was his favorite film. He was absolutely charming, said Chick Crumpacker, winning in a way that didn't fail to take into account the reaction of his audience.

It was a gloomy day — rain had been pouring down in the aftermath of a storm that had blanketed the East Coast — but when the rehearsal was over Elvis was not averse to doing some sightseeing with Grelun Landon and his son. They bought a ball to toss around in a sporting goods store near Madison Square Garden, stopped off at a coffee shop and ordered milk shakes, and happily soaked up the hustle and bustle of the city. Back at the hotel Scotty and Bill reminisced about some of the early tours, and Bill talked about all the things they had done when they first started out to bolster Elvis and support the act. Scotty was characteristically reserved, while Bill was full of beans in describing some of the scrapes they had gotten themselves into, but with Elvis, said Landon, you simply couldn't tell how relaxed he really was or to what extent he was simply brazening it out. "He knew," said Landon, a sophisticated observer of human nature and, at thirty-three, a music-industry veteran, "what he was doing at all times. I really believe he was like a novelist — he studied and watched what was going on, it was really just second nature with him." There was some talk about "Heartbreak Hotel," which had been released with considerable misgivings by the RCA brass the day before. "I Forgot to Remember to Forget," in its new RCA pressing, was still riding high on the charts, and probably there was no one at RCA, including

Steve Sholes, who wouldn't have picked its clear, crisp, snappy sound over the murky mix and message of the new song. But RCA needed fresh product, they needed to demonstrate their commitment to their new artist, they needed to prove that they had not made a mistake of monumental proportions; they were not about to become the laughingstock of the industry. Just before it was time to go over to the theater Elvis Presley took a nap.

T HE SHOW THAT NIGHT, wrote Chick Crumpacker, was not marked by any foreshadowings or harbingers of great success. It was broadcast from CBS' Studio 50, between Fifty-third and Fifty-fourth, and "few had braved the storm. The theater was sparsely filled with shivering servicemen and Saturday nighters, mostly eager for the refuge from the weather. Outside, groups of teenagers rushed past the marquee to a roller-skating rink nearby. Just before showtime, a weary promoter [Crumpacker himself] returned to the box office with dozens of tickets, unable even to give them away on the streets of Times Square."

The series itself was on rather shaky ground; ratings were poor, and in many quarters it was seen simply as the indulgence of one of television's biggest stars, who happened to love the sweet sound of swing. *Stage Show* had started out the previous fall as a half-hour lead-in to Jackie Gleason's *Honeymooners,* which had previously occupied the full hour as *The Jackie Gleason Show.* It proved so weak a lead-in that by March the order would be switched, and the show itself dropped after a single season. Other guests on the night of Elvis Presley's television debut included Sarah Vaughan, whose manager-husband George Treadwell refused to let her follow some untalented "hillbilly" singer, and comic-banjoist Gene Sheldon. In the paper the previous morning it had been announced in Nick Kenny's *New York Daily Mirror* column that "Bill Randle, one of the country's ace disc jockeys, makes a guest appearance on the CBS-TV 'Stage Show' tomorrow night at 8. Bill will present his new pop singing discovery Elvis Presley." It was not Elvis Presley, then, whom Tommy Dorsey introduced but "special guest" Bill Randle, who had been plugging the television appearance on his Saturday-afternoon New York radio network show. "We'd like at this time," said Randle, "to introduce to you a young fellow who, like many performers — Johnnie Ray among them — came out of nowhere to be an overnight big star. This young fellow we saw for the first time while making a movie short. We think tonight that he's going to make television history for you. We'd like you to meet him now — Elvis Presley."

Then Elvis came out looking as if he'd been shot out of a cannon. Wearing a black shirt, white tie, dress pants with a shiny stripe, and a tweed jacket so loud that it almost sparkled, he launched into the first song with no more than a toss of his head to Scotty and Bill, but much to Randle's surprise the song that he launched into was not his new RCA single but Big Joe Turner's "Shake, Rattle and Roll." When it came to the instrumental break, he drew back into the protective shelter of the band, got up on the balls of his feet, spread his legs wide, and let loose.

The reaction of the audience, as Chick Crumpacker recalled it, was something between shock and interest, "a kind of amusement. People tended to laugh as much as applaud at key moments." His hands never stop moving, it looks as if he might be chewing gum, there is a twitchiness to his whole aspect — and yet there is a boundless confidence, too, and his mascaraed visage appears to scan the audience as he seeks . . . connection. In the middle of the song he segues into "Flip, Flop and Fly," another Big Joe Turner number, and you're not sure if it's planned or unplanned, but there is the feeling of something fierce and uncontrolled. Scotty concentrates intently on his guitar playing; Bill — who *is* chewing gum — shouts encouragement: "Go, go, go." And Elvis is gone. At the end of the performance he almost staggers back from the mike, takes a deep bow, and waves, all in one instant. What you take away from it, no matter how many times you watch or how much you are aware of the fluttery movement of the hands, is the sheer enjoyment of the moment. *Elvis Presley is on top of the world.*

"Daddy just sat there," said Jackson Baker, Elvis' fifteen-year-old next-door neighbor of the previous summer, "and he said, 'Elvis is going to be a big star.' We all watched, and it was just so obvious that he was." Bob Johnson wrote in his notes for a future story: "Presley puts intensity into his songs. Over-emotional? Yes. But he projects. He 'sells.' Elvis has arrived. . . . But you can't throw that much into something without it telling. It'll wear him out. It will exhaust him emotionally and physically. He's 20 now [actually he was twenty-one]. If he's wise, he'll slow down a little and live another 20 years."

Probably there were few in Memphis who did not watch — Bob Neal, the mayor, the Lansky brothers, Dixie and her family, Elvis' boyhood friends, all were rooting for him, no doubt. And yet the stars didn't fall from the sky, the ratings didn't even go up appreciably, there was certainly no great press notice of Elvis Presley's television debut, and on Monday morning he was back in the studio recording.

S TEVE SHOLES once again had a session in mind that was not going to take place anywhere *but* in his mind. He had lined up a good boogie-woogie piano player named Shorty Long, currently featured on Broadway in the musical *The Most Happy Fella,* to fill out the band, and he had done his best once again to prep Elvis for the session, but he sensed that something was missing. For while he never got any back talk from the boy, and he could sincerely offer nothing but praise to Colonel Parker with respect to the attitude and deportment of his young charge, he suspected that some connection was not being made, that the boy's politeness masked a distance or another point of view that he could not, or would not, articulate.

At Sholes' instigation, in what amounted to standard record company procedure, they started off with "Blue Suede Shoes," the new Sun release that was climbing the charts and provoking such galling afterthoughts at RCA. Recording conditions here in New York were far more satisfactory than in Nashville, the studio on the ground floor of the RCA building on East Twenty-fourth that had once housed the old police academy stables was a comfortable one for Sholes to work in, and the musicians were certainly familiar with the material. After thirteen takes, though, they still hadn't come up with a version to rival the authority of the original, and Sholes could scarcely have been reassured when the boy declared that it was no use doing any more, they couldn't do better than Carl's anyway. Next, at Presley's urging, they launched into a song with which Sholes was surely familiar because it came from an artist with whom he had worked extensively in Victor's "race" series, blues singer Arthur "Big Boy" Crudup. Crudup had written "That's All Right," Presley's first song, and now they did a masterful version of his "My Baby Left Me," in which for the first time the band really started to sound like a unit. D.J.'s drums and Bill's descending bass introed the song. In contrast to the rushed rhythms of the Perkins number or the murky echo of "Heartbreak Hotel," this sounded deliberate, thought out, a vibrant companion piece to the Sun recordings. And yet it can hardly have been of much consolation to Sholes, to whose way of thinking an Arthur Crudup blues was not what they were looking for, no matter how good it might be. *This* was not the potential new pop artist that RCA had signed, this was not the revolutionary new sound that RCA was looking for.

The afternoon session brought more of the same, another wonderful Crudup number, "So Glad You're Mine," plus one of the six songs that Sholes had suggested, a honky-tonker called "One Sided Love Affair" that was particularly suited to Shorty Long's barrelhouse style. If he could get three or four more, Sholes figured, along with the five unissued Sun titles that he had acquired, he would have just enough for an album.

At some point in the process he called Sam Phillips in Memphis and, under the pretext of informing him that they had cut "Blue Suede Shoes" (which he assured Sam he would not put out as a single), sought advice and reassurance concerning the course he was following. He even put out feelers, according to Phillips, for Sam to produce Elvis for RCA on a free-lance basis. "I told him he hadn't bought the wrong person. And I told him what I told him when he bought the contract in the first place, just don't try to make Elvis what he's not instinctively. The worst mistake you can make is to try to shape him into some damn country artist, or anything else, if it just doesn't naturally flow that way. I told him to keep it as simple as possible, and I happen to be the greatest admirer of Steve Sholes — he was a person of the utmost integrity and how he could be that way when he was with a major label, quote unquote, I really don't understand — but he was *not* a producer. Steve was just at every session, and he kept his fucking mouth shut."

On the second day of recording a young wire reporter named Fred Danzig showed up for an interview, the first fruits of Anne Fulchino's publicity campaign. "I wrote a thing called 'On the Record' for the radio wire, and I did another version for the newspapers for what was called the United Press Red Letter. I would interview singers and composers and record producers and just give them stuff like that. At some point in 1955 Marion Keisker started writing me from Memphis about this kid, Elvis Presley, who was doing such marvelous things down there, and then he placed ninth in our third annual Disc Jockey Poll. So I knew about him when Annie called me up and told me that he was going to be in New York to do the Dorsey show."

Danzig watched the show on TV and showed up at Fulchino's office at 11:00 A.M. the following Tuesday. She took him down to the recording studio where he found, he later wrote, "a tall, lean young man standing in the hallway waiting for us." He was wearing "a shirt the likes of which I had never seen before. It was a ribbon shirt, light lavender in color. Elvis said it cost $70. I also noted that his blue alligator loafers were scuffed and worn-down at the heels. He had on a gray sports jacket and dark gray slacks. His fingernails were chewed down to where there was no biting room left." His presence was compelling, Danzig said, "just for that face alone. If you saw him on the street, you'd say, 'Wow, look at that guy.' "

They went into the control room to do the interview. In response to a question about his music, the boy started naming blues singers with whom Danzig was somewhat familiar but who "obviously meant a lot to him. I was very surprised to hear him talk about the black performers down there and about how he tried to carry on their music. He talked about how he wanted to buy his parents a house and make life easier for them. I asked him about the shaking and the wiggling, and he told me they hadn't wanted him to jump around so much on TV but that he had told them it was the way he had to perform, it was just the way he did it. He showed me his leather-covered guitar and explained that there was only one other leather guitar case like it. Hank Snow had given him the idea, he said. 'It keeps the guitar from getting splintered when I swing it around and it hits my belt buckle.' " They talked about the movies and how he "wanted to go out to Hollywood and become the next James Dean. And I thought, 'Yeah, well, come on, kid . . .' But that was obviously his goal.

"We talked for about twenty or twenty-five minutes — he wasn't the most articulate kid in the world, but he answered all the questions — when Steve Sholes came in and said they were ready to begin." Elvis invited Danzig to stick around and watch him work, and the first number they tried was "I'm Gonna Sit Right Down and Cry (Over You)," a 1954 r&b number for Roy Hamilton (it was the B side of Hamilton's smash inspirational hit, "You'll Never Walk Alone"). "Gee, those sideburns bother me," Sholes remarked to Danzig wryly. "I wonder if I should get him to the barbershop." But, he added with a mirthful chuckle, "I guess you don't tamper with success. I guess we'll leave them on the kid."

* * *

THE NEXT COUPLE OF DAYS were taken up with sightseeing and a scattering of promotional activities, mostly organized by Anne Fulchino and Chick Crumpacker, with Hill and Range representative Grelun Landon along for the ride. The Colonel by now had gone home to Tennessee, presumably to oversee, in his meticulous fashion, the multiplicity of details surrounding the start-up of the upcoming tour. With his "keepers," Elvis drove out to Trenton to do an interview on perhaps the only station in the New York metropolitan area to air country music. They got lost looking for the station, and Elvis slept all the way out and back. The William Morris people threw a party for him; so did Julian Aberbach, the president of Hill and Range, who had a dinner in Elvis' honor at his home. Julian's wife, Anne Marie, served lamb cooked rare, and Elvis almost gagged on it, explaining that he was not used to "bloody" meat; his taste ran more to hamburgers, well done. "He was extremely polite," said Freddy Bienstock, Julian's cousin, who was also present, "but he was completely lost."

Chick, in what he later came to see as a case of enthusiasm overrunning judgment, scheduled a reception at the Hickory House, on Fifty-second Street above Times Square, but made the mistake of failing to secure a private room. "It might as well have been Grand Central Station the way people were milling in and out, but the savior of the situation was Elvis, who looked around, took stock of things, and then took charge with such aplomb and such charm that he made everybody feel like they were alone with him in the room." He was wearing a hand-painted tie that he had gotten for a dollar in Times Square and the same lavender ribbon shirt that Fred Danzig had remarked upon. What was his reaction to success? he was asked. "It's all happening so fast," he said, "there's so much happening to me . . . that some nights I just can't fall asleep. It scares me, you know . . . it just scares me."

THE SECOND DORSEY SHOW went fine. He sang "Tutti Frutti" and "Baby, Let's Play House," once again failing to plug his new single, which according to *Billboard* was "a strong blues item wrapped up in his usual powerful style and a great beat. . . . Presley is riding high right now with network TV appearances, and this disk should benefit from all the special plugging." Evidently something was bothering Elvis about the show, though, because when Sholes wrote to Parker three days later he said: "I thought Elvis did even better Saturday night than he did on the previous week's show. I understand he was not so pleased but I think he had every right to be happy. You should be very proud of the boy," Sholes went on,

> because as far as I can find out he conducted himself very well after you left. At the press party he mingled with all the guests and made a very good impression there. As a result he is very hot material here in New York and with any luck at all I think we all should do extremely well. . . .
>
> On Friday we didn't have any new material that suited Elvis so we recorded LAWDY MISS CLAWDY and SHAKE RATTLE AND ROLL. Neither one of these would be suitable for single release but I know they will make good selections for the second album.

On Sunday night Elvis was back in Richmond with an Opry troupe assembled by the Colonel that included the Carter Sisters and Mother Maybelle, Ernest Tubb's son, Justin, and Charlie and Ira Louvin, who had already played a good number of dates with Elvis and were Mrs. Presley's favorite country singing group. They were booked every night — in Greensboro, High Point, and Raleigh, North Carolina, then in Spartanburg and Charlotte the first week, with Saturday night off for Elvis to go up to New York to play the third Dorsey brothers show. Oscar Davis acted as the advance man, and the Colonel came in behind him to set up the show, hauling pictures, programs, and all the concessions that he was now personally peddling, taking away a lucrative source of outside income from Bill. Oscar's expansive manner charmed every local newspaperman, promoter, desk clerk, and bellhop in sight, while the Colonel's scrupulous, almost compulsive attention to detail, at such striking odds with the casualness of his appearance, his almost contemptuous dismissal of the niceties of human behavior, virtually guaranteed that everything would be just so. "The Colonel embarrasses me," Oscar frequently complained to his cronies. "Goddam, he embarrasses the hell out of me — runs around like a goddam carny, with his damn shirttail hanging out and no necktie." Parker could become no less infuriated by the way that Oscar threw his money around, but they were the perfect team so long as Oscar didn't quit or the Colonel didn't fire Oscar for giving a stagehand a fifty-dollar tip at any given show.

"We were working near every day," said Scotty. "We'd pull into some town, go to the hotel room and get washed up or go right to the auditorium or movie house, and after we played our shows, we'd get back in the cars and start driving to the next town. We never saw any newspapers. . . . And we didn't hear much radio, because it was drive all night, sleep all day. . . . All we knew was drive, drive, drive." It was, said D.J., like being in a fog.

On Saturday night the whole troupe watched the third *Stage Show* appearance, when Elvis for the first time sang not only "Heartbreak Hotel" but his newly recorded version of "Blue Suede Shoes." The performance of "Heartbreak Hotel" was something of a disaster, with Scotty and Bill hidden away in the shadows, the Dorsey brothers' orchestra contributing an arrhythmic arrangement that Elvis was unable to move or cue, and Charlie Shavers taking a trumpet solo that left the singer with a sickly smile on his lips.

With the exception of the Carter Sisters, the troupe was probably not unhappy to see the young phenom fall on his face. There was a considerable amount of envy already over the attention that Elvis had been getting not just from audiences but from the Colonel himself, who was clearly focusing almost all of his energies and interest on his new acquisition. To Justin Tubb, who had grown up in the business and at twenty had already had three country hits and was a member of the Opry in his own right, everything about the tour was different right from the start. "The audiences were a lot younger, and it was the first time I'd ever seen them start screaming and waving their arms and hollering. You know, country singers and pickers had always been [considered] almost second class, pop musicians looked down on us. The kind of feeling you got was that here was somebody who was kind of using country music to get going, and yet he would go out and do his rockabilly stuff, his real raunchy stuff, and that's what the girls wanted to hear.

"I'm sure there was some real — not jealousy, but envy, because he was happening and you could feel it. Not only in the audiences but in the importance of 'Heartbreak Hotel' just being released and RCA buying his deal and him flying to New York to do the TV show and our all sitting there watching him.

"He was like a diamond in the rough. When he walked offstage, he would be just soaked, just dripping. He worked hard, and he put everything he had into it, and everything he did worked, because the audience just didn't care — we had never seen anything like it before. My feeling was that they didn't capture him on the television show — of course we had already seen him in action, and it could have been envy, but he seemed a little reserved from what we had seen, he seemed a little nervous, they didn't seem to get his magnetism or charisma."

The tour continued. Elvis and Scotty and Bill kept pretty much to themselves, according to Justin. "Elvis always stood in the wings and watched everybody, especially the Louvins, he was a *fan*." Once in a while he would go out to eat with the others, but Red West, who was doing most of the driving, and D.J. were the ones who were more likely to be hanging out. At the end of the second week, Elvis and his three band members flew back to New York from Winston-Salem, North Carolina, to play the TV show with borrowed instruments, while Red loaded up theirs on a little trailer cart that Vernon had had made up and painted pink ("It looked more like a rolling toilet than anything else," said Red in his book, *Elvis: What Happened?*, "[but] the way Elvis' dad went on about that thing, you would have thought it was a goddamned yacht") and took off on the fifteen-hour drive to Tampa. By now the record was finally starting to show some movement. It was just about to debut on the pop charts and had been steadily gaining attention in *Billboard*, particularly in its country and western "Best Buys" column, which declared that sales had "snowballed rapidly in the past two weeks, with pop and r.&b. customers joining Presley's hillbilly fans in demanding the disk." Perhaps as a result of this new flurry of activity, Jackie Gleason Enterprises had picked up the option on Presley's contract and scheduled two more appearances on *Stage Show* for the end of March at the agreed-upon $1,250 each.

Meanwhile on the tour things had already reached something of a boiling point. A few days before that fourth Dorsey appearance, in Wilson, North Carolina, the promoter oversold the show, and the Colonel told the troupe they would have to work a second one at no additional pay that night. Exasperated by Colonel Parker's increasingly peremptory manner (they were beginning to feel as if they were being treated not just as "entertainers," a necessary nuisance in the Colonel's book, but as second-class citizens, little more than stage props on this tour), they banded together and refused to do it. Ira Louvin, who could charitably be described as hot-tempered even under the best of circumstances ("My brother didn't get along with a lot of people," said Charlie Louvin understatedly), went on and on about who did this Presley kid think he was, that no-talent sonofabitch, trying to take over their music — and fuck the Colonel anyway, he was going to go to the Colonel and let him know they weren't going to take this shit anymore.

They had a meeting, with Ira moderating his demands only slightly and Justin Tubb, who had known the Colonel since he was a child (and whose father was as widely respected and loved as anyone in the country music community), making a calmer and more reasoned presentation. But if they thought that Tom Parker was going to be moved by sentiment, or backed into a corner by a unified stand, they had made a serious miscalculation. The Colonel was appalled — *appalled,* he said — that his motives should be questioned in this way. He had heard that Ira was mouthing off and saying, "Fuck the Colonel." "Why did you say that, Iwa?" said Tom Parker in his unmodulated, Elmer Fudd accent. "Why did you say, 'Fuck the Colonel'?" And as for Justin, the Colonel shook his head, the Colonel was surprised at Justin. The Colonel had known Justin's mother, known his father, even given him a little Shetland pony for his birthday when Justin was a small child ("It was old and nearly blind," said Justin, but not to Tom Parker's face), what did Justin mean by coming to him and making these outrageous demands? The Colonel's eyes alternately flashed with fire and filled with tears. As Justin recognized, "he was an old carny, and he grew up the rough, tough way, he was a self-made man — he was brusque, but, I mean, he was the Colonel, I think most of us expected that of him. We didn't bear him any ill will, we just had to make a stand."

In the end the Colonel capitulated — all the performers got paid, and the show went on. But feelings definitely lingered, tempers continued to fester, there was no question in anyone's mind that the Colonel was mad and that Ira Louvin, who sniffed out slights even when there were none, was seething. A couple of days after the incident in Wilson, things came to a head backstage between shows. Elvis was hanging around the dressing room with the Louvins, singing hymns and playing the piano when, in the recollection of Ira's younger brother, Charlie, "Elvis said, 'Boy, this is my favorite music.' Well, Ira walked up and said, 'Why, you white nigger, if that's your favorite music, why don't you do that out yonder? Why do you do that nigger trash out there?' Presley said, 'When I'm out there, I do what they want to hear — when I'm back here, I can do what I want to do.' " Ira flashed and "tried to strangle him," according to Charlie, "and they were very distant from that point on."

In Jacksonville on February 23, Elvis collapsed. He had completed the first night's show at the Gator Bowl and they were loading up the instruments in the parking lot when, in Bill's account, he "fell out cold." They took him to the hospital, where he was kept under observation for a couple of hours and told by a doctor that "I was doing as much work in twenty minutes as the average laborer does in eight hours. He said if I didn't slow up, I'd have to lay off a couple of years." But he checked out of the hospital before morning, because, he told his friends with a wink, the nurses wouldn't give him any rest. And besides, he said to Red, it was all just a stunt to impress Anita Carter. He played the Gator Bowl again that night with undiminished energy and effect. He had no intention of slowing down.

They were back on the Hayride the following week for the first time in a month. A lot had happened in that month, but for Elvis and Scotty and Bill there had been no time to gauge it, and it didn't appear all that different from everything else that had been building and going on for the last year. They did "Heartbreak Hotel" for the first time, said Scotty, "and that damn auditorium down there almost exploded. I mean, it had been wild before that, but it was more like playing down at your local camp, a home folks–type situation. But now they turned into — it was different faces, just a whole other . . . That's the earliest I can remember saying, *What is going on?*"

WITH COLONEL PARKER, LAS VEGAS, APRIL 1956. (JAMES REID)

THE WORLD TURNED
UPSIDE DOWN

THE ELVIS PRESLEY who made his sixth and final appearance on the Dorsey brothers' *Stage Show,* on March 24, 1956, was a far cry from the ill-at-ease, fidgety, almost manic gum-chewing figure who had made his television debut just two months before. He strode out purposefully, leaned into "Money Honey," and just poured it on without ever letting up. Even his hair was different, less obviously greasy, more carefully sculpted, and where in earlier appearances his vocal energies appeared to wax and wane and that moment when he pulled back into the shelter of the little group to do his dance seemed as much an attempt to incite a response from the crowd as to invite one, now he regarded the adoring multitudes with a look of amused — not so much contempt as authority. He took their adulation gratefully as his due . . . and then just poured it on some more. When he announced that he would do one side from his latest record, there were screams from the crowd, and "Heartbreak Hotel" took on a sensuous intensity that was dispelled only when he slipped into the small, childish voice he used to break up Scotty and Bill at unpredictable moments. This time it was little more than an allusion, betrayed by the slightest self-amused smile, before he jauntily went on with the show. And then he was gone, coolly, casually striding off the stage and skipping out again for a deep bow. Elvis, as Jimmy Dorsey had announced at the beginning of the show, was off to Hollywood for a screen test.

The band left that night, driving into a snowstorm but stopping off in Dover, Delaware, to visit Carl Perkins in the hospital where he was recuperating from a bad automobile accident in which his two brothers (who played bass and rhythm guitar in his band) were also seriously injured. His song "Blue Suede Shoes" was competing furiously with "Heartbreak Hotel" in the charts, and he had been on his way to New York to appear on *The Perry Como Show,* opposite the Dorsey brothers, when the accident occurred. Elvis meanwhile remained in New York that evening to complete an interview with *Coronet* magazine reporter Robert Carlton Brown in which he mused on his current success. He called his parents every day, he said, because "my mother is always worried about a wreck, or me getting sick. So I have to let her know, because she's not in real good health anyway, and if she worries too much, it might not be good for her." He had just bought his parents a new house, he informed Brown; as a matter of fact "they moved in Tuesday. It's a ranch-type, seven-room house. Three bedrooms, a den, playroom, it's a pretty nice place." As for his father, "he doesn't do any — he takes care of all my business. In other words, he's much more important to me at home than he is on the job. Because I have so much stuff piling up for me when I'm gone, and if he wasn't there to help, when I got home I wouldn't get a bit of rest. He takes care of everything — you know, any business that pops up, any insurance, or just oodles of things that I could mention." And the Colonel? "I read," said the interviewer, "that Colonel Tom Parker has given you a lot of advice and help. What kind?" "Everything," said Elvis without hesitation. "He's the one guy that really gave me the big breaks . . . I don't think I would have ever been very big with another man. Because he — he's a very smart man."

Bob Neal watched bemusedly from the sidelines, now that he was completely, and formally, out of the picture. On March 15, his own contract with Elvis had run out and as per his November 21 agreement with the Colonel, he chose not to exercise the option. On March 26 the Colonel's new status as "sole and exclusive Advisor, Personal Representative, and Manager in any and all fields of public and private entertainment" was formally ratified and his 25 percent commission reaffirmed at the same time. "I suppose," Neal said to Jerry Hopkins in 1971, "really, in many ways, I — felt that I should try to continue in the picture, but at the same time with the things that I had going in Memphis — with my radio show and the promotions, and we owned a record shop . . . had a big family, kids in school and so forth . . . I decided to more or less let things go." While he was undoubtedly gratified by Elvis' own success, it must have galled Neal nonetheless to see the headlines in the trades week after week and to realize that he could, and perhaps should, have been a part of it. "A WINNAH! Presley Hot as $1 Pistol" was the headline in *Billboard* on March 3.

The hottest artist on the RCA Victor label this week has been none other than the amazing young country warbler, Elvis Presley, who has been on the label for only about two months.

Presley has six hit singles in the company's list of top 25 best sellers, five of which had been previously issued on the Sun label. . . . The coupling of "Heartbreak Hotel" and "I Was the One," cut by Victor, is the label's No. 2 seller, right behind Perry Como's "Juke Box Baby."

By the end of March the single had sold close to a million copies and, in an unprecedented achievement (mirrored only by Carl Perkins' "Blue Suede Shoes" at virtually the same time), was closing in on the top of all three charts: pop, country, and rhythm and blues. Moreover, the new album, released on March 13, stood at nearly three hundred thousand sales, making it a sure bet to be RCA's first million-dollar (at $3.98 retail) album, and the EP containing "Blue Suede Shoes," which RCA had released on the same date as the LP and which was also simply entitled *Elvis Presley* without any additional credit or qualification (as per the Colonel's instructions, neither musicians nor recording supervisors were named), had already started up the charts itself. Steve Sholes, as another *Billboard* headline trumpeted a few weeks later, was definitely having the last laugh.

O N SUNDAY, MARCH 25, after a few hours' sleep, Elvis flew out to the West Coast. He was scheduled to appear on *The Milton Berle Show* the following Tuesday, and his screen test with producer Hal Wallis had been hurriedly set up for the week in between. Wallis, a fifty-six-year-old veteran of the movie business who had made such well-known pictures as *The Maltese Falcon, Casablanca, Yankee Doodle Dandy,* and *The Rose Tattoo* and currently had N. Richard Nash's play *The Rainmaker* in preproduction, had first heard about Presley at the beginning of February from his partner in New York, Joseph Hazen. Hazen's sister-in-law, Harriet Ames, one of the seven wealthy Annenberg sisters, was a "television addict" who happened to be watching the Dorsey show. She called Hazen, who lived across the street from her at 885 Park Avenue, "and I called my partner in California," Hazen remembered. "I said, 'Turn on the television and look at the show. This kid is terrific.'"

Wallis was impressed, he later wrote, with Presley's "originality," but he was probably more impressed with the sales figures and the stir he was creating (not to mention the clear potential to tap into the new youth market, which was crying for a successor to the late Jimmy Dean), factors that were pointed out to him forcefully by Abe Lastfogel of William Morris. The screen test was scheduled to coincide with the Berle appearance, and the Colonel waved off any RCA efforts to set up press or radio promotion for the West Coast trip until all the details with Wallis were nailed down. From Anne Fulchino's point of view, "That's when we really lost control. I remember the Colonel came up to me [just before he went out to Hollywood], and he put his arms around me, and I smelled a rat right away. He said, 'You know, I want to apologize to you for what I did in Jacksonville [this was the incident that took place with Chick Crumpacker on the RCA Country Caravan two years before].' Boy, did I smell a rat then, because he never apologized, even if he was dead wrong, so now I *knew* something was coming. And he said to me, 'You did a tremendous job on Elvis. But,' he said, 'now you can rest.' "

Although Elvis himself had made it plain to the Colonel that he had little interest in just "singing in the movies" — if he was going to do anything in the pictures, he wanted to be a movie *star,* a serious actor like Brando, Dean, Richard Widmark, Rod Steiger — the screen test that he took consisted of two parts. In the first he was given what looked like a toy guitar and told to mime a performance to his recording of "Blue Suede Shoes." The idea, according to screenwriter Allan Weiss, who was present for the test and cued up the record as a then-member of the sound department, was to see if the "indefinable energy" that had showed up on television would translate to film.

There was never any doubt, wrote Weiss, as Presley stepped in front of the camera:

> The transformation was incredible . . . electricity bounced off the walls of the soundstage. One felt it as an awesome thing — like an earthquake in progress, only without the implicit threat. Watching this insecure country boy, who apologized when he asked for a rehearsal as though he had done something wrong, turn into absolute dynamite when he stepped into the bright lights and started lip-synching the words of his familiar hit. He believed in it, and he

made you believe it, no matter how "sophisticated" your musical tastes were. . . .

The number was completed in two takes, and they moved in for close-ups. He protested mildly that he hadn't been "dead-on" in a couple of places. It was explained that the closer shots would be inter-cut to cover it. I don't think he understood, but with characteristic trust, he did what he was told. No stand-in was provided, and he stood uncomplainingly while the lights were being adjusted — bathed in perspiration.

Then he did two scenes from *The Rainmaker,* a period comedy-drama set in Kansas in 1913 that was scheduled to start shooting in June with Burt Lancaster starring opposite Katharine Hepburn, in which he played the younger brother, a kind of male ingenue role. "I knew my script," Elvis said proudly later that year. "They sent it to me before I came to Holly-wood . . . and I got out there and just tried to put myself in the place of the character I was playing, just trying to act as naturally as I could." He had never been in a play before; he had never spoken a single line onstage. He came across, wrote Weiss, "with amateurish conviction — like the lead in a high school play," but if he was wooden from lack of dramatic training, that didn't stop him from telling Mr. Wallis that he didn't think the part was right for him when Wallis sat down with him sometime later to dis-cuss his celluloid future. This character was "lovesick, real shy. I mean, he wasn't real shy. Real jolly. Real happy, real jolly, real lovesick. It wasn't like me. . . . Mr. Wallis asked me what kind of a part I'd like to play, and I told him one more like myself, so I wouldn't have to do any excess act-ing." But that wasn't what he meant exactly. When the producer laughed, the boy just grinned and let it go, because he couldn't say what he really meant: he couldn't say that he *knew* he could do it, it would be like saying that he knew he could fly. And while he might never have been in a high school play, he had imagined himself up on the screen, he had studied the movies, he studied the actors — the way they presented themselves, the way they cocked their heads, the way they won the audience's sympathy. He had imagined himself a singing star, and it had come true — so why not this, too?

Wallis for his part was struck by the young man's polite, well-mannered demeanor. After dealing with Jerry Lewis for seven years, it would come as a relief to work with such a tractable, essentially malleable young man. And Wallis and the Colonel (whom Wallis found "as fascinating as Elvis" in his own right) were both well aware of the long and profitable tradition by which virtually every popular male singing star, from Rudy Vallee to Bing Crosby to Frank Sinatra, ended up in Hollywood and, if he was lucky, was transformed into a movie star. This rock 'n' roll might not last, but the boy was a real phenomenon, and if he was able — like Crosby and Sinatra before him — to turn that magnetism into the warmth of the all-around entertainer, then they would be able to make a lot of money together.

He and the Colonel quickly came to an understanding that would be formalized over the next few weeks in what Wallis characterized — accurately or flatteringly, it would be impossible to say — as "one of the toughest bargaining sessions of my career." It was a one-picture deal with options for six more, with the first picture paying just $15,000, the second $20,000, and the sum gradually escalating to $100,000 for the last. The Colonel reserved the right to make one picture each year with another studio, though that picture could be preempted by Wallis for a comparable fee. It was by no stretch of the imagination (except a studio PR man's) a blockbuster deal, but at its heart was the Colonel's fixed determination to sign with a legitimate filmmaker and, above all, to keep his options open, a strategy based as much upon his belief in his boy's unlimited potential as upon his confidence that every deal could be improved once you got in the door.

There was no time to savor the triumph. Elvis was due in San Diego for the Berle show, which was scheduled to be broadcast on April 3 from the deck of the U.S.S. *Hancock,* docked at the San Diego naval station. *The Milton Berle Show* was a definite step up from the Dorseys. Milton Berle, the original "Mr. Television," was still a major star and had booked Presley only as a favor to his agent, Abe Lastfogel. Berle met Elvis and the Colonel for the first time at the airport. "I sat in the middle and Colonel Parker was on the other side and Elvis was on my right. So I said, 'Oh, here's the contract for the show,' and I was about to hand it to Elvis when Colonel Parker grabbed it, says, 'Don't show that boy that contract!' So Elvis didn't know what he was getting. Colonel Parker held a hard hand!"

They went directly to rehearsal, where Scotty and Bill and D.J. met them, having just rolled into town themselves after an arduous cross-country trek. D.J. was thrilled at the presence of the great drummer Buddy Rich, a member of the Harry James Orchestra, but Rich did not return the compliment. The musicians all sniffed when Elvis did not produce any charts, and when he launched into "Blue Suede Shoes," Rich rolled his eyes at Harry James and said, audibly, "This is the worst."

The show itself was one more unmitigated triumph. It was a windy day, and flags were flying in the breeze, with the ocean as backdrop and an audience that was as good-natured as it was enthusiastic. Elvis opened with "Heartbreak Hotel," naturally, after an elaborate introduction by Berle, who came out onstage dressed in an admiral's uniform with plenty of gold braid. The performer that television viewers saw appeared in yet another stage of radical metamorphosis, more self-assured by half, more in command of his look and style than he had been just ten days before — but it is the stark visual imagery that sets off his performance most, as he stands, all in black save for white tie, white belt, and white bucks, legs spread wide apart and at a point of hitherto-unremarked stillness, just inviting the crowd to come to *him*.

They did. The song was greeted by an audience made up predominantly of sailors and their dates with an appropriate mixture of screams and laughter — because it is clear by now that the performer is playing with them. It may not be as clear to the little girls, but there is no aggression in this act, he is teasing them, fooling with them, his laughter is their laughter, for the first time in his life he is one of them. He then introduced "my latest release, 'Blue Schwede Shoes,'" and launched into the song in a loose, carefree manner that far surpassed any of his previous televised efforts. The crowd was with him all the way, and when he went into the repeated, almost mantra-like coda, Bill got on the bass and rode it for all it was worth, hands up in the air, legs sticking out, and whooping as the crowd whooped happily back. It was a moment, a picture, a perfectly lit snapshot, that the Colonel vowed was never going to be repeated: Bill Black was never going to take attention away from his boy again.

Next was a comedy sketch with Berle in which the comedian came out dressed identically to his guest star, only with his pants rolled up and looking like a rube in oversize blue suede shoes. He was, he declared in the broadest Catskills cornpone accent, Elvis' twin brother, Melvin, who had taught Elvis everything he knew. They played with that for a while, with Elvis declaring, "I owe it all to you, Melvin," and then they went into a reprise of "Blue Suede Shoes," which Elvis flung himself into as good-naturedly as he had the earlier rendition, while Berle pranced about the stage and did a limber send-up of his enthusiastic young friend. It would have been hard to detect any sign of resentment, if resentment existed, on the part of "America's newest singing sensation," whether because Berle was spoofing his act or because of the twin-brother routine; it was all just show business, after all — Gladys was probably laughing at home with some of the cousins and Grandma Minnie. They had always enjoyed Uncle Miltie, ever since they got their first television set; he was, of course, a very important and powerful figure in the business, said Colonel Parker, and Elvis should never forget, Mr. Berle was doing them a favor by having him on the show.

There was an appearance the next day at a San Diego record shop and a riot the next night at the conclusion of the first of two appearances at the San Diego Arena. At one point Elvis had to admonish the crowd mildly to "sit down or the show ends," and the girls went back to their seats, but the musicians couldn't get out of the building for a full forty-five minutes after the show was over, and Elvis sat around backstage with some local musicians, talking about the Hayride and his rapid rise to fame. "The crowd was too noisy for most of the numbers to be heard," sniffed the San Diego paper, which noted that his brief appearance followed "a woman vocalist, an acrobatic dance team, a comedian, and a xylophone player," a far cry from the all-star country packages on which he had been appearing. "I changed my whole style," said Glen Glenn, a twenty-one-year-old committed country singer from just outside Los Angeles who had driven down for the show with his guitar player and was introduced backstage by bass player Fred Maddox of the Maddox Brothers and Rose. "We all wanted to be like Elvis after that."

There was no stopping the juggernaut now. Elvis had made his last regular Hayride appearance on Saturday, March 31, flying in from Hollywood in the midst of the Hal Wallis negotiations. The Colonel had extricated Elvis from his contract by paying a penalty of ten thousand dollars and promising that he would do a benefit concert in December for free. The Sunday after the Berle show they played Denver, then flew to Texas for the start of a two-week tour that would be interrupted by a recording session on Saturday, April 14. It had reached the point where no one even knew any longer what day it was; they drove through the night because it was impossible to get to sleep until 9:00 or 10:00 in the morning anyway, Elvis said, he was just too keyed up. There were girls everywhere; more time was spent hiding from them than looking for them. There was, of course, at least one call a day home. He had yet to spend a single night in the new house on Audubon Drive.

Everywhere he went, everyone wanted to know everything about him. They wanted to know how he got started in the business. They wanted to know about his mother and father. They wanted to know about the movies, naturally. He deflected every question with that unique combination of deference and candor. He answered every question with the truth. Yes, he was very excited about his Hollywood contract, it was a dream come true, it just showed that you could never tell what was going to happen to you in your life — but no, he wasn't going to sing in the movies. No, he didn't have any special girl, he had thought he had been in love, he had been in love once, in fact it was only when he started singing that they broke up. He still heard from her, she wrote to him sometimes. Did he still go to church? "I haven't since I been singing, 'cause Saturday night is usually our biggest night, and almost every Sunday we have a matinee or we're on the road . . ." Are you taking good care of yourself? There are rumors that you've been carousing around and don't really know where you're going. "Well, that's about the truth. It really is. I can't deny it, because half the time I — I don't know from one day to the next where I'm going. I have so much on my mind, in other words, I'm trying to keep with everything, trying to keep a level head. . . . You have to be careful out in the world. It's so easy to get turned." And what did he like best about being so successful, aside from the money? "I would say the money in a way, of course that, like you said, is the biggest part, but actually the thing I like about it better is to know that people like — that you've got so many friends."

It was hard work — and it never let up. But no matter how hard he worked, he didn't work any harder than the Colonel. Colonel was up at 5:30 every morning when they were just getting in, and he was there until the last ticket was counted, the last picture sold. He was in everybody's face, it seemed, he didn't let a promoter get away with a single unsold ticket, and he was always on Scotty and Bill about something they had or hadn't done onstage. "He was working for Elvis, period," said D.J., more of a disinterested observer than either of the other two. "He didn't care what you did. That's all he knew, twenty-four hours a day, Elvis. That was his boy." Sometimes, it seemed, Elvis would test the Colonel — he would arrive late for one show after another and then, said D.J., when the Colonel was ready to jump down all their throats, "he'd say, 'Don't you worry about the Colonel. I'll take care of it.' And then the Colonel would

jump us and say, 'Hey, you guys have got to get here a little bit earlier.'
And we'd say, 'You tell *him*,' and that was the end of it. I think he done it
just to make the Colonel mad sometimes."

Scotty and Bill knew the Colonel would just as soon cut their throats
as look at them. They'd be gone in a minute, they both agreed, if it was up
to the Colonel; he had long ago made that plain. They never really
brought it up directly with Elvis, though — they knew Elvis would never
consider anything that would change his music, and they doubted that
Colonel would ever push him on this point. It was clear what happened if
anyone pushed Colonel. Red had had a blowup with the Colonel, and it
didn't escape anyone's attention that Red was gone, at least for this tour.
In Red's account Elvis had been with a girl, and he wouldn't get out of
bed with her.

> When he finally emerged, he looked like he had been mixed up with
> an eggbeater. . . . Well, we're really late now. It's winter time, and it's
> sleeting and raining colder than hell. We jump in the car, I drive like a
> madman through snow and everything to Virginia to this audito-
> rium. . . . We arrive there, I guess we're fifteen minutes late, or some-
> thing like that. Now it's still snowing like hell, but out in front of the
> auditorium I see this crazy guy in a T-shirt. I get out of the car, and I
> notice he is puffing on this cigar, and he has got an expression on his
> face like he is going to kill me . . . kill *me*, not Elvis. Then I notice that,
> despite the fact he is wearing a T-shirt in this damn snow, he is so
> worked up he is sweating. . . . He just looks at me as if he was going
> to rip a yard from my ass. Right away he starts in, "Where in the hell
> you been? Do you know what time it is? I got these people waiting,
> and you're damn well late. You can't keep people waiting. Who do
> you think you are?"

There was little room for sentiment in the new order of things. The
business was changing, the mood was changing, and the show was necessarily changing, too. The crowds were so frenzied by now that you could
no longer hear the music. The screams that started up from the moment
they took the stage, the tortuous faces and blinding tears — Scotty and
Bill watched it all with something like disbelief, playing as loud as they
could while all they could hear over the din was the occasional sound of
D.J.'s drums. "We were the only band in history," Scotty frequently

joked, "that was directed by an ass. It was like being in a sea of sound." It was true, but as intently as they watched him, they could never really tell what he was going to do next. "I'll bet I could burp," said Elvis impishly, "and make them squeal." And then he burped and did.

They chartered a plane out of Amarillo in the middle of the night so that they could get to Nashville in time for the recording session at 9:00 the following morning. Just before dawn they got lost and landed at an airstrip outside of El Dorado, Arkansas, to refuel. It was chilly, and the musicians huddled together in the little coffee shop, yawning and making desultory conversation. It was just light when they took off again. Scotty was sitting beside the pilot, who asked him to hold the wheel for a minute while he studied the map. Just as Scotty took the wheel, the engine coughed and died and the plane started to lose altitude. There was a good deal of confusion, and Bill pulled his coat over his head and cursed the day he had ever let himself be persuaded to go up in this rickety machine, before the pilot discovered that when they refueled they hadn't switched over to the full tank and the airstrip attendant hadn't bothered to refill the empty one. When they finally got to Nashville, Elvis announced half-jokingly, "Man, I don't know if I'll ever fly again."

The session reflected the edginess of everyone's mood. They worked from 9:00 till 12:00, did close to twenty takes of a single song, and ended up with only that one song, a ballad called "I Want You, I Need You, I Love You" that Steve Sholes had come up with for the date. Once again the backup singers were the same mismatched trio that had been assembled for the first Nashville session: Ben and Brock Speer of the Speer Family, and Gordon Stoker of the Jordanaires. Where were the other boys? Elvis asked Stoker during a break. He had played with the Jordanaires in Atlanta just a month before, on the same bill with country comedian Rod Brasfield, Mississippi Slim's cousin, and his brother, Uncle Cyp, and they had made plans to get together in the studio sometime soon. This gave Stoker, who was fuming over the other Jordanaires' exclusion, just the chance he needed. "It was the worst sound on any of Elvis' records. It was a strained sound and a very bad sound. We didn't have a full quartet. Chet didn't even honor Elvis enough to get him a full quartet. Brock was a bass singer, a real low bass singer, and Ben is middle-of-the-road, and here I am first tenor. Elvis was not knocked out by it. He was extremely courteous about it and tactful in everything he said, but he knew exactly what he wanted. So I let him know that I was the only one of the Jordanaires that was asked. Elvis never really had much time for chatting, and that could have been one reason he never had any time to chat after that. But he asked me, 'Can the Jordanaires work with me [from now on]?' And I said, 'We sure can. We'll be there!' "

Steve Sholes was practically beside himself when he heard how the session had gone. He had told the Colonel, how many times had he told the Colonel, he had told Tom over and over again that more preparation time was needed, RCA had a schedule to maintain, he was under increasing pressure to have the second album ready by April 15 for scheduled fall release. "I know you have Elvis on a heavy personal appearance program and I certainly can't blame you," he had written back in February, "but the main purpose of this letter is to point out that we still must get a number of additional recordings from Elvis in the near future." They had gotten not a single one in the intervening months, and now here it was mid April and Tom was still not listening, it was obvious that the boy was not listening (if he was even capable of listening), and Sholes wondered more and more if Nashville was the right place to even try to record him. Chet was his protégé, he had made Chet his Nashville a&r man, but it was obvious that Chet and the boy were not hitting it off at all; he could tell from Chet's noncommittal report, not to mention the fact that they had gotten only the one song, that something was wrong. He waited a couple of weeks, then fired off yet another letter to Tom, complaining once again that attention should be turned to the recordings — but it was like trying to stop a runaway train. At the Nashville session Elvis had been presented with a gold record for "Heartbreak Hotel," and the album had already sold more than 362,000 copies: Sholes was being strangled by his own success.

The session might have continued if there had been a better feeling to it, but Elvis and the boys were anxious to get home for a few hours after being away so long, and Chet just had the one three-hour slot booked anyway. They took their chartered plane back to Memphis that afternoon and on the way ran into some turbulence. This time, Scotty said, "Bill's going berserk. He's scared to death, really he would have jumped out of the plane if he could have. Elvis said, 'Just hang on, Bill, when we get to Memphis we're turning this thing loose.' Then we caught a commercial flight to wherever we had to be the next day."

They continued their Texas tour: San Antonio, Amarillo, Corpus Christi, and Waco, where Elvis gave a brief interview on Tuesday night, shortly before going onstage, to *Waco News-Tribune* reporter Bea

Ramirez. "What do you want to know about me, honey?" he said as he stared out at the four thousand screaming teenagers from backstage, "half scared," wrote Ramirez, "and half unbelieving.

"Elvis, have you any idea just what it was that started the girls going crazy over you?"

"No, I don't. I guess it's just something God gave me. I believe that, you know. Know what I mean, honey? And I'm grateful. Only I'm afraid. I'm afraid I'll go out like a light, just like I came on. Know what I mean, honey?"

Presley has a way with that "honey" business. When he talks, he looks straight ahead, or sort of dreamy like in no direction at all. Then he turns with that "know what I mean, honey?" His face is close, real close. Right in your face — almost. . . .

"Elvis, I hear you walk in your sleep."

"Well, I have nightmares."

"What kind?"

"I dream I'm about to fight somebody or about to be in a car wreck or that I'm breaking things. Know what I mean, honey?" (I don't have any idea what he means.)

"Where are you from?"

"From Memphis, Tennessee."

"Oh yes, that's where all the hillbilly singers come from, isn't it?"

"Maybe so, but I'm no hillbilly singer."

"Well, have you typed yourself, I mean your type of singing?"

"No, I don't dare."

"Why?"

"Cause I'm scared, know what I mean, honey? Real scared."

"What of?"

"I don't know . . . I don't know. Know what I mean, honey?"

At this point I thanked him for his time and started to make a beeline for the door. He grabbed my hand, sat there looking sleepy-eyed into my face and fanned his long lashes while he said:

"Write me up good, will you, honey?"

On Saturday night, April 21, they played two shows at the City Auditorium in Houston. At the end of the first show, when the crowd wouldn't leave, Elvis left the predominantly female audience with the thought that "it's been a wonderful show, folks. Just remember this. Don't go milking the cow on a rainy day. If there's lightning, you may be left holding the bag." As the *Houston Chronicle* reported, "Four thousand females just died." After the show, with the first open date in weeks in front of them. Scotty and Elvis and Bill headed for the Club El Dorado across town, where blues singer Lowell Fulson was headlining. Fulson, who had had a big hit the previous year with "Reconsider Baby," was a regular at the Club Handy and the Hippodrome in Memphis and a big favorite of Dewey Phillips'. During the break Scotty introduced himself and Elvis, and Fulson called them up onstage for a couple of numbers during the next set. For Scotty it was a highly memorable experience. "I remember me and Lowell standing up toe to toe, getting down on some blues." One of those, recalled Lowell, was Big Joe Turner's "Shake, Rattle and Roll." "I don't know what the other one was. Anyway, Elvis sounded good, and the house accepted it, so he [Scotty] said, 'What do you think of him, what do you think of the boy?' I said, 'Well, one thing, he's a pretty boy, and the women will make him. He won't have to work too hard.' He got a big bang out of that. He laughed for a good while."

On the next day, a Sunday, they boarded a flight to Las Vegas.

T HE LAS VEGAS BOOKING appears to have come about as something of a last-minute arrangement, since there were no advance notices in the trades. Elvis was booked in for the first two weeks of a four-week Freddy Martin engagement in the thousand-seat Venus Room, at the New Frontier Hotel, at $7,500 a week, which the Colonel was said to have demanded in cash because, as he told *Time* magazine, "no check is good. They got an atom-bomb testing place out there in the desert. What if some feller pressed the wrong button?" Bill Randle, the Cleveland DJ who had remained in the picture up to this time (Steve Sholes pointed out to the Colonel in March what a great job Randle was doing for them, to which the Colonel responded somewhat acerbically that he had eyes of his own), occasionally claimed credit for setting up the contract, and he may well have had a hand in it, but the Colonel had his own contacts, and even with so little lead time the Colonel left nothing to chance. When Elvis arrived in Las Vegas, there was a twenty-four-foot-high cutout of Elvis Presley standing out in front of the hotel beside the casino entrance — it was the same action photograph, taken in Florida in the summer of 1955, that graced the cover not only of his first album but of the song folio and any number of additional publicity items. His name was up on the marquee, just below comedian Shecky Greene's, as "Extra Added Attraction Elvis Presley," and in the print ads as "The Atomic Powered Singer."

It was the first sit-down gig of his career. As fellow promoter Gabe Tucker wrote, even the Colonel appeared to be taken in by this newfound elevation in status, which followed statements to his colleagues that he needed to find a whole new kind of venue for his act suitable to Elvis' phenomenal success. Bandleader Freddy Martin, who specialized in pop arrangements of the classics (he started with Tchaikovsky but branched out to Grieg, Rimsky-Korsakov, movie themes, and Khachaturian as well), had been enjoying hits consistently since 1933 and featured a $40,000 floor show, including a seventeen-piece orchestra, twenty-eight singers, twin pianos, dancers, ice skaters, and selections from *Oklahoma!* On opening night, New Frontier vice president T. W. Richardson, who according to Gabe Tucker had first heard Elvis in his hometown of Biloxi and contacted the Colonel about the booking the month before, invited a bunch of friends up from Houston to catch the show. Elvis was the closing act, and as the Freddy Martin Orchestra played their arrangement of "Rock Around the Clock," the curtain rose to reveal a very nervous, very out-of-place hillbilly quartet. Scotty and D.J. and Bill were all wearing light-colored sports jackets, dress pants, bow ties, and white shirts, while Elvis was dressed neatly in loafers, dress pants, and black bow tie, with a light-colored, western-cut checked sports jacket with a dark-cowled collar. From the opening notes of the song that he introduced as "Heartburn Motel" to his stammered attempts to thank Freddy Martin for the nice introduction, you could hear a pin drop. When Elvis started singing, Tucker related, one of Richardson's guests "jumped up from their ringside table and shouted, 'Goddamn it, shit! What is all this yelling and screaming? I can't take this, let's go to the tables and gamble.'"

"For the first time in months we could hear ourselves when we played out of tune," said Bill Black plaintively. "After the show our nerves were pretty frayed, and we would get together in pairs and talk about whoever wasn't around to defend himself." "They weren't my kind of audience," said Elvis. "It was strictly an adult audience. The first night especially I was absolutely scared stiff [but] afterwards I got a little more relaxed and I finally got 'em on my side." "We didn't even know we were failures," said Scotty, but after that night, reported *Billboard,* they no longer closed the show.

Nonetheless he persisted. He played out the full two weeks, and as hometown reporter Bob Johnson wrote, "Elvis, who has played hard audiences before, kept right in there busting guitar strings and shaking his legs and the rafters. . . . And the ice began to break." Bill Randle, who viewed the engagement almost as a social "embarrassment," had arranged to have some of the performances filmed, and Hal Wallis showed up to check out his investment. Judy Spreckels, the attractive twenty-four-year-old divorced sixth wife of sugar king Adolph Spreckels II, whom Elvis had met briefly in California, showed up and served as his "secretary" and aide-de-camp. Curiosity-seeking celebrities like Ray Bolger, Phil Silvers, and Liberace were prominent in the audience, and there is even a film of Elvis and Liberace clowning it up for the cameras. Liberace, one of his mother's favorite performers (Elvis made sure to get the flamboyant showman's autograph), is pretending to play Scotty's guitar, while Elvis flings himself into it, throwing his head back and laughing easily as he sings, perhaps, "Blue Suede Shoes." Not about to be upstaged, Liberace draws a square in the air, pointing at his brother George. It is, in many ways, a picture of perfect innocence.

They played what Elvis calculated to be twenty-eight twelve-minute shows (two shows a night, at 8:00 and midnight, for fourteen nights), and the rest of the time he was free to do as he liked. He and his cousin Gene, whom he described as his "utility man" and who had replaced Red on this tour, rode the Dodgem cars at the local amusement park almost every day, and in two weeks Elvis estimated that he spent more than a hundred dollars on rides for himself and his friends. He lounged around at poolside, flirted with the girls, went to the movies, caught as many acts as he could, stayed up all night long, and if he felt any doubts he kept them to himself. "One thing about Las Vegas pleased Elvis," wrote Johnson, who went out to report on the event, "it never goes to sleep. He had company during those long night hours, and night had become like day to him." It was like being in a city where you played dress-up all the time. Every time he entered a room he created a stir, the showgirls fawned on him, you never knew what was going to happen next. But he didn't drink, he didn't gamble ("It don't appeal to me," he said, explaining why he "never dropped a nickel in a slot machine"); whatever he was doing, whether it was what his mother had raised him to do or not, he wasn't hurting anybody. One time he missed an appointment with United Press reporter Aline Mosby because he was at the movies, a Randolph Scott western, but he made it up to her. He saw the Four Lads again and met former teen sensation Johnny Ray for the first time (both were discoveries of Bill Randle's; Elvis had met the Four Lads at the Cleveland show that Randle had filmed). He caught a little bit of Liberace's show at the Riviera, and he went back again and again to catch the lounge act at the Sands, Freddie Bell and the Bellboys.

The Bellboys, a highly visual act who provided both action and comic relief, had had a minor hit the previous year with a song that had been a huge rhythm and blues success for Duke/Peacock artist Big Mama Thornton in 1953. "Hound Dog" had been written by two white teenagers, Jerry Leiber and Mike Stoller, who specialized in rhythm and blues, and was a very odd choice for a male performer, since it was written from a female point of view. Nonetheless, it was the showstopper of Bell's act, even retaining some of the original's rhumba-flavored beat, and it sparked a determination on Elvis' part to incorporate it into his own show. "We stole it straight from them," said Scotty. "He already knew it, knew the song, but when we seen those guys do it, he said, 'There's a natural.' We never did it in Las Vegas, but we were just looking on it as comic relief, if you will, just another number to do onstage."

On the first Saturday of the engagement the New Frontier scheduled a teenage matinee especially for Elvis Presley fans. Proceeds from the show were to go toward lights for a youth baseball park, and finally there was some semblance of Elvis Presley normality. "The carnage was terrific," wrote Bob Johnson in a story that was headlined "The Golden Boy Reaches for a Star While the Music Goes Round and Round and—": "They pushed and shoved to get into the 1000-seat room, and several hundred thwarted youngsters buzzed like angry hornets outside. After the show, bedlam! A laughing, shouting, idolatrous mob swarmed him. . . . They got his shirt, and it was shredded. A triumphant girl seized a button, clutched it as tho it were a diamond."

They played out the rest of the engagement with increasing confidence. Mr. Martin was more respectful, even if he retained a little bit of a tongue-in-cheek attitude toward the whole thing. "We should have five minutes' silence now," he announced after Elvis' act. "Makes me wonder if I've been wasting my time for the last twenty years." One of the casino owners, Mr. Frank Williams of Osceola, Arkansas, gave him an eight-hundred-dollar watch with diamonds for the numbers, and Elvis reciprocated with half a dozen letters of thanks. Even the Colonel, who was initially discomfited by what amounted to the first misstep in a series of otherwise perfectly calculated moves, seemed finally to have come to terms with the value of the experience. In Scotty's view, "I think in one sense it was good, because it was completely different. That's what's funny about Vegas. People that were there, if you'd lifted them out and taken them over to San Antonio, the big coliseum, they'd have been going crazy. It's just a different atmosphere. But we had a ball out there. We really did."

On the last night, which was recorded by a member of the audience and released by RCA twenty-five years later, Elvis still sounds nervous, self-conscious, glad to be done with it all — but aware that he has carried it off. "Thank you very much, ladies and gentlemen," he says as the polite applause dies down. "I would like to tell you, it's really been a pleasure being in Las Vegas. This makes our second week here, and tonight's our last night, and we've had a pretty hard time — stay . . . ah, had a pretty good time while we were here." He introduces "Blue Suede Shoes" by saying, "This song here is called, 'Get out of the stables, Grandma, you're too old to be horsing around,'" and when that doesn't get much of a laugh he turns to the orchestra leader and says, "Do you know that song, Mr. Martin? You do? You know that one about 'Take back my golden garter, my leg is turning green'?" When Martin calls him back graciously for an encore, he says, "Thank you, friends, I was coming back anyway."

"Like a jug of corn liquor at a champagne party," declared *Newsweek*. "Elvis Presley, coming in on a wing of advance hoopla, doesn't hit the mark here," reported *Variety*. *Life* headlined its April 30 story "A Howling Hillbilly Success." Any publicity, said the Colonel, was good publicity. "Heartbreak Hotel" was at number one; "I Want You, I Need You, I Love You" had just been released to advance sales of 300,000; RCA Victor reported that Elvis Presley's records accounted for half of their pop sales; and he was going home to the new house he had been able to purchase with his earnings for himself and his parents. They could write whatever they liked, there was no stopping him now. He really believed that.

He was back in Memphis two days later and stopped by the newspaper office on Tuesday night. "Man, I really like Vegas," he announced. "I'm going back there the first chance I get." He was nettled at a report that a Halifax radio station had given all of its Elvis Presley records away

MARCH–MAY 1956 ∾ 275

in hopes that it would hear no more. "I didn't know that there were any radio stations in Nova Scotia" was his first reaction, reported the newspaper. "The more they try to ban the stuff, man, the more they'll have to listen to. I mean, man, a lot of people like it, man, it's really hot right now." Then he reminisced about his start in the business just two short years ago. "I was strumming the guitar in Mississippi before I ever came to Memphis," he said. "My father bought one for $12 — it was the best investment he ever made." And then he was off into the night in his "Kelly green frontiersman shirt, black trousers and doeskin loafers," whether on his Harley motorcycle, one of his three Cadillacs, or the three-wheeled German Messerschmidt he had recently purchased, the paper didn't report. He was going to be headlining the big Cotton Carnival bill at Ellis Auditorium one week from tonight, and he had gigs booked in Minnesota and Wisconsin starting on the weekend, but for now he was just going to ride around town.

RUSSWOOD PARK, JULY 4, 1956. (ROBERT WILLIAMS)

"THOSE PEOPLE IN NEW YORK ARE NOT GONNA CHANGE ME NONE"

FOR HIS MAY 15 APPEARANCE on opening night of Memphis' twenty-second annual Cotton Carnival, in which a king and queen were crowned and a midway set up on Front Street, both sides of Ellis Auditorium were opened up for a performance for the first time since Liberace had played the hall. The show was scheduled to begin as close to 7:30 as possible but had to await the landing of the Royal Barge at the foot of Monroe, where the reigning monarchs were to take part in opening ceremonies before traveling to the nearby auditorium to signal the start of the show. Bob Neal was master of ceremonies, and Hank Snow and the Jordanaires were featured, while Eddie Fisher appeared on the Royal Barge and the Carter Sisters, George Morgan, and a host of other country stars were headlining an all-star event at the festival tent on the midway. There was little question, though, that the hometown boy was the focus of this "new and open-to-the-public feature of the Carnival season [that] helps add excitement to its opening night." Country comedian Minnie Pearl flew in for the occasion at the urging of her husband, Henry Cannon, a charter pilot who had recently been flying Elvis all around the country and who had flown him in from La Crosse, Wisconsin, early that morning. "Henry introduced me to him, and he was such a nice man. I always kidded him that he treated me like an old-maid schoolteacher, he was so overly polite — but he always was."

For Elvis, though, this homecoming was a chance to prove himself. " 'More than anything else,' " he had told the *Press-Scimitar*'s Bob Johnson earnestly in Las Vegas just two weeks before, " 'I want the folks back home to think right of me. Just because I managed to do a little something, I don't want anyone back home to think I got the big head.' He wants almost desperately," added Johnson, perhaps not really needing to, "to be thought well of at home."

He arrived accompanied by a police escort to find the usual waiting throng in front of the auditorium. One girl said, "I grabbed his hand, and he grinned and he said, 'Cut me loose,' so I cut him loose. It was heavenly." Vernon and Gladys were already present, seated in a box above the stage on the north side of the hall, eagerly anticipating their first opportunity in some months to see their son perform. In his role as MC Bob Neal whipped up the crowd with sly references to Elvis' upcoming appearance, and one time he even put the spotlight on Elvis' mother and dad, who smiled nervously and took a polite bow. The other acts had a good deal of trouble trying to figure out how to deal with both sides of the auditorium at once, a problem that Hank Snow solved to no one's satisfaction by singing one song to one side, the next to the other. When Elvis came bounding out, however, in black pants, white shirt, and kelly green jacket, he seemed to give the matter no thought at all but, in the words of one thirteen-year-old spectator, simply "staggered all over the stage. Up until he came out I remember thinking, this is a lousy show," recalled Fred Davis, an eighth-grade student at Messick High School where Elvis, Scotty, and Bill had appeared as part of Sonny Neal's student council campaign the previous year. "Then I'd seen him at Ellis with Carl Perkins in November, and he was all over the stage, riding Bill's bass, popping three or four strings, but there was no climax, it didn't seem really practiced, there were just a few screams. This time it was solid noise from start to finish, there were girls in hysterics, I never heard a word he said. No one rushed the stage, no one stood in the aisle, but the flashbulbs were going from start to finish, and I just remember thinking, 'What have I seen?!' "

He opened with "Heartbreak Motel," introduced "Long Tall Sally" as a song by a friend of his whom he had never met (Little Richard), brought the Jordanaires out for "I Was the One," called out to Scotty to "go wild" on "Money Honey," pretended to burp as he introduced "I Got a Woman," on which Bill joined in with a high-pitched call, introduced "Blue Suede Shoes" to wild applause, and then announced that he would be back in just a few weeks in a benefit performance for the *Press-Scimitar*'s Cynthia Milk Fund. And for anyone who wasn't planning to be there, "just remember this one thing, friends, if you're not there, friends, just remember this one thing . . ." At which point he launched into the opening bars of his final song, the still unrecorded "(You Ain't Nothin' But a) Hound Dog." When he got to the end there was even more wild applause, and he looked back at D.J., repeated slyly, "Ladies and gentlemen, remember this one thing," and kicked into a half-time coda, declaring over and over again to the audience the simple one-line message of the song. It was a curious performance, far removed from the loose spontaneity of his Hayride shows of just six months before, but after twenty minutes both he and his fans were exhausted. The last time he had appeared at Ellis he had come out onstage afterward and patiently signed autographs, but with that no longer a possibility, this time he was whisked away into the night before the applause had even died down.

The next day he played Little Rock, then Springfield, Missouri; Des Moines; Lincoln and Omaha, Nebraska. In Kansas City there was a riot: the band was overrun, D.J.'s drums and Bill's bass were smashed, and D.J. was thrown into the orchestra pit, but everyone escaped with their lives and aplomb intact. In Detroit he was billed as "the atomic explosion," but back home in Memphis the review of the Cotton Pickin' Jamboree appearance declared more meaningfully, "Only a few times previously (Billy Sunday, Eddy Arnold, Liberace at his height) have so many persons gathered under one roof in Memphis for one attraction, and the reception had a fire and enthusiasm never in memorable history granted a native son."

Hank Snow meanwhile was finally beginning to accept the conclusion he had long since come to: he was never going to see any money from this deal. It had been six months now since they had signed the contract with RCA, and while some tour money had come to him initially through the Hank Snow Enterprises–Jamboree Attractions booking agency, he had seen not a penny from the RCA deal or the phenomenal RCA sales. He had been to his attorney some months before, who was shocked to discover that there were no formal papers of incorporation and urged Snow to insist on this at least as a first step toward straightening out the partnership's tangled affairs. But when he had approached his partner and pressed him on this point, "Parker immediately flew into a rage. Pacing up and down my office floor, he told me he thought we should dissolve our relationship in every aspect of our business. . . . I thought for several minutes and then asked him, 'If we do, what happens to our contract with Elvis Presley?' He twirled his big cigar back and forth in his mouth, pointed his finger at his chest, and said, 'You don't have any contract with Elvis Presley, Elvis is signed exclusively to the colonel.'"

*　*　*

ELVIS WAS DUE to make his return appearance on *The Milton Berle Show* on June 5. He spent most of the previous week at home for what amounted to the longest extended period of time off he had had (six days) since the beginning of the year. He was too jittery to stay home — after all this time on the road he couldn't really sleep more than three or four hours a night, and Gladys was worried almost constantly that he was just going to burn himself up. "I'm so proud of my boy," she said over and over again, and she would get up early in the morning to run off the fans so Elvis could sleep. Still, there was no escaping them: they lined up politely by the carport from morning till night in the manicured residential neighborhood that the Presleys had moved into at the end of March. All they wanted was a glimpse of Elvis, or any of the family, for that matter. Mrs. Presley answered the doorbell in her housecoat and slippers every time it rang, and sometimes she let them borrow the phone if they said they needed to call their mama and daddy. On a hot day she might even have the new maid, Alberta, bring them a glass of ice water — after all, she said, "they like my boy." Sometimes, she would confide to a friend, she just wished that Elvis would quit right now. He could have a good living, buy himself "a furniture store . . . marry some good girl and have a child — where she would see it and be with it. And she'd be the happiest person in the world," she told Mrs. Faye Harris, an old Tupelo neighbor, "if he would [just] quit and come home and stay with them there in Memphis."

Mr. Presley on the whole was less sanguine about it all. "I wish," he said to a contractor friend named Carl Nichols who was doing some work around the house, "they would all go away." "You wouldn't be here if they did," said his friend. But he still felt like they were all taking advantage of him — of him and his family. He enjoyed playing skill pool in the game room with his son or his brother, Vester, or the various in-laws and cousins, who had virtually moved into the house since they had come up in the world, and he was in the process of having Nichols build him a pool out back because Elvis thought they would all enjoy the chance to cool off in the hot Memphis summertime. But he watched every nickel, and he regarded every newcomer with glowering suspicion, and Elvis had to explain to his friends sometimes that that was just the way his father was.

It wasn't that it didn't feel like home — Gladys had filled the house with what Elvis called "a museum of me," and bought so much furniture that they'd had to pile up a lot of their old things out on the sunporch.

When he surveyed his life, he liked what he saw. He liked the pale green, seven-room ranch house that sat here "out east" in the kind of affluent tract development that he could never have imagined living in back when he was going to Humes High. He was proud of his mama and his daddy — his mama would never change, she never wanted anything for herself, and she was just happy with her kennel and vegetable garden in the backyard. And if the people who lived out here in this nose-up-in-the-air neighborhood didn't think she was as good as any of them, well, they could just kiss his ass. They were all right, though, he supposed. It was just that there was increasingly little differentiation between his public and private lives. Bob Neal had told him it was going to get like this. He hadn't really believed him, but now he didn't know if he cared. It wasn't all that different, as he pointed out to Mr. Johnson at the paper, than the way it had been all along. "It didn't happen all at once," he explained. "Since the beginning, when I first began, it was just the same. The only difference, the crowds are bigger now."

He liked it in a way. The fans were the living representation of his success. Other stars, he read in the movie magazines, resented the demands that were made on them, but he couldn't understand that. The fans, he said over and over again, were his life's blood. Sometimes he stood out in the driveway for hours signing autographs — they were polite for the most part, and besides, he told *Seventeen* magazine reporter Edwin Miller, who was researching a story on him in Memphis that week, "you say no to one person because you had a hundred autographs to sign, they just know you're saying no to them. I never refuse to do anything like that, no matter how tired I am." Sometimes Gladys would have to call him two or three times to get him to come in for supper.

ON THE SECOND DAY that he was home, almost on a whim, he stopped by Dixie's house on Lucy Street. She had just come from rehearsal for her high school graduation that night and was wearing her graduation dress, but when he suggested that they go for a ride she pulled on a pair of jeans, hopped on his motorcycle, and left her parents to explain her absence to her boyfriend when he arrived. That evening he attended her graduation, and on Friday he went out to the Overton Park Shell to catch the show that Sam Phillips and Bob Neal were putting on, under the banner of their newly formed partnership, Stars, Inc., with Sun artists Carl Perkins, Johnny Cash, Warren Smith, and the recently signed Roy Orbison.

Elvis was called upon to take two bows from the audience and signed autographs afterward with Carl, who was by now fully recovered from his automobile accident.

Then on Saturday, June 2, he flew out to California with his cousin Gene, where he met Scotty and D.J. and Bill, who had driven out earlier in the week. On the way they had heard a song called "Be Bop A Lula" on the radio for the first time, and they were sure that Elvis had recorded it behind their back. As soon as they saw him, they jumped all over him for going into the studio without them, but he assured them that it wasn't his record, it was by a cat named Gene Vincent. There were shows scheduled in Oakland at 3:00 and 8:00 on Sunday, and then they flew into the Inglewood airport at 4:00 in the morning, leaving little time for sleep before a Berle show rehearsal called for 10:30 A.M.

Elvis felt considerably more at ease with Mr. Berle this time and ran through the material confidently, lounging in the orchestra seats between takes with Irish McCallah, the exotic-looking star of the popular TV series *Sheenah Queen of the Jungle* and meeting the beautiful film star Debra Paget for the first time. There was an opportunity to catch up on business with the Colonel — there was to be a formal presentation of the double Triple Crown Award from *Billboard* for "Heartbreak Hotel" (this meant that the record had topped sales, jukebox, and disc jockey lists in both the pop and c&w categories), he had been signed for Steve Allen's newly announced Sunday-night show, opposite Ed Sullivan, in just a month's time, and an Elvis Presley record was currently number one on each of the three in-store charts, pop ("I Want You, I Need You, I Love You"), r&b ("Heartbreak Hotel"), and country (still "I Forgot to Remember to Forget").

The Colonel's steely gaze bore in on him; it was as if he could read his mind. "If you ever do anything to make me ashamed of you, you're through," the Colonel had said to him more than once already, and he worried that the Colonel might bring up the pretty blond dancer who had promised to go on the road with him for the rest of the week. Hearing about the success they were having, though, and feeling the Colonel's reassuring hand on his shoulder, he cast his doubts aside — he knew the difference between a good girl and a bad girl, and the way you treated each. The Colonel was just a cranky old man who worried too much sometimes, things had been going so smoothly lately nothing could seriously go wrong.

H E OPENED WITH "Hound Dog," the song with which he had been closing his act ever since Las Vegas. He was wearing a light-color checked jacket, dark pants, a two-tone polo shirt, and white socks, and for the first time, surprisingly, he was not even cradling a guitar. Perhaps to make up for its absence he seemed to have carefully worked out new moves, wrists splayed out almost limply in seeming contrast to the ferocity of his vocal attack, fingers fluttering, arms outspread. With Scotty's solo he lurches backward in what might be interpreted as an upbeat adaptation of the shrugging, stuttering, existential hopelessness of a James Dean, there is a jittery fiddling with his mouth and nose, and as the song comes to an end he is dragging the microphone down to the floor, staggering almost to his knees. Scotty and D.J. and Bill keep their eyes glued on him, there is only the slightest flicker of surprise as he points at the audience and declares emphatically, *You* ain't nothin' but a hound dog, then goes into his patented half-time ending, gripping the mike, circling it sensuously, jackknifing his legs out as the audience half-screams, half-laughs, and he laughs, too — it is clearly all in good fun.

"How about my boy?" says Milton Berle with obvious pride and affection as he musses up his hair. "How about him?" Elvis is clearly pleased but does his best not to show it: he yawns, grimaces, rolls his tongue around in his mouth, touches his ear, mugs, and ducks his head as if to say, Who is this guy?, doing everything that he can not to laugh at Berle's nonstop clowning. Before this part of the show is over, Berle, playing the part of the Dutch uncle, seeks to dissuade Elvis from thinking that he could ever get an "ultrasophisticated" movie star like Debra Paget with his sex appeal ("She's not in your league. Stick to Heartbreak Hotel, and stay away from the Waldorf"), then calls Debra out onstage and "introduces" her to Elvis Presley. Whereupon, to Berle's delighted double take, Debra screams, flings her arms around the new teenage idol, and bends him backward in a kiss.

The Milton Berle Show topped Phil Silvers' *Sergeant Bilko* in the ratings for the first time all season, and *Variety* reported that "it was a relaxed and therefore more effective Milton Berle who signed off his program for the season last week with one of his better NBC-TV efforts." But while the immediate response was for the most part favorable and Elvis went on to wildly successful appearances in San Diego, Long Beach, and the Shrine Auditorium in Los Angeles, another reaction was setting in, a reaction that had been building for some time and that culminated now in personal attacks and cries of moral outrage unlike anything that Elvis had encountered to date. "Mr. Presley has no discernible singing ability," declared Jack Gould in the *New York Times*. "The sight of young (21) Mr. Presley caterwauling his unintelligible lyrics in an inadequate voice, during a display of primitive physical movement difficult to describe in terms suitable to a family newspaper, has caused the most heated reaction since the stone-age days of TV when Dagmar and Faysie's necklines were plunging to oblivion," wrote Jack O'Brian in the *New York Journal-American*. "[Popular music] has reached its lowest depths in the 'grunt and groin' antics of one Elvis Presley," fulminated Ben Gross in the *Daily News*. "The TV audience had a noxious sampling of it on the Milton Berle show the other evening. Elvis, who rotates his pelvis, was appalling musically. Also, he gave an exhibition that was suggestive and vulgar, tinged with the kind of animalism that should be confined to dives and bordellos. What amazes me is that Berle and NBC-TV should have permitted this affront." And, under the banner "Beware Elvis Presley," the Catholic weekly *America* suggested that

if his "entertainment" could be confined to records, it might not be too bad an influence on the young, but unfortunately Presley makes personal appearances.

He recently appeared in two shows in the Municipal Auditorium of La Crosse, Wisconsin. According to the La Crosse paper, his movements and motions during a performance, described as a "strip-tease with clothes on," were not only suggestive but downright obscene. The youngsters at the shows — 4,000 at one, about 1,200 at the second — literally "went wild," some of them actually rolling in the aisles. . . .

Yet the National Broadcasting Company wasn't loath to bring Presley into the living-rooms of the nation on the evening of June 5. Appearing on the Milton Berle show, Presley fortunately didn't go so far as he did in La Crosse, but his routine was "in appalling taste" (said the San Francisco *Chronicle*) and "his one specialty is an accented movement of the body that hitherto has been primarily identified with the repertoire of the blond bombshells of the burlesque runway" (New York *Times*).

If the agencies (TV and other) would stop handling such nauseating stuff, all the Presleys of our land would soon be swallowed up in the oblivion they deserve.

Juvenile delinquency, a widespread breakdown of morality and cultural values, race mixing, riots, and irreligion all were being blamed on Elvis Presley and rock 'n' roll by a national press that was seemingly just awakening to the threat, the popularity of the new music among the young, and, of course, the circulation gains that could always be anticipated from a great hue and cry. In an age which attached little or no value to vernacular culture in any form and had always focused its fiercest scorn upon the South ("Dogpatch" was about as sophisticated a concept as existed for an appreciation of southern culture), the level of vituperation should perhaps have come as no great surprise — but, after the warm reception that Elvis had gotten almost everywhere that he had appeared throughout the South, and the generally indulgent one that he had received elsewhere, it clearly did. Mrs. Presley was beside herself with anger and shame ("She'd get mad and cuss sometimes, say some low-down things," said Vernon's brother, Vester), and even Elvis seemed taken aback by the onslaught of the debate. "I don't do any vulgar movements," he protested weakly to Aline Mosby, the UP reporter he had stood up in Vegas. "I'm not trying to be sexy," he told Phyllis Battele of the International News Service. "It's just my way of expressing how I feel when I move around. My movements, ma'am, are all leg movements. I don't do nothing with my body."

Only the Colonel kept his cool. Back in Madison the letters were pouring in by the truckload, most of them accompanied by dollar bills for the picture packets that were offered through the fan clubs. After the Berle appearance, Charlie Lamb, the veteran PR man whom Colonel Parker had left in charge back home, hired twenty girls to take care of the overflow: "I hired a doctor's wife to handle the money and keep records of what's coming in with the mail, and I called the bank and told them, 'I got so much money I can't bring it in.' " What did Colonel Parker think about it all? "I'm going to get a wiggle meter to time the wiggles," said the Colonel with imperturbable calm. "When Elvis stops singing, we'll put him on the stage and just let him wiggle!" Only his cigar hid the smirk of the jovial Colonel, "who was the exact opposite," Miss Mosby reflected, "of the serious singer."

Elvis flew home to Memphis early on the morning of Monday, June 11, for the funeral of his cousin Lee Edward Smith, Gene and Junior's brother, who had drowned. Coming back from the funeral with his parents, he drove up to the house and found June Juanico, a pretty little girl he had dated one night when he played Keesler Air Force Base, in Biloxi, almost a year before, standing in line with all the others. He recognized her right away and they started talking, and when he found out that she was in Memphis for the week with some girlfriends, he said he'd call her at her hotel and maybe they could get together later.

Over the next two days he showed June a month's worth of Memphis sights — he took her by Humes, stopped by the Memphis Recording Service, went up to the Hotel Chisca, where he introduced her to Dewey, showed her the Courts where he had grown up, and Crown Electric across the street, with the truck he had driven sitting out in the yard. He introduced her to Bernard and Guy Lansky and bought her a motorcycle cap just like his. Then they went out to Mud Island, where he drove his motorcycle so fast that they both got scared, and he made her put her hand on his chest so that she could feel his heart pounding. It was like the first night they had met, the previous June in Biloxi, when they sat out on the White House Hotel pier until 3:00 or 4:00 in the morning, "and I was very nervous — I was afraid of myself. My mother used to tell me, 'Keep a good head on your shoulders. When you get in a compromising situation, think: "What would my mother think of me if she could see me right now?" ' So here's this beautiful boy with his luscious lips kissing me on the back of my neck, and he turns me around gently, and I don't know if he's going to start fondling on me and I felt like it would be all right if he did, so I was trembling, and then when he held me close I could feel him trembling, too. And so we laughed, and he said, 'Which one is more nervous, you or me?' and then we laughed about that."

Mr. and Mrs. Presley couldn't have been nicer. June felt right at home — with Mrs. Presley anyway. She fussed so over June and showed her how Elvis liked his chicken prepared, and when his daddy told him that his new Cadillac was ready for delivery, it didn't surprise her one bit that Elvis asked her if she would go pick it up with him. It did surprise her when it turned out that they had to go to Houston to get it, but June bravely asked her girlfriends to pack a bag and bring it out to the house, and she went on her first plane ride ever, after first swearing to Mrs. Presley that she really was eighteen. In Houston they were booked into separate rooms on separate floors, but she stayed with him after he assured her that he would never hurt her. "Trust me, baby," he said, and she did. They drove the white Cadillac El Dorado back to Memphis the next day, and when they pulled into the driveway, "Mrs. Presley came out and hugged him like he had been gone for weeks." Before they parted on Friday she made him promise that

he would come down to visit her in Biloxi, and he said he had some vacation coming up in July, so he thought maybe he would. They exchanged
vows of undying love, and while June worried on the one hand that "I
might never see him again," she was in fact as confident of his character as
she was of his continued success.

NBC, on the other hand, had its doubts. Not sure quite how to react to
the furor that had surrounded the most recent *Milton Berle Show* appearance, the network put out conflicting press releases, and Steve Allen, who
had already signed Elvis to a one-shot appearance at $7,500 (he had received
$5,000 apiece for his two Berle appearances), stated on his late-night *Tonight*
show that "there has been a demand that I cancel him from our show. As of
now he is still booked for July 1, but I have not come to a final decision on
his appearance. If he does appear, you can rest assured that I will not allow
him to do anything that will offend anyone." An NBC spokesman said, "We
think this lad has a great future, but we won't stand for any bad taste under
any circumstances." On June 20 a compromise of sorts was reached when
NBC announced that Allen would be presenting a new, "revamped, puri-
fied and somewhat abridged Presley. He'll wear white tie and tails, glory
be," wrote columnist Harriet Van Horne with understandable skepticism.
"And he'll stand reasonably still while singing. . . . With so much Bowdler-
izing, he may well sing 'Come, Sweet Death' as far as his career is concerned."

It was, said Allen, reflecting back on the experience, "a way of saying
something comic." It was also a way, of course, of getting around the Mrs.
Grundys of the nation with a big wink. The irony, unfortunately, was lost
on Elvis, who seemed bewildered at the force and ferocity of the criticism
that continued to be directed at him and his music. It seemed as if all the
pent-up forces of puritanism and repression had been unleashed simultaneously to discover in rock 'n' roll the principal source of America's growing
moral decadence and the world's ills. What hurt most of all were the
denunciations from the pulpit, but even the newspaper articles stung. He
said for the record that the critics had a right to their opinions, they were
only doing their job, and Elvis was always the first to disparage himself and
his talents — but it wasn't fair. He didn't drink, he didn't smoke (except for
the little cigarillo Hav-a-tampas that he increasingly enjoyed, though not in
public), he did his best to make sure that the boys always conducted themselves like gentlemen. It wasn't supposed to matter how you *looked*.

It was just like in high school — he might have appeared one way, but
he was really another. He had always believed that what was important

was who you were underneath, but now he was beginning to have his doubts. He treated every girl who deserved to be treated with respect with the respect that was due her, didn't he? And he tried not to swear too much in public and generally set a good example. But when in Charleston he nibbled a reporter's fingers just to get her attention, it made national headlines — "Girl Reporter Bitten by Elvis" — and his mother was upset that now he was being accused of some new form of moral degeneracy until he reassured her that there was nothing to it. In Charlotte on June 26, on the same tour, he uncharacteristically exploded at all the criticism that had been coming at him for the last month and talked seriously about what his music meant to him.

Elvis Presley is a worried man. Some, that is, for a man with four Cadillacs and a $40,000 weekly pay check. Critics are saying bad things about him. It has been especially rough during the past three weeks. And that is why he bucked his manager's orders to stay away from newsmen in Charlotte Tuesday until showtime. That is why he refused to stay in the seclusion of his hotel room. At 4:10 he couldn't stand it any longer, and with "Cousin Junior" left the room.

He walked quickly to a restaurant a few doors away for a barbe-cue, flirtation with a few women and a 30-minute round of pool next door.

"Sure I'll talk. Sit down. Most of you guys, though, been writin' bad things about me, man!"

His knees bounced while he sat. His hands drummed a tattoo on the table top.

Eyes, under long lashes, darted from booth to booth, firing rapid winks at the girls who stared at him. "Hi ya, baby," he breathed. And she flopped back in the booth looking like she'd been poleaxed. "This Crosby guy [the critic for the *New York Herald-Tribune*], whoever he is, he says I'm obscene on the Berle show. Nasty. What does he know?

"Did you see the show? This Debra Paget is on the same show. She wore a tight thing with feathers on the behind where they wiggle most. And I never saw anything like it. Sex? Man, she bumped and pooshed out all over the place. I'm like Little Boy Blue. And who do they say is obscene? Me!

"It's because I make more money than Debra. Them critics don't like to see nobody win doing any kind of music they don't know nothin' about."

And he started to eat. The waitress brought his coffee. Elvis reached down and fingered the lace on her slip.

"Aren't you the one?"

"I'm the one, baby!"

Presley says he does what he does because this is what is making money. And it is music that was around before he was born.

"The colored folks been singing it and playing it just like I'm doin' now, man, for more years than I know. They played it like that in the shanties and in their juke joints, and nobody paid it no mind 'til I goosed it up. I got it from them. Down in Tupelo, Mississippi, I used to hear old Arthur Crudup bang his box the way I do now, and I said if I ever got to the place where I could feel all old Arthur felt, I'd be a music man like nobody ever saw."

Yep, some of the music is low-down.

"But, not like Crosby means. There is low-down people and high-up people, but all of them get the kind of feeling this rock 'n' roll music tells about."

Elvis says he doesn't know how long rock and roll will last. "When it's gone, I'll switch to something else. I like to sing ballads the way Eddie Fisher does and the way Perry Como does. But the way I'm singing now is what makes the money. Would you change if you was me? . . .

"When I sang hymns back home with Mom and Pop, I stood still and I looked like you feel when you sing a hymn. When I sing this rock 'n' roll, my eyes won't stay open and my legs won't stand still. I don't care what they say, it ain't nasty."

It was all strangely familiar and yet at the same time surprisingly revealing, the sort of interview he might have given in high school, perhaps, if anyone had thought to interview the strange, silent boy who had attended Humes High, and it was filled with the same odd mixture of crudeness and sensitivity, truculence and hurt. He still seemed to enjoy the anomaly created by the gulf between character and appearance, but it was no longer working in quite the way that he wished. Perhaps this was what he had been thinking of when he confided to Bob Johnson the month before, "Mr. Johnson, you know some things just change when something like this happens. I can't just do like I did."

H E A R R I V E D at NBC's midtown rehearsal studio on Friday morning, June 29. He had played Charleston, South Carolina, the night before and was scheduled to play Richmond the following evening, with rehearsal for the Sunday-night show sandwiched in between. Other than the Colonel, only his cousin Junior Smith had accompanied him on the train ride north, and Junior stood staring out at the street while Elvis fooled around at the piano beside him and the Colonel talked business with two William Morris agents and representatives of RCA and Hill and Range. A young photographer named Al Wertheimer, who had taken some publicity shots for RCA at the time of Elvis' fifth Dorsey brothers appearance three months earlier and, in the wake of all the bad press, had been contacted by RCA's Anne Fulchino to take some more, asked if he could shoot some pictures. "Sure, go ahead," said Elvis diffidently. "I couldn't tell if he recognized me," wrote Wertheimer, an admirer of the David Douglas-Duncan school of eloquent, documentary realism, "or if he was just keeping up his side of the conversation." Elvis went on playing as Steve Allen entered, surrounded by his entourage. He was then introduced to the star, who gave him a rather flippant greeting ("Allen eyed him much as an eagle does a piece of meat," recalled Hill and Range rep Grelun Landon, to whom the offbeat, hip-talking comedian had always been "one of my gods") and was handed a script for a "western" skit called "Range Roundup." Playing the part of "Tumbleweed," Elvis rehearsed with Allen, Andy Griffith, and Imogene Coca. "A secretary whispered to Steve as they wrapped up the rehearsal," recorded Wertheimer. "He turned to Elvis, who was studiously flipping back and forth through his script, and said, 'The tailor's here.'

Elvis looked up, confused, and replied, "Yes, sir? What about?"
"Remember, you're wearing tails while you're singing to the hound dog."
"Oh yeah, I remember."
Elvis stepped into a broom closet and reappeared in baggy pants and floppy tails. With the same unlit cigar jammed in a corner of his

mouth, Colonel Parker stepped forward to make sure his boy got a custom job. After the tailor made his last chalk mark, Elvis turned to the mirror across the room, snapped the lapels and checked his hair with that half-leer, half-smile that kept me guessing.

The room returned to a chapel-like serenity when the door slammed closed on the last of Allen's group. The Colonel instructed Junior about hotel accommodations and train schedules for a concert in Richmond, Virginia, the following day. Elvis didn't pay any attention. He was back at the piano playing another spiritual.

On a whim, Wertheimer accompanied him to Richmond. Just as in New York, not simply at the Steve Allen rehearsal but on an earlier occasion, when Wertheimer had captured him shaving and sculpting his hair ("Sure, why not?" Elvis had replied when the photographer asked if it was okay to come in the bathroom and shoot some pictures), Elvis was "the perfect subject for a photographer, unafraid and uncaring, oblivious to the invasion of my camera." Perhaps because he was so easily bored, but even more due to his quick inventiveness and tongue-in-cheek humor, "if you just stuck around with him for five minutes there was something happening."

In Richmond there were two shows scheduled, at 5:00 and at 8:00, and after a breakfast of bacon and eggs, milk, home fries, and cantaloupe à la mode, Elvis went up to his room. Wertheimer didn't see him again until about an hour before the start of the first show, when he found him eating a bowl of chili at the Jefferson Hotel coffee shop.

I was hot and sweaty, and he was cool and clean, looking almost dignified in a slate-grey suit, pressed white shirt and white knit tie. It was the white bucks that gave him away.

A woman was with him. She wasn't interested in a quick lettuce and tomato. She was dressed for Saturday night. . . . She was trying to appear casual, not an easy task since a photographer was on the other side of the salt and pepper. Elvis was cool, "Oh, he's the photographer, that's okay, he's with me," as if to say it's only natural to have a photographer on a date. . . . She crossed her legs and in a soft Southern accent asked what he was reading. He was only too happy to oblige, telling her it was the script for the "Steve Allen Show" — "It's gonna be on tomorrow night, are you gonna see the show?" — and

talking about learning his lines. . . . Elvis set the script aside and finished his chili, and when he set that aside he turned his full attention
to her, talking about how nice her hair was and how pretty her earrings were. He was sweet and natural.

Junior, who had been sitting glowering at the far end of the counter
the whole time, tapped his fingers impatiently and said it was time to go.
"Go where?" said Elvis. But Junior wasn't in any mood for a joke.

When they got to the theater, Elvis checked out the stage, "feeling its
size like a builder inspecting a piece of land." Girls screamed through an
open window as Elvis and the Jordanaires tried to rehearse. The Colonel's
assistant Tom Diskin was handling the box office while the Colonel was
"hunched over [in the lobby] in the middle of the crowd, breaking open
bundles of souvenir programs and glossy photos suitable for framing. He
gave a handful to a kid.

" 'Got enough change on ya, son? Make sure you count your
change.' "

The lobby, Wertheimer noted, was papered with glossies. "Nowhere
did I see pictures of any other performers. It was wall-to-wall Elvis."

Backstage there was the usual complement of opening acts milling
around: Phil Maraquin, the magician; the dancing team of Doris and Lee
Strom; a local square-dancing troupe; and the Fliam Brothers, musical
comedians. This was the show with which the Colonel had replaced the
more traditional country and western caravan of just two months before.
A lackluster brass band was rehearsing onstage, and Wertheimer decided
it was a safe time to go to the bathroom, but when he heard what he took
to be the sound of the show starting, he raced down the staircase to the
stage area. There on the landing he discovered Elvis and the blonde from
the coffee shop engaged in a ritual dance of courtship, with Elvis "slow,
natural, insistent. He slid his arms around her waist. She pressed her arms
against his shoulders, pinning the purse between them. He inched forward, she retreated." The photographer snapped picture after picture
until at last, in an image destined to become as memorable as Doisneau's
classic "The Kiss," "she stuck her tongue out at him and he playfully returned the gesture. The tips of their tongues touched." At this point Wertheimer discreetly withdrew, and not long afterward Elvis faced his loyal
fans.

At the end of the second show Elvis left while the band was still playing, and the photographer rode to the train station with the other musicians in a police paddy wagon. There they caught the 10:50 sleeper back to New York; Elvis was already on the train, in an upper berth, "his hand on his forehead, his eyes on the ceiling, watching his own movie."

THEY ARRIVED back in New York early Sunday morning and promptly took a taxi to the Hudson Theater, on Forty-fourth Street, for a full day of rehearsals for the live broadcast that night. They did a quick run-through in which Elvis sang his latest hit, "I Want You, I Need You, I Love You," on a Greek-columned set (it was all part of Allen's comedic concept of presenting low culture in a high-culture setting). "He sang without . . . passion," Wertheimer noted. "He didn't move, he didn't touch the microphone, he stood square, both feet spread and stuck to the ground. After he had finished . . . Steve patted him on the back and told him it was great. Elvis smiled and in a slow, modest voice, he said, 'Thank you, Mr. Allen.' "

Then he met the dog, a female basset hound dressed in collar, bow tie, and top hat. In further keeping with the theme of the show he was going to sing "Hound Dog" to — who else? During the first run-through the dog ignored him. Allen "suggested that they get to know each other." Elvis petted her, sang to her, and in the end prevailed, to the applause of the assembled stagehands and professionals. They then went into the rehearsal of the sketch. At the dress rehearsal, as Elvis stood uncomfortably in his dress shirt and tails waiting to go on, Milton Berle, who was making a cameo appearance on the show, walked by. "Good luck, kid," he said, straightening Elvis' bow tie. "Thank you, Mr. Berle," said Elvis gratefully.

"Well, you know, a couple of weeks ago on *The Milton Berle Show,* our next guest, Elvis Presley, received a great deal of attention, which some people seem to interpret one way and some viewers interpret another. Naturally, it's our intention to do nothing but a good show." There is a yelping sound from backstage. "Somebody is barking back there. We want to do a show the whole family can watch and enjoy, and we always do, and tonight we're presenting Elvis Presley in his, heh heh, what you might call his first comeback . . ." — Allen laughs again self-consciously, prompting scattered laughter from the audience — ". . . and at this time it gives me extreme pleasure to introduce the new Elvis Presley. Here he is."

If Allen was experiencing extreme pleasure, it was clear that Elvis was experiencing the opposite. He sidled out to the accompaniment of dreamy music, holding the guitar by the neck out from his body, almost as if he were dragging it. He bowed stiffly from the waist, then wiped his nose on his top hat, hiding his face as he handed it to Steve. "Elvis, I must say you look absolutely wonderful," said Allen with a straight face while Elvis tugged at his white gloves, shifted nervously, and looked away. "You really do. And I think your millions of fans are really going to get kind of a kick seeing a different side of your personality tonight."

"Well, uh," said Elvis almost somnambulistically, "thank you, Mr. Allen, uh . . ."

"Can I hold your guitar here?"

"It's not often that I get to wear the, uh, suit and tails . . ."

"Uh-huh," said Allen encouragingly, perhaps wondering if they were ever going to get through this sketch.

". . . and all this stuff. But, uh, I think I have something tonight that's not quite correct for evening wear."

"Not quite formal? What's that, Elvis?"

"Blue suede shoes."

"Ooh yes," said Steve with a double take. The audience laughed and applauded encouragingly.

With his opening number, "I Want You, I Need You, I Love You," for the first time he appeared if not comfortable, at least involved, even in tails. He sang the song with sincerity and feeling, hunching his shoulders, loosening his tie, but for the moment lost in the private reverie which his music provided. The Jordanaires dooh-wahed behind him, out of the picture, as were the musicians, save in silhouette. Even as the last notes were still ringing, Steve Allen bustled out onstage again, this time wheeling the basset, and announced that Elvis was now going to sing "Hound Dog," his next big hit, which he would record the next day. The dog started to look away, Elvis cupped its chin, and there was sympathetic laughter as Elvis glanced balefully, as if sharing a joke with a friend, at the audience. The camera was on the dog as Elvis pointed at her and declared the obvious with a playful snarl. When the dog started to tremble, he held her affectionately and in the course of the song even kissed her once or twice. Apart from nervous titters, there was little response from the audience, but Elvis was a good sport about it all ("He always did the best he could with whatever situation he was given," said Jordanaire Gordon Stoker of the appearance, "and he never, ever insulted anybody"), walking the mike around into the basset's line of vision whenever its attention wandered, sharing his discomfiture openly and amiably. There was a sense of almost palpable relief on the part of all concerned when the song ended and he could finally march offstage after a long, lonely moment in the spotlight.

The embarrassment was only heightened when, after a commercial break, the "Range Roundup" skit (with "Big Steve and the Gang") opened to the strains of "Turkey in the Straw." "Big Steve" was carrying a toy guitar, Andy Griffith had a fiddle and was wearing furry chaps, Imogene Coca was dressed up in a Dale Evans cowgirl skirt, and "Tumbleweed" Presley, looking extremely abashed, was shadowed, like everyone else, by his cowboy hat. At first he literally lurked in the background, throwing in his shouts of agreement in unison with the others with some diffidence and having a good deal of difficulty getting his own lines out (even "You tell 'em, Big Steve" came out in a garbled Memphis accent). But gradually he warmed to the task, and by the time they sang their little western ditty at the end, with each actor taking a verse and all joining in the chorus, he seemed to have entered into the spirit of fun, beating out a rhythm easily on the body of his guitar, throwing a couple of patented, self-referential moves into his cowboy sashay, and singing out his lines with good humor if not abandon. "Well, I got a horse, and I got a gun / And I'm gonna go out and have some fun / I'm a-warning you, galoots / Don't step on my blue suede boots." "Yeah!" said Steve, with the cast ending on a chorus of "Yippy-i-oh, yippy-i-yay, yippy-i-oh-i-yay."

"On his way to the dressing room," reported Wertheimer, "Elvis was intercepted by the William Morris agent with the wire-rimmed glasses whom I had seen Friday morning at the first rehearsal. Shaking Elvis' hand, he said, 'I think the show was terrific. You did a marvelous job. We really ought to get a good reaction to this one.' Tom Diskin, the Colonel's lieutenant, stood by with a wide smile."

Back at his room at the Warwick, Elvis was still not done with his official duties. It had been arranged for him to do an interview on *Herald-Tribune* columnist Hy Gardner's program, "Hy Gardner Calling!," which broadcast locally on WRCA-TV, channel 4. The peculiar conceit of the program was that both parties were filmed "at home," and the show was broadcast "live" at 11:30 P.M. as a split-screen telephone conversation. This particular conversation must have been even more awkward than most. Gardner came across as the ultimate square, while Elvis, perhaps as a result of his experience that evening, suggested more of the James Dean aspect than ever, looking weary and, at times, genuinely lost. Frequently a fluttering hand would drift up to a furrowed brow, his eyes were heavily made up, and overall he presented a perplexing mix of rebellious image and conventional values, resentful truculence and hurt misunderstanding.

Was he getting enough sleep? Gardner wondered. No, not really, "but I'm used to it, and I can't sleep any longer." What would go through his mind to keep him awake? Some of the songs he was going to do, "or some of your plans, or what?" "Well, everything has happened to me so fast during the last year and a half — I'm all mixed up, you know? I can't keep up with everything that's happened." Slightly nonplussed, Gardner asks him about some of the criticism that has been directed at him. Does he feel any animosity toward his critics? "Well, not really, those people have a job to do, and they do it."

But has he learned anything from them?

"No, I haven't."

"You haven't, huh?"

"Because I don't feel like I'm doing anything wrong."

It was not the words so much as the affect — the generational stance not so much that he doesn't understand as that he isn't understood. Over and over again he rejects the rebel label ("I don't see how any type of music would have any bad influence on people when it's only music. . . . I mean, how would rock 'n' roll music make anyone rebel against their parents?") while adopting the stance. Gardner was clearly taken with him and concluded the interview with fatherly advice, suggesting that even the bad publicity may have helped him; it's "made it possible for you to do the kind of things for your folks that you always wanted to. So I sort of think I'd look at it that way, Elvis." "Well, sir, I tell you," said Elvis, repeating words he has said many times but which part of him clearly believes, "you got to accept the bad along with the good. I've been getting some very good publicity, the press has been real wonderful to me, and I've been getting some bad publicity — but you got to expect that. I know that I'm doing the best that I can, and I have never turned a reporter down, and I've never turned a disc jockey down, because they're the people that help make you in this business. . . . As long as I know that I'm doing the best I can." "Well, you can't be expected to do any more," says Gardner reassuringly. "I want to tell you it's been just swell talking to

MAY–JULY 1956 ∾ 297

you, and you make a lot of sense." With that the interview concluded, and Elvis was able to set aside the ambivalent feelings and experiences of the last two days and, perhaps, finally, get some sleep.

T HE NEXT DAY he seemed hardly the worse for wear. He arrived at the RCA building to find fans carrying picket signs that declared "We Want the Real Elvis" and "We Want the GYRATIN' Elvis"; held yet another press conference, in which he announced that "Barbara Hearn of Memphis and June Juanico of Biloxi, Miss. . . . are the two girls he dates. Miss Hearn has the added distinction of being a good 'motorcycle date' "; and recounted the story of his life once again in painstaking, and painstakingly accurate, detail. Then he entered the studio, shortly before 2:00, and settled down to work.

The studio, according to Al Wertheimer,

> looked like a set from a 1930's science fiction movie. It was a large rectangular space of acoustical tile walls ribbed with monolithic half cylinders. These ran vertically on the long sides of the rectangle and horizontally on the short sides. The high ceiling was rippled with more parallel cylinders and two pipes of fluorescent light. The floor was a series of short strips of wood scaled in a sawtooth pattern of right angles. In the center of the room lay a patch of carpet on which the musicians had placed their instruments.

This was a different kind of session. For one thing, "Hound Dog," the one song they knew they were going into the studio to get, was a number that Elvis and the band had been polishing in live performance for two months now. For another, it was the first session to be attended by Freddy Bienstock, the twenty-eight-year-old Viennese-born "double first cousin" and protégé of the Aberbach brothers, in his capacity as Hill and Range's representative. It was also, of course, the first time that a full complement of Jordanaires was present in the studio. More significant than anything else, though, for the first time the twenty-one-year-old singer was clearly in charge.

They started with "Hound Dog," but perhaps not surprisingly it proved more difficult to capture on record than anyone had anticipated from its easy onstage success. Engineer Ernie Ulrich, as cynical about rock 'n' roll as anyone else in the building, got a good sound mix early on, but then there were seventeen takes without a satisfactory master. The drums, always the driving force in the live show, weren't working right, Scotty was groping toward his guitar solo, the Jordanaires were having some difficulty finding their place, and Shorty Long, the boogie-woogie piano player who had filled in on the last New York session, was just looking for his cues. Steve Sholes was getting visibly discouraged — he was desperate to get material for the second album, and here they were wasting all their time on a single song — but Elvis, who exhibited few points of stillness in any other aspect of his life, maintained absolute concentration. "In his own reserved manner," wrote Wertheimer, "he kept control, he made himself responsible. When somebody else made a mistake, he sang off-key. The offender picked up the cue. He never criticized anyone, never got mad at anybody but himself. He'd just say, 'Okay, fellas, I goofed.'"

On the eighteenth take they finally got something. By now the beat had changed considerably from the way they did it in live performance, and the phrasing of the lyrics had changed even more. It had veered still further from Big Mama Thornton's original Latin-flavored "rhumba-boogie" feel (preserved mainly in the repetition of the final words, *hound dog,* at the end of the opening lines) and become a hard-driving number powered by D.J.'s tommy-gun attack and a solo that Scotty later labeled "ancient psychedelia." With the twenty-sixth take Sholes thought they had it, but Elvis wanted to keep going. After the thirty-first take Sholes announced over the PA, "Okay, Elvis, I think we got it."

Elvis rubbed his face, swept back his hair and resigned. "I hope so, Mr. Sholes." . . .

The recording had taken over two hours and without the air conditioner turned on (the mikes would have picked up the noise), the air in the room hung low and close. The double doors were opened, admitting cool air, the noise of vending machines and visitors with glowing compliments. Elvis combed his hair, drank the Coke offered by Junior and shrugged in reply to comments about how good the music was. Steve trod lightly. "Elvis, you ready to hear a playback?" As if bad news never had good timing, he said, "Now's as good a time as any."

Elvis sat cross-legged on the floor in front of the speaker. The engineer announced the take over the PA and let the tape roll. Elvis winced, chewed his fingernails and looked at the floor. At the end of the first playback, he looked like he didn't know whether it was a good take or not. Steve called for take eighteen. Elvis pulled up a folding chair, draped his arms across its back and stared blankly at the floor. . . . The engineer racked take twenty-eight.* Elvis left his chair and crouched on the floor, as if listening in a different position was like looking at a subject from a different angle. Again he went into deep concentration, absorbed and motionless. At the end of the song he slowly rose from his crouch and turned to us with a wide grin, and said, "This is the one."

They ate a late lunch, with Junior taking orders for sandwiches and drinks, and then they began to look for something else to record. Freddy Bienstock had brought in a stack of acetate demos with lead sheets from Hill and Range, and Elvis sorted through them, picking out several by title alone, then listening to them on the studio speaker as Steve broadcast them out from the control room. When he heard the second one, he instantly brightened. "Let me hear that again," he said. "Something I like about that one."

The song was "Don't Be Cruel," a number that Bienstock had acquired through Goldy Goldfarb, a song plugger at booking agent Moe Gale's Shalimar publishing company. It was written by rhythm and blues singer Otis Blackwell, who had enjoyed some success as an artist but was just beginning to enjoy far greater prominence as a writer (his "Fever" had just reached the top of the r&b charts in Little Willie John's classic version). Bienstock, whose principal administrative background had come in running Hill and Range's rhythm and blues division, St. Louis Music, for the past couple of years, was immediately taken with the song. However, he let Goldfarb know in no uncertain terms that if he wanted to get a song recorded by the hottest new act in the business, he would have to give up half the publishing (to Hill and Range) and half the writer's share (to Elvis). As Otis Blackwell later said, "I was told that I would have to make a deal" — but there was little question that it was worth it.

---

*Wertheimer appears to be mistaken in his count, since it was actually the final take that was selected.

Elvis had the song played back for him again and started working it out on the guitar while the others listened for the first time. Then he sketched out a rough arrangement on the piano, which he showed to Shorty Long, who made notes on the lead sheet. By this time he had memorized the lyrics. Scotty tried out a couple of openings, and Elvis suggested that he leave a little more space and told D.J. to "come in behind Scotty and slow it down a little"; then the Jordanaires worked out their arrangement, and after about twenty minutes they were ready for a run-through. After a single rehearsal, Sholes was ready to record, but Elvis wanted to rehearse some more, so they did. The song continued to evolve through twenty-eight takes. It took on a lilting, almost casual, off-hand kind of feel, as Scotty virtually sat out except at the beginning and the end, Gordon Stoker of the Jordanaires came to sing a duet with Elvis on the chorus, and D.J. laid Elvis' leather-covered guitar across his lap and played the back of it with a mallet, to get an additional snare effect. It was hardly a formulaic approach, and it was clearly one that left the nominal a&r director baffled. When they finally got the sound that he was looking for, Elvis pronounced, "That felt good," and, though it was late, called for another playback on "Anyway You Want Me," a pleading ballad that he had listened to at the beginning of the session. There was just one rehearsal. "At the fourth take," Wertheimer wrote, "Steve said they had it. Elvis said again, 'That's fine, Mr. Sholes. Let's try it one more time.' "

"I wasn't all that impressed with him, *as a singer*," said Gordon Stoker. "I mean, I kind of got a kick out of 'Don't Be Cruel,' I was entertained, so to speak, but then with 'Anyway You Want Me,' all of a sudden I took an entirely different attitude, the feeling that he had on that particular sound made the hair on my arm come up. I said to the guys, 'Hey, men, this guy can sing!' "

It was 9:00 by the time the session was over, and the studio was deserted. The guys were talking about going home by train the next morning; they were going to be playing that Milk Fund benefit at the ballpark in town, and then they were going to have the rest of the month off, their first extended break in six months. Everybody was looking forward to it, and Junior was laughing his evil little laugh, his hooded eyes regarding his famous cousin with what seemed like only thinly veiled jealousy. Steve Sholes had some songs he wanted Elvis to hear, but Elvis said he'd have to take them home with him if he was going to get a chance to listen to them at all. Anyway, he'd want acetates of the three songs they'd recorded that day — he wanted to learn the songs exactly the way they'd recorded them so he could do them that way in his shows. Sure, Sholes said, a little reluctantly, he'd get a package over to the hotel in the morning.

There were still some fans waiting outside when they came out of the studio, and Elvis patiently signed autographs while the others waited. By now *The Steve Allen Show* seemed like a million years ago, and the verdict was long since in. Allen had trounced Ed Sullivan in the ratings, the reviews were no more kind toward the stationary Elvis than they had been toward the gyrating one ("A cowed kid," declared the *Journal-American*, "it was plain he couldn't sing or act a lick"), and Sullivan had publicly reiterated that he would not have the singer on his show at any price ("He is not my cup of tea") while privately he had already been in touch with the Colonel. "Hey, Elvis, we gotta get back to the hotel," said Junior. Elvis got into the car. It had been a long day, and now he was hungry again.

H E RAN INTO GENE VINCENT at Penn Station the following morning as they were leaving the city. One of the boys pointed the new rock 'n' roll star out to him, and Elvis walked over and introduced himself, congratulating him sincerely on the success of "Be Bop A Lula." To his surprise Vincent immediately started to apologize. "The first thing he said was, 'I wasn't trying to copy you. I wasn't trying to sound like you.' Just right off the bat, without even being asked. I told him, 'Oh, I know that, it's just your natural style.'" And then the two twenty-one-year-olds compared notes on success.

He spent most of the twenty-eight-hour train ride home relaxing and fooling around. The photographer Al Wertheimer, convinced that this was an historic opportunity that would not pass his way again, took the trip at his own expense and got shots of Elvis catching some sleep, flirting with girls, reading *Archie* comic books, contemplating a giant teddy bear that the Colonel had given him, and listening to the acetates of his songs on a portable record player, over and over again, with obsessive concentration. "How'd it go yesterday at the recording session?" the Colonel asked him in the restaurant car, as Wertheimer recorded the event.

Elvis replied blandly, "It went pretty well." The Colonel carried on the conversation. "The reaction was terrific on the 'Steve Allen Show.' Better than I thought." Elvis shrugged. He seemed unimpressed. "Glad to hear it." This appeared to be a routine. The Colonel would start a conversation and Elvis would end it. "It's gonna be good to get back home. I'm sure your folks'll be mighty glad to see you," said the Colonel. "Yeah, it'll be good to see 'em."

That was the end of the conversation. The Colonel looked out the window. Tom [Diskin] talked shop. Junior talked to Elvis, and Elvis ate his sandwich. It was two generations sitting at separate tables.

When they finally reached the outskirts of Memphis, Elvis got off at a small signal stop called White Station, made his way across an empty field, inquired for directions to Audubon Drive, and, "still dressed in his suit and white knit tie," Wertheimer noted, "with a wave to us, and a smile that could be seen for a hundred yards, Elvis walked home alone."

He spent the rest of the afternoon at home, signing autographs for the fans, going for a ride on his motorcycle, splashing in the new pool (which Vernon was only filling just now with a garden hose), and playing the RCA acetates for his nineteen-year-old "Memphis girlfriend," Barbara Hearn, an advertising copywriter whom he had known since South Memphis days (she had been going out with Dixie's friend Ron Smith when he first met her) and with whom he had renewed his acquaintance early that spring. Wertheimer got pictures of Vernon shaving, Gladys handing her son a fresh pair of jockey shorts, and the family album, with the only demurral coming from Vernon, who said, " 'But I got shaving cream on.' I told him it was all right. He rinsed off his razor and smiled. . . . 'Well, if that's what you want, okay.' . . . I wondered," wrote Wertheimer, "how a house this open could remain a home."

THE COLONEL ARRIVED sometime after 9:00 with a police escort. He deputized Tom Diskin to take care of the family and Barbara, while he and Elvis rode to the midtown ballpark, home of the Memphis Chicks, in a white squad car. It was a hot night, 97 degrees, and the show had been going on for almost three hours at the old wooden stadium when the police car finally delivered Elvis to the performers' tent at third base. Not a few in the crowd of seven thousand (by comparison, an anti-integration rally led by Mississippi's senior senator James O. Eastland at the Overton Park Shell that afternoon drew thirty-five hundred) had shown up as early as 9:30 that morning, with lunch and supper packed, so as to be sure to get good seats. "The roaring was so loud and long," reported the *Commercial Appeal,* that "extra rations of sleeping pills were passed out to the patients of the four hospitals near the field," with Elvis' name receiving mentions twenty-nine times in advance of his arrival and each mention eliciting uncontrollable screams and squeals.

There was a "bop-dancing" contest, Elvis' signature fourteen-diamond horseshoe ring (worth six hundred dollars) was won in a drawing by seventeen-year-old Roger Fakes, the Colonel sold out the five thousand souvenir programs he had personally donated to the event (when asked by Al Wertheimer why the programs didn't come with a price tag, the Colonel pointed out, "You never want to put a price on anything"), and Dewey Phillips was "cotton-pickin' cute," reported the paper, and "worked like a Trojan" as MC. Among the more than one hundred performers — including four bands, the Dancing Dixie Dolls, the Confederate Barbershop Quartette, the Admiral's Band of Navy Memphis, and a surprise appearance by the Jordanaires, who had flown in from Nashville — was Jesse Lee Denson, who sang Gogi Grant's "Wayward Wind" and with his brother Jimmy told everyone backstage who would listen how he had taught Elvis Presley to play guitar back in the Lauderdale Courts.

Then it was finally time for Elvis to go on, and Dewey did a good imitation of the "old" Elvis and the "new" Elvis, as a squadron of police, firemen, and shore patrol escorted him to the stage. He was dressed all in black save for red socks and the red tie which he and his father had picked out just before the show, and as he sauntered out and greeted Dewey with casual grace, saluting his fans and acknowledging his family in the front row, the place literally exploded. The fans "broke from their seats, swept like a wave up to the stage. . . . Elvis pleaded with them as pleasantly as he could to sit down, but it was like Canute telling the tide to stop. . . . What made [it] all the more remarkable," reflected Bob Johnson in the *Memphis Press-Scimitar,* "was that he had previously played to a packed house in the Auditorium during the Cotton Carnival less than two months ago." To sixteen-year-old Jack Baker, who had been living next door to him just nine months before, "there was this keening sound, this shrill, wailing, keening response, and I remember thinking, That's an amazing sound, and then I realized I was making it, too." When the furor finally died down, and Elvis had graciously accepted a city proclamation designating Wednesday, July 4, as Elvis Presley Day, he turned to the crowd and announced, with that inscrutable mixture of boyish charm and adult calculation, "You know, those people in New York are not gonna change me none, I'm gonna show you what the real Elvis is like tonight."

And he did. After all the personal changes that had taken place, and the dramatic evolution that his career had witnessed in the previous few months, it was perhaps not surprising that the "real Elvis" should be, in Bob Johnson's description, "about halfway between the 'old' Elvis and the 'new' Elvis," but what this really meant was that he was able to control the crowd, to tantalize and manipulate them in a manner that differed significantly even from his appearance a few short weeks before. "He rocked 'em," wrote Johnson, "socked 'em, set them screaming with delight as his sensational individualistic song style throbbed out over the frenzied stadium." He opened with "Heartbreak Hotel," threw in "Mystery Train" and "I Got a Woman," brought out the Jordanaires for "I Want You, I Need You, I Love You" and "I Was the One," roared back with "Blue Suede Shoes" and "Long Tall Sally," and ended, of course, after half an hour, with "Hound Dog."

"When it was time to go," Johnson noted, "he made a quick retreat thru a phalanx of police and Shore Patrolmen to a squad car backed right up to the stage. The excited fans rolled around the car like a wave. Two Shore Patrolmen and a policeman were picked up and carried back as tho they were feathers, but [Police] Capt. Woodward got him in the car all in one piece, and Elvis grinned as the car pushed thru the crowd."

It was a moment of unmitigated triumph, a moment of pure and unsullied splendor that would be forever frozen in time. All Elvis wanted, Bob Johnson had written, was to be "thought well of at home," and now here he was succeeding in front of his family and his hometown in a style, and on a scale, that to anyone else would have been utterly unimaginable.

WITH JUNE JUANICO, 505 FAYARD STREET, BILOXI, SUMMER 1956.
(COURTESY OF JUNE JUANICO)

ELVIS AND JUNE

T HE FOLLOWING MONDAY, July 9, he arrived in Biloxi, unannounced and somewhat unexpected. He showed up in his white El Dorado convertible at June Juanico's house on Fayard Street with Red, his cousin Junior, and his friend Arthur Hooton, whose mother had worked with Gladys at Britling's Cafeteria. They waited in the driveway while some neighborhood kids went looking for June. When she got back, she and Elvis made a date for that night, and he left to register at the Sun 'N' Sand Hotel, whose courtyard quickly filled with fans as news of his arrival spread.

That night they went out on the town with June's mother, Mae, and her boyfriend, Eddie Bellman. On their own they revisited many of the sights June had shown him on his visit the previous year. They stayed out late, talking excitedly and making plans. Elvis wasn't sure how long he would be staying this time, he told her; he guessed she would just have to wait and see. All he knew was that he was on vacation for three weeks, footloose and fancy-free. He didn't know what he wanted to do exactly, but he wanted to do *something*. A few days before, he had wheeled into Tupelo on a whim and gone to see both his aunt and his fifth-grade teacher, Mrs. Grimes, who had originally been responsible for his entering the singing contest at the Mississippi-Alabama Fair. Now, it had just been announced, he was going to be returning to headline the fair in September. He was being written up in all the major newspapers and national magazines, and he was going to star in a movie soon. He could buy his mama and his daddy anything they needed, whatever they might want.

The next day he and June spent the whole day together. That afternoon they heard reports on a New Orleans radio station that Elvis Presley had become engaged to a Miss June Juanico of nearby Biloxi, and on the spur of the moment they jumped in the car and drove to New Orleans to dispel the rumors. Elvis got the address of the station at a pay phone, and they just showed up at WNOE, at the St. Charles Hotel, pressing their noses to the plate glass until DJ Hal Murray noticed them, did a double take, and then announced to his amazed listeners that "the man of the hour" had just walked into the studio and hurriedly switched to an interview format.

The only thing he was serious about at this point was his career, Elvis told the radio audience. He didn't have time to even think about getting engaged; right now he was just thinking about his vacation, which he was planning to spend in Florida. "You probably won't have too much of a vacation," interpolated the DJ, "because of the tremendous amount of kids who will be down there and fans — " "Well, I don't mind," he said. "Without them I'd be . . . lost." By the time they left the studio, the hotel lobby was full, and a girl fainted from the excitement and the heat.

From there the party of seven went on to Pontchartrain Beach, where they wandered the midway. Elvis won a host of stuffed animals to join the panda he had won for June at the Memphis Fairgrounds which they had christened Pelvis. In the course of the evening, it was reported in the press, Elvis consumed three halves of fried chicken and June three soft-shell crabs. On the way home they stopped off for a snack, and Elvis ordered his eggs over hard with the bacon burnt. When the eggs weren't cooked to his satisfaction, he sent the order back, and when the waitress brought it back again and it still wasn't right, she said, "What do you want, special treatment because you're Elvis Presley?" "No," he said, "I'd just like to be treated like a regular customer," and dumped the plate at the waitress's feet. They got home at 3:45 in the morning, and June responded from her bed to a *New Orleans Item* reporter's queries the next day. "Did I kiss him good night? What do you think? Certainly I kissed him good night. We were standing on the porch. No, not by the garden gate; on the porch. He's wonderful!"

THEY SAW EACH OTHER every night and spent almost all of each day together. Elvis kept telling the press that he was leaving for Florida any day, but he never left. On Thursday they went deep-sea fishing with June's mother and Eddie Bellman, and they had so much fun that he called his parents from the pier and told them to come down. In the meantime, with Eddie Bellman's help, he rented a villa out at the Gulf Hills Dude Ranch, in exclusive Ocean Springs. The crowds at the beachfront hotel had become impossible; there were close to five hundred people waiting for them when they returned from their fishing expedition, and Elvis' Cadillac was constantly covered with addresses, phone numbers, and love notes written in lipstick. When asked by the same reporter who had interviewed him earlier in the week when he was planning to leave for Florida, "keeping a sardonic smile on his lips," Elvis replied, "Well, if this keeps up, probably tonight." By the time that Vernon and Gladys arrived in their pink Cadillac and checked in at the Sun 'N' Sand on Friday, it didn't even matter that Elvis was no longer around; a crowd surrounded the car and grew bigger and bigger as Mrs. Presley stared out silently in curiosity and fear. When they went deep-sea fishing on Saturday, neither of the elder Presleys could have been any happier — Mr. Presley just liked being out on the water, with nobody to bother him or tear at his boy, and Mrs. Presley made Elvis peanut butter and banana sandwiches and fed them to him while he trolled for fish, wiping the crumbs away from his lips when he was done. It was a bright sunny day with a deep blue sky and not a cloud in sight.

On Monday they all drove to New Orleans. They went to the zoo, walked around in a cemetery overhung with Spanish moss, visited June's grandparents, who used to manage the Astor Hotel on Royal Street, and drove by some of the beautiful antebellum mansions in Pass Christian. Mr. and Mrs. Presley held hands, and Gladys asked Vernon if he wouldn't like to live in a big house like that someday. Mrs. Presley obviously liked June. She said, "You know, I've never seen my boy so taken with a girl. You two are planning to get married one of these days, aren't you?" They didn't have to answer, she said. She knew, she just had a feeling. "You just better not let Colonel Parker know how serious you are about June," she told her son. "You know how he feels, especially about marriage." Gladys called June "Satnin'," and June, who had not been able to bring herself to call Mrs. Presley "Gladys" even after she was asked, started calling her "Lovey" for her middle name, Love. "You know, my son's going to make me very proud of him," she confided to June — as if he hadn't made her proud already!

The Presleys returned to Memphis, and Elvis rented a four-bedroom house from the Hack family on Bayview Drive, just on the edge of the Gulf Hills resort, which afforded a greater measure of privacy than the villa could offer. It was a summertime idyll such as neither he nor June had ever experienced before. The next few weeks went by as if they would never end — and as if they would end before they had even begun. Mr. and Mrs. Presley came down again, one or another of the boys would go off from time to time to take care of unspecified business, and occasionally Elvis returned to Memphis, presumably because he had business to take care of, too. Sometimes June suspected that his business had to do with his "Memphis girlfriend," Barbara Hearn — but she didn't care. Not really. For Elvis and June a moment was an eternity, when he was with her he was with her alone, and as she told a reporter mischievously, "It'd be a sin to let something like that go to waste."

At Gulf Hills they rode, they water-skied, they played shuffleboard on a concrete court, they were in and out of the water all day long. At the "Hack House" they had fireworks battles at night behind the high hedge and on the golf course across the street, with everybody running around with little cigars in their mouths to light the fireballs that they threw at one another. Even at the resort they were pretty much left to themselves, so after waterskiing, they might all have dinner in the hotel dining room with June's mother and Mr. Bellman, then walk over to the Pink Pony Lounge and gather around the piano, where Elvis would entertain everyone, and they would all join in on familiar old standards until he ended the evening with a spiritual. He wanted June right there with him all the time and complained when she kept her distance. "He said, 'Other girls I've dated are always right next to me. They act like they're proud to be with me. If I say something, they listen. If I want to say something to you, I have to find you first.' " She knew exactly what he was talking about. Sometimes she would even hang back on purpose, just to see if he would look for her — and he always did. "I said, 'I'm not like your other girlfriends, Elvis, I'm not going to hang on your every word. When we first met, you said, "I like you, June, you're different." Now all of a sudden you want me to be like everybody else.' " No, he protested, but why was she spending so much time talking with the ski instructor when he wanted her to watch *him* ski? "Oh, really," said June. "All you care about is how many guys I've made out with. But, you know, I've gone out with a lot of guys and never really done anything."

"He said, 'Does that mean you're still a cherry?' I said, 'I'm not only a cherry, George. I'm the whole pie.' "

* * *

THEY WERE PERFECTLY MATCHED. June loved to cut up and fool around, and he was surprised to discover that she loved to sing, too. When they went riding, they sang "Side By Side," "Back in the Saddle Again," and "Let the Rest of the World Go By," with June contributing the tenor harmony, and when they were swimming there was always a phonograph sitting beside the pool. Elvis played "My Prayer," a hit by the Platters that summer, over and over again until, just at the point when the lead singer was approaching the climactic high note, "Elvis would always say, 'I'm gonna get that note, I'm gonna get that note, one of these days I'm gonna get that note, here it comes, here it comes . . . ' And he'd try to relax and just let it out, and it just wouldn't happen, and he'd scream and go under." He sang all the time — sometimes it seemed he'd rather sing than breathe. June was not particularly a fan of his records, so they stuck mostly to old tunes like "That's My Desire" and "Over the Rainbow" or big-voiced r&b hits like "Ebb Tide" and "Unchained Melody." Not surprisingly, June didn't hesitate to let him know her reservations about his music. "I thought most of his records sounded like he was singing in a tin can. I said, 'Why don't you let some of those guys who do your records hear you sing like this and see if they can find you some of this kind of material? You know, you have a wonderful voice.' "

Most of all, though, they shared a sense of humor. Nearly all the pictures from that time show a smiling, laughing Elvis, relaxed in a way that reveals little self-consciousness, only youth and pride. Healthy, innocent, brimming with energy and a sense that he has arrived, he clowns around in these photographs in a way that the grave-faced youngster of Tupelo days never would, and the rising young star never could, his hat tilted back on his head, his hair mussed up, looking for all the world like the Greek god Pan.

Newsweek ran a column by John Lardner on July 16 excoriating Steve Allen for his attempt to "civilize" Elvis, "to mute and frustrate Presley, for the good of mankind. . . . Allen's ethics," declared Lardner, "were questionable." Ed Sullivan announced on the twelfth that he had changed his mind and was booking Elvis at an unprecedented fifty thousand dollars for three appearances in the fall and winter. The Colonel was also working out a deal with Twentieth Century Fox after Hal Wallis informed him that he would not have a property ready for Elvis until the beginning of the following year. The deal was for $100,000, with co-star billing and options for two additional pictures at $150,000 and $200,000. The film was a western called *The Reno Brothers* which would start shooting at the end of August. Meanwhile, RCA was getting an almost incredible response — even judging by the tumultuous reaction to every other Elvis Presley record they had put out that year — to the coupling of "Hound Dog" and "Don't Be Cruel," which was released on July 13 and within a week was on the verge of going gold.

Meanwhile, Elvis got so sunburnt he was forced to water-ski in long pants and a long-sleeved jersey for a day or two (despite his incongruous dress, "his skill," according to water-ski instructor Dickie Waters, "was almost professional-looking"), and June was in and out of the water so much that she finally just got fed up with fixing her hair and, at Elvis' suggestion, had it all cut off. The world seemed far away, and when it intruded in unwanted fashion there was likely to be a spontaneous response. Elvis for some reason detested Teresa Brewer's "Sweet Old Fashioned Girl," which was popular that summer, and one time after they'd been horseback riding and were sitting around afterward with a giant pitcher of ice water, the song came on the radio. "I told him, 'Here's your favorite song,'" June said, and mischievously turned the radio up. "He took that entire pitcher of ice water and dumped it on his head! That was a typical Elvis thing to do."

The only sobering notes were Elvis' all-too-imminent departure at the beginning of August for yet another Florida tour and the occasional intrusion of others — Red and Junior and sometimes Arthur, whom June called "Arthritis" — on their almost perfect happiness. It wasn't that June didn't like his friends, although she sensed a meanness on Junior's part, not to mention a coarseness on Red's, that flourished when the elder Presleys were away. That she could certainly have lived with — she was confident that she could give as well as she got. What disturbed her far more was their effect on Elvis: he seemed to need their approval so much that he became like them. Her friends didn't have that effect on her, or on him; they were just fun to be around. But Elvis seemed to lose his confidence as well as his temper when he was around his gang. On the one hand, he desperately wanted to be a good influence on them, he shot them a look of sharp rebuke if they ever really got out of line, and he was good to them, too, he was always showing that wonderful generosity of spirit that she loved so much in him. On the other hand, she hated it when he showed off in front of them, when he tried so hard to act like one of the boys that he was no longer even himself. She was a person, too, she told him. She wasn't a possession. She didn't belong to anyone.

"He always wanted me right there, right under his thumb. He'd always be looking for me, and when he found me, it was always, 'Where the hell have you been? Who the hell do you think you are?' This is in front of the guys. He was quick to fly off the handle, and I could be stubborn at times, too! So this one time he's saying, 'You're not going to talk to me like that, you're not going to treat me like that,' and I chewed on his ass in front of them all. Well, he grabbed me — 'Come on!' Just grabbed me by the arm like he was really going to read my beads and pulled me into the bathroom. But when we got in there, I mean he would just take my face in his hands and kiss me and say, 'Baby, I know it. I know you're right . . . and I'm sorry.' But he would not show that to the guys. The guys just did not know that he had a tender heart."

June did, though. She sensed his spiritual side from the first, and she gave him a copy of *The Prophet*, by Kahlil Gibran, a graduation present from a former boyfriend the previous year. "He loved it. I would tell him my favorite chapters — my favorite was on love and friendship, and there was even a little bit on marriage." They read it over and over and talked about it at length, and June thought it calmed him down some — though she doubted that anything would ever really do that. One night they stopped by the hospital to visit a little girl with leukemia whose mother June knew, and then they went to the pier where they had sat out till almost dawn the night they first met. Elvis told June to look up at the moon, to let herself totally relax and not think about anything else, just let herself float in the space between the moon and the stars. If you relaxed enough, he told her, you could get up right there next to them. "How long have you been doing this?" she asked him. "Since I was a little boy," he told her. But he didn't tell just anyone about it. "I learned a long time ago not to talk about it. People think you're crazy when you talk about things they don't understand." His mother, he said, was the only one he had ever really trusted to understand.

She understood. She understood that when she was with him she had something that others couldn't break. And she understood that when he was in public he had something that she was not allowed to threaten. It would be three years, he told her a little apologetically, before he could have a life of his own. Then he could do whatever he wanted to do. Then he would be free to marry, have children, admit in public that he did not simply belong to the public, but until then he had promised the Colonel, this mysterious personage she had never met, that he would never do anything detrimental to his career.

For all of that, though, life in Biloxi was tucked away enough so that they could almost pretend to be leading normal lives, and the town itself was sufficiently accustomed to celebrity that after a while it could simply pretend to ignore them. They went to see *The King and I* at the Saenger Theatre downtown and walked out because, Elvis said, he thought movie musicals were ridiculous, people bursting into song at the drop of a hat just when things were getting serious. They hung around with June's friends, Patty Welsh and Patsy Napier and Buddy Conrad, who drove a sharp new mint green Lincoln Continental, and they went to Gino's Pizza and King William's Cellar in Ocean Springs and, of course, the Pink Pony, typical teenagers, just having fun. All of her friends adored Elvis and wouldn't hear a word against him. One time, as a favor to Eddie Bellman, Elvis made an appearance at Dave Rosenblum's clothing store, where Mr. Bellman owned the ladies' shoe department with Lew Sonnier, and the crowd was so large, the newspaper reported, that it stopped traffic downtown. One night they went to Gus Stevens' famous Supper Club, "the nightclub of the Coast," because Elvis wanted to see the comedian Brother Dave Gardner, and Mr. Gus made a big fuss over them, put them in a private dining room, and had his picture taken with the rising young star.

Toward the end of July Elvis had to go back to Memphis for a week, and when he returned he had a brand-new Lincoln Premiere with a wisteria purple bottom and a white top, which he said would be "less conspicuous." He couldn't get back into the "Hack House," so he rented both sides of a villa which would ordinarily be shared by two families, allowing June and Elvis to maintain their privacy from the guys. With the time of Elvis' departure rapidly approaching, they clung to each other more and more — neither one of them, it seemed, could imagine it ever ending. Finally he said couldn't she just go with him? She asked her mother, and her mother said no, but then Elvis said to just leave everything to him. He had his mother call Mrs. Juanico and assure her that June would be properly chaperoned. Then he went out to Keesler Air Force Base and persuaded the father of June's seventeen-year-old friend Patsy, Sergeant Napier (who June thought would never go for it, not in a million years), to let his daughter accompany them. Then, when Sarge agreed, he enlisted their friend Buddy to drive.

On the last night at the villa, with the older Presleys down for one final visit, June stayed the night, falling asleep in his arms. When she woke up early and started to get dressed, he pulled her back into bed, and they started fooling around, as they frequently did, wrestling and giggling and carrying on. "We had spent night after night falling asleep in one another's arms without anything beyond a lot of kissing and a little touching. Elvis respected women, I think because he respected his mother so much, and he always stopped before I would ever have to say no. But this one time I didn't want to say stop, and I don't think he wanted to stop either, so I got hysterical with giggling — that's what I do when I get nervous — and then my giggling rubbed off on him, and here we were rolling over and over on top of one another without any clothes on just laughing our asses off, because we were both afraid of what we were about to do. And then we stopped, and all of a sudden there was a little tap at the door, and it was Mrs. Presley. She said, 'I heard it was quiet in here, and then I heard giggling, and then I heard quiet again. So I thought I'd better come see. You know, maybe we'd better get June on some pills to keep her from having too many babies.'

"Neither one of us ever said anything about it like 'I'm sorry it went almost that far.' It was more like, 'Boy, we almost did it, June, didn't we?' That was his comment. 'We almost did it, didn't we, baby?' And I said, 'We almost did.' He said, 'That was close, wasn't it?' Like it was fun for him, and it was fun for me, too, and it was close. After that, we really didn't have too many more occasions when we were totally alone. There was only a few times — but it never really got as close as it did that night."

Then he was gone. He would meet them in Miami, he said. Just look for Red or Junior or Gene — any one of those three would take care of them.

THEY ARRIVED in Miami on Friday, August 3, just as Elvis was going on for the first of three daily shows at the Olympia Theatre, a vaudeville redoubt from the 1920s still resplendent with stuffed peacocks and a ceiling twinkling with painted stars in a painted sky. June was immediately ushered backstage, where a *Miami News* reporting team discovered her and recorded that

she reportedly stroked [Elvis'] brow between stage shows. . . . Furthermore, June Juanico, 18, the Biloxi beauty whom Presley evidently prefers to aspirin, admitted that Elvis is as unsteady in love as he is on the stage. "It would be nice if Elvis loved me as much as I love him," June sighed. "But right now he's married to his career and he isn't thinking of marriage." June, whose hair is bobbed Italian-style, said she's going on the Presley tour of six [additional] Florida cities and New Orleans. But when he returns to Memphis, she said, "I don't know just what I'll do."

Interviewed in the tunnel underneath the Olympia stage, June recounted the story of their meeting and subsequent courtship.

"Well, you know how love is. Eight months went by, and I never heard from him." . . . Overhead, while June was talking and posing for us deep down under the stage, Presley was warming up and she didn't want to miss even one performance. . . . We asked why the girls, especially the younger set, threw such hysterics — and how come she didn't scream. Without missing a knee jerk or bounce June replied: "If you were a member of the opposite sex you'd appreciate him, too. And I do feel like screaming."

They went back to the Robert Clay Hotel after the final performance. Elvis' two-week-old Lincoln was covered with names and messages and phone numbers. There had been reporters underfoot all day, and Elvis was irritated both with himself and with them. At a press conference that afternoon he had stumbled over a question about the Suez Canal crisis, and he felt like he had made a fool of himself. He told June, "Well, I shouldn't have said anything then. I should have waited and thought about it for a second and not come out with anything so dumb." June and Patsy had their own room, of course, and after taking a shower Elvis came back to see them — and to get away from the Colonel and the boys. He lay down on the twin bed with June, touched her as if he couldn't believe she was really there, fooled around with Patsy, a mischievous little sister as no-bullshit and sharp-tongued as June, murmured sweet nothings in June's ear, and then, before she knew it, was fast asleep.

The next day June's interview ran in the newspaper, and the Colonel came storming into the dressing room before the first show. His gaze went first to June, then back to Elvis, and he had the paper in his hand.

"Son, we can't have this kind of publicity," he declared, face red, eyes flaring, rapping the newspaper loudly against his palm. "You've got to do something about this, son," he announced again meaningfully. For the first time since she had known him, Elvis looked really scared. "What is it, Colonel?" he asked, stuttering the way he always did when he was agitated. "Read it yourself, son, and make damn sure you do something about it."

Elvis was still upset after the show — he seemed to blame her for giving the interview, he seemed to feel like if she hadn't talked to "that damn reporter," no one would ever have noticed her presence here in Miami. He was obviously just frustrated and upset, and when he finally calmed down he decided to go car shopping with his manager while June went back to the hotel. On a whim he plunked down $10,800 for a white Lincoln Continental just like Buddy's, with his brand-new lipstick-covered Premiere used as a trade-in. A reporter tracked him down as he lingered in the showroom and asked about June. "Now this is the way it is," Elvis declared nervously. "I got twenty-five girls I date regular. She's just one of the girls." "They show up sometimes eight at a time," chimed in the Colonel, seemingly restored to good humor, "all claiming they're his 'steadies.' One girl even claimed she was my daughter, and I don't have a daughter."

Later, when the Colonel came to Elvis' hotel room, he barely gave June a look. "Here, I thought you might want to see this," he said, handing Gene a copy of the script for the picture they were going to start filming in Hollywood in three weeks. Then he turned on his heel and slammed the door. Elvis grabbed at the script eagerly, and he and June started reading through it, but he got impatient and couldn't resist turning the pages to find out how it ended. He was keenly disappointed when he discovered that the character he played was going to die. "He said, 'June, I don't want to die in my first movie.' I said, 'Why not? I think it's a good idea. I always remember the character who dies. Happy endings you forget. Sad endings stay with you longer.' "

For the final show Elvis told everyone to be sure to be in the cars when he started the last song, not when he finished. He told June to stay away from the Colonel, who would be preoccupied with selling his pictures and souvenirs anyway; after all, he had to feel like he was doing something. In the car as they traveled through the night, they held each other. He put an unlighted cigar in his mouth and made fun of the Colonel, bravely declaring, "You're seeing too much of this girl from Biloxi. She's not good for you, son. You can't be linked to any one girl. For God's sake, don't get her pregnant. You do, and you're through in this business, that's for sure." They laughed till the tears streamed down from their eyes, but June knew his bravery in the dark would never see the light of day. He was trying to look out for them all, Red and Junior and Gene and June and her friends, his family, his fans, they were all counting on him, they were all looking up to him, and some part of him felt like none of this would have been possible, all of it could end in a minute, without the Colonel. So he tried to take care of the problems he could take care of, he did all he could to keep Red and Junior in line, he wanted, thought June, to make everything come out all right.

The next day, in Tampa, the shit really hit the fan. The Miami paper had interviewed June's mother over the telephone and then set her quotes against Elvis' and the Colonel's. Under the headline "Elvis Denies Biloxi Beauty Is His 'Steady,' " Mrs. Mae Juanico was quoted as saying "— in no uncertain terms — that 'The Pelvis' had asked her daughter to be 'his permanently' in three years. . . . 'I don't object to her making the trip,' Mrs. Juanico said. 'He's a nice boy, and June is a good girl. I talked to his parents and they said Elvis would take good care of her. . . . He said he can't get married for at least three years, and he asked her to wait for him.' " The Colonel was rigid with rage, the boys reacted to Elvis' quote that he had twenty-four other girlfriends by saying, "Yeah, that's why he takes us along, we take care of the overflow," and Elvis wanted June to call her mother right away and tell her not to talk to anyone else — he didn't want to hear about her defending her daughter's honor, he just didn't want any more of this shit.

There were two shows that day at the Fort Homer Hesterly Armory, sponsored by the Seratoma Civic Club, with seats at $1.50 and $2.00. There were boxes set up for a stage, no house PA, two microphones, and two amps, with the same incongruous procession of vaudeville acts that Al Dvorin, the Chicago booking agent, had been supplying since the spring, amounting to an hour and a half of mediocre warm-ups preceding the main twenty-minute show. "Fuck you very much," Elvis said over the din, but no one could make out the words, the music, or the remarks. "It was more than obvious," wrote Anne Rowe, a reporter for the *St. Petersburg Times* who was there for an interview, "that he loved every scream and yell . . . and every minute on that stage. He wrestled with the mike, breaking two apart in his frenzy, and finally, with perspiration pouring down his face, he practically tore his jacket off and let go on two more numbers."

He felt like a different person, he told June, when he was onstage: "I don't know, it's hard to explain. It's like your whole body gets goose bumps, but it's not goose bumps. It's not a chill either. It's like a surge of electricity going through you. It's almost like making love, but it's even stronger than that." Did it happen to all entertainers? June asked him. "I don't know. The few I've talked to experience excitement and nerves, but they must not feel the way I do. If they did, they would say more about it, don't you think? They say they get nervous, but after they sing a few lines they calm down. Hell, I don't calm down till two or three hours after I leave the stage. Sometimes I think my heart is going to explode."

H E PLAYED LAKELAND, St. Petersburg, and Orlando, using Tampa as his home base for the first two. When he played Lakeland on Monday, he did an interview backstage with *Tampa Tribune* reporter Paul Wilder, which was scheduled to run the following month in *TV Guide*. Wilder had been with the paper for years and in fact had covered Tom Parker on a regular basis in his column "In Our Town" when the Colonel was merely Tampa's inventive animal-control officer. He had reviewed Elvis' show in Tampa with relative indifference (his daughter, Paula, had covered the teenager's angle with considerably more fervor), but he began his interview, with unimaginable insensitivity, by reading lengthy excerpts from one of the most vicious write-ups Elvis had ever received.

" 'The biggest freak in show business history,' " Wilder read, from Herb Rau's column in the *Miami News,* in a flat, droning voice. " 'Elvis can't sing, can't play the guitar — and can't dance. He has two thousand idiots per show, yet every time he opens his mouth, plucks a guitar string, or shakes his pelvis like any striptease babe in town. . . .' Do you," he asked the startled performer, "shake your pelvis like any striptease babe in town?"

For one of the few times in his career Elvis actually showed anger, not just for himself but for his fans. After first stipulating that Wilder probably knew about striptease babes because that's where he must hang out, he protested the slur on his audience. "Sir, those kids that come here and pay their money to see this show come to have a good time. I mean, I'm not running Mr. Rau down, but I just don't see that he should call those people idiots. Because they're somebody's kids. They're somebody's decent kids, probably, that was raised in a decent home, and he hasn't got any right to call those kids idiots. If they want to pay their money to come out and jump around and scream and yell, it's their business. They'll grow up someday and grow out of that. While they're young, let them have their fun. Don't let some old man that's so old he can't get around sit around and call them a bunch of idiots. Because they're just human beings like he is."

Okay, said Wilder, returning to his readings. But what did he think about Rau suggesting that what his female fans really needed was " 'a solid slap across the mouth?' Have you any comment to that?" "Yeah, but I don't think I should say it." "Okay, okay, this isn't over the air, this is for *TV Guide*," Wilder inexplicably persisted, but Elvis continued to show a remarkable degree of restraint. He still didn't think he should voice his reaction. "Okay —," said Wilder. " 'Cause I'm a singer, not a fighter," said Elvis, to a background of sardonic laughter. What about all this talk about his gyrations? Wilder asked him. "I read a clipping, somewhere you were attributed as saying that Holy Roller —"

"I have *never* used that expression," Elvis exploded angrily. "That's another deal. See, I belong to an Assembly of God church, which is a Holiness church. I was raised up in a little Assembly of God church, and some character called them Holy Rollers —" "Oh, I see. Well, you —" "And that's where that got started. I always attended church where people sang, stood up and sang in the choir and worshiped God, you know. I have never used the expression 'Holy Roller.' " What about the music in his church? Wilder wondered innocently enough. "Do you think you transfer some of that rhythm into your —"

For the first time Elvis seemed to lose his composure altogether. "That's not it. That's not it at all," he practically shouted, obviously stung by an implication far more sweeping than the dismissal of his music. "There was some article came out where I got the jumping around from my religion. Well, my religion has nothing to do with what I do now. Because the type of stuff I do now is not religious music, and my religious background has nothing to do with the way I sing."

After that even Wilder seemed to get it, and he backed off on his questioning, so much so that by the end of the interview he appeared to be totally disarmed. Then, with the show going on in the background, he interviewed his old friend the Colonel, but it was obvious that he never had a chance. Was there a possibility of more frequent television appearances? "I think one of the main reasons that I don't book Mr. Presley on television more often is that to my way of thinking many of the artists today are overexposed on television. . . . My way of thinking may be wrong on this. However, I'll have plenty of time to find out next year. If it doesn't work this way, we'll try something new." The wiggling, and the criticism it provoked? "I have tried to figure out many angles. First of all, for many months we were touring the country, and Elvis had never appeared on television, and the only way people would know about Elvis was by his records. And I have tried repeatedly to play his records and figure out some way where I could see him wiggle while listening to his records. Which is impossible." Elvis' future as an actor? "Well, Mr. Wilder, when we made the screen test for Mr. Hal Wallis at Paramount Studios in Hollywood, they tested Mr. Presley in a singing role, and also, while he was there, they gave him a short story or some play — whatever you call it — and Mr. Wallis decided after seeing the test that Mr. Presley was capable of starring in a dramatic production. When and how I don't know, but Mr. Presley had no training in acting, and I saw the test, and if I was not his manager, I could not be more excited about a new personality than I am now being Elvis Presley's manager, for his acting ability was the greatest. . . . I think Elvis Presley could play any role he makes up his mind to play."

He did three shows in Lakeland, three in St. Petersburg (renamed "St. Presleyburg" for the day), two in Orlando, and two in Daytona Beach. By the time that he arrived in Jacksonville on Friday, August 10, the town had taken on all the trappings of a religious revival. The faithful were gathered as always in a long line in front of the box office from the predawn hours before the first show; a minister was offering up prayers for Presley at the Trinity Baptist Church after declaring that the singer had "achieved a new low in spiritual degeneracy"; reporters from two national magazines, *Life* and *Collier's,* were on hand to cover his every move; a contest winner named Andrea June Stephens was flown in with her mother from Atlanta by *Hit Parader* magazine for a date she had won with an essay entitled "Why I Want to Meet Elvis"; June Juanico was hissed at and gossiped about and cursed as a whore by girls who had read about her or just didn't like the confident way she stood at "his" side; and Judge Marion Gooding,

who was determined not to see a repeat of the previous year's performance when "aroused fans ripped nearly all [of Elvis'] clothes off," met
with the Optimist Club and prepared warrants charging Presley with im-
pairing the morals of minors, which he said he would serve if the singer
acted in a fashion that "put obscenity and vulgarity in front of our children."

Judge Gooding was at the first performance at 3:30 Friday afternoon
and subsequently invited the singer to a meeting in chambers. There Elvis
expressed his shock at the judge's reaction ("I can't figure out what I'm
doing wrong," he said to reporters; "I know my mother approves of what
I'm doing"), and the judge repeated his determination to serve the warrants if the show were not toned down. A compromise was reached, and
Judge Gooding was satisfied that Presley complied with the agreement,
"judging from reports of the later shows." Meanwhile, the *Jacksonville
Journal* informed its readers, a representative of the American Guild of Variety Artists told Presley that, because of his suggestive body movements,
it would be necessary to post bond and join the guild (which represented
exotic dancers, among others), or they would block the show. The Colonel took care of that, and Presley, noted the paper, "kept a nonchalant
attitude throughout the day," answering reporters' questions, taking Andrea June Stephens out for a cheeseburger (which Andrea June declined),
and, in place of the body movements, wiggling his little finger lasciviously
in a move that sent his audience into paroxysms of ecstasy. Back in the
hotel room afterward he told June, "Baby, you should have been there.
Every time D.J. did his thing on the drums, I wiggled my finger, and the
girls went wild. I never heard screams like that in my life. I showed them
sons of bitches — calling me vulgar. Baby, you don't think I'm vulgar, do
you?" And he put a pair of June's underpants on his head and glided
around the room.

WITH THE TOUR'S triumphant conclusion in New Orleans, he returned to Memphis, while June went home to Biloxi. The *Life*
magazine team was still with him, and he was never far removed from a
reporter's question or a photographer's flashbulb. The *Life* photographer
got a picture of the fence that had been installed just a few weeks before,
complete with musical staff and notes. It didn't really keep the fans out —

Life also ran a picture of some girls plucking blades of grass from the lawn, and the newspaper reported lines of cars so long that the neighbors called the police. Vernon's brother, Vester, still working full-time at Precision Tool, was now moonlighting as a kind of security guard, but mainly he just chatted with the fans or tried to get them to keep their racket down so Grandma and Gladys could get some rest. There was no question of running them off: Elvis wouldn't hear of it. He knew who he owed his success to.

There were only four days left before his scheduled departure for Hollywood, and he had a lot to pack in. On the first night he went out to the Fairgrounds, and Red got into another fight. The next day Vernon told Red that he didn't want him around anymore, that Red wouldn't be going out to Hollywood with Elvis, because they just didn't need that kind of bad publicity. Red got pissed off and said he was going to join the Marines; he was mad because he didn't hear Elvis speaking up for him, and what else was he going to do, anyway? Elvis saw a lot of Barbara Hearn, and he stopped off to see Dewey down at the radio station almost every night — they laughed and talked about the old days. Dewey was just about to start a TV show, which would go on at 8:00 on Saturday night, just after Lawrence Welk. "You better warn those Welk listeners to grab that dial quick," Dewey told Bob Johnson at the paper, " 'cause if they don't switch quick, I'll be right there at 'em."

Everyone was talking about Hollywood, and no one who knew him doubted that he would make a big success. Sam Phillips told him that he would be another James Dean, and Dewey figured he would just nail all the little starlets he met. He heard from the Colonel out in Hollywood that there were going to be one or two songs in the picture, and that was all right, as long as they didn't take away from the dramatic impact of the role. Was he going to take acting lessons? the reporters all asked. No, he told each and every one, although he had not recited so much as a single line onstage in his life, "I don't think that you learn to become an actor, I think you just, maybe you've got a little bit of acting talent and develop it. If you learn to be an actor, in other words, if you're not a real actor — you're false." On the precipice of something he had never experienced before, he seemed strangely serene — but then why shouldn't he be? Everything he had ever dreamed had come true, so far. "I've made a study of Marlon Brando," he confided to Lloyd Shearer when Shearer had come down to Memphis to do a story for Sunday *Parade* the month before. "I've made a study of poor Jimmy Dean. I've made a study of myself, and I know why girls, at least the young 'uns, go for us. We're sullen, we're broodin', we're something of a menace. I don't understand it exactly, but that's what the girls like in men. I don't know anything about Hollywood, but I know you can't be sexy if you smile. You can't be a rebel if you grin."

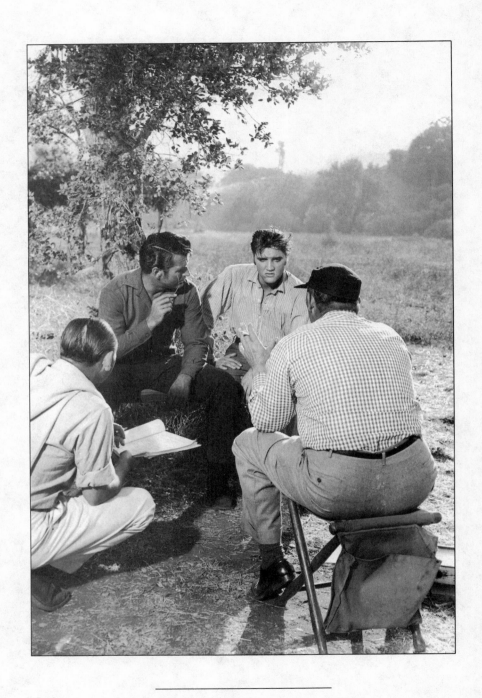

STUDYING LINES WITH COSTAR RICHARD EGAN AND
DIRECTOR ROBERT WEBB, RIGHT. (MICHAEL OCHS ARCHIVES)

LOVE ME TENDER

H E ARRIVED IN HOLLYWOOD on Friday, August 17. There were signs as he got off the plane at the Los Angeles airport announcing "Elvis for President," but when reporters asked him about it, he indicated no serious interest in the post, declaring, "I'm strictly for Stevenson. I don't dig the intellectual bit, but I'm telling you, man, he knows the most." With that he was off to his hotel, the Hollywood Knickerbocker, on Ivar off Hollywood Boulevard, where the Colonel was already staying and where he and his cousin Gene occupied a spacious suite on the eleventh floor.

He reported to the studio for meetings and costume fittings at the beginning of the following week. Unsure exactly what preparations were required, he had memorized the entire script, not just his own part but everyone else's, too. "I have no trouble memorizing," he told a reporter proudly. "I once memorized General MacArthur's farewell address, and I can still reel off Lincoln's Gettysburg speech from when I memorized it in school." He met his costars, Richard Egan and Debra Paget (to Egan he confided that he had never acted before and that he was "plenty scared"), as well as director Robert Webb, a fifty-three-year-old veteran of the system who was understandably concerned that, with Elvis' late entry, the film, a modest B western, might be turned into a sideshow. To Mildred Dunnock, who was to play his mother in the film, he was a nice boy whose extremely polite and deferential manner indicated an obvious willingness to learn. The person he was most excited about meeting, though, was forty-one-year-old producer David Weisbart, who had produced James Dean's *Rebel Without a Cause* the previous year. Weisbart was talking about filming a documentary-style *James Dean Story*, something, Elvis blurted out to Weisbart, he would like to do "more than anything else." He sat with his legs tucked under him, chewing gum and stroking his chin nervously. "I'd sure like to take a crack at it," he said. "I think I could do it easy."

It was like a magical kingdom, with famous stars constantly strolling by, cowboys and Indians making casual conversation in the commissary, and everyone sneaking a peek out of the corner of their eye to get a look at the latest arrival on the lot. Gene seemed a little bit overwhelmed by it all and took to whittling or retreating to the big dressing room where the Colonel conducted business while Elvis was on the set. For his part Elvis couldn't seem to get enough — it was like the playing out of a childhood fantasy, he just didn't want to reveal by an inadvertent glance or blurted-out words how excited he really was.

On his second day on the set he met twenty-five-year-old Nick Adams, a Hollywood hustler who had originally brazened his way into the cast of *Mister Roberts* two years before by doing impressions of the star, Jimmy Cagney, for director John Ford. Adams, a coal miner's son from Nan-ticoke, Pennsylvania, had had a supporting role in *Rebel Without a Cause* and was, he announced to all and sundry, currently writing a book about his "best friend," Jimmy Dean. Desperate for success and recognition, he was known to keep meticulous notebooks on Hollywood social life and never failed to send thank-you notes and congratulatory messages to pro-ducers, directors, and people of influence in the industry. On this particu-lar day he was roaming the lot, looking to make a connection for the "bad guy" role in *The Reno Brothers* that Cameron Mitchell had just dropped out of. That was when he ran into Elvis. "It's no secret around town that Nick's a go-getter," wrote Army Archerd in *Photoplay*, but "before Nick knew what had hit him, Elvis was saying, 'Gee, I think you're a swell actor.' It didn't take Nick long to tell Elvis how much he'd like to be in his film. He told Elvis how he'd played a 'heavy' in 'The Last Wagon.' 'Gee,' said Elvis, 'I'll tell Mr. Weisbart to look at "The Last Wagon." ' " Though nothing came of it, the point was made, and when Nick offered to intro-duce Elvis to some more of his, and Jimmy's, friends, their friendship was sealed. Had Elvis met Natalie Wood? He had to meet Natalie. And, of course, this being Hollywood, there were always lots of girls . . .

It was hard to keep track of everything, it was all happening so fast. Every night he called home to tell his mother the latest news. Almost every night he called June. Three songs were now set for the picture, and Colonel was making deals for their delivery to RCA, working out the pub-lishing, and making sure that Elvis got coauthorship. Colonel Parker was staying up nights, Elvis told a reporter, "thinking up ways to promote me." In the midst of it all, Scotty and Bill and D.J. showed up after driving cross-country from Memphis. They had been promised a tryout for the picture, and there was an RCA recording session with Mr. Sholes scheduled for the following weekend.

The tryout was held in the music bungalow on the west end of the lot where Elvis was rehearsing his three songs with Mr. Darby, the musical director. They were asked to play their regular show, but when they got done they were told they were not "hillbilly" enough for the picture. Scotty was furious — if they had known the musical director wanted "hillbilly," he fumed, they would have given him banjos and jugs and Roy Acuff music, that was what they had grown up on, after all. Elvis' mind was somewhere else, though, and the Colonel was certainly not going to stick up for them. As far as the Colonel was concerned, Scotty knew, they might just as well never have showed up.

It was a minor setback — the next picture, Elvis promised them, he would make sure that they were used. He had finally gotten to renew his brief acquaintance with Debra Paget, he told June on the telephone. She was even more beautiful than he had first thought, she was really nice, and . . . Well, who else had he met? June wondered. When Elvis didn't answer, June asked, Well, what did you talk about with Debra? After a long silence he finally said he didn't remember, but he had met Richard Egan. "Oh, I *love* Richard Egan," June simpered. "Oh, really? And just how much do you love Richard Egan?" About as much as he loved Debra Paget, she supposed. Now who else had he met?

On Wednesday the picture started shooting, but Elvis was getting ready for the soundtrack session the following day. On the day of the session Elvis was eager to perform the ballad that would provide a running theme for the movie (and was even then under discussion as a new title for the picture) for Army Archerd, who was on assignment for *Photoplay*. He took Archerd back to the music bungalow, where Ken Darby accompanied him on the grand piano, and Elvis stood "erect, as if he were in a choir," in front of a tall stained-glass window and sang "Love Me Tender." Archerd was astonished both at the stillness of his manner and the straightforwardness of his treatment of the song, which was a rewrite of the Civil War ballad "Aura Lee." "When he finished," wrote Archerd, "it seemed only normal to express our amazement. 'People think all I can do is belt,' he said. 'I used to sing nothing but ballads before I went professional. I love ballads,' " he insisted to the Hollywood columnist with utter sincerity. He was going to start introducing them more into his live act. This was the kind of music he had grown up singing in church.

The session itself went off without a hitch. The film-studio setting may have been a little intimidating at first, with the distinguished conductor-orchestrator Lionel Newman counting off the beat for the little combo and the Ken Darby vocal trio not really up to the kind of support on Brother Claude Ely's "There's a Leak in This Old Building" (retitled, and recopyrighted, as "We're Gonna Move") that the Jordanaires would have provided. Elvis poured himself into "Love Me Tender," though, and when the session was over went off happily with his new pals, Nick Adams and Nick's roommate, Dennis Hopper.

It was a relief once the real work of acting finally began. It was a job like any other — he was up at 5:30 every morning, he told Dewey on the phone, and sometimes he fell asleep talking to June on the phone at night. "This place isn't anything but a workshop," Elvis declared to the Memphis DJ. "I spent one whole day plowing mules. Man, that was rough!"

Richard Egan told him that the trick was to just be yourself, and David Weisbart insisted that acting lessons would probably ruin him, because his greatest asset was his natural ability. The director, Robert Webb, was very patient, taking him aside before the start of each scene and going over it with him so that he could visualize the action and emotion. Webb would break down the lines, too, giving the fledgling actor points of emphasis and breathing points, talking to Elvis in private and showing him the kind of respect that always allowed him to take direction. Everyone liked the kid — they had all thought he would be some kind of hillbilly freak, but he had won them over with the same combination of humility and deferential charm that had worked for him in every other situation in which he had found himself in his twenty-one-year-old life. "I had a nice talk with him one day," Mildred Dunnock recounted to writer Jerry Hopkins, "and he told me a little bit about how he got started. He evidently played the guitar and was very anxious to get on a recording — this was in Memphis. So he kept approaching the man that had the [studio] and just simply couldn't get on it. One night this man took pity on him, or got bored with his asking, and felt finally he'd give him a try. . . . [The night that the disc jockey played the recording] Elvis told me he was so nervous he went to the movie house. He said to his mother, 'I can't listen to this, I just can't listen to it.' So he went down to see the movie, and at about twenty minutes after eleven his mother came rushing down to the movie, to the aisle seat where he was sitting, and said, 'Elvis, come on home, the telephone is ringing like crazy.' And that was the start of his real popularity."

"Before I met him, I figured he must be some sort of moron," said Debra Paget, voicing what she said was a commonly held assumption on the set, but once she got to know him, she, too, came to find him "very sweet, very simple," just not the kind of boy she would care to date. Trude Forsher, a Viennese émigrée, mother of two, and distant relative of the Aberbachs, who had just gone to work for the Colonel as his West Coast secretary, hosted informal meetings in his dressing room in which the Colonel and Abe Lastfogel, the head of William Morris, talked business and Elvis drank milk and fooled around with Gene. Between takes Gene and Elvis would pester her to teach them German and reminisce about their childhood when they played underneath the house in Tupelo with a little toy car. "Gene was just so happy to be with Elvis." The two of them followed her around the lot singing "Trude Frutti."

He was constantly busy with visitors and reporters on the set. He flirted openly with the women reporters and trusted them to see through his bravura facade. "I could make you like me if I tried," he told one reporter. "I'm just teasin' now, but I'd be sweet, and you'd like me because I was sweet, wouldn't you?" With the men he was equally forthright, and he was open about his hopes and fears with one and all. "I'm so nervous," he said in response to a question about biting his fingernails. "I've always been nervous, ever since I was a kid." "From the time I was a kid, well, I knew something was going to happen to me," he told another interviewer. "Didn't know exactly what." To *True Story* staff writer Jules Archer he confessed his genuine disturbance at the reaction to his Jacksonville shows and the preacher who asked his congregation to pray for Elvis' salvation. "I think that hurt me more than anything else at first. This man was supposed to be a religious leader, yet he acted that way without ever knowing who I was or what I was like. I believe in the Bible. I believe that all good things come from God. . . . I don't believe I'd sing the way I do if God hadn't wanted me to. My voice is God's will, not mine."

He signed autographs willingly and met with studio executives' daughters. He and Gene spent $750 on a Saturday night at a Long Beach amusement park. Meanwhile, the Colonel was working without letup to promote his boy, to make sure that the film's title was changed and that the title song, with Elvis' name on the copyright, would run all the way through the picture, to solidify his merchandising deal with marketing king Hank Saperstein, to earn his own newly conferred title (and salary) as "Technical Adviser" to the film. He wore his pink Elvis Presley button everywhere he went on the set and, when asked by a reporter how to obtain one, said, "We'll have to check you over. It's not that easy, you know."

Back at the hotel Elvis was exhausted, frequently by 8:30 or 9:00 at night. Sometimes he and Nick went out together. Mostly he and Gene ordered in room service. He kept June up-to-date on how the movie was going. One night he told her in some wonderment how William Campbell, who played his brother, Brett, had refused the director's orders to wear a hat, because he was so vain about his hair. "He combs his hair even more than I do," he told her — if she could believe that. He was lonely, he missed her, he wanted her to come out. He would arrange for a screen test. What was she up to back home in Biloxi, what was she doing without him?

Everything was going pretty much according to plan. He put himself into the scenes the same way he put himself into the music. He listened intently to the other actors saying their lines, and then he reacted — the character that he played was an innocent, almost a child as he portrayed him, full of hurt and rage and indignation. The only thing that gave him away was his hands. If he didn't have something to do, his hands betrayed him. You could see it in the rushes: his fingers fluttering, just as they did when he was onstage, as he waited for the other actor to get through with his lines, revealing the same lack of training that Mr. Weisbart told reporters was a virtue. "Presley has the same smoldering appeal for teenagers, and the same impulsive nature [as James Dean did]. In his singing style Elvis often expresses the loneliness and yearning of all teenage kids as they break away from childhood and become adults. . . . Elvis is simply a kid who is emotionally honest, and honestly emotional."

On the Friday before Labor Day weekend, Mr. Sholes visited the set, and Colonel got him into a broad-brimmed straw hat while donning a fake goatee and mustache himself for a photograph with other RCA executives to commemorate the occasion. Sholes had flown out the day before with Bill Bullock, manager of RCA's singles division, for the recording session he had been importuning the Colonel for ever since the spring. It was *imperative*, he argued, that they have material for the second album, which was scheduled for November, and Colonel had finally, grudgingly, conceded the point and scheduled a session for Saturday, Sunday, and Monday of the holiday weekend. Also flying out for the session was Freddy Bienstock, and the three men, plus the Colonel's assistant Tom Diskin, met for breakfast each morning in the hotel dining room, with Sholes dressed in his somber suit and tie while the Colonel was suitably decked out for the California sunshine in a colorful western or Hawaiian shirt that barely tucked into his ample waistband.

Sholes had sent out a bunch of songs and arranged with Henri Rene, an arranger-producer at RCA's West Coast office, to make sure that Elvis was supplied with a phonograph player, but every time he made inquiries as to whether or not Elvis had selected material, he was rebuffed with a corny joke or enigmatic double-talk. Freddy Bienstock, the junior member of the trio and the Hill and Range representative who had brought "Don't Be Cruel" to the last session, had arrived with material of his own, and Sholes grew impatient as Bienstock and the Colonel bantered back and forth and spoke with evident good humor of Freddy's cousins the Aberbachs, with whom Steve had been doing business for years. It was a most uncomfortable situation but one he was going to have to get used to: no matter how much bullshit there was to get through, *he* was the one who was responsible in the end for delivery of the product, and he was going to make sure that he delivered.

Since RCA did not have studio facilities of its own in Hollywood, the session was booked into Radio Recorders, an independent studio on Santa Monica. There had been a problem with the Jordanaires' schedule, but that was worked out, and when Elvis walked in the door shortly after 1:00, everyone was there and all set up. The engineer in charge of the session was a twenty-nine-year-old mixer from Dundee, Michigan, named Thorne Nogar who had been assigned the RCA account a year or two before. A quiet man of Scandinavian background and dour mien, he resembled Scotty somewhat in temperament and was neither impressed nor unimpressed by this kid from Memphis, "awful nice kid — he come in there with no pretensions, just a kid off the street." Elvis in turn warmed to the sound recordist's equally unpretentious manner from the start. He liked Nogar's assistant, too, a soft-spoken young jazz drummer named Bones Howe who had just gone to work for the studio and did everything that needed doing, from getting Thorne coffee to cueing up the tape on the reel.

They started off with "Playing for Keeps," a number that Elvis had gotten from Stan Kesler in Memphis (Kesler had written "I Forgot to Remember to Forget" and "I'm Left, You're Right, She's Gone" for him at Sun), and then Bones played the acetate demos, as Freddy handed them to him, over the PA that boomed into the studio. Freddy had a new song "from the pencil of" Otis Blackwell, and, after the great success of "Hound Dog," he had solicited a number from the songwriting team of Leiber and Stoller, too. They had submitted an old tune called "Love Me," which they had originally written as a kind of hillbilly send-up, to their mind "what Homer and Jethro might have done to a legitimate lyric." On this first day Elvis also responded favorably to both "How Do You Think I Feel," which he already knew from Jimmie Rodgers Snow's rhumbaized version (Snow had also recorded a perfectly sincere version of "Love Me"), and a beautiful Eddy Arnold ballad, "How's the World Treating You?" When he liked a song he touched the top of his head so as to hear it again, *from the top.* When he didn't like a number, he simply drew his finger across his throat. By the end of the day they had three songs wrapped and a fourth (Blackwell's "Paralyzed") well in hand. More significantly, there was an overall spirit of optimism and a new order of ascendancy in the studio.

There was no longer any question of who was in charge. Mr. Sholes might still call out the take numbers; he recorded all the session information meticulously in his notebook; he might even request another take or mildly interject a suggestion here and there — but the pace, the momentum, the feel of the session, were all with the boy. Maybe it was his sense of dislocation (Sholes did almost all of his recording at this point in Nashville and New York), and certainly the presence of Freddy Bienstock in the control room, and the central role that Bienstock had assumed, changed things in a fundamental way. It could have been a combination of the Colonel's constant needling and a recognition on his own part, without ever really acknowledging the full truth of it to himself, of the limited, somewhat peripheral and demeaning role of company watchdog into which he had been thrust. Whatever the reason, Steve Sholes seemed at this point to subside into a role of almost avuncular disinterest.

Meanwhile, Elvis ran through the material with the musicians the same way that he always had, he worked out head arrangements for the songs by having Freddy play the dub over and over again, he listened carefully to the final mix with Thorne — whom he called "Stoney," either as a joke or because of a misunderstanding that no one wanted to bother to correct in case it *was* a joke — but he did it all at a pace, and in a manner, different from that of any other RCA session to date. As Bones Howe remarked: "It was always about the music. He would keep working on a song, and he would listen to it played back, and his criterion was always: did it make him feel good? He didn't care if there were little mistakes, he was interested in anything that would make magic out of the record. The sessions were always fun, there was great energy, he was always doing something that was innovative. It was always about whether you had a feeling for music or not, whether you felt what he felt. That's why he liked Thorne so much. Thorne was a very genuine, sincere person, and he wanted Elvis to be completely happy with the records. The trick was that there was no trick. Thorne was there, and the studio was there — it was a level playing field. So he could just come in and do what felt good."

On the second day he recorded two of the songs that Mr. Sholes had brought to the "Hound Dog" session, "Too Much" and "Anyplace Is Paradise," as well as "Old Shep," the Red Foley tale of a boy and his dog with which he had won his first public recognition, at the Mississippi-Alabama Fair, in 1945. At his own insistence he played the piano on this number for the first time on an RCA session, and you can hear in the halting chords and the somewhat stumbling rhythm both the unmistakable emotion and the equally unmistakable valuing of emotion over technique. He nailed down "Old Shep" on the first take, while "Too Much," an oddball piece of pop construction that aimed to emulate "Don't Be Cruel" without either the craft or the charm, took twelve takes and still failed to achieve a satisfactory guitar solo ("It was in an odd key, and I got lost," Scotty confessed, "but it felt good") and "Anyplace Is Paradise," a jaunty, upbeat bluesy number, took twenty-two. He cut three songs by Little Richard (for which Freddy had secured co-publishing), an old tune by Wiley Walker and Gene Sullivan called "When My Blue Moon Turns to Gold Again," which with its lilting country rhythms and easy, unforced fervor would have been equally at home on Sun, and a new song by Aaron Schroeder and Ben Weisman, two of Hill and Range's top young contract writers. He fooled around with some gospel numbers with the Jordanaires and sang "Love Me Tender" to everyone over and over again.

Time meant nothing to him in the studio. If he felt like singing spirituals, he would sing spirituals to his heart's content. It was his way of finding his place; it was all part of the creative process as he had learned it in the Sun studio. If the feeling wasn't there, you waited until it *got* there, you didn't try to define it too precisely before it showed up — and if something else happened to show up while you were waiting, well, then, you took advantage of that. "He ran the session," said Thorne. "He would be right in the center of everything. Like with the Jordanaires, when he sang, we would set it up with a unidirectional mike, so he would be standing right in front of them, facing them, and they would have their own directional microphone, and they would be singing to one another. He could spend two hours on a tune and then just throw it away." If the band wasn't able to do it the way he wanted, said Scotty, he'd just say, "Well, do whatever you can do, then." "He was very loyal," observed Thorne. And he was a movie star.

On Tuesday he was back on the set, working first on the soundtrack, then on the picture, which had now been officially renamed to accommodate the Colonel's marketing plans. He had a number of difficult emotional scenes, but he handled them in stride. When he had to beat up Debra, to prepare the audience for his own obligatory death (the story was a muddled Civil War drama in which Elvis, playing the youngest of four sons and the only one left at home, marries his oldest brother Vance's fiancée, thinking Vance dead. Naturally, when Vance comes back . . .), Webb worked with him extensively on his motivation, and when in another scene Mildred Dunnock as his mother said, "Put that gun down, son," according to Dunnock he was so deep into his character that he dropped the gun right away. "Oh my God, what in the world were you doing?" said the director. "You were supposed to keep on going." "Well, she *told* me to put it down," said Elvis, who may have been fooling — but Dunnock didn't think so. To her: "For the first time in the whole thing he had heard me, and he believed me. Before, he'd just been thinking what he was doing and how he was going to do it. I think it's a funny story. I also think it's a story about a beginner who had one of the essentials of acting, which is to believe."

Meanwhile, he was growing more accustomed to the Hollywood life. He changed hotels, moving to the Beverly Wilshire, along with the Colonel, because his gang of fans had simply overwhelmed the Hollywood Knickerbocker. He was hanging out more and more with Nick and his friends and, through Nick, Natalie Wood, another in the "Rebel" crowd. The gossip columnists reported it as a sizzling romance, and Natalie, who presented him with matching red and blue velvet shirts from her dressmaker, was quoted by the wires as saying, "He's a real pixie and has a wonderful little-boy quality." But while he continued to pester Debra Paget fruitlessly for dates — and had to keep a careful eye (and ear) on his cousin Gene, who was still gawking around like a tourist — with Natalie and Nick, and sometimes Dennis Hopper, he felt more like he was part of a real gang; they all went around together, shared innocent enthusiasms, appreciated one another's work, and disdained pretentiousness and "swank places." One night they descended en masse on the home of Louella Parsons, who had been trying to get an interview with Elvis for some time and who reported with agreeable surprise: "Finally met Elvis Presley, who called on me accompanied by Natalie Wood, Nick Adams and his cousin, Gene Smith, who is a character straight out of a book. Elvis and his gang drink only soft drinks. . . ." In an interview with Albert Goldman years later Natalie described herself, a child of Hollywood, as intrigued by his very conventionality. "He was the first person of my age group I had ever met who said to me: 'How come you're wearing makeup? Why do you want to go to New York? Why do you want to be on your own?' . . . It was like having the date that I never ever had in high school. I thought it was really wild!

"I hadn't been around anyone who was [that] religious. He felt he had been given this gift, this talent, by God. He didn't take it for granted. He thought it was something that he had to protect. He had to be nice to people. Otherwise, God would take it all back."

On September 9 he was scheduled to appear on the premier *Ed Sullivan Show* of the season. Sullivan, however, was recuperating from an August automobile accident and, as a result, was not going to be able to host the program, which Elvis would perform from the CBS studio in Los Angeles. Elvis sent Sullivan a get-well card and a picture autographed to "Mr. Ed Sullivan" and was thrilled to learn that the show would be guest-hosted by Charles Laughton, star of *Mutiny on the Bounty*. Steve Allen, who had presented him in his last television appearance, was not even going to challenge Sullivan on the night in question: NBC was simply going to show a movie.

He opened with "Don't Be Cruel," strolling out alone from the darkened wings onto a stage spotlighted with silhouettes of guitars and a bass fiddle. He was wearing a loud plaid jacket and an open-necked shirt, but his performance was relatively subdued, as every shoulder shrug, every clearing of his throat and probing of his mouth with his tongue, evoked screams and uncontrolled paroxysms of emotion. Then he announced he was going to sing a brand-new song, "it's completely different from anything we've ever done. This is the title of our brand-new Twentieth Century Fox movie and also my newest RCA Victor escape — er, release." There was an apologetic shrug in response to the audience's laughter, and then, after an altogether sincere tribute to the studio, the director, and all the members of the cast, and "with the help of the very wonderful Jordanaires," he sang "Love Me Tender." It is a curious moment. Just after beginning the song he takes the guitar off and hands it to an unseen stagehand, and there are those awkward moments when he doesn't seem to know quite what to do without his prop and shrugs his shoulders or twitchily adjusts his lapels, but the moans which greet the song — of surprise? of shock? of delight? most likely all three — clearly gratify him, and at the end of the song he bows and gestures graciously to the Jordanaires.

When he comes back for the second sequence, the band is shown, with Jordanaire Gordon Stoker at the piano and the other Jordanaires in plaid jackets at least as loud (but nowhere near as cool) as his own. They rock out on Little Richard's "Ready Teddy," but when Elvis goes into his dance the camera pulls away and, as reviews in the following days will note, "censors" his movements. It doesn't matter. The girls scream just when he stands still, and when he does two verses of "Hound Dog" to end the performance, the West Coast studio audience goes crazy, though the *New York Journal-American*'s Jack O'Brian, after first taking note of Presley's "ridiculously tasteless jacket and hairdo (hairdon't)" and granting that "Elvis added to his gamut (A to B) by crossing his eyes," pointed out that the New York audience "laughed and hooted." "Well, what did someone say?" remarked host Charles Laughton, with good humor, at the conclusion of the performance. "Music hath charms to *soothe* the savage breast?"

The show got a 43.7 Trendex rating (it reached 82.6 percent of the television audience), and in the Colonel's view, which he shared gleefully with Steve Sholes, really boosted Presley's stock with an adult audience for the first time. A number of disc jockeys around the country taped the performance and started playing their tape of the new ballad on the air, and that undoubtedly hastened the release of the single, which came out about three weeks later. In the meantime prerelease orders built up to close to a million, and the Colonel pushed RCA to find that millionth customer not only as a confirmation of Elvis' well-established popularity but as a credit to Ed Sullivan, and the power of his show, which could then be proffered to Sullivan as a gratuitous gift.

There were just two more weeks of shooting before Elvis was scheduled to leave for the Tupelo homecoming concert that had been booked in July. Filming was originally supposed to be over by then, but now he was going to have to come back for a few more days after the concert. That was all right. He was enjoying himself now. They had filmed his death scene, which the director said was really going to touch audiences everywhere. Colonel was busy making deals and keeping everyone on the set off balance in a way that irritated some but always tickled Elvis. "We're the perfect combination," Elvis often told friends. "Colonel's an old carny, and me, I'm off the wall." At one point the would-be producers of a rock 'n' roll pastiche called *Do Re Mi* approached Colonel about getting Elvis to sing a couple of songs in the picture for $75,000. Colonel professed to be insulted, then offered to roll the dice for his boy's salary, double or nothing. Other members of the *Love Me Tender* cast claimed to be shocked, and William Campbell was convinced that Elvis' lack of reaction as Colonel told the story indicated an acceptance of his role as chattel or worse, but in Elvis' view, the Colonel was simply a very smart man: "He's a very amusing guy. He plans stuff that nobody else would even think of." And as he made clear to more than one interviewer who tried to cast the Colonel in a Svengali role, "We more or less picked each other." What people didn't understand was that Colonel mostly kept out of his hair. He took care of business, and he left Elvis to take care of his private life. Oh, he could be a pain in the ass sometimes, and he expected Elvis to keep his nose clean in order to maintain his end of the bargain. But for the most part he just left him alone — and he did his best to help Nick out, too. Elvis was glad Colonel liked Nick. Nick didn't have anything better to do, so he was going to come to Tupelo with them. Elvis was looking forward to showing him Memphis for the first time.

They flew into Memphis on Saturday, September 22, and went out to the fair briefly that night. On Monday they visited Humes, where Elvis introduced Nick to his old homeroom teacher, Miss Scrivener, who had sponsored the talent contest in which he had first performed in front of all his classmates senior year. Nick did impressions for Miss Scrivener's class, and Elvis beamed as the kids broke up. He presented the ROTC drill team with $900 for uniforms and gave another teacher a television set "to be used for educational purposes." They visited the Tiplers at Crown Electric, too, and Nick put his feet up on Mr. Tipler's desk while Elvis explained, said his former employer, "how he had his money arranged so he wouldn't get it all at one time." They even went by Dixie's house one afternoon, and she told Elvis she was getting married, and he congratulated her and wished her well.

On Wednesday they left for Tupelo around noon. Mr. and Mrs. Presley, Nick, and Barbara Hearn all drove down with Elvis in the white Lincoln, missing the parade that was being held in his honor but not missing any of the hoopla. Main Street was decked out in bunting and a giant banner that proclaimed "Tupelo Welcomes Elvis Presley Home," while every store window was decorated at the suggestion of fair manager James M. Savery with an "Elvis theme." The fact that it was Children's Day, too, the very day that the children of East Tupelo had been transported to the fair eleven years earlier and Elvis had quaveringly sung "Old Shep," only made the symbolism complete.

Vernon and Gladys were practically overcome. She wore a brocade dress and a locket with a photograph of Elvis around her neck. "It made me feel bad," she told a friend afterward, "to go back there like that and remember how poor we was." Vernon, on the other hand, was practically exuberant. He was wearing a dark suit, white shirt, and tie, with the tie loosened and slightly askew on this very hot day. Outside the big tent in back of the stage he spotted Ernest Bowen, for whom he had had a delivery route when he was working for L. P. McCarty and Sons, the last job he had held before leaving Tupelo. Bowen was now general manager of WELO and trying fruitlessly to gain entry to the tent so he could get an interview for his announcer, Jack Cristil. "All of a sudden this guy hollers at me — I didn't even recognize him, but it was Vernon, all cleaned up and greeting me like a long-lost friend. He wanted to know if he could do anything, and I said, 'Yeah, get me in the tent.' He said, 'Just follow me,' and he just like parted the waves. I asked Vernon, 'How are y'all doing?' He said, 'Oh, we doing just great.' Said, 'The boy is really taking care of us.' And I said, 'Good!' "

Inside the tent, while June Carter was performing, or maybe it was Mississippi Slim's cousin Rod Brasfield, telling jokes for the hometown crowd about his experiences on the Opry or making a Hollywood picture, Elvis told James Savery, with some exaggeration — but probably not much — that this was the first time he had actually been through the main gate; as a kid he had always had to climb the fence. "And just think, you're paying me for it, too!" There was a host of friends, relatives, and acquaintances (and would-be acquaintances) wanting to catch up on old times, with every one of them, seemingly, reminding him of how poor they had all been, of how they, too, had snuck into the fair with him. Elvis graciously received them all, passing off his success, for the most part, as a simple twist of fate, but with the father of one old schoolmate who was attending the University of Mississippi school of pharmacy "so he could amount to something," his answer was a little more revealing. In the account of a New York reporter, "Presley grinned at the older man and replied: 'Shucks, why don't you tell him to just get himself a guitar. That's all he needs.' "

There was an informal press conference before the afternoon show, and Elvis returned to the same theme repeatedly. He couldn't "hardly remember how I looked in overalls," he said. "It's all great," he responded good-humoredly to another question. "I've been looking forward to this homecoming very much. I've been escorted out of these fairgrounds when I was a kid and snuck over the fence. But this is the first time I've been escorted in." How about Natalie? someone called out. "I worry about her when I'm out there where she is," replied Elvis nonchalantly. "I don't think about her when I'm not." The reporters tried in vain to get Colonel Parker to say something, but Mr. and Mrs. Presley, who according to the *Tupelo Daily Journal* seemed "a little bewildered by all the commotion . . . but smiled pleasantly for photographers," expressed their gratitude first to a reporter from the *Journal* and, later, to a radio interviewer. What were their favorite records? the radio interviewer wanted to know. " 'That's All Right,' " said Mr. Presley. " 'Baby, Play House,' " said Gladys. "That's a good one," said Mr. Presley. "And 'Don't Be Cruel,' " added Mrs. Presley. "There's so many of them I can't remember the names," said Vernon. "It was terrific," said the interviewer in summation about the parade he had just determined that they had missed, "and everyone was having such a fine time and I know that you're sorry you missed it and I know that you've heard it was a wonderful parade. . . . Well, I'm sure that you know that the whole town is just wide open to the Presley family."

Mississippi governor J. P. Coleman, whose car had been mobbed by fans who mistook his arrival for their idol's, was backstage, and while they were taking a picture together, Elvis told the governor he thought he might go into politics himself. Oh, what would you run for? asked the governor. "The city limits," said Elvis affably. A highway patrolman asked Elvis to autograph a pile of pictures, and he signed away. Then it was time to go out and do the show, and he manfully made his way into the sea of sound.

He was wearing the heavy blue velvet shirt that Natalie had given him, even in all this heat, and Colonel had arranged for a ceramic model of the RCA dog, Nipper, to be placed onstage. Fox Movietone News was filming the show, and from the first notes of "Heartbreak Hotel" the crowd of five thousand — mostly teenagers, mostly girls — went crazy. There were forty city police and highway patrolmen on hand, but "reporters and photographers had to scramble up on the stage to safety," reported the *Journal*, "when Elvis first opened his mouth and a yelling wave of teenage girls broke for the guitar king." At the conclusion of "Long Tall Sally," Governor Coleman was announced, and after Elvis quieted the crowd ("Excuse me, Governor," he apologized to the startled chief executive), Coleman read off a text that proclaimed the young Tupeloan "America's number-one entertainer in the field of American popular music, [our] own native son." Then Tupelo mayor James Ballard presented him with a key to the city in the shape of a metal-sculpture guitar and declared, "The people of this community and of this city admire you and certainly are proud of you." "Thank you, Mayor, and thank you, ladies and gentlemen, very much, and, uh, and uh —" The crowd's screams drowned out any further comments he might have had in mind.

"I was right at the back of the stage watching him," said Ernest Bowen. "I saw him bring that crowd to hysterics, and he did it by teasing. He knew just how far to walk to the end of that stage, he would lean just far enough so that they could touch the tip of his finger." One time he leaned too far and had a silver button torn from his bright velvet blouse. In the middle of "Don't Be Cruel," fourteen-year-old Judy Hopper, from Alamo, Tennessee, scaled the five-foot-high stage to throw her arms around her idol, who only appeared amused. After that six policemen stayed onstage with Elvis. He ended up with "Hound Dog," naturally, at which point pandemonium really broke loose. "Elvis," shrieked the girls in the front row, among them fourteen-year-old Wynette Pugh, later to become famous as country star Tammy Wynette. " 'Elvis,' they shrieked," reported the *Journal*, "tearing their hair and sobbing hysterically, 'Please, Elvis.' "

After the show photographers got some more shots of Elvis with his mother and father, and a British journalist named Peter Dacre from the London Sunday *Express* ascertained that he would like to go to England, so long as he didn't have to fly ("If something were to go wrong on a plane, there's no land under you. That's a long swim"). Then he was escorted back to his hotel by the four highway patrolmen assigned to him to get some rest for the evening performance.

Fifty National Guardsmen were added for the evening show, which was anticipated to draw half again as many spectators. There must have been close to fifty thousand visitors to town, including sightseers and lookers-on, the biggest crowd that anyone could remember since Roosevelt had visited at the height of the Depression. Elvis was relaxed and chewing gum but disappointed that he wasn't feeling better for the occasion. "I've looked forward to this day for a long time," he said, "and the heck of it is, I'm sick today." He asked for the girl who had crashed the stage that afternoon and was introduced to Judy Hopper, who had her picture taken with him and said, "It was even more thrilling than I dreamed it would be."

The evening performance was, if anything, less inhibited on the part of the audience than the earlier one. At one point Elvis stopped the show to admonish the crowd in a good-natured way that little kids were getting hurt and that he wouldn't go on if they didn't sit back down. They were back up again for "Don't Be Cruel," though, and by the end they were almost out of control. "As howling sirens carried Elvis away, the fairgrounds were wild with crying teenagers," declared the *Journal*, "who fought for a chance for a last look at the boy who put burlesque back in business in a big way."

Elvis and Nick had returned to Hollywood by the weekend, and the film finished shooting within a week, with a Thanksgiving release date planned and more prints expected (575) than for any other film in Twentieth Century Fox's history. Then he was briefly back on tour, with Nick accompanying him and, with the Colonel's blessing, doing impressions to open the show; in Dallas Nick was even served with a summons in a breach-of-contract suit by a Fort Worth process server who didn't know what Elvis Presley looked like.

The Dallas show, which opened the four-day Texas tour on October 11, marked a watershed for the group. There were 26,500 on hand at the Cotton Bowl, which according to the *Dallas Morning News* had not witnessed such hysteria "since a December day in 1949 when a crazy-legged

Mustang named Kyle Rote tied the score against the heavily favored Fighting Irish of Notre Dame." It was the largest paying crowd ever to see an entertainer perform in Dallas (Elvis took home $18,000 out of a $30,000 gross), and from the moment Elvis appeared, waving to the crowd from the back of a Cadillac convertible as he circled the field, a kind of high-pitched, earsplitting, seismic wail went up, there were "screams of anguish" and "shrieks of ecstasy," the papers reported, that never wavered or stopped. The musicians couldn't hear a thing, apart from the crowd, and Elvis, dressed in his kelly green coat and navy blue pants with a black and gold cummerbund, sang by instinct alone, dropping to his knees over and over again, and ending the show by jumping off the stage with the microphone and falling to the ground at the fifty-yard line before being whisked off in a limousine. "It looked like a war out there," said drummer D. J. Fontana. "That's when it really hit me: we went around the park on the back of that Cadillac, and all you could see was just thousands of bulbs going off. I thought, What's this guy done? I just sat on the stage and looked around and thought, This guy draws more than the football players do. One man, and, you know, this park is full of people."

It was the same everywhere he went on this tour. There were riots even when they didn't show up, as teenagers in Temple tore up the Kyle Hotel because they had heard he might be staying there (he was thirty-five miles away, in Waco, at the time). The next night, in Houston, he begged the crowd three times to quiet down and listen, but with little success.

Meanwhile, the single of "Love Me Tender," which had already been certified gold, was about to enter the *Billboard* charts, and Elvis' next movie, a Hal Wallis production called *Lonesome Cowboy*, had been announced to the trades with a projected starting date of December or January. Reporters were pestering him about his draft status (he had gotten his pre-induction questionnaire in Hollywood around the first of the month, but, he said, he didn't know what that meant in terms of being called up, or how soon that might be expected to happen). Everyone wanted to know about his love life, of course. He was getting only four hours of sleep a night, he conceded, but when reporters asked why he didn't take it easier, he suggested that "the Lord can give and . . . the Lord can take away. I might be herding sheep next year." He arrived home exhausted on Monday, October 15, immediately went to see Barbara, and then called June about her upcoming visit at the end of the week. "Well, it won't be long now," he said for what must have been the thousandth time and couldn't resist repeating the joke that Richard Egan pulled on him when he expressed the same sentiment one too many times on the set. "You remind me of that damned monkey," Egan had said. "What monkey is that, Mr. Egan?" Elvis blundered innocently along. "The monkey that was sitting on the railroad track, and the train come along and cut off his tail. That's what he said. 'It won't be long now.'" Elvis laughed and laughed — he loved the joke, and he loved being considered one of the boys enough by Richard Egan that Egan would pull it on him. Then he told June to be packed and ready; he would wire her the money for her flight in a couple of days.

EVERYONE IN BILOXI knew about June's trip, and everyone was excited about it. The owner of Rosie's Dress Shop gave her a new outfit to wear, and the beauty shop trimmed her new pixie hairdo for free. When she went to Western Union on Thursday, she and her friend Patsy announced proudly that they were waiting for a money order from Elvis Presley, but they needn't have bothered — everyone at Western Union already knew she was Elvis Presley's girl from the telegrams they had delivered from Hollywood. She and Patsy waited and waited, going next door to Klein's Bakery, trying to mask their growing discomfiture with cream puffs and coffee. Eventually June went home, utterly humiliated. She was there only a few minutes when the phone rang. It was Elvis, who told her that he had run into a little trouble and would send her the money as soon as he could. She didn't know what to think — she was worried and pissed off — and when her friend Buddy Conrad came by later, the three of them, June, Patsy, and Buddy, proceeded to get drunk.

Only on the next day did she find out what had happened. It was in all the papers. Elvis had been in a fight with a filling-station manager. He had stopped for gas in his Lincoln at the Gulf station at the corner of Second and Gayoso. He asked the attendant to check his tank for a leak — he was getting a gas smell in the air-conditioning vents. When a crowd formed, the manager, Edd Hopper, asked Elvis to move along; he had other customers to take care of, too. By Elvis' account he was unable to move, because of the crowd surrounding the car, and he explained that to Mr. Hopper, but Hopper got mad and reached inside the car and slapped Elvis on the back of the head. With that Elvis leapt out and decked the forty-two-year-old Hopper, who then pulled a knife. By this time there were two policemen on the scene, and one of them restrained Hopper's six-foot-four attendant, Aubrey Brown, who had gone after Elvis and been on the receiving end of a punch himself. "I'll regret this day as long as I live," Elvis was quoted as saying. "It's getting where I can't even leave the house without something happening to me." On his way to the police station, where all three were booked on charges of assault and battery and disorderly conduct, Elvis said, "Maybe you'd better put down Carl Perkins," when asked to state his name.

Western Union called June shortly after she read the account in the paper: the money was finally there. When she went to sign the order, she noticed it had been sent by Vernon, and when she and Patsy arrived at the Memphis airport the following day, it was the elder Presleys who picked her up in the pink Cadillac, not Elvis. Elvis had been acquitted of all charges and advised by Acting Judge Sam Friedman that because of his "avocation" and the fact that "wherever you go you have a large following . . . [you should] try to be considerate and cooperate with businessmen. Avoid crowds where business will be interrupted." The two gas-station employees were fined $26 and $16 apiece, but for Mrs. Presley this was not the end of it. She was frightened of Elvis even going out of the house, she said. She knew her boy, and she knew he could take care of himself, but what if some crazy man came after him with a gun? she said to June, tears streaming down her face. "Now, Mama, he's gone be just fine," said Mr. Presley reassuringly, patting her on the leg. "That was the biggest black eye I ever saw," Patsy declared of the picture of Edd Hopper she had seen in the paper, and that broke the ice a little as Mr. Presley chuckled, but Mrs. Presley was still visibly shaken.

They stayed around the house for most of the first couple of days. They played darts and bumper pool, and Elvis shadowboxed with June in the empty swimming pool, with one hand behind his back. He was clearly feeling restless and trapped, and his mother got mad at him when, in sheer frustration, he flung some darts up at the ceiling, where they stuck until she knocked them down with a broom. "Next time I'm going to use the broom on you," she said with grim affection, but everyone knew she was just worried about him. She fixed his favorite fried chicken and little treats like peanut butter crisscrosses out of her *Better Homes and Gardens New Cookbook*. June and Patsy occasionally went out to the fence, where the fans patiently waited, and they saw Bitsy Mott, the Colonel's brother-in-law, whom they knew from Florida, working security there. They were allowed to talk to the fans from their side of the fence but not to go out on the street and mingle. "You're so lucky," some of the girls said. They all wanted to know what he was really like, they wanted to know what it was like to kiss him. Elvis conscientiously came out two or three times a day to chat and sign autographs, and Gladys sometimes had to call him two or three times to get him to come in.

Finally on Sunday night he couldn't stand it any longer: they were going to go out, he didn't care what his mama thought. One of the local theaters was running the Fox Movietone newsreel of the Tupelo concert, and he wasn't just going to let himself become a *prisoner*. Nothing was going to happen, anyway.

They took the band's black Cadillac limo so as to be less conspicuous, and June paid for the tickets before they dashed inside to watch the picture from a private viewing room. They hadn't been in the theater twenty minutes when two policemen came in to get Elvis' car keys. A crowd had formed outside the theater and was tearing the car apart, scratching names into the paint, breaking windows, ripping out upholstery, and denting the fenders. The policemen moved the car, then came back for Elvis and the two girls, escorting them through an inflamed mob that tore at their clothes and, for the first time, really frightened June. Elvis didn't want his parents to know what had happened, so they left the car at Dewey's and Dewey drove them home. Gladys was surprised to see them back so early, and the next morning Vernon cut the story out of the paper — it had Barbara Hearn as his date and the white Cadillac vandalized — in hopes that Gladys would not learn of the incident.

That afternoon Scotty and Bill and D.J., along with the Jordanaires, came by for a brief rehearsal for the next Ed Sullivan appearance, which was coming up on the weekend. After a brief run-through of the four songs they were going to do on TV, they all sat in a little circle on the floor singing spirituals, with Gladys beaming on the couch. Every so often she would join in and softly sing a line, while June, never shy about her singing, took the alto part on "In the Garden," which had been part of her high school graduation ceremony. Later that night she and Elvis drove out to Mud Island, where they had ridden Elvis' motorcycle at what seemed like 100 miles an hour on her first trip to Memphis.

It was a more contemplative visit this time, sadder somehow; for June there was a sense of almost ominous foreboding. She didn't doubt that he loved her, she knew he was there with her — and yet she didn't know if she could ever get him back. Elvis told her he had just heard from Nick and that Nick was coming to town tomorrow or the next day. He started telling her all about Nick and Nick's friends and Jimmy Dean, but she didn't want to hear. On their way home they passed a milk truck making deliveries. Elvis swung around and waited for the milkman to come back to his truck. He asked the man if he could buy some milk but then found he had no money. The milkman said that was all right, and Elvis just auto-graphed an IOU. They drank the cold milk out of the bottle, and Elvis wiped the milky mustache off his upper lip with the back of his hand, just like James Dean, June thought, in *Rebel Without a Cause*.

It was all right when Nick arrived, but it was somehow, and not all that subtly, different. They drove around town together and talked about many of the same things, but she felt as if, without even bothering to dis-guise it all that much, she and Nick were competing for his attention. Nick was talking about Natalie all the time — he had even brought a dress of hers as a kind of souvenir and made a big point of how Natalie really filled it out. "I wish you could have invited him some other time," June said to Elvis in a rare moment of privacy, but Elvis insisted that he hadn't invited Nick, Nick had more or less invited himself. "He's just a lonesome little guy struggling to make it in Hollywood," Elvis said, with compas-sion, of his friend. But Mrs. Presley seemed to sympathize with June. "He sure is a pushy little fellow," she said; she just wished Elvis could be a lit-tle more careful in his selection of friends.

One night they went down to the radio station to see Dewey and ran into Cliff Gleaves, a DJ from Jackson, who had met Elvis in passing seven months before. He had just gotten back into town and was hanging around the station on the off chance of seeing Elvis again. Afterward they all went out to Dewey's house, on Perkins, and played pool for a while, but then the men went off into the den, where a movie projector had been set up, while Patsy and June stayed in the living room with Mrs. Phillips. At one point one of the men came out and, with the door mo-mentarily ajar, June saw flickering images of naked bodies. Furiously she marched up to the door, knocked, and then flung it open. She stood in what she called her "Elvis position," her arms folded in front of her, star-ing blankly ahead. "What the hell are you doing, June?" Elvis said, leaping up in acute embarrassment. "I don't want you watching that shit."

"You can watch that shit as long as you want, Elvis," she said, "but first you can take me and Pat home." And if he thought she was just being a prude, she added, "then y'all can kiss my ass."

The night before she was scheduled to return to Biloxi and Elvis was due to go to New York for the Sullivan show, they all went out to dinner with some wealthy acquaintances of the older Presleys who wanted to provide a special occasion for Vernon and Gladys. It seemed like Gladys was going to fuss with them forever about their manners and their appearance, but then at dinner Elvis gave June his new temporary tooth caps to hold, and she started fooling with them so she looked like a vampire, and soon their hosts were as broken up as they were. "It's about time you kids relaxed and had some fun," said the husband approvingly, as Gladys laughed until the tears ran down from her eyes. Afterward they went to a private screening of a rough cut of *Love Me Tender*. Everyone thought it was wonderful except for Elvis. When June tried to tell him how good he was, he made it clear that he did not want to be just "good." "Quit being so damn hard on yourself, man," Nick muttered, "and give it some time." He had been working for years, he said, to try to get to the point where Elvis was now. "You've proved yourself as an actor, man. Don't worry about it." Elvis took Nick's remarks as highly complimentary, but June put them down more to jealousy.

In the end he wanted her to fly up to New York with him, and if she wouldn't do that, why couldn't she just stay here in Memphis with his parents? He would be back in a few days, and Natalie was going to come visit next week: he wanted her to meet Natalie. Wait a minute, Nick protested, if June was going to stay, he would just call Natalie and tell her to come some other time — there wasn't enough room in the house for everyone. "Don't worry, Nick, I'm not staying," June announced, leaving the room. When Elvis followed her, she told him she wanted to go home, and she wasn't interested in meeting Natalie anyway. "Baby, I didn't invite Natalie," Elvis protested, it was *Nick* who had invited Natalie, and he could just as easily uninvite her.

It was a sour note on which to end the week, and when she got back to Biloxi and went to have her picture taken for the studio portrait that she had promised Elvis, she told the photographer she thought she wanted something really different. They talked about it for a while and finally decided on a picture the photographer had never taken before: the subject in tears. The photograph won second prize in an exhibit sometime later.

WITH NATALIE WOOD OUTSIDE THE HOTEL CHISCA, OCTOBER 31, 1956.
(ROBERT WILLIAMS)

THE TOAST OF THE TOWN

I T WAS A RELAXED, confident, and very much at ease Elvis Presley who made his second appearance on *The Ed Sullivan Show,* still popularly known as the *Toast of the Town,* on the evening of Sunday, October 28. Gone were the explosive nervous energy, the involuntary mannerisms, that had dominated his television appearances of just a few months before; even the self-abashed, somewhat shambling manner of his Sullivan debut had been replaced by a good-natured, almost studied and bemused *playfulness,* a kind of good-humored recognition of common cause both with his audience and that of his host. When he appeared following Sullivan's characteristically stiff, almost wooden introduction, his hair high and a pleased, slightly embarrassed look on his face, it was as if for the first time he really took it all as his due — there appeared to be no rage hiding behind the mask, there was no caged tiger desperate to get out, he acknowledged the response with the deferential distraction of the grand seigneur. He was a recording star, he was a movie star, he was a servant of the Lord and the master of his own destiny; for one brief moment there was not even a hint of imposture in his mind.

He had spent the day primarily fulfilling professional responsibilities and doing good works. After a couple of nights on the town with Nick, Dewey, his cousin Gene, and his new friend, Cliff Gleaves, all of whom he had invited to come up to New York at his expense, he reported for rehearsal at noon, while the Colonel handed out "Elvis for President" buttons at the unveiling of a forty-foot "statue" of the new Hollywood star above the marquee of the Paramount Theatre in Times Square, where *Love Me Tender* would premiere in a little more than two weeks. "The idol of the rock 'n' roll juveniles also surprised an afternoon press interview by demonstrating to adult reporters that he is a polite, personable, quick-witted and charming young man," reported the *New York Times.* "Teenagers are my life and triumph," he declared to the assembled reporters. "I'd be nowhere without them." He wished he could sit down with some

351

of those parents who saw him as a bad influence, "because I think I could change their minds and their viewpoint. Ever since I got to be a sort of name I've examined my conscience and asked myself if I led anybody astray even indirectly, and I'm at peace with my conscience." Somebody asked him if it wasn't teenagers that had recently ripped his car apart. "That means nothing to me, sir. That's a car and I've got other cars, but the idea of doing to others what you'd like them to do to you is what's in my craw. It's in the Bible. . . . I read my Bible, sir, and this is no story just made up for now. My Bible tells me that what he sows he will also reap, and if I'm sowing evil and wickedness it will catch up with me. I'm right sure of that, sir, and I don't think I'm bad for people. If I did think I was bad for people, I would go back to driving a truck, and I really mean this."

At the end of the afternoon, in a public ceremony just as extensively covered by the media, he received an inoculation of the newly developed Salk polio vaccine. He was doing so, he said in a public service announcement he recorded for the March of Dimes, because "so many kids and adults, too, have gotten just about one of the roughest breaks that can happen to a person. . . . We can help these people. And the way to do it is this: join the 1957 March of Dimes." "Halo, Everybody, Halo: Latest Presley Pitch" had been the headline for a recent *Variety* story, which suggested somewhat cynically an "institutional build-up to re-create the rock 'n' roller into an influence for the good" — but that was really missing the point: Elvis didn't need an institutional push, this was what he believed was truly intended for him, this was the real function of fame.

The streets that night were so crowded you could barely get to the studio. There were policemen on horseback, and thousands of fans clamoring to get past the barricades, but Elvis insisted on signing autographs anyway, to the acute discomfiture of his traveling companions. Mr. Sullivan complimented the youngsters in the audience on their comportment; he had asked them not to yell during the songs themselves, he said, and they had kept their promise. A number of the reviews suggested that Elvis had been pressured to tone down his act, that either he or the cameras had been urged to restrain his body movements, but there is no evidence of that: mainly what you see is great good humor, a manner that exudes utter confidence, and a sense of vast amusement both at himself and, lovingly, his audience. Over and over again he stops in the midst of a practiced gesture and shrugs his shoulders, audibly exhales, rolls his eyes, *freezes* — just waiting for the wave that has been momentarily stilled to roll back over him. His eyes twinkle; he smiles and then catches himself and sneers (but affably); he listens to Mr. Sullivan say that Elvis will return for his second appearance on the show in just a couple of minutes and he impishly demurs, then after a brief colloquy agrees that yes, he'll be back. At the conclusion of his third and final segment, he announces the scheduled opening of his new picture and his next appearance on *The Ed Sullivan Show* in January. "And, uh, and uh," he says, momentarily stuck, then recovers with a sincere "Until we meet you again, may God bless you as he has blessed me."

The ratings were not quite as spectacular as they had been for the first show, but Sullivan still beat the principal competition (Mary Martin and Paul Douglas in a special television production of the play *Born Yesterday*) by a margin of two to one and gained an overall 34.6 (57 percent share) Trendex rating.

Elvis shot a new ending for the film the following day at the Junco Studio on East Sixty-ninth Street. Pressure had been building ever since it had been announced he would perish in his first screen role, and there had been pickets all week in front of the Paramount Theatre with suspiciously uniform printed signs that pleaded, "Don't Die! Elvis Presley." Whether prodded by public pressure or perhaps just acceding to the publicity value of the occasion, the studio had acknowledged the protest and flown in director Robert Webb, cameraman Leo Tover, and a crew of technicians. It was going to be a simple shot of the image of Elvis Presley superimposed over the dying Clint Reno and singing the title song of the film as the character expires. There was no need even to change his shoes, and he played the scene in the white bucks he had worn on the television show the night before.

On the next day the new RCA contract which the Colonel had been negotiating for the last couple of months was announced: royalty payments were to be spread out in such a way that Elvis would be guaranteed $1,000 a week for the next twenty years. He had at this point sold well over ten million singles for RCA (this would compute to a record royalty of roughly $450,000), which represented approximately two thirds of RCA's singles business. In fact, *Variety* had declared him a millionaire just the previous week on the basis of their unofficial computations of record royalties, movie income ($250,000, figuring in the new movie that was coming up in a couple of months), song publishing, TV appearances, and personals. It was a situation virtually unprecedented in the record business, rivaling anything that had ever been seen in the larger world of show business, and it didn't even take into account merchandising.

Just three short months before, the Colonel had entered into a deal with a thirty-seven-year-old merchandiser from California named Hank Saperstein for the exclusive right to exploit and commercially promote the Elvis Presley image. Saperstein, who had offices in Beverly Hills, had been in the business for seventeen years and had previously conducted highly successful campaigns for *Super Circus, Ding Dong School,* Lassie, the Lone Ranger, and Wyatt Earp, but, as *Variety* noted, this was the first all-out merchandising campaign in memory aimed at teens, not "moppets." By the time that *The Reno Brothers* started shooting, Saperstein's campaign was fully operational, with something like eighteen licensees and twenty-nine products, many of which (belts, scarves, skirts, jeans, lipstick, lockets, charm bracelets, publications, and western ties) were laid out on the hood of Saperstein's car in a publicity shot taken on the movie set. By the end of October the program was really getting into gear, with thirty licenses and fifty products to be marketed through Sears, Montgomery Ward, W. T. Grant's, and Woolworth's, among others, and *Variety* was endorsing Saperstein's prediction of $40 million in retail sales over the next fifteen months. This would come to $18 million wholesale, which at the customary 5 percent licenser's royalty would mean $900,000, to be split between Saperstein and Elvis Presley Enterprises equally.

In the offing were hound dogs and houndburgers, and Saperstein, clearly a realistic man, who advertised "promotion in depth," foresaw at least a two-year life to the market. It was just the kind of deal the Colonel loved, and one he knew how to exploit the hell out of both for himself and his boy. In a *Look* magazine article about the Elvis Presley phenomenon, the author, Chester Morrison, quoted the title song of the movie and then remarked:

> There are two grown men who love him true and tender and hope that they will never have to let him go. They are the two who operate the Great Elvis Presley industry, and, Lord, how the money rolls in! . . . Hank Saperstein and Tom Parker are a great pair. They are sardonically gay, as Fred Allen used to be. The Colonel sometimes drops absent-minded ashes from his good cigar onto the folds of his plumpness. Hank is younger, handsomer, taller and he doesn't sag any-

where. Both of them have a reverence for money and work hard for it. But both of them give the impression that if they didn't get any fun out of making money, the hell with it.

The Colonel was a former carnival man, Morrison noted, who "is happy, but he is certainly not unsophisticated, and he has seen the Tattooed Lady. He genuinely loves those people who come to the carnival, because every last one of them buys a ticket. He is writing an autobiography that should find a place in every home. He calls it *The Benevolent Con Man*, but his alternate and better title is *How Much Does It Cost If It's Free?*"

NATALIE ARRIVED for her Memphis visit on Halloween night. Elvis and Nick picked her up at the airport and showed her the sights, then took her back to the house, where Elvis promised the fans they would come out again in half an hour to talk and sign autographs. After supper they drove around town some more, got ice cream cones, and ended up at the Chisca, where they went up to the "magazine floor" (the mezzanine, in other words) to see Dewey. By the time they came out, hundreds of fans had collected in the street, and they were barely able to recapture the white Lincoln.

The next day Elvis bought himself a new motorcycle, and that night they went for a long ride, with Natalie clinging to Elvis and Nick "chugging along behind," the newspapers reported, on Elvis' old Harley. In the next few days Elvis took Natalie on the standard tour: she met his family, she met his friend George Klein, they drove by Humes, they went out to the Fairgrounds and stopped by Sun, he introduced her to a few of his policemen friends, they even stopped in to see Bob Neal at the new Stars Inc. management firm he had set up in partnership with Mr. Phillips. To Natalie, who was accustomed to celebrity, it was both an eye-opening, and a somewhat numbing, experience. It was, she told a reporter some years later, "like a circus come to town the minute I got off the plane. A mob of people stood outside his house night and day. Someone sold hot dogs and ice cream from a wagon. . . . When we went out on Elvis' motorcycle, we had an instant motorcade behind us. I felt like I was leading the Rose Bowl parade." Elvis was sweet, she told friends and reporters alike, but, she suggested, maybe there was such a thing as being too sweet. According to her sister, Lana, she called home in the middle of her

visit and begged her mother to get her out of this. "He can sing," Natalie
confided to Lana afterward, as recorded in Lana's memoir, "but he can't
do much else." On Saturday Nick and Natalie headed back to Hollywood,
after a visit on Natalie's part of only four days.

For Elvis, though, it was good just to have some time to himself. Colonel thought it would be something like two months before they started
work on the new picture, and with *Love Me Tender* scheduled to open in
ten days, on November 15 in New York, and the day before Thanksgiving
in Memphis and everywhere else, he was perfectly happy to be able to
concentrate on more mundane matters, like the Beginner Driver Range,
"the nation's first police-sponsored behind-the-wheel driving school,"
whose opening Elvis attended on Monday, November 5, as a past finalist
in the annual Road-E-O safe-driving contest for teenagers four years
before. " 'If there is anything I can do to set an example, I want to do it,'
Presley said to the new class of 31 students, mostly teenagers. No one
shrieked or swooned," reported the *Press-Scimitar*. "They did look serious
and determined. . . . It was a community project, designed to make Memphis a safer place to live."

Meanwhile, Cliff Gleaves was back in town after his fantasy trip to
New York, a tale so improbable that even Cliff, who was accustomed to
putting an optimistic spin on the truth, with his DJ's wit, comedian's flair,
and philosopher's penchant for positive thinking, was having a difficult
time believing it. When he got back, he couldn't seem to run into Elvis
again, though, let alone find the opportunity to thank him. He went by
the Chisca on a number of occasions, but he never saw him there. He
missed him the whole time that Natalie was in town. He started showing
up at WMC every afternoon, just as George Klein was finishing his shift as
host of *Rock 'N' Roll Ballroom,* and dropped broad hints to George about
getting together with Elvis sometime. But while George sprang for dinner
almost every night, he never picked up on the hints.

There was another guy, a big fat jolly young fellow named Lamar
Fike, who had started hanging around George lately, too, and was interested in getting into radio. He drove a brand-new '56 Chevy, talked like he
knew everything about everything, and was desperate to meet Elvis. Cliff
was on the verge of telling him to get lost when Lamar happened to flash
his billfold, and Cliff, always quick on his feet, said, "Yeah, man, I guess
you can come to dinner with us." After that he let Lamar bug them for
radio pointers on a regular, paying basis, which didn't get either one of

them any closer to Elvis, and Cliff finally came to the conclusion that if this thing was going to happen, it was just going to have to happen on its own. He was nearly at the point of giving up hope, and his room at the YMCA, when he finally ran into Elvis again, and this time turned out to be the charm.

He was on his way to the Chisca on a Monday night, ostensibly to see Dewey, when he saw a pink Cadillac coming toward him on Union. "Hey, Cliff, follow me," Elvis said, leaning out the window and leading him to Madison Cadillac, just a few blocks away.

"At that point my life changed. At that point I made a 180-degree turn with old Elvis. Understand: we pull in. He says, 'I got this car for my mother, and she doesn't have a license, and I don't want to touch it anymore, but I like to keep it tuned. I just bought an El Dorado, but they still got the masking tape on it, and I want to know if you'll do me a favor.' I said, 'Elvis, are you serious?' I had already thanked him for the weekend, and he just said, 'If you can't have fun, what is it? If enjoyment is not in there, what is it worth?'

"He said, 'Cliff, can you take me a couple of places?' Well, no sense in going into the petty details, but about five-thirty he says, 'Cliff, I'd like to invite you home to meet my parents. I'd like you to have dinner with us.' Boom! I said, 'Great!' and we drive out to Audubon Drive, where he lived. After dinner he said, 'Cliff, you know Red West?' I said, 'No, I don't.' He said, 'He was with me, and he joined the Marine Corps.' He said, 'I'm alone now.' He said, 'I like you, my mama and daddy like you' — you see, dinner is over, and we're in the living room now. 'I'm alone now, and I'd really like for you to be with me. When I invited you to New York, I really wasn't thinking that way.' I said, 'Elvis, I'll tell you what. I have obligations here and there.' I said, 'To do that, you know — the obligation factor, I really can't take that offer. I have to be a free agent, free spirit, I can't be obligated. But as a *friend* — that's a different ball game.'

"He said, 'You mean the only thing stopping you from joining me is that?' I said, 'That's about it.' He said, 'Cliff, let's go get your clothes.' That night I moved into my bedroom on Audubon Drive. Elvis' bedroom is down at the end, down the hallway is what they call Natalie's room, because that's where Natalie Wood stayed when she was there, and Elvis' mother and father are at the other end of the house. Three bedrooms, two baths — no problem. I moved in bag and baggage. His mother said,

'That was Natalie's room, now it's yours.' From that point on, he always wanted me there."

Cliff found life with the Presleys utterly beguiling. Elvis, as he saw it, was "an innocent. He didn't know about the tricks, the 'worldly ways'; he operated on sheer instinct. Never was there any arrogance — he was simply not going to let people trying to get to him be denied. He did not have the 'informal schooling' of being out in the world too long. He wasn't out there just a little bit when he walked into Sun Records: only thing he knew was his parents' home to Sun to making money to fame. He had no introduction to the world." His parents? "Vernon was not an innocent, 'cause he'd been burned. Vernon was finely tuned to the world, a dollar was a dollar to Vernon, a quarter is a quarter. One night at dinner Elvis said, 'Daddy's a hard man, but you can't blame him. You got to know what happened to him.' Then they explained it all. Vernon said, 'Hey, Cliff, I offered to work as long as the man would let me work it off — but he refused.' He said, 'Cliff, that was hard.' "

Gladys, on the other hand, was simply proud of her boy — no more, and no less, than when he had won the singing prize at the fair. "It wasn't that [she knew that] he was going to come along and tear the world up, it was just something that was in him. Vester came along and taught him a couple of chords, nobody paid much attention, it was just an isolated event, but she was very proud of him. She said, 'I just hope to hell we all live.' 'Cause it upset her, she was not thrilled with his big-time success, she was not carried away by the fame, the only thing that counted was Elvis."

At night they would frequently sit around listening to gospel music: the Blackwood Brothers, Sister Rosetta Tharpe, the Clara Ward Singers, the Statesmen Quartet — Elvis would always point to the singing of Jake Hess as they listened. Often he would sit at the organ and sing the songs himself, as Mr. and Mrs. Presley nodded appreciatively. For Cliff it was something of an education, because though he considered himself a "spiritual" person, he had never heard this kind of music before. For Cliff it was something of a trial, too. There was no smoking or drinking allowed in the house, and Cliff was not by nature an abstemious person, but he abided by house rules. "Elvis did not want to be around people when they were drinking. He had tremendous willpower, and he just felt like people who were out of control — how many times did he say,

'Cliff, I just can't afford being around people who are not in control of themselves.' "

One night they were invited over for "cocktails" by a wealthy young couple with "old Memphis" roots who lived up the street. Frank Pidgeon, whose family owned the Pidgeon-Thomas Iron Company, had written the insurance on the house, and Betty Pidgeon was the granddaughter of E. H. "Boss" Crump, who had virtually ruled Memphis from his election as mayor in 1910 until his death in 1954. Elvis was reluctant to go at first — the neighbors had been unremitting in their rejection, he felt, not just of him and his family but of his fans. He could understand their being upset at the disruption which his presence had caused the once-quiet little street, and he had done everything he could to accommodate their concerns, but there had even been public discussion of buying the Presleys out, which Elvis had countered by offering to buy the neighbors out in turn. As one Memphian wrote to Elvis biographer Elaine Dundy, "From the point of view of the world I was born and raised in, the world of the country club etc., he was referred to . . . as an embarrassment."

Cliff recalled the social occasion vividly. "Elvis said, 'Mama, I don't want to go, these people got a lot of money, and I don't fit in, I don't feel comfortable, I just don't want to do it.' She said, 'Son, these people don't want anything from you. They've already made their mark in the world, and they are prominent people from two prominent families here — you know that she's a Crump. What they are doing is welcoming you to the neighborhood, that's all. You can't give them anything, they are just proud of you, another Memphian who is making his own mark in the world.' "

They drove the short distance up the street, arrived a little late, and declined the bourbon and sodas they were offered, taking Cokes instead to wash down their Cheez Whiz crackers. Elvis seemed "a little nervous at first" to Pallas Pidgeon, who was eight at the time, "but he was very nice, very friendly and accommodating. Daddy asked if he would mind calling my father's first cousin, who lived in Plainfield, New Jersey, and she was a great fan of his. So we put the long-distance call through to her. Then we called my aunt, the youngest daughter of my grandparents, who were also there — she was at St. Catherine's School in Richmond, and her whole dorm went crazy. Then I asked him if he would mind calling my best friend, Louise, and he did the same thing. 'Louise, this is Elvis.' It was just incredible. Then we went on a tour of the house, and we went in the bedroom, he and Cliff and my mother and I, and I had a lot of stuffed animals on the bed, and he asked me when my birthday was, and he said he would send me a teddy bear, which he never did, but at least I could dream about it for a few months."

He was hurt that people judged him without knowing him, he told Marion Keisker one day when he stopped off at Sun. Mr. Phillips was busy a lot of the time — Johnny Cash was really hot now, and he was trying to get Carl back on track, and he had some new boys he was excited about — but Elvis always felt comfortable just stopping by and talking to Marion with the sun beating down on the blinds and the sights and sounds of a recording session coming through the window cut into the partition wall. He was still upset by that Jacksonville preacher who had been written up in *Life* magazine, he told her. "The only thing I can say is they don't know me."

As the date of the movie opening approached, he became more and more nervous, he felt increasingly on display, even in his own hometown. He finally took the Colonel's advice and got out of town for a little while, taking a vacation in Las Vegas, which saved him from having to make excuses when the reporters inevitably asked for his reaction to the reviews. It was all in keeping with the new management strategy of removing him from the public eye (the Colonel indicated that he might have to start charging reporters for interviews with Elvis soon), but at the same time it suited the very impulse that had led him to duck into the Suzore No. 2 the night that Dewey played his record for the first time.

In Vegas he was a celebrity among celebrities, and while his comings and goings were duly noted, it was from a distance, and with a casual disinterest, that left him pretty much on his own. He stayed at the New Frontier with his cousin Gene and attended all the shows. At the outset of his visit he dated Marilyn Evans, a dancer at the New Frontier, and invited her to come see him in Memphis in December. Then he met Dottie Harmony, a blond eighteen-year-old dancer from Brooklyn who had come to town to do a show at the Thunderbird and who had a girlfriend at the Frontier who was getting married. He kept sending emissaries over to her table to see if she would join him, but she told them to get lost "until all of a sudden I looked over, and there was Elvis on his knee, saying, 'Ma'am, you're the most beautiful woman I've ever seen in my life.

Would you have a drink with me?' " They started seeing each other almost exclusively, he came to see her show, "we spent almost every single day and evening together, except for when I worked." On November 14, the night before the *Love Me Tender* premiere in New York, he attended Liberace's opening at the Riviera and was introduced from the front row by the flamboyant entertainer, who was dressed in gold-sequined cutaway and matching pants. Afterward they exchanged jackets and instruments, cutting up for the cameras and singing and playing songs like "Girl of My Dreams" and "Deep in the Heart of Texas." "Elvis and I may be characters," commented Liberace, "but we can afford to be."

He and Dottie were totally caught up in each other. "He was just the nicest guy. He used to call his mother every night, and he made me call mine. He would tell me stories about how his family had all lived together in this one room and how his father used to pray every night that things would get better and how happy he was now that he could make it better for his parents. It's a little hard to believe, but we mainly just hung around. We would go out to the airport and watch the planes take off. One night we stopped and helped an old man change a tire. You know, we were just kids." They would fight on occasion, usually about the attention Dottie got from other men ("I knew everybody in town, and I think that bothered Elvis, but I said, 'What's good for the goose is good for the gander' "). Sometimes when they fought, Elvis would rip the phone out of the wall, "but next thing I knew it was always fixed again." One night they went to see Billy Ward and His Dominoes, one of Elvis' favorite r&b groups, whose young lead singer, an unbilled Jackie Wilson, in addition to reprising the various Dominoes hits ("The Bells," "Rags to Riches," "Have Mercy Baby"), also did an Elvis Presley medley in his act. He did "Hound Dog" and one or two other numbers that didn't impress their originator all that much, but then he did "Don't Be Cruel," slower and with more dramatic impact than the record, and Elvis went back to see him four nights running. Nick came into town to visit, and a couple of other Hollywood pals, too, but mostly it was just the two of them doubledating with Gene, and before Elvis left he made Dottie promise that she would spend Christmas with him in Memphis.

June had read about Natalie and him in the Memphis papers. He had telephoned her the day that Natalie left, but by the time she called back, Gladys said he was in Las Vegas and she wasn't sure when he'd be home.

The two of them had a nice long chat anyway, but Elvis didn't call when the movie opened, he missed her birthday on November 19, and she was less and less inclined to blame it on the Colonel.

The movie premiered with great hoopla on the fifteenth. There were fifteen hundred teenagers lined up when the doors opened at the New York Paramount at 8:00 A.M. for the first show, and there would have been more in attendance if truant officers hadn't combed the lines. When the film opened on November 21 at Memphis' Loew's State and 550 other theaters across the country, it did record-breaking business and by the end of the month was reported by *Variety* to be enjoying "sock grosses," which "underscored the need for the industry to develop players and subject matter to bring out the juvenile audience sector." It outperformed Marilyn Monroe's earlier *Bus Stop* and *The Seven Year Itch* in the same or similar locations, was running neck and neck with *Giant* and *The Ten Commandments,* which opened around the same time, and, it was reported, the concession business was "astounding."

The reviews were for the most part extremely condescending, if occasionally granting Elvis a certain measure of grudging respect. *Time* was particularly derisive, asking, "Is it a sausage?" of the new, sleekly packaged Hollywood image, while the *New York Times* gave Elvis backhanded credit for failing to recognize the film's limitations and providing an animated performance in the midst of a lusterless vehicle. "Richard Egan is virtually lethargic as the brother who comes home from war," Bosley Crowther wrote, "and Debra Paget is bathed in melancholia," while "Mr. Presley . . . goes at it as though it were 'Gone With the Wind.'" Perhaps the most interesting review appeared in *The Reporter,* which led an all-out assault on popular culture with a vilification of Elvis Presley ("Presley resembles an obscene child") and his so-called "music" (a "vacillation between a shout and a whine") but posed the pertinent question: "Who is the new hero? How does he look, move, talk and dress?" And went on to answer it by comparing Elvis with Brando and James Dean, and characterizing the new hero as possessing

> mannerisms by Brando out of the Actor's Studio. . . . First of all he does not walk: he slouches, ambles, almost minces. His hand gestures are all tentative, incomplete, with arms out in front as though he were feeling his way along a wet-walled underground passageway, or folded back against the body as though he were warding off a blow.

. . . The new hero is an adolescent. Whether he is twenty or thirty or forty, he is fifteen and excessively sorry for himself. He is essentially a lone wolf who wants to belong.

The Colonel's only public comment was his advice to theater operators to be sure to empty the house after every matinee showing. Otherwise, the Colonel said, Elvis' fans would stock up on food and camp out in the theater all day, thereby depriving theater owners of a valuable source of revenue.

Elvis himself was embarrassed, according to Cliff, both by the inadequacy of his own performance and by the reaction of his fans. " 'I'll never make it,' he said, 'it will never happen, because they're never going to hear me 'cause they're screaming all the time.' He really meant that." At the same time he was what he had always wanted to be: a movie star. Critics might tear him apart, he told reporters at the Ed Sullivan news conference just two and a half weeks before the movie's opening, and if they did he might have to rethink his approach, but he could see a lifetime career in the movies, long after he had stopped singing. "I'm not going to quit," he said, "and I'm not going to take lessons because I want to be me."

WITH B. B. KING AT THE WDIA GOODWILL REVUE, DECEMBER 7, 1956.
(ERNEST WITHERS. MIMOSA RECORDS PRODUCTIONS INC./MICHAEL OCHS ARCHIVES)

THE END OF SOMETHING

I T WAS A TUESDAY AFTERNOON in early December. Cliff and Elvis were cruising down Union Avenue with Marilyn Evans, the dark-eyed dancer from Las Vegas whom he had dated before meeting Dottie Harmony. As they drove by 706, it looked, in the words of Marion Keisker, like a "chicken coop nested in Cadillacs." There was obviously a session going on, and on an impulse Elvis wheeled the car around and parked out in front of the studio. Once inside, he found Carl Perkins and his brothers Jay and Clayton, with "Fluke" Holland on drums and a new blond-haired boy on piano, working on a couple of Carl's new tunes. The session quickly broke up — they were just listening to playbacks at this point anyway — and, after general greetings all around, Mr. Phillips introduced him to the piano player. His name was Jerry Lee Lewis, he was from Ferriday, Louisiana, and he had a new single just out, his first on the Sun label — but, it turned out, he didn't really need much of an introduction, he wasn't shy in the least. As a matter of fact, he would have talked Elvis' ear off if Elvis hadn't already been talking with Carl and Mr. Phillips about Hollywood and Las Vegas and the new RCA single that was coming out in January: the B side would definitely be Stan's song "Playing for Keeps," on which Mr. Phillips had the publishing. Sam was pleased to hear that, and Elvis and Carl were enjoying catching up on old times, but the piano player was getting impatient with all this small talk — he just wanted to get back to the piano.

Eventually a jam session did develop. They fooled around with "Blueberry Hill" and "My Isle of Golden Dreams," and then someone provided an acoustic guitar out of the trunk of his car, and Elvis began to warble "You Belong to My Heart," a 1945 Bing Crosby hit from the Disney animated feature *The Three Caballeros,* rolling his rs in the Latin manner with exaggerated, eye-rolling passion. Next they launched into a bunch of spiritual numbers with Carl and the band pitching in and the new boy echoing Elvis high-spiritedly on every number and taking the lead on some. "This

365

is fun!" says Jerry Lee. "You ought to get up a quartet," someone suggests, and a woman — maybe Marilyn — requests "Farther Along" from this "Rover Boys trio." Elvis does imitations of Bill Monroe, and of Hank Snow singing an Ernest Tubb song. Has he heard the new Chuck Berry single? someone asks him. Yes, he likes "Brown Eyed Handsome Man" better than "Too Much Monkey Business," and without further ado they are off and running on that. Carl has just gotten back from being out on tour with Berry, he says. Man, he just set out behind the stage and — he shrugs helplessly at Berry's prolific genius and creativity. Which just sets them off again on another pass at "Brown Eyed Handsome Man."

Almost from the start Sam had the tape recorder turned on. He was all set up for a session anyway, and he realized immediately that this could be an historic occasion. "I told Jack Clement [who was in the control room, too], 'Man, let's just record this. This is the type of feel, and probably an occasion, that — who knows? — we may never have these people together again.'" He didn't fail to recognize the potential for publicity either, and he called Johnny Cash, currently Sun's biggest star, who showed up briefly with his wife, and Bob Johnson at the *Press-Scimitar,* who came by with a UP reporter and a photographer in tow. "I never had a better time than yesterday afternoon," wrote Johnson, a little disingenuously, in the paper the next day, as he added: "If Sam Phillips had been on his toes, he'd have turned the recorder on when that very unrehearsed but talented bunch got to cutting up. That quartet could sell a million." Phillips himself sent the write-up out to DJs with a note headlined "Our Only Regret!," the regret being that "each and every one of you wonderful D.J.'s who are responsible for these boys being among the best known and liked in show business could not be here *too!*"

If they had, they would have been amazed. "I heard this guy in Las Vegas," Elvis reports to his captivated audience, "there was a guy out there [with Billy Ward and His Dominoes] that was doing a takeoff on me — 'Don't Be Cruel.' He tried so hard till he got much better, boy, much better than that record of mine." There are polite murmurs of demurral. "No, wait now, I mean, he was real slender, he was a colored guy, he got up there and he'd say —" And here Elvis begins to perform the song in imitation of the singer imitating him. "He had it a little slower than me. . . . He got the backing, the whole quartet, they got the feeling on it, he was hitting it, boy. Grabbed that microphone, and on the last note he went all the way down to the floor, man, looking straight up at the ceiling. Man, he was cutting out. I was under the table when he got through singing. . . . And all the time he was singing, them feet was going in and out, both ways, sliding like this. . . . He's a Yankee, you know," said Elvis, remarking with bemusement upon the singer's strange pronunciation of "tellyphone" and coming back to the song yet again, even trying "Paralyzed," the Otis Blackwell song he had recorded in September, in similar fashion. "All he needed was a building or something to jump off of," says someone, won over by the sheer enthusiasm of Elvis' description. "That's all he needed," agrees the unknown singer's foremost admirer, "that would have made a big ending."

They sang "No Place Like Home" and "When the Saints Go Marching In" with the blond-haired boy on piano ("The wrong man's been sitting here at this piano," said Elvis when Jerry Lee took his place. "Well, I been wanting to tell you that all along," responded Jerry Lee without missing a beat. "Scoot over!") and "Is It So Strange?," the number Faron Young had given him some months ago which he and June had taken as a twisted symbol of their love. He didn't know if he was going to record it, though, he said; Faron didn't want to give him any of the publishing. When he sang "That's When Your Heartaches Begin," the song he had cut in this very studio the summer after his senior year, he told everyone, "I recorded the sonofabitch and lost the dub on it." He thought it could still be a hit, he said. With the right arrangement and the same kind of deep baritone voice that had been featured in the background of the Ink Spots' original, he thought it could still sell.

Throughout the session people drift in and out, the guitar is passed around, while Snearly Ranch Boys piano player and sometime session musician Smokey Joe Baugh contributes his gravelly comments and harmonies. You can hear comments by unidentified women and children, doors slamming, and musicians departing (the Perkins brothers exit fairly early in the proceedings), which leaves a clear field for singers and piano pickers almost exclusively. At the end of the day Jerry Lee Lewis finally gets a chance to really show off his wares as he storms through both sides of his new single as well as "You're the Only Star in My Blue Heaven" and "Black Bottom Stomp." "That's why I hate to get started in these jam sessions," says Elvis affably, "I'm always the last one to leave. . . .

"Jerry, it was good to have met you," he says to the brash newcomer, inviting him to come out to the house sometime, while good-byes are being exchanged all around. "It was totally extemporaneous," said Sam Phillips, the proud progenitor, "everything was off mike, if it was on mike it was by accident — I think this little chance meeting meant an awful lot to all those people, not because one was bigger than another, *it was kind of like coming from the same womb.*" "I never saw the boy more likeable," wrote Bob Johnson, "than he was just fooling around with those other fellows who have the same interests he does."

Three nights later Elvis was among other fellows with much the same interests, but under entirely different, if no less newsworthy, circumstances. WDIA, which had been broadcasting since 1949 with programming aimed exclusively at Memphis' black population, but with white management, news announcers, and engineers, had established a Goodwill Fund almost from its inception with the goal of helping "needy Negro children." Each year the station put on a revue on the first Friday of December, which for the last several years had taken place at Ellis Auditorium. In 1956 the headliners were Ray Charles, former WDIA disc jockey B. B. King, the Magnificents, and the Moonglows, along with a gospel segment that featured the Spirit of Memphis Quartet and the Happyland Blind Boys. Each year's show featured a theme acted out by the current DJ staff, and this year's had to do with a contingent of "hep Choctaws," led by Chief Rockin' Horse (Rufus Thomas) and his bride, Princess Premium Stuff (Martha Jean the Queen), who are determined to introduce rock 'n' roll to a recalcitrant, and hopelessly square, rival tribe.

One of the engineers at the station, Louis Cantor, who doubled as a part-time gospel and r&b announcer under the names of Deacon and Cannonball Cantor, had graduated from Humes a year ahead of Elvis and George Klein and was a fellow student with Klein at Memphis State, as well as a fellow congregant at Temple Beth El Emeth. Wouldn't it be something, the powers that be at WDIA speculated, if they could get Elvis Presley to make a guest appearance on the show? Cantor approached Klein, who spoke to Elvis about it. He would be thrilled, he said, to put in an appearance, but he couldn't, of course, perform — that was something the Colonel had drilled into him since the very beginning of their association.

He and George showed up on the night of the show and stood quietly in the wings as some of his biggest heroes appeared onstage. Ray Charles sang "I Got a Woman" to Princess Premium Stuff; Phineas Newborn, Sr., led an all-star pit band dressed in Indian costumes of its own; and the ubiquitous Professor Nat D. Williams, master of ceremonies both here and at the amateur talent shows at the Palace Theatre as well as a popular columnist in the Negro press, crowned the station's "Miss 1070," as he did every year. "I was fourteen," said Carla Thomas, Rufus' daughter, a member of the highly disciplined Teen Town Singers, who sang backup for many of the singers on the show and had a performing spot of their own, "and I told my girlfriend, 'That's Elvis Presley back there in the wings.' We were on the completely other side, but I could see it was Elvis. She said, 'That's not Elvis Presley, he's not on the show.' I said, 'I know.' He was just watching from the wings. They didn't announce him until the very end, because they didn't want everybody to get carried away, and when they did and he came out and did his little 'How you doing?' everybody said, 'More! Do a little something for us.' So he did a little shake, and he tore everybody up."

"I told them, If you put Elvis into the front of the show, the show is over," said Carla's father, Chief Rockin' Horse for this evening, "so they took me at my word and put Elvis on near the end. I took Elvis onstage by the hand, I had this great big headdress with all the feathers, and when I took Elvis out there and he did that little wiggle that they wouldn't let him do on television, the crowd just went crazy. They stormed all backstage, beating on the doors and everything!"

After the show was over he stood backstage talking quietly and having his picture taken with B.B. and Miss Claudia Marie Ivy, the newly crowned WDIA queen. "To all who were in earshot," reported the *Tri-State Defender* to its black constituency proudly, "Presley was heard telling King, 'Thanks, man, for the early lessons you gave me.' Arthur Godfrey would surely call that 'humility.'"

"He stayed around a long time after the show," said Carla. "My sister Vaneese and I had our pictures taken with him, and there was an old piano backstage and he played some little runs on it. The audience was gone, and there were just the people getting dressed, and finally the stage manager said, 'All right now, y'all got to go.' He stayed that long, and we were just having a lot of fun. I remember *that* Elvis."

The accounts in the Negro press in succeeding weeks and months were just as positive, with one exception. Various reports pointed out that Elvis freely acknowledged not only his debt to B.B. but, implicitly, to black music in general, and the *Memphis World* cited an account of six months earlier that had Elvis "crack[ing] Memphis segregation laws [on June 19] by attending the Fairgrounds Memphis amusement park on East Parkway, during what is designated as 'colored night.' " For the most part there was little question that he was a hero in the black community. Nat D. Williams alone demurred. In his column in the December 22 issue of the *Pittsburgh Courier*, he wrote:

> Maybe it's the Indigo Avenue's blase blues sophistication, native ig-norance of the important, or just pur-dee meanness, but ordinarily nobody generally excites Beale Streeters enough to cause them to cue up to buy tickets or crash lines for autographs. . . . But Elvis Presley has 'em talking. And they ain't talking about his "art." You see, some-thing happened the other night that the average Beale Streeter doesn't altogether dig or appreciate.

What the average Beale Streeter didn't dig or appreciate, Nat D. went on, appeared to be a variation on the same thing that so disturbed the white middle-class (and middle-aged) mainstream.

> A thousand black, brown and beige teen-age girls in the audience blended their alto and soprano voices in one wild crescendo of sound that rent the rafters . . . and took off like scalded cats in the direction of Elvis. It took some time and several white cops to quell the melee and protect Elvis. The teen-age charge left Beale Streeters wondering: "How come cullud girls would take on so over a Memphis white boy . . . when they hardly let out a squeak over B. B. King, a Memphis cullud boy?" . . . But further, Beale Streeters are wondering if these teen-age girls' demonstration over Presley doesn't reflect a basic inte-gration in attitude and aspiration which has been festering in the minds of most of your folks' women folk all along. Huhhh?

Just six days later, on December 13, Hal Kanter, the screenwriter and director for *Lonesome Cowboy*, Elvis' first Hal Wallis production, which was scheduled to start shooting in mid January, flew into town. Kanter, a thirty-seven-year-old native of Savannah, had started out writing comedy skits in the pioneer days of TV, worked on a couple of Bob Hope movies, directed television's top-rated *George Gobel Show,* and most recently writ-ten screenplays for Tennessee Williams' *Rose Tattoo* and Dean Martin and

Jerry Lewis' *Artists and Models* for Hal Wallis — but this would mark his celluloid directorial debut. Elvis was slated to make his final appearance on the Louisiana Hayride two days later, the charity performance at Hirsch Coliseum that the Colonel had worked out back in April (along with the ten-thousand-dollar buyout) so as to free him of all contractual obligations, and Wallis thought it would be a good idea for Kanter to get a sense of the flavor of his star performer's life, since *Lonesome Cowboy* was intended to be something of a rock 'n' roll biopic.

Elvis met Kanter at the airport with Cliff and Gene and Freddy Bienstock, too, the dapper twenty-eight-year-old Hill and Range representative with the pronounced Viennese accent. Bienstock wasn't quite sure what he was doing there, except that he sensed that Elvis was a little nervous about Kanter coming to visit his home and he wanted to make an impression on the "Hollywood director." The first thing he did once they got to the house was to put Kanter in the same vibrating chair in which he had installed Bienstock upon *his* arrival, flipping the switch that set the chair in motion without any warning, which gave Kanter something of a surprise. Then he proudly showed off the house before his mother announced it was time for dinner. They had fried chicken and okra and greens, but Alberta, the maid, had forgotten to put any water on the table, and Kanter was parched, so he asked if he could please have some water. Elvis, being, naturally, a little embarrassed, "started screaming for the maid," Freddy recalled, "and he yells 'Alberta, some water please!' So she comes in with a pitcher of water and puts it in the middle of the table, but she didn't bring any glasses. So Kanter was looking at the water, and Elvis screams, 'Alberta, you forgot the glasses!' And Kanter says, 'It's all right, a straw will do.' Which I thought was very funny — but Elvis resented it. He didn't take to strangers easily, and later on in the evening, when I was getting ready to go back to New York, he came to me and said, 'Listen, man, you got to come with me [to Shreveport]. This director, I don't really know how to approach him — he's supposed to be directing my next movie, and he turns out to be a fucking comedian!' "

Things weren't beyond salvaging, though — Elvis was simply embarrassed, and Kanter was understandably feeling his way. After dinner they sat around in the recreation room, shot some pool, and talked about the movie. Hal Wallis had specifically enjoined the director from bringing a script, but after Elvis had expounded on his theory of screen acting (the ones who lasted were the ones who didn't smile much), Kanter hastened to reassure him that this wasn't just another "jolly" film where Elvis would sit around grinning all the time; in fact he wouldn't have to smile at all if he didn't really want to. You know, Elvis is a really good actor, Gene volunteered to Kanter. I'm sure he is, said Kanter agreeably. He had seen the screen test and he thought it was very good. " 'Man, that screen test ain't nothin'. You oughta hear him do his piece. Elvis, do that piece of yours for him.' Elvis said, 'Naw, I don't want to, I don't —' He said, 'Go ahead, do the piece.' I said, 'What piece are you talking about?' He said, 'Oh, it's a little something I learned.' And I said, 'What is it?' He said it was General MacArthur's speech to Congress, his farewell address. I said, 'Why did you learn that?' He said, 'I don't know. I just wanted to see if I could memorize it, and I did.' "

The next day Elvis gave Kanter a tour of Memphis, and that night they left for Shreveport in the Lincoln, with Scotty and Bill driving the instruments in the big yellow Cadillac limo. Kanter rode with Elvis in the front seat, while cousins Gene and Junior and the Colonel's brother-in-law, Bitsy Mott, rode in the back. At one point everybody was asleep except Elvis and the director, "and we passed a dog, an old dog howling in the night, and he said how much he envied that dog. That dog had a life of his own. He said, 'He goes out at night, and he's doing this, and he's doing that, and nobody knows what he's up to, but he's having more fun — and when the sun comes up he's back under the front porch, just thinking, and nobody knows the life he's been living during the night.' "

They pulled in to Shreveport at 5:00 A.M. and registered at the Captain Shreve, where the fans were already gathered in force and making enough noise that Elvis had to stick his head out of his room window to ask them to please let him get some sleep. "He awoke in late afternoon and breakfasted with two travelling companions," wrote Kanter in an article entitled "Inside Paradise," which was published in *Variety* some three weeks later. The story bore no specific reference to Elvis Presley, but it could have been about no one else, starting with its striking lead about "the young man with the ancient eyes and the child's mouth . . . [who] awoke from the nightmare of poverty to find the brilliant sun of Fame suddenly burst in his eyes. . . .

The lobby of the hotel had been swarming with camera-equipped hordes waiting for his brief flight to the auditorium; police had been detailed to keep order; one was posted at his door in the hallway. . . .

Now, the hours drag by for the young man. He reads a magazine, plays some records, chats with his travelling companions, looks over the newspapers, signs a few autographs for the hotel manager. Now it is time to dress. He takes his time, stretching out every movement to consume more minutes, to eat away the hour remaining.

On schedule the assistant manager arrives with the two burly police who escort him to the waiting patrol car. Down the service elevator, through the kitchen, into the alley where the patrol car hums, poised for immediate flight. . . .

Another squad of police wait at the stage entrance of the auditorium, leaning heavily against the throng of fans straining for a glimpse of their hero. A shout goes up as the car wheels into view. It turns into screams, high-pierced, splitting the night air, beseeching, fanatic, as he leaps from the car and hurdles himself past clutching hands into the comparative safety of the auditorium.

Backstage there are milling scores who want to slap his back, shake his hand, "remember me" him. Then the reporters, the photographers, the disk jockeys with their tape-recorders, city officials, civic dignitaries, fan club presidents, business associates. Talk. Laugh. Shake. Smile. Pose. Answer. Listen. Stand. Sit. Walk. See. Sign. Hear. Acknowledge. Deny.

A nerve-shattering hour and then the moment to appear onstage. The introduction is drowned by the shout that goes up at the merest hint he is next on the bill. The shrill, deafening, roof-lifting screams continue.

"That's the night my car got stomped in," said Horace Logan, the head of the Hayride, who introduced Elvis wearing his trademark Stetson hat and pearl-handled six-guns. "I parked it right behind the dressing room behind the Coliseum, and the little old girls stomped the roof in standing on top of it trying to see Elvis. That was the night they had roped off the front of the stage, about twenty-five feet. Nobody was supposed to get down there, and when we got there, they were jammed up against the stage. And the fire chief said, 'Get them to move back or there is no show.' Well, you're talking about eight thousand people on the lower floor, they had to move their chairs back, all eight thousand of them would have had to move. Now how am I going to do that? I told the fire chief, I said, 'I'll tell them there is not going to be any show, but I'm going to tell them who canceled it — and they'll kill you!' Then I got an inspiration. We had some kids out there in iron lungs, and I told them, 'Folks, I'm sorry to have to do this, but these young people over here in the iron lungs are the only ones I'm going to allow down here. Every one of you has got to back up and move over, so we can put those kids in the front.' And they did it."

The show itself lasted for about half an hour, and there was screaming from start to finish. Hal Kanter, who had admittedly come to scoff, came away a true believer. When he had driven out to the Coliseum earlier in the day with Bill, the fans had converged on the car, thinking it was Elvis', and he thought he was going to be torn apart. Then, after they realized their mistake, he saw something he could scarcely believe. "I saw a young girl open her purse and take out a Kleenex, and she wiped her hand on the car, took some dust, put it in the Kleenex and folded it and put it back in the purse. I thought, 'My God, I've never seen any kind of devotion like this anywhere, about anything.' "

At the show that night he saw further evidence of this same strange sense of almost trancelike absorption. He saw a young girl who looked as if she were about to strangle herself by swallowing her hand. "She appeared to have her hand in her mouth all the way down to her wrist, and I was wondering, how can a little girl like this get her whole hand down her throat? And then at one point she pulled her hand out of her mouth, and I found out she didn't have a hand at all. She was just sucking on the stump. And I thought, 'God, I've got to get that in the picture!' " He saw twins clapping to the music, one twin using her left hand, the other using her right. Most of all, he saw a kind of mass hysteria, and a mass adulation, that he had never seen before or since. "I'm a man who saw Al Jolson on the stage, and I never saw anything like the reception that Al Jolson got until Elvis Presley — and he made Al Jolson seem like a passing fancy."

Nobody had seen anything like it before. If there had been any doubt that Elvis Presley had outgrown the Hayride, that doubt was now erased. It was, in a way, the end of the Hayride itself. Though it would limp along for another few years, how could it follow an act like this? Webb Pierce had succeeded Hank Williams, Slim Whitman and Faron Young had succeeded Webb Pierce, and Elvis Presley had succeeded them all — but who was going to succeed Elvis Presley?

Backstage there was an uproar of activity. Paul Kallinger from 150,000-watt station XERF in Mexico, which broadcast unimpeded, and essentially unregulated, just across the border from Del Rio, Texas, got Tillman Franks to introduce him, but Elvis spent at least an equal amount of time with Tillman's daughter, Darlene. Even Sandi Phillips, a reporter for the Broadmoor Junior High School student newspaper, got an interview. She was there with a group of girls from Broadmoor, and they all went backstage after the show. "I said I was a reporter for the *Bulldog Bark,* and there were all these guards, and they weren't going to let me in, and then all of a sudden this man says, 'Let her in,' *and it was him* — I'm getting goose bumps just telling this — and he said, 'Hey, little lady, you want an interview or something?' Something like that. And his hair was flopping around, and he was sweating, and he had a towel around his neck, and I had a little pad and pencil and I was wearing jeans and a Levi shirt and I had a ponytail, and I asked him a few questions (who knows what in hell I asked him?), and he answered whatever I asked, and he kissed me on the cheek, and I remember going out into the hall and all my girlfriends were just screaming at the top of their lungs and I just fell into their arms and, of course, I wouldn't let anyone touch me or wash that spot for weeks."

DOTTIE HARMONY FLEW IN from Hollywood the following week to celebrate Christmas with the Presley family. There had been a snowstorm, and her plane was delayed, so when she got to Memphis there was nobody at the airport to meet her, and she fell asleep disconsolately next to a heater. "The next thing I knew, I heard a whole bunch of kids shouting, and I open up my eyes, and there are a bunch of girls with banners that say, 'Go home, Dottie Harmony.' Then I heard screams, and in comes Elvis, who proceeds to pick me up and carry me out to the Lincoln, and we went home, where he introduced me to his mom and dad."

Dottie found Mrs. Presley a totally sympathetic figure — Gladys hugged her and made a big fuss over her — and while Vernon didn't show anywhere near as much personality, "they were very affectionate with each other, and he was very much so with Elvis, too." Within an hour of her arrival Gladys had bundled her up and given her a Christmas list. "Mind you, I'd never met any of the people on this list, and I don't know what I'm supposed to get them. I got the female list, and Elvis took the males, and we went to this big department store downtown, walked in, and he tells me, 'We'll meet here when we're done.' So I went about my business, bought gifts left and right, and I had a whole bunch of presents stacked up and waiting when all of a sudden I saw him running right past me, out the door to the car — 'cause he had a whole bunch of fans running after him. About twenty minutes later, Cliff came back and got me, and we went home and had dinner."

Dottie spent a little over two weeks at the house, sleeping in Elvis' room while he stayed down the hall. He spoke to her parents in Brooklyn several times on the phone to reassure them that she was all right; they rode around town in matching motorcycle outfits, and he introduced her to his friends and showed her where he had grown up and gone to school. The Colonel came by on a number of occasions, but he barely acknowledged her presence. "He acted like I wasn't even there. I remember one time, he wanted to talk to them about some kind of money deal and he asked me to leave, and Elvis' mother said, 'Doroty' — she always called me Doroty — 'stays right here. Doroty is part of the family.' He didn't like that one bit."

Mrs. Presley talked about her garden ("Doroty, we've got tomatoes as big as your two fists") and cooked black-eyed peas and greens and a coconut cake for Elvis almost every night. The fan magazines had a field day, but it wasn't, said Dottie, "anything like you might think. We used to read the Bible every night, if you can believe that — he used to read aloud to me and then talk about it. He was very religious — there was nothing phony about that at all. At six o'clock at night he made me go out and sign autographs with him, which I thought was so ridiculous. I said, 'I mean, what do people want my autograph for, Elvis?' He said, 'Just sign it.' He said he wouldn't be where he was if it wasn't for his fans. He really felt that way."

Elvis tried to get Dottie to give up smoking ("I knew I didn't have to worry about that, because he promised to stop chewing his nails if I did"), and he lectured her frequently on the "many lives he had seen ruined by drink." One time she and Gladys managed to get him out of the house, "and we cracked a beer. One beer!" On Christmas Day they all exchanged gifts under a white nylon Christmas tree. Gladys wore her brocade dress and a red Santa hat, and there were pictures in the newspapers of Elvis and Dottie, of Elvis surveying his presents (including any number of stuffed animals and teddy bears), of Dottie opening *her* presents, even of a touch football game at the Dave Wells Community Center two days later, with Red home on leave and Elvis wearing tennis shoes and rolled-up dungarees, hair flopping across his forehead and a determined expression on his face.

June saw the pictures in the paper and fumed. "Here I am, I'm being good, I'm being faithful, I'm not doing anything — and I've had lots of offers to go out. And then Christmas Day we were home till about noon, but then we were invited to some friend's house. I even made myself a brand-new blue velvet dress to wear for Christmas Day, and I felt really pretty. I'm thinking, This is Christmas, and he's got to call. When I woke up on Christmas Day, I was thinking about Elvis Presley — but he wasn't thinking about me. Because Dottie Harmony was there. Well, that really clinched it for me, it really broke my heart, I had no idea it was all just this game. He called me afterwards and said that he had called and we didn't answer, and that's probably true, but right after that I met someone and started going out with him, and he just swept me off my feet, eased my heartache, and asked me to marry him, and I said yes."

Scotty and Bill saw the pictures, too, and it only reinforced their growing feeling that they were on the outside looking in. Christmas was a bleak season for them that year. Although they had worked a lot of dates the first half of the year, since August there had been no more than two weeks' worth of work, and this didn't add up to much on a $100-a-week retainer (even when they were working, they were earning $200 a week tops and were enjoined from making any product endorsements or taking any free goods). "We were broke, flat broke," said Scotty's wife, Bobbie. After living in Elvis' old house on Getwell for a few months, they had moved in with her three sisters and a brother-in-law in a big house on Tutwiler, near Sears, and Bobbie was having to hide money from Scotty in a jewelry box just to be sure to have enough to pay the bills. Scotty and Bill (and D.J., too, in a good-humored subsidiary role) gave an interview to the *Press-Scimitar* in mid December in which they spoke in only slightly veiled terms of their straitened financial and social circumstances. They didn't see as much of Elvis as they once had, they conceded — "just can't be that way." He was still fun to be around, though; "[he's] always got some jazz going, likes to keep up chatter and joking," said Bill. "I don't think anyone should criticize him until they try to put themselves in his shoes and figure out what they would do." They used to split the money three ways before D.J. came into the group, reported the newspaper, but "when [Elvis] hit the real big time, they realized that different financial arrangements would have [to be] made, and were happy that they came out of it as well as they did." The real purpose of their "press conference" was to announce that they had just been given permission by management (which explicitly did not permit them to work with anyone else or "appear as a unit without Elvis in between tours") to make a record of their own, an instrumental that RCA would put out sometime after the first of the year. They were very excited about this new opportunity. "We don't even know how they will title us yet," said Bill. "Maybe as 'Elvis' Boys.'"

On January 4, 1957, Elvis' new single was released, and he reported for his pre-induction physical. He asked Dottie if she could stick around and go in with him, and she and Cliff accompanied him to the examination center at Kennedy Veterans Hospital, on Getwell, where he had performed in the rec room not long after his first record came out. Ordinarily there would have been forty or fifty men processed on any given day, but the army had decided that Elvis should be put through on an "off day," all by himself. No one was supposed to know about it (the notice had been telephoned, not mailed), but there was a legion of photographers and reporters waiting when they pulled up in the rain. Dottie waited in the car at first, then joined Cliff inside, and Elvis announced to them both with a broad smile that he thought he had passed the intelligence test. Then she flew back to California, and Elvis left for New York on the train later that evening to play *The Ed Sullivan Show* for the third and final time.

The Ed Sullivan appearance could best be described as the triumph of inclusion over exclusion, the boldfaced embrace and declaration of respectability that civilization inevitably has to offer. With the gold lamé vest that Barbara had given him for a Christmas present worn over the blue velvet blouse that he had worn for his appearance in Tupelo, Elvis looked something like a Middle Eastern pasha, while the Jordanaires, dressed in checked salesmen's sports jackets, gave their booster's all behind him. For his first segment he delivered an easygoing medley of his biggest records (it was not that they were any bigger in *size*, he hastened to kid his totally rapt audience, as per custom), concluding with a rendition of "Don't Be Cruel" that owed everything, from finger rolls to his pronunciation of "tellyphone" to the big pumped-up ending, to the per-

formance by Jackie Wilson he had witnessed in Las Vegas. Then he did
"Too Much" and "When My Blue Moon Turns to Gold Again," the lilting 1941 hit that he had included on his second album, and thanked his
thoroughly mesmerized audience for the best Christmas he had ever
had — and for the 282 teddy bears that they had sent him. After another
break he came out again, this time dressed in one of his loudly tweedy
sports jackets and, with eyes closed, straining up on his toes, he sang a
song that Ed Sullivan introduced as "sort of in the mood that he'd like to
create," the spiritual "Peace in the Valley."

"Elvis, ladies and gentlemen," said Ed, "inasmuch as he goes to the
Coast now for his new picture, this will be the last time that we'll run into
each other for a while, but I —" Screams from the audience. Elvis laughs.
"Now wait a minute." Ed holds up his hand. "I wanted to say to Elvis
Presley and the country that this is a real decent, fine boy, and wherever
you go, Elvis, all of you . . . we want to say that we've never had a pleas-
anter experience on our show with a big name than we've had with you.
So now let's have a tremendous hand for a very nice person." Elvis is
clearly gratified and, with a generous gesture, includes both the band and
the Jordanaires in his circle of acclaim, as Ed shakes the hand of each
backup singer. There will be no more appearances on the show, the Colonel has made that clear by setting what amount to prohibitive terms for
all three networks: if they want Elvis in the future, they will have to pay a
$300,000 fee, which will cover two guest appearances and an hour-long
special. But Ed's gesture does not seem to be motivated by the normal
show business considerations; he appears genuinely taken with the young
man. And Elvis for his part is just as genuinely thrilled — he says as much
to friends and fellow musicians — to receive recognition and validation
from someone so widely respected, so experienced in the business. "This
is a nice boy, and I want you to know it," Ed repeated that same night in a
television interview with Hy Gardner, on *Hy Gardner Calling!* "He could
so easily have his head turned by all that's happened. But it hasn't. . . ."

By then, though, Elvis was already on the long train ride back home.
He wanted to spend his twenty-second birthday with his mother and father before leaving for the Coast in a couple of days. On Tuesday he celebrated quietly at the house and made plans with his parents to join him in
California several weeks later. The draft board announced that same day
that he was an "A profile," which meant that he would be classified 1-A,
or draftable, as soon as his local board received the report, though he

would probably not be called up for six or eight months. It didn't matter, Elvis told reporters who telephoned, he was happy to serve, he would simply go whenever he was called. He knocked around Memphis for the next couple of days, got a haircut at Jim's Barber Shop, on the corner of Beale and Main, stopped by the police station just to shoot the bull (in December it had been reported that he told his "home town police friends" that he thought Debra Paget was the prettiest of the Hollywood stars, but Kim Novak was a good-looking girl with a good figure, and Rita Moreno really knocked him out), saw Dewey and George at their respective radio stations, and briefly dropped by the place that Dixie worked. She was married now, she told him. She had gotten married not long after the last time she had seen him with Nick. "Well, I'll see you around," he said, and then he was on the train to California with Cliff and Gene, stocked up with Reese's peanut butter cups and comic books and movie magazines, and looking forward to making what he felt would amount to his real movie debut, his first chance at a genuine starring role.

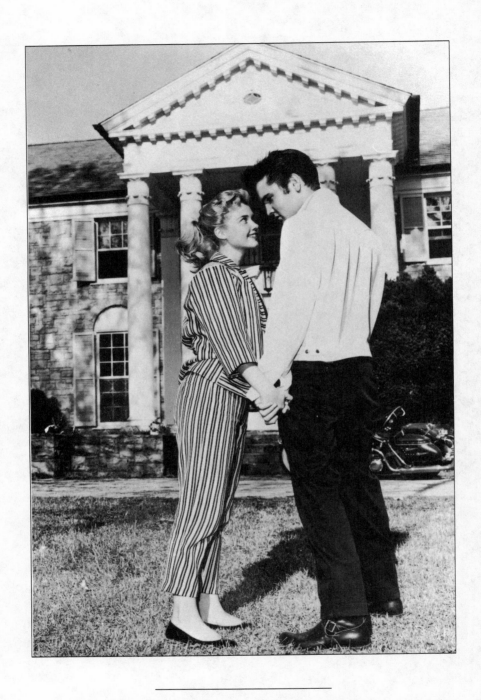

WITH YVONNE LIME, IN FRONT OF GRACELAND, EASTER WEEKEND, 1957.
(ROBERT WILLIAMS)

LOVING YOU

THE MOVIE HAD BEEN RETITLED *Loving You* (after a new Leiber and Stoller ballad of that name, expressly written for the
picture) by the time that Elvis arrived in Los Angeles by train
on January 11. It had been planned with all the characteristic
care and attention to detail of a typical Hal Wallis production, with the
casting of seasoned stars (Wendell Corey and Lizabeth Scott) who were
unlikely to overwhelm the new "singing sensation," the secondary interest of another Hal Wallis discovery (eighteen-year-old Dolores Hart, née
Hicks, whom Wallis was said to have found in a campus production of
Joan of Lorraine just weeks before), colorful contract players like James
Gleason in significant minor roles, a carefully prepared script, and an experienced studio crew. It was, in short, the kind of lighthearted, fresh-
faced picture with which a major studio might have introduced an exciting new star twenty, or even five, years before, but it was worlds away
from the flurry of rock 'n' roll exploitation features that had sprung up in
the previous year to fill the void that *Variety* had pointed to in its review
of *Love Me Tender.*

With a customary two-month studio shooting time and its newly
commissioned score alone, *Loving You* would have differed substantially
from *Rock Around the Clock* or *Don't Knock the Rock,* for example, the two
1956 quickie productions by exploitation master Sam Katzman which set a
rock 'n' roll movie trend for even more rudimentary filmic exercises like
Rock, Rock, Rock (filmed in less than two weeks) to follow. Each of these
movies presented stars like Bill Haley and DJ Alan Freed who, in the face
of adult opposition, conspire to put on a show that inevitably includes a
panoply of rock 'n' rollers — from Little Richard, the Platters, and Fats
Domino to such Las Vegas staples as the Treniers and Freddie Bell and
the Bellboys — trotted out on a soundstage to lip-synch their latest hits.

What the Colonel and Hal Wallis had in mind was something quite
different. Their idea, linked by a partnership of convenience and a shared

canniness which had approached similar challenges and similar partnerships in the past, was to build a career that would last, a career that could
survive musical trends, which inevitably come and go, while permitting
an incandescent talent to continue to shine. In keeping with that goal, the
Colonel knew, it was necessary to *distance* his boy from the hurly-burly;
he was becoming increasingly concerned that the very controversy that
had originally fueled Elvis' fame was now serving to limit it. He had
worked hard to get his boy on Ed Sullivan and pointed with pride not
only to the ratings, which clearly reflected a substantial, and substantially
growing, adult audience, but to Sullivan's public endorsement and embrace — and he was now determined to work just as hard to achieve success in the movies.

The Colonel had always paid close attention to newspaper accounts
and never failed to note criticism. In Elvis' case he had exploited it for a
time, assuring RCA that he knew what he was doing and that, if they
didn't like it, they could just step off the merry-go-round. Now it was time
for them *all* to step off the merry-go-round. The criticism had simply
become too intense, and it was becoming all too clear that rock 'n' roll
now served as a lightning rod for a more and more sharply divided society. Denounced from the pulpit, derided in the press, increasingly linked
to the race issue, and even subject to congressional hearings, the music
was being used to stigmatize a generation. New York congressman Eman-
uel Celler, chairman of the Antitrust Subcommittee of the House Judi-
ciary Committee, which was looking into the issue of "payola," declared
that while "rock 'n' roll has its place [and has given] great impetus to talent, particularly among the colored people," the music of Elvis Presley
and his "animal gyrations . . . are violative of all that I know to be in good
taste."

To the Colonel it was all business. The attacks, the whipped-up emotion, the moral outrage — these were simply the actions of concerned
businessmen, secular and ecclesiastic, determined to protect their investment in society. But the Colonel was determined to protect his investment, too, and to that end, without ever announcing his policy or spelling
it out in specific detail, he was prepared to remove Elvis from the fray, he
was committed to the idea of getting him off the road and out of the glare
of needless, negative publicity. Elvis' business was communication, after
all, and what better way to communicate with his audience all around the
world than from the silver screen, where the image always flickered, the

candle burned but never flamed — and fame, carefully nurtured, need never go away?

Meanwhile, Wallis, a veteran of seven of the first eight Martin and Lewis pictures and one of the most careful polishers of image and fame, however unlikely the source, was not about to overlook his own investment. He recognized in the Colonel a kindred spirit. "He was a genius," he said of Parker in a quote that might well have been applied to himself, "at getting every possible inch of financial mileage out of his astonishing protégé," and he was somewhat taken aback by Hal Kanter's rather cavalier take on the whole phenomenon. When Kanter, in recounting his experiences on the road, mentioned the girl he thought had swallowed her hand and suggested that perhaps they could find an attractive amputee from central casting, Wallis, who had thoroughly enjoyed the recitation up to that point, reacted with horror. "Oh God, you can't put *that* in the picture," he said. Leave the satire to Frank Tashlin, whose *The Girl Can't Help It* at Twentieth Century Fox was a clever takeoff on rock 'n' roll, with Edmond O'Brien, as a love-struck gangster, warbling songs like "Rock Around the Rock Pile" and Jayne Mansfield competing for attention with Gene Vincent and Little Richard. Hal Wallis was not simply in the business of exploiting fads, and he was as determined as Tom Parker to see to it that Elvis Presley's career was a long, and mutually profitable, one. As far as he was concerned, *Loving You* was going to be good entertainment, a typical name-above-the-title Hollywood production, with the best of the "new music," a clever (but not too clever) script, and a wholesome Hollywood patina to spread over any recognizable real-life details. It would be a picture you could take the whole family to.

N OT DUE AT THE PARAMOUNT STUDIO until the beginning of the week, Elvis reported to Radio Recorders at noon on Saturday, January 12, the day after his Hollywood arrival, for his first RCA session since September. He might more easily have recorded in Nashville during his time off in November and December, but he was adamantly opposed to working anymore under such uninspired conditions, unless he absolutely had to. With the second album out and nothing of any substance left in the can, Steve Sholes had been begging the Colonel for more studio time, and Parker had at last grudgingly conceded it to him on the two weekends that framed the start of the picture — *unless* Paramount should happen to change its plans. The principal purpose of the session was to record an extended-play "inspirational" album of four or five titles, something Elvis had publicly stated to be his ambition since his start in show business, along with a follow-up single to "Too Much," which was currently number two on the charts. In addition, it appeared that he would cut studio versions of several of the songs intended for the motion picture, so as to avoid the problem they had run into with *Love Me Tender* and be able to offer recording-quality sound on at least some of his RCA movie soundtrack releases.

Steve Sholes would be present, of course, but with Freddy Bienstock serving as de facto a&r man, he had been virtually relegated to a timekeeper's role, and he was fed up with being the constant butt of the Colonel's jokes. On principle he refused to address Parker by any other title than his Christian name. Still, he was a good company man, and that was the limit of his personal rebellion, until, on the second or third day of his visit, he told the Colonel that he wouldn't be able to join him and Bienstock and Tom Diskin for their daily breakfast meeting, due to an unavoidable early meeting at RCA. "That sonofabitch just doesn't want to have breakfast with us," declared the Colonel indignantly to Freddy Bienstock. The next morning Colonel had everyone there an hour and a half early, and they caught Sholes sneaking into the dining room. "Must have been a short meeting, Steve," remarked the Colonel caustically. "And, of course, Steve had to sit down at the table," recalled Bienstock, "and he hated all of it. He felt perhaps that he was too important an executive to play along with Colonel Parker. You know, the Colonel knew a lot of practical jokes and so forth, and he was a difficult man and had, always, all kinds of demands and requests, and Steve was just too impatient a man to put up with all of this."

The sessions themselves went smoothly enough. In addition to the religious and movie titles, Elvis recorded "That's When Your Heartaches Begin," the Ink Spots number which he had spoken of at the "Million-Dollar Quartet" session in December, as well as Otis Blackwell's latest, "All Shook Up," which Elvis thought was a good phrase for a refrain. For this he received a co-writing credit, his last (after the one third Mae Axton had given him for "Heartbreak Hotel" and the songwriter's share Hill and Range had insisted on for "Don't Be Cruel" and the *Love Me Tender* soundtrack) for a long while.

Hill and Range had its own deal in place by now, which got around the question of credit by simply getting a one-third cut-in from every songwriter who wanted to have his song recorded by Elvis Presley. What this meant was that the songwriter signed a document surrendering one third of his songwriter's royalties, which were paid by the record company to the song publisher. Once the publisher received them, they were split, under ordinary circumstances, 50–50 with the writer(s), but in this case one third was to be reserved out, to be "paid to Elvis Presley personally." As a result the writer, or writers, ended up getting 33⅓ percent, instead of 50 percent, of these "mechanical royalties." The performance royalties, on the other hand (which were calculated on the basis of live performance and jukebox and air play) were not affected. They were collected by the performing-rights societies ASCAP and BMI and paid directly to songwriter and publisher alike. The understanding was that this agreement would apply only to songs first recorded by Elvis Presley and only in their original version. This got around Elvis' embarrassment at taking credit for something he didn't do ("I've never written a song in my life," Elvis insisted vociferously on a number of public occasions, going on to declare in one interview, "It's all a big hoax . . . I get one third of the credit for recording it. It makes me look smarter than I am") while at the same time neatly sidestepping his contractual agreement with RCA to give the record company a reduced publishing rate on all songs authored, or coauthored, by him.

It would be virtually impossible at this point for a non–Hill and Range song to find its way to a session — unless, of course, Elvis introduced it, and then Hill and Range was bound to secure a substantial piece of the publishing before RCA might see fit to clear it for release. Still, the publishing house liked to cover all bets, and on the second day of the session, after Elvis had recorded "Peace in the Valley" and "Precious Lord, Take My Hand" — two staples of the Hill and Range religious catalogue by Thomas A. Dorsey, the father of modern black gospel music — there was a suggestion from Jean Aberbach, the younger of the two brothers who had founded the firm. Since Elvis was recording religious music anyway, offered the debonair forty-five-year-old Aberbach, why not try a holiday release like "Here Comes Peter Cottontail," with which the firm had had great success? Freddy, somewhat more attuned to the likes and dislikes of their successful young partner-client, was horrified, but Jean, for the first and only time in what would turn out to be a very long association, persisted. "I mean, you had to be mad to think Elvis is going to record 'Peter

Cottontail,' " recalled Freddy, "and I told him that, but Jean had no sense for songs and he insisted. So he brought a lead sheet down to Radio Recorders, and he put it on Elvis' stand while Elvis was having something to eat, and Elvis comes back and looks at it and said, 'Who brought that Bre'r Rabbit shit in here?' " Whereupon Jean conceded defeat ("Jean could laugh at himself, and when he saw Elvis' reaction, he died laughing — he just disappeared"), but he got the last laugh anyway when he snuck an instrumental version of the song onto the motion picture soundtrack.

On Monday Elvis reported to the studio for makeup and wardrobe tests. This would be his first Technicolor film, and he'd always thought that actors with dark hair, like Tony Curtis, lasted the longest and looked the best. The makeup man said that with his eyes he should photograph well with black hair, so they dyed it and Mr. Wallis liked the way it looked, and they went with the darker coloring. From the start he felt more comfortable on the Paramount lot than he had ever felt at Fox. Mr. Wallis treated him with affectionate respect, and it was clear he was not being seen as just the latest freak, to be trotted out and eyed suspiciously by the rest of the cast and crew until he had proved himself. Hal Kanter greeted him with the fond familiarity that only shared experience can bring, and he immediately took to the music director, an easygoing guy with a pencil-thin mustache named Charlie O'Curran, who was married to Patti Page (he had previously been married to Betty Hutton) and who rolled up his sleeves and went to work with Scotty, D.J., and Bill.

They spent the week first rehearsing, and then recording, the film soundtrack on the Paramount soundstage. It quickly became evident that Elvis was uncomfortable in the big open space, with people wandering in and out, but whether because Radio Recorders was all booked up or because Hal Wallis truly believed that he had the best facilities for motion picture recording, with a two-track 35-millimeter sound system that allowed you easily to bring up the vocal, tone down the instrumentation, and introduce ambient sound, they persisted at Paramount throughout the week. There were moments of exasperation when, for example, sultry Lizabeth Scott, the thirty-four-year-old smoky-voiced heroine of countless films noirs, strolled in during a take, perhaps to get a closer look at her costar. Songwriter Ben Weisman, too, showed up unannounced at a session. Weisman, a protégé of Jean Aberbach's who had gotten his first Elvis cut a few months earlier with "First in Line" and had then written

"Got a Lot O' Livin' to Do" for the film, was tipped off to the recording session by Aberbach and flew in from New York with his songwriting partner, Aaron Schroeder — at their own expense — to make sure that the song got cut. On the afternoon that Weisman and Schroeder arrived, Elvis was struggling with the movie's title cut, and it didn't seem like he would ever get to their song. He had already recorded a version of it at Radio Recorders, but Weisman was getting increasingly worried that the number wouldn't make it into the movie.

"So I do things sometimes that are very unorthodox, I've learned sometimes you've got to do things that are a little off-the-wall. Aaron and I were sitting in the control booth waiting for our song to be recorded, and I told Aaron during an intermission that I was going out there to meet him. Aaron says, 'Don't go. You don't belong out there.' But I went anyway, and it happened that Elvis was sitting in the corner of this big studio with nobody around him, playing guitar, and there was a piano right next to him. So I sat down at the piano — he was playing the blues — and I jammed with him. He didn't look up. After a chorus or two, he looks up and says, 'Who are you?' I said, 'My name is Ben Weisman.' He said, 'Ben Weisman. Didn't you write . . .' He said, 'Wow.' He was so impressed. He liked the way I was jamming with him. He got up, and he yelled out, 'Guys, get out here,' and on the spot they all got together again, and I was there watching, and I went back in the control room, and they did the tune."

Because Wallis had so little faith in Elvis' musicians ("I need them like I need a hole in the head," Wallis told Elvis, who insisted that he needed his boys behind him), he made sure to have a couple of experienced studio musicians for the session. Hilmer J. "Tiny" Timbrell, an affable native of British Columbia in his mid thirties, played rhythm guitar, while Dudley Brooks, forty-three-year-old assistant music director at Paramount and an alumnus of the Lionel Hampton band, played piano and served as de facto arranger of the sessions. "Dudley was a little, short, heavyset guy, black as the ace of spades," said Radio Recorders engineer Thorne Nogar, who met him at the recording studio just a few days later. "For some reason Elvis took a liking to him, and he would sit there at the piano, and Dudley would say, 'Well, El, you play it this way — no, use that finger.' He kind of taught Elvis."

The band gelled, but the sessions didn't, and even Wallis was forced to admit that the studio soundstage was not the ideal setting for an Elvis

Presley recording. They went back to Radio Recorders the following week to fix up the soundtrack (in the end they wound up using a judicious mix of studio and soundstage recordings), but Wallis was hooked by now and even attended some of the sessions. "I was fascinated by the way Elvis recorded," he wrote in his autobiography. "Never bothering with arrangements, he and his boys noodled around, improvised, ad-libbed, and worked out numbers for hours. Finally, he would rehearse a number straight through. Night after long night I watched and listened, fascinated." What he did not put into his autobiography was the almost daily pressure to which the Colonel was subjecting him to bring Elvis' pay up to a more suitable level. In the end Wallis reluctantly came up with a bonus of $50,000 on top of the agreed-upon $15,000, which did not quite equal Elvis' Twentieth Century Fox salary but certainly bore out the Colonel's belief that everything was negotiable.

By then production had started up, and some of Wallis' genuine faith and fascination with his star carried over into the actual filming. Hal Kanter had adapted what might have been a conventional Hollywood musical ("Hey, kids, let's put on a show") into a witty treatment of fame and disaffection. Here the wily manager was transformed from a cigar-chewing carny into a beautiful, if inaccessible, woman (Lizabeth Scott); the faithful musicians, who might have been left behind but in the end were warmly reembraced, became, in this version, Wendell Corey alone; and Elvis' character was rendered with faithful perplexity as a pained innocent in a Technicolor world. The music was incorporated into the script in a way that celebrated its wholesome joyousness, the very "spirituality" that Sam Phillips had spoken of from the start, without confronting any of its troublesome social, or generational, implications. Ben Weisman and Aaron Schroeder's "Got a Lot O' Livin' to Do" ran like a trouble-free theme throughout the film, and there was lots of snappy repartee playing off its audience's, or its author's, knowledge of the real-life drama. The Trouble in Jacksonville, for example, is put up on the screen in the form of a campaign to ban Deke Rivers' music, while The Gas-Station Fight in Memphis — or perhaps it is The Hotel Fight in Toledo — here is transformed into a café fight in which Elvis is goaded into performing a wonderful version of "Mean Woman Blues," then knocks his tormentor into the jukebox which has, miraculously, provided his musical accompaniment.

Elvis was seemingly attuned throughout, in character in a way that he had been able only fitfully to achieve in his debut film, and his musical performances were marvelous representations of his stage act, not the real thing exactly but close enough to leave no one in the audience in any doubt as to what the fuss was all about. What was most striking, however, was not his energy, which was considerable, nor his very convincing representation of emotion (mostly inner turmoil and wounded pride, in the manner of James Dean) but the occasional indication of a stillness at the center, those rare moments of true ease which gave promise of the kind of long-term career that a Spencer Tracy, or even a Bing Crosby, could enjoy and that Hal Wallis could well envision for his latest discovery.

He felt at ease with his fellow actors as well. He liked Wendell Corey, whose acting tips he appreciated (and for whom he later named a cat), and he felt perfectly comfortable with Dolores Hart, who was younger and did not have even *his* experience in the movies. His romance with Dottie seemed to be cooling, helped along by the Colonel's obvious skepticism of her motives ("The Colonel never wanted anyone to get close," Dottie felt, though she continued to remain in touch with Elvis' mother), and the Colonel stepped in on one or two other occasions, too, when he felt that one of Elvis' Hollywood acquaintances might be "unsuitable." But for all that, there was no question he felt more at home in Hollywood, dating starlets like Rita Moreno, with whom he went to see Dean Martin at a Hollywood nightclub, and Yvonne Lime, a Paramount player who had a small part in the picture and who was more like a hometown date, "a lot of fun to be with," Elvis told *Press-Scimitar* reporter Bob Johnson. "Mostly we'd go to movies or just ride around looking at things. Sometimes we would play records."

Less idyllic was the situation that seemed to be developing with Scotty and Bill, and with D.J. to a lesser extent. They didn't like Hollywood, they were bored just sitting around waiting to be called, and they couldn't help but feel the slights, real or imagined, that they saw continually coming their way. To relieve the boredom on the set they would jam with Elvis between takes. An electrician would plug them in, and they always drew a crowd, up to the point that Kanter had to beg, "Will you please stop? We're trying to do some work here!" Off the set they hung around with Charlie O'Curran, a man who enjoyed his liquor and could ask them out to his house in Santa Monica without even calling his wife, Patti. For the most part, though, they were on their own, seeing little of Elvis even though they were only two or three floors below him at the Hollywood Knickerbocker and, in Scotty and Bill's case in particular, hurt and resentful at the separation. Aspiring rockabilly singer Glen Glenn (né Troutman), who had first met Elvis in San Diego in April 1956 and had subsequently become good friends with the band, came by often to see Scotty and Bill, and Bill would frequently bring him up to see Elvis, who was his main inspiration.

"Lots of times Bill would go up with us, knock on the door, and then he would go back down. It wasn't that easy to get in, but he always made sure. There were always a lot of girls sitting around on the couch and stuff, talking. One night I remember Elvis had all the acetates for the soundtrack from *Loving You,* and he had that old Smiley Lewis song, 'One Night,' too — that wasn't in the movie, but he cut it at Radio Recorders at the same time — and he was bragging on it 'cause he played guitar on that. We sat there listening to every one of those songs, and the girls were setting around and Black had already left — he kept playing 'One Night' over and over. 'That's a good fuckin' record,' he said.

"Bill got real mad one time, 'cause they wouldn't let us in upstairs — I think it was mainly the Colonel didn't want Elvis to see anybody that night, but Bill said, 'I ought to go up there and just hit him right in the nose.' He knew I loved Elvis, and it meant a lot to Bill that he could actually take me up there to meet him. He was very bitter, because he thought that Elvis could have put his foot down and done more. Scotty never would say much, but Bill felt like him and Scotty was the band, they should be with Elvis, these other guys were just along for the ride."

That was the only real cloud on the horizon, though. Cliff and Gene ("Cuz") were getting to feel more at home in Hollywood, too, so much so that Elvis was embarrassed at times and felt compelled to restrain their more unencumbered speech and behavior, his cousin's in particular. His father had shipped out his new white Cadillac so that he could cruise around town in style. All in all, despite "a little homesick[ness]," he felt like he was fitting in just fine.

About three weeks into filming, Vernon and Gladys Presley came out with their friends the Nicholses for an extended stay. They had been scheduled to arrive sometime earlier, but Gladys had not been feeling well and checked into Memphis' Baptist Hospital for a series of tests. It was an undefined ailment, a kind of general malaise, brought on perhaps by worry. "I was suffering some nausea and pain in my left shoulder," she told the newspaper, but after the tests had been carried out, she announced with some relief, "There is no surgery in sight." On their first morning at the lot, reported a somewhat disingenuous press release, "the officer of duty at the main studio gate was approached by a . . . man [who] said, with a Southern accent, 'Howdy, officer, can you tell me how to get into this place? We've got a boy working here?' " Vernon was wearing a light-colored suit, round-brimmed, pushed-back hat, and a too-short tie bunched up by an ornamental tie clip, while Gladys wore a simple pinned-back hat and an elegant new jacket over a dark dress. After it was ascertained what exactly their boy did on the lot, they were ceremoniously ushered in. Elvis showed them all around, and within days of their arrival both they and their friends bought poodles, whom they named Pierre and Duke (Gladys led Duke, named for John Wayne, around by a fake diamond necklace collar), and Vernon introduced Carl Nichols to one and all as his "decorator," which puzzled Hal Kanter until it dawned on him that Nichols was by profession a housepainter.

Gladys was entranced. She had worried before coming out that her boy might be made fun of, but she delightedly told friends and relatives afterward, "There's somebody to comb his hair for him and even a man to help him get dressed and another man to ask him if he's ready to work." On weekends they went sightseeing, touring neighborhoods dotted with imposing mansions, as Elvis pointed out Debra Paget's house, Red Skelton's showplace, the homes of the stars. One time they went to the movies, and he took eighteen-year-old Paramount contract player Joan Blackman to see *The Ten Commandments*, but Gladys had to keep shushing him as he enthusiastically explained every scene from a biblical or "technical," cinematic point of view. Scotty Moore's wife, Bobbie, came out for a week, and she and Scotty took the elder Presleys to Burbank for the filming of Tennessee Ernie Ford's popular weekly show, where Vernon and Gladys were introduced from the audience and later met Tennessee Ernie and his wife backstage.

One day when they visited the set, on a whim Hal Kanter shot some film of them and then invited them to come back to see themselves in the daily rushes the next day. Gladys was concerned that she looked fat, but Vernon reassured her that she looked fine, and overall they were so delighted with the results that Kanter got the idea of including them in the audience in the climactic show scene. When he broached the idea to Elvis, Elvis said he was sure that they would love it. So in the final Coast-to-Coast broadcast that caps the picture and refutes all the mean-spirited critics of rock 'n' roll, there is Elvis rocking away onstage, and there is Gladys seated on the aisle — with Vernon beside her, and the Nicholses beside *him* — clapping away in time to the music, intent on nothing but her boy. It is perhaps the musical high point of Elvis' career in films, yet another reprise of "Got a Lot O' Livin' to Do" which combines illusion and reality in such a way as to heighten the attraction of each. Elvis swivels his leg sharply, then good-naturedly drags it behind him. He stands at the lip of the stage and, along with the Jordanaires, who are dressed in matching cowboy outfits, leads the audience in hand clapping, then jumps down and comes dancing up the aisle. Gladys' gaze never wavers. For a moment he is standing to her left, and as she claps along she never takes her eyes off her son. Then he backs away, climbs back up on the stage, and the number is over, the studio audience is still applauding, Gladys along with all the rest — but for her it is different, different even than for the man beside her. For her it is the pinnacle of everything she has ever dreamed or imagined. Her gaze is transformed by love.

They returned home in mid March with the Nicholses after a month-long stay in Hollywood. Elvis would be coming home in about a week — but then he would be off again in May, to make the new picture that the Colonel and MGM had jointly announced would make Elvis Presley, by one manner of accounting anyway, the highest-paid star in motion picture history. For his new movie, tentatively entitled *The Rock*, Elvis would get $250,000 up front plus a range of additional benefits (office, travel, staff, not to mention the Colonel's fee for technical assistance), with 50 percent of the film's net profits assigned to Elvis on the back end. It was, remarked *Time* magazine in its May account, "unheard of."

Elvis handled it all with the utmost good grace and aplomb; everyone on the set agreed that he remained the same simple, thoughtful, almost unnaturally controlled and polite young man you might ever hope to meet — but there were at the same time unmistakable signs of pressure. He blew up at Gordon Stoker of the Jordanaires, who had come to Hollywood to record with him and be in his picture, for making a record with Tab Hunter (whose "Young Love" had just beaten out "Too Much" for the number-one pop position) — even though he had always said the Jordanaires were free to record with whomever they pleased. The next day he apologized, and apologized profusely. You don't have to do that, said Stoker, taken a little bit aback. " 'You don't have to apologize to me or to anybody,' I told him. 'Yes, I do,' he said. I never will forget it as long as I live. He said, 'See that man sweeping the floor right there?' We were on the movie set. 'If I hurt his feelings, it would bug me till I went and apologized to him. I guess I'm a weird guy.' " He supposed he was just getting antsy; he was really beginning to miss his road trips, and he was just looking forward to getting back out there and working off some of this excess energy.

At the wrap party Hal Kanter put a good deal of effort, and not a little of his own money, into thanking a cast and crew who he felt had given their all on this, his first picture. Due to some last-minute business involving a two-shot with Elvis and Lizabeth Scott, he was late getting to the party, and when he arrived he found the Colonel operating out of a booth decorated with RCA promotional material and a banner declaring "Elvis and the Colonel Thank You." Colonel Parker was handing out Elvis Presley albums which had been provided by the record company and publicity pictures of Elvis with his autograph printed on them, and he was raffling off an RCA Victrola, giving everyone a number. "It cost me several thousand dollars, but it turned out to be *his* party!" remarked Kanter. The Colonel greeted him warmly, welcoming him to the festivities, and Kanter was reminded once again of the book that Parker had asked him to help write. "All I have is the title," the Colonel had told him, recapitulating a familiar theme, "but I guarantee that it's gonna be a best-seller." What was the title? Kanter asked, going for the bait. "It's called *How Much Does It Cost If It's Free?*" The reason he knew it would be a best-seller, the Colonel hastened to assure the movie director, was that RCA had guaranteed to buy ten thousand copies of the book the moment it was published.

E LVIS SPOKE TO HIS PARENTS on the telephone on Saturday just before boarding the train for home. They were both excited. They had just seen a house, an estate, really, and they thought he would be excited about it, too. They had made an appointment to go back to see it again on Tuesday after he got home. He sent a telegram to June to meet him when the train stopped in New Orleans. She went with some ambivalence but with more of an intention to pay him back for all the hurt that he had caused her, and when he told her that he wanted her to accompany him to Memphis — he had a surprise that she would really love — she told him that she was engaged. He didn't believe her at first, but then he never told her his surprise, just looked at her blankly as the train pulled away.

Graceland turned out to be beyond his wildest expectations. Built in 1939 in Whitehaven, about eight miles south of downtown Memphis, it was written up by Ida Clemens in the *Memphis Commercial Appeal* in the fall of 1940 as the new country home of Dr. and Mrs. Thomas D. Moore. "Located well back from Highway 51 in a grove of towering oaks, it stands proudly on land that has been in the family nearly a century. . . . As you roll up the drive you sense its fine heritage from the past in its general feeling of aristocratic kindliness and tranquillity." The facade of Tishomingo limestone and the Corinthian columns of the entrance portico were remarked upon. "Polished with the quiet manners characteristic of today's beauty, the palatial home is a noteworthy example of the Georgian colonial style" with an "air of subtle luxury that pervades the exterior [and] seeps through the walls and penetrates every room in the house. . . .

" 'Our entire home is centered around music,' " Mrs. Moore told the *Commercial Appeal* reporter, alluding to her fourteen-year-old daughter, who went on to a distinguished career as harpist for the Memphis Symphony, and proudly showing Miss Clemens around the eighteen-room house, with its parlor that opened up for entertainment to a full seventy-five-foot length and its beautifully planted 18¼ acres. This was what remained of Mrs. Moore's family's almost 500-acre Hereford cattle farm after her great-aunt Grace (for whom the house was named) sold off much of the rest of the land for a subdivision and shopping center and Mrs. Moore herself subsequently gave away another 4½ acres to the Graceland Christian Church just before putting her home on the market.

Elvis got in after midnight Monday night and went out to see the estate first thing on Tuesday with his parents and a reporter in tow. Accompanying the family was Mrs. Virginia Grant, a young real estate agent whom Gladys had met early in February in the parking lot of Lowenstein's East department store. Mrs. Grant had had a number of properties to show them, but they were leaving for California the next day and didn't contact her again until their return. They didn't like the first house, a sprawling ranch on seven acres, and Mrs. Grant was feeling a little bit discouraged when Gladys said, "Don't you have anything to show us with a Colonial home?" All of a sudden the image of Graceland, which had only recently come on the market and which she had never been inside, popped into her head, and though Vernon at this point thought that he might like to move to California, Gladys prevailed upon him to look at the property.

"This is going to be a lot nicer than Red Skelton's house when I get it like I want it," Elvis told the *Press-Scimitar* reporter enthusiastically after going through the house for the first time, and before the deal was done or a firm offer even made, everyone in Memphis knew that Elvis Presley was going to pay $100,000 for Mrs. Moore's beautiful old southern mansion. "We've found a house that we like very much, and we will buy it if we can come to terms," said Vernon, ever cautious and aware that the price was not going to come down if they did not indicate some reluctance. Elvis was simply not one to negotiate, though. He knew how happy the house would make his mother ("I think I am going to like this new home," Gladys announced publicly. "We will have a lot more privacy and a lot more room to put some of the things we have accumulated over the last few years"), and within a week the deal was done. The price was $102,500. Hugh Bosworth, the listing agent, took their old house at an assigned value of $55,000 in trade, and the Presleys put down $10,000 cash and took out a mortgage of $37,500. In fact, the only barrier to really cashing in on the deal was the Colonel's decision that they would have to turn down a bubble gum manufacturer's bid at a "fabulous" price to strip the newly installed wood paneling from the house on Audubon, chop it up, and distribute it as prizes with his bubble gum. The Colonel said this would conflict with merchandising deals they already had in place.

Within a couple of days renovations had begun. Sam Phillips had just moved into *his* new house, out east in the higher-priced Memphis suburbs, earlier in the year, and on Sam's recommendation Elvis contacted Sam's decorator, George Golden, a forty-three-year-old former Lipton tea salesman with a taste for the eclectic and a flair for self-promotion. To advertise his business, Golden had several flatbed trucks cruising around Memphis, day and night, decked out with illuminated "three-foot-wide miniature rooms, built to scale, complete with carpet, wallpaper and a two-foot sofa, upholstered in chartreuse satin. That sofa with the shiny satin really caught everyone's eye." It evidently caught Elvis' eye, or at least the futuristic touches and bold "lush life" style that marked Sam's house did, and he wanted something on an even grander scale for himself. For his bedroom, he told the newspapers, he was going to have "the darkest blue there is . . . with a mirror that will cover one side of the room. I probably will have a black bedroom suite, trimmed in white leather, with a white [llama] rug [like Sam's]." The entrance hall, he said, would be decorated with a sky effect, with tiny lights for stars and clouds painted on the ceiling, and he intended to build "a swimming pool on the south side of the house with a large sunken patio leading up to the pool," a six-foot pink stone wall, purple walls with gold trim for the living and dining rooms, and a number of other resplendent touches.

When it actually came down to it, he gave up the purple for pavilion blue at his mother's request (her son, like most young people, she said understandingly, liked "dark, cozy colors"), and according to Golden, there were two priorities that asserted themselves most strongly. "One was that he had the most beautiful bedroom in Memphis for his mother. Number two, he wanted a soda fountain — a real soda fountain with Cokes and an ice cream thing — so his young friends could sit and have a soda." He had an eight-foot-square bed built for himself and a fifteen-foot sofa custom-built for the living room, and with all the other touches that were planned — the swimming pool, the gates with the musical motif which Golden would have custom-made, the chicken house that Gladys wanted, the painting that Mr. Nichols was going to have to do throughout the house, and the structural repairs that were needed — he seemed ready to pay as much again for the renovations as he had paid already for the house. He just wanted it all to be ready by the summer, when he got home from making his next movie.

For now he scarcely had time to think. He had another disturbing run-in downtown when he was accused of pulling a gun on a nineteen-year-old Marine who claimed that he had insulted his wife. The gun turned out to be a prop Elvis had brought back from Hollywood, Elvis had never even met Private First Class Hershel Nixon's wife, and the whole thing was settled in Judge Boushe's chambers the day before he went back out on the road, but it was beginning to seem like he couldn't go anywhere in Memphis anymore without something happening.

On the same day as the incident with the Marine, there was an announcement in the paper that Elvis would be returning to Tupelo for an appearance at the Mississippi-Alabama Fair in the fall. "The fair wanted Elvis back," the *Press-Scimitar* reported, "[and] offered his manager, Col. Tom Parker, a guarantee of $10,000 for an appearance. Parker turned [them] down. 'Elvis has been thinking about returning to Tupelo ever since last year,' Parker said. 'He has spoken about it a number of times. We'll come to Tupelo, but all money over actual expenses will go to build a youth recreation center for boys in the East Tupelo section, where Elvis grew up.' " He was excited about that, and he was excited about the upcoming tour, too. Cliff had remained in California to try to promote his "career," and Elvis was increasingly disinclined to take along his cousin Junior, whose behavior was becoming more erratic — but Gene, of course, would be with him, as always, and Arthur Hooton would be going out again for the first time in a while, and his friend George Klein was going to be accompanying him for the first time ever.

"I had gotten fired from WMC because they quit playing rock 'n' roll. One night I was up at HBQ visiting Dewey, and Elvis dropped by and said, 'What are you doing, GK?' And I said, 'Well, I got fired, Elvis.' He said, 'You want to come work for me?' I said, 'What do I do?' He said, 'Nothing.' I said, 'Really, what do I —' He said, 'You're just my traveling companion.' I said, 'Elvis, you know I'll just go along for the ride.' He just wanted some hometown guys with him so he wouldn't get lonesome.

"Mrs. Presley always liked me, I don't really know why — she liked my mother, too. She told me, 'George, when you go out on the road with Elvis, he has some bad habits, so please watch him because he's my baby.' She said, 'Make sure you go through his pockets before you send his clothes to the wash because he'll leave money in his pants. And he has a bad habit of walking in his sleep.' She told me how to handle it. She said, 'He's a very nervous young man, and when he gets up to walk in his sleep, you talk to him real soft. And when he talks back to you, you talk back to him real soft: "That's right, Elvis, now why don't you come back to bed?" ' So then I knew how to handle it."

The first date on the tour was in Chicago on March 28. Elvis had a press conference at the Saddle and Sirloin Club at the Stockyards Inn in the afternoon, and that night he unveiled the $2,500 gold-leaf suit that the Colonel had had made up for him. The idea had come from the gold cutaway that Liberace wore in Las Vegas, and the Colonel had Nudie Cohen, Hollywood tailor to the stars (or perhaps a certain kind of star, including all the bespangled country and western luminaries), come out to the movie set in his steer-horn-decorated Cadillac to measure him for it. There were twelve thousand in attendance at the International Amphitheatre, with a $32,000 gross, and thirteen girls passed out during the performance, but what stood out most for the Colonel was the first time Elvis fell to his knees like Al Jolson and left fifty dollars' worth of gold spangles on the floor. He went up to Elvis after the show and asked him please not to do it again. Elvis wore the suit the following night at the Kiel Opera House, in St. Louis, which sold out for only the second time in its history (the first was for Liberace), but after that for the most part he stopped wearing the suit pants, substituting dark slacks to set off the jacket, sometimes wearing the gold slippers and bow tie, sometimes not. After a while he came to be embarrassed by it — it was as if he were advertising the suit rather than the other way around.

For his part, George was having a ball. The shows themselves were outrageous, there were bomb threats and riots, the atmosphere was charged, and after the show there were always girls to "promote." George served as a kind of scout and advance man ("Elvis knew I could talk"). But after a while he was forced to carry identification with him — a picture of Elvis and him together — just to prove he was who he said he was. The Colonel didn't much like it, George knew; what was he going to do about it, though? Colonel was always worrying about potential trouble, and George tried to be careful in his selection process. He told the girls they had nothing to worry about, it was a good bunch of guys, no drunken orgies or wild sex scenes, but in the end who was he going to please, Elvis or the Colonel? There was only so much the Colonel could expect from Elvis, and the Colonel understood that, too.

"Hysterical Shrieks Greet Elvis in His Gold Jacket and Shoes" read the headline in the Detroit paper, which complained that "the trouble with going to see Elvis Presley is that you're liable to get killed." "Convent Suspends Eight Elvis Fans," declared the *Ottawa Citizen* with reference to the expulsion of eight girls from the Notre Dame Convent school for attending the Ottawa show. In Philadelphia, in his first major appearance in the Northeast, he was pelted with eggs by Villanova University students, and in a headline that could have summed up the general journalistic reaction, under the sarcastic banner of "Music (?) Review," the *Toronto Daily Star* trumpeted, "All Too Plainly Visible Elvis Is Barely Audible."

In Canada, Oscar Davis finally made his move. Playing on the split that had clearly grown up between Elvis and his musicians, Davis, who was still doing all the advance work for his onetime protégé but dreamt of a day when he could once again operate on his own, approached first Scotty and Bill, then D.J., and then the Jordanaires, about having him represent them. *They* were not tied to the Colonel, he argued, but they were clearly being exploited — and he could just about guarantee them that the boy would not risk losing his entire musical troupe over a matter of a few dollars. His importunings did not fall on deaf ears. Scotty and Bill were more than ready to make the leap, and in the end D.J. was, too: Presley was making millions, and they were still on $200-a-week pay when they were working, $100-a-week retainer when they were not. In the end the Jordanaires were the lone holdouts, but without them there was simply not enough leverage. "He offered us a better deal than what the Colonel had offered us," said Gordon Stoker, "but I think we more or less didn't trust him. He was beautifully dressed, and he didn't have the bull that the Colonel had, but he was a con artist, too. A beautiful con artist, immaculately dressed, always sharp as a tack — but that's the reason we didn't fall for it."

They played ten cities in ten days — big cities, far removed from their former regional base — and the tour grossed more than $300,000 with a commensurate sale of programs and souvenirs. It generated coverage, controversy, and cash, and from nearly every point of view could not fail to be accounted a success, but if anything was needed to confirm the Colonel's growing conviction that this was a phenomenon that had orbited out of control ("All those sweet little girls out there, they're fucking animals," he had told Hal Kanter), this tour served to do it. It wasn't just the riots, egg throwing, and ridicule, nor even the concerted effort by the Catholic Church to paint Presley as some kind of a moral pariah (in St. Louis, Catholic schoolgirls had burned him in effigy and recited prayers "as public reparation for excesses committed by teenagers"). It was just too damn out of control — and it was becoming increasingly impossible even to do the show. "Girls screamed and hundreds of flash bulbs were discharged," reported the *St. Louis Post-Dispatch* of a typical scene, "making the hall look as if it were under an artillery barrage. Presley clung to the microphone standard and staggered about in a distinctive, distraught manner, waiting for the noise to subside a bit. . . ." *He couldn't even hear himself.* Perhaps thinking of this, Gordon Stoker came to feel that he sought protection in the group; "on some numbers he worked almost just up in our face because he would feel more secure this way."

In Philadelphia, speaking to a group of high school newspaper reporters, Elvis expressed suitable humility in the face of a flurry of not particularly respectful questions ("Is it true you can't get married before you're twenty-three — that it's in your contract?"). What were his most memorable high school experiences? he was asked. When he didn't answer, the reporter persisted: "Well? Didn't you have any?" What did he think of his first movie? "It was pretty horrible. Acting's not something you learn overnight. I knew that picture was bad when it was completed. I'm my own worst critic. But my next picture is different. I know I done a better job in it." And what of the future? "I just take every day as it comes," Elvis told the teenage reporter, who identified herself as Rochelle. "I don't plan too far ahead. There'll be record albums, of course, and movies, too. Don't know anymore; maybe I'll go back to driving a truck."

And then he was home. The work on Graceland was proceeding, but the house wasn't close to ready and the Presleys were still living on Audubon when Yvonne Lime came to visit the Friday of Easter weekend. The first thing that Elvis did was to take her out to see his new home, and he proudly showed both it and her off on Saturday as a newspaper photographer snapped pictures. In one photograph, which went on the UP wire, they are standing in front of the mansion holding hands, the pillars and the portico in the background. Yvonne is wearing a striped, pajamalike outfit and looking up adoringly at an Elvis who appears studiedly sincere. In another shot they are clowning around, holding up a window frame in front of them, Yvonne more animated but still wholesomely perky. Yvonne was surprised to discover how small and cramped the house on Audubon Drive was, she reported in *Modern Screen* magazine, made even more cramped by all the furniture Elvis had bought and all the fan mail that was boxed up on the porch. They ate meat loaf and mashed potatoes and after dinner sat out on lawn chairs in the back. Elvis held Yvonne's hand and Gladys' and declared that they were his "two best girls."

On Saturday night they went over to Sam's new house for a party, and Elvis checked out the decor. Sam's wife, Becky, a DJ and big band authority on WHER, was the perfect hostess; Dot and Dewey Phillips were there; and, of course, Sam's eleven- and nine-year-old sons, Knox and Jerry, immaculate in their Lansky's-bought clothing and carefully sculpted DAs, hung on Elvis' every word and gesture. Elvis introduced Yvonne to many of his old friends and acquaintances, and as the evening wore on and it started to rain, the party gravitated to the living room, where he began to sing spirituals and hymns. "It was a thrilling experience," Yvonne wrote. He sang "on and on, until day began to break and it was Easter morning." For Dot Phillips, who had known Elvis informally ever since her husband had played the first record, it was one of the most moving moments of a long acquaintance. They ended up out by the pool as the sun came up on Easter morning, with Elvis singing and Becky serving scrambled eggs just as hard as Elvis liked them.

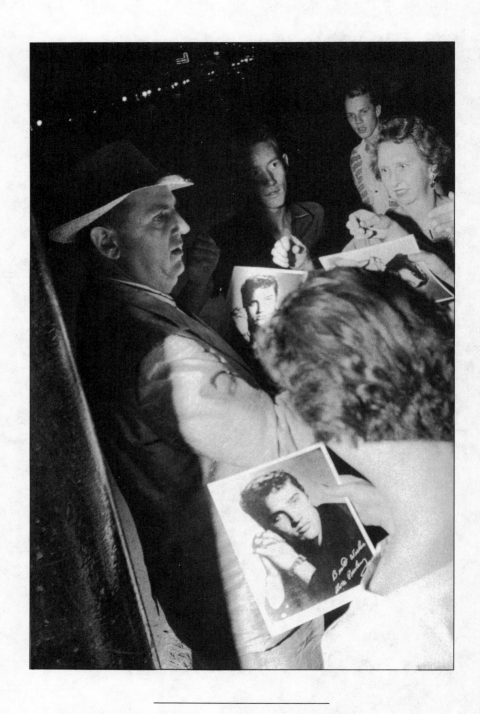

COLONEL PARKER, WITH FANS. (ALFRED WERTHEIMER)

JAILHOUSE ROCK

H E WAS STAYING at the plush Beverly Wilshire, occupying the penthouse apartment plus the Presidential Suite. Scotty and D.J. and Bill tried it, but they didn't like it — it was too far removed from the hustle and bustle — so they moved back to the Knickerbocker, in the heart of downtown Hollywood. Elvis had plenty of friends to keep him company in any case. George and Gene and Arthur Hooton ("Arthritis") had ridden out with him on the train, and Cliff, of course, was there to meet them when they arrived. Junior had wanted to come, too, and Elvis had told him that he could join them in a little while — if he didn't fuck up. The Colonel's brother-in-law, Bitsy Mott, had a single just down the hall, and Colonel and Mrs. Parker were staying on another floor. There were always girls at the soda fountain downstairs looking for dates — pretty little starlets, beautiful girls looking to break into the business, it was known for that reason as "the Mink Farm" to some. It was nice.

It had been the usual long, boring train ride out. Gene and Arthur slept most of the time, but George was excited just to be going to Hollywood. He read lines with Elvis until he knew most of the script himself, and they talked about a lot of things. What was success, Elvis wondered aloud, if you couldn't share it with your friends? Part of him still couldn't believe it was real. "One time he turned to me, and he said, 'I wonder how the people feel, George.' I said, 'What do you mean?' He said, 'When I went to audition for Arthur Godfrey, they told me to watch the mailbox. Well, man, every day for two weeks I met that mailman — I couldn't wait. And I never got a response. I wonder how they —' I said, 'Well, Elvis, I guess they're kicking themselves in the seat of the pants.' . . . He kind of laughed about it, and then he told me about a couple more gaffes, but the thing about it was, he had so much drive, so much determination and energy, he just knew he was going to make it and nothing was going to stop him."

He reported to the recording studio on Tuesday, April 30, with Freddy, Steve Sholes, a number of other RCA officials and MGM executives, plus the band (augmented once again by Dudley Brooks on piano) and Thorne Nogar all in attendance. It was a good, productive session, going from 10:00 in the morning till 6:00 at night. The only thing that made it different from previous sessions — aside from the fact that there was no battle over using the movie studio soundstage, once the Colonel had made it clear that there was not going to *be* any battle — was the presence, and the contributions, of the film's two principal songwriters.

Jerry Leiber and Mike Stoller had been commissioned, more or less, to write the score. Just two years older than Elvis, but with a string of r&b hits (including "Hound Dog") going back into their teens, they had not exactly leapt at the opportunity. In fact, Jean Aberbach had practically had to lock them in their New York hotel room the month before just to get them to settle down long enough to write four songs (the other two had then been farmed out). As hipsters of long standing and deep-seated belief, their attitude, simply stated, was: who was this lame ofay moving in on their territory? They had hated the job he had done on "Hound Dog"; "Love Me," the second song they gave him, was their idea of a joke; and they hadn't been particularly impressed by the two songs of theirs that he had recorded for *Loving You* either. They were scarcely prepared, then, for the person they actually met at Radio Recorders, where Big Mama Thornton's original version of "Hound Dog" had been cut four years earlier, with the same songwriters present and the same recordist, Thorne Nogar, engineering.

"We thought we were the only two white kids who knew anything about the blues," said Mike Stoller, "but he knew all kinds of stuff." "We thought he was like an idiot savant," echoed Jerry Leiber, "but he listened a lot. He knew all of our records. He knew Eddie 'Cleanhead' Vinson. He loved Ray Charles' early records. And he was a workhorse in the studio — he didn't pull any diva numbers." They fenced warily for a while, trading enthusiasms, and Elvis and Mike sat down at the piano to play some four-hand blues. Afterward, Jerry and Mike ran through the title song they had written for the new picture, and Elvis smiled approvingly at Leiber's hoarse, knowing vocal and said, "Okay, let's make it."

They got three songs on the first day, but then, on the following day, their luck ran out. The movie studio was concerned, evidently, at the amount of time that had been spent recording three titles, and someone spoke to the executive in charge of production about it. As Elvis warmed up at the piano singing spirituals with the Jordanaires ("The thing that really surprised us was that there was no clock," said Mike Stoller. "It was amazing—Jerry and I just weren't used to that"), the studio man prodded Thorne and asked him if he couldn't do something. Then at lunchtime, in Gordon Stoker's recollection, he approached the Jordanaires and told them, " 'Get him off this stuff. In fact, if he starts singing [gospel], don't sing with him.'

"So Elvis came back from lunch and started at the piano and we didn't sing. And he said, 'Hey, what's wrong with you guys?' And it fell to my duty to say, 'Elvis, they told us we couldn't sing with you.' He got up and said, 'If I want to bring you guys out here and sing the entire week of spirituals, this is what we'll do.' And he left, just walked out and left."

Elvis didn't come back into the studio at all on the following day, but when he returned on Friday it was as if nothing had happened, except that, seemingly by the tacit consent of all concerned, Leiber and Stoller were now in charge. To Freddy Bienstock it was a logical enough progression: "They came in because we pushed them in, and they were certainly more talented as record producers than Steve Sholes was." And whatever reservations Elvis might have felt, he was now completely caught up in the enthusiasm of the moment, in Leiber's manic flood of ideas ("Elvis thought Jerry was completely crazy," said Bienstock, "with those two different-color eyes, one brown, one blue"), in Stoller's patient musical coaching of Scotty and the other musicians, in the inspired lunacy that for the moment seemed to have come back into the recording studio. "He was completely open," said Mike Stoller. "I played piano to demonstrate—in fact I played piano on some of the sides—and Jerry would sing. And then we would stay on the floor while he was recording, with Jerry sort of conducting with body English. Frequently we'd have what we thought was a take, and he would say, 'No, let me do it again,' and he would just keep doing it. As long as he *felt* like doing it. Sometimes it got better, but other times we knew we had it, and he would just enjoy himself, and then he would say 'Let's hear it,' and then, 'Yeah, that one had it.' In many ways he was a perfectionist, and in other ways he was very relaxed in the studio—a strange combination."

However relaxed he may have been feeling at this point, though, there was an incident toward the end of the session that betrayed some of the longtime tensions in the group. Bill Black was feeling increasingly frustrated not just at the indifference with which he saw himself and Scotty being treated but by his own difficulties in trying to learn how to play the electric bass (the electric bass had just come into common use, achieving almost instant adoption in all fields but bluegrass, because it was compact, amplified, and for the precise fretting it allowed). Bill had only recently gotten a Fender bass of his own, and he couldn't get the ominous, rhythmic intro to Leiber and Stoller's "(You're So Square) Baby, I Don't Care," one of the highlights of the film score. He tried it again and again, got more and more pissed off and embarrassed by his failure, and finally just slammed the bass down, slid it across the floor, and stormed out of the studio, while everyone watched in disbelief. "Most artists," said Gordon Stoker, "would have said, 'You pick that bass up and play it, buster, that's your job,' but not Elvis. You know what Elvis did? Elvis thought it was funny. He picked it up and played it himself. He just picked up that bass, put his foot up on my chair, and played that song all the way through."

They were in the studio for more than seven hours altogether, and when they were done they had virtually completed the entire soundtrack. There were still overdubs to do (like the vocal for "Baby, I Don't Care"), but they had recorded a typically witty, specially commissioned, more than slightly cynical set of songs "mostly by Jerry Leiber and Mike Stoller," as the film credits would declare, a set of self-contained "playlets" of the tongue-in-cheek variety (listen to "Jailhouse Rock" sometime if you doubt the satiric intent) that Leiber and Stoller had pioneered in their work with the Coasters. They had done different versions for different stages of the character's musical evolution (Vince Everett, whom Elvis played, was, needless to say, a singer), some intentionally flat in their affect, some with the undeniable Presley touch. It was, all in all, an exciting enterprise and the kind of thing that could at least make the musical interludes endurable — so long as it was necessary to make musicals at all.

On Monday he reported to the studio for costume fitting and met some of the cast and crew. It was a different kind of studio, and a different kind of set, than the Loving You shoot at Paramount — MGM seemed a little more imposing, and the set, without the presence of Hal Wallis constantly hovering over the proceedings, a little more impersonal — but in the end people everywhere were pretty much the same, and the similarities were bound to outweigh the differences. Elvis was assigned the Clark

Gable dressing room, and when they drove in through the Thalberg Gates for the first time, secretaries and executive secretaries and office workers poured out of their offices in such numbers that security had a real problem on the lot. Richard Thorpe, the sixty-one-year-old director, a veteran of scores of low-budget pictures delivered on a tight schedule from 1923 on, showed no great personal enthusiasm (he was known as a man who refused to discuss anything to do with the film in progress over lunch) but was cordial enough, and Elvis had little doubt that he could win him over, whether by charm or by persistence. He was getting to know the game. His mother had taught him these people weren't any different than anyone else, and Colonel had certainly reinforced the lesson.

He met his leading lady, Judy Tyler, who had played Princess Summerfall Winterspring on the children's show *Howdy Doody* and had more recently appeared as a regular on *Caesar Presents,* Sid Caesar's comedy-variety hour, and in the Rodgers and Hammerstein musical *Pipe Dream,* on the Broadway stage. Judy had just gotten married to a young actor named Gregory Lafayette, so that eliminated any chance of anything going on there, but he liked Judy, and he liked Mickey Shaughnessy, his costar, who had played strong secondary roles in a number of pictures (including *From Here to Eternity*) and did an imitation of Elvis in his nightclub act. He met the choreographer, too, Alex Romero, who was already planning the big dance sequence that was scheduled to be shot at the beginning of the following week. Romero had a dub of the song for the sequence, "Jailhouse Rock," and showed Elvis some of the steps that he had devised for it along the lines of a typical Gene Kelly or Fred Astaire number.

"Elvis looked at me, and I looked at Elvis and Cliff," said George Klein, who had gone to the rehearsal room with the others, "and — Alex Romero was a really nice guy, and he said, 'Elvis, will you please try it?' And Elvis got up to copy his steps, and, just from the first instant, you could tell it wasn't going to work. And Elvis said, 'Man, it's not me.' So Alex, being such a sharp guy, said, 'Have you got any of your records in your dressing room?' And we put the records on — 'Don't Be Cruel' and 'Hound Dog' and 'All Shook Up.' And Alex said, 'Would you just show me what you do onstage?' Well, Elvis would go along if he thought you knew what you were doing, so he went through about three songs, and Alex Romero said, 'I got it. See you later, Elvis.' And Elvis said, 'What do you mean you got it?' He said, 'Elvis, what I'm going to do is I'm going to go home tonight and I'm going to take what you do and work it into the routine, and it's going to be you, what you normally feel comfortable doing onstage, but I'm going to choreograph it.' The next day we came back to that same little rehearsal hall, and Alex Romero's choreographed the scene so it looks like you're watching Elvis. He put 'Jailhouse Rock' on and put little markings on the floor, and said, 'Elvis, just do what you feel comfortable doing.' So Elvis whipped through it, and, man, he had it. And then he couldn't wait to do the dance sequence!"

He liked show people. He enjoyed being back in Hollywood. It was good running around with Nick again — there was always something happening, and the hotel suite was like a private clubhouse where you needed to know the secret password to get in and he got to change the password every day.

On the weekend Nick called up his friend Russ Tamblyn, who had a small, one-bedroom beach house on the Pacific Coast Highway just south of Topanga Canyon, and asked if he could bring his friend Elvis over. Tamblyn, who at twenty-two had been in the business from early childhood on, both as an actor and as a dancer, and who saw Nick as something of a hustler, said sure, come on out.

"I'll never forget it. I mean, no one could forget it. First, because Elvis was so big at the time. And, second, when he came, they drove up in three limousines, and there were Elvis and all of his cousins and hangers-on and girls — it was like fifteen or twenty people pouring out of these limos, and then they came in. It was nuts — I thought Nick was just going to bring Elvis over, and it ended up like twenty people came pouring into the room. They brought in soft drinks, and I had a record on, it was a Josh White record, that Elvis just flipped over. I can't remember the title, but it was a weird song, it was a good one with a real low, gutty guitar sound — I could never quite figure what it was about — and we played it about ten times in a row until Elvis finally asked if he could borrow it. Everybody else was sort of partying out on the porch, which was right out on the beach, and Elvis and I were over in front of the record player, and as he listened to the music, he started doing his dance with his knees like he does, and I said, 'Great.' I said, 'Throw those knees.' I guess just being a dancer, I could see where a couple of suggestions might help, so I said, 'Throw those knees out more.' So I showed him, and he said, 'What did you do? Show me again.' So the music was on, and we were standing there dancing in front of the record player, and I remember a girlfriend I had at that time was coming over that night and she told me later she came in and she couldn't believe it, 'There you were dancing with Elvis!' But he was really interested. It wasn't that I technically knew that much, but I was a street dancer, and I understood what he was doing, and I could see right away where with little exaggerated movements it would look better — it would just put it on another level and make it a little stronger, and he got some of that in *Jailhouse Rock*."

Principal shooting started the following Monday, May 13, and began with the dance sequence that Alex Romero had worked on with Elvis the previous week. The set was a skeletal scaffolding with barred doors suggesting cells on two levels. There was a fireman's pole for the inmates on the upper level to slide down, and a cast of professional dancers was outlined in silhouette behind bars at the start of the number. The dancers then swing out on the cell doors in their striped prison shirts and white-stitched denims and jackets. Miming the song's story line, they escape, only to return in the end to their cells, because the party that the warden has thrown — the "Jailhouse Rock" of the title — is so much fun that who would ever want to leave? Elvis flung himself into the number with utter abandon ("He couldn't wait to do it," said George Klein), so much abandon, in fact, that on Tuesday he swallowed one of the temporary caps for his teeth as he was sliding down a pole. He told the assistant director, Bob Relyea, that he thought he could feel something rattling around in his chest, and Relyea called a doctor to the set, but after examining him the doctor reassured Elvis and Relyea that it was just Elvis' imagination, no more than a scratch. "So now we get the entire crew and all the dancers down on their hands and knees looking for the [cap], 'cause it's very very small and it must be on the floor someplace, and we decide it's all in his mind. About an hour later he comes up after a take and says to me, 'You know that scratch that I think I feel? It's moved. It's over to the left now.' And I said, 'No, no, it's all in your mind.' So about an hour later, after a take he came up and said, 'Ah, it's in my mind? Listen to this.' And then, when he was breathing, you could hear a whistling sound!"

Elvis called George Klein from the Cedars of Lebanon Hospital. It turned out that he had aspirated the cap, which had lodged in his lung, so the next day a surgeon went in and got it out. Oddly enough, there was a scene just like this in the movie, where Vince Everett, the character Elvis played, is punched in the throat by his former cellmate, Hunk Hogan, and everyone is gathered around him toward the end of the picture anxiously waiting to see if he will ever sing again. In this case, according to Relyea, the scene in the recovery room was not much different, with Colonel Parker present and the doctor coming in to announce that everything was fine. " 'We got it,' he said, 'we just had to, we had to part the vocal cords and put the tool through and get in the lung.' And he said, 'Then the darn thing broke in two, and we had to get one piece out and then — it's like arthroscopic surgery — get the other piece out.' When he got to the part about separating the vocal cords to put the instrument through, it got Colonel Parker's attention!"

Elvis was a little hoarse for a couple of days, and when he got back on the set he ran into Russ Tamblyn, who was getting ready to go out on location for *Peyton Place.* "I remember they were rehearsing, and I watched a little bit. When he got done with what he was doing, he came over and got me and said, 'I want to show you something.' And he took me back to his dressing room, and we went inside and he shut the door and said, 'I've been working on this,' and he started going into this dance, and sure enough he had really gotten his knees out further and gotten his elbows back and was doing more with his arms. He wanted to show me how he had been practicing, *but he didn't want anybody else to see."*

Meanwhile the retinue had grown by the addition of one. Lamar Fike, who had been hanging around with George and Cliff in Memphis the previous fall in hopes of an introduction, was down in Texas visiting his mother when he read in the newspaper that Elvis was in the hospital. He had been calling George regularly for the past couple of weeks suggesting that he might like to come out, and George had been telling him things were kind of tight, everybody was busy, "in other words I didn't want to be responsible for him." At this point Lamar took matters into his own hands, jumped into his '56 Chevy, and drove straight to the Beverly Wilshire, without asking permission of anybody. When he showed up, all three hundred pounds of him in chartreuse shorts and yellow cowboy boots, George wasn't there, but according to his understanding, Cliff met Lamar at the door. "He went into his con, and Cliff went into his con, and Lamar said, 'Man, can I come in?' And Cliff said, 'Man, it's kind of tight. I mean, Elvis is real particular here in Hollywood.' So, finally, Cliff goes and tells Elvis, he says, 'Elvis, there's a guy here from Memphis. He's hung out with me and George, and he's kind of jolly and he's kind of funny and he drove all the way from Texas. Can he come in tonight and party with us?' So Elvis said yeah, and Lamar made an impression like he always does and that's how he worked his way into the group."

ONCE THE DANCE SEQUENCE was finished, the picture moved along at a brisk pace. There were none of the relatively complicated setups of *Loving You*, and Richard Thorpe worked fast anyway. For George, just being on the lot was like a fantasy come true. "Cliff, Arthur, and I were on the payroll now — of course Gene was already on the payroll. I'll never forget, he said, 'I'll pay all you guys' expenses, if you need any money you know you can always come to me. But Colonel says we're making a movie so I've got to put you on salary for tax purposes.' So he put us on salary at fifty dollars a week. Gene and Cliff and Arthur, they'd get bored on the set and would just lay down and go to sleep in the dressing room, but I was all over that lot like crazy, I didn't want to miss a thing. The first day we got there Glenn Ford was there, he'd just finished a picture for MGM. And he was talking to Elvis, he was telling Elvis something — he was a real nice guy — and he was going through these motions just like he did in movies, and I said, 'God, he acts just like he does in the movies, Elvis!' And Elvis says, 'Shut up, shut up.' He didn't want me to sound like I was starstruck, but me and Cliff were, you know.

"Whenever there was a break in the action, I'd jump off this sound-stage and run over to another soundstage and watch Yul Brynner work or John Ford or Kim Novak — she was unloading some stuff from her car, and I told Cliff, I said, 'Shit, I'm going to go over and talk to her. She might not say a word to me, but I got to talk to Kim Novak!' I remember, they were making *Saddle the Wind* with Robert Taylor and Julie London, and one day I go over to the set 'cause Anne Francis was on the set and I wanted to see what she looked like. So I'm on the set standing in the background watching — it was an open set — and Vince Edwards walks over to me and starts talking. He said, 'Hey, man, ain't you with Presley?' 'Cause I guess everybody on the lot noticed who was with Elvis. And I said, 'Yeah,' and he introduced himself, and we start talking and he said, 'Man, I'm a big fan.' Now he was just starting out in Hollywood, but he'd been a big swimming champion at Ohio State, and he said, 'You want to meet Anne Francis?' And I said, 'Sure.' So when they took a break, he said, 'This is Elvis' buddy.' And he said, 'I'd like to meet Elvis,' so I said, 'Come over to the set.' Well, Vince came over, and immediately Cliff liked him and Elvis liked him and I liked him, so Elvis invited him up to the Beverly Wilshire and he started coming every now and then."

Edwards became a regular member of the group, and he introduced them to an actor named Billy Murphy, who had been in *Sands of Iwo Jima* with John Wayne, and to Sammy Davis, Jr., too, who came up one night and scared the hell out of Elvis with his impression of Dr. Jekyll and Mr. Hyde. Murphy was a Hollywood character, a few years older than the others, who walked up and down Hollywood Boulevard dressed in black — black pants, black shirt, black hat, black gloves — and carrying an unproduced screenplay that he had written about Billy the Kid in a bold, illegible script. "Elvis was just infatuated with him," according to George, "we all were, because he was just so colorful and interesting. Some directors were scared of him, I think, because he was very physical, even threatened one or two of them. He was friends with Robert Mitchum and Rory Calhoun on a first-name basis, he had a certain way of walking, kind of like Mitchum, and he had a pet phrase that we all picked up: 'You bet your life, mister, and you may have to.' It came out of an old Clark Gable movie, really, but we picked it up from Murphy. Nick Adams would tell us wild stories about him. I think he just became a little too erratic for Hollywood."

Mitchum himself stopped by one afternoon, because he wanted Elvis to play the part of his brother in the upcoming production of *Thunder Road,* a moonshiner's tale which he was producing and for which he had written the story. Elvis was thrilled at the visit, and at the offer — Mitchum had gotten him "all shook up," he told Russ Tamblyn, who arrived just after Mitchum's departure — and listened enthralled to Mitchum's real-life tales of growing up hard in the South and doing time on a Georgia chain gang.

In the evenings they would go to the movies sometimes, the whole gang of them; it was, according to Vince Edwards, like "The Clan of Elvis Presley," with the limos pulling out of the Beverly Wilshire full of cousins and kin. "When we got to the theater," said Russ Tamblyn, "we all got out and bought our tickets and formed a line. Now by this time a crowd has formed, you know, they'd see all these strange-looking characters get out of the cars and wonder, who the hell is this, so if there wasn't a problem before, there is now. Anyway, there would be two lines right up to the ticket taker, and Elvis would be the last one, or if he had a girlfriend, the girlfriend would come out with him, and Elvis would go right between the two lines, and everybody would be so blown away they'd just move back. I always thought Elvis loved the entourage, and he loved playing the part — he seemed to have an instinct for entrances."

They went out to Russ' beach house one or two more times, and with Russ on the verge of leaving to shoot his new movie in Maine, Elvis asked if he could rent it for the next couple of months. He was still seeing Yvonne Lime occasionally, but he was dating Anne Neyland, a former Miss Texas whom he had met on the MGM lot, and Venetia Stevenson, too, when a rumor that he was about to marry Yvonne in Acapulco broke at the end of May. "When I get married," he told the press, after the Colonel's official denials, "it'll be no secret. I'll get married in my hometown of Memphis, and the whole town'll be there."

He wasn't really serious about anyone for the time being, though. He was enjoying the single life, and when he got bored he just had to tell the guys to hunt up some girls in the lobby of the hotel. He would have them brought up to the suite, offered one observer, "and Elvis would go in the other room, he'd go in the bedroom or somewhere, and then when they came back with the girls, the girls would sit there for maybe ten or fifteen minutes, and finally one of the cousins would go in the bedroom and come out himself and another ten minutes would go by — and then in would come Elvis. And there would be like a silence, and then the cousins would say, 'Oh, Mary Jane, this is Elvis,' and the girls would be totally gone." For the more experienced girls it wasn't like with other Hollywood stars or even with other more sophisticated boys they knew. They offered to do things for him, but he wasn't really interested. What he liked to do was to lie in bed and watch television and eat and talk all night — the companionship seemed as important for him as the sex — and then in the early-morning hours they would make love. "He had an innocence at that time," said one of them. "I'm sure it didn't last. But what he really wanted was to have a relationship, to have company. He was very clean-cut about it. There were a lot of things that he didn't like. And another thing that you could not do around him was mention drugs, he was dead set against it. There was a lot of grass around in Hollywood at that time, and what the cousins said was, 'If you got any dope, don't bring it out around Elvis.' If anyone wanted to turn on, they had to go away and not do it around Elvis."

In a wholly unlikely turn of events, one of the newcomers to the scene was songwriter Mike Stoller. Stoller had gotten a part in the movie when

Jerry Leiber, who, in the eyes of the film's casting director, *looked* more like a piano player than his piano-playing partner, begged off film work for a dentist's appointment. Stoller shaved off his goatee to play the part, looking exceedingly uncomfortable on-screen without it. He found film work boring but, to his surprise, enjoyed the opportunity it gave him to get to know Presley a little better. "He was very comfortable in the recording studio, but not so much on the set. I remember one time a couple of extras were sitting around, and I witnessed this whole thing — these two guys were playing cards and talking about their families, you know, the baby, the car payments, that kind of stuff. And one of them said something to the other, and they started laughing. Elvis came through at that moment, and he turned around and zap, right on them, and he said, 'Boy, you think you're so hot, huh?' They didn't know what he was talking about, and he was already in a sense omnipotent — but he thought they were laughing at him.

"I know he was very insecure, and I think that he used the Colonel in this as protection in a different way than the Colonel was using him. My own feeling was that he felt comfortable surrounded by his friends, and I think that also worked to the Colonel's idea of keeping him exclusive, keeping him isolated and insulated so that no one could get to him and he could never become too commonplace. I felt a little sorry for him because he didn't have a shot at becoming a whole person: in twenty minutes he would go from being arrogant and high-handed to frightened. He would order people about, and the next minute he would be saying, 'Can I get you a sandwich? Do you want some pie?'

"I used to hang out in the dressing room with the entourage, and one day we were horsing around, and Elvis said, 'You know, Mike, I'd really like you to write a ballad, a real pretty ballad, for me,' and that week Jerry and I wrote a song called 'Don't,' and we made a demo of it up at Hollywood Recorders with [rhythm and blues singer] Young Jessie singing, and I came back to the set and gave him the record and he loved it and eventually recorded it. But we caught hell for not going through the proper channels. I was supposed to tell Jean and Julian [Aberbach] and to play it for Freddy — and then *Freddy* was supposed to play it for Elvis. The Colonel was very upset — it was supposed to work the way it always worked, they didn't want any loose cannons around.

"One day after the shooting he invited me up to the hotel — I think we had a Coke downstairs, and then we went up to his suite on the top floor. And we went in and shot some pool and ate some peanuts, and we're kidding around and talking about songs and music, and then the Colonel came in and it was like a scattering of birds: they all flew away. I was in the middle of a pool shot and looked up and nobody was there. When Elvis came back, he looked terrible. He said, 'Mike, the Colonel's all upset because you're here, and I guess you gotta go.' I said it was all right and took off. They just didn't want anybody around, especially a songwriter — it was okay to work with him in a controlled area, but to be able to get to him and perhaps influence him, present him with a song. . . . That was the kind of control the Colonel had."

"I don't feel like I'm property," Elvis told columnist Joe Hyams, while lunching alone in his dressing room on a bowl of gravy, a bowl of mashed potatoes, nine slices of well-done bacon, two pints of milk, a large glass of tomato juice, lettuce salad, six slices of bread, and four pats of butter. "I can't get it into my head that I'm property. People tell me you can't do this or that," he went on, "but I don't listen to them. I do what I want. I can't change, and I won't change." He was a hard worker, he said, he had worked hard all his life, and even though he got lonely as hell sometimes ("A lot of times I feel miserable, don't know whichaway to turn"), he still loved every minute of it. "If I had to drop it all I could do it, but I wouldn't like it." And what about the Colonel? Hyams asked. "I've got an idea of how to handle me better than anyone else has as far as keeping me in line," said Elvis. "Colonel Parker is more or less like a daddy when I'm away from my own folks. He doesn't meddle in my affairs. Ain't nobody can tell me 'you do this or that.' Colonel Parker knows the business and I don't. He never butts into record sessions, I don't butt into business. Nobody can tell you how to run your life."

He studied the daily rushes religiously every night. He was still dead set against acting lessons — it was like the difference between an opera singer and a singer who sang from the heart, he explained to George Klein; formal study might rob him of his spontaneity. But, as a great believer in self-improvement and self-education, he never left the studio at night without carefully scrutinizing his performance. "I always criticize myself in films," he told an interviewer a few months later. "I'm always striving to be natural in front of a camera. That takes studying, of a sort."

He was serious about it, and he felt like he was getting somewhere. Mr. Thorpe wasn't very approachable, but he sought tips wherever he could get them, asking assistant director Bob Relyea for suggestions, thanking character actor Glenn Strange for his patience in a difficult scene. "He interacted with everybody," said Relyea. "One of the first days we were shooting a scene, and we were held up — and one of the crew just said, 'Well, we should have a song.' So he got his guitar out and played a song. It wasn't any, 'No, no, I don't do that, uh, don't embarrass me.' He just said, 'Give me my guitar!' He had all these qualities that you knew that he could succeed at whatever he wanted to do. He probably would have been good as a schoolteacher, he would have been a good mechanic. He was so dedicated and focused, he knew what it was about: he knew what tomorrow's work was going to be."

It was into this volatile mix of work and play, of desperate deal making and disingenuous denial, that Dewey stepped when he arrived for a Hollywood vacation several weeks into filming. He was all excited about the trip, which Elvis had even offered to pay for because, Bob Johnson wrote in the *Press-Scimitar,* "he wanted Dewey to spend a lot of time with him, and to watch him at work at MGM. . . . He didn't put him in with the other fellows, but put Dewey up in a room in his own personal suite. . . . Elvis took Dewey to his dentist and spent about $400 getting Dewey some of those fancy porcelain caps just like Elvis' for his teeth. He took him around to the various studios and stars' homes, proud of his strange friend from Memphis."

Unfortunately, "strange" appeared to be the operative word. Dewey, as Scotty said, "acted just the way he did around Memphis. Of course everyone in Memphis knew him, but out there he was just out of his league." He showed up on the set on the first day, got bored, and left after fifteen minutes. He got thrown off another set for taking pictures. Elvis took him over to the soundstage where they were making *The Brothers Karamazov* and introduced him to Yul Brynner, whereupon Dewey spontaneously observed, "You're a short little mother, aren't you?" and Elvis, mortified, apologized for his friend. "It was a star-crossed situation," observed George Klein. "Elvis loved Dewey for what he'd done for him, but by the same token he was embarrassed by what Dewey was doing in Hollywood. We went to see Sammy Davis, Jr., at the Moulin Rouge, and they introduced Elvis, and Dewey jumped up between Elvis and the spotlight and said, 'Dewey Phillips, Memphis, Tennessee,' and there's Elvis standing up to take a bow. We didn't get mad. We just said, 'That's crazy Dewey.' I mean, Elvis knew how Dewey was."

Before he left, Elvis played him a dub of his new single, "Teddy Bear," from *Loving You,* and Dewey flipped over it, it was a damn hit, he said and asked to hear it again. When he got on the plane, according to Dewey's report to Bob Johnson, "we even shed a few tears. I told him I'd never be able to repay him for all the nice things he'd done for me. His last words to me were, 'Phillips, be sure and say a prayer before you get on that plane.' "

Unfortunately Dewey had taken some stowaway luggage on board: against Elvis' explicit instructions, he had appropriated a copy of the new single, which was not due for release until June 11 and which, against all protocol and advice, he played on the air immediately upon his return. The Victor people were furious, the Colonel was furious — it only vindicated what he had been saying about Elvis' Memphis friends all along — and Elvis was furious, too. The headline in the *Press-Scimitar* was "These Reports True — Elvis and Dewey Had a Falling Out."

In the meantime shooting on the movie was rapidly coming to an end. When it was finished, it offered a neat little parable in black and white on the debilitating effects of fame (Vince Everett turned bigheaded before fate intervened) and the discrepancy that could exist between a truculent and much-criticized exterior and the essential sweetness that might lie underneath. It was a point Elvis had been arguing by deed, if not by word, for years, and one to which he clearly took, in a performance that marked an even further advance over the significant progress shown in *Loving You.* You couldn't really say that he had achieved an acting style, because in each scene he was a little different: there were traces, of course, of Dean and Brando — Brando particularly in the penitentiary scene where Elvis was flogged and registered silent suffering while naked to the waist — but, not surprisingly, the most striking resemblance was to a young Robert Mitchum, or perhaps it was Billy Murphy he was thinking of. In any case, it was a most creditable performance, and one of which Elvis could be proud as he departed for home at the end of June.

The train ride home was relatively uneventful, though it might have been less boring for Elvis if he had been aware of the behavior of his increasingly erratic cousin Junior Smith. Junior bunked with George, because at this point no one else could stand him. "He was drinking a lot, and when he'd get drunk he'd get mean. And he smoked in bed at night, and everyone was afraid he'd set the cabin on fire. So Elvis said, 'George, do you mind if Junior stays with you?' And I said no, because for some reason Junior and I hit it off, we'd kid around and tell old stories and it was fine. Well, this particular night he'd had a few drinks and he gets up and starts packing his bag, and it's about three-thirty in the morning, and I said, 'Junior, where in the shit are you going?' And he said, 'I'm getting off this fucking train.' I said, 'Junior, what are you going to do?' He packed his bag, and I said, 'Man, don't wake up Elvis, Junior.' He said, 'I ain't gonna wake up Cuz.' So he pulls that fucking cord that stops the train, and the conductor comes running down to our little booth, and Junior says, 'Stop this motherfucker, I want to get off.' And I started talking to him, and the conductor started talking to him, and we finally calmed him down and got him back to bed.''

Elvis couldn't wait to get home to see the renovations and stay overnight at Graceland with his parents, who had already moved in. So impatient was he that, after trying to get June to meet him in New Orleans, only to find out that she had been married on June 1, he got off the train in Lafayette, Louisiana, rented a car with Cliff, and drove the rest of the way home. "When we got there, the wall, the limestone wall, was not finished, and the gate was not up, and these little sticks guided you up the driveway with these orange markers because the asphalt was not fixed yet. Well, we made the little curve, got out, and went up to the door, and he stopped — it was about eleven-thirty at night, and he says, 'Well, Cliff, here goes.' He opened the door, and there was a little foyer there, and he went in, and, standing under the chandelier in the extended part of the foyer, were his mother and father. And she said, 'Welcome home, son.' And we talked for most of the night. It was not the excitement you might expect. Not, you know, 'Hey, we made it. We're on top of the world.' That never came out of that family — it was against their nature. They just talked. 'It's nice.' 'They've done a good job.' Elvis' father explained to him, 'We've still got to do this or that . . . I think this man here charged a little too much. I think we ought to change this guy, get another contractor . . .' That kind of talk." Had they completed the hog pens and chicken coop out back? Elvis wondered. Elvis' mother told him she had put in the garden.

THERE WAS NOTHING PLANNED, there was nothing that he had to do, there was nowhere that he needed to be. "Teddy Bear" and "Whole Lotta Shakin' Going On," the new song that Sam had put out on

Jerry Lee Lewis, were vying for number one, "Love Letters in the Sand" was still going good for Pat Boone, seventeen-year-old Ricky Nelson was doing all right with his first record, and he liked Tommy Sands, too — "There's plenty of room for all of us," he reassured his friends when they started running down one artist or another, though he didn't ever want to be taken for granted, either. The world premiere of *Loving You* was scheduled to be held in Memphis on July 9 at the Strand Theatre on South Main, and he was planning to attend. In the meantime he wanted to make sure that everything at Graceland was just right. He had heard that geese were good for keeping down a lawn, so he took one of the Cadillacs, drove it down to Mississippi, and filled up the backseat with sixteen geese, which, not surprisingly, left a substantial deposit. Another time he took over from Vernon on the driving mower, heading straight for his mother's tulip bed. He was just fooling around, but then his mother started to yell, "Elvis, Elvis, don't!" and a look of panic came over her face, which only added to the temptation. Tulips flew everywhere, and his mother eventually started laughing, too, but Mr. Presley was worried that he was going to be blamed.

Then on the night of July 3 he heard that Judy Tyler had been killed with her husband in an automobile crash out west. She had played the record company girl who became his manager and love interest in *Jailhouse Rock,* and he was devastated. He showed up at George's house with Arthur at 10:00 the following morning, an unheard-of hour. "I was still living across from Humes with my mother, and she came into the bedroom and said, 'Elvis is at the door.' I said, 'No, Mom, Elvis is not at the door.' He was real serious, so I said, 'What's wrong, man?' but he just wanted to take a ride. So we got in the car and he said, 'Hey, man, Judy got killed.' So we drove around for a while and he explained it to me, he just felt so bad."

He was determined to go to the funeral, he told the newspapers later in the day, even if it meant missing the premiere. "She was at the peak of success," he said, fighting back tears. "Nothing has hurt me as bad in my life. . . . I remember the last night I saw them. They were leaving on a trip. Even remember what she was wearing." He didn't know if he could stand to look at the movie now, he said. "I just don't believe I can." In the end he didn't attend the funeral. It was his mother, not the Colonel, who told the papers a couple of days later that he would just send flowers, he didn't want to disrupt the service.

That Sunday he met a girl he had been seeing on TV ever since getting home. Anita Wood was nineteen, a beauty-contest winner, blond, pert, and talented, who had been appearing with Wink Martindale on the *Top Ten Dance Party* on WHBQ for the past few months. She was from Jackson, Tennessee, originally, like Wink, and Cliff knew her from there, while George knew her through Wink. Elvis had George check the situation out, and when George came back and said she'd like to meet him, he had George call her up. The first time she was busy, and when she had to decline a second time, she thought he would never call again, but the third time George called she was free. They drove by the Strand to see the cutout of Elvis that the theater had put out in anticipation of the movie opening in two days. George and Cliff were in the backseat, and Lamar, too, and they went out for hamburgers at Chenault's afterward. Then he gave her a tour of his new home and its grounds: the swimming pool, the six cars, his collection of teddy bears, from which he lightheartedly selected one as a gift. He showed her his bedroom, but she told him she didn't feel comfortable there, so they went back downstairs and spent the rest of the evening talking and playing records and singing at the piano. At the end of the night he took her home to the room she rented in Mrs. J. R. Patty's house, and they chastely kissed good-night.

After that they kept almost constant company. Elvis didn't attend the *Loving You* premiere, which set box office records in Memphis and, a few weeks later, across the country, but he took Anita and his parents to a special midnight showing, which they all enjoyed. During the day they frequently drove around in an old panel truck that guaranteed anonymity, as Elvis showed her all the places that meant something to him in his life. He was painstaking, almost compulsive, about pointing out to her the route he had walked to the store, where he had played as a child, where his friends and cousins lived, the places where he had worked and played. He dreaded going into the army, he told her, and started calling her "Little" because of the size of her feet. Sometimes he would talk baby talk to her the same as he would talk to his mother. It was all very down-to-earth and flattering, too, if only for the way he simply adored her. He didn't play the big star, he was just like a boy that you would meet and fall in love with and then expect to marry — and his family was so welcoming, too. "I just can't wait," Gladys told her, not long after Anita had become a regular fixture, "to see that little ol' baby walking up and down the driveway." She had been sick a lot lately and stayed up in her room. "She had a heart problem, I think, and she was overweight with fluid — her ankles and her legs would swell a lot. . . . She never ceased to worry about Elvis."

They drove all around on his motorcycle and went horseback riding and played badminton out on the lawn. There was a special dining room reserved for them in the back room at Chenault's Drive-in; they went out to McKellar Lake on occasion or to the Fairgrounds to ride the Dodgems and the Pippin, the oldest operating wooden roller-coaster ride in the country. The guys were with them almost constantly, George or Cliff, Lamar, Arthur, the cousins. Once in a while Elvis would run into one of his old friends and invite him up to the house. Buzzy Forbess from the Courts came by one evening, and Elvis surprised him by fooling around with a classical harp he had just bought, but to Buzzy there were just too many people sitting around holding out their hands, and the atmosphere was kind of forced, so he didn't go back for a while. George Klein brought around a friend named Alan Fortas, who had been an All-City tackle at Central High, then went on to Vanderbilt University and Southwestern before dropping out and going to work at his father's junkyard. George, who knew him through the temple and a number of other Jewish organizations, needed a ride out to Graceland one night.

"George didn't drive, he was one of the few people who didn't, so he asked me if I'd like to go out to meet Elvis. Of course I was an Elvis fan, I had seen him in a couple of shows at the Overton Park Shell and Russwood Park, and I had been out to the Eagle's Nest. So I said, 'Man, I'd love to,' and I picked George up, and we went out there and, of course, Elvis was a big football fan and he remembered me from high school and showed me all around the house. Well, I left after a couple of hours, I didn't want to overstay my welcome, and when I left, he said, 'Well, I'll see you again, Alan.' So a couple of nights later George called and said, 'Elvis asked about you and wanted to know why you hadn't been back.' 'Well,' I said, 'I didn't want to press my luck.' He said, 'Oh, he liked talking to you. Come back out.' So I went out, and when I left that night, he said, 'I'll see you tomorrow night.' One thing led to another, and every night I left he said, 'I'll see you tomorrow night, Alan.' "

Elvis seemed to really take to him. Before long he started calling him "Hog Ears," just as he called Lamar "Mr. Bull" and George "GK." It was cool going out to Graceland — you never knew what was going to happen. Where else were you going to find donkeys in the swimming pool (courtesy of Colonel Parker) and peacocks on the lawn? As the summer wore on, Elvis started renting out the Fairgrounds through a friend of George's named Wimpy Adams, and they would have it to themselves from midnight till sunrise. They rented out the Rainbow Rollerdrome, too, from Joe and Doris Pieraccini, and had skating parties where the guys put on knee and elbow pads and divided up into teams, playing rough games of tag and roller derby, with one of the cousins acting as referee. One night, Alan recalled in his memoir of that time, Elvis was "more keyed up than usual" when they piled in the car to go home.

> Lamar and I climbed in the front seat, and Elvis and Anita sat in the back. We were just tooling along, when all of a sudden Anita announced in a loud voice, "My cunt hurts!" What? My mouth dropped down to my ankles. Maybe I misunderstood. I cleared my throat, Lamar did the same, and we drove on a little farther. Then Anita burst out again. "Did y'all hear me? I said, 'My cunt really hurts!' " . . . It wasn't until we got back to Graceland that I found out that Elvis had told Anita the whopping lie that "my cunt hurts" is a Hollywood expression for "my rear's sore." And every time she yelled it out, it was only because Elvis nudged her. . . . She had no idea what it meant.

Alan didn't think much of the cousins and the uncles and the aunts — they were, he wrote, "an odd lot. . . . Sometimes I'd talk to Gene and it was almost like talking to a retarded person. I didn't know if he was acting or whether he was really that dumb." Mostly they just had a helluva time, though. They went everywhere and they did everything on the slightest whim. The only place they didn't go was to the Hotel Chisca. Ever since getting back, Elvis had studiously avoided the radio station, and now he wouldn't even come to the phone when Dewey called. Dewey had apologized right after he got back — almost under duress, it seemed — and there had even been a brief period of rapprochement, but then Dewey began to feel aggrieved that Elvis wasn't coming by with a sack of Krystal-burgers anymore, and he started telling anyone who would listen that he thought Elvis had the big head.

One night he came by the house at 3:00 in the morning, ranting that Elvis had forgotten his old friends, and when he was turned away at the gate, he "climbed the fence," the paper reported, "and went in and roused the household shouting: 'I'm through with you, Elvis.' Elvis is said to have doubled him in spades. One person close to Elvis said, 'What made it especially bad is that Mrs. Presley is so nervous, especially since Liberace's mother got hurt.'" The story was quite different, according to an obviously remorseful Dewey. It was only about 1:00 A.M., he thought, and he'd gone out there to retrieve a Polaroid camera that Sam Phillips had given him for Christmas. He needed it back, because he was about to take the rest of his vacation and he wanted to take some pictures. "It wasn't really late for Elvis," he said. "They wouldn't let me in and I still haven't got my camera. I said some things I shouldn't have said. . . . I still love that boy like a brother. Or maybe it would be better to say like a son."

There were lots, of course, of other nights at Graceland. One night the great rhythm and blues singer Ivory Joe Hunter, whose anthemic 1950 hit, "I Almost Lost My Mind" (remade with even greater success as "Since I Met You, Baby" in 1956), was one of Elvis' favorites and whose "I Need You So" Elvis had recorded in February, came out to the house. Brother Dave Gardner, the comedian whom Elvis had first met in Biloxi the previous summer, was in town recording a follow-up to his unexpected pop hit, "White Silver Sands." Somehow or other he had hooked up with Ivory Joe, and he called up Elvis and asked if he could bring him over. Elvis was thrilled, and they were all sitting on the white couch in the living room swapping stories when, according to George Klein, "Elvis said, 'Ivory Joe, I sure do like your songs. You ain't got any more of them for me, do you?'

"Now Ivory Joe was a real friendly guy. Great big 'Hey, baby, how you doing, baby?' kind of guy. You just immediately liked him. And he said, 'Well, baby, I just have — I got one just for you.' So we went in the piano room, and he sang 'My Wish Came True,' and Elvis said, 'Shit, I'm cutting that at my next session!' Which he did, even though it didn't come out for a couple of years. And they sat there for hours, mostly singing Ivory Joe's songs, a few of Elvis' — man, I just wish I'd had a tape machine."

"He is very spiritually minded," said Hunter, who had felt some trepidation to start off with because, "frankly, I'd heard he was color prejudiced." The rumor had been circulating throughout the Negro community that spring and summer, in fact, that Elvis Presley had said, "The only thing Negroes can do for me is buy my records and shine my shoes." After determining that "tracing the rumored racial slur to its source was like running a gopher to earth" (the remark was said to have been made either in Boston, which Elvis had never visited, or on Edward R. Murrow's national television show, on which he had never appeared), *Jet* magazine sent a reporter to the set of *Jailhouse Rock* to confront the singer himself. "When asked if he ever made the remark, Mississippi-born Elvis declared: 'I never said anything like that, and people who know me know I wouldn't have said it.'" The reporter, Louie Robinson, then spoke to some people who *were* in a position to know and heard from Dr. W. A. Zuber, a Negro physician in Tupelo, that Elvis used to "go around with quartets and to Negro 'sanctified' meetings," from pianist Dudley Brooks that "he faces everybody as a man," and from Elvis himself that he had gone "to colored churches when I was a kid, like Reverend Brewster's," and that he could honestly never hope to equal the musical achievements of Fats Domino or the Ink Spots' Bill Kenny. "To Elvis," *Jet* concluded in its August 1 issue, "people are people, regardless of race, color or creed." And to Ivory Joe Hunter, who verified the matter for himself, "he showed me every courtesy, and I think he's one of the greatest."

All in all it was a peculiarly lazy, idyllic kind of existence, an adolescent daydream that seemed like it could go on forever. In the basement the jukebox was playing all the time, and the soda fountain was fully stocked. If he felt like it, he might fix a visitor a milk shake, and with no fans around to observe him, he could smoke the little Hav-a-tampas that he and the guys all enjoyed without compunction — but without inhaling either. According to Bettye Maddox, a DJ at WHER whom Elvis met after seeing her do a commercial for Honeysuckle Cornmeal on Dewey's *Pop Shop* TV show, "It was like a magic spell — it was like each night you knew something magic was going to happen, but you didn't know what it was." Some nights Anita would call and Bettye would be out there, and he would just tell the guys to say that he was busy. Venetia Stevenson flew in from Hollywood to stay with him, and there was a trio of fourteen-year-old girls that he had known since the previous fall (one of their fathers operated a garage that Vernon patronized); they came around from time to time, and he roughhoused with them and had pillow fights and kissed and cuddled some ("We'd tickle, fight, laugh, mess around," said one, "but all you'd have to say is 'Stop!' and he'd roll over and quit"), until Lamar had to drive them home. But mostly it was Anita. She saw him almost every night, though she told a reporter a couple of months was much too early to tell whether there was anything really "serious" to it.

From Alan Fortas' perspective there was a quality of wholesomeness, whether internally or externally determined, that was almost unreal, and largely attributable to Mrs. Presley's presence. "It never got wild at Graceland," he wrote. "People respected Graceland as the Presleys' home. And the language never got [too] rough around there, either. . . . If anybody said 'goddamn,' he erupted in a rage . . . 'You can use any other word you want to, but don't use the Lord's name in vain!'" He had his high school class picture up on the wall, and he would point it out to everyone, in George's presence, saying, "Look who's up there at the top." And they would always say, "Who is that, Elvis? It's hard to see." He would say, "That's George Klein. He was one of the few guys that was nice to me in school," to George's acute discomfiture and radiating pride.

Vernon couldn't have been happier — everybody came to him for decisions, he had plenty to do, Elvis deferred to him on money matters, he was as proud as one of the peacocks on the lawn. For Gladys, on the other hand, there was a clear sense of resignation, a pervasive air of sadness; she didn't seem able to ever really settle in to her new home. "She never did go nowhere after they moved out there," said her sister Lillian. "She used to go to the grocery store, but she quit going to the grocery store. She never was satisfied after she moved out there — I think the house was too big, and she didn't like it. Of course she never told Elvis that." When her cousin Frank Richards visited with his wife, Leona, that summer, Gladys confessed to her, "I'm the most miserable woman in the world," and Alan always recalled her "sitting by the window in the kitchen, daydreaming, or looking out in the backyard at her chickens." Every so often she'd have a beer or two with Cliff. "We never did that at Audubon, but up at Graceland we'd be sitting and chatting in the kitchen, maybe two or three times a week in the afternoon — that was it — and Elvis would come in and shake his head like, 'My God, you people are going to hell, drinking beer like this.' I'm serious! She just said, 'Son, Cliff and I are going to have a beer, whether you like it or not.' And he'd turn around and shake his head and just walk out without saying another word." It was all right, she told Lamar, if Elvis blew up at him, or at any of them, once in a while. " 'When Elvis gets mad at you,' she said, 'always remember, it's from the mouth out.' That was one of her expressions. She knew him better than anybody. She could tell what he was going to do before he did it. She was scared to death something was gonna happen to him. She used to say, 'I hope I'm in the grave before he is. Because I could never stand to see him dead before me.' "

Toward the end of the summer Freddy Bienstock came down to go over material for the upcoming session in Hollywood in September. "It was the second time that I went to Memphis, ostensibly to play songs for him. I was told that he wasn't going to get up till about three o'clock, and it was a hot day, so I went into the swimming pool and a couple of ducks jumped in and one of them clipped me on the ear, and I jumped out of that pool so fast. . . . He had all kinds of animals around, and he had built columns around the pool — he told me afterwards that he had the idea of building these columns from seeing the movie *The Philadelphia Story*. Anyway, he showed me around — he was very proud of Graceland without putting on any airs about it — and in the evening we all went out to dinner. I hadn't eaten very much, so I was really looking forward to a terrific dinner. We were driving in two limousines, and he said to Lamar, who was an endomorph for sure, to call the restaurant on the car phone — they were very rare in those days — he wanted a private dining room reserved for him. So I thought this is really going to be a lovely dinner. He said, 'We may as well order now, so when we get there the food will be ready and we don't have to wait.' The first order was a hamburger and an orange pop, and, you know, then a ham and cheese sandwich and a Pepsi-Cola, a bacon sandwich and a glass of milk, and so forth, and when it came to me I didn't want to be different, so I ordered another cheese sandwich and an orange pop. And then, when it came to paying the bill, the whole thing came to, I think, fourteen or fifteen dollars, and Elvis pulled out a twenty and grandly says, 'Keep the change.' "

THE SCENE AT THE TRAIN STATION as he left for the Coast at 11:00 on the night of August 27 threatened to get out of hand. The Colonel had set up a whirlwind tour of the Pacific Northwest (five cities in four days) to precede the September 5–7 recording session that Steve Sholes had finally gotten him to allow Elvis to do. George, Lamar, and Cliff, who would once again be his traveling companions, had all driven to the station with his parents and him, while his uncle Travis and aunt Lorraine had come in their own car, but Anita was without question the center of attention. "Anita is number one with me — strictly tops," Elvis told the small crowd of fans and reporters who had gathered to see him off. He then embraced his mother several times, reported the paper faithfully, and she reminded him to 'Be good, son,' as he boarded the train. 'Take care of yourself, boy,' said Mr. Presley. . . . Elvis kissed Anita twice for photographers (and about five times for himself) before hopping aboard. As the train moved away, Anita burst into tears and Mrs. Presley put her arm around her. The Presleys and Anita walked arm in arm out of the station to the Cadillac again, with Uncle Travis, himself moist-eyed, following."

And then they were gone. Anita had just won the Mid-South Hollywood Star Hunt the previous Thursday and was traveling to New Orleans to take part in the finalists' competition, which promised a small movie role to the winner. He was keeping his fingers crossed, he told her, but for himself Elvis was just looking forward to getting back to work. The promoter for the tour was Lee Gordon, the same flamboyant Detroit-born entrepreneur who had booked them into Canada and the Midwest the previous spring and was now imprecating Colonel Parker — so far without success — to agree to an Australian tour. Jerry Leiber and Mike Stoller, the songwriters, were all set for the Hollywood session. And Elvis was going to have Millie Kirkham, the soprano who had done a good deal of Nashville session work with the Jordanaires and whose backup vocals he had admired recently on a Jimmy "C" Newman release, flown in specially for the session. He hadn't heard anything from the draft board lately, though there were rumors in the papers every day, and maybe that would work out, maybe the Colonel could fix it — why would the government want to give up all those millions of dollars in taxes?

The tour went pretty much according to plan. There were riots in virtually every city, but security was generally good, and he enjoyed teasing the crowd, dancing suggestively and lying down and writhing on the stage, sometimes with a model of RCA's trademark dog, Nipper. "A chunky, effeminate-looking man with long hair, later identified as a member of Presley's entourage, seemed almost in a trance as he snapped his fingers, wiggled his body and shouted over and over: 'Yeah man, yeah man, yeah, yeah, yeah,' " reported the *Tacoma News Tribune*. "I lose myself in my singing," Elvis told one press gathering. "Maybe it's my early training singing gospel hymns. I'm limp as a rag, worn out when a show's over." His first love was "the old colored spirituals," he told a press conference in Vancouver. "I know practically every religious song that's ever been written," he boasted proudly.

He ended every show with "Hound Dog," which he had taken to introducing as the "Elvis Presley national anthem." Meanwhile, the Colonel, never one to miss a trick, was selling nearly as many "I Hate Elvis" buttons as "I Love Elvis" ones. In Vancouver a small contingent of Canadian Mounties was not up to the task of holding back a crowd of almost twenty-five thousand at Empire Stadium, and for the first time the Colonel, who had protested bitterly over the size of the force, Mounties or no Mounties, was impelled to actively intervene.

"The Colonel came out and pulled Elvis offstage," said George Klein, "and the MC said, 'You are going to have to get back in your seats, or we can't go on with the show.' Meanwhile, the Colonel told Elvis, 'Elvis, don't tease this crowd. These people are crazy.' Well, if you tell Elvis not to do something, that's the surest way you're going to get him to do it, so he goes back onstage and the first thing he does is, 'Wellllllll . . .' And here come fifty thousand more people! So the Colonel runs out again — this is the first time I ever saw Colonel Parker go out onstage — he got mad, and he went onstage because he was protecting his property. And he said, 'Okay, you can stay on the field if you act right and you don't tear the stage up. Otherwise Mr. Presley's not going to be performing.' And he says to Elvis, 'Elvis, please don't do an hour. Do thirty minutes tonight.' So Elvis did about forty-five or fifty minutes, and when we left that stage the last thing we saw was the stage being turned over — sheet music flying up in the air, they grabbed music stands, instruments, drumsticks, everything they could get. That was a pretty scary night."

"A gang moved into our town," declared the *Vancouver Province*. It was nothing more than "subsidized sex," sniffed the paper's music critic, Dr. Ida Halpern. The performance "had not even the quality of a true obscenity: merely an artificial and unhealthy exploitation of the enthusiasm of youth's body and mind." Meanwhile, Elvis heard from Anita that she had won the talent contest in New Orleans. She told him excitedly that she would join him in Hollywood the following week, and he sounded really happy and told her not to be nervous and said that he was really looking forward to showing her around.

The session went smoothly enough. Mr. Sholes had just been promoted to head of pop a&r — it hadn't been announced yet, but he and Mr. Bullock were celebrating. That still didn't stop Colonel from getting in his little zingers every chance he got. The principal aim of the session was to record a Christmas album, and Elvis wanted to get in the right mood, so Mr. Sholes arranged to have a tree in the studio and made sure that there were wrapped presents under it. Elvis had never been satisfied with the version of "Treat Me Nice" he had recorded for the movie, so he did it again, and he cut "Don't," the ballad that Jerry and Mike had written for him in June, as well as a beautiful version of Ivory Joe Hunter's "My Wish Came True," on which he coached the Jordanaires to mimic the harmonies of the Statesmen and in particular Jake Hess' habit of crisply enunciating his syllables. Freddy tried to sneak in a song that he had pitched without success back in January — he figured Elvis would never remember it — but he didn't get more than eight bars into it when Elvis said, "I've heard that song before, and I don't like it any better now than I did then."

They recorded a number of Christmas standards, including a re-creation of the Drifters' arrangement of "White Christmas" from a couple of years before and the Ernest Tubb country standard, "Blue Christmas." With "Blue Christmas" Elvis wanted the sound that Millie Kirkham had created on Ferlin Husky's "Gone," and he had her singing a soprano obbligato all the way through. "It was horrible," said Kirkham, who was six months pregnant at the time. "It was sort of comical. It wasn't supposed to be, but the longer it goes the funnier it gets — but he liked it. He was a star, but he was so much fun to be around. He was very polite to everybody, amazingly so to me. When I walked in, he said, 'Get this woman a chair!' I was the only female, of course, but if one of the guys happened to say something off-color he would just say, 'Wait a minute, guys, we got a lady in the room,' and they were never offended. We always used to say they laughed on cue." Toward the end of the session they ran out of material, and Jerry and Mike went back into the mix room, where they concocted "Santa Claus Is Back in Town," a wonderful double-entendre blues that Elvis delivered with great panache.

Scotty, D.J., and Bill were watching the clock with increasing apprehension as the three-day session came to a close. They had been promised the opportunity to record some instrumentals on Elvis' time when the session was over. Actually, the idea had been kicking around for close to a year now, but this time they had a firm commitment for studio time, and they had worked up some tunes, and Elvis was even talking about playing piano on one or two. When it came down to it, though, Elvis felt tired, or was simply not in the mood, and Tom Diskin came into the studio and said, "That's it." Scotty and Bill protested that they had a deal, but Diskin told them Colonel said they could do it another time and told everyone to pack up, unmoved by either their anger or protestations. Bill hit the roof, muttering to himself and slamming his electric bass into its case, while they waited for Elvis to stand up for them — but he never did. He didn't say a word, in fact, and, as had so often been the case, seemed to slide out of the situation without even acknowledging that he knew what was going on.

Scotty and Bill went back to the hotel, but the gnawing feeling of resentment wouldn't go away; it just grew stronger and stronger until, finally, later in the evening, they wrote up a letter of resignation which each of them would personally sign and send. They had expected more from Elvis, they had expected to *share* in his success, and here they were still only making two hundred dollars a week on the road and responsible for their own expenses. They were in debt, they needed financial help, they just wanted some fucking respect. Within the formal constraints of a letter they were barely able to touch on their long-standing feelings: the fact that they had had only one raise in two years; the cutback in personals to the point that they had played only fourteen dates so far this year; the way in which the Colonel had prevented them from making any endorsements and, as they saw it, simply "squeezed us for a matter of dollars"; the way in which they had been cut off from all access to Elvis — it was almost as if, Bill felt, they were no longer even permitted to talk to him.

When they approached D.J. with the letter, he declined to sign it. He felt that he had been treated fairly, he explained; he had come in as a salaried employee, he had always gotten paid, he had no real complaints. "Bill was pretty pissed, but I explained my reasons, and they said, 'Okay, don't worry about it.' " Then they had the letter delivered to Elvis at the Beverly Wilshire Hotel.

Elvis read the letter, shook his head, said "Aw, shit," and passed it around. He obviously couldn't believe that Scotty and Bill would do something like this to him, that they would humiliate him, in front of the world, in this fashion. It flashed through his mind that maybe this was the beginning of the end: first Dewey, then them. *Where was their fucking loyalty?* Then he was pissed off. If they had just come to him, he told the guys and anyone who would listen, they could have worked something out. Now he would *never* take them back. They had probably been hired by someone else — Ricky Nelson or Gene Vincent or one of them. He was wild with grief. Anita, who had arrived from Memphis only that evening, tried to console him. Colonel and Diskin stayed out of his way — the boy would work it out for himself, Colonel said, while Steve Sholes expressed the hope, several times, that the separation would be permanent. In Sholes' view Elvis could do better, he could get better musicians, brighter musicians, quicker learners, any day of the week.

The last couple of days in Hollywood were bittersweet. Elvis showed his girl the sights and, before he left, gave her a ring to signify his feelings. He bought it in the Beverly Wilshire jewelry shop, and it was described as eighteen sapphires surrounding a diamond and "very expensive" by "bug-eyed" hotel employees. It was just a "friendship ring," Anita said, showing it off proudly to reporters, but, secretly, she felt differently.

The news of the split with Scotty and Bill had reached Memphis by the time Elvis got home on September 11. He called Scotty the following day and offered a raise of $50 across the board, but Scotty said that he would need $10,000 in addition to the raise, if only "out of the kindness of [Elvis'] heart," just to get out of debt. Elvis said he would think about it, but in the meantime Bob Johnson sniffed out the story and interviewed Scotty and Bill for a feature that ran the next day in which both musicians expressed their disappointment, and described the disagreement, in sorrowful but explicit terms. The crux of the matter, said Scotty, was that "[Elvis] promised us that the more he made the more we would make. But it hasn't worked that way."

Elvis' reaction was not surprising: he felt even further betrayed and released a statement to the newspaper to accompany an interview in which he told *his* side of the story.

"Scotty, Bill, I hope you fellows have good luck," Elvis' statement read. "I will give you fellows good recommendations. If you had come to me, we would have worked things out. I would have always taken care of you. But you went to the papers and tried to make me look bad, instead of coming to me so we could work things out. All I can say to you is 'good luck.' " So far as promises were concerned, Elvis said, "I have a good memory and I don't remember ever telling them [anything like] that." To *Press-Scimitar* reporter Bill Burk, Elvis spoke of "certain people close to him who have tried to persuade him to drop his musical group during the last two years. He would not name these people, but said he told them he would not because they were good musicians and because of sentimental reasons. 'We started out together,' he said, 'and I didn't want to cut any-one out of anything. . . . These boys could have had a job with me as long as I was making a dime.' "

Their resignations, he told Burk, came at a particularly crucial time. "He plays the Tupelo Fair (which he called 'my homecoming') Sept. 27. He said he just received the dates of his next tour, which will be in Octo-ber. . . . Elvis said he would immediately begin auditioning for a new gui-tar player and bass player during the two weeks before the Tupelo Fair. 'It might take a while,' he said, 'but it's not impossible to find replace-ments.' "

"We're both pretty stubborn," Scotty conceded to the press. "I guess he can be stubborn longer because he's got more money."

He arrived in Tupelo with Anita and his parents, along with Cliff, George, Lamar, Alan, and another friend, named Louis Har-ris. There was as much excitement in town about his upcoming appear-ance as there had been the previous year, but it was of a different sort, and mindful of his generous donation toward a youth center, the lead editorial in the paper offered an admonitory note to the community to "Let Our Welcome for Elvis Be Truly Warm." Elvis had been "the best ambassa-dor any town could have," declared the *Tupelo Daily Journal,* and "he needs to feel appreciated in at least one community in America for just being himself." The paper was full of stories about the riots in Little Rock over school integration, and there was even a story with a Memphis date-line about white students from still segregated Humes High School jeer-ing at Negro students on their way to nearby Manassas, but in Tupelo, the paper noted on the front page, while the annual 4-H Club style show would be held in front of the grandstand, "the Negro junior Jersey show will start at 10 A.M. in the Negro section of the fairgrounds."

Mr. Savery, the fair manager, had them all over to dinner, and Jack Cristil from WELO spent as much time interviewing Anita as he did Elvis.

Did they have marriage plans? the reporters all shouted at him at the press conference in the tent before the performance. "I haven't found the girl yet," he said, staring straight at Anita with a look meant just for her. After a slow advance sale, the grandstand was filled to capacity; the band — with Nashville's Hank "Sugarfoot" Garland on guitar and Chuck Wiginton, a friend of D.J.'s from Dallas, on bass — sounded tight; Colonel made sure that they put up a big banner announcing that *Jailhouse Rock* was coming soon; and he worked the crowd, and himself, up into the usual frenzy. But somehow it wasn't the same. It didn't feel right, he told D.J. afterward. Garland was a helluva guitarist, but you could tell the difference on "Don't Be Cruel"; Garland could really *play*, but he didn't hit that intro the way that Scotty did.

A feeling of melancholy had stolen over him, as if, somehow, it was all coming to an end. He felt badly let down by Scotty and Bill — he didn't understand why they had done this to him. And even though things were back to normal with Dewey as of last week, he wasn't sure they could ever really be the same again. He had stopped by Sun, but things were different there, too, with Marion gone. She and Sam had had a big fight, and she had gone off and enlisted in the air force. The draft was hanging like a dark cloud over his head. Every day there were stories in the paper about it, and reporters wanted to know what he was going to do.

The week after the Tupelo homecoming, he decided to take them back. Scotty and Bill played a miserable two-week engagement at the Dallas State Fair and then formalized the arrangement, with everyone swallowing his pride a little and the Blue Moon Boys returning on a per diem basis. There were no hard feelings, Scotty said. It was a matter of money all along. For Elvis, though, it would have been hard to say what it was exactly. One day he heard "Jailhouse Rock" on the radio and declared, "Elvis Presley and his one-man band," with a rueful shake of his head. It seemed like everything was plunging headlong forward, and he didn't know how to hold it back.

PORTRAIT. (ALFRED WERTHEIMER)

WALKING IN A DREAM

"HERE. READ THIS!" said a reporter, shoving a magazine article into Elvis' hands. "Rock 'n' roll smells phony and false," declared Frank Sinatra in the story's text. "It is sung, played, and written for the most part by cretinous goons and by means of its almost imbecilic reiteration, and sly, lewd, in plain fact, dirty lyrics . . . it manages to be the martial music of every sideburned delinquent on the face of the earth. . . . [It] is the most brutal, ugly, desperate, vicious form of expression it has been my misfortune to hear."

And what was Elvis Presley's response to that? he was asked, standing in front of a roomful of reporters. It was an hour before his October 28 performance at the Pan Pacific Auditorium, which would mark his Hollywood debut. "I admire the man," said Elvis. "He has a right to say what he wants to say. He is a great success and a fine actor, but I think he shouldn't have said it. He's mistaken about this. This is a trend, just the same as he faced when he started years ago. I consider it the greatest in music," Elvis added mischievously, throwing the reporters a little off balance. "It is very noteworthy — and namely because it is the only thing I can do. . . ."

"Is that all you have to say?"

"You can't knock success," declared Elvis and went on to answer questions about his income, his sideburns, his draft status, and any plans he might have for marriage, before taking the stage in gold jacket and dress pants at 8:15.

He was determined to impress his celebrity-studded audience, and he did. In front of a sold-out, paid attendance of more than nine thousand (at the Colonel's insistence, even Hal Wallis was required to buy his own ticket), he flung himself about, "wiggled, bumped, twisted," and at the conclusion of the fifty-minute performance rolled around on the floor with Nipper in a manner longtime critic Jack O'Brian of the *New York*

Journal-American declared "far too indecent to mention in every detail."

The audience went wild, but the newspapers took a somewhat dimmer view. "Elvis Presley Will Have to Clean Up His Show — Or Go to Jail," declared one headline, while O'Brian characterized the music as "a terrible popular twist on darkest Africa's fertility tom-tom displays" and *Los Angeles Mirror-News* entertainment editor Dick Williams noted: "If any further proof were needed that what Elvis offers is not basically music but a sex show, it was proved last night." His performance, wrote Williams, resembled "one of those screeching, uninhibited party rallies which the Nazis used to hold for Hitler," and many parents who had attended with their children, including actors Alan Ladd and Walter Slezak, expressed equal outrage to authorities and the newspapers. The result was that the Los Angeles Vice Squad contacted the Colonel, who told Elvis that he would have to cut out some of the dancing and in general tone down his act. What was Elvis' reaction? the Colonel was asked. "This isn't the first time," said the Colonel. "You know, they done it a couple of times before." Did Elvis complain about not being able to dance? "Naw, he didn't complain. . . . He just said, 'Well, if I don't dance tonight, maybe I don't have to take a shower tonight.' " "Colonel Parker said that?" declared Elvis incredulously. "He couldn't have! You see," Elvis explained, genuinely upset, "I take a shower every night, whether I dance or just sing."

When the police showed up with movie cameras on the second night, the show *was* considerably toned down, and the only person to object was Yul Brynner, "whose bleeding heart," wrote Jack O'Brian, "led him to protest [the censorship] as if it were an invasion of someone's privacy." Brynner, declared O'Brian olympianly, was "ridiculous." Elvis, for his part, kept his own counsel.

Still, he felt good about it. He had done what he did best in front of a town in which he was only beginning to feel comfortable — and it had caused just as much of a stir as it would have in Memphis or Saskatchewan. The single of "Jailhouse Rock" was currently at number one, the film had just had its world premiere in Memphis at the same theater where Elvis had ushered as a teenager and was scheduled to open in theaters throughout the country the following week, and the Colonel had estimated that, with the deal they had with MGM, Elvis was likely to make more than two million dollars when it did. As he said to one reporter who raised the question of what he would do if his popularity were to decline,

"You can't stay on top forever. Even if I stopped singing tomorrow, I'd have no regrets. I had a ball while I was there."

There was a party that night at his suite, and everyone was there: Sammy, Nick, Vince Edwards, Venetia, Carol Channing, Tommy Sands, a whole bunch of pretty girls, even seventeen-year-old Ricky Nelson showed up, riding the crest of his first big Imperial hit. Elvis knew that Ricky was friendly with Scotty and Bill, but he and Ricky had never really talked, and Ricky was just hanging around on the edge of the party when Elvis pushed his way through the crowd, picked him up in the air, and said, "Man, I just love your new record." He loved *The Adventures of Ozzie and Harriet,* too, he watched it all the time, he told Ricky, and he wondered whether Ricky's brother, David, was here tonight. When *Photoplay* editor Marcia Borie told Elvis that Ricky was about to go out on tour for the first time and could use some advice, Elvis took Ricky aside and filled him in. "You'll never know how much tonight has meant to me," Nelson told Borie later in the evening. "Imagine Elvis Presley watching our show. He repeated episodes I'd even forgotten about. He remembered them word for word. And he gave me some great tips about things to do on my tour. I still can't believe it." Cliff, Nick, and Sammy Davis, Jr., entertained the guests with impressions, and Elvis' date for the evening was Anne Neyland.

One week later he sailed for Hawaii. The three shows scheduled there were the last of a broken six-day tour (San Francisco, Oakland, Hollywood, and Hawaii) that seemed to have been arranged at the last minute and was elongated even further by the four-day boat ride. The Colonel and the Jordanaires and the band, of course, all flew over, but Elvis stuck to his promise to his mother not to fly unless it was absolutely necessary. There was one small surprise at the dock: Billy Murphy showed up with his bags packed just as the ship was about to sail. Elvis had invited him sometime earlier, but there had been no further discussion of the subject, and now a mild flurry of confusion arose before someone finally purchased a ticket for him. Other than that, the cruise was a dull one, made up of typical tourists and retirees and a notable absence of eligible girls. Cliff, who continued to aspire to Hollywood hipness, followed Billy around to the point that Murphy finally told him, "Cliff, you're colorful and you're interesting, but you're ninety percent exaggeration and ten percent lies." Which kind of took the wind out of Cliff's sails and gave the others something to chew on. When they finally arrived, Elvis enjoyed his first view of Hawaii; the Colonel's old pal, Lee Gordon, who still had hopes of getting Elvis to Australia, promoted the shows with his usual flamboyance; and Elvis even went down to the beach in shorts on the last night to sign autographs.

They were back in Hollywood by November 17, with nothing, really, to do. The Colonel didn't want him making any recordings — RCA had more than enough in the can — and the new movie deal with Twentieth Century Fox had fallen through when Hal Wallis refused to release Elvis from his contractual obligation to make another picture with Paramount first. There was no further touring planned, and he had no particular reason to be home, so he returned to Las Vegas, where he had spent a couple of weeks in October going out with showgirls and catching every act in town. On this visit he met a fresh-faced, twenty-one-year-old singer named Kitty Dolan, whom he formally "dated," as he had dated Dottie and June before, as well as the stripper Tempest Storm, to whom he announced, at an appropriate moment, "I'm as horny as a billy goat in a pepper patch. I'll race you to the bed."

It was a strangely unsettled time. The draft wasn't going to go away, his career seemed to be in a temporary state of limbo, even the tour — with the exception of his appearance at the Pan Pacific — had been without any real luster. There had been the usual riots, there had been the usual challenge of provoking the crowd into a frenzy, of teasing them until they were aroused past the point of turning back — *but there was nothing new*. It was all something he had done before, all just the playing out of a masquerade. For the first time in a long time he was no longer sure what was supposed to happen next. Perhaps the one real surprise had come in San Francisco when security guards came backstage to tell him that there was a rabbi outside insisting that he had to see Elvis. George scrutinized the scribbled note and realized to his astonishment that it was Rabbi Fruchter, his old rabbi from Temple Beth El Emeth, but he couldn't for the life of him figure out how Rabbi Fruchter would know George was there or what the connection with Elvis might be. "Elvis said, 'Oh, we used to live underneath him on Alabama Street, he was really nice to me, he'd loan me money, and sometimes he'd ask me to turn on the lights for him on Saturday.' So I went and got him, and Elvis hugs him and shakes hands with him, and at the press conference he introduces Rabbi Fruchter, and the reporters all look at this rabbi, and they just couldn't relate!"

Some guys from Tupelo showed up at the same performance, and Elvis recalled them, too, riding on a train with George sometime later. "We'd be going through some little country town, and he'd say, 'Shit, this reminds me of Tupelo.' He said, 'You remember when we were in San Francisco, George, and those guys came up to us, and all they wanted to talk about was Tupelo? They kept saying, "Elvis, remember back in Tupelo?" And all I was thinking was, "Fuck Tupelo. I want to forget about Tupelo." ' He wasn't putting down Tupelo. He just meant he was glad to get out. Tupelo was a little small town where there really wasn't much to do. Memphis was where everything had happened for him."

BACK HOME IN MEMPHIS the same overhanging miasma continued to prevail. In the midst of public celebration an unsettling sense of spiritual malaise would overtake him, which he might share, occasionally, with friends or reveal, almost despite himself, in public statements. After the Easter service at First Assembly, for example, which he had proudly attended with Yvonne Lime, he had sought out the Reverend Hamill. "He said, 'Pastor, I am the most miserable young man you have ever seen. I have got more money than I can ever spend. I have thousands of fans out there, and I have a lot of people who call themselves my friends, but I am miserable. I am not doing a lot of things that you taught me, and I am doing some things that you taught me not to do.' " To *Photoplay* magazine he announced, in what the magazine described as a state of dejection and what might more accurately be seen as a moment of near-desperation: "I never expected to be anybody important. Maybe I'm not now, but whatever I am, whatever I will become will be what God has chosen for me. Some people I know can't figure out how Elvis Presley happened. I don't blame them for wondering that. Sometimes I wonder myself. . . . But no matter what I do, I don't forget about God. I feel he's watching every move I make. And in a way it's good for me. I'll never feel comfortable taking a strong drink, and I'll never feel easy smoking a cigarette. I just don't think those things are right for me. . . . I just want to let a few people know that the way I live is by doing what I think God wants me to. I want someone to understand."

He visited Lansky's one night at 9:00 or 10:00, "and we had a big feast for him," said Guy Lansky. "I went down to the deli to pick up corn beef

and salami, we had a beautiful spread for him, and all he wanted was po-
tato salad. He reached over and got that quart of potato salad and said,
'That's all I'm going to eat.' And I said, 'How about a corn beef sandwich,
Elvis?' And he said, 'No, Mr. Lansky, this is all I want. Give the rest to
Lamar. He's my garbage disposal.' He got a big laugh out of that, but
Lamar didn't take it so pleasantly. There were still some customers in the
store, and Elvis said, 'Give them anything they want' — I mean, up to a
certain limit. I said, 'You're on, Elvis. Whatever they want.' Man, they
couldn't get over it, the customers — and of course it was mostly black
customers in Lansky's at that time — but for his entourage he didn't buy
them anything, he never bought them anything. I couldn't figure that one
out."

On December 6 he attended the WDIA Goodwill Revue once again.
His appearance didn't cause the commotion that it had the year before,
but he had his picture taken with Little Junior Parker (the originator of
"Mystery Train") and Bobby "Blue" Bland, and he was quoted in the
paper as saying that this music was "the real thing. . . . Right from the
heart." You couldn't beat it, he said, watching from the wings and smiling
and swaying to the music. "The audience shouted in time to the solid
rhythm," reported the paper. " 'Man,' grinned Elvis, 'what about that!' "

It was a strangely desultory Christmas. The tree was taken down out
of storage, Elvis distributed a considerable amount of money to local
charities as well as the United Fund and the March of Dimes, the Christmas album reached the number-one chart position even as it encountered
vicious criticism (from Irving Berlin, among others) for what was seen as
a desecration of the traditional Christmas spirit. The Colonel told him he
had two more movies definitely lined up upon the completion of the new
Hal Wallis production, a specially tailored adaptation of the Harold Robbins novel *A Stone for Danny Fisher*. The first of the outside projects was an
unnamed picture for Twentieth Century Fox, the other a Hank Williams
biopic for MGM — both, if he bothered to read the trades, at enormous
sums of money — but he doubted somehow that either was ever going to
get made.

About ten days before Christmas he started getting serious pitches
from the army, the navy, and the air force about what they could do for
him. They had suggestions for various kinds of deals — the navy proposed
an "Elvis Presley company" that could be specially trained, and the air

force offered a deal where he would merely tour recruiting centers around the country — but when he and the Colonel talked it over, he could see that the Colonel was right once again, it would merely serve to inflame public opinion and create a vicious backlash if he did not go in and receive the same treatment as every other citizen.

Then, on December 19, he got word informally from Milton Bowers, chairman of the draft board since 1943 and former president of the Memphis School Board, that his induction notice was ready and that he could simply stop by the draft board to pick it up. Bowers didn't want to put it in the mail, he said, for fear that the news would be leaked by someone who saw the letter addressed in an official Selective Service envelope.

Elvis dropped in at the Sun studio the next day, just after picking up his notice, and announced cheerfully, "Hey, I'm going in," but with George and Cliff and the other guys he was somewhat more revealing. "We were at Graceland," said George, "and I walked in. First thing he did was hand me the note. I said, 'What's this?' He said, 'Read it.' And I opened it up, and it said: 'GREETINGS.' I said, 'Oh no, Elvis.' He said, 'Yeah, I've been drafted.' He was devastated — just down, depressed. I said, 'Damn, what are we going to do?' He said, 'Man, I don't know.' He said, 'The Colonel says we might could get a deferment to make *King Creole,* but he says I probably got to go.' I said, 'Well, man, there's no war going on' — we were trying to make him feel better, me and Cliff and Arthur, and Gene. Cliff said, 'Wait a minute, Elvis, they'll never take you. You're too big! You're the biggest thing in show biz. They won't let them take you, the kids won't let them. Elvis, just think' — and Cliff's a real quick thinker, and he said, he immediately zeroed in, 'Elvis, you're paying the government ten million dollars a year in taxes, you know there's no war going on. It's all —' And so he kind of got Elvis' mind off it, but the last thing Elvis said when he got on the damn bus to go in the army was, 'Fuck Cliff Gleaves!' "

James Page, a *Press-Scimitar* reporter, caught up with him well after midnight as he was coming in from a night on the town. There were dozens of fans still at the gate maintaining a mournful vigil when Elvis roared up in his Continental. He professed himself relieved to have the situation finally resolved and expressed sincere feelings of gratitude for "what this country has given me. And now I'm ready to return a little. It's the only adult way to look at it."

"Would you like to go into Special Services?"

"I want to go where I can do the best job."

"What about your movie contracts?"

"Don't know — just don't know."

"How about a look at your draft notice?"

Elvis grinned sheepishly: "Man, I don't know what I did with it."

The search was on.

"Maybe in the kitchen," someone suggested. It wasn't.

"Last time I saw it, it was right there," said Elvis and pointed to a place in the front hall. No notice.

Finally: "Here's the envelope — the notice must be in my parents' bedroom."

One thing sure: There is a notice for Elvis and "I'll do what I have to — like any American boy."

He left for Nashville that same night to deliver his Christmas present to the Colonel. It was a little red Isetta sports car, and he loaded it onto a rented truck, which he drove, with Lamar and Cliff following in the Lincoln. They arrived at the Colonel's home in Madison early the next morning, but there was already a gang of reporters and photographers waiting. He and the Colonel posed for pictures in the car. "It is snug," observed Parker. "It is only a small, small way of showing my feelings for you," replied Elvis on the record. "Now isn't he a sweet kid?" Colonel said to the newspapermen, his eyes "dewing up." "He could have just sent something in the mail." In addition, Elvis answered questions about the draft (who knew, he said, he just might reenlist when his hitch was up) and even tried on an army surplus set of fatigues, which a photographer thoughtfully provided and in which he looked exceedingly uncomfortable. " 'I guess I'll be wearing this stuff for real, soon,' he said, looking ruefully down at the green twill." Whatever private feelings he had he kept to himself or reserved for the private conference that he and the Colonel had, as per custom, behind closed doors.

Gordon Stoker came out at the Colonel's direction to pick up the Jordanaires' four thousand dollars in Christmas bonuses, and Elvis asked if he'd be going to the Opry that night. "He told me, 'If I had some kind of clothes, I'd go with you guys. Well, I called Mallernee's down on Sixth — I happened to know the man who owned the store — and I told them, 'I'm going to bring Elvis Presley in there to get something to wear down to the Grand Ole Opry tonight, but if any of the salesmen or anyone makes anything over him, he'll walk right out in the middle of a fitting, so don't tell anyone he's coming.' Anyway, surprisingly, he picked out a tuxedo with a tux shirt, tux tie, even tux shoes. I was shocked. I thought he'd just buy a suit or a sports coat. But that's what he wore down to the Opry that night."

His draft situation was really bugging him, Stoker felt; he still couldn't understand why the Colonel hadn't fixed things better, but he didn't say much about it. At the Opry that night he just walked out onstage and waved and visited with old friends backstage. How were things going? asked T. Tommy Cutrer, who had promoted him in Shreveport and was announcing the Opry now. "He said, 'It's lonesome, T.' I said, 'How can you talk about that, with thousands of people . . .' He said, 'Well, I can't go get a hamburger, I can't go in some little greasy joint, I can't go water-skiing or shopping' — and he loved to go shopping. By this time he'd dyed his hair and had on makeup, which was strange to me. The only one of the Opry stars that would make up back then was Ferlin Husky, and that was to go onstage. So I said, 'Cat, why you got that shit on you?' He said, 'Well, that's what the movies want.' But he never changed a bit, he was always the same."

He had his picture taken with old friends and current Opry stars: he and the Colonel posed with the Duke of Paducah and Faron Young and booking agent Hubert Long, and he was pictured with his arm around an absolutely thrilled-looking Brenda Lee (who at thirteen looked no older than ten), with Johnny Cash, Ray Price, Hawkshaw Hawkins, the Wilburn Brothers, even Hank Snow, who seemed to hold no grudge against his onetime protégé even if his feelings toward his former partner were less than mixed. Jimmie Rodgers Snow, too, came by with his fifteen-year-old fiancée to say hello, "and he asked me what I was doing. I said, 'Nothing special, why?' And he said, 'Why don't you come over to Memphis around the first, we'll have some fun.' And I said, 'Fine.'" Then he changed back into the clothes he had worn on the trip over and, according to Gordon Stoker, threw his new tux into a barrel full of stage ropes before setting off on the 230-mile drive back to Memphis.

By Monday morning the draft board had received a letter from Paramount studio head Y. Frank Freeman requesting a sixty-day deferment for Elvis on the basis of financial hardship: the studio had already spent between $300,000 and $350,000 in preproduction costs for King Creole (formerly *Sing, You Sinners*) and stood to lose that amount or more if Elvis Presley were not permitted to film it. That was all very well, declared draft board chairman Milton Bowers, the board might very well look favorably upon such a request, but the request had to come from the inductee. On Tuesday, December 24, Elvis wrote to the draft board, explaining that as far as he was concerned he was ready to enter the army immediately, but he was requesting the deferment for Paramount "so these folks will not lose so much money, with all they have done so far." He concluded by wishing the three board members a merry Christmas. Three days later the request was granted, which the Colonel called "very kind," adding, "I know of nothing that would prevent his induction when his deferment is up. And I don't think Elvis would consider making another request, because I know how he feels personally about it." "I'm glad for the studio's sake," Elvis said. "I'm glad they were nice enough to let me make this picture because I think it will be the best one I've made."

Jimmie Rodgers Snow arrived on the afternoon of New Year's Day, and Lamar picked him up at the airport. Snow had been undergoing something of a spiritual crisis of late, brought on by his recognition of an increasing dependence on pills and alcohol, but he and Elvis just picked up where they had left off a year and a half before. "When I first arrived there was somebody at the door getting his signature on a special delivery. He just tossed it on the couch, didn't even open it until much later when he said, 'Oh yeah, my gold record.'

"He introduced me to all his friends, and we ran around all night and slept all day. When we would come downstairs probably at two or three in the afternoon, his mother would always be there, sitting in the kitchen drinking a beer. He'd go up and kiss her, and we'd go down and shoot pool or sing at the piano, talk about what we were going to do that night, which was either go see his movie, *Jailhouse Rock,* at the theater with a bunch of girls or go roller-skating, things like that. When we went to the movies, he rented the whole theater, and he'd sit beside me and say, 'What did you think of me in that scene? How'd I do? Was I flat on that note? Did I hold it too long?' He was just the same. He used to love for me to imitate Winston Churchill, put a cigar in my mouth and sound just like Churchill — he'd want me to do that for everybody, and he loved it every time. It was nothing for him to be driving down the street at night and all of a sudden put his brakes on, open the car door up, jump out, make a face back at the cars behind him, and get back in and drive off and laugh.

"Sometimes he'd get serious and sit down at that white piano, and we'd sing gospel songs. And, of course, I'd been a Christian in 1950, '51, I didn't stay with it very long but I was being tugged on at that time by God to go into the ministry, get married and give up my career. So we'd get serious, which I didn't really want to because I was fighting it then, but we'd talk about the Lord and he would voice his feelings, and then we would get off of it and go into fun things."

Cliff and Lamar got into a fight that week over a badminton game, and Lamar finally egged Cliff to the point that Cliff hit him over the head with his racket. Mr. Presley was pissed off, and Mrs. Presley got so upset that Elvis had to fire the two of them. He apologized as they were packing, trying to sort out what was theirs and what was his ("Oh, just keep it," he said of every item), and he told them he was sure that once things had cooled down he could hire them back. It was just that his mama was so nervous with everything that was going on that she couldn't have that kind of uproar around the house. "She just couldn't cope with [the idea of] him being gone," her sister Lillian said. Vernon was tight-lipped about it, but Gladys' mood was increasingly somber, and her eyes were limpid pools of sadness.

He asked George to accompany him once again to California, but George had just started a new job deejaying at WHUY out in Millington, so he couldn't go. He gave Jimmy Snow the script for *King Creole*, "because he wanted to know if I'd be interested in going out to California with him and maybe do a part in the film. And it was in the bedroom upstairs as I was reading the script that I made my decision, which I told him about the next day. I told him I really appreciated the opportunity. It was something I had wanted to do all my life. 'But,' I said, 'strange as it may seem, I think I'm going to go back and quit the business and go into the ministry.' Which he thought was wonderful, he was very complimentary and wished me a lot of luck and anything he could do, just let him know. So that's what I did."

He celebrated his twenty-third birthday on January 8 with a party at home and asked Alan Fortas if he would accompany Gene and him to California. "I was working for my father in the junk business, and Elvis asked me if I thought I could get off for a little while. I said, 'You know how that is, Elvis. You work for your father, you can do what you want to.' He said, 'Good, we leave for California in two days.'" At the last minute he took Cliff back, but Lamar remained in the doghouse for the time being, so when they embarked on January 10 it was just Gene, Cliff, and Alan, plus the Colonel, "security chief" Bitsy Mott, Freddy Bienstock, and Tom Diskin. There were huge crowds at every stop, alerted, Alan felt sure, by an intentional leak from the Colonel's organization. "That was the first time I'd been around the Colonel, and I thought, 'Man, this guy is tough.' He was just — he didn't trust anybody. Didn't like anybody. At least that was the impression he gave. You didn't know if he was serious or kidding — of course he was just looking out for one person: Elvis. He just didn't want people taking advantage."

They arrived in California on January 13 and reported immediately to the studio, with soundtrack recording scheduled to begin at Radio Recorders two days later. This time there was no question of where they were going to record. Hal Wallis was finally convinced that Elvis knew what he was doing, and Jerry Leiber and Mike Stoller, at Elvis' request, were in charge. Leiber and Stoller had been hired by RCA the previous fall as perhaps the first independent a&r men in the business (while they were on salary with RCA, they also continued to maintain a profitable relationship with Atlantic, producing the Coasters, along with numerous other side ventures). Elvis was clearly their primary responsibility at the label, and it had been suggested that they would have a relatively free hand, but so far it hadn't worked out the way they had hoped.

Jerry was living in New York at this point and going out with former MGM board chairman Nick Schenck's daughter, Marty Page, whose best friend was divorced from the well-known agent Charlie Feldman. "Charlie was very much connected to people like Moss Hart and Cole Porter, and he took a shine to me and was going to try to groom us as Broadway writers. He liked what we did, but he thought it was kind of kid stuff and now we were ready for the big time, which was Broadway and film. He said to me, 'You know what would be marvelous? I have a property that would make an incredible musical motion picture. It's called *A Walk on the Wild Side* [the celebrated novel by Nelson Algren], and it would be great for Elvis Presley.' He said, 'I'm sure I can get Elia Kazan to direct, and I think we might get Budd Schulberg to write the screenplay, and you two guys would write the book.' He said, 'It's perfect. He's handsome, he's innocent, and he's a victim.'

"I took the idea to the Aberbachs, who were the closest to Colonel Parker. They watched me in complete silence as I spun this story for about twenty minutes and made the pitch, and finally Jean said in his

Viennese accent, 'If you ever try to interfere with the business or artistic workings of the process known as Elvis Presley, if you ever start thinking in this direction again, you will never work for us again.'

"It wasn't long after that, to be very frank, that we both got bored, because we knew there were no possibilities left. It was just going to be another one like the last one, every movie the same. I mean, you had three ballads, one medium-tempo, one up-tempo, and one break blues boogie, usually for a production number. It was too fucking boring. I told Stoller, 'If I have to write another song like "King Creole," I'll cut my fucking throat — maybe theirs first.' We talked about — you know, maybe we're burning up a license to print money. I said, 'You know what? Burn it up.' 'Cause we could have made fucking history, and those assholes only wanted to make another nickel the same way."

The sessions proceeded without incident. Leiber and Stoller contributed three songs, plus a fourth that wasn't used, and for the first time experienced session players were employed to create a semiauthentic Dixieland sound. Perhaps the two most interesting songs were "Crawfish," a duet with rhythm and blues singer Kitty White, which was written by songwriters Ben Weisman and Fred Wise as a street vendor's cry, and Leiber and Stoller's "Trouble," a Muddy Waters–styled blues intended somewhat tongue in cheek but delivered by Elvis with untempered ferocity. In Jerry Leiber's view, " 'Trouble' was the same kind of song as 'Black Denim Trousers.' They're both send-ups, and the only people who are going to take them seriously are Hell's Angels and Elvis Presley. I suppose there was a bit of contempt on our part. You know, when the guy sang, Ba boom ba ba boom, 'If you're looking for trouble,' you know, 'just come looking for me' — there's something laughable there. I mean, if you get Memphis Slim or John Lee Hooker singing it, it sounds right, but Elvis did not sound right to us. But I would be tolerant. Just like [rhythm and blues bandleader-arranger] Maxwell Davis was tolerant of me when I first walked in, this little white kid with a twelve-bar blues, and he said, 'That's nice.' He said, 'I think that's nice.' He didn't say, 'That's full of shit, you don't know what you're doing.' He said, 'That's nice.' It's a sort of tolerant attitude with a little bit of tongue in cheek. So in the early days that's where we were coming from. It sounded sort of comical to us, but strangely enough to the mass market it wasn't. It was somewhat generational and somewhat cultural, but they bought it."

They wound up the session in two days. In reality, the score was independent of the picture; the character that Elvis played was a singer, it was true, but the story was up-from-poverty, and the protagonist might better have remained the boxer that he was in the novel in terms of the dramatic impact of the story.

Elvis had read the book in preparation for making the film. He was determined to do his very best, because, he told Alan Fortas, this could be it for him. He got together with his new friend Kitty Dolan to run lines with him and spoke with concern of what his absence from the scene for two years might mean. The director, Michael Curtiz, was a sixty-nine-year-old Hungarian émigré who had been directing films since 1919 and had made such notable pictures as *Casablanca*, *Mildred Pierce*, and *Young Man with a Horn*. Elvis was a little taken aback at first when Curtiz told him he would have to cut his sideburns and lose fifteen pounds for the role, and he had a great deal of trouble initially understanding Curtiz's accent. "You just didn't have a lot of fooling around with Curtiz — I mean, he would embarrass the hell out of you," said Jan Shepard, who played Elvis' sister in the movie. "But no matter what Curtiz would ask of Elvis, he would say, 'Okay, you're the boss.' Curtiz said he thought Elvis was going to be a very conceited boy, but when he started working with him, he said, 'No, this is a lovely boy, and he's going to be a wonderful actor.'

"The first time I met Elvis was when we went to the doctor's office for the insurance. I was sitting there, and he walked in with his little group from Memphis, and then we worked together alone for about a week, because we did the opening of the show. He was just really young, care-free — it was like letting a kid loose in a candy store, he was just a lot of fun and buoyant, not guarded at all. There was a five-and-dime store on our set, and in the morning I would find earrings and little bracelets, little five-and-dime stuff on my dressing room table. I used to call him the last of the big-time spenders!

"He was very concentrated, very focused on playing Danny. For a kid coming in and just beginning his career he had a great sense of timing; there was great honesty in his acting. He was a very good listener, and he just became that young boy, he became Danny in the show. Just like in his music, he really got involved in his acting, you'd look in his eyes and, boy, they were really going."

With Walter Matthau as the heavy, Dolores Hart once again as the fresh-faced ingenue, Carolyn Jones as the offbeat vamp, and Dean Jagger as the weak, ineffectual father (a stock-in-trade for every teen picture since *Rebel Without a Cause*), the cast that Wallis had assembled was a uniformly good one, and there was a uniformly positive spirit on the set. "I almost hesitate, I creep up to the sentence," Walter Matthau told a BBC interviewer, "he was an instinctive actor. Because that almost is a derogation of his talents. That's saying, 'Well, you know, he's just a dumb animal who does it well by instinct.' No, he was quite bright, too. He was very intelligent. Also, he was intelligent enough to understand what a character was and how to play the character simply by being himself *through* the means of the story. Michael Curtiz used to call him Elvy, and he'd call me Valty. He'd say, 'Now Elvy and Valty, come here, now, Valty, this is not Academy Award scene. Don't act so much. You are high-price actor. Make believe you are low-price actor. Let Elvy act.' But Elvy didn't *over*act. He was not a punk. He was very elegant, sedate . . . refined and sophisticated."

In Carolyn Jones' observation "he was always asking a lot of questions. God, he was young! I didn't think anybody could be *that* young! He was always talking about his folks and about the house he'd just bought them." Jones suggested that in order to really learn his craft he should consider taking acting lessons, and the guys picked up one of her lines in the film, "Take a day out of your life and love me," as a kind of sardonic commentary, to be trotted out on any number of occasions, in a wide variety of social settings.

One Sunday when he was feeling blue, he told Jan, he spent most of the day just talking to his mother on the phone, and he was both saddened and amused as he and the guys retold the story over and over again of how Dewey had been fired from his new midnight television show on the eve of their departure from California. The show had commanded a number-one rating in its afternoon slot, until it had been forced off the air to make room for Dick Clark's network-syndicated *American Bandstand*. It was in the fourth night of its present incarnation when Harry Fritzius, a noted young abstract painter who appeared in an ape suit on the air, explicitly fondled a life-size cutout of Jayne Mansfield in an altogether human way. "He embarrassed the station, and he embarrassed me personally," said station manager Bill Grumbles. Dewey would continue on the air with a Saturday-evening show and his nightly radio spot, but his sidekick Harry Fritzius was finished, "probably the best thing that ever happened to me," declared Fritzius. "I'm twenty-five, and it's time I found something to do with my life."

Crazy old Dewey, the guys all said, and Elvis was tempted to join them. He thought about giving Dewey a call, but he knew the complications that could cause, and he wasn't sure that he wanted to deal with them now, when everything seemed to be spinning out of control. And yet, for all of his worries, he had probably never felt more relaxed or at home on a set. He saw Pat Boone on the Paramount lot one day and greeted him smilingly with an impromptu rendition of "April Love"; on the soundstage he serenaded cast and crew alike; and he even got to meet Marlon Brando, after a fashion. He and Jan Shepard were in the commissary. "Sophia Loren and Carlo Ponti were sitting at a table next to us, and I remember Cornel Wilde came over and asked for an autograph for his daughter. Elvis said, 'Can you believe that Cornel Wilde wanted my autograph?' He was stunned by it. Then I said, 'Elvis, did you know Marlon Brando is sitting right behind you?' He had his back to him, and he almost started shaking, and I said, 'You know, he keeps looking over.' He was just like, you know, 'I couldn't, oh I couldn't, you know, it's Marlon Brando' — like that. So I said, 'Well, when we get up, all you have to do is push your chair back and you're going to go right into him.' So as we got up to go, he bumped into Brando, and Brando got up, of course, and then they shook hands, and when we went out he said, 'Oh my God, I shook hands with Marlon Brando!' "

February 1 was the only day open for RCA recording, and with his induction date rapidly approaching, Steve Sholes was desperate to get a final studio session in. Elvis had rehearsed two numbers for the upcoming date at a January 23 soundtrack session, but he was insistent that Leiber and Stoller, who had returned to New York after the initial session the previous week, be there. Dutifully, the Colonel had Tom Diskin inform Sholes that their presence was required — Elvis by now considered them a kind of "good-luck charm." Sholes wrote, telegrammed, and attempted to call, but all to no avail, because Stoller was unable to locate his partner, who was lying incommunicado in the emergency ward of a Harlem hospital with pneumonia. "Nobody knew where I was, I didn't know where I was for a couple of days. When I came to my senses, I started calling around. I called Mike, and I got out of the hospital, and when I got home there was a stack of telegrams jammed under my door, and they were all about the same thing: 'You must come to L.A. immediately.'

"I called the Aberbachs, and I got Julian on the phone. He said, 'You must come to California immediately. Presley is ready to record, and he will not go in the studio without you.' I said, 'I don't think I can come immediately, but I'll see.' So I called my doctor, and he told me absolutely not to go anywhere for two weeks, and I called them back and they started to get real nasty. Finally, Parker got on the phone and said, 'Boy, you better get your ass out here or else.' He said, 'By the way, did you get my contract for the new projects?' I said, 'No, it might have slipped by. I opened up about eight telegrams, and they were all the same, so I figured the rest weren't any different.' He said, 'You better open up the rest.'

"So I opened them up, and there was in fact another piece of mail from Colonel Parker's office, and it said, 'Enclosed you'll find the contract. Please execute and return.' And I looked at the piece of paper, and it had nothing on either side, but it had a line at the bottom with a space for my signature. And on the right-hand side was a line for Tom Parker that was signed by him. So I got on the phone and said, 'There must be some kind of mistake, Tom. There's just a blank piece of paper here with a place for my name.' He said, 'There's no mistake, boy, just sign it and return it.' I said, 'There's nothing on the paper.' He said, 'Don't worry, we'll fill it in later.'

"We never worked with him again. That was it. We never talked to each other again."

The session was a disaster. They spent eight hours in the studio and got two barely usable tracks. Elvis was a wreck — it was as if the magic had worn off, and for the first time the Colonel was embarrassed both for his boy and for the waste of RCA's (and Elvis' and his own) time and money. Two weeks later Elvis wanted to go back into the studio to repair the damage, and there was some talk among all the parties about arranging another session, but that would have meant Colonel acknowledging some degree of failure to Steve Sholes, and he was not prepared to do that. So in the end Sholes had to make do with what he had. For the Colonel the whole experience underlined one fundamental point: never let *anyone*, let alone a songwriter, get in the middle of your business. In future, he stressed emphatically to his brother-in-law, Bitsy Mott, keep those people away from Elvis, watch very carefully *anyone* who got anywhere near him, and, for God's sake, keep them away from the suite.

Toward the end of February, just before most of the cast and crew were scheduled to depart for New Orleans for a week of location shoots, Dolores Hart staged a surprise birthday party for Jan Shepard at her home. Although Elvis was invited, no one expected him to show up, and Jan was surprised enough just to discover most of her fellow cast members, along with young Paramount contract players like Ty Hardin and Edith Head's assistant, Pat Richards. "But I was really shocked when Elvis walked in, and he had this big stuffed tiger cat on his shoulders. We named it 'Danny Boy,' because he always used to sing that song on the set. The other thing was, I had all these little kids in the neighborhood who wanted pictures of him, and we had this running gag, where I kept saying, 'Elvis, bring some pictures in for my birthday.' So his *second* gift to me was a movie camera with a light bar and, I think, three rolls of film, and he said, 'Go ahead, take your pictures now.' Which I did, even though I'd never used a movie camera before!

"It was wonderful. Everyone was cooking and helping out in the kitchen, and we all had dinner, and Ty Hardin, who had studied to be an engineer, made a cake that looked like a theater, with a marquee and everything. Then after dinner we sat in the living room, and Elvis sat down at the piano and Ty had brought his guitar and started playing, and then Elvis took the guitar and Dolores had her clarinet, and Dolores' mother was dressed up like Topsy and was doing a number from Topsy. It was kind of a free-for-all, just, you know, just a very relaxing time, and he stayed till the end, which was really amazing, but there was nobody there that was going to interfere with him. It was really nice."

Red West showed up the next week on a two-week leave from the Marines. He had stopped by Graceland to pay his respects, and Mrs. Presley called Elvis on the phone, and Elvis invited him to fly out the next day. "When I got up to say goodbye," Red wrote in *Elvis: What Happened?*, "she just sort of called me back, and I heard her say what she had said a hundred times: 'Bob, look after my boy.' " Red arrived in Hollywood, "a crew-cut hick sonofabitch in a Marine uniform on a Paramount movie set," they had their first extended reunion in more than a year, and Elvis asked him if he wanted to go to New Orleans with the troupe two days later.

While most of the film company flew, Elvis and his friends rode the train. Red, Cliff, Gene, and Alan all accompanied him, along with Carolyn, her husband, Aaron Spelling, and Nick Adams, whom Red met for the first time and who amused everyone with his impressions on the long trip. In New Orleans, the Colonel, who had argued bitterly against a location shoot for security reasons, was, not surprisingly, proved right. "Hal Wallis loved locations," said Alan Fortas, whose opinion of the Colonel was considerably higher than it had been at the start. "He said, 'I had

Dean Martin and Jerry Lewis in their prime. I had this star and that star . . .' Colonel said, 'I don't care who you had, Wallis, you never had Elvis Presley.' "

Cliff was given a line in the picture ("See you next week, baby," he said to a prostitute while dressed up in a sailor's uniform), and the guys got a big kick out of kidding Alan that he would soon be making his movie debut as well. They had him walking around in makeup all day with Kleenex stuck into the collar of his shirt, convinced that his scene would be coming up any minute. Meanwhile, Cliff met a kid whose father owned a clothing store and conned him out of blazers for the whole gang. According to George, who joined the group in New Orleans, "Cliff said we worked for Elvis, and it would be real sharp if all of Elvis' guys wore blazers, uniform-style. The guy said, 'Yeah?' Cliff said, 'Man, I'll tell you what, what do those blazers sell for?' The guy says, 'About fifty dollars apiece.' Cliff said, 'There are five guys that work for Elvis, there's Elvis and Colonel Parker. We need seven blazers, but we ain't gonna pay for them. Here's what we are going to do for you. You give us the jackets, and you can advertise that Elvis' traveling companions and Elvis Presley are wearing clothes from your clothing store.'

"We said, 'Cliff, Colonel Parker is going to have a fit, Elvis has never endorsed anything.' Cliff said, 'Don't worry about it,' and next day, man, everyone has a brand-new blazer, and the guy even has one for Colonel Parker. So Cliff tells him, 'There's Colonel Parker, you just go over there and say, "Colonel Parker, I'm so-and-so, and I'd like to present you with this blazer as a gift." ' Well, he goes over and presents the blazer, and Colonel immediately picks up something is wrong, and he comes over and says, 'Cliff, what the hell are you doing? You know Elvis doesn't endorse anything. He never has, and we don't intend to start now.' And Cliff says, 'Wait a minute, Colonel, look, Elvis wanted us to have these blue blazers, and Elvis wanted one, so if Elvis went down and bought one, Colonel, and he bought one for all of the guys, the guy is going to say the same thing anyway, so we might as well just get them for free.' The Colonel said, 'That makes sense,' and he just kind of shook his head and walked away. But we all got blue blazers."

They took the train back to Hollywood, and Hal Wallis threw a breakup party at the studio commissary. He wasn't worried about the army, Elvis told columnist Vernon Scott, who was present. It couldn't be any worse than the merry-go-round he'd been on for the past two years, and he certainly knew what hard work was — he'd been working since he was fourteen. "Had to. Got a job at Loew's State Theatre in Memphis as an usher. They fired me for fighting in the lobby. . . . I've worked in factories, drove a truck, cut grass for a living, and did a hitch in a defense plant. I'll do whatever they tell me, and I won't be asking no special favors." It was going to be harder on his folks, he said, than it would be on him.

Just to get everyone in the spirit of his usual "pull-out-all-stops" promotion campaign, the Colonel had a big bunch of balloons made up with "King Creole" written on them, and he led Trude Forsher, the William Morris agents, and everyone else he could commandeer around the lot carrying the balloons before marching into the commissary and releasing them to the ceiling. Elvis posed politely for pictures, showed off the prop Civil War blunderbuss that he had been given as a gift, and ate a little bit of cake decorated with the figure of an army private peeling potatoes.

Then he was off to Memphis, with less than two weeks until his formal induction. He was so impatient to get home that, once again, he got off the train, this time renting a fleet of Cadillacs in Dallas. He was met by a *Commercial Appeal* reporter when he arrived at Graceland at 6:30 on Friday night, March 14. The questions were all about his new movie and the army. How did his parents feel about his going in? "Well, my mother hates to see her son go in service," he said candidly, but added: "My mother is no different from millions of other mothers who hated to see their sons go, though." As far as the movie went, he had reason to be proud. "It was quite a challenge for me because it was written for a more experienced actor," he said. It was, he felt without false modesty, his best performance to date, one in which he had acquitted himself well in truly distinguished company. But what about his popularity? asked the reporter. Did he think it would slip while he was in the army? "That's the sixty-four-dollar question," replied Elvis plaintively. "I wish I knew."

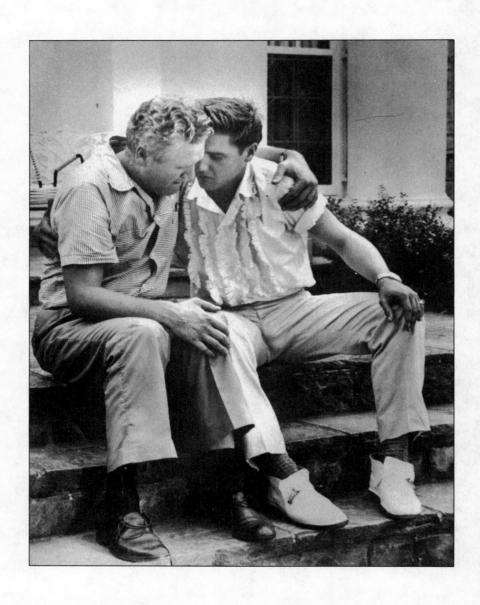

ON THE STEPS OF GRACELAND, AUGUST 14, 1958. (JAMES REID)

"PRECIOUS MEMORIES"

THE TEN DAYS that he had left before going in were a blur of
activity. On Monday he met Dewey down at Poplar Tunes,
and a lot of misunderstandings, reported Bob Johnson, seemed
to just fall away. Elvis bought Dean Martin's "Return to Me,"
Nat King Cole's "Looking Back," Pat Boone's "Too Soon to Know," Jo
Stafford's "Sweet Little Darling," Don Gibson's "I Can't Stop Loving
You," and "Maybe" by the Chantels. He got a haircut at Jim's Barber
Shop, his second in less than a month, and declared that he liked the new
crew cut style so much he intended to get it cut even shorter before induction.

On Wednesday he looked at cars with Anita, who was now customarily described in the national press as both a "Hollywood starlet"
and a "frequent companion," but it was also reported in the papers that
he was entertaining a parade of women, "no fewer than twelve beautiful
girls," by one count. "I screwed everything in sight," he told a friend
years later in an uncharacteristic, and perhaps inaccurate, display of sexual
bravura, while to reporters he simply commented, "I'd be crazy to get
married now. I like to play the field."

Whoever his companion for the evening, every night he would go in a
group to the movies, to the skating rink after it was closed, back to Graceland after all other sources for fun were exhausted, in what seemed like an
almost desperate attempt to pack in every last element of civilian experience, a vain effort to stave off the inevitable moment by hiding himself in
the crowd.

Over the course of the week he let the last of the boys go, wrote Bob
Johnson, about to be without their company for the first time in more
than two years. He had "fed them, clothed them, paid them in return for
simple duties, but mostly their job was just to keep him company in a
rather extraordinary world where new friends could have no understanding of a world he knew." He said good-bye to Scotty and Bill: "It was just

459

'So long, see you when I get out,' " said Scotty, who detected little nervousness. "We were just like two mules turned out to pasture." Over the weekend he gave Anita a 1956 Ford. She felt he was dreading the army, "because it was something unknown to him, he didn't know what to expect, but it was something that he had to do — he could have gotten out of it, but he wanted no part of that." He told her that he had to do what was expected of him and reassured his mother that he was going to be all right. "I can make it," he said. "I can do this." To Barbara Pittman, who had known him from childhood, he was somewhat more unbuttoned. "He was very upset about it. He kept saying, 'Why me, when I can stay here and make so much more money? My taxes would be more important than sticking me in the service.' He was crying. He was hurt. He couldn't understand why he had to go." Judy Spreckels, who described herself as "like a sister" ("Girls come and go," she said, "but sisters stay forever"), flew in from the Coast to provide support.

On his last night of freedom he was up all night with his friends. He and Anita and some of the boys went to the drive-in to see Tommy Sands in *Sing, Boy, Sing,* the story of the rise and fall of a rock 'n' roll star told in somewhat harder-hitting terms than any of Elvis' movies. Sands, just twenty but a recording artist from the age of fourteen, and a longtime protégé of Colonel Parker's, had gotten the role, originally written for Elvis, only through the intercession of the Colonel. "We pulled in to the drive-in in the Cadillac limousine," said George Klein, "and Nick Adams was playing a combination of all of Elvis' sidekicks in the movie — he played me and Gene and Cliff and Arthur, all rolled into one. It was kind of cold, and we all wanted to stay up with him until the last minute, you know, and keep his mind occupied so he wouldn't have to think about leaving the next day. And I think he appreciated that, but we got quite a kick not so much out of Tommy Sands as out of Nick Adams playing all the other guys." Afterward they went to the skating rink for the eighth night in a row, and when it finally came time to leave, "he got in and out of the panel truck three times," the owners told writer Vince Staten. "He didn't want to go."

He hadn't eaten or slept when dawn came up. "Overnight," he said, "it was all gone. It was like a dream."

* * *

H E SHOWED UP at the draft board in the M&M Building at 198 South Main at 6:35 the next morning and parked just south of the Malco Theatre. He was accompanied by several cars full of friends and relatives and was greeted by a couple of dozen photographers and reporters, including representatives of the British press. It was raining lightly, and he was half an hour early. He was wearing dark blue trousers, his loud gray-and-white-checked sports jacket, a striped shirt, and pink and black socks, and he was carrying a pigskin shaving kit. Gladys looked as if she were about to cry, while Vernon gripped her hand tightly. Lamar gave everybody a laugh by pretending that he wanted to enlist, too, but at 270 pounds there was little likelihood that he would be taken. Anita looked prettily composed while Judy remained in the background and the Colonel hovered on the edge of the proceedings, making sure that everything went off without a hitch. Among the recruits was an old friend from Lauderdale Courts, Farley Guy, who told reporters it was "the same old Elvis." "If I seem nervous," said Elvis, "it's because I am," adding that he was looking forward to the army "as a great experience. The army can do anything it wants with me. Millions of other guys have been drafted, and I don't want to be different from anyone else." At 7:14 the thirteen inductees left the draft board in an olive drab army bus. They were bound for the Kennedy Veterans Hospital several miles away, where they would be examined and processed. The army of newsmen, friends, fans, and relatives all followed, but not before Anita got special permission from Recruiting Sergeant Walter Alden to visit Elvis at the induction station that afternoon in order to say a special good-bye.

At Kennedy he was examined, weighed, and pronounced fit, all under the scrutiny of reporters' pencils and pads, microphones, and cameras. The picture of him in *Life* magazine the following week revealed a well-nourished white male, still showing some evidence of baby fat, standing on the scale in his underpants with his eyes on either side of the height-measuring extender. His gaze is distracted, his mouth is downcast, and you could imagine either that he was momentarily lost in thought or frozen in fear. To the *Life* reporter he simply said, "Heaven knows I want to live up to what people expect of me." In conversations with other photographers and newsmen "Elvis recalled that in the days before he became famous, he pawned his old guitar for $3 'five or six times.' Also, he remember[ed] that in 1952 he sold a pint of his blood to Baptist Hospital for $10. Elvis said his has always been a happy family and is happy today, but that money brings a lot of headaches. . . .''

The army provided a box lunch of a ham sandwich, a roast beef sandwich, a piece of apple pie, an apple, and a container of milk, which Elvis wolfed down, explaining that he hadn't eaten since the previous night. ''Man, I was hungry,'' he said. Then he lay down on a rec room couch and took a nap for half an hour. More friends and relatives continued to show up, and a telegram from Governor Frank Clement arrived, declaring that ''you have shown that you are an American citizen first, a Tennessee Volunteer, and a young man willing to serve his country when called upon to do so.''

Outside, the Colonel was marching around handing out more balloons that advertised *King Creole,* while the crowd grew larger and larger and the Presleys looked increasingly stricken. The army brass were growing nervous that they would not fulfill the quota of twenty (including volunteers as well as draftees) necessary to requisition a bus and get out of Memphis *today.* Finally a draftee named Donald Rex Mansfield, who had just arrived on the bus from Dresden, Tennessee, and was not slated to go in until the following day, was rushed through processing, and Private Elvis Presley, serial number 53 310 761, was put in charge of the 150-mile bus trip to Fort Chaffee. He rapidly embraced his mother, who was virtually inconsolable by now, and his father, who was openly weeping. ''Good-bye, baby,'' he said to Anita as the bus was about to pull out. ''Good-bye, you long black sonofabitch,'' he said, referring to his black Cadillac limousine standing at the curb. The other recruits laughed nervously. That, reported Rex Mansfield, broke the ice. After that he was, at least nominally, ''one of the boys.''

A CARAVAN OF CARS containing newsmen and fans followed the army bus out of Memphis, and when it made its regular scheduled stop just across the Mississippi at the Coffee Cup restaurant in West Memphis, there was a crowd of close to two hundred already assembled, and the bus driver had to bring sandwiches and drinks back to the bus. At Fort Chaffee, the information officer, Captain Arlie Metheny, a native Arkansan and twenty-year vet, had been anticipating the arrival since January, but nothing in his previous experience (not even his stint as information officer during the Little Rock integration crisis) could have fully prepared him for the mob scene that erupted when the bus finally pulled in at 11:15 that night. More than a hundred civilian fans, forty or fifty newsmen, and another two hundred dependents of military personnel descended on the hapless new recruit, with the Colonel leading the greeting committee. The newsmen followed Elvis into a reception room for roll call and photographed him making his bed over and over again for the cameras, though when a photographer hid in the barracks to get a shot of a sleeping Private Presley, that was too much for even the army's tolerance, and Captain Metheny had the photographer thrown out. Throughout it all Elvis bore up with extraordinary patience, presenting a bright, cheerful exterior, offering up quips and self-deprecating statements, entertaining all requests without demurral, refusing only to sign autographs while he was "in ranks."

He estimated that he slept no more than three hours and was up well before 5:30 reveille the next morning, dressing and shaving while the others were just waking up. The Colonel and twenty photographers joined him for breakfast at 6:00 ("It was good, but I was so hungry I'd eat anything this morning," he was reported as saying), and then he was scheduled for five hours of aptitude tests, a two-hour postlunch lecture on a private's rights and privileges, a brief classification interview, the issuance of seven dollars in partial pay (What are you going to do with all that money? reporters shouted. "Start a loan company," Elvis replied good-humoredly), and, finally, the bestowal of the standard-issue GI haircut. There were fifty-five reporters and photographers standing around waiting to record this historic moment. "Hair today, gone tomorrow," said Elvis, holding some of the hair in his hand and blowing it away for photographers, but he was flustered enough that he forgot to pay the barber the sixty-five-cent fee and, to his embarrassment, had to be called back. He spotted a phone booth and went off to telephone his mother. When reporters sprinted after him, Colonel Parker blocked their way. "I think a boy's entitled to talk to his mother alone," said the Colonel.

On Wednesday he was issued his uniform, and the Colonel, clowning for the cameras, tried to get him to try on a western string tie with it. "No, sir. If I wore a string tie in here, I'd have to take the punishment, not you," Elvis replied, as the Colonel declared to the photographers, "I wish you boys would stop taking pictures of yourselves." That afternoon there was an announcement (surprising only because it came sooner than expected) that Elvis Presley would be assigned to the Second Armored Division — General George Patton's famous ''Hell on Wheels'' outfit — at Fort Hood, just outside Killeen, Texas, for basic training and advanced tank instruction. He had been a good soldier so far, announced post commander General Ralph R. Mace; ''at least in my opinion, he has conducted himself in a marvelous manner.'' And Hy Gardner wrote a column in the form of a letter to Elvis' fellow soldiers, proclaiming Elvis a credit to his country:

> Where else could a nobody become a somebody so quickly, and in what other nation in the world would such a rich and famous man serve alongside you other draftees without trying to use influence to buy his way out? In my book this is American democracy at its best — the blessed way of life for whose protection you and Elvis have been called upon to contribute eighteen to twenty-four months of your young lives. . . . I hope you go along with my sentiments.

S IX OF THE THIRTEEN original Memphis draftees were assigned to Fort Hood, including Rex Mansfield and William Norvell, whom Elvis immediately dubbed ''Nervous'' Norvell. After being chased for more than two hundred miles by a convoy of devoted fans (''I'd hate to see anyone get hurt,'' said Elvis worriedly. ''Maybe if I wave . . .''), the chartered Greyhound bypassed the usual stops in Dallas and Waxahachie, where hundreds of people had already gathered, finally stopping for lunch in Hillsboro, Texas, at 1:30. Captain J. F. Dowling assigned two of his largest men to sit on either side of Elvis: ''I think we must have set some kind of record. We went twenty-five minutes before anyone recognized him.'' When they finally did, there was a small riot, and it took at least another twenty-five minutes before they could make their way out of the restaurant. ''Elvis was very nice about the whole thing,'' said Captain Dowling. ''Some of the men ordered meals that exceeded the allowance on the meal ticket, but Elvis said he'd pick up the check for the difference. And before we got him on the bus, he managed to buy cigarettes and candy, which he passed out to the boys. As we left Hillsboro, the girls were fighting over who would keep the chair that Elvis had sat in.''

At Fort Hood things were under substantially more control from the start. The information officer, Lieutenant Colonel Marjorie Schulten, had already made the determination, before the bus arrived, that she was going to take a different approach than the one that had been tried at Fort Chaffee. "He was due in on [March] twenty-eighth about four P.M.," she told writer Alan Levy. "Beginning at eleven A.M. the media people started to come in here. I've never seen so many people. . . . When I saw a Fort Worth editor with a reputation for never leaving his swivel chair, I knew this was an event." Colonel Parker stopped by not long afterward to offer, Levy observed, "his services, advice, and moral support. Lieutenant Colonel Schulten turned to 'Colonel' Parker and, couching her words in the respect accorded a higher-ranking person — particularly one who made all his rank 'on the outside' — she told him: 'Colonel Parker, the Second Armored Division will not be able to train this boy at the rate these requests are coming in. You have an enormous investment, so you may not like what I'm about to do here and now.' Parker, whose most detailed pre-induction plans had never anticipated a woman officer, . . . surrendered to the inevitable with a meek, 'Well, Colonel, you're the boss.' "

What she was about to do was declare Elvis Presley off-limits to newsmen and photographers after his first day at Fort Hood. "You will have carte blanche as promised," she said, "but just this one day. After today, nothing!" And that was the policy she stuck to.

The first few days were extremely difficult for a very homesick, very isolated Elvis Presley. The others just watched, some of them ragged on him a little ("Boy, you ain't wiggling right," someone was likely to call out as he ran past, and "Miss your teddy bears, Elvis?" was a common put-down), but mostly it was Elvis' own private battle, Rex Mansfield observed, as he struggled desperately to find his equilibrium and be accepted as one of the guys. Gradually he was, and gradually he relaxed a little, too, but recruit instructor Sergeant Bill Norwood, who befriended him and allowed him to make private calls from Norwood's home, witnessed his homesickness and tears at first hand and worried what would happen if the others saw him like this. "When you come in my house," he told Elvis, "you can let it all out. Do whatever you want to, and don't worry about anything. But when you walk out of my front door, you are now Elvis Presley. You're an actor. You're a soldier. So, by God, I want you to act! Don't let nobody know how you feel on the inside."

He got his marksman medal with a carbine, sharpshooter with a pistol, and he was named acting assistant squad leader for his squad along with Rex for his squad and "Nervous" Norvell for his. Gradually, he said, he came to be accepted. "I didn't ask for anything, and they didn't give me anything. I just did the same thing everybody else did. I made it very well." He just didn't know who to trust.

The Colonel came to see him once or twice to get his signature on some pieces of paper and report to him on sales and strategy. It was reassuring to hear news of his career, even if he cared little about the facts and figures, but when a Waco businessman named Eddie Fadal, whom he had first met during a five-day Texas tour in January 1956, came to see him two weeks into basic, it was as though he had found a long-lost friend. Fadal, in his thirties, married with two daughters, was one of those not so rare individuals who had responded more than instantly to Elvis' appeal. He had in fact quit his job as a Dallas DJ after Elvis' spur-of-the-moment invitation to go out "as a general flunky," in Fadal's words, on that brief 1956 tour, and he had rejoined him for another few days when Elvis returned with Nick Adams for a performance at Waco's Heart O' Texas Coliseum later that year. "I thought, he probably won't remember me, but I'm going over to the base and see. I went through a lot of red tape at the gate, and I went to see the sergeant of the day room, and he gave me a lot of flak, too, but finally he went to get Elvis for me. And sure enough, he did remember me. I invited him to come to our house when he could get away, told him that we'd give him a home away from home, provide him with privacy and home-cooked food and all of those things, and he said, 'Sure, I'll be there.' He said, 'I can't come for another two weeks, but I'll be there.' I thought to myself, 'Yeah, I'll bet you will,' but, true to his word, in two weeks my telephone rang. . . ."

In the meantime Anita had come down at the invitation of Sergeant Norwood and his wife, who made their home on the post available to her. When she first arrived, Elvis was assigned to guard duty for twenty-four hours, but Sergeant Norwood suggested that, according to army regulations, he could get out of the assignment if he could find a substitute of equal rank. Elvis approached Rex Mansfield and offered him twenty dollars to take his place. "I told him straightaway that I would be glad to pull his guard duty, but in no way would I take his money," wrote Rex, who had observed with distaste the competition for Elvis' attention. "I said to him that I would do this for any other GI whose girl was waiting to see him. . . . This was the real beginning of our friendship."

Elvis brought Anita with him to Waco to visit Eddie Fadal. "He called me from the circle at the confluence of all the highways that come into Waco, and I had a hard time finding him because he didn't stay right where I thought he would be. But he followed my car and he followed me out to my house, and from then on it was every weekend." Nervous Norvell accompanied him once or twice with his wife, who had come to Texas to keep Anita company. But mostly it was just Elvis and Anita and the Fadals. They sang and played records, and Elvis called home at least once a day. "He'd say, 'Mama,' and I imagine she would say, 'Son.' And then it would just go on from there — it was weeping and sobbing, and crying. He thought his career was over. He told me many times, 'It's all over, Eddie.' He told me, 'They aren't going to know me when I get back.' I said, 'Elvis, it's not over. It's just beginning. You're never going to be forgotten.' He said, 'Naw, it's all over. That's it.' He firmly believed that."

Toward the end of basic, Anita got word that she would be recording in New York during the first week of June, and one night as they sat around the piano, Elvis prompted her to sing Hank Williams' "I Can't Help It (If I'm Still in Love with You)" and Connie Francis' brand-new hit, "Who's Sorry Now?," while he mostly sang gospel. Someone turned on a tape recorder, and you can hear Eddie saying to Anita, "I can't wait till your first record comes out." "It better be a good one," Elvis jumps in. "I wish they'd let me pick it." If they did, he says, it would be a song like "Happy, Happy Birthday, Baby," which the whole gang has just been singing. Or it might be something like "Cold Cold Heart," something with some heartbreak in it. "What I'm afraid of is they're going to put her on something a little too modern, a little too popular, you know what I mean?" "It will just die out quick?" "No . . ." "It'll catch on and then fade?" "No, what I'm talking about — they're gonna give her some music I'm afraid is more of a Julie London type. They got to give her something like Connie Francis sings. Something with some guts to it." Anita demurely assents to any and all suggestions, and they go back again and again to "Happy, Happy Birthday" as Elvis sings along with the Tune Weavers' record and ends the impromptu recital with a beautiful, self-accompanied version of "Just a Closer Walk with Thee" while one of the Fadals' daughters cries in the background. Eddie had little doubt that Elvis was going to marry Anita someday. They were so comfortable with each other, and he was so obviously at home in her company and in the Fadals' house. "His mother said to me later that he told her the Fadals had provided him with a home away from home."

Furlough was scheduled to begin at 11:00 A.M. on Saturday, May 31, but at the last minute it was moved up to 6:00 A.M., and Anita and the Colonel were waiting at the post gate. Elvis dropped them in Dallas, where they caught planes to Memphis and Nashville respectively, and then continued on his way with Rex Mansfield and "Nervous" Norvell. He dropped Nervous off on Lamar Avenue and then took Rex to Graceland, where hundreds of fans were waiting at the gate when they arrived. Elvis didn't stop the car, wrote Rex, because he was tired and impatient to see his folks, but he promised to come out later to sign autographs. "The treatment which I received from Elvis upon our arrival . . . was really amazing to me. After the usual hugs and kisses to his mother and dad and the warm welcome to his old friends, he turned all of his attention to me." He showed Rex around the mansion, which Rex in his memoir sought to describe, "but mere words have limitations and seeing is better for believing. . . . I had never before seen the inside of any house, even in the movies, that was as beautiful and luxurious as Graceland Mansion. . . .

"Elvis then amazed me further by, personally, going to the trouble to take me to my parents [when they arrived at his brother-in-law's house in Memphis]. We went out the back gate of his home through a big field in one of his many other limousines (a black Cadillac). Two of his best friends . . . went with us, Lamar Fike and Red West [who] was in the Marines at that time but had taken a leave to be with Elvis during his leave. . . . In parting . . . Elvis asked me to spend [the last] few of my fourteen days' leave with him at Graceland and I could travel back to Fort Hood with him. I eagerly accepted his offer."

HE FELT AS IF he had been transported back into the world to which he truly belonged — but it was no more than a tantalizing vision, he knew it was all destined to disappear. Everything seemed just the same, it was like old times, with everyone gathered at Graceland, friends, family, the fans at the gates. So what's it like in the service, *Cuz*? Junior asked with that slightly malevolent sneer. Now you boys be careful, his mother said, as they all went off to go roller-skating or to the Fairgrounds, now that the weather was warm again. There were business meetings with the Colonel, the Colonel was talking to him all the time about boring business matters, decisions that had to be made.

And what about Anita spending so much time with him in Texas?

hometown reporters asked. "Well, I know the papers had us engaged, married, and everything else, but it just looked that way." How did he like army food? "I've eaten things in the army that I never ate before, and I've eaten things that I didn't know what it was, but after a hard day of basic training, you could eat a rattlesnake." Army hours? "I'm used to them. I don't sleep more or less than I used to, just do it at different hours. Here on leave, I'm having trouble staying awake after midnight, where I used to stay up all night." Had he written many letters home? "I've never written a letter in my life." Why was he wearing his uniform the whole time he was on leave? "Simple. I'm kinda proud of it." And his overall impression of the army? "It's human nature to gripe, but I'm going ahead and doing the best job I can. One thing: the army teaches boys to think like men."

He went with his parents to a specially arranged screening of *King Creole,* got a haircut at Jim's, and bought a new red Lincoln Continental convertible. He had a recording session scheduled in Nashville for the following week, which the Colonel had finally granted in the face of Steve Sholes' near-hysterical pleas. Sholes saw them going into the wilderness for two years with no more than four releasable songs in the can and only himself to be blamed if the whole thing should suddenly fall apart. The Colonel practically made him crawl — it is evident from their correspondence that Sholes had to virtually tie himself down to keep from expressing his true feelings — but, ironically, as frustrating as the last session had been, this time everything gelled and in ten hours, over the course of a single night, they got five nearly perfect sides. For the first time Scotty and Bill were not in the studio with him, and D.J. was relegated to a supporting role, but they were scarcely missed, as top Nashville session players took their place and the session exploded with a kind of live-wire energy and musical humor that hadn't been present for a while. There was Hank Garland on guitar, bassist Bob Moore, Floyd Cramer playing piano, and Buddy Harman on drums, while Chet Atkins came out of the booth to contribute rhythm guitar. In addition, the Jordanaires had a new member, Ray Walker, singing bass, and every time his part came up, "[Elvis] tried to throw me every way he could. He'd move his lips and not say anything, and then he'd say his line. He was giving me a rough way to go!" Tom Diskin, speaking for the Colonel, expressed his concern that the instruments were coming through too loud and might override Elvis' voice, but Sholes reassured him that it would all be balanced out in the mix.

By the time that Rex returned to Graceland, the whole gang was assembled, including Nick Adams, who had flown in from Hollywood, and Rex felt a distinct chill in the air. "I could feel their mistrust and resentment," he wrote. "Later on I caught myself having those same resentments. . . . It was a jealous feeling like maybe Elvis would not pay as much attention to me and more attention to the new guy. Anyway, I made up my mind these guys had better accept me because I was planning to be around for a while." Anita, too, had returned by now ("Naturally we both just felt awful when I had to go to New York for my recording session just when he came home on furlough, but we both knew it had to be"), and it was reported that she spent the last hours alone with him "without friends or parents around."

When he left to go back to the base in the new red Lincoln early Saturday morning, he felt both exhilarated and depressed: exhilarated because it had been so easy to slip back into the old life, depressed for much the same reason, because he couldn't stand to let it go just like that. The Colonel had been making a study of army regulations, and back at Fort Hood, Elvis conferred with Sergeant Norwood, who advised him that once basic training was completed, permission would customarily be granted for a soldier to live off-post — *if* he had dependents living nearby. Within days Vernon and Gladys, who were indeed Elvis' legal dependents, had packed up and were en route in the white Fleetwood with Vernon's mother, Minnie, while Lamar led the way in the Lincoln Mark II. By June 21 they were ensconced just outside the Fort Hood gates in a rented three-bedroom trailer, and when, almost immediately, that proved a little cramped for five adults, they rented a house in the middle of Killeen from Judge Chester Crawford, who was planning on taking a two-month vacation, starting July 1.

Elvis brought his parents over to meet the Fadals the first weekend they were in town and then, again, for a Fourth of July cookout the following week. His mother took immediately to Eddie's wife, LaNelle. "She and my wife would go to the grocery store and purchase the things that Elvis liked. And then she would put on her little apron and go in the kitchen and start fixing it. She was jolly, just home folks, and we had a merry time." Eddie had by now added on a wing to his house with its own customized hi-fi, decorating it in pink and black so that Elvis would feel more comfortable on the weekends when he came to stay. During the week, Eddie visited with the Presleys while Elvis was on duty.

"Gladys would be sitting there in a rocking chair wearing a housecoat and barefoot, just as homey as anybody could be. Elvis loved banana cream pies, and there was a restaurant here that made them called the Toddle House. I'd take him a couple of those pies on a Tuesday or a Wednesday along with the latest magazines and a batch of 45s. A good friend of mine, Leonard Nixon, owned a record store, and every new 45 that came out he would call me and say, 'Elvis would like to hear this one, I know.' He'd just give them to me, the newest things by Connie Francis and Fats Domino and Sam Cooke, artists that Elvis really liked. We'd visit for an hour or so before Elvis got there, and then everything started jumping. They had to start fixing dinner, and the fans would gather at the door, and, you know, it was just a lot of hectic times, because they knew when he'd be home."

It was good times again for the Presley household, even though Gladys was not particularly looking forward to going to Germany when Elvis' company was shipped overseas ("I just can't see myself over there in a foreign country," she told Lamar. "I've left nothing over there, and I'm not trying to find anything"), and Vernon was primarily concerned with the impact that all of this might have on his son's career. For himself, during the week Elvis remained totally taken up with advanced basic, which consisted of training to become a tanker — Elvis placed third in tank gunnery, and occasionally he took over the company drum for marching — but he lived for the weekends. Anita came down some, but mostly he and Lamar and Rex ("Rexadus," as he dubbed him) and a bunch of other guys headed out for Dallas or Fort Worth, where there was an airline stewardess school, or just hung out at the Fadals' in Waco, where they would eat and fool around and play touch football. "There was always a parade of cars," said Eddie proudly. "Every time my wife would see him driving up, she'd say, 'Oh oh, I've got to feed twelve or fifteen people.' But only Elvis would stay over."

Gladys was unfailingly gracious to the stream of visitors who arrived in Killeen on official business, social business, or no business at all. The Colonel came several times and closeted himself with Elvis and Vernon. "He would come into the living room," said Eddie, "and talk with whoever was there, me and Gladys and Lamar mostly, but they talked their business behind closed doors. We never knew what went on in there, but sometimes Elvis would come out mad, and after the Colonel would leave he would cuss and fume, but other times it was amicable and he came in with a good feeling and a smile on his face. There were times that they disagreed, but [it] had nothing to do with Elvis' artistic endeavors. The Colonel had nothing to do with that, but he had everything to do with the business side, which I think was the way it should be."

A DJ named Rocky Frisco showed up one time after bicycling five hundred miles from Tulsa on a publicity stunt. When he arrived in Killeen, it was only to discover that Elvis was out on bivouac, but Gladys invited him to visit with them every day, and "I was made to feel every bit as welcome there as if I were family." Vic Morrow, who had played the gang leader in *King Creole,* stopped by one time, and Vince Edwards and Billy Murphy detoured through Killeen on their way to Dallas, knowing only that Elvis was stationed there but not where he lived. They had just pulled into a service station to ask directions when Lamar ("We called him 'Old Elephant Ass' ") spotted the Hollywood plates and took them out to the house. Elvis was still on duty, Gladys told them. She insisted that they stay for dinner, though, and Vernon set them up in a little tin trailer out back. Elvis finally arrived home, and they had a happy reunion, but then Vince and Billy got increasingly spooked in the trailer after everyone else had gone to bed. Around one in the morning, said Vince, "we didn't care what he would think, the goddam animals started making so much noise we just had to get our ass out of there and get to a motel." So they left without even saying good-bye.

Fans showed up at their doorstep, neighbors complained about the traffic, some girls set up a booth by the side of the road on Elvis' route home with a sign declaring "Please Stop Here, Elvis," and one day Elvis did. Eddie Fadal ferried fan club presidents back and forth to the bus stop in Temple, and Mrs. Presley was never less than courteous, but as the summer wore on she started to feel more and more poorly, her color was bad, and she wasn't able to keep anything down. She called her doctor in Memphis, Dr. Charles Clarke. "She said to me, 'Dr. Clarke, tomorrow's Wednesday.' I said, 'Yes, ma'am.' She said, 'Ain't you off on Wednesday? Well, I want you to fly out here to see me, 'cause I'm sick.' I said, 'Mrs. Presley . . .' I jumped around for some excuse. I said, 'I'm not licensed to practice in Texas.' She said, 'You ain't?' She said, 'Well, I'll just have to get somebody to drive me up there. I need to get Elvis a mess of greens out of the garden anyway.' That was just the way she talked. She was a very sweet person. I remember sometime back she was having a lot of stomach trouble, and I had put her on what we called a 'soft diet.' She came back sometime later and said, 'Doc, I done just what you told me. I ain't put nothing in my stomach. I've been very careful — I ain't put nothing but Pepsi-Cola and watermelon.' That was her soft diet!"

Elvis put his parents on the train for Memphis in Temple on August 8, a Friday. On Saturday Gladys was admitted to the hospital. Dr. Clarke was not sure just what was the matter with her: "It was a liver problem, but she was not jaundiced, as I recall. It wasn't a typical hepatitis. I called every consultant we could latch on to, and we tried our best to diagnose it. Apparently she had some sort of clotting phenomenon that involved her liver and internal organs."

By Monday he was still unsure of the diagnosis, but he knew that it was serious. He telephoned Elvis, who had just begun his six weeks of basic unit training and was unable initially to get leave. Elvis called practically every hour for news of his mother, and "finally he said, 'If my leave doesn't come through by tomorrow morning, I'll be there tomorrow afternoon anyway.' I said, 'Now, Elvis, don't go AWOL. All the young men in the world are watching you. You're a model. Don't do that.' I said, 'Give me the name of your colonel, and I'll get you out if it's come to this.' I said, 'I know the chairman of the Military Affairs Committee. I'll call him.' So he gave me the name of his colonel, and I called the colonel. The colonel said, 'Well, Doctor, if it was anyone but Elvis Presley, we'd let him go, but let Elvis go and they'll say we're giving him special privileges.' I simply said to the colonel — these are my very words — I said, 'Look, Colonel, I'm having to sit down with the press of the whole world here and talk to them every day. Now if they say you gave him special privileges, I will back you to the hilt if you let him go.' But I said, 'Furthermore, Colonel, if you *don't* let him go, I'm going to sit down with them, and I'm going to burn your ass.' I told him that in so many words. I spent five and a half years in the army myself. I was chief of cardiac surgery at Walter Reed during World War II, and I knew how to handle colonels. Elvis was here in a matter of hours. The colonel saw the handwriting on the wall."

Elvis and Lamar flew from Dallas on Tuesday evening, August 12, and Elvis went straight to the hospital. "Oh my son, oh my son," exclaimed Gladys, who had already expressed concern about his flying to come see her. He spent an hour or so in the hospital room and found her a little better than expected. Her condition was still grave, said Dr. Clarke, but his visit had done her a world of good. He left his father at the hospital, where Vernon was camped out on a folding cot beside Gladys' bed. The pink Cadillac was parked so she could see it from her window. "I walked in one morning," said Dr. Clarke, "and she said, 'Look at that pink Cad out there in the parking lot.' She said, 'I like that special, 'cause Elvis give it to me.' The thing she was proudest of in her whole life was working as a nurse's aide at St. Joseph's Hospital."

Elvis came back early the next morning and spent several hours with her, then returned in the late afternoon with a bunch of friends, who hung out in the waiting room while he visited with his mother. She was in better spirits than the day before and spoke volubly about a wide range of subjects. He stayed till nearly midnight and promised her he'd be back early the next morning to take some of the flowers home.

At 3:30 A.M. the phone rang at Graceland. "I knew what it was before I answered the telephone," Elvis said. Vernon had been awakened by what he described as his wife "suffering for breath." He propped up her head and called for a doctor, but before the doctor was able to get there she was gone. Elvis arrived within minutes and sank to his knees, with his father, beside the bed. When Lamar brought Vernon's mother, Minnie, to the hospital just minutes later, "we got off the elevator, and I could hear Elvis and Vernon wailing. I had never heard anything like it before in my life — it was like a scream. I came down the hall, and Elvis saw me and he grabbed hold of me and said, 'Satnin' is gone.' "

They waited at the hospital for the hearse to come and take her away. Elvis was inconsolable, touching the body over and over, until hospital attendants had to ask him to stop. From the hospital Elvis called Sergeant Norwood at the base, and Anita Wood, who was in New York to do *The Andy Williams Show*. It was 5:30 in the morning, and her mother answered the phone. Elvis could barely speak, said Anita. She promised she would come right after the show that night.

When reporters came to the house at mid morning, they found Elvis and his father sitting on the front steps of Graceland, utterly bereft. They had their arms around each other and were sobbing uncontrollably, oblivious to the presence of anyone else. Elvis was wearing a white ruffled dress shirt with the sleeves rolled up, khaki continental pants, and unbuckled white buck shoes. His mother's death, he told reporters without embarrassment or shame, had broken his heart. "Tears streamed down his cheeks," wrote the *Press-Scimitar* reporter. "He cried throughout the interview. 'She's all we lived for,' he sobbed. 'She was always my best girl.' " Looking down the curved driveway, he said, "When Mama was feeling bad we used to walk with her up and down the driveway to help her feel better. Now it's over."

Hundreds of fans had assembled outside the gates and were keeping vigil when they moved the body to the house in the early afternoon. Elvis had announced that he wanted the funeral at home, in the traditional manner, because his mother had always loved his fans, and he wanted them to have a chance to see her. The Colonel overruled him, however, citing security, and the viewing at Graceland was limited to friends and family. The body was placed in a 900-pound copper, steel-lined coffin and lay in state in the music room. Gladys was clothed in a baby blue dress which her sister Lillian had never seen her wear, and Elvis struggled with tears once again as he recalled his mother's simplicity, her imperviousness to the blandishments of wealth and fame. "My mama loved beautiful things, but she wouldn't wear them," he declared with bitter emotion.

Nick Adams was flying in from the Coast, Cliff Gleaves was coming from Florida, and Vernon's father, Jessie, was riding the bus from Louisville. When Dr. Clarke arrived at the house ("I mean, they insisted that I come out and be with them at the home"), he found a chilling scene. "The expression of grief was just profound. He and his dad would just be pacing around, walk up to the front door with their arms locked around each other, and I remember the father saying, 'Elvis, look at them chickens. Mama ain't never gonna feed them chickens no more.' 'No, Daddy, Mama won't never feed them chickens anymore.' Just that sort of abject grief."

All day there was a mounting crescendo of tears and emotion. Some of Elvis' relatives, according to one source, were dead drunk in the kitchen. As Dr. Clarke saw it, the Colonel was doing his best "to make an extravaganza out of it." When Alan Fortas came in, "Elvis was in a daze. His voice was small and strained. 'My baby's gone, Alan, she's gone!' 'I know, Elvis,' I said. 'I'm sorry. She was a nice lady.' Then he took me over to view the body. . . . Except when he got up to greet visitors, he just sat there with her, almost as if they were the host and hostess of their own little party. It was a pitiful thing to watch." Junior picked up Eddie Fadal at the airport, and Elvis led him to the casket. "Just look at Mama," he said. "Look at them hands, oh God, those hands toiled to raise me." He couldn't stop touching her, Gladys' sister Lillian said. He would hug and kiss her and rock back and forth, whispering endearments, pleading with her to come back. "They couldn't get him to stop, until they were afraid for him, you know, and finally they had to cover over the coffin with glass." Telegrams arrived from Dean Martin, Marlon Brando, Ricky Nelson, Sammy Davis, Jr., Tennessee Ernie Ford, and present and soon-to-be Tennessee governors Frank Clement and Buford Ellington.

In the evening Sam and Dewey Phillips both came out to the house. Dewey was a mess. He had been fired from WHBQ the month before, and his behavior, under the influence of drink, pills, and congenital eccentricity, was becoming more and more erratic, but he and Sam stayed the whole night and did their best to comfort Elvis, who would not leave his mother's side. "After a time," said Sam, "I persuaded him to come to the kitchen, and we sat down, and I just listened to him. He knew I wasn't going to give him any damn bullshit or try to make him artificially feel good about it. . . . Elvis kept talking about the body and how he didn't want to give it up to anyone else. I eventually got Elvis away from the casket and we sat down by the pool. I'll never forget the dead leaves by the pool. I was able to convince him that he should let his mother go. I knew just enough to know which part of him to touch and in what way."

Anita finally arrived at 2:30 Friday morning. Everybody was camped out in the kitchen and living room. Nick, who had arrived with a cut over his eye from a fight scene with Frank Lovejoy, set up a makeshift bed next to Elvis' so he could keep him company through the night. George, Alan, Lamar, and a bunch of the other guys, too, were all set for the duration. Anita found Elvis and Vernon sitting on the steps in front of Graceland. He hugged her when he saw her, and they both cried, and he said, "Come in, Little. I want you to see Mama." She didn't really want to, because she'd never seen a dead body before, but he said, "Come on in, Little, Mama loved you. I want you to come and see her, she looks so pretty." He took her to the music room, "and there was a glass over her covering her up, but the top was up all the way so that the entire length of her body was exposed, and he took me over there and started talking about how pretty she looked, and then he patted on the top of the table where her feet were, and he said, 'Look at her little sooties, Little, look at her little sooties, she's so precious.'"

The Colonel cleared out most of the stragglers at that point, and Dr. Clarke administered a sedative to Elvis. The Memphis Funeral Home came for the body at 9:00 that morning while Elvis was still asleep.

The funeral was scheduled for 3:30 that afternoon, with the Reverend

Hamill presiding. By the time the service started, close to three thousand people had filed by the body, and there were sixty-five police outside to control the crowds. The chapel was filled to overflowing with nearly four hundred mourners jamming the three-hundred-seat hall. Chet Atkins attended, but Bill and Scotty did not. Elvis was wearing a dark brown suit and tie and had to be helped from the limo. Before the service started, Dixie, married and a mother by now, arrived with her aunt and entered the little alcove where the family sat, to pay her respects. "When I went in the room, Elvis and his dad were sitting there, and he just burst up out of his chair and grabbed me before I was in the door: it was like, 'Look, Dad, here's Dixie.' Like I was going to save the world. And we just hugged and comforted each other for a minute — there were twenty or thirty people sitting there, and it was almost time for the service to start — but it was a very emotional thing for both of us, and for his dad, and he said, 'Will you come out to Graceland tonight? I just need to talk to you.' And I said, 'Well, I'll try.' He was just so shaken over it. It just broke my heart to see him like that." When the Blackwood Brothers, who were stationed behind the altar room, sang "Precious Memories," Vernon could be heard to exclaim, "All we have now are memories," with Elvis sobbing out, "Oh Dad, Dad, no, no, no. . . ." The Blackwood Brothers had been Gladys Presley's favorite quartet, and Elvis had arranged for them to fly in from South Carolina. Every time they finished a song, said J. D. Sumner, who was singing bass, "he would send a note back for us to sing another one. We were supposed to sing three or four songs, and we wound up singing something like twelve. I never seen a man suffer as much or grieve as much as he did at the loss of his mother."

The Reverend Hamill preached on a theme suitable to the occasion. "Women can succeed in most any field these days," he said, "but the most important job of all is being a good wife and a good mother. Mrs. Presley was such a woman. I would be foolish to tell this father and this son, 'Don't worry, don't grieve, don't be sorrowful.' Of course you will miss her. But I can say, with Paul, 'Sorrow not as those who have no hope.' "

Several times during the service he almost collapsed. "I sat right behind him during the ceremony," said Anita, "and he would just cry out." When the service was over and the mourners had filed out, he and Vernon and James Blackwood and his friend Captain Woodward, of the Memphis Police Department, stood by the coffin alone. "He went over to the casket," said James, "and kissed his mother and said, 'Mama, I'd give up every dime I own and go back to digging ditches, just to have you back.' He was sobbing and crying hysterically. He came over and put his arms around me and just laid over on my shoulder and said, 'James, I know you know something of what we're going through.' He said, 'You don't know it, but I was in the audience at R.W. and Bill's funeral at Ellis Auditorium after the crash. So you know what I've been experiencing.' And I said, 'Yes, I do,' but I hadn't known that he was there until that day."

The scene was no less emotional or chaotic at the cemetery. The streets were lined with onlookers as the funeral procession left town on Bellevue, becoming Highway 51 as it reached Forest Hill Cemetery two or three miles short of Graceland. The grave site was crowded with an additional five hundred onlookers. "Some spectators," wrote Charles Portis in the *Commercial Appeal* the next day, "seemed to be honestly bereaved, but the majority craned their necks and chattered." Mr. Presley tried to comfort Elvis, but every time he did, he would himself dissolve in a paroxysm of grief. "She's gone, she's not coming back," he declared hopelessly over and over again. Elvis himself maintained his composure a little better until, toward the end, he burst into uncontrollable tears and, with the service completed, leaned over the casket, crying out, "Good-bye, darling, good-bye. I love you so much. You know how much I lived my whole life just for you." Four friends half-dragged him into the limousine. "Oh God," he declared, "everything I have is gone."

It was a mob scene back at Graceland, with friends and relatives milling around in helpless confusion, Elvis inconsolable, and the Colonel at his command post in the kitchen, when Dixie came out early that evening. She had no intention of intruding on his grief. "I didn't mean to see him that night, because he was already surrounded by people. I was wearing shorts, and I had my hair in rollers, and I was just going to tell him I'd see him the next night. I stopped at the gate, and none of the Presleys were down there — it was like Grand Central Station, and all these little girls were trying to get in, and I sat there for a minute and watched all the commotion. And I went up to the guard — it was somebody I didn't know — and said, 'Will you just call up to the house and tell Elvis that I'm down here, and that I'll come out tomorrow night to visit with him, if that's good.' So the guy says, 'Okay, I'll tell him,' but I was sure he wasn't going to give him the message.

"Then I went back to get in the car, and my car wouldn't start, and while I was sitting there one of Elvis' cousins came up and said, 'Aren't you Dixie?' And I said, 'Yes.' He said, 'Elvis is waiting on you at the house.' I said, 'No, I don't want to see him tonight. I've got my hair rolled up, and I'm not dressed. I was planning to see him tomorrow night.' He said, 'No. You'd better come up. He's already called down to see if you're here at the gate.' He took my keys to the car, and he took me up to the house, and Elvis came out the front door and just enveloped me. We went in the house, and the only person we saw was his grandmother. I said, 'Where is everybody? I thought you had all these people.' Because, I don't think this is an exaggeration, I think there were at least twenty or thirty cars out front. He said, 'There were — but I told them to get lost.' And I did not see or hear a soul the whole time we were there, except the maid was in the kitchen and he went in and asked her to bring us some lemonade, and we went in the wing where the piano was and we talked and he sang 'I'm Walking Behind You on Your Wedding Day,' and we sat there and cried.

"We talked about his mother and rehashed from the time that I'd met her and all the things that we'd done that were funny and silly. And he expressed how special it was just to be with somebody you knew from those many days back that loved you and accepted you for just what you were back then. He said, 'I wonder how many of my friends that are here now would be here if it were five years ago.' He said, 'Not very many, because they are all looking for something from me.' And he told me about one of the guys who was singing backup for him at the time who had just given his heart to the Lord. He had been in the world for a long time and was just really messed up, and he told Elvis that he was having to walk away from the life that he was leading, and Elvis said, 'I wish I could do that.' It was just so sad. I said, 'Why don't you? You've already done what you wanted to do. You've been there, so let's just stop at the top and go back.' He said, 'It's too late for that. There are too many people. There are too many people that depend on me. I'm too obligated. I'm in too far to get out.'

"That was the last time I saw him. Well, not the last time, because I went back the next night, all dressed up, but, you know, the next night the house was all full of people. You know, it was like, this is the way it will always be. That was his lifestyle. That was his life. It just reinforced to me that what I was seeing that night was really it. We both realized that.

He was in it, and there was no way out. He couldn't come back to my lifestyle any more than I could have gone on to his."

He was grieving almost constantly, the papers wrote. "He'd cry all day," said George, "and we'd get him calmed down, and the next day it would start all over again." On Saturday he returned once again to the Memphis Funeral Home, this time for the funeral of Red West's father. Red, who was still in the Marine Corps and stationed in Norfolk, Virginia, had requested emergency leave as soon as he heard of Gladys' death. It was denied, but then he heard of his father's illness that same morning. He was on his way home when he got word of his father's death. He was forced to miss Gladys' funeral because he had to attend to the details of his father's the next day, and he was flabbergasted when Elvis showed up at the funeral home. "Man, he had gone through a trial the day before. . . . He was out of it. But just before the service started Elvis appeared at the doorway. He was with Alan Fortas and Gene Smith and Lamar Fike. They were all very respectfully dressed. Elvis almost had to be carried over to me. . . . He came over to me and sort of half fell into my arms. 'My mama was here yesterday just where your daddy is, Red,' Elvis told me. He couldn't say too much more."

That afternoon they went out to the cemetery to visit Elvis' mother's grave, which couldn't have seemed like much of an idea to any of his friends but which none of them could talk him out of. "After a near emotional breakdown," reported the *Press-Scimitar*, "Elvis had a fever of 'near 102,' his doctor reported. 'I went down and checked him over and gave him some cold drugs,' the doctor said. 'I called again Sunday and he was feeling better and eating a little, so I didn't go down.' "

His leave was extended by five days, and his friends tried to cheer him up. He bought a new van, and the whole gang traveled with him around the countryside — they went to the movies and the Rainbow Rollerdrome — but it wasn't the same. Even the Tennessee Highway Patrol got into the act, as they took him on morning helicopter rides over Memphis and taught him how to operate the controls. All of Memphis, the whole world, in fact, grieved with him, as more than a hundred thousand cards, letters, and telegrams came into the Colonel's headquarters in Madison. None of it made any difference. One day he ran into an old schoolmate and neighbor from the Courts, George Blancet, driving down Bellevue. "He rolled his window down, and his eyes were teary and he called me by name. I told him I was sorry his mother had died. He just said, 'I don't know how I'm gonna make it.' Something like that. It was a statement of desperation."

Toward the end of the week his dentist, Lester Hofman, came by with his wife, Sterling, to pay their respects. "This was the first time we had been there. I was racking my brain about what to do — should I send flowers? I really didn't know — when I got a call saying, 'Dr. Hofman, can you come out to the house? Elvis would like to see you.' When we got there, the room was full of all his buddies. We looked around and we didn't see a face we knew. I sat next to this young fellow, and he said, 'Who are you here to see?' I said, 'We're here to see Elvis.' He said, 'Well, you're not going to see him. He hasn't been out of his room.' I said, 'Well, that's his privilege. It's up to him whether he wants to see us.' Then we were talking with Vernon, and Vernon said, 'Just a minute, I'll get Elvis.' Five minutes later Elvis walked in, and he went like this and the room cleared. We told him how sorry we were, and he said to Sterling, 'Mrs. Hofman, I don't know if this is the right time, but the newspapers have made my house so laughable' — that was the word. He said, 'They have made it sound so laughable, I would love to have your opinion of my home.' She said, 'Elvis, I really didn't come here to go through your home. We came here to be with you.' He said, 'But I want your opinion.' He took us all through the house, my taste is not so marvelous, but it was very attractive, it all fit — there was a modern sculpture on the chimney over the fireplace, and I had the same sculpture in my office, it was called 'Rhythm.' Anyway, when we got back to the living room, he said, 'What do you think?' and Sterling said, 'If you give me the key, I'll swap you. And I won't even move a dish!' Then Sterling said to him, 'Did you ever think one day, you might have all of this, it's just so beautiful.' He said, 'Mrs. Hofman, I never thought I'd get out of Humes High.'"

On Sunday he returned to Fort Hood. He left instructions that nothing was to be changed, nothing was to be the least bit disturbed in his mother's room, all was to be kept exactly as it had been. The simple inscription on his mother's grave was to read: "She was the sunshine of our home."

THE LAST FEW WEEKS at Fort Hood went by in a haze. Vernon, Elvis' grandmother Minnie, Lamar, Junior, and Gene were all living at the house in Killeen, and Red joined them when he got out of the Ma-

rines in the first week of September. It was, as Red described it, a kind of
''open house'' atmosphere in which everyone tried almost desperately to
cheer up Elvis. They'd stay up all night occasionally; ''sometimes a whole
team of us would sit around with a guitar and sing ourselves hoarse.''
Things were never again the same, wrote Rex Mansfield in his memoir of
army days. ''We all suffered (his whole outfit) with and for Elvis' great
loss . . . and there remained a certain sadness with all of us throughout the
rest of our training.''

The Colonel came down a couple of times to huddle with Elvis over
embarkation plans and future RCA releases. Anita, who was constantly
fending off rumors of impending marriage (''Heavenly days, I just can't
imagine it''), visited frequently in between performance dates and television appearances. Elvis' grandmother, she noted, was doing her best to
take Gladys' place. She fixed all his favorite foods: sauerkraut and crowder
peas, sliced tomatoes and brown gravy, and bacon cooked till it was
burnt. Whatever he liked she would fix for him, and there was still an extraordinary sense of closeness among Elvis, his father, and his grandmother, but now it was a closeness tied to grief. Sometimes he and Anita
talked about her coming to see him when he was in Germany, but the
thought existed more in the realm of fantasy than reality.

Once in a while they would go to the drive-in in Waco with Eddie
Fadal, and Elvis and Eddie attended an r&b revue in Fort Worth (''I don't
remember who they all were, but we parked by the stage door, and they
all came out to the car and greeted him'') and almost caused a riot at a
Johnny Horton show in Temple. ''It was at the auditorium in downtown
Temple,'' said Shreveport native Jerry Kennedy, still in his teens but playing guitar for Horton at the time. ''I was sitting on those big doors that
used to come up at the back of auditoriums, where you can back a truck
into, and this car pulled up, and all these guys bailed out of it with Elvis in
uniform, and they said, 'Hey, can you let us in the back door?' I said, 'I
guess. Since it's you.' So I went down and opened the back door, and he
came in, and then we went onstage. Johnny did four or five songs, and
then he said, 'I want to extend a warm welcome to somebody who is visiting me backstage.' He said something about his mother, and so forth, and
I remember, I was standing there thinking, 'Don't do this. Oh God, he's
not going to do that.' And he did, and then he said, 'I'd like for him to step
out and take a bow. Elvis . . .' And the people got up and just rushed the
stage, and I grabbed my guitar and got away!''

The last weekend that he was at Fort Hood, Kitty Dolan, the young singer whom he had met in Las Vegas the previous fall, came for a visit. When she arrived, she found the living room full of girls. "I Was One Girl Among Many" read the headline over her article in *TV and Movie Screen*. She fully appreciated the sincerity of the others, though, and their genuine desire to try to alleviate his grief. One fan told of visiting Graceland and how Gladys had proudly shown her the home and the pink Cadillac that her son had given her. "What other boy would love his parents so much?" Gladys had said to her, the girl reported, as tears came to Elvis' eyes. After dinner they sat around singing songs, ending with a gospel session with a bunch of the guys. "At two A.M. we said good night," Kitty told columnist May Mann. "When he kissed me, I said with a little laugh, 'What is this with you and Anita Wood? I've been reading all the stories.' Elvis smiled and said, 'She has a good press agent.' And then he kissed me again."

There is a group picture from Elvis' last night in Killeen taken with Vernon, Lamar, Eddie, Junior, and Red, along with two or three of the fan club presidents. Elvis has his arms around Eddie's and his father's shoulders. He is wearing his marksman and sharpshooter medals, and he is surrounded by friends, but he looks alone and lost, his eyes blank, his mouth downturned, as if he were about to cry. After the picture was taken, he asked Eddie if he would lead the group in prayer, and then they left to take him to the troop train in the drizzling rain. "He shipped out that very night," said Eddie. "I rode with Elvis and Anita in his new Lincoln Continental, with Elvis driving. Then Anita and I drove home and we sat there with Vernon for a while. We were really in mourning, he'd never been out like that before, and we were [worrying]: how are they going to treat him, are they going to resent or embrace him, you know, how is he going to take it?"

T HE TRAIN RIDE to New York was uneventful for the most part. One of four special troop trains moving approximately 1,360 soldiers to the Brooklyn Army Terminal to ship out for Germany as replacements for Third Armored Division troops, it was, ironically, routed through Memphis, and word got out. When the train pulled in, there was a crowd of fans already waiting, along with George Klein, Alan Fortas, and several other of Elvis' friends. The train took about an hour to refuel, "and this gorgeous brunette came up to me," said Klein, "I don't know if she went to Ole Miss at the time, but she was a typical Ole Miss beautiful girl, and she said her name was Janie Wilbanks, and she asked if I would introduce her. I did, and about two weeks later I get this call from Germany saying, 'Who in the hell was that girl? Man, she was good-looking! Tell her to send me some pictures and write to me.' That was when I first got the indication that it might not be all that serious with Anita."

One of his fellow soldiers gave Elvis a book called *Poems That Touch the Heart,* compiled by A. L. Alexander ("Creator of Radio's GOOD WILL COURT"), and he leafed through it, reading several of the poems, including "Mother" ("Again your kindly, smiling face I see"), "Friendship," and "One of Us Two" ("The day will dawn, when one of us shall harken / In vain to hear a voice that has grown dumb"), but one in particular really hit home. It was called "Should You Go First," and he stared at it for some time, until he practically knew it by heart: "I'll hear your voice, I'll see your smile / Though blindly I may grope / The memory of your helping hand / Will buoy me on with hope. . . . "

Mostly, though, he didn't like to be alone with his thoughts, and the other boys wanted to hear about Hollywood and Hollywood starlets and the movies. The train was delayed several times as it ran into commuter traffic, and somewhere in Delaware or New Jersey a brash, pint-size young soldier named Charlie Hodge, who had done everything he could to get together with Elvis at Fort Hood but had never really gotten the chance, showed up in the train car that Elvis and Rex and Nervous Norvell were riding in. Charlie had sung with the Foggy River Boys on Red Foley's Ozark Jubilee and had even met Elvis once backstage at Ellis Auditorium in 1955. He was not at all shy about drawing on mutual show biz connections, and before long they were talking about Wanda Jackson and country comedian Uncle Cyp and the passion that they shared for quartet music. Charlie was "bound and determined to meet Elvis," observed Rex, but he "really was one of the funniest guys you could meet; the type you could not help but like and Elvis liked him instantly." They spent the rest of the train ride trading stories and separated only when the train finally got into the Brooklyn Army Terminal at Fifty-eighth and First Avenue, a little after 9:00 A.M. There Elvis Presley, the public figure, became the center of attention once again.

It was a scene worthy of P. T. Barnum, Cecil B. DeMille, or the Colonel at his most extravagant. There were 125 newsmen waiting impatiently, all of RCA's top brass, Elvis' father, his grandmother, Anita, Red and Lamar, the Aberbachs and Freddy Bienstock, plus the Colonel with his full entourage. Elvis would be out shortly, army spokesman Irving Moss explained, but in the meantime he wanted to go over protocol: for the first ten or fifteen minutes still photographers would be permitted to take pictures; then there would be a press conference proper; following that, the newsreel and TV cameras would have their chance; then Pfc. Presley would board the ship's gangplank for photographers, with eight buddies selected at random from off the train; finally, there would be a small group of newsmen permitted on board. Would he be carrying a duffel bag? someone asked. No, said Moss, his duffel bag had already been loaded on board, but when that answer didn't satisfy the press, the army spokesman proposed that a duffel bag could be *borrowed*. "I want to say one more thing, ladies and gentlemen. Since this terminal has been established, [during] World War I and through World War II and to date, there have been millions of troops going through here and among them have been thousands of celebrities in the various fields of the arts, sciences, sports, and the entertainment field. It has not been, nor is it, the policy of the army to single out any of these people for press conferences. However, in this particular instance . . ." "What are we waiting for?" called out one reporter as it became evident that Elvis Presley had arrived. "All right, bring him out." "Let's go, for heaven's sake," came the "angered squawks from photographers, desperately shoving each other to get a clear shot at Presley."

Then, at last, Elvis emerged from behind the blue backing where he had been chatting with the Colonel, stood for a moment for photographers, smiled graciously for the cameras, signed autographs, kissed a WAC named Mary Davies whom the army had produced for the occasion, did his best to oblige every shouted request, and finally sat down at the table with Information Officer Moss in front of a cluster of microphones. He was carrying a shiny calfskin attaché case and clutching the book of poems he had had on the train. What was the train ride like? he was asked. What were his medals for? What did the *a* in his name stand for? "A-ron," he explained, pronouncing the *a* long. Yes, his father and his grandmother and Lamar were going to accompany him to Germany. Would he ever sell Graceland? "No, sir, because that was my mother's home." The guys in his outfit had been great. "If it had been like everybody thought, I mean everybody thought I wouldn't have to work, and I would be given special treatment and this and that, but when they looked around and saw I was on KP and I was pulling guard and everything, just like they were, well, they figured, he's just like us, so . . .''

He'd come in for a lot of criticism in his career. What did he think of the charges that his music had contributed to juvenile delinquency? ''I don't see that. Because if there is anything I have tried to do, I've tried to live a straight, clean life, not set any kind of a bad example.'' ''Elvis —'' ''I will say this, excuse me, sir, I will say there are people who are going to like you and people who don't like you, regardless of what business you are in or what you do. You cannot please everyone.'' What about his great success? Did he feel that he'd been lucky, or that he had talent? ''Well, sir, I've been very lucky. I happened to come along at a time in the music business when there was no trend. The people were looking for something different, and I was lucky. I came along just in time.'' And did he miss show business? ''I miss my singing career very much. And at the same time — the army is a pretty good deal, too.'' But surely he didn't miss the fans grabbing at his clothes, invading his private life, threatening his safety? He did, he said, he missed even that, ''because that is my great- est love — like I said, entertaining people. I really miss it.''

And marriage? Did he think there was an ideal age to get married? ''Well, as you're growing up, a lot of times you think you're in love with someone, and then later on in your life you find out that you're wrong. Actually you didn't love them, you only thought you did. And I was no different. Several times as I was growing up I would have probably mar- ried, and my mother and dad talked to me and told me, 'You better wait and find out that this is just what you want,' and I'm glad that I did.'' When was the last time he thought he was in love? ''Oh, many times, ma'am, I don't know, I suppose the closest that I ever came to getting married was just before I started singing. In fact, my first record saved my neck.'' There is general laughter, and then someone asks him if he'd like to say something about his mother.

''Yes, sir, I certainly would. Ahhh, my mother . . . I suppose since I was an only child we might have been a little closer than — I mean, everyone loves their mother, but I was an only child, and Mother was always right with me all my life. And it wasn't only like losing a mother, it was like losing a friend, a companion, someone to talk to, I could wake her up any hour of the night if I was worried or troubled about something, well, she'd get up and try to help me. And I used to get very angry at her when I was growing up. It's a natural thing — a young person wants to go some-where or do something, and your mother won't let you, and you think, 'Why, what's wrong with you?' But then, later on in the years you find out, you know, that she was right. That she was only doing it to protect you and keep you from getting into trouble or getting hurt. And I'm very happy that she was kind of strict on me, very happy that it worked out the way it did."

The press conference went on for nearly an hour, and when it was over, he posed for more pictures and signed more autographs as Informa-tion Officer Moss tried to extricate him from the crowd. The people would get mad if they were turned down, Elvis said in an aside to the army information officer. "Come on," said the Colonel, urging the RCA executives forward. "We all eat off him, let's get in the picture. The boy is mighty sad." Then there were more photographs to be taken outside on the dock and activities to be staged for the newsreel cameras. "I think I'm talking for all the guys," said one of the eight army "buddies" picked at random for the task, "when I say that we learned a lot about people in general when we were lucky enough to have Elvis with us. . . . He gives so much of himself to all the people around him that you just can't help but improve a little through the association. He's a lonely guy in many ways, and a little afraid of what tomorrow will bring for him and his loved ones."

He marched up the gangplank with a borrowed duffel bag slung over his shoulder as the army band, under the direction of Chief Warrant Offi-cer John R. Charlesworth, struck up "Tutti Frutti." He did it not once but eight times for news crews and photographers, with the two thousand rel-atives who were there for their own leave-takings waving and screaming on cue. Once on board, he was closeted in the ship's library with the Col-onel, Steve Sholes, Bill Bullock, and various other members of the indus-try entourage. He recorded a brief Christmas message for the fans, which, together with an edited version of the press conference, to be entitled "Elvis Sails!," would help keep him in touch with his public. He conferred anxiously with the Colonel, Freddy, and the Aberbachs and promised them that he would do his very best. "He was resigned," said Anne Ful-chino, the RCA publicity chief, who had scarcely seen him since launch-ing that first national publicity campaign for a bright-eyed youth in early 1956. "He was concerned about interrupting his career, he was worried that his records would stop selling. I said there was no reason they should, but I know he was thinking about that.'' He took out one of the postcards with which the Colonel had supplied him to present to fans and fellow soldiers alike. ''May God bless you,'' he wrote on it as he handed it to her. He seemed trapped, cornered, she thought, his eyes frantically searched the room. Why don't you come along, too? he said, suddenly, to Red, who was just standing there with Lamar. Red could fly over with Vernon and Grandma and Lamar. ''Daddy will fix up the tickets,'' he said. They would have themselves a ball.

Then there was a brief interview in the library. For the first time that day, in public he sounds tired, even a bit downcast. He hasn't eaten since early morning, he says, but he doesn't feel like he could eat anything right now. What are his thoughts? he is asked, as the time for departure approaches. ''Well, I'm going to be very honest about it,'' he says haltingly. ''I'm looking forward to Germany, I'm looking forward to seeing the country and meeting a lot of the people, but at the same time I'm looking forward to coming back here, because here is where I started. Here's where all my friends, my business and so forth . . .'' Would he like to send any special message to his fans? ''Yes, I would. I'd like to say that in spite of the fact that I'm going away and will be out of their eyes for some time, I hope I'm not out of their minds. And I'll be looking forward to the time when I can come back and entertain again like I did.'' ''Well, thank you, Elvis,'' the interviewer concludes, with fifteen minutes left before departure. ''I know you want to talk to Colonel Parker, your close friend and your manager. All we can do is wish you a wonderful trip and all the best luck in the world and come home soon.''

The band played ''All Shook Up,'' ''Hound Dog,'' and ''Don't Be Cruel'' as the ship got under way. Elvis stood out on deck handing out pictures and postcards to his fellow servicemen and throwing kisses back to the pier but stopped for a moment ''to rotate his shoulder, snap his fingers and buckle his knees. His admirers shrieked,'' reported the *New York Herald-Tribune*. ''Colonel Parker beamed. The Department of Defense man from Washington who had overseen the operation wiped his brow and sighed.'' And Elvis waved. And waved again for the cameras. And again, and again.

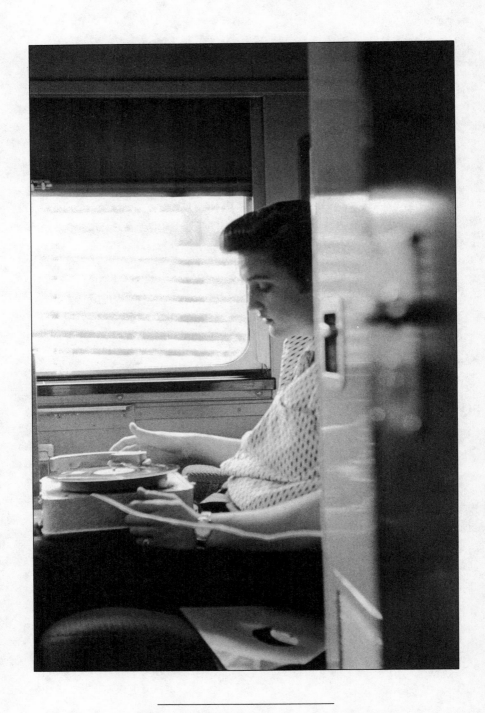

ON THE TRAIN TO MEMPHIS, JULY 3–4, 1956. (ALFRED WERTHEIMER)

Notes

THE MAJORITY OF THE INTERVIEW MATERIAL is my own, but Jerry Hopkins' interviews of various figures for his 1971 biography, *Elvis,* have been a unique, and invaluable, resource. They were made available by the Mississippi Valley Collection at Memphis State University (MVC/ MSU) through the kind efforts of Dr. John Bakke. In addition, Stuart Goldman and Adam Taylor were good enough to share information and interview material assembled for their 1993 film, *Elvis in Hollywood.* Many other people contributed their time and resources, and I have tried to indicate my thanks and indebtedness both in these notes and in the acknowledgments that follow.

PROLOGUE: MEMPHIS, 1950

3 the Mississippi Delta begins: David Cohn, *Where I Was Born and Raised,* p. 12.

4 The newcomer, Dewey Phillips, is twenty-four years old: Much of the account of Dewey Phillips' early background comes from " 'Phillips Sent Me' Has Become Vital Part of City's Lexicon" by Ida Clemens, *Memphis Commercial Appeal,* June 9, 1950.

4–5 That is why Sam Phillips: Sam Phillips' early background, as well as his account of his first meeting with Dewey Phillips, comes from interviews with Sam Phillips, 1979–93. All subsequent quotes are from these interviews, unless otherwise specified.

5 "Negro artists in the South who wanted to make a record": "Man Behind the Sun Sound," *Melody Maker,* c. 1957, as cited by Mike Leadbitter in "Memphis," *Blues Unlimited* Collectors Classics 13.

5–6 "genuine, untutored negro" music; "Negroes with field mud on their boots": Robert Johnson, "Suddenly Singing Elvis Presley Zooms into Recording Stardom," *Memphis Press-Scimitar,* February 5, 1955.

6 The ostensible reason: Interview with Sam Phillips, 1988; letter from Sam Phillips to "Mr. J. Edward Connolly, June-bug, 8 — 50," published in *Kicks* 7, 1992. The letter to Connolly seems to belie Phillips' contention that he was not trying to sell Dewey to Connolly, but this was at the very beginning of their acquaintance, and by August, Dewey and Sam had their first (and last) release out on the aptly named "The Phillips" label.

8 "so nervous he was bug-eyed": Vernon quoted in *Elvis Presley,* prepared by the editors of *TV Radio Mirror,* 1956, p. 10.

8 the Presleys gave the impression: "Elvis by His Father Vernon Presley" as told to Nancy Anderson, *Good Housekeeping,* January 1978.

8 In February 1949: All information on the Presleys' housing from the time of their arrival in Memphis comes from Memphis Housing Authority records, kindly made available by Rick Hawks, whose "adoptive aunt" was Housing Authority adviser Jane Richardson.

11 "industry rising in the midst of agriculture": *Mississippi: The WPA Guide to the Magnolia State.*

11 "Over the years": Dale Dobbs, "A Brief History of East Tupelo, Mississippi," *Elvis Presley Heights, Mississippi, Lee County, 1921–1984,* compiled by members of the Elvis Presley Heights Garden Club.

12 Gladys Presley, everyone agreed: The best printed source for background information on Gladys and Vernon Presley, and the Smith and Presley family backgrounds, is Elaine Dundy's *Elvis and Gladys.* Vernon's employment and financial records, however (made available by the Elvis Presley Estate), have been illuminating.

13 Aron (pronounced with a long *a*): This is how Elvis pronounces it at his army press conference on September 22, 1958.

13 "when one twin died": "Elvis Presley Part 2: The Folks He Left Behind Him," *TV Guide,* September 22–28, 1956.

13 Gladys was never able to have another baby: In *Elvis Presley Speaks,* the book-length bio by Memphis reporter Robert Johnson that came out in 1956, Vernon says, "That was just one of those things that couldn't be. . . . We spent a lot on doctors trying to change it, but there wasn't anything we could do."

13 The physician's fifteen-dollar fee: William Thomas, "Delivering Elvis Paid $15 — From Welfare," *Memphis Commercial Appeal,* January 6, 1980.

13 "she worshiped him": Jerry Hopkins interview with Faye Harris (MVC/MSU).

13 "Elvis was so sure": *Elvis Presley,* prepared by the editors of *TV Radio Mirror,* 1956, p. 6.

13 "My mama never let me": C. Robert Jennings, "There'll Always Be an Elvis," *Saturday Evening Post,* September 11, 1965, p. 78.

14 "common laborer": This was Elvis' own phrase in a number of interviews.

14 In 1937 Gladys' uncle Gains: Dundy, *Elvis and Gladys,* p. 72.

14 "when Elvis was just a little fellow": *TV Radio Mirror,* p. 8.

14 "My daddy may seem hard": Both Cliff Gleaves and Charlie Hodge cited this phrase in separate interviews, and George Klein alluded to similar conversations.

14 "It was no big disgrace": Interview with Frank and Corene Randle Smith, 1990.

14–15 "afraid that he would get run over": Interview with Corinne Richards Tate, 1990.

15 "crying his eyes out": Dundy, *Elvis and Gladys,* p. 84.

15 "Though we had friends": "Elvis by His Father Vernon Presley" as told to Nancy Anderson, *Good Housekeeping,* January 1978, p. 156.

15–16 "Mrs. Presley would say": Interview with James Ausborn, 1990.

16 "[one time] I asked him": *Good Housekeeping,* p. 157.

16 " 'When I grow up' ": Recollected by both Gladys (in Martha Lopert, "The Boy with the Big Beat," *Celebrity,* winter 1958) and Vernon (in Edwin Miller, "Elvis the Innocent," *Memories,* May 1989, from a May 1956 interview). This story combines the two accounts.

16 "an average student," "sweet and average": Dundy, *Elvis and Gladys,* p. 107; Pat Chism, "Teacher Recalls Elvis' Favorite Tune While at Lawhon Was 'Old Shep,' " *Tupelo Daily Journal,* July 28–29, 1956; Kathy Jarman, "Milam Report Card Reveals Elvis as an 'Average' Student," *Tupelo Daily Journal,* October 6, 1977.

16 "and we couldn't": Larry Geller and Joel Spector, *"If I Can Dream,"* p. 288.

16 The picture that you see of him: This picture was in the Tupelo Museum in 1989.

16 "I'd tramp all over town": *TV Radio Mirror,* p. 8.

16–17 In May of 1943 the whole family moved: Dundy, *Elvis and Gladys,* p. 87; Vernon's employment records; friendship with Sales and Annie Presley documented in *Elvis Presley Heights,* p. 47.

17 On August 18, 1945: Dundy, *Elvis and Gladys*, p. 108.

17 became a deacon in the church: Ibid., p. 109; *Good Housekeeping*, p. 157.

17 the Presleys, like every other member: Interview with Frank and Corene Randle Smith.

17 "I sang some": *Saturday Evening Post*, p. 78.

17 he "trioed" with his mother and father: Army Archerd, "Presley Takes Hollywood," *Photoplay*, December 1956, p. 94.

18 two doors down from the Presleys: *Elvis Presley Heights*, p. 156.

18 the two couples would share: Ibid., p. 48.

18 The newspaper did not cover: In 1994 Bill Burk discovered a photograph of a ten-year-old Elvis Presley standing onstage after the contest, wearing glasses and flanked by the first-, second-, and third-place winners. Elvis, as he always said, had come in an unofficial fifth. The photograph and accompanying interviews will appear in Burk's *Early Elvis: The Tupelo Years*.

18 "I'll never forget": *TV Radio Mirror*, p. 26.

19 (the tornado of 1936): *Mississippi*.

19 "Son, wouldn't you rather": *TV Radio Mirror*, p. 26.

19 "I always played the guitar": Interview with Frank and Corene Randle Smith.

20–21 the hillbilly star of the station: Background on the Brasfield family of comedians, Rod, "Boob," and Cyp, from Linnell Gentry's *A History and Encyclopedia of Country, Western, and Gospel Music; The Country Music Story* by Robert Shelton; *Nashville's Grand Ole Opry* by Jack Hurst; and 1989 and 1990 interviews with Charlie Hodge and James Ausborn respectively.

21 "He was a good entertainer": Interview with Bill Mitchell, 1990.

21 Archie Mackey's memory: Interview with Archie Mackey, 1990.

21 "He was crazy about music": Interview with James Ausborn.

22 "He always knew": *Elvis Presley Speaks!*, p. 16.

22–23 Tex Ritter was making a personal appearance: The Tex Ritter story is from a 1990 interview with James Ausborn.

23 "I took the guitar": 1972 interview.

24 To Ernest Bowen: Interview with Ernest Bowen, 1990.

24 "All of us were country kids": Interview with Willie Wileman, 1990.

25 "It was unbelievable": Interview with Roland Tindall, 1990.

25–26 "Elvis would bring": Ibid.

26 "He brought his guitar": Interview with James Ausborn.

26 A classmate, Shirley Lumpkin: Dundy, *Elvis and Gladys*, pp. 120–121.

26 "All the socializing": Interview with Roland Tindall.

27 You walked by the Elks Club: My tour guide for the North Green Street area of Tupelo was Jimmy Young, a lifelong resident, who was good enough to drive me around and point out all the sights.

27 Several times a year: The basis for this description of a revival on North Green Street comes from Ernest Bowen, although I have taken the liberty of adapting it and introducing an eyewitness. In the August 1, 1957, edition of *Jet* magazine, Dr. W. A. Zuber, a black Tupelo physician, spoke of Elvis going "to Negro 'sanctified' meetings."

28 On his last day of school: Vince Staten, *The Real Elvis: Good Old Boy*, p. 42; Dundy, *Elvis and Gladys*, pp. 124, 132. The date is based on the fact that Elvis' first day in the Memphis school system, as recorded on his high school record, was November 8, 1948. Also, see below.

28 They moved on a Saturday: *TV Radio Mirror*, p. 9.

28 "We were broke, man, broke": James Kingsley, "At Home with Elvis Presley," *Memphis Commercial Appeal, Mid-South Magazine*, March 7, 1965.

28 According to Gladys: *TV Radio Mirror*, p. 9.

28–29 "I told Elvis": Ibid., p. 8.

29 "There were times": *Good Housekeeping*, p. 157.

MEMPHIS: THE COURTS

33 putting in an application for public housing: This, and all subsequent information on the Presleys' living situation, is from Housing Authority records, as supplied by Rick Hawks, and Jerry Hopkins' interview with Housing Authority adviser Jane Richardson.

33 ("We always found"): Jerry Hopkins interview with Jane Richardson (MVC/MSU).

34 "like we'd come into the money": Interview with George Blancet, 1989.

34 you just did it: Interview with Buzzy Forbess, 1991.

34 Stanley Products (Tupperware-like) parties: Interviews with Barbara Pittman and Jimmy Denson, 1989.

34 "They treated him": Jerry Hopkins, *Elvis*, p. 38.

35 "He was particular": Interview with Lillian Fortenberry, 1988.

35 "He never spent": "Elvis by His Father Vernon Presley" as told to Nancy Anderson, *Good Housekeeping*, January 1978, p. 157.

35 "If one has no scruples": *Humes Herald*, 1953.

35 At first Gladys: Joseph Lewis, "Elvis Presley Lives," *Cosmopolitan*, November 1968, p. 94.

35 "He was a gentle, obedient boy": Robert Johnson, *Elvis Presley Speaks!*, p. 18. (Miss Susie Johnson was *Press-Scimitar* reporter Bob Johnson's aunt.)

35 "He was during his first years": Ibid., p. 18.

36 According to a classmate: Elston Leonard, "Elvis Presley: The New Singing Rage," *Tiger*, c. 1956. George Klein, another student in the class, also tells this story to date the beginning of his friendship with Elvis.

36 "My older brother": Interview with Barbara Pittman.

36 Gladys was working: *Elvis Presley Speaks!*, p. 17.

36–37 "Paul lived on the third floor": Interview with Buzzy Forbess.

37–38 "The first evening he came in": *Elvis Presley Speaks!*, p. 17.

38 "With the three of us": Interview with Buzzy Forbess.

38 One time Farley's mother: Vince Staten, *The Real Elvis: Good Old Boy*, p. 44. The quote from Jane Richardson comes from Jerry Hopkins' interview.

38 "He even practiced two or three songs": Interview with Buzzy Forbess.

38 In one typical 1951 segment: Air check, *Red Hot and Blue*, December 2, 1951.

38 "If you have a song": Lydel Sims, "Rocket Becomes Flying Disc, Spins Toward Record Glory," *Memphis Commercial Appeal*, March 28, 1951.

38 "Do like me": This is an adaptation of one of Dewey Phillips expert Charles Raiteri's fine evocations of Dewey's patter and style.

40 He had run away from home: Various interviews with Jimmy Denson, 1989–92.

40 made the papers for performing: Rhea Talley, "Early A.M. Audition Needed by Lee Denson, Guitarist," *Memphis Commercial Appeal*, August 5, 1956.

40 He didn't want to teach Elvis: Interview with Lee Denson, 1989.

41 Lee's friends Dorsey Burnette and his younger brother, Johnny: Background information on the Burnettes comes from interviews with Jimmy and Lee Denson, 1989; Johnny Black, 1990, 1991; Evelyn Black, 1993; also Ian Wallis interview with Paul Burlison, 1989.

41 In the summertime there were informal dances: Interview with Jimmy and Lee Den-

son. This is supported by interviews with various other Courts residents, including Johnny Black, 1990, and Evelyn Black, 1993.

41 "We would play under the trees": Interview with Johnny Black, 1990.

41 When he missed a note: Interview with Jimmy and Lee Denson.

42 "She used to come out": Michael Donahue, "Elvis: The Project Years," *Memphis Commercial Appeal, Mid-South Magazine,* August 11, 1985.

42–43 "Elvis was a great kisser": Bill E. Burk, *Early Elvis: The Humes Years,* pp. 110–111.

43 "He tried not to show it": Robert Palmer, "Sam Phillips: The Sun King," *Memphis,* December 1978.

43 He sings Eddy Arnold's: The repertoire was specified in an interview with Buzzy Forbess. Buzzy also mentioned Bing and Gary Crosby's catchy (and up-tempo) "Play a Simple Melody."

44 ("Wild-looking guys"): 1972 interview.

44 ("It was just something"): Ibid.

44 she was very proud of the job: Interviews with Gladys' physician, Dr. Charles Clarke, 1989, and Ronny Trout, 1991.

44 a 1941 Lincoln coupe: This has been described on some occasions as a 1942 model (and, more specifically, as a Lincoln Zephyr), but it is specified as a '41 Chrysler in the Housing Authority report.

44–45 "My daddy was something wonderful": Edwin Miller, "Elvis the Innocent," *Memories,* May 1989, p. 13.

45 One time, Vernon recalled: *Elvis Presley,* prepared by the editors of *TV Radio Mirror,* 1956, p. 17.

45 "Elvis saw the street": *Elvis Presley Speaks!,* p. 26.

45 the firemen, who welcomed any diversion: Ibid.

45 "One time we were hanging around": Interview with Johnny Black, 1990.

46 "we don't have any Negro conductors": David Tucker, *Lieutenant Lee of Beale Street,* p. 146.

46 "He came down": Interview with Guy Lansky, 1990.

46 "I suppose that was where I saw him": Jerry Hopkins interview with Bob Neal (MVC/MSU).

46–47 "I mean, we didn't know Elvis Presley": Interview with Jake Hess, 1991.

47–48 Once a month Ellis was filled: A great deal of the background on the All-Night Singings, and quartet singing in general, comes from extensive interviews with Jake Hess and James Blackwood; early videos of the Blackwood Brothers and the Statesmen supplied by Mary Jarvis, James Blackwood, and Jake Hess; various writings by Charles Wolfe (including "Presley and the Gospel Tradition" in *Elvis: Images and Fancies*) and *The Music Men* by Bob Terrell.

47 "the big heavy rhythm beats": C. Robert Jennings, "There'll Always Be an Elvis," *Saturday Evening Post,* September 11, 1965, p. 78.

48 "He went about as far as you could go": Interview with Jake Hess.

48 "Oh, no, not again": Interview with Johnny Black, 1990.

48 "I moved everything": Interview with Lillian Fortenberry, 1988.

48 He sang quite a few: Elvis' musical repertoire is supplied from interviews with Buzzy Forbess, Lee Denson, Johnny Black, and Ronald Smith, as well as various published interviews with Paul Burlison.

48 Some evenings Vernon and Gladys: "Elvis by His Father Vernon Presley" as told to Nancy Anderson, *Good Housekeeping,* January 1978, p. 157.

48 "He grabbed it out of my purse": Billie Wardlaw quoted in Bill E. Burk, *The Young Elvis*, pp. 111–112.

48 Occasionally Buzzy and the other boys: Interview with Buzzy Forbess.

49 According to a teacher, Mildred Scrivener: Mildred Scrivener, "My Boy Elvis," *TV Radio Mirror*, March 1957.

49 "It got so hard on him": *Elvis Presley*, prepared by the editors of *TV Radio Mirror*, 1956, p. 10. Actually Gladys went back to work at St. Joseph's in August, but the same principle applied.

50 "I really felt sorry for him": Red West et al., *Elvis: What Happened?*, p. 17.

50 "He would wear dress pants": Interview with Ronny Trout.

51 One time he got a home permanent: The "permanent" was described in various manifestations in interviews with Ronny Trout, Jimmy Denson, Barbara Pittman, and "Mary Ann," a neighbor in the Courts, who is quoted in Jane and Michael Stern's *Elvis World*, p. 151.

51 he stopped by St. Joseph's: Interview with Ronny Trout.

51 Perhaps he attended the Midnight Rambles: Interviews with Ronny Trout, George Blancet, George Klein, et al.

51–52 "the same place," he later recalled: 1972 interview.

52 "We just thought he was pretty": Interview with Evelyn Black.

52 Rabbi Alfred Fruchter and his wife, Jeanette: Staten, *The Real Elvis*, p. 61.

52–53 On April 9, 1953: Interviews with George Blancet, George Klein, Buzzy Forbess, Ronny Trout, and Red West, as well as the program of the event.

53 "I wasn't popular in school": 1972 interview.

53 "While other students were dashing around": Scrivener, "My Boy Elvis," *TV Radio Mirror*, March 1957.

53 Toward the end of the school year he took: "Elvis's Prom Date Remembers a Shy Guy in Blue Suede Shoes," *People*, 1989; also *The Young Elvis* by Bill E. Burk and "Elvis: Wallflower at Own Prom," *Fort Lauderdale News and Sun Sentinel*, May 23, 1989.

54 "we are reminded at this time": *Humes Herald*, 1953, p. 33.

"MY HAPPINESS"

All quotes from Sam Phillips and Marion Keisker are from the author's interviews, 1979–93 (Phillips) and 1981–89 (Keisker), unless otherwise noted.

57 On July 15, 1953: Clark Porteous, "Prison Singers May Find Fame with Record They Made in Memphis," *Memphis Press-Scimitar*, July 15, 1953. Further information on the Prisonaires from interviews with Sam Phillips; "The Prisonaires," *Ebony*, November 1953; and Colin Escott's liner notes, and research for, *Just Walkin' in the Rain*, the Prisonaires' album on Bear Family, and his own history of Sun (written with Martin Hawkins), *Good Rockin' Tonight: Sun Records and the Birth of Rock 'n' Roll*.

58ff Sun Records, and the Memphis Recording Service, were a two-person operation: Background on the Memphis Recording Service and Sun Records stems, primarily, from numerous interviews with Sam Phillips and Marion Keisker over the years and Escott and Hawkins' *Good Rockin' Tonight*.

58 renting for $75 or $80 a month: Interview with Sam Phillips, 1990. Vince Staten sets it at $150 a month in *The Real Elvis: Good Old Boy*, and various other figures have been suggested.

59ff Marion Keisker would have been: Background on Marion Keisker from interviews and conversations, 1981–89; obituary by Colin Escott, *Goldmine*, February 9, 1990.

59 and where Jake Hess (later to join the Statesmen) got his start: Interviews with Jake

Hess, 1991, 1994. Jake continued to cross paths with the Phillipses and in Memphis sang on WREC with the Daniel Brothers Quartet, which Jud managed. Hess was so impressed with the warmth and kindness of Sam's future wife, Becky, who was working at WLAY when he first met her, that years later he named his daughter for her.

60 He was inspired equally: Interview with Marion Keisker, 1981.

60 Hoyt Wooten, who had started the station: Robert Johnson, "Wooten Sells T-V, Radio Stations," *Memphis Press-Scimitar*, November 3, 1958.

60 he remained quiet and reserved: This surprising self-description of a young Sam Phillips was borne out in interviews with Marion Keisker, Biff Collie, Jake Hess, and T. Tommy Cutrer, among others.

60 "some of [the] great Negro artists": "Man Behind the Sun Sound," *Melody Maker*, c. 1957, as cited by Mike Leadbitter in "Memphis," *Blues Unlimited* Collectors Classics 13.

60 "As word got around": Robert Johnson, "Suddenly Singing Elvis Presley Zooms into Recording Stardom," *Memphis Press-Scimitar*, February 5, 1955.

62 the partnership with Jim Bulleit: Interviews with Sam Phillips and Marion Keisker; Escott and Hawkins, *Good Rockin' Tonight*.

63 "to surprise my mother": March 24, 1956, interview.

63 "I just wanted to hear": Robert Johnson, *Elvis Presley Speaks!*, p. 8.

63 "we had a conversation": Jerry Hopkins interview with Marion Keisker (MVC/MSU).

64 "sounded like somebody beating on a bucket lid": *Time*, May 14, 1956, and *passim*.

64 "We might give you a call sometime": C. Robert Jennings, "There'll Always Be an Elvis," *Saturday Evening Post*, September 11, 1965, p. 78.

64 He even had Miss Keisker: This is a combination of Marion's story as related in Jerry Hopkins' biography (here Sam comes in after the recording is done) and Robert Johnson's account in *TV Star Parade* (September 1956), where it is Sam who takes the boy's name.

It must be noted that this is one scenario, and one scenario only. Over the last twenty years there has sprung up a raging controversy. The nub of the controversy consists of a dispute between Sam Phillips and Marion Keisker over who actually recorded Elvis Presley that first time, which in essence boils down to who turned on the tape recorder when he walked in off the street to make a "personal" record for his mother. The first detailed published version that I am aware of, Bob Johnson's 1956 *Elvis Presley Speaks!*, based on extensive reporting by Johnson since early 1955, was clearly Marion's version. In it she had Sam Phillips coming in "before the record session was completed. It took about fifteen minutes." Subsequent stories by Johnson (and other newspaper and magazine stories) fudged the issue with language that *could* have indicated the presence of both parties. Marion's account remained the same, however, until her death, with minor variations, which occasionally offered explanations for Sam's absence and, in her well-known interview with Jerry Hopkins, had her making a tape copy of the young singer partway into his performance so that she could play it for Sam afterward. As she said to me in 1981, disclaiming credit for anything other than thinking of Sam: "I knew nothing about r&b, I knew nothing about country, and I didn't care whether I did. I was totally enamored of Sam. All I wanted was for Sam to do whatever would make him happy." And it clearly hurt her, as she said, to be branded a liar.

I knew Marion for the last ten years of her life. In our friendship I knew her to be a truthful person, always, but Marion would have been the first to tell you that memory is a creative function, and many aspects of her story contradicted others: for example, if the waiting room was full of people and she got acquainted with Elvis while others were taking their turn, who was recording the others? These internal contradictions in no way disprove her story; they only indicate the difficulties of ascertaining "the truth."

Sam didn't weigh in with his version until 1979, when he broke what amounted to two decades of silence and spoke first to Robert Palmer, then to me and, subsequently, to many others. Sam's version, essentially, claimed credit for the recording (he didn't need to claim credit for the discovery, since that was not the issue here) and registered first disbelief, then indignation, that Marion's story should indicate an ability on her part to operate the delicate disc-cutting machinery, let alone Sam's permission to do so. Marion, who referred to herself as a "mechanical idiot," described to me just how she operated the lathe when I first met her — before I ever spoke about it with Sam or was fully aware of the controversy, though not before Marion and Sam had discussed the matter thoroughly between themselves. Marion said, "Who do you think recorded Buck Turner [Sam's first partner, who had a daily radio show that was frequently transcribed in the studio] when Sam wasn't there? You know, everything didn't just stop during his absence. It couldn't."

I've spoken to numerous people familiar with the Sun operation over the years. All agree, from what they know of Marion and the technical operation of the lathe, that not only could Marion have operated it, she probably did. But none could recall ever seeing her do so. I tried to contact her son, who she said was frequently in the studio with her, but was unable to get a response from him. I've spoken to a number of people — though not a great number — who made "personal" records in those years, and all of them recall Marion out front and Sam doing the recording.

None of which proves anything.

Toward the end of Marion's life there was some talk of a compromise between the two versions, and I've often felt that Marion was offering an olive branch by bringing Sam more frequently into the studio at the conclusion of the session (upon his return from Miss Taylor's restaurant). Sam has remained steadfast that he alone operated the lathe. Whatever version one would like to choose, I don't think any proof is possible in the absence of a credible, impartial witness, and I honestly don't think it makes any difference. I would like to think that this is simply a dispute on a specific point of fact between two honorable people who simply have remembered a scene, which could scarcely have had much significance to either one until long after the event, in different ways. The reason that I have chosen the version that I have presented is that it best fits Marion's "crowded room" scenario, while allowing both Sam and Marion to fulfill the roles that were clearly theirs: Marion, as Elvis portrayed her, was the one who listened, the one who responded to his need, and he was always grateful to her for this. Sam, as Marion conceded in every word, gesture, and deed, and as Elvis himself consistently indicated over the years, was solely responsible for the music. Sam possessed the vision. That is the nub of both Sam's and Marion's version. Who flicked the switch simply should not represent an issue of earthshaking importance.

65 Miss Keisker was always very nice: The picture here of Elvis tentatively putting himself in the way of discovery is based on Marion's impressionistic portrait, not a chronological sequence that recalled him coming into the studio on specific occasions. It makes sense to me in terms of the person that both she and Sam portrayed as well as the aspirations he possessed and the skeletal chronology of events.

"WITHOUT YOU"

All quotes from Dixie Locke are from the author's interviews, unless otherwise noted.

67ff the Assembly of God Church at 1084 McLemore: Background information on the First Assembly of God Church comes from James Blackwood; Dixie Locke; Vince Staten's *The*

Real Elvis: Good Old Boy; Bill E. Burk's *Early Elvis: The Humes Years;* Ronald Smith; and Bill E. Burk.

74 One time there was a crisis at work: Interviews with Lillian Fortenberry, 1988, and Dixie Locke, 1990.

75 the colored church at East Trigg: Background information on the East Trigg Baptist Church and the remarkable Dr. William Herbert Brewster comes from "William Herbert Brewster, Sr.," *We'll Understand It Better By and By,* edited by Bernice Reagon; *The Gospel Sound: Good News and Bad Times* by Tony Heilbut; also Horace Boyer's 1979 interview with Dr. Brewster; Bill E. Burk's interview with the Reverend James Hamill in *Early Elvis,* p. 117; and my own interviews with Sam Phillips, James Blackwood, Jack Clement, George Klein, Lamar Fike, et al.

76 Charlie had put it on the jukebox: There are a number of different versions of this story. Johnny Black remembered clearly hearing the record in Charlie's; Ronald Smith recalled just as clearly Elvis bringing him to see it on the jukebox at the Pantaze Drug Store, opposite Ellis Auditorium; and Elvis' aunt Lillian Fortenberry placed it in a drugstore near Sun.

77 "They told me I couldn't sing": Elaine Dundy, *Elvis and Gladys,* pp. 175–176.

77 "Elvis, why don't you give it up?": Jimmy Hamill quoted by his father in Burk, *Early Elvis,* p. 118.

78 Pastor Hamill wouldn't approve: Ibid.

79 Sometimes while Bob was doing the commercials: Interview with James Blackwood, 1988.

80 ("If you can't drink it, freeze it"): Dewey's pitch adapted from Randy Haspel's version in "Tell 'Em Phillips Sencha," *Memphis,* June 1978.

80–81 Toward the end of April, Elvis got a new job: Background information on Crown Electric and James and Gladys Tipler comes from Elston Leonard's "Elvis Presley: The New Singing Rage," *Tiger,* c. 1956; *Elvis* by Jerry Hopkins; Jerry Hopkins' interviews with the Tiplers (MVC/MSU); the 1987 BBC television documentary *Presley: "I Don't Sing Like Nobody";* and "Elvis Presley Part 2: The Folks He Left Behind Him," *TV Guide,* September 22–28, 1956.

81 Dorsey told him about one night: Interviews with Scotty Moore, 1990, and Bobbie Moore, 1992; Ian Wallis interview with Paul Burlison, 1989.

81 Dorsey and Paul invited Elvis: This is an imagined conversation, but it is based on interview material — with Ronald Smith, Paul Burlison, Jimmy Denson, and Barbara Pittman, as well as a 1963 *New Musical Express* interview with Johnny Burnette — that makes it clear that he played places like the Home and the Girls' Club, the basement rec room of St. Mary's across the street from the Courts, on an increasingly regular basis. In addition, both Dixie Locke and Ronald Smith felt certain that he did not, and *would* not, play "joints" at this time. He even made this distaste clear to Sam Phillips and Bob Neal when he was embarking upon his professional career.

81 his parents were getting older: Jerry Hopkins interview with Bob Neal (MVC/MSU), in addition to interview with Dixie Locke.

82 (a Lodge banquet at the Columbia Mutual Towers): Interview with Ronald Smith, 1993; Buzzy Forbess, too, spoke in a 1991 interview of Elvis playing guitar at a number of dances put on at the Columbia Mutual Towers building by the Junior Order of the Oddfellows Lodge, to which Buzzy belonged.

82–83 The featured performer, Eddie Bond: The experience with Eddie Bond was described by Dixie Locke and Ronald Smith in separate interviews, while Elvis' recollection of the event in later years comes from an interview with George Klein. Eddie Bond's take on the incident is described somewhat differently in "Eddie Bond: A Reluctant Rockabilly Rocker Remembers" by Charles Raiteri, *Goldmine,* August 1, 1986.

As a final footnote, the Hi Hat was, evidently, a "higher class of joint," and the reason for the tryout in the first place, according to Ronald Smith, was that the owners, Tom and Mary, an older couple who had formerly been Arthur Murray dance instructors, wanted to institute a classier policy of entertainment, featuring waltzes and popular music. Since Eddie Bond by his own admission was strictly a country singer, and Elvis at this stage was strictly a pop singer, it seemed to be a perfect fit. Ron put the dismissal down to jealousy to some degree, but Eddie told Charles Raiteri in the *Goldmine* interview, "The big shots that run this place . . . sat at the front table like they was runnin' the Peabody and just stared at us. . . . I called 'em the 'Board of Directors.' [That] night . . . [the] old lady says, 'I'll tell you what you gone do. You gone get rid of that snaky-lookin' fella. If you don't, I'm gone fire all of you.' " Bond thought it was something of a matter of personal hygiene as well. "Elvis wasn't the cleanest guy you'd find, I'll guarantee you," he told Raiteri, further explaining the owners' distaste.

83 "We came very close": Elvis, too, spoke of how close the couple came to marriage. "I got out of school, and I was driving a truck. I was dating a girl and waiting for her to get out of school so we could get married," he said in a 1972 interview, only one of many times he referred to Dixie in similar fashion in subsequent years.

84 "I was in doubt": March 26, 1956, interview.

84 "She said, 'Can you be here?' ": 1972 interview.

84–85 Sam had picked up an acetate: This account is based primarily on interviews with Sam Phillips in 1979 and 1990. In the 1990 interview Sam told me that Wortham had an uncle who was a guard at the prison, and the uncle steered Wortham toward another prisoner, a short-termer, perhaps white, who recorded the acetate.

The role that this one-sided acetate has been assigned in history is quite different than the actual song will bear. Marion, I'm sure putting together two different stories, and knowing Sam's evolving thinking nearly as well as Sam himself, always said that this was the moment at which Sam realized his vision: "If I could find a white man who had the Negro sound and the Negro feel, I could make a billion dollars," she quoted Sam correctly, though, as she always said, the quote was missing Sam's underlying vision and irony ("Sam could not have cared less about the money") when it subsequently appeared in print. Far more misleading, however, is the context in which the quotation has generally been placed. All it takes is one listen to the acetate (which is in the possession of Dr. John Bakke at Memphis State and which was heard in part in the BBC documentary *Presley: "I Don't Sing Like Nobody"*) to realize that there could have been nothing less overtly African-American-sounding than this particular acetate or this particular song. Moreover, Elvis had given no one, least of all Sam Phillips, reason to think that he was drawn to black music in particular at this point.

Unquestionably, Sam Phillips heard something different in his voice, and there is equally little question that Phillips was coming to recognize at this time both the limitations of the "race" market and the unlimited possibilities, and untapped potential, in the popular appetite for African-American culture. One other side note of contention: Marion always said that Sam wanted to put out the demo as it was but couldn't find the singer. Sam has consistently denied that. You couldn't put out a record in that form, he has said, and the singer was secondary to the song in this case anyway. Listening to the demo tends to confirm Sam's view, though who knows — Sam Phillips prized originality above all else, and he may have heard something sufficiently different here to tempt him to put it on the market.

85 "I guess I must have sat there": Robert Johnson, *Elvis Presley Speaks!*, p. 10.

86–87 On the evening of Wednesday, June 30: In addition to interviews with Dixie Locke, James Blackwood, and Jake Hess on the crash and their own (and Elvis') reaction to it, I have relied on the accounts in the *Memphis Press-Scimitar* and *Commercial Appeal*, July 1–3, 1954.

All quotes from Sam Phillips, Marion Keisker, Scotty Moore, and Dixie Locke are from the author's interviews, unless otherwise noted.

89 The group, which had existed in various configurations: Background on the Starlite Wranglers from interviews with Scotty Moore, Bobbie Moore, and Evelyn Black, as well as Colin Escott and Martin Hawkins' *Good Rockin' Tonight: Sun Records and the Birth of Rock 'n' Roll.*

89 how they "could get on MGM": The quotation is from "Scotty Moore: The Guitar That Changed the World," interview by Robert Santelli, *Goldmine*, August 23, 1991.

91 Sometime around the middle of May: The dating, and the circumstances, are primarily from interviews with Scotty Moore.

91 "I told him I was working": Jerry Hopkins interview with Scotty Moore (MVC/MSU).

92 After a few minutes: The repertoire is based on various interviews with Scotty Moore over the years, the conversation on Scotty's description of Elvis' manner, with likely topics supplied in interviews with Scotty, Bobbie Moore, Evelyn Black, and Johnny Black. The whole question of whether Elvis knew Bill (he was certainly meeting Scotty for the first time) before they got together on this occasion is a somewhat vexed one. By all logical standards he *should* have known Bill, having lived across the street from Bill's mother for the past year or so and having known Bill's brother Johnny for quite some time. There is no question that Bill's wife, Evelyn, recognized Elvis, but neither Scotty nor Bobbie was aware of Bill's knowing Elvis, and Elvis always denied any prior acquaintance in his early interviews. It certainly seems possible that theirs was a nodding, but not a speaking, acquaintance. "[He] intended to use my brother on the fiddle," Bill told Bob Johnson in 1956 (*Elvis Presley Speaks!*, p. 10), but whether this was the literal truth or simply family politics is impossible to say.

93 The next night everybody: This description of the first night in the studio is based primarily on extensive interviews with Scotty Moore and Sam Phillips. The actual order of recording is impossible to determine, but Lee Cotten makes a good case for "Harbor Lights" coming first in his *All Shook Up: Elvis Day-by-Day, 1954–1977*, and there is little question that "I Love You Because" was recorded at the first session, prior to "That's All Right." Interestingly, Elvis' friend from the Courts, Buzzy Forbess, was under the impression that Elvis recorded "Blue Moon of Kentucky" first, a piece of misinformation fostered by Elvis when the record came out in what must have been a moment of embarrassment. "I never sang like [that] in my life," Elvis told *Jet* magazine in 1957, "until I made that first record. . . . I remembered that song because I heard Arthur (Big Boy Crudup) sing it and I thought I would like to try it. That was it."

95 "This is where the soul of man never dies": Robert Palmer, *Deep Blues*, p. 233.

95 It was a slap beat: Colin Escott, liner notes to Bill Black Combo album.

96 "we couldn't believe it was us": *Elvis Presley Speaks!*, p. 10.

96 "It just sounded sort of raw": Trevor Cajiao interview with Scotty Moore for "We Were the Only Band Directed by an Ass," *Elvis: The Man and His Music* 10, March 1991, p. 19.

96 "We thought it was exciting": Jerry Hopkins interview with Scotty Moore (MVC/MSU).

96 "It got so you could sell a half million copies": Edwin Howard, "He's Made $2 Million on Disks — Without a Desk," *Memphis Press-Scimitar*, April 29, 1959.

96–97 The next night everyone came to the studio: The exact chronology of these two nights is guesswork to a certain extent. There are no written records. I have Elvis singing "Blue Moon" (though he probably did not record an acceptable take of it until mid August), because he was singing the song when he first met Scotty and Bill, and at this point they were casting about, somewhat desperately, for a second side. We know that Dewey broke the record on the air at least by the Friday after it was first recorded, but which night exactly is somewhat open to conjecture. I have tried to follow what seemed to me the most logical progression, based primarily on the most persuasive of Sam Phillips' accounts of how, and why, he contacted Dewey.

98 "Dewey [was] completely unpredictable": Johnson's comments are constructed from columns in the *Press-Scimitar* on August 22, 1956; October 1, 1968; and June 20, 1972, all of which cover much the same ground.

98 "Dewey loved to argue": Interview with Dickey Lee, 1988.

99–100 Dewey opened a Falstaff: This account of Dewey and Sam's meeting is based primarily on interviews with Sam Phillips in 1988, 1989, and 1991.

100 "He fixed the radio": *Elvis Presley*, prepared by the editors of *TV Radio Mirror*, 1956, p. 21.

100 The response was instantaneous: Carlton Brown, "A Craze Called Elvis," *Coronet*, September 1956. This seems the most considered account of the overwhelming reaction.

100–101 "hearing them say his name": Elaine Dundy, *Elvis and Gladys*, pp. 180–181.

101 "Mrs. Presley, you just get": Elston Leonard, "Elvis Presley: The New Singing Rage," *Tiger*, c. 1956, p. 13.

101 "I was scared to death": Elvis interviewed on Dewey's death in the *Memphis Commercial Appeal*, September 29, 1968.

101 "Sit down, I'm gone interview": Stanley Booth, "A Hound Dog to the Manor Born," *Esquire*, February 1968.

101 It was Thursday, July 8: The story has been told many times, but this seems to me the most logical date by the sequence of events described. Recording would appear to have definitely taken place on Monday, July 5. Leaving some time for it all to settle in, one would imagine that Sam's meeting with Dewey would logically wait until Wednesday, which would leave Thursday for the actual making of an acetate before the Thursday-evening show. But obviously, this is only informed conjecture, and likely to remain so.

101 "I told him I loved it": Larry Johnson, "Memories of Elvis Shared by Close Friend," *Trenton Herald Gazette*, August 17, 1978.

102 "Sometime during the evening": Bill E. Burk, *Early Elvis: The Humes Years*, p. 131.

102 Another classmate, George Klein: Interview with George Klein, 1989.

102–103 "We spent three or four nights": Jerry Hopkins interview with Scotty Moore (MVC/MSU).

103 "All right, boys": Interview with Carl Perkins, 1979.

103 "That's fine now": This can be heard in conversation between takes on the album, *The Complete Sun Sessions*.

105 "like a little kid at Christmas": Telephone interview with Ed Leek, 1988.

105 Jack Clement, who was singing: Interviews with Jack Clement, 1978, 1989.

105 On Saturday, July 17: This can be dated because it was Dewey and Dot Phillips' sixth anniversary.

107 Dixie rode with him on his route: Various interviews with James and Gladys Tipler, including *Elvis* by Jerry Hopkins; Jerry Hopkins' interviews with the Tiplers (MVC/MSU); the 1987 BBC television documentary *Presley: "I Don't Sing Like Nobody"*; and "Elvis Presley: The New Singing Rage" by Elston Leonard in *Tiger*, c. 1956.

108 She had hoped: Interview with Marion Keisker, 1981.

108 "I'll never forget": Burk, *Elvis: A 30-Year Chronicle*, p. 7.

110 "I was scared stiff": Paul Wilder interview, August 6, 1956.

110 "It was really a wild sound": 1972 interview.

110 "I came offstage": Paul Wilder interview.

When Elvis referred to "my manager," the interviewer asked him who his manager was at the time. Momentarily flustered, Elvis stammered, "Bob . . . Bob Neal," who became his manager several months later. It's hard to say for sure whether it was in fact Neal or Sam Phillips, who clearly was there to provide reassurance and inspiration, who explained the crowd reaction to him, but given the context, and the fact that Neal was the "manager" of the show, it seems likely that it was Neal who, essentially, pushed him back out onstage.

110 Elvis sang "Blue Moon of Kentucky" again: What he sang for his encore is purely supposition at this point. Scotty said they *could* have sung "I Love You Because," because they had rehearsed it — but he doubted that they did. In his recollection "That's All Right" and "Blue Moon of Kentucky" were not simply the only songs that they knew well enough to perform in this kind of setting, they were the only songs that the audience would have wanted to hear. No one else that I have interviewed to date, or whose interview I have read, has offered persuasive testimony to the contrary, but there may well be someone out there who actually knows!

110–111 "It was a real eye-opener": Jerry Hopkins interview with Bob Neal (MVC/MSU).

111–112 he had traveled between sixty-five thousand and seventy-five thousand miles: Trevor Cajiao, "The Most Important Man in the World: Sam Phillips Talks to *Now Dig This*," pt. 2, *Now Dig This* 84, March 1990, p. 17.

112 "I remember talking": Escott and Hawkins, *Good Rockin' Tonight*, p. 67.

112 "He played my r&b records": Escott interview of Sam Phillips as quoted in ibid. and Charles Raiteri liner notes to the Dewey Phillips air checks album, *Red Hot & Blue*, on the Zu Zazz label.

112 "Paul Berlin was the hottest": *Now Dig This*, p. 20.

113 "One night I left Houston": Ibid., edited down from a more discursive account, with permission.

114 "The current greeting": *Cowboy Songs*, June 1955.

114–115 "I thought, Surely, no": Interview with Ronny Trout, 1991.

115 Johnny Black was in Texas: Interview with Johnny Black, 1990.

115 Ronnie Smith called up for Eddie Bond: Interview with Ronald Smith, 1993.

115 he brought the record out to the Rainbow skating rink: Vince Staten, *The Real Elvis: Good Old Boy*, p. 92.

116 The Songfellows, Elvis told her: There are persistent rumors that Elvis tried out again for the Songfellows at around this time. Neither Sam nor Scotty nor Dixie nor James Blackwood recalled a specific tryout, but it would not be unlike Elvis to compartmentalize his activities in such a way that they would not be aware of it.

Vernon Presley offered the most specific recollection. "Later, after he made a couple of records professionally," Vernon declared in his January 1978 *Good Housekeeping* article with Nancy Anderson, "Elvis came to me and said, 'Daddy, you know the Song Fellows? They want me to join them now.' My answer to that was, 'To hell with the Song Fellows! You're doing good with what you've got going, and I don't believe I would change.' "

116 "They taught him how to stand": Interview with Bobbie Moore and Evelyn Black, 1993.

116–117 "It was kind of like we adopted him": Interview with Bobbie Moore, 1992.

117 they played out at the Kennedy Veterans: Ibid.

117 "My mother brought a group out once a month": Interview with Monte Weiner, 1993.

119 "He wanted us to come out": *Tiger*.

119 According to Reggie Young: Interview with Reggie Young, 1989.

119–120 "Sleepy Eyed John was all into Ray Price's": Interview with Jack Clement, 1989.

120 "he didn't play with bands": Elizabeth Kaye, "Sam Phillips: The *Rolling Stone* Interview," *Rolling Stone* 467, February 13, 1986, p. 56.

121 On the strength of these credentials: Jim Denny's role was detailed in interviews with Sam Phillips in 1979, 1988, and 1990.

121–122 Others were noticing: Mike Seeger interview with Carter Stanley, spring 1966, as quoted in *Bluegrass: A History* by Neil V. Rosenberg, with additional material from Rosenberg; also, "Joe Meadows: Mountain State Fiddler" by Ivan M. Tribe, *Bluegrass Unlimited*, October 1978.

122 "All of our distributors": Interview with Chick Crumpacker, 1989.

122–123 "My bell-cow area": Interview with Brad McCuen, 1988.

124 "This was the first we could see": Jerry Hopkins interview with Scotty Moore (MVC/ MSU). In addition I interviewed Scotty, Dixie Locke, George Klein, and a number of bystanders about the performance.

124–125 In Florida, Lee Denson: Interview with Jimmy and Lee Denson, 1989.

GOOD ROCKIN' TONIGHT

All quotes from Sam Phillips, Marion Keisker, Scotty Moore, and Dixie Locke are from the author's interviews, unless otherwise noted.

127 Jim Denny had finally succumbed: Sam first met Jim Denny in 1944 when he applied for a job as an announcer at WSM, the Opry's mother station. When he didn't get the job, and his future partner, Jim Bulleit, did, Bulleit sent him down the street to WLAC, where Bulleit had already won a job that he was now going to pass up.

127–128 In the meantime Sam had also heard: Interviews with Sam Phillips, 1979, 1990, 1991.

128 Twenty-one-year-old bass player Buddy Killen: Interview with Buddy Killen, 1989.

128 Marty Robbins saw evidence: Alanna Nash interview with Marty Robbins in her book *Behind Closed Doors: Talking with the Legends of Country Music*, p. 443.

128 when Elvis spotted Chet Atkins: Interview with Chet Atkins, 1988.

128 Probably of all the Opry legends: Interview with Sam Phillips, 1988.

128–129 But when they met Monroe: Interviews with Sam Phillips and Bill Monroe, 1980. Also Neil Rosenberg's *Bluegrass: A History* describes the meeting, as does *Bluegrass 1950–1958: Bill Monroe,* the Charles Wolfe and Neil Rosenberg booklet that accompanies the Bear Family boxed set of Monroe's music of the same name.

129 There were two additional surprises: Interviews with Marion Keisker, 1981, and with Bobbie Moore and Evelyn Black, 1993.

129–130 Before leaving, Sam conferred briefly: Interview with Sam Phillips, 1988.

This contradicts the well-known version that has Denny telling Elvis to go back to driving a truck — but then so does the account of every eyewitness that I have interviewed. The almost universal acceptance of the story by members of the music community who were not present appears to be based on two factors: Denny's personal chilliness and somewhat autocratic manner, and Elvis' genuine dislike of the man for that reason. But Denny, if anything, was giving Elvis a break, not denying him one, and if it would not have been out of character for him, in another well-known part of the story, to have referred slightingly to Elvis' music as "nigger music," such attitudes were common, as Chet Atkins has frequently pointed out, in many segments of the country music community at that time. The story that Elvis cried all the way back to Memphis is based on thirdhand testimony; as Marion Keisker said, "There was only Sam and Elvis and me in the car. We were in good spirits. I'd like to see where that other person was sitting."

130 They left not long afterward: Interview with Ernest Tubb, 1976; also interviews with Justin Tubb, 1989, and Bobbie Moore, as well as the *Ernest Tubb Discography (1936–1969)* by Norma Barthel. According to Tubb and his son, Justin, Elvis wrote a note to Ernest afterward, thanking Tubb for his kindness and advice. It should perhaps be borne in mind that what Elvis said to Ernest Tubb, a childhood idol, might have been more in the nature of politeness, an unerring instinct for deference, or, as Marion said, never putting a foot wrong. It is not necessarily a statement to be taken literally, though Ernest obviously did.

132 as good as it was "humanly possible": Jerry Hopkins interview with Marion Keisker (MVC/MSU).

132 the Shelton Brothers had originally recorded: The Shelton Brothers were originally the Attlesey brothers. The song is credited to the Attleseys and guitarist Leon Chapplear, but it clearly goes back to an earlier blues and "minstrel" tradition. The Attlesey lineage is spelled out in Billy Altman's liner notes to *Are You from Dixie? Great Country Brother Teams of the 1930's,* on RCA.

133 With the last song of the session: This more or less follows the order suggested by Lee Cotten in *All Shook Up: Elvis Day-by-Day, 1954–1977* (Cotten appears to have been working from RCA executive Steve Sholes' notes), and Ernst Jorgensen's definitive discography. It must be emphasized, however, that there can be no certainty as to order in the absence of a true recording log.

133 To Marion Keisker it was like: Jerry Hopkins interview with Marion Keisker (MVC/MSU).

135ff Sam called Pappy Covington: This account is based on interviews with a myriad of sources, including Sam Phillips, Scotty Moore, Tillman Franks, Billy Walker, Frank Page, and Horace Logan. Unfortunately, there is nearly as much dispute over Elvis' arrival at the Hayride as there is over his arrival at the Memphis Recording Service, or at the Opry, for that matter. According to Horace Logan, it was he who first contacted Sam Phillips (though Tillman Franks, with whom he fell out just around this time, played an unspecified part), and it was he who first introduced Elvis onstage. Both Slim Whitman and Billy Walker, who appeared on the bill at Overton Park, have suggested credibly in published interviews that they brought the news of the young Memphis phenomenon back to the Hayride, while Tillman's story seeks credit for nothing but the need to find a substitute for Jimmy and Johnny on the Hayride bill. From talking with most of the principal players, I think the scenario I have presented is as logical a version as one might come up with, but that doesn't mean it happened that way.

136–137ff The Hayride was a little over six years old: Background information on the Hayride comes from interviews with Horace Logan, Tillman Franks, Frank Page, T. Tommy Cutrer, Merle Kilgore, and Alton and Margaret Warwick, among others. Also the 1984 PBS documentary *Cradle of the Stars* and "Saturday Night Live" by Joe Rhodes in *Westward* (the *Dallas Times-Herald* magazine), October 10, 1982.

138 He stopped by Stan's Record Shop: Interview with Stan Lewis, 1990; also Robert Trudeau, "Stan the Record Man," *Upstate,* December 8, 1983.

138 He walked out on the stage: Interview with Horace Logan, 1991.

138–139 He was wearing: This is a composite picture put together from descriptions of Elvis' appearance that evening and contemporaneous photographs. I don't know of a photograph from that first performance itself.

139 Horace Logan was out onstage: Interview with Horace Logan. Logan fully described his working methods.

140 "Elvis, how are you this evening?": This dialogue, which prefaces performances of "That's All Right" and "Blue Moon of Kentucky," appears on *Elvis. . . . The Beginning Years,* on the Louisiana Hayride/RCA label. Despite Horace Logan's claim, the interlocutor appears to be Frank Page (though it's always possible that Logan preceded Page). The tape seems to be authentic, and I don't know any reason to question its dating (the dialogue is certainly awkward enough to signal a first appearance). In any case, it's well worth a listen.

140–141 The cheers that went up: Interviews with Sam Phillips, Merle Kilgore, Tillman Franks, Jimmy "C" Newman, Curley Herndon, et al., 1989–92.

142 "I'd never seen anything like it before": Interview with Jimmy "C" Newman, 1990.

142 "I think he scared them": Interview with Merle Kilgore, 1989.

143 "My daddy had seen": 1972 interview.

143 He missed the Hayride for the next two weeks: There has been some debate over this issue. There is no question that Elvis returned to the Hayride and signed a contract on November 6, 1954, or that he missed the October 30 broadcast. I had believed from oral testimony, and from a story in *"The Cashbox* Country Roundup" of November 6, 1954 (which quoted Marion Keisker on the success of his second week's appearance), that he played the Hayride on October 23. But he does not appear to have been listed in the lineup, and Scotty's recollection is that there was at least a two-week gap while Sam was "negotiating the contract — not that there was all that much to negotiate, at twenty-four dollars a week or whatever it was." Sam, meanwhile, recalls clearly that they did *not* return until at least three weeks later, after the contract had been arranged.

144ff That Friday night Bob Neal brought a visitor: This account of Oscar Davis' discovery of a fresh young talent is based on several interlinked sources: Jerry Hopkins interviews with Oscar Davis and Bob Neal (MVC/MSU); a joint interview with both Colonel Parker and Oscar Davis carried out briefly in the aftermath of Elvis' well-known interview in August 1956; Gordon Stoker's recollections to me (and others) of meeting Elvis backstage at the Eddy Arnold show, long before Elvis had made his mark; my interview with Hoyt Hawkins' widow, Dot Hawkins; ads and a review in the *Memphis Press-Scimitar* of Eddy Arnold's October 31 show; and the documented fact that by early January the Colonel was well aware of exactly who Elvis Presley was.

At the time of that first meeting, Oscar Davis told Hopkins, "Scotty Moore was acting as [Elvis'] manager. . . . They were somewhat excited about getting me in the picture with them, and we agreed to meet the following Sunday when Eddy Arnold would be in town and I would be in town." In the 1956 interview Parker credited Davis with "introducing" him to the boy (he refused to acknowledge that Davis actually discovered him), though it is unclear whether he actually met Presley at the time, and Davis made a point to Hopkins that he tried to keep his find secret from the Colonel. Both Parker and Davis stipulated that an Eddy Arnold concert in Memphis was the occasion, and Davis declared that "I called him to the Colonel's attention on the Sunday which we played [there]." The working out of this scenario has involved some guesswork, obviously, but the only discrepancy that I am aware of is that Davis remembered going to see Elvis perform at a little "airport inn." The fact that Elvis was advertised at the Eagle's Nest the weekend of the Eddy Arnold show seems to resolve the discrepancy.

Background on Oscar Davis and Tom Parker stems from numerous interviews, including invaluable ones with Grelun Landon, Gabe Tucker, and Sam Phillips, as well as extensive documentation in Marge Crumbaker and Gabe Tucker's *Up and Down with Elvis Presley; Elvis* by Jerry

Hopkins; *It's a Long Way from Chester County* by Eddy Arnold; *Elvis and Gladys* by Elaine Dundy; *Elvis and the Colonel* by Dirk Vellenga; and *Elvis* by Albert Goldman.

145–146 he introduced him to Eddy and to Hoyt Hawkins: Interview with Gordon Stoker, 1989.

146 they had enjoyed *his* singing, too: Jerry Hopkins interview with Neal Matthews (MVC/MSU).

146 The following Saturday night: Interview with Horace Logan. The actual contract is available and has been widely reproduced.

147 They stopped by the Chisca to visit: Elvis' relationship with Dewey was documented in interviews with Sam Phillips, Dixie Locke, June Juanico, and Dickey Lee, among others, as well as by Jonnie Barnett's extensive interviews with Harry Fritzius and Charles Raiteri's exhaustive research for his fine screenplay on Dewey.

So far as the issue of Elvis on Beale, this is an old, and much-debated, question. I have spoken with innumerable Beale Streeters, and read the testimony in *Beale Black & Blue* by Margaret McKee and Fred Chisenhall. Although Rufus Thomas has adamantly insisted he never saw Elvis on Beale until the December 1956 WDIA Goodwill Revue, I don't have any problem placing Elvis on Beale; it is just a question of when. From speaking with Elvis' childhood friends, and considering the nature of the young man, I find it far more likely that he would start going down to the clubs once he had achieved a certain measure of confidence and respect, and if WDIA's Professor Nat D. Williams was Beale Street's uncrowned mayor, Dewey Phillips was something like a roving ambassador from another galaxy. There is nothing in the interviews with Beale Street habitués that I have conducted or read that would indicate a distinction in the mind of the speaker between a young Elvis Presley who had not recorded at all and a young Elvis Presley who had simply recorded locally but was not widely known, at least not in the black community. That, as I see it, is the cause of the confusion. Robert Henry, for example, who is quoted in *Beale Black & Blue* as having "taken him to the Hotel Improvement Club with me," was cited in much the same role in the *Press-Scimitar* on Elvis' death with one telling exception: "I met him through Dewey Phillips," Henry said. You can read the interviews with Billy "The Kid" Emerson (*Living Blues* 45/46, spring 1980), Sunbeam Mitchell (by David Less, unpublished), and Calvin Newborn with this chronology in mind, and I don't believe there is anything in any of them that would sharply contradict it. And when an even younger, even less well known white boy is recalled hanging out in the clubs at a presumed earlier date, the question naturally arises: How did you know it was Elvis? In the absence of an introduction, the presumption must be that the name was attached retrospectively. This is all, in other words, inductive (but not, I hope, circular) reasoning, and persuasive only to the point that it is actually proved, or disproved, by documented events. Putting the description in the form of a dialogue with Dixie is a narrative device, however: the conversation may have happened, but it is not a memory that I have gotten from Dixie, and it is simply a means of threading together a chronological story in a manner that seems to me reasonably plausible.

148 Toward the end of football season: Jerry Hopkins interview with Red West (MVC/MSU); Red West et al., *Elvis: What Happened?*; Trevor Cajiao interview with Red West for *Elvis: The Man and His Music* 22, March 1994; interview with Buzzy Forbess, 1991.

148 "He would look in the papers": Interview with Guy Lansky, 1990.

148 Ronnie Smith recalled running into Elvis: Interview with Ronald Smith, 1993.

148 Sometimes old friends passed him: He speaks of this happening, at a later date, to Bob Neal in Robert Johnson, *Elvis Presley Speaks!*, p. 30.

148 he didn't know if they were laughing: He cites this fear in his Warwick Hotel interview in March 1956.

149 In between shows at the auditorium: Interview with Maylon Humphries, 1991.

149 With Merle Kilgore: Interview with Merle Kilgore.

149–150 Sometimes they would go: Interview with Maylon Humphries.

150 They worked one night: Interviews with Curly Herndon, 1991; Scotty Moore; D. J. Fontana, 1988, 1991; and Tillman Franks, 1991–93.

150–152 Pappy called Tom Perryman: Interview with Tom Perryman, 1989.

Scotty Moore confirmed how the connection came about and the nature of the relationship. "A lot of times," Perryman recalled, "the boys would come by after the show. Elvis would look after our three kids when we took the baby-sitter home. Hamburgers and banana pudding."

152–153 On Thursday, November 25: Interview with Biff Collie, 1990.

In addition to the quotes, much of the background material on Biff Collie comes from this same interview. Additional information on Collie from interviews with Tillman Franks and T. Tommy Cutrer, while the Eagle's Nest incident was illuminated by Franks as well as by the story "The Notorious 'Country' Johnny Mathis" by Bill Carpenter, which appeared in *Goldmine,* May 28, 1993. The telegram was on display for a time at the Elvis — Up Close Museum, across from Graceland, and was published in *Goldmine,* August 10, 1990, in a story by Joe Haertel, "Retracing Elvis's Memphis and Tupelo Footsteps."

153–156 Meanwhile, Bob Neal was looking on his new project: Jerry Hopkins interviews with Bob Neal (MVC/MSU).

154 "they didn't know exactly how to take him": This description of Elvis' development as a stage performer is assembled from various points in Jerry Hopkins' interviews with Bob Neal (MVC/MSU).

154–155 Sometimes Bill would come out of the audience: Interviews with Bobbie Moore, 1992, and Bobbie Moore and Evelyn Black, 1993.

156 Elvis had already given himself: *Elvis Presley Speaks!,* p. 16; Robert Johnson, "Suddenly Singing Elvis Presley Zooms into Recording Stardom," *Memphis Press-Scimitar,* February 5, 1955; *Country & Western Jamboree,* April 1955.

157 a new song by a Covington, Tennessee, theater manager: Colin Escott and Martin Hawkins, *Good Rockin' Tonight: Sun Records and the Birth of Rock 'n' Roll,* p. 72.

FORBIDDEN FRUIT

All quotes from Sam Phillips, Marion Keisker, Scotty Moore, and Dixie Locke are from the author's interviews, unless otherwise noted.

160 "They did a lot of their harmony gospel songs": Interview with Tom Perryman, 1989.

160–162 In Corinth, Mississippi: Interviews with Buddy and Kay Bain, 1989, 1990, 1994.

162 It was all like a dream: Elvis referred to this fear again and again, that somehow his success would turn out to be all an illusion, from his earliest recorded interviews on. "I think about things that have happened," he told Edwin Miller in May 1956 ("Elvis Presley," *Seventeen,* fall 1956), "and it's kind of like a dream. A year and a half ago, I was nothing." To Bob Johnson he insisted that, despite this dreamlike atmosphere, he would never forget "who I am and where I came from and my friends and how this all happened."

162–163 there was a full, four-column spread: *Memphis Press-Scimitar*, February 5, 1955.

163 He was fascinated, too: Interview with Martha Carson, 1989; Dave Byers, "Martha Carson: 'The Rockin' Queen of Happy Spirituals,' " 1983.

163–164 In between shows he and Scotty went across the street: Scotty recalled the experience in 1988, 1989, and 1992 interviews; Sam Phillips spoke of it in 1989 and 1990 interviews; the date in New Boston in early January has been confirmed by a January 24, 1955, letter from the Colonel to Robert Shivers, a promoter in Hope, Arkansas, in which the Colonel states: "Presley alone did over $500 in New Boston a few weeks ago."

164–165,169–170 The meeting at Palumbo's: This account has been put together primarily from interviews with Sam Phillips and Scotty Moore, along with Oscar Davis' colorful, if somewhat confused, description to Jerry Hopkins (MVC/MSU). Davis gives the most vivid account by far of the Colonel's frontal assault, but both Scotty's and Sam's impressions of Tom Parker in the aftermath of the meeting, and the Colonel's subsequent attempt to sell Tommy Sands, not Elvis Presley, to RCA as a harbinger of the new music, bear out the somewhat unfortunate contretemps that resulted, at least initially, from this meeting.

165 Thomas A. Parker on first impression: Much of the specific background on the Colonel here comes from Marge Crumbaker and Gabe Tucker's *Up and Down with Elvis Presley*; Dirk Vellenga's *Elvis and the Colonel*; and Albert Goldman's *Elvis*.

165–166 Acuff, then known as: Elizabeth Schlappi, *Roy Acuff*.

166 According to Oscar Davis: This description of Colonel Parker has been put together from various points in Jerry Hopkins' interview with Oscar Davis (MVC/MSU).

166 To Biff Collie, the Houston DJ: Interview with Biff Collie, 1990.

166 Gabe Tucker, who met Parker: Interview with Gabe Tucker, 1990.

167 "When Tom's your manager": Eddy Arnold, *It's a Long Way from Chester County*, pp. 46–47.

167 From now on, he told Gabe Tucker: Crumbaker and Tucker, *Up and Down*, p. 74.

167–168 In 1953, in an episode: Jerry Hopkins, *Elvis*, p. 101.

168 Arnold and Parker "were dissipating": Crumbaker and Tucker, *Up and Down*, p. 71.

168 making his office in the lobby: Jerry Hopkins interview with Bill Williams (MVC/MSU); the story is told in Hopkins' *Elvis*, p. 102.

168 By the spring of 1954: *Billboard* passim.

168 "No one knows very much": Jerry Hopkins interview with Oscar Davis (MVC/MSU).

168–169 "You have one fault": Vellenga, *Elvis and the Colonel*, p. 126.

169 As Gabe Tucker observed: Interview with Gabe Tucker.

169 everyone else in the Colonel's estimation: "Everyone has weaknesses," Oscar Davis told Jerry Hopkins (MVC/MSU). "He'll read you very quickly. Helluva guy."

171–175 Snow was bowled over by his first exposure to this kid: Interviews with Jimmie Rodgers Snow, 1990, 1993, 1994.

A note on the spelling of Jimmie Rodgers Snow's name. Snow was named, obviously, for his father's musical idol. He came to identify himself, however, as "Jimmy," both as an artist and, in later years, as a minister. Hence the discrepancy in spelling.

One final note. Jimmy Snow believes that he played Lubbock with Elvis a month earlier than this booking, operating as a kind of scout for his father and Colonel Parker. After extensive interviews with Billy Walker, who headlined Elvis' first, brief West Texas tour; Tillman Franks, who booked it; and "Pappy" Dave Stone, who booked the Lubbock gigs in both January and February (not to mention Bill Griggs' article "Elvis Presley in Lubbock" in *Rockin' '50s*, August 1992), I have come to the conclusion that this is just a matter of the normal telescoping and expansion of memory — but I remain open to correction.

171 "His energy was incredible": Nick Kent, "Roy Orbison: *The Face* Interview," *The Face,* 1989.

172–173 "He was this punk kid": Ibid.

173 "There never was a country act": Jerry Hopkins interview with Bob Neal (MVC/MSU).

173 The trouble was: Robert Johnson, *TV Star Parade,* September 1956, p. 65.

174 "I see people all different ages": 1972 interview.

174 "He would study a crowd": Interview with Tillman Franks.

174 "He was always unhappy": Jerry Hopkins interview with Bob Neal (MVC/MSU).

175–176 the startling success of Alan Freed: My primary source for background on Alan Freed was John Jackson's biography *Big Beat Heat: Alan Freed and the Early Years of Rock & Roll.*

176–177 "For the past year the top U.S. deejay": *Time,* February 14, 1955, © 1955. Reprinted by permission.

177 ("It was a tremendous emotional problem"): *Cleveland Plain Dealer,* September 15, 1956.

177–178 "He was extremely shy": This and subsequent quotes by Randle are from Ger Rijff and Jan van Gestel, *Memphis Lonesome.*

178 On March 15: Jerry Hopkins interview with Bob Neal (MVC/MSU); also Report of Guardian Ad Litem re the Estate of Elvis A. Presley, Deceased, in the Probate Court of Shelby County, Tennessee (this reproduces the Colonel's agreement with Neal on November 21, 1955).

179 While they were out: Interview with Stan Kesler, 1987.

179 this new boy Perkins: Colin Escott and Martin Hawkins, *Good Rockin' Tonight: Sun Records and the Birth of Rock 'n Roll,* p. 130.

180 Jimmie Lott was a junior: Ibid., p. 73.

181 Some two weeks later: Both the date and the background have been established by correspondence between Colonel Parker and Bob Neal, and Colonel and the William Morris Agency, which ultimately set up the audition. The information on the trip itself is from Jerry Hopkins' interviews with Bob Neal and mine with Scotty Moore, while Bill Randle's perspective is described in Rijff and van Gestel, *Memphis Lonesome.*

182 a 1951 Cosmopolitan Lincoln: Interview with Merle Kilgore, 1989. Information on the Cadillac comes primarily from records made available through the Elvis Presley Estate.

182 "It was always exciting": 1972 interview.

182 "He's the new rage": Jules J. Paglin, "Louisiana Disc Jockeys," *Melody Maker,* December 31, 1955 (as reprinted in *Blues World* 31, June 1970).

182–183 "This cat came out": Paul Hemphill, *The Nashville Sound: Bright Lights and Country Music,* pp. 272–273.

183 The Miller Sisters, the performing duo: Hank Davis, "The Miller Sisters," *DISCoveries,* June 1989.

184 "one of the newest": Souvenir program accompanying the "Hank Snow All Star Jamboree" tour.

184 Johnny Rivers saw the show: Steve Roeser, "Johnny Rivers: The Man Who Made the Whisky," *Goldmine,* September 6, 1991.

184 Jimmy Snow roomed: Interview with Jimmie Rodgers Snow, 1990.

185–186 He met Mae Boren Axton: Interview with Mae Boren Axton, 1988.

186–188 In the interview he persisted: Mae told me about this interview before I heard it, and we spoke about it afterward. Actually putting a date on it has proved to be a persistent problem. In the course of the interview Mae refers to Elvis having previously played Florida, which would lead one to wonder about its actual date. It certainly *sounds* like a first meeting, and my best guess about the somewhat tentative references to earlier touring is that this was a way to indicate a wider celebrity than the singer actually possessed. The evident intention of the interview was to publicize his appearances throughout Florida over the next week; at least that is the most logical explanation I can come up with. The fact that the Jacksonville riot of May 13 is not referred to indicates to me that the interview predates the actual tour.

188 "and she was just right into it": Interview with Mae Boren Axton.

189–190 "Skeeter Davis was there": Ibid.

191–192 Parker had accused publicist Anne Fulchino: This account and the subsequent quotes by Crumpacker are from interviews and letters, 1989–94.

192 Chick finished up his trip: The next time Chick saw Elvis was at the third annual Jimmie Rodgers Festival in Meridian, Mississippi, on May 25. Founded to honor the "Singing Brakeman," who was widely hailed as the Father of Country Music, the festival also served as a kind of trade convention about midway between one annual DJ convention in Nashville and the next. Elvis and Scotty and Bill made a big impression on the '55 festival, practically causing a riot in their appearance at the football stadium and coming to the inescapable attention of Steve Sholes, Chick's boss at RCA. Hill and Range was also represented in the person of Grelun Landon, and there were innumerable other performers and industry figures getting a look at this new phenomenon for the first time.

The reason I mention all this is that in recent years a story has sprung up that this was not Elvis' first trip to Meridian. In 1953, so the story goes, Elvis hitchhiked to Meridian two days short of high school graduation, performed in an amateur contest to some acclaim, and then borrowed ten dollars from a festival official to get back home. I first heard this story in 1980 when I was in Meridian for the festival and have tried to track it down ever since. I have never found any evidence to support the story, and, while it is always possible that hard evidence will turn up, it seems more likely that this is yet another case of two stories merging: the first that of an unknown young singer who appears hungry and talented (and anonymous) in 1953, the second the appearance two years later of a rapidly gathering sensation still largely unknown to an older generation. It would not be at all inconceivable that these two stories could become legitimately confused. In any case, Elvis enjoyed a real triumph at Meridian in 1955 among both his peers and his elders.

All quotes from Sam Phillips, Marion Keisker, Scotty Moore, and Dixie Locke are from the author's interviews, unless otherwise noted.

195 a man who had it in his power: Neal and Parker conferred in Memphis all day on June 17, just one month after the Jacksonville "riot." According to the July 2 *Cash Box*: "Bob Neal . . . flew into Nashville last weekend for a meeting with Col. Tom Parker . . . [and] signed an exclusive contract with Hank Snow Enterprises, allowing the company to represent Presley in all phases of the entertainment field. Neal, however, will continue as exclusive manager of Presley."

195–204 On balance Bob Neal was well satisfied: Not only the quoted material but the appraisal of Elvis' career, his listening habits, and avidity for knowledge, all stem from Jerry Hopkins' interviews with Bob Neal (MVC/MSU).

196 "I was, I think, a year or two": Neal was in fact about a year younger than Vernon.

196–197 Then on July 4 he found himself: Information on the De Leon date from interviews with James Blackwood and J. D. Sumner in 1988, 1990, and 1991: also *Country & Western Jamboree,* October 1955 , as supplied by Wayne Russell, Lee Cotten's *All Shook Up* (second edition), and Bob Terrell's *The Music Men.* Colin Escott's biography, *Hank Williams,* points out that Hank Williams was booked in 1950 but showed up drunk and didn't perform.

197–199 The next-door neighbors, the Bakers: Interviews with Jackson Baker in 1989, 1990, and 1992, as well as a joint telephone interview with Jack, his sister, Sarah, and their mother, Eve, in 1990. Just when the Presleys got their phone became a matter of some debate among the Bakers, but even if the Presleys had their own line by July, as might well be expected, both Jackson's and Sarah's memories of him on their hall phone are so vivid that it seems clear that he must have continued to make some calls from their home even afterward.

199 "He told me to drive it": Interview with Guy Lansky, 1990.

201 He kept telling them about Colonel Parker: "Elvis by His Father Vernon Presley" as told to Nancy Anderson, *Good Housekeeping,* January 1978, p. 157.

202–203 Meanwhile Bob Neal was fielding offers: Jerry Hopkins interviews with Bob Neal (MVC/MSU).

Additional information on the other labels' interest in Elvis comes from interviews with Jerry Wexler, Jerry Leiber and Mike Stoller, Grelun Landon, and Sam Phillips, as well as Colin Escott and Martin Hawkins' *Good Rockin' Tonight: Sun Records and the Birth of Rock 'n' Roll* (the MGM telegram); Arnold Shaw's *The Rockin' '50s;* Bill Randle in *Memphis Lonesome* by Ger Rijff and Jan van Gestel; Vince Staten's *The Real Elvis: Good Old Boy* (on Randy Wood's offer); and Albert Cunniff, "Muscle Behind the Music: The Life and Times of Jim Denny," pt. 3, *Journal of Country Music,* vol. 11, no. 3 (on the involvement of Jim Denny, Jud Phillips, and Decca Records).

206 "Elvis Presley on Beale Street": Margaret McKee and Fred Chisenhall, *Beale Black & Blue,* p. 95.

206 "before he could be rescued": *Cash Box,* August 13, 1955.

206–208 Vernon seemed pretty much ready to sign: The account of this Little Rock meeting is based primarily on Vince Staten's interview with Whitey Ford in *The Real Elvis,* Vernon Presley's testimony in his *Good Housekeeping* story, and — for the specific context in which the Colonel's wooing of the Presleys was taking place — my own interviews with Sam Phillips, Marion Keisker, Jimmie Rodgers Snow, Hank Snow, Gabe Tucker, Mae Boren Axton, Lillian Fortenberry, and Scotty Moore, as well as Jerry Hopkins' interviews with Marion Keisker and Bob Neal (MVC/MSU).

207 maybe her boy was being overworked: Jerry Hopkins interview with Marion Keisker (MVC/MSU).

207 spending a few days with Colonel and Mrs. Parker: Jerry Hopkins, *Elvis,* p. 117.

207 "He seemed like a smart man": *Good Housekeeping,* p. 157.

208 she "heard someone screaming": Jerry Hopkins interview with Marion Keisker (MVC/MSU).

208 "Of course I never actually met the Colonel": Interview with Marion Keisker, 1988.

209–210 a document that named "Col. Thomas A. Parker": Report of Guardian Ad Litem re the Estate of Elvis A. Presley, Deceased, in the Probate Court of Shelby County, Tennessee.

THE PIED PIPERS

All quotes from Sam Phillips, Marion Keisker, Scotty Moore, and Dixie Locke are from the author's interviews, unless otherwise noted.

213 When Arnold Shaw, the newly named general professional manager: Arnold Shaw, *The Rockin' '50s*, pp. 4–7. Shaw had accompanied Chick Crumpacker to Meridian in May.

213 The contract stipulated: The contract that I have seen does not stipulate the four-hundred-dollar penalty, but Horace Logan has referred to it frequently in interviews and in his interview with Rob Finnis said of Elvis, "He probably thought I pocketed it!" In any case, it clearly came into effect in the spring of 1956, when Elvis in effect left the Hayride, and it clearly stymied the Colonel. The Colonel's role, and his frustration with Vernon, were clearly delineated by the Colonel to me, within the context of a story about Vernon signing the renewal while the Colonel was in New York trying to sell Elvis' contract. Since the Hayride contract is dated September 8, and the Colonel was in New York a month and a half later, I can only think that this is another case of memory telescoping events — unless, of course, the renewal was backdated. But Bob Neal's pride in negotiating that renewal ("We negotiated a deal that was quite a thing then," he told Jerry Hopkins [MVC/MSU]) would suggest otherwise.

213 share the cost of [D.J.'s] $100-a-week salary: Max Weinberg, *The Big Beat: Conversations with Rock's Great Drummers*, p. 115.

213 he kept saying he couldn't afford it: Jerry Hopkins interview with Scotty Moore (MVC/MSU).

214 "The eventual basic decision": Jerry Hopkins interview with Bob Neal (MVC/MSU).

214 Scotty and Bill were inclined: Scotty has always spoken of a royalty understanding that would have gone into effect at some undefined (but clearly indicated) point in the future, but I don't think that is what came into play here.

Scotty's expectation was based on conversations at the very outset of Elvis' career. "It was never on paper. Bill and I would split half of one percent, one quarter percent each. Strictly on record royalties. This came about from several conversations sitting on the steps in front of the house on Alabama just pipe-dreaming, a few weeks, I'm guessing, after the first record came out. [We were thinking]: 'With all the commotion going on in Memphis, we better tighten up our business stuff here. We're liable to have to go across to West Memphis!' We had already agreed to a three-way split, with expenses equal. He said, 'Okay, we'll do this on everything [including record royalties].' I told him, from what little I knew about the music business, 'No, that won't work. 'Cause if we do anything, you'll be the headliner, you'll be the main guy. There will be problems down the road if we go into anything like this on record royalties.' I said, 'If you want to give us a *token* — ' And that's what it would have amounted to. But it never did start."

In later years, understandably, this became a source of considerable bitterness, but at the time I would guess it was as much a case of legitimately hurt feelings as of financial claims.

215 "when Elvis went up into the control room": Colin Escott and Martin Hawkins, *Good Rockin' Tonight: Sun Records and the Birth of Rock 'n' Roll*, p. 83.

215–216 Hill and Range, one of the most prominent: Information on the folio deal comes specifically from interviews with Sam Phillips, Grelun Landon, and Freddy Bienstock. Information on the Aberbach family and Hill and Range from Russell Sanjek, *American Popular Music and Its Business*, vol. 3; *Billboard Music Week*, January 30, 1961, as cited in *Country Music, U.S.A.* by Bill Malone; and research generously provided by Tony Scherman. Bill Randle's views are articulated in *Memphis Lonesome* by Ger Rijff and Jan van Gestel.

216 Randle's belief, fostered by the Aberbachs' desire: The political intricacies of all this are somewhat unclear. Randle spoke of the specifics of the Hill and Range connection in an interview with the *Cleveland Plain Dealer*, December 6, 1984, and is quoted to this effect in Rijff and van Gestel, *Memphis Lonesome*, as well. There seems little question that he fully believed that, had he taken the Aberbachs' offer, he would have become Elvis Presley's manager — though perhaps this is another instance of memory cropping and enlarging to some degree (possibly the Aberbachs offered him the position of Elvis' song manager, which Freddy Bienstock later became). In any case, when I tried a blunter version of this scenario on the Colonel, he professed utter ignorance of any part that Bill Randle may have played and deemed it the most ridiculous thing (my scenario) he had ever heard — at least from me. I hope I have improved on it since then.

217 "the folk music world": "Rockin' to Stardom," *Country Song Roundup*, winter 1955–56.

217–218 The Colonel had approached Haley's manager: John Swenson, *Bill Haley*, p. 66.

219 "Now this was a long time": Ken Terry interview with Bill Haley, as cited in ibid.

219 "Elvis was one of those guys": Peter Mikelbank, "Elvis '86: Myth and Memory," *Washington Post*, August 3, 1986.

220 they were angry at their former landlord: Interview with Eve and Sarah Baker, 1990.

221 "Called 'Top Jock' ": The title was subsequently changed to, alternatively, *The Pied Piper of Cleveland* or *A Day in the Life of a Famous Disc Jockey*, with the latter also used as a subtitle to the former.

221 the idea was for this one: "Randle Short Scuttled by IBEW Ruling," *Billboard*, December 3, 1955.

221–224 According to Randle: Rijff and van Gestel, *Memphis Lonesome*, pp. 19–20.

222–223 Pat Boone never forgot: The information on Pat Boone's meeting with Elvis Presley comes from "Pat Boone" by Jeffrey Ressner, *Rolling Stone*, April 19, 1990; Dave Booth's interview with Boone; and an unsourced clipping included in Ger Rijff and Poul Madsen's *Elvis Presley: Echoes of the Past*. In each interview Boone discusses exactly the same moment in virtually the same language, but each offers a slightly different emphasis with more, or less, detail at certain points. The two quotations that I have included here are edited versions combining elements of all three interviews.

222 he hoped these Yankees liked his music: John Haley and John von Hoelle, *Sound and Glory*, p. 109.

224 if they could successfully negotiate union problems: They didn't. Filming was shut down in New York by an International Brotherhood of Electrical Workers dispute on November 29. What was shot in Cleveland had yet to be seen as of spring 1994.

225 "I have told you repeatedly": Escott and Hawkins, *Good Rockin' Tonight*, pp. 80–81.

226 "ladylike tardiness": *Memphis Press-Scimitar*, October 28, 1955.

227–228 "Elvis did ask me once or twice": Jerry Hopkins interview with Bob Neal (MVC/MSU).

228–229 The convention itself: Interviews with Chick Crumpacker, Grelun Landon, Buddy Bain, Buddy Killen, Mae Boren Axton, Galen Christy, et al.

230 On Sunday he played Ellis: The description of the concert comes primarily from Fred Davis, who was there.

231–232 The purchase price was $35,000: This is my understanding of the deal. RCA paid

Sam Phillips $35,000 as specified, beyond the initial $5,000 deposit which Tom Parker had made (and for which he was reimbursed). Presumably, the $5,000 represented the back royalties that Phillips owed Elvis, who was specifically exempted from any future royalty payments. Beyond that, RCA and Hill and Range kicked in an additional $6,000 total as a signing bonus for the artist. This was paid to Parker, who deducted a 25 percent commission, which he split, after expenses, with Bob Neal. It has been speculated for years that Hill and Range put up a substantial amount of the purchase price itself, up to $15,000, but I have found nothing either in the contract or in the negotiations that led up to it to confirm that arrangement, nor has anyone I have spoken to confirmed it from a position of knowledge. At the same time it remains a logical possibility.

STAGE SHOW

All quotes from Sam Phillips and Scotty Moore are from the author's interviews, unless otherwise noted.

235 *The last admonishment I had:* Interview with Sam Phillips, 1992.
235 About a week before the session: Interview with George Klein, 1988.
236 At the DJ convention: "What Has Happened to Popular Music?," *High Fidelity Magazine,* June 1958; "Sholes Has Last Laugh," *Billboard,* April 21, 1956, covers much the same ground.
237 The room was big, high-ceilinged: Chet Atkins, *Country Gentleman.*
238 Tommy showed her a Miami newspaper story: The story appeared in the *Miami Herald* of October 1, 1955, as documented in Arena Television's *Tales of Rock 'N' Roll: Heartbreak Hotel,* broadcast in 1993.
238 Mae promised the song to Buddy: This account is based primarily on interviews with Buddy Killen, 1989, and Mae Boren Axton, 1988. Buddy's account is at odds with Mae's mainly in terms of the availability of the song prior to Elvis' recording of it. In Buddy's recollection he got the song from Mae in July, at the same time that she introduced him to Elvis, but the date of the *Miami Herald* headline would seem to disprove that scenario.
239 a "morbid mess": *New York Post,* October 3, 1956.
239 Stoker, who had met the boy: Interview with Gordon Stoker, 1989.
239 "They all told me": Tandy Rice interview with Steve Sholes, Country Music Foundation collection, used by permission.
239 a father's night show at Humes: Robert Johnson, *Elvis Presley Speaks!,* p. 44.
239 a Christmas show produced by Miss Scrivener: "Elvis Presley," prepared by the editors of *TV Radio Mirror,* 1956, p. 31.
240 "I think there was a big difference": Shelley Ritter interview with Minnie Pearl, 1990.
241–242 According to Maylon Humphries: Interview with Maylon Humphries, 1991.
242 Steve Sholes introduced: Interview with Chick Crumpacker, 1992; additional interviews with Arlene Blum and Lorene Lortie, 1993.
242 "Steve brought Elvis in": Interview with Anne Fulchino, 1992.
242ff introduced Elvis to the Dorseys: Interviews and correspondence with Grelun Landon, 1988–94; also, unpublished manuscript by Landon.
242–243 "and Elvis exhibited a kind of deference and courtesy": Arnold Shaw, *The Rockin' '50s,* p. 11.
243 ("We didn't know what to expect"): Jerry Hopkins interview with D. J. Fontana (MVC/MSU).

243 talking to Grelun and Chick Crumpacker: Interview with Chick Crumpacker, 1989.

244 The show that night: Chick Crumpacker liner notes to *Elvis* (RCA LPM 1382) and interviews and correspondence, 1989–94.

245 "Daddy just sat there": Interview with Jackson, Sarah, and Eve Baker, 1990.

245 Bob Johnson wrote in his notes: *Elvis Presley Speaks!*, p. 45.

246 it was no use doing any more: Grelun Landon, "Elvis Presley: The Tape Keeps Rolling," RCA publicity package, 1984.

247 On the second day of recording: Interview with Fred Danzig, 1993.

248 "a tall, lean young man": Manuscript copy of "The Day No One Wanted Elvis — But Me" by Fred Danzig.

248 They went into the control room: Interview with Fred Danzig.

249 The William Morris people threw a party: Interviews with Freddy Bienstock and Grelun Landon; also Martha Lopert, "The Boy with the Big Beat," *Celebrity*, winter 1958, p. 62.

249 a reception at the Hickory House: Interviews and correspondence with Chick Crumpacker; also interviews with Arlene Blum and Fred Danzig.

250 "I thought Elvis did even better": Booklet for *Elvis: The Complete 50's Masters*.

250 "The Colonel embarrasses me": Interview with Gabe Tucker, 1990.

251 "We were working near every day": Jerry Hopkins, *Elvis*, p. 125.

251ff To Justin Tubb: Interview with Justin Tubb, 1989, and subsequent correspondence.

252–253 ("My brother didn't get along"): Jimmy Guterman interview with Charlie Louvin, 1987.

253 "Fuck the Colonel": Interview with Chet Atkins, 1988.

253 "Elvis said, 'Boy' ": Howard Miller, *The Louvin Brothers*, p. 47.

253 Ira flashed: Jimmy Guterman interview with Charlie Louvin.

254 In Jacksonville on February 23: Robert Johnson, "Elvis Himself," *TV Star Parade*, September 1956, p. 65; also *Elvis Presley Speaks!*, p. 45. Other sources include the *Jacksonville Journal* (as cited in Morrie and Virginia Kricun, *Elvis: 1956 Reflections*); my interview with Justin Tubb and Jimmy Guterman's with Charlie Louvin; also James Poling, "Elvis Presley: Go, Cat, Go," *Pageant*, July 1956, p. 12, and Red West et al., *Elvis: What Happened?*, p. 109.

THE WORLD TURNED UPSIDE DOWN

All quotes from Scotty Moore are from the author's interviews, unless otherwise noted.

258 "I suppose," Neal said: Jerry Hopkins interview with Bob Neal (MVC/MSU).

259 Hazen's sister-in-law: Interview with Joseph Hazen, 1993.

260 Wallis was impressed: Hal Wallis and Charles Higham, *Starmaker*.

260 From Anne Fulchino's point of view: Interview with Anne Fulchino, 1993.

260–261 "The transformation was incredible": Allan Weiss, "Elvis Presley: Rock Music Phenomenon," in Danny Peary, ed., *Close Ups: The Movie Star Book*. Used by permission.

261 "I knew my script": August 6, 1956, interview.

261 This character was "lovesick": Will Jones, "Squeals Drown Presley's Songs," *Minneapolis Tribune*, May 13, 1956.

Just when Elvis delivered this opinion is a matter of conjecture. As of April 13, he evidently still believed he would be making *The Rainmaker* starting in June (this is borne out by an interview with Jay Thompson in Wichita Falls, Texas, on April 9 and his interview in the *Press-Scimitar* four days later), but whenever he spoke to Wallis, and whatever words he actually used, I believe that the feelings represented here — not to mention the combination of verbal confusion and emotional assurance — ring true.

261–262 Wallis for his part: All Wallis quotes from Wallis and Higham, *Starmaker;* further information gleaned from interviews with Joseph Hazen and William Morris agent Leonard Hirshan, and correspondence with Nick Tosches.

262 The Colonel reserved the right: Just for the record the strategy worked, and the Colonel continuously improved every aspect of the deal, getting Elvis $65,000 for the first Wallis picture (1957's *Loving You*) after making *Love Me Tender* in 1956 for Twentieth Century Fox at a salary of $100,000.

262 Berle met Elvis and the Colonel: Andrew Solt interview with Milton Berle.

264 At one point Elvis: *Variety,* April 11, 1956.

264 "The crowd was too noisy": San Diego newspaper story, as quoted in Ger Rijff, *Long Lonely Highway,* p. 78.

264 "I changed my whole style": Interview with Glen Glenn, 1990.

264 The Colonel had extricated Elvis: Interview with Horace Logan, 1991. In Elvis' interview with Jay Thompson on Monday, April 9, he speaks of his final night on the Hayride as being "last Saturday night," but March 31 was advertised as his final appearance. The figure of ten thousand dollars is stipulated in the revision of his Hayride contract.

264 a recording session on Saturday, April 14: This session has always been listed as taking place on April 11, but Ernst Jorgensen called my attention to a number of discrepancies in scheduling, and a story in the *Press-Scimitar* on April 13 makes it clear that Elvis recorded on the fourteenth.

265 everyone wanted to know everything: All quotes are from Elvis' interview at the Warwick Hotel on March 24 but reflect fairly both the kind of questions he continued to be asked and the answers that he gave.

265–266 "He was working for Elvis, period": Interview with D. J. Fontana, 1991.

266 Scotty and Bill knew the Colonel: One of the Colonel's early schemes, according to both Scotty and D. J., was to replace them with Hank Snow's band for the ostensible purpose of saving money. The difference in musical styles was of little or no concern to him, they felt.

266 In Red's account Elvis: Red West et al., *Elvis: What Happened?,* pp. 120–121.

267 "I'll bet I could burp": Interview with Gordon Stoker, 1989.

267 They chartered a plane: Interviews with Scotty Moore, 1988, 1989; also *Memphis Press-Scimitar* account, May 4, 1956.

267 "Man, I don't know if": Interview with Chet Atkins, 1988.

267–268 "It was the worst sound": Interview with Gordon Stoker.

268–269 Elvis gave a brief interview: "Elvis Gives Out with Crazy Cool Interview," *Waco News-Tribune,* April 18, 1956.

270 Scotty and Elvis and Bill headed for the Club El Dorado: Interviews with Scotty Moore and Lowell Fulson, 1989.

270 "no check is good": *Time,* May 16, 1960.

271ff It was the first sit-down gig: Principal sources for this account of the Las Vegas booking are interviews with Scotty Moore and D. J. Fontana; stories in the *Memphis Press-Scimitar* and *Commercial Appeal;* Robert Johnson, *Elvis Presley Speaks!; Billboard* and *Variety* coverage; Marge Crumbaker and Gabe Tucker's *Up and Down with Elvis Presley;* Bill Randle's comments as detailed in Ger Rijff and Jan van Gestel, *Memphis Lonesome;* RCA's recording of the final show as presented on *Elvis: The Complete 50's Masters;* various contemporary interviews with Elvis Presley; Bill Dahl's story on Freddie Bell ("Remembering Rock" *Chicago Tribune,* December 5, 1990); and Jonny Whiteside's interview/memorial to Johnnie Ray, "Who's Crying Now," *LA Weekly,* March 9–15, 1990.

It should be noted that it has frequently been assumed that Elvis was fired from this engagement because he left after two weeks and Freddy Martin stayed on. In fact it would appear from all indications that Elvis was hired for the first two weeks of Martin's engagement only. He went on to regular scheduled gigs starting in St. Paul on May 12 and going through the entire next week, which included a headlining appearance at the Cotton Carnival in the middle of what would have been his fourth week in Vegas. I think the confusion initially arose from trade accounts that had him "replaced on the bill by Roberta Sherwood" (*Variety*, May 9, 1956). This came in the midst of a negative article, and indeed in the midst of a negative sentence ("The more sophisticated gambling clientele didn't dig his frenzied antics, and Presley was replaced . . . "), but I believe from interviews and all other indications that it was booked as a two-week engagement from the start and that the announced replacement was a planned one, the conjunction ("and") merely sequential. This, too, however, is subject to revision.

271 one of Richardson's guests: Crumbaker and Tucker, *Up and Down*, p. 38.

271 "For the first time in months": *Elvis Presley Speaks!*, p. 53.

271 "After the show our nerves": Elston Leonard, "Elvis Presley: The New Singing Rage," *Tiger*, c. 1956, p. 14.

271 "They weren't my kind of audience": *Elvis Presley*, prepared by the editors of *TV Radio Mirror*, 1956, p. 43.

271 "It was strictly an adult audience": May 14, 1956, interview, La Crosse, Wisconsin. See the *Memphis Commercial Appeal* of May 9 for a similar interview, in which he declares, "Man, I really liked Vegas. I'm going back there the first chance I get."

272 "Elvis, who has played hard audiences": Robert Johnson, "The Golden Boy Reaches for a Star While the Music Goes Round and Round and — ," *Memphis Press-Scimitar*, May 4, 1956.

272 They played what Elvis calculated: Richard Lyons, "Presley Irked by Overtime — Even at $4000 an Hour," *Memphis Commercial Appeal*, May 9, 1956.

272 "One thing about Las Vegas": *Elvis Presley Speaks!*, p. 55.

273 "The carnage was terrific": *Memphis Press-Scimitar*, May 4, 1956.

274 eight-hundred-dollar watch with diamonds: The gift is shown in a photograph accompanying the *Press-Scimitar* story. The thank-you notes are specified by Marge Crumbaker and Gabe Tucker in *Up and Down with Elvis Presley*.

274 "Like a jug of corn liquor": "Hillbilly on a Pedestal," *Newsweek*, May 14, 1956.

274–275 He was back in Memphis: *Memphis Commercial Appeal*, May 9, 1956.

"THOSE PEOPLE IN NEW YORK ARE NOT GONNA CHANGE ME NONE"

277 this "new and open-to-the-public feature": *Memphis Commercial Appeal*, May 13, 1956.

277 "Henry introduced me to him": Shelley Ritter interview with Minnie Pearl, 1990.

277–278 "I grabbed his hand": *Memphis Commercial Appeal*, May 13, 1956.

278–279 Vernon and Gladys were already present: This account is based primarily on Fred Davis' firsthand testimony, as well as the *Press-Scimitar* story of May 16 and a fortuitous recording of the Little Rock concert the following day, which followed virtually the same format.

279 Hank Snow meanwhile was finally beginning: Hank Snow with Jack Ownbey and Bob Burris, *The Hank Snow Story*, p. 390. Used by permission. The chronology of Snow's understanding is somewhat difficult to understand. In a March 2 letter to his attorney, the Colonel explained that a "recent unpleasantness" with Snow had been resolved by the dissolution of their management and booking agency contracts, but clearly Snow could not at first fully accept that he would see nothing from the deal. In his book, *Up and Down with Elvis Presley*, coauthored with Marge Crumbaker, Gabe Tucker posits that this all stemmed from a trap the Colonel laid when the idea

of selling Elvis' contract first came up. "Hank, you put in everything you make," Tucker has the Colonel saying, "and I'll put in everything I make, and we'll buy this boy's contract. . . . " When Snow demurred, as Parker knew that he would, Parker cut him out of the deal.

One essential factor not to be discounted is that Snow was a proud man and would never have been able to brook the idea of being "taken." In the other words of his son: "I don't think that my dad realized at that time what had happened," and certainly Snow's explanations to this day do not fully explain the matter.

280 "I'm so proud of my boy": Interview with Cliff Gleaves, 1990.

280 Mrs. Presley answered the doorbell: Interview with Pallas Pidgeon, 1990; Robert Johnson, *Elvis Presley Speaks!*, p. 64; Jerry Hopkins interview with Faye Harris (MVC/MSU).

280 "I wish," he said to a contractor friend: Interview with Guy Lansky, 1990.

280–281 Gladys had filled the house: Edwin Miller, "Elvis the Innocent," *Memories,* May 1989. Miller's account of his visit at precisely this time was written up first in a 1956 issue of *Seventeen* and, later, in this more reflective article.

281 "It didn't happen all at once": *Memphis Press-Scimitar,* May 4, 1956.

282 On the way they had heard a song: Peter Cronin interview with Scotty Moore, 1992.

282 "If you ever do anything to make": Albert Goldman, *Elvis,* p. 505.

283 "it was a relaxed and therefore more effective": *Variety,* June 13, 1956.

284 "Mr. Presley has no discernible": *New York Times,* June 6, 1956.

284 "The sight of young (21) Mr. Presley": *New York Journal-American,* June 9, 1956.

284 under the banner "Beware Elvis Presley": *America,* June 23, 1956.

285 ("She'd get mad and cuss"): Shelley Ritter interview with Vester Presley, 1991.

285 "I don't do any vulgar movements": Aline Mosby, "Presley Sexy? He Denies It," *New York World Telegram,* June 15, 1956.

285 "I'm not trying to be sexy": Phyllis Battele, *New York Journal-American,* June 18, 1956.

285 "I hired a doctor's wife": Interview with Charlie Lamb, 1990.

285 "I'm going to get a wiggle meter": *New York World Telegram,* June 15, 1956.

285–287 He drove up to the house and found June: Interview with June Juanico, 1991.

287 a one-shot appearance at $7,500: Allen indicated this figure in his interview with Andrew Solt, though the amount has also been cited as $5,000. The higher figure would seem to explain Ed Sullivan's unprecented bid ($50,000 for three appearances) after the Allen broadcast.

287 "there has been a demand that": *New York Journal-American,* June 13, 1956.

287 On June 20 a compromise of sorts was reached: Ibid., June 21, 1956.

287 It was, said Allen: Andrew Solt interview with Steve Allen.

288–289 Elvis Presley is a worried man: Kays Gary, "Elvis Defends Low-Down Style, *Charlotte Observer,* June 27, 1956.

290 "Mr. Johnson, you know some things": *Memphis Press-Scimitar,* May 4, 1956.

290–295 He arrived at NBC's midtown rehearsal studio: This particular detail, along with extended and attributed quotations, comes from Alfred Wertheimer's book *Elvis '56: In the Beginning,* © 1979, and is used by permission. All observations are from Wertheimer's point of view, unless otherwise specified, and are used with grateful acknowledgment. This credit carries through to the end of the chapter, wherever noted.

291 "if you just stuck around with him": Anita Houk, "Lensman's Early Look at Elvis Was Rare, Personal," *Memphis Commercial Appeal,* August 11, 1991.

294 ("He always did the best he could"): Peter Cronin interview with Gordon Stoker, 1992.

297–302 The next day he seemed: Once again Alfred Wertheimer's firsthand observation (in words and pictures) was an invaluable source of visualization, information, and insight. In addition, interviews with Freddy Bienstock and Chick Crumpacker were of great help, along with Grelun Landon's, Scotty Moore's, and D. J. Fontana's recollections. Finally, Chick Crumpacker took Ernst Jorgensen and me on a guided tour of the old RCA neighborhood and building, which is now a division of Baruch College, in which Studio B has been astonishingly preserved as a television teaching studio.

297 "Barbara Hearn of Memphis": Rhea Talley, "Memphis, Biloxi Girls Share Top Spot in Elvis' Date Book," *Memphis Commercial Appeal*, July 8, 1956.

299 As Otis Blackwell later said: "Otis Blackwell: The Power Behind Elvis," *Essence*, May 1978. For additional information on Otis Blackwell, see Gary Giddins, "Just How Much Did Elvis Learn from Otis Blackwell?," *Village Voice*, October 25, 1976.

300 "I wasn't all that impressed": Peter Cronin interview with Gordon Stoker.

301 He ran into Gene Vincent: New Orleans radio interview, July 1956.

302–304 It was a hot night, 97 degrees: Most of the detail on the Russwood Park show comes from *Press-Scimitar* and *Commercial Appeal* coverage the next day. Early editions of the *Press-Scimitar* had attendance at fourteen thousand, but the figure was corrected by the end of the day. Robert Johnson's account in the *Press-Scimitar* was particularly vivid, as was Alfred Wertheimer's in *Elvis '56*.

303 The fans "broke from their seats": Robert Johnson, "Elvis Sings and Thousands Scream," *Memphis Press-Scimitar*, July 5, 1956.

303 "there was this keening sound": Interview with Jackson Baker, 1990.

304 "He rocked 'em"; "When it was time to go": *Memphis Press-Scimitar*, July 5, 1956.

304 All Elvis wanted: Ibid., May 4, 1956.

A note on the title of this chapter: The quotation comes from Jackson Baker's recollection of the event in a 1989 interview. Stanley Booth uses a variant of the same quote in his classic February 1968 story for *Esquire*, "A Hound Dog to the Manor Born." The only reference in newspaper accounts is in Bob Johnson's July 5 story in the *Press-Scimitar*, which states: "Elvis joked about his recent appearance on the Steve Allen show, when he had to restrain some of his wriggling," but no direct quotation is made.

ELVIS AND JUNE

All quotes from June Juanico are from the author's interviews, telephone conversation, and correspondence, 1991–94, unless otherwise noted. June's own unpublished manuscript gives a wonderful picture of the period and should not remain unpublished for long.

307–308 they just showed up: Thomas Sancton, "Elvis Dates Biloxi Girl," *New Orleans Item*, July 11, 1956; also interviews with June Juanico.

308 In the course of the evening: Ruth Sullivan, "Slim Elvis Presley Is Heavy on the Diet," "The Grapevine" (column in a New Orleans newspaper), July 1956.

308 "Did I kiss him good night?": *New Orleans Item*, July 11, 1956.

308–309 The crowds at the beachfront hotel: Kay Freeman, "Elvis Presley Catches Spanish Mackerel; Dodges Crowd of 500 Coast Rock, Roll Fans Thursday," *Biloxi Daily Herald*, July 15, 1956.

310 "It'd be a sin to let something like that go to waste": *Miami News*, August 4, 1956.

312 Meanwhile, Elvis got so sunburnt: Harry Reeks, "During Vacation on Gulf His 'Mob' Proves Active," publicity handout, July 1956.

314 Toward the end of July: *Memphis Press-Scimitar*, July 23, 1956.

315 a vaudeville redoubt from the 1920s: Philip Chapman, "The Girl Who Got Presley," *TV Radio Mirror*.

315–316 she reportedly stroked [Elvis'] brow: Sandy Schnier and Damon Runyon, Jr., "Hey, Gals! Elvis Has 2 Steadies," *Miami News*, August 4, 1956.

317 "Now this is the way it is": Bella Kelly, "Elvis Denies Biloxi Beauty Is His 'Steady,' " *Miami News*, August 5, 1956.

318 Mrs. Mae Juanico was quoted: Ibid.

319 "The biggest freak in show business history": *Miami News*, August 4, 1956.

322 "aroused fans ripped": "Elvis — a Different Kind of Idol," *Life*, August 27, 1956.

322 a fashion that "put obscenity and vulgarity": *Jacksonville Journal*, August 10, 1956 (as quoted in Morrie and Virginia Kricun, *Elvis: 1956 Reflections*).

322 ("I can't figure out what I'm doing"): Ibid., August 11, 1956.

323 Dewey was just about to start: *Memphis Press-Scimitar*, August 22, 1956.

323 "I don't think that you learn to become an actor": August 6, 1956, interview.

LOVE ME TENDER

All quotes from June Juanico and Scotty Moore are from the author's interviews, unless otherwise noted.

327 "I'm strictly for Stevenson": *New York Herald-Tribune*, August 18, 1956.

327 "I have no trouble memorizing": Harold Stone, "Meet Mr. Rock 'N' Roll," *Top Secret*, November 1956, p. 54.

327 he was "plenty scared": Army Archerd, "Presley Takes Hollywood," *Photoplay*, December 1956.

327 Elvis blurted out to Weisbart: Ibid.

328 On his second day on the set: Ibid. There is also a charming account of his friendship with Elvis by Nick Adams in the May 1957 issue of *16* (vol. 1, no. 1), begun under the editorship of Memphis' Robert Johnson.

328–329 Colonel Parker was staying up nights: Martha Lopert, "The Boy with the Big Beat," *Celebrity*, winter 1958.

329–330 Elvis was eager to perform: *Photoplay*.

330 It was a job like any other: *Memphis Press-Scimitar*, September 1, 1956.

330 The director, Robert Webb: *New York Post*, October 3, 1956.

330–331 Webb would break down the lines: Jerry Hopkins interview with Mildred Dunnock (MVC/MSU).

331 "Before I met him": Albert Goldman, *Elvis*, p. 218.

331 Trude Forsher, a Viennese émigrée: Interview with Trude Forsher, 1993.

331 "I could make you like me if I tried": Joe Hyams, "All Alone with Elvis Presley," *New York Herald-Tribune*, September 23, 1956.

331 "From the time I was a kid": Atra Baer, "The Real Presley," *New York Journal-American*, September 23, 1956.

331 To *True Story* staff writer Jules Archer he confessed: Jules Archer, "Is This Unassuming Rocker America's Newest Rebel?," *True Story*, December 1956, as reprinted in *DISCoveries*, January-February 1988.

331 He and Gene spent $750: *New York Journal-American*, September 23, 1956.

332 "We'll have to check you over": *Photoplay*.

332 "Presley has the same smoldering appeal": *True Story*.

332–336 On the Friday before Labor Day weekend: Interviews with Freddy Bienstock, Scotty Moore, Thorne Nogar, Bones Howe, Gordon Stoker, D. J. Fontana, and Trude Forsher.

336 "Well, do whatever you can": Peter Cronin interview with Scotty Moore, 1992.

336 the picture, which had now been officially renamed: Bob Thomas, "Vul-gah? Not Me," *New York Post*, September 4, 1956.

336 Mildred Dunnock as his mother: Jerry Hopkins interview with Mildred Dunnock (MVC/MSU).

337 "He's a real pixie": *Tupelo Daily Journal*, September 13, 1956, as quoted in Morrie and Virginia Kricun, *Elvis: 1956 Reflections*.

337 "Finally met Elvis Presley": *New York Journal-American*, September 20, 1956.

337 "He was the first person": Goldman, *Elvis*, pp. 219–220.

337 Elvis sent Sullivan a get-well card: *Photoplay*.

339 "We're the perfect combination": Interview with Cliff Gleaves, 1991.

339 sing a couple of songs in the picture: This was cited as a hundred-thousand-dollar offer on occasion.

339 William Campbell was convinced: Goldman, *Elvis*, p. 201.

339 the Colonel was simply a very smart man: March 24, 1956, interview.

339 "He's a very amusing guy": August 6, 1956, interview.

339 "We more or less picked each other": Ibid.

339 Colonel liked Nick: Sidney Skolsky, "Tintyped: Elvis Presley," *New York Post*, November 21, 1956. Skolsky had Colonel and Nick writing a book together called *Elvis Presley: Actor, Singer and Man*.

339 On Monday they visited Humes: Mildred Scrivener, "My Boy Elvis," *TV Radio Mirror*, March 1957. On December 1 the *Memphis Press-Scimitar* ran a picture of the drill team modeling the new equipment and carrying a banner which stated the band's new name, the EP Rebels.

340 Nick put his feet up: Jerry Hopkins interview with James and Gladys Tipler (MVC/MSU).

340 "It made me feel bad": Elaine Dundy, *Elvis and Gladys*, p. 260.

340 Bowen was now general manager: Interview with Ernest Bowen, 1990.

340–341 "And just think, you're paying me": *New York Post*, October 2, 1956.

341 He couldn't "hardly remember": *Tupelo Daily Journal*, September 27, 1956.

342 "The city limits": Peter Dacre, "Eyewitness to Presleymania."

342 There were forty city police: *Tupelo Daily Journal*, September 27, 1956.

342 "I was right at the back of the stage": Interview with Ernest Bowen.

343 in Dallas Nick was even served: *Dallas Morning News*, October 12, 1956.

344 "It looked like a war out there": Interview with D. J. Fontana, 1988.

344 teenagers in Temple: *Memphis Press-Scimitar*, October 13, 1956.

344 Reporters were pestering: *Dallas Morning News*, October 12, 1956.

345–346 Elvis had been in a fight: *Memphis Press-Scimitar*, October 19, 1956.

346 "I'll regret this day as long as I live": *New York Post*, October 19, 1956.

346 advised by Acting Judge Sam Friedman: *Memphis Commercial Appeal*, October 20, 1956.

THE TOAST OF THE TOWN

351 "The idol of the rock 'n' roll juveniles": *New York Times*, October 29, 1956.

351–352 "Teenagers are my life and triumph": Gordon Sinclair, "Sinclair Says Elvis 'Fine Lad,' Hopes to Last for 40 Years," *Toronto Star*, October 29, 1956.

353 The ratings were not quite as spectacular: *Variety*, October 31, 1956.

353 he played the scene: There are pictures of Elvis shooting the scene in his white bucks in Ger Rijff's *Faces and Stages*.

354–355 In the offing were hound dogs and houndburgers: Chester Morrison, "The Great Elvis Presley Industry," *Look*, November 13, 1956; additional background on merchandising in Mike Kaplan, "Elvis a Millionaire in 1 Year," *Variety*, October 24, 1956, and Louis M. Kohlmeier, "Heartbreak Hound Dogs Put Sales Zip into Presley Products," *Wall Street Journal*, December 31, 1956.

355 "like a circus come to town": Joseph Lewis, "Elvis Presley Lives," *Cosmopolitan*, November 1968.

355–356 According to her sister, Lana: Lana Wood, *Natalie*, p. 45.

356 "the nation's first police-sponsored behind-the-wheel driving school": *Memphis Press-Scimitar*, November 6, 1956.

356–357 Meanwhile, Cliff Gleaves was back in town: Interviews with Cliff Gleaves, Lamar Fike, and George Klein. Needless to say, Cliff, Lamar, and George do not agree on every detail.

357–359 "At that point my life changed": Interview with Cliff Gleaves, 1990.

359–360 Elvis seemed "a little nervous at first": Interview with Pallas Pidgeon, 1990.

360 "The only thing I can say is they don't know me": Jerry Hopkins interview with Marion Keisker (MVC/MSU).

360 (the Colonel indicated): Dick Kleiner, "20 Questions with Elvis Presley," *Memphis Press-Scimitar*, December 1, 1956.

360–361 Then he met Dottie Harmony: Interview with Dottie Harmony, 1993.

361 he attended Liberace's opening: *Memphis Press-Scimitar*, November 15, 1956.

362 Perhaps the most interesting review: Gerald Weales, "Movies: The Crazy, Mixed-up Kids Take Over," *The Reporter*, December 13, 1956.

363 The Colonel's only public comment: *New York Journal-American*, October 8, 1956.

363 Elvis himself was embarrassed: Interview with Cliff Gleaves.

363 "I'm not going to quit": *Toronto Star*, October 29, 1956.

THE END OF SOMETHING

365 a "chicken coop nested in Cadillacs": Jerry Hopkins, *Elvis*, p. 107.

366 Sam had the tape recorder turned on: Interviews with Sam Phillips, Jack Clement, Carl Perkins, and Johnny Cash, 1979.

366–368 "I heard this guy in Las Vegas": *The Million Dollar Quartet* (RCA 2023-2-R).

368 One of the engineers at the station: Interviews with George Klein and Louis Cantor, 1993. Cantor's *Wheelin' on Beale* is an invaluable source of information on the radio station and the era.

369 "I was fourteen," said Carla Thomas: Interview with Carla Thomas, 1980. Sam Cooke's brother L.C., then a member of the Magnificents, also remembers the show, and Elvis' enthusiasm for his brother's gospel singing, vividly.

369 "I told them, If you put Elvis": Interview with Rufus Thomas, 1988.

369 "To all who were in earshot": *Tri-State Defender*, February 2, 1957.

369–370 the *Memphis World* cited an account: *Memphis World*, June 23, 1956, and July 6, 1957, as supplied by Louis Cantor.

370 "Maybe it's the Indigo Avenue's blase blues": *Pittsburgh Courier*, December 22, 1956, as cited in *Beale Black & Blue*, by Margaret McKee and Fred Chisenhall, and *Wheelin' on Beale*, by Louis Cantor.

371–372 Elvis met Kanter at the airport: Interviews with Hal Kanter, 1993, and Freddy Bienstock, 1992.

372 "'Man, that screen test ain't nothin'"': Interview with Hal Kanter for *Elvis in Hollywood*, 1993.

372–373 "He awoke in late afternoon": Hal Kanter, "Inside Paradise," *Variety*, January 9, 1957.

373–374 "That's the night my car got stomped in": Interview with Horace Logan, 1991.

374 "I saw a young girl open her purse": Interview with Hal Kanter for *Elvis in Hollywood*, 1993.

375 Even Sandi Phillips: Interview with Sandi Phillips Kallenberg, 1992.

375–376 Dottie Harmony flew in: Interview with Dottie Harmony, 1993.

377 June saw the pictures in the paper: Interview with June Juanico, 1991.

377 "We were broke, flat broke": Interview with Bobbie Moore, 1992.

377–378 an interview to the *Press-Scimitar*: Robert Johnson, "These Are the Cats Who Make Music for Elvis," *Memphis Press-Scimitar*, December 15, 1956.

378 his pre-induction physical: Interviews with Dottie Harmony and Cliff Gleaves, 1990.

378 the gold lamé vest that Barbara had given him: "Elvis Likes Barbara," 16, May 1957.

379 they will have to pay a $300,000 fee: *Newsweek*, October 8, 1956; see *Time*, November 4, 1957, for a slight variation.

379 Elvis for his part is just as genuinely thrilled: Interview with Gordon Stoker, 1989.

379 "This is a nice boy": *TV Star Parade*, April 1957.

380 he was happy to serve: *Memphis Press-Scimitar*, January 8, 1957.

LOVING YOU

384 while "rock 'n' roll has its place": John Jackson, *Big Beat Heat: Alan Freed and the Early Years of Rock & Roll*, p. 146.

385 "He was a genius": Hal Wallis and Charles Higham, *Starmaker*, p. 148.

386–388 on the second or third day of his visit: Interview with Freddy Bienstock, 1992.

386 Elvis thought was a good phrase: October 28, 1957, interview.

388 On Monday Elvis reported to the studio: There has always been a good deal of controversy about when exactly Elvis started to dye his hair. Given his experimentation with hairstyles from high school on, this confusion is certainly understandable, and not of any great critical importance, but according to George Klein, he had never seen Elvis with black hair before he came back from the filming of *Loving You*, and this was the story that Elvis told George of how it came about.

388–389 Songwriter Ben Weisman, too, showed up: Interview with Ben Weisman, 1989.

389 ("I need them like I need a hole in the head"): *Memphis Press-Scimitar*, September 14, 1957.

390 "I was fascinated by the way Elvis recorded": Wallis and Higham, *Starmaker*, p. 151.

391 He liked Wendell Corey: Interviews with Glen Glenn, 1990, and Hal Kanter, 1993.

391 "a lot of fun to be with": Robert Johnson, "Elvis' Hollywood Diary," 16, July 1957.

391–392 the situation that seemed to be developing: Interview with Glen Glenn; also interviews with Scotty Moore.

392 "a little homesick[ness]": *Memphis Press-Scimitar*, March 7, 1957.

392 "I was suffering some nausea": *Memphis Press-Scimitar*, January 29, 1957.

392–393 On their first morning at the lot: Dick Williams, "Behind the Scenes with *Loving You*," as cited in Bill DeNight et al., eds., *Elvis Album*, p. 90.

393 "There's somebody to comb his hair": C. Robert Jennings, "There'll Always Be an Elvis," *Saturday Evening Post*, September 11, 1965, p. 79.

393 One time they went to the movies: Albert Goldman, *Elvis*, pp. 231–232.

393 Scotty Moore's wife, Bobbie, came out: Interview with Bobbie Moore, 1992.

393 One day when they visited the set: Interview with Hal Kanter.

394 It was, remarked *Time* magazine: *Time*, May 27, 1957.

394 He blew up at Gordon Stoker: Interview with Gordon Stoker, 1989.

395 he was really beginning to miss his road trips: *Memphis Press-Scimitar*, March 19, 1957.

395 At the wrap party Hal Kanter: Interview with Hal Kanter.

395 He sent a telegram to June: Interview with June Juanico, 1991.

395–396 Built in 1939: Ida Clemens in the *Memphis Commercial Appeal*, October 27, 1940, as cited in Jane Brown Gillette, "Elvis Lives," *Historic Preservation*, May / June 1992.

396 Accompanying the family was Mrs. Virginia Grant: *Graceland*, pp. 30–31.

396–397 "This is going to be a lot nicer": "Singer Is Interested in Purchasing Graceland," *Memphis Press-Scimitar*, March 23, 1957.

397 ("I think I am going to like this new home"): William Leaptrott and Tom Johnson, "Presley Is Eager to Redecorate," *Memphis Press-Scimitar*, March 26, 1957.

397 Sam Phillips had just moved into: Interview with Knox Phillips, 1989.

397–398 "the darkest blue there is": *Memphis Press-Scimitar*, March 26, 1957.

398 there were two priorities: Shelley Ritter interview with George Golden, 1993; additional information on Golden from Dewey Webb, "Goodness Graceland! Elvis' Interior Decorator Tells All!" *Phoenix New Times*, July 28–August 3, 1993.

398 He had another disturbing run-in: *Memphis Press-Scimitar*, March 22–26, 1957.

398 Elvis would be returning to Tupelo: *Memphis Press-Scimitar*, March 22, 1957.

399 "I had gotten fired": Interview with George Klein, 1991.

400 "Hysterical Shrieks Greet Elvis": Press coverage from this tour is extensively documented in Ger Rijff, *Faces and Stages*.

400–401 In Canada, Oscar Davis finally made his move: Interviews with Scotty Moore, Gordon Stoker, and D. J. Fontana.

401 ("All those sweet little girls out there"): Interview with Hal Kanter.

401 ("as public reparation for excesses"): *New York Journal-American*, March 31, 1957.

401–402 In Philadelphia, speaking to a group: Carol Gelber, "Press Conference: High School Reporters Keep Their Poise Interviewing Elvis," *Philadelphia Evening Bulletin*, April 6, 1957.

402 Yvonne Lime came to visit: Yvonne Lime, "My Weekend with Elvis," *Modern Screen*, 1957.

402 On Saturday night they went over to Sam's new house: Ibid.; interviews with Sam and Knox Phillips; Dot Phillips' recollections in "Memories of Elvis Shared by Close Friend" by Larry Johnson, *Trenton Herald Gazette*, August 17, 1978.

JAILHOUSE ROCK

All quotes from Scotty Moore, George Klein, Russ Tamblyn, Cliff Gleaves, and Jerry Leiber and Mike Stoller are from the author's interviews, unless otherwise noted.

405 He was staying at the plush Beverly Wilshire: Interview with George Klein, 1993.

407 " 'Get him off this stuff' ": Jerry Hopkins interview with Gordon Stoker (MVC/MSU).

407 "They came in because we pushed them in": Interview with Freddy Bienstock, 1992.

408 "Most artists," said Gordon Stoker: Interview with Gordon Stoker, 1989.

409–410 "Elvis looked at me": Interview with George Klein for *Elvis in Hollywood*, 1993.

411–412 He told the assistant director: Interview with Bob Relyea for *Elvis in Hollywood*, 1993.

412–413 Cliff met Lamar at the door: Cliff's account essentially bears out George's.

413 "Cliff, Arthur, and I": Interview with George Klein for *Elvis in Hollywood*, 1993.

413–414 "Whenever there was a break": Interview with George Klein, 1993.

414 scared the hell out of Elvis: Sammy Davis, Jr., et al., *Why Me? The Sammy Davis, Jr., Story*, pp. 77–81. This is supported by interviews with George Klein et al., as well as newspaper accounts.

414 Mitchum himself stopped by: Interviews with George Klein, Russ Tamblyn, and D. J. Fontana.

414 "The Clan of Elvis Presley": Interview with Vince Edwards, 1990.

415 "When I get married": AP report, June 6, 1957.

417 "I don't feel like I'm property": Joe Hyams, "The Highest Paid Movie Star Ever," *New York Herald-Tribune*, May 16, 1957.

417 "I always criticize myself": October 28, 1957, interview.

417–418 he sought tips: Interview with Bob Relyea for *Elvis in Hollywood*, 1993.

419 Before he left, Elvis played: Robert Johnson, "These Reports True — Elvis and Dewey Had a Falling Out," *Memphis Press-Scimitar*, summer 1957.

421 "There's plenty of room for all of us": *Tacoma News Tribune*, September 2, 1957.

421 He had heard that geese: Shelley Ritter interview with George Golden, 1993.

421 "I was still living across from Humes": Interview with George Klein for *Elvis in Hollywood*, 1993.

421 "She was at the peak of success": *Memphis Press-Scimitar*, July 5, 1957.

422 At the end of the night: *Memphis Press-Scimitar*, September 14, 1957.

422–423 After that they kept almost constant: 1987 BBC television documentary *Presley — "Cut Me and I Bleed."*

423 They drove all around on his motorcycle: *Memphis Press-Scimitar*, September 14, 1957.

423 Buzzy Forbess from the Courts came by: Interviews with Buzzy Forbess, 1991, 1994.

423–424 "George didn't drive": Interview with Alan Fortas, 1990.

424 One night, Alan recalled in his memoir: Alan Fortas, *Elvis: From Memphis to Hollywood*, p. 61.

424 Alan didn't think much of the cousins: Ibid., p. 56.

425 One night he came by the house at three: Robert Johnson, "These Reports True," *Memphis Press-Scimitar*, summer 1957.

425–426 One night the great rhythm and blues singer: Interviews with George Klein, Barbara Pittman, Quinton Claunch, and Bettye Berger.

425–426 "He is very spiritually minded": Mike Hellicar, "Elvis Sings Spirituals Like a Negro, Says Ivory Joe Hunter," *New Musical Express*, c. May 1961.

426 The rumor had been circulating: Louie Robinson, " 'The Pelvis' Gives His Views on Vicious Anti-Negro Slur," *Jet*, August 1, 1957.

426 "It was like a magic spell": Interview with Bettye Berger, 1989.

426–427 a trio of fourteen-year-old girls: Albert Goldman, *Elvis*, pp. 252–254.

427 a couple of months was much too early: *New York Journal-American*, September 11, 1957.

427 "It never got wild at Graceland": Fortas, *Elvis*, p. 58.

427 "She never did go nowhere": Interview with Lillian Fortenberry, 1988.

427 "I'm the most miserable woman in the world": Elaine Dundy, *Elvis and Gladys*, p. 292. In Dundy's book the visit is dated earlier, but Corinne Tate, the Richardses' daughter, told me that it took place just after Judy Tyler's death.

427 "sitting by the window": Fortas, *Elvis*, p. 79.

427–428 Every so often she'd have a beer: Interview with Cliff Gleaves, 1990.

428 It was all right, she told Lamar: Interview with Lamar Fike, 1988.

428 Toward the end of the summer: Interview with Freddy Bienstock.

428–429 The scene at the train station: *Memphis Press-Scimitar*, August 28, 1957.

429–430 "A chunky, effeminate-looking man": *Tacoma News Tribune*, September 2, 1957.

430 "A gang moved into our town": *Vancouver Province*, September 3, 1957, as cited in AP report, September 3, 1957.

431 the harmonies of the Statesmen: Jerry Hopkins interview (MVC/MSU) and 1992 Peter Cronin interview with Gordon Stoker.

431 Freddy tried to sneak in a song: Interview with Freddy Bienstock.

431 "It was horrible": Interview with Millie Kirkham, 1989.

431–434 Scotty, D. J., and Bill were watching the clock: This articulation of Scotty and Bill's feelings, and their subsequent playing out, is based on stories that ran in the *Memphis Press-Scimitar* on September 13 and 14, 1957, as well as numerous interviews with Scotty Moore, Bobbie Moore, Evelyn Black, Reggie Young, Glen Glenn, D. J. Fontana, Alan Fortas, and George Klein.

432 "squeezed us for a matter of dollars": Interview with Scotty Moore, 1989.

432–433 Elvis read the letter, shook his head: Interview with George Klein, 1990.

433 a ring to signify his feelings: *Memphis Press-Scimitar*, September 11, 1957.

433 He called Scotty the following day: *Memphis Press-Scimitar*, September 14, 1957.

433 "[Elvis] promised us": *Memphis Press-Scimitar*, September 13, 1957.

434 the lead editorial in the paper: *Tupelo Daily Journal*, September 27, 1957.

435 It didn't feel right: Interviews with D. J. Fontana, 1991, and George Klein, 1990.

435 "Elvis Presley and his one-man band": Interview with George Klein, 1990.

WALKING IN A DREAM

All quotes from George Klein, Cliff Gleaves, and Jerry Leiber and Mike Stoller are from the author's interviews, unless otherwise noted.

437 "Rock 'n' roll smells phony and false": Frank Sinatra, as quoted in Linda Martin and Kerry Segrave, *Anti-Rock*, pp. 46–47.

437 And what was Elvis Presley's response?: Press conference, as reported in the *Los Angeles Times*, *New York Post*, *New York Journal-American*, *New York Herald-Tribune*, October 29–30, 1957.

437–438 "wiggled, bumped, twisted": Jack O'Brian, "L.A. Outraged at Presley," *New York Journal-American*, November 8, 1957.

438 including actors Alan Ladd and Walter Slezak: Carla Phillips, "My Story of Elvis," fan club publication.

438 What was Elvis' reaction?: *New York Post*, October 30, 1957.

439 even seventeen-year-old Ricky Nelson showed up: Joel Selvin, *Ricky Nelson;* Philip Bashe, *Teenage Idol, Travelin' Man;* Albert Goldman, *Elvis.*

439–440 One week later he sailed for Hawaii: Interviews with George Klein, Cliff Gleaves, and Vince Edwards, in addition to press coverage in the *Honolulu Star Bulletin.*

440 "I'm as horny as a billy goat": Tempest Storm, *The Lady Is a Vamp,* p. 168.

441 After the Easter service: Bill E. Burk, *Early Elvis: The Humes Years,* p. 118; also Alanna Nash interview with the Reverend James Hamill; Steve Turner's *Hungry for Heaven,* pp. 33–34; and Yvonne Lime, "My Weekend with Elvis," *Modern Screen,* 1957.

441 "I never expected to be anybody important": Louis Larkin, "God Is My Refuge," *Photoplay,* July 1957.

441–442 He visited Lansky's: Interview with Guy Lansky, 1990.

442 this music was "the real thing": *Memphis Press-Scimitar,* December 7, 1957.

442–443 About ten days before Christmas: Robert Johnson and Thomas N. Pappas, "Army, Navy Recruiters Make Offers to Elvis," *Memphis Press-Scimitar,* December 1957; additional *Memphis Press-Scimitar* articles, December 1957; interview with George Klein, 1993.

443 Elvis dropped in at the Sun studio: Interview with Jack Clement, 1989.

443 "We were at Graceland": Interview with George Klein for *Elvis in Hollywood,* 1993.

443–444 James Page, a *Press-Scimitar* reporter: *Memphis Press-Scimitar,* December 21, 1957.

444 He left for Nashville that same night: *Nashville Tennessean,* December 22, 1957; also *Nashville Banner,* December 21, 1957.

444–445 Gordon Stoker came out: Interview with Gordon Stoker, 1993.

445 How were things going?: Interview with T. Tommy Cutrer, 1990.

445 Jimmie Rodgers Snow, too, came by: Interview with Jimmie Rodgers Snow, 1993.

446 On Tuesday, December 24, Elvis wrote: *Memphis Commercial Appeal,* December 28, 1957.

446 He concluded by wishing Alan Levy, *Operation Elvis,* p. 14.

446–447 Jimmie Rodgers Snow arrived: Interviews with Jimmie Rodgers Snow, 1990, 1993.

446–447 an increasing dependence on pills and alcohol: Interview with Jimmie Rodgers Snow, 1990; Jimmy Snow, *I Cannot Go Back,* pp. 57–58ff.

447 "She just couldn't cope": Interview with Lillian Fortenberry, 1988.

447–448 "I was working for my father": Interview with Alan Fortas, 1990.

450 Elvis had read the book: Both Alan Portas and George Klein spoke in separate interviews of Elvis' unusual preparations for the role.

450 He got together with his new friend Kitty Dolan to run lines: May Mann, *Elvis and the Colonel,* pp. 47ff.

450 "You just didn't have a lot of fooling": Interview with Jan Shepard, 1992.

451 "I almost hesitate, I creep up to the sentence": BBC interview with Walter Matthau, as quoted in Gerry McLafferty, *Elvis Presley in Hollywood.*

451 In Carolyn Jones' observation "he was always": Joseph Lewis, "Elvis Presley Lives," *Cosmopolitan,* November 1968.

451 Jones suggested: Interview with Cliff Gleaves, 1991.

451 One Sunday when he was feeling blue: Interview with Jan Shepard.

451 It was in the fourth night: *Memphis Press-Scimitar,* January 14, 1958.

452 He saw Pat Boone: Interview with Jan Shepard.

453–454 Toward the end of February: Ibid.

454–455 "Hal Wallis loved locations": Interview with Alan Fortas.

455–456 He wasn't worried about the army: Vernon Scott, "Elvis at Home, Awaits Clippers," *New York World-Telegram,* March 15, 1958.

456 the Colonel had a big bunch of balloons: Interview with Trude Forsher, 1993.

456 Elvis posed politely for pictures: Levy, *Operation Elvis*, p. 21.

456 He was met by a *Commercial Appeal* reporter: James H. White, "Elvis Back in Town, with Sideburns Clipped and the Army on His Mind," *Memphis Commercial Appeal*, March 15, 1958.

''PRECIOUS MEMORIES''

459 On Monday he met Dewey: *Memphis Press-Scimitar*, March 18, 1958.

459 "no fewer than twelve beautiful girls": Alan Levy, *Operation Elvis*, p. 22.

459 "I screwed everything in sight": Larry Geller and Joel Spector, *"If I Can Dream,"* p. 236.

459 He had "fed them": *Memphis Press-Scimitar*, March 18, 1958.

459–460 "It was just 'So long' ": Interview with Scotty Moore, 1989.

460 he was dreading the army: BBC interview with Anita Wood.

460 To Barbara Pittman, who had known him: Interview with Barbara Pittman, 1989.

460 ("Girls come and go"): *Memphis Press-Scimitar*, March 24, 1958.

460 "We pulled in to the drive-in": Interview with George Klein for *Elvis in Hollywood*, 1993.

460 "he got in and out": Vince Staten, *The Real Elvis: Good Old Boy*, p. 139.

460 "Overnight," he said, "it was all gone": 1972 interview.

461–462 He showed up at the draft board: *Memphis Press-Scimitar*, March 24, 1958; additional sources are Alan Fortas' *Elvis: From Memphis to Hollywood*; Levy's *Operation Elvis*; and *Elvis the Soldier* by Rex and Elisabeth Mansfield.

461 not before Anita got special permission: *New York Post*, March 24, 1958.

461 The picture of him in *Life*: *Life*, April 7, 1958.

461–462 "Elvis recalled that in the days": *Memphis Press-Scimitar*, March 24, 1958.

462 The army provided a box lunch: *New York Post*, March 24, 1958.

463 refusing only to sign autographs: *New York Journal-American*, March 25, 1958.

463 "Start a loan company": Levy, *Operation Elvis*, p. 51.

463 He spotted a phone booth: Ibid., p. 52.

463 "No, sir. If I wore a string tie": Ibid., p. 54.

464 Hy Gardner wrote a column: *New York Herald-Tribune*, March 28, 1958.

464 After being chased for more than two hundred miles: Levy, *Operation Elvis*, pp. 61–63.

464–465 At Fort Hood things were under substantially: Ibid., pp. 59ff.

465 recruit instructor Sergeant Bill Norwood, who befriended him: Albert Goldman, *Elvis*, pp. 278–279.

465–466 "I didn't ask for anything": 1972 interview.

466–467 a Waco businessman named Eddie Fadal: Interview with Eddie Fadal, 1993.

466 Elvis approached Rex Mansfield: Mansfield, *Elvis the Soldier*, pp. 16–18.

467 Someone turned on a tape recorder: This has been available on a number of bootlegs over the years, starting off with *An Evening with Elvis* (Memphis Flash 92447).

468 "The treatment which I received": Mansfield, *Elvis the Soldier*, pp. 20–21.

469 "Well, I know the papers had us engaged, married": *Memphis Press-Scimitar*, June 3, 1958; UPI reports, June 3; Levy, *Operation Elvis*, p. 69.

469 He went with his parents: UPI report, June 14, 1958.

469 "[Elvis] tried to throw me every way": Jerry Hopkins interview with Ray Walker (MVC/MSU).

470 By the time that Rex returned: Mansfield, *Elvis the Soldier,* pp. 22–23.

470 Anita, too, had returned by now: Levy, *Operation Elvis,* p. 71; "Anita Wood Reveals — Why Elvis and I Couldn't Marry," fan magazine article excerpted in Bill DeNight et al., eds., *Elvis Album;* and UPI report, June 14, 1958.

470–472 Elvis brought his parents over: Interview with Eddie Fadal.

471 ("I just can't see myself over there"): Goldman, *Elvis,* p. 280.

472 A DJ named Rocky Frisco: Bill E. Burk, "Rocky Road Led to Meeting Elvis," *Elvis World* 20, June 1991.

472 Vince Edwards and Billy Murphy detoured: Interview with Vince Edwards, 1990.

472–473 She called her doctor in Memphis: Interview with Dr. Charles Clarke, 1989. Dr. Clarke's account of his forcefulness with army authorities is supported by news clippings of the time.

474 She was in better spirits: UPI report, August 14, 1958.

474 "we got off the elevator": Interview with Lamar Fike, 1988.

474 When reporters came to the house at mid morning: UPI report, August 14, 1958.

474–475 "Tears streamed down his cheeks": *Memphis Press-Scimitar,* August 14, 1958.

475 "When Mama was feeling bad": UPI report, August 14, 1958.

475–476 Hundreds of fans had assembled: This account of Gladys' "waking" draws on news accounts, Goldman's *Elvis,* and Elaine Dundy's *Elvis and Gladys,* as well as interviews cited.

475 When Dr. Clarke arrived at the house: Interview with Dr. Charles Clarke.

475 "Elvis was in a daze": Fortas, *Elvis,* pp. 91–92.

475 Junior picked up Eddie Fadal: Interview with Eddie Fadal.

476 "They couldn't get him to stop": Dundy, *Elvis and Gladys,* p. 325.

476 In the evening Sam and Dewey Phillips: Colin Escott and Martin Hawkins, *Good Rockin' Tonight: Sun Records and the Birth of Rock 'n' Roll,* p. 90.

476 "Come on in, Little": BBC interview with Anita Wood.

477 "When I went in the room": Interview with Dixie Locke, 1990.

477 "All we have now are memories": *Memphis Press-Scimitar,* August 16, 1958.

477 Every time they finished a song: Interview with J. D. Sumner, 1990; also interviews with James Blackwood, 1988, 1991.

477 The Reverend Hamill preached: *Memphis Commercial Appeal,* August 15, 1958.

477–478 "He went over to the casket": Interview with James Blackwood, 1991.

478–480 "I didn't mean to see him that night": Interview with Dixie Locke.

480 "He'd cry all day": Shelley Ritter interview with George Klein, 1993.

480 On Saturday he returned once again: Red West et al., *Elvis: What Happened?,* pp. 153–154.

480 "After a near emotional breakdown": *Memphis Press-Scimitar,* August 18, 1958.

480 his friends tried to cheer him up: Interview with Eddie Fadal; Fortas, *Elvis,* p. 93.

480–481 "He rolled his window down": Interview with George Blancet, 1989.

481 Toward the end of the week his dentist: Interview with Lester and Sterling Hofman, 1989.

482 It was, as Red described it: West et al., *Elvis,* p. 155.

482 Things were never again the same: Mansfield, *Elvis the Soldier,* p. 29.

482 ("Heavenly days, I just can't imagine it"): *New York Journal-American,* August 28, 1958.

482 Elvis and Eddie attended an r&b revue: Interview with Eddie Fadal.

482 a Johnny Horton show in Temple: Interviews with Jerry Kennedy, 1990, and Eddie

Fadal; also 1993 interviews with Galen "Corncob" Christy, who promoted the show and played on it, and Tillman Franks, who managed Johnny Horton and played bass in Horton's band.

Christy did not remember the exact date of the concert but thought it was just before he went into the army himself, in mid September. His recollection was of asking Elvis how things were going. " 'It's like prison,' " said Elvis, who had met Christy at the 1955 DJ convention in Nashville. "He said, 'I tried to go to church the other day, and I disrupted the church service.' He thought that was not right: that a human being would disrupt the worship of the Lord."

483 The last weekend that he was at Fort Hood: Kitty Dolan, "I Shared Elvis' Love," *TV and Movie Screen,* March 1959.

483 "At two A.M. we said good night": May Mann, *Elvis and the Colonel,* p. 68.

483 he asked Eddie: Interview with Eddie Fadal.

483–484 The train took about an hour: Interview with George Klein, 1990.

484 One of his fellow soldiers gave Elvis a book: Elvis named the book, and the poem "Should You Go First," at his pre-embarkation press conference. He said that he had read several other poems, and I have taken the liberty of guessing which ones. He said that he preferred poetry to short stories.

484 Charlie was "bound and determined": Mansfield, *Elvis the Soldier,* p. 33; also interview with Charlie Hodge, 1989.

484–487 It was a scene worthy of P. T. Barnum: The scene is fully audible in recordings of the press conference — and visible to a degree as well in film clips. It is particularly well described in Ren Grevatt's "On the Beat," *Billboard,* September 29, 1958.

487 "Come on," said the Colonel: *New York Journal-American,* September 28, 1958.

487 "I think I'm talking for all the guys": Ibid.

487–488 "He was resigned": Interview with Anne Fulchino, 1993.

488 Why don't you come along, too?: In West et al., *Elvis: What Happened?,* Red has Elvis asking both him *and* Lamar at this point, but since he had already announced in the press conference that Lamar would be accompanying him, this is my best guess at the actual scenario.

Bibliography

REFERENCE

Cotten, Lee. *All Shook Up: Elvis Day-by-Day, 1954–1977*. Ann Arbor, Mich.: Pierian Press, 1985.

———. *Shake, Rattle & Roll: The Golden Age of American Rock 'n' Roll*. Vol. 1, *1952–1955*. Ann Arbor, Mich.: Pierian Press, 1989.

Dellar, Fred, Roy Thompson, and Douglas B. Green. *The Illustrated Encyclopedia of Country Music*. New York: Harmony Books, 1977.

Elvis: Like Any Other Soldier. Reprint of the 1958 2nd Army Division Yearbook. Port Townsend, Wash.: Osborne Productions, 1988.

F.B.I. Files for Elvis A. Presley. Released under the Freedom of Information Act.

Federal Writers' Project of the Works Progress Administration. *Mississippi: The WPA Guide to the Magnolia State*. Golden anniversary ed. Jackson: University Press of Mississippi, 1988.

———. *The WPA Guide to Tennessee*. Knoxville: University of Tennessee Press, 1986.

Gart, Galen, comp. and ed. *First Pressings: Rock History as Chronicled in Billboard Magazine*. Vol. 1, *1948–1950*. Milford, N.H.: Big Nickel Publications, 1986.

———. *First Pressings: Rock History as Chronicled in Billboard Magazine*. Vol. 2, *1951–1952*. Milford, N.H.: Big Nickel Publications, 1986.

———. *The History of Rhythm & Blues*. Vols. 1–7 (*1951–1957*). Milford, N.H.: Big Nickel Publications, 1991–1993.

———. *The History of Rhythm & Blues, Special 1950 Volume*. Milford, N.H.: Big Nickel Publications, 1993.

Gentry, Linnell. *A History and Encyclopedia of Country, Western, and Gospel Music*. Nashville: Linnell Gentry, 1961.

Hardy, Phil, and Dave Laing. *Encyclopedia of Rock, 1955–1975*. London: Aquarius Books, 1977.

The 1953 Senior Herald. Humes High School Yearbook. Reprint, Port Townsend, Wash.: Osborne Enterprises, 1988.

Report of Guardian Ad Litem in re the Estate of Elvis A. Presley, Deceased, in the Probate Court of Shelby County, Tennessee. Number A655.

Stambler, Irwin. *Encyclopedia of Pop, Rock and Soul*. New York: St. Martin's Press, 1977.

Stambler, Irwin, and Grelun Landon. *Encyclopedia of Folk, Country and Western Music*. New York: St. Martin's Press, 1969.

Whisler, John A. *Elvis Presley: Reference Guide and Discography*. Metuchen, N.J.: Scarecrow Press, 1981.

Worth, Fred L., and Steve D. Tamerius. *All About Elvis*. New York: Bantam Books, 1981.

———. *Elvis: His Life from A to Z*. Chicago: Contemporary Books, 1988.

DISCOGRAPHIES, SONG AND RECORD GUIDES

Blackburn, Richard. *Rockabilly: A Comprehensive Discography of Reissues.* N.p.: Richard Blackburn, 1975.

Cotten, Lee, and Howard A. DeWitt. *Jailhouse Rock: The Bootleg Records of Elvis Presley, 1970–1983.* Ann Arbor, Mich.: Pierian Press, 1983.

The Elvis Presley Album of Juke Box Favorites, No. 1. New York: Hill and Range Songs, 1956.

Escott, Colin, and Martin Hawkins. *Sun Records: The Discography.* Vollersode, West Germany: Bear Family, 1987.

Hawkins, Martin, and Colin Escott. *Elvis Presley: The Illustrated Discography.* London: Omnibus Press, 1981.

Jancik, Wayne. *Billboard Book of One-Hit Wonders.* New York: Watson-Guptill, 1990.

Jorgensen, Ernst, Erik Rasmussen, and Johnny Mikkelsen. *Elvis Recording Sessions.* Stenlose, Denmark: JEE Productions, 1984.

Jorgensen, Ernst, Erik Rasmussen, and Roger Semon. Sessionography and Discography for *Elvis: The King of Rock 'N' Roll: The Complete 50's Masters* (RCA 07863-66050-2), 1992.

Kingsbury, Paul, ed. *Country on Compact Disc: The Essential Guide to the Music.* New York: Grove Press, 1993.

Pavlow, Big Al. *The R & B Book: A Disc-History of Rhythm & Blues.* Providence: Music House Publishing, 1983.

Tunzi, Joseph A. *Elvis Sessions: The Recorded Music of Elvis Aron Presley, 1953–1977.* Chicago: JAT Productions, 1993.

Weisman, Ben. *Elvis Presley: "The Hollywood Years."* Secaucus, N.J.: Warner Brothers Publications, 1992.

Whitburn, Joel. *Pop Memories, 1890–1954: The History of American Popular Music.* Menomonee Falls, Wis.: Record Research, 1986.

————. *Top Country Singles, 1944–1988.* Menomonee Falls, Wis.: Record Research, 1989.

————. *Top Pop Records, 1955–1972.* Menomonee Falls, Wis.: Record Research, 1973.

————. *Top R & B Singles, 1942–1988.* Menomonee Falls, Wis.: Record Research, 1988.

BOOKS OF MORE GENERAL INTEREST

Alexander, A. L., ed. *Poems That Touch the Heart.* Garden City, N.Y.: Doubleday, 1941.

Amburn, Ellis. *Dark Star: The Roy Orbison Story.* New York: Lyle Stuart, 1990.

Arnold, Eddy. *It's a Long Way from Chester County.* Old Tappan, N.J.: Hewitt House, 1969.

Atkins, Chet, with Bill Neely. *Country Gentleman.* Chicago: Henry Regnery, 1974.

Atkins, John, ed. *The Carter Family.* London: Old Time Music, 1973.

Bane, Michael. *White Boy Singin' the Blues: The Black Roots of White Rock.* New York: Penguin Books, 1982.

Bane, Michael, and Mary Ellen Moore. *Tampa, Yesterday, Today and Tomorrow.* Tampa: Misher and King Publishing, 1981.

Banks, Ann, ed. *First-Person America.* New York: Vintage Books, 1981.

Barthel, Norma. *Ernest Tubb Discography (1936–1969).* Roland, Okla.: Ernest Tubb Fan Club Enterprises, 1969.

Bashe, Philip. *Teenage Idol, Travelin' Man: The Complete Biography of Rick Nelson.* New York: Hyperion, 1992.

Benson, Bernard. *The Minstrel.* New York: G. P. Putnam's Sons, 1977.

Berry, Chuck. *Chuck Berry: The Autobiography.* New York: Harmony Books, 1987.

Biles, Roger. *Memphis in the Great Depression*. Knoxville: University of Tennessee Press, 1986.

Black, Jim. *Elvis on the Road to Stardom*. London: W. H. Allen, 1988.

Blaine, Hal, with David Goggin. *Hal Blaine and the Wrecking Crew*. Emeryville, Calif.: Mix Books, 1990.

Blumhofer, Edith L. *Restoring the Faith: The Assemblies of God, Pentecostalism, and American Culture*. Urbana: University of Illinois Press, 1993.

Booth, Stanley. *Rythm Oil: A Journey Through the Music of the American South*. London: Jonathan Cape, 1991.

Bowles, Jerry. *A Thousand Sundays: The Story of the Ed Sullivan Show*. New York: G. P. Putnam's Sons, 1980.

Branch, Taylor. *Parting the Waters: America in the King Years*. New York: Simon and Schuster, 1988.

Braudy, Leo. *The Frenzy of Renown: Fame and Its History*. New York: Oxford University Press, 1986.

Buckle, Phillip. *All Elvis: An Unofficial Biography of the "King of Discs."* London: Daily Mirror, 1962.

Burk, Bill E. *Early Elvis: The Humes Years*. Memphis: Red Oak Press, 1990.

———. *Early Elvis: The Tupelo Years*. Memphis: Propwash Publishing. Forthcoming.

———. *Elvis: A 30-Year Chronicle*. Tempe, Ariz.: Osborne Enterprises, 1985.

———. *Elvis Memories: Press Between the Pages*. Memphis: Propwash Publishing, 1993.

———. *Elvis Through My Eyes*. Memphis: Burk Enterprises, 1987.

Cain, Robert. *Whole Lotta Shakin' Goin' On: Jerry Lee Lewis*. New York: Dial Press, 1981.

Cantor, Louis. *Wheelin' on Beale*. New York: Pharos Books, 1992.

Capers, Gerald M., Jr. *The Biography of a River Town: Memphis, Its Heroic Age*. 1966. Reprint, Memphis: Burke's Book Store.

Carr, Roy, and Mick Farren. *Elvis Presley: The Illustrated Record*. New York: Harmony Books, 1982.

Cash, Johnny. *The Man in Black*. New York: Warner Books, 1975.

Cash, June Carter. *From the Heart*. New York: Prentice Hall Press, 1987.

Cash, W. J. *The Mind of the South*. 1941. Reprint, New York: Vintage Books.

Chapple, Steve, and Reebee Garofalo. *Rock 'n' Roll Is Here to Pay*. Chicago: Nelson-Hall, 1977.

Choron, Sandra, and Bob Oskam. *Elvis! The Last Word*. New York: Citadel Press, 1991.

Cocke, Marian J. *I Called Him Babe: Elvis Presley's Nurse Remembers*. Memphis: Memphis State University Press, 1979.

Cohn, David. *Where I Was Born and Raised*. Notre Dame, Ind.: University of Notre Dame Press, 1967.

Cohn, Nik. *Rock from the Beginning*. New York: Pocket Books, 1970.

Conaway, James. *Memphis Afternoons*. Boston: Houghton Mifflin, 1993.

Country Music Foundation. *Country: The Music and the Musicians*. New York: Abbeville Press, 1988.

Country Music Magazine, editors of. *The Illustrated History of Country Music*. Garden City, N.Y.: Doubleday, 1979.

Crumbaker, Marge, and Gabe Tucker. *Up and Down with Elvis Presley*. New York: G. P. Putnam's Sons, 1981.

Dalton, David. *James Dean: The Mutant King*. New York: Dell, 1974.

Dalton, David, and Lenny Kaye. *Rock 100*. New York: Grosset and Dunlap, 1977.

Daniel, Pete. *Standing at the Crossroads*. New York: Hill and Wang, 1986.

Davis, Jr., Sammy, Jane Boyar, and Burt Boyar. *Hollywood in a Suitcase*. New York: William Morrow, 1980.

———. *Why Me? The Sammy Davis, Jr., Story*. New York: Farrar, Straus and Giroux, 1989.

DeCosta-Willis, Miriam, and Fannie Mitchell Delk. *Homespun Images: An Anthology of Black Memphis Writers and Artists*. Memphis: LeMoyne Owen College, 1989.

Delmore, Alton. *Truth Is Stranger than Publicity*. Edited by Charles K. Wolfe. Nashville: Country Music Foundation Press, 1977.

DeWitt, Howard A. *Elvis — The Sun Years: The Story of Elvis Presley in the Fifties*. Ann Arbor, Mich.: Popular Culture, Ink., 1993.

Dollard, John. *Caste and Class in a Southern Town*. 3d ed. New York: Doubleday Anchor, 1957.

Dundy, Elaine. *Elvis and Gladys*. New York: Macmillan, 1985.

———. *Ferriday, Louisiana*. New York: Donald Fine, 1991.

Dunne, Philip. *Take Two: A Life in Music and Politics*. New York: McGraw-Hill, 1980.

Elvis Presley. Prepared by the Editors of *TV Radio Mirror Magazine*. New York: Bartholomew House, 1956.

Elvis Presley Heights, Mississippi: Lee County, 1921–1984. Compiled by Members of the Elvis Presley Heights Garden Club. Tupelo, Miss., 1984.

Elvis Presley Speaks! Text by Robert Johnson. New York: Rave Publishing, 1956.

Escott, Colin, and Martin Hawkins. *Good Rockin' Tonight: Sun Records and the Birth of Rock 'n' Roll*. New York: St. Martin's Press, 1991.

Escott, Colin, Martin Hawkins, and Hank Davis. *The Sun Country Years: Country Music in Memphis, 1950–1959*. Vollersode, West Germany: Bear Family Records, 1987.

Escott, Colin, with George Merritt and William MacEwen. *Hank Williams: The Biography*. Boston: Little, Brown, 1994.

Falkenburg, Claudia, and Andrew Solt, eds. *A Really Big Show: A Visual History of the Ed Sullivan Show*. Text by John Leonard. New York: Viking Studio Books, 1992.

Farren, Mick, ed. *Elvis in His Own Words*. London: Omnibus Press, 1977.

Finnis, Rob, and Bob Dunham. *Gene Vincent and the Blue Caps*. London: Rob Finnis and Bob Dunham, n.d.

Fortas, Alan. *Elvis: From Memphis to Hollywood*. Ann Arbor, Mich.: Popular Culture, Ink., 1992.

Fowler, Gene, and Bill Crawford. *Border Radio*. Austin: Texas Monthly Press, 1987.

Fowles, Jib. *Star Struck: Celebrity Performers and the American Public*. Washington, D.C.: Smithsonian Institution Press, 1992.

Frady, Marshall. *Southerners: A Journalist's Odyssey*. New York: New American Library, 1980.

Gabree, John. *The World of Rock*. Greenwich, Conn.: Fawcett, 1968.

Gaillard, Frye. *Watermelon Wine: The Spirit of Country Music*. New York: St. Martin's Press, 1978.

Garbutt, Bob. *Rockabilly Queens: The Careers and Recordings of Wanda Jackson, Janis Martin, Brenda Lee*. Toronto: Robert Garbutt Productions, 1979.

Gart, Galen, and Roy C. Ames. *Duke/Peacock Records: An Illustrated History with Discography*. Milford, N.H.: Big Nickel Publications, 1990.

Gelatt, Roland. *The Fabulous Phonograph, 1877–1977*. New York: Collier Books, 1977.

Geller, Larry, and Joel Spector with Patricia Romanowski. *"If I Can Dream": Elvis' Own Story*. New York: Simon and Schuster, 1989.

Gibson, Robert, with Sid Shaw. *Elvis: A King Forever*. London: Elvisly Yours, 1987.

Gillett, Charlie. *The Sound of the City: The Rise of Rock and Roll*. Rev. ed. London: Souvenir Press, 1983.

Goldman, Albert. *Elvis*. New York: McGraw-Hill, 1981.

————. *Elvis: The Last 24 Hours.* New York: St. Martin's Paperbacks, 1991.

Goldrosen, John, and John Beecher. *Remembering Buddy: The Definitive Biography of Buddy Holly.* New York: Penguin Books, 1986.

Graceland: The Living Legacy of Elvis Presley. San Francisco: Collins Publishers San Francisco, 1993.

Green, Douglas B. *Country Roots: The Origins of Country Music.* New York: Hawthorne Books, 1976.

Greenwood, Earl, and Kathleen Tracy. *The Boy Who Would Be King.* New York: Dutton, 1990.

Gregory, James, editor. *The Elvis Presley Story.* New York: Hillman Periodicals, 1960.

Gregory, Neal, and Janice Gregory. *When Elvis Died.* Washington, D.C.: Communications Press, 1980.

Grissim, John. *Country Music: White Man's Blues.* New York: Paperback Library, 1970.

Gruber, J. Richard, organizer. *Memphis: 1948–1958.* Memphis: Memphis Brooks Museum of Art, 1986.

Guterman, Jimmy. *Rockin' My Life Away: Listening to Jerry Lee Lewis.* Nashville: Rutledge Hill Press, 1991.

Hagarty, Britt. *The Day the World Turned Blue: A Biography of Gene Vincent.* Vancouver: Talonbooks, 1983.

Haining, Peter, ed. *Elvis in Private.* New York: St. Martin's Press, 1987.

Halberstam, David. *The Fifties.* New York: Villard Books, 1993.

Haley, John W., and John von Hoelle. *Sound and Glory.* Wilmington, Del.: Dyne-American Publishing, 1990.

Hammontree, Patsy Guy. *Elvis Presley: A Bio-Bibliography.* Westport, Conn.: Greenwood Press, 1985.

Hand, Albert. *Meet Elvis.* An Elvis Monthly Special: Manchester, 1962.

Harbinson, W. A. *The Illustrated Elvis.* New York: Grosset and Dunlap, 1976.

Harbinson, W. A., and Kay Wheeler. *Growing Up with the Memphis Flash.* Amsterdam: Tutti Frutti Productions, 1994.

Hawkins, Martin, and Colin Escott, comps. *The Sun Records Rocking Years.* London: Charly Records, 1986.

Hemphill, Paul. *The Nashville Sound: Bright Lights and Country Music.* New York: Simon and Schuster, 1970.

Hill, Wanda June. *We Remember, Elvis.* Palos Verdes, Calif.: Morgin Press, 1978.

Historic Black Memphians. Memphis: Memphis Pink Palace Museum Foundation, n.d.

Hodge, Charlie, with Charles Goodman. *Me 'n Elvis.* Memphis: Castle Books, 1988.

Holmes, Richard. *Footsteps: Adventures of a Romantic Biographer.* New York: Viking, 1985.

Hopkins, Jerry. *Elvis.* New York: Simon and Schuster, 1971.

————. *Elvis: The Final Years.* New York: St. Martin's Press, 1980.

————. *The Rock Story.* New York: Signet Books, 1970.

Horstman, Dorothy. *Sing Your Heart Out, Country Boy.* Rev. Ed. Nashville: Country Music Foundation Press, 1986.

Hurst, Jack. *Nashville's Grand Ole Opry.* New York: Abrams, 1975.

The Impersonal Life. Marina del Rey, Calif.: DeVorss, 1988.

Jenkins, Mary. *Elvis: The Way I Knew Him.* Memphis: Riverpark Publishers, 1984.

Jenkinson, Philip, and Alan Warner. *Celluloid Rock.* New York: Warner Books, 1976.

Jones, Ira, as told to Bill E. Burk. *Soldier Boy Elvis.* Memphis: Propwash Publishing, 1992.

Juanico, June. *Elvis — In the Twilight of Memory.* Unpublished manuscript.

Kienzle, Rich. *Great Guitarists: The Most Influential Players in Blues, Country Music, Jazz and Rock.* New York: Facts on File, 1985.

Killen, Buddy, with Tom Carter. *By the Seat of My Pants*. New York: Simon and Schuster, 1993.

Kirby, Edward "Prince Gabe." *From Africa to Beale Street*. Memphis: Music Management, 1983.

Lacker, Marty, Patsy Lacker, and Leslie S. Smith. *Elvis: Portrait of a Friend*. New York: Bantam, 1980.

Laing, Dave. *Buddy Holly*. London: Studio Vista, 1971.

Langbroek, Hans. *The Hillbilly Cat*. Self-published, n.d.

Latham, Caroline, and Jeannie Sakol. *"E" Is for Elvis: An A to Z Illustrated Guide to the King of Rock and Roll*. New York: New American Library, 1990.

Lemann, Nicholas. *Out of the Forties*. New York: Simon and Schuster, 1983.

————. *The Promised Land*. New York: Alfred A. Knopf, 1991.

Levine, Lawrence W. *Black Culture and Black Consciousness: Afro-American Folk Thought from Slavery to Freedom*. New York: Oxford University Press, 1977.

Levy, Alan. *Operation Elvis*. New York: Henry Holt, 1960.

Lewis, Myra, with Murray Silver. *Great Balls of Fire: The Uncensored Story of Jerry Lee Lewis*. New York: Quill, 1982.

Lichter, Paul. *The Boy Who Dared to Rock: The Definitive Elvis*. New York: Doubleday Dolphin, 1978.

Lornell, Kip. *"Happy in the Service of the Lord": Afro-American Gospel Quartets in Memphis*. Urbana: University of Illinois Press, 1988.

Loyd, Harold. *Elvis Presley's Graceland Gates*. Franklin, Tenn.: Jimmy Velvet Publications, 1987.

Lydon, Michael. *Rock Folk: Portraits from the Rock 'n' Roll Pantheon*. New York: Dial, 1971.

Lytle, Clyde Francis, ed. *Leaves of Gold: An Anthology of Prayers, Memorable Phrases, Inspirational Verse and Prose*. N.p., n.d.

Malone, Bill C. *Country Music, U.S.A.: A Fifty-Year History*. Austin: American Folklore Society, University of Texas Press, 1968.

————. *Southern Music: American Music*. Lexington: University Press of Kentucky, 1979.

Malone, Bill C., and Judith McCulloh. *Stars of Country Music: Uncle Dave Macon to Johnny Rodriguez*. Urbana: University of Illinois Press, 1975.

Mann, May. *Elvis and the Colonel*. New York: Drake Publishers, 1975.

Mansfield, Rex, and Elizabeth Mansfield. *Elvis the Soldier*. Bamberg, West Germany: Collectors Service GmbH, 1983.

Marcus, Greil. *Dead Elvis*. New York: Doubleday, 1991.

————. *Mystery Train*. 3d rev. ed. New York: Dutton, 1990.

Marsh, Dave. *Elvis*. New York: Times Books, 1982.

Martin, Linda, and Kerry Segrave. *Anti-Rock: The Opposition to Rock 'n' Roll*. Hamden, Conn.: Shoe String Press, Archon Books, 1988.

Matthew-Walker, Robert. *Elvis Presley: A Study in Music*. London: Omnibus Press, 1983.

McIlwaine, Shields. *Memphis Down in Dixie*. New York: E. P. Dutton, 1948.

McKee, Margaret, and Fred Chisenhall. *Beale Black & Blue: Life and Music on Black America's Main Street*. Baton Rouge: Louisiana State University Press, 1981.

McLafferty, Gerry. *Elvis Presley in Hollywood: Celluloid Sell-Out*. London: Robert Hale, 1989.

McNutt, Randy. *We Wanna Boogie*. Hamilton, Ohio: HHP Books, 1988.

Michael Ochs Archives. *Elvis in Hollywood*. Text by Steve Pond. New York: New American Library, 1990.

Miller, Jim, ed. *The Rolling Stone Illustrated History of Rock & Roll*. New York: Random House, Rolling Stone Press, 1976.

Miller, William D. *Memphis During the Progressive Era: 1900–1917*. Memphis: Memphis State University Press, 1957.

——. *Mr. Crump of Memphis*. Baton Rouge: Louisiana State University Press, 1964.

Morris, Willie. *North Toward Home*. Boston: Houghton Mifflin, 1967.

Morthland, John. *The Best of Country Music*. Garden City, N.Y.: Doubleday Dolphin, 1984.

Muir, Eddie, ed. *'Wild Cat': A Tribute to Gene Vincent*. Brighton, U.K.: Self-published, 1977.

Murray, Albert. *South to a Very Old Place*. New York: McGraw-Hill, 1971.

Nash, Alanna. *Behind Closed Doors: Talking with the Legends of Country Music*. New York: Alfred A. Knopf, 1988.

Palmer, Robert. *Baby, That Was Rock & Roll: The Legendary Leiber & Stoller*. New York: Harcourt Brace Jovanovich, 1978.

——. *Deep Blues*. New York: Viking, 1981.

——. *Jerry Lee Lewis Rocks!* New York: G. P. Putnam's Sons, 1981.

——. *A Tale of Two Cities: Memphis Rock and New Orleans Roll*. I.S.A.M. Monographs: Number 12. Brooklyn: Institute for Studies in American Music, 1979.

Palmer, Tony. *All You Need Is Love: The Story of Popular Music*. New York: Viking Press, Grossman Publishers, 1976.

Parker, Ed. *Inside Elvis*. Orange, Calif.: Rampart House, 1978.

Parker, John. *Five for Hollywood*. New York: Lyle Stuart, 1991.

Passman, Arnold. *The Deejays*. New York: Macmillan, 1971.

Pearl, Minnie, with Joan Dew. *Minnie Pearl: An Autobiography*. New York: Simon and Schuster, 1980.

Peary, Danny, ed. *Close Ups: The Movie Star Book*. New York: Workman, 1978.

Percy, William Alexander. *Lanterns on the Levee: Recollections of a Planter's Son*. Baton Rouge: Louisiana State University Press, 1973.

Perkins, Carl, with Ron Rendleman. *Disciple in Blue Suede Shoes*. Grand Rapids, Mich.: Zondervan Publishing House, 1978.

Pleasants, Henry. *The Great American Popular Singers*. New York: Simon and Schuster, 1974.

Poe, Randy. *Music Publishing: A Songwriter's Guide*. Cincinnati: Writer's Digest Books, 1990.

Porterfield, Nolan. *The Life and Times of America's Blue Yodeler: Jimmie Rodgers*. Urbana: University of Illinois Press, 1979.

Presley, Dee, Billy Stanley, Rick Stanley, and David Stanley, as told to Martin Torgoff. *Elvis, We Love You Tender*. New York: Delacorte Press, 1980.

Presley, Priscilla Beaulieu, with Sandra Harmon. *Elvis and Me*. New York: G. P. Putnam's Sons, 1985.

Presley, Vester. *A Presley Speaks*. Memphis: Wimmer Brothers Books, 1978.

Presley, Vester, and Nancy Rooks. *The Presley Family Cookbook*. Memphis: Wimmer Brothers Books, 1980.

Quain, Kevin, ed. *The Elvis Reader: Texts and Sources on the King of Rock 'n' Roll*. New York: St. Martin's Press, 1992.

Raines, Howell. *My Soul Is Rested*. New York: G. P. Putnam's Sons, 1977.

Reagon, Bernice Johnson, ed. *We'll Understand It Better By and By*. Washington, D.C.: Smithsonian Institution Press, 1992.

Rheingold, Todd. *Dispelling the Myth: An Analysis of American Attitudes and Prejudices*. New York: Believe in a Dream Publications, 1993.

Rijff, Ger. *Faces and Stages: An Elvis Presley Time-Frame*. Amsterdam: Tutti Frutti Productions, 1986.

——. *Long Lonely Highway*. Amsterdam: Tutti Frutti Productions, 1985.

——. *Memphis Lonesome*. Amsterdam: Tutti Frutti Productions, 1988.

————. *The Voice of Rock 'n' Roll: Elvis in the Times of Ultimate Cool.* Rotterdam: It's Elvis Time, 1993.

Rijff, Ger J., and Jan van Gestel. *Elvis: The Cool King.* Amsterdam: Tutti Frutti Productions, 1989.

————. *Fire in the Sun.* Amsterdam: Tutti Frutti Productions, 1991.

————. *Florida Close-Up.* Amsterdam: Tutti Frutti Productions, 1987.

Roark. Eldon. *Memphis Bragabouts.* New York: McGraw-Hill, Whittlesey House, 1945.

Rodriguez, Elena. *Dennis Hopper: A Madness to His Method.* New York: St. Martin's Press, 1988.

Rosenberg, Neil V. *Bluegrass: A History.* Urbana: University of Illinois Press, 1985.

Rovin, Jeff *The World According to Elvis: Quotes from the King.* New York: HarperCollins, Harper Paperbacks, 1992.

Russell, Tony. *Blacks Whites and Blues.* London: Studio Vista, 1970.

Russell, Wayne. *Foot Soldiers and Kings.* Brandon, Manitoba: Wayne Russell, n.d.

————. *Foot Soldiers and Kings.* Vol. 2. Brandon, Manitoba: Wayne Russell, n.d.

Sanjek Russell. *American Popular Music and Its Business: The First Four Hundred Years.* Vol. 3, *From 1900 to 1984.* New York: Oxford University Press, 1988.

————. *From Print to Plastic: Publishing and Promoting America's Popular Music (1900–1980).* I.S.A.M. Monographs: Number 20. Brooklyn: Institute for Studies in American Music, 1983.

Sawyer, Charles. *The Arrival of B. B. King.* Garden City, N.Y.: Doubleday, 1980.

Schlappi, Elizabeth. *Roy Acuff: The Smoky Mountain Boy.* Gretna, La.: Pelican Publishing, 1978.

Schroer, Andreas. *Private Presley: The Missing Years — Elvis in Germany.* New York: William Morrow, 1993.

Selvin, Joel. *Ricky Nelson: Idol for a Generation.* Chicago: Contemporary Books, 1990.

Shaw, Arnold. *The Rockin' '50s.* New York: Hawthorne Books, 1974.

Shelton, Robert, and Burt Goldblatt. *The Country Music Story: A Picture History of Country and Western Music.* New York: Bobbs-Merrill, 1966.

Siegel, Don. *A Siegel Film: An Autobiography.* London: Faber and Faber, 1993.

Sigafoos, Robert A. *Cotton Row to Beale Street.* Memphis: Memphis State University Press, 1979.

Smith, Wes. *The Pied Pipers of Rock 'n' Roll: Radio Deejays of the 50s and 60s.* Marietta, Ga.: Longstreet Press, 1989.

Snow, Hank, with Jack Ownbey and Bob Burris. *The Hank Snow Story.* Champaign: University of Illinois Press, 1994.

Snow, Jimmy, with Jim Hefley and Marti Hefley. *I Cannot Go Back.* Plainfield, N.J.: Logos International, 1977.

Stanley, Billy, with George Erikson. *Elvis, My Brother.* New York: St. Martin's Press, 1989.

Stanley, David. *Life with Elvis.* Old Tappan, N.J.: Fleming H. Revell, 1986.

Stanley, Rick, with Michael K. Haynes. *The Touch of Two Kings: Growing Up at Graceland.* N.p.: T2K Publishers, 1986.

Staten, Vince. *The Real Elvis: Good Old Boy.* Dayton: Media Ventures, 1978.

Stearn, Jess, with Larry Geller. *The Truth About Elvis.* New York: Jove Publications, 1980.

Stern, Jane, and Michael Stern. *Elvis World.* New York: Alfred A. Knopf, 1987.

Storm, Tempest, with Bill Boyd. *The Lady Is a Vamp.* Atlanta: Peachtree Publishers, 1987.

Sumner, J. D., with Bob Terrell. *Elvis: His Love for Gospel Music and J. D. Summer.* N.p.: The Gospel Quartet Music Company and Bob Terrell, 1991.

Swaggart, Jimmy. *The Campmeeting Hour: The Radio Miracle of the 20th Century.* Baton Rouge: Jimmy Swaggart Evangelistic Association, 1976.

Swaggart, Jimmy, with Robert Paul Lamb. *To Cross a River.* Plainfield, N.J.: Logos International, 1977.

Swenson, John. *Bill Haley: The Daddy of Rock and Roll.* New York: Stein and Day, 1982.

Terrell, Bob. *The Music Men: The Story of Professional Gospel Quartet Singing.* Asheville, N.C.: Bob Terrell Publisher, 1990.

Tharpe, Jac L., ed. *Elvis: Images and Fancies.* Jackson: University Press of Mississippi, 1979.

Thompson, Charles C. II, and James P. Cole. *The Death of Elvis: What Really Happened.* New York: Delacorte Press, 1991.

Thompson, Sam. *Elvis on Tour: The Last Year.* Memphis: Still Brook Publishing, 1992.

Tobler, John, and Stuart Grundy. *The Record Producers.* New York: St. Martin's Press, 1982.

Toll, Robert. *Blacking Up: The Minstrel Show in Nineteenth-Century America.* New York: Oxford University Press, 1974.

Torgoff, Martin, ed. *The Complete Elvis.* New York: G. P. Putnam's Sons, 1982.

Tosches, Nick. *Country: The Biggest Music in America.* New York: Stein and Day, 1977.

———. *Dino.* New York: Doubleday, 1992.

———. *Hellfire: The Jerry Lee Lewis Story.* New York: Dell, 1982.

———. *Unsung Heroes of Rock 'n' Roll.* Rev. ed. New York: Harmony Books, 1991.

Townsend, Charles R. *San Antonio Rose: The Life and Music of Bob Wills.* Urbana: University of Illinois Press, 1976.

Tribute: The Life of Dr. William Herbert Brewster. 2d ed. Memphis: Brewster House of Sermon Songs, n.d.

Tucker, David. *Lieutenant Lee of Beale Street.* Nashville: Vanderbilt University Press, 1971.

———. *Memphis Since Crump: Bossism, Blacks, and Civic Reformers, 1948–1968.* Knoxville: University of Tennessee Press, 1980.

Turner, Steve. *Hungry for Heaven: Rock and Roll and the Search for Redemption.* London: W. H. Allen, 1988.

Van Doren, Mamie, with Art Aveilhe. *Playing the Field: My Story.* New York: G. P. Putnam's Sons, 1987.

Vellenga, Dirk, with Mick Farren. *Elvis and the Colonel.* New York: Delacorte Press, 1988.

Vernon, Paul. *The Sun Legend.* London: Paul Vernon, 1969.

Vince, Alan. *I Remember Gene Vincent.* Liverpool: Vintage Rock'n'Roll Appreciation Society, 1977.

Wade-Gayles, Gloria. *Pushed Back to Strength.* Boston: Beacon Press, 1993.

Wallis, Hal, and Charles Higham. *Starmaker: The Autobiography of Hal Wallis.* New York: Macmillan, 1980.

Ward, Ed, Geoffrey Stokes, and Ken Tucker. *Rock of Ages: The Rolling Stone History of Rock & Roll.* New York: Summit Books, 1986.

Weinberg, Max, with Robert Santelli. *The Big Beat: Conversations with Rock's Great Drummers.* New York: Billboard Books, 1991.

Wertheimer, Alfred, with Gregory Martinelli. *Elvis '56: In the Beginning.* New York: Collier Books, 1979.

West, Red, Sonny West, and Dave Hebler, as told to Steve Dunleavy. *Elvis: What Happened?* New York: Ballantine Books, 1977.

Westmoreland, Kathy, with William G. Quinn. *Elvis and Kathy.* Glendale, Calif.: Glendale House Publishing, 1987.

White, Charles. *The Life and Times of Little Richard: The Quasar of Rock.* New York: Harmony Books, 1984.

Wiegert, Sue. *Elvis: For the Good Times.* Los Angeles: The Blue Hawaiians for Elvis, 1978.

Wiegert, Sue, with contributions by Elvis friends and Elvis fans. *"Elvis: Precious Memories."* Los Angeles: Century City Printing, 1987.

————. *"Elvis: Precious Memories."* Vol. 2. Los Angeles: Century City Printing, 1989.

Williams, William Carlos. *In the American Grain.* New York: New Directions Press, 1956.

Winters, Shelley. *Shelley II.* New York: Simon and Schuster, 1989.

Wood, Lana. *Natalie: A Memoir by Her Sister.* New York: G. P. Putnam's Sons, 1984.

Woodward, C. Vann. *The Burden of Southern History.* Rev. ed. Baton Rouge: Louisiana State University Press, 1968.

————. *Thinking Back: The Perils of Writing History.* Baton Rouge: Louisiana State University Press, 1986.

Wren, Christopher S. *Winners Got Scars Too: The Life of Johnny Cash.* New York: A Country Music/Ballantine Book, 1971.

Wynette, Tammy, with Joan Dew. *Stand By Your Man: An Autobiography.* New York: Simon and Schuster, 1979.

Yancy, Becky, and Cliff Linedecker. *My Life with Elvis.* New York: St. Martin's Press, 1977.

Yogananda, Paramahansa. *Autobiography of a Yogi.* Los Angeles: Self-Realization Fellowship, 1974.

Zmijewsky, Steven, and Boris Zmijewsky. *Elvis: The Films and Career of Elvis Presley.* New York: Citadel Press, 1991.

CLIPPINGS, COLLECTIONS, PICTURE BOOKS, AND MEMORABILIA

Burk, Bill E. *Elvis: Rare Images of a Legend.* Memphis: Propwash Publishing, 1990.

Clark, Alan. *Buddy Holly and the Crickets.* West Covina, Calif.: Alan Clark Productions, 1979.

————. *Elvis Presley Memories.* West Covina, Calif: Leap Frog Productions, 1982.

————. *The Elvis Presley Photo Album.* West Covina, Calif.: Alan Clark Productions, 1981.

————. *Gene Vincent: The Screaming End.* West Covina, Calif: Alan Clark Productions, 1980.

————. *Legends of Sun Records.* West Covina, Calif.: Alan Clark Productions. Various volumes, 1986 to present.

————. *Rock-a-billy and Country Legends.* West Covina, Calif: Alan Clark Productions.

————. *Rock and Roll in the Movies.* West Covina, Calif.: Alan Clark Productions. Various volumes.

————. *Rock and Roll Legends.* West Covina, Calif: Alan Clark Productions. Various volumes.

————. *Rock and Roll Memories.* West Covina, Calif.: Alan Clark Productions. Various volumes.

Cortez, Diego, ed. *Private Elvis.* Stuttgart: FEY Verlags GmbH, 1978.

Curtin, Jim. *Unseen Elvis: Candids of the King.* Boston: Little, Brown, 1992.

DeNight, Bill, Sharon Fox, and Ger Rijff. *Elvis Album.* Lincolnwood, Ill.: Beekman House, 1991.

Esposito, Joe. *Elvis: A Legendary Performance.* Buena Park, Calif.: West Coast Publishing, 1990.

Fox, Sharon R., ed. *Elvis, His Real Life in the 60s: My Personal Scrapbook.* Chicago: Sharon Fox, 1989.

Hannaford, Jim. *Elvis: Golden Ride on the Mystery Train.* Vols. 1 and 2. Alva, Okla.: Jim Hannaford, 1986.

Kricun, Morrie E., and Virginia M. Kricun. *Elvis: 1956 Reflections.* Wayne, Pa.: Morgin Press, 1991 and 1992.

Lamb, Charles. *The Country Music World of Charlie Lamb.* Nashville: Infac Publications, 1986.

Life: 1946–1955. New York: Little, Brown, New York Graphic Society, 1984.

Loper, Karen. *The Elvis Clippings.* Houston: "The Elvis Clippings," n.d.

Michael Ochs Rock Archives. Garden City, N.Y.: Doubleday, 1984.

Now Dig This. *The King Forever.* Wallsend, Tyne and Wear, U.K.: Now Dig This, 1992.

O'Neal, Hank (text). *A Vision Shared: A Classic Portrait of America and Its People.* New York: St. Martin's Press, 1976.

Parish, James Robert. *Solid Gold Memories: The Elvis Presley Scrapbook.* New York: Ballantine Books, 1975.

Rijff, Ger, and Poul Madsen. *Elvis Presley: Echoes of the Past.* Voorschoten, Holland: "Blue Suede Shoes" Productions, 1976.

Tucker, Gabe, and Elmer Williams. *Pictures of Elvis Presley.* Houston: Williams and Tucker Photographs, 1981.

Tunzi, Joseph A. *Elvis '69: The Return.* Chicago: JAT Productions, 1991.

———. *Elvis '73: Hawaiian Spirit.* Chicago: JAT Productions, 1992.

PERIODICALS

I couldn't begin to list all the periodicals, past and present, that I have consulted. Just for the briefest of references, I have found *Now Dig This, Goldmine, DISCoveries, New Kommotion, Kicks, Country Music,* and *Picking Up the Tempo* particularly useful (and frequently invaluable) over the years. In addition, I have consulted the following Elvis publications extensively: *Elvis: The Man and His Music; Elvis: The Record; Elvis World; Because of Elvis; Elvis International Forum;* and *Graceland Express. Musician's* special 1992 report, "Elvis Presley: An Oral Biography," with interviews conducted by Peter Cronin, Scott Isler, and Mark Rowland, offered an insightful portrait. Finally, Orbis' *History of Rock,* vols. 3 and 5, published in 1981 and 1982, has good pictures and interesting background on the early career, and life and times, of Elvis Presley.

For detailed reference to specific articles and periodical sources, however, please see the Source Notes (page 491).

A Brief Discographical Note

MUCH OF THE WORK THAT would once have gone into pointing people toward the best of Elvis Presley on record has finally been done (or is in the process of completion) by RCA/BMG. Thanks to the efforts of Ernst Jorgensen and Roger Semon, the vast majority of Elvis' essential performances are now available on three 5-CD sets. *Elvis: The King of Rock 'N' Roll: The Complete 50's Masters* (RCA 66050), *Elvis from Nashville to Memphis: The Essential 60's Masters* (RCA 66160), and *Walk a Mile in My Shoes: The Essential 70's Masters* (RCA 66670) contain nearly everything in the way of studio masters (the '60s and '70s boxes leave out all the movie soundtrack material), together with some wonderful, frequently enlightening surprises along the way.

The Complete 50's Masters alone could, really, serve as the soundtrack to this book, including everything from the first acetate to the last in-uniform '58 session, with such bonuses as Elvis' embarkation press conference, his 1956 Las Vegas show, and a number of impromptu 1955 performances, both live and in the studio.

In addition, *Amazing Grace* (RCA 66421) is the definitive 2-CD compilation of Elvis' gospel recordings, and no respectable record collection should be without either it or *Sunrise* (RCA 67675), a 2-CD set of the Sun sides, various alternate takes and Hayride performances, and not just the first but the *second* pre-professional acetate that Elvis recorded at his own expense at 706 Union Avenue. The only other truly essential purchases that I can think of are *The Million Dollar Quartet* (RCA 2023), which offers a fascinating, unbuttoned view of the creative process at work, with powerfully ragged harmonies from Elvis, Jerry Lee Lewis, and Carl Perkins (the one-man-short but scarcely overvalued quartet) and the incomparable audio spectacle of Elvis imitating Jackie Wilson imitating him; *Elvis/NBC-TV Special* (RCA 61021) and *Tiger Man* (RCA 67611), which represent, respectively, the soundtrack for the '68 comeback special and the second live sit-down show complete; and *Suspicious Minds* (RCA 67677), a 2-disc set which includes all the masters cut at the American studio in 1969, along with a generous assortment of outtakes from what may have been the single most productive session undertaken by Elvis after Sun. With that said, however, I should mention that Elvis' initial post-army session, whose eighteen cuts were dispersed among three singles (including "It's Now or Never" and "Are You Lonesome Tonight?") and the only album that could arguably be compared with *From Elvis in Memphis* (the first LP to present the American material), has now been released as a complete eighteen-track CD under the same name as the original twelve-track album, *Elvis Is Back* (RCA 67737). Presented in its entirety for the first time, that album is, I think, a true revelation.

There are lots of other avenues to explore — the movie songs, live performances, alternate takes (*The Essential Elvis* series, of which Volume 2, *Elvis Presley Stereo '57* [RCA 9589] is the most consistently engaging), theme- and chronology-linked compilations — but for these and numerous other permutations, I'll leave you to your own devices. The only other suggestion that I have (though this is one that could sustain almost endless exploration) is the music from which Elvis derived his inspiration: music from sources as varied as Roy Hamilton, Hank Snow, Arthur Crudup, Martha Carson, Eddy Arnold, Ray Charles, Bing Crosby, Little Junior Parker, the Ink Spots, the Statesmen, the Blackwood Brothers, and Sister Rosetta Tharpe. There are two albums out featuring original versions of some of Elvis' better-known songs (*The King's Record Collection*, volumes 1 and 2 [Hip-O 40082 and 40083]), and they are certainly a good start, but if Elvis' music moves you, it's worth more than a leisurely stroll along the frequently diverging paths of great American vernacular music. There's a wealth of inspiration to be found for music still to be made.

Acknowledgments

IN WRITING A BOOK over so long a period (and one that stretches back well beyond its formal start), one incurs debts that one can never repay. Literally hundreds of people have helped me with my research and my interviews, and I thank them all. The following are just some of the people who gave me a hand over the weeks, months, and years:

Mrs. Lee Roy Abernathy, Curtis Lee Alderson, J. W. Alexander, Hoss Allen, Terry Allen, Chet Atkins, James Ausborn, Mae Axton, Buddy and Kay Bain, Eva Mills Baker and Sarah Baker Bailey, Jimmy Bank, Jonnie Barnett, Dick Baxter, Bob Beckham, Fred and Harriette Beeson, Bill Bentley, Bettye Berger, Freddy Bienstock, Steve Binder, Evelyn Black, Johnny Black, James Blackwood, George Blancet, Arthur Bloom, Arlene Piper Blum, Barbara Bobo, Barbara Boldt, Dave Booth, Stanley Booth, Joella Bostick, Ernest Bowen, Horace Boyer, Will Bratton and Sharyn Felder, Avis Brown, Jim Ed Brown, Monty and Marsha Brown, Tony Brown, James Burton, Sheila Caan, Trevor Cajiao, Louis Cantor, Jerry Carrigan, Martha Carson, Johnny Cash, Anne Cassidy, Marshall Chess, Gene Chrisman, Galen Christy, Dr. Charles L. Clarke, Quinton Claunch, Rose Clayton, Jack Clement, Jackie Lee Cochran, Jim Cole, Biff Collie, L. C. Cooke, Al Cooley, Daniel Cooper, X. Cosse, the Country Music Foundation, Floyd Cramer, Jack Cristil, Peter Cronin, Mike Crowley, T. Tommy Cutrer, Bill Dahl, Pete Daniel, Sherry Daniel, Fred Danzig, Fred Davis, Hank Davis, Richard Davis, Joan Deary, Bill Denny, Jesse Lee Denson, Jimmy Denson, Howard DeWitt, Jim and Mary Lindsay Dickinson, Duff Dorrough, Carole Drexler, Vince Edwards, Leroy Elmore, Sam Esgro, David Evans, Eddie Fadal, Charles Farrar, Charlie Feathers, Robert Ferguson, Lamar Fike, D. J. Fontana, Buzzy Forbess, Trude Forsher, Alan Fortas, Lillian Fortenberry, Fred Foster, Sharon Fox, Ted Fox, Andy Franklin, Ann Freer, Donnie Fritts, Anne Fulchino, Lowell Fulson, Ray Funk, Marty Garbus, Honeymoon Garner, Galen Gart, Gregg Geller, Larry Geller, Gary Giddins, Homer Gilliland, Cliff Gleaves, Glen Glenn, Billy Goldenberg, Stuart Goldman, John Goldrosen, Kay Gove, Betty Grant, Sid Graves, Tom Graves, Alan Greenberg, Bob Groom, Jimmy Guterman, Joe Haertel, Rick Hall, Jim Hannaford, Terry Hansen, Glenn D. Hardin, Gary Hardy, Sandy Harmon, Dottie Harmony, Phyllis Harper, Homer Ray Harris, Randy Haspel, Dot Hawkins, Martin Hawkins, Rick Hawks, Joseph Hazen, Skip Henderson, Curley Herndon, Lamar Herrin, Jake Hess, Leonard Hirshan, Charlie Hodge, Lester and Sterling Hofman, Bones Howe, Eliot Hubbard, Tom Hulett, Maylon Humphries, Nick Hunter, Bill Ivey, Mark James, Roland Janes, Jim Jaworowicz, Jimmy Johnson, Sandi Kallenberg, Hal Kanter, Jerry Kennedy, Stan Kesler, Merle Kilgore, Buddy Killen, Paul Kingsbury, Millie Kirkham, Pete Kuykendall, Sleepy LaBeef, Charlie Lamb, Guy Lansky, Dickey Lee, Mike Leech, Ed Leek, Lance LeGault, Jerry Leiber, Barbara Leigh, Ed Leimbacher, David Leonard, Stan Lewis, Horace Logan, Mary Logan, Larrie Londin, Lorene Lortie, Bill Lowery, Archie Mackey, Kenneth Mann, Brad McCuen, Judy McCulloh, Charlie McGovern, Gerry McLafferty, Andy McLenon, John and Pat McMurray, Scott McQuaid, Sandi Miller, Bill Mitchell, Bill Monroe, Sputnik

Monroe, Bob Moore, Bobbie Moore, Steve Morley, John Morthland, Joe Moscheo, Alanna Nash, David Naylor, Jimmy "C" Newman, Thorne Nogar, John Novarese, Herbie O'Mell, Jim O'Neal, Sean O'Neal, Michael Ochs, Bob Oermann, Jay Orr, Terry Pace, Frank Page, Colonel Tom Parker, Ed Parker, Pat Parry, Judy Peiser, Carl Perkins, Millie Perkins, Tom Perryman, Brian Petersen, Pallas Pidgeon, Bob Pinson, Barbara and Willie Pittman, Randy Poe, Gail Pollock, Doc Pomus, Steve Popovich, Bill Porter, John Andrew Prime, Mark Pucci, Ronnie Pugh, Norbert Putnam, Pat Rainer, Charles Raiteri, Jerry Reed, Eleanor Richman, JillEllyn Riley, Fran Roberts, Don Robertson, Jeffrey Rodgers, Steve Rosen, Neil Rosenberg, John Rumble, Wayne Russell, Ben Sandmel, Johnny Saulovich, Jerry Scheff, Tony Scherman, Tom Schultheiss, Joel Selvin, Jan Shepard, Barbara Sims, John and Shelby Singleton, the Reverend and Mrs. Frank Smith, Myrna Smith, Ronald Smith, Hank Snow, the Reverend Jimmy Snow, Jessica St. John, Kevin Stein, Jim Stewart, Alan Stoker, Gordon Stoker, Mike Stoller, Dave Stone, Billy Strange, Peter Stromberg, Marty Stuart, J. D. Sumner, Billy Swan, Russ Tamblyn, Corinne Tate, Bob Terrell, Rufus and Carla Thomas, Linda Thompson, Sam Thompson, Roland Tindall, Nick Tosches, Ruth Trussell, Ernest Tubb, Justin Tubb, Gabe Tucker, Cindy Underwood, Billy Walker, Slim Wallace, Jan Walner, Dick Waterman, Monte Weiner, Ben Weisman, Alfred Wertheimer, Kathy Westmoreland, Jerry Wexler, Jonny Whiteside, Tex Whitson, Willie Wileman, Jimmy Wiles, Charles Wolfe, Gloria Wolper, Terry Wood, Eve Yohalem, Chip Young, Jimmy Young, Reggie Young, and Mrs. W. A. Zuber.

Once again Bill Millar generously provided tapes, clippings, insights, and information, as did Ger Rijff, Karen Loper, Poul Madsen, Stephen Stathis, Rich Kienzle, and Diana Magrann. Robert Gordon energetically uncovered all kinds of arcane Memphis information and lore (and accompanied me to Riverside Park, the site of Rocky's Lakeside refreshment stand); I'm looking forward to reading Robert's take on some of this same material in his forthcoming book, *It Came from Memphis*. Other gracious Memphis hosts and guides were Bill Burk, Shelley Ritter, David and Angela Less, Jackson Baker, Ronny Trout, and the South Memphis gang to whom Ronnie Smith introduced me. In Nashville, too, I couldn't begin to name all my unflagging guides and personal sponsors, but Mary Jarvis and David Briggs in particular went out of their way to vouch for me and set me off in the right direction on my travels. Elaine Dundy, whom I first met when I began work on the book, soon became a fast friend and introduced me to all of *her* friends in Tupelo (whom she had met in the course of writing her own book, *Elvis and Gladys*). Those she didn't introduce me to personally, local historian and genealogist Roy Turner, who helped Elaine with her research and is Tupelo's resident expert on Marilyn Monroe, did. In Shreveport, Alton and Margaret Warwick and Tillman Franks fulfilled much the same function, doing everything in their power to provide me with all the background on the Hayride that I could absorb and introducing me cheerfully to many of its key figures.

I am greatly indebted to John Bakke, chairman of the Department of Theatre and Communication Arts, for making available to me both the resources of the Mississippi Valley Collection at Memphis State University and the tapes of the annual memorial service program, which was cosponsored by Dean Richard Ranta of the College of Communication and Fine Arts each August for ten years after Elvis' death. Andrew Solt and Malcolm Leo each helped immeasurably in opening up to me the resources, contacts, and files (not to mention knowledge, insights, and goodwill) that they developed initially in making *This Is Elvis* and in their subsequent work both together and individually over the years.

Both Dixie Locke and June Juanico were more than generous in their sharing of personal memories and thoughtful insights. Jerry Schilling, George Klein, and Joe Esposito gave freely of their time, reflection, and good offices. Chick Crumpacker and Grelun Landon were my unfailing guides and friends, taking me down various obscure and pleasurable paths, generally in the way of reminiscence but, in Chick's case, in semi-corporeal reality, too, when we revisited the old RCA building, studio, and environs with Ernst Jorgensen.

Scotty Moore patiently submitted to interview after interview (over the passage of more than fifteen years), finally played me his Josh White records, and said "Ouch, that hurts!" only often enough to point out what painful brain twisters the past can inevitably present. The late Marion Keisker, too, was the best of friends, always kept me abreast of the latest Memphis news, and was quick to share her views on everything from theater and film (in which she was an active participant) to feminism (ditto) to the Memphis Pyramid. I can't overstate my thanks to Sam Phillips, Knox Phillips, and the entire Phillips family, for their unstinting friendship and dedication to helping in this project in every way, down to the last, most infinitesimal detail. Sam, Marion, and Scotty all came together at a moment in history, and while their recollection of that moment has sometimes differed sharply, their commitment to its unblinking portrayal, whether presenting them in a flattering or unflattering light, and their sense of its significance independent of their own role in it have remained unswerving.

Kit Rachlis once again provided the most helpful (not to mention annoyingly perceptive) editorial suggestions and advice, and Alexandra Guralnick patiently read, transcribed, debated, and imagined the details of the story every step of the way. Colin Escott read the manuscript for accuracy and supplied clippings, information, and advice toward that end, while Ernst Jorgensen, co-compiler of Elvis' *Complete 50's* and *Essential 60's Masters,* RCA's two definitive five-CD sets, proved even more obsessive than I in running down obscure facts, upsetting theoretical applecarts, and refusing to allow a dream scenario to get in the way of the real one. My thanks to past and present editors Jim Landis and Michael Pietsch; to Dick McDonough; to Debbie Jacobs for her tireless, sympathetic, and cheerfully stringent copyediting; and, once again, to Susan Marsh, not just for her fifteen-year partnership in design but for all her help, encouragement, perspective, and unflaggingly professional passion for the work.

Thanks to all, and to all those not named, from whom I drew encouragement, sustenance, and inspiration, not to mention the courage (and enthusiasm) to begin Volume II!

Index

Page numbers in *italic* type refer to illustrations.

547

ALSO BY PETER GURALNICK

FEEL LIKE GOING HOME
Portraits in Blues and Rock 'n' Roll

With portraits of Muddy Waters, Howlin' Wolf, Jerry Lee Lewis, Charlie Rich, the Chicago blues scene, and the legendary Chess record label in its final days — a vivid celebration of the artists who were the building blocks of blues and early rock 'n' roll.

"Brings it back alive better than any book of its kind ever published . . . . Guralnick has a lover's passion, a novelist's sensitivity to nuances of character and event, a musician's ear, a historian's insatiable appetite for detail and fact." — Charles Shaar Murray, *New Musical Express*

"The most loving book I have ever read about American popular music." — Greil Marcus, *Rolling Stone*

LOST HIGHWAY
Journeys and Arrivals of American Musicians

With profiles of Ernest Tubb, Charlie Feathers, Rufus Thomas, Big Joe Turner, Bobby "Blue" Bland, Merle Haggard, Sleepy LaBeef, and others — a stirring tribute to American roots music: country, rockabilly, and the blues.

"Guralnick consistently gives us scenes along the road that are so strange and haunting, or touching, that they make the whole trip worthwhile. . . . You put the book down feeling that its sweep is vast, that you have read of giants who walked among us."

— Lester Bangs, *Los Angeles Herald Examiner*

"A book not just for fans, but for anyone interested in music, American popular culture, and quietly eloquent writing." — John Rockwell, *New York Times*

SWEET SOUL MUSIC
Rhythm and Blues and the Southern Dream of Freedom

The story of the legendary artists — Sam Cooke, Ray Charles, James Brown, Solomon Burke, Aretha Franklin, Otis Redding, and Al Green among them — who merged gospel and rhythm and blues to create Southern soul music.

"One of the best books ever written on American popular music. . . . A stunning chronicle."

— Jim Miller, *Newsweek*

"The best history of '60s soul music anyone has written or is likely to write, but it is much more than that. . . . *Sweet Soul Music* is as important for what it says about America, class and race issues, and the '60s as for its outstanding musical insights. . . . A classic."

— Robert Palmer, *New York Times*

Available in paperback from Back Bay Books

PRAISE FOR

CARELESS LOVE

"Nothing written about Elvis Presley comes close to the detail, authority, and uncondescending objectivity that Peter Guralnick has brought to his two-volume biography. . . . Hypnotic." — Andy Seiler, *USA Today*

"Assiduously researched, meticulously written, and beautifully assembled, equal parts Shakespearean tragedy and psychological mystery."
— Richard Harrington, *Washington Post*

"Majestic. . . . The most meticulously researched and sympathetic, honest portrait of Elvis we are likely to see." — *Kirkus Reviews*

"Definitive . . . scrupulous. . . . An epic American tragedy, captured in all its complexity." — *Publishers Weekly*

"Guralnick is one of our best nonfiction writers. He's also one of our most trustworthy citizens — inherently, defiantly decent. His voice is plain-spoken but elegant, holy without being holier-than-thou, reverent while recognizing his subject's intrinsic irreverence. . . . *Careless Love* . . . is a more staggering achievement than *Last Train to Memphis* — which is saying something. Though the first book was more lovable, it was also an easier story to tell. *Careless Love* requires guts from the author, a kind of relentlessness and no small amount of faith." — Sarah Vowell, *Los Angeles Times Book Review*

"Possibly the greatest biography of an American musician ever penned. For those who never saw Presley perform live, Guralnick offers something just as galvanizing: front row center to a life."
— Bill Ellis, *Memphis Commercial Appeal*

"*Careless Love*, a chronicle of shadows and sadness, is no sentimental epitaph. It is the fine and careful measure of a pilgrim traveler . . . in Guralnick's thorough and compassionate telling."　　　— Jay Cocks, *Time*

"Mr. Guralnick's book is a labor of love, and of profound respect. What's remarkable is how he manages to be simultaneously compassionate and dispassionate, truthful, unflinching, and nonjudgmental. His (all too rare) refusal to criticize, second-guess or gloat . . . lends the entire enterprise an aura of capaciousness, generosity and even transcendence. . . . Everything in the biography strikes you as fitting seamlessly together. . . . Mr. Guralnick's book enlarges your imagination for the extremes and marvels, the highs and lows that can occur within a single lifetime."

— Francine Prose, *New York Observer*

"Guralnick has done a masterful job of synthesizing information into a nuanced, deftly paced narrative. He brings long-overdue subtlety and insight to one of the most overscrutinized characters in American popular culture."　　　— Tom Moon, *Philadelphia Inquirer*

"We all know how the story ends, but Guralnick still manages to break our hearts in the telling. . . . *Careless Love* is the toughest book about Elvis ever written, but it's also one of the loveliest. . . . One of the saddest stories ever told."　　　— Stephanie Zacharek, *Newsday*

"Remarkably, Mr. Guralnick neither moralizes about Elvis' actions nor opines about his place in history. . . . The result: a crystalline focus on the man and his music that offers up Elvis' life as a sort of Rorschach test for the late 20th century. . . . Together the two volumes make up an 1,100-page masterwork — a streamlined and riveting narrative tracing the rise and fall of arguably the most important entertainer of the century."

— Craig Havighurst, *Wall Street Journal*

"*Careless Love* restores the flesh to Elvis' beleaguered bones. . . . Guralnick writes with such profound sympathy for his subject that Elvis' fate, though excruciating to read about, isn't *shocking*, as it was, for example, in Albert Goldman's loathsome 1981 biography. . . . Guralnick, working with the same basic material, shows us a terribly unhappy and frustrated man. I know which version I believe."　　　— Terrence Rafferty, *GQ*

"With the intense and objective eye of a master biographer . . . Guralnick takes the reader into the underlying issues of class, race, and the American desire to transform who we are into something better. . . . Monumental."
— Lucinda Ebersole, *Chicago Tribune*

"Narrative biography at its absolute zenith. A stunning literary achievement."
— Douglas Brinkley, director, The Eisenhower Center for American Studies, University of New Orleans

"Tracing what seems a grand and irrevocable arc through an American life that finally became an American tragedy, Peter Guralnick has produced the second half of his colossal biography of Elvis Presley. . . . Depressing as the story is, Guralnick's approach redeems Elvis as a human, not a myth or a punch line, and calmly, methodically makes coherent what often has been obscured by the almost *X-Files* level of paranoid fantasy associated with the King's Final Years."
— Steve Dollar, *Atlanta Journal-Constitution*

"Guralnick gives even the most familiar parts of this story fresh life. And as with any rendering of experience that attempts to understand the motivations of the people involved without judging them, the life described takes on an irreducible mystery."
— Charles Taylor, *Salon*

"A brilliant, beautifully written biography. . . . With sentences built simply and carefully, yet containing ideas that are intense and true . . . Guralnick has created a masterpiece."
— Robert Santelli, *Cleveland Plain Dealer*

"Essential reading not only for fans . . . but for anyone curious about the process and price of fame in America."
— Curtis Ross, *Tampa Tribune*

"A mythic tale of the American experience. . . . Guralnick tells the tale with a profound sensitivity and a depth of detail that is unsurpassed."
— Joel Williamson, *Raleigh News & Observer*

"The great triumph of *Careless Love* is that it celebrates, amid an unflinching portrait of personal and creative deterioration, the immutable innocence of Elvis' aspiration."
— Joan Anderman, *Boston Globe*

CARELESS LOVE

THE UNMAKING OF ELVIS PRESLEY

October 1958 — Summer 1977

PETER GURALNICK

BACK BAY BOOKS

BOSTON · NEW YORK · LONDON

Originally published in hardcover by Little, Brown and Company, 1999

First Back Bay paperback edition, 2000

FRONTISPIECE: GRACELAND, FALL 1960. (ROBERT WILLIAMS)

Permissions to quote from copyrighted material appear on page 767.

Library of Congress Cataloging-in-Publication Data

Guralnick, Peter.
    Careless love : the unmaking of Elvis Presley / Peter
Guralnick. — 1st ed.
        p.   cm.
    Includes bibliographical references and index.
    ISBN 0-316-33222-4 (HC) 0-316-33297-6 (PB)
    1. Presley, Elvis, 1935–1977. 2. Rock musicians — United
States — Biography. I. Title.
ML420.P96G85   1998
782.42166'092 — dc21
[B]   98-25778

10 9 8 7 6 5 4 3 2 1
MV-NY

DESIGNED BY SUSAN MARSH

Printed in the United States of America

For Jacob and Nina
and for Alexandra

Contents

Author's Note

It's difficult to be a legend. It's hard for me to recognize me. *You spend a lot of time trying to avoid it. . . . The way the world treats you is unbearable. . . . It's unbearable because time is passing and you are not your legend, but you're trapped in it. Nobody will let you out of it except other people who know what it is. But very few people have experienced it, know about it, and I think that can drive you mad. I know it can. I know it can.*

— James Baldwin, interviewed by Quincy Troupe

THIS IS A STORY of fame. It is a story of celebrity and its consequences. It is, I think, a tragedy, and no more the occasion for retrospective moral judgments than any other biographical canvas should be. "Suspending moral judgment is not the immorality of the novel," Milan Kundera wrote in what could be taken as a challenge thrown down to history and biography, too. This suspension of judgment is the storyteller's *morality*, "the morality that stands against the ineradicable human habit of judging instantly, ceaselessly, and everyone; of judging before, and in the absence of, understanding." It is not that moral judgment is illegitimate; it is simply that it has no place in describing a life.

Elvis Presley may well be the most written-about figure of our time. He is also in many ways the most misunderstood, both because of our ever-increasing rush to judgment and, perhaps more to the point, simply because he appears to be so well known. It has become almost as impossible to imagine *Elvis* amid all our assumptions, amid all the false intimacy that attaches to a tabloid personality, as it is to separate the President from the myth of the presidency, John Wayne from the myth of the American West. "It's very hard," Elvis declared without facetiousness at a 1972 press conference, "to live up to an image." And yet he, as much as his public, appeared increasingly trapped by it.

The Elvis Presley that I am writing about here is a man between the ages of twenty-three and forty-two. His circumstances are far removed from those of the boy whose dreams came true in the twenty-second year of his life. It is not simply that his mother has died, testing his belief in the very meaning of success. With or without his mother by his side, he would have had to grow up; he would have had to face all the complications of adulthood in a situation of almost unbearable public scrutiny, a young man little different in temperament from the solitary child who had constructed a world from his imagination. The army was hard for him not just because he was temperamentally unsuited to it but because it was something he knew he had to succeed at, both for himself and for others. The artistic choices he faced when he returned to an interrupted life were far more ambiguous than the good fortune he had so innocently embraced, and he never came fully to terms with the burden of decision making that those choices placed upon him. His natural ability to adapt, his complex relationship with a manager whom he perceived not just as a mentor but as a talisman of his good luck, served him in both good and bad stead. He constructed a shell to hide his aloneness, and it hardened on his back. I know of no sadder story. But if the last part of Elvis' life had to do with the price that is paid for dreams, neither the dreams themselves, nor the aspiration that fueled them, should be forgotten. Without them the story of Elvis Presley would have little meaning.

I've tried to tell this story as much as possible from Elvis' point of view. Although he never kept a diary, left us with no memoirs, wrote scarcely any letters, and rarely submitted to interviews, there is, of course, a wealth of documentation on the life of Elvis Presley, not least his own recorded words, which, while seldom uttered without some public purpose, almost always offer a glimpse of what is going on within. I've pursued contemporary news accounts, business documents, diaries, fan magazines, critical analyses, and the anecdotal testimony of friends and eyewitnesses not with the intention of imposing all this on the reader but simply to try to understand the story. In the end, of course, one has to cast aside the burden of accumulation and rely on instinct alone. There is always that leap of faith to be made when you accept the idea that you are painting a portrait, not creating a web site. Certainly you have to allow your gaze to wander, it is essential to take every possibility into account, not to prejudge either on the basis of likelihood or personal bias — but you also have to recognize that with the angle of perception changed by just a little, with a slightly different selection of detail, there may be an altogether different view. This is where the leap of faith comes in: at some point, you simply have to believe that by immersing yourself in the subject you have earned your own perspective.

I have spent eleven years with Elvis. Much longer if I go back to the pieces I originally wrote to try to tell the world why I thought his music was so vital, exciting, and culturally significant, how it was part of the same continuum of American vernacular music that produced Robert Johnson, Hank Williams, Sam Cooke, the Statesmen, Jimmie Rodgers, and the Golden Gate Quartet. I still think that — but immersion in the subject has changed my view in other, more subtle ways. Once I saw Elvis as a blues singer exclusively (that was my own peculiar prejudice); now I see him in the same way that I think he saw himself from the start, as someone whose ambition it was to encompass every strand of the American musical tradition. And if I am still not equally open to his approach to every one of those strands, I can at least say that I have awakened to the beauty of many of the ballads I once scorned and come to a new appreciation of the gospel quartet tradition that Elvis so thoroughly knew.

In the course of writing these two volumes, I interviewed hundreds of people, some dozens of times. There were moments, certainly, when I felt as if I had at last gained access to Elvis' world; just as often, I was made aware that no matter how long one peers in from the outside, it is never quite the view from within. That's why it's so important to keep going back — not just to try to understand the sequence of events but to give the picture a chance to come into deeper focus. You want to try to capture the chipped paint on the doorknob, the muted conversations in the hall; you want the reader to hear the carefree exuberance of Elvis' laugh — even if none of these things ever fully emerges from the background. Perhaps there is no need to point out that this is a task that can drive both writer and interview subject almost mad. But what struck me again and again, as it has struck me with every book that I have written, was the graciousness of the participants, their own curiosity about *what actually happened,* about others' perspectives on events in which they themselves had participated. There was no question in my mind that almost without exception everyone I interviewed was telling the truth as he or she saw it. Interpretations might be shaded, time frames telescoped — but there was no conscious attempt at distortion, save for the universal human impulse to see oneself at the center of the picture.

I have tried to respect those truths. I have tried to understand each of the witnesses' stories. But most of all I have tried to understand Elvis', and to give the reader, too, a new basis for understanding by delineating the *context* in which frequently well-known events occurred. That search for context — sometimes it can be not much more than how the weather was — is, as much as anything else, at the heart of my own deep-seated belief in research. Not that ultimate meaning can ever be uncovered (I must admit, I have my doubts about ultimate meaning), but, on the most basic level, how are we ever to understand cause and effect if we don't know which came first? History may well be, as Arthur Schlesinger, Jr., has suggested, "an argument without end," but it can provide fruitful grounds for debate if certain rules of evidence are observed. There is room for the widest variety of interpretation, Schlesinger points out, so long as we recognize that we are establishing "small truths [in order] to place them in larger contexts and perspectives," that "we are prisoners of our own time and our own experience." So, too, are the protagonists. "Thomas Jefferson and Benjamin Franklin did not sit around a table and say, 'Isn't it great living in the past?'" in the formulation of historian David McCullough. "They didn't know any more how it was going to come out [than we do]." Which to me means that one must respect not just the story but the way in which it develops; judging the past by the standards of the present sheds little light on understanding, it represents no more than the I-told-you-sos of history.

There are no villains here. The story of Elvis' inexorable decline — what could almost be called the *vanishing* of Elvis Presley over a period of time — is neither a simple nor a monolithic one, and it may have no greater moral than the story of Job or Sophocles' *Oedipus Rex:* Count no man lucky until he has reached his journey's end. The kind of fame that Elvis experienced requires constant reinvention if one is to escape its snares — and, as more than one friend of Elvis remarked, his desire to escape was ambivalent at best; as much as he may at times have been tempted, he was not about to throw away the identity he had so assiduously created, he *enjoyed* being Elvis Presley.

The last few years of his life amounted to little more than a sad diminution; this is what has become the basis for the caricature that we so often see repeated in our pathographic times. More significantly, the music with which he made his mark has become a battleground for competing ethnocentric claims: Elvis Presley, whose democratic vision could not have been broader or more encompassing, is used as the centerpiece for accusations of cultural theft. This is a misunderstanding not just of Elvis Presley but of popular culture, which even in its purest forms cannot help but represent the polyglot borrowings that radio and the phonograph record first introduced almost a century ago. You don't have to *like* Elvis Presley — but it's impossible, if you listen to his music, not to recognize both his achievement and his originality. He was no more a copy of blues singer Arthur "Big Boy" Crudup than he was of bluegrass pioneer Bill Monroe — though they, along with a far-flung range of influences (Roy Hamilton, Mario Lanza, Dean Martin, Clyde McPhatter, Jake Hess), were among his heroes, and he unquestionably absorbed their music into his own. That music exists, like all art, without explanation (if it could be formulized, why wouldn't everyone do it?), but it came about no more by accident than Duke Ellington's carefully worked-out compositions or Robert Johnson's blues. That is what the story keeps coming back to in the end — the music. That is the mystery that will continue to reward repeated explorations, long after the frenzy of fame is finally gone.

CARELESS LOVE

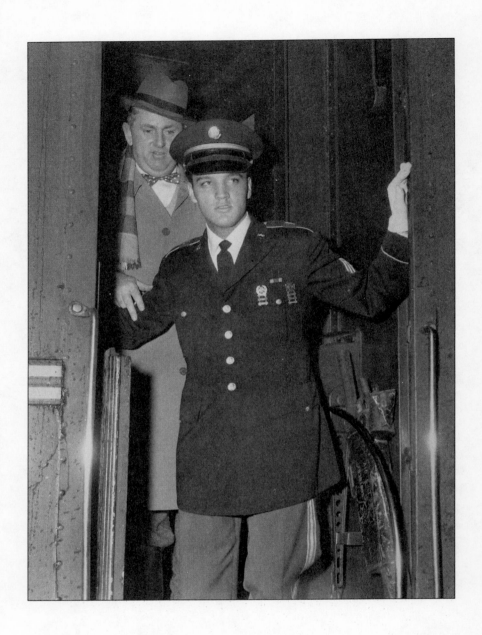

UNION STATION, MEMPHIS, MARCH 7, 1960. (JAMES REID)

PROLOGUE: HOMECOMING, MEMPHIS, MARCH 1960

THEY LEFT IN THE AFTERMATH of a blustery winter storm. The newly promoted sergeant emerged from the Fort Dix, New Jersey, paymaster's office with a mustering-out check of $109.54 for travel expenses, food, and clothing. "Don't forget my commission," growled his manager, Colonel Tom Parker, loud enough for newsmen to hear, and Elvis Presley smilingly handed him the check. He then strode toward a chauffeur-driven limousine surrounded by six MPs, as the post band played "Auld Lang Syne." Six teenage girls emerged from the crowd and the MPs closed ranks, but the young soldier slowed down, smiled, and stopped to chat with his fans. He reached into his traveling case and pulled out six autographed pictures, one for each girl, then disappeared with his manager into the limo as his army buddies yelled, "Go get 'em, Elvis."

It was two years since he had left civilian life, seventeen months since he had last set foot on American soil. He leaned back in the seat, a broad smile illuminating his handsome twenty-five-year-old features, and cast a backward glance at the forty-car caravan of reporters, photographers, and fans that fell in behind them on the snowy highway. It seemed in some ways as if he had never been away, in others that he was still a stranger in a foreign land. His fingers drummed nervously on the plush upholstery — he had scarcely slept the previous night, and even now he felt such a mix of emotions that it would have been impossible for him to express them all. He had told reporters that the only thing on his mind was to rest up at home for the next few weeks, but that was not in fact true. He had an RCA recording session coming up on which he knew everyone was pinning their hopes; his guest appearance on "Frank Sinatra's Welcome Home Party for Elvis Presley," a television special, was scheduled in less than a month; and Hal Wallis, who had signed him to his first motion picture contract just four years earlier, was planning to start production on *G.I. Blues* the moment these other obligations were fulfilled.

If he was certain of one thing, it was that his manager had a plan. The Colonel, heavy, saturnine, his hooded eyes veiling an expression of amused avidity that Elvis sometimes thought he alone could read, had stayed in constant touch with him throughout his army hitch. He had never come to see him in Germany — he was too busy orchestrating all the elements necessary to sustain his single client's career — but he had maintained almost daily communication and provided a steady stream of encouragement, both strategic and paternal, even in the darkest days. No detail was too small for the Colonel to take up. He had continued to promote Elvis Presley merchandise, devised sales campaigns for each new record release, and hustled small-time theater owners when Paramount rereleased *King Creole* and *Loving You* the previous summer. He had fought the army to a standstill over plans to enlist Elvis as an ambassador-entertainer, refused to cave in to RCA's increasingly importunate demands to have him record something — *anything* — while stationed in Germany, and then used the shortage of product to improve their bargaining position. He had negotiated movie deals in a climate of doubt (*Will Presley's Appeal Last?* was a typical headline, and a typically voiced studio sentiment whenever money was being discussed) and had been so successful at it that they now had three starring vehicles lined up for this year alone, including two "serious" pictures for Fox.

Above all he had kept Elvis' name in the headlines for the entire two years, a feat that Elvis had never believed possible — and he had shared every detail of the campaign with his protégé, confiding his strategy, describing his "snow jobs," bolstering the homesick soldier when he was down, praising him for his courage and forbearance, making him feel like a man. They were an unbeatable team, a partnership that no one on the outside could ever understand, and Elvis was well aware that Colonel had not taken on one new artist in the time that he was away.

The present plan was more in the nature of a diversion, and Colonel was having fun with it. They were heading for New York, he had informed the press; they were going to have a big news conference at the Hotel Warwick and then spend the weekend there. But that, of course, was nothing like what he had in mind. He had in fact worked out five fully developed alternate routes and schemes, with any number of decoy vehicles and even a helicopter on standby if need be — but, really, his only intention was obfuscation, at which he was preternaturally adept. They lost the caravan of accompanying vehicles somewhere in New Jersey. "Elvis Presley mysteriously vanished from a snow-packed fan-laden highway," it was reported in the newspapers the following day, but in actuality they simply retreated to a hotel hideout in Trenton, where they rendezvoused with the rest of the group: three-hundred-pound Lamar Fike, who had accompanied Elvis to Germany and remained faithfully by his side the entire seventeen months; Rex Mansfield, Elvis' army buddy from Dresden, Tennessee, to whom the Colonel had gladly agreed to give a lift home; the Colonel's chief lieutenant, Tom Diskin; and assorted other record company representatives and members of the Colonel's staff. For most of the day they holed up in Trenton, with Colonel relaying confusing messages to the world at large through his secretary in Madison, Tennessee. That evening they took a private railroad car to Washington, where they boarded the *Tennessean,* scheduled to depart at 8:05 A.M. Once again they occupied a plush private car, attached to the rear of the train, but now their schedule was known to the world, published by the Colonel with the idea of giving his boy the kind of welcome a home-coming hero deserved.

There was a crowd of fifteen hundred in Marion, Virginia, twenty-five hundred in Roanoke, and substantial turnouts at smaller stops along the way. Elvis emerged on the observation platform at every one, slim and handsome in the formal dress blues he had had made up in Germany with an extra rocker on the shoulder designating a higher, staff sergeant's rank. It had been, he explained embarrassedly when challenged about the extra stripe, a tailor's mistake, but some of the more cynical reporters put it down as the Colonel's work, or, simply, Elvis' vanity. He never said a word at any of the stops, merely waved and smiled, and, in fact, somewhere in Virginia, Rex took his place on the platform at the Colonel's insistence, and with the Colonel's assurance that the fans would never know the difference.

Inside the car the Colonel and Elvis were rolling dice at $100 a throw, and Elvis gave Rex and Lamar enough money so they could play, too. When Rex tried to return the several hundred dollars that he subsequently won, Elvis offered him a job as his chief aide. There would be lots more money, he said, if Rex would just stick with him, and a glamorous life to boot. Talk to the Colonel, he suggested, if Rex had any doubts.

To Rex's surprise the Colonel, whom he had been hearing about from Elvis ever since they had first met at the Memphis induction center two years before, advised against it. After listening carefully to Rex's well-formulated plans for the future and what he considered to be his prospects for business success, Colonel Parker "told me that he thought I was good enough to make it on my own and that I did not need to hang around Elvis. He said that I was not like most of the other guys that hung around and that his best advice was not to take the job. Then the Colonel told me not to tell Elvis what he said, because it would make Elvis mad. . . . He said he had given me his honest, sincere advice, but the final decision was still mine. Again, he said to me, 'If you tell Elvis that I told you not to take the job with him, I'll deny it.'"

In Bristol, Tennessee, a young reporter from the *Nashville Tennessean* got on, alerted by a collect call from the Colonel's staff. Presley, wrote David Halberstam, was "like a happy young colt. . . . He wrestled with some of his bodyguards, winked at the girls in the station, and clowned with his ever-faithful manager and merchandiser, Col. Tom Parker. 'Man, it feels good to be going home,' Presley said. 'So good.' Then he put a hand over the Colonel's receding hairline and said, 'Andy Devine [a portly Hollywood character actor], that's who it is. Andy Devine.' 'Quit pulling my hair out,' the Colonel said. 'I'm just massaging it for you,' Presley said. 'Every time you massage,' [the Colonel replied], 'I have a little less left. . . .'

"The Colonel, both remarkably excited and unshaven after the cloak and dagger days on the east coast . . . was pleased. Pleased with his boy, and pleased with the hordes of youngsters that he had to fight off. 'As many or more than before,' he said, pointing to the mobs. 'Better than ever.'"

Halberstam observed three thousand teenagers in Knoxville waving banners and signs, as the train made its stop at 8:55 P.M., less than eleven hours from Memphis. He could feel the excitement mounting, the young singer's nervous energy would allow him neither to sit still nor to sleep all through the long night. He continued roughhousing with his companions, practiced his quick draw, and threw in an occasional demonstration of the Oriental discipline of karate, which he had been studying seriously in Germany for the past few months. If he ever lost his voice, the Colonel remarked dryly, "we could make money with his wrestling." When Memphis reporters joined the party in Grand Junction at 6:15 A.M. and then at Buntyn Station a little more than an hour later, he was still wearing his dress uniform with Good Conduct ribbon and Expert's medal for marksmanship prominently displayed, but by now he had donned one of the two formal lace shirts that Frank Sinatra's nineteen-year-old daughter, Nancy, had presented to him at Fort Dix on behalf of her father. "If I act nervous, it's because I am," he told *Press-Scimitar* reporter Bill Burk. "I've been gone a long time, a long time," he muttered almost to himself, as the train pulled into the station. What had he missed most about Memphis? he was asked. "Everything. I mean that — everything."

Two hundred fans, reporters, and the just plain curious were waiting when the train arrived at 7:45. It was snowing, and there was an icy wind, but the crowd chanted, "We want Elvis," as they massed behind a six-foot-high wrought-iron fence. "It was nice to have you aboard," said the conductor, H. D. Kennamer, shaking his hand. "Thank you, sir," said Elvis Presley, squaring his shoulders and plunging back into the life he had once known. He walked along the fence, shaking hands through the bars and recognizing familiar faces. He spoke briefly with various friends and fans, then indicated to the Colonel's brother-in-law and aide, Bitsy Mott, that he wanted to confer with Gary Pepper, a twenty-seven-year-old cerebral palsy victim who had recently taken over the Tankers Fan Club (Elvis had been assigned to a tank corps) and was holding a "Welcome Home, Elvis, The Tankers" sign above his head. Bitsy wheeled Pepper through the crowd, and they had a brief meeting, with Pepper apologizing that there wasn't a bigger turnout, it was a school day, after all. "Elvis bit his lip," reported the newspaper, "seemed to be trying to repulse tears, and said, 'I'll see you later, pal.'"

Then he was gone, scooped up in his old friend police captain Fred Woodward's squad car, arriving at Graceland less than thirty minutes later with lights flashing and siren screaming. "The gates swung open," reported the *Memphis Press-Scimitar,* "and Woodward's car . . . shot through at nearly 30 miles per hour. Then the gates closed. The king was once again on his throne."

AT HOME, GERMANY, 1959: VERNON, GRANDMA, ELVIS.
(COURTESY OF THE ESTATE OF ELVIS PRESLEY)

GERMANY: MARKING TIME

H E ARRIVED IN BREMERHAVEN on October 1, 1958, as a member of the 750-man Thirty-second Tank Battalion, Third Armored Division, part of the fabled "Mailed Fist of Europe." He was met at the dock by fifteen hundred fans, five television news teams, two newsreel operators, and reporters and photographers representing virtually every major European periodical and newspaper. It was a well-planned operation, with only one autograph seeker breaking through police cordons, and one young woman, a German reporter, presenting Private Presley with a bouquet of flowers.

He was subdued on the troop train to Friedberg, just north of Frankfurt, some two hundred miles away, eating with the cooks in the kitchen car so as to have a moment or two of privacy, thanking each one individually for their hospitality. Military plans called for him to interact with the press and the public for the next few days — but *only* for the next few days, while he was still undergoing processing. A press conference was scheduled for the following morning, and he would undoubtedly be faced with the same kinds of questions that reporters came up with everywhere else. Did he still want to meet Brigitte Bardot now that she was formally engaged? What did he think of German girls, even if he had never met any? Would his music change? Would his popularity remain the same? Colonel said he just had to get through it; he had his job, the press had theirs, and there was no reason that they couldn't serve each other's needs. It was his job to be *like any other soldier,* and once this initial flurry of attention was over that was just what he would be.

It had been a strange and solitary crossing. Not so much because he was alone on the transport ship — he had made friends with a number of the guys — as because, with his mother gone, he was truly alone in the world. Seeking solace, he read and reread some of the poems about death and motherhood in the book he had been given by a fellow GI just prior to his departure, an anthology called *Poems That Touch the Heart.* He sought out

9

the companionship of sympathetic souls, requesting to bunk with Charlie Hodge, the little guy he had met on the train to the Brooklyn Army Terminal who was a fellow southerner, singer, and veteran of show business himself. At night, Charlie said, he could hear him thinking about his mother — he could tell by the way Elvis breathed, and he would try to cheer him up, telling him jokes, running through old vaudeville routines, until at last his friend dropped off to sleep.

Several days out to sea, Elvis and Charlie were put in charge of a talent show on the U.S.S. *Randall,* and they held auditions and staged the program, with Charlie MCing and telling jokes and Elvis playing piano in the backup band. Although he threw himself into the entertainment, he would not take the spotlight, saying that he didn't want to steal attention from any of the other GIs but giving rise at the same time to rumors that he had been forbidden to perform by his manager. He was generally liked by, but distant from, his fellow soldiers, who observed him with the same understandable mistrust that he might just as well have felt for them. "Charlie," he told his new friend, "you keep me from going crazy."

In Friedberg he was stationed at Ray Kaserne, a barracks for German SS troops during the Second World War. He got through the obligatory press briefings (he *was* interested in German girls; he planned to buy a guitar in Frankfurt, since he had not brought one with him on the ship; he would like to see an opera and attend some classical concerts while stationed in Germany). He was initally designated jeep driver for the commanding officer of Company D but was quickly transferred to Company C, a scout platoon, where he was assigned to drive for Reconnaissance Platoon Sergeant Ira Jones. Not only was Jones, a tough, no-nonsense enlisted noncom, deemed to be the man for the job; the fact that the company spent much of its time in the field on maneuvers might help to remove Private Presley from the public eye.

His family arrived on Saturday, October 4, and Elvis had dinner with them at their hotel in Bad Homburg that evening. It was a strange grouping, the young towheaded soldier, his handsome forty-two-year-old father and gaunt sixty-eight-year-old grandmother, plus two buddies from home, Red West and Lamar Fike. He was avid for news of Memphis, almost desperate to *connect*. He needed people he knew, people he could trust, and to Lamar there was no great mystery as to why any of them were there; "Elvis always kept his own world with him; he kept his own bubble." After dinner he posed for photographs with his father and grandmother, then reluctantly returned to camp. He was exhausted, he told reporters; he just wanted to get back to the barracks and get some sleep.

I T WAS HARD, harder perhaps than anything he had ever done — and army life was only part of it. Two days after his family arrived they changed hotels, and three weeks later, after Elvis had received permission to live off base with his two family dependents, they moved again, to the elegant Hotel Grunewald in Bad Nauheim, just twenty minutes from the base. There they had the whole top floor to themselves, but it was still cramped, with Red and Lamar sharing a bedroom and, more significantly, feeling distinctly out of place in the subdued setting of a European health spa for wealthy, primarily elderly visitors.

Red reacted, as he generally did, by blowing up at anyone and everyone who got in his way. Elvis wasn't paying either one of them anything, they were there as his *friends,* but he did tell his father to give them enough money to have a good time — a couple of hundred marks, or roughly $50, a week apiece. Vernon, who couldn't see what either one of them had done to deserve such largesse, doled out no more than two or three marks a night to each, and they nursed their money, and their resentment, at Beck's Bar around the corner, where Red was prone to sharp altercations with fellow drinkers and local policemen. There had never been any love lost between Red and Vernon anyway, and with Vernon doing his share of drinking, there was the constant possibility that things could really get out of hand. For Elvis the only truly peaceful time of the day was when he was with his grandmother, "Dodger," who never judged him, who wanted nothing from him, who called him "Son" and recalled every day of his childhood with the clarity and wonder generally reserved for chronicling the lives of the saints.

There was a moment of confusion just after his arrival, when it seemed as if the army was breaking its agreement with Colonel Parker not to put any pressure on Elvis to perform. The Colonel had waged an extensive campaign to develop contacts in Washington and then to persuade them that it would be against the interests of the armed services for Elvis to appear as anything but an ordinary soldier, while remonstrating at the same time to Elvis that he should resist any such opportunities, however innocent they might at first appear. Nonetheless, John Wiant, the European editor of *Army Times,* approached Elvis and Vernon about a Christmas benefit for German orphans and pursued the matter with Colonel Parker after Vernon explained that he had no authority to accept or decline such an invitation. Even the Colonel was panicked for a moment, since clearly the pressure was coming from above, but he counseled Elvis to *make no commitments* and immediately advised his principal contact in Washington, E. J. Cottrell, the assistant chief of information at the Department of the Army, that not only would this be against everything they had both been working for, it would also end up costing the army money to provide the security necessary for a show of this sort — and if such security were not provided, it would look very bad for the army. Cottrell responded in an amused but sympathetic vein, and while the story got into the newspapers and continued to surface in one form or another for some weeks, it seemed to reflect little more than an ongoing struggle between the State Department and the army over the correct deployment of Private Presley, with the outcome all but conceded to Colonel Parker.

Gradually things began to settle into a routine. Because Elvis was up at 5:30 A.M., the rest of the household was, too, though they could go back to sleep, of course, once he left for the base at 6:30 in the black Mercedes taxi he had hired to take him back and forth. Many days he was home for lunch, and he never returned later than 6:00 P.M. except on Friday, which was "GI party night," when they scrubbed the latrines and cleaned the barracks, often until ten o'clock, in preparation for Saturday morning inspection. It was for the most part congenial enough work; he was improving his map- and compass-reading skills in preparation for maneuvers and keeping his jeep in top condition. And he had a little girl — she was sixteen, but she looked older — a typist with an electrical supply company in Frankfurt who had just showed up with a photographer the day after Elvis' family arrived in Bad Homburg. She and the photographer waited outside the hotel until Elvis emerged with his father, and when she approached him on the pretext of getting his autograph, not only the photographer that she was accompanying but all the other photographers who had staked out the hotel clamored for the two of them to kiss. Elvis was only too happy to oblige, and the papers were full of news of Elvis Presley's "German girl-friend," Margit Buergin, the next day. Lamar got her number for him, and he saw her a few times. She was a nice girl who lived with her mother and had to be home every night. Sometimes she even brought her little German-English dictionary along on their dates.

Home was a nagging memory that on occasion he could barely sustain.

He called some of his pals and told them how much he missed Memphis, kidding around about the German "chiclets"; he had his father call home on October 15 to order a generous supply of alfalfa pills from a Memphis pharmacy because he had heard that that was a good way to help keep your weight down. He wrote breezily to a few girls, confiding his unease but acting as if he could *handle it*. But Anita Wood was the only one to whom he truly unburdened himself — even though he was not exactly sure how he really felt about her.

He knew how he was *supposed* to feel. The papers had linked them almost from the day they met in the summer of 1957, and he knew that Anita was certainly expecting that they would get married someday. In fact, in a moment of desperation, just before he left, he had even spoken to her about bringing her over to visit once things got sorted out. He wrote to her now that she should keep herself clean and wholesome, that he had never, and would never again, love anyone in his life as he loved her, that he looked forward to their marriage and "a little Elvis." In another letter he referred to himself as a "lonely little boy 5000 miles away," even as he was denying the newspaper stories about Margit (referred to as Margrit in the American press), and added in a self-conscious p.s.: "No one ever reads this, OK?"

But even as he wrote and tried to communicate some of his feelings of helplessness and isolation, things were actually starting to look up. He heard from Janie Wilbanks, the girl he had met at the train station in Memphis when the troop train had pulled in on its way to the Brooklyn Army Terminal, that she was going to be coming over to visit her uncle, an army chaplain in Germany, sometime around Christmas and couldn't wait to see him again. His buddy Charlie Hodge, from the U.S.S. *Randall,* showed up at the hotel on his first weekend leave and fit right in with the rest of the group. Elvis prompted him to tell Vernon the same jokes he had told on their crossing, and his daddy got a good laugh for what seemed like the first time since Mama died. Red and Lamar obviously liked Charlie, too, and they all harmonized on some old gospel numbers, which they sang a cappella or accompanied by the guitar that Elvis had gotten on his first leave in Frankfurt, with Vernon, too, joining in on more than one occasion.

There was a flurry of activity just before the company went out on maneuvers at the beginning of November that reinforced this growing semblance of normality. Elvis heard that Bill Haley was going to be performing in Frankfurt and Stuttgart on October 23 and 29, and went to see him both times, with happy reunions backstage at which Elvis confided to the older star that if it hadn't been for Haley's help and encouragement, he might still be driving a truck. A few nights later, on the Saturday night before departure, he had another date with Margit, who told the press that he was "a very nice boy" and she liked him very much. The following night, November 2, according to a wire-service report, he threw a "noisy pre-maneuvers party in his hotel, where the sounds of his guitar and singing bounced down to the sidewalks below and caused a crowd to collect. Between plunks on his guitar he confessed he liked Margit 'very much' and added, 'And I'm glad her parents like me as well.'"

He got a peculiar call from a woman named Dee Stanley around this time; she was the wife of a master sergeant stationed in Frankfurt, she explained to him, and she just wanted to invite him to dinner with her family. She knew he must be lonely, and she wanted to show him that a foreign country didn't have to be so cold and inhospitable. After spending a few minutes trying to figure out what she was driving at, he eventually told her to call on Monday, when he knew he would be on maneuvers and Daddy could just handle it.

Then they were off to Grafenwöhr, a cold, dismal location near the Czech border. At first reporters hounded him for pictures, and soldiers and officers who hadn't seen him before asked for autographs. But then the reporters were banned, and the soldiers got used to his presence, and things settled down into a predictable routine over the next seven weeks. This was where he finally proved himself to his platoon sergeant's satisfaction, enduring the same harsh conditions as everyone else, showing himself to be a resourceful soldier in field exercises as his reconnaissance unit took eight prisoners thanks to a clever ruse that he had worked out, finally becoming one of the boys. The first weekend that they had leave to go back to Friedberg, a notice was posted that buses would be available at a cost of $6 round-trip. When a number of his fellow soldiers didn't have money for the fare, Elvis told Sergeant Jones that he would like to help out, giving Jones money to loan out to the soldiers, who eventually repaid Jones without ever learning the identity of their benefactor.

About two weeks into maneuvers he wrote Alan Fortas, his friend back in Memphis, a letter which, if it wasn't exactly cheery, could at least be described as more chipper than previous communications. After complaining about the weather and indulging in an uncharacteristic daydream that "a miracle" might happen to get him home sooner than March of 1960 ("Boy it will be great getting out"), he sent personalized greetings to friends and wrote of his social life, "I have been dating this little German 'chuckaloid' by the name of Margrit. She looks a lot like B.B. [Brigitte Bardot]. It's *Grind City*." Then, after declaring that he had to go off and "wade in the mud," he signed off as "Your Pal, Elvis Presley," with "Eri Viar Ditchi [Arrivederci]" scribbled on the back of the envelope as a postscript.

Almost every night he and Rex Mansfield and another friend, named Johnny Lange, went to the post theater, frequently viewing the same movie several nights in a row at Elvis' instigation. They would generally slip in late to avoid the gawkers and autograph seekers and leave early for the same reason, before the show was finished. Rex was the boy from Dresden, Tennessee, he had originally met at the Memphis induction center who had served with him at Fort Chaffee and Fort Hood, probably his best friend in the army. Even Red, suspicious of all outsiders, had to acknowledge that Rex was a regular guy, neither starstruck nor stuck on himself, someone who could fit into their world as if he had always belonged.

One evening at the post theater, just before Thanksgiving, Johnny came back from the lobby, saying there was a girl who wanted to get Elvis' autograph. Elvis asked if she was pretty, and when Johnny said she was, he had Rex bring the girl into the theater to sit beside him. The girl was practically petrified. All she had wanted was an autograph, but he treated her with such gentleness and respect, put his arm around her and asked for her name, "and from that moment on," she later wrote, "I was floating. . . . After the movie, Elvis walked me home, which was only about ten minutes from the theater. On the way home that first night we talked about the Army, what I was doing in Graf, and about my family. It seemed to me that Elvis was very interested in me personally and wanted to know all about me. We were standing by this tree, which was in sight of our dependent apartment house, when he kissed me for the first time. It was a goodnight kiss, and I asked him if he would like to come in and meet my parents, but he said some other time please."

Her name was Elisabeth Stefaniak, she was just nineteen years old, the daughter of a German mother whose husband had deserted her during the war; her stepfather, Raymond McCormick, was a U.S. Army sergeant stationed at Graf, and now she had a little half sister, Lindy, who was six years old. They dated practically every night for a week, and then on Thanksgiving Day he showed up unexpectedly at her house and stayed for Thanksgiving dinner. He impressed her parents with his manners, spoke with deep emotion of his mother, and then sang to them all with a guitar borrowed from a neighbor. On December 19, the last day of training, he told her parents that he needed a secretary with a good knowledge of German and

English and that Elisabeth would exactly fit the bill. "He wanted me to come to Bad Nauheim and live in his home. He said he, his father, and his grandmother would take full responsibility for me." To Elisabeth's astonishment her parents consented, and it was agreed that she would join him in Bad Nauheim sometime after the New Year.

Upon his return home he rapidly made up for lost time. The day after his arrival he leased a white BMW sports car to go with the old Cadillac he had bought from the company commander for his father to use and the beat-up Volkswagen bug he had gotten for the boys. Back at Ray Kaserne he threw himself into preparations for a Christmas party at the local orphanage and made a sizable financial contribution to the effort. In addition, the recon platoon was designated to clean the company area and decorate the Christmas tree for any visitors who might come in during the holidays. After working all day, everyone was getting ready to go on leave when one of the soldiers picked up a guitar and started to sing a Christmas song. One by one others joined in, and then the soldier with the guitar asked Elvis if he would like to take part, too. "'Yeah, all right,'" said a subdued Elvis, in Sergeant Jones' account, and he led the soldiers in song. At the end everybody else stopped as he performed "Silent Night," singing "as if in a trance, totally oblivious" to his surroundings. "Those going on pass didn't interrupt. They simply walked silently by Elvis, touched his shoulder, and walked out the door. Not another word was spoken after the song until Elvis broke the spell. 'Merry Christmas, everyone,' he said. 'Merry Christmas, Elvis!' they replied in unison."

I T WAS CHRISTMAS at the Hotel Grunewald, too. Vernon gave Elvis an electric guitar, and they had a special holiday meal, but it didn't erase the bad feelings that Elvis continued to have about what was going on between his daddy and that woman Dee, who had called him out of the blue just before he left for Grafenwöhr. He blamed himself in a way; he should never have palmed her off on Vernon, who had accepted her invitation to dinner in the name of "downhome hospitality" and become a frequent visitor in her home. There he had met her three little boys, palled around with her husband, Bill, a sergeant with wild and woolly tales from his days as General Patton's personal bodyguard and a drinking problem that anyone could see, and eventually found his way into her bed. Now Vernon was behaving like a love-struck teenager, and Elvis could barely restrain his feelings of resentment when they met — it was too soon, she wasn't the right kind of woman, it was an insult to his mother's memory. She tried to play up to him, just like so many of them did. She wondered coquettishly if Elvis remembered her from the time he had appeared in Newport News in 1956. She had only been a member of the audience, she said, but it had seemed as if he were singing directly to her. "Of course I remember you, Mrs. Stanley," he replied in his usual gracious fashion. "How could I ever forget someone so beautiful?" But he didn't like the way she put on a show for him any more than he liked what Vernon was doing, and he couldn't get it out of his mind that he might still be the one she had in her sights.

It seemed like they were all feeling the pressure of living at such close quarters. Red and Lamar were increasingly at Vernon's throat, and when Elvis found out that Vernon still had them on an allowance of a few marks a night, he spoke to his father sharply about giving them the amount that had previously been agreed upon. "Let them go out and try to get some money on their own," Vernon said angrily, expressing his own frustration at how out of hand the boys were getting now that Elvis was home and warning Elvis that their antics were going to get the whole party, including Grandma, thrown out of the hotel. Elvis didn't take any more kindly to his father's criticism than his father did to his and simply reminded Vernon of who was paying the bills. So he and the guys continued to chase each other around the hotel corridors with water pistols and set off fireworks whenever they felt like it, with Elvis generally taking the lead, just like he did at home.

It was the shaving-cream fight at the end of January that proved to be the final straw. Red was chasing Elvis, and Elvis locked himself in his room, so Red put paper under the door and lit it, trying to smoke him out. The fire got a little out of control, and they were just in the midst of putting it out when the manager, Herr Schmidt, appeared and informed them that their continued presence was no longer desired and that they should perhaps start looking for a new home without delay. No one was too unhappy about this outcome, not even Vernon, so long as any scandal that might get back to the Colonel could be avoided. They clearly needed a house of their own, where they would have the room and the freedom to be themselves without the scrutiny of outsiders, and where Grandma would be able to prepare a home-cooked meal and they wouldn't have to eat this damned German food and worry about any crotchety old convalescents having heart attacks whenever they felt like fooling around.

*　*　*

E LISABETH MOVED WITH THEM when they finally found a place. She had showed up, as promised, right after the first of the year, occupying the large corner room in their hotel complex that had until then been used as storage space for fan mail. Red and Lamar had set her up to answer the mail, instructing her in the fine art of forging Elvis' signature, which she could soon do almost as well as they. Mrs. Presley took to her right away, insisting that she call her "Grandma," Mr. Presley was always perfectly courteous and polite, and she liked the boys well enough, even though she knew that by Elvis' rules she could scarcely so much as glance at them, let alone have a private conversation — he said that any attention she paid to them would make him look like a fool. She accepted that even if she didn't understand it, just as she accepted all the other confusing elements that seemed to go with the situation. On the first night he came to her room and said that he would be spending the night with her, even though at Graf there had never been anything beyond kissing, and she was unclear as to what their romantic status was exactly. He explained to her that she didn't have to worry, that they wouldn't have full intercourse because he didn't do that with any girl that "he was going to see on a regular basis," because he couldn't risk getting her pregnant. "Such a risk would damage his reputation and image. That first night we sort of played around. Over the course of the next weeks and months, I went to bed with him almost every night."

But, she soon realized, she was not the only one. Within days of her arrival he took another girl to bed, then after Lamar took the girl home, Elvis knocked three times on the wall between their bedrooms, summoning her to him. Margit Buergin continued to be a frequent visitor, and within a week or two Elvis announced that Janie Wilbanks, the girl from the Memphis train station, was coming for a visit — but she came to accept that, too, and in time she and Janie would actually become friends.

Often she could hear him with his girls through the wall of her room, and while she doubted that Elvis did any more with the others than he did with her, it didn't really make her feel any better. "There would be at least a couple of girls each week, more on weekends. . . . These were often very beautiful girls [but] although I resented them, I knew they were not staying. I was. I did not let him see me cry [and] all the time I was telling myself how lucky I was. . . . He never apologized. I guess he never felt he owed me an explanation. I do remember the pain of getting into bed with him maybe ten or twenty minutes after another girl had left. Many times we never made love; he would sometimes just give me a good-night kiss and go to sleep. It was like a comfort thing for him."

THEY MOVED INTO THE TRIM, neatly kept, three-story white stucco house at Goethestrasse 14, just ten blocks from the Hotel Grunewald, in early February. They were paying the equivalent of $800 a month, several times the going rate, but it more than met their needs. It came equipped with a kitchen for Grandma to cook in, five bedrooms, a spacious living room for entertaining, and a landlady, Frau Pieper, who stipulated as a rental condition that she would maintain a room in the house both to serve as housekeeper and to oversee her American tenants. Frau Pieper and Grandma made an oddly matched pair — they shopped together, cooked together, drank together, clearly were fond of each other but frequently had fierce disagreements, though neither understood the other's language.

It was a less-than-perfect arrangement, but it was home, removed from the prying eyes of outsiders except at certain designated hours. At Elvis' direction a sign was immediately put up indicating AUTOGRAMME VON 19:30 20:00, and Elvis would emerge promptly at 7:30 in the evening to sign autographs with much of the neighborhood looking on. Grandma made biscuits and eggs and burnt bacon for breakfast every morning, and they all had a big family meal before Elvis went off to the post and everyone else went back to sleep. By now Elvis had bought at least ten pairs of nonissue tanker boots (which had to be special-ordered at the PX at $45 a pair), and Red and Lamar were kept busy spit-polishing the boots and keeping the dozens of extra uniforms he had purchased as well pressed and clean. Elvis now came home for lunch almost every day, climbing over the fence in the back but after a while fooling almost none of the fans, who anticipated his arrival like clockwork.

It was in the evening, though, and on weekends that Goethestrasse 14 really began to feel like home. With the curtains drawn and the world shut out, lots of girls around, and the radio tuned to the Armed Forces Network playing the latest American hits, sometimes it could almost seem like there was not all that much to distinguish Germany from Graceland, except for the accent of some of the visitors. Elvis kept the record player constantly spinning with records by the Statesmen, the Harmonizing Four, Marty Robbins, Jackie Wilson, and Peggy Lee singing "Fever," and when they weren't listening to music, Elvis, Charlie, Red, and Rex would frequently gather around the piano that Elvis had rented in Frankfurt to sing gospel, old sentimental favorites, and rock 'n' roll. Not long after they moved in, Charlie brought Elvis an album of jubilee spirituals by the Golden Gate Quartet that he flipped over. It contained such classic numbers as "Blind Barnabus" and "Swing Down, Chariot" as well as an infectious up-tempo number that caught his fancy, "Born Ten Thousand Years Ago," along with a single pop song, "I Will Be Home Again," which he and Charlie began singing as a duet. Charlie, who had studied voice with Professor Lee Roy Abernathy of Canton, Georgia (Abernathy was the author of "Gospel Boogie" and a beloved figure in the gospel field), worked with him some on his technique, encouraging him to develop a greater fullness in his vocal tone, helping him to "sing out" more toward the top of his almost three-octave range.

Music almost inevitably led to reminiscences of show business and thoughts of home. In his first extended interview since arriving in Germany, a telephone hookup with Memphis DJ Keith Sherriff just before they moved into the house, Elvis confessed that he could no longer imagine himself doing anything at this point other than show business. "That's probably it, one way or another, whether it's singing or working as a stagehand. You know, once it gets in your blood, it's hard to stay away from it." Asked for a greeting for his many friends in Memphis, he declared, "I'd like to say they'll never know how wonderful good old Memphis is until they get away from it for quite a while, and I'm just counting the days and the hours until I can return and sort of pick up where I left off because that's all [that's] on my mind, that's all I think about, that's all my heart is set on — and I'll make it!"

For his friends in Germany he had less disingenuous memories. He talked to them about the movie contracts the Colonel was negotiating and the deal he had with RCA, which would pay him $1,000 a week for the next twenty years. He even bragged that the Colonel's 25-percent commission was greater than that paid by any other star to his manager — and was well worth it. He frequently recited the Colonel's nostrum "Human nature says that people want most what they cannot have," as if that went a long way toward explaining at least part of his appeal. When he sang, though, he explained, he held back nothing; that was when he offered himself up exactly as he was, whole and without calculation.

They had fireworks battles with the local kids and played football with a select group of invited friends on an empty lot at the end of the street every Sunday afternoon. Elvis had his own private barber, his own dentist, who would open up his office at night for this very special patient, and his own personal driver-messenger, Joseph Wehrheim, who had once performed the same function for William Randolph Hearst. For the first time since he had arrived in Germany Elvis was beginning to feel like he was really in control: he had a house to go home to; he had a girl who was crazy about him and would do anything he asked; and with the pills that a sergeant had introduced him to when they were on maneuvers at Grafenwöhr, he was so full of energy he never had to slow down.

They all took them, if only to keep up with Elvis, who was practically evangelical about their benefits. According to Rex, who was introduced to their use right after the move to Goethestrasse, "Elvis would say, 'These little pills will give you more strength and energy than you can imagine.' It was better to take the pill with coffee, Elvis would say, because the hot coffee and caffeine would tend to make the pill work a lot quicker. Elvis assured me these pills were completely harmless, and when I would eat anything the effects [would be] gone immediately. . . . Elvis also informed me that these pills would keep a person slim and trim because they were appetite suppressants prescribed by doctors to millions of overweight people every day. . . . I honestly believed every word Elvis said and gladly received my little bottle of amphetamines from his supply."

The pills did prove miraculous both for keeping weight off *and* for extending your weekend without any diminution of energy on Monday morning, and it seemed like half the guys in the company must have been taking them, but Rex still wondered where Elvis was getting his enormous supply. One Friday he was riding home with Elvis, and they stopped at the post dispensary, where Rex observed one of the clerks hand over four quart-size bottles of amphetamines in exchange for some "large bills." When Elvis returned to the car, he said with a wink, "Rexadus, it ain't what you know but who you know that counts in this old world." And Rex couldn't help but think, "And if you got lots of money it helps."

As for Elisabeth, she, too, was getting an education of her own. Still plainly in love with Elvis, she adored being a part of this self-contained little world, basking in Elvis' attention and cherishing the pet names he came up with for her: Miss Foghorn (for her voice), the Belle of East Overshoe (for her footwear), or Miss Sneeze of '59 (for obvious reasons). She never found it any less painful to observe the attentions he paid to other girls, but she grew used to making herself scarce when they were around and to obscuring the role that she herself played in Elvis' life. She had no trouble with his prohibition of any dating for herself; she grew accustomed to the strange, brusque, sometimes harsh ways of a household full of men; and she came to like Red and Lamar, seeing another side of Red and feeling sorry for poor, garrulous three-hundred-pound Lamar, who was always falling for girls who were clearly using him just to get to Elvis. She and Grandma became great friends, and Grandma taught her to cook biscuits southern-style, just the way Elvis liked them. Sometimes Grandma would talk about Elvis when he was a little boy, how different he was from all the other children, how he was the one member of the family who had ever really amounted to anything, and the two women shook their heads indulgently over some of the boys' carryings-on.

The one thing that Elisabeth found most difficult to accept was Elvis himself — the gulf that frequently existed between the public and the private personalities, the extreme mood swings that he would sometimes experience and the cruelty that he could exhibit. One time she went shopping with him, and he asked her to tell the saleslady that he was looking for a small wastepaper basket for his bedroom. Without thinking, she reminded him that he already had a wastebasket, and he turned on her in an instant. "Don't you ever tell me what or what not to buy," he said. "If I want a thousand trash cans in my bedroom, that's my business." They left the store without buying anything, and in the car Elvis told her "that he had planned to buy me a lot of clothes this day but [that] I had ruined it." From that experience she learned that "no matter what you thought, you don't tell Elvis what to do." And you made sure never to show anything but a positive demeanor.

He was, she finally came to realize, jealous of virtually any personal relationships among those around him that did not directly revolve around him. "One had to be very careful of what [one] said around Elvis, because he could turn on you in a second. [He] was suspicious of everybody, and yet his ego caused him to be naive in many situations." If you fell afoul of him, you were threatened immediately with expulsion, especially if you were male. And yet "he had a way of making anyone feel they were the most important person in the world to him."

There was never any question that she would stay.

I N MARCH HE DECIDED to venture to Munich on a three-day pass. A couple of months earlier he had done some publicity shots for the March of Dimes, and the photographer, seeing an opportunity to place the pictures with a movie magazine as well, brought along a pretty eighteen-year-old actress from Munich named Vera Tschechowa, who spoke English and whose grandmother, Olga, was a renowned figure on the German stage. Evidently they hit it off, or at least Elvis was sufficiently attracted by Tschechowa's exotic good looks that he decided to pay her a visit, unannounced, two months later. Through her mother, Ada, a well-known theatrical agent, he discovered that she was performing with a small theater group in an experimental work and, undeterred by the fact that the play was being put on in German, said that he would like to see it for himself. "So he hired the whole theater and came together with his two fat and nasty bodyguards," said Tschechowa, who obviously was not impressed either by this "incredibly shy, typical American middle-class boy, well bred with a crease," or with his "hooligan [bodyguards] who were standing around him like walls, and I have to say that they were really ordinary, with [their] belching and farting and everything that belongs to it. I believe that he never went without them even to the toilet."

After the performance, which Vera deemed a "miserable" presentation, with only three, nondiscerning spectators, they spent much of the next two days together, visiting a movie set where a Viking film was being made, taking a boat ride, going to the zoo, having dinner with Vera's mother and various theatrical friends.

After dinner on the first night, Elvis indicated that he'd like to go to a nightclub, and Walter Brandin, a songwriter who was serving as Vera's "chaperone" for the evening with his wife, Elisabeth, suggested the Moulin Rouge, a sophisticated striptease club that he knew well. Some of the women in the party had never visited a striptease club before, but everyone was enthusiastic about the prospect, and they set off for the club in the big four-door Mercedes, which had replaced the Cadillac a couple of months before. Almost from the moment he arrived, the band started playing Elvis Presley songs and doing their best to coax their famous guest up onstage. According to Toni Netzel, a public relations manager for Polydor and one of the party, "he began to sing, and one of his bodyguards said that he should stop — he should know that he is not allowed to sing, it is forbidden. Then he was singing at the table, and that wasn't allowed either. So then he beat the time, and that wasn't allowed either."

In photographs from that evening he is wearing a dark suit, a narrow tie, his hair is upswept, and he looks alternately innocent and hungry for sin. With Vera and the rest of the theatrical party, he looks strangely jaded, his face a churlishly proprietary, almost dissipated mask, while with the half-naked strippers and some of the garishly made-up show people, he appears almost lost, an American abroad with an appetite so variously stimulated he does not even know where to begin. Elisabeth Brandin was impressed with his modesty, if not his independence: "We had a totally different version of Elvis Presley. I mean, we thought that he was crazy or that he would be flipped out in the same way as any other young singer. We were really surprised about his naturalness." She was also surprised, she said, by his meekness. He did everything that his bodyguards told him to do. When he went to the bathroom, his bodyguards went with him. It was because of the threats on his life, Lamar explained to her. "He answered that I should understand because they have so many contracts for the time after the army, that when a flipped-out woman gets the idea to throw some hydrochloric acid into his face or some other crazy shit, it would be over. . . . There was too much money to lose if something happened to him."

Elvis stayed at Vera's that night, while Red and Lamar remained at the Hotel Edelweiss. He rejoined them the following night because, he implied, Vera's mother had caught him in bed with her daughter. According to Vera, however, her mother just got tired of all the fans camping out in their garden and the restless, pent-up energy that Elvis seemed unable to control. "After he had bothered our animals, canaries, dogs, and cats long enough, my mother said to him, 'Now you better leave. There is the door. Bye!'" To reporters Ada Tschechowa simply remarked, "Elvis is a simple, intelligent boy, who, though he is rich, never forgets he once drove a truck for thirty-five dollars a week. He does his work as a soldier without whining. Teenagers do not have to be ashamed of such a hero."

He spent the next two days in Munich — and the next two nights at the club. After the first such evening, he joined Vera at breakfast with "bits of tinsel everywhere, in his hair and his eyebrows. I asked him what happened, and he only said, 'I stayed there.'" That was the last she saw of him in any case; "including the shooting [for the March of Dimes], I saw him three times." That didn't stop the press, which had covered their every move, from blowing it up into a full-scale romance. Vera was Elvis' "mystery date," and Vera's own sixty-five fan clubs protested her alliance with this boorish American. To his friends back home Vera became a symbol of his enviable new lifestyle; as Lamar said, "In some of the pictures he looks like a guy who's been having nonstop sex for six months." Elvis never went into a lot of detail with Red or Lamar or any of his other friends about the things he did with any of these girls. He never boasted except by implication, but they still felt like they were getting a pretty good idea, and among themselves they frequently wondered if he would be doing anywhere near as well if he were not Elvis Presley; if there were ever a fair contest, Red for one had little doubt as to who would get the girl.

HE WAS A GOOD SOLDIER. On maneuvers he continued to show his ingenuity as a scout, but more important, he was by now firmly entrenched as one of the guys, and if another soldier gave him a hard time over his wealth or celebrity, he could give as good as he got. Sometimes he told them about his experiences in Hollywood, like the time he got a hard-on doing a love scene with Debra Paget in *Love Me Tender,* and he was uncanny at imitating his sergeant — but his sergeant was his biggest fan. To the executive officer of Company B, Lieutenant Taylor, who had previously served as commander of the scout platoon himself, he was "a gentleman . . . a guy who cared a lot about other people" and, without much in the way of formal education, could speak intelligently both about world issues and about his own life. Nothing came without hard work, he stressed to the lieutenant; in this life you made your own luck. Once in a while he would express self-doubt, but then it was almost as if he would will himself to overcome it. "Sometimes I feel like just quitting," he said — but he couldn't do that; there were "too many people depending on me. Too many people think I'm going places. Too damn many people."

He loaned out money cheerfully, without a second thought, and brushed off the inconveniences of fame, whether it was being pestered in the chow line by guys he didn't know or followed by fans who always seemed to figure out exactly where he was going to turn up. *He was making the best of it,* the Colonel told him over and over again in the phone calls and letters that never ceased to give him a boost on an almost daily basis. He was making everyone proud of him, Colonel said to cheer him up, *things were working out exactly as they had planned.* And Elvis believed that was just about the truth.

Colonel on his end was waging a fierce, multifronted attack, holding off on one flank impatient RCA executives, challenging on another the massed forces of Hollywood, finally — and most important — devising new and ingenious strategies to satisfy the fans. With RCA he had successfully withstood every pressure that a&r director Steve Sholes and vice president Bill Bullock had come up with *to get Elvis to record;* he had even turned down their invitation to him to travel to Germany at RCA's expense so that he could personally oversee a session which Sholes would produce. He had steadfastly refused to allow the overdubbing of unfinished recordings like "Your Cheatin' Heart" and "Tomorrow Night," which Elvis had deemed unsatisfactory for release; he had turned a deaf ear to Sholes' importunings that Elvis make a personal appearance at an industry function in Frankfurt; he had imperturbably resisted all of Sholes' dire warnings of what his stubborn strategy could do to Elvis Presley's career — what if sales of one of the new singles should dip under a million? Sholes demanded. This way lay ruin.

Nonsense, the Colonel responded, bedeviling Sholes by his very assurance. RCA knew exactly what it had in the can when Elvis went into the army, and Colonel had even bowed to Sholes' logic when he allowed Elvis to record in Nashville while on furlough the previous June. Surely the label didn't want to *flood the market*. RCA simply had to learn to harvest wisely what it had — and wouldn't now be a good time, in any case, to start thinking about putting out a second album of gold records, seeing the great success that they had enjoyed over the past twelve months with the first?

The record company simply had to stay the course, Colonel lectured Sholes with infuriating regularity, relaying to Elvis in Germany every twist and turn of their exchange, missing few opportunities to undermine Sholes' dignity and authority while at the same time making it clear that these were decisions for Elvis alone to make; it was up to Elvis to assess the material and determine what was suitable for the next single release. Over and over he emphasized that he — Colonel — knew nothing about the music, that he was merely supporting Elvis' judgments — but that Elvis was *right* not to want to record in Germany, where he was under so much pressure already, where he would necessarily be forced to make do with unfamiliar surroundings, where he already had *a job to do*. Not to mention the fact that this very absence of surplus material, the reality that in no time at all RCA would be scraping the bottom of the barrel, couldn't hurt their bargaining position in the slightest when they returned to the negotiating table.

What Sholes and all the other RCA executives missed, Colonel insisted in letter after letter, was that it was Elvis alone that the fans wanted, not all these other singers and musicians with whom RCA wanted to clutter up the sessions. As early as January 9, Colonel came up with the idea of Elvis simply recording himself. All he had to do was to go out and get a tape recorder and then record one or two of those sacred songs that he did so well with just his own voice and piano. It could be done strictly on the q.t., without any publicity and without RCA having to know anything about it in advance — he wasn't sure if it made as much sense to Elvis as it did to him, but he *knew* the fans would be "wild" about it. Seemingly on little more than the strength of his own enthusiasm, Colonel wrote to Sholes five days later, hinting that he might have a surprise for the a&r director before too long, and the subject was revisited with Elvis from time to time, but there is no record that Elvis ever seriously responded to the proposal or did anything more than smile indulgently at his manager's touching faith in his powers.

In Hollywood negotiations were considerably more hard-boiled and frequently fraught with threats of litigation and counterlitigation. To begin with, in the fall of 1958, Colonel had planted a flurry of confusing, and sometimes contradictory, items in the trades about the likelihood of Elvis making his first post-army movie at Twentieth Century Fox. Hal Wallis naturally took strong exception to this stance, since by his interpretation of their contract Elvis was obligated to make his next movie for Wallis at Paramount, as the Colonel well knew. After fighting a furious rearguard action with Wallis and his partner, Joe Hazen, on various technical issues (such as whether army service merely delayed picking up an option or could actually cancel it) and even citing an unnamed German producer who wanted to pay them $250,000 plus 50 percent of the profits for Elvis' services in a European production, Colonel finally bowed to what he surely knew to be inevitable, but not before extracting from Wallis $175,000 plus a small profit participation for a picture for which they had no reason to expect anything more than $100,000, including bonuses *and* profit participation. At this point Fox, far from withdrawing from the fray, indicated its intention to exercise its option not just for one but for two additional pictures, prompting the Colonel to remark, "Some snow job," when he reported these developments to Elvis and Vernon at the beginning of November. With Fox formally picking up both options by the end of the year, Colonel could barely restrain his jubilation. This would give Elvis three pictures in 1960 alone (one for Wallis, two for Fox), with a guaranteed income of over half a million dollars and negotiations with MGM still on the horizon. It should prove to Elvis once and for all, Colonel declared, that his fears about being forgotten were groundless, his career was not going to go away. In fact, this brought their picture setup into line with what the Colonel had been seeking all along. "The facts are now we do not have to call on Wallis every time with our hat in our hands."

It also seemed to bring out the Colonel's creative side. Not content with having virtually humiliated Wallis in business, the Colonel continued to

pepper the veteran showman with various demands, hoaxes, and suggestions, including an unsolicited scenario, which he said he was happy to submit free of charge — though he would gladly accept a retainer's fee if in
Wallis' judgment he was deserving of it. In Colonel's scenario the action
would take place on the Hawaiian Islands, because Hawaiian music looked
like it might be the coming trend and Elvis clearly had the voice for it.
The story line focuses on a gang of promoters who con Elvis into singing
with some native Hawaiians — he is running away from his fans perhaps,
his record company is frantically looking for him because they need material — but the promoters snow Elvis into singing for free, then surreptitiously record and bootleg the performance, to the natives' (and Elvis')
financial disadvantage. In the end, Colonel assures Wallis, Elvis will bust
open the conspiracy — but he hasn't gotten that far in his story yet, and in
the meantime he has come up with another approach. In this one, Elvis is a
foundling brought up by a traveling band of gypsies who live in wagons,
sleep outdoors, and have the kind of lifestyle that will provide Elvis with
the perfect opportunity to show off his rugged versatility and stay free of
the goody-good image that is killing Pat Boone.

Wallis, it must be noted, remained patiently forbearing throughout,
acknowledging the appeal of the Hawaiian angle but suggesting that the
story line might be a trifle melodramatic. By January in any case he had settled on the almost inevitable first post-army picture, a comedy that would
focus on Elvis' GI experience and that at this point was to be called *Christmas in Berlin*. Michael Curtiz, the much-respected director of *King Creole*
and a longtime associate of Wallis, read the script and agreed that with certain minor changes this could be the best Presley picture yet, and the
Colonel graciously accepted the verdict — for the time being anyway.

With the fans he was an altogether different figure. Like a gruff uncle
able to let down his guard only when he is sure that he will not be perceived
as "soft," the Colonel and his chief lieutenant, Tom Diskin, remained in
constant touch with the loose confederation of fan clubs, extending little
courtesies, bringing them up to date on the latest news and letting them
know in one form or another that Elvis and the Colonel recognized and
appreciated their loyalty. There were fan club contests in Europe, movie
magazine contests at home, and stories planted in the press about everything from a one-hundred-city closed-circuit broadcast that would make
history to the even more unlikely prospect of an Australian tour to a movie
magazine story, "The Persecution of Private Presley," that the Colonel
secretly encouraged for all the obvious reasons.

On a more formal basis, Colonel Parker sent out over four thousand telegrams and congratulatory gifts and messages to fellow performers and show business eminences in his and Elvis' name on the occasion of openings, career milestones, or any other opportunity for mutual snowing. He traveled to theaters throughout the South to promote the rerelease of Elvis' movies, blanketed the Country Music Disc Jockey convention in Nashville, the Cotton Carnival in Memphis, and the Music Operators of America convention in Chicago with Elvis' name and achievements, and even put together an Elvis Presley Midget Fan Club to draw attention to his client. He did everything, in short, to keep Elvis' name in front of the public, *without ever actually exposing Elvis himself,* and at a time when other big-name artists' sales were dropping and the industry itself was in a slump, so far, he assured Elvis, his organization and hard work, together with Elvis' talent, had been able to keep them on top.

And he was right. For all of Steve Sholes' doom-filled prognostications, despite all of the nay-saying critics and all of the adversity they had to contend with, the Colonel's carefully conceived strategy of scarcity value and the painfully negotiated release schedule he had worked out with RCA was actually succeeding, and each of Elvis' new singles, spaced roughly four months apart, went at least as high as number four on the pop charts, while album sales for *King Creole* and *Elvis' Golden Records* more or less kept pace. He had succeeded, Colonel reassured him over and over again, by sticking to his guns and refusing to do anything but his duty to his country. He had proved all the doubters wrong, and with less than a year to go, they had only to stick to their plan.

VERNON AND ELISABETH were in an automobile accident on March 26, just after the photographer Colonel had dispatched from the States to take exclusive publicity pictures of PFC Elvis Presley, from which he expected they could pick up several thousand dollars profit (Do not under any circumstances, the Colonel admonished, let anyone get any free shots of you in uniform), had gone home. Vernon was driving when he lost control of the wheel, rolling over several times and ending up upside down on the other side of the autobahn. He was unhurt, but the Mercedes was a total loss, and Elisabeth had to be taken to a nearby hospital. Elvis' first reaction upon seeing the car was that he had lost his daddy now, too, but after determining that his father was all right, he went immediately to the hospital, where he found Elisabeth bandaged, medicated, and in a good deal of pain. Without even asking her how she was feeling, "he wanted to know [if] Mr. Presley and I were engaged in advances toward each other. . . . This was why he thought the accident occurred." Elisabeth was shocked at first. Mr. Presley had always been a perfect gentleman toward her. But, she realized, it was merely one more indication of Elvis' pervasive mistrust and insecurity; "[he] was suspicious of everybody around him, even including his own dad."

Nor did it escape any of their attention that he was not especially pleased at his friend Rex's military success. The fact that Rex had been assigned to a more rugged outfit in the first place had always stuck in his throat, and now that Rex had achieved the position of tank commander, or acting sergeant, allowing him to wear sergeant's stripes before actually being promoted, Elvis' jealousy was plain for all to see. Plain enough that Rex never wore his uniform when he came around the house, despite the obvious pride he felt in his advancement.

As for Red, life in Bad Nauheim became more and more burdensome, as he grew restive under what he felt to be an increasingly arbitrary and autocratic reign. He had come to Germany strictly on impulse, on a wave of feeling precipitated by the deaths of Elvis' mother and of his own father within days of each other, just before his release from the Marines. But it hadn't really worked out from the start. Red was a hard-ass, and he chafed under the restrictions imposed not just by Vernon's penny-pinching ways but by what seemed like Elvis' own growing need to have everyone around him bow and scrape to his whims. Red felt like he had done the best he could — and he would have been the last to deny that he had caused more than enough trouble on his own. But the way that Elvis had started acting, the big-shot airs that he was always putting on, the way that he had come to believe his own publicity just pissed Red off and reminded him more and more of the reasons that he had quit originally in the summer of '56. From Red's point of view, this was a very different Elvis than the scared kid he had known in high school, or even the budding star that he had accompanied on his early travels in 1955 and 1956. That Elvis didn't think he was so high and mighty; he was grateful for the attention he got and didn't parade around like he thought he was God's gift to women and everyone else. That was the reason, Red theorized, that he took so readily to uppers: they "[brought] out a personality that he didn't have."

And then there was the other situation — Red didn't like taking orders from Elvis or anyone else, but he'd be damned if he'd take orders from that hypocrite Vernon. Watching Vernon mooning over that drunken sergeant's wife, the three of them going around together like they were the best of friends while Vernon was fucking the wife — the worst of it came one night when they all went out and everybody got pretty smashed, "but Vernon and Bill really got drunk. We all ended up at Sergeant Bill's apartment. Luckily [he] passed out in his chair, because things were getting rough. Vernon was mouthing off. [Dee's kids] were crying, and I put them to bed." Vernon protested mightily when Red and Lamar carried him out and put him in a taxi. "He was cursing and yelling that he was going to have us on the first plane back to the States. But just as well we got out of there, because if Bill Stanley had woken up and heard all this going on, it might have got out of hand. He didn't know that Vernon and Dee were more than just seeing each other." And it wouldn't have done for Elvis to have found out about this drunken spree either: he had made it clear that he didn't like Dee, he didn't like his daddy to drink, and the thought of anyone replacing his mother, Red knew, was the one thing that was guaranteed to send him around the bend.

In the end Red simply announced that he was going home. Whether he jumped or was pushed (opinion was equally divided on the subject), he departed at the beginning of May, just around the time that Dee Stanley returned to Virginia with her boys "to get away and think." Whatever Red's private feelings, his public loyalty was unwavering, as he painted a rosy picture of Elvis and Vernon's experience in Germany in an on-air interview with Memphis DJ George Klein, a high school classmate and longtime friend of Elvis', shortly after his arrival home. Elvis' favorite off-duty activity was touch football, Red declared. His army life was a far cry from the night-owl existence he had lived as a civilian. His father, too, had made a good adjustment. "He has met a lot of people who speak English — soldiers' families mostly — and they visit quite a bit back and forth."

Elvis for his part could understand Red's feelings, but he needed someone from home besides Lamar. The first person he called was Alan Fortas, who might have given the matter more serious consideration except that he had already spoken to Red about the subject ("Red kept telling me, 'Whatever you do, don't go. I promise you, you'll hate it, and you and Elvis will never be the same'"). For a period of time he focused on Anita once again, and Colonel even set up a tentative date for her to visit, using her aunt as a cover — but the more Elvis thought about it, the less it seemed like a good idea, and even in his bluest moments, he was aware that it

wouldn't answer his need for constant companionship. So he called Cliff
Gleaves, not without a certain amount of trepidation but knowing that
Cliff was always good for a laugh and had proved his loyalty if not his
responsibility in the year and a half that he had palled around with them all
prior to Elvis' army induction.

Cliff was in Baton Rouge trying his hand at show business when he got
the call. A former DJ and natural entertainer who had blown his one line in
King Creole out of stage fright, he was promoting his first record, "Love Is
My Business," on Jack Clement's fledgling Summer label and working some
Brother Dave Gardner comedy material into his act, "when the phone rings,
and it's Elvis. He says, 'Cliff, I got a two-week leave in Paris coming up.' I
didn't even ask him how are you or nothing. I said, 'Elvis, I'm on my way.'"

Not so fast that he actually got to go to Paris with them. With the tickets that Elvis supplied, Cliff managed to remain in transit for some time,
stopping off in Memphis, New York, London, and one or two other points
along the way before finally arriving in Germany at the beginning of June.
When he did, he promptly took off again, upon his introduction to an airman named Currie Grant, who served as assistant manager of, and produced a variety show for, the Eagle Club in Wiesbaden, the largest air force
club and community center in Europe.

Grant had originally met Lamar, Vernon, and Elisabeth the previous
month when they attended a benefit for crippled children that he was hosting in Giessen. He hit it off with Lamar right away, and in exchange for an
invitation to the Eagle Club, Lamar in turn extended an invitation to Currie
and his wife Carol to come visit Bad Nauheim sometime after Elvis got
back from maneuvers. The Sunday that Currie took Lamar up on his invitation just happened to coincide with the weekend of Cliff's arrival, and Rex
noted the almost instantaneous reaction on Cliff's part to the news that
Currie, too, was in show business. Within a matter of days, Cliff was off to
Wiesbaden, having first secured a booking at the Eagle Club, and both he
and the Volkswagen he had borrowed for transportation stayed gone for
some time. Which was why Rex, and not Cliff, got to go to Paris.

I T WAS ELVIS AND LAMAR, Charlie and Rex who made the trip. First
they stopped off in Munich, where they revisited the Moulin Rouge, and
Elvis had his picture taken with Marianne, a stripper who had developed
a routine, as the wire services gleefully reported, wearing "nothing but a
standard-size Presley record." Then after two nights it was off to Paris in

a private train car, where they were met on June 16 by Hill and Range co-head Jean Aberbach, a Viennese refugee who with his brother, Julian, had pioneered in the field of country and western song publishing before fate, in the person of Colonel Parker, brought them together with Elvis Presley.

Jean was prepared to take care of everything. He had made reservations for them at the plush Prince de Galles (Prince of Wales) Hotel, where they would occupy a suite on the top floor with a panoramic view of the Champs-Elysées and the Arc de Triomphe and he would be just down the hall. In addition, Freddy Bienstock, the Aberbachs' cousin and principal publishing go-between at recording sessions, was at their disposal, as was Ben Starr, the Hill and Range lawyer whom Elvis knew from his original RCA signing. Anywhere he and the boys wanted to go, anything they wanted to do could be arranged by Aberbach, a sophisticated and urbane forty-eight-year-old bachelor who with his brother maintained apartments and offices throughout the world; he and Freddy and Ben were just there to show the boys a good time. They brought regards from the Colonel, of course, who was sorry he could not be there himself, and from Hal Wallis, with whom Jean and his brother were already working on the upcoming motion picture, now retitled *G.I. Blues,* and who would, as Elvis knew, be arriving soon himself in Germany to shoot exteriors and army footage. If they wanted to see the sights, if they would like a guided tour of the city, they had only to ask.

Rex and Lamar were definitely curious, but Elvis was interested strictly in the activities after dark, so it was arranged that they would go to the Lido that night. After a brief press conference, which he handled with his customary aplomb ("In the spotlight he seemed to turn into another person," remarked Rex, who had never witnessed his friend in this kind of setting before), Elvis decided to give the famed sophistication of Paris a try. Here, reporters reassured him, he would not be bothered by the vulgar crowd; he could go out on the street without fear of being recognized, let alone accosted. The experiment lasted about ten minutes. That was how long it took a crowd of two hundred to swarm all over them at a sidewalk café just blocks from the hotel. It was over an hour before they were able to get back to the Prince de Galles, and while Rex and Lamar subsequently took advantage of Jean's offer to show them the sights, Elvis henceforth stuck to his original resolve.

Nights were a different matter altogether. The Lido was like a more licentious Las Vegas, and after one night the pattern was pretty much set. They woke up late in the day to have their one full meal, a huge 8:00 P.M.

breakfast. Then they would catch the first show at the Carousel or the Folies Bergère, and from there go on to the Lido, where the statuesque chorus line, the Blue Belles, were all English girls eager to make Elvis Presley's acquaintance. After the Lido closed, they would proceed to Le Bantu, a late-night club which didn't open until 4:00 A.M., bringing with them as many of the Blue Belles as wanted to come along. At the end of the evening Elvis would take his pick from among all the girls, leaving the rest for Rex, Charlie, and Lamar to choose from. One memorable night the entire chorus returned to the suite with them, and everyone was still asleep the next evening at 9:30 when the phone rang. It was the manager of the Lido, who announced to Lamar that he would like to begin his first show. Lamar told him to go right ahead and hung up without thinking any more about it. A moment later the phone rang again, and the same message was repeated. "Lamar got angry," observed an amused Rex, "[and] this time . . . told the Lido manager . . . to quit bothering us. The manager then told Lamar that he could not start his show, because we had his entire chorus line in our hotel suite. Needless to say, Lamar was a little embarrassed," concluded Rex, who in later life was at least as embarrassed by the recollection of his own actions, "but at the time it seemed to be all right."

That was how it went, a kind of Arabian nights existence in which they were shepherded from one improbable fantasy to another. One night at the Lido Elvis got up and sang "Willow Weep for Me" alone at the piano. He was scared to death, he told reporters afterward. "For the first time in 15 months there I was in front of an audience. Then it flew all over me, boy — sudden fear." As for his army experience, "I had got used to a certain way of life. It's hard for anybody to adjust to the Army, and maybe it was harder for me than for most. But I was determined to adjust, because any other way I would only have hurt myself."

They were like a pack of schoolboys, whipping out their butane lighters (just recently introduced on the market) to see who could raise the highest flame should anyone be unwary enough to request a light. Poor Lamar, who had already lost his passport on the train, became the subject of even greater ridicule when he insisted that he had fallen in love with one of the dancers at Le Bantu. Elvis quickly investigated, invited the girl to join Lamar outside in their car, and almost fell over when Lamar discovered to his great surprise that his "'she' was a 'he.'" Elvis loved to tell the story about Lamar's great passion and how when all was said and done, "she had one bigger than he did!"

At the end of their stay they were having such a good time that Elvis decided to give up their train reservations for one more night in Paris. He hired a limousine on the following day, and they arrived at the barracks in Friedberg just in time for the three soldiers to report back at midnight on the fifteenth day of their leave.

V ERNON MEANWHILE WAS TAKING an indefinite leave of his own. He had sailed from Bremerhaven the day the boys left for Paris, arriving in Memphis eight days later, on June 24. He had some business to take care of, he told reporters who noted his presence; he wanted to get the cars registered and ready for Elvis' homecoming in nine months; and he had a tooth that needed to be extracted while he was in town. But, of course, the real reason for his return was Dee, whom he was determined not to let go.

He had accompanied her to the airport with her husband, Bill, and afterward the two men sat around drinking in the Stanleys' apartment, each of them despondent in his own way. He was afraid he might have lost his wife, Bill Stanley confessed, unaware of whom he had lost her to, and he asked Vernon to try to help him get her back. "You're my dearest friend," he declared in Dee's version of the story. "You took her shopping and gave her so much that I didn't. She loved you, you know. She'll listen to you. . . ." That was finally too much for Vernon, and he called Dee even before she arrived at her sister's home.

He stayed for a month and a half, attending the Colonel's fiftieth birthday party in Madison, Tennessee, visiting his father in Louisville for the first time in quite a while and taking the opportunity to introduce him to Dee, mostly just trying to persuade her that they could really have a life together. In the *Memphis Press-Scimitar* it was reported that he was "so changed you wouldn't know him. . . . A friend said, 'He just goes around crying. He is so lonesome that sometimes he has one of his brothers spend the night in the house with him.'" And, it was further reported, he left untouched a broken windowpane that Gladys had fallen against — out of the deep grief that he and Elvis shared. But he brought Dee to Graceland. And he promised that he would provide a home there for her and her boys. "I got sent home from school," he told a local friend and fan, Dotty Ayers, leaving no question as to why Elvis was angry with him. "I don't think that it's this woman in particular," he said. "I think it would be any woman right now." By the time that he sailed from New York in early August, Dee had placed her boys, now eight, six, and three, in a home called Breezy Point Farms and made plans to join him in Germany.

HAL WALLIS ARRIVED in Frankfurt in mid August with a full crew for a couple of weeks of location shooting in Germany. He had gotten the Third Armored Division's permission to film tank maneuvers, along with more informal scenes at the base — all, the Paramount publicity apparatus hastened to assure the American people, at studio, not government, expense. Elvis was clear on his instructions — he was not to participate in filming in any way — but he did go to dinner with Wallis on several occasions and spoke excitedly about the upcoming production. He had put in a lot of time just preparing for this role, he declared, about seventeen months so far, and he thought he would have it just about right by the time he got out in March. Elvis even asked him for a script, Wallis told gossip columnist May Mann, but he was forced to refuse because he knew his star would have just gone ahead and memorized it on the spot.

At just about the time of Wallis' visit, on August 15, Captain Paul Beaulieu and his family arrived at the Rhine-Main air base and traveled from there to Wiesbaden, where Captain Beaulieu was to be stationed. Like most military families, the Beaulieus had moved around a good deal, but they had spent most of the past four years at the Bergstrom Air Force Base in Austin, where their oldest child, Priscilla, just fourteen, had been elected "Most Beautiful" and "Best Dressed" by her graduating classmates at Del Valle Junior High School the previous semester. Four years older than her brother Don, with a little sister of four and a newborn baby brother, Priscilla had only recently discovered that Paul Beaulieu, the man she had always assumed to be her father, had in fact adopted her after marrying her mother when Priscilla was three. Her real father, her mother explained in response to Priscilla's frantic questioning when she came upon a baby picture of herself with her parents, was a navy pilot who had died in an airplane crash when she was only six months old. She thought it would be best, she told her distraught daughter, if they kept this secret to themselves and didn't tell the other children — in fact, she thought it would be a good idea not to let Priscilla's father, who loved her very much, know that she had found out. Priscilla bowed to her mother's judgment, although she didn't understand her reasoning, and she couldn't help but feel like something of an outsider in the family from that point on. Which made it seem all the more unfair the following year to be forced to move *again* — and to Germany, of all places, this time.

For the first few days after their arrival she didn't do much of anything, refused to be appeased, rejected all offers of help. She was a beautiful girl with a snub nose, a childlike freshness of appearance, but a fully formed, adult expression and a mind of her own. Her mother did everything she could to coax her out of her mood of sullen resentment, and her father, who was strict but fair, tried to kid her out of it, but she continued to sulk with resolute determination, until at last she grew bored with the part herself. The family moved out of the hotel they had been living in and into a pension, and Priscilla started dropping by the nearby Eagle Club, which served as a kind of community center for air force families, every day on her way home from school. She would sit in the snack bar, listen to the jukebox, and write letters to friends at home. It was there that she met Currie Grant.

She didn't know who he was at first. He was just this good-looking, older guy in his twenties staring at her — but she was used to that. One day, while she was sitting with her ten-year-old brother, Don, he came up and introduced himself. She gave her own name with some misgivings and listened even more suspiciously as he explained that he was the entertainment director here at the Eagle Club, and was she by any chance a fan of Elvis Presley? She just stared at him — of course she was, who wasn't? She and her friend Angela had located Bad Nauheim on the map when she found out she would be going to Germany, and when they saw how close it was to Wiesbaden she told Angela she was going to meet Elvis over there. "I'm a good friend of his," said Currie Grant. "My wife and I go to his house quite often. How would you like to join us one evening?"

Eventually, her father agreed to it. After meeting Currie and getting Currie's assurances that his daughter would be well chaperoned by both him and his wife, Captain Beaulieu next contacted the airman's commanding officer and then — and only then — let her go, with the promise that she would be home by eleven o'clock without fail; the next day was a school day.

She wore her navy-and-white sailor dress with white socks and shoes. Brenda Lee's "Sweet Nothin's" was on the record player when she entered the room, and Rex thought she was a vision of loveliness. Elvis was sitting in his easy chair, with one leg thrown carelessly over the arm. He was

ELVIS AND PRISCILLA. (COURTESY OF THE ESTATE OF ELVIS PRESLEY)

wearing tan slacks and a red sweater and smoking one of his little cigars. To Rex it was obvious that Elvis was immediately smitten, but the fourteen-year-old was nearly struck dumb in her tracks.

> As Currie led me over to him, Elvis stood up and smiled. "Well," he said. "What have we here?"
>
> "Elvis," Currie said, "this is Priscilla Beaulieu. The girl I told you about."
>
> We shook hands, and he said, "Hi, I'm Elvis Presley," but then there was a silence between us until Elvis asked me to sit down beside him, and Currie drifted off.
>
> "So," Elvis said. "Do you go to school?"
>
> "Yes."
>
> "What are you, about a junior or senior in high school?"
>
> I blushed and said nothing, not willing to reveal that I was only in the ninth grade.
>
> "Well," he persisted.
>
> "Ninth."
>
> Elvis looked confused. "Ninth what?"
>
> "Grade," I whispered.
>
> "Ninth *grade*," he said and started laughing. "Why, you're just a baby."
>
> "Thanks," I said curtly. Not even Elvis Presley had the right to say that to me.

He played the piano for her, singing some of his own songs but also, to her surprise, big, expressive numbers like Tony Bennett's 1953 hit, "Rags to Riches," and Mahalia Jackson's "I Asked the Lord," and, with the others joining in, Earl Grant's Nat "King" Cole–like ballad, "The End." The way he looked at her, it was obvious he was trying to impress her, but she didn't really know how to respond as she looked around the room, checking out the poster of Brigitte Bardot, watching all these adults competing for his attention and approbation. He took her into the kitchen, where she met his grandmother, and he consumed the first of five bacon sandwiches smothered with mustard. She tried to think of things to say, but for some reason it didn't matter, he just seemed to want to pour out his feelings to her, and when Currie came into the room and said it was time to go, Elvis begged her to stay a little longer. When Currie explained that she couldn't, Elvis said maybe she could come by again, but Priscilla doubted that he would remember, and she didn't get home till 2 A.M. anyway when they got held up by an impenetrable fog on the autobahn to Wiesbaden.

It was only a few days before she got another call from Currie: Elvis wanted to see her again. She couldn't believe it, and it threw the rest of the household into some consternation, but her parents eventually agreed to let her go, and before she knew it she was back in the house on Goethe-strasse. This time it was clear from the start that she was the one: after playing the piano and singing to her, Elvis said, "I want to be alone with you, Priscilla." She looked around; there was no one near them.

> "We are alone," I said nervously.
>
> He moved closer, backing me against the wall. "I mean, *really* alone," he whispered. "Will you come upstairs to my room?"
>
> The question threw me into a panic. *His room?* . . .
>
> "There's nothing to be frightened of, Honey."
>
> As he spoke, he was smoothing my hair. "I swear, I'll never do any-thing to harm you." He sounded absolutely sincere. "I'll treat you just like a sister." Flustered and confused, I looked away.
>
> "Please."

She preceded him up the stairs, so it would "look better," and explored his room, finding letters from Anita and other girls carelessly strewn about, examining his books and records, all his uniforms, waiting almost breath-lessly for him to appear. At last, after what seemed like forever, he did, took off his jacket, turned on the radio, and sat down on the bed. Why didn't she sit down beside him? he said, as she imagined all kinds of unimaginable conclusions, but she was won over by his sweetness, his sincerity, his eyes, and they fell into a conversation from which she could scarcely be roused to go home. He was just like her, he felt things just like her, underneath "he was just a boy, he was afraid, he didn't know if he was going to have a career or not, he didn't know if he was going to come back to [his] fans — he was *stripped*, he was vulnerable." At the end of the evening he kissed her good night, and she clung to him desperately, not wanting to let him go. He was the one to pull away. They had plenty of time, he told her, kissing her on the forehead and addressing her for the first time as "Little One."

* * *

O N THEIR FOURTH DATE he met her parents, at Captain Beaulieu's insistence. Up till then Currie had been taking her back and forth to Bad Nauheim, but Priscilla told Elvis that if he wanted to see her again, he was going to have to pick her up himself. He arrived with his father in the white BMW and sat nervously in the Beaulieus' living room waiting for her parents to enter. When they did, he jumped up and said, "Hello, I'm Elvis Presley, and this is my daddy, Vernon," as if they might not know who their visitors were. They made small talk while Priscilla nervously fretted; she knew what her father could be like, and she had seen and heard things at Bad Nauheim that she knew her father would never approve of. But Elvis was on his best behavior — he talked about his assignment with the scouts and looked smart in his army uniform. When Captain Beaulieu told him he would have to pick up Priscilla and bring her back himself from now on, just like a regular date, Elvis explained that by the time he got off duty and cleaned up, much of the evening was already gone, and would it be all right if his father picked their daughter up, he would bring her home.

Captain Beaulieu seemed to mull over this compromise solution, then posed the question directly: What was it exactly Elvis wanted with his daughter? After all, he had all these girls throwing themselves at him. Why Priscilla? Elvis seemed to really squirm at that one — Priscilla felt even more sorry for him for a moment, being subjected to this kind of inquisition, and Vernon, too, shifted uncomfortably in his seat. But then he declared, "Well, sir, I happen to be very fond of her," in that forthright manner of his that could make you believe just about anything he said. Priscilla was very mature for her age, he stated, and it got kind of lonely for him, being stationed so far away from home. "I guess you might say I need someone to talk to. You don't have to worry about her, Captain," he declared. "I'll take good care of her."

F ROM THAT POINT ON they saw each other almost every night. He *didn't* take her home all the time, or even most of the time, and Vernon didn't always pick her up; it was Lamar as often as not who acted as the chauffeur, but that was no longer an issue. Her parents had been mollified, convinced for the time being anyway that he really was a nice, well-mannered young man.

Every night they ended up in his bedroom. Every night they ended up in each other's arms. He proved true to his promise: he didn't harm her, he wouldn't harm her even if she begged him to — she was too young, he told her; he wanted her to remain pure. Someday the time would be right, but for now there were lots of other things they could do. She felt closer to him than anyone she had ever known in her life. Through Grandma, whom she called Dodger now, just as he did, she got to hear all about what he was like as a child, she learned all the family stories, she heard how hard his mother could be on him sometimes but how she protected him from all harm. She felt totally a part of him, and yet she didn't know what her own role was supposed to be. She knew he had other girls, much as he might deny it. When she told him that she loved him, he put his fingers to her lips and said he didn't understand what he was feeling himself. "Daddy keeps reminding me of your age and that it can't be possible," he stumbled on. "When I go home. . . . Only time will tell."

It was worst when they were around the others. Earlier in the evening, before Priscilla preceded him upstairs, they were constantly surrounded, and he could be so different when other people were around, hiding the little boy that had been revealed to her, brutally brushing aside their secret life. She didn't know how she was supposed to be with him then. Then she was just the same as all the rest, waiting for him to reveal his mood, laughing when he laughed, sitting silently with a blank expression until he had something to say.

"I really felt I got to know who Elvis Presley was during that time. Not with ego — not the star that he felt he should portray. I saw him raw, totally raw, I saw him as he really was after he lost his mother. We talked so much, he shared his grief with me, he was very insecure, and he felt very betrayed by his father, that he would even fall for such a woman [as Dee Stanley]. He used to literally babble about how this couldn't be his father, about how 'This will pass, once we get away from Germany, this will go away. . . .' He was at his most vulnerable, his most honest, I would say his most passionate during that time."

About his career he expressed trepidation, but he had utter faith in the Colonel. He showed her letters Colonel had written him, letters detailing *their* plan, showing how he was keeping the fans' interest alive, running down the list of all his pitches and promotions, telling Elvis not to worry. "He talked about how I'd meet the Colonel one day, how Colonel was working on a film project for him as soon as he got back and he was going to be in more films [after that]. He spoke of him very endearingly." And it was obvious that he trusted him implicitly, because, he told Priscilla,

Colonel was the whole reason he hadn't performed the entire time he was in the army, and, as in every other career decision, *Colonel had been right.*

She soaked it all in, no more surprised by his conviction on this subject than by his almost evangelical espousal of the benefits of yogurt, which he had only recently discovered and ate by the gallon. At the end of the evening they would listen to "Goodnight, My Love," the sign-off number on the armed forces radio station every night, and then Lamar would drive her home.

E VERYONE COULD SEE it was different right from the start. To Charlie there was no question that he had fallen in love at first sight. "Did you see the bone structure in her face?" Elvis demanded of his friend, as if somehow he had to explain it. "It's like the woman I've been looking for all my life." To Joe Esposito, a newfound army buddy from Chicago who had recently started playing touch football with them on the weekends, the source of the attraction was obvious ("Every Sunday afternoon Priscilla sat by herself on the sidelines watching the football games. I still have that image clear in my head. I've never seen anyone before or since so absolutely fragile and beautiful"), even if the underlying explanation might have been more mundane. "He knew she was young, and he was going to train her to be just the way he wanted her to be."

Even Elisabeth, who continued to sleep with him every night and was, of course, intensely jealous, knew immediately that this was something of a different order from all the other dalliances, from all the other girls who passed in and out of his life. She had thought for the longest time that he would never leave Anita; she passed on Anita's letters without comment and expected, like everyone else, that they would probably get married someday — but with this quietly pretty, petite brunette she sensed all certainty evaporating. "I often wanted to ask Elvis if he had fallen in love with Priscilla, but I knew better than to ask that question."

Otherwise, almost all of the talk, all of the focus was now, suddenly, on going home. Elvis spoke sometimes about bringing Elisabeth back to Memphis as his secretary. Sometimes he talked about taking them *all* home with him. But even as he was waxing nostalgic about how much they had all been through together, it was perfectly clear where his attention was increasingly directed, even when he was with Priscilla, who saw her dream evaporating before she had even been able to fully formulate it, who was growing more and more certain that he would go back to the States, and it would be *as if it had never happened.*

Communications from the Colonel were arriving at an ever accelerating pace — calls, telegrams, letters. The Frank Sinatra television special, which had first been announced in July, was now all worked out: it was to be subtitled "Frank Sinatra's Welcome Home Party for Elvis Presley," and Elvis would be receiving $125,000, the highest fee ever paid for a guest appearance on television — and, the Colonel made sure to point out, for singing only two songs. The recording session that would take place just prior to the special was on his mind as well. He would debut his new single on the show, Colonel said, so he should be thinking about that — that would be their first order of business at the session, and it had to be right. Otherwise they had RCA just where they wanted them. They couldn't write a new contract until certain tax issues had been cleared up, but the record company had already agreed to pay a full, "favored nations" publishing royalty on all songs in which they had a copyright interest, an important modification of the existing contract that stipulated a three-quarter rate on all such compositions, according to standard company policy. What this meant in light of Elvis' publishing partnership with Hill and Range, the Colonel was quick to point out, was a 25-percent upgrade in payment on virtually every song that he would record. Not only that, if any other RCA artist were to get a better deal, Elvis' deal would automatically kick up to the same level due to the "favored nations" clause in the contract. They had RCA practically eating out of their hand, the Colonel crowed — and it was all because they had stuck to their guns.

Elvis' mind for the most part, though, was on other things. He enjoyed Colonel's running account of his business successes, he loved to hear how Colonel had all the big shots jumping to his tune, and he certainly appreciated the way in which his manager was always looking out for him, the extent to which Colonel had provided a measure of insurance against the future — but what concerned him most of all, what Colonel had *freed* him to be able to concentrate on, was the music. That was what he focused on each night as he sat down at the piano, that was what he dreamt about more and more — the songs that he would actually record when he got home, the music with which he would once again be able to communicate to the world. There were a number of songs that he had been considering for some time: the Four Fellows' 1955 hit, "Soldier Boy," an understandable refrain ever since he had joined the army; "I Will Be Home Again," the old

Golden Gate Quartet number that he and Charlie sang as a duet; classic r&b material like Clyde McPhatter's "Such a Night," and Vikki Nelson's "Like a Baby." He *knew* he was going to do a gospel album before the year was out, and to that end Charlie kept feeding him jubilee material, while Gordon Stoker of the Jordanaires sent him records by everyone from the black gospel group the Harmonizing Four, with their great bass singer Jimmy Jones, to the latest releases by the Statesmen and the Blackwood Brothers. Good old Dewey Phillips back in Memphis kept tipping him to songs he probably would never get around to recording, and Freddy Bienstock kept up a steady flow of Hill and Range material.

None of them seemed to fully recognize the new directions he wanted to explore — but then, how could they when it was territory he had always tended to shy away from since he had begun making records himself? He had always been drawn to the big-voiced, inspirational, near-operatic ballad singing of Roy Hamilton, for example, nominally an r&b artist whose "You'll Never Walk Alone" had shot to number one in 1954. He had recorded Hamilton's bouncy "I'm Gonna Sit Right Down and Cry (Over You)" upon his arrival at RCA in 1956, but he hadn't thought he was even close to ready to tackle Hamilton's more ambitious numbers — and who knew what Steve Sholes, the man who signed him, would have thought if he had? Now, with Charlie's encouragement, he worked constantly on improving his vocal technique — Charlie continued to show him tricks to help with his breathing and expand his range, and he employed those lessons on numbers like Hamilton's "Unchained Melody" and "I Believe," as well as the lilting Irish air "Danny Boy" and one of his other longtime favorites, Tony Martin's "There's No Tomorrow," a 1949 English-language adaptation of "O Sole Mio," which was itself based upon an Italian folk melody forever immortalized in the great opera singer Enrico Caruso's 1916 recording.

At first it frightened him to think what his fans' reaction might be. But then he fell back on the one precept that had guided him throughout his recording career: what you sang had to come from the heart; it couldn't just be a matter of following trends, because then the public would never believe you. Up till now he had relied on instinct alone, and his instinct had proved as reliable in music as the Colonel's in business. It wasn't as if he was putting on airs; this was music he had always loved — he could remember listening to Caruso's records as a child. So he pursued these new directions with the same unfaltering zeal that he always showed for a fresh

idea, picking up tips from Charlie, studying familiar records by the Ink
Spots and the Mills Brothers minutely for clues as to how to phrase, how to
hit the note, preparing himself for the challenge.

Freddy did his best to get a cut-in on "There's No Tomorrow" so that
they would be able to participate in publishing royalties, but when he
failed, he came up with the idea of commissioning new lyrics, since the
melody was already in the public domain. Elvis was open to the idea — it
was the *song* he cared about, not the words — and they talked about it
some more when Freddy came to Bad Nauheim to deliver acetates for
Elvis' consideration. Everything was falling into place for the upcoming
session. They would use most of the same musicians from the last session
in Nashville in June of 1958, and even Scotty Moore, Elvis' original guitarist, was back in the fold — he had a song on which he wanted to make a
deal. That was just the way things ought to be, Colonel said, a good business relationship, and if the other original trio member, Bill Black, was
playing hard to get (Black had recently formed his own combo, which was
starting to enjoy a little bit of success), well, there were plenty of good
bass players in Nashville, Colonel declared, and it never did to beg. There
was no question in Freddy's mind of Elvis' enthusiasm about getting back
to work — he had never seen him anything less than 100 percent committed, but now he was practically champing at the bit. At the same time,
Freddy's sardonic view of human nature was also satisfied during his visit
as he observed Elvis' increasing discomfiture and watched him turn the
record player up louder and louder to try to drown out the sounds of Vernon and his blond girlfriend in the next room.

IN OCTOBER ELVIS saw a magazine notice advertising the services of a
South African doctor who specialized in dermatology and owned the
patent rights to a unique method of treatment guaranteed to reduce
enlarged pores and acne scars, which he felt might greatly improve his
appearance in front of the movie cameras. He had Elisabeth get in touch
with the doctor, Laurenz Johannes Griessel Landau, and they had an immediate reply from Johannesburg proposing a course of treatment which
would remain entirely confidential ("Boy Scout's honor," promised the
doctor), and would cost Elvis nothing except the dermatologist's expenses
unless, and until, it proved successful. It would be Dr. Landau's pleasure to
work with such an eminent patient, he suggested in the course of his initial

ten-page letter, and in a four-page p.s., he mentioned that he would be bringing with him recordings of some of his own musical compositions. The correspondence continued while Elvis was on maneuvers in Wildflecken, and then Dr. Landau himself showed up in Bad Nauheim with no advance notice before Elvis had even returned from the field.

Treatments began on November 27 and continued several times a week for roughly two hours at a time for the next four weeks. Elvis was positive that he could see results and pointed them out to everyone around him, though no one else recognized any change and Vernon was convinced that the eccentric South African was going to bankrupt them. In early December Elvis began formal karate lessons as well after witnessing a demonstration by Jurgen Seydel, "the father of German karate," whom he sought out at his studio in Bad Homburg. He and Rex went twice a week at first, and before long Elvis was demonstrating what they had learned to Priscilla and everyone else in the household and giving lectures on the discipline required to master the art of karate and its superiority to other, cruder forms of self-defense.

Then on the day before Christmas Elvis emerged from a session with Dr. Landau in his bedroom with a look of horror on his face. The sonofabitch was queer, he told Lamar and Rex, he was going to kill the fucking sonofabitch. Landau was hustled out of the house right away, if only to keep Elvis from actually following through, but the South African reappeared that night with a letter that threatened to go to the press with photographs and tape recordings and accounts of "compromising situations" of which he had direct personal knowledge, including an illicit relationship with a "16-year-old" [sic] American girlfriend.

Vernon was utterly panic-stricken; he was convinced that this could mean the end of Elvis' career, and there were emergency calls to the Colonel and general consternation all around. Colonel remained unfazed, however, consulting with some of his high-level army contacts in Washington, and on his advice Elvis and Vernon got in touch with the army's Provost Marshal Division, which in turn referred the matter to the FBI. On January 6 Laurenz Johannes Griessel Landau (who turned out, not surprisingly, *not* to be a medical doctor) was on a plane to London, having received a small amount of money for his troubles but never to be heard from again.

* * *

A LL OF THIS EXCITEMENT cast something of a pall over the holiday
season, but it didn't spoil the Christmas party that Elvis threw for
some of the guys at his home, and by the time he had his twenty-fifth
birthday party on January 8 at the local recreation center, Dr. Landau was
little more than a memory. It was a gala affair, with close to two hundred
in attendance, and the room filled with attractive women, but Elvis had
eyes only for Priscilla. Charlie sang and Elvis joined in; Cliff, who had been
AWOL for much of the last few months, put in a rare appearance; Joe
Esposito and a bunch of the "regulars" presented a trophy inscribed ELVIS
PRESLEY. MOST VALUABLE PLAYER. BAD NAUHEIM SUNDAY AFTER-
NOON FOOTBALL ASSOCIATION, 1959; and Vernon and Dee, who had
brought Priscilla to the party, acted like an old married couple, proudly surveying the scene.

Earlier in the evening Elvis had spoken to Dick Clark, the Philadelphia-
based host of *American Bandstand,* by telephone, touching on his upcoming
television and motion-picture appearances, all part of the stepped-up publicity campaign that the Colonel had been waging ever since November.
For the first time, full-length features were beginning to crop up regularly
in the American press; RCA put out a carefully orchestrated series of press
releases and planted stories that posed the question, Will Elvis Presley
Change His Style?; and there was a whole series of interviews scheduled
over the next two months, which would climax, according to the Colonel's
plan, in an avalanche of coverage of Private Presley's Triumphant Return
Home. The reality of the life that he had left behind was beginning to impinge more and more on even his everyday activities, he had already begun
to think about packing — but he still didn't know what he was going to do
about Priscilla.

Grandma had seen where things were going almost from the start, and
she felt very bad for Elisabeth, who had been her best friend in this godfor-
saken land. She didn't blame Elvis for it exactly, but she didn't like to see the
girl left dangling on a string — and she saw the way that Rex was looking at
her out of the corner of his eye. So she brought the two of them together,
dropping oblique hints at first, then inviting them surreptitiously to her
room, where she told them both exactly what she thought they should do.

At first they met at the apartment of a service couple who were part of
the whole gang — the wife even helped Elisabeth with the fan correspondence. They had to be very careful, because Elvis seemed able to keep track
of where everyone was at all times. Lamar and Cliff knew about the rela-

tionship and to Rex's surprise "seemed to really enjoy the intrigue of the situation. . . . Maybe it was their way of getting back at Elvis for some of the things that Elvis had done to them." Once they almost got caught, but a friend said that he was the one who had been seen with Elisabeth, so he, instead of Rex, was banished from the house. They had been seeing each other in this manner for a little over two months when the birthday party took place, and Rex could only observe helplessly as Elvis showered all of his attention on Priscilla while he could not so much as ask Elisabeth for a dance.

Finally, it was just too much for him, watching Elisabeth besieged by dancing partners, with one in particular making a blatant play for her. Out of sheer frustration he informed Elvis that this guy was trying to hit on Elisabeth, and he took a small measure of satisfaction when Elvis blew up, as Rex knew he would, and told the guy to get lost.

Elvis went to Paris a second time shortly after that, taking Joe and Cliff and his karate instructor, Jurgen Seydel, with him this time in addition to Lamar. The evening activities remained much the same, but during the day he now studied shotokan technique with a Japanese karate teacher that Jurgen Seydel introduced him to. Joe held the money for them on this trip, paid all the bills, and on Vernon's instructions collected all the receipts, impressing Elvis with his organizational skills. One night they went to the Café de Paris to hear the Golden Gate Quartet, and Elvis went backstage and sang spirituals with them for hours, dredging up songs that even the group had trouble remembering on occasion.

He was promoted to acting sergeant on January 20, two days after his return. It was somewhat of a bitter pill, since Rex had long since gotten his full promotion, and Elvis even took the occasion to state that Rex had probably made sergeant only because of his association with Elvis. "Rexadus," he said, "see what good things can happen to you because you know me."

He finally got his full sergeant's stripes on February 11 and threw a little party at the house, where everything was in a flurry of preparation, with Grandma busily packing, Vernon and Dee making plans for the future, and Priscilla desperately clinging to him every night, not wanting to go, not wanting him to go, ever — but if he did, why couldn't he take her with him? She didn't care about her parents, school wasn't part of the picture, and she couldn't even let on that she was tired, because one night when she fell asleep waiting for him to finish his karate class, he asked her how many hours of sleep she was getting. "After a second, I said, 'About four or five hours a night. But I'll be fine.'

Elvis looked thoughtful and said, "Come upstairs a minute. I have something for you." He led me up to his room where he placed a small handful of white pills in the palm of my hand. "I want you to take these; they'll help you stay awake during the day. Just take one when you feel a little drowsy, no more than one, though, or you'll be doing handstands in the hallway."

"What are they?" I asked.

"You don't need to know what they are; they give them to us when we go on maneuvers. If I didn't have them, I'd never make it through the day myself. But it's okay, they're safe," he told me. "Put them away and don't tell anyone you have them, and don't take them every day. Just when you need a little more energy."

She trusted him, she believed him implicitly, but she put the pills away in a little box she had for her keepsakes — cigar holders, the sweet little notes he wrote her, things that would remind her of him when he was gone. And she tried to stay awake from then on.

Meanwhile, Elvis had business to take care of. In interview after interview he stressed that he felt as if he had really accomplished something. "People were expecting me to mess up, to goof up in one way or another. They thought I couldn't take it and so forth, and I was determined to go to any limits to prove otherwise. Not only to the people who were wondering but to myself." He couldn't wait to resume his career, he said. He didn't know what was going to happen, but whatever it was, the Army had been an invaluable experience and his manager, Colonel Parker, an unfailing source of support and sound advice. Yes, he expected to tour Europe, definitely. Maybe next year, though the timing was up to his manager. He would never change his style; he chose all his own songs by instinct, as though he was the one buying the record himself; more than anything, he wanted to be taken seriously as a dramatic actor.

As the day of departure drew near, he found to his surprise that it got harder and harder to let go, and he talked to each of the boys individually about staying in touch, about not allowing friendship to fade, about maybe going to work for him when they got home. Joe was the first to ship out, leaving a week before Elvis and Rex and promising at Elvis' last-minute urging that he would give up the bookkeeping job that he had been planning to go back to and report for duty as soon as Elvis called. Lamar and Cliff, of course, would continue in their familiar roles, Cliff as the comedian always good for a laugh until you got tired of him, Lamar the loyal butt of all jokes. Charlie promised he'd come by as soon as he'd had a chance to visit his mama and daddy in Decatur, no more than a hop, skip, and a jump away. Elisabeth would continue as his private secretary; there was no question of her loyalty, and he knew he could trust her to keep her mouth shut when she was around Anita. Rex was the one he really wanted, though. Rex had been with him all the way and was the lieutenant he needed, the most practical, the best-educated, in his own quiet way the most independent of the group.

Rex for his part was racked with guilt. After breaking off with Elisabeth in a series of painful confusions and misunderstandings, he had finally gotten back together with her just a week before they were scheduled to go. But then Grandma had become ill and Elisabeth had had to take charge of the preparations, so they had less time to themselves than ever, with more than two dozen trunks and suitcases and over two thousand records to pack. They could scarcely look at each other when they were around Elvis without immediately looking away again. Both of them were aware that if either one of them was to work for Elvis Presley, they could not continue their relationship, but Elisabeth was in no mood to go back to her family, who had just been reassigned to the States, and each remained confused and conflicted about how things were going to end.

March 1 dawned raw and gray. There was a press conference scheduled for Elvis at 9:00 A.M. in the enlisted men's club at Ray Barracks in Friedberg. Over one hundred reporters and photographers were present, flinging questions at Elvis almost as he walked in the door seventeen minutes late in a hand-tailored uniform. For the most part the questions were the usual ones: what did he think of his army experience ("I've learned a lot"); any prospects of marriage in the near future (Not really); had he kept a diary ("I haven't kept a diary, but I can tell you any date you would like to know. I would like to write a book"); what about his movie and recording plans? He even received a special certificate of merit from his commanding officer, General Richard J. Brown, citing his "cheerfulness and drive and continually outstanding leadership ability."

All in all, it was a masterful, utterly disarming performance, with the only sign of nervousness on Elvis' part the constant jiggling of his leg under the table. The one hitch came when he was asked about the air force captain's daughter, Priscilla Beaulieu, who was generally believed to be his "16-year-old [sic] girlfriend." Yes, he acknowledged, he had seen her a number of times over the last few months, she was a very pretty brunette with beautiful blue eyes. "She is a very nice girl. Her family is nice, and she is

very mature for her age." That sent reporters rushing to the phones immediately to call the girl's father, who, before making any comment, asked to
know exactly what Sergeant Presley had said, since he wasn't going to say
anything to embarrass either Elvis or his daughter. "There is nothing serious about this," Captain Beaulieu finally declared, after being debriefed.
"The two of them have been great friends. They have had a real nice time
knowing one another. But that is all there is to it."

Toward the end of the news conference Elvis spotted an old friend in
uniform. "Marion!" he called out in utter surprise, recognizing Air Force
Captain Marion Keisker MacInnes, whom he had not seen since she left
Sun Records in the summer of 1957 and who was now stationed in Germany. "Marion," he repeated as she drew closer, "I don't know whether to
kiss you or salute!" "In that order," replied Sam Phillips' former assistant,
who had been the first to welcome him to his original label. When, a little
later, he saw her being reprimanded by an army captain for overfamiliarity
with a noncom, he rushed over to explain that they wouldn't even be having this press conference if it weren't for this lady. "This WAC captain,"
replied the army officer without so much as glancing at her, Marion later
recalled. "Elvis said, 'Well, it's a long story, but she wasn't always a WAC
captain.' Then he held my hand. He was determined that the army wasn't
going to throw me out. That was a very significant thing for me; that was
the first and only time that Elvis indicated publicly that he recognized the
role that I had played."

The calls about Priscilla kept coming in all day. Elvis had lunch and
returned briefly to the barracks to finish up some business, but he was back
at Goethestrasse signing autographs by 5:40 P.M., emerging from the
house several more times in the course of the evening to try to calm his
near-hysterical fans. Priscilla stayed with him till late that night, pleading
with him one last time to consummate their love. He told her that he loved
her and promised that someday they would, when the time was right —
but not now, she was still too young. She returned from Wiesbaden early
the next morning after a sleepless night, and the two of them emerged
from the house at 11:10 A.M. to be hustled past a clutch of screaming fans,
some of whom had never abandoned their post over the course of the long
night. Then Elvis bade a temporary farewell to Priscilla and the rest of the
family — Daddy and Grandma and Elisabeth and Lamar would all be flying out of Frankfurt by commercial airliner later in the day — joining his
fellow GIs on a military bus that would transport them to the air base at

Rhine-Main. Reporters were already lying in wait by the time Priscilla arrived at the base, hurling questions at her, snapping her picture. She was wearing a kerchief knotted around her chin and a demure, high-necked, checked dress under a plain winter coat. She was very fond of Elvis, she repeated over and over again in response to their questioning, but that was all there was to it. "I'm too young for marriage," she had told one reporter the day before, "but I think Elvis is a wonderful boy — so kind, so considerate, such a gentleman. . . . He doesn't drink or smoke and doesn't even use bad words, like some boys do."

At the airstrip she was held back by a cordon of MPs, who would not permit her to say good-bye. Reporters picked up every nuance of this lover's farewell. "More than ten tall Air Force police surrounded Priscilla," reported the *New York Mirror*.

> She cried. She ran towards Elvis, but the policemen pulled her back. . . . "They won't let me see her, they won't let me see her," said Elvis, disappointment written all over his tanned face.
>
> Priscilla fondled the gold wristwatch with a large diamond that Elvis gave her for Christmas.
>
> "He has promised to telephone me as often as he can. Elvis said he would rather telephone than write because he can hear my voice," the Air Force captain's daughter said.

The plane lifted off at 5:25 P.M. and *Life* magazine got a shot of Priscilla waving good-bye. "Girl He Left Behind," was the caption, and it was accompanied by another photograph of "16-year-old" Priscilla in the backseat of the car that had taken them to Ray Barracks, about to bestow "a last kiss [before] they separated."

"When he left, the car ride home was extremely painful. I didn't know if that was the last time I was going to see him, if he would ever call. It was always in my head, you know, why would he even call me? He was going back to Hollywood, and his days would be filled, where I'd be at home, I'd be at school, thinking of nothing but him, writing his name down on a piece of paper every day like a kid. Was it infatuation? Was it illusion? At the time it was very real for me. I was in love, and these were the first [deep] emotions I had ever felt. I wasn't sure if it was a good feeling or not, in a way I didn't like these feelings because I couldn't control them, I just knew they were very painful and very real."

FRANK SINATRA SHOW, MARCH 26, 1960.
(COURTESY OF THE ESTATE OF ELVIS PRESLEY)

ELVIS IS BACK

I T WAS LIKE COMING HOME to a party for which all the places have been laid, all the guests provided with noisemakers and party hats, and only the occasional look of bewilderment on the guest of honor's face betrays a fear that he may somehow have wandered into somebody else's dream.

He was dressed all in black, with just a gold medallion around his neck to provide color and his light brown hair dramatically upswept, at the press conference that took place on the very day of his homecoming. Some fifty reporters crowded into the little building behind the main house at Graceland, which ordinarily served as his father's office. More than one reporter remarked upon the white nylon Christmas tree standing off in a corner with its lights twinkling and what looked like gifts still piled up beneath it, a memento of his last Christmas at home.

"Now, gentlemen," he announced from behind an austere metal desk with a sign that read "The Boss" on it, "I have called you here to discuss a very important matter." He chuckled as the assorted reporters picked up the allusion to one of President Eisenhower's televised news conferences. Then the questions came fast and furious. Had he chosen his first single yet? What had he learned from army life? Was his music going to change?

He carried it off with the same aplomb that he always seemed to keep in reserve for public occasions, declining only to pose with a doll that was thrust upon him from a pile of stuffed animals and other fan tributes. "It would look a little silly for a twenty-five-year-old man home from the army to be playing with dolls," he said, considerably more interested in sharing with reporters his knowledge of karate and more than ready to split a board for them if one could be obtained. "I just can't get it in my mind that I'm here," he said between questions. "I'm hungry, but I haven't even taken time to eat. I just keep walking around and looking." Behind him was a plaque that read, "Let not your heart be troubled. Ye who believe in God believe also in Me," and he smilingly posed for photographers as he cut and sampled a giant white guitar-shaped cake, said to have been baked by fans, that declared "Welcome Home Elvis," with "Hound Dog" and other song titles written in script on the side. He had no immediate plans other than to catch up on his sleep (he hadn't slept in twenty-four hours, he said, he had been so excited about getting home) and to renew old acquaintances. With that, Colonel Parker declared the press conference over, and Elvis retired to his bedroom upstairs in the main house, leaving Colonel to point out the financial intricacies of some of the deals he had made to the reporters who remained.

Anita came over after dinner. He had written to her "that the first night he got home we would not see each other because his family and friends and fans might be offended. So I was at his cousin Patsy Presley's house — I knew Patsy and Aunt Clettes and Uncle Vester were going out there, and I wanted to go so bad, but I knew what he had said. Then he called [and said], 'Come on out, Little, I want to see you.' So I went flying out there — I just can't explain, there are no words to explain the feeling that I had when I saw him again; it was like he'd never left."

Anita quickly made Elisabeth's acquaintance, and, after getting over her initial surprise that the drab, practically orphaned secretary that Elvis had described in phone calls and letters should turn out to be this pretty young girl, immediately started pumping her for information. She invited Elisabeth to spend the night with her sometime soon, and Elisabeth, barely acclimated to her new surroundings and still unsure what to feel about the position Elvis had put her in when he asked her to hide a half-gallon jar of amphetamines in her luggage, happily accepted — but not without hearing from Elvis right away that she had better be careful what she said.

He went to the cemetery the following day to visit his mother's grave. It was the first time that he had seen the Italian statuary that he and his father had commissioned as a monument, with an open-armed Jesus and two kneeling angels at his feet. The inscription on the gravestone read, "She was the Sunshine of Our Home." Afterward he was subdued and depressed, the visit brought back "memories and sadness," but he returned again and again.

He was almost as upset about his father. Vernon had been dodging the press ever since he had arrived in Memphis four days earlier with Grandma, Elisabeth, and an unidentified Dee, who had picked up the train in Virginia. At first denying that he even knew "the mysterious blonde" in dark glasses, kerchief, and a cream-colored coat, he was soon confounded by reporters who had eyes of their own and within a day had admitted to

Press-Scimitar photographer James Reid, "Well, you know I'm not being honest with you. . . . I just can't talk about it yet." Dee stayed out of the way during the press conference and for the next few days, but Elvis could barely wait for them to leave for her brother's house in Huntsville. It was obvious even to reporters that they were planning to get married ("Let's not talk about that just now," Vernon was quoted as saying with a warm laugh), but for now Elvis simply didn't want to think about it. He tearfully visited his mother's room, which on his instructions had been kept exactly as she had left it. "He didn't seem like Elvis," said his aunt Lillian, who came by the house with the rest of the relatives looking for a job two days after his return and went back to work for him the following Monday.

But he *was* Elvis. And if his mother never entirely left his mind, other things were beginning to crowd in on it, too. He felt like a man who had been let out of prison. Just riding around town with Elisabeth on his motorcycle gave him a sense of freedom that he had sometimes thought he would never experience again. On Thursday night he went to the ice show at Ellis Auditorium accompanied by nine or ten girls and half a dozen guys. It was the same company he had seen in Frankfurt the previous year, Holiday on Ice, and he spent most of the evening reminiscing backstage with various members of the troupe. On Friday he dyed his hair black in preparation for the television filming just two weeks away, and he went out motorcycle riding with Lamar. Charlie and Joe showed up at the house, Red and Cliff were scheduled to arrive at any moment, and Anita, Alan Fortas, and George Klein came by after work every day. His cousins Gene and Billy and Junior Smith were constantly at his side, with Gene chattering away in his secret language, somewhere between pig Latin and double-talk, that only Elvis could understand.

The fans, too, were back at the gates. The whole gang in fact was reunited, except for Rex, who had not yet returned from visiting his family to give Elvis his decision about heading up the team. Toward the end of the week Elvis surprised Elisabeth with a car that he had picked out for her, a pretty yellow Lincoln, and even gave her driving lessons in it himself. He also told her she was free now to date others, and for the first time she saw her choice clearly: "I could stay with Elvis and be, only, his private secretary — or I could go with Rex." Without hesitation she called Rex ("I explained to him that I was calling from one of the Graceland phone lines . . . so I couldn't say everything I felt on the phone"), and he promised he would be there in just a few days.

Saturday night Elvis had a big party for all of his friends, taking time out to greet students from the Arkansas School for the Deaf who had shown up at the gate. On Sunday he returned to Ellis and watched the ice show's "performance for Negroes," spending most of his time backstage chatting and signing autographs but mounting the podium briefly in his formal dark suit to conduct the seventeen-piece orchestra with a lighted baton. He surprised everyone by extending an invitation to the entire sixty-member company to come out to Graceland the next day, and when they arrived in the two buses he had rented for the occasion, he greeted them at the door in black slacks and a maroon jacket, presenting each of the children in the troupe with a signed stuffed animal before taking everyone on a personal tour of his home. "If you'd rather just wander around the house, why, that's fine, too," he said. The only rule was that they had to "check [their] flash guns at the door." He was clearly proud of Graceland and proved to be an exemplary host, showing them his bedroom, with its carved figure of an Indian chief, its formal portrait of his mother and father, and Dr. Norman Vincent Peale's *The Power of Positive Thinking* and Dr. John A. Schindler's *How to Live 365 Days a Year* on the bed table next to his oversize bed. He pointed out his gold records and the soda fountain downstairs and proudly declared that there had been talk of Khrushchev coming to visit his home "to see how in America a fellow can start out with nothing and, you know, make good."

Rex showed up that evening while he was dressing to go to the movies, having rented the Memphian Theatre for himself and his friends from eleven o'clock on. "I was very serious about everything as I proceeded to tell him my decision to go to work again for the firm I had left when drafted into the army. I thought Elvis would be very upset with me, but instead he said he understood and wished me the best of luck. . . . I said I would like to spend a couple of days, and he said I could stay as long as I wished, and I would be welcome to come back anytime." Emboldened by his success, Rex next brought up the subject of Elisabeth while helping Elvis with his suspenders. Without alluding to any past connection, he said he would like to ask her out for the evening, maybe take her to a drive-in where they could be apart from the crowd. "Elvis was completely silent for a minute or so, and I held my breath. Finally, he said, 'Rexadus, you know Elisabeth will never love anybody but me,' still looking at himself with great pride and ego." Rex didn't reveal any reaction of his own, simply saying that he figured Elisabeth needed a break every once in a while. Elvis nodded thoughtfully and said he was glad it was Rex taking her out, since he knew he could count on Rex to always treat her like a lady.

Elisabeth left the next day. She told Elvis that she was going to see her parents, who were vacationing in Florida, even though by now everyone in the household knew that she was going off with Rex to meet his family. To throw Elvis even further off the scent, she arranged for Janie Wilbanks, the girl from Mississippi who had visited in Germany, to pick her up at Graceland, but just as they were leaving, Elvis came running out of the house and asked her to come back inside. Elisabeth's heart was pounding, as "Elvis looked [me] straight in the eye and asked if [I] was going to meet Rex." Evidently Cliff had been unable to keep her secret past the moment that she walked out the door, but Elvis chose to believe her when she told him he was just being silly; he knew that she was going to see her parents in Hialeah.

Rex and Elisabeth married less than three months later, sending Elvis a telegrammed invitation. Elisabeth remained in touch with Grandma, but except for a signed photo that he sent the following Christmas, neither she nor Rex ever heard from Elvis again.

ON SUNDAY, MARCH 20, the whole gang left for Nashville in the Greyhound bus the Colonel had chartered for the occasion. The studio was booked under a false name, and some of the musicians were initially told that they would be working a Jim Reeves session. In addition to guitarist Scotty Moore, drummer D. J. Fontana, and the vocal backup group the Jordanaires, who had worked almost every RCA session from the beginning, the band consisted of the same group who had backed Elvis on his last session, while on furlough, in June of 1958. This was Nashville's A team of studio players, made up of pianist Floyd Cramer, brilliant country-jazz guitarist Hank Garland, stand-up bass player Bobby Moore, and percussionist Buddy Harman, who would once again double with D.J. on drums. With RCA executives Steve Sholes and Bill Bullock joining Colonel Parker, his assistant Tom Diskin, Nashville a&r head Chet Atkins, publisher's rep Freddy Bienstock, and engineer Bill Porter in the control booth, the anticipation bordered on outright tension, and it seemed almost eerie, according to Jordanaire Ray Walker, when Elvis finally walked in the back door. "He hadn't made a sound — you couldn't have heard it if he had — but everybody, just like we were on pivots, turned, and there he was."

The first order of business, as it often was at any Elvis session, was to get something to eat, and Lamar was sent out to Krystal's for hamburgers, sweet milk, and fries. There was plenty of time to get reacquainted while they were waiting for the food, and they all listened to acetates and caught up as they ate. "Of course he talked to the guys about Germany and tank battles and all that kind of stuff," observed twenty-eight-year-old newcomer Bill Porter, who had arrived at RCA as chief engineer the previous year after five years of audio engineering on Nashville television station WLAC. "And karate demonstrations. Bobby Moore, the bass player, was also into karate, and he and Elvis got into a demonstration in the studio. This went on for about forty-five minutes." When Elvis finally started on the first tune, Porter sensed the Colonel, Sholes, and Bullock almost breathing down his neck. "They didn't say anything, but they wouldn't sit down until he got it down. [After that] they all started talking about other things."

The first tune, a rousing Otis Blackwell gospel-flavored number called "Make Me Know It," actually required nineteen takes, which must have prolonged the suspense a little, and the second, "Soldier Boy," which Elvis had brought home with him from Germany, took fifteen. With the third, "Stuck On You," a somewhat pedestrian mid-tempo rocker along the lines of "All Shook Up," they hit a groove, and even the difficulties that they encountered nailing down "Fame and Fortune," a kind of doo-wop ballad that Elvis could really sink his teeth into, didn't take away from the overall good feeling of the session.

By this time Porter had recognized that, for all of the big shots in the booth and the veteran musicians on the floor, it was Elvis who was calling the shots. The next-to-last number of the night, "A Mess of Blues," was probably the highlight of the session. Written by Doc Pomus and Mort Shuman, a new Hill and Range team who specialized in rhythm and blues material, it was the one song of the evening to escape formulaic predictability, and its sly sense of having fun with the genre suggested some of the very sense of freedom that had animated all of Elvis' best music from the first. Unlike "Stuck On You," for example, it was tailored to his image without being confined to it, and Elvis' high-spirited whoop at the end, a kind of wobbly falsetto, is almost reminiscent of his joyous exclamation at the conclusion of "Mystery Train." But there was nothing on the session that could not be said to be of a very high standard, and they concluded with an exuberantly dirty "It Feels So Right," whose dissonant chords matched its sexual message, just as the sun was coming up.

RCA wasted no time in capitalizing on the session's success. Within little more than forty-eight hours they had pressed 1.4 million advance orders for the new single ("Stuck On You" and "Fame and Fortune") and shipped them out in preprinted sleeves that announced only "Elvis' 1st New Recording For His 50,000,000 Fans All Over the World" in the absence of definitive titles at the time they had gone to press. They finalized arrangements, too, for a second session to follow the Sinatra taping, which would ensure completion of the album, already entitled *Elvis Is Back* and scheduled for mid-April release, before Elvis' departure for Hollywood. After all the frustrations of dealing with the Colonel, and all the worries that he had caused them, whether intentionally or just for sport, RCA executives Steve Sholes and Bill Bullock finally felt as if they had some breathing space. Judging by his attitude and performance, there seemed little question: *Elvis really was back.*

THE TRAIN TRIP TO MIAMI to tape the television show was little less than a repetition of the triumphant journey home just two weeks earlier. To Scotty Moore, who had seen the crowds from the beginning, "it was just unreal. The only thing I can relate it to was reading about Lincoln's body going back to Springfield or seeing movies of Roosevelt — his body coming out of Georgia after he died. Every little crossroads, every little town; you just can't imagine — they were *lined* with people. Even though you knew the Colonel had gone ahead and let all those little places know, still it was thrilling, just all the way down."

For Scotty the experience so far had had all the characteristics of a true reunion, with the stirring up not only of old memories but of some of the painful confusion that old memories necessarily involve. The train ride was simply more of an extended opportunity to try to recapture some of the feelings of easygoing good fellowship that he and Elvis and D.J. had shared on the road. "Everybody would just get in his car and be kibitzing. At one point it was getting late, it was like two or three in the morning, and he gave D.J. and myself a couple of little white pills and said, 'Here, these'll keep you awake, it's what they use in the army, driving tanks.' I never did take mine — couldn't have been very much. But I had never known him to do that before."

For the rest of the guys there was more of a sense of restless anticipation. For Joe and Lamar, Elvis' cousin Gene, and Peck's bad boy tagalong Cliff Gleaves, there was no question of not staying awake, even if all they were doing was playing cards, eyeing girls, or cracking jokes throughout the long night. For Joe, regarded with some mistrust by Elvis' Memphis sidekicks as a "slick operator" from Chicago, this was in reality his first taste of the big time. The session had introduced him to a whole new world, and now here he was on his way to Miami with the possibility of actually meeting Frank Sinatra. The Colonel, whom he had just met in Nashville, was obviously keeping an eye on him, and he felt in many respects as if he were auditioning for a job whose description he had not yet been given. But he was determined to keep on his toes and take care of business just like he had in Paris, and he figured the old man would accept him in the end. The Colonel for his part stayed mainly within his own little coterie, taking in everything that was going on around him, brusquely making his presence felt — but quietly exulting in the triumph that *his boy* had achieved in Nashville, confident now that nothing was going to stand in their way.

E LVIS AND JOE SHARED a two-bedroom penthouse suite at the Fontainebleau, with everyone else in adjoining rooms and the Colonel just down the hall. The first meeting between host and guest star in the Grand Ballroom was carefully staged, with Elvis dressed jauntily in a beige sports jacket and black fedora and Frank studiedly cool in baseball cap and sweater. Sinatra's pal, comedian Joey Bishop, unctuously requested an autograph for his niece and got word back from the Colonel that there would be a charge of $1, while Sammy Davis, Jr., who had hung out with Elvis when he first came to Hollywood, greeted his old friend with undisguised, and unabashed, delight. Elvis spent the week nightclubbing and rehearsing, with the guys in constant attendance, but Scotty and D.J. and the Jordanaires (the rest of the band was picked up in Miami) were specifically excluded from all social activities by order of the Colonel.

The night of the taping, it was Frank, forced after all to swallow his intemperate criticism of rock 'n' roll to build a show around its principal representative, who appeared the more embarrassed of the two. It was not so much that he had changed his mind about the music, he was at pains to reassure the press. "But after all, the kid's been away two years and I get the feeling he really believes in what he's doing." As for Elvis, faced with a situation which could very well have become a repetition of the Steve Allen debacle, where he sang "Hound Dog" to a basset while dressed in top hat and tails, he carried himself with dignity, anchoring a creaky, almost painfully self-referential "Rat Pack" reunion (only Dean Martin was missing from the Sinatra gang) with an eight-minute appearance almost forty minutes into the show.

"Well, Elvis, that's our little welcome home gift," Sinatra declares. "All you seem to have lost is your sideburns." And then, turning to the audience: "Now, folks, what would you say if I was to sing another song now?" "No," come the carefully cued screams from the four hundred fan club presidents and members who have gotten their tickets from the Colonel. "WE WANT ELVIS!!" And with that the man of the hour comes slinking out from the wings, ducking his head and laughing self-consciously, his hair piled up like a waterfall, looking impossibly fresh, impossibly elegant in his perfectly draped tuxedo.

It is a marvelous performance of two fairly mediocre songs, his movements so subdued during the ballad ("Fame and Fortune") that even the planted audience does not know quite how to react. But then as he launches into "Stuck On You," we do, indeed, see a new Elvis, a modified Elvis, who suggests motion without precipitating it, who elicits genuine screams by indirection rather than assault. Sinatra at this point comes out for what is undoubtedly intended to be the knock-out punch, a two-song medley, with Frank singing one of Elvis' songs, Elvis one of Frank's. The older man opens with "Love Me Tender" and, by attempting to parody it, merely parodies himself; then Elvis launches into Sinatra's sophisticated "Witchcraft," for which he shows utter respect, indicating by a shake of his shoulders, the limp extension of his wrists, his bemused acceptance of a task which he is prepared to perform with elegance and humility. They conclude by harmonizing on the last lines of "Love Me Tender," then repeat the harmony after Frank declares, "Man, that's pretty." And that's it, except for a little additional comic dialogue and a plug that the Colonel has arranged for the upcoming production of *G.I. Blues.* It is, all in all, an amazing performance, and one that must have been deeply satisfying to a performer who had been worried whether he still had a place in show business. The subsequent ratings (the show broadcast a month and a half later, on May 12, with a 41.5 Trendex rating, representing a 67.7-percent audience share) can only have made the triumph all the sweeter.

And then it was back to Memphis — by chartered bus this time, as the Colonel felt the train gimmick had been played out, and funds were not unlimited. There was a week to go before the follow-up session in Nashville, and Elvis got a letter from the Colonel not long after getting home, running down some of the things that he should keep in mind when he went back into the studio. All that he had to deliver in order to fulfill his contractual obligation to RCA were eight additional tracks. With four cuts in the can and a single already released, this would give the record company everything that it needed to put out an album, and *he should record no more.* It was the same set of rules that had always guided them; they didn't want to give RCA any more leverage in future contract negotiations than they had in the past. So far as material went, Scotty had made the standard deal required of any outside musical contractor: he had given up half the publishing to Elvis Presley Music and assigned one-third of the writer's royalties to Elvis Presley himself. Under these circumstances, Colonel advised, Elvis should do all he could to record Scotty's song. Also, Colonel had directed Freddy to clear "Fever" at a favorable royalty rate, along with "Are You Lonesome Tonight?," the first song that Colonel had ever directly asked Elvis to record. He knew it was old-fashioned, he told Elvis, a ballad with a dramatic recitation that had first been a hit in 1927, but he thought it could be right for Elvis' "new style," and he had a hunch that it could be a hit all over again. Elvis knew how much it meant to the Colonel both because Gene Austin, the first singer Colonel ever managed, used to feature it in his stage act and because it was his wife, Marie's, favorite song — he probably would have done it just as a sentimental gesture. But he actually liked the song. The rest of the content of Colonel's letter left him less sanguine. The press had gotten wind of the fact that Dee and her children were living at Graceland, the Colonel advised him soberly, so it would probably be better not to set up any appointments at the house. He also wanted to call Elvis' attention to the fact that Joe's record keeping for the Miami trip had been sloppy and inefficient, and while this was entirely Elvis' business, if Colonel were to run *his* business this way, he wouldn't last very long.

The second session, on April 3, started once again at 7:30 on a Sunday evening and went straight through till morning. It was the same lineup of backing musicians as the last time, with the addition of saxophonist Homer "Boots" Randolph, a regular member of the Nashville A team who could double on percussion if saxophone wasn't called for on a song. Elvis' old drummer, D. J. Fontana, and Buddy Harman both continued to play drums, with Harman steadying D.J.'s time, and on the first track, "Fever," it was just bassist Bobby Moore and the two drummers providing a seductive backdrop for Elvis' interpretation of the 1956 Little Willie John r&b hit, which had enjoyed even greater success as a torch song for Peggy Lee two years later. Elvis' version falls somewhere in between the two, with a warmth and intimacy that stems not just from the erotic suggestion of the song but from a new vocal confidence and a new vocal control. By the time that they got to "It's Now or Never," the rewritten version of "O Sole Mio" that Freddy had commissioned, it was obvious that Elvis was reaching for something more than he had ever attempted before, and he delivered several performances that were impressive right up till the moment that he had to achieve the full-voiced operatic cadence with which the aria concludes. Trying to be helpful, Bill Porter suggested that they could always splice the ending on. "I said, 'We don't need to do the song all the way through.' He said, 'Bill, I'm going to do it all the way through, or I'm not going to do it.' And he finally did."

Over the course of the long evening they cut an extraordinarily diverse range of material — blues, ballads, standard pop fare from Hill and Range that he elevated by his passion, "Such a Night," done as a lilting tribute to Clyde McPhatter, much in the manner of "White Christmas," the Drifters homage on his 1957 Christmas album, for which he had been so roundly reviled by the critics. It was only as the session wound to a close, and with the Colonel's requisite eight cuts already under his belt, that he finally got around to the number that his manager had requested, along with the song Scotty had brought in, "Girl Next Door Went A'Walking," and the Golden Gate Quartet tune he had promised Charlie they would sing as a duet despite Colonel's opposition.

He started with "Are You Lonesome Tonight?" at around 4:00 A.M., with just acoustic guitar, drums, and bass, the mood of the song strikingly similar to "My Happiness," the very first song he had ever recorded. He asked Chet Atkins if the lights could be turned down. "He chased everybody out of the studio, all the guests and everything — you know, studios back then were like supermarkets with bright fluorescent lighting, but he was singing in the dark." As this was going on, Bill Porter was editing the master take off the last reel and splicing it onto a master reel so that at the end of the session all the agreed-upon versions would be in a single place. "Well, I turned around and looked in the studio, and the lights were all out, and I couldn't see what the hell was going on, and then I hear the guitar and the bass and the Jordanaires humming a little bit, and Elvis started to sing. And then suddenly he starts talking right in the middle of it! If you listen closely, you'll hear them bumping the microphone stands because there were no lights out there. So we started the take again, and he got about, oh, maybe two or three bars into it, and Elvis said, 'Mr. Sholes, throw that tune out, I can't do it justice.' Steve looks at me and says, 'Don't you dare, that's a hit, Bill.' He pushed the talkback button and said, 'The Jordanaires made a mistake, and I'd like to get one good take all the way through.'" So they did that, and that became the master, right up to the final bar.

After that he made short work of Scotty's tune, then summoned Charlie into the studio for their touching duet on "I Will Be Home Again." With eleven cuts in the can and the musicians almost out on their feet (this was not the end but the beginning of their working day: they had at least three Monday sessions scheduled), Elvis was in no mood to quit. He began strumming Lowell Fulson's "Reconsider Baby," an old blues that he had fooled around with at Sun, on his Gibson J-200, and despite themselves, everyone just fell in. Just as on the Sun sides, Elvis' rhythm guitar takes the lead, and piano, sax, and guitar all get gritty solos, but what carries the song is the manner in which Elvis' voice soars, giving the blues a kind of harmonic freedom that recalls no one so much as Little Junior Parker but in the end is Elvis' mark alone.

WITH JUST TWO WEEKS to go before leaving for Hollywood, Elvis occupied himself mainly with roller-skating wars at the Rainbow Rollerdrome, touch football games, moviegoing, and dating Anita. One night he called up gospel singer James Blackwood, one of his earliest inspirations, who used to admit him to the all-night singings at Ellis Auditorium for free when he was a teenager and with whom he had always stayed in touch. "He said, 'First night y'all have off and are not doing a concert, why don't you come out and let's sing?' We sang most of the night, all gospel, he wouldn't do anything else. I think he knew every song we ever recorded." He spoke of the gospel album he was planning to make before the year was out. He only hoped he would be worthy of the task.

The first Saturday after the session, he went on a $4,000 shopping spree downtown, looking for a birthday present for his father. Somehow the fact that one of his purchases was a diamond necklace for Anita was immediately picked up by the papers, and both he and Anita spent much of the next few days denying that the gift meant anything special. He was in fact already dating another Memphis girl without Anita's knowledge, a nineteen-year-old singer and beauty contest winner named Bonnie Bunkley, whom he had met when she arrived at Graceland with her voice teacher to collect a teddy bear he had donated for a benefit at Whitehaven High School, her alma mater. They hit it off right away, and she would come by sometimes when he told Anita that he wanted to spend time by himself. He had an aquarium in the music room upstairs, and often they would just sit by themselves and listen to records and watch the fish in the tank. He got depressed sometimes for no reason, he said, his mother's memory was always with him. He was moodier than she would ever have thought from observing him in public, but he was always considerate of her and her feelings. Anita was never mentioned when she was around, and he asked if she and her mother might come to visit while he was making his movie in California.

Anita dyed her hair black to match his, and on Easter Sunday, April 17, the day before his scheduled departure, they attended the First Assembly of God Church together, where Elvis' presence caused such a commotion that they had to leave the service. Then it was off to Hollywood on another triumphant three-day whistle-stop trip, this time aboard the Southern Pacific's *Sunset Limited*. The party of eleven occupied two private cars at a cost of $2,424.41 and, in addition to the Colonel's three-man staff, incorporated a personal retinue of six, including Joe, Gene, and Lamar, with newcomer Sonny West (Red's cousin) and last-minute addition Charlie Hodge. Charlie had been visiting for the last couple of weeks and accompanied them to the train. "We hadn't talked about me working with him or anything. So Mr. Presley and I are standing there and Elvis was standing at the door of the train, and he was waiting on his cousin Gene. And Elvis looked down and said, 'You want to go with me?' and I looked at him and I said, 'Why not?' And he said, 'Daddy, put him on salary!'"

Elvis had made it clear from the beginning that it was loyalty he was concerned about most of all. "What he said on the ship over to Germany was, 'Charlie, as long as you're cool' — he was talking about the press and all kinds of things like that — 'we can be friends for a long time.'" With Sonny and the others the same consideration applied. Sonny, three years younger than Elvis and just behind Red, with whom he was raised almost as a brother, at Humes High, had first met Elvis in March 1958 a few weeks after his discharge from the air force and just days before Elvis went into the service himself. His initiation had come in one of those vicious games of roller mayhem at the Rainbow, with Junior Smith refereeing and Sonny, a rugged ex-football player and boxer, ending up on the floor, decked by a girl. By the time that Elvis got out of the army, Sonny was dating Elvis' double first cousin Patsy Presley, and it seemed only natural that he would start coming around. Elvis liked him from the start. He could use another good-natured, down-to-earth, physical type of guy to help take care of some of the simple tasks and problems that were always coming up; his only reservation about Sonny, he told Red at the time, was Sonny's language. "He's a heck of a nice guy . . . but he never stops saying 'sonofabitch.' He calls everyone 'sonofabitch.' I just [wish] he would stop saying it all the time."

Elvis took special pride in the guys he had around him. They proved you didn't need to surround yourself with college-educated "intellectuals." These down-home southern boys (with Joe the only exception — and he had Chicago "street" connections) were all smart, dedicated, and could take care of themselves. Cliff was a "character"; Red (who, like Cliff, was waiting for them in California, where he was working on Nick Adams' new television series, *The Rebel*) was a good old boy; Lamar capably filled the role of court jester; Charlie had show-biz connections; and Gene was family. Elvis tried to get Alan Fortas to come along with them on this trip, too, but Alan's family was still opposed. Elvis knew he would join up before too long, however; Alan wanted to be a part of things too much to risk being permanently left out.

They all had their individual identities, they all had their personal idiosyncrasies and specially delineated roles. Elvis was proud of having assembled a team much like the Colonel's, a group of guys with whom he could be comfortable and share some laughs and not have to worry about who he was or where he fit in. From Sonny's point of view, "I guess you could say we were a bunch of hicks, [but] there was a great warmth between us. No pettiness, just a bunch of young guys setting out for some excitement and going to conquer the world. It was fantastic, and the guy who was most fantastic was Elvis."

In his own role as leader Elvis maintained a somewhat different perspective. A leader, he knew, had a different role; a leader had to provide direction, inspiration, coalescence; most of all a leader had to believe in himself. He was aware, certainly, of the personality conflicts within the group. Joe had a very low opinion of Lamar; Charlie was seen as little more than a know-it-all by a number of the guys; Lamar was so devoted as to be jealous of anybody else who got Elvis' attention; and nobody but a blood relative would ever have understood Gene. Others might take this division as a drawback, but Elvis saw it as what the Colonel called "creative conflict." In an imperfect world one basic principle always applied: divide and conquer. This was his world, a comfortable space with a rattle and clatter all its own, its own constant hum of anticipation and excitement. When asked by a former girlfriend, Barbara Hearn, to name his pet likes and dislikes for a column she was now writing for the fan magazine 16, he came up with enthusiasm for sports, staying up all night, fried foods, listening to old rhythm and blues 78s, Marlon Brando, making movies, and, above all, "having lots of people around me at all times." Among his dislikes were conformists, humorless sourpusses, insincerity, being alone, and not being able to attend church regularly. "I hate it most of all that my mother was not at home on my discharge from the Army. She prayed for that day so many times. It didn't seem right to return to a home without her."

THE CROWDS ON THE WAY out to California were almost as overwhelming as on his two previous train trips, and Elvis had to disembark at a siding outside Union Station in Los Angeles, for fear that some of his fans might get hurt. He reported for preproduction on April 21 and that night went out to a club in the Valley, the Crossbow, to see Lance LeGault, a Louisiana boy who Red said was a great rhythm and blues singer. They sat up in the closed-off balcony digging the music — Ray Charles, Jimmy Reed, Fats Domino, all the good old sounds — and in between sets Red introduced him to club owner Tony Ferra. There was a picture of Tony's pretty fourteen-year-old daughter, Sandy, on the club owner's desk, and when Elvis asked about her, Tony picked up the phone and gave her a call. "My dad said, 'I want you to meet Elvis Presley,' and put him on the phone, and he said, 'Your father told me about you, and I'd like to meet you.' It was ten o'clock at night, and I had school the next day, so I said, 'I'm sorry, I can't tonight.' And he said, 'Well, maybe some other time.'" Then he and the guys went back to the hotel, and Sandy Ferra thought she would never hear from him again.

"Stuck On You" hit number one the following week, a foregone conclusion after the preshipment of over a million copies to dealers, which was more a statement of confidence on RCA's part than a true reflection of sales, since the dealers could always ship them back. Elvis made his initial recordings for the soundtrack of G.I. Blues, too, but due to a new union agreement, he was forced to record at the RCA studio on Hollywood Boulevard rather than at Radio Recorders, where he knew the room, liked the people, and had grown to feel comfortable. For Elvis it was an altogether unsatisfactory situation, and on May 6 he went back to the old studio to redo half the songs after a week's worth of shooting on the film.

To assistant engineer Bones Howe it was a very different Elvis who returned to Radio Recorders than the one who had left two years before. "He came to the studio in full-dress uniform, with the piping around the sleeves [presumably his costume for the film], and all these guys around him, a whole new cast of characters. I was flabbergasted. He looked great, he had everything he could want, all the same people were there — but it just wasn't the same." Howe detected an absence of spontaneity, a searching for the spark rather than its actual presence. "It was like, 'Wait a minute. How did I do this? What was it I did?' Maybe through being away all that time he'd had [too much of] a chance to think about what he'd been doing and tried to figure out what it was. But something was gone."

Elvis himself seemed to sense that there was something missing from the movie from the start. With the exception of Pomus and Shuman's "Doin' the Best I Can," written in conscious emulation of songwriter Don Robertson's elegantly austere style, the songs for the most part were an undistinguished lot, and Elvis was disappointed at the exclusion of Jerry Leiber and Mike Stoller's compositions from the soundtrack for what the Colonel described as "business" reasons. In a phone call to Priscilla in Germany, amid fond endearments, he expressed his bitter frustration about the score. He had just had a meeting with Colonel Parker, he said, and informed him that half the songs in the picture should be cut. What did the Colonel say? Priscilla wondered. "Hell, what could he say? I'm locked into this thing," Elvis replied miserably, and they went back to talking about how someday she would be able to come over and see all of this for herself, dreamily planning for a future that was hard for either of them to believe would ever really exist.

By this time, though, he had met Sandy Ferra, and he was intrigued. He had called her a second time from her father's nightclub and got the same answer as the first: it was late, it was a school night, there was no way she could come out to meet him at this hour. Well, how about if they made a date for the *next* Thursday? he asked. Maybe her mother could drive her over. "So I asked my mom, and she said okay. They had the whole upstairs roped off for him, and he had a date that night with an actress named Kathy Kersh. So there I was with my little ponytail, and he held my hand and smiled at me. And I don't remember exactly what our conversation was, because this very attractive woman was on the other side of him. But then he said, 'I'd like to see you again,' and he kissed me good night on the cheek when my mom took me home.

"A few days later Red West called and said, 'Elvis is having a party at the Beverly Wilshire Hotel, and he'd like you to come.' My mom said, 'No way. I don't care who he is — you're not going.' She talked to him and said, 'I don't care if you're King Farouk; my daughter is more important to me.' And he said, 'You know, I have a career, and I know your daughter is underage, and I promise you I'll respect her.' So my mom came on the date — I mean, she came with me. I thought, Well, you know, he's probably never going to want to talk to me again. I mean, how embarrassing! But he *liked* my mom. We sat in the kitchen in his Beverly Wilshire Hotel suite, and we had banana splits. And he was talking to my mom and telling her how much he missed his mom. He really liked talking to her; they had this great understanding.

"A few days later he called again. I thought he'd never call, and he called again, and my mom said, well, I could go, as long as I took another girl with me. So I would invite one or two girlfriends to go with me, and that was okay for a while, and then eventually she trusted him and let me start seeing him by myself, and I dated him for years."

The age difference never really struck her, though the difference in their professional circumstances did. Sandy was enrolled at the Hollywood Professional School, and she was flattered when he told her that she was a better dancer than his beautiful twenty-three-year-old South African co-star, Juliet Prowse, whose ballet training had led to her discovery by Hollywood choreographer Hermes Pan. She never thought of visiting him on the set, though, and she was under no illusions about using their friendship to advance her career. At the same time she felt perfectly comfortable in his company. "He was a very *young* twenty-four. I mean, he and the guys played like teenagers, they'd have water fights and chase each other through the halls and play hide-and-seek — kid stuff. So he didn't really seem older, and he didn't *act* older. We danced a lot — we'd dance and neck for hours, and then I'd go home. Sometimes we'd kiss for so long that my skin would be bright red, and I'd have to put makeup on my face for school the next day.

"You know, it was really strange. There were always all these other women. On nights when we had dates, I would be sitting there in my frilly little dresses, and girls would come in that would be half undressed, they'd tremble and they'd shake and they'd cry and they'd just go bonkers. But I felt pretty secure sitting there because he'd called *me,* because he wanted to see *me.* I mean, it never really bothered me, because the way I was raised, these other girls could do things that I wasn't going to do — nor did he ask me to. So I figured, *somebody's* got to be there for him to date in a more adult fashion, because I wasn't ready for anything like that. So we just had fun, and I think — I don't know, maybe he dated me because he didn't feel he had to be this Valentino, he didn't have to perform for me other than just to have fun, kiss me good night, then he could go to sleep and get up and go do his movie the next day. Whereas when he was dating these other women that were really women, I'm sure they expected more of him than I did. He told me that he felt very relaxed — tranquil — when he was with me."

Bonnie Bunkley, the girl he'd met in Memphis, came out with her mother for a weeklong visit, and he took them on the set where Dean Martin and Shirley MacLaine were filming *All in a Night's Work.* She met Currie Grant, too, the airman who had introduced Elvis to Priscilla in Germany, and Elvis said to him, "Doesn't she look like Priscilla?" Which kind of made her mad, even though she didn't know who Priscilla was. But otherwise he was a model host and never gave her reason to think he was anything but a perfect gentleman.

For Elvis and the guys on their own, on the other hand, Hollywood was just an open invitation to party all night long. Sometimes they would hang out with Sammy Davis, Jr., or check out Bobby Darin at the Cloister. Nick Adams and his gang came by the suite all the time, not to mention the eccentric actor Billy Murphy, longtime friend of John Wayne and Robert Mitchum, who traveled up and down Hollywood Boulevard invariably clutching the battered script about Billy the Kid that he had been working on for years. Elvis outfitted all of the guys in sunglasses and dark clothing, and they carried around briefcases so it would look like they had something to do. Gene's briefcase contained a hairbrush and a doorknob, and he had taken to wearing makeup and calling himself by a stage name, El Gino Stone; if anyone ever asked him about his duties, he said, "I don't do a goddamn thing. I'm Elvis Presley's cousin."

"None of us," by Joe's account, "slept more than a few hours at a time. We lived on amphetamines. We woke at five o'clock each morning to report to the set, then spent the rest of our time screwing around." Just as at the Hotel Grunewald in Germany, their escapades were beginning to grate on other residents of the hotel. Joe was not surprised. "Music blared

continuously. . . . We ferried Hollywood starlets up and down in the elevators all day and all night. Elvis was breaking boards in his suite and trying to
teach the rest of us karate, [and] when we weren't trying to break boards,
we were running around the halls, waging water-gun fights that escalated
into full-scale battles."

With the idea of pursuing his karate studies more assiduously, Elvis
attended a demonstration by kenpo karate master Ed Parker at the Beverly
Hills Hotel. Parker, a twenty-nine-year-old native of Honolulu with a
degree in sociology from Brigham Young University, had developed a flexible new "street" approach to the art, and after his demonstration to a group
of doctors, Elvis came up to him. "He said, 'I don't think you know me, but
my name is Elvis Presley,' and I kind of laughed." He told Parker that he
had studied karate while he was in the army and that he had subsequently
been in contact with Hank Slamansky, an American karate pioneer, but
that he saw in Parker's methods real creativity and innovation.

"He felt like I was kind of a rebel in my field, as he was in his. I didn't
accept a lot of the Oriental methods, because I knew they didn't work on
the street, but a lot of the other aspects could be revamped so they would
be applicable." They spent some time out by the pool, talking about karate
and the Islands, about Parker's royal Polynesian heritage and his Mormon
beliefs. "His mother meant an awful lot to him, and he talked about how
she kept him from physical activity for fear he might get injured or hurt.
Now that she was gone, he found karate to be an avenue of pursuit that he
wanted to be involved in, because he wanted the activity and the knowledge that stemmed from it. He talked to me about the fact that he was different than others. He was basically a very shy guy." Parker offered to give
him lessons, and they discussed technique ("He was intrigued with the
logic of what I taught"), but despite occasional contact over the succeeding
months, and despite Elvis' continuing passion for the sport, it would be
years before he finally applied to Parker for formal instruction.

He remained resolutely professional in his commitment to the film,
though it became harder to hide his underlying resentment with each passing day. Colonel kept reassuring him that it was going to be a big success,
that it would enable him to reach an older audience at a time when his own
audience was growing older — but that didn't make him feel any better
about the script, or the image of him that the script presented, which were
the key elements that Colonel and Mr. Wallis were counting on to allow
this expansion to occur. The character that Elvis played was at odds not just

with the characters that he had played in all of his pre-army films but with the very image of rebellion that had always defined him. Far from being an outcast, this Elvis Presley was safe, "social," and cheerfully domesticated, a conventionally bland Hollywood stick figure whose principal conflict comes in the ethics of "dating" a nightclub dancer (Juliet Prowse) in order to win a bet. The girl turns out to be unexpectedly down-to-earth, the army tank corps man that Elvis portrays proves as adept at baby-sitting as at seduction, there is plenty of sightseeing footage of Germany, and the highlight of the score comes at a puppet show for children when Elvis' character improvises a song. It is, in other words, a genuinely *wholesome* entertainment, a motion picture for the entire family, and not really all that far removed from those aspects of the real Elvis Presley that aspired to middle-class respectability. But it did not even begin to suggest the complexity of either the real Elvis or the real world that Elvis had come to know, and his feelings of foolishness and humiliation were not helped by the guys smirking over some of the "cute" bits he was given to do and his ineffectual attempts to control his amphetamine-racing speech.

They observed his romantic escapades with a somewhat keener degree of interest and respect. He was dating Judy Rawlins, an actress with a small part in the picture, and he met Tuesday Weld, the sixteen-year-old "sex kitten" who was about to start shooting *Return to Peyton Place,* around this time as well. But it was his relationship with Juliet Prowse, his co-star and Frank Sinatra's unofficial fiancée, with which his growing entourage was most intrigued at this time. Elvis made a big point of withdrawing to his dressing room with her every day, and before long the guys started banging on the door and yelling that Frank was on his way. One day Sinatra actually did show up, but Elvis emerged unruffled and unmussed after first telling Red to go fuck himself when he heard the same tiresome message once again. They were all intrigued by Elvis' stories of Juliet's athletic limberness, Lamar perhaps most of all. "He said Juliet liked to grab her ankles and spread her legs real wide. But then [later] he said it about another girl, too. I said, 'I thought that was Juliet.' And he said, 'Well, a lot of 'em do different things like that.' And I said, 'Oh, okay.'"

There was a steady stream of visitors on the set, arranged for the most part by the Colonel: Elvis greeted the king and queen of Thailand, Tennessee Ernie Ford and Minnie Pearl, the wife and daughter of the Brazilian president, Pat Boone, and three Scandinavian princesses in one day. The Colonel made a particular point of claiming credit for the royalty, citing it to Wallis as an example of the kind of tireless dedication he gave to thinking up new ways to promote the film. As he sat in the headquarters which Paramount had given him free of charge and surveyed the three rooms plastered with Elvis Presley album covers and sheet music, life-sized cutouts of the boy, and various items of merchandise large and small, the record player that he had gotten from RCA never ceased its steady stream of Elvis Presley hits. He had his own "wall of fame," on which he was pictured with celebrities from every walk of life, and his sense of overall well-being is reflected in interviews that he gave out at this time which for the first time focused on the Colonel alone.

Grizzled, unshaven, dressed in an untucked Hawaiian shirt, sandals, and a whimsical beanie, he made no apologies for himself as he entertained reporters' questions and detailed the business successes that he had achieved in guiding his boy's career. Yes, they were asking $150,000 for television guest shots now, but he didn't expect to do any, he didn't want Elvis competing with his own movies. As far as the movies themselves went, he doubted that they would win any Academy Awards. "All they're good for is to make money." As for the money, "He relies on straight income, and so do I. When he works, he knows that about 90 cents out of every dollar that he earns goes to the government and a dime to him." The Colonel was in the 90-percent tax bracket, too, he implied, but, far from looking for any loopholes, he and Elvis took the attitude that "We're luckier than a whole lot of people, even as things are. . . . Somebody's got to pay the government for the country we've got."

It was almost as if he were speaking to an unseen audience; crude, blustering, crassly honest to a degree that appears as defiant of public opinion as reflective of it, he seems bound to proclaim his patriotism, his integrity, his *honesty* in a subtext that underscores every wisecrack he throws out. There was no question of his gruff affection for his client, but he made clear that they did not socialize, and he didn't handle Elvis' finances either. That was his father, Vernon's, job. "I'm not his father. . . . Our interests are different. And he doesn't need a nursemaid. . . . I just tell him, 'Don't forget to pay your taxes.' I tell him that every week when he's working. I've seen too many people get into bad trouble by forgetting to pay their taxes." And if the balloon ever burst? "He could go back to driving a truck. And I could always go back to being a dogcatcher. Head dogcatcher, that is."

Elvis must have smiled when he read some of the stories, if he even bothered to follow all the "snow jobs" the Colonel was handing out. He had heard it all before: the pet cemetery in Tampa; the Snowmen's League, the phantom organization in which Colonel had enlisted half of Hollywood;

the carny stories where the customer was always the mark; the movie that would someday be made of the *Colonel's* life (it would probably be produced by Bob Hope, he told Louella Parsons); all the ways in which he managed to bedevil poor Mr. Wallis and Mr. Hazen and then just flung it back at them when they finally capitulated to his demands. Colonel was a funny duck, there was no doubt about that — it was Elvis' little joke to call him Admiral, since he had no more claim on one title than on the other. He had his own ways and he stuck to them, you had to admire that about him. But more than anything else, *it had all turned out exactly like he said it would.* Elvis knew that Colonel was just having fun now, and his attitude was, Let the old man have a good time. He certainly was having a good time himself.

They took off for Las Vegas on the weekend that they finished shooting. The studio would not release Elvis until the following week, after all the footage had been screened, so he decided they should treat themselves to a little vacation. They had visited once during filming, and the boys were all excited about going back, but they had only gotten as far as Barstow when Elvis asked Gene for his kit bag. He mumbled something about wanting to brush his teeth, but everyone knew that was where he kept his pills, and when it turned out that Gene had forgotten the bag, Elvis got so angry that he had the whole caravan turn around and head back to L.A., cursing and yelling at Gene and the rest of the guys all the way.

Everyone was tired and depressed. Sonny, who had been as excited as any of them, watched while Elvis drove and smacked Gene in the chest every time he dozed off. "There will be no goddamn sleep, do you hear?" he announced as Gene jerked awake and indicated assent. "Joe in the back is dozing off," recalled Sonny, "and chewing gum at the same time. 'Joe, goddamnit, I said no sleeping.' Joe replies, 'I wasn't sleeping, just looking out the window.'" By the time they got back to the Beverly Wilshire, everybody had pretty much had it. It was early in the morning, and they all drifted off to bed. Just as they started to fall asleep, the phone rang. It was Joe. Now that he had retrieved his bag, Elvis had changed his mind; they were going to Las Vegas after all.

It was a long weekend. Elvis dropped $10,000 at the crap tables, and they went to all the shows, catching Billy Ward and the Dominoes at the Dunes, Della Reese at the New Frontier, and Red Skelton at the Sands. The guys all wore their black mohair suits and sunglasses, there were more girls than you could trip over, and they got maybe two hours' sleep the whole weekend. The joke around town was that they were Elvis' "Memphis Mafia."

He was finally released by the studio the following Wednesday, June 29, and was so impatient to get home that he and Gene took a plane to St. Louis late that night, then rented a Cadillac and arrived at Graceland at three o'clock the following afternoon. Anita came over as soon as she was done with work, the papers reported, and they had a quiet evening at home with Gene and his wife, Louise, and Vernon, who was for the moment on his own but left the following day to join Dee at her brother's house in Huntsville. They were going to get married, he told Elvis. They were going to do it in Huntsville to try to throw reporters off the track. Elvis shrugged and wished him luck. He wouldn't attend the ceremony, he said, because he didn't want to take away from the attention that should go to Dee. Both of them knew that what he said wasn't what he really meant, but neither of them knew how to address their true feelings. They spoke briefly of transferring ownership of the house, so it would be in Elvis' name alone, but mostly they communicated in nods and silences, and in a shared sadness which neither could express.

Vernon and Dee got married that Sunday, July 3. The following day Elvis went to the cemetery on his motorcycle and was almost run down by a girl who spotted him kneeling by his mother's grave in prayer. "She spoke to me using a lot of jive talk," he was quoted in the *Press-Scimitar.* "She asked me where I would be later. I told her that she didn't need to use that kind of language, especially in the cemetery. I guess I was feeling a little depressed. As I was leaving a little later, she came back in the cemetery and swerved toward my motorcycle." She was smiling, he said, as if it were all a joke.

He bought a boat, went waterskiing out on McKellar Lake, just like he used to with his first love, Dixie Locke; he did all the same things, went to the movies, rented the Fairgrounds, took over the Rainbow for roller-skating parties — it wasn't the same. Toward the end of the month Vernon and Dee came home from their honeymoon and moved into Graceland with her three kids. He continued to speak well of Dee for public consumption. "She seems to be a pretty nice, understanding type of person," he had said when news of the marriage first began to leak out. "She treats me with respect, just as she does Daddy. She realizes she could never be my mother. I only had one mother and that's it. There'll never be another. As long as she understands that, we won't have any trouble." As for Vernon, "If he can find happiness in some way, I'm all for him. . . . He is my father, and he's all I got left in the world. I'll never go against him or stand in his way. He stood by me all these years and sacrificed things he wanted so that I could have clothes and lunch money to go to school. I'll stand by him now — right or wrong."

He felt sometimes as if there were a weight pressing down on him that he could no longer bear. He was surrounded by friends and relatives, all dependent on him, all looking to him for help, for guidance, for hand-outs — for something. He could give them jobs, he could dispense money and favors, on the surface they all deferred to him, and he was clearly the one in charge — but in his darkest moments he suspected that it was all a masquerade, they were like bluebottle flies buzzing around a dung heap, with no more loyalty to him than a fly would feel. His uncles Travis, Johnny, and Vester, his aunt Lillian, his cousins Harold Loyd, Gene, Junior, Bobby, and Billy Smith, even his daddy, were in a state of constant con-tention, it sometimes seemed — Bobby using his name to pass bad checks, Daddy falling out with Travis and Vester over one thing or another, Lillian accusing Daddy of being tight with his money, one uncle getting drunk and opening the gates, inviting everyone in off the street, other relatives just taking the money he offered them without thanks, blowing it, and then coming back for more. With his father's new wife in the house, he felt as if there were a cloud hanging over him and over his mother's memory, and he left almost as soon as they arrived.

H E SPENT A WEEK in Las Vegas before having to go back to work. The new picture, *Black Star* (it was retitled *Flaming Star* after shoot-ing had been completed), was the first of the two back-to-back productions the Colonel had sold to Twentieth Century Fox, and was a straight dra-matic role. Originally intended as a vehicle for Marlon Brando, with a script by respected writers Clair Huffaker (author of the novel on which it was based) and Nunnally Johnson (screenwriter of *The Grapes of Wrath*), it reunited Elvis with producer David Weisbart, who had shown such faith in him in his first movie, *Love Me Tender,* and brought in talented forty-eight-year-old Don Siegel (who had made the original *Invasion of the Body Snatch-ers*) to direct. Everyone connected with the production saw it as a serious picture; Siegel in fact had initially objected to the selection of a leading man who in his view was widely considered to be "a laughingstock," until Weisbart, whose great success had come with James Dean's *Rebel Without a Cause*, overcame his objections. There was to be a minimum of songs (four were recorded at the soundtrack session on August 8, and in the end only two were used); there was a socially progressive, if somewhat confusing, story line in which Elvis played Pacer, a "half-breed" caught between two worlds; there was extensive location shooting scheduled and a fine supporting cast, including veteran actors Steve Forrest, John McIntire, and Richard Jaeckel, and the fiery fifty-five-year-old Delores del Río, playing Pacer's Indian mother, in her first Hollywood role since 1942.

From the start, though, there were problems in almost every aspect of the production. Not surprisingly, the Colonel contributed to them by insisting on every advantage he could get, and studio production head Buddy Adler's death in mid July was something of a factor, but the principal stumbling blocks were the relationship of star and director and the confusion of purpose that lay at the heart of the script itself. Elvis had gone into the picture with the idea that it could be his dramatic breakthrough, and he threw himself into it at first without reservation, but he felt little warmth coming from Don Siegel, and in fact he sensed that the director was laughing at him. Siegel's own recollection was that he "had a problem communicating with [Elvis]" because he could never get him alone, but Elvis was convinced the older man was looking down on him, that he was patronizing him about his karate, his cars, and his gang, and it only motivated Elvis to play the yokel with Siegel all the more. Every morning when he and the guys arrived on the set, they started off with karate exercises as though they were doing their daily calisthenics. He generously loaned Siegel his brand-new Rolls-Royce but allowed the director to think that it was his "childlike" way of bribing him to put off a difficult scene. And constantly during the breaks he and the guys would play nonstop games of touch football in one-hundred-degree weather at the Conejo Movie Ranch in Thousand Oaks, somewhat to the director's amazement and consternation. "[He] didn't know how we did it," recalled Sonny. "It was because of the uppers."

Unfortunately, this same ambivalence showed up in his performance. For all of his sincerity of commitment, for all of the tributes that he garnered from fellow actors and grips with respect to his thoughtfulness and cooperation, he never seems at ease in his on-screen role: he is stiff and unsure and forever gulping his words, and this most instinctive of performers ("Acting skill will probably ruin him," Weisbart had said when Elvis first arrived in Hollywood, "because his greatest asset is his natural ability") seems to have no instinct to fall back upon but flounders about instead for some stock theatrical gesture. The film itself would not have won any awards, with or without Elvis; there is a great deal of undifferentiated action, and it is confused in its message, which veers between the tragedy of being an "invisible" member of society, deprived of history and roots, and a fairly insipid plea for racial tolerance. Perhaps most surprising, it never really gives Elvis a chance to rise above a style of ensemble acting for which he is clearly not suited; whatever his billing, he is unquestionably playing a supporting role with few lines or situations that allow him to go beyond a somewhat passive, reactive response. At the end Pacer, desperately wounded and having seen "the flaming star of death," rides off into the desert to die alone. "Maybe someday, somewhere," he says, "people'll understand folks like us."

In the midst of shooting, Elvis was forced to find new living quarters, having finally been asked to leave the Beverly Wilshire after a number of incidents, culminating in Tuesday Weld throwing a fit in the hotel lobby when security wouldn't allow her to go upstairs. Joe looked at four houses and found one on Perugia Way, in Bel Air, overlooking the Bel Air Country Club. The house, owned by the Shah of Iran, was available on a six-month lease that could be extended and was perfect for their needs: it afforded privacy, space, and the opportunity for more and better parties. Elvis put up a painted photograph of himself, his mother, and father over the fireplace in the living room, and it was home.

THE PICTURE WRAPPED ON October 7, and after a weekend in Las Vegas they started off on the seventeen-hundred-mile drive home. There was less than a month to go before the start of the next picture, but Elvis missed Memphis, and there was no question that he wanted to record his gospel album in Nashville, not Hollywood. At Graceland he quickly settled into his old routine but made little secret of just how conflicted he continued to feel about his father's remarriage and the presence of Dee and her boys in his home. "When I first came back," he told the Press-Scimitar's Bob Johnson in an interview from Hollywood the previous month, "everything was strange. Now I'm lonesome, and so homesick it hurts. In some ways what I've got is good, and in some ways it isn't. I'd like to get back home again. But even that will never be the same."

Not long into his three-and-one-half-week stay, he heard from the Tau

Kappa Epsilon fraternity at Arkansas State College that they would like to induct him as a member. The letter came from chapter president Rick Husky, who had dreamt up the idea as a stunt, following in the wake of the bonanza of publicity their house had gotten when movie actor Ronald Reagan, passing through town in his role as corporate spokesman for General Electric, genially agreed to pose for pictures with the officers of the local chapter of his college fraternity. Husky, in the midst of a recruiting drive, saw Elvis Presley as a way of making TKE the most successful house on campus and concocted "a heartfelt memo about how we'd like to initiate him in the fraternity and give him an award as man of the year. Two days later there's a telegram slipped under my door from Elvis' secretary, Pat Boyd, saying that Elvis would be at Graceland at eight o'clock on Tuesday night. 'He'd love to see you and accept his award.'"

There was no award. There had been no thought of doing anything more than putting out the publicity announcement as a news item — but Husky, a resourceful young man majoring in journalism, wasn't going to allow that to stop him. He devised some appropriate wording, sketched out a design, and went to the local sporting goods store to have a trophy made up. They told him it would take at least two weeks, but when he explained his dilemma, somehow they came up with a plaque in time for the Tuesday appointment.

"We took an adult adviser to the fraternity, myself, and two other guys. We were cleared through the gate and went up; it was like a postcard — you just drove up and there's this gorgeous building, like the White House, with a black Rolls-Royce parked outside. Joe Esposito opened the door and said, 'Elvis will be down in a minute,' and we go into the music room and look around. By now I'm getting totally nervous, but then Elvis came down and was absolutely terrific. He was just so genuine and sincere. And so we just very sincerely initiated him into the fraternity. He put his hand on the skull and swore an oath; we gave him the secret word, and I pinned him. He was really great."

In a way they were embarrassed by the very ingenuousness of his response. He told them how he had always wanted to go to college but couldn't afford it; he asked about the Arkansas State football team and said he hoped maybe he could attend some games. "My great love is football," he told them. "I always wanted to play, but I couldn't because I had to work." He reminisced about dances he had played in Jonesboro and other small Arkansas towns just a few short years ago. Wealth was in the eye of the beholder, he declared, proudly showing off his Rolls-Royce. "You know, when I first got home with the car I was pretty proud of it," he said. "The first day I arrived, I left it parked outside, alongside my Cadillac limousine. The maid came in, and the first thing she said was, 'Mr. Elvis, I heard you got yourself a new car. I'd sure like to see it.' I told her that it was parked right outside and she said, 'Well, I just came from outside, and all I saw out there was some big, long white Cadillac and some old black car.'" When they were leaving, he told them, "This is one of the nicest awards that I've ever received. The plaque is certainly beautiful, and you can be sure that it will occupy a place of honor in my home."

FREDDY BIENSTOCK SHOWED UP on the afternoon of October 29 to go over songs for the gospel session that was scheduled to start at 6:30 the following evening. Once again recording was to be confined to a single all-night session, and although the Colonel wanted to make sure that Elvis had the afternoon cleared for Freddy, there really wasn't all that much to go over, given that Elvis knew what he wanted to record and Freddy had already made cut-in deals on the publishing for many of the songs. Freddy did bring one new nongospel song with him, which he had commissioned Doc Pomus and Mort Shuman to adapt from another Neapolitan ballad ("Torna a Surriento") in the public domain. Elvis liked the new Pomus and Shuman number, "Surrender," very much. It offered him the opportunity to prove to his critics that the ambitious new direction he had first embraced with "It's Now or Never" (which had gone to number one the previous summer, far outstripping "Stuck On You" in sales) and "Are You Lonesome Tonight?" (due to be released as the new single within the next couple of weeks) was no fluke. He could not have been more excited about the gospel session either. But he shocked Freddy when he confessed to him about a recurring nightmare he had been having. In this dream there were no fans outside the gates, there was no Colonel Parker, and he felt alone, helpless, and deserted. The debonair young Viennese businessman didn't know how to react or what to say to Elvis, except to suggest that it was natural to doubt the reality of success when attempting to deal with such unimaginable popularity at so early an age. But it struck him as a curious confession nonetheless and a telling parable of the extent to which Elvis saw his own success linked to the continuing presence of his mentor.

The session itself was as inspiring as its genesis, as much a promise that Elvis was keeping to himself as a tribute to the quartet tradition on which he had grown up. From the first confident, lightly swinging notes of the Trumpeteers' classic "Milky White Way," there was no question of either his fervor or his confident sense of just what he wanted to do, and it translated instantly to the background singers and the band. Charlie joined in on the next three numbers — "His Hand in Mine," "I Believe in the Man in the Sky," and "He Knows Just What I Need," each a Statesmen standard on which Jake Hess, perhaps Elvis' most direct vocal influence, had provided the original stirring lead. The session went off without a hitch, concluding at eight o'clock the following morning with a rousing version of "Working on the Building" and a grand total of fourteen sides. By then Chet Atkins had long since gone home, the musicians were all exhausted, and Bill Porter was feeling violently ill ("I had food poisoning that night and was throwing up; around five in the morning I said, 'Mr. Sholes, I've got to quit. I can't keep this up.' He said, 'One more song, Bill, one more song. Just hang in there.' I heard that about four times"). To Gordon Stoker and the Jordanaires the highlight came toward the end of the evening with "Known Only to Him," another of Jake Hess' virtuoso performances, on which *all* the singers got inspired, to the point where it was almost like having church.

One week later Elvis caught a flight to L.A., where he was scheduled to record the soundtrack for his next picture, *Wild in the Country,* on Monday, November 7. Advance notices for *G.I. Blues* (scheduled to open at Thanksgiving) were just beginning to come in and only echoed the enthusiastic embrace of the "new" Elvis which had first greeted the success of "It's Now or Never." Moreover, the soundtrack album, just out, gave every evidence of far outstripping *Elvis Is Back* in sales (surprisingly, that eclectic, and truly adult, album had not sold even half a million copies), while Colonel was in the first flush of his all-out campaign to promote the movie with an "exploitation" that involved distributing more than one hundred thousand paper army hats, which he had gotten RCA to pay for after Paramount turned him down ("We are always promoting," Colonel flung back defiantly at Hal Wallis).

At RCA, meanwhile, there was no question that the Colonel had won the war. To begin with, he had succeeded in undermining Steve Sholes' authority by persuading new RCA president Bob Yorke to move the decision-making process into marketing, where Bill Bullock, Sholes' nominal superior and the man responsible as much as anyone else for signing Elvis Presley to the label, was not inclined to challenge his authority. The result was that nothing happened without the Colonel's okay: he dictated copy, he approved the artwork, by now he had even taken over the files that publicity director Anne Fulchino had painstakingly assembled and was charging RCA a licensing fee for the very photographs that had in most cases originally been paid for by the label. He had in addition convinced RCA to cede to Elvis the authority to run his sessions, pick his singles, select album cuts, and approve the sound mix, none of which would be formalized until the renegotiation of the contract option at the beginning of the new year but all of which was in place by the time that Elvis completed his gospel album, which would be titled *His Hand in Mine* and would be rushed out for Christmas release. RCA appeared to be so well trained at this point that they even offered to build Elvis a studio in his home so he could record whenever the inspiration took him — but the Colonel wisely urged him to turn the company down, seeing their generosity for what it was, a desperate attempt to generate more product and thereby undercut the Colonel's unassailable bargaining position.

W*ild in the Country* started shooting on location in Napa, California, on November 9. Taken from J. R. Salamanca's well-regarded 1958 first novel, *The Lost Country,* the script had been written by prizewinning playwright Clifford Odets *(Waiting for Lefty, Awake and Sing!);* the director, Philip Dunne, was the author of such notable screenplays as *How Green Was My Valley* and *The Ghost and Mrs. Muir;* and the older woman, one of three principal love interests in the story, was to be played by the distinguished French actress Simone Signoret. Unfortunately, Signoret fell through, Odets was fired just as filming was about to begin, and studio head Spyros Skouras, in agreement for once with the Colonel, insisted that the number of songs in the picture had to be expanded in order to make it more of an "Elvis Presley" picture. There was the usual confusion of studio politics, there was the somewhat less common confusion of a script that appears to have been cobbled together just ahead of the actors' delivery of their lines, but it was on the whole a creditable venture with a good cast, a trio of women to fall in love with Elvis and vice versa (Tuesday Weld was the hoyden, Millie Perkins the dewy-eyed innocent, and twenty-six-year-old Hope Lange capably, if somewhat improbably, filled in for Simone Signoret), and what appear to have been altogether honorable intentions.

Of all the principals, the only one who seems to have taken a dim view of the proceedings was Millie Perkins, and her reservations centered more on pretense than lack of aspiration. Perkins, a twenty-two-year-old who had been discovered and generally acclaimed for her only other previous acting role, the title part in *The Diary of Anne Frank,* saw the whole enterprise, probably with some discernment, as intellectually dishonest. She had no reservations about Elvis Presley as a person, and given the manner in which she had been plucked from a modeling career and awarded the starring role in a major motion picture, she could have had little objection to an attempt to do the same for a popular singer. But she saw Dunne as the kind of intellectual poseur who took pride in playing the Fifth Brandenburg Concerto for some of the love scenes ("I think I won a unique place in the directors' pantheon as the only director ever to make Elvis Presley listen to Bach. As a matter of fact, he loved it," Dunne wrote in his memoirs). And, whether out of dissatisfaction with a movie career that had just happened to her ("I had never even thought of being an actress. I didn't know the movie business. I was very shy, very opinionated — I wanted to be in Paris"), or with a clarity of vision that came from being an outsider, she saw the entire enterprise as hopelessly compromised from the start, a phony attempt to dress things up in a self-serving way that kept stressing the lofty mission of art.

"I think that everybody making the movie thought, 'We're classier than all those other Elvis Presley movies. We're so much better.' Everyone was going around patting themselves on the back for being artists; they were going to do something with Elvis that other people couldn't, or didn't want to, do — and I think they didn't come up with the goods at all.

Elvis turned out to be someone I liked very much. I felt there was a man with a heart and soul there who truly cared about people. Certainly he treated me as if he cared about me; there was a mutual respect between us. But his life was on a level that my life was not on. I was married to Dean Stockwell at the time, and he was — I felt like he was drifting. The guys were on the set every day, you know, wrestling on the floor. I didn't even know what girls he was dating at the time, because it didn't interest me, his personal life seemed so silly. And yet I knew he was a victim of it. I felt like Philip Dunne fawned all over Elvis. Elvis' attitude was — I saw Elvis looking around that set and summing up people faster than anyone else could have, and I felt that after a short period of time he was disappointed in Philip Dunne, but he was too polite and well behaved to say anything.

He tried very hard to make this film better than his other movies, and you saw him trying and asking questions. And I just believe the sad thing is that [the director] did not have the ability to help Elvis through it. I remember doing this one scene; we were sitting in the truck, and we were supposed to be driving home from a dance or going to a dance, and in the script he was supposed to break into song, turn on the radio and start singing. And to me it was like, "Yuck," I was very young, and I thought, "My sisters are going to tease me, this is so embarrassing and tasteless." You see, I was a snob, too. But — and this was the nicest thing — while we were rehearsing, finally the director walked away, and Elvis looks at me and says, "God, this is so embarrassing. Nobody would ever do this in real life. Why are they making me do this?" So there we were, both of us having to do something and we just wanted to vomit.

He never used his star power — never. Maybe he should have. Maybe he did it on some other level, but he sure didn't do it on the set. I felt like he was younger than me, this very humble person who would make statements about what he believed in. And I would think, "He's saying that to show me he's a fine human being." All I know is that there was a person there with a refined heart and soul, and I say refined on any level you want to look at it. When you meet someone like that, you know they're there, even if they're sitting there eating fifteen lollipops — that's beside the point. That's just what they're doing at that time, but that's not the essence of the person. The essence of Elvis was as fine a person as I've ever met; he treated me as well as anyone has ever treated me in this business.

Her explanation of the failure of the film may well be correct, and certainly her insights into the ambivalent impulses of Elvis' nature are prescient, but they still don't explain what we see on the screen. If you were to pick out the one thing that is desperately wrong with *Wild in the Country*, leaving aside a script that is freighted with all the "sensitive young man" clichés of its time — it is Elvis Presley. He simply seems lost in the role, ambling his way through it, alternating between bouts of sullenness that start and end with bombastic declamation and equally silly posturings of trembling sensitivity.

You look at the actor up on the movie screen, and he is simply not engaged. There is one moment early in the film when the character speaks of his dead mother, and a sense of genuine sorrow and regret seems to come through. Elvis is clearly visualizing his own experience, using emotions that he has himself felt to summon up a wellspring of conflicting feelings. But otherwise — nothing. He is flat, he blurts out his lines, there is an almost total absence of timing, conviction, commitment, tone. If you doubt your eyes, contrast this with his performance in *King Creole,* full of jauntiness, assurance, an ease and melodiousness of nuanced approach. Here, just two and one-half years later, there is no pulse, no beat between the lines, there is simply the sense of a young man running, in many cases racing, through his lines.

What role amphetamines may have played in this dramatic deterioration of affect and attitude is impossible to say. To Millie Perkins the waiting-around moments were always the most important moments on the set, a time when "your training as a human being to discipline yourself to do what you really believe in or do what you *say* you believe in" should kick in — and they represented Elvis' most conspicuous failure. She put it down to externals, the guys around him who kept him from growing, the lack of formal education that only added to his natural insecurity. The guys themselves, meanwhile, watched with a growing sense not so much of alarm as bemusement at the increasingly violent mood swings that Elvis sometimes exhibited, not always recognizing their employer as he gave in to sudden fits of unpredictable rage.

One time, on a weekend excursion to San Francisco, he pulled a derringer on a carful of guys who gave him the finger; another time, back in Hollywood, he flared up at Christina Crawford, who had a bit part in the picture and was dating Joe at the time, dragging her by the hair and cursing her out because she objected to Joe's lighting his cigar. It was not that they did not understand the reasons for his anger. Christina had no business knocking the boss's cigar out of his mouth; he was within his rights to get pissed off at her, and he'd always had a pretty hot temper anyway. But they noticed the differences, too, not just the loss of control but the absence of remorse in a nature that each of them saw as essentially soft-hearted, for good or for ill. They were all taking pills to keep going; they were all under stress, Elvis most of all, and in the end they just accepted his behavior as something that grew out of his role. It was like getting first choice of the girls, an unquestioned prerogative that went with the territory.

Otherwise, it was the same old Elvis, the same kind of hijinks and good times that they always had on the set. Alan Fortas had finally rejoined the group for this film, lured by the promise of meeting Tuesday Weld, and he and Tuesday actually got to be good pals, the other guys all jibing at him for the puppy-dog devotion he showed the seventeen-year-old blond actress. Hope Lange liked to drink vodka, and Elvis uncharacteristically joined her throughout the filming, for the first time allowing the guys to have liquor in the house.

When they got back to Hollywood, it was just more of the same, except that Anita came out for a brief visit and started snooping around and found a recent letter from Priscilla in Germany. "In the letter there was something to the effect of — 'You need to call my daddy and talk him into letting me come over. I want to come really bad.' When Elvis came home from the studio, I confronted him with the letter, and we had a terrible argument. He said, 'She's just a young, fourteen-year-old [actually fifteen now] child, and she just has a bad crush on me. She wants to come over. We're family friends, army buddies, her daddy's a good friend of mine.' He just tried to smooth it over that way. Well, I did not understand, because I had seen pictures of Priscilla waving 'good-bye.' She was waving 'good-bye' like I was waving 'good-bye' when he left Memphis. Elvis kept saying, 'She's just so young. It means nothing.' But I was still perturbed. So, I went back to Memphis."

As soon as she left, he went back to dating Nancy Sharp, a wardrobe girl on the picture, and he continued to see Sandy Ferra, with whom he remained fascinated. "We'd just spend hours dancing in the living room, and then he would sit down at the piano sometimes and sing spirituals, and it was just beautiful. Cliff was around all the time at that point; he had 'Long Black Hearse' out — his 'big record!' — and a lot of times he'd get up and sing. I lived in the Valley, and different guys would pick me up in either the Rolls or a limo, and we'd go up to the house. There was always a line of girls standing outside, and we would drive through the gates, and usually the guys would have dates, and we'd sit in the den, or the maid would make up something for dinner, and we'd sit and watch TV and eat.

"One time I wore pants, and Lamar picked me up and didn't say anything, we drove out to the house and I walked in and Elvis was all dressed up, because he always got dressed up for our dates. So he said, 'Hi, baby,' and he kissed me on the cheek, and we sat down on the couch, and he did not speak to me for the next three or four hours. It seemed like an eternity.

Then he kissed me good night, and he said, 'Don't ever wear pants again.' I said, 'Oooooh, I won't.' 'Cause he said he got all dressed up for me, and he expected me to get dressed up, too. So I always wore my prettiest party dresses from then on. No more pants."

The movie was briefly threatened by a new studio policy limiting shooting time to thirty-seven days instead of fifty, even for those shows currently in production. Philip Dunne threatened to quit several times before that problem was resolved, but the picture was still over schedule, and cast and crew were given just one week off for Christmas before shooting once again resumed. Elvis was just as glad to get back to California after discovering the changes that his father's wife had made in his home, and he and his daddy quietly agreed that no more changes would be made without his explicit approval.

The Colonel meanwhile had preceded him to Memphis to join the mayor in making an announcement about the big Memphis Charities show that he had been hinting at all year. Elvis would headline at Ellis Auditorium on February 25, the performance would benefit some two dozen Memphis charities plus the long-dormant Elvis Presley Youth Center in Tupelo, and, as per his long-standing policy with respect to benefits, even the Colonel would be buying his own ticket. "There will be no passes," he said. "This is going to be 100% charity."

Flaming Star opened strongly nationwide on December 21, though not as strongly as *G.I. Blues,* which had risen as high as number two on *Variety*'s weekly list of top-grossing films, ranking number fourteen overall for 1960 and grossing $4.3 million in the last six weeks of the year alone. For Elvis' twenty-sixth birthday, on January 8, there was a small party on the set, and cast and crew presented him with a plaque portraying a cartoon Elvis clad in a karate ghi and breaking blocks of wood. "Happy Birthday, 'King Karate,'" was the message. On January 20 he was finally released by the studio and permitted to go home, though he was recalled briefly two and one-half weeks later to reshoot the ending when studio executives decided that Hope Lange's suicide after her abortive romance with Elvis' film character was "too bitter an ending." By this time, though, Elvis was busily preparing for his return to live performance, which was now scheduled to include not just one but two big charity shows that the Colonel was promoting with all of his customary flair and zeal.

THOMAS A. PARKER, HAWAII, CIRCA 1930.
(COURTESY OF THE ESTATE OF ELVIS PRESLEY)

THE COLONEL'S SECRET

THE SECOND CHARITY CONCERT had come about as a result of a story the Colonel read in the *Los Angeles Herald-Examiner* on December 4, 1960, prompted by the nineteenth anniversary of the Japanese bombing of Pearl Harbor. The piece centered around stalled plans to erect a memorial to the victims of that bombing on the site of the U.S.S. *Arizona*, whose 1,102 officers and men remained entombed beneath the water. Three hundred thousand dollars had been raised over the course of the past fifteen years, but the War Memorial Commission was still $200,000 short of the funds necessary to construct a monument in time for the twentieth anniversary of the attack the following year.

The story was prompted by a letter sent out to over sixteen hundred mainland newspapers by George Chaplin, editor of the *Honolulu Advertiser,* asking that they consider running an editorial on or about December 7 with an appeal for funds. The appeal brought in about $20,000 from all around the country, but it also brought a telephone call to Chaplin from the Colonel. "Parker said Elvis was coming to Hawaii to make the film *Blue Hawaii* — and that if we could get an appropriate arena, and the tickets, ushers, lights, et cetera were for free, then Elvis would donate his services." Chaplin seized on the Colonel's offer, cleared it with the navy, explained that if they were able to raise $50,000 they would have enough to complete the "bare essentials" necessary for a Memorial Day dedication, and issued an official invitation to the Colonel to come to Hawaii.

The Colonel arrived on January 7 to solidify arrangements with H. Tucker Gratz, chairman of the Memorial Commission, and held a press conference at the Hawaiian Village Hotel on January 11. Every penny that was raised would go to the fund, Parker announced, while stipulating that he and Elvis would pay for the talent on the show out of their own pockets. "This is the real McCoy, fellas. This is no gimmick. . . . You know, Elvis is twenty-six (last Sunday was his birthday), and that's about the average age of those boys entombed in the *Arizona.* I think it's appropriate that he should be doing this." And then, once again, he reminded every dignitary present, along with all potential attendees, that "everyone's gotta buy a ticket — the governor, Admiral Solomons, Admiral Sides, commissioners — everyone, even me. Everyone in that hall will be a contributor to the *Arizona* fund."

The Colonel was riding high. The Memphis benefit on February 25 had already drawn an avalanche of publicity for what Colonel had billed as "the greatest one-day charity show box office in the country's history." With his return to Hawaii in this new public-spirited guise, made possible by Hal Wallis' embrace of the "Hawaiian story" (albeit without gypsies) that he had first proposed over two years ago, the Colonel couldn't have helped but feel a little smug. He had always believed that you made your own destiny, and while he remained a notorious disrespecter of nearly every form of social convention, he prided himself on his patriotism and public-spirited generosity, too. It was something he was convinced paid off in any number of different ways, and if one of those could be further proof of his boy's good character — and it could help the new picture in the process — well, so much the better.

Meanwhile, he had unfinished business to attend to. On January 6 he had completed yet another renegotiation and contract extension with Hal Wallis, raising the price per picture once again, to $175,000 for the next three Paramount outings, $200,000 for the two beyond those. At the same time he was vigorously pursuing the deal which, as he saw it, would ensure Elvis' future: a multi-picture arrangement with MGM for far more money than he could ever have hoped to squeeze out of Wallis, but, more important, one which would announce to Hollywood that Elvis Presley was a major motion picture star. On January 12, the day after the Hawaii press conference, he returned to the mainland and plunged back into the MGM negotiations, emerging on January 20 with a guaranteed four-picture deal at $500,000 per picture and 50 percent of the profits. This meant, he announced jubilantly to RCA vice president Bill Bullock, that they were "sold out for motion pictures through 1965, which of course enhances the value of this great artist for your company also. The confidence shown in him by the motion picture industry undoubtedly will rub off to the benefit of all of us." And in a rare visit, he stopped by the house on Perugia that same day to deliver the news personally to Elvis, then accepted congratulations from all the guys as Elvis explained to them how the deal worked. "Just remember, boys," pronounced the Colonel, no doubt tamping his cigar vigorously to emphasize the point, "if we didn't have Elvis, I couldn't make these deals, and we wouldn't be having dinner in this beautiful home."

By now he had come up with yet another twist on the Hawaiian scheme, retaining the nonprofit principle at its core but proposing that an NBC television special be structured around the concert (the taped broadcast would combine documentary touches with the live performance) in a package for which Elvis would receive $50,000 to recoup costs, the *Arizona* memorial would realize another $100,000, and ownership of the program would revert to Elvis after a single showing. Like most of the Colonel's projects, eleemosynary and otherwise, this one was brilliant in its simplicity, simultaneously burnishing Elvis' image and benefiting the fund, and while in the end it fell through, it prompted venerable William Morris Agency head Abe Lastfogel to recognize the distance the Colonel had brought his single client. At one time, the diminutive talent agent pointed out to a small group of agency and NBC representatives studying the feasibility of this new proposition, Elvis Presley was seen by most people as an "oddity," with little staying power and less broad-based appeal. Now, Lastfogel declared, with the conviction of one who had had to be converted initially himself, that phase was finished. After the army experience, with this magnificent charity concert that the Colonel was putting on, the world could see Elvis Presley for who he truly was.

The work continued on various fronts, with Colonel shuttling back and forth between his various projects and Elvis returning home for a brief vacation. The house continued to feel strange to him — nothing more had been physically altered, and his father's new family was now living in the apartment that had been constructed from the garage behind the kitchen, but it remained unsettling, not just for him but for Vernon, too, who continued occasionally to sleep in his old bedroom, its closets still filled with Gladys' clothing. Elvis stopped by the cemetery almost every day, fussing with the flowers that were delivered each week on a standing order and cleaning up the area around his mother's grave. On February 2 he drove down to Tupelo with Anita and Joe and Gene, revisiting the scenes of his childhood, stopping by the Lawhon School to see his fifth-grade teacher, Mrs. Grimes, showing Joe, who had never seen Tupelo before, all the different places he had lived, the Negro community of Shake Rag, the Fairgrounds where he had sung in public for the first time, talking all the while about the world he had left behind. When they got to his birthplace on Old

Saltillo Road, they found the sign marking the site of the Elvis Presley Youth Center fallen down and tried without success to prop it back up. Elvis was visibly angry: the house, which was intended to be the centerpiece of the park, was still occupied, the fourteen-acre location had barely been cleared, the guitar-shaped swimming pool that Elvis had stipulated for East Tupelo's youth was not even on the architectural drawing board. He couldn't help but feel that if the park were in a more fashionable part of Tupelo, plans would have been much further along by now, and he and the Colonel had never been able to satisfactorily determine what had become of the $14,000 he had donated from his performance at the 1957 fair. But he was not about to give up; he was *determined* to see this project through to completion — it was just as important as the Colonel's thing in Hawaii; there would be ball fields and recreational facilities and a teen center here someday.

On Saturday Gene's brother, Junior, died. Though he was only twenty-eight, it came as no great surprise. Junior had been on a downward path ever since he had come home shell-shocked from Korea in 1953; he had always been unpredictable and moody, but he had become more erratic since Elvis' discharge from the army and was no longer even able to travel with them. Evidently he had been up all night drinking with his (and Elvis') uncle Travis, passed out in his cousin Billy's room, and suffocated on his own vomit.

Elvis went to Travis' house practically beside himself with anger and grief over a life so senselessly thrown away. Junior had been weak, but he understood Junior, and he understood how easy it was to lose control. "I can see him just standing there," said Eddie Fadal, Elvis' friend from Waco who happened to be visiting Graceland and accompanied Elvis to the house. "He just kept saying, 'It's all over, Junior, it's all over.'" Late that night he and his seventeen-year-old cousin Billy visited the funeral home, the same one that had interred his mother, and he got someone to let them in so they could view the body. At Elvis' instigation they took a tour of the premises and encountered two morticians, one working, one snoring in a casket. Elvis introduced himself, explained about his cousin, then interrogated the mortician who was awake about the mechanics of his work, about what happened to the body after death. It was, Billy thought, a little creepy — he himself was not particularly comfortable surrounded by all these corpses laid out on their slabs — but he thought he understood what Elvis was doing. "He had a fear . . . and he wanted to face that fear. And I think he was just trying to bridge that gap and hold on a little longer."

THE COLONEL WAS IN the midst of a fever of preparations for the two charity shows, throwing out promotional challenges and hustling $100 celebrity tickets, when he received the latest in a series of letters from his brother Ad in Holland. Ad and an older sister had seen a photograph in the Dutch magazine *Rosita* the previous spring, showing Elvis Presley, just out of the army, standing at the opening of a train door. Behind him, wearing a hat and a long winter coat, was a man identified as his manager, Colonel Thomas A. Parker. To Ad and his sister the man in the photograph looked very much like their brother Andreas ("Dries"), whom they had not heard from since 1937, when the last of his letters from America arrived. The similarities were striking, and any doubt they might have had that this heavyset middle-aged man really was the same person as the brother they had last seen in 1929 was immediately erased by his uncanny resemblance to another brother, Jan, a policeman, as he looked today.

Ad contacted *Rosita*, whose editors were naturally skeptical at first. But Ad persisted, writing first to the Dutch Elvis Presley fan club, then to the fan club in Memphis, sending family pictures and news of their mother, who had died in 1958, heartbroken, Ad said, that she had never seen her son, Dries, again. Eventually he got a response of sorts, a perplexing letter that began in the third person but slipped into a first-person account midway through. Ad showed the letter to *Rosita* editor Leo Derksen, who concluded that "there was no doubt that Parker had written the answer personally. He denied everything. It was all a mistake, he wrote."

With that, Ad was able to persuade *Rosita* to sponsor him on a trip to America for a reunion with his famous brother, and at this point he started bombarding Dries with one letter after another, until finally the Colonel, with the pragmatism on which he had always prided himself, responded that yes, he would welcome Ad's visit but that he was very busy right now, he was scheduled to leave for Hawaii any day, but when he got back, Ad should contact him and he would be glad to see him. To his brother-in-law, Bitsy Mott, who worked security for Elvis, he grumbled that he had heard from a brother whom he hadn't seen in years, and now all of a sudden this brother was talking about coming to visit. "He wants something from me," the Colonel complained. "What's he up to?" But he never mentioned that his brother was Dutch.

> The Chief Potentate of the Snowmen's League of America, Col. Tom Parker was on the phone from his suite in [Memphis'] Hotel Claridge, and he was joking and in fine fettle.
>
> "That Mayor of yours, he's learning and he worked hard and one of these days he's going to make the grade," the Colonel said happily, "but I already made good on my end of the deal."
>
> The Colonel was referring to his challenge to [Memphis] Mayor Loeb yesterday that if Loeb in 20 minutes would sell 10 of the $100 tickets to the luncheon honoring Elvis Presley at Hotel Claridge at 12:30 P.M. tomorrow, the Colonel would match it by selling 10 himself. Mayor Loeb got on the phone, altho he said he was handicapped because in his position as Mayor he had to be careful to whom he made his appeals, and got 10 promises to buy the gold luncheon tickets, and two "almost certains." It took him 27 minutes.
>
> "I just sold 14 more tickets," the Colonel said, "and it took me seven minutes on the phone. How many calls? Two. I sold eight on one call and six on another.
>
> "Well, maybe it did run a little over seven minutes . . . maybe eight minutes. The long distance operator had trouble getting one number.
>
> "So now that makes 96 tickets I sold."
>
> — from Robert Johnson's "T-V News and Views,"
> *Memphis Press-Scimitar,* February 24, 1961

There was very little left to be done when the great day finally arrived. Saturday, February 25 had been declared Elvis Presley Day throughout the state of Tennessee; not only the mayor but the governor was scheduled to attend, and comedian George Jessel was flying in from Hollywood to MC. All the top RCA executives from president Bob Yorke, Bill Bullock, and Steve Sholes on down would be there, not to mention William Morris Agency head Abe Lastfogel, the Aberbach brothers (Jean was flying in from Rome, where he had been conducting Hill and Range business), the Colonel's first show business client, Gene Austin, of "My Blue Heaven" fame, and virtually every Memphis civic leader you could name. Because the first show had sold out in less than twenty-four hours, a matinee performance had been added, and the Colonel was hustling unreserved $3 seats to that. The Colonel in short was everywhere, "snowing" everyone from the highest lord high-muck-a-muck to the humblest citizen alike with his unique application of the salesman's credo: "There is nothing I can give you which you have not. But there is much, while I cannot give you, you can take."

Elvis held a rehearsal at Graceland on Friday, February 24. Various session musicians arrived from Nashville, along with Scotty, D.J., veteran Memphis guitarist Brad Suggs, and the Jordanaires, and they ran through a program which combined some of Elvis' biggest early hits ("That's All Right," "Heartbreak Hotel," "All Shook Up," and, of course, "Hound Dog") with a judicious selection of recent recordings ("Such a Night," "Fever," "It's Now or Never," "Swing Down, Sweet Chariot," "Are You Lonesome Tonight?"). Elvis was visibly nervous but clearly excited, and they rehearsed late into the night.

The matinee performance, which began at 4:23 P.M., was characterized by the *Commercial Appeal* as bringing together elements from "Negro cottonfield harmony, camp meeting fervor, Hollywood showmanship, beatnik nonchalance, and some of the manipulations of mass psychology." At the evening show, the crowd grew restive during the Colonel's usual parade of tap dancers, acrobats, jugglers, and comedians, though they woke up a little for Boots Randolph's "yackety sax" and Brother Dave Gardner's sharp-edged satire. Then after a brief intermission Elvis came out, and MC George Jessel flung himself, palms down, at Elvis' feet, as wave after wave of screams and applause washed over the singer for a full three minutes.

"[He] grabbed the mike as if he were trying to eat it," the *Press-Scimitar* reported, remarking on his nervousness and evident rustiness after more than three years away from live performing. The *Press-Scimitar* reporter noted something else, too: there appeared to be a new edge of irony to his performance. He seemed more confident in some ways, indicating his amusement "at the frenzied zeal which some of his fans show for him. He would make it apparent when he twitched a hip or made one of those sudden gestures which cause the screaming excitement, that he was laughing at the response. He went out of his way several times to let photographers get a good picture. He would go all the way across stage and make a gesture to accommodate a photographer whom he knew." At the same time there was no question of his utter seriousness, his total immersion in the moment. "He mixed his numbers beautifully. . . . It was easy to see by the smile on his face . . . that he knew he had the crowd going his way."

The transformation was something that he could never have anticipated, said the newest Jordanaire, Ray Walker, who hadn't sung onstage with Elvis before. "He just had kind of an effervescence about him. He would do some unexpected things and do them so well we'd forget to come in. Then he'd turn around and grin and call us a name." When Scotty, acting as bandleader, forgot a song that was supposed to have been on the program, or Elvis himself messed up some lyrics, he just went right on: he was masterful, in command, *he was where he was supposed to be.* For forty-nine minutes he commanded the stage, as comfortable in this role as the Colonel was in his, removed for just a moment from all the strain of pretending, from all the uncertainty of manufacturing an image, simply doing what he was meant to do. The following day it was announced that he had raised $51,612 for twenty-six Memphis charities and the Elvis Presley Youth Center in Tupelo, which with a contribution of $3,789.80 would receive the single largest share.

On March 8, he made another appearance, this time at the Tennessee State Legislature, where he was a special guest of a joint session of both houses, convened to honor him for "bringing fame to Memphis and Tennessee throughout the nation." He drove up with Joe and Sonny and Alan in the Rolls, disarmed the legislators and a gallery full of "truant teens" with a speech in which he called this recognition "one of the nicest things that has ever happened to me," proclaimed that he would never live in Hollywood, and got a "$.10 tour" of the governor's mansion from Governor Ellington's attractive daughter, Ann, with whom he then sped off and spent much of the rest of the day. On the way back to Memphis he and the guys stopped off for forty-five minutes at the Tennessee State Prison, where Johnny Bragg, lead singer of the Prisonaires, the group Sam Phillips had brought to national fame on the Sun label in 1953, was incarcerated for a parole violation. Elvis toured the various workshops, prison dining hall, and death house, and spoke briefly with Bragg, asking if he needed a lawyer or if there was anything at all he could do for him. Then it was back to Memphis, a return to Nashville on the weekend for a quick recording session at RCA's behest, and more marking time.

* * *

H E FLEW OUT TO THE COAST on March 18 in preparation for the
Arizona benefit on the twenty-fifth and the start of shooting on *Blue
Hawaii* two days later. The Colonel had already been in Honolulu for ten
days, talking up the benefit, buying a half hour on all thirteen Oahu radio
stations to advertise the concert with selections from Elvis' religious
album, hustling the $100 tickets (he sold seventy-four before even leaving
the mainland), thoroughly enjoying himself and the rare opportunity to
get generals and admirals to jump at his command. Elvis was scheduled to
record the *Blue Hawaii* soundtrack in Hollywood, and he had flown the
whole band out from Nashville for the session and the concert. They
relaxed and rehearsed at the house on Perugia, then went into Radio
Recorders on March 21 to record a full fourteen-cut soundtrack album
under the watchful eye of Hal Wallis over the next three days.

The song selection included everything from a number originally
recorded by Bing Crosby in 1937 for another Paramount motion picture
("Blue Hawaii," the title cut) to several Hawaiian standards to the usual
assortment of contemporary adaptations from the Hill and Range stable
("Rock-a-Hula Baby," "Beach Boy Blues"). Among the Hill and Range contributions was a pretty ballad based on an eighteenth-century French
melody, "Can't Help Falling in Love," and yet another number in Elvis'
recently acquired Mediterranean manner, "No More," adapted this time
from the classic Spanish folk melody "La Paloma" and co-written by songwriter Don Robertson, two of whose more contemporary compositions
Elvis had just recorded in Nashville the previous week.

The Nashville session had been scheduled strictly to fulfill a contractual
commitment to RCA: twelve songs were required to make up a new studio
album, and as per the Colonel's instructions just twelve songs were
recorded, with the title assigned to the album that came out four months
later, *Something for Everybody,* reflecting some of its compromised origins.
The two songs that Robertson contributed, however, "There's Always Me"
and "Starting Today," struck a fresh note, coming as close as you could get
to the kind of moody late-night ballad one might expect from Frank Sinatra (if Frank Sinatra were to adopt country chord changes) and offering
Elvis a rare opportunity for introspection and serious interpretation. After
the session he told Freddy he'd like to meet Don Robertson if he ever got
the chance, and Freddy and Julian Aberbach invited Robertson, a Chicago
psychiatrist's son whose country and western compositions consistently
reflected a profundity born of determined simplicity, to the first night of

the *Blue Hawaii* soundtrack session, when his new song was scheduled to be recorded.

"I sat in the control room, and he came in during a break and introduced himself (he was standing there in his little captain's hat), and we talked some, and he told me how he got started in the music business. He was very charming, very humble, sweet, an altogether appealing person. That night, before I left he told me that some of the musicians and the Jordanaires were going to be coming up to his house after the session, and would I like to come? While I was there, he played me his version of 'There's Always Me' — it was the first time I heard it, and we listened on headphones because he didn't want the rest of the people in the room necessarily to hear it. I remember, he got almost operatic at the end, just like he did on 'It's Now or Never,' and he said, 'Listen to this ending.' He was very proud of it. And he talked with me about the lyrics, he was very interested in the lyrics. It was almost like he wanted me to know that he understood everything that was going on, everything that was intended in the lyric. I don't think I was overawed by him, but I was totally disarmed. He had this talent for making people feel comfortable, for letting you know that he really liked and respected you. And, you know, he told everyone that night that I was the one that had started Floyd Cramer's 'slip-note' style [the grace-note approach to country and western piano that was sweeping Nashville at the time]. I think he was kind of proud of me on that account."

Back in the studio the session proceeded along admirably professional lines. Joseph Lilley, the music supervisor, was a veteran of numerous Paramount musical productions, including five Bing Crosby pictures, and he was a stickler for an authentic Hawaiian sound, employing various top Los Angeles studio musicians and well-known steel guitarist Alvino Rey. When they finished, Hal Wallis was convinced that he finally had what he had been looking for all along: the soundtrack for a Bing Crosby picture, starring Elvis Presley.

ELVIS AIRPORT ALOHA IS WILD
"Hi, E-L-V-I-S . . . !"

The roaring greeting rolled like thunder across Honolulu International Airport at noon yesterday as 3000 teenage fans (and some not so young) greeted their hero, Elvis (The Man) Presley. Some had been waiting as long as 3½ hours.

A moment before at 12:15 P.M. the big Pan American Airways jet touched down. The other passengers got off — and then at 12:27 Elvis appeared at the rear door.

Actor Jimmy Stewart, his wife and four children
came in yesterday on the same plane that brought Elvis Presley.
But nobody noticed Jimmy.

He was dressed in a black suit and tight-fitting pants, with a ruffled white shirt and dark-patterned tie, broad-shouldered coat and black shoes with sidebuckles.

Screams filled the air. . . .

For 10 minutes the handsome lad with the baby blue eyes passed in review — just like they do in the Army — up and down in front of the crowd with the wire screen and a cordon of Honolulu military police between him and the fans. . . .

Presley and his party didn't venture into the crowd. Looking pale, Elvis paused only twice in his march up and down outside the fence.

Once he stopped to let a little girl give him a lei and he rewarded her with a sweet smile. And once he stopped to tell disc jockey Ron Jacobs of radio station K-POI that he was "happy to be back, and thank you all."

Well, thank you, too, Elvis Presley, for coming here on behalf of the Arizona Memorial Fund.

— *Honolulu Sunday Advertiser,* March 26, 1961

Veteran country comedian Minnie Pearl, a featured performer on the show, who had once briefly been managed by the Colonel and whose husband, Henry Cannon, had piloted Elvis frequently early in his career, was practically in shock at the reception. Colonel Parker had met them on the plane and told her that he wanted her to stick right by Elvis' side, so that she could be in all the pictures. "I didn't know what staying with Elvis involved. If I had, I wouldn't have [done it]. There is no way to describe the pandemonium. I never saw as many women in my life. They were screaming. They were yelling. I was just horrified. I thought, 'They're going to kill him.' And they would have if they could have gotten loose, I'm afraid.

"Well, we [finally] got in the limos — they parked them right up next to the plane — and we got to the hotel, the Hawaiian Village. There's sort of a lanai overhang at the hotel, and when we got there, there were five hundred screaming women and no fence like they had at the airport. So it was very dangerous. Elvis and I got out of the limo — I never will forget, the police had this cordon of arms together holding the crowd back, but the crowd burst through, these women, screaming women, all ages, they burst through the police and started grabbing at Elvis, and, of course, that scared Tom Parker to death. We finally escaped and got inside the hotel, and I said to Elvis, 'How do you stand it?' And he said, 'I just got used to it.' And I said, 'You know, those women could kill you.' And he said, 'They're not going to hurt me.'"

The press conference was scheduled for 3:30 that afternoon, and the Colonel not surprisingly was everywhere. The press was represented, of course, by the two dailies, the *Advertiser* and the *Star-Bulletin,* but also by nearly one hundred student reporters from all twenty-seven Oahu high schools and middle schools. Elvis was laden down with leis and honors (one girl would not let go of him until the Colonel firmly disengaged him from her grasp) and politely answered all the usual questions about movies, touring, girlfriends, and karate. What about his army status? he was asked. "I'm in the stand-by reserve. They could call me up in an emergency." But not until after the show, the Colonel hastened to add. Did he have *any* plans to travel? "I might go to South Africa to catch wild buffalo," he said, as if in competition for laughs. But if he was, it was a competition he could not win. "Elvis answered questions with a matter-of-fact mumble," the *Sunday Advertiser* concluded its account. "Colonel Tom Parker, his manager, supplied the punch lines that brought laughter and applause from the students."

The show that night was another story. Even with the very poorest home recorder–quality sound, you have only to listen to the tape of the performance that has survived to sense the energy that was coming off the stage, to get a whiff of the ferocity of feeling that the music unleashed. There is certainly the same irony that *Press-Scimitar* reporter Bill Burk had remarked upon in his account of the Memphis show, the same playful toying with the audience, but there is something else besides: there is a sheer joyousness, a guttural exuberance of expression that refuses to be denied. By now the band had been playing together off and on for just over four weeks, and Elvis eggs them on with an enthusiasm not just for what they are able to do but for what they are able to permit *him* to do. Again and again he urges guitarist Hank Garland to solo, indicating his appreciation with grunts and exclamations that have nothing to do with the audience. The music crests and surges with an impulse all its own, and Elvis calls for Hank to solo again, he *demands* another sax solo from Boots, he forgets the words, even loses the structure of the song, but embraces the moment with pure, uninhibited feeling. To Boots it was "one of the highlights" of his life, and to Jordanaire Gordon Stoker, who had worked with Elvis steadily since 1956, there was a spontaneity to his performance that most closely resembled a man being let out of jail.

Listening to the recording, though, raises a question: you wonder why this quality couldn't have translated for Elvis into film. It was certainly present when he made *King Creole;* you even sense it in the tentative, wildly erratic groping for emotion that is his performance in *Love Me Tender* — in this first attempt at acting, in the absence of either knowledge or experience, there is a self-contained assurance that allows him effectively to bypass technique, even as you are aware of his technical limitations. He seemed, then, to have confidence in himself and in his mission. Now, as many people were coming to observe, he mouthed that confidence in any number of public situations, but it did not appear to be truly present.

It was not there, certainly, for the shooting of *Blue Hawaii.* The picture was intended to be a bright, fast-paced musical comedy, with a formulaic Hollywood approach. It had a good supporting cast portraying the usual stock characters, including thirty-five-year-old Angela Lansbury as Elvis' birdbrained southern mother. Elvis himself played Chad Gates, a rich boy who wants to throw aside his privileged status and embrace Island culture. There is the usual tri- or quad-angle romance, with an older woman, a younger true love (Joan Blackman playing Maile Duval, half Islander but, perhaps in a bid to mitigate any suggestion of miscegenation, also half French), and a much younger woman/misunderstood brat. Journeyman director Norman Taurog, a big hit with Elvis and the guys for his relaxed tolerance of their hijinks on *G.I. Blues,* was once again in charge, and Elvis has clearly loosened up enough to try some conventional bits of comedy at Taurog's instigation — there are playful double takes, lots of brisk and energetic business, and even some genial self-mockery to go with the spectacular Hawaiian sights and sounds and "production values" that are the hallmark of any Hal Wallis picture.

It is in nearly every way a direct answer to the two previous movies at

Fox, which Wallis detested and which for all of their serious aspirations had clearly not achieved what they set out to do. With *Blue Hawaii* there is little question that Wallis and the Colonel's intentions are fully realized, and if Elvis were merely to be considered as an agreeable presence on the screen, an innocuous addition to the scenery, the picture would have to be judged a success. He moves easily from scene to scene, delivers all fourteen songs with charm and panache (even the worst of them is beautifully sung), and for the most part gives the appearance of having a good time. And yet, underneath, one can sense the confusion and the fear — many of the lines once again are garbled or delivered with indifferent intensity, as if they were an embarrassment to get through; the familiar movements that Elvis has always claimed are *natural* to his music are appended to silly songs, as if they were a joke — one feels for him, one squirms with an embarrassment of one's own as he is asked to stand still for the trivialization of his music, as he is forced to publicly repudiate his commitment to rock 'n' roll.

The confusion expressed itself off the set in more hijinks, more conquests, more seeming need to declare out loud just who he was and who he was not. He was constantly surrounded by girls, and he and the guys partied every night to such an extent that eventually Hal Wallis had to move the female cast to another wing of the hotel, placing them on a ten o'clock curfew. Wallis had little use for the guys, but the Colonel needled him that he was just getting old, didn't he remember what it was to be young himself? On several occasions Elvis got together with Patti Page, who was married to Charlie O'Curran, Wallis' longtime choreographer of musical numbers (O'Curran went back to the first Paramount picture with Elvis, *Loving You*, and had worked most recently on *G.I. Blues*), and they harmonized on country songs far into the night.

The Colonel remained in imperturbable good humor. It seemed as if Hawaii had brought out all of his impishness, and he interviewed tourists, using the aluminum tube from his cigar as a microphone and identifying himself as a representative of Radio Pineapple; hypnotized the boys for Hal Wallis' amusement; and halted shooting one day by walking in front of the cameras and demanding a conference with Wallis. Wallis, who thought something really was wrong at first, anxiously inquired as to what the problem was. "Read the contract, read the contract," the Colonel angrily replied, although by now even Wallis was beginning to catch on. "You know, if Elvis provides his own clothes, he gets ten thousand dollars more."

Wallis surveyed the scene, in which Elvis was wearing nothing but a bathing suit and riding a surfboard, and arched his eyebrows. "He's wearing his own watch," declared the Colonel without batting an eye. And the scene did not proceed until he took off the watch.

Just before they were scheduled to leave, Elvis and the guys were having dinner in the hotel dining room in Kuaui. Sonny got drunk at the bar, and when he saw a man and woman standing on the bridge that faced the dining room singing "Hawaiian Wedding Song," he was so overcome with good feeling that he joined them, unaware that they were part of the hotel floor show. Elvis and the guys got a big laugh out of that, but from then on Elvis gave Sonny the cold shoulder, "and he [was] telling all the crew what I had done as if it was a big crime. . . . I started to think he was a pretty phony bastard."

Instead of dissipating, the ill feeling only intensified once they got back to the mainland. Elvis was still seeing Tuesday Weld occasionally at this point, and one night she brought a girlfriend over to the house, whom Sonny started to promote for himself. "We had all been drinking a bit, so had Elvis. Tuesday and Elvis are on the couch, and I am talking to this girl. Elvis leans over and kisses her and says, 'You're really cute.' Well, I knew that was the end of me trying to score with this chick, because whatever Elvis wants in the way of women, he gets. . . . He has Tuesday there, and he wants this girl, too. Later on, he comes over and really plants a kiss on her." Sonny chose this as a good strategic moment to withdraw, and he and Gene began a private dialogue in whispered tones about which girl they'd rather have if both were available, with the vote pretty much going to Tuesday. Elvis for some reason assumed they were talking about him and demanded to know what Sonny had said, while Sonny for his part declined to reveal the true subject of their conversation until Elvis picked up a Coke bottle and said, "Tell me or I'll break your goddamn head open with this bottle." Sonny just stared at him. Elvis wasn't going to hit him, he said. And besides, he quit. He couldn't quit, Elvis declared. He was fired. "Then he drew back and punched me in the face. I didn't move. I didn't even feel the blow, but I could feel the tears of emotion coming out of my eyes, and I said quietly, 'I didn't think you could do that to me.'" Elvis gave him $200 before he left and got him into the screen extras guild two weeks later, but he didn't apologize.

To Hal Kanter, the writer-director of *Loving You,* and the principal script writer on *Blue Hawaii,* it was a very different Elvis Presley on this picture than on the 1957 Hal Wallis production, and the difference could not just be explained away by age. To Anne Fulchino, the young RCA publicity director who had helped Elvis draw up a long-range plan for success when he first joined the label, the contrast was even more striking. Recently transferred to Los Angeles, she was brought to the set by Tom Diskin. "It was a while before he came over and talked to us, and when he did — you see, at the beginning I used to call him Chief, and I said, 'Hi, Chief,' and he just looked at me like he wished I hadn't come. We made some small talk, and then he said something like, 'This isn't what we had in mind at Klube's [the German restaurant across from RCA, where they had drawn up their plan], was it?' I said to myself, 'If I was making these crappy pictures, I wouldn't want to see anybody from my past either.' That's the reason I didn't hang around. Tom said, 'We can stay all day,' and I said, 'No, why don't we just take off?' He was obviously uncomfortable with what he was doing, he was frustrated and disgusted — it was all in his face. The emotion that I respected most was that he was ashamed of it, which meant that he knew better — but you could see that he was trapped. It was kind of like when your own child goes wrong, and you can't help feeling it — and I did."

Anita came out to see him while they were still filming, and she and Elvis gave the guys a dose of their own medicine, when they pulled off one of those tricks that Elvis and the guys generally liked to play on outsiders. They were all riding in the Cadillac limousine when Elvis decided to play dead, and she went along with him, crying out, "Elvis isn't breathing! He isn't breathing!" By the time that they pulled up in front of the house on Perugia, the guys were in a state of panic, and Lamar ran into the house yelling for someone to call an ambulance, but Elvis sat up at this point and confessed, "I just wanted to see what you guys would do."

Not everything went as smoothly. Patti Parry, an eighteen-year-old hairdresser who had met Elvis on Sunset Boulevard the previous October and had been hanging around in the role of everybody's little sister ever since, let her guard down one time when Anita asked nonchalantly, "Who's he been dating lately?" "Just Sandy Ferra," Patti responded innocently, and Anita was off, until Elvis calmed her down and convinced her that Patti was just a goofy kid who didn't know what was going on.

With Patti, though, he really blew his top. If she wanted to hang out with them, he told her, the first, last, and only rule that she had to remember was *deny everything*. What went on in the confines of his home, *anything* that she observed at any time, was privileged information, not to be shared with anyone from the outside world, no matter how knowledgeable they might appear. Patti got the message: it was her choice to make, but if she wanted to continue to be part of things, she had to be loyal to him exclusively. Which she accepted, so she remained a member of the family.

That wasn't the only source of friction with Anita. Once again she came across evidence that he was staying in touch with that girl in Germany; there were more letters from her, more indications that she was still trying to get Elvis to bring her over to this country. He continued to deny it, he insisted that this was just a lovesick teenager's fantasy, he asked Anita to give him a little more credit, but he also pleaded with her not to say anything to anybody, and they made up for the time being. So she went back to Memphis, where she kept Grandma company at Graceland and waited for the record she had recorded the previous Christmas for Sun Records to come out. It was called "I'll Wait Forever," with a flip side that declared "I Can't Show How I Feel."

I have never seen Bob Hope as intrigued with anyone as he was with Col. Tom Parker at the MGM party honoring Bob and Lana Turner. The Colonel stood at the back door handing out pictures of Elvis Presley and on the back it said, "Elvis is now in 'Blue Hawaii,' a Hal Wallis picture." Mind you — a Paramount picture at an MGM party.

Bob wants to do a picture based on the life of the Colonel, who admits he's the greatest con man since Barnum. The Colonel gave Bob a citation on which all of Elvis' pictures made at other studios were mentioned.

Mrs. Parker, who is as quiet as the Colonel is lively, was with him and she seemed to enjoy meeting Bob, Lana and Janis Paige.

Bob wants Elvis to play himself in the life of Col. Parker, but the Colonel says, "No money, no deal."

— Hollywood gossip column item, May 1, 1961

The Colonel seemed without a care in the world. Everything was clicking: "Surrender" ("Torna a Surriento") had succeeded "Are You Lonesome Tonight?" at number one on the charts in March; the *G.I. Blues* soundtrack, out since the previous November, continued to alternate between number one and number two on the LP charts; and they had another movie starting up — for United Artists this time — in July. There had been an almost uninterrupted flow of publicity off the back-to-back charity concerts, and Colonel had recently written to Vice President Lyndon Johnson announcing their availability for other worthy causes in the future. They had raised over $62,000 for the U.S.S. *Arizona* memorial, he informed the vice president. Now, more than ever, he declared, "we feel it proper to let you know that we are willing, able and available to serve in any way we can our country and our President in any capacity, whether it is to use our talents or help load the trucks."

He had created his own world, which even included his own club, the Snowmen's League, a W. C. Fieldsian celebrity roll without meetings or reality outside the Colonel's sardonic imagination, which cost nothing to get into and $10,000 to get out of ("We've never lost a member," boasted the Colonel). It was nothing more in short than a celebration of the age-old concept of "snowing," somewhere between selling and conning, to which the Colonel had dedicated his life, its name a take-off on the Showmen's League of circus owners and carnival operators from whom the Colonel had taken his inspiration, its membership booklet a map of the League's method of doing business. The table of contents gave a hint of methodology, with references to the "melt and disappear" technique and the concept of "directional" snowing (which required the ability to make one's approach simultaneous with one's departure) as well as consequences of the snowing life ("with sufficient training one can develop the ability to go nowhere with devastating results") — but the real core of the book was the thirty-two blank pages and Complete Listing of Paid-Up Members in Alphabetical Order (also blank) at its center. Over the years induction into the Snowmen's League had come to be taken as a high honor in Hollywood, and its bemused membership included everyone from Hal Wallis and Joe Hazen to RCA executives, William Morris agents, newspaper columnists, and such prominent show business personalities as Frank Sinatra, Milton Berle, Bing Crosby, and Bob Hope. It was the Colonel's sole concession to social climbing, and, inevitably, one in which he dictated all the rules.

Meanwhile his brother Ad was scheduled to arrive any day now. Much to the Colonel's annoyance, he got a call from *Time* magazine around this time asking what the story was with this guy who claimed to be his brother from Holland; he didn't have a secret stash of wooden shoes, did he? The Colonel harrumphed and spluttered, effectively putting the reporter off, but he was furious at his brother: What was the matter with him, letting everyone know his business? Didn't he realize you could get more with honey than you could with vinegar? When he met him at the airport, he let him know just what he thought of such behavior — but in English, not in Dutch. He had forgotten all his Dutch, he claimed, and as he drove Ad back to his Beverly Hills apartment he laid down the rules of the game: he was to be addressed as Colonel at all times; now that their mother was dead, he was *not* interested in any of their other brothers and sisters; he was no longer the man his brother had once known, he had created not just a new life but a new identity.

T HE MAN KNOWN AS Colonel Thomas A. (for Andrew) Parker had been born Andreas ("Dries") Cornelis van Kuijk in Breda, Holland, on June 26, 1909, to a father who was a liveryman and a mother whose parents were floating peddlers, traversing the Netherlands by its waterways and setting up a booth to sell their wares at local fairs and markets throughout the country. He grew up the fifth in a family of nine children, loving horses and animals generally, so fascinated by the circus, his siblings recalled, that he trained his father's horses to put on one of his own. When the van Bever family circus came to Breda as part of the great October carnival, Dries was captivated, volunteering to do odd jobs just so he could hang around. He taught his pet crow to sit on his shoulders and a goat to climb stairs.

He dropped out of school at thirteen or fourteen, helping out at the stable until his father's death in July 1925. Then the family dispersed, and he became a ward of his uncle in Rotterdam, going to work on the docks until, he said later, he got a job working for the Holland–America line. The next his family heard of him was a letter they got from a Dutch family in New Jersey declaring that Dries was living with them and doing well; he had been reluctant to write himself, but he was such a nice boy and they didn't want his uncle and aunt to worry.

He reappeared in Breda on September 2, 1927, his mother's birthday, remaining in town for a while and going to work on a shipping line between Breda and Rotterdam, before he disappeared again in May of 1929. The family didn't hear from him for a good while after that and never found out what the course of his wanderings had been. But it seemed clear that he had worked his way over to America once again on a freighter and found his way to Atlanta, where he enlisted in the army under the name of Andre van Kuijk, as part of a widespread recruiting drive to find volunteers to serve in Hawaii.

He was stationed at Fort de Russy at first, near Waikiki, then transferred to Fort Shafter, just outside Honolulu, as part of the Sixty-Fourth Regiment, an anti-aircraft unit, of the Coast Artillery. It was at Fort Shafter that he came under the command of Captain Thomas R. Parker, and it was from Fort Shafter that his family first heard from him again with a note that contained virtually no information but that was written in English and signed, inexplicably — *Thomas Parker.* His mother started getting bank drafts for $5 apiece shortly thereafter; seventeen of them arrived between January 1930 and February 1932, all originating in Washington, D.C., and going directly into the Frank Laurijssen Bank in Breda with no name of sender attached. He wrote occasionally, sent one or two pictures with no explanation of where he was or what he was doing. ("Never an address," recalled one family member, "only funny pictures. In one Dries was standing next to a big American car, maybe a Buick, and it was taken in Honolulu. In another, Dries was sitting by a swimming pool. We figured that he was a chauffeur for a rich man.") In February 1932 the bank deposits stopped, and there was one final letter to his mother. After that, the family never heard from him again.

What probably happened was that he left the army at this point. He was, evidently, transferred, back to the mainland, to Fort Barrancas in Pensacola, Florida, and sustained a knee injury, which earned him an honorable medical discharge. Somehow at this point he found his way to Tampa, where the carnival folk all wintered, and in 1932 he joined up with the Johnny J. Jones Exposition, signing on with the much bigger Royal American Shows a year or two later. That was where he met his wife, Marie — twice married and four years his senior, with a child from her first marriage — working the Hav-a-Tampa cigar stand on the grounds of the South Florida State Fair. He seems to have quit the carnival not long after meeting Marie and settled down in Tampa, where he became well known as the city's resourceful chief Dog Officer and where he, quite naturally, gravitated into show business, doing promotions first for Gene Austin and Roy Acuff and gradually expanding his show-business activities until, in 1944, he hooked up with Eddy Arnold and, with Arnold as his client, moved to Nashville at the end of the following year.

* * *

WHY HADN'T HE WRITTEN over all the years? Ad asked. Because, the Colonel said without blinking an eye, he and his wife had been destitute for much of that time. "Sometimes we had to live on a dollar a week. We slept in horse stables behind the horses. I did all kinds of things then. I went to the Indian territory, where I pretended to be a big wise white man. It so happened that sometimes I really predicted the future. I also had a canary and a few sparrows that I sprayed yellow and then sold. After a couple of weeks the people came back to me and said, 'This bird only says, "Peep!"' 'That's right,' I told them. 'It takes six weeks. It's got to feel at home.' I've been a dogcatcher, and I sold hot dogs. But I didn't want you to know all the things that I did. Besides, most of the time I didn't even have the money for stationery and a stamp. After that, the war came. I organized parties for the army, and that's how I got into the world of show business. At the end of the war I met a guy from Tilburg who served in the Princess Irene Brigade. He told me that Mother had died. She was in fact my only true tie with Holland, and when she was dead Holland was dead for me."

His brother accepted the account in the spirit in which it was offered, informing Dries that their mother had not actually died until 1958 but getting no visible reaction. He stayed in the storeroom of the Colonel's modest apartment, where he slept surrounded by stuffed animals, promotional items, and Elvis Presley merchandise. He was unable to penetrate his brother's elaborate web of fanciful inventions and was alternately intimidated by the manner in which Dries would bark orders into the phone and, as an entrepreneur of sorts himself, bemused by his brother's sheer audacity. Twenty-five percent of everything Presley made disappeared into the pockets of "the old Colonel," his brother boasted. "It fills 'em up nicely," Parker added, echoing an old Dutch saying.

Ad's visit lasted for seventeen days. In the course of his stay he met a number of the Colonel's friends and associates, including his wife's brother, Bitsy Mott, and he and Dries even went out to Elvis' home in Bel Air, where the Colonel simply introduced Ad as "my brother." When he returned to Holland, he had very little of a personal nature to convey to the rest of the family, and his other brothers and sisters suspected that Ad might have made his own deal with their wily "American" brother. His story ran in *Rosita* on July 1, 8, and 15, 1961, but no U.S. newspaper picked it up. The family made attempts to get in touch with the Colonel from time to time in subsequent years, but the only acknowledgment they ever got

was an Elvis calendar, the occasional streamer, or some other equally
impersonal promotional item.

Elvis returned home at the beginning of June. There was another
session coming up, precipitated once again by pressure from Steve
Sholes and Bill Bullock on behalf of RCA. The idea of a home studio had
been broached once again a number of months earlier; this time Elvis actually indicated his interest in building a recording facility at Graceland, and
initial plans were drawn up, but in the end Bullock was forced to make
excuses for RCA's unwillingness to finance it. They would gladly make their
Nashville or L.A. studios available to Elvis anytime, Bullock wrote to the
Colonel in May even as he was pointing out the need for a new session. The
Colonel countered with cold fury. Bullock should get used to the idea: they
were not going to deliver any more product than the contract called for,
with or without a studio to fool around in.

The session, on June 25 in Nashville, was limited to the recording of five
titles, but these were five titles for the most part of a very high order. There
were three by Doc Pomus and Mort Shuman, including "Kiss Me Quick,"
an up-tempo Italian-flavored r&b number, somewhat on the model of
"Save the Last Dance For Me" (and originally intended for the Flamingos)
with which the session kicked off. It was by far the most disposable of the
songs on the session, but Elvis carried it off with panache and really sank
his teeth into two other Pomus-Shuman contributions, "Little Sister," a
cheerfully nasty blues, and "(Marie's the Name) His Latest Flame," an
utterly charming demonstration of his mastery of pure pop, with a Latin-
flavored, Bo Diddley beat. Don Robertson's single offering, on the other
hand, "I'm Yours," was open-ended in a manner that encouraged Elvis
to express his full range of emotions and show off his vocal technique. It
came complete not only with a recitation but with the rare opportunity to
hear Elvis harmonize with himself, and had it not been for an unfortunate
roller-rink organ accompaniment, it might have taken its place among his
finest recordings. Just as remarkable, however, was the one song on the session that did not come from a professional songwriter, a moody piece
called "That's Someone You'll Never Forget." It was the second number
to be put down on tape, and its writers were listed as Red West and Elvis
Presley.

Red had actually been writing songs for some time now and had even gotten a few recorded (including sides by Pat Boone and Johnny Burnette) in addition to putting out a number of little singles of his own. But he had never been able to get a cut on Elvis Presley, or to get Hill and Range interested in his songs (to some extent one and the same thing), and he might not have been able to do so now if Elvis hadn't given him the phrase that became the song title earlier that spring. He had fooled around with it for a while, working out the melody first, then coming up with the lyrics. The song he had eventually come up with contained sentiments that under ordinary circumstances would have been assumed to be about an ex-lover, but in this case it wasn't much of a stretch to imagine that Elvis might be singing of his mother, an ambiguity that Red encouraged by the lack of specificity in his writing. It was a song about longing, and Elvis poured himself into it in a way that had nothing to do with craftsmanship, nothing to do with professionalism, and nothing to do with the territorial wars that Colonel and RCA continued to fight.

Red got married on July 1, to Elvis' pretty blond nineteen-year-old secretary Pat Boyd. There was the usual informal get-together at Graceland the night before, as friends started arriving at ten-thirty, a number of guests were tossed in the pool, and the party didn't break up until four. Elvis and Anita were late to the wedding the next day, late enough that Elvis' place as best man had to be taken by Joe Esposito — but when he arrived, he was resplendent, like the groom, in white tuxedo jacket, white ruffled shirt, paisley bow tie, and dark pants. After a reception in the church hall, most of the wedding guests drove out to the Fairgrounds, which Elvis had rented out for the occasion from midnight until six-thirty the following morning. The next day Elvis had to go to Nashville to record the soundtrack album for his new picture, and after a riotous Fourth of July fireworks fight, he and the guys all left for Crystal River, Florida, where *Follow That Dream* was scheduled to start shooting, trailing Elvis' new twenty-foot Coronado powerboat behind them.

Follow That Dream was a Mirisch Brothers/United Artists production, for which Elvis was to get $600,000 plus 50 percent of the profits, an offer too rich for Hal Wallis, who had the option of preempting it, even to think about matching. Elvis' nineteen-year-old cousin Billy Smith accompanied the group for the first time, and the Colonel arranged for a special event to honor Elvis' achievements in show business on the last Sunday of the month in Weeki Wachee Spring. Over three thousand solid citizens showed up, including the hastily convened Elvis Presley Underwater Fan Club, which put on a show in a large tank while Elvis and the guys, attired identically in cool dark continental suits, appreciatively looked on. Elvis attended with his co-star Annie Helm, as well as his father and stepmother (who had come down with the kids for a visit), while the Colonel orchestrated the bizarrely paranormal proceedings. This was the Colonel's old stomping grounds, and he demonstratively renewed acquaintanceships, as old friends from dogcatcher and carnival days constantly stopped by to wish him well throughout his Florida stay. At one point he even visited an elephant from the Royal American Shows, too old for the carnival now, whom the Colonel fed and clowned around with and encouraged to remember him.

Elvis enjoyed having his new boat on the river, went waterskiing frequently, and gave a good comic performance as idiot savant (and instinctive moral arbiter) Toby Kwimper. There was a decent screenplay for once, a good supporting cast, and the usual friction among the guys, as Joe got fired briefly for conspiring with the Colonel to get rid of a recent addition, Ray Sitton, known as "Chief," whom no one much liked to begin with but who, after Joe's reinstatement, became an accepted member of the group. The director, Gordon Douglas, invited Elvis to dinner one night, throwing him into a fit of consternation until the Colonel suggested that he bring all of the guys with him, explaining to Douglas afterward that Elvis was not comfortable except within his own circle.

Annie Helm, who was playing the ingenue role, observed it all with wide-eyed wonder. She was twenty-two years old, a seven-year veteran of television, modeling, and ballet, who had made one previous movie, but this was her big break. "I was not really a fan of Elvis' — I was so caught up in my own career I was almost like an old lady in my view of him — but I loved the part. I met him on location. He came over to my cabin on the day that I arrived and brought me a flower. He may have just picked the flower on the way over to the cabin, who knows? But we went for a drive and turned the radio on — and he was on the radio. It was a very bizarre date. I mean, I felt like I was in a small town with the poodle skirt and sneakers, like a little kid going out for a milkshake with my date. But we hit it off right away. He was so much fun, and there really was nothing to do down there except play cards at night and go out on the boat — I mean, we were all very bored."

They quickly drifted into a romance that seemed to her strangely impersonal in a way. "He loved to hang out with the guys. They made his word good. No one questioned what Elvis wanted. It wasn't that his demands were out of line — he just didn't want to put up with any nonsense. He had a lot of patience, he was always very polite, but he wanted things a certain way. It wasn't my idea of a fun date after a while. It was just me and the guys. That's sort of a strange way to spend your evenings with a person you care about.

"I always had fun with the Colonel. He liked to joke around, and that's the kind of relationship that I saw between Elvis and the Colonel. I think Elvis really cared about the Colonel. I remember the difference between Elvis' relationship with the Colonel and with his father. It was sort of like there was more of a reserve with his father. He was very polite, but I was shocked when I [first] found out that this was Elvis' father.

"When we were on location, we all took Dexedrine. I mean, in those days it wasn't considered drugs, I had doctors giving me Dexedrine diet pills from the time I was fourteen, because they wanted me to be emaciated as a model. You know, we used to stay up late at night, playing cards and goofing off until one in the morning, and then we'd have to be up early, so if I wanted a Valium to go to sleep, it was there, and then there was speed to keep us going during the day. I really was amazed at his talent — I used to tell him that. I don't remember him talking [much] about his feelings, but he did share with me that he was offered a part in *The Fugitive Kind* that was based on Tennessee Williams' play, with Elia Kazan directing. It was a wonderful movie, I mean, it was almost written for Elvis. He didn't say he had regrets, but my feeling was that he did.

"It was just never quite comfortable for me — I mean, it's abnormal to have a relationship with seven or eight guys. Naturally, they disappeared when we had romance, but then they came back again. In those days we were very promiscuous, and of course [I knew] he was having a lot of affairs, but we really adored one another, I mean, I really loved him. I just sensed that his life was very compartmentalized."

THEY SHOT THE INTERIORS in Hollywood. Elvis and Annie continued to go out for a while, but she knew instinctively that it was all over. Much of September was spent in Las Vegas, holed up at the Sahara, the casino owned by the Colonel's friend Milton Prell. Every night they went to the shows, Elvis and his guys, dressed identically in their dark glasses and dark mohair suits. The Colonel joked that they looked like a bunch of old men, but the Memphis Mafia had become almost as well known around town as Frank Sinatra's Rat Pack. They were living on speed and tranqs; for Joe, who liked to portray himself to Elvis as Broadway Joe, a sophisticated man-about-town, "it was a party like you wouldn't believe. Go to a different show every night, then pick up a bunch of women after-wards, go party the next night. Go to the lounges, see Fats Domino, Della Reese, Jackie Wilson, the Four Aces, the Dominoes — all the old acts. We'd stay there and never sleep, we were *all* taking pills just so we could keep up with each other."

The next picture started at the end of October after a brief return to Memphis and a four-tune Nashville session on October 15. *Kid Galahad*, the second in the two-picture deal with Mirisch, turned out to be a very differ-ent experience from the one he had in *Follow That Dream*. Once again he was playing a kind of idiot savant — an instinctively gallant boxer this time — but without the comic touch, or script, of the previous film. He was unhappy with his appearance (his weight had ballooned to nearly two hundred pounds), unmotivated about the film, and he felt generally put-upon — just about the only consolation was taking boxing lessons from former world welterweight champion Mushy Callahan, who treated him with deference and for whom Elvis felt great respect. He was stung, on the other hand, by the indifference of Charles Bronson, who played the part of his tough but kindly trainer. Bronson, one of fifteen children of a Lithuanian-born coal miner and a combat veteran of World War II, made it very clear that he was unimpressed by Elvis' karate exhibitions. Elvis for his part indi-cated to Red, and to Sonny, too, now back from exile with no apparent hard feelings on either side, that he had no use for Bronson, whom he uncharac-teristically dismissed as "a muscle-bound ape."

After three weeks of location work, they moved into a new house on Bellagio, just around the corner from Perugia. It was a Mediterranean villa with more room for the guys, and Elvis brought the husband-and-wife butler-and-cook team with them from Perugia. There were the usual fam-ily squabbles: Joe and Chief still didn't get along; Elvis took a liking to Sonny's girl with predictable results; a new guy, Marty Lacker, a friend of George Klein's who had come out with them for the first time, seemed to conceive of himself as Joe's assistant and rubbed everyone, including Joe,

the wrong way; Elvis was always encouraging Lamar to spout off on subjects he knew nothing about, just setting him up for the kill; and Gene was
feeling more and more left out.

About the biggest excitement was a chimpanzee named Scatter, whom
Elvis had bought in October from a Memphis TV personality named Captain Bill Killebrew. Scatter was only the latest in a long line of simians that
went back to Jayhew, a spider monkey who lived in a cage on the glassed-in
porch on Audubon Drive in 1956. Killebrew had taught Scatter how to
"drive" (Killebrew sat behind him with a setup that enabled him to steer,
accelerate, and brake from the backseat), and Alan got him a chauffeur's
cap and drove around in the Rolls with Scatter sitting on his lap, ready to
duck below the dashboard whenever he saw anyone that might be
impressed by the sight of a monkey at the wheel. Scatter introduced an
unpredictable element into their lives: shortly after his purchase in Memphis, he bit Vernon's wife, Dee; he wrecked a hotel room in Flagstaff on the
way out; best of all, he loved to look up girls' dresses, and he was an exhibi-
tionist in the manner of all chimpanzees. The guys taught him to drink,
too, and there was no end of Scatter stories, from his tearing out of all the
phone lines in the house to his having simulated sex with a former stripper
named Brandy to various hair-raising (and skirt-raising) escapades with
nearly every other girl who came to visit. When there was nothing else to
talk about, there was always Scatter.

E LVIS FINISHED UP THE MOVIE on December 19, which would have
given them more than enough time to get home for Christmas — but
what was the point? Vernon and Dee were still living at the house, though
they had just purchased a three-bedroom, split-level ranch around the corner — but even if they had been able to move before the holiday, there was
still no real reason to go home. The original plan, promoted by the
Colonel, had been to go to Vegas for a few days of R and R. Billy and Marty
returned to Memphis to see their families, and some of the other guys took
off for varying lengths of time. But then Joe started dating Joanie Roberts,
a twenty-year-old dancer at the Sands, and soon everyone else seemed to
have found more than enough diversions of their own. Elvis flew in Bonnie
Bunkley, his "other" Memphis girlfriend, for a few days, and he and Bonnie
and Joe and Joanie frequently double-dated in the Rolls, with one of the
guys driving and the rest tagging along.

To Joan, who had come out to Vegas after completing her reign as Miss Missouri the previous summer but was as notable for her perky good humor as for her blond good looks, "Elvis was so wonderful and warm — he was always more than polite. I can remember him yelling at the guys if any of them started to call somebody by their first name, 'I call him Mister, so you better call him Mister, too.' I don't know, I really accepted it all as normal. It was exciting to walk in and have everybody turn — he had so much mystique about him. You would walk into all the shows and get the first-class treatment: 'Come right here to the front row.' Everything was yours. Anything you wanted. All of that was exciting."

To Joe it was not quite so wholesome a vision. His own view of Elvis was an increasingly conflicted one, colored by his view of himself as a person with more street smarts and greater sophistication. "Elvis was very insecure. He knew nothing about the street. All he knew about was what he read in books." And his insecurity, Joe felt, led to weakness, fear of confrontation, an inability to assume responsibility, and a need to surround himself with potential scapegoats, whose number, Joe recognized, would always necessarily include Joe himself.

On New Year's Day they ran into the songwriter Don Robertson, in town to get married and also staying at the Sahara. "Elvis had met my wife, Irene, before, she had gone with me up to the house and he liked her a lot. Anyway, we sat in the coffee shop at the Sahara, Irene and me and Elvis and Joe or Lamar, just the four of us, and we got on the subject of weight. I had always had a struggle with my weight, and Elvis had, too — and Lamar was this wide. And Elvis said, 'I've got something for you. I've been taking some pills, and they just work great.' So after we parted company, one of his guys came down to where I was in the lobby and said, 'Elvis asked me to give this to you.' It was a big bottle of one thousand Dexedrine pills, and I started on them right away." Later Robertson spotted Colonel at the roulette wheel, losing what looked like thousands of dollars, "and we ended up sitting and talking very briefly. He said, 'You've been pretty lucky with Elvis, haven't you?' That was all he said, but the implication was that there was no talent involved on my part. I was just lucky."

Days stretched into weeks, weeks into a month and more. People came and went, Elvis celebrated his birthday on January 8 with a big cake supplied by the Colonel's friend Milton Prell — it seemed sometimes as if there was something almost holding him there. Three times they set out to leave, and three times they were forced to turn back on icy, snow-packed roads. He loved Las Vegas for one reason above all: time was meaningless here, there was no clock, there were no obligations. It was a place where you could lose yourself, a place you could indulge your every fantasy — it was, for Elvis, momentary respite from all the self-doubt, from all the questions lying in wait, lurking in the shadows, waiting to assault him.

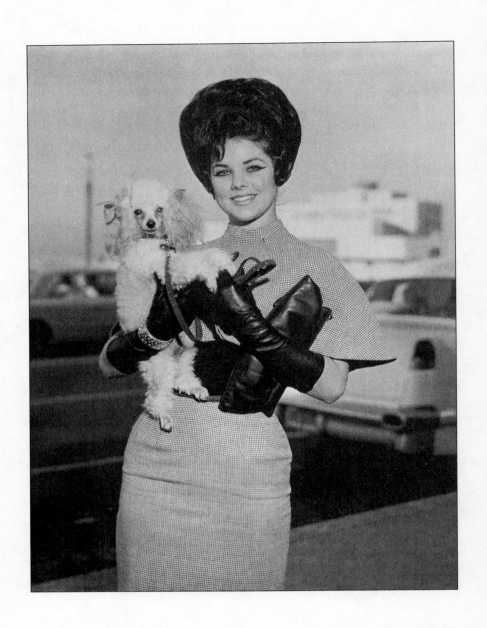

PRISCILLA, WITH HONEY, 1963. (MICHAEL OCHS ARCHIVES)

NEGLECTED DREAMS

HEY FINALLY PICKED UP CAMP and returned to Memphis at the end of January. Vernon and Dee had by now completed their move, taking up quarters in their new house on Hermitage, just behind Graceland, and life soon returned to the normal round of moviegoing and other recreational activities. There was another session in Nashville, on March 18 and 19, at which Elvis cut ten new sides. With five tracks still in the can from the previous session plus one unused number from *Blue Hawaii*, this constituted precisely half of the 1962 contractual commitment to RCA, and there was little doubt that the rest would be taken care of by soundtrack recordings. Elvis threw himself into a number of Doc Pomus and Mort Shuman songs, including "Suspicion," the latest in a growing line of Italianate offerings. There was one particularly moving ballad in the Don Robertson tradition ("She's Not You," written by Pomus in collaboration with Jerry Leiber and Mike Stoller), but once again the most arresting element of the session was a song that Elvis brought to it himself, which he only got around to at the end of the first long night of recording.

"You'll Be Gone" was a number that he and Red had been working on, writing and rewriting it in informal jams for over a year now. Originally they had set it to the tune of Cole Porter's "Begin the Beguine," but then Porter's publishing company refused them permission to alter his composition in any way and Charlie Hodge suggested a basic, two-chord "Spanish" melody, to which they continued to add new lyrics. In the end the song that they came up with was musically melodramatic and narratively murky, a tale of dark passions and dawn partings (because of the murkiness, it's hard to be any more specific: whether the singer was abandoning or being abandoned by his lover remains, for me anyway, a moot point), but it was one into which Elvis poured all of his emotions, climaxing in an all-out musical crescendo that all but overwhelmed the song.

It might well have offered a lesson. Had there been anyone to analyze the nonsoundtrack sessions of the last two years, they would certainly have noticed that new directions were being explored, that Elvis appeared tentatively to be trying to forge a new artistic identity composed of equal parts bravado (the aria-like quality of many of his most ambitious songs) and vulnerability (the utterly naked, painfully wounded fragility of some of the Don Robertson and Doc Pomus ballads). His very willingness to put his name on two of the songs, to claim actual authorship for the first time since 1956 (and not for business reasons this time), might have seemed to an outside observer evidence of a barely cloaked desire to reveal himself. But there was no such person. The Colonel increasingly saw these nonsoundtrack sessions as a waste of time, a diversion from their principal business of making movies. Steve Sholes and Bill Bullock, far from influencing anything going on in the sessions, were, by the Colonel's machinations, occupied almost exclusively just with getting Elvis into the studio. Freddy Bienstock was no more than a gatekeeper at this point, charged with shepherding properly credentialed songs in and out of the sessions. And the guys, with the notable exception of Red and Charlie, who were themselves actively involved in the music, and Lamar, who remained Elvis' biggest fan, just wanted to get the session over with and get back to Graceland.

Sometimes the studio players sensed what they took to be almost a soul weariness on Elvis' part, an acceptance of things as they were which, while it never compromised his professionalism, led to a numbing sense of defeat. In the view of Jordanaire Gordon Stoker, "he always tried to make the best out of any situation. Sometimes he'd walk over to us [at the soundtrack sessions] and say, 'Man, what do we do with a piece of shit like this?' Sometimes he'd back up so far from the microphone that they would say, 'Elvis, you've just got to get closer to the mike'; they'd put a soundboard around him just to try to pick him up. But most of the time he would console himself with the idea of, 'Well, regardless of what I say, [they're] going to demand that I do this song, so I'll just do the best I can.'"

They returned to California right after the session for the new Paramount picture. There was no doubt in Hal Wallis' mind what image of Elvis *he* intended to convey. He would give the public what it wanted, Elvis the entertainer over Elvis the actor — a course that in his mind was only reinforced by the relative failures of Twentieth Century Fox's *Flaming Star* and *Wild in the Country*. His own *Blue Hawaii*, by way of contrast, had gone straight to number two on *Variety*'s weekly list of top-grossing films upon its Thanksgiving release and continued to do business well into the new year (it ended up as the fourteenth-highest-grossing film of 1962, doing a total of $4.7 million worth of business for the two years). Meanwhile the album from *Blue Hawaii*, like *G.I. Blues* before it, shot to number one on the LP charts, far outstripping any studio album Elvis had released to date (with sales of over one and one-half million, it sold close to five times the number of *Elvis Is Back*, for example) and further confirming the wisdom not just of Hal Wallis' strategy but of the Colonel's grander plan.

To the Colonel the movies were just one more plum in the pudding, a promotional tool which could sell the music and which the music in turn could sell. Nothing could be simpler or more logical: the soundtrack album promoted the movie release, the movie release guaranteed a certain level of sales and publicity for the album. And as the Colonel perfected his own brand of synergistic opportunity (there were balloons, calendars, radio ads, photo opportunities, and a deluge of press releases to go with each sales campaign, every aspect of which the Colonel personally oversaw), it began to become apparent that there was no real need for anything *but* the soundtrack music. Why record separate singles and albums when the movie material sold better, was more easily controlled (there was no reason ever to go outside the Hill and Range catalogue; every song originated with Elvis Presley and Gladys Music and came complete with all the financial concessions that were a sticking point for so many outside songwriters), and could serve to fulfill all their commitments to RCA? It was a perfect setup in almost every way, and with the clause giving RCA nominal control over song selection long since deleted from the contract, and royalties and guarantees substantially improved as of the beginning of 1962 (Elvis and the Colonel were now to realize $200,000, split 75 percent–25 percent between them, as an annual advance payment against royalties through 1966), there was little to spoil the Colonel's overall sense of well-being, save for the one thought never far from his mind, that even a good position could be improved.

For *Girls! Girls! Girls!,* Hal Wallis took the company to Hawaii once again for beautiful vistas, beautiful sunsets, and, needless to say, beautiful girls. It was a highly forgettable production, a decided step back artistically not just from the two United Artists films that immediately preceded it but even from *Blue Hawaii*. Norman Taurog was directing once again, and there were lots of familiar faces among the crew, but even the soundtrack seemed somewhat of an afterthought, with only Otis Blackwell's "Return to Sender" rising above a level of dreary mediocrity.

They returned from Hawaii at the end of April and finished principal shooting on the Paramount lot on June 8. There were lots of parties and, *always,* lots of girls, but to Sandy Ferra, about to graduate from Hollywood Professional School at the age of sixteen, there remained a kind of innocence at the core. Even though she knew she was far from the only girl in his life, she didn't date anyone but him. Sometimes when they talked about the future, he told her that she was the kind of girl that he would like to marry, if and when the time came to get married. He remained very tender and protective of her, he never ever pressured her, but he could be jealous, too. When she went with a classmate to her senior prom, he became very upset, "so I had my mom come pick me up at the Beverly Hills Hotel, and she drove me up to the house, and then he drove me home."

Sometimes, she knew, his temper could flare up, and you just had to stay out of his way. Everyone talked about the girl that Sonny brought out to the house one time who decided that she wanted to leave while Elvis and Sonny were playing pool. She asked Sonny if he could move his car because she was blocked in, and Elvis got annoyed and told her to get somebody else to move the car, didn't she see they were in the middle of a damn game? The girl didn't know anybody else and, failing to recognize the familiar signs, asked Sonny again. "Goddamnit!" Elvis exploded. "Didn't you hear what I said? Get someone else to move it." The girl, embarrassed now and mad, cursed Elvis and called him a sonofabitch. That was when Elvis hurled his pool cue at her, striking her in the breast. It was probably because she had called him a sonofabitch, they all theorized afterward — you couldn't say that to Elvis, he took it as a slur on his mother. But how could Sonny's girl, how could *any* outsider have known that? It was just lucky she wasn't more badly hurt; it was fortunate, the guys all agreed when they discussed it among themselves, she didn't sue.

He was curiously inept in certain basic social ways. "He was so retarded," remarked one of the girls, who came up to the house regularly dressed in "my nice little tweed skirt, with my white blouse, black bolero jacket, stockings and heels — you didn't just go up in your blue jeans and T-shirt. All the girls dressed the same. The guys were more aggressive; they scored because a girl always had the idea that eventually she would get to Elvis [through one of them]. Elvis himself had nothing to say; if Scatter hadn't been there, we probably would have sat there all night looking at each other. The chimp became the focus of attention, all the conversation was centered on the activities of the chimp — it was like a buffer.

"One time Elvis took a friend of mine out of the room and made out on a couch upstairs — it was like heavy teen petting, and he got totally aroused, and all of a sudden he came all over his pants. He got embarrassed and said, 'Oh, look at all the babies we killed.' I'll never forget that statement. If he got involved [with some girl] on a casual basis and she put out really quickly and went to bed with him, I really don't think he'd see her again. Because that meant she was a bad girl. I don't know any of my friends who [had sex] with him. A lot of them made out with him, but they didn't go to bed with him, and one, who was just the ultimate good girl — I mean, she came from a Catholic family on the East Coast and was one of the few virgins in town — spent the night with him all the time but remained totally unsullied, because he just really respected her."

Few of the girls knew about the two-way mirror he had installed in the swimming pool cabana that served as a ladies' dressing room. Sonny had originally gotten a smaller version for the house on Perugia, where they had used it in the den for shows put on by the guys and their unsuspecting dates. The only way to gain access to the new one was by crawling under the house, but Elvis and the guys just took that as part of the game.

On Sunday afternoons all the girls came over to watch them play football at the little park on Beverly Glen, just off Sunset, five minutes from the house. They would play half a dozen games in a row, two or three touchdowns declared the winner, and Elvis' team always won. They played against teams made up of other young actors and singers, like Pat Boone, Jan and Dean, Ty Hardin, Bob Conrad, Ricky Nelson, and Bing Crosby's son Gary, while Elvis' team included Red and Sonny and the rest of the guys, plus ringers like Max Baer, Jr., the giant star of *The Beverly Hillbillies,* whose father had been heavyweight champ. Elvis always played quarterback, throwing himself into the fray with genuine abandon but taking the game utterly seriously, too, diagramming elaborate plays for his team, following developments in the National Football League religiously, and deeming the sport "a gift of the gods."

He was almost as excited about his new Dodge motor home, taking frequent trips out to George Barris' Kustom Automotive Products in North Hollywood, where he was having it tailored to his specifications. Barris, the thirty-seven-year-old "King of the Kustomizers" and car designer to the stars, had already fixed up his black 1960 Cadillac limousine with two telephones, an entertainment console, a refreshment bar, and a little electric shoe buffer, all gold-plated with a golden guitar insignia, while the car itself was painted in a white-gold Murano pearl with gold-plated trim and Elvis' name written in gold. He and Barris frequently conferred on the motor home, seeking some of the same "luxury yacht" feeling for a vehicle that Barris personally considered a piece of shit. "He'd be very much involved. He liked to make a selection of materials. He liked to see sketches. He was not some guy who would write up a ticket and then say, 'No, no, not that way.' He was excited every time he got something new, and he never was pushy to put himself on a different level from everybody else." He eagerly pointed out all the little conveniences and innovations (what Barris called the "toys") to the guys, oblivious of how many times he might have shown them off before. He kept checking about when the motor home would be ready — and then he practically floored Barris when he asked if he and Mrs. Barris might be willing to do Elvis a special favor and put up a houseguest for a few days: his girl was coming over from Germany for a visit.

I T WAS SOMETHING HE had been planning for quite some time now. He had started talking to Priscilla about it in March, two years after they had last seen each other and months since their most recent telephone conversation. Priscilla had continued to write nearly every day; she continued to voice her hope that her parents would allow her to visit and that they would be reunited someday, but she had just about given up the thought of ever hearing from him again when he called and said that he wanted to make arrangements for her to come to L.A.

Her parents were, naturally, somewhat apprehensive about the prospect, and her dad set all kinds of conditions once he was even willing to discuss it. She had to finish her school year, he said, he wanted a complete itinerary, and he wanted to know where she was going to be staying and who would be chaperoning her (it would, of course, be out of the question for her to stay with Elvis). And she would need a first-class round-trip ticket.

She was sure that Elvis would be insulted and tell her to forget about the whole thing, she was furious at her parents and sulked in her bedroom for days — but Elvis only seemed to see each of the requirements as a challenge to get by, and one by one, in a series of phone calls and negotiations, he overcame each of the objections, until, in the end, a day was set. It all had to be carried out with the precision and hush-hush secrecy of a military operation, and maybe that was one of the things that appealed to him most. Not only was there Captain Beaulieu to mollify and security to be maintained (the Colonel didn't have to tell him what the consequences would be if the press ever got hold of this), there were Anita's acute suspicions to allay as well. With Joe's cooperation, he came up with a plan to throw her off the track, dispatching Joe's new wife, Joanie, to Memphis — which, with the movie done, couldn't help but convince Anita that they would be home soon. Elvis even enlisted his father and Dee to divert her attention by taking the girls to look over a fishing camp that he said he was planning to buy.

The motor home was ready, the Barrises had prepared a room for Priscilla at their duplex in Griffith Park, Captain Beaulieu's conditions had all been met — everything was in readiness. One night Elvis sat all the girls down at the house on Bellagio and announced that there would be no more parties, that nobody would be allowed up at the house for the time being. This little girl who was coming to visit was very special, he said; they had been talking on the phone all these months, and now she was traveling all the way from Germany to see him.

JOE PICKED HER UP at the airport, pointing out some of the sights to her on the way back to the house. They were met at the door by Jimmy the butler, who informed her that "Mr. P. is in the den," and she followed Joe down the stairs to the source of the music and laughter she had heard when she entered the house. She didn't see Elvis at first; there were a bunch of people standing around a jukebox. But then she spotted him dressed in dark pants, a white shirt, and a dark captain's hat, leaning over the pool table, lining up his shot. She stood there for a moment, until at last he saw her, too. "There she is!" he shouted, throwing down his pool stick. "There's Priscilla!"

It wasn't the way she had envisioned it — candlelit, hesitant, intimate, alone. He kissed her in front of everyone, murmured how much he had missed her, and took her around the room to introduce her to all of the guys and their girls. She tried not to shrink from the attention, his and everyone else's; he told her she looked great and she wondered if she really did — and she wondered for the first time if she had made a big mistake. She wondered who was this confident, dark-haired twenty-seven-year-old man whom she had known as an insecure, fearful, fair-haired boy, and how could he possibly be interested in her?

The rest of the evening passed in a blur. He went on playing pool, coming back to her from time to time to give her a kiss, as if to make sure she was really there — but continuing to play the star role, while treating her like a prize possession meant to be casually shown off. He was no more at ease than she was herself, she realized, but he was not willing to admit it and covered his fear with a boastfulness that she failed to recognize at first. "It was a shock to me, he wasn't someone that I could just say, 'Gee, I'm feeling insecure now because I don't know anybody, because everyone is older and I'm the only girl here who is sixteen.' I didn't feel that I could confide in him; he had a wall put up, not from me, but he had his entourage around. I think he felt like he had to lock himself up into another person that was confident, I think for the boys he had to show that he wasn't about to let a woman control him or make decisions for him, that he was in charge."

It was only when they got behind closed doors that she saw the sweet, frightened, vulnerable boy that she had known. Then the barriers came down, just like they had in Germany, he revealed himself to her in a way that gradually allowed her to quiet her own fears. In his bedroom, in the early hours of the morning, they kissed and kissed, until she made it clear to him that she didn't want to stop with kissing. "Wait a minute, baby," Elvis remonstrated. "This can get out of hand."

> "Is there anything wrong?" I was fearful that I wasn't pleasing him. He shook his head, kissed me again, then gently put my hand on him. I could feel for myself just how much he desired me. . . .
>
> "Elvis, I want you."
>
> He put his fingers to my lips and whispered, "Not yet, not now. We have a lot to look forward to. I'm not going to spoil you. There'll be a right time and place, and when the time comes, I'll know it."
>
> Although confused, I wasn't about to argue. He made it clear that this was what he wanted. He made it sound so romantic, and, in a strange way, it *was* something to look forward to. . . .

In the early-morning hours, he had Joe drive her over to the Barrises, so as to be sure to keep his promise to her father.

* * *

THE NEXT DAY HE WAS like a kid, showing her all around: he pointed out the houses of the stars, the movie lots, places that he knew, places that he'd been. "We drove all over for hours, he was just so happy to see me — and that threw me, too. Because I couldn't understand: here he was doing what he loved — he could be with whoever he wanted to be with — and yet here he was showing such enthusiasm and boyishness around me, trying to show me Hollywood." Later in the day he got the idea of going to Las Vegas. They had the motor home, it wasn't that much of a drive anyway, and Alan could take her shopping for something to wear — if she would just pre-write a series of postcards before they left, Jimmy could mail her parents one a day, with the appropriate Los Angeles postmark. The guys spent the rest of the afternoon and evening loading up, and around midnight they all piled in, with Elvis driving, Priscilla beside him, and Gene riding shotgun and babbling away in a language that only his cousin could understand. Every so often Gene would pounce on Elvis in an alarming sneak attack, but then he would scuttle to the back of the bus, where he was protected from reprisal by the rest of the guys, whose loud guffaws made Priscilla feel as if she would always be an outsider.

They arrived at the Sahara at 7:00 in the morning, and, after getting the room set up just the way Elvis liked it, with his RCA stereo system assembled, the lights turned down, and all the TV sets on low to provide an illusion of constant muted conversation, they went to bed. Elvis stared at her for a while before the sleeping pills took effect. "Do you believe this, baby?" he said. "After all this time, here you are. Who'd ever have thought we'd pull this off?" Then his words began to slur, as he said, "Let's not even think about you going back. We'll think about the other when the time comes."

ELVIS SPENT THE NEXT TWO WEEKS showing her the town. She had as hard a time getting used to the upside-down hours at first as she did to the celebrity life, but gradually she grew accustomed to both. She took amphetamines along with the others to wake up in the late afternoon, and she took sleeping pills in the early-morning hours to get to sleep. She was, in her own words, "adapting"; the uppers, she felt, allowed her to be more assertive, she had a whole new wardrobe and a whole new sophisticated, heavily made-up and beehive-coiffed image — what she was having the most trouble with was *Elvis,* getting used to him, getting used to his moods, just trying to figure out where she fitted in.

"[It was like] he'd decided he was going to take me to Vegas and dress me up and show me to everyone, introduce me because he'd been talking about me to everybody for so long. It was just so hard for me to understand this, as a kid. I started looking at myself: 'What is it about me?' You know, I didn't quite understand it: 'What *is* it?' He showed me the best time, took me shopping, picked out everything for me, bought me everything — I couldn't look like a seventeen-year-old, that was one of the things he was trying to do. And the night was always for courting, he was always pursuing me, always trying to impress me. In a sense it was so normal; it was the exact same thing a seventeen- or eighteen-year-old would be doing in high school — he didn't have to do any of those things, but he was pursuing me as if there was still doubt: Will she still like me? — you know. Or: Am I impressing her enough? It was like he never really felt as if he had me, it seemed."

One time, early in the visit, he played her some acetates from his most recent recording session with a bunch of the guys around, and she made the mistake of giving him her honest reaction. She liked them, she said, they were really pretty, but she wished he would do something more in his old rock 'n' roll style, something like "Jailhouse Rock" — that was what the kids really went for. "Goddamnit," he exploded. "I didn't ask for your opinion on what style I should sing. I asked if you like[d] the songs, that's all — yes or no. I get enough amateur opinions as it is. I don't need another one."

He marched into the bedroom and slammed the door, leaving her mortified and confused: How could she have been so stupid? It was just one more illustration of why she didn't really belong. There was nobody else around, and eventually the bedroom door opened, and she saw Elvis standing there in the doorway. He motioned to her to come inside, closed the door, and sat her down on the edge of the bed. To her surprise not only did he apologize, he spent the rest of the day trying to make up to her for it. But she learned to keep her mouth shut from then on whenever anyone else was around, she saw the others subjected to the same whims and flashes of temperament, and she learned that "there were definitely rules. You had to play by the rules. The more you knew, the longer you lasted."

On their last night together she begged once more for him to consummate their relationship, and while he still refused to deflower her, "he fulfilled my every desire. 'I want you back the way you are now,'" he told her. "'And remember, I'll always know.'"

She returned to her parents transformed. When she first saw them, "my mother was crying with joy . . . and my father was wearing a big welcome-home smile. But as I came nearer, their expressions changed from delight to absolute horror. My father turned away angrily. For a moment my mother just stared. Then she reached into her purse, pulled out a mirror, and thrust it at me. 'Look at yourself. How could you walk off the plane like that?'" She immediately understood. Her makeup was smeared, her beehive hairdo was unkempt, she was not their little girl anymore. She felt ashamed and defiant. All she could think about was how she was going to get back to her lover.

E LVIS AND THE GUYS RETURNED to Memphis just after Priscilla's departure at the beginning of July. Memphis didn't really offer much in the way of diversion — not after Vegas. They rented the Memphian whenever Elvis wanted to go to the movies; they rented the Fairgrounds three or four nights a week; and Elvis proudly showed off the motor home to anyone and everyone who expressed an interest. There were lots of pills and lots of parties, and that was the summer that he and Anita finally broke up.

She would have had to be blind to have missed the change in him. There wasn't any need for anyone else to tell her, Elvis was the last person able to keep a secret himself. There was all this talk and all this scurrying around and all this plotting — and it was becoming increasingly obvious that Elvis was never going to marry her anyway. "I wanted a husband, and I wanted a home and a family — you know, some people might not have wanted that, but that's what I wanted, and I saw that girls were there continuously and that was not going to change. He led me to believe, and I *did* believe, that they were not important to him, but [that] because they were his fans he always treated them nice and that he would always come back to me; always, you know, after every episode he would just smooth things over, and there I'd be.

"[But at] this time, I was in my young twenties and I was ready to get married and have a family, and then the fact that this little girl [had come] all the way over from Germany — I mean, I couldn't believe it. So I just made the decision. It was a very *difficult* decision because I loved him, he was my first love and I hated to give up being with him, enjoying the fun and the super things that we did, because I knew there would never be anyone like that again or any way of life like that again — but I was ready for that step. So one afternoon, he was eating breakfast, Elvis and Mr. Presley were at the dining table, and I just shared with him that I was going to leave, that there was no future there, and we both cried, and Mr. Presley was very touched and said, 'I see things like this on TV, you know. Maybe you'll get back together sometime.' And I [said], no, I didn't think that would ever happen, and Elvis said, 'Oh, Little, I pray to God I'm doing the right thing by letting you go.' And I said, 'It's got to be that way,' and I went and called my brother because I had a lot of things out at Graceland, and he [came] and got all my things from Grandma's room and we loaded them up and I went home to Jackson and stayed there for quite some time."

Not before she released a statement to the paper on August 6, though, in which she announced that she was ready "to pick up the pieces of my career." Elvis was not ready to settle down, she told the *Press-Scimitar* reporter, and she had to start thinking about what she was going to do herself. She had a recording date coming up in Nashville, she said; the song's title was "Love's Not Worth It." Her previous release, the paper pointed out with some asperity, was entitled "I'll Wait Forever."

Elvis for his part felt both guilty and relieved. Some of the guys thought Anita was too focused on her career, he knew; even Colonel felt she sometimes liked seeing her name in print too much — but that wasn't the problem. He just couldn't give her what he knew she had every right to expect. Anita was the last link to Mama — Mama had really loved her, and if he had to be honest, that was probably what hurt the most. He had always told his mother that he would get married and have children someday, and he didn't like the feeling that her dream was still lingering like a broken promise in the air. But otherwise he didn't have any regrets. Not really. He knew that he had always treated Anita like a lady. And besides, he couldn't get that little girl in Germany out of his mind.

THE NEXT MOVIE, tentatively titled *Take Me to the Fair*, took them to Seattle, Washington. MGM, stealing a page out of Hal Wallis' book, decided that shooting in a semi-exotic setting was the key to a successful Elvis Presley film, so for the first picture under their new 1961 contract they borrowed Norman Taurog to direct his fourth Elvis Presley vehicle and spent three weeks filming at the Seattle World's Fair. For a time there was talk of a live performance at the fair, but that fell through and life on the set was pretty dull, with the exception of the cream-pie and water fights that livened up the action and the elaborate practical jokes with which Elvis and

the guys, their number now swollen to nine, sometimes amused themselves. (One of Elvis' favorites on this trip was calling for hotel room service after removing all the furniture from the room, then having it all back
in place by the time the astonished bellboy returned with the manager.)
Colonel saw any location shoot as a good opportunity for publicity, so he
allowed a number of photographers on the set, planted a story on the new
continental wardrobe that Elvis would be sporting in the picture (Elvis had
grown up, said Hollywood couturier Sy Devore, who allowed that the
entire wardrobe cost $9,300 and included everything but underwear, because
Elvis, Devore said, never wore any underwear), and, when they returned
to the Hollywood lot, set up interviews with two trusted national reporters, Lloyd Shearer and Vernon Scott, for stories in *Parade* and *McCall's*
magazines.

Shearer, who had first met a twenty-one-year-old Elvis Presley in Memphis in the summer of 1956 as he was about to make his first movie (this
was the interview in which Elvis explained his theory of lasting motion picture appeal; he was not going to smile too much, he said, because if you
smiled, you forfeited credibility: "I know you can't be sexy if you smile. You
can't be a rebel if you grin"), encountered the same disarmingly honest
approach the second time around. Although Elvis Presley was now a movie
star who, Shearer noted somewhat credulously in his lead, "earned the
staggering sum of $2,800,000 on which he cheerfully paid, after all deduc-
tions, a federal income tax of $1,700,000 [the previous year]," he remained
"one of the most considerate, well-mannered young gentlemen in the
movie community." Colonel Parker, too, remained the same, "a razor-
sharp mountain of a business manager," who happily confided all the financial details of his client's success.

What was changed, oddly enough, was the *effect* of the young man's
candor. Where once it had protected him and prevented him, in the formulation of Sun Records office manager Marion Keisker, from "ever making a
wrong move," now it unmasked him, revealing an uncertainty, an almost
fatalistic sense of dissatisfaction which, while it never appeared in the published story, verged occasionally on a kind of wounded truculence.

He had been motivated from the beginning, he said, by respect for his
fans. "I don't assume the attitude of, 'Get these people out of here,' like I
have heard of being done. I don't just sign the autographs and the pictures and so forth to help my popularity or to make them like me. I do it
because they're sincere, and if you don't do it, you hurt their feelings. Once

you get involved in this business, your life is not your own, really, because people are going to want to know what you're doing, where you are, what you wear, what you eat — and you have to consider that these people are sincere."

As far as his own career went, there remained a lot to do, "but I feel that it takes time to accomplish certain things, you can't overstep your bounds." In that same vein, he wouldn't want to remain at a standstill. "I'd like to progress. But I realize that you can't bite off more than you can chew, you have to know your capabilities. I have people say to me all the time, 'Why don't you do an artistic picture? Why don't you do this picture [or] that picture?' Well, that's fine — I would like to. I would like to do something some day where I feel that I really done a good job. I think it will come eventually — you know, that's my goal. But in the meantime, if I can entertain people with the things I'm doing — well, I'd be a fool to tamper with it, to try to change it. It's ridiculous to take it on your own and say, 'Well, I'm gonna change, I'm gonna try to appeal to a different-type audience.' Because you might not. You might not. And if you goof a few times, you don't get many chances in this business. That's the sad part about it. So you are better off — if what you are doing is doing okay, you're better off sticking with it, till just time itself changes things. I mean, that's the way, I believe, really."

He spoke of his mother, whom Shearer had met ("Funny, she never really wanted anything — anything fancy. She just stayed the same all the way through"), his loneliness, and his guiding philosophy and motivation. "I like to entertain people. The money, or the financial end, is not the greatest aspect as far as I'm concerned. It can't be. Because if it was, it would show, and I wouldn't care about the other people, I wouldn't care about a performance that I gave. That's why I pick all my records and try to pick the best songs possible. I tried to do the best I can in the movies, you know, with the experience I've gotten, but looking at myself strictly as a human being, who's like I said been very lucky but whose life has blood running through my veins and it can be snuffed out in just a matter of seconds, not as anything supernatural or better than any other human being —"

But did he like himself? Shearer cut in, which seemed to bring him up short. "Sometimes," he said with a laugh. "No, what I mean by liking myself, I'm proud of the way I was brought up to believe and to treat people and have respect for people. I — when I am pushed to a certain point, I have a very bad temper, so much to the point that I have no idea what I'm doing." Did he blow often? the reporter asked. "Not very often. In fact, I could probably count the times. But when I have, it's always been pretty bad — but that doesn't happen very often, and, of course, everyone has a temper — and then I don't like myself, you know, later."

If he could have done anything differently, he would like to have gone to college, but, he quickly suggested, one of the principal reasons was that he wanted to play football, he had had "a great ambition to play football — and I still [do], believe it or not." He had a touch football league back home, and he liked contact sports, where you dealt with your opponent "as a man, you know." He wasn't knocking people who liked golf or tennis or other things, but he liked rugged sports such as boxing and football and karate. He knew the numbers of all the NFL players, he watched as many games as he could, even got film from some of the NFL teams to study the action more closely.

What about these eight or nine guys that he had around him all the time? What exactly was their function?

Well, Elvis said, hedging on exactly who was and wasn't a member of the group, there really weren't eight or nine, there were just five, really, the others came and went. And they all had *jobs:* one was an accountant, his cousin Gene took care of the cars, and he felt sorry for his little cousin, Billy, who had had trouble finding a job because of his size. . . . But what about intellectual growth? Shearer said, coming back to the topic. Didn't he find some of these guys he had grown up with somewhat lacking?

No, he didn't, Elvis said with more than a touch of annoyance. He had thought about this question before, and he had his own approach to learning; it didn't necessarily depend on them. But they were all different, they had their own little tics, they were not dummies by any means. "I don't have them around because they're idiots. But now you can surround yourself with intellectuals or people [who are] your so-called equal[s], and there can be dissension, there can be jealousy, and that's bad. The only thing you can learn there is to become bitter. I have my own way of learning. I learn from the people I work with. I learn from everyday life itself. I mean, I'm not trying to impress anybody by having a group of intellectuals around — not that I'm knocking [intellectuals], but you can be fooled by having a group of people that you think you're learning something from, and you're not learning a damn thing. I had a girl say to me one night, 'Don't make the mistake, Elvis, of surrounding yourself with people you can't learn something from,' and the girl never caught it, but I got up and walked away from her. I never said a word, but in so many words I was saying, 'I can't learn anything from you.'

"You can't fool yourself. I have my own way of thinking, and nobody else, regardless of their belief, can change me or make me think a certain way if I don't feel that it's right. There's not an intellectual son-of-a-gun walking the face of the earth that could make me believe a certain thing unless I really thought [it was right]. It's more important to try to surround yourself with people who can give you a little happiness, because you only pass through this life once, jack, you don't come back for an encore."

While his friends snickered in the background, he told Shearer that he wanted to marry ("I mean, who wants to grow old and be alone?"), that he might have liked to become a doctor if he had had the money to go to college ("I keep up with modern medicine, medical discoveries, diseases, I get doctor's handbooks, the *PDR,* which is [the] *Physicians' Desk Reference,* things like that"), and that he read philosophy and poetry, particularly a book called *Leaves of Gold,* which contained "different men's philosophy of life and death and everything else."

At the end of the interview Shearer asked him if he would do anything differently if he were entering the entertainment world today. No, Elvis said, "I would do exactly what I felt. I wouldn't make it a point to do a certain thing. I've got to do just like I've always done, going by impulse and the spur-of-the-moment. That's the only way I can operate." And if he had one lesson to impart to a son? He seemed taken aback, he didn't have a son, that was a difficult question to answer theoretically. But if he did? "I think my biggest thing would be consideration for other people's feelings," he said, whatever could keep you "from becoming hardened," whatever could make you "a better human being."

T HERE WERE NO MORE MOVIES scheduled for the last two months of the year. There were no more recording sessions, because with the movie soundtracks all of his obligations to RCA had been fulfilled. And the tour that the Colonel had been talking about for the past year had never worked out; he wasn't sure exactly why. The original idea had been for RCA to finance it; he would appear in forty-three cities under the sponsorship of RCA's forty-three distributors, with a press conference in each city and a guarantee of over $1 million. Colonel had even turned down a second

MGM picture for this year so they could do it. But RCA had evidently lost some of its enthusiasm, and Colonel wasn't interested in their proposal to scale the tour down to eleven cities for a flat $500,000. It wasn't worth doing if it wasn't going to be done right, Colonel said, and if RCA lacked the nerve to back what would undoubtedly have been one of the Biggest Tours in Show Business History, it was better to wait. Other opportunities would come along.

In the meantime, they were sitting pretty. They had three more MGM movies coming up, at a salary of $500,000 per picture *plus* 50 percent of the profits after Elvis' salary earned out (this was at a time when a top money-maker like Elizabeth Taylor might get $750,000 for a picture — but one that cost twice as much and took twice as long to shoot). They had their old reliable Hal Wallis contract, which would once again pay $175,000 for the next picture, presently scheduled to be filmed on location in Mexico. And in August Colonel had induced RCA to upgrade the contract, which had been renegotiated as recently as January, with a three-year extension (plus an additional two-year option, through 1971); two more nonrecoupable royalty points (to be divided equally between Elvis and the Colonel); a guarantee of $320,000 a year against royalties, with $240,000 to Elvis and $80,000 to Colonel; and a nonrecoupable signing bonus of $50,000 for each, with that bonus repeated for two years, then reduced to $37,500 apiece for the next four years of the contract, which added up to nonrecoupable payments of $600,000, split 50–50 between manager and client.

Colonel explained it all patiently to Elvis and Vernon, drawing a careful distinction between the 25-percent management fee he would continue to take on all formal contractual guarantees (both royalty payments and advances against royalties) and the special partnership arrangement that applied to bonus payments, as much a fruit of the Colonel's salesmanship as of Elvis' talents, which the Colonel (and the Colonel alone) could have gotten out of RCA. Elvis had no quarrel with his manager; he fully grasped the concept of what Colonel sometimes referred to as their "joint venture," and he took almost as much satisfaction in hearing all the details of how Colonel had put it over on RCA as the older man took in recounting them. But he had no one to share the story with. Vernon was never one to dwell on such matters, and though he dropped veiled allusions to the guys, they didn't really show much interest, and in the absence of anything better to do, they all headed for Las Vegas again when filming was over at the beginning of November.

They stayed for just two weeks this time, with a wearying sense of frag-mentation and déjà vu. For all of his brave words to Lloyd Shearer, Elvis felt frustrated and bored, tired of the same situations, the same conversations, the small dramas of petty jealousy, endlessly repeated, that seemed to make up his daily life. Lamar had left in June; there had been a big blowup right after *Girls! Girls! Girls!*, and he was now road-managing for Sandy Ferra's friend and Hollywood Professional School classmate Brenda Lee. Red and Sonny were in and out of the group, trying to make their way in Hollywood; Charlie was off with veteran country singer Jimmy Wakely half the time; and he was increasingly worried about his cousin Gene, who seemed to be getting goofier by the minute and had almost ODed on their trip out to California in August. Gene had been driving for two days straight and was completely wired on uppers, so Elvis prescribed 500 mil-ligrams of Demerol to calm him down. When that didn't work, Elvis gave him 500 milligrams more, but Gene mixed that with sleeping pills, and when Billy found him, he was passed out and barely breathing in the back of the motor home. Somehow they managed to revive him — but it was becoming increasingly clear that Gene could no longer fit in.

The way that Billy saw it, Elvis promoted conflict just to keep himself amused. He'd ostracize one of them for weeks at a time over an imagined slight, he'd fantasize that "there was a Judas among us . . . and he'd play one of us against another. This always happened when he heard that one of the guys had said something about him. And we were all guilty of that." Things always picked up a little whenever a new guy came into the group — that was what happened when Richard Davis and Jimmy Kings-ley, who had hung around with them in Memphis, came out to California on vacation and Elvis invited them to stay, at first just for the shooting of *It Happened at the World's Fair*, then indefinitely. He didn't necessarily think about who might fit into the framework of the overall group, it seemed sometimes like he was just looking for a breath of fresh air.

The only thing he could really focus on now, in any case, was Priscilla's upcoming visit. He hadn't really thought a lot about what was going to happen next when she left in July, he hadn't been home for any length of time at Christmas himself since his mother died five years before, and he didn't have much of a plan when he first suggested that she come see him at Graceland — but it seemed like the more her parents resisted, the more determined he became, until finally they agreed to let her go *if* she were to be strictly chaperoned, as she had been in California when she stayed at the

Barrises' house. Elvis immediately said that she could stay with his father and stepmother, at their new home on Hermitage, and that he would even have them meet her plane in New York so she would not have to travel to Memphis alone.

He grew more and more excited as the day drew near, and he had Vernon call the moment they arrived at Hermitage so he could come over and drive Priscilla through the gates of Graceland himself. The annual Christmas display was fully mounted, the house was ablaze with lights, and there were fans at the gate snapping pictures of the life-sized Nativity scene on the lawn, but she could only think that she was finally here with him, after all these years she was actually about to see his home. The whole gang was waiting when she arrived — some of them she recognized, and some of them she was meeting for the first time — but Elvis whisked her away to his grandmother's room, and they had a brief but happy reunion. How had things been for Grandma since she'd been home? the seventeen-year-old girl asked her after Elvis left them alone. Grandma shook her head. She was worried about Elvis, she said. She thought he was still upset about his father's marriage. "He don't spend much time at Graceland anymore, and his Daddy's worried. . . . I don't know if he'll ever accept [the marriage]."

Later that night she was so worked up that Elvis gave her two big red pills to relax. She didn't wake up for two days, and when she did, it was to discover that everyone had been worried to death about her; Vernon and Grandma had wanted to call in a doctor right away, Elvis told her, but he had vetoed that. From her point of view, she was more concerned about the two days she had lost.

The whole visit was frustrating not just for its brevity but for the hint of domestic bliss that it suggested but could not deliver. Of course she didn't stay any longer at Hermitage than she had at the Barrises', and they tried to cram everything into the two weeks they had, as he introduced her, seemingly, to everyone he had ever met, took her roller-skating at the Rainbow, arranged for all-night screenings at the Memphian movie theater, and proudly showed her his hometown. He gave her a toy poodle that she promptly named Honey, they had a Christmas party for the whole gang, and then they celebrated New Year's Eve at a private party for friends, relatives, and fan club presidents at the Manhattan Club on Bellevue, where, to her embarrassment, she got drunk and had to be taken back to Graceland early. Later, when Elvis returned home, inebriated himself, they came closer to actually going all the way than they ever had before, until he reasserted that maddening self-control and withdrew at the last minute, saying, "No. Not like this."

It was over almost before it started. At the end of her visit, he tried to get her to stay, talking wildly, saying that he couldn't live without her. He even prevailed upon her to call her father, against her better judgment, and then he got on the extension to plead with Captain Beaulieu himself just to give them a few more days. Her father was obdurate, as she knew he would be, and Elvis was furious, calling his own father to come up to his office and cursing Captain Beaulieu in front of his daughter. Where did this two-bit army officer get off with his "cocky attitude [and all] his jargon about making agreements"?

"Now calm down, Son," Vernon told him, in Priscilla's account. "It ain't that bad. He was probably just concerned about her being home in time for school."

"School, what the hell do I care about school?" Elvis snapped, ignoring Vernon's efforts to soothe him. "Put her into school here, that'll solve everything. She doesn't need school. Hell, they don't teach you anything nowadays anyway."

"Well, Son, she's gonna have to go back. There ain't no two ways about it. . . ."

Gradually he calmed down, and Priscilla returned to her parents on the appointed day, but she made it clear to them she was returning as someone different: she was all grown up now, she was no longer going to be treated like a child. It was no longer the way it had been when she used to wonder if Elvis would even remember to call her, sometimes for weeks at a time; now she and Elvis were on the phone for hours practically every night, and he had only one thing on his mind: how to get her back. The key element of his plan, he told her, was surprise: she had to sugarcoat everything, be a good girl, get good grades in school, and *then* they would spring it on her parents that she wanted to come back to him and finish her senior year in Memphis.

She hadn't even been able to carry out the first phase of the plan. "From the moment I got off the plane my attitude was one of defiance," and against Elvis' advice she continued to maintain the posture of a daughter who had gone on strike. In the end she gave her parents an impossible choice: they could either let her go or watch her three younger siblings and the year-old twins get caught up in the maelstrom, too. Through her mother's reluctant intercession, Elvis was at last permitted to address her father on the subject. He turned on all his charm and assured Captain Beaulieu that if he were to allow his daughter to return to Memphis, the Vernon Presleys would provide her with a good home and she would get a good Catholic education *and* he would make sure that she graduated. "He said I'd always be chaperoned and that he'd take care of me in every way. Declaring his intentions honorable, he swore that he loved and needed and respected me. In fact, he couldn't live without me, he said, intimating that one day we'd marry."

In the end her parents capitulated. In early March, it was decided, she and her father would fly to Los Angeles, where Elvis was already working on his new movie. There Elvis and Captain Beaulieu would have a chance to talk man to man, and her father could get a few things straight; then she and her dad would go on to Memphis, where he would see to it that she got settled in with Vernon and Dee Presley and was properly enrolled at her new school before returning to Germany.

Elvis was halfway through *Fun in Acapulco* when she arrived. He had been excited about the foreign setting when he first got the script and started practicing his Spanish for the soundtrack, taking to wearing a cape around the house in preparation for a bullfight number. Early on there had been talk about location shooting in Mexico, but the Colonel put the kibosh on that, citing security concerns and his sense that there was "a lot of unrest down there."

Elvis took some time out from the movie to show Priscilla and Captain Beaulieu around. Every day he picked them up in the Rolls or his customized gold Cadillac and enthusiastically pointed out the sights, but then she was gone and he was left with the uneasy feeling that he had somehow charted a course whose outcome he could not fully predict or control. Sometimes he grew resentful at what he imagined Priscilla and Captain Beaulieu had forced him to do. He was only twenty-eight years old. Why should he be stuck with just one girl when he could have any woman in the world at the snap of his fingers? But then when he thought of who she was and what she had done — and what she was still prepared to do — he knew that he had done the right thing. Priscilla had given up everything for him, and she was now ready to be everything that he wanted her to be. She was too young to have gotten her values all screwed up or to harbor any false expectations of him — he would teach her to be the kind of woman that he needed, and as a result she would be the first to fully understand his needs. She was the one — if there was ever going to be a "one."

I N MEMPHIS PRISCILLA HARBORED doubts of her own. Without Elvis, and after the excitement of insisting on, and getting, her own way, she felt alone and more like a child than ever. Vernon drove her to school every day, imposing the same strict rules on her that he did on Dee's three little boys, and he was *very* tight with his money, forcing her to go back to him for even the smallest expense. She sensed that he was still suspicious of her; she recognized that "it took a while for Vernon to trust you, you didn't just walk in and be his best friend," but still it hurt. She hated school, she couldn't have any friends over to the house, and socially she was regressing to the level of the Stanley boys, getting into stupid squabbles with them *over nothing.* She was jealous about what she read about Elvis and his co-star Ursula Andress in the movie magazines, she didn't believe him when he said that he could never fall for a girl whose shoulders were broader than his, but she just waited for his calls.

Gradually she started spending more time with Grandma and became friends with one of the secretaries, Becky Yancey, and Elvis' cousin Patsy Presley, who also worked in Vernon's office behind the house. Soon she was spending so much time there that Vernon put up a sign: NO ONE BELONGS IN THE OFFICE UNLESS THEY WORK THERE, OR HAVE AN APPOINTMENT. She moved into Graceland not long after that, whiling away the hours in Grandma's room, as Grandma would reminisce about Elvis and Gladys and dip snuff or play hymns on the little organ that Elvis had given her as a present.

It seemed to Priscilla as if they all lived for his calls, every one of them. "Any time Elvis failed to call home for two days in a row, they worried that something terrible had happened to him in California. Elvis' enormous success and wealth notwithstanding, they were convinced that some misfortune was going to snatch it all away from them." Even Grandma was subject to the gloomy sense of foreboding that seemed to hang over all the Presleys' lives. If Priscilla went off with Becky or Patsy, "Grandma complained that she was being neglected. She reminded me that Elvis' old girlfriends used to stay with her every single night he was gone." Was it any wonder, then, that she felt miserable and abandoned? She couldn't wait for his return.

*   *   *

I T ALL CHANGED THE MOMENT he got home. He rushed back from California as soon as shooting was finished at the end of March and bought her a pretty little bright red Corvair a few days later so she wouldn't have to rely on Vernon or Dee to drive her to school anymore. A reporter from the *Commercial Appeal* happened to spot him with Priscilla on his motorcycle the following day, and seized the opportunity for an impromptu interview in the parking lot of Chenault's restaurant after Elvis had dispatched his "pert . . . motorcycle partner" for milkshakes. Elvis proved to be in an unusually expansive mood. He gave the reporter Priscilla's name and age, explaining, in a variation of the story that she herself had given to a *Press-Scimitar* reporter the day before, that she was the daughter of an army officer that he had met in Germany whose family would be returning to the States soon.

"They sent her ahead because she wanted to graduate on time and she's attending Immaculate Conception High School now." People kept wanting to link him to her romantically, he explained, but she was just a friend. "I couldn't get married right now. It wouldn't be fair to the girl. Since I got out of the Army, I've been busy all the time making movies." Making movies, he acknowledged, was not really such hard work, "but I try to get better roles all the time. I always look over the scripts in advance, and I choose all my own songs. . . . I've gone through more than 100 numbers to get just one that I thought was right."

And what had he been doing since he got back to Memphis? Going to the movies mainly, he said. "I've seen *Lawrence of Arabia* and *To Kill a Mockingbird* since I've been home. Which one do you think will win the Academy Award? *Lawrence*, I'll bet, because more money was spent on it, but I think *Mockingbird* was really better — that's a wonderful movie."

He talked about his motor home and his own just-released film, *It Happened at the World's Fair*, which was the most expensive picture he had made to date and one of the best. "He discussed his career with concentration, carefully pondering his statements. Then he pushed his [familiar yachting] cap back on his head and said with a relaxed smile, 'It's great to be back in Memphis.'"

It *was* great to be back in Memphis. He and Priscilla frequently went motorcycle riding together, they attended the movies or went out to the Fairgrounds with the gang, he took her shopping and bought her clothes at various shops on Union Avenue, getting the store owners to open up after closing time and pointing out all the ways in which she could improve her appearance. He took her to his dentist to have porcelain caps put on her teeth, she dyed her hair to match his, he gave her extensive instruction in what he liked and what he didn't like in his "ideal woman."

Sometimes they'd go over to Vernon's in the early evening and just watch TV, and she would sit there watching "father and son relaxing, puffing on cigars, discussing the state of the world" or something less weighty, like the latest car that Vernon was restoring. Sometimes they stopped by the Memphis Funeral Home, where Elvis would show off his knowledge of embalming and ask questions prompted by his fascination with medical texts. Almost every night they stayed up till dawn, and then she would drag herself out of bed and off to school, drowsing through her half day of classes until at last she could drag herself home again and get some sleep until he woke up, with her still beside him, late in the afternoon.

She objected at first to the exotic menu of uppers and downers he prescribed for them both, but he overcame her objections by pointing to the *Physicians' Desk Reference* and declaring that there was nothing in it that he didn't know, or couldn't find out, about the medications. His total familiarity, not just with their effects but with their complicated medical names and ingredients, soon overcame her inhibitions, because, after all, as he pointed out proudly to her, it wasn't as if he *needed* the pills, they weren't anything habit-forming like heroin, he could *never* become dependent on them. Besides, if she didn't take them, how was she going to keep up with him? And if she didn't keep up with him, she was just going to get left behind.

It was a little like playing house — except it wasn't a house, it was a mansion, and it wasn't a family, it was a bunch of guys coming and going as they pleased. That was the hardest part. "None of them felt comfortable with me. He didn't want me looking at anyone else, not even the guys that worked for him. I was not to go in a room if one of them was there by himself, I was afraid to say anything to any of them for fear he would hear me and reprimand me later: What was I doing down there in the first place? What did you talk about? What were they talking about? I was with *him*.

"It was an emotional roller coaster, what to do and what not to do, what was right and what wasn't right. I'm sure I appeared cold, but I wasn't used to dealing with any of this. There was a pecking order there unbeknownst to me; there was a whole other world when women weren't around. I mean, I came from a family that was very traditional, very close — and to be thrown into a situation where I had to always be suspicious of who was thinking what, what was being said, how do I look?, who do I look to? I'm sure that they came up with the idea that I was very reserved. I was *petrified*. I did not want to do the wrong thing, because he couldn't — once he was upset, he wasn't the easiest person to live with."

Joanie Esposito, who was her best friend among the wives and girl-friends, felt sorry for her. "It was not that she was immature. She was quiet, and that's what gave her a leg up. But no one had taught her how to do [a lot of things], and it was hard, because she didn't have anyone to ask." Joanie tried to help her, and to cover for her as best she could. But Joanie was a married woman of almost twenty-two with a six-month-old child and her own home in Memphis, now that Grandma had moved downstairs to make room for Priscilla. And besides, the only person she really felt comfortable with was Elvis.

No one else really understood them; the life they led together was a secret life, and no matter how much the others might think they knew Elvis, she was the one who saw him without defenses, she was the one who had to deal with his true, unvarnished feelings, she was the one to whom he confessed all his secret fears and desires. More and more she pressed him to consummate their relationship, but he refused; it was a very sacred thing to him, he told her. "I want it to be something to look forward to. It keeps the desire there."

> I sat up in anger. "What about Anita?" I yelled. "You mean you didn't make love to her the whole four years you went with her?"
>
> "Just to a point. Then I stopped. It was difficult for her, too, but that's just how I feel."

There was more than one way to satisfy each other, he told her. "Instead of consummating our love in the usual way, he taught me other means of pleasing him." One of those ways was taking pictures. She dressed up in her schoolgirl uniform, sometimes she was the teacher seducing her student, "we were always inventing new stories, and eventually I learned what stimulated Elvis the most." They documented those stories with a Polaroid camera; Priscilla was mortified at first to have to keep going back to the drugstore for more film; she was sure that others suspected what they were using the film for, but Elvis just laughed. "It might create some excitement around here," he said. "This town's dead. Memphis needs a little gossip!"

Gradually she grew accustomed to it, it became *her* world, too. There were lots of laughs and plenty of good times. She resented the thoughtlessness of the guys; sometimes they were just so inconsiderate, but after a while she came to the conclusion that they were basically good-hearted, and she didn't feel quite so threatened. The best part was that Elvis was around almost the entire time. About the only time he was gone was when he went to Nashville for two nights at the end of May to cut what was intended to be his one studio album for the year, and then at least she was able to catch up on her sleep.

She paid attention to everything he said and did, laughed when he laughed, and kept out of the way when he was brooding; it was a way of life that simply required *alertness* at all times. The only thing really bad about it was school — it was just a total waste of time, a meaningless distraction, and she couldn't stand to have any of the guys see her in her little Catholic girls' school uniform. All she wanted was to graduate and get out, and she ensured that by persuading the girl sitting beside her in algebra to let her copy off her exam in exchange for an invitation to Graceland.

To her surprise, on Graduation Day, May 29, Elvis all of a sudden started acting like "a proud parent." While she tried on her cap and gown, he debated what he should wear to the ceremony, finally deciding on a blue suit. Priscilla eyed him nervously. If he were to attend, she knew, it would be a circus, all eyes would be on him, it would just be a *joke*. "Finally I worked up enough courage to ask him to wait outside, and explained why. Smiling his funny little grin, the one that came to his lips when he was hurt or upset, he agreed without hesitation. 'I hadn't thought about that,' he said. 'I won't come in. I'll just be outside in the car waiting for you. That way I'll kinda be there.'"

Afterward he threw a party for her, and she cast aside her cap and gown with the alacrity of someone more than ready to embrace her freedom. In snapshots taken at the time she appears ladylike and wary, her hair piled up in a huge black beehive that almost totally obscures her delicate features and might even suggest a kind of sullen indifference if it were not for the effort involved in the pose. For much of the next three weeks they shut themselves off in Elvis' bedroom and never even went downstairs. With the windows covered over with tinfoil and blackout drapes, it made no difference whether it was night or day. They called down to the kitchen for their meals, listened to gospel music, made sure not to miss *The Untouchables* or *The Tonight Show* on TV, and watched some of Elvis' favorite movies, classics like *Wuthering Heights, It's a Wonderful Life, Les Misérables,* and a sentimental 1940 remake of the Emil Jannings silent *The Way of All*

Flesh, in which a good man is ruined and, too ashamed to admit his failure to his wife and children, embarks upon a life of aimless wandering. Years later he returns to his hometown and finds himself outside his old house, watching his family open their Christmas presents. Though she doesn't recognize him, his wife invites the lonely old man in to share their good fortune, but the old man refuses and marches off into the snow alone. They both cried when the movie ended. Elvis had thought of doing it as a remake, he told her; he had even toyed with the idea of casting his father, Vernon, in the leading role.

It was their own private world, and in that world "Elvis could become a little boy again, escaping from the responsibilities of family, friends, fans, the press, and the world. Here, with me, he could be vulnerable and childlike, a playful boy who stayed in his pajamas for days at a time." They had pillow fights and played hide-and-seek, they retreated to a world of childlike fantasy. And she tried to put it out of her mind that he would be leaving her again right after he and the guys had their big annual fireworks war on the Fourth of July.

THE MOVIE THAT HE was returning to Hollywood to shoot, *Viva Las Vegas,* was the first of two he was scheduled to do back-to-back for MGM this year. The Colonel had been working since January to get this second MGM production, not just for the substantial addition that it would make to their combined income but to hasten the renegotiation of a contract which, even at $500,000 and 50 percent of the profits, he felt could stand some improvement. Elvis had had three top-grossing films in 1962, with *Blue Hawaii* leading the way. He had been ranked the fifth-most popular star in the *Motion Picture Almanac's* annual poll of exhibitors, and MGM said they were really excited about this new film; they thought the chemistry between Elvis and his co-star was going to create a whole new market for Elvis Presley pictures. Elvis didn't know about that, but he knew he was really looking forward to meeting his co-star.

Twenty-two-year-old Ann-Margret was just coming off the explosive success of *Bye Bye Birdie,* the film version of the 1960 Broadway musical which told the story of an Elvis Presley–like rock 'n' roll singer who gets drafted. Pretty, vivacious, a gifted singer and dancer whose personal magnetism and bubbling energy overwhelmed even her substantial talents, she had been discovered in Las Vegas by George Burns three years earlier and

REHEARSING WITH ANN-MARGRET.
(COURTESY OF THE ESTATE OF ELVIS PRESLEY)

subsequently appeared in two other films. It was *Bye Bye Birdie* that put her on the map, though, and it was the director of *Bye Bye Birdie*, George Sidney, who had previously directed such lavish MGM musicals as *Annie Get Your Gun, Show Boat,* and *Kiss Me Kate,* who introduced his two stars on the MGM set. There was some polite small talk. Elvis, dressed formally in a dark suit and tie, said how much he'd enjoyed her in her latest film, and the two of them went their separate ways, though not before each sensed, according to Ann-Margret's later account, that the other was a true kindred soul.

Much of the first three days was spent in the recording studio. The score was, for once, something of a challenge, with a clever title track by Doc Pomus and Mort Shuman; a thoughtful, deeply romantic ballad, "I Need Somebody to Lean On" — on which Elvis lavished some twenty takes — by the same pair; Red's first movie cut, "If You Think I Don't Need You"; and three duets with Ann-Margret, recorded live in the studio on the third day of sessions. Then on the weekend the whole troupe moved to Las Vegas to begin location shooting on July 15.

Elvis and the guys, along with the Colonel and his staff, all stayed at the Sahara, just as they always did. On the first day of shooting, a reporter from *McCall's* magazine observed a rehearsal and noted that "Elvis makes a face and shakes his head. It is a flirty, cute expression that isn't in the script, but it delights Ann-Margret. She laughs and flirts right back. Whenever the dialogue brings Ann-Margret and Presley together, their roles suddenly become more than play-acting. An electricity from the two charges the crew with alertness."

By the time they returned to Hollywood two weeks later they were an item. "This is news to make the younger set flip," reported columnist Bob Thomas in an AP dispatch on August 6. "Elvis Presley and Ann-Margret are having a romance. At least that's the way it looks," wrote Thomas, who conceded that you couldn't always be sure with Hollywood romances but then went on to describe their behavior on the set. "They hold hands. They disappear into his dressing room between shots. They lunch together in seclusion." In short, it appeared that this was the real thing.

It was. The chemistry that was evident from their first moment together on-screen was borrowed from real life. From Ann-Margret's point of view, music was the catalyst. "Music ignited a fiery pent-up passion inside Elvis and inside me. It was an odd, embarrassing, funny, inspiring, and wonderful sensation. We looked at each other move and saw virtual mirror images." She was, Joe Esposito told Elvis, "a female you," and soon she was at the house almost every night, or he was over at the apartment she shared with her parents. They drove around listening to tapes in his new Rolls-Royce limousine, they rode motorcycles together (she shared his passion for Harleys), the guys always knew enough to disappear at the right moment — and if they didn't, Joe let them know. Everybody liked Ann — they all referred to her by the name of the character she played in the movie, Rusty, but Elvis called her Rusty Ammo. She was funny, she was sexy, she was never anything less than a good sport, she was one of the guys. One night she and Elvis were sitting around watching TV with the gang, "an average, lazy night at home," when she and Elvis put on an impromptu show.

We snuck out of the living room. Then, without warning, he pushed open the big double glass doors. Everyone turned and looked. We were both on the ground, stretched out like cats, and in a husky growl he sang, "You got me runnin'." I answered in a similar voice, "You got me hidin'." [These are the first lines of the Jimmy Reed blues "Baby What You Want Me to Do?"] As we traded lyrics, we crawled across the carpeted room in time with the music while everyone clapped and laughed.

To Joanie Esposito, "Ann was wonderful. She would make him pick her up, and the four of us would go to a movie together, no one else. He didn't have to have everyone else with him to do things. It was a much more normal situation." From everyone else's standpoint she was just lots of fun. Sandy Ferra, who was working on the show as a dancer, was not jealous in the least, because they were such a great personality fit. "She was his alter ego; he just really liked her." George Klein, one of Memphis' most popular DJs by now, who was taking his annual two-week vacation in Hollywood to permit a walk-on appearance in another of Elvis' movies, couldn't fail to notice the spark. He had been around a lot of Elvis' girls — he had in fact introduced Elvis to many of them — but he had never seen Elvis act happier. To Patti Parry, who came around almost every night after getting off from her job at Neil Sloane's hairdressing salon, "She had spirit, and she wasn't afraid of him. They just had the best time."

It was against everything he had ever held — he was the one who was always criticizing show business marriages, telling Priscilla or Sandy Ferra that they shouldn't even be thinking about a career in entertainment, there wasn't room enough in one household for two performers. But maybe there were different rules for people like him and Ann; maybe, with all the energy she had, she could play every role without faltering; maybe, it began to occur to him, he had made a terrible mistake. He talked to her about his mother. "He'd describe her in the most heartfelt, childlike manner and talk about what a plain, simple woman [she] had been. He explained how she'd never been interested in the luxuries his money could buy. She didn't care. She only wanted to be able to love him and see him truly happy." Sometimes they talked about marriage, even though they both knew it could never be: "Elvis and I knew he had commitments, promises to keep, and he vowed to keep his word."

At one point he was so overwhelmed with his feelings for Ann-Margret, and so guilty over his inability to do anything about them, that he even approached the Colonel for help. One of the boys called to say that Elvis was on his way over to the Colonel's place at the Wilshire-Comstock Apartments, which told the Colonel right away that something was wrong because Elvis never just stopped by to visit. Elvis was obviously agitated when he arrived, but even if he had possessed true extrasensory powers, Colonel could never have guessed what was on his mind. He had a big favor to ask, he confessed hesitantly to his manager. He had Ann-Margret waiting outside in the car; he wanted the Colonel to manage her.

For once Parker was stymied. What the outside world failed to understand was that you didn't just say no to Elvis Presley, even if you were Colonel Parker; the boy was very persuasive and very determined and very accustomed to getting his own way. Above all, Parker was aware, you didn't embarrass him in front of others. And if he had promised his co-star that he could deliver the Colonel, there was no way that Parker was going to just turn him down flat. Instead he instantly agreed. He would be delighted, he said, to manage the young lady. Ann-Margret was a wonderful talent, and he believed he could really do something for her. The one thing that Elvis would have to understand was that this would take time and effort; Ann-Margret was not yet a star of Elvis' magnitude, and to get her the kind of deals that Colonel was able to get for Elvis would take — well, he wasn't going to shortchange Elvis; he hoped Elvis knew where his first loyalties were, but Elvis would surely understand that he would have to devote 50 percent of his time to his new client, at least at first. They talked for a little while more, but when Elvis went back to the car he was no longer so sure of himself, and he never brought up the subject again.

The Colonel saw bigger problems on the horizon. To begin with, the director was giving the girl too many close-ups; some of the boys said it was because he was in love with her, but if that was the case, everyone else on the picture was in love with her, too. Colonel was embroiled with the studio in disputes over budget, over publicity, even over the soundtrack. They had a clause in all of their contracts that prohibited anyone else in the cast from singing without the explicit permission of the star. Of course, with the cute story the scriptwriter had come up with, which pitted the two co-stars against each other in an employee talent contest, and with all the publicity the girl had gotten from her last picture, there was no question that she should have one or two numbers, but then against his better judgment Colonel had let himself be persuaded to allow her to do those three duets with Elvis — and the way things were going, it looked like she might steal the picture if he didn't step in and put a stop to it. No one at the studio seemed to remember that *this was an Elvis Presley picture* — that's what they were paying for, and that's what was going to be delivered. Colonel was already deeply embroiled in a dispute with the publicity department over that very issue — they couldn't seem to grasp who was the star; they couldn't stop talking about the special quality that the girl brought to the picture and how they were going to expand Elvis' audience by putting the spotlight on her. What kind of a fool did they take him for? Were they all forgetting that *Elvis Presley pictures always made money?*

Colonel Parker fought back with every resource at his command, killing one of the duets completely and recasting another as a song for Elvis alone, vigorously protesting the way in which the director was favoring Ann-Margret and making sure that Elvis knew about it, letting MGM know that he would be perfectly happy to sit at home and forgo his own proven methods for promoting a picture (which, as MGM was aware, had always paid off in the past and which he was glad to deliver for a fraction of the cost) if the studio was really convinced that they had discovered a new way of minting money. In short, he fiercely defended the interests of his client at every turn.

What galled him most was the disregard that everyone seemed to have for the bottom line. No Elvis Presley picture had ever been budgeted at more than $2.5 million in production costs, and his and Elvis' profit participation began only after all postproduction costs (roughly twice the production budget) had been recouped as well. But in this case for the first time they were going well over budget, and Parker realized he had no protection against the rising costs. No matter how successful the picture was, their share was necessarily going to be diminished by all the unnecessary frills and fancy production numbers that would not add a penny to the box office and that Hal Wallis would have known how to strictly control. It was all a rear-guard action by now, he realized; there was nothing he could do to make this picture right. On August 15 he finalized arrangements for the next film, to be produced by Sam Katzman, a veteran B movie producer currently operating out of MGM, who assured him that on his set costs would be carefully controlled, shooting time would be halved, and quality would not be sacrificed — and put all but the last in writing.

Meanwhile, Priscilla waited patiently at home. At first Elvis told her he thought she could come out at some point during the filming, but then he kept putting her off, and she saw the pictures and stories in the papers, and she was worried and confused. There was nothing to do in Memphis: she was bored to death. She had taken some modeling classes at the Patricia Stevens School and even did a little modeling during lunch hour at the Piccadilly Cafeteria, until someone told Elvis about it and he told her to stop. Now she was taking modern dance classes and working very hard at it, but she didn't know how Elvis felt about that. She kept trying to figure out different ways of reintroducing the idea of her coming out to see him, but every time she brought up the subject, he came up with another story of "problems on the set." What kind of problems? she ventured tentatively. Oh, you know, the usual kind, he said, as if she should know all about that sort of thing. The director was in love with his co-star, she was getting all of the close-ups, and Colonel warned him that if they didn't watch out she was going to steal the picture. Well, how about Ann-Margret — how did he get along with her? Priscilla asked sweetly. Oh, she was all right, he said, just "a typical Hollywood starlet," the kind he had often described when he was trying to reassure her, as "into their careers and their man comes second. I don't want to be second to anything or anyone. That's why you don't have to worry about my falling in love with my so-called leading ladies."

But she *did* worry. And she did keep pestering him. And she did keep seeing the stories. And she didn't know what to do.

They finished shooting on September 16, and whether to assuage his own guilt or to allay Priscilla's suspicions, Elvis came straight home. For all of Colonel's concerns, the picture was probably Elvis' best since *Follow That Dream,* and the first since he had gotten out of the army to exploit his genuine sex appeal — even if it did run in tandem here with Ann-Margret's. Some of the production numbers may have been a little over the top, but there was no need to worry about losing the fans through "arti-ness." In fact, this was perhaps Elvis' first legitimate Hollywood musical, in which the songs actually served the purpose of advancing character and plot, however skimpily developed those areas might be. There was even a big production number added at the end of shooting, in which Elvis and Ann-Margret attend a Vegas show, dance to a black quartet's version of a Leiber and Stoller tune called "The Climb," and Elvis gets up onstage and launches into an incendiary, if somewhat incoherent, version of Ray Charles' "What'd I Say." It's hard to imagine what may have prompted this last-minute addition, other than the sparks that Elvis and Ann-Margret were giving off on-screen and George Sidney's penchant for off-the-cuff musical inspiration. The song was not recorded in any case until August 30, five days before it was to be filmed. Completed in four quick takes, it might well have benefited from a more tempered approach, and despite the pres-ence of the Jubilee Four, a black gospel group that included two members of the original Golden Gate Quartet, it comes across as a frenetic, irretriev-ably wholesome mess. Nonetheless, it gives a sense at least of Elvis Presley unleashed, as he mumbles — and on-screen Ann-Margret poutily mimics — Ray Charles' orgiastic moans, and the camera pans a soundstage full of all the frenetic activity of a Busby Berkeley water ballet.

Perhaps the most telling moment in the movie, though, was its most atypical, as the Elvis character, troubled over the failure of his relationship with Rusty, wanders in a kind of dream sequence in which the beautiful Doc Pomus–Mort Shuman ballad "I Need Somebody to Lean On" becomes his inner voice. It is his purest acting in the entire picture, as we see him in an overhead spotlight shot, singing now with a quiet, earnest sincerity that belies the surface charm of the rest of the show. It is a sequence that would not have been out of place in a Gene Kelly musical, and you can sense the quiet satisfaction that Elvis must have felt as words, music, and image all come together for once.

H E HAD A MONTH IN MEMPHIS before the next movie, *Kissin' Cousins*, was to start. Priscilla kept after him about what she had read, but he was steadfast in his denials, giving no ground but at the same time talking to Ann-Margret almost every night on the phone. Colonel told the movie people that Elvis wouldn't have time to go out to Hollywood to cut the soundtrack for the picture, so Gene Nelson and Freddy Karger, the director and musical director respectively, flew in to Nashville at the end of September and ran through ten tracks in two nights, with Nelson contributing percussion on a few of the numbers which he and Karger had preselected and sent on to Presley for approval ten days earlier. For the first time Elvis didn't record his vocals with the band and in fact did not do them at all until he got to California, though he was in Nashville and stopped by the studio briefly to say hello. To Boots Randolph, who played jug as well as saxophone on the session, while others contributed banjo and fiddle to emphasize the "hillbilly" flavor of the picture, it was all just part and parcel of the prevalent Hollywood view of Elvis Presley as "product," and guitarist Jerry Kennedy, who had been working sessions for two years now, felt sorry for Elvis, trapped in an atmosphere that more and more resembled a zoo. Two weeks later the film had started production on location in Big Bear in the San Bernardino Mountains, one hundred miles from the MGM lot in Hollywood.

The Colonel had sought out Sam Katzman to produce this picture for one very simple reason: he admired his work. The sixty-two-year-old Katzman, who had made the first rock 'n' roll picture, *Rock Around the Clock*, for $300,000 in 1956 (Katzman liked to boast that it grossed $4 million, giving it one of the highest margins of profit in Columbia Pictures' history), was known as the "King of the Quickies." Colonel had run into him at MGM while he was working on *Hootenanny Hoot*, which presented fourteen musical acts and was filmed in eight and one-half days. "It seems they were spending an awful lot of money on the Presley pictures, and me being a frugal producer, the Colonel figured we could save a few dollars. His last few pictures before I took over hadn't been going so good. The grosses had been dropping." And so the Colonel and Katzman talked business.

For once the Colonel felt like he had run into a kindred soul. Katzman prided himself on his ability to deliver a picture on budget; he had what he called a "below-the-line set limit, and we never [went] over our below-the-line." Which to Gene Nelson, who had won his spurs as a director with *Hootenanny Hoot* and was just the right man, Katzman felt, to direct an Elvis Presley picture, was not an inconsiderable ability. "The man knew how to make pictures," said Nelson, who had embarked upon directing after a career as an ice skater, a dancer, a character actor, and an occasional leading man. "The fact that he had lousy taste has nothing to do with it. He knew every angle, every possible way to 'cheat'; he could have done a good picture the same way and he would have been even more of a hero. He just had lousy taste in writers, and he wouldn't know a story if it hit him in the face."

The more the Colonel and Katzman talked, the more they hit it off, and the Colonel even tried to get Katzman interested in one of his pet projects, the life story of Hank Williams, which he had been trying to sell MGM on for years, with Elvis in the leading role. It was a natural. It was a dramatic story, and MGM owned the recorded masters, which would make for a natural tie-in — and besides, the Colonel had a plan for promoting it by block booking it throughout the South. If Katzman were interested, he said, he would volunteer his promotional services even without Elvis involved, and when the producer indicated that he was ready to take him up on his offer and arranged to make *Your Cheatin' Heart* his next picture (after *Kissin' Cousins*) at MGM, that pretty much won the Colonel over and solidified the deal.

Katzman, Nelson, and the Colonel went location scouting before Elvis came out to California, and Colonel regaled his companions with tales of the carnival days. He described to them how his operation worked as well, and Katzman noted admiringly how he handled "all the exhibitors, all the publicity, all the sales, all the records — everything comes through his office. I don't know any campaign [that] he hasn't added to and improved." He indicated no interest in the script, other than whether or not there would be any writer's fees to pay, and since it was based roughly on a story by Bret Harte, who had been dead for over sixty years, he was satisfied on that point.

Gene Nelson was itching to get going, though first "I had to really talk myself into liking that kind of music. I couldn't stand it then, and I can't now. But if I was going to do this shit, you either fall in love with it or you don't do it at all — and I got myself very involved with Elvis. I mean, I began to listen to him; I ran all his pictures and really tried to see where he was coming from, what the attraction was. He was the handsomest sonofabitch that ever walked across a screen, you know. I mean, he couldn't dance worth a shit, he really couldn't, but he had these weird wiggles that he produced, which was — okay, that was part of his creativity." Nelson rewrote the script ("it was a little square"), and "just before Elvis arrived, I packed it up and sent it over to the Colonel. It wasn't the first time I'd ever written a script — it was the second — so I'm concerned. I sent a nice note. 'Dear Colonel, The script is finished. I hope you like it. If you have any suggestions, please feel free to call me.' The next day I get a call from the Colonel. 'I got your script. If you say it's okay, it's okay with me. As far as suggestions are concerned, for consultations I get $25,000.' I was in shock. I mean, he was a big teaser. He really put me on!"

Production began in Big Bear on October 14 and, except for the weather and Nelson's understandable concern about keeping to the schedule (fifteen days had been allotted for the shooting), everything went well. To his great relief Nelson couldn't have found his star more cooperative. "I was quite nervous [about working with him]. He and Red, whenever there was nothing going on, would start doing karate, and everyone would gather around and watch. Then one day we were lighting the set for the big dance number, and I'm sitting in my chair facing the area that they're lighting, checking my script, and I hear, 'Uh, Mr. Nelson, can I talk to you for a second?' I say sure, so he sits down, and he says, 'I just want to tell you, I've been a big fan of yours for a long time.' I said, 'Really?' He said, 'Yeah, the first time I saw you in person was when I was fifteen or sixteen years old and I was an usher at this movie theater in Memphis, and you were in town with Virginia Mayo, and I heard music blasting in the street, and I left my post and ran out of the theater and sat on the curb with everybody else as this white Lincoln convertible went by, and you were sitting on the back with Virginia Mayo waving.' This was *She's Working Her Way Through College*. I did a one-of-a-kind dance number, a gym number that'd never been done before, where I used every [piece of equipment] in the gym; it was 1952, and Virginia and I were doing a kind of southern tour, there was a big banner on the side of the car with the name of the picture on it. He said, 'You know, I really love the stuff you do.' He didn't have to say that, but he wanted me to know that he was not unaware of my status."

The Colonel was all over the set, clowning, entertaining, donning Elvis' blond wig (Elvis played look-alikes in the picture, one dark-haired, one blond, and *hated* the wig), from Nelson's point of view generally defusing any tension on the set — and there was a good deal of that. "There got to be some really high-powered tension between me and Sam Katzman, because I'm busting my butt trying to get this thing finished in fifteen days, and Sam was really giving me a rough time. I remember one time the Colonel came on the set with an old-fashioned white car coat all the way down to his ankles, with the names of all of Elvis' pictures sewed on it and a funny hat, and he walked in and said, 'Well, fellas, what do you think of this?' Just, you know, trying to get us to relax and forget about whatever it was we were angry about."

Even Elvis was infected with the tension. "He'd never worked this way before. But the Colonel explained how he would make more money [this way], and I explained that it was more like shooting a TV show than a movie, and he went along with it." For the most part Elvis and the guys seemed to be having a good time, there were lots of pranks and water balloon fights, but Nelson couldn't be bothered — "my mind was filled with meeting schedules." And whatever the guys might get up to as they were setting up for a shot, Elvis himself was never less than cooperative, always on time, eager to please and easy to direct.

Nonetheless, Nelson never felt like he really got to know him. "He was just so enigmatic. I mean, you felt compelled to try to figure out what really made him tick, because what he presented was not really Elvis, at least not all of it. I mean, why would he isolate himself with this bunch of idiots? What is going on? Well, I finally came to the conclusion that Elvis had no [insecurity] about what he was in the media, absolutely none. He knew he was great. He knew he could do anything he wanted. He knew the value of his status, and there was never any shyness or awkwardness about his persona onstage. However, I thought he suffered an acute lack of self-esteem as a human being. I found, not once but a number of times, that he felt that he was uneducated and had nothing to contribute in a conversation. As a performer, he wasn't adventuresome, he didn't really want to learn, because he was embarrassed and, besides, what he was doing worked, so why change it? I don't think he was ever involved to his full potential as an actor, but I could see moments when he would get involved in a scene. I think he could have been a very good actor, but mostly he would just be his charming self and get away with it — because he was Elvis Presley."

In four weeks the production was completely wound down. As Nelson recalled it, there were seventeen days of actual shooting, and Katzman was angry with him even then for going two days over schedule. There was unquestionably a science to it. When they got back to the studio, they started out on MGM's huge Stage 25 or 26, shooting exteriors to match the location shots, with giant pines, hills, and a farmhouse front. Then gradually they shut down the set, putting up an accordion wall as less space was required, letting electricians go "as we needed less lights, so that in a week's time we had maybe three guys up high." Toward the end the schedule was so hectic that Elvis offered to get sick. "I hadn't learned the patience and control that I have now, and I'd get uptight — and this upset Elvis. He came to me the last week and said he didn't like to work this way, it wasn't worth it. He said he knew what kind of pressure I was under, and he volunteered to get sick or show up late if it would help. I thanked him and said to hang in, it was *my* problem."

They finished shooting on November 8. For all of Elvis' good-sport attitude toward the movie, and for all of Nelson's cheerful energy and inventiveness, it was probably the film that most embarrassed Elvis in his career to date. He knew the story was ridiculous, he hated the way that he looked (some mornings, according to his co-star Yvonne Craig, he didn't even want to come out of the dressing room he was so embarrassed), the processing technique which enabled the audience to see two Elvises on-screen at the same time was laughably amateurish, and in the musical grand finale you can spot Lance LeGault, as Elvis' double, walking toward the camera. He was obviously not intended to be seen from the front, but, Yvonne Craig noted, "Sam said it was too expensive to shoot over."

As perceived by LeGault, who had now made three pictures with Elvis as double and special choreographer's assistant assigned to the star, *Kissin' Cousins* marked a turning point in Elvis Presley films. "Up until that time certain standards had been maintained, but it seems to me from *Kissin' Cousins* on, we were always on a short schedule. It was like, 'It's good enough because it's Elvis, and it's in color, and we're gonna make two and a half times negative cost plus another two and a half times.' Sometimes [Elvis might] comment about this, that, or the other — but he'd go ahead and do it. Very seldom he might go over and say something to the director — but very seldom: he just kind of went along with it. I don't remember how long I was on *Viva Las Vegas,* but it seems like it was ten or eleven weeks, a long time. We weren't off a [few] weeks when, boom, we jumped back into *Kissin' Cousins,* which was shot in seventeen days. When they realized they could take this guy and do a film that quickly with him, from then on we were on quick pictures."

PRISCILLA HAD GROWN TIRED of waiting at home. There was nothing to do, and besides, she kept reading about Elvis and Ann-Margret riding around Bel Air on their motorcycles. More disturbingly, she kept picking up hints that something was going on. No one would say anything to her outright, but all the denials — even Elvis' — were less and less convincing. Finally, she insisted on coming out. Elvis kept saying he didn't have time for her, she didn't understand, he was completely tied up making a movie, and this movie in particular took *all* his time with the schedule they were on. She told him she didn't care, she didn't need to be amused, she just wanted to be near him. Besides, she hadn't been out to California since she and her father had stopped off on their way to Memphis, and she'd hardly seen the house on Perugia, which he had moved back into at the beginning of the year; she just wanted a chance to visit.

Finally, she came out while they were still shooting the movie. She met Mr. Nelson and Mr. Katzman briefly on the set, the Colonel smiled at her benevolently without revealing a thing, and she realized that the guys were even more uncomfortable around her than ever. Then on November 8, the same day that production ended and Elvis signed a new deal to make a picture with Allied Artists for $750,000 in 1964, there was a UPI story in the paper headlined "Elvis Wins Love of Ann-Margret." The story was filed from London, where Ann-Margret was attending the royal premiere of *Bye Bye Birdie,* and according to the wire-service report, "Ann-Margret says she's going steady with Elvis Presley, and 'I guess I'm in love.' . . . The red-haired 22-year-old beauty says she doesn't know yet if they will get married. 'Nothing has been fixed,' she said. Ann-Margret says she and Elvis have lots of fun together riding motor bikes. . . . 'But I cannot say when, or if, we will marry.' Added Ann-Margret, 'He's a real man.'"

Elvis came home from the studio with a newspaper that contained the story. "I can't believe she did it," he declared without preamble. "She had the goddamn nerve to announce we're engaged." For Priscilla it was as if her world had suddenly collapsed. All her suspicions, all the rumors and insinuations that he had so vehemently denied were true. Every major newspaper had picked up the story, he told her with an anger that barely masked his embarrassment and guilt. She would have to go home. The press would be all over him, Colonel thought it would be best if she were not around to complicate the matter even more.

I couldn't believe what I was hearing. Suddenly all the months of unbearable silence broke and I screamed, "What's going on here? I'm tired of these secrets. Telephone calls. Notes. Newspapers." I picked up a flower vase and hurled it across the room. . . . "I hate her!" I shouted. "Why doesn't she keep her ass in Sweden where she belongs?"

Elvis grabbed me and threw me on the bed. "Look, goddamnit! I didn't know this was going to get out of hand. I want a woman who's going to understand that things like this might just happen." He gave me a hard, penetrating look. "Are you going to be her — or not?"

Eventually they both calmed down. "Elvis was very honest and very blunt with me: he told me in detail what their relationship had been. Basically, he said that she had paid him the highest compliment that a woman can give a man: here she was imitating him, and he was intrigued by it. He was *fond* of her as a person; he told me explicitly and in detail what the relationship was. But as far as it going anywhere, it could never have gone anywhere, because her career meant a lot to her, and his career meant a lot to him, and he wanted to have a family and a home with me. It was *very* hard to take. I was very hurt by it, because I didn't understand it at the time, but what he was relating seemed to me very truthful and very honest; [maybe it was] just the fact that he told me. . . ."

He promised that he would never see Ann-Margret again, but he and Priscilla had to be apart for now. His resolve lasted as long as it took to get Priscilla to leave. At her parents' urging, Ann-Margret called him from London. She had never said any of those things to the British press, she swore. She never would. Elvis said that he believed her and he wasn't surprised or upset, that was just the way reporters were — but was *she* hurt? She told him she was "terribly hurt by the lies."

Just after Ann returned home from England, President Kennedy was assassinated. She heard the news on the car radio, listening numbly to the minute-by-minute reports. "I drove to Elvis' house and found him glued to the TV. I sat down next to him. We stayed like that for the entire weekend, for what seemed an eternity — watching, waiting, and crying over the President's death. . . . [We] clung to each other, tried futilely to make sense of what had happened, and prayed for the future."

He returned to Memphis two weeks before Christmas, and although they continued to see each other and exchange secret messages well into the next year, soon she began thinking of him in the past tense. As for Elvis, he never made it clear exactly what he was thinking; some of the guys felt that he was simply too much of a coward to do what he really wanted to do, but he never confided his feelings to any of them. At home he continued to do exactly what he always had: he rented out the Memphian, listened to his gospel records, and he and Priscilla watched movie after movie on Graceland's home projection system; he made his customary Christmas charity contribution — $55,000 this year to fifty-eight mostly local charities — and received a plaque in a modest ceremony at the mayor's office; he sent $1,000 to his cousin Gene, who had left his employ the previous spring under somewhat shadowy circumstances and was having a difficult time catching on. He even purchased a wedding ring, which had the jeweler, Harry Levitch, a kindly man who had befriended him when he was just out of high school, all excited — until he found out it was to replace a ring that Elvis' grandmother had lost. On January 8 he celebrated his twenty-ninth birthday quietly at home, and then on the twelfth he traveled to Nashville to do a nonsoundtrack session for the first time since the previous May.

The May session had originally been intended to yield an album and a single, but as the Colonel's plan to concentrate exclusively on soundtrack recordings took greater hold, the album was set aside and the fourteen tracks dispersed among single releases ("Witchcraft," for example, became the B side of *Fun in Acupulco*'s "Bossa Nova Baby" in October 1963) and "bonus cuts" on soundtrack albums. Elvis understood that this was merely good business; the Colonel had explained it all to him before, just as he had explained about the publishing: they had Hill and Range's top writers all vying for a spot in their motion pictures in a competition that prohibited anyone from taking advantage of the system. There were times when songwriters like Don Robertson or Doc Pomus and Mort Shuman might be favored, certainly, but they were well aware that they could just as easily be replaced (and frequently were) if they ever got too big for their britches. It might seem harsh, the Colonel conceded, but this was a dog-eat-dog world in which they were only doing what everybody else did before the other guy did it to them first.

Still, Elvis could not help but notice that sales were substantially down: "Return to Sender" had been his last million seller, in 1962, and if he had studied the matter more closely, he would have discovered that overall sales for this year's three new singles releases amounted to less than two-thirds of 1962's total, while album sales hovered in the 300,000 range. Nor did the quality of the movie songs or the declining standard of the new material that Freddy Bienstock brought to the sessions escape his notice. They might still have some of the top writers in the business, but it seemed like they weren't getting their best songs.

The reason for Elvis' return to the studio in January of 1964, however, had nothing to do with Freddy or the Colonel or song publishing but, rather, with a song in which he truly believed, Chuck Berry's "Memphis, Tennessee," which he had attempted at the last session but which he knew he could do better — in fact, he felt like it could be one of his strongest singles in years.

"Memphis" had first been released in its composer's version in 1959 with no great chart success. Then in the spring of 1963, just before the last Nashville session, Lonnie Mack had come out with his instrumental interpretation of the song, which ultimately was a number-five pop hit. Elvis' version was different from either one. With the heavy double drumming intro of Buddy Harman and D. J. Fontana, you would think that you were in for the kind of "jungle rhythms" and unrelenting vocal attack that Elvis brought to Little Richard's "Long Tall Sally" some years earlier, but instead, with his vocal entrance we hear a sweet-edged, delicate, almost keening plea as he recounts Berry's tale, in which the singer appears at first to be trying to call a wife or girlfriend in Memphis but then in a clever, and poignant, twist reveals that it is his six-year-old daughter whom he is attempting to reach ("We were pulled apart because her mom did not agree / And tore apart our happy home in Memphis, Tennessee").

The idea for the last session had been to achieve a true pop sound, and while not every song was worthy of the effort and not every arrangement did justice to every song, Elvis had worked out a consistent approach that pitted light, airy, almost ethereal vocals against fuzztone guitars and a heavily emphasized rhythm track for what seemed like a curious and deliberately incongruous effect. That was the tack he had taken with the Berry tune in May, and to a large extent it was the one he carried out now, in a version considerably more nuanced than Berry's, with the rhythm never faltering as Elvis maintains a tone of underlying wistfulness and deep melancholy through six highly focused takes.

The first and the last were clearly the outstanding performances (as with any Elvis recording session, the differences were relatively minor, with the aim being to get *inside* the song rather than to develop radically different variants), and while in the end it was hard to say whether he had surpassed the May version, he had at least satisfied himself that he had explored the song to the fullest. With that he went on to the only other scheduled business of the day, "Ask Me," an English-language adaptation of yet another Italian song, which he had also attempted at the last session. Here the instrumental approach was not so sure, with Floyd Cramer's roller-rink organ once again taking the lead, but Elvis contributed a stunning vocal that alternated between the top of his tenor range and a falsetto of almost heartbreaking fragility, adding eleven more takes to the six he had tried at the previous session.

There was clearly a certain amount of frustration, a continuing sense that the arrangement did not do justice to the Italian ballad's broad romantic sweep, but as you listen to the session develop, you become aware of a serious musician who remains unfazed and fully focused on his vision, one that he alone may grasp but that he will not relinquish until he has seen it through. Save for his unfailing politeness and the thoughtful deference he shows at all times to his fellow musicians, it's hard to reconcile this Elvis with the Elvis who is used as little more than a cardboard cutout or a piece of moving scenery in films like *Girls! Girls! Girls!* or *Kissin' Cousins* — but perhaps that is the point. For this one fleeting moment he, and we, are aware of the goal, for this single instant he is able to shed the trappings of fame and recognize, briefly, what it was he was seeking in the first place.

And then it is gone. Though there appear to have been no formal plans to record any additional material, Elvis did go on to record one more song, "It Hurts Me," a quietly passionate and beautifully articulated ballad pitched by Freddy and seconded by Lamar Fike, who had reconciled with Elvis at the recording session the previous May and was now working for Hill and Range in Nashville. The session ended before midnight, and he was back in Memphis by early the next morning. It might have crossed his mind how much more could have been accomplished, but then what would have been the point? The Colonel had his proven game plan, and Elvis had long since reconciled himself to his own need for going along with it.

THE COLONEL, FOR HIS PART, was reasonably well satisfied. The kids still loved Elvis, and if they didn't love him as much as they once had, with a guaranteed income from RCA for the next seven years and an increasingly lucrative schedule of movies to keep them busy at least through 1964, there was no immediate cause for concern. His promotions continued to make money for him and Elvis; through controlled on-set interviews and photo opportunities he was able to keep Elvis' name constantly in the news; "Our gimmicks work," the Colonel boasted whenever he was challenged by any of the record company or movie studio college boys with their fancy suits and college degrees. "Look, you got a product, you sell it," he told *Variety* with a pride that was not at all belied by the disingenuousness with which it was put forth. There was no one capable of beating him at his own game, there was no one with a greater knowledge of the science of exploitation. No matter what changes in tastes or trends might lurk on the horizon, he was confident he could keep Elvis and himself in the 90-percent tax bracket for years to come. He didn't doubt his own abilities for a moment; he was getting just a little bit apprehensive about the boy keeping up his end of the bargain.

Wallis had written to him toward the end of the year to express his own apprehensions about Elvis' appearance. He had screened *Viva Las Vegas* at home, and Elvis to him looked "fat," "soft," "jowly." His hair was "atrocious": with its inky-black coloring, it looked like a bad wig. He had no business critiquing the MGM picture, Wallis admitted, that was not his concern — but Elvis' career was, and Wallis at this point was very concerned about that. For their upcoming picture, *Roustabout,* in which the Colonel had taken such an interest, Elvis had to understand that as a carnival roustabout he was playing a "rough, tough, hard-hitting guy." If he didn't change his appearance, the character would be completely unbelievable, and to that end Wallis wanted the Colonel to speak to Elvis about letting the studio hairstylist cut, color, and comb his hair the way they wanted for the character rather than come in with his own barber, haircut, and dye job.

He reiterated his concerns at the end of January, and no doubt to his surprise the Colonel agreed with him. The Colonel would convey his message to Mr. Presley just as it had been expressed, with full support, but in addition, the Colonel suggested to Wallis that he should "strongly impress" upon his production people that they convey their desires to Elvis simply and clearly, because if Elvis wasn't clear what was expected of him, he would naturally gravitate back to his own tastes and inclinations. Everyone would have to be instructed in this approach, Colonel wrote; proper coordination was necessary in order to ensure success.

The new picture itself was, as Wallis suggested, something very near and dear to the Colonel's heart. After first getting Wallis to agree to a production schedule that cut nearly two weeks out of the normal eight-week shooting schedule, and then eliciting $45,000 in bonus payments (to be split equally between Elvis and himself, with an additional $25,000 going to him as Technical Adviser), the Colonel devoted himself exclusively to his consultant duties, which for once had a creative, as well as a marketing, bent.

The idea for a picture with a carnival background went back to early 1961 and was, not surprisingly, the Colonel's — at least in part. More recently, as the studio had developed a script, the Colonel had come up with all kinds of suggestions, from toning down some of the more high-flown language to injecting many notes of actual "business" into the story. In his communications with Wallis, he was very careful to stress that he would not be party to a picture that cheapened carnival life, that this was a wholesome way of life in which the participants had a legitimate pride — and, it was clear, Colonel did, too. When *New Musical Express* ran a story on September 9, 1963, indicating that *Roustabout* would be based on the Colonel's own life story, the Colonel reacted with the kind of righteous indignation that was always good for business (if the world was to understand that this was his life story, then he should be paid for it), but on this occasion, for once, his response seemed to reflect an underlying insecurity, an unacknowledged fear of accepting responsibility for something that he might truly be seen to be responsible for. It was as if, for the first time, the Colonel were exhibiting a creative nervousness of his own.

E LVIS RETURNED TO LAS VEGAS at the end of January. He wasn't scheduled to report for the picture until the beginning of March, but he was bored in Memphis, he was tired of playing the good boy — he was pissed off at feeling like he was somehow trapped and didn't know what to do.

It was Marty Lacker's first trip to Vegas. Marty had rejoined the group after they got back from California. With Gene gone, and Elvis' cousin Billy a new father at twenty and temporarily on the outs with Vernon over the cost of long-distance calls home, there was room in the organization, and Marty hadn't had much luck with any of the radio jobs he had picked up since leaving in early 1962. Elvis felt sorry for him, and he was an organized little guy — some of the others didn't much like him, but he was *different* — so Marty signed on, leaving his wife and one-year-old son back home in Memphis for a life of adventure that promised to be footloose and fancy-free.

He found it without any delay. Vegas was like nothing he had ever experienced. Elvis built it up to him as they drove cross-country in the motor home, with a caravan of cars trailing behind. "Elvis kept telling me how much I would enjoy Vegas and that the greatest thrill was to see the city, for the first time, all lit up at night.

We were about thirty miles outside Boulder City, Nevada, when the mobile home broke down. It was daytime, and Elvis kept insisting we would wait in the mobile home until it got dark because he didn't want me to see Vegas for the first time in the daylight. Twenty minutes later he said, "Let's get in the damn car and go to the nearest motel and wait 'till it's dark and then go into Vegas. . . .

We weren't in the motel more than a minute when we discovered they had no television. That blew the whole thing, and Elvis said, "Moon [his nickname for Marty because of his bald head], I'm really sorry, but let's get out of here and get the comforts of Vegas." It made not the slightest bit of difference to me, but he was really disappointed that his plan didn't work.

They stayed up all night and slept through the day. They went to all the shows, saw Fats Domino and Della Reese, insult comedian Don Rickles (who would not cut Elvis because, like Rickles, he was devoted to his mother), and Tony Martin, whose "There's No Tomorrow" Elvis had adapted as "It's Now or Never." Elvis dated Phyllis McGuire of the McGuire Sisters and refused to be put off by the fact that she was mobster Sam Giancana's girlfriend. One night they went to the Stardust, and just before leaving the suite Elvis handed Marty a box. Marty asked what was in it, and Elvis told him to open it. "The damn thing was packed so full of pills I spilled some on the floor when I raised the lid. It was like giving a baby a box of candy. I'd never seen so many in one place."

The opening act of the show they went to see was a sleight-of-hand artist billed as "the world's greatest pickpocket." They were sitting to the side as usual so they could make a quick exit, and Marty was sitting on the aisle. The featured performer walked around the club talking with individual members of the audience. While he was talking, he would pilfer a necktie or a wallet or a piece of jewelry, which the audience member would not miss until he held the item up in the air to general applause.

> I had never seen the guy before, and I believed all of it. Well, I'm sitting there with this box of pills in my pocket and I begin to worry. What the hell would I do if he came over and managed to get the box?
>
> I really started to get worried as the guy got closer to where we were sitting. I slipped the box of pills out of my coat pocket and held it under the table. I tried to kick Joe to get his attention, but he was watching the act and not concerned with me or the box. I finally leaned over to him and said, "Joe, take this damn box, man, that son of a bitch is liable to pick my damn pocket."

NOT LONG AFTER THEY ARRIVED in Vegas, on January 30, Elvis' purchase of the U.S.S. *Potomac* for $55,000 was announced. The *Potomac*, known as President Roosevelt's "floating White House" during the Second World War, had been operational up until the previous year and had most recently served as a tourist attraction in Long Beach. Its current owners, however, decided to auction it off on the eighty-second anniversary of Roosevelt's birth, and the Colonel persuaded Elvis on the spur of the moment that it might create the same kind of splash as the *Arizona* benefit in 1961 if they bought the boat and gave it to the March of Dimes.

Almost right away they ran into trouble. The March of Dimes didn't want the boat (they had no use for it, and it was too expensive a gift to maintain); on February 11 Colonel tried to give it to a Coast Guard unit in Miami, but the Coast Guard turned it down for similar reasons. The newspapers picked up the story and began to ridicule the purchase, referring to the yacht as a "white elephant" that nobody wanted and the singer and his manager couldn't unload.

Finally, on February 14, Colonel succeeded in giving the damn thing away to St. Jude Hospital in Memphis, a research center "dedicated to finding cures for catastrophic diseases of children" that had been founded and championed by comedian Danny Thomas. He had the boat towed to a new mooring and arranged to have one side painted in a hurry, in order to make a good impression on the press. Elvis and the guys drove in from Vegas the next day for the dedication ceremony at Long Beach, the guys all looking somber in their dark suits, Elvis dapper in a light continental suit, narrow patterned tie, and forelock of hair falling carelessly across his brow. Danny Thomas accepted the gift for St. Jude's, citing Elvis as a true humanitarian, and Elvis pointed out accurately that St. Jude stood near the spot on Alabama Street where he once had lived.

In the end the event generated a good deal of publicity, but Elvis was furious nonetheless. What had the old man been thinking, buying this piece of shit that nobody wanted and turning him into a laughingstock in the eyes of the world? He had agreed to it, it was true; as a student of history, and as an admirer of Roosevelt and Churchill and General MacArthur, he had been proud to purchase the boat on which great issues of the Second World War had been discussed. But the way this thing had gone, he was beginning to wonder if maybe Colonel was slipping. And besides, what did the old man mean, interrupting his Las Vegas vacation?

THE NEW SINGLE CAME OUT on February 15, three weeks prior to the release of *Kissin' Cousins,* which had been rushed out ahead of *Viva Las Vegas* and block booked into five hundred theaters around the country. After a good deal of consideration, Elvis had finally decided to pair "It

Hurts Me" with the movie's title song — he preferred to wait for a better opportunity for "Memphis," which he continued to believe would be his best single in years. Preproduction on *Roustabout* was not scheduled to start until March 2, so they took their time coming back from Vegas, spending the greater part of the month there and only emerging groggily a few days before Elvis was booked into Radio Recorders for the soundtrack recording.

Filming started up the following week. Wallis had put together a good cast, with veteran character actor Leif Erickson playing the sentimental heavy (he's a drunk with an oppressive burden of guilt and a pretty daughter who fights Elvis at every turn but eventually comes around) and Hollywood legend Barbara Stanwyck, in a rare sixties screen appearance, deftly playing the part of the beleaguered carnival owner, a role originally offered to Mae West. The director, John Rich, was a television pioneer who had started out in comedy *(Our Miss Brooks)*, graduated to westerns like *Gunsmoke* and *Bonanza,* and had just finished directing the first three seasons of the highly successful *Dick Van Dyke Show* when he signed with Wallis the previous year to make feature films. "I didn't know too much about the musical theater, I knew nothing about Elvis, I said, Why me? I had visions of doing rather grandiose pictures like *Becket,* but I was going to do the very best I could and [try to] catch up as quickly as possible."

The guys looked at Rich with suspicion; he was not the affable, easygoing sort of director that Norman Taurog was, and the atmosphere on the set was different from the start. Then Elvis injured himself on the third day, doing his own fight scene against Rich's better judgment.

"He came to me and said, Could he please do the stunt himself? I said, 'My God, no. What happens if you get hurt?' He said, 'I'm not going to get hurt. I really know how to do this stuff. You see, I'm a black belt in karate.' I said, 'Well, congratulations, I think that's wonderful, I suppose that's good in life, but this is a movie. And God forbid that you get hit in some way.' He said, 'I won't. I know these people, and they know me. I really want to do this.' He begged. He really did. And, finally, he said, 'I'll be totally responsible for this if anything happens.' Well, what do you do in a situation like that? I finally gave up and said okay. But it was a mistake, because he got clipped severely in the head, and it was like, 'Oh, God, there goes my life in the theater.' To tell Hal Wallis that I allowed the star to do a fight. I thought, This is not going to go down well.

"Of course we had to stop shooting, and I sent him off to the hospital, and he had four or five stitches in his forehead, but fortunately I had a way out. The script called for Elvis as a motorcycle rider to be run off the road [by Leif Erickson in an early scene], and I thought, There's no reason we can't put a Band-Aid over Elvis' eye. Wallis was quite pleased. He thought it was a damn good idea — as long as I could keep shooting. And Elvis was all right as soon as he got back. He was a little subdued, having caused all this trouble — he was *very* apologetic. But once I told him what I'd like to do, he said, 'Oh, that's great, because we can keep shooting.' He was just afraid we'd have to shut down."

The rest of the show was without incident. Under Rich's direction it had a better look than most of the Paramount pictures, and Rich was particularly proud of the authenticity of the carnival, which he set up on a huge cattle ranch in the Valley with over a thousand extras, and of several rather difficult, unbroken tracking shots that had Elvis singing one song while riding on his motorcycle, another to his girl as they spun around on the Ferris wheel. Rich substituted these, at no additional cost and with considerable technical ingenuity, for the conventional matte shots (a stationary Elvis against a moving background) that were called for in the script. He worked with Elvis on his lines, too, and Elvis did a decent job of recapturing some of his old rebel image, though the score was almost embarrassingly bad and the surliness that Elvis was called upon to exhibit, like the music, was clearly more synthetic than felt. There was, as well, continued friction between Rich and the guys, who fiercely resented their exclusion from the action, while Rich for his part had little use for them.

"I'm not one for fraternizing too much with the group that are around the players, but they were around quite a bit, and you couldn't ignore them. One thing that comes to mind that really troubled me: Somewhere in the middle of the picture I was in the editing room, looking over the cuts, and Elvis dropped by and started looking over my shoulder. I was working over the Moviola with my editor, and he became so fascinated with what I was doing that I showed him how we go from a long shot to a close-up, or why I was cutting something around something. He said, 'Can I come and look at this more often?' And then the guys said, 'Aw, come on, this is nonsense' — only they didn't use the word 'nonsense.' And they took him away, and he never came back to the cutting room after that."

In the end probably the greatest problem was with the script, which, like the last three Paramount pictures, had been written by Allan Weiss to Hal Wallis' specifications ("Wallis kept the screenplays shallow. I was asked to create a believable framework for twelve songs and lots of girls") and once again presented an Elvis who appeared only marginally less bored and listless than in any of his other recent ventures. On April 20, the last day of principal shooting, a story appeared in the *Las Vegas Desert News and Telegram,* which was headlined "Elvis Helped in Success of Burton-O'Toole Movie" and went on to explain just how:

> Would you believe that Richard Burton and Peter O'Toole owe part of their current success to Elvis Presley? These two brilliant Shakespearean-trained actors, winning worldwide acclaim for their performances in *Becket,* might not have had the opportunity to star in the picture, were it not for Sir Swivel Hips. Don't laugh, it's not that Elvis refused either the role of Henry II or Becket. No, Elvis helped finance *Becket* indirectly. Producer Hal Wallis, who has made Presley's biggest hits, also produced *Becket.* And were it not for the revenue from Elvis' movies, there might not have been the wherewithal to film *Becket.* Says Wallis, "In order to do the artistic pictures, it is necessary to make the commercially successful Presley pictures. But that doesn't mean a Presley picture can't have quality, too." . . . At the moment Wallis is shooting *Roustabout,* starring Elvis. This story may not be the greatest, but then O'Toole and Burton can't sing like Elvis either.

It confirmed all of Elvis' worst fears. From the moment that he first became aware of the story, which appeared in one form or another all over the country, he freely expressed his anger and hurt. He was never going to be taken seriously as an actor; Wallis was just a double-dealing sonofabitch, and the Colonel wasn't any better — he was *never* going to get the opportunity to prove himself. The guys all nodded their heads in vociferous agreement, but if they'd thought about it, they might have recognized that most of all he was expressing his disappointment in himself. He was unhappy and disillusioned, profoundly dissatisfied with the way his life was going. He was ready for a revelation.

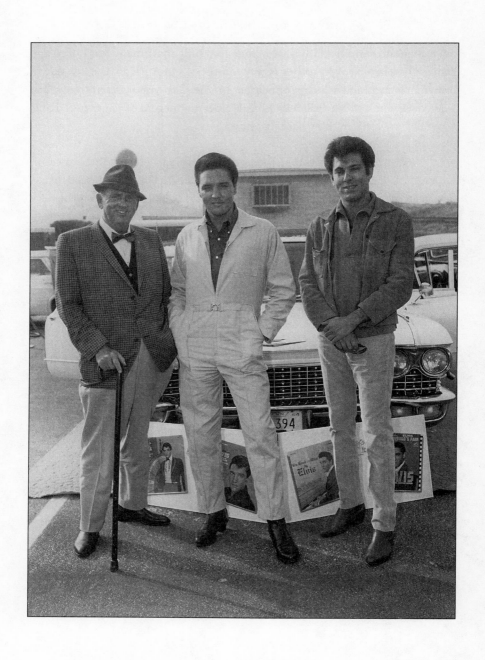

COLONEL PARKER, ELVIS, LARRY GELLER ON THE SET OF "SPINOUT."
(COURTESY OF THE ESTATE OF ELVIS PRESLEY AND LARRY GELLER)

SPIRITUAL AWAKENINGS

THE REVELATION CAME in the form of a twenty-four-year-old hairdresser named Larry Geller, who arrived on Elvis' doorstep at 4:00 P.M. on the afternoon of April 30. Elvis' regular hairstylist, Sal Orifice, had just quit Jay Sebring's fashionable salon but told his client that Geller, a colleague for the last five years, would make a suitable replacement. Larry, who was working on their friend singer Johnny Rivers' hair when Alan Fortas called, jumped at the chance. He was met at the Bel Air gates by Jimmy Kingsley and guided back to the house on Perugia. There he was shown into the den, where he met Elvis, who was wearing a motorcycle cap perched at a jaunty angle on his head and who stuck out his hand and introduced himself, as if Larry would have no idea who he was. Why didn't they go back into the bathroom, Elvis suggested, where Larry could work undisturbed and they could talk a bit, too?

For the first hour or so the talk was little more than polite conversation. Elvis had heard a lot of good things about Larry from Sal, he told the young hairstylist. He explained that he had just finished shooting his new movie and was going to the studio the next day for publicity stills, so they couldn't do much other than maintain his present appearance. What he needed was a light trim and a little tinting just to match the way he looked in the picture. Larry was impressed with his courtesy, his thoughtfulness, his "common touch" — but he was not sure what lay behind the reticent manner. Then, just as Larry had finished spraying and shaping his hair, Elvis suddenly turned to him and said, "Larry, let me ask you something. . . . What are you into?"

Larry, who had devoted himself seriously to spiritual studies for the last four years, had no doubt that there was something out of the ordinary in the question and didn't hesitate in his response. "I said to him, 'Obviously, I do hair, but what I'm really more interested in than anything else is trying to discover things like where we come from, why we are

173

here, and where we are going.' As I'm saying this, I'm thinking he might think I'm some kind of a kook, but while I was talking, I noticed that Elvis' eyes were lighting up. . . . He said, 'Man, just keep talking, just keep talking.'

I talked about how, five years before, I had begun to wonder about life. Why? Is there a purpose to all this, or are the materialists and atheists right? . . . And what was *my* purpose?

Engrossed, Elvis hung on to every word. "What *is* your purpose?" he asked, looking into my eyes.

"If there is a purpose . . . then my purpose is to discover my purpose. It doesn't matter to me if that takes years or a lifetime. That's what we're born to do."

Elvis looked as if he'd been slapped. As he shook his head from side to side, he said, "Whoa, whoa, man. Larry, I don't believe it. I mean, what you're talking about is what I secretly think about *all the time*. . . . I've always known that there had to be a purpose for my life. I've always felt an unseen hand behind me, guiding my life. I mean, there *has* to be a purpose . . . there's got to be a reason . . . why I was chosen to be Elvis Presley."

For the next four hours he was like a parched man in the desert: he bared his entire soul. He told Larry about his mother; he told him about the hollowness of his Hollywood life; he told Larry all the things he secretly thought and could share with no one around him. "Man, Larry," he said, "I swear to God no one knows how lonely I get. And how empty I really feel." With that he burst into tears.

Larry was initially taken aback; he wondered if Elvis did this with everyone he met, if this was some kind of game. But then, as Elvis kept talking, exposing his innermost feelings in an almost painful rush of words and emotions, his suspicions were allayed, and *he* began to wonder, Why me? After a couple of hours there was a knock on the door. It was one of the guys concerned whether everything was all right — what was going on in there? Everything was *fine*, Elvis shouted through the closed door. "Leave us alone! I'll be out soon enough." Before Larry left, he had promised to quit his job with Jay Sebring and bring some of the books that he had been talking about to the studio the next day.

*   *   *

H E WAS AS GOOD as his word. He arrived on the Paramount lot at
8:00 A.M. the following morning with copies of *The Impersonal Life,*
Autobiography of a Yogi, The Initiation of the World, and *Beyond the Himalayas.*
By that evening, when Larry came out to the house with a King James version of the Bible, Elvis had devoured all of *The Impersonal Life,* and if the
connection had not been made before, it was now written in stone. This
was the book he had been looking for all his life, Elvis announced to Larry.
This was the confirmation that he had needed.

The Impersonal Life had first been published in 1917, produced by a man
named Joseph Benner who claimed not to have written it but merely to
have been the vehicle for its transmittal, which came from a higher divine
self. Its message, essentially, was that the truth lies within us all, that God is
in fact "the divine I." "Are you ready?" came the question in the first few
pages of the slender volume. "Do you *want* to go? . . . In order that you
may learn to know Me, so that you can be sure it is *I,* your own True Self,
Who speak these words, you must first learn to *Be Still.*"

The book struck any number of chords for someone to whom it had
been impossible to voice such questions or even to be sure that others
asked them, too. It took into account human weakness and folly, saw these
as equal parts of the divine plan. It offered hope, process, a path to self-
improvement, and redemption. It engaged a mind hungering for knowledge and lacking any clear focus, or even a true confidant, since the death
of his mother. "It is really I, Who cause your personality thus to rebel; for
your personality with its proud sense of individuality is still needed by Me
to develop a mind and body strong enough that they can perfectly express
Me. . . . [That individuality] is nothing but your personality still seeking to
maintain a separate existence." All earthly events and conditions "have
been but a Dream, from which you will fully awaken only when You
(Humanity) again become wholly conscious of Me within."

Finally, as if anything else were needed to cement the bond, Benner
declared: "I may be expressing through you beautiful symphonies of sound,
color or language that manifest as music, art, or poetry . . . and which so
affect others as to cause them to acclaim you as one of the great ones of the
day . . . [and] hail you as a wonderful preacher or teacher." The book,
which abounded in illustrations of the true connections between those
things that passed for coincidence in this life, was copyrighted by the Sun
Publishing Company.

"I don't believe that book," Elvis declared in wonderment to Larry.
"Bring me more books like it. Whatever you think I need."

They spent the evening largely in discussion of *The Impersonal Life*, talking about its meaning, talking about it specifically as it related to Elvis. The inner voice, he told Larry, was one he had been hearing since he was four or five years old; it had come to him first in the form of his dead brother Jesse's invocation "to care for other people, to put myself in their place, to see their point of view, to love them. It was like the voice of conscience." The book's message that "I will cause even you who thus seek to serve me to do many wondrous things towards the quickening and awakening of your brothers . . . I will cause even you to influence and affect the lives of many of those whom you contact, inspiring and uplifting them to higher ideals," really struck home. Once again they retreated for hours into the bathroom, where Larry washed and styled Elvis' hair; once again the guys grew impatient, querulous even over this bizarre and inexplicable diversion which their boss had chosen to take up.

Over the course of the next month Larry would arrive in his battered Volkswagen nearly every night, and they would consume the evening in extended bouts of philosophical discussion that excluded everyone else not just intellectually but physically as well. Quickly the whole tone of life at Perugia changed, and a grumbling mentality took hold among most of the guys. Why weren't they heading home for Memphis? they complained. They had a month between pictures. If there wasn't time to go home, why didn't they take off for Las Vegas and have some fun? If anyone suggested inviting some girls over or throwing a football around, Elvis appeared to be totally indifferent. Joe Esposito, whose primary concern was to make sure that things ran smoothly, was willing to give him the benefit of the doubt initially. "I liked Larry at first. He was a nice, good-looking guy, very polite — but *strange*. To me it was almost like he was brainwashing Elvis. He'd get him into that bathroom and cut and dye his hair, and they'd talk for hours at a time and go into all these things. We were having fun, and now all of a sudden Elvis is outside looking at the stars all night or reading these books — you get up in the morning, and he's sitting there reading a book and asking questions about religion. Hey, what about the football game that happened last weekend? We used to sit and watch football games. All that stuff was gone."

As far as Joe was concerned, Elvis was easy pickings for a self-styled guru like Larry; his passive personality played right into Larry's hands. "He was always gullible when it came to those things. He was always trying to figure out why he was the one picked to be who he was, why he was the one chosen — he was into all these things that you couldn't solve. He liked to show his intelligence by trying to find the answers that no one else knew."

The other guys almost universally agreed. Some of them started referring to Larry as the Swami or Rasputin or the Brain Scrambler and making cracks to his face as well as behind his back. Some of them referred to him as the Wandering Jew, but mostly what they felt was a seething, undifferentiated resentment. Elvis made a few perfunctory attempts to get Larry to explain to the guys what they were studying, even to get them to read some of the books, but with the exception of his cousin Billy and Charlie Hodge, who was at this point only an intermittent presence in the group and who had recently discovered *Autobiography of a Yogi* on his own, he was met for the most part with sullen indifference. To Sandy Ferra, on the other hand, Larry was like a breath of fresh air in a frequently suffocating environment. In Sandy's view, "The spirituality was always there, but Larry brought it out when he brought the books to him. I think it gave him some peace. I was eighteen, and I had read Gibran, I had read the Buddhist Bible, because I liked to look at other philosophies. Elvis gave me a copy of *The Impersonal Life,* and he said, 'You *have* to read this.' He had underlined it himself."

Larry, for his part, was getting to know a witty, insightful, impractical man riven with contradictions. The Elvis that Larry saw was shy, he didn't trust himself, he was afraid people might laugh at him, but he also possessed a quality of inner calm that permitted him to study himself minutely, without self-consciousness or vanity. "When Elvis appreciated something, when he appreciated beauty, he just appreciated it; it was timeless to him. Like a flower — a flower just exists now, it doesn't exist yesterday. It just is. If Elvis loved something, it just was. [That kind of appreciation] is different, perhaps 'abnormal.' But there's something beautiful and interesting about it." To Larry, Elvis possessed an uncanny ability to "read" people, too. "His intuition was highly developed, and very little escaped his notice." And yet, Larry felt, he had surrounded himself with people who had no sympathy for his spiritual needs or aspirations.

Larry was amazed not only at Elvis' desire for knowledge but at his aptitude for it. For someone who had never been exposed to any sort of formal study before, he seized upon the reading that Larry gave him with an unquenchable thirst. In addition to *The Impersonal Life,* which he kept going back to over and over again, he devoured Paramahansa Yogananda's *Autobiography of a Yogi,* Krishnamurti's *First and Last Freedom,* Madame Blavatsky's translation of *Voice of Silence, Leaves of Morya's Garden,* and dozens of other books on numerology, cosmology, and metaphysics over the course of the succeeding weeks and months. "[He] was requesting a new book almost every other day. . . . It was never enough for him to simply read a book; he had to absorb it, think about it, question it, link its thoughts and ideas with all he had read before and things he had heard people say. Elvis dog-eared pages, highlighted passages, and jotted notes and questions on the endpapers and throughout the margins. For Elvis, reading wasn't a passive activity; each book promised a new adventure, a new way of viewing things."

THE NEW MGM PICTURE, *Girl Happy,* the last in his 1961 contract, began with a recording session at Radio Recorders on June 10. Freddy Bienstock had assembled what was by now a typically desultory grab bag of songs, and Elvis was sufficiently embarrassed, while recording the title song on the first day, to beg the movie producer, Joe Pasternak, not to bring his vocal up in the mix. On the second day he walked out in the middle of the session after thirty-six takes of a number called, with no apparent attempt at irony, "Do Not Disturb."

The film itself was no better. Joe Pasternak, a sixty-three-year-old native-born Hungarian with a career in pictures dating back to 1929 in Europe, was a longtime Hollywood operator who had come to MGM in 1942, after first saving Universal with a string of Deanna Durban musicals. His original idea, while at Columbia briefly in 1957, was to cast Elvis Presley in *Gidget,* the first "beach movie." The studio turned him down, and he went back to MGM, where he had a hit in 1960 with a wholesome picture about college kids on spring break in Florida. That was what gave him the idea for *Girl Happy.* "Metro had signed him for four, and I was at Metro as an independent producer. I went to them and told them I had an idea for Elvis Presley. I knew he was a young guy and that he could sing well, and I did [this] picture, *Where the Boys Are,* with the same background, Fort Lauderdale — and I was crazy about the background. [So] they said, 'Go ahead and make it.'"

Like *Kissin' Cousins, Girl Happy* was done on a short production schedule. Elvis was to be paid his usual $500,000 for six weeks' work and would get 50 percent of the profits after the first $500,000 in profits had been recouped by the studio. The rest of the budget came to less than two times the star's salary, and the finished picture had a bargain-basement look, with no location shooting and poorly matched matte shots. On the set Elvis seemed uncharacteristically subdued, almost dispirited. There were the usual celebrity visits; Ann-Margret came by from time to time to say hello, and the guys all liked co-star Gary Crosby, Bing's son, who had often played football with them at De Neve Park. Plus, they got a kick out of facing down the Secret Service detail accompanying Lynda Bird Johnson, the president's daughter, when she visted the set, as each group stood screened by dark glasses and impenetrable expressions, waiting for the other to blink.

Their old pal movie actor Nick Adams showed up for the Colonel's fifty-fifth birthday on June 26, and there was a cake and the usual celebration, but Colonel was absent with back trouble for much of the picture. On one of the few occasions that he was present, he gave an interview to gossip columnist Earl Wilson, throwing off the usual lines in typically boisterous and undiminished fashion. "Do you remember when we came out here?" he asked of no one in particular. "They didn't give us six weeks." What about marriage? Wilson asked. "There's a rumor, Colonel, that if Elvis ever gets married, you're going to have it in the Hollywood Bowl and sell tickets." "Untrue!" the Colonel responded with animation. "I always figured on a nice quiet wedding on top of an elephant."

Elvis, Wilson noted, was "as quietly non-circusy as his manager was the carnival barker when I found him in his portable dressing room." He had little to say about marriage or anything else other than to concede that he probably would get married someday as he glanced down embarrassedly at the floor.

I T WAS A TIME IN WHICH he felt oddly distanced from his old life. Between his reading and his daily obligations at the studio, there was little time for anything else. Elvis was just counting the days till the movie was done; he wanted more time to devote to his spiritual studies and was impatient with the progress he was making. Larry told him that you needed to assimilate the lessons, that there were no shortcuts. But Elvis was sure that he could go faster once he got home to Memphis. Each night on the phone he told Priscilla excitedly about his new discoveries, he couldn't wait for her to meet Larry, he said; he knew the two of them were really going to get along.

Early in the summer Johnny Rivers' version of "Memphis" hit the charts. It took everyone by surprise, because Johnny had been a frequent visitor at the house over the last three years. He had played football with them, been accepted as one of the gang, and even jammed with Elvis on the Chuck Berry number after Elvis played him a test pressing of his own recording of the song. There was no question among any of the guys that Johnny had known Elvis was planning to put it out as his next single. Elvis should just release his version now and kill the little cocksucker's, they all muttered angrily among themselves. But Elvis would not; he just shook his head sorrowfully and said he didn't want to see Johnny anymore. And in July RCA quietly put out "Such a Night" from his first post-army session in March of 1960 (it had originally been released on the album *Elvis Is Back*), after Conway Twitty had enjoyed some chart action on the song in a version produced by Nashville newcomer Felton Jarvis for ABC Records.

With sales of little more than three hundred thousand, "Such a Night" barely outsold Elvis' last single, "Suspicion," another old album cut which had been rushed into release when Terry Stafford had a number-three hit with his version of that song earlier in the year. In fact, with the exception of "Kissin' Cousins," none of the four singles released so far in 1964 had sold half a million copies, not even the title cut from *Viva Las Vegas*. It might have been a more sobering time if the movie itself had not opened at number fourteen on *Variety's* July 1 box-office survey, with glowing reports coming in from New York, Atlanta, Omaha, Cedar Rapids, and all over the country. But even if the movie had not done such reassuring business, it probably wouldn't have mattered all that much to Elvis. His mind was clearly elsewhere.

Colonel asked to meet with him just before he left for Memphis in mid-August. Larry and some of the guys accompanied him to the lot, waiting in the car while he talked with the old man. After about half an hour, Elvis emerged, "his face red," Larry later wrote, "his jaw clenched in anger. He quickly stepped into the car, and after one of the guys slammed the door behind him, he started screaming. 'How dare that sonofabitch!' Elvis shouted. 'He doesn't know the first thing about my life. He doesn't know anything about me. He said I'm on a kick, a religious kick. It's not a kick, it's my life. And my life is not a kick. It's real.'" He then glared at each of the guys except for Larry and declared meaningfully, "I wonder who gave him that idea. What happens in my house is my private business. It is none of the Colonel's affair, nor anybody else's."

For all of his brave words, though, Larry knew that the Colonel had gotten to Elvis and that this would not be the end of it. The Colonel had always been perfectly polite on the few occasions that they had met, almost excessively so, as if he were observing the newcomer, coolly taking his measure. But now it was clear that he had made up his mind and that, one way or another, battle was soon to be joined.

THE TRIP HOME WAS as unusual as every other aspect of their two-and-one-half-month relationship. Larry sat up front beside Elvis in the motor home. "Elvis is driving, the guys are in the back, and we're all talking, and I'm just yacking about everything, metaphysics and God and life. But then every hour or so he'd pull over and start reading *The Impersonal Life* or some other book, and the guys started getting angry at me, 'cause they knew I'd started this. We got to the outskirts of Oklahoma City, and all of a sudden Elvis pulled over into a big lot. I'm sitting right there, and he turns to me and says, 'Would you step outside with me?' And I'm thinking, 'What the heck is going on?' He says, 'Okay, tell me the truth, who sent you here to give me this material? Where do you come from?' I'm about to open my mouth, and a car pulls up, and two guys jump out. Reporters. And they say, 'Can we have a picture?' And he says, 'Sure. If you take one with my friend.' He put his arm around my shoulder, and I'm thinking, 'I don't believe this. What's really happening behind this picture?' Anyway, they shake Elvis' hand, get in their car, and he turns to me and says, 'All right, answer me, who sent you?' I said, 'Elvis, *you* sent me. You know that.' He looked at me with a big grin and said, 'You're right.' "

Larry had come upon one big surprise already. A sometime recreational drug user, Larry had never taken pills of any kind, or, up to this point, seen any evidence of Elvis taking pills. Just outside of San Bernardino, though, Elvis offered him a couple of Dexedrine tablets, with the explanation that they were going to be driving through the night and that they wanted to be alert at all times. Larry took the pills with some misgiving, figuring that it *was* a long trip and they had so much to talk about.

> And what a trip it was. As Elvis sat listening intently, I talked, and talked, and talked. I literally could not shut up, and while Elvis enjoyed hearing me ramble on and on about every spiritual book I'd ever read, every idea I'd investigated, by the next day my jaw was killing me. Only later did I learn that Elvis didn't want to "loosen me up," as he so delicately put it, for his benefit alone, but for the guys'. From the moment Elvis embarked on his spiritual studies, he never totally relinquished the idea that he could teach [the] others by his example. . . . That he

had some inkling of the guys' reaction was obvious. And just as Elvis set me up as the mouthpiece to say to the guys things he wanted to say himself, many of them answered him by making me a sort of walking effigy of the spiritual Elvis, the guy they didn't like. The wisecracks and insults they didn't dare hurl at their boss were aimed squarely at me.

The bad karma came to a head in Amarillo, where, as was common, a crowd gathered outside the motel where they had stopped to sleep for a few hours during the day. The guys all knew that this was a result of the Colonel leaking the location just to create a little excitement, but this time Elvis pointed the finger squarely at Joe. "It was about four o'clock in the afternoon, and there was this roar of kids outside. Hundreds of kids outside the motel room yelling, 'Elvis! Elvis!' What had happened was that they were announcing on the radio that Elvis was in town at this motel. I knew what had happened. Every time we'd stop, I'd check with Colonel and say, 'Okay we're here.' And Colonel called the radio station. But Elvis got pissed off at me, and we had a big fight, and I quit on the spot, and Jimmy Kingsley quit with me. I didn't leave, but I didn't ride with Elvis for the rest of the trip, I just stayed in the Pontiac station wagon pulling a trailer."

Everyone was a little taken aback, but this kind of thing happened all the time, and as they made their way back to Memphis the mood was subdued; they were more fed up than anything else at the constant, incomprehensible dialogue that continued to go on between Elvis and Larry. If things had been anything like normal, Joe would probably just have been hired back on the spot before they even got home, or Elvis would simply have acted like nothing had happened, but by the time they rolled through the gates of Graceland, Marty Lacker was firmly ensconced as the new foreman and Joe returned to Hollywood a couple of days later, still pissed off, a little fearful, but confident that he could find work based on all the connections he had made in the last four years.

In Memphis Elvis had to show Larry everything. They drove out Bellevue to Forest Hill Cemetery to see Gladys Presley's grave, and Elvis stood silently for fifteen minutes communing with his mother's spirit. One day Elvis gave Larry a car and told him to drive to Tupelo to see with his own eyes what Elvis had been telling him about. They drove around Memphis, and Elvis pointed out Humes High School, the public housing project where he had grown up, the various places he and his parents had lived, the places where memory resided. Elvis' father, Vernon, appeared reserved and suspicious, but that didn't really surprise Larry from the way Elvis had described his father. "I'm sure Vernon saw me not as his son's employee or friend, but as another weekly expense." It was Priscilla who came as the surprise. Far from being the warm, welcoming presence that he had expected, she appeared disinterested, dismissive, almost jealous of his role. She read Vera Stanley Alder's *Initiation of the World,* but with little interest or pleasure; her eyes glazed over when Larry started to talk of the Oneness of Being; she seemed to display a kind of unreasoning animosity toward him that bordered on fear.

"Larry was a total threat to us all. He would spend hours and hours and hours with Elvis, just talking to him, and he wasn't *anything* that Elvis represented; he didn't represent anything that Elvis had believed in prior to that time. Everyone wondered who he was, what he was doing there, what they talked about. When I first met him, I thought, Well, he's not so bad, he's really harmless. But then Elvis went the other way and became harmless, unthreatening, energyless — he became passive. Which was the total opposite of what he had been before. He read books studiously for hours and hours. He had conversations with Larry for hours and hours — he was going on a search for why we were here and who we were, the purpose of life; he was on a search with Larry to try to find it. You know, Larry would bring him books, books, books, piles of books. And Elvis would lay in bed at night and read them to me. That was the thing when you dealt with Elvis: if he had a passion for something, you had to go into it with him and show the same love he had for it. Or at least you had to pretend to."

To make him feel more at home, Elvis flew Larry's wife, Stevie, in, along with their two kids, Jova and Kabrel, and put them up with Larry at the Howard Johnson's just down the street. He continued to rent out the Fairgrounds, where Red went after Larry one time on the bumper cars. "He came at me as if he were protecting Elvis from me. Maybe in his mind he was. 'I'm going to kill you, you motherfucker!' he screamed. 'I'm going to get you!' And he did." At the Memphian they saw *Dr. Strangelove* three times in a row, then watched the final reel an additional three times before Elvis was satisfied. Peter Sellers was so subtle an actor, he had so many different bits of business going on in a single scene, Elvis told Larry, "that you don't always get him the first time, or even the second or third." They watched the Hal Wallis production of *Becket,* too, and Elvis once again wondered if he would ever get to play a substantial dramatic role in his own film career.

* * *

I T WAS A VERY DIFFERENT GROUP under Marty's leadership. For
sometime there had been serious division among the guys, and an
undercurrent of resentment against Joe in particular for the way he
acted — like he thought he was better than everyone else. Red had never
liked him, and Elvis' cousin Billy Smith dismissed him as "a big college
man" who established class separations within the group, even though Joe
had never finished high school. Most of all, though, Marty, a brooding, naturally choleric man whose anger was fueled by amphetamines, just
couldn't abide taking orders from Joe, and he encouraged everyone else to
feel the same. There was never any question in his mind that given the
same position, he could do it better, and even though he had railed at Joe's
"military" organization, he unveiled a fussy eccentricity of his own as he
swiftly established a new order in the Elvis world. With a nod from Elvis,
he made up lists of duties for everyone: it was up to Marty to "call Mrs.
Pepper [for] Movie Times (As Early As Possible); Transact Business and
Correspondence with the Colonel's office for Elvis," and maintain a purchase order system for all charges in Elvis' name. Alan Fortas got the
assignment to, "along with Marty, be responsible for Organization both in
good and bad situations," maintain Elvis' scrapbook, and "be in den with
Elvis as much as possible." Marty and his family (his pregnant wife, Patsy,
and two small children) moved into the garage apartment behind the house
that Vernon and Dee had once occupied, and in every way he tried to make
himself as indispensable to Elvis as he could.

T WO DAYS BEFORE THEIR scheduled departure for California, on the
evening of September 21, Elvis was appointed deputy sheriff of Shelby
County, a promotion over his previous title of "honorary chief deputy," by
newly elected Sheriff Bill Morris. He was photographed and fingerprinted
for his official badge, and he reminisced with Morris, a fellow native of
north Mississippi whose wife, Ann, had been a classmate of Elvis' at
Humes High, about "the good old days" they had both known and how far
they had both come. He told Morris that he had "always been interested in
law enforcement" and, according to a *Press-Scimitar* account of the meeting, that he had "once applied for a job as a Memphis policeman but been
turned down because he was too young — only 19." After a pleasant visit in
which Elvis reiterated that he was still "crazy about Memphis" and that
Ann-Margret was "great," he rejoined the guys outside and went off with
them to the movies.

That Friday night, after postponing his scheduled midweek departure by two more days, he went to the movies one more time, screening *Dr. Strangelove* for the fifth time on this visit, along with two other pictures. There was still one opening on the staff left to fill after Elvis hired Mike Keaton, who had been hanging around in much the same way that Chief and Richard Davis and Jimmy Kingsley did a few years earlier. Keaton was quiet, introspective, a member of the First Assembly of God Church, and his wife's name was Gladys — he looked like a good fit, though no one was quite sure what his connection was. Then, on the evening of the twenty-fifth, Elvis gave the nod to a considerably more familiar but, at the same time, less predictable choice.

Jerry Schilling was twenty-two years old and in the first semester of his senior year at Memphis State, where he was studying to be a teacher. A big, square-jawed ex-football player, he had left Arkansas State College when he lost his football scholarship due to a back injury, then followed his girlfriend to New York for a time and come back to Memphis the previous year to finish his education. Raised by his grandparents from the time of his mother's death when he was only one, he grew up shy and insecure, barely knowing his father, brought out of himself — like many of the guys — by his talent and love for sports. In 1954 he had been introduced to Elvis by Red, who had grown up with his older brother, Billy Ray, now a Memphis policeman. They were playing football at Guthrie Park in Elvis' old neighborhood, where Jerry, too, grew up, and they needed an extra player, so Elvis invited the shy twelve-year-old to join.

He had been hanging around the fringes of the group ever since, going out to the Fairgrounds with them, returning from Jonesboro, Arkansas, his first couple of years in college every weekend that he could, just to see what was going on. Elvis talked to him in a way that no one else ever had; "you just felt when he talked to you, it was like you were the most important person in the world. I mean, he knew how shy I was and that I really admired him, but people just didn't take time to go and talk about life with you like that. The feeling you had was that he felt like you understood him, and that's why he talked to you this way."

For all of his credentials, though, Jerry didn't seem to fit in with the rest of the group. He was perceived as a "liberal" in a world where the prevailing views were presumed to be conservative in terms of race and southern values; he was seen as something of a hothead by Marty in particular, who resented his youthful presumption and intellectual pretensions; and he was generally believed to be a Catholic (an equal sin among both the Jews and the Protestants in the group) because he had attended parochial school, even though his family background was as Southern Baptist as the majority of them. At this point he had been hanging around for so long that his presence was taken almost for granted, and everyone knew that Jerry really wanted it, but no one thought he was quite right for the job until Elvis finally gave him the nod, practically out of the blue.

Jerry was down at the Film Exchange with Richard Davis, returning the evening's viewing when he got a telephone call from Elvis. "It was almost four in the morning by the time I went out to the house, and he told me he needed me to go to work for him. I said, 'When?,' and he said, 'Now.' I said, 'Can I go home and get my clothes?,' and he said, 'We won't be leaving till this afternoon.' So I went home and got my stuff and came back and just sat out on the back porch thinking until they were ready to go. We left late that day."

The trip out was an education. Larry had already returned to California with his family, so even with the two new additions there were only five or six guys, and Elvis did most of the driving. Every time they pulled into a truck stop, they would toss a football around under the lights, with everybody diving for the ball and running around, until Jerry, who was still in shape for college football, was worn out. "I never could figure out how Elvis could play so damn long, seven or eight hours at a stretch, and then I found out that night, literally. He didn't give me anything himself, but he gave it to someone else, and then they gave it to me. I mean, I had never taken a pill in my life, but pretty soon I was playing like he was, and when we got to the hotel to rest for a few hours, I couldn't even go to sleep, I was so wide awake. The rest of that trip I don't think I ever ate. I ran after footballs, I was diving for the ball. I just thought, 'This is great' — 'cause I figured anything that he did had to be great, there couldn't be anything wrong with it. By the end of the trip, I think I'd lost about twenty pounds, and he was probably saying, 'What happened to the big guy I hired?' "

If that was a revelation, the arrival in California offered an even more graphic introduction into Elvis' world. When they got to the house on Perugia, Jerry was assigned Billy Smith as his roommate, but he was too excited to go to bed. "Everybody was beat and went to sleep, but I'd never been in a place like this before — there was a pool in the backyard, there were all these colored lights, and I was just sitting there in the den pretty much in the dark just looking around, when all of a sudden I hear the front door click, as if somebody's got a key, but everybody's in their room asleep.

Anyway, I'm sitting there, and I see this woman with long hair walking across the room towards Elvis' bedroom, and she knocks on the wall, and I go, 'Miss?,' and she turns and screams, and the wall opens up, and Elvis is standing there, dying laughing. He says, 'It's okay, Jerry, it's Ann [Margret],' and she goes into the bedroom, and the next night he's telling everyone else the story!"

They began work on the new film, *Tickle Me,* for Allied Artists ten days later, on October 6. From Jerry's point of view, there was nothing about the new life that was not in some way enchanting. It was a dream beyond imagining to drive to the studio every morning with Elvis summarily reviewing his day's dialogue, then watch him deliver it letter-perfect on the set. Jerry was alternately fascinated and puzzled by Larry Geller, whom he had scarcely met before coming out to California, and he took to reading some of the books that Larry recommended with keen interest. Even shopping with Marty became a kind of surreal adventure, after Marty decided that the maids were spending too much money on food and assigned Jerry to follow him up and down the supermarket aisles, checking prices against the interminable lists he had compiled.

Most of all, though, what he hungered for was Elvis' approbation. "I practically didn't speak for the first few weeks. He knew I was sensitive, and sometimes he'd get pissed at the other guys just because they'd been around so long — but then he'd wink at me, like 'Don't worry about it.' After a while I realized he was almost as shy as I was; there were days when he would just brood over things, because he was so unhappy with the reality of his accomplishments. Then one day you'd see nothing but anger — and I've never seen anyone with an anger stronger than his. If he had been just a nice guy, I don't know if I would have loved him as much, but the fact was that he had all this power; he had such extreme power that he could have gotten away with anything at this point. *And yet he chose to be sensitive* — most of the time. And those times that he didn't, you knew that they were very important to really understanding him."

The making of *Tickle Me* went no better and no worse than any of the other recent movies. Elvis' $750,000 salary made up more than half of the $1,480,000 budget, and with the star's 50-percent profit participation, Elvis and the studio were truly partners. This was Elvis' first picture for Allied Artists, and Colonel was well aware of the financial difficulties the studio was in. Earlier in the year he had magnanimously offered to let Allied head Steve Broidy out of their agreement, and when Broidy demurred, pinning the studio's hopes for survival on the success of the new Elvis Presley picture, Colonel encouraged Norman Taurog, back at the helm for the fifth time and always an efficient worker, to do his best to bring the picture in under budget.

It was in August, just a month before the film's scheduled start, that the Colonel came up with his most ingenious ploy of all. In a dense two-page letter, dictated on August 21 "from the hospital bed at the apartment" (Colonel was still laid up with a bad back), he reported to Elvis on a three-hour meeting he and Abe Lastfogel had just had with Broidy and Ben Schwalb, the picture's producer. He had proposed to them what he had already discussed with Elvis: that they forgo any original soundtrack recording for this movie and substitute instead a dozen songs already recorded by Elvis and proven by LP release. Each of the songs would be owned by Elvis Presley or Gladys Music and would never have appeared on a single or EP. In this manner they could bypass all the problems and expenses associated with soundtrack recording (finding the right songs, paying for musicians and studio time, pinning Elvis down on a date) and yet retain a majority of the benefits (having a single, or even an EP, to promote the picture).

Mr. Broidy and Mr. Schwalb immediately grasped the advantages of such a setup, Colonel wrote to Elvis; it was now merely up to Elvis to endorse it. And to that end he was including a list of twenty-two songs that he thought might fit the bill. It was entirely Elvis' decision, of course, and he could select any ten or twelve other songs that he liked, if he so chose — the producers just had to know by August 25, or else Elvis would have to come back to California a week or two early to record a fresh soundtrack.

Elvis did not object, though he did not respond until well after the Colonel's firm deadline. "Arrangements with records okay," was his terse, telegraphed conclusion. So for the first time, Elvis did not record a single new song for one of his motion pictures, and perhaps just as significantly, Colonel did not deliver a single tape to RCA.

Colonel was, as always, looking to the future. Under the amended 1961 agreement with Hal Wallis, there was just one picture to go at a salary of $200,000, though the Colonel was confident that this, like every other aspect of their deal since 1956, could be upgraded. To that end he bombarded Wallis with a blizzard of complaints and correspondence all through the fall of 1964, prepared, as always, to give Wallis and his partner, Joe Hazen, the opportunity to show their appreciation for Elvis and the Colonel's loyalty to their original benefactors, despite the niggardly pay.

Roustabout opened to fairly tepid notices on November 11, just three months after the Beatles' *A Hard Day's Night* premiered in this country to rave reviews (it was called "the *Citizen Kane* of jukebox movies" in the *Village Voice*) and brisk summer business. This was one of the few things that the Colonel didn't note in his extremely active correspondence with Wallis that fall, which seemed aimed almost as much at bedeviling Wallis and Hazen as improving his client's working conditions.

Meanwhile, the Colonel was also in negotiations with MGM, and as the year wore on, he closed in on the $1 million fee he had been seeking as a benchmark all along. It was part of a new three-picture deal in which only the first picture actually delivered the $1 million, while the last two paid $750,000 apiece, with profit participation for each at 40 percent from the first dollar. It was an unquestionable financial coup, but perhaps just as significantly, it explicitly embraced the principle established by *Kissin' Cousins:* that fewer shooting days promised greater potential profits for all.

He had the MGM deal wrapped up just before Christmas, even as he was concluding yet another agreement, this one with United Artists, for two pictures at $650,000 apiece. Thus, by the end of 1964, Elvis was in effect the highest-paid star in Hollywood, not on a per-picture basis (though figuring in the profits, he might even have been in the running for that), but on the basis of his ability to make a minimum of three pictures a year at $500,000 and up, *with profits virtually guaranteed.* By the time the Colonel had completed his negotiations, he had eight pictures scheduled over the next three years (at guaranteed salaries adding up to $5,350,000), with new possibilities opening up seemingly every day. It was little wonder, then, that Colonel should express a certain sanguinity when he was interviewed in November on the set of *Tickle Me* by *New York Times* reporter Peter Bart. "We're doing all right the way we are going," he drawled to the reporter, lighting his cigar with a foot-high silver beacon. "Every year more money rolls in."

THEY RETURNED HOME at the end of November for the usual three-month break. There was a brief contretemps among the guys over their Christmas present to Elvis: Marty went out and got a deluxe leather-bound white Bible and then had a sketch he had drawn of the "Tree of Life," with Elvis' name on the trunk and each of the guys' names on a separate branch, printed at the front of the book. Underneath the tree was one of Elvis' favorite quotations: "And ye shall know the truth, and the truth shall set you free," written in English, Latin, and Hebrew "to represent the religions of all the men who were his friends." Somehow, though, Marty neglected to inform Larry of the gift, an omission that Elvis immediately picked up when he failed to see Larry's name inscribed upon it. He refused to accept their present until Larry signed one of the branches that was still available at the bottom of the tree.

This wasn't the only snub that Larry was forced to endure. He continued to be made fun of for his lack of interest in contact sports (he preferred tai chi), his musical tastes (Bach), and his predilection for recreational drugs — and there were few tears shed when he was busted for marijuana by the Memphis police, a mess from which Larry was extricated only by the direct intervention of Elvis and his friend Sheriff Bill Morris. Even Larry's Jewishness was grist for the mill as the guys referred to him to his face as "Lawrence of Israel," but here, too, there was a clear sense of rivalry as well, particularly with Marty, who was at least as proud of his Jewish heritage.

Larry had introduced Elvis to new ways of thinking about Judaism early on when he had drawn a connection between Judaism and numerology (Larry contended that "rabbis change people's names according to numerological principles"), and Elvis had taken to wearing a gold chai around his neck when Larry explained to him that *chai,* in Hebrew, meant "life." Both Larry and Marty claimed credit for encouraging Elvis' decision that Christmas to have a new headstone placed on Gladys' grave — with a Jewish star on one side, a cross on the other — and while George Klein and Alan Fortas, the other Jewish members of the group, wholeheartedly approved, there was no question that some of the other guys remained skeptical of the whole enterprise. According to Marty it was not long afterward that he and Elvis came up with an idea for a watch that would alternate the cross and the Star of David on its face, as a symbol of universal brotherhood. He took a sketch to the jeweler Harry Levitch, who created a prototype from which he subsequently manufactured hundreds of the watches for Elvis to give to friends.

Clearly Vernon could not have been altogether pleased with these developments. Both Marty and Larry were well aware from talking with Elvis that Vernon was less than totally understanding of the need for such ecumenicism, and Marty was convinced that Vernon and everyone else in the family were anti-Semitic — and that the rest of the family was crazy, too. In the short time that the Lackers had been living at Graceland, Elvis' uncle Johnny Smith (Gladys Presley's brother) had threatened Marty's wife and come at Marty himself with a knife, while Clettes Presley (Vester's wife, and Johnny and Gladys' sister), who drank as heavily as her brother, had made it clear that she had little use for him, too. Marty didn't think much of Elvis' retarded uncle, Tracy, who went around saying, "I got my nerves in the dirt" and made noises "like he was getting ready to explode"; overall, it could be said that he took a pretty dim view of the whole clan.

Larry's perspective was somewhat more benign; he saw the family as victims of a general benightedness and lack of education, subject to the same opportunism that preyed upon the guys and doomed his own relationship with them, the fear that some undeserving newcomer was going to take away from them what was rightfully theirs. Mostly, though, the tensions were relatively muted, with Elvis and Vernon finally settled into a more comfortable relationship in which Vernon's life with Dee and her boys was simply an accepted fact and Vernon could walk from their new house on Dolan to his office behind Graceland through the back pasture gate, have a companionable breakfast in the Graceland kitchen, or come to visit at a moment's notice at any time, day or night.

In fact, the one abiding source of tension between father and son was money: Elvis had no idea what anything cost and couldn't care less, Larry observed; Vernon, on the other hand, "lived in constant fear that something . . . would befall them, and that one day he and Elvis would find themselves back in Tupelo . . . [a prospect that] struck terror in Vernon's heart."

Far more disturbing was Priscilla's fierce, undiminished, and virtually undisguised hostility toward him. Larry put it down to a lack of spiritual awareness on Priscilla's part, but for Priscilla it was a more visceral concern, in terms of her relationship with Elvis virtually a matter of life and death. Under Larry's influence, as she saw it, Elvis no longer took any interest in her. At night he would read to her in bed, but he simply refused to indulge in any of the sexual pastimes which they had substituted for actual lovemaking. He was, he told her, "going through a cleansing period, physically and spiritually. Any physical temptations were against everything he was striving for."

"Cilla," he said one night before we went to bed. "You're going to have to be pretty understanding these next few weeks, or however long it takes. I feel that I have to withdraw myself from the temptations of sex."

"But why? And why with me?"

He was quite solemn. "We have to control our desires so they don't control us. If we can control sex, then we can master all other desires."

When we were in bed, he took his usual dose of sleeping pills, handed me mine, and then, fighting off drowsiness from the pills, pored over his metaphysical books.

As his soul mate, I was expected to search for answers as fervently as he did, but I just couldn't bear reading the ponderous tracts that surrounded us in bed every night. Usually within five minutes of opening one, I'd be sound asleep. Annoyed at my obvious disinterest, he awoke me to share an insightful passage. If I voiced the slightest protest, he'd say, "Things will never work out between us, Cilla, because you don't show any interest in me or my philosophies." Then, pointedly: "There are a lot of women out there who would share these things with me."

[At one point] I could bear it no longer. I lost control and started screaming.

"I can't stand it! I don't want to hear any more! I'm sick and tired of your voice going on and *on*! It's — driving — me — crazy!" I was hysterical, pulling at my hair like a wild woman.

"What do you see?" I demanded. "*Tell* me, what do you see?"

He stared at me, his eyes half-closed. "A madwoman, a goddamn raving madwoman," he answered, slurring his words because of the sleeping pills.

I fell on my knees beside him, crying. . . . By the time I'd finished my tirade, all I could hear was the faint sound of religious music playing on the radio. I looked up at him. He had fallen into a deep sleep.

On January 8 Elvis celebrated his thirtieth birthday. The guys gave him a tree of life medallion, and he spent the day at home, reading his books and quietly contemplating the past that had brought him to this point and the future that lay ahead. Before he left for Hollywood at the beginning of March, he reflected a little to *Commercial Appeal* reporter James Kingsley on the meaning of it all. "We have come a long way from Tupelo," he told Kingsley, who, next to Bob Johnson, had known him probably as well as any of the Memphis reporters. "I know what it is to scratch and fight for what you want." He could never forget the longing to be someone, he said, as he gave an outsider a rare glimpse of Graceland. "Behind the enormous white couch," Kingsley wrote, "were floor-to-ceiling red drapes, hung on push-button, electric traverse rods. A fireplace of smoky, molded glass dominates the opposite wall. Scattered around it are white chairs and multicolored cushions on a deep, white carpet. To the left is the dining room, where a star-shaped chandelier hangs above a walnut table. The chair seats, repeating the color theme, are covered in red velvet.

"Opening off the other end of the living room is the music room, with an ivory grand piano and an ivory TV set. . . . 'Do you think that house in Tupelo would fit in this room?'" he mused, proudly showing Kingsley the rest of the house (though it remained off-limits to the *Commercial Appeal* photographer), his seven or eight cars, motor home, and three motorcycles — and a way of life that was as deliberately unpretentious as it was whimsical. "His idea of an elaborate meal is a small steak and potatoes. Breakfast generally is well-done bacon, scrambled eggs, toast and coffee. . . . For snacks he fancies sandwiches made with jelly or peanut butter and mashed bananas." He was aware of his reclusive reputation, reported Kingsley, but was at pains to point out that "I certainly haven't lost my respect for my fans. . . . I withdraw not from my fans but from myself." He hoped to have children, he said, if he could only find the right girl. If he did, he said, "I would name my first daughter Gladys, after my mother."

Then he looked at his watch and turned to the reporter with a smile. "Look, let's quit this business. It's after eight, and the night's pretty outside. After all, I am one of the night people. The sun's down, and the moon's pretty. It's time to ramble."

B Y THE TIME THE STORY came out on March 7, he was back in Hollywood, but for all the contentment that he had shown the reporter ("Elvis is as gracious as the caricature of the Southern gentleman . . . [his language] a mixture of colloquialisms strangely juxtaposed with the words of an intelligent man who was not content to let his education end with his graduation from Humes High School"), he was no longer the same man that he had been. For he had finally had his vision on the road to Damascus.

He had been waiting for it for so long that he thought it would never come. Larry kept telling him that he simply had to be patient, that you couldn't force these things, but he was not easily assuaged. He had been dedicating himself to his studies for almost a year now, he had read over a hundred books, and if something was going to happen, *it should have happened by now.*

He had it out with Larry just before they got to Amarillo, pulling suddenly into a motel as Marty complained that they didn't have time to stop, they were scheduled to be in L.A. on the weekend to be ready for preproduction starting on Monday. Larry found Elvis in his room "looking worn and depressed. Without speaking, he rose, and, while pacing back and forth, kept shaking his head in dismay. Finally he declared firmly, 'All right, all right, Larry. Just tell me the damn truth, man. What am I doing wrong, huh? What's wrong with me? Maybe God doesn't love me or something. . . . All I want is to know the truth, to know and experience God. I'm a searcher, that's what I'm all about. You woke that up in me, and ever since I started, I haven't had one experience — nothing. I really believe in all the spiritual teachings. I really believe, only nothing happens, and I want it to. Oh man, I want it so bad. What the hell is wrong?'"

Larry was taken aback by the pain and confusion in Elvis' voice, "but I tried to keep calm while explaining how each idea we had discussed over the past months had its place among the others, how each built upon the others and together they formed something very beautiful. The spiritual readings, the meditation, our conversations — all these contributed to our development, but they were just parts, stages of a process that might continue for the rest of our lives. No one knows when that moment of revelation may come; it's not a 'prize' one 'earns.' For some, it never comes, but that is all the more reason to continue working toward God."

The conversation continued, as Larry attempted to show him that this was the one area in his life where it made no difference that he was Elvis Presley, that before God everyone was the same, and to experience God it was necessary to empty oneself of all expectations and preconceptions. "You have to drop your ego, Elvis," Larry told him, "and make room for God." He had to "forget the books, let go of your knowledge [and] become empty so God can have a place to enter." Finally, Elvis was mollified. "[He] looked down at the floor, then back at me, then grinned. Nodding in agreement, he said softly, 'Well, you're right.' He chuckled softly to himself. 'I guess I needed that. Let's hit it.'"

They set off across New Mexico and Arizona, into the desert; "an iridescent blue sky seemed to drape itself over the sacred mountains of the Hopi Indians and color everything in view with a peaceful, heavenly shade." Elvis drove without speaking, with Larry beside him and some of the guys in the back. Then outside Flagstaff it happened.

Elvis suddenly gasped and cried, "Whoa!"

When I turned to him, he was slumped back in his seat, slack-jawed, staring at the horizon. Following his gaze, I saw a cloud, a single white mass floating in the sky. From the clouds emerged a clear, definite, recognizable image.

"Do you see what I see?" Elvis asked in a whisper. I looked again. "That's Joseph Stalin's face up there!"

Try as I might to see it any other way, there was no denying that it was Stalin's face in the cloud.

"Why Stalin? Why Stalin?" Elvis asked, his voice breaking. "Of all people, what's he doing up there?"

Before I could answer, the cloud slowly turned in on itself, changing form and dimension until the image faded and gradually disappeared. I knew we had witnessed something extraordinary and turned to say so, but stopped when I saw Elvis, staring into the cloud, his eyes open wide and his face reflecting wonder. It's almost impossible to describe how he looked . . . but Elvis' expression was the one that you read of in the Bible or other religious works: the look of the newly baptized or the converted. He appeared so peaceful, so accepting, so open, so happy. It was something I had never seen before and I would never see again. . . .

Elvis swung the bus over to the roadside and brought it to a violent halt. "Just follow me, Larry!" he shouted as he bolted out the door and began running across the sand. I finally caught up, and as we stood in the cool desert breeze Elvis' face beamed with joy.

"It's God!" he cried. "It's God!" . . . Tears streamed down his face as he hugged me tightly and said, ". . . I thank you from the bottom of my heart. You got me here. I'll never forget, never, man. It really happened. I saw the face of Stalin and I thought to myself, Why Stalin? Is it a projection of something that's inside of me? Is God trying to show me what he thinks of me? . . . And then it happened! The face of Stalin turned right into the face of Jesus, and he smiled at me, and every fiber of my being felt it. For the first time in my life, God and Christ are a living reality. Oh, God. Oh, God," Elvis kept saying. Then he paused and added a peculiar aside. "Can you imagine what the fans would think if they saw me like this?"

"They'd only love you all the more," I said.

"Yeah," he said, "well, I hope that's true."

The rest of the trip was not without its awkward moments. Elvis basked in his newfound bliss, while the guys all fumed at this latest evidence of the boss's weirdness and almost perverse dedication to the bizarre. If they had had reason to mistrust Larry before, they were practically ready to kill him now. It seemed only appropriate to the fucked-up nature of the trip when the motor home, which had become separated from the rest of the group, caught fire in the Mojave Desert, just outside of Needles, California. Somehow Elvis and the guys on the bus found two taxis to take them back to L.A., and everyone naturally wanted to hear what had happened to them when they finally got home. All Elvis wanted to do, though, was to talk to Larry by himself. He shut the louvered doors to the den, and though he could hear the guys standing just outside trying to listen in on his conversation, he didn't seem to care — he had been up for thirty-six hours straight now, and he was still in the grip of his revelation. He just wanted to quit the business, he told Larry with a kind of certitude that he had never shown before. He wanted to become a monk.

JOE REJOINED THEM in California. He had not found it as easy as he had imagined it would be, striking out on his own; film industry connections that had seemed rock solid when he was working for Elvis Presley dried up when he was looking for work, phone calls that once would have been routed right through were not returned, and by Christmas he was practically broke. Then Elvis sent him a holiday check, and Joe called to thank him, and one thing led to another, and finally Joe swallowed his pride and asked if he could come back. Eventually it was worked out that Joe and Marty would be co-foremen, a state of affairs not really comfortable for either one but that both were for the moment prepared to accept.

On March 15 production began on the first film in the new three-picture deal with MGM, a light-hearted desert epic called *Harum Scarum,* with Sam Katzman back at the helm. Elvis had relinquished his plans for going into a monastery for the time being, won over by a combination of common sense, a couple of nights' good sleep, and Larry's argument that he had a responsibility to share his gift with the world. He had already recorded an embarrassingly mediocre soundtrack in Nashville, and he was frustrated that once again Katzman had allotted only fifteen days for production, but he was looking forward to resuming his collaboration with director Gene Nelson. And he was excited about the costumes that Nelson had designed for him, which were consciously intended to evoke Rudolph Valentino.

Whatever enthusiasm he felt pretty much evaporated on the first day of shooting, as it became instantly clear that the story was a joke, the sets shoddy, even Nelson was apologetic about the haste and slapdash quality of the production. The Colonel had a small marquee with flashing lights set up in front of his office on the MGM lot, but it seemed like an act of empty bravado, as its fifty-six-year-old occupant, still laid up with a bad back, rarely appeared on the set, relying on daily reports from his lieutenant, Tom Diskin, as to how the picture was progressing. At the end of the shoot, Elvis presented cast and crew with the Star of David watches that Harry Levitch had created, and he gave Gene Nelson an autographed picture that declared, "Someday we'll do it right."

I T MIGHT ALL HAVE GOTTEN to him more if he had not been so immersed in his new life. While he was still making *Harum Scarum*, he started going out to the Self-Realization Fellowship's Lake Shrine retreat in Pacific Palisades just a few blocks from the ocean, and there he discovered an inner peace and a new mission in his quest for spiritual enlightenment.

The Self-Realization Fellowship was founded in 1920 by Paramahansa Yogananda, an Indian holy man who came to the United States in 1920 at the invitation of the International Congress of Religious Liberals in Boston and soon became a sensation on the Chautauqua circuit. By 1931, when he gave a series of lectures in Salt Lake City, he had been widely recognized as a unique phenomenon, "a Hindu invading the United States to bring God in the midst of a Christian community, preaching the essence of Christian doctrine." It was in Salt Lake City that Faye Wright, a seventeen-year-old free thinker, first heard him speak and informed her parents shortly thereafter that she had found her life's calling and was going to Los Angeles to serve Yogananda at the Fellowship's International Headquarters on Mount Washington. Three years after Yogananda's death in 1952, Wright became president of the Self-Realization Fellowship, under her adopted name of Sri Daya Mata. Yogananda's crowning work, *Autobiography of a Yogi*, a record of his spiritual search and encounters with remarkable men and women, from Luther Burbank and Rabindranath Tagore to Gandhi, "Therese Neumann, the Catholic Stigmatist," and "The Woman Yogi Who Never Eats," had long since been established as a spiritual classic, and the inexplicable manner in which the Master's body failed to decay during the three weeks it was displayed in an open coffin after his death ("The absence of any visible signs of decay in the dead body of Paramahansa Yogananda offers the most extraordinary case in our experience," wrote the mortuary director of Forest Lawn) provided yet another example of his own remarkable powers.

For all of the vaguely "spiritualist" trappings of the movement, though, what was most remarkable about Yogananda was the commonsense quality of his teachings. They took a singularly ecumenical approach, far removed from the ideological purity of fundamentalist movements or the cult of personality celebrated by many charismatic orders. Yogananda's teachings offered an umbrella under which the seeker of any persuasion (Christian, Jewish, Buddhist, Hindu) could find spiritual solace — as well as a step-by-step program of meditation technique called Kriya Yoga that required dedication, discipline, and a commitment to process not necessarily exclusive of religious belief but not requiring it either. Elvis was fascinated from the moment he first read *Autobiography of a Yogi* at the start of his studies, and when he learned from Larry of Yogananda's "incorrupted" body, an element that seemed to tie in directly with his own obsession with mortality, he was all the more intrigued.

At the park in Pacific Palisades he met a monk named Brother Adolph, well into his eighties now, with whom Elvis frequently conversed and indulged in long philosophical discourses. Brother Adolph gave him further readings and referred frequently to Sri Daya Mata, who had returned from India the previous summer after a pilgrimage of nearly a year. Did Brother Adolph think Sri Daya Mata would consent to speak with him? Elvis asked. He was but a humble seeker and would value the opportunity to talk with her. Brother Adolph brought the request to Daya Mata, and she agreed to see him; she would be glad, she said, to meet with the famous entertainer, depending upon the exigencies of her schedule.

In the spring of that year, Elvis traveled to the Fellowship's headquarters, up the winding little roads that traversed Mt. Washington, a sharp rise dotted with modest bungalows on the outskirts of Los Angeles overlooking Pasadena. There he discovered a spacious, rambling estate, with beautifully maintained, tree-lined grounds and an open light-filled building that had once been a luxury hotel and spa to the burgeoning local film industry. There, too, he met fifty-year-old Daya Mata, whose calm, soft-spoken manner immediately impressed itself upon him, much as he had imagined that it would. What he had not been able to anticipate was the extent to which her serene, reassuring presence would remind him of his mother, Gladys Presley.

Daya Mata, whose followers referred to her affectionately as "Ma," was impressed for her part not just by the performer's evident humility but by his genuine dedication and thirst for knowledge as well. "I saw in him someone who was full of innocence, if you can understand the way I mean that. He was a naive, somewhat childlike individual who was caught up in the adulation of the world and enjoyed it, but, more than that, he felt a deep bond with his public; he was carried away by them and didn't want ever to disappoint them. That was what I noticed. Then we proceeded to talk about matters that were of great concern to him. He had done some reading. He was sinking. Here was someone who had everything the world could offer, [but] it didn't satisfy him. There was still an emptiness, and the only way to fill it was to turn within."

He spoke to her as he had spoken to no one in years. "When he came in, I could see that he was shy. I said, 'Now, Elvis, just relax. You've come to see me; just sit and talk. You can think of me as an old shoe if you want.'" As he got to know her, he unburdened himself more and more, confessed fears, acknowledged doubts that he would have been reluctant to voice explicitly even to Larry. The guys around him, he told her, didn't understand. "They didn't share his interests, they felt he was getting too involved, it was a threat to them, and it created a rift between them. They couldn't really relate to him, they didn't really understand his need, and evidently he couldn't confide it to them." Only when he was speaking about the Colonel did his characteristic caution reassert itself. "He was very careful about anything pertaining to his manager. I think he felt that Parker was a very important part of his life and as long as he was going to be an entertainer he had to follow [his advice], because he had steered him so well for so long. The only thing that concerned him was that the Colonel did not seem to understand his need to nourish his soul. He was nourished in every other way, *but where was the nourishment for his soul?*

"My point was to urge him to take a little time for himself. I didn't want to be the cause of any problems between him and his manager, but he was giving so much of himself away that he didn't have anything left for himself. My argument has always been, if you have twenty-four hours in a day, a man is pretty foolish if he can't even give half an hour out of the twenty-four to God. I urged him to take time for himself and his spiritual well-being, but he was very much pulled toward his following, he wished to please them, they gave him love."

Daya Mata saw in him the same impatience for "results" that Larry had observed, but she had seen this in others as well. He spoke to her about being given a "shortcut" to attain the enlightenment of Kriya Yoga, but she just shrugged it off. "Oh, well, that I didn't give him. I wouldn't do that. I've had that come to me from so many people, and I just said, 'Well, that's — just set back a little. Just because someone has a name, that doesn't impress me. I'm not interested in that side of your nature. I'm interested in your soul.' There was one point where he wanted to wholeheartedly [join the movement], he wanted to teach the teachings, be more involved — but I told him that wouldn't be right because I could see his nature. He might be enthusiastic for a while, but then he would cool back and lean towards his other activities, [because] that was his life, he had another mission than that. Once, going out through the door, he came back just like a child, so sweet, and said, 'Oh, Daya Mata, I want you to know I love you.' And he meant it, just as he would if he was talking to his mother. He said, 'If only you could have met my mother.' I said, 'Oh, Elvis, I wish I had.'"

He felt a new serenity in his life. To the guys it seemed more like madness, and they felt increasingly alienated, resentful, bewildered, and angry all at once. Elvis appeared to be leaving them with his almost daily visions, his tales of going off in a spaceship, his delusions of being able to turn the sprinkler system of the Bel Air Country Club golf course behind the house on and off with his thoughts, his conviction that he could cure them of everything from the common cold to more serious aches and pains by his healing powers. To Marty he announced that a bird's song had turned into the voice of Christ, and under other circumstances they might have been tempted to commit him to a doctor's care, but reason told them that he would come out of this obsession, too, just as he had come out of all of his other momentary impulses and infatuations.

To Joe it was mainly a matter of the pills he was taking and his intense, unrealistic desire for something more — but that didn't make it any more palatable as their regular nightly parties became alcohol-free evenings of philosophical discussion, and Timothy Leary's *Psychedelic Experience* became prescribed reading for all. There was still the occasional football game, and there were still those rare times when they all went to Sandy Ferra's father's new club on Sunset, the Red Velvet, but it just wasn't the same; all the fun seemed to have gone out of it. The guys themselves were still alternating uppers and downers, and Marty and Alan in particular were developing substance-abuse problems of their own. When Marty did the expense reports, not infrequently he would stay up for two or three days at a time. "And one night, after I'd probably been up three days — I was sitting in the middle of the bed, writing. I had all the books and receipts around me. And I was so screwed up on pills that the last thing I remember, I looked at the clock and it was like two-thirty or three o'clock. The next morning I woke up and I was still in the same position, right in the middle of the bed. . . . But you couldn't help doing stuff like that when you were doing as many uppers as I was."

It was Marty, too, who principally reported to the Colonel, letting him know all the latest examples of Elvis' increasingly bizarre behavior. Marty conveyed the news with the same zeal with which he compiled all his other lists and reports, but it could not have been lost upon him that Colonel for once was baffled as to how exactly to proceed. Still virtually bedridden by his persistent back problems, he spent more and more time at the Palm Springs home that the William Morris Agency supplied him free of charge, where he could take daily steam baths at The Spa Hotel, reorganize his wife's freezer, or simply sit out in the sun by his pool and barbecue to his heart's content. Mixing and mingling in his eccentric way with Hollywood's most exclusive elite, he put on a good front to the world, but for the first time his patented combination of carnival sideshow and unassailable conviction was beginning to fray, his familiar braggadocio was starting to sound more and more like whistling in the dark.

To C. Robert Jennings, doing a story for the *Saturday Evening Post* around this time, he declared that his own seedy appearance and all the midway trappings of his offices (with their gaudy display of stuffed animals and Elvis pennants, posters, records, and merchandise) were aimed at discouraging all the stuffed-shirts and studio phonies from seeking him out. "The big shots are afraid to be seen with me," he said. "Saves a whole lot of time." As far as rumors of marriage were concerned, he denied them but noted that "Elvis promised to give me three weeks' notice if he ever gets married, so I'd have time to tie down some pretty good promotional deals." His personal credo, Jennings noted, was "Don't try to explain it, just sell it," though English music reporter Chris Hutchins, who interviewed him just a few months later, detected a considerably more chastened mood lurking beneath the rodomontade.

The world should not be surprised if he retired before too long, the

Colonel declared, noting the difference in age between himself and his boy. "Sooner or later someone else is going to have to take the reins." During the same visit the reporter sat in on a merchandising conference with two New York "tycoons" that offered the potential of $80,000 in licensing fees. Just before the businessmen arrived, an old friend of the Colonel's from his carnival days showed up.

> The friend had fallen on hard times and had with him a box containing several hundred balloons, which he offered to sell the Colonel for forty dollars. To help the man keep his pride, the Colonel bargained with him for half an hour, and finally bought the balloons for thirty-eight dollars.
>
> As he closed the deal, the Colonel invited in the tycoons who had been waiting in an outer office. When the man had gone, one of them stormed at the Colonel: "You kept us waiting twenty minutes to buy thirty-eight dollars' worth of balloons when we have a deal worth eighty thousand to discuss?" Replied the Colonel: "It so happens that his deal was more vital to him than yours would be to you. I say 'would,' gentlemen, because I've just decided not to do business with you. Good afternoon."

He was, without question, a peculiar mix. For all of his unflagging desire to run things and his almost perverse need to keep colleagues off balance at all times, observed Gabe Tucker, a longtime associate who had just returned to the Colonel's employ after an absence of nearly a decade, Parker was more than capable of many equally impulsive acts of generosity. It was "one of the quirks of his personality to disguise his acts of kindness," Tucker noted, but it was loyalty and long-term relationships — not religion nor belief in the future nor faith in human nature — that were his only yardsticks. And it was loyalty that he was concerned about now.

Not that he suspected Elvis of disloyalty exactly; it was simply that for the first time in their long relationship he could not really tell where Elvis' loyalties lay. All this talk that he heard about the boy quitting the movie business — it had never come directly to him, and he didn't think it ever would. He and Elvis had an understanding — and he believed that Elvis would always try to live up to that understanding — that Elvis would not set out to deliberately embarrass him in any way. But at the same time, memories of his devastating split with Eddy Arnold in the summer of 1953 cannot have been far from his mind. The Colonel was a thoroughly pre-pared man — he prided himself on his ability to get the jump on his com-petitors by *knowing the territory:* that was what had made him such a great advance man, and if he had had to point to one reason for his success in a difficult and always unpredictable business, that would have been it. Prepa-ration. Anticipation. Always staying two moves ahead of the other guy. But Arnold's defection was something that had caught him by complete sur-prise; Eddy's unilateral decision to leave him after nine years of unswerving loyalty simply as a result of differences of "style" had come like a bolt out of the blue. And while he had recovered almost instantly — never showing weakness, never admitting to error, teaming up with Hank Snow by the end of 1954 and finding his boy almost immediately thereafter — the mem-ory of its suddenness, the fact that he had never seen it coming could not help but affect his demeanor now.

He couldn't see where Elvis was going. They were a team, but *he didn't know what was on the boy's mind.* And in the absence of knowledge, he retreated to familiar ground. He didn't want a confrontation with Geller; if he was confident of one thing, it was that Geller would eventually reveal his con, or else that Elvis would simply tire of it and move on to something else. In the meantime he would show that he could still deliver, just as he always had.

To that end, all through the spring he vigorously promoted *Tickle Me* — it was, he loudly proclaimed, his biggest and most effective exploitation yet. On May 19 he sent Gabe Tucker to Atlanta for the picture's premiere with the gold Cadillac, which he had recently persuaded RCA to buy and put out on tour. If Elvis couldn't be there in person to promote the picture, at least his customized luxury car could. He put together fifty thousand publicity packages for local RCA tie-ins, purchased a hundred thousand balloons, and approved the two singles releases to be culled from the movie's sound-track of old songs (the Colonel's favorite, "I'm Yours," was the B side of the second single) while directing an all-out campaign to sell the movie as "a wholesome family picture — downplay the sex." At the end of the day the picture saved Allied Artists, achieving the third-highest gross in the company's history (behind *55 Days at Peking* and *El Cid*) and making a handy profit for Elvis and the Colonel to boot.

At the same time, he realized that something had gone seriously wrong with *Harum Scarum.* After viewing the first cut on June 17, he fired off a let-ter to MGM, stating that it would take "a 55th cousin to P. T. Barnum" to sell this picture and that, given the artistic debacle that had taken place, maybe the best thing to do would be just to "book it fast, get the money, then try again." As an afterthought, he added with uncharacteristic intro- spection, perhaps more time should be spent on the next picture to ensure a better result. To try to cram everything into a fifteen- or eighteen-day pro- duction period, with the star included in virtually every scene, was, the Colonel concluded, nothing less than a recipe for disaster.

A month later, still trying to salvage what he regarded as an essentially unsalvageable situation, he suggested that perhaps they should add a talk- ing camel as narrator; at least that way the ridiculousness of the scenario might seem intentional, and the kids might see the camel as cute. It was a rare instance of the Colonel suggesting that he might have made a mistake and, while he continued to maintain a cheerful bluff, not a particularly happy one. But he forged ahead. The picture might still make money; for all its faults, it might do as well as *Kissin' Cousins,* maybe even a little better. By this time, though, he already had his eye on the next goal, which was — as always — to make the biggest and best deal yet.

IN APRIL JERRY SCHILLING got a Triumph 650 motorcycle. It took a few days before Elvis, who had always ridden a Harley himself, noticed it, but when he did, he asked if he could take it for a spin. He was so tickled by the way the Triumph handled that he decided everyone should have one. George Barris started calling around to dealers, and before long they were assembling nine Triumphs in the yard at three o'clock in the morning. Marty didn't want to ride a motorcycle, so Elvis bought Marty a car. Even- tually he bought everyone else a car, too. But for the next couple of weeks they rode their motorcycles everywhere, roaring in and out of the Bel Air gates at all hours, until the neighbors got up a petition about the noise. Jerry was furious at this abridgement of their civil liberties, but Elvis just laughed it off and got a trailer to take the bikes back and forth to the gates.

His concern for civil liberties aside, Jerry was not a conventional part of the extended family in any way. In pursuit of his education, he was taking history courses at UCLA; he showed a broad curiosity about the world, from spiritual studies to current events; and in general he displayed an idio- syncratic mix of wholesome naivete, genuine loyalty, and stubborn inde- pendence that was not lost upon anyone in the group. Joe and Joanie Esposito called him "Mr. Milk," and Joanie saw him as very different from the others. "He was so funny. He would eat a doughnut with a knife and fork. And he wouldn't let any one type of food touch another on his plate. But he was open. And he would listen. And he was very sensitive. That's why I think there was a good relationship with Priscilla. And that's why I think there was jealousy on Elvis' part."

Jerry had already found out about the jealousy. Just before they left for California, he had been in the kitchen when Priscilla came down from the bedroom, obviously distraught. "I didn't realize they'd had a big fight — I guess he'd thrown a lamp, and the room was all torn up — but I just thought she was sick, and I asked her how she was feeling. We hadn't spoken all that much before because I was so shy, but I just kind of talked to her and then she went back upstairs, and I guess they got back into it and she said, 'Well, at least Jerry Schilling cares how I'm feeling.' And that's what did it. He came down and said, 'I don't need any goddamn guys asking Priscilla how she's feeling,' and all this stuff — and I was crushed. This was the first time he'd ever said anything upsetting to me, and I didn't know what to say. But the next day he just said, 'Let's go for a ride,' and he never mentioned it to me again, it was like, 'It's cool. I'm not pissed off at you.' And it was all right. But it left kind of a taste."

To the others Jerry was a little bit of a wild card who had the annoying habit of letting Elvis know exactly what was on his mind at any given moment. "Joe would say to me, 'Jesus, Jerry, why the hell did you have to say that? He was in a good mood.'" But Jerry fit in more with Elvis' own moods by his very openness and by his boundless admiration not just for Elvis' accomplishments but for his *character*. "I worked for this guy that I thought the world of, and he treated me better than I'll ever be treated in my life, but then there would be time periods when nothing would be happening, and there you were in this vacuum, and you would get moody and insecure, and I'll never forget Elvis telling me one time — he just picked up on my thought; we were sitting on the couch watching TV, and he said, 'You know, one of the most important things to learn in life is to be able to cope with not having anything to do.'"

T HEY BEGAN THE NEW MOVIE, *Frankie and Johnny*, for United Artists, at the Sam Goldwyn Studio in mid May. It was another dreary enterprise, offering little hope of satisfaction beyond contractual items of profit and loss to any of the parties involved. The soundtrack was done in a new way to minimize time wasting and overcome Elvis' increasing distaste for the material. Instrumental tracks were recorded in the evening, Elvis' vocals the following day. The official rationale was that this was a more efficient, modern method of operation, but according to Alan Fortas the real reason was that Elvis threw a temper tantrum in the studio on the first night and this was the result.

The movie itself, a remake of a 1936 release with Helen Morgan, was directed in pleasant enough fashion by Fred De Cordova, who had directed Ronald Reagan in *Bedtime for Bonzo*, done *Leave It to Beaver* and *The Jack Benny Program* on television, and several years later would become the long-standing producer of *The Tonight Show*. The cast was competent, Elvis was visibly overweight, and perhaps the most notable aspect of the filming was the spiritual connection that he made with his co-star Donna Douglas. Instead of dating her, according to Sonny West, he took a genuine intellectual interest in her. They exchanged books and ideas, spoke of Daya Mata and the Self-Realization Fellowship to which she, too, belonged, and meditated together. He showed her many of his books, Larry noted proudly, "and they would go over his marked passages together."

At the conclusion of filming, once again he gave away dozens of the trademark "brotherhood" wristwatches and, while still on the set, donated $50,000 to the Motion Picture Relief Fund in a special ceremony that the Colonel had arranged, with Frank Sinatra and Barbara Stanwyck showing up to accept the check. Even his generosity was viewed cynically and taken as further evidence of the boss's hypocrisy by some of the guys, who just as cynically took advantage of that very quality as they competed for financial assistance of their own, whether in the form of cars, cash, or jewelry.

To Joe there was no question of Elvis' charitable impulse: it was the thrill of seeing the expression on the recipient's face that motivated Elvis most of all. "Elvis was crazy about a TV show . . . called *The Millionaire*. Each week an ordinary person with a problem answered a knock at his door to find a messenger in a suit who announced that he was presenting the person with one million dollars from an anonymous donor." Elvis wanted to make a difference in people's lives, Joe believed, whether it was a close friend or a total stranger, and this was the simplest, most direct way he had figured out of doing it. To Lamar, though, it was also "a Band-Aid for the abuse he heaped on you the rest of the time. That was the blessing and the curse of Elvis."

The one real bright spot on the musical horizon was the success of

"Crying in the Chapel," his first top-ten hit in two years and his first million-seller since "Return to Sender" in 1962. And while it was true that the song had been recorded almost five years earlier for Elvis' gospel album (it had been held up all this time because Elvis had not been satisfied that his version matched Sonny Til and the Orioles' r&b original), it was gratifying nonetheless to be back on top, with three hundred thousand more sales than his last number-three hit, 1963's "Devil in Disguise."

It was all the more gratifying when the record reached number one on the British charts "for the first time," wire service reports pointed out, "since the Beatles rose to fame nearly three years ago" — and with a *spiritual* number to boot. Because, however sincere his public pronouncements that there was room for everyone in this business, however carefully phrased his well wishes for the Beatles' success, none of the guys missed that he saw the Beatles and the whole British invasion as a threat and that it galled him to be widely perceived as passé. It was clear that he himself was neither interested in, nor satisfied with, the music that was being released in his name, and for all the Colonel's pep talks and recitations of figures, numbers, and deals, there was no getting past the fact that the records were no longer selling as they once had, they no longer *mattered* as they used to. He admired the Beatles, he felt threatened by the Beatles, sometimes it made him angry how disrespectful the Beatles and Bob Dylan and the Rolling Stones were toward the public and their fans — but most of all he was envious of the freedom that they evidently seemed to feel and to flaunt. He, too, had once enjoyed that freedom, he, too, had once been in the vanguard of the revolution, and now he was embarrassed to listen to his own music, to watch his own films.

THE CHARACTER THAT ELVIS was to play in *Paradise, Hawaiian Style,* Rick Richards, a pilot who operates a helicopter charter service, was intended to recap some of the rugged qualities of his *Roustabout* role. Norman Taurog's one-time assistant, Mickey Moore, who had worked with Taurog on *G.I. Blues, Blue Hawaii,* and *Girls! Girls! Girls!* as well as serving as assistant director on *Roustabout* and *King Creole,* was a familiar face in the director's chair, and with Allan Weiss as scriptwriter and the third Hawaii location shoot in five years, the feeling was more one of extreme déjà vu than the mere revisiting of familiar ground.

After much harassing, the Colonel had finally gotten Wallis to come up with a $90,000 bonus on top of Elvis' $200,000 salary, with the bonus to be split 50–50 between Elvis and the Colonel. Nevertheless, he continued to convey a degree of disappointment that money alone could not assuage and immediately began his new campaign, which was the contract for the *next* picture.

Elvis was ill the week that he recorded the soundtrack, which Wallis might have deduced was the reason that he refused to bark like a dog during one of the songs. *Movie News* correspondent Derek Hunter reported that the star was "too sick to present himself for wardrobe fittings" and that when he arrived in Hawaii, it was "without his usual smiling face. . . . When Elvis finally went to work in front of the cameras, he was not his usual patient and polite self. He continually grumbled about the way his privacy was always being disturbed. He beefed about the circus that always surrounds him, and how he'd hoped to be able to get away from it all in Hawaii."

The ten guys that he brought along with him, together with his father and stepmother, might well have disputed that account, but the very fact that Elvis was for the first time being characterized in such terms is indicative of the extent to which he was allowing his feelings to show. He was as polite as ever to film crew and actors, he and Vernon and the Colonel laid a wreath on the monument to the U.S.S. *Arizona* that his efforts had helped to build, and he found himself fascinated by the lessons in Hawaiian customs, music, and culture provided by the Polynesian Cultural Center, a Mormon-founded college and retreat in Oahu that served as both a location and cultural adviser to the film.

Probably the most notable event that took place on location was that Jerry Schilling fell in love. Sandy Kawelo was a student at the center and one of the dancers who was being used in the picture. Jerry scarcely spoke to her during the week or so that they spent at the center, but on the final night there was a special party with elaborate floral arrangements for the departing film crew and a special dance recital. That was the first time that Jerry spent any real time with Sandy, and they discovered almost instantly how much they had in common.

"It was just a really moving experience in every way — the whole presentation. Elvis left with tears running down his face. Then when we walked out to the plane the next day, Sandy brought me a flower lei that she had made for me herself, and I wrote her a letter on the plane telling her how much I loved her. Elvis thought it was great and encouraged me to keep in touch with her, which I did, but I think I just moped around the rest of the time we were making the picture."

The general mood on the Paramount lot was not much different than Jerry's. To Jan Shepard, who had played Elvis' older sister in *King Creole* and had a small part in the new picture, the difference in the person she encountered now after an absence of seven years was almost heartbreaking. "He was not unfriendly, just very withdrawn and kept to himself in between takes — really, we scarcely saw him. Of course there was a whole different group of guys — he was now surrounded by an entourage — [but he] seemed very within himself, not as outgoing and fun-loving as before. He was preoccupied with theology books and seemed to be questioning his role in the scheme of things. One time he asked about Dolores Hart [his co-star in *Loving You* and *King Creole,* and a good friend of Shepard's, who had given up her film career to become a nun], and we had a little bit of a conversation. In the quiet moments he was still very sweet. When we reminisced about *Creole,* he said, 'Honey, that was my favorite picture.'"

May Mann, the Hollywood gossip columnist who had enjoyed good entree to Elvis ever since his arrival in Hollywood, noted the rumor that Elvis had left his own faith "to join an occult church." How can such a rumor grow? she asked herself, then Elvis, who explained that it was because of all the books he had been buying at an occult bookstore across the street from Paramount (actually Pickwick Books, on Hollywood Boulevard). "Some of the boys bought some of the books," Mann reported him as saying. "I began reading and . . . became very interested reading about religions. I was interested in self-realization — in finding one's true self. Who isn't? [But] I have never left my own church."

It is scarcely surprising that the Colonel should have felt it incumbent upon himself at this point to finally confront Larry, if only to let him know that he *knew* what was going on, whether or not he chose to do anything about it. The guys were all sitting around on the set one day when Colonel came by and indicated that he was going to "hypnotize" them. This was one of his favorite parlor tricks, though it was never clear whether he was indulging them or they were indulging him. In any case, soon he had Billy scratching like a monkey, Charlie barking like a dog, and one of the other guys impersonating yet another member of the animal kingdom. Larry watched and wondered: "What were the guys responding to? Hypnotic suggestion? Fear of the consequences if they didn't play along? The point is that Parker got people to do things they didn't necessarily want to do, a very powerful ability regardless of its source.

"See," he said, his face in a grin while his eyes seemed to bore through my head, "they're all hypnotized. But no," he added, as if answering a question no one else could hear or talking to himself, "we won't do one on Larry, because Larry knows hypnotism."

With that he gave me a conspiratorial smile and said to no one in particular, "Where's a chair for the Colonel?"

Several guys rushed over with chairs for the Colonel.

"And get one for Larry," Parker added, knowing that there was probably nothing the guys would rather do less.

Not too many days later, he announced in full hearing of everyone, "Larry, you missed your calling in life. You should have been on the stage. I'm telling you. I know. You should have been on the stage." And not long after that he inducted Larry into the Snowmen's League of America, ordinarily a much sought-after honor in the Colonel's circle ("A good Snower does not praise his own Snow ability," the Colonel was accustomed to advise the too-ardent suitor). Larry, however, did not take membership as a compliment. In fact, if he was interpreting it correctly, he saw it as a distinct insult. "Parker's actions always spoke louder than his words, and this gesture summed it up. In Parker's eyes, he and I were in the same league, so to speak, and I was a good enough snowman to earn his respect. I was working for Parker now." One time when Larry visited The Spa Hotel in Palm Springs, the woman who collected the steam room fee registered immediate recognition. "'Oh, *you're* Larry Geller!' she exclaimed, as if she had been looking for me. 'Yeah,' I answered, confused. 'I heard about you,' she said. 'I understand that you're a magician. Colonel Parker told me so.'"

O N AUGUST 27, A WEEK AFTER Elvis' return from Hawaii, the Beatles came to visit. The Colonel had been well aware of their impact on the popular scene ever since their first appearance on *The Ed Sullivan Show* the previous year when he had sent a telegram in his and Elvis' name wishing them success and a pleasant visit. Subsequently he had met with their manager, Brian Epstein, and brought presents for his boys (covered-wagon table lamps and gun belts personally selected by Mrs. Parker) from

Elvis and him. There had even been some talk about trying to get the British group to sing one song with Elvis at the conclusion of *Paradise, Hawaiian Style* until Hal Wallis discovered that their United Artists movie deal precluded that. The meeting was something that the Colonel had long seen as a valuable publicity coup — *if* it could be arranged on his and Elvis' terms. He and Brian Epstein had been fencing over the details for some time, but in the end Epstein capitulated and Colonel presented it to Elvis as an opportunity to snow the world with very little expenditure of time or effort, though Elvis remained at best lukewarm about the prospect of hosting some kind of formal get-together for people he didn't know.

The Beatles arrived at 10:00 P.M. amid a flurry of switched cars, special police details, and elaborate security arrangements masterminded by the Colonel — but with hundreds of fans still gathered at the Bel Air gates. The whole gang (Joe, Marty, Alan, Red, Sonny, Larry, Jerry, Billy, Richard, Mike, and Chief, along with Priscilla, Joanie, and assorted other wives and girlfriends) was waiting anxiously at the house. Everyone was excited about meeting the Beatles, it seemed, except for Elvis, who was sitting on the long, L-shaped white couch in the den, watching a soundless TV when his guests arrived. He rose to greet them, introduced them to Priscilla and some of the guys, and then, when conversation flagged, picked up the bass that was plugged into an amp set up in front of the TV. Charlie Rich's "Mohair Sam," which had just entered the charts, was on the jukebox and Elvis played along with it over and over again, fingering the bass absentmindedly as if nothing more were on his mind than simply working out his part.

In the end everyone seemed to settle down a little, and events just took their own course. Ringo played pool with Richard Davis and Billy Smith; George, who looked to most of the guys to be stoned when he arrived, smoked a joint with Larry Geller and spoke to him about Hinduism out by the pool. John and Paul, after some desultory small talk, eventually picked up a couple of guitars and jammed a little with Elvis, while the Colonel and Brian Epstein gambled at a coffee table that converted into a roulette table.

The Beatles' overall reaction was one of disappointment, their response to Elvis a prickly mix of anger and disillusion ("To be honest," said their press officer Tony Barrow afterward, "I'd describe Elvis on that showing as a boring old fart — but I do know Ringo enjoyed his game of pool"). Nonetheless, they reciprocated with an invitation of their own: Why didn't Elvis and the guys stop by and visit *them* on the weekend? Elvis almost immediately demurred; he didn't know what his schedule was like, he said, though he would see if he could work something out. The next day Joe called Beatles road manager Malcolm Evans to formally decline, but a number of the guys were still excited about the invitation, and on Saturday Jerry went up to the rented house in Benedict Canyon on his own, returning with Marty and Richard on the following day. John Lennon went out of his way to tell Jerry how much the evening had meant to him and that he would appreciate it if Jerry could tell Elvis "if it hadn't been for him I would have been nothing." Jerry carried the message back. "I was just thrilled, of course, and I told Elvis, but he didn't say anything, he just kind of smiled. That was it."

Before the end of filming, Tom Jones, the Welshman who had recently topped the charts with "What's New, Pussycat?," one of Elvis' favorite recent records and movies (he liked almost anything with Peter Sellers in it), stopped by the set and was practically tongue-tied with excitement. "[Elvis] was sitting in a helicopter. He sort of waved over in my direction, and I thought, 'Is he waving at me?' Just in case he was, I waved back. . . . Then he came over and said hello and said he knew every track on my album. We chatted for a while, and I asked him, 'Any chance I can get a photo together with you for the British newspapers?' . . . Then, as we were doing the photographs, he started singing songs off my album! I was really dumbfounded."

The remainder of filming proceeded uneventfully, and Elvis was finally released by Paramount on October 1, arriving home in Memphis six days later. He had made three movies in seven months, filming virtually without interruption and with very little to show for his efforts other than the deals and the money that the Colonel boasted about so incessantly. He was fed up with Colonel's way of thinking, he complained to Priscilla. He wanted to do straight dramatic roles, he told her with some bitterness, and all Colonel could talk about was the need to fulfill his current obligations. "He kept thinking that he was going to get good scripts. Elvis was very loyal. I would never have seen him breaking off with Colonel, but there were a couple of occasions when they both went at it on the telephone and didn't speak for a week or two. It all basically related to career."

THE COLONEL, MEANWHILE, had his own concerns about Elvis' career. He was concerned about record sales, but his policy of using up every conceivable scrap in the can, with only the movie soundtracks offering new product (and in the case of *Tickle Me* not even that), had put him in the same position he was in when Elvis got out of the army: if RCA wanted this artist, and there was no question that they did, then they would have to pay him his true worth, in 1965 dollars.

All through the summer Colonel had been patiently negotiating with Harry Jenkins, Bill Bullock's replacement as RCA's executive in charge of Elvis Presley, and on September 21 the deal was finally concluded, with Elvis committed through 1972, a year beyond his present obligations, and the record company retaining a two-year additional option on his services. In exchange for what amounted, really, to a one-year extension, RCA would raise its guaranteed annual payments to Elvis from $200,000 a year to $300,000 (there was currently about $1 million owed in back royalties, so the total would come to $2.1 million in guaranteed payments over the next seven years, with $1.1 million left to be recouped), with all of these payments split 75–25 between artist and manager. RCA would in addition pay out a $300,000 nonrecoupable bonus, to be split 50–50 between Elvis and All Star Shows (the Colonel), along with an additional $25,000 bonus to each party on January 1, 1966. The basic 5 percent royalty arrangement that had been established with the original 1956 contract remained in place; these royalties went against the $1.1 million that had to be recouped. The "bonus" royalties, on the other hand (2 percent domestic, 1 percent foreign), which the Colonel had first negotiated at a lower rate in 1960 and which were split 50–50 because of their definition as special payments outside the scope of the regular contract, were free of any encumbrance and were to be paid out, no matter how much in arrears Elvis' recoupments might be. Finally, the $27,000 annual payment that RCA had made to the Colonel since March 1, 1960, for consultation, promotion, licensing of photographs, and general counsel and advice, was upgraded to $30,000, with all arrangements explicitly acknowledged and signed off on by Elvis.

All in all it was a remarkable contractual upgrading for an artist who was no longer selling that many records — *and* for his manager. According to Alan Fortas, Colonel was openly jubilant. RCA, not surprisingly, put the best face on the deal, declaring 1965 to have been Elvis' biggest year ever, and pointing to the fact that "his sales reached an all-time high in 1965," which was in no way true, whether you were looking at singles, albums, a weighted combination of singles and albums together, or merely Elvis' sales since his release from the army (by comparison, he had sold approximately 40 percent more records in 1960). When *Elvis For Everyone*, a collection of leftovers and rejected takes still left in the can, came out in August, the press release trumpeted, "This is the first Elvis Presley album since 1962 that is not a movie soundtrack."

For all the rhetoric, though, it seems clear that this new contract did come burdened with expectations and that all parties were in essential agreement, however different their interpretation of that agreement might be: something clearly had to be done. Colonel had gambled in his negotiations that RCA would do all that they could to hold on to their brightest star; now, with an incentive-laden new contract in hand, he was gambling that Elvis was prepared to deliver. For while it was against the Colonel's nature ever to concede a point, after the experience of the last couple of years, he had at last come around to the realization that Elvis had to go back into the studio and do what he did best: make records. About this there could be no debate.

He was busy on other fronts as well. From September on he negotiated seriously with Hal Wallis for one more picture, and by November they had finalized an arrangement whereby Elvis would receive an unprecedented $500,000 plus 20 percent of the profits (a bargain price he would offer no other studio, Colonel hastened to remind the producer), and Wallis, exhausted, confided to his partner, Joe Hazen, that he would never do business with the Colonel again. Meanwhile, Colonel began talks with MGM about a new four-picture deal at $850,000 per picture and 50 percent of the profits, up $100,000 plus 10 percent in profits from the three-picture contract he had negotiated only last year.

With the promise of other deals for comparable sums, it looked as if he would soon have Elvis tied up through 1968, at a guaranteed income of nearly seven million dollars for the next three years *for pictures alone*. And this at a time of distinctly diminishing returns, when the motion picture companies, like RCA, might very well have been expected to question the reason for their continuing commitment. Elvis, Colonel was convinced, simply did not understand the forces that his manager had to contend with, but this did not give him pause for thought. With his relentless drive, his almost obsessive need to see every cautionary signal as a challenge, every relationship a game (the Colonel, Eddy Arnold had long ago observed, was missing an off-switch), Colonel had little doubt that Elvis would someday come to his senses and appreciate his efforts. When the MGM deal was finally worked out in January, he announced to Elvis with characteristic pride, and equally characteristic indirection, that as soon as the formal contract was drawn up he would deliver the rest of the cake, but that Elvis already had the icing.

Within twenty-four hours of his return to Memphis, Elvis had gone motorcycle riding, rented out the Memphian, visited his mother's grave, and several days later was pictured in the paper "roaring around the drives of his Graceland estate in a low-slung Go Cart" after midnight. He bought a brand-new 1966 red Oldsmobile Toronado, and he bought a new Harley, too, arranging to have Priscilla's little white Honda motorcycle shipped in from the Coast so she could go riding with him. On October 22 his original bass player, Bill Black, died of a brain tumor at the age of thirty-nine, and Elvis was quoted in the *Commercial Appeal* to the effect that Black was "a great man and a person that everyone loved. . . . I can hardly explain how much I loved Bill." But he did not attend the funeral.

That fall, too, the Meditation Garden was completed. The previous year Marty Lacker's brother-in-law, Bernie Grenadier, who had an interior decorating business with his wife, Marty's sister Anne, had reconstructed the waterfall in the den, and Elvis had been so pleased with the job he did that, before they left for California, he gave Bernie the assignment to refurbish the gardens along the lines of the Self-Realization Park in Pacific Heights. It would be great, he said, just to have a place where he could meditate, "some place that's really pretty and peaceful where I could think and be by myself."

Bernie set out on the project right away, but actual construction didn't get going until well into the spring. According to Marty's highly detailed reports, Bernie was working on it night and day. He went to Italy to purchase marble statues of ancient Roman soldiers, and stained-glass windows were obtained from Spain to be set into a brick wall. He found brick for the wall in Mexico, commissioned arches and plantings, and built a fountain with fourteen different sprays and underwater light formations. It was to be a work of art.

Even after they returned home, Bernie made Elvis promise not to view it until everything was ready. At last Bernie told Elvis that he could take a look, and Elvis and Priscilla went out to the garden by themselves to survey the work. When he came back in, Marty recounted, there were "tears of joy in his eyes, [though] as was his way, he avoided Bernie for the rest of the evening. It was never easy for Elvis to express his appreciation." Appreciation aside, it became the source of considerable contention as well, according to Marty, when Vernon refused at first to provide final payment on

Bernie's bill of $21,000. It was typical of the way things were done in the Presley household, Marty sniffed, and he took it as one more example of Vernon's underlying anti-Semitism, a view not calculated to endear him to Vernon's son.

For Christmas the guys gave Elvis a statue of Jesus for the garden. Marty commissioned John McIntire, an instructor at the Memphis Academy of Arts, whom Jerry knew from taking classes there, to sculpt the statue. According to McIntire, "Jerry Schilling, Larry Geller, and Marty Lacker came in this big black car. They said, 'We want to do Elvis a Christmas present. Could you make a statue?' Marty posed, a short, little fat guy, with his arms sticking out. He said, 'Something like this. About four foot high. Could you do it? We only have five hundred dollars.' I said, 'No way.' They wanted marble. I had four weeks, it was December 6, 1965, when they came. I carved it in the front living room; it's the world's largest plastic Jesus (they [still] think it's marble). On the plaque on the bottom of the sculpture the bodyguards made this little poem up; the wording on it put [Elvis] on the same level as God."

Jerry got an even better present for Christmas. Sandy Kawelo came over from Hawaii to join him. He had been moping around for most of October when Elvis finally came to him one day and said, "You're no good to me anymore." Jerry was totally shocked. "I was just crushed. I said, 'What do you mean?' Then he smiled and gave me a round-trip ticket to Hawaii. He said, 'Go over there and get her and bring her back.'" Jerry followed the instructions he had been given to a T, staying in Hawaii for several weeks, persuading Sandy's family that his intentions were honorable, and finally meeting her at the Memphis airport one chilly afternoon just after Christmas. Jerry had been telling Grandma Presley for weeks all about his beautiful Hawaiian girlfriend. "I really loved Grandma — she was a very wise and great woman — but she would say, 'Son, why don't you get yourself an American girl?' Then Sandy came to Memphis, and we moved into the apartment complex right across the street — and Grandma just fell in love with her."

To Larry, Elvis seemed increasingly restive, which was hardly surprising, given the extent to which his world continued to be constricted, almost calcified. "In Elvis' life the outside world was a distant place he ventured out into but never really lived in. To outsiders, Elvis' observations on philosophy and religion were interesting; to most insiders, they were annoying. . . . The routines [were] immutable. The occasional employee might leave or come back again; Elvis might move from one house in Los Angeles to another; his recreational interest[s] . . . might shift, but these were imperceptible ripples in an otherwise static existence. Things happened, of course, but even the most dramatic event assumed the texture of an episode on a television series." To Jerry it was like they were all being drawn into a virtual world in which gradually the courtiers became as isolated as the king. "We were all together so much; we were all very much influenced by Elvis, because, let's face it, he was the center of everything that went on. It became normal to us to get up late in the afternoon and go to bed at sunrise, and because of that we became isolated from our families, our friends. We found ourselves relating to each other but not to anybody else. It was like you were in somebody else's environment. There was friction sometimes over salaries or over who did this or that, but Elvis always remained in control. It was a family; we all had our one-on-one relationships with Elvis, and everybody thought that was *the* special relationship. Elvis had a spiritual charisma about him that made you feel like he was your best friend, and you could always depend on him."

They celebrated New Year's Eve at the Manhattan Club once again, with bandleader Willie Mitchell playing his instrumental hits and various vocalists singing r&b songs of the day. Elvis had George Klein clear the dance floor at one point so he could get a better view of Vaneese Starks when she sang "Hound Dog," and he and Priscilla danced a couple of slow dances and one fast one before he said good night to his guests — over one hundred friends, family, and fans.

He didn't see as many movies as usual over the holiday season, because much of his time was consumed with the slot-car track that Priscilla had given him for Christmas. He and the guys had discovered slot car racing in California and started renting out the Robert E. Lee Raceway almost as frequently as they had once rented the Rainbow Rollerdrome. Priscilla got the home racing set from the proprietor of the Robert E. Lee, and it was such a success that Elvis almost immediately started talking about adding another room on to the house to accommodate an expanded setup, something Marty volunteered his brother-in-law could very easily take care of.

It was during this same extended Christmas break that Elvis finally tried LSD. They had all tried marijuana brownies the previous August, and Elvis' interest in consciousness-expanding drugs had been stimulated by his reading, particularly Aldous Huxley's *Doors of Perception* and Timothy Leary's 1964 psychedelic manual. Some of the guys in fact had already taken acid at Elvis' urging, and under his supervision, but the fact that he himself had remained an observer occasioned a good deal of cynical commentary on their part. In Alan Fortas' view, "he was too scared to take it himself, and we were stupid enough to be his guinea pigs," and Red speculated that he wanted to see the effect of the drug on their creativity. In any case his interest in psychotropic effects was not lessened by observation, and when a fan gave him several hits of windowpane acid, he and Larry made plans to take a trip, under carefully controlled conditions.

That day finally came several months after their return to Graceland, and with Sonny (who had been part of the original experiment) as their monitor, Elvis, Priscilla, Larry, and Jerry all embarked upon the experience. They sat at the conference table in the room adjacent to Elvis' bedroom and started out soberly talking about the Leary book and the whole psychedelic experience. Larry, who was the only one with any direct knowledge of the drug, observed with interest as it gradually began to take effect.

About an hour and a half later, we stood up to walk around. Suddenly I noticed that we had lost Jerry. No one knew where he was, and I didn't know whether Jerry was actually missing or whether I was imagining it. Nevertheless, I joined in the search, and we found him lying in a closet, under a pile of Elvis' clothes. Through all this, Elvis obviously was really fighting the effects of the drug, trying his best to make it appear that he was not getting high.

We were having a pleasant, mellow trip when suddenly Priscilla began sobbing. She fell to her knees in front of Elvis and cried, "You don't really love me, you just say you do." . . . Next thing we knew, she was saying to Jerry and me, "You don't like me." When she started telling us that she was "ugly," I worried she might be having a bad trip [but] fortunately she soon snapped out of it. . . .

Like anything else Elvis did, he tripped Elvis-style. No beaded curtains, incense or Indian sitar music for us. Several hours after we had started, we turned on television and watched a science-fiction movie, *The Time Machine,* and sent out for pizza. As we were all coming down, we walked out behind Graceland and marveled at the beauty of nature, talked about how lucky we were to have such good friends and how much we cared about one another. As far as I know, it was the only time Elvis took acid.

When they returned to California, they moved into the new house on Rocca Place. Less than a mile from Perugia, it had been purchased and then rented out to them once again by Mrs. Reginald Owen, the widow of the British film actor, with whom Joe had been doing business ever since they moved to Bellagio in 1961. The new ranch-style home afforded considerably more room and privacy than the house on Perugia, and Joe and Marty got it ready for Elvis' arrival at the beginning of February. Marty took the bedroom next to Elvis' and decorated it with red-flocked wallpaper and black silk hangings draped from the walls; the rest of the house was decorated according to Marty's tastes in dark, solid colors, with Elvis' favorite color, blue, predominating.

Charlie Hodge came back just in time for the move. He had continued working for veteran country entertainer Jimmy Wakely off and on all these years, but now he had made up his mind to return for good. He was present for the recording of the soundtrack for the new picture, even playing some piano on the session, and his presence restored not just a lot of laughter but a lot of music to the house. Charlie was not really one for factions. He had a single loyalty, and while his undeviating devotion to it got on some people's nerves, he was just as capable of getting along with Larry, whom he genuinely admired, as he was with Red, who didn't admire Larry at all but whose love of music Charlie could equally well appreciate. Charlie was emotionally high-strung, he drank too much, and he was dismissed in some quarters as little more than a sycophant — but those quarters were hardly free of the same taint themselves, and overall, Charlie's renewed presence made a difference in the day-to-day mood of the house.

In addition, Rocca Place was meant at last to provide Priscilla with a California home. Some of the guys saw this as the first sign of capitulation in a "struggle of the will" in which "Priscilla very much wanted to get married and [Elvis] was not prepared to sacrifice his enviable bachelor status." She had always been excluded from their Hollywood trips, the ostensible reason being that she would be a distraction to Elvis in his work. But now here she was flying out to join them and doing her best to take over, to establish rules and standards of domestic behavior that could never have been contemplated, let alone enforced, so long as their Bel Air home remained a boys' club exclusively. Naturally, it was resented and perceived as yet another sign of the kind of weakness that had started to manifest itself when Larry first came on the scene. There were personal causes for resentment as well, which, even if they did not originate with Priscilla, ended up in her lap. As Billy Smith saw it, "Elvis basically told her to exert more control over the wives *and* the guys. He said, 'They work for me, so if you tell one of the guys to do something, he'd better do it.' She thought it was easy. She'd tell somebody to get her something, and if he didn't, she'd tell Elvis, and Elvis would blow up. The majority of the guys went along with it, but they left a lot of things unsaid."

Not surprisingly there was no end to the gloating when Priscilla got anything that could be perceived as a comeuppance. One time, for example, she suggested that she might like to visit the set in order to meet Elvis' co-star Shelley Fabares, about whom she had been hearing so much. Elvis said he didn't think that was such a good idea, but she persisted. The guys could hear every word of the argument; they could hear angry shouting and furniture being overturned. Priscilla was beside herself. Was there something going on on the set that he didn't want her to see? "I don't have a goddamn thing to hide," he announced. "You're getting a little too aggressive and demanding. It might be a good idea if you visited your parents for a while."

Shocked, I yelled, "Well, I'm not going!"

"I think you should. In fact, I'll help you." He walked over to my closet and proceeded to throw every piece of clothing I had on the floor, hangers included, along with my suitcase on top of the clothes.

"All right, woman. Start packing!" . . .

Sobbing, I started to pack, as he turned and strode out of the room. Moments later, I heard him yelling for Joe to make a reservation. "Get her on the next flight out. She's going back to her parents." There was a finality in his voice that I had never heard before. Hysterical, I began folding my clothes as he continued yelling in the other room. I packed slowly, stunned by the blow-up.

When he came back into the room, I felt humiliated. I continued folding clothes, sobbing uncontrollably. . . . I got up slowly and started toward the door. Just as I reached it, I felt his hand on my shoulder, turning me around, and then, miraculously, I was in his arms, and he was holding me tight.

"Now do you understand? . . . Do you see that you need this? You need someone to take you right to this point and put you in your place."

I was relieved and happy to be back in his arms. Anything he'd have said would've made sense to me in that moment. . . . This was Elvis' technique of keeping me under control.

He was equally capable, though, of defending her and turning that same controlling fury on the others. Larry and Charlie watched him fire every one of the guys in sight after one of the wives told Priscilla Elvis didn't want her there because he wanted to be free to have his other women. "That's it, that's it," he announced to the room at large. "I'm fed up with you guys and all the small talk, gossiping and bullshit. Now fuck off, all of you. I don't want to see your faces anymore. Call Daddy, tell him every word I said. This will make him real happy."

For the most part, to his surprise Elvis did not find Priscilla's presence as trying as he had thought it might be. Perhaps he simply enjoyed the diversion of a different situation, whatever its attendant difficulties. He took Priscilla out to the Self-Realization Park and even introduced her to Daya Mata, who, Priscilla agreed, bore a striking resemblance to Gladys Presley. If his life lacked a clear center (the new MGM picture, *Spinout,* once again directed by Norman Taurog, was as slight as anything else in which he had appeared, with a racing-car driver replacing the pilot hero of *Paradise, Hawaiian Style*), it at least had its peripheral pleasures. And he was very excited about the bus that George Barris was customizing for him, which Barris had promised they would have for the trip back to Memphis in April. It was a retired Greyhound D'Elegance coach, fully outfitted, its rear engine lined with lead to minimize noise, with a hydraulic driver's seat molded to Elvis' body, an elaborate stereo, full kitchen and sleeping quarters, and portholes once again to simulate that "luxury yacht" feeling. He went to Barris' North Hollywood shop several times a week to check on its progress, and was so impatient to try it out that on February 17, the night they finished the soundtrack recording, he induced Barris to break into his own shop (the Kustom King had forgotten his key) so that he and Elvis and Joe could take it on a trial spin to Las Vegas.

He also got a brand-new reel-to-reel Sony video camera and recorder, only recently introduced into the United States for home use. It didn't take him long to figure out the possibilities, and soon he was staging his own private dramas, just as he had with the Polaroid camera a year or two before. Sometimes he used Priscilla alone, sometimes in Priscilla's absence he got girls to wrestle for him wearing only white bras and panties, and occasionally he included Priscilla, too, in an expanded scenario. As to why exactly the underwear had to be all-white no one was altogether clear, but everyone knew that was the way Elvis liked it — it was just his thing. The tapes, too, were strictly for Elvis; sometimes the guys would see them lying around, but Elvis would just say they were TV shows he had recorded. "Okay," Joe once challenged him. "Show us what you recorded." In some embarrassment Elvis declined.

One day Elvis brought the bulky video camera to the set to show it to Norman Taurog. When Taurog responded politely to Elvis' enthusiastic sales pitch for the machine (it would be handy, he agreed, to have something like that for instant playback of scenes they had just done), Elvis gave it to him in an impulsive burst of generosity, even though he knew there was a long wait for the average customer for a new machine. He had no intention of waiting, however, as he made clear to Marty; it was up to Marty to find him an immediate replacement.

In keeping with the Colonel's newfound embrace of production values, the picture was filmed on seven soundstages, with five location sites, including Dodger Stadium. Tempers flared at one point when Red, who had never made any secret of his contempt for Larry, took a swing at him before being restrained by the other guys. Elvis on the other hand maintained spirited philosophical dialogues with several of his co-stars. He genuinely liked Shelley Fabares, with whom he had worked on *Girl Happy;* he gave Diane McBain an underlined copy of *The Impersonal Life* and spoke with her of the spiritual precepts of Yogananda; and he set out to save Deborah Walley, who had previously played the leading role in *Gidget Goes Hawaiian* and was presently lost in a sea of spiritual doubt and confusion. He told her, "Look, we've only got this moment together, so let's have it completely. No holding back. No wasting time on trivialities. I've got the word; I want to give it to you. I'm not a man, I'm not a woman — I'm a soul, a spirit, a force. I have no interest in anything of this world. I want to live in another dimension entirely." It was, according to Walley, the turning point of her life.

To movie columnist May Mann he spoke at length of his mother, of his upbringing, of their last Christmas together. When he was home, he went to the cemetery at least once a week to visit her grave, he told Mann, and he had flowers placed there weekly. The dreams he had of his mother were happy ones: "it's like seeing and being with her again." Graceland was the place he would always maintain as his home because of his memories of her. It was more than just a house to him; it represented "the residence of the heart. It is far more than a place of physical needs. . . . To me my home is all wound up with all the acts of kindness and gentleness that my mother and my grandmother and my daddy lovingly provided. . . . All of this love still remains within its walls. It's an enduring way of life for me." He wanted to get back to going to church, he said. "Church was our way of life since I can remember. The last time I went, there was so much confusion, and autograph-seeking, that out of respect I've stayed away. . . . I've been working on religious songs for an album. I feel God and his goodness, and I believe I can express his love for us in music."

That was, in fact, exactly what he was doing: immersing himself once again in the music. RCA had stipulated that it needed a new album, two new singles, and a Christmas single, to come out of a session tentatively scheduled for May. Perhaps with the idea of capitalizing on the success of "Crying in the Chapel," the album was specifically designated as a religious one, and Elvis and Charlie and Red started working informally on material almost from the moment of Elvis' arrival in California. Somewhat coincidentally, Red had recently added a second tape recorder to the one he had long owned in order to further his ambitions as a songwriter. He wanted to be able to produce his own rough demos without having to go into a studio, and with two reel-to-reel recorders, he felt, he could learn to overdub voices and instrumental parts. He got singers like Glen Campbell, whom he knew from the Red Velvet and the Hollywood musical scene, to demo some of his compositions for just a few bucks a session, but at the same time, he and Charlie started taping songs that they thought Elvis might be interested in — and not just religious ones either.

Almost as if to certify the wisdom of the Colonel's strategy, there was a growing renewal of interest within the entire household in music in general; every morning, before going to the studio, they listened to *Peter, Paul & Mary in Concert* or the trio's latest, *See What Tomorrow Brings,* and *Odetta Sings Dylan* was never far from the turntable. Elvis showed a keen interest in Ian and Sylvia as well, along with his usual gospel, blues, and rhythm and blues favorites, and when they all got together to sing, he was as likely to suggest Bob Dylan's "Blowin' in the Wind" as a Statesmen number, much as he may have detested Dylan's abrasive vocal quality and equally abrasive cultural politics ("My mouth feels like Bob Dylan's been sleeping in it," he frequently said, and Dylan's "Rainy Day Women #12 and 35," currently on the radio, infuriated Elvis, with what he saw as its casual advocacy of the drug culture).

These informal sessions drifted all over the place, just as easily jogged by a casual phrase or a recollected note as by sustained musical logic. What they came back to over and over again were the close harmonies with which Elvis had grown up, in which Charlie or Red would frequently take the lead and Elvis as often as not sang the bass part on gospel songs, Hawaiian numbers, and western classics like the Sons of the Pioneers' "Tumbling Tumbleweeds" or "Cool Water." Sometimes the whole gang got into the act, with even Sonny or Priscilla providing an impromptu, if uncertain, lead; Red and Charlie occasionally came up with song ideas of their own; and once in a great while Elvis just might try a demo that Freddy had sent him, singing against the recorded number, then working out his own approach to the song on piano, as Red faithfully documented the process.

It was, really, akin to a reawakening of the soul; just rediscovering the joy of singing led Elvis to further expand his listening tastes, which in turn motivated him to undertake greater vocal challenges. He listened to Caruso, Mario Lanza, and Hank Williams, Judy Garland, Aretha Franklin, and the Rolling Stones. He grew so consumed with admiration for Jimmy Jones, the bass lead for the black gospel group the Harmonizing Four, that he became determined to have Jones on his upcoming session and informed the Colonel and Freddy Bienstock to institute a search.

Colonel felt vindicated. He was under substantial pressure from RCA at this point to deliver; he had in fact been getting persistent telephone calls and letters from RCA vice president Harry Jenkins, somewhat nervous reminders of what they were all hoping would come out of this session, the high expectations that had been raised with the new contract. These were the kind of letters that in the past Colonel might have written to the company. They reminded him of his obligations, and under any other circumstances he would certainly have blown up at the unwonted presumptuousness of their tone. But he put up with Jenkins' reminders with remarkable equanimity, because he was convinced that until Elvis delivered, this was the only way for the game to be played.

He even put up with the recurrent rumor that he was about to sell Elvis' contract and retire with a forbearance that could only have been engendered by his growing confidence that they were past the worst of it. Just after Elvis' February arrival in Hollywood, he gave his good friend Jim Kingsley of the *Memphis Commercial Appeal* an interview that was intended to reassure Kingsley, and the world, that the reports of his demise were not to be believed. "Heck yes, I would retire, and so would my boy, Elvis — if we received enough money," he declared. "But if we retired, who in the heck would want us?" There were hundreds of people who depended on Elvis for their livelihood, he pointed out, as if speaking to a secret listener.

"The bigger an attraction you become, the more responsibilities you face. . . . Elvis is big enough to bear up under [those] responsibilities . . . and he also loves to work. I honestly believe that he will become one of the industry's great actors in the future."

It was a masterly performance, a perfect example of the good Snowman's last resort, his ability to hypnotize even himself. And now, as work on the film concluded, he could more honestly have stated his belief. He had always known that Elvis would tire of Geller's mumbo jumbo, at least as an exclusive diet; he might never let go of it altogether, but the boy's mind jumped around too much ever to settle on any one thing. That was where all these Johnny-come-latelies made their miscalculation: they all counted on the spontaneous enthusiasm, the heart brimming with love, the momentarily sunny day. But they didn't see the clouds on the horizon, they didn't understand the rules of the game, they didn't make provision for an uncertain future — that was what the Colonel was determined to do, for himself and for his boy.

E LVIS AND THE GUYS left for Memphis on the weekend of April 16, arriving home at 9:00 P.M. the following Saturday. Elvis drove the refurbished bus practically all the way himself, wearing his driver's cap and thin leather racing gloves. They made music much of the way, laughing and singing and listening to the tapes that Charlie and Red had put together. Whenever they got to a motel where they were going to stay for the night, someone had to lug the heavy video recorder to Elvis' room so he could watch his private tapes. The trip took a little longer than usual, because in Albuquerque Elvis suddenly got the urge to call one of the girls who had performed for him on some of the tapes to come and replicate her performance. The guys all groused as they waited first for her to fly in, then for Elvis to finish doing whatever he was doing with her. Everyone was impatient to get home to their wives and children and girlfriends. They were well aware that there was no contradicting the boss; every one of his whims had to be satisfied. But at least now those whims were finally getting back to something they could all understand.

WITH MOTORCYCLES, 1966: LARRY GELLER, MARTY LACKER, ALAN FORTAS,
JOE ESPOSITO, ELVIS, ACTRESS DEBORAH WALLEY, JERRY SCHILLING.
(COURTESY OF THE ESTATE OF ELVIS PRESLEY)

FAMILY CIRCLE

THE NEW WAVE of musical enthusiasm that had engulfed him in California continued with his return home on April 23. Within a week of Elvis' arrival in Memphis, three days had been set aside at RCA's Studio B in Nashville, starting on Wednesday, May 25. The seriousness with which this first nonsoundtrack session in two and one-half years was being taken was evident from the preparations that went into it. There was a flurry of correspondence between the record company and the Colonel, the Colonel and his assistant Tom Diskin, Diskin and Freddy Bienstock. Freddy in turn contacted Red West, who with Charlie Hodge now screened all of Freddy's demos for Elvis and passed along the title of every non–Hill and Range number for which Elvis exhibited any enthusiasm so that Freddy could make a deal on it before Elvis went into the studio. In addition, Red and Charlie continued to supply Elvis with tapes of songs in which they thought he might take an interest (Charlie, for example, supplied Elvis with the Sons of the Pioneers' version of the popular hymn "How Great Thou Art"), with Red on occasion pitching songs of his own. They continued to get together for impromptu singing sessions with no focus other than to go wherever the feeling took them, and they continued to talk excitedly about the gospel album that was to be the centerpiece of the upcoming session.

Elvis was disappointed when, despite all of Freddy's and Mr. Diskin's efforts, nobody was able to locate Jimmy Jones, the great black bass singer on whom he had set his heart for the session, but his disappointment was mitigated when Diskin suggested that they substitute the Imperials, a new all-star quartet put together by Jake Hess, former lead singer of the Statesmen and Elvis' boyhood idol. In addition to the Imperials, Elvis made sure that the Jordanaires, soprano Millie Kirkham, and two other female backup singers were all contracted for the session, bringing the total number of singers to eleven and making it possible to achieve the kind of massed choral effect that he had come to envision for the album. For all of the care put into these preparations, and with all of the expectations on every side, there was one key element that came about strictly by chance, when Elvis' nominal Nashville producer, Chet Atkins, asked a newcomer on the RCA staff if he would mind taking Atkins' place in the control room. Chet had never been one for all-night sessions, and he thought Elvis and this young firecracker would get along well. That was how Felton Jarvis became Elvis' producer.

Jarvis, a thirty-year-old staff producer whom Atkins had brought over from ABC Records the previous year, jumped at the chance. Although he had cut his teeth producing r&b groups like the Tams in his native Atlanta, it was Elvis Presley who had first inspired him to go into the business. A printer by trade, he had seen Elvis while he was stationed at the Marine base in Norfolk, Virginia, in 1955, and it had changed his life. When he got out of the Marines, he recorded an Elvis imitation record ("Don't Knock Elvis") and went to work as a sheet music printer at Bill Lowery's NRC (National Recording Corporation) studio/label/publishing complex. NRC at the time was recording Joe South, Ray Stevens, Mac Davis, Freddy Weller, and Jerry Reed, all of whom would become bona fide stars in the next decade, and Felton hung around the studio so much that when the engineer quit he was hired. In 1961 he recorded a number-one r&b hit on a then-unknown group called Gladys Knight and the Pips. That led to a job doing promotion for ABC, which he parlayed into an a&r position when, in 1962, he produced a split session on an Elvis imitator named Vince Everett (whom he had discovered performing under his real name of Marvin Benefield in a talent contest and then renamed for the lead character in *Jailhouse Rock*) and Tommy Roe, another NRC alumnus, who had been kicking around on the fringes of the music industry for the last three or four years. Everett's version of "Such a Night," recorded by Elvis in 1960 but released only as an album cut, was a regional hit, but it was Tommy Roe's "Sheila" that made Felton's career. When it went to number one on the pop charts, Felton renewed his suit to join ABC's a&r department, and when the label indicated that it might be willing to entertain the idea if he were willing to forgo producer's royalties on his number-one hit, he seized upon the opportunity. His friends weren't sure he even knew what he was signing, but he knew what he wanted, and when ABC opened up a Nashville office the following year, he moved like a shot.

It was his enthusiasm, not his technical expertise, which everyone who came into contact with Felton first remarked upon. "Every man a tiger," was Bill Lowery's frequently repeated motto, but Felton carried it to a new extreme. In Atlanta Felton had owned a tiger, or at least a pet ocelot; in Nashville he soon acquired an anaconda, which he took swimming with him in the pool of his apartment complex until an elderly couple, out for an early-morning walk, noticed his unusual swimming companion, and he was forced to find new quarters. In Nashville, too, he quickly fell in with a group of young guys who hung out at the Pancake Pantry and traded stories of their adventures in the music business and their dreams of achieving success within it. No one could top Felton's stories for sheer irrepressible buoyancy, and everyone loved to hear him tell about his encounters with r&b stars like Lloyd Price and Fats Domino, whom ABC was bringing in to Nashville to record at that time. "Fel-tone, my man," Fats' invariable greeting to him, became a byword in certain circles in Nashville, and Felton soon acquired an industry-wide reputation for eccentricity, affability, and imagination.

In 1965 he came to RCA at Chet's invitation, co-producing Willie Nelson with Atkins, then recording Mickey Newbury, Jim Ed Brown, Floyd Cramer, and Cortelia Clarke, an old blind blues singer whom he recorded live, with traffic sounds and background noise, on the streets of downtown Nashville. He had an office right across the hall from Chet's, in which he constructed a tropical hut with a grass roof to house his snake, and there was no question that he tried his boss's patience on occasion. But Chet, who was himself of a drier, more phlegmatic nature, got a real kick out of Felton and, less than a year after his arrival at RCA, came up with the idea of connecting him with another decidedly antic spirit. A few days before the Presley session he came into Felton's office. "He just said, 'I'm going to carry you over, and maybe you all will hit it off.' And so we did."

F ROM THE MOMENT that Elvis first arrived at the studio at around 8:00 P.M., there was no question that he was taken with the hopped-up, almost hyperactive enthusiasm of this skinny young producer — it was a hell of a relief after Chet's damned indifference. At first conversation was somewhat strained. They talked a little about the material, they talked about some of the records that Felton had produced — Elvis couldn't get enough of hearing about Felton's experiences with Fats Domino, and Lamar, who hung out with Felton and his friends on a semiregular basis, goaded Felton to reveal more of himself.

They talked, too, about the sound of the records that Elvis had been putting out lately. As an Elvis Presley fan (Felton might very well have said, as Elvis Presley's *biggest* fan), Felton was well aware that "for a while before I started working with him, what they were doing was turning the band way down and Elvis way up, and it sounded like — it was just bad. It wasn't exciting. There was no excitement on the records. This is what I was trying to correct [because] Elvis had nobody to communicate with at RCA — somebody in New York that didn't know anything would just mix it, and it wasn't mixed properly."

What Elvis wanted, he explained to Felton, was the kind of sound the Beatles and some of the other English bands were getting: it was a hotter sound; it jumped out at you, you got the sense that something was really happening. Felton eagerly nodded assent. It was a matter of feel, he told Elvis. "You get your excitement from the drums and the bass getting real funky — you got to have all that stuff up — and it's got to be mixed properly." And it became clear almost immediately that they would become not only friends but musical allies. Felton was, Elvis quickly realized, one of them. Chet recognized just as quickly that the two of them *had* hit it off and went home before a note was struck. The singers all gathered around Elvis at the piano and felt each other out — there was an edge of expectation in the air, and the new producer was in no hurry to get down to the business of recording, he was having so much fun just being a part of it all.

It was well after ten o'clock before they finally got to work, starting out with "Run On," a traditional number in the black spiritual tradition. Elvis took it in the manner of the Golden Gate Quartet, lightly swinging, coolly elegant — from the very first notes he was clearly in command, and Felton was just as clearly second in command, soothing, encouraging, carefully picking his way among potentially bruised egos, urging another take when he felt he could comfortably do so, holding back a little at first but always providing encouragement and reassurance.

To Jake Hess, who took a backseat to no one both as a pure singer and as a gospel music innovator, there was no way they could miss with all the positive energy in the room. "Elvis just really loved that sound; the adrenaline really pumped in him when he heard it. He wanted a big sound, and we sung like Elvis wanted it sung. We all had our parts written out, the chords, and we all stayed in the same chord, even though we stacked our harmony different than the Jordanaires. I don't think he cared so much [how] we blended, he just wanted that big sound."

After seven takes they had a master ("Swing!" Felton urged, to kick off the final take), and they moved on to "How Great Thou Art," the nineteenth century Swedish hymn that had been popularized in its English translation by George Beverly Shea in Billy Graham's sixteen-week 1957 Crusade at Madison Square Garden. It was a bravura showpiece, and Elvis and Charlie and Red had been working on it all spring, though not off of Shea's rather formal model. Elvis saw the song, as he saw every number with which he made a passionate musical connection, as his opportunity to pour out his entire heart and soul, with no holding back, and that is what he did here. To Jerry Schilling, it was as if he had been taken over by another spirit as he built to a vocal crescendo that left him visibly shaken.

"He didn't do a lot of takes, but something almost frightening happened on that song; it was like he was just *drained* — he turned white and almost fainted when he finished. I wish I could verbalize it better, and I don't know if I'm talking about three minutes or three seconds, but it was as if something happened outside the normal experience. And I don't really think like that ordinarily — and it's not even my favorite song! But there was no question that for Elvis something really happened."

The rest of the night maintained the same high spirits, if not the transcendent aspect, of that moment. They ran into a little bit of trouble on "Stand By Me," a staple of the black gospel tradition, but aided by Felton's increasingly vocal encouragement, Elvis was able to overcome some difficulties with the feel and the lyrics and deliver a beautifully articulated, almost nakedly yearning performance on the eleventh take. The warmth of his voice, his controlled use of both vibrato technique and natural falsetto range, the subtlety and deeply felt conviction of his singing were all qualities recognizably belonging to his talent but just as recognizably not to be achieved without sustained dedication and effort. Perhaps even more instructive was his approach to the next song, "Where No One Stands Alone," one of Jake Hess' most challenging showpieces. The song was, really, beyond Elvis' range; it required a kind of projection that was not within his power at this stage. And yet he persisted, as if to underscore his commitment to the moment, taking the bridge over and over until at last, without ever quite getting it right (he was reduced to a kind of inelegant bellowing to push out a sound that appears to have been effortless for Jake Hess), with Charlie's coaching and Felton's encouragement, and the chorus obscuring some of his greatest difficulties, he achieves a hard-won but satisfactory result. It is a genuinely heroic effort, the very attempt in and of

itself as touching as anything else to come out of the session — and it did
not go unnoticed among many of the participants.

To Jake Hess it was one more example of the conviction of Elvis'
singing. "Elvis was one of those individuals, when he sang a song, he just
seemed to live every word of it. There's other people that have a voice
that's maybe as great or greater than Presley's, I don't know, but he had that
certain something that everyone searches for all during their lifetime. You
know, he sang a lot with his eyes closed, and I think the reason for that was
because he [wanted] to have a picture in mind at all times; if something was
distracting him to where he couldn't put his heart into what he was doing,
he would close his eyes, so he could get that picture of what he was talking
about. That's the reason he communicated with the audience so well."

It was 4:00 A.M., and the Imperials were done for the night, but Elvis
and Felton and the rest of the session singers and musicians never flagged.
For Felton, actually working with Elvis merely served as proof of everything
he had taken from Elvis' music in the first place. Felton's entire philosophy
of recording rested on creating a sense of enthusiasm and spontaneity in
the studio, and now to discover the man he had idolized for so long equally
focused in his beliefs, equally committed to working all night if necessary
until the feeling was right, made him feel in a way as if their meeting must
have been fated. To guitarist Chip Young, working his first Presley session,
Felton and Elvis were like mirror images of one another. Young, another
native Atlantan, who had recorded Tommy Roe in the first place and then
brought him to Felton, saw the effect the two of them had on each other.
"Everything just started getting electrified when they came into the room."
There was never any question, working with either one, that a musician
was prepared to give his all, and then some.

Without hesitation, and with no apparent sense of any disparity between the sacred and the profane, they launched into "Down in the Alley,"
a raucous r&b hit by the Clovers which had been a favorite of Elvis' since
its original release in 1957. "Funksville, Take One," announced Felton, as
Elvis gave the backup singers their lyrics, and the good feeling in the studio
was almost palpable. For this song Bobby Moore, who had been playing
stand-up bass all night, switched to electric, Boots Randolph took a bleating
saxophone solo, and they ran through nine quick takes, interrupted only by
Elvis' uncontrollable laughter at Charlie's jokes and familiar hijinks. Everyone remained in high spirits all the way through, and while the results may
not have been art, or even the equal of the Clovers', we get a sense of Elvis'
untrammeled r&b side for the first time since 1960.

In an even more improbable programming twist, Elvis announced that for the final song of the evening they would do "Tomorrow Is a Long Time," a Bob Dylan composition which had yet to be recorded by Bob Dylan but which Elvis had picked up from one of his favorite current albums, *Odetta Sings Dylan*. They took just three passes at it, including one false start, with a dobro part at the center of a lovely, lilting arrangement that was the antithesis of the pounding, not very subtle attack of the previous number. Elvis' vocal was focused exclusively on the lyrics, with very little in the way of stylistic embroidery or emotional interpolation, and the result is a delicacy and purity of tone rivaled only by some of his best early-sixties recordings.

At the end of the evening Elvis and Felton sat around, exhausted but feeling good. They talked about the all-night gospel singings that both had grown up with, and Elvis confessed that it had been his childhood ambition to join one of those great quartets. "We stayed," recalled Felton, "till the secretaries started coming in. Everybody else had gone but me and him. I said, 'Elvis, we better go; the people are starting to come to work.' He said, 'Lord, is it that late?,' and I carried him back to his motel."

T HE FOLLOWING EVENING pianist Floyd Cramer had another session booked from 6:30 to 9:30, so Chet's secretary, Mary Lynch, arranged for a twenty-three-year-old piano player named David Briggs, who had arrived in town the previous year, to fill in during what was sure to be a largely wasted time slot. Briggs, like Chip Young, had known Felton from the early days, when Felton brought many of his Atlanta acts to Muscle Shoals to record with a rhythm section that included David. Felton had in fact encouraged the entire rhythm section to move to Nashville for better working conditions and better pay, but it was Mary Lynch, in her position as Chet's studio booker, who had been throwing session work David's way and to whom he was now grateful for the chance at least to meet one of his idols.

No one expected there to be any need for Briggs' services, since Elvis rarely even showed up for the first couple of hours, but for some reason this time not only did he show, he came to work. "I was just there as a substitute, and they said, 'You know, Elvis, Floyd couldn't be here for a while, so this is David, and he's going to play whatever.' And he said, 'Yeah, okay, fine,' and he sat down beside me at the piano, and then, of all things, he wanted to do 'Love Letters' [a big r&b hit for Ketty Lester in 1962, and a pop hit for Dick Haymes two decades earlier], which is all piano. I mean, we were supposed to be doing a gospel album, and here Elvis was sitting beside me, wanting to do 'Love Letters' — and that was a hard song to play!

"I was scared to death. I mean, I had done a Beatles tour with Tommy Roe, but Elvis was something else. And then he wants the piano pulled up in front of him. He had all the lights turned out, put candles on the piano so he could see the lyrics, and he made everybody lay out except the bass player and D.J. on drums and Buddy Harman on tympani, I think. He had the piano moved up so he could be right on top of it — there was just that six-foot piano between us; man, it was a pretty tense situation."

Floyd showed up by the time they were actually ready to record. "I said, 'Great! Come in, Floyd, you've got it.' And I went back to the organ. Floyd ran through it once, and Elvis said, 'Where is that boy?' And I said, 'Oh, shit.' He was looking for me — he didn't even know who I was, and Floyd could have played it better, but he had gotten used to the way I was doing the song. That's just the way Elvis was. If he got used to something, and if he liked you, then you were just better than the next guy, even though you might not be a tenth as good. So — now talk about pressure. Not only was it Elvis, it was Floyd, who was probably the number-one keyboard player in town, sitting behind me on organ and laughing because he didn't give a shit; he'd been working all day and was sick of it. So that was my first encounter with Elvis. I probably had knots coming out of the back of my neck."

Elvis sang the song with delicacy and feeling, and they got a master on the ninth take, even if Briggs was never satisfied with his part, which he felt came out too saccharine. The rest of the session may not have offered quite as much offstage drama, but it was certainly as successful, with an easy-going, up-tempo black gospel number ("So High"), a mournful version of the quartet standard "Farther Along" that could very well have been offered as a tribute to Elvis' mother, and an interpretation of "In the Garden," a classic gospel piece that for Jake Hess was the highlight of the session. Elvis, Charlie, and Red closed out the evening with a trio version of "Beyond the Reef," with Red taking the lead, Charlie singing high tenor, and Elvis on second tenor and playing piano. It was one of the songs they had sung together all spring, a sweetly sentimental Hawaiian number popularized by Bing Crosby in 1950 (it was the B side of Crosby's "Harbor Lights," one of the first songs Elvis had attempted at Sun), and they imparted to it a freely nostalgic, almost spiritual quality, as they wrapped it up in two takes.

The next night was the final one planned, and the last on which the

Imperials could participate, since they were taking off on a Canadian tour early the next morning. Once again Elvis seemed to be simply following his instincts, choosing songs with little regard for prearrangement or publishing, and no doubt causing "the mighty Freddy," as the Colonel ironically referred to the song plugger, paroxysms of anxiety. The music didn't come easy; in fact they got only two songs in the first six hours. But it continued to reflect some of Elvis' warmest, most profoundly felt work. Toward the end of the evening, casting about for a fast number to offset the many slow, almost dirgelike tunes they had already cut, Elvis requested a lead sheet for "If the Lord Wasn't Walking By My Side," a recent Imperials release, which he then went on to record as a straightforward duet with his mentor, Jake Hess. Here for the first time we can hear Jake's voice truly unleashed, as the two singers toss phrases back and forth, and the clear lineage of Elvis' music unmistakably emerges. Listening to the first playback, Jake was a little taken aback. "I said, 'Man, I'm too loud, I've got to back out.' Elvis said, 'No, you don't back out. If anything, you step in and sing loud.' He said, 'This is your song. I'm recording with you, and I want to enjoy singing it like you're singing it.' The way it finally came out, my voice was not as strong as it was in the recording session. But it's still ridiculous."

A fourth night provided little more than a disappointing coda. For all the success of the gospel recordings, and all the good feeling engendered by the session, it had become obvious by now that the two new singles and Christmas record that the Colonel had promised RCA were unlikely to materialize. With the exception of "Love Letters," there was nothing even remotely resembling a single (the Dylan cut could scarcely qualify, since Freddy had no chance of making a publishing deal, and "Down in the Alley" and "Beyond the Reef" were more in the nature of personal indulgence than commercial product). The result was that another night was tacked on in hopes of fulfilling the RCA quota, but with little preparation and less suitable material, Felton had to scramble just to get the session off the ground. In the end much of the good feeling of the first three nights appears to have dissipated, and there is an edge to Elvis' voice in the between-takes chatter that seems to reflect a general change of demeanor. When they knocked off at ten o'clock, it was with little fanfare or regret, but Elvis did sign a photo to Felton that said, "You make me look forward to the next time."

The next time came sooner than either one of them expected. Two weeks later, on June 10, Felton had the whole group back together again to

try to get the sides that were contractually required. Virtually all the participants from the first session were present, with one exception: Elvis was
not there. He may have simply felt that he was being pressured; it may have
been, as Red West believed, that he was just not in a "recording mood" —
whether due to a bad throat, an excess of pills, or even surreptitious advice
from the Colonel. Whatever the case, Elvis was in a foul temper and
refused to leave the motel room, dispatching Red, armed only with
amphetamines to bolster his confidence, to go into the studio and cut reference vocals. "I was a nervous wreck, and I'm in there singing 'Indescribably
Blue,' 'I'll Remember You,' and [my song] 'If Every Day Was Like Christmas.' And he's calling every hour and half, two hours, and saying, 'How's it
going? How's it going?' And after we finished the third, he said, 'Come on,
bring what you got, that's it.' We were going to do a lot more, but we did
those three, and that was the end of it."

Of the three, two came with obligations attached, and the third, Don
Ho's "I'll Remember You," was another of those achingly romantic Hawaiian numbers that Elvis loved so much and would continue to sing for the
rest of his life but that fell into the same noncommercial category as some
of his other equally whimsical choices. "Indescribably Blue," on the other
hand, was a pretty, somewhat insipid ballad that Lamar had brought to the
first session and, spurred on both by his belief in the song and by the fact
that in his three years of employment at Hill and Range he had never gotten an Elvis Presley cut on his own, had been pushing for Elvis to record
ever since. Of course, to be fair, for two and one half of those years, Elvis
had been recording nothing but movie material, but Lamar was never one
to take a backseat to anyone, and it must have galled him to see the Imperials get a cut at the previous session, to know that Red and Charlie all
of a sudden had gained the inside track, when he had a song that he *knew*
could be Elvis' first number-one hit in years, not to mention his own ticket
to music industry respectability. Red, meanwhile, had been pushing Elvis to
cut his Christmas song for close to a year, finally recording it on his own
Brent label in the fall of 1965 only after it became obvious that Elvis was not
going to get around to it in time for Christmas that year himself.

Listening to Red's scratch vocals on the songs is something of a revelation. "Indescribably Blue" is sung breathily in Elvis' key, but with a feeling
that must have revealed hitherto unsuspected depths to some of the session
musicians who knew Red as nothing more than a hulking, somewhat men-
acing self-described "bodyguard." The resemblance to Elvis' voice is uncanny, almost eerie in its precision, but what is even more remarkable is the

tender quality of the performance not just on this song but on the two others that follow. With the completion of the third, his own composition, Red
picked up a copy of the tape from Felton and, following Elvis' instructions,
brought it back to the Albert Pick Motel. They listened to it a number of
times, and Elvis expressed his satisfaction with the results, but he didn't
show up at the studio the next night either, and the session was canceled.
When he finally appeared on the third night, it was only to overdub his own
voice, and whatever hopes Felton had for recording any additional material
were dashed when Elvis took off for Memphis later that evening.

It was a puzzling end to a first meeting that had begun so promisingly
just two weeks before, and no one knew quite what to make of it, least of
all Felton. But if Felton was perplexed, RCA's Harry Jenkins must have
been even more disturbed. After all the talk, after all the precise spelling
out of obligations, after all the Colonel's lulling reassurances, the record
label in the end was still left with an unsatisfactory result. They had their
gospel album, to be sure, and maybe they could piece together two
singles — though it seemed unlikely that there was any hit material from
either session. They still had only half a Christmas single, and perhaps not
surprisingly there was nothing left in the can. It seemed evident, too, that
Freddy, after years in the Hollywood desert, could no longer deliver tunes
to Elvis' taste or inclination, and it was hard to say what the long-term
implications of that were likely to be. And, of course, the way that it had
ended simply left everyone with a bad taste in their mouths. No one could
fully interpret events, except to wonder if this wasn't Elvis' way (and perhaps the Colonel's as well) of saying that he wasn't going to be pushed
around.

Elvis for his part must have thought better of his actions. Back home in
Memphis he wrote Felton a warm letter of appreciation. "Please convey
how much I deeply appreciate the cooperation and consideration shown to
me and my associates during my last two trips to Nashville," he declared. "I
would like to thank you, the engineers, musicians, singers, and everyone
connected with the sessions. Please see that every one of them know my
feelings. And as General MacArthur once said, 'I Shall Return.'"

TWO WEEKS LATER, on June 28, he was back in Hollywood recording
the soundtrack for his latest motion picture, *Double Trouble,* an MGM
release with Norman Taurog once again at the helm. It was a full eight-
week shoot in the course of which he presented his leading lady, Annette

Day, with a blue-and-white Mustang, but undoubtedly the two most memorable events of the summer had nothing to do with the movie but instead revolved around visits from George Klein and Cliff Gleaves.

George was out for the start of filming, planning his two-week summer vacation as usual around Elvis' shooting schedule (this would be the sixth Elvis movie in which he would appear). Coincidentally, one of Elvis' favorite entertainers, rhythm and blues singer Jackie Wilson, was appearing at a club on Sunset called The Trip from June 30 to July 10. George knew Jackie, renowned almost as much for his acrobatic stage act as for his near-operatic voice, from promoting some of his headlining Memphis appearances on the television show that George hosted, a local version of Dick Clark's *American Bandstand* called *Talent Party*. Elvis had even seen Jackie perform while he was still working as lead singer for Billy Ward and the Dominoes ten years earlier in Las Vegas. So it was with Elvis' eager assent that George arranged for them all to attend Wilson's show.

Everyone was in a great state of excitement. With the exception of their occasional trips to the Red Velvet, it was almost unheard of for the whole gang to get out in L.A., and there was a flurry of preparations and security precautions to be carried out. George and Richard Davis went down to the club as a kind of advance party, and George called up James Brown, another frequent guest on his show, who was in town to give a concert of his own. Brown knew through George how big a fan Elvis was of his spectacular performance on *The T.A.M.I. Show,* a filmed concert that had been released in movie theaters in late 1964, and he had sought an introduction from George on numerous occasions, including his latest Memphis appearance just two months earlier. Every time he called, though, he got word that Elvis was asleep — it became a running joke between him and George, and a source of embarrassment to the DJ, who was known as one of Elvis' best and oldest friends. Seizing the opportunity that this occasion provided, George issued Brown a special invitation to come see Jackie perform, and this time he guaranteed him an introduction.

The show was electrifying. Wilson, whom Elvis had recognized as a premiere performer when he first saw him in Vegas in 1956 ("I was under the table when he got through singing"), was no less mesmerizing now. There were a number of prominent contemporary rock musicians in the audience, including members of the newly formed Buffalo Springfield, and expatriate Elvis imitator P. F. Sloan, but it was James Brown that Elvis instantly sought out as soon as George told him that Brown was present

and would like to say hello. George thought Elvis might stand on ceremony, "but he got up and went over to [Brown's] table. Me and Richard
went through the introductions, and they go through some small talk —
this is before showtime — and James Brown says, 'Man, Elvis, you sure do
sleep a lot.' And Elvis almost fell on the floor, laughing. He said, 'Aw, James,
you know how it is, being a night person. . . .' And James said, 'I know,
brother,' and slapped Elvis' hand."

In between sets he finally got the opportunity to meet Jackie, too, and
express his unreserved admiration for Wilson's talent. With what he had
going for him, Elvis said, there was no reason Jackie shouldn't be the
number-one singer in the world today, and he invited him out to the film
set the following week. Larry Geller's particular memory of the meeting
was that Elvis asked Jackie "about his profuse sweating. 'Man, I'll tell you,'
[Wilson replied] 'the chicks really dig that.' Elvis said, 'How do you do it?'
Wilson grinned and said, 'Hey, that's simple.' He showed us a large bottle
of salt tablets and then revealed his secret. Each night before a show, he'd
swallow a handful of tablets, guzzle a few quarts of water, then go onstage.
Once he got moving, the sweat would wash off him like rain. Soon Elvis
started incorporating this trick into his weight-loss regimen. It was dangerous, it depleted potassium and overtaxed the heart, but it produced one of
Elvis' favorite things: an instant result with minimal effort."

It was a memorable evening in every respect, and undoubtedly one of
the reasons that it loomed so large in everyone's respective (and sharply
diverging) memories was that evenings like this happened so seldom.
There was some of the same sense of excitement — or maybe it was just
relief at anything resembling a break in the usual routine — when Cliff
Gleaves showed up later in the summer with nothing more than a flight bag
and a Water Pik for luggage, all the way from Florida by way of Arizona.
Some of the younger members of the group who had never met him but
had long known him by reputation were at first enthralled. Cliff, Red's successor in Germany, where he had pursued a career as a singer and comedian, had by now pretty much given up any real show business ambitions
and was living with his mother and father in Fort Lauderdale, Florida, occasionally entertaining in piano bars for the wealthy older ladies who wintered in the area. He continued to be the kind of self-styled free spirit
who could still give everyone a good laugh, but the laughs tended to wear
off after the first two or three days of a visit. And he had begun to encounter certain problems of his own, problems that he was surprised to

recognize for the first time in a friend he had always viewed as something of an "innocent."

"I was aware that the prescriptions that Elvis was taking — I did not know the names of the medications — were beginning to affect his personality. I saw the change, be it ever so subtle. Slight touches of the Colonel that were negative. Sense of danger that was never there before. All of a sudden the snake was down around his leg. *And he did not know.* If he had been aware, he would have had someone get that damn snake off of him.

"During this period I was taking pills, too, mostly Dexedrine. And if I was tired I'd just say, 'Have you got any more of these red ones?' Or, 'You got any more of those pink ones?' Sometimes he'd just grin and say, 'Here's the bottle.' I'll tell you this: Elvis didn't care if anyone else took them or not. He was getting off on them. He loved to sit there high and wiggle in the chair, just wiggle his legs with a big pitcher of ice water in front of him — he'd drink tons of water 'cause you could see it dehydrating him — just sit there and watch TV. He didn't give a damn whether you did anything. He was going to do what he wanted to do anyway."

PREPRODUCTION for what was to be the final Hal Wallis picture, *Easy Come, Easy Go*, was scheduled to begin on September 27, just three weeks after the conclusion of *Double Trouble*. The Colonel had already given Wallis no end of trouble himself, bedeviling him to the point of demanding a chair similar to one in Wallis' office as part of his final negotiations. Wallis had at last resigned himself to the end of a highly profitable, if highly stressful, ten-year relationship, and he said as much to John Rich, the director, who at this point was almost as disillusioned with Wallis as Elvis was. Rich had originally balked at the idea of working with Elvis on *Roustabout* but had made the best of it and even come to respect Presley for his professionalism and musical talent. Now after a disappointing two and one-half years in Hollywood, it was a different story.

"Wallis was really tightening up. He wanted everything done rapidly. [That was the attitude] from the word go. I remember telling him, 'Hal, I appreciate having done *Roustabout*. It came out rather well. But I would prefer not to do this picture.' And he said, 'Oh, just put them through their paces.' It was not my finest moment, but that was his assessment as to how the picture was to be made."

For somewhat similar reasons, all that Elvis seemed to bring to the picture was an accumulation of resentment. When it came to the soundtrack, he simply turned the job of song selection over to Red, and he arrived uncharacteristically late on each of the first two days of shooting — and with a haircut that Larry had given him at home, against Wallis' explicit instructions. He was overweight, Wallis complained to the Colonel, and the "inky-black" color of his hair dye made it look like he was wearing a wig. The Colonel offered no objections, but neither did he do anything to alleviate Wallis' concerns.

The picture dragged on almost interminably in a test of wills that had little to do with actual results. With the new stepped-up shooting schedule, production was completed in six weeks, but Elvis was not released until his contractual deadline a full two weeks later. He occupied much of the time in Palm Springs, where he had rented a house at the Colonel's suggestion just a week before the movie began. He needed a "getaway" retreat, Colonel told him, somewhere that he and Priscilla and one or two of the boys could just relax and get away from it all.

The house that they found, at 1350 Ladera Circle, was just around the corner from the one that William Morris furnished to the Colonel, a brand-new, ultra-modern structure (the design incorporated "glass and peanut-brittle stonework to inscribe four perfect circles on three levels," boasted a 1962 squib in *Look* magazine) built by Palm Springs developer Robert Alexander originally as a residence for his family. It had a tennis court, a waterfall, a free-standing fireplace in the living room, and, best of all, a wing that could serve as a private apartment for Elvis, with entry only from the outside off the circular pool. With neighbors like Frank Sinatra, Dean Martin, Bob Hope, and Bing Crosby, not to mention studio heads and powerful behind-the-scenes figures like William Morris founder Abe Lastfogel and Hal Wallis himself, it might have seemed that Elvis was at last joining the Hollywood establishment. With the exception of shopping sprees and occasional trips to the Spa Hotel, where the Colonel took his daily steam bath, however, he kept as much to himself in Palm Springs as he did in Bel Air. Indeed, he appeared more comfortable with the policemen who worked the security detail at his house or the air-conditioning servicemen who installed a powerful hotel-sized unit to keep the temperature at the meat-locker chill that Elvis preferred than he did with the movie-town high society all around him.

In fact, he felt more estranged from Hollywood than ever, as he stoically endured a movie that no one seemed to want to make and faced the

242 of FAMILY CIRCLE

inescapable conclusion that, after all these years, to these people he was nothing more than a joke. Most of the time he just followed directions; he had learned long ago that it was all about finding your mark, and then just having whatever fun there was to be had along the way. But even the fun was drying up. He was sick of all the turmoil around him, he confessed to Daya Mata on one of his still-frequent visits to the Self-Realization Center on Mt. Washington. He was sick of all the infighting that was increasingly coming to dominate his life. RCA had sent him a telegram on August 30 renewing the option that had not been scheduled to be picked up for another year and a half ("Because of our confidence in you, we decided not to wait until 1968," it read in part. "Your complete cooperation and understanding over the last eleven years has been most sincerely appreciated"). He supposed that that was good — it was, as Colonel pointed out, a form of insurance — but he was as aware as anyone that his records still were not selling as they should ("Love Letters" from the May session got no higher than number nineteen and failed to sell half a million copies), his movies were not doing any business, and although the old man continued to keep up a good front, you could see that even he was beginning to wonder.

All this seemed only to exacerbate the tensions within the group. There was jealousy on every side, and Priscilla's growing role at Rocca and the new Palm Springs house just inflamed those tensions. Marty in particular raged at the way that Joe and Joanie alone were included in the Palm Springs plans every weekend and that the two couples seemed to socialize with each other more and more, even joining the Colonel and Mrs. Parker for Sunday dinner on occasion. Marty and Joe were barely speaking to each other at this point, Red and Sonny set themselves apart, Alan had gone home to be with his father, who was gravely ill, and Marty and Priscilla were squabbling all the time.

Meanwhile, the Colonel had stepped up his campaign against Larry; it was finally out in the open now, and where Elvis might once have spoken up in Larry's defense, now he no longer seemed to have either the energy or the belief for battle. One time in Palm Springs the Colonel got Elvis to tell Larry that the beard that he was growing was an embarrassment to the Colonel and Hal Wallis. They had seen Larry in the swimming pool at the Spa Hotel, Elvis dutifully reported, and "Colonel said that when you stood up in the pool you looked just like John the Baptist."

Another time, Larry was convinced, Colonel tried to set him up by having a mutual acquaintance, who was homosexual, ask Larry out to dinner and then hit on him. The inclusion of the musical number "Yoga Is As Yoga Does," which Elvis performed as a duet in *Easy Come, Easy Go,* was no accident, Larry felt, but intended, rather, as a direct insult to Elvis' (and Larry's) beliefs — but Elvis went ahead and recorded it anyway. Only after the scene in which it was included was shot did Elvis finally react. It was then, in Larry's account, that Elvis "stormed into his trailer, shouting, 'That son of a bitch! He knows, and he did it! He told those damn writers what to do, and he's making me do this.'"

The final indignity, according to Larry, came when the Colonel invited Larry and his family to visit for the first time at his home in Palm Springs. There he entertained Larry and his wife, Stevie, treated the kids to ice cream, and put on what Larry deemed a good, if somewhat puzzling, show of sociability. Upon their return to Los Angeles, however, "I saw that the back door was open. . . . Two large garbage cans had been upended, and trash was strewn throughout the house, along with human urine and feces. My initial impression was that a thief had broken in. But when I looked around, I could see that most of our portable valuables were still there. Only a reel-to-reel tape, along with some tapes Sister Daya Mata had made for me, my files containing palm prints and numerological and astrological charts on Elvis and other friends were missing." In addition, all of Larry's clothes had been taken, except for his underwear. Although there could certainly have been other explanations, Larry was led to one inescapable conclusion. When he shared it with Elvis, "our eyes met, and he looked away. . . . Shaking his head, he kept repeating, 'Damn! Damn!' Then he stared me straight in the eye, his way of telling me things he couldn't articulate. After a moment, he said, 'Lawrence, it's a dangerous fuckin' world. . . .'"

Whether or not he actually believed the Colonel would orchestrate so blatant an attack (and it seems as unlikely that Elvis would have believed this literally as that the Colonel — with his fine regard for legality and his almost compulsive need, in all of his affairs, to dot all his i's and cross all his t's — would have left himself exposed in this manner), he had his own reasons for mistrusting his manager. He was sick of being caught up in the petty politics of the business, and he was angry at Colonel for not protecting him better — there was nothing in the contractual arrangements that should have permitted either the studio or the record company to take their pound of flesh. As the days dragged on and he realized that Wallis wasn't going to release him anytime soon, he grew increasingly sullen, and even as he accepted the old man's invitation to spend Thanksgiving with him and Mrs. Parker in the desert, he seethed inside. This was not the kind of life he had set out to lead.

The Colonel, for his part, kept his thoughts largely to himself, except in those rarest of moments when he might let down his guard a little with a close business associate whom he could rely upon never to break the trust. There were problems, he confessed to Roger Davis, the forty-three-year-old William Morris attorney who had been delegated an increasing amount of Elvis Presley business as some of the more senior agents either phased out or concentrated on handling just a few oldtimers' accounts. "The Colonel would say to me, 'I'm having trouble with the boy.' You see, he couldn't control him [anymore]. I said, 'What's the matter?' And he said, 'Well, he's changing, you know. He's not the way he used to be.'"

THEY FINALLY ARRIVED HOME on November 29, just after *Spinout* opened nationally. It wasn't doing any real business, and the title track never rose above number forty on the charts, but Elvis was still in a pretty good mood as they got closer to Memphis. Just outside Little Rock they picked up George on WHBQ's 560 radio frequency. He was playing the country tearjerker "Green, Green Grass of Home" by Tom Jones, whom they all liked, and Elvis stopped the bus and had one of the guys call George and ask him to play the song again. When they got a little further down the road, Elvis put in another call, and this kept up the rest of the way to Memphis, with George dedicating each play to Elvis and all the boys and Elvis growing visibly more affected by the song's portrait of a condemned man's imagined reunion with his loved ones and the idealized small-town life he has forever left behind. Everyone got a good laugh out of the incident except for Red, who had brought Elvis the song the year before and been told by Elvis it was far too country for him to even consider recording.

When they finally arrived at Graceland in the usual caravan, the Nativity scene was illuminated, the house was alight, and — just as in the song — everyone was outside to greet them, as they drove around the circle honking their horns. Elvis immediately went upstairs to survey the renovation of his quarters, which Marty's brother-in-law, Bernie, had once again supervised. He came back down with a broad smile. It was beautiful, he pronounced. He loved the black-and-red Spanish motif of the walls, and Bernie had upholstered the ceiling with green Naugahyde, with two television sets imbedded in the material at an angle, so he could just look up and watch from his bed. Unfortunately, the redecorating had led to further financial strain between Bernie and Vernon, who was overseeing the work, and accusations had once again been made and names called. When Marty came back the following day, he thought he would be in line for more compliments, but instead "in front of a couple of the other guys, Elvis started screaming, calling my whole family names. . . . At first I was going to let it slide. But then he started getting really nasty. And it burnt a hole in me. I got up, and I said, 'Hey, fuck you! And fuck your father, and fuck your whole goddamn family! You don't talk about my family that way. They haven't done anything but good here. And you can kiss my damn ass.' . . . I was so upset that I took three sleeping pills and stayed in bed for three days."

It was a somewhat cheerless season around Graceland. Elvis made his usual Christmas contributions to virtually every Memphis charity of every color and denomination, bringing his total up to $105,000 over the course of the year. On December 15 he gave George Klein a new canary yellow Cadillac convertible and then arranged for George to give his old Impala to Tankers Fan Club president Gary Pepper's father, Sterling, now a guard at Graceland. Alan's father was dying of cancer, and Elvis visited him at the hospital several times. They went to the movies most nights, but Elvis spent a good deal of time by himself upstairs, and his generally autumnal mood was reflected in an interview with Jim Kingsley of the *Commercial Appeal* at this time.

He liked to read, he told Kingsley, mainly religious works and medical textbooks, and he listened to gospel music a lot. He recalled one time, in 1954, when he and Scotty and Bill had played a club date outside of Shreveport just before Christmas and then were stopped for speeding on the way home. "It was cold, and I was sleepy. I woke up, and the officer asked, 'Who are you?' 'Elvis Presley, a singer.' The officer looked puzzled. Of course he had never heard of me. Hardly anyone had. I thought, 'Here goes my Christmas money for a traffic ticket.' But the officer let us go with a warning. . . . I gave a big sigh of relief. After the officer left, the three of us got out of the car and counted our money by the car headlights. The money was mostly in dollar bills. Man, that was the most money I ever had in my pockets at one time! I blew the whole bundle the next day for Christmas presents. . . .

"There is a lot of difference in Christmases today and when we were growing up in East Tupelo. [But] honestly, I can't say these are any better. We are just in a better position to spend. But that's not the important thing. It's the friendships and the devotion that really count. Everything is so dreamy when you are young. After you grow up it kind of becomes — *just real.*"

W HAT FINALLY DISTRACTED HIM were the horses. First he decided to get one for Priscilla, next he asked Jerry Schilling if Jerry would mind his buying Sandy a horse so Priscilla would have someone to ride with, and then he got one for himself. After that, he decided everybody should have a horse, and there was a flurry of activity around Graceland as the old barn was renovated, Elvis bulldozed the little house out back where Billy and his family had once lived so that they could have a riding ring, and he started buying farm equipment at Sears and fancy saddles and western wear at the Ben Howell and Son Saddlery in Whitehaven. "Elvis would go out in the barn every day and every night," Marty noted with approval. "This barn, which he called House of the Rising Sun, a pun on the name of his horse, hadn't been used in years. He fixed up a little office for himself and wrote the names of the horses on the stalls with a big red marking pen. He'd write notes to himself like 'What I'm Going to Buy Tomorrow' and 'What I'm Going to Do Tomorrow.' And he would clean up the barn and buy new tack. He just loved it."

He took in his aunt Delta (Vernon's sister) after her husband, Pat Biggs, died of a heart attack. Not everyone liked Delta; even Elvis' cousin Billy Smith conceded that she "had a horrible temper, and she drank too much." But Pat, a former nightclub owner and big-time gambler, had always been one of Elvis' favorite relatives, someone who encouraged him to believe in himself, and as a result, according to Billy, "he felt like he needed to take Delta in." He set her up in the former maid's quarters by the kitchen, put her in charge of Grandma, and made sure that the funeral arrangements allowed everyone in the household, including the cooks and the maids, to attend.

All of a sudden it was starting to seem as if Elvis was reestablishing control; with the horses and the home improvements, with the decisiveness that he showed in taking charge of Pat Biggs' funeral and finding a place for his aunt, the guys all felt like they were beginning to see the old Elvis again, and it became open season on Larry. Just as the Colonel seemed to have sensed his new vulnerability, the guys gave Larry a harder time than ever, first for failing to share their enthusiasm for the cowboy life, then with renewed gibes at Lawrence of Israel and the Wandering Jew. Priscilla barely bothered to conceal her contempt, and while Elvis tried to make it right with Larry and explain her actions, just as he had tried to indicate his private disapproval of the Colonel's, he did nothing to stop them. Larry felt more and more left out by all this macho posturing. And now Elvis was talking about getting married.

I T WAS SOMETHING ABOUT which he clearly continued to feel a deep, almost physical ambivalence. Some months earlier he had asked jeweler Harry Levitch to make up a set of rings but then had him keep them at the store. "I put them in the safe, and [something like] six months went by, and nothing happened. So I asked Elvis, 'Did you change your mind?' And he said, 'No, I just can't make up my mind. It's just — it's a big step, Mr. Levitch.'" He confided his misgivings to Larry, too. "More than once Elvis remarked, 'Look at Jesus. He never married.' [And] I don't think that this necessarily pointed to a Christ complex, although certainly Elvis suffered from that to a degree. . . . But at age thirty-two Elvis sensed that a real marriage involved commitments he wasn't sure he could meet."

Rumors had been circulating for months, though, and Elvis had been getting clear signals from Priscilla, not to mention her father, about the promises he had made. The Colonel, too, was urging him to fulfill his obligations — and even if no one had said anything to him, he knew what he had to do. So just before Christmas he proposed. He came to her room with "his old boyish grin on his face and his hands were behind his back. 'Sit down, Satnin', and close your eyes.' I did. When I opened my eyes, I found Elvis on his knees before me, holding a small black velvet box. . . . I opened the box to find the most beautiful diamond ring I'd ever seen. It was three and a half karats encircled by a row of smaller diamonds, which were detachable — I could wear them separately. 'We're going to be married,' Elvis said. . . . 'I told you I'd know when the time was right.'" They showed the ring to Vernon and Grandma, but Elvis said they should wait to inform her parents. He wanted to tell her father in person.

Every day and night they would go riding en masse, and afterward they would all huddle together in the barn, in smaller or larger groups, conferring about the horses, talking about necessary improvements and repairs, just enjoying each other's company. For the first time in a long time there was a sense of a future to be shared and a feeling on almost everyone's part that they were embarked on a common enterprise. It wasn't like the slot cars, long since abandoned after Marty and Red got into an argument over the performance of their respective cars. This was different somehow, reminiscent of the good times they had had before Larry Geller ever came along. To Jerry Schilling, who had joined only in the aftermath of Larry's arrival and Joe's brief period of exile, "it was just really fun. We'd sit out in the barn talking until the sun came up. It was really like a family."

E LVIS' NEW DEAL with the Colonel went into effect on the first business day of the new year. They had initially spoken of it on the phone several weeks before, and the way that Colonel explained it, everything would just go on as it always had: the Colonel would continue to take care of business, with Elvis as his only client. The only difference was the new contract would recognize for the first time in businesslike fashion that Elvis *was* his only client, that they had formed, without ever really explicitly acknowledging the fact, a kind of partnership, and that what was called for now was a *partnership agreement*. Colonel would go on taking his 25-percent management fee on all existing contracts, and on all future contract guarantees as well — but that managerial split would apply only to the "flat payments" that derived from those contracts.

For example, if Elvis were contracted to MGM for a picture for which he was to receive $750,000 plus 50 percent of the profits, Colonel would take his normal 25-percent management fee on that portion of the deal that represented salary, but on the profits there would be a 50–50 split, since, in essence, with all the work Colonel put into publicity and promotion on the picture, its success represented, really, a joint venture. Similarly, on the current RCA deal, the $300,000 annual payment was subject to the usual 25-percent commission, but any additional payments or profits beyond that guaranteed amount would be split 50–50.

There were various minor permutations as set forth in letters that went out under Elvis' signature to RCA and William Morris (future profits from past film ventures would be split on the new 50–50 basis; merchandising, of course, was as always a 50–50 deal; and publishing remained unchanged), but the basic principle was a simple one: the embrace of a partnership concept that, as Colonel Parker explained it, had evolved over the years to the point that it existed in all but fully recognized contractual fact.

It was a partnership that existed in far more than contractual fact. Managers since time immemorial have sought financial advantage through the kind of partnerships, joint ventures, and side deals on which it might have been thought the Colonel wrote the book. Popular soprano Kate Smith's manager, Ted Collins, for example, had created a partnership with his client in 1930 and maintained it for over thirty-three years, and Patti Page and her manager, Jack Rael, had had a 50–50 deal since her early days of stardom. Even Bob Dylan, who in 1967 might have seemed the antithesis of Elvis Presley in terms of music business expertise and cultural sophistication, appears to have permitted similar opportunities for self-aggrandizement to his manager Albert Grossman, who, like the Colonel, took a 25-percent manager's share but, probably unbeknownst to his client, received a 50-percent share of the publishing from the firm to which he first brought the Dylan song catalogue.

To say that a practice is not without precedent does not, of course, condone it, but the Colonel had reasons of his own to seek a modification of terms at this juncture. The most compelling had to do with the notorious unpredictability of the business, compounded by the increasing unpredictability of his single client. If he was going to tie his future and devote all of his considerable energies to one performer, there was little question in his mind that he should be getting some equity, too, and he didn't hide his thinking either from his client or from anyone else with whom he did business.

For all of his reputation for deviousness among those who chose not to listen to what he was saying, in certain respects he could be the most straightforward of men, and what he was looking for now, perfectly straightforwardly, was some kind of insurance. At fifty-six he didn't know how many years he had left. His own health was not so good, his wife, Marie's, worse. If Mr. Presley wanted to take off in new and unproven directions, that was up to him, of course, but Colonel, for all of the relative simplicity of his living arrangements, had never pretended to aspire to the ascetic life. He enjoyed Palm Springs, he liked the comforts of the Spa Hotel steam room, he had come to appreciate the company of the rich and famous, and he felt he had earned his place among them. Perhaps the most compelling element of his thinking stemmed from the philosophy embodied in the title of the book he was always threatening to write, *How Much Does It Cost If It's Free?*: nothing was worth anything unless you placed a value on it. His services, he felt without any self-consciousness whatsoever, were worth 50 percent.

Elvis would have had no problem assenting to that proposition, and he indicated no compunction about signing the agreement. If it made the old man happy, then he was happy. Marty and the others could grumble and act like they knew what was going on, but only he and his father really *knew* what it took to sustain this kind of enterprise, how much faith Colonel had shown not just at the beginning of his career when everyone else said he was a flash in the pan but during those dark days when he was in the army and only the Colonel's ingenious schemes could sustain not just the business but Elvis' own faith in himself. Colonel had outwitted the sharpest Hollywood operators, and *he had never become like them*. There were no phony Hollywood affectations or social hypocrisies, no apologies for who he was or where he came from — the one obligation that he acknowledged was to *show up and do the job,* and in that he made no more demands of his star than he did of himself.

When, in the wake of their new arrangement, Colonel revamped the agreement with RCA to extend through 1980 — with the guaranteed payment of $300,000 a year extending only through 1970 and subsequently reduced to $200,000 a year for the next five years of the contract (one year beyond the term of the option that had been picked up in August) and nothing for the last five — Elvis never questioned the basis for the revision but instead sent telegrams to RCA expressing his gratitude "that it will be at least 1980 before there is a divorce" and declaring his faith that by then "we will have such a large catalog family that it will be cheaper to stay together." His wire to the Colonel simply acknowledged "the greatest Snowman on earth," seemingly taking as much delight in his mentor's exploits as the Colonel did himself. Others could talk and might well have pointed out that the new agreement actually reduced the guaranteed payment schedule substantially, thereby allowing Colonel's profit sharing to kick in that much earlier — if they had known any of the details of the deal. But they did not, and it was by intent that Elvis chose to leave them out of the picture. This was his secret life, if he could be said to have a secret life at all. He didn't need to scrutinize the fine points of a contract to know that he was being fairly dealt with. Two days after the RCA transaction went through, Colonel delivered a deal memo for another Allied Artists picture, this one to be made in 1968 at a salary of $900,000. Elvis never doubted that there was something in it for the Colonel. But there was plenty in it for him, too.

*   *   *

BESIDES, HIS MIND was elsewhere. The number of horses had quickly outstripped the number of stalls, and when Red ran down Elvis in the field one day playing out a Wild West scenario, it was apparent that Graceland's thirteen and three-quarter acres had grown too small. At the same time it was equally apparent that nothing was going to discourage Elvis' zeal for acquisition, and he just kept purchasing more horses and more equipment until one day, as they were returning from a horse-buying trip in Mississippi, he and Priscilla spotted an immaculately maintained 160-acre cattle ranch called Twinkletown Farm, with a lighted sixty-five-foot-high white cross overlooking a small man-made lake, outside of Walls, Mississippi, just across the state line.

Not long afterward, they were out driving with Alan Fortas and a couple of the guys, when Fortas spotted a "For Sale" sign on the property. They turned around to read the sign and then drove out to the Twinkletown Airport, where Jack Adams, the ranch owner and one of the biggest used-aircraft salesmen in the world, had his headquarters. Ever the canny businessman, Elvis sent Alan in to inquire about the property (the idea was that if the owner knew it was for Elvis Presley, the price would immediately be jacked up), but Alan barely had time to introduce himself before "here comes Elvis walking in the door. Shit. Well, Adams was a smooth operator and a good salesman, and he said, 'Look, don't ask me how much I want for it; I'll give you the keys. Why don't you just spend the night?'

"Elvis said, 'But we got horses.' He said, 'Bring your horses down, get everybody, keep the place as long as you want. Then if you like it we can talk.' So we haul the horses down there, sit around, party all night, like typical cattlemen! Next day Elvis wakes up. He said, 'Alan, that was the best night's sleep I ever had in my life. Let's go buy this goddamn place.' I said, 'Elvis —' He said, 'Go buy it.' So I called Mr. Adams, and he said, 'I'll take so much for this and so much for that, and that includes everything — the cattle, the house, the furnishings and everything, except a few personal items and some clothes.' I said, 'Okay, I'll call you back,' and I went and told Elvis. Now I had had some experience in real estate. I knew we could beat him down. But Elvis just said, 'Look, goddamnit, how much does he want?' I told him. He said, 'Ask him how long it will take to get his stuff out of there.' I called Mr. Adams back, and he said, 'About fifteen minutes.' I said, 'Elvis wants to buy it.' And that was it, no negotiating, nothing."

On February 8 he put down a deposit of $5,000 against the sale price of $437,000. Within a week he had purchased at least five pickup trucks and a '63 Cadillac, and by the time the deed was filed on February 22 he had bought more than two dozen vehicles, half a dozen house trailers, and six horse vans, not to mention numerous tractors, miscellaneous ranch equipment, septic tanks and water lines, and a quarter mile of temporary plywood fencing which would have to serve until the $12,000 eight-foot-high wooden fence that he had contracted for could be built. In all he managed to pay out well over $100,000 in approximately two weeks, an orgy of spending that seemed to momentarily pacify Elvis but horrified Vernon, who was sure that they were all going to end up in the poorhouse. According to Priscilla, who was no more sanguine about Elvis' spendthrift ways but found it easier to act like a good sport, "Vernon literally begged him to stop, but Elvis said, 'I'm having fun, Daddy, for the first time in ages. I've got a hobby, something I look forward to getting up in the morning for.'"

He *was* having fun. "He liked it when everyone was together," Priscilla observed, "and he got upset when they wanted to leave." He named one of the new horses Mare Ingram for the Memphis mayor who kept trying to name a building or a highway after him, his latest effort — to call the Mid-South Coliseum the Elvis Presley Coliseum — shot down by a unanimous vote of the city commission. (This civic endeavor would not bear fruit until 1972, when a section of Highway 51 South running by Graceland was officially christened Elvis Presley Boulevard.) He named the ranch the Flying Circle G and put its brand (the letter G with a pair of wings) on every horse, every piece of livestock, and every pickup truck on the property. "It wasn't unusual," Priscilla noted, "to see him walking around the property, knocking on doors, waking everyone up, or checking on the horses in the early-morning hours. He was having a ball, and there were days he didn't even want to take time out to eat — he'd walk around with a loaf of bread under his arm in case hunger pangs struck. . . . On Sundays we had picnics, and all the girls chipped in on potluck. . . . We rode horses, held skeet-shooting contests, and combed the lake for turtles and snakes. There was fun, laughter, and a lot of camaraderie."

Out of that spirit of camaraderie he got the idea of deeding over an acre apiece to each of the guys. After all, if it was a commune in spirit, why shouldn't it be a commune in fact? He went so far as to draw up plans with Marty, but Vernon quickly put a stop to that. Vernon had always fancied himself a gentleman rancher, and if he could have restrained some of his son's excesses, he might have come to enjoy the role. But he was as helpless to control him as anybody else, and when he contacted the Colonel for advice, Colonel could offer nothing more than the familiar bromide that

Elvis would soon tire of his new plaything. In desperation he even tried to enlist Joe. "Vernon is coming to me and saying, 'Joe, he's spending too much money. I tried to tell him, and he said, "Hey, I'll get more if I need it." You've got to tell him.' So I talked to Elvis. I said, 'What are you doing with all this stuff?' Went on and on. And he said, 'It's okay, I want it now.' Sometimes he'd listen, sometimes he wouldn't. Sometimes he'd just get mad. He'd say, 'You don't like it? There's the fucking door.'"

Every day, according to Alan Fortas, was like the last day. To Mike McGregor, a saddle maker and rodeo rider whom Elvis had met the previous month while buying riding apparel and equipment at the western-wear shop on Millbranch, then put on salary to help take care of the horses, it was an experience never to be repeated. Mike told Elvis straight off that he couldn't work on Sundays because he had church, but Elvis said that was fine, as long as he could feed the horses first thing Sunday morning. "He was very thoughtful and very much a gentleman. He never told me, 'Go get this horse'; he always asked me did I have time to get him. I can never remember the man giving me a direct order. One of the fun times on the ranch was when it snowed down there, and they took the tractors and sleds and drove around and tore them up. One night one of the cows had a calf, and they were so excited everyone had to go see the calf." When one of the horses had a colt, "you would have thought [it was] royalty."

For Jerry Schilling, on the other hand, it was a deeper, darker dream, a dream of almost Edenic innocence and loss. "It was really beautiful at first. Sandy and I had a little trailer in front of the lake — it was the first real place of our own that we ever had. You'd wake up in the morning, the horses would be drinking out of the lake; Elvis and Priscilla would ride over, and we'd go for a ride, then have breakfast.

"But then Elvis got really busy, and it lost that overall good feeling. It got so competitive with all the trailers and trucks: who got this, who got that. And it got to the point where you began to feel that Elvis was just caught up in it, there was all this buying and giving with no real meaning behind it. Looking back on it, I have to think drugs were a part of it. I guess the climax came when Elvis showed up at our trailer one night; it was 2:00 A.M. and pouring down rain, and he's standing in the doorway, looking like an old cowboy, rain pouring off his hat, just standing there with a loaf of bread in his hands! He told me he needed to go somewhere. 'I need you to go with me.' We ended up going to the house of this pharmacist back in Whitehaven that we knew. Elvis just wanted to fill a prescription —

whether it was Darvon or Tuinal or Dexamyl or Placidyls I don't know. The pharmacist didn't really care; I guess he should have, but, I mean, this was Elvis Presley. The point was, Elvis didn't even make any excuses. And up till then he had always been pretty secretive with the heavyweight stuff around me — like he didn't want me to know. That was when I thought it started to change."

Things once again had begun to get out of control. All of a sudden Elvis was incommunicado to the Colonel. The session for his upcoming picture, *Clambake,* had been moved to Nashville for the convenience of the star, but when it took place on February 21, the star flew back to the ranch after the first night and didn't even bother to show up on the second. Red, who had once again picked all the songs, covered for him, telling the music director that Elvis had a cold and doing the scratch vocals, which Elvis over-dubbed on the third night, wearing a cowboy outfit and chaps.

It was just a few days until his scheduled departure for California, and Colonel was getting increasingly worried. He was frustrated with Marty, who had sunk into a miasma of pills and sullen noncommunication, and he finally fired off a letter to Mr. Lacker effectively relieving him of his co-foreman duties. He knew all about the weight gain from Joe, and he was furious when Elvis finally worked up the nerve to tell him what he had suspected the boy was going to inform him of all along: that he needed more time, that he wasn't feeling well, that he would not be able to report for preproduction on schedule on March 3. This would have to stop, the Colonel thundered in reply; the movie companies had a great deal of money invested in their product and little patience with stars who took that money and then didn't deliver on their promises. He would have to obtain a doctor's certificate if he intended to postpone filming.

That was how Dr. George Nichopoulos first came into the picture. On Sunday, February 26, Elvis tried to contact his regular physician, but when he was not available, George Klein's girlfriend, Barbara Little, who was out at the ranch for the weekend with George, suggested Dr. Nick, one of the physicians in the medical group for which she worked.

Nichopoulos, the thirty-nine-year-old son of Greek immigrants who operated a restaurant in Anniston, Alabama, had graduated from Vanderbilt Medical School after completing all the course work for a Ph.D. in clinical physiology at the University of Tennessee in Memphis. In 1963 he had moved to Memphis permanently to take a position with the Medical Group, a consortium of physicians offering patients a full range of interlocking specialties. A soft-spoken man and a good athlete (he had played tailback on the Sewanee football team at 150 pounds), he had a modest, self-effacing manner and a nice appearance, with a full head of white hair making his otherwise youthful looks particularly striking.

"I didn't know what to expect, I didn't know the kind of illness or what the problem was, but when I got there, he was complaining about saddle sores. They had been riding the last couple of days, and he was supposed to be in L.A. to do a shoot. Well, after I saw him, it seemed like his saddle sores were not all that bad; I think he just wanted to stay home for a few days. So we spent more time chit-chatting than treating his saddle sores.

"[My first impression of him was that] he was very polite, very humble. He was very respectful. In fact, during our whole relationship, he never called me by my first name; it was always Dr. Nick or Dr. Nichopoulos. And he would always raise hell with anybody that he interpreted as being disrepectful toward me [in that regard]. That night he seemed kind of depressed and lonely; he just wanted to talk. Even with everybody that was out there, to me he just sort of remained a lonely person. It seemed like they didn't have new things to talk about; everything was old hat.

"Of course, he liked to talk about medicines and the *PDR*, and what kind of symptoms do you get with this and what have you — I was amazed at how much he had educated himself. Anyway, I gave him some ointments to use on the sore places, and then he asked me if I could stop by his house and check on his grandmother on the way back. She had been sick with a cold, and she had heart trouble, too, so I said, okay, I'd stop by and check her out. Well, while I was there, one of the guys called for Elvis and said he had forgotten to ask me something; could I come back out to the ranch? I said, 'Can't we just talk about it over the telephone?' And whoever I was talking to came back and said, 'He'd like for you to come back out if you would.' So I went back out there [it was about a fifteen-minute ride], and we talked about nothing, really; he just wanted to talk. And he gave me something else he wanted me to do at the house on the way back into town, so I stopped back by the house and had another phone call from him. I played this game three times, and I wasn't very happy about it, but I called the Colonel and got a letter off. The Colonel questioned me [pretty closely]. 'You sure he can't do this? You know, as soon as he gets back in Memphis, he likes to hang around. We've got everything set up, the crews and everything, he needs to be here.' And I said I really didn't feel like he was going to be able to do it, there was a lot of action in the movie, and I felt like he might have some difficulty."

The conversation left the Colonel fuming, but there was nothing to be done about it. He got the studio to revise their schedule, pushing back the start of preproduction to the following Monday, March 6, but he continued to worry that things were falling apart. He had thought that Elvis would come to his senses with Larry out of favor and things finally worked out with the girl. There were problems within the organization, to be sure. Some of the boys were no longer capable of pulling their weight (Alan, of whom Colonel was genuinely fond, was going to have to be left behind in Mississippi because of his drug problems, and Mr. Lacker's usefulness was plainly at an end), and this ranch business was going to have to be addressed if it did not swiftly run its course. But more than that, he needed an excuse to get matters out in the open with Elvis once and for all — and in a way that would assure him of the boy's attention. Because things couldn't go on like this much longer.

ELVIS ARRIVED IN CALIFORNIA on Sunday, March 5. On the sixth he reported to the studio for wardrobe fitting, as planned, and that evening completed most of the one vocal overdub that remained to be done at Thorne Nogar's Annex Studio. Everything seemed normal, except for his weight, which was going to necessitate some costume changes. On Thursday, though, when Joe came to pick him up to go to the studio, there was clearly something wrong. The guys were just sitting around, and Elvis was nowhere in sight. He had staggered in woozily a few minutes earlier, they reported to Joe, and told them he had fallen during the night. He had hit his head on the bathtub and thought he might need to see a doctor, but they had simply gotten him back to bed and were waiting for Joe to take command.

Joe called the Colonel right away. There was no doubt in anyone's mind that it was the pills, and when Colonel arrived he closeted himself with Elvis in the bedroom, then came out looking grim and arranged for Elvis' regular physician, Dr. M. E. Gorsin, and a radiologist, Dr. George Elerding, to come over with portable X-ray equipment. Then he lit into the guys. What was the matter with them? he demanded. What did they think their job was? Why did they let him get this way? Someone was going to have to be with Elvis twenty-four hours a day — even if they had to go to the bathroom with him. From now on, he declared, things were going to be different around here.

The doctors' report was not so bad: Elvis had suffered a minor concussion; no evidence of fracture could be identified. Additional X rays of the cervical spine indicated no fracture there either, though there was considerable limitation of motion due to muscle spasming. He was, in other words, bruised and in a good deal of pain, but with rest he should be fine. Everyone was looking daggers at Larry as Colonel announced that he wanted all of Elvis' books removed forthwith. "And don't you dare bring him another one."

Two days later Colonel called a series of meetings at which Elvis was present. First he met with Joe; then he met with Marty, whom he informed officially that he was no longer co-foreman, that he would no longer be writing checks, and that he would in future be in charge of "special projects." Although he went on to say that the first of these special projects was to be the upcoming wedding, for Marty this was little consolation. "I thought it was a joke, because the Colonel and Joe had already planned the wedding." He looked over at Elvis, but Elvis wouldn't look back at him. "To see Elvis acting that way, and to hear this old, fat bastard spewing edicts like he was Elvis' ruler just made me sick. In fact, it destroyed my desire to be part of the group."

To the rest of the guys Colonel simply laid down the law. With Elvis sitting there, he announced that there were going to be some big changes. From now on they would not be going to Mr. Presley with their personal problems and concerns. If they had any concerns they needed to address, they would go to Mr. Esposito, who was now the sole person in charge, and he would take care of them. "Some of you," he said, looking at Larry, "think maybe he's Jesus Christ, who should wear robes and walk down the street helping people. But that's not who he is."

There were going to be economies as well. Some salaries and expenses were going to have to be cut. Mr. Presley couldn't afford to just throw his money away, and everyone was going to have to earn his keep. For the present everyone would remain on payroll, but when they got back to Memphis, some of them would probably be let go. "It's nothing personal," Colonel declared. "It's just business." In addition, he said, with another meaningful glance at Larry, there would be no more discussions of religion, there would be no more books, and if anyone didn't like it, they knew where the door was. Larry felt sick. "Throughout Parker's tirade, Elvis never looked at me once." On the other hand, there was an aspect of it that didn't surprise him. "I knew this wasn't Elvis. I mean, obviously it was Elvis, but he looked very strange, as if he were under the influence of something, and there's no doubt in my mind that he was drugged. . . . His eyes were glazed, haunted looking. And I don't think it's any coincidence that Elvis' descent into experimenting with the next level of psychoactive medication, very heavy downers and synthetic narcotics, followed his 'recovery.' "

Afterward everyone was in a state of shock. Jerry Schilling, sure that the Colonel had been looking directly at him while he was speaking about cutbacks, was already packing his suitcase when Elvis walked into his room and reassured him, "He wasn't talking about you." Billy, too, took it very personally. "I thought I was going to be one of the ones terminated. Or if not terminated, I knew I'd have to quit. Because me and [my wife] Jo were getting an apartment in California . . . and with cutting down on expenses there wouldn't be any rent money for the ones who wanted to stay." He offered Elvis his resignation, but once again Elvis reacted with surprise. "He said, 'Why?' I said, 'Because I can't afford to keep a home in Memphis and an apartment out here.' Elvis said, 'That doesn't apply to you. You'll get your apartment out here, and it'll be paid for.' "

C*lambake* started up two weeks later under familiar enough auspices, but true to the Colonel's instructions Larry was no longer allowed to spend any time in private with Elvis. Haircutting sessions, once the occasion for grand philosophical discussions, were now limited to half-hour time periods that were strictly chaperoned. Hostility from the guys reached new and undisguised heights, and Elvis didn't even bother to indicate secret sympathy. "You know," he said to Larry one day out of the blue, "those masters of yours have hidden motives. They're trying to control people's minds and use them for their own damn purposes."

The atmosphere on the set was one of almost enforced gaiety. Once again there were practical jokes, cherry bombs, cream pie and water balloon fights, with even the director, Arthur Nadel, getting into the act. It was like a staged remembrance of things past — but there was a wistful note, too, that did not escape some members of the cast. And it hardly seemed coincidental that Elvis kept listening to a single album over and over throughout the filming, a collection of song lyrics recited in heavily accented English by the French actor Charles Boyer. The album was titled *Where Does Love Go?*, and the fully orchestrated arrangements were as lushly romantic as Boyer's recitations, with melancholy spoken versions of "What

Now My Love," Edith Piaf's "La Vie en Rose," Charles Aznavour's "Venice Blue," and "When the World Was Young." Elvis' favorite song by far was "Softly As I Leave You," a dying man's profession of love for his wife, and he gave the album to various members of the cast and crew while playing it again and again for the guys, who could not understand what he saw in its morbid mood.

Elvis and the Colonel, too, seemed back on the same old footing. To Bill Bixby, the second lead in the picture, who was meeting them both for the first time, "They were like Frick and Frack when they'd get together — they really were. They were great put-on artists. The Colonel got me in on a mind-reading gag, and we worked it out with signals, Elvis and the Colonel and me. One of the guys would tell me a word that he was thinking of, and I'd never go near the Colonel, but he would get it [with these indicators]. It was a great way of entertaining ourselves."

The Colonel still had serious obstacles to overcome. If there was one thing Colonel hated, it was to be on the defensive, but with all these recent downturns in business, and now this latest embarrassment, which all the studio heads were bound to hear about sooner or later, it was no longer possible simply to paper over some of the problems with which they were faced. He had movie contracts that carried them through 1968, maybe into 1969, but he didn't know what he could look forward to after that.

He had gotten a taste of the new climate in which they would be operating when Paramount refused to release any money to him for the usual exploitation campaign on the final Hal Wallis picture, *Easy Come, Easy Go*, scheduled for Easter release. Wallis was embarrassed but couldn't pry any money loose, and on February 20 Colonel had angrily told Wallis' loyal lieutenant, Paul Nathan, that he wasn't going to do a goddamn thing for the picture. Three days later he found occasion to rethink his stance, as he informed "Colonel Wallis" in one of his masterful pieces of diplomatic correspondence. The average guy, he said, under these circumstances, would simply pull out. But he was not the average guy. He knew that Wallis always honored his promises and non-promises, and he was convinced that in the end Wallis would probably be overcome with "a warm feeling of generosity towards the good old Colonel." He could count on the fact that any evidence of such generosity would be gratefully accepted by the Colonel, and it was — when Wallis and his partner, Joe Hazen, coughed up $3,500 from their personal funds. But Colonel was shaken nonetheless, and when Nathan wrote to Wallis in Spain after the film's opening, he underscored the legitimacy of the Colonel's concern: "Obviously the star is not as big an attraction as he was."

Things were no more sanguine for Elvis at home. Marty, whom in a fit of remorse he had asked to be his best man, was at constant odds with Priscilla, who couldn't for the life of her understand why someone with such utter contempt for her should play so important a role in their wedding. Then, as if to make up for his own lapse of judgment, Elvis asked Joe to be co–best man, and he left it to Joe and Marty to work out the details. Billy Smith saw Elvis' behavior as increasingly erratic, though he was not sure of the underlying cause. More and more he saw his own role, and that of the other guys, as simply not to let things bother Elvis too much, "but we had our work cut out for us. And it got to be more than most of us could handle."

On March 15, during the enforced film break, Jerry and Sandy got married in Las Vegas. Jerry had wanted to get married for some time, and he definitely considered himself to be engaged, but at the same time he was very much aware of the less than subtle pressure he was getting from the Colonel, and he began to wonder if this might not have something to do with Elvis' evident reluctance to go through with the ceremony himself. He knew Colonel believed in marriage and propriety, and he accepted to a degree Colonel's professions of concern for his and Sandy's well-being, but still he couldn't help but feel that his own marriage was designed in some respects as a "trial run."

It was only after Jerry's wedding that Elvis finally agreed to a date — as soon as the movie was over — and almost immediately Colonel started going to Las Vegas on weekends to tie up all the loose ends. Charlie Hodge drove him most of the time, and as they drove, Colonel would expound upon his thoughts about matrimony. "'Now, Charlie,' he said, waving his big cigar, 'when you finally decide to get married, let me handle it.' He shot an amused glance at me. 'When are you going to get married?'

"Not yet, Colonel," I said. "I'm still practicing."

He laughed.

"When you do decide, let me know," he said. "Charlie, we could make some money on it."

"Make money?" I said. "On my own wedding?"

He nodded. "Yes, we can. Now you listen to the old Colonel."

He outlined his plan as we sped along. . . . "I'll rent a football stadium, and you and your bride will ride in to the altar, located on the fifty-yard line, on a pair of big elephants." He smiled and pulled out a fresh cigar. "We'll charge admission for it."

I laughed. "Colonel, that's wild."

He waved the cigar at me like a magic wand. "It's not wild. There's money in it. Now you listen to the old Colonel."

He'd take me into the casinos with him when he wanted to gamble. I couldn't spend a dime of my own money. He knew I loved to gamble almost as much as he did.

He'd sit down at a roulette wheel and start putting out chips for both of us.

"Let's put a $25 chip on this square for you, Charlie," he'd say. "And some here and here and here."

Whenever I won, it would be $200.

The Colonel would say, "Now you'd better go wire Mrs. Parker some flowers."

He winked. "Listen to the Colonel. Go wire Mrs. Parker some flowers when you win."

I NVITATIONS WERE SENT OUT under a veil of secrecy: Lamar and Alan were omitted simply because they were not part of the group that was in California. In addition to the guys on the movie, it was just family, plus Colonel and Mrs. Parker, George Klein, and, unaccountably, Elvis' jeweler, Harry Levitch.

Rona Barrett sniffed out the news on April 27, stalking Joe and Joanie in the local market even as everyone was converging on Palm Springs. They flew out of Palm Springs in two chartered planes at around two o'clock Monday morning, May 1, with Elvis and Priscilla taking Frank Sinatra's private jet. The engaged couple paid $15 for a marriage license at the Clark County Courthouse at 3:00 A.M., then drove to the Aladdin Hotel, a four-hundred-room re-creation of the English Tudor style across the street from Caesar's Palace, recently purchased by the Colonel's friend Milton Prell, who had previously owned the Sahara, where they always stayed. For the next few hours they waited nervously in their suite until the Colonel finally indicated it was time, and then they were married in an eight-minute ceremony conducted by Nevada Supreme Court Justice David Zenoff that commenced at 11:41 A.M.

Just before the ceremony was about to begin, Red went to Joe's room to find out when he and his wife, Pat, and the rest of the guys and their

MAY I, 1967: RICHARD DAVIS, JERRY SCHILLING, GEORGE KLEIN,
FREDDY BIENSTOCK (IN BACKGROUND), JOE ESPOSITO,
PRISCILLA AND ELVIS PRESLEY, CHARLIE HODGE, MARTY LACKER.
(COURTESY OF JERRY SCHILLING)

wives, should get ready. With some embarrassment Joe told him what he had just learned himself: that with the exception of the two best men and Elvis' cousin Billy, none of the guys or their wives were to be included in the actual ceremony. The wedding was scheduled to take place in the relatively confined space of Mr. Prell's private living quarters, and since there wasn't room for everyone, Colonel had decided the only way to avoid accusations of favoritism was for none of the guys to attend — they could all just go to the reception afterward.

Red hit the roof. He had never made any secret of his feelings about Joe, but now he cursed him out as a chickenshit brownnose and came close to hitting him. What did Elvis know about all this? he demanded. The motherfucker didn't have any balls and never had. Red was fucked if he was going to attend the reception if he wasn't welcome at the ceremony itself. This was the so-called friend whom Red had asked to be best man at his own wedding. He hadn't asked to be here — he had come at Elvis' invitation. And he hadn't brought his wife to be humiliated by some asshole who didn't have the guts to tell him what he needed to tell him face-to-face. Colonel just better stay out of his way. He would beat the shit out of that sonofabitch if he so much as saw him. Fuck him. Fuck Joe. Fuck Elvis. Fuck them all. He was finished with all this bullshit.

The rest of them took it a little more diplomatically. There was the same feeling of resentment, there was the same sense of being let down, but mostly they put it on the Colonel, muting their disappointment for Elvis' sake — after all, it was his day, it wasn't his fault, he had never really had the guts to stand up to the Colonel anyway. Jerry Schilling saw denial almost as a matter of self-preservation. Elvis had given him so much, *as a friend,* and he had looked up to Elvis in such a way that he just wasn't prepared to deal with his own conflicting emotions at this point. "I don't think I even recognized how I really felt till years later."

As for Elvis, for all of his inner turmoil, and for all of the anger and ill feeling that were roiling around just outside the range of his vision, he still retained all of his ability to charm. Judge Zenoff wanted to meet separately with both the bride and the groom before the ceremony. "Colonel Parker brought Elvis off to the side of the room to meet me, and I chatted with him a few moments. My pre-ceremony meeting with Elvis was probably the most impressive part of the whole experience. I was simply amazed at the boy's modesty. He was low-key, handsome as a picture, very respectful and very intense . . . and so nervous he was almost bawling. Then I was taken over to meet Priscilla. She was absolutely petrified. She couldn't open her mouth — just stood there staring at me and nodding a little bit when I explained things to her."

Priscilla would not have disagreed with his description. "We were both so nervous, I don't think either of us was aware of who was there and who was not. We hadn't slept all night long and were escorted into the room with the judge and everyone already there. We should have had Red there. Elvis agreed [afterward]: that was not right. And he understood how Red felt. But never did he think it would not be forgiven. It was an oversight. Now it could have been manipulative; I wouldn't put it past Colonel. And I think, too, from Red's point of view, this was a time when Elvis should have taken a stand. There were all those times he didn't as far as business was concerned. But this was personal, and he should have said, 'You get in here. I have a choice of who I want to be at my wedding.' I think basically that's where Red was coming from. Elvis didn't take a stand."

With the brief ceremony over, they snuck through the pool area to the Aladdin Room, where a press conference had been scheduled by the Colonel. In response to reporters' questions, Priscilla's father, Colonel Beaulieu, said that he had "known from the beginning" that Elvis and his daughter would be married someday. "Our little girl is going to be a good wife." When asked what had caused him to finally tie the knot, Elvis said, "Well, I guess it was about time," then turned disarmingly to his father. "Hey, Daddy, help me," he said. "I can't reach you, son," kidded Vernon with a proud grin. "You just slipped through my fingers." "Remember," said the Colonel, getting his two cents in, "you can't end bachelorhood without getting married."

There were about a hundred people at the reception, reported the *Commercial Appeal,* "a buffet banquet that by one estimate cost $10,000 and featured such things as: ham and eggs, Southern fried chicken, roast suckling pig, clams Casino, fresh poached candy salmon, eggs Minette, oysters Rockefeller, and champagne. . . . A string trio played romantic ballads, including 'Love Me Tender.' . . . There was also a strolling accordionist."

Red held true to his vow, remaining in the hotel room with his wife and watching news of the wedding on television as the reception was taking place. He just wanted to catch the first flight back to Los Angeles, and he wasn't going to accept any more damn charity, but when it came time to purchase the plane tickets, he discovered that he had to borrow the money from Harry Levitch, the Memphis jeweler whose acts of civic philanthropy had originally helped Red get through high school. Then on the flight to L.A., Red found himself in the midst of half the wedding party, including Vernon and Dee. He didn't say two words to anybody, refusing even to give Vernon a glance. As far as he was concerned, this was it; he was never going to go back to work for Presley, that fuck.

Ironically, at almost that very moment, Red's principal nemesis, Larry Geller, was learning of the wedding through a newspaper headline. Larry had been feeling the cold wind of rejection ever since the Colonel's edict of two months before. It was, as Larry noted in his memoir, *"If I Can Dream,"* "open season on the Swami," and he had made up his mind to quit when, at the end of April, he called Elvis' house "to tell him that I wasn't coming back. Jerry got on the line and said, 'Larry, you'd better come to the house right now. We're all going to Vegas.' I didn't respond. So they were all going to Vegas. What else was new? 'We're all going to Vegas,' he repeated, as if I would pick up on his meaning. 'No, Jerry,' I answered. 'I can't go.' . . . The next day when I went to the market, to pick up some groceries and the paper, I saw the front page headline, ELVIS PRESLEY IS MARRIED, running above a large photograph of Elvis and Priscilla smiling happily in their wedding attire."

M OST OF THE GUESTS flew back to Los Angeles after the reception, while Elvis and Priscilla returned to Palm Springs. Three days later, on May 4, they flew to Memphis, leaving early the next day for the ranch. They were planning a reception at the end of the month for all of their hometown friends, but for the time being they had at least three weeks free and clear. Most of the guys accompanied them, but even so, it was, for Priscilla, a rare chance to be "alone" with her husband. "I loved playing house. I personally washed all his clothes, along with the towels and sheets, and took pride in ironing his shirts and rolling up his socks the way my mother had taught me. Here was an opportunity to take care of him myself. No maids or housekeepers to pamper us. No large rooms to embrace the regular entourage. . . . Although the rest of the group traveled with us, they respected our privacy as newlyweds and, for the most part, left us alone."

Some of the rest of the group adopted a more cynical view. Lamar, who had not even heard about the wedding until after the fact, drove over from Nashville and joined the newlyweds in the trailer they had commandeered from Alan, who moved into the ranch house. "I guess you could say I went on their honeymoon with them. . . . I'd been with him from the beginning, so nothing had changed, really." Alan, for his part, goaded on by the pills, scarcely bothered to hide his resentment of Priscilla. He blamed her for exiling him to the ranch and felt that she was "conspiring with Vernon to find a way to get rid of us [the guys] or at least reduce our numbers. It wasn't that she didn't like us as individuals. She just felt threatened by our presence. I think she had a fantasy of a normal home life with [Elvis], one in which he went to work like other husbands, came home in the evening, helped her cook dinner, and then sat around with her at night. . . . 'We never have any privacy!' she told me once. And it was true. Just as she couldn't believe Elvis would want to take all of us and our wives down to the ranch, I found it odd that Elvis often circumvented her plans to be alone with him by inviting an entire herd of people to come along."

Still, it was an idyllic time. Elvis had had a porch and steps built for his trailer and a white picket fence around it. They rode horses and relaxed, and, in Jerry Schilling's view, "it was like we were all just friends. They spent a lot of time by themselves, and when they came over it was more like neighbors dropping by. We'd go out riding and maybe have a little picnic, and it was as if things had kind of calmed down for a little while." It was, said Priscilla, "almost like a commune effect."

At the end of the month, on May 29, they had the reception for their Memphis friends in the former slot-car room. Elvis and Priscilla dressed in the same formal clothing they had worn for the wedding, but it was an informal affair, with Elvis' doctor, dentist, painter, horse trainer, and electrician, all of his uncles and aunts and cousins and most of the guys, along with the entire Graceland staff making up the greater part of the small guest list. Priscilla felt a new sense of security not just as a young bride but as someone who had finally managed to put history behind her. One night when they were at Graceland, just before the reception, she persuaded Elvis to burn the books that the Colonel had banned. At three in the morning they dumped a large box filled with books and magazines into an abandoned well, poured gasoline over the pile, "and kissed the past good-bye."

Everyone remarked on how serene the newlyweds looked. Elvis' dentist, Dr. Lester Hofman, and his wife, Sterling, savored the moment as something very special. "There was a beautiful, lavish buffet. We figured if we were invited, the whole world would be there, but I don't think there were more than forty or forty-five people. Tony Barrasso [a well-known society bandleader who was dating Bonnie Bunkley, Elvis' former girl-friend, and would eventually marry her] was playing the accordion. I said, 'I am so thrilled you got married. I was about to give up on you.' He said, 'Mrs. Hofman, I wanted to be sure. Because I cannot imagine ever loving somebody enough to marry them and then falling out of love.' He said, 'That would just kill me.'" No one was prouder than Vernon, though. He practically beamed as he surveyed the festive scene, the head table deco-rated in green and white with white carnations, the grounds all decked out, his son looking handsome with his beautiful bride. Not at all characteristi-cally, Vernon just kept pouring the champagne. He was very drunk and very happy.

ELVIS AND FELTON JARVIS: "GUITAR MAN" SESSION, SEPTEMBER 1967.
(COURTESY OF MARY JARVIS AND JOSEPH A. TUNZI, J.A.T. PUBLISHING)

THE LAST ROUND-UP

HEY LEFT MEMPHIS on June 10 in the big Greyhound bus that George Barris had customized so lavishly for Elvis. For the first time, in honor of his own marriage, wives were included on the cross-country trip, though, of course, children were not, and a long, leisurely, sight-seeing drive was planned. It was like a much-anticipated family vacation, with a visit to the Grand Canyon giving everyone a chance to act like typical tourists, and Joe's home-movie camera recording events in the same random manner that might memorialize any other kind of domestic event. Mostly they just enjoyed each other's company in an atmosphere that appeared to combine a newfound embrace of maturity with an almost desperate determination not to let go of their youth. Joe's movies show men performing self-consciously for the camera, feinting and dodging and taking occasional karate swipes at one another, as the women gaze on approvingly, pick wildflowers, and play the familiar role of wife, lover, friend. At the center of it all is Elvis, looking sober and silly at the same time, wearing a porkpie hat and seemingly suspended for a moment from the action as he quizzically contemplates just what could have caused all of this to come about, then once again throws himself back into the fray.

The MGM picture they were going out to do, *Speedway*, featured Elvis as a race-car driver for the third time and was to be director Norman Taurog's eighth Elvis Presley picture. Nancy Sinatra was the love interest; the guys played various roles; even Taurog's one-and-one-half-year-old granddaughter was given a small part. In keeping with his renewed commitment, Elvis actually worked till four in the morning on one of the two nights dedicated to soundtrack recording, completing two versions of "Suppose," the romantic ballad he had been experimenting with at home for over a year, but occupying himself for the most part with dispiriting material like "He's Your Uncle, Not Your Dad," the most egregious, but by no means the only, example of the standard to which Freddy Bienstock, and Hill and Range, had been reduced.

Life at Rocca Place was fraught with some of the same tensions and contradictions that continued to be reflected in his career. It was a somewhat reduced retinue, with Red and Sonny and Alan all gone, though Gee Gee Gambill, who had married Elvis' cousin Patsy, filled in as best he could, moving into the house with Patsy, who had worked in the office at Graceland for years. There was no mistaking the difference in mood. Everyone recognized the inevitable changes that marriage, not to mention the Colonel's edict of three months before, was bound to bring, and everyone made their own adjustments. Jerry planned to stay in L.A. when the movie was done, making his living as an extra and bit player until he could figure out exactly what he wanted to do with his life. Billy was chafing to get home, looking to spend more time with his family and increasingly resentful of the arbitrary demands that his cousin so often put on him. Joe intended to make a more permanent home for himself out on the Coast with his wife and daughters, while Marty was definitely out of favor and Charlie tended to get under everyone's skin with his ceaseless chatter, his emotional fragility, and his sycophantic ways.

To Joan Esposito it was an incestuous world in which Elvis could be "so wonderful and warm — I always respected who he was, regardless. But as close as you could be as friends, he was still signing the paycheck." Nor was there ever any question as to who was calling the shots or the extent to which "you lived your life around their lives." Priscilla would probably not have disagreed — though she might have changed the possessive to the singular. "It was the whim of the moment. It was who was around at the moment, and that's why everyone wanted to be around. It was like some of the guys would say, 'You got to be around for the gravy.' Elvis was funny — he would tell one person one thing, and then he would tell another person something else. [And they all thought] they knew him so well. I'm sure they knew parts of him that I didn't know, just like I as a woman knew parts of him they would never know — but a lot of times they just couldn't see him as a man."

Priscilla had her own reasons for resentment. Just before they left on the cross-country trip she found out that she was pregnant. Her first reaction was one of anger. Before the wedding she had asked Elvis if she should start taking birth-control pills, but he was adamantly opposed because, he told her, they had not yet been proven to be medically safe. She saw pregnancy as the end of all their dreams. "If I were pregnant, I knew that our plans to travel would have to be postponed. . . . For the first year I truly wanted to be alone with Elvis, without any responsibilities or obligations." She approached Elvis with a considerable degree of trepidation. "I expected him to react with the same mixed reactions I felt, but he was ecstatic . . . and immediately wanted to tell everyone." The instant that it was confirmed, he informed his father that he was going to be a grandfather. "You're going to be a gray-headed granddaddy," he teased him in the doctor's waiting room, as father and son shared a moment of unalloyed joy.

Priscilla was determined not to let pregnancy interfere with her normal life; "as far as I was concerned, the less people mentioned about my looking pregnant, the better," and she went on a program to lose, rather than to gain, weight. She experienced periods of despondency nonetheless, and she made no attempt to hide her deepest feelings from Joanie Esposito, who observed that "it just took all the glow off." For all of Priscilla's deepseated ambivalence, Elvis' own feelings seemed to run remarkably true. When Priscilla, in a moment of despair, confessed that she was contemplating abortion, Elvis said he would support her in whatever she chose to do. Brought face-to-face with the necessity of actually making a decision, she realized she couldn't go through with it. "'It's our baby,' I said, sobbing. 'I could never live with myself, neither could you.' There were no words, only his smile of approval; he held me tightly in his arms as I cried." And when he announced her pregnancy on the movie set, handing out cigars to cast and crew, he showed nothing but paternal pride, mixed with the understandable bewilderment of most first-time fathers. "This is the greatest thing that has ever happened to me," he told reporters. "We really hadn't planned to have a baby this soon. [When] Priscilla told me the good news . . . [at first] I was so shocked I didn't think I could move for a while. Then it began to dawn on me this is what marriage is all about." The Colonel confessed that he, too, was surprised, "but I've already got a contract drawn up for the new Presley singer."

MARTY WOULD BE DISMISSED before the movie was over, sent back to Mississippi to join Alan on the ranch. There, under the increasing influence of pills and depression, "all I really did was sleep," working as a caretaker and relief guard before going off the payroll for good in September. To Marty it was all part of an alliance of convenience between Vernon and Priscilla, cleverly encouraged by the Colonel, to cut spending and place Priscilla's friends in positions of power. There was no longer any question of who was mistress of the house, and Elvis and Priscilla spent the rest of the summer finishing up the movie, enjoying a long visit from Vernon and Dee, and on weekends getting away to Palm Springs with Joanie and Joe, where they relaxed and enjoyed themselves under the Colonel's watchful eye.

The Colonel continued to violate his own long-standing rule never to mix business and pleasure. Whether out of concern for Elvis' narrow escape from the clutches of mystical messianism, or out of approval for Elvis' newfound matrimonial state, the Colonel and his wife continued to socialize openly with the young people, frequently including Joe and Joanie in their Sunday dinner invitations. After dinner, in time-honored fashion, the men would talk among themselves, puffing on their cigars, while the women more often than not played Yahtzee with Mrs. Parker, who made up her own rules and never stopped complaining about being abandoned by her husband all week while he was off on a Hollywood movie lot.

Joan Esposito appreciated Colonel's sense of humor and his affection for her children, whose bedroom was filled with stuffed animals from his office. "One night in L.A. Joe called and said, 'Colonel wants to come home for dinner.' I said, 'We're having sloppy joes.' He told Colonel, who said he was so tired of restaurant food that would be perfect. So he came over and ate with us, and he just made you feel like he really appreciated it." Another time, driving back from Palm Springs with Joe, he suggested that they stop and split a beer. "I realized I'd never seen him drink before — not once. So I said, 'Did you ever drink, Colonel Parker?' He said, 'I can't drink.' He said, 'I completely change when I drink, my personality does, I get very mean. That's why I don't drink.'"

It was a whole different view of the Colonel than either Joe or his employer had ever seen, watching him putter endlessly around the pool area to which Mrs. Parker had banished him from the fussy plastic-wrapped neatness of the house, pointing out some new feature on the out-door barbecue that was his pride and joy. There was a little rock waterfall garden with a miniature Dutch windmill; he had a stove and a fully stocked refrigerator, another windmill on top of a white trellis, and everything was painted blue and white. It was never too hot for him; he loved to sit out in his deck chair, baking like a lobster in the hot, dry desert sun and telling them of his dogcatcher days in Tampa or life with the carnival, explaining once again the disappearing hot dog trick or (Elvis' favorite) how you took the customer for twenty-five cents on every ticket by pretending to make change with a quarter welded to the inside of your pinky ring.

As fond as he sometimes felt toward the old man, however, and as much as he appreciated his antics, Elvis was under no illusions as to why the Colonel wanted him in Palm Springs, and there was no question in anyone else's mind that he resented it. Everyone had the same sense of being under scrutiny, but for Elvis it was particularly acute since he was the prime object of observation. Jerry was the Colonel's principal driver to and from Palm Springs at this point. If he were not down for the weekend himself, Jerry would leave Los Angeles early Monday morning, arriving two hours later to collect the Colonel for his four- or five-day work week. "Lots of times I'd have breakfast with the Colonel when I got there or chitchat with Mrs. Parker — she was always saying, 'I just wish the Colonel would stay here.' Then I'd load up the car, and we'd drive back to L.A. with the windows rolled up and Colonel smoking cigars. And that's when he would start probing me about what was going on. It was the scariest thing in the world to me at first. I mean, he would always say he had nothing to do with Elvis' personal life. He had *everything* to do with Elvis' personal life, from our going to Palm Springs in the first place, where he could come and check up on us to — everything." Jerry didn't pretend to understand it all, but he knew that if Colonel had come right out and said what was on his mind, Elvis would probably just have blown. And if Elvis had expressed any of his own resentment, Colonel might have said things he could never take back. So they continued to circle each other warily, like an old married couple locked in a relationship from which neither could see any escape.

Business showed no signs of picking up. *Easy Come, Easy Go,* the picture made at Paramount the previous fall, had confirmed all of Hal Wallis' worst fears, failing even to recoup its costs (it grossed less than $2 million when it came out in March), with the soundtrack EP bottoming out at 36,000 sales. *Double Trouble,* released in April, did little better, with the soundtrack album selling approximately 185,000 but topping out in the high forties on the charts (in comparison, say, to 1964–65's *Roustabout,* which sold nearly half a million and went to number one on the charts). There was some consolation in the steady sales of the gospel album, *How Great Thou Art* (on its way to nearly three-quarters of a million units sold over the next few years), and in the moderate success (400,000 sales) of the year's first single, the song Lamar had originally brought to the first Felton Jarvis session, "Indescribably Blue." In addition, with only three pictures left on the MGM contract and National General alone exhibiting any real interest in future projects, the movie cupboard was just about bare. Others might have sought solace or found false hope in the occasional success, the unreadable blip on the horizon, but Colonel was never one to hypnotize himself with pipe dreams. It was clear that changes were going to have to be made — by both Mr. Presley and himself. Figures, as the Colonel well knew, didn't lie.

The first result should not have been unexpected, though it may well have been coincidental: by the end of the summer Elvis had virtually shut down the Circle G ranch. Expenses, of course, had long since spun out of control, but the principal factor in his decision seems to have been that after six months Elvis had simply grown tired of the cowboy life. Most of the Ranchero pickups were gone by now; the mobile homes that were to have been the basis for his commune were being sold off one by one; the Santa Gertrudis cattle that Vernon had dreamed would make him a gentleman rancher were on the block; even Alan had been given notice that his days as ranch foreman were numbered. The word among the guys and all the various Presley and Smith relatives who depended upon Elvis for their living was that Colonel had warned him that he was going broke; Gladys' brother Travis, a gate guard like Vester Presley, said that he had heard that Elvis was spending $500,000 a month just to keep things running. And even though no one really believed that Elvis would ever run out of money, least of all Elvis himself, he appeared for once to be acting on prudent financial advice.

Of greater long-term consequence was the whole business of his recording career. In June the decision had been made not to return to Nashville but to record in Los Angeles instead. It was a decision that may well have been taken principally for reasons of geographical convenience, but it seems more than likely that ditching the Nashville musicians with whom Elvis had become so comfortable, as well as the familar surroundings of RCA's Studio B, was part of the same attempt to "modernize" his sound that had begun with the introduction of Felton Jarvis the year before. Moreover, although Felton was still slated to produce the August session, and RCA's principal Nashville engineer Jim Malloy was being flown in to work the board, a new arranger-contractor had usurped much of the function that a producer ordinarily serves, hiring the musicians, helping to choose the material, and generally taking part in areas in which no one but Elvis or RCA had previously been involved.

Billy Strange, a flamboyant, thirty-seven-year-old session guitarist and entrepreneur who had grown up in the music business (his father was a well-known California country radio personality), had gained a foothold with Elvis and the Colonel, both from past soundtrack session work and from his connection with Elvis' most recent co-star, Nancy Sinatra. A big bluff man, not at all shy about proclaiming his qualifications, he was tied in with the new wave of Hollywood writers, producers, and studio players that in 1966 had helped create Nancy Sinatra's brief but explosive hit-making career. Billy shared with Elvis a taste for motorcycle riding and got along well with the guys, but mostly he just seemed like the right kind of person to accommodate himself to a situation that called for a different approach — but not a radically different one.

The aim of the session was straightforward enough: two singles, four or five "bonus" tracks for the upcoming *Clambake* album (which would have only seven songs from the actual soundtrack), and an Easter single if possible. Billy's conception of the sound was contemporary country as played by crack L.A. musicians, with a brass section and fully worked-out arrangements, but he was as confounded as any of his predecessors by Elvis' all-over-the-map approach. Every time he thought he had the reper-toire worked out and started to sketch in some arrangements, the lineup was apt to shift radically once again, and Elvis' enthusiasms (communi-cated now via Charlie Hodge) sent him scurrying to run down titles he might up till that moment never even have heard of.

Elvis resurrected Della Reese's "After Loving You" (originally an Eddy Arnold number) and Ray Peterson's "The Wonder of You" for the session. Both had been strong contenders the previous May, and he added to them such old favorites as Sanford Clark's rockabilly classic from 1956, "The Fool," Johnny Ace's posthumous 1955 r&b chart-topper, "Pledging My Love," and the Golden Gate Quartet's "Born Ten Thousand Years Ago," to which Charlie had introduced him in Germany. That summer he heard a new song on the radio called "Guitar Man" by fellow RCA artist Jerry Reed, and Freddy was instructed to work out the publishing on that, too, as well as on the old Jimmy Reed blues "Baby What You Want Me to Do?" and one of Vernon's all-time country favorites, "From a Jack to a King." Freddy's mind unfortunately wasn't really focused on the business at hand. Hill and Range had recently been forced to divest itself of its foreign publishing, and Freddy had been chosen to take over his cousins' holdings in Great Britain, with the presumption that his interests would be their interests. He appar-ently saw this as an opportunity to establish an independent identity, and as a result he was even less responsive than usual to the Colonel's and Tom Diskin's constant prodding. Nonetheless, the session took shape, and Billy

Strange felt that he was prepared for any eventuality as they got ready to go into the studio on the evening of Tuesday, August 22. That very day, however, Richard Davis ran over and killed a Japanese gardener who stepped out from behind a hedge on a curve that screened any view from the road. It was too late to notify Felton and Jim Malloy, who were already on flights coming into L.A., but Colonel, sensing that there might be a lawsuit brewing, and wanting at all costs to keep Elvis out of it, canceled the session, suggesting to Joe that it might be better for them all to get out of town for a few days. So Elvis, Joe, Priscilla, Charlie, Billy, and Gee Gee all headed for Las Vegas, where they remained for a couple of days before returning to Memphis without the session ever taking place at all.

I T WAS RESCHEDULED FOR NASHVILLE on September 10, with all thought of Billy Strange's participation evidently forgotten and, in its place, a new focus, the recording of the Jerry Reed song whose driving acoustic sound Elvis couldn't get out of his head. Felton at this point was feeling increasingly hamstrung in his role as producer without portfolio, a kind of glorified cheerleader who could suggest neither material nor direction. As much as he loved Elvis and as thrilled as he still was by being in a position to contribute anything to the music, Felton couldn't help but conclude that he was in a box. He couldn't call a rehearsal session, he couldn't get Elvis to learn the material ahead of time, he couldn't even be sure that Elvis would show up. The only thing he felt confident of was his ability to establish an atmosphere that allowed Elvis to sound like he did "when he was just in there singing to himself" — and he was frequently thwarted even in that by the politics of the situation. As second engineer Al Pachucki saw it, it was like a marbles game, with everyone competing on one level or another for Elvis' attention, to the detriment of the business at hand. "That was a scene to see. Freddy would have his stack of records, and Lamar would walk in and slip his record on top. And then Freddy would do the same thing. And I would say, 'Man, I don't believe it. Look at these dudes, man, trying to get their material cut.'"

At least this time there was some clear sense of direction, as the session kicked off with a rundown of "Guitar Man" — but it soon became apparent that there was no way they were going to get the Jerry Reed sound without Jerry Reed himself. Someone said they thought Reed had gone fishing, but nobody was sure how to get hold of him until Chet's assistant,

Mary Lynch, was finally able to locate him on the phone, and he agreed to come in. When he arrived, he looked, said Felton, "like a sure-enough Alabama wild man. You know, he hadn't shaved in about a week, and he had them old clogs on — that was just the way he dressed. He come in and Elvis looked at him and said, 'Lord, have mercy, what is that!'"

Reed was a genuine individualist, even in Nashville terms. Thirty years old, like Felton a native of Atlanta and a graduate of the Bill Lowery School of Music, he had been writing songs and making records off and on for over ten years. He got session work through an admiring Chet Atkins after moving to Nashville in 1962, but he had not really enjoyed any recording success until signing with RCA in 1965. "Guitar Man," which had reached number fifty-three in the country field just a few months earlier, was his first record even to chart. Nonetheless, Reed, a whirlwind of energy with a ready supply of infectious charm and irrepressible enthusiasm, was never bashful about his talent. He had strong opinions of his own from the start and never wavered in his belief that if he was going to make it, he was going to make it *his* way. "I never thought of myself as a Nashville record-ing musician. 'Cause I was a stylist. I [could] only play my stuff. And I wasn't worth a damn playing all that other stuff.

"See, I had my own tuning, and they were trying to record 'Guitar Man,' and they couldn't make it feel like my record. And I forget if it was Pete Drake or Charlie McCoy or Chip Young — one of those musicians said, 'Well, these guitar players in here are playing with straight picks, and, you know, Reed plays with his fingers.' So they called me, and I went down, and I hooked up that electric gut string, tuned the B-string up a whole tone, and I toned the low E-string down a whole tone, so I could bar straight across, and as soon as we hit the intro, you could see Elvis' eyes light up — he knew we had it."

Reed immediately took over the session. You can hear it from the first notes of the first take — Reed is coaching the musicians, encouraging them, egging them on, with Felton happy just to be presiding over some-thing that is actually *happening*. There is a bright, shimmering surface to the music different in many respects from anything Elvis has ever recorded before but providing, at the same time, the kind of churning, driving rhythm that has characterized Elvis' music from the first. There is not the slightest question of Elvis' engagement. There is no self-deprecation, there is no wisecracking; all of the singer's attention is focused on the music. By the fifth take he has started to fool around with the song, introducing a hint of Ray Charles' "What'd I Say" on the outro, which by the tenth take has evolved into a full-blown quote so infectious that everyone just bursts out laughing.

Reed himself felt nothing but pure delight. "It was just a jamming session. I thought I was going to be so damn nervous I couldn't play, but it was right the opposite. I got pumped, and then Elvis got pumped, and the more he got pumped up, the more I did — it was like a snowball effect. To tell you the truth, I was on cloud nine. And once Elvis got the spirit, things really began to happen. When the guitars and the rhythm sounded right, I guess the guitar lick kind of reminded him of 'What'd I Say,' and he just sort of started testifying at the end. That was how it happened — one of those rare moments in your life you never forget."

They jumped, almost without pausing for breath, into the Jimmy Reed blues standard "Big Boss Man," and once again you can hear the "Alabama wild man" pushing, prodding, encouraging, contributing his exuberant personality and musicianship to every note. The whole room is reverberating by now, and Elvis is obviously totally at ease. On the seventh take he yells out, "Go apeshit!," and it is clear that everyone is relaxed and having fun. "That's a gas, man," Felton announces at one point. Elvis has roughened his voice for the blues, a tactic of which Felton obviously approves. He adjures Elvis to sound "like you're mad, like you're mean." By the time that they nail the song in eleven carefree takes, it feels like everyone is ready to go on all night long.

But then politics entered the picture once again. Freddy was supposed to have cleared the publishing on "Guitar Man" for the Billy Strange session, but whether due to the exigencies of his new business situation or because it had simply slipped his mind when he went on vacation the previous month, he had somehow neglected to approach Jerry Reed about it, a situation of which he now became embarrassingly aware. He got Lamar to try to deal with the songwriter (who held his own publishing), but Reed was in no mood to be bullied or sold out. "I remember saying, 'Why didn't you tell me this before I come here? I could have saved you all a lot of effort.' I started to get emotional now. I said, 'You done wasted Elvis' time. You done wasted all these musicians' time, and RCA's time: I'm not going to give you my soul.'" At this point Freddy got into it. Session leader Scotty Moore, who had witnessed his share of confrontations over the years, and even been involved in one or two, observed the scene admiringly. "They got Jerry off in a corner, but he wouldn't sell."

Of course, it helped his position to know the song had already been cut and that Elvis loved it. Even for as independent a spirit as Jerry Reed, that knowledge could only have been emboldening. "I said, 'I know how important it is to have an Elvis Presley cut. I mean, I'm thrilled to death. And we can work out a split on this record — because I do appreciate the importance of it, and what it means. But,' I said, 'you are not going to get any of the copyright on this damn song.' He said, 'You know, it will be an important copyright.' And I said, 'I understand that, Mr. Bienstock.' But I wasn't really listening, because I had my side of the argument in concrete anyway. I can remember him saying, 'You know the record is not going to come out if we can't work out some kind of an arrangement here.' And I said, 'Mr. Bienstock, I'll put it to you this way. You don't need the money, and Elvis don't need the money, and I'm making more money than I can spend right now — so why don't we just forget we ever recorded this damn song?'"

The musicians watched practically open-mouthed. Nobody could recall a time when business had intruded so nakedly into an Elvis Presley session; everyone was aware of the arbitrariness of the rules, but no one had ever seen them challenged so boldly before. The upshot was that Reed left in high dudgeon and the session stumbled on, but the heart had long since gone out of it when they finally gave up at 5:30 in the morning. The next night they were back to the same old grind, fumbling around for songs, settling for the best of a mediocre lot, trying somehow just to get Elvis through. Elvis himself remained thoroughly professional, he didn't complain and did all that he could to work up some kind of enthusiasm, even on the most stubbornly recalcitrant material. It wasn't a bad session, and Elvis took over the piano bench for "You'll Never Walk Alone," the Rodgers and Hammerstein ballad which had been one of his favorites ever since Roy Hamilton's inspirational r&b version in 1954. He sang with all the full-throated fervor of Hamilton or Jake Hess, and although his playing remained necessarily limited, both rhythmically and melodically, it was always a measure of his engagement when he sat down at the keyboard to play. There was a moment when session guitarists Chip Young and Harold Bradley tried to get things going by playing a few bars from "Hi-Heel Sneakers," a 1964 Tommy Tucker hit with much the same bluesy appeal as "Big Boss Man." Elvis leapt to the bait, and they did a fine version of the song, but afterward Harold was told by Felton never to do that again. "I said, 'Do what?' He said, 'Pitch any songs.' He said Freddy Bienstock went bananas. I said, 'Okay, I didn't know, I thought we were making records.

If I had known we were playing games, I wouldn't have pitched it.' I said I wouldn't do it again."

The session broke off at 3:30 in the morning, with everyone feeling more than a little dispirited. On balance they had achieved what they set out to do: in two nights they had recorded nine separate songs, including a couple of singles, some B sides, and some album filler. But they never came close to recapturing the feeling they had glimpsed for the few hours that Jerry Reed was in the studio the previous night; it had slipped through their fingers, and no one knew how to get it back.

THERE WAS ABOUT A MONTH before the next film was scheduled to begin, and Elvis spent most of it watching two or three movies a night at the Memphian Theatre, traveling back and forth to the ranch on many days but doing more shooting than riding. Friday, September 29 was declared Elvis Presley Day by Tennessee Governor Buford Ellington, and Elvis celebrated by shooting off fireworks at Graceland all day (Billy got burned and Elvis did, too) and getting drunk at the Memphian that night, seemingly embarrassed, even while he was in the midst of the experience, by his public loss of control. Priscilla was supervising the upstairs redecoration of Graceland in preparation for the baby's arrival and remained determined not to let her condition restrict her in any way. An accomplished (and highly competitive) rider, she insisted on continuing to ride bareback until one day, as stable manager Mike McGregor watched, her horse, Diamond, swerved, and she went flying through the air. By the time that Mike got to her, "she was sitting in a mud puddle, a streak on her cheek . . . laughing." Priscilla told everyone about her adventure, and everyone marveled at her gutsiness and determination to keep going, even if some wondered about her common sense. Elvis tried to get her to promise to be more careful in future, but in Priscilla's mind it was part of a pact she had made with herself: she was going to have to show the same kind of reckless abandon that Elvis did if she wanted to be able to maintain any degree of self-respect.

ELVIS WAS BACK IN NASHVILLE on October 1 for the soundtrack re-cording of his new MGM picture, Stay Away, Joe. Scheduled to go into production the following week, it seemed at first glance a complete change of pace, a social satire that pitted Indian ingenuity against government bureaucracy and was to be shot entirely on location in Sedona, Arizona.

Elvis' character was an Indian rodeo rider named Joe Whitecloud, "a wheeler-dealer who's always promoting something," from Elvis' point of view. He had high hopes that this film would provide him with "a more grown-up character," a role that he could play in sophisticated fashion somewhere between Paul Newman's Hud and Michael Caine's Alfie. That they were recording only three titles for the picture might have added to his overall optimism, except for the fact that one of the numbers, "Dominick," was written to be sung to a bull.

In a rare moment of candor Elvis told Harry Jenkins, the RCA vice president in charge of Elvis Presley product, who was present at the session, "God, Harry, I don't want to record this." He begged Felton, only half-jokingly, that if he ever died, "Promise me they won't put this out." Even Colonel was aware that Freddy had achieved a new low in terms of supplying soundtrack material, a fact of which he informed MGM marketing vice president Clark Ramsay somewhat obliquely in a telephone conversation the following day. Elvis had simply come up against "a blank wall" in the studio, Colonel apprised the MGM executive, and while he had done everything that was asked of him, and done it without complaint, the Colonel just wanted to go on record as to what the creative situation really was. It was as close to outright criticism in nonbusiness affairs as the Colonel was ever likely to come, but it was addressed to the wrong party. The Colonel might better have directed his criticism at himself.

The picture started a week later in Sedona, after Elvis had detoured for a few days with some of the guys to Las Vegas. The director, Peter Tewksbury, had a long and successful track record in comedy, though mostly in television (he had directed the long-running situation comedies *Father Knows Best* and *My Three Sons*), and the cast was somewhat better than usual, with veteran actors Burgess Meredith, Thomas Gomez, and Katy Jurado lending a touch of professionalism to the proceedings. Elvis rose to the occasion up to a point, offering his warmest and most relaxed performance since *Follow That Dream,* one of his last out-and-out attempts at an actual movie rather than an *Elvis Presley* movie, and perhaps his only legitimate comedy. Unfortunately, *Stay Away, Joe* lacked the earlier movie's coherence, story line, and point of view. It was a disaster, and everyone knew it was a disaster, a fireworks display without a payoff.

Still, they had fun on location. The Colonel clowned around, having his picture taken in the pool with several days' growth of beard and a mean snarl on his face, then getting the picture printed up in the same form as the Elvis pocket calendar that RCA gave out as a staple of its promotional material and proudly presenting it to fans, friends, and business acquaintances. The Colonel bought some ponies, too, and presented them to Elvis as a gift, with Alan Fortas and Mike McGregor coming out to pick them up and take them back to Memphis. More significantly, Elvis worked out an effective rapprochement with Sonny by getting him a speaking part in the picture, which certainly erased some of the resentment engendered by the wedding snub — even if Red continued to maintain his distance.

He repeated his hopes for the film in the form of the slightly shopworn mantra that he delivered to one of Colonel's chosen reporters, Joseph Lewis, on the set doing a story for *Cosmopolitan*. "I guess I'd like to prove myself as an actor, and to do that I'll have to take more chances. You can learn an awful lot just by hanging out with real good professionals, and there isn't a day that goes by that I don't pick up on something from the other actors. Right now, I'm still taking little steps because I'm not all that sure of my ability. There's a lot more I want to do before I call myself an actor." For all of the brave talk, though, the sympathetic reporter saw Elvis as "bored and bemused," a paradox combining a "plastic grin" with an "orgiastic fury of movements." He came alive, Lewis concluded, only in the fight scenes, "all sinew and cartilage exploding with kinetic energy. . . . At the end of the day, he nurses a bruised cheek and a sore shoulder, but he is happy."

THERE WAS AN ANNOUNCEMENT in the Memphis newspapers during the first week of filming that there would be a public auction at the Circle G on November 4. Tractors, trailers, television sets, and miscellaneous farm equipment were to be sold off, and eventually $108,000 was raised, with two thousand potential buyers and fans in attendance at the auction. Colonel meanwhile was in a frenzy of activity, completing details on the upcoming Christmas radio special (he was buying a half hour of airtime on twenty-four hundred stations nationwide to play a selection of Elvis' Christmas and sacred tunes, "just our way of saying Merry Christmas"), completing the deal for next summer's picture with National General, and beginning negotiations with NBC on a new deal that seemed to be turning into something different from anything they had ever done before.

The radio special was straightforward enough, just a take-off on the Mother's Day specials they had done the previous two years, something for the fans. The National General contract had worked out pretty much the way that he had wanted, $850,000, plus 50 percent of the profits from the first dollar, but, according to Roger Davis, the William Morris lawyer who formally represented the deal, when Colonel tried to get the press to pick up on it as a significant industry story, he couldn't find any takers. Nor was he able to find any other studio willing to meet his asking price. "The aim was always the same: money," Davis observed. "The pictures weren't making any money, and nobody [else] was willing to come up with the kind of money the Colonel thought he should have. It was a matter of pride."

So he went to NBC. In October he contacted West Coast vice president Tom Sarnoff with the idea for a 1968 Christmas special. He had been in touch with Sarnoff off and on since 1965, when he proposed a picture that would premiere domestically with an NBC broadcast, then have a theatrical release throughout the rest of the world. Now he had come up with a scheme whereby NBC would get Elvis for his first television appearance in eight years, and in exchange the network would finance a motion picture which it could either produce itself or farm out to a mutually agreed-upon studio. The entire package would come in at the bargain price of $1,250,000 ($850,000 for the movie, plus an additional $25,000 for the music; a mere $250,000 for the special, with $125,000 reserved for a second showing). What this all meant, the Colonel said to Sarnoff, was that he would be getting for his client the $1,000,000 that he saw as a simple mark of respect, but NBC would be getting Elvis Presley at a steal.

Priscilla meanwhile had found a new home. Not content with either the privacy or the security arrangements that Rocca Place afforded, she had found a house atop a hill in the exclusive Trousdale Estates development. It offered a view overlooking all of Los Angeles, a location more discouraging of fan access, and, best of all, only four bedrooms, thereby ensuring some privacy for Elvis, Priscilla, and the baby. It would be their first real home, the first house in which they would live in Los Angeles that was not a rental; it would mark, Priscilla believed, a whole new beginning.

They bought it for something in excess of $400,000, and Priscilla began remodeling right away with the idea of moving in the following spring, after the baby was born. Elvis seemed genuinely enthusiastic, and they spoke more and more of making their home in California for most of the year. When they returned to Memphis, though, in mid December, Elvis shocked Priscilla by announcing that he thought maybe they should consider a trial separation. He needed some space, he said, he needed a chance to think, and he felt like they could both benefit from some time apart. At first she was completely taken aback. She was devastated, bewildered, and seriously questioned her self-worth. But then when nothing else happened and the subject was dropped, never to be brought up again, she decided it must have been something he felt guilty about, whether a thought or a deed — with her husband there was never any simple way of telling.

"Elvis would do things like that when he didn't feel worthy, or he felt that he'd been bad and he didn't want to hurt me. He seemed to feel better after he said it. He had so many ups and downs; life would basically inter-fere with his emotions, [sometimes] on a daily basis. If his father upset him, or one of the guys, sometimes he'd go upstairs and not come down for two or three days. He'd remove himself, stay in his room and not come down; he had a very difficult time confronting his emotions, confronting conflicts. But eventually he'd come out of it.

"You went with the ride. Basically, you just went with it. One thing that I realized was that he loved the chase. And once the chase was over, I knew I didn't have to worry on anything — whether it was a new game or a girl or somebody new coming into the group. He would always come home. And once you realized that about him, you knew it was just a matter of time; it just depended on how long he wanted to play the game, and whether you wanted to wait."

They spent much of the Christmas season saying good-bye to the Circle G. The horses that Elvis had decided to keep were being shipped back to Graceland, but for the time being they all continued to ride at the ranch, where hayrides and snowball fights were organized as part of an extended farewell. On New Year's Eve Elvis rented out the Thunderbird Lounge for a party that once again included fan club presidents, relatives, and friends. There was a strange mood at the party this year, as Flash and the Board of Directors, Vaneese Starks, and Billy Lee Riley all entertained with a pro-gram of Memphis rock and rhythm and blues. Early in the evening Elvis started drinking Bloody Marys and mocking Lamar mercilessly. By the end of the night Elvis, Vernon, and Lamar were all drunk, and Elvis was rag-ging Lamar that he couldn't even hold his head up straight. As if to prove his point, he grabbed an ice bucket and stuck Lamar's head in it, then called out, "Hey, Lamar," and laughed some more as Lamar half-lifted his head out of the bucket and gave Elvis a sheepish grin.

* * *

THERE WAS ANOTHER NASHVILLE session scheduled for January 15 and 16 to record a new title track and one additional number for *Stay Away, Joe* (MGM agreed in exchange to underwrite $10,000 of the session), along with some new material for RCA. In addition to session work, Scotty Moore had been running his own studio in Nashville for the last few years, mostly engineering sessions, and Elvis now asked him if he could transfer some of Elvis' old r&b and hillbilly 78s to tape. Nothing could be easier, Scotty told him, all he had to do was bring them over, so he carried them to the session in a specially made-up carrying case designed to reduce breakage, all the brightly colored discs of his youth. It must have brought back poignant memories to both men, as their minds were cast back momentarily to a time when they were just starting out, when there was no way of telling how it was all going to end. Big Joe Turner, Ray Charles, Fats Domino, Hank Snow's "I'm Gonna Bid My Blues Goodbye," The Dominoes, Ivory Joe Hunter, The Four Lads. Here were the originals of "Lawdy, Miss Clawdy" by Lloyd Price, Big Mama Thornton's "Hound Dog" and "Baby, Let's Play House" by Arthur Gunter (both cracked), Lowell Fulson's "Reconsider Baby." A lifetime of experiences, a lifetime of memories — another lifetime.

Jerry Reed was back for the session, strictly as a guitar picker this time — everyone had gotten such a kick out of his playing, and Felton, for one, had quietly appreciated the stand he had taken, as he let Jerry know some weeks after the September date. Freddy had eventually worked out a cut-in deal with him on the publishing, with Elvis Presley Music participating only in Elvis' version of the song, which was about to come out as the new single that very week. No new material had been requested from Reed, however, and he was under no illusions that he would be asked for any.

They had a hard time settling on anything at first. That wasn't unusual in and of itself, but Elvis was in an odd mood — seemingly preoccupied one minute, belligerent the next, revealing himself in a fashion that few of the musicians had witnessed before. For all of the scrutiny that he was constantly under, Elvis ordinarily showed as little of his hidden self to these men as he did to the casual outsider. Just as on the movie set, he was invariably observed to be polite, deferential, soft-spoken — to the less sympathetic observer somewhat passive perhaps, definitely immature. Now, on the contrary, he was swaggering, boastful, profane, in a way that many of them didn't fully recognize. To Ray Walker, who had come in for his first session with the Jordanaires in 1958, it was a perplexing turnabout. "Presley had such a unique way of becoming what you needed him to be at the moment. That's where it really kind of surprised us. Because there were two terms that just made him furious in his early life: 'bastard' and 'sonofabitch.' He just couldn't stand them. And he never took the Lord's name in vain. In fact, around us he would never use 'slang' until this session, [but here] things got jokingly rough; there was some language going on."

There appeared to be very little suitable new material — once again Freddy had failed to do his job, and Elvis amused himself by chucking the acetates that Freddy and Lamar had submitted one after another up against the wall. Finally, after several hours, they settled on an old favorite, Chuck Berry's "Too Much Monkey Business," on which there was clearly no chance of a publishing deal. Elvis jumped into the song with both feet, egged on by Jerry Reed's guitar. Just as he had with "Guitar Man," Reed took a fresh, fundamentally acoustic approach, with an emphasis on the kind of light, dancing rhythm that drew as much from bluegrass and Elvis' Sun sides as it did from either contemporary country or rock 'n' roll. Evidently emboldened by their success, they next took up "Goin' Home," a tune Lamar had come up with for the picture, and struggled through thirty torturous takes. Over and over you can hear Elvis break off singing to the accompaniment of raucous laughter and forced hilarity from the guys. Over and over he fails to get past the first verse, declaring at one point, "I just don't know what I can do to improve this except *go home*." When they finally broke off at five in the morning, they had an acceptable master take but not much else, certainly nothing in the way of either good feeling or any sense of accomplishment.

The next night started out even worse. "Stay Away," the new title track, written to the melody of "Greensleeves," was no improvement on "Goin' Home," and Elvis continued to explode with inappropriate profanities and inexplicable displays of temper for the four hours that it took to get through it. There was more ridicule, more scornful rejection of Freddy and Lamar's offerings, until, finally, with the session in utter disarray and the participants in various stages of desperation, Jerry Reed was induced to submit a song that Felton thought might be suitable for Elvis, a talking blues called "U.S. Male" that had come out on an album that spring. Reed was, naturally, reluctant to repeat his previous experience, but by this time Freddy was so anxious for anything to come out of this session he probably would have offered Reed a cut-in on one of *his* songs. Jerry played the song for Elvis out in the hallway, and Elvis liked it, so they set out to get it on tape.

There was no doubt about the immediate pickup of energy that the song provided, and the braggadocio quality of its lyrics turned out to be a good match for Elvis' mood. But the strange vibes persisted, and after just one take, Elvis drifted off into a "blue" version of "The Prisoner's Song," which began "If I had the wings of an angel and the balls of a big hairy coon/I'd fly to the highest mountain and cornhole the man in the moon." On the next take, he declares, "I'm a fucked-up U.S. Male," which at this point he may very well have been. Two more songs like that, declared Felton, unable at this point to hide his exasperation, and they could have a complete "party album." And so it went, until they finally got a successful take, one that could certainly join "Guitar Man" and "Big Boss Man" in its brightness, differentness, and overall sense of engagement, but one that came from a very different place.

What could have been bothering Elvis so? Perhaps it was no more than what Priscilla observed when she made note of her husband's constant up-and-down mood swings, a tendency not helped by his constant intake of "medication." But in some ways it appears to have been something more than that. The Colonel was unquestionably taking care of business — Elvis could *see* that, if only by the flurry of promotional activity that surrounded each new movie, every new single release. The problem was that this single-minded "exploitational" approach was no longer working. Because of the quarrel over publishing, "Guitar Man" had not initially come out as a single, and when "Big Boss Man" took its place in October, it sold no more than any other single, a disappointing 350,000 copies. It didn't sound the same to Elvis either, it didn't sound anything like the acetate RCA had shipped him: the bass wasn't as strong, the vocal had been pushed too far out in front. The Colonel, Elvis was convinced and told anyone who would listen, was continuing to mess with his music. He became almost obsessive on the subject, carefully comparing the acetate that the record company sent him with his memory of how the song had sounded in the studio and then with the record that was ultimately released, refusing to listen to RCA vice president Harry Jenkins' arguments that nothing had been altered, recordings simply sounded different depending on time, place, even mood, and, of course, equipment.

It had become an almost symbolic argument that required no response, as Elvis focused more and more on differences of vision between his manager and himself, and what had come across for so many years as benign encouragement now sounded more and more like woeful ignorance on the

Colonel's part. Colonel's uncritical embrace of his music, his assertion that the fans just wanted to hear Elvis' voice, not all this instrumentation and fancy arrangements, was just one more maddening proof that the old man didn't know what he was talking about. It was the same argument that almost every artist has had with himself at one time or another, and deep down Elvis may well have known that what he was most frustrated by was his own inability to follow through, his own inability to commit to a sustained work process. But the Colonel remained an easy target, and there must have been a sense of panic on Elvis' part as the one thing the Colonel had always stood for, an unwavering instinct for business and its payoff in cold hard cash, was no longer proving effective.

It was little consolation, then, when Colonel told him right around the time of the session that the NBC deal had gone through. From Elvis' point of view this was just another one of the Colonel's schemes. He knew Colonel's mind: all Colonel wanted to get out of it was another fucking Christmas album, and what did he want to stand up and sing a bunch of Christmas carols on national TV for? He felt angry and frustrated, he felt like Colonel was turning him into a joke. The one person he could talk to about his doubts and fears, Sri Daya Mata, had been declared off-limits, and he had been made to feel ashamed of his association with her. If he could have expressed anything of his feelings to his manager — but Colonel didn't want to hear about his feelings, because that would have meant that Colonel had to reveal feelings of his own. Even his father, as close as they were, couldn't fully understand. He was alone.

PRISCILLA GAVE BIRTH to a baby girl at 5:01 P.M. on February 1, after nine hours of labor. Elvis paced the waiting room just like any other expectant father, except the waiting room was a doctors' lounge specially set aside for Elvis and his entourage, and he had well over a dozen friends, family, and police security in attendance. Their arrival had been something of a comedy of errors. They had a carefully worked-out plan, with a decoy car to divert reporters, but when it came time to put the plan into action, someone forgot to tell the driver, Jerry Schilling, that they had switched hospitals, and Charlie had to convince him that it was Baptist General, not Methodist, where Priscilla would be having the baby. Elvis, too, was in something of a state of nerves. He was practically beside himself when Priscilla insisted on taking a shower and carefully applying her makeup after her water broke, but then he wasn't ready himself even after she was standing at the door, and he had to be reminded by his grandmother that it was Priscilla, not he, who was having the baby. When the doctor came out and told him he was the father of a girl, he passed out cigars and declared himself to be the happiest man in the world.

The baby was named Lisa Marie. If it had been a boy, the proud parents said, they would have called him John Barron, and while Priscilla denied that there was any particular significance to either name — and there may well not have been — it could not have been lost upon Elvis that the Colonel would take the baby's middle name to be a tribute to his wife. There was no further talk, in any case, of naming the baby Gladys after his mother, as he had told friends over the years that he might and declared to reporter Jim Kingsley that he planned to do in a 1965 interview in the *Commercial Appeal*.

They left the hospital four days later. Elvis was wearing a pale blue suit with a paler blue turtleneck, Priscilla a pink mini-dress, with her hair set in a big bouffant that had required the arrival of a hairdresser before she was ready to leave. There were about a hundred fans and student nurses gathered outside the hospital entrance, with patients and other nurses craning out the windows to get a glimpse of the celebrity couple as they left in a caravan of Cadillacs and Lincolns, Elvis and Charlie and Jerry and Joe and all the rest. "She's a little miracle," he told his dentist, Les Hofman, when Hofman came out to the house a few days later with his wife, Sterling, to visit. During the day, the Hofmans noted, the baby was kept in a crib downstairs between the kitchen and the back den, and Elvis could scarcely leave her alone — he kept picking her up so much that Priscilla finally had to tell him to put her down. But later in their visit, when Elvis started talking about going back to work, maybe even going out on tour, "Priscilla said, 'I'm going with you, wherever you go.' And he said, 'You're not dragging that baby around.' She was eleven days old," Sterling Hofman observed, "and I saw a look right then."

On February 14 he and Priscilla placed a wreath of red roses and another of white carnations on Gladys' grave with a card signed "Elvis-Priscilla-Lisa Marie." He left orders at the office that the card should be burned along with the flowers once the flowers wilted. They had a steady stream of visitors at the house, and Elvis went riding almost every day, spending more time with the fans at the gate than he had in many months. Priscilla's family stayed for three weeks, and he presented her eighteen-year-old brother Donnie with a brand-new Mustang before they left.

He remained at home for most of the month before flying out to California to start the next picture, which would eventually be called *Live a Little, Love a Little* and was based on Dan Greenburg's well-received comic novel *Kiss My Firm but Pliant Lips*. Like *Stay Away, Joe,* it was an attempt to cast Elvis in a somewhat unfamiliar role (he played a successful photographer) and show off his comedic talent, but it was as tired and stale as any of the other recent pictures, and with Norman Taurog directing once again and Michael Hoey, who had written the screenplay for *Stay Away, Joe,* performing the same function here, it wasn't any funnier. The soundtrack consisted of only four songs, with recording overseen by Billy Strange, the arranger-contractor for the canceled August session. No Nashville musicians were used; in fact, Strange called upon virtually the same lineup of top L.A. studio players that he had booked in August. Not surprisingly, the sound was altogether different from Felton's sessions — with elaborate orchestrations and a score that ranged from sophisticated Sinatra material to Danny Kaye children's songs to Jimmy Webb–influenced folk funk. The results were no more successful (almost all of the songs were wordy and awkward in the extreme), but they did represent a different direction, and Billy Strange brought in a talented young songwriter named Mac Davis, whose work gave promise for the future. Perhaps the only other notable aspect of the picture was that Red, working regularly as a stuntman and actor now both in television and the movies, played a bit part and staged one of his famous fight scenes with Elvis. They still kept their distance — Red was still hurt about the wedding — but his presence on the set represented a kind of silent acknowledgment on Elvis' part. It was as close to an apology as he could come.

Elvis and Priscilla, meanwhile, were enjoying a newfound domesticity in their hilltop home in Trousdale Estates. Only Charlie and Gee Gee and Patsy lived with them now, and as Charlie described it, the arrangement was idyllic. "Joe and Joanie had their own place. They came by the house a lot. So did the Colonel and his aide, Tom Diskin. The dining room table was one of the Colonel's favorite places. He loved to sit there and puff on a big cigar and tell Elvis stories about his past exploits. . . . It was a happy time for all of us."

Not so happy for Priscilla, though there was no question of who was in charge now. Most of the guys had been banished or had left; even Billy Smith had departed that spring to start a new life with his family in Memphis, and the fans who used to hang out at Perugia and Rocca Place were in some disarray under Priscilla's new rule. One weekend in April they all traveled to Las Vegas to see Tom Jones, who introduced Elvis warmly from the stage even as Elvis carefully studied his act. The following weekend they spent Easter at the new, more "secure" house they were renting in Palm Springs, with an Easter egg hunt on the front lawn (Elvis cheated) and, of course, a visit with Colonel and Mrs. Parker. Everything looked just the way it was supposed to look. But this vision of cheerful domesticity was not anything like the reality that Priscilla knew.

Since the birth of their child, Elvis had refused to make love to her. Not only that, he was making it more and more plain that he was no longer attracted to her physically in any way. "He is still withdrawn," she wrote in her diary. "It's been two months, and he still hasn't touched me. I'm getting concerned." "I embarrassed myself last night," she wrote on April 20. "I wore a black negligee, laid as close to Elvis as I could while he read. I guess it was because I knew what I wanted and was making it obvious. I kissed his hand, then each finger, then his neck and face. But I waited too long. His sleeping pills had taken effect. Another lonely night."

Elvis had told her before they were married that he had never been able to make love to any woman he knew to have had a child — but she had never thought that stricture could apply to her. Now, she wrote, she was beginning to question "my own sexuality as a woman." Her physical and emotional needs were unfulfilled. Not long afterward, in doubt and desperation, she embarked upon an affair with her dance instructor. It was the ultimate act of defiance in the Elvis world, where the men were permitted to do whatever they wanted but the women were always expected to know their place. Some of the guys raised questions with Elvis about all the time Priscilla was spending at the dance studio, but he didn't want to hear about it. It was impossible, he exploded. Why didn't they just leave her alone? She tried to keep it a secret even from her best friend, but Joanie Esposito knew there was definitely something going on. "She was taking so many classes, and then there was an incident at the house when I came over one Sunday afternoon and rang the bell and wasn't invited in. But, you know, I think it was almost an innocent thing that occurred, if you can call it that. She didn't have anyone else. Her family wasn't there. Everyone in the world is telling her how lucky she is, and, you know, it didn't mean a thing. She was very lonely." It was, Priscilla realized, a turning point in her life; it wasn't what she wanted, but it was what she needed. She needed to remind herself that she was still *there*.

"IF I CAN DREAM," JUNE 30, 1968.
(COURTESY OF JOSEPH A. TUNZI, J.A.T. PUBLISHING)

THE BLUEBIRD OF HAPPINESS

LVIS LEFT FOR HAWAII on May 17, the same day that he met the director and musical director of his upcoming television special for the first time. He had been talking with executive producer Bob Finkel, the man who had put together the package for NBC, for the past week, and gradually his feelings about the show had begun to shift. Finkel, after a series of meetings with the Colonel, had finally persuaded the sponsor (the Singer Sewing Company), the network, and, most important, the Colonel himself, to abandon the original plan of simply presenting an hour of Elvis singing Christmas songs on a bare stage. The Colonel, who Finkel sometimes thought just liked to make them all jump through hoops, was the last to give in, but in the end he conceded the point with relative equanimity: so long as the production remained a one-man show, and the record company was able to get a soundtrack album and Christmas single out of it, he would trust Mr. Finkel to make the creative decisions.

Finkel's talks with Elvis began immediately after his release from *Live a Little, Love a Little* on May 8, coincidentally the same day that the executive producer got all parties to agree on the new format for the show. At first he found Elvis "as most people who dealt with him on this kind of basis found him, very courteous and kind and respectful, as I mentioned to him what I thought we would do." At their initial encounter he got no indication of Elvis' true feelings about the show one way or another, but then, as they continued to meet, Finkel informed the network and Singer, he sensed a real change in Elvis' attitude, to the point where he made the "rather revealing statement . . . that he wants this show to depart completely from the pattern of his motion pictures and from everything else he has done." He even implied to Finkel that he was "not interested in what Colonel Parker has to say about this show; he 'wants everyone to know what he really can do. . . .'" This led Finkel to the question, "Who was I going to get to do it?"

He had had his eye on a young director named Steve Binder for some time now. Barely out of his twenties but already a veteran of close to a decade of television production, Binder had gone to work for Steve Allen after graduating from USC, then directed *Hullabaloo* (NBC's answer to *Shindig,* the highly successful prime-time weekly rock 'n' roll show) and a 1966 Leslie Uggams special, as well as the 1964 theatrical release *The T.A.M.I. Show,* one of the first concert films to be shot with light hand-held equipment, which had featured James Brown and the Rolling Stones, among others.

More recently, in association with his new partner, audio engineer Bones Howe, Binder had shot a bright, splashy, "mod" special starring Petula Clark, which had attracted a good deal of controversy when its pretty, blond British star embraced her principal guest, black singer and civil rights activist Harry Belafonte. To Finkel, Steve Binder was right in the thick of things. "I thought this was a guy who knew and understood the new music, so I decided, This is the guy for the job."

Binder was reluctant at first — Elvis didn't mean all that much to him. He was a fan of contemporary music: the Beatles, the Beach Boys, Jimmy Webb. But then when he talked to his partner about it, he discovered that Bones had worked with Elvis at Radio Recorders in 1956 and 1957 and was really excited about the idea: he thought Steve and Elvis would really hit it off. Elvis' approach to recording was very much like Steve's to doing a show, he told his partner — they both relied almost totally on feel. So a meeting with the Colonel was arranged.

That first meeting at MGM struck them both as a little bit like entering Ali Baba's cave. There were posters and flashing marquee signs and promotional material covering every wall of the Colonel's outer office. Everywhere you looked, Bones realized with a start, it said Elvis, "or there's his face or a catalogue or a gold record." Then when you went back through a maze of hallways, you arrived at the Colonel's private office, which consisted of a huge desk covered with papers and memorabilia and surrounded by giant pictures of Elvis, Elvis and the Colonel, the Colonel dressed up in a Snowman's outfit, the Colonel and Lyndon Johnson, the Colonel and Bob Hope. Tom Diskin's desk, much neater and about half the size of the Colonel's, was off to one side, and there was an enormous shipping room in which signs of busy activity could be glimpsed.

The meeting, like so many of Colonel's business get-togethers, was a 7:00 A.M. breakfast conference in his kitchen/"canteen," with its big stove, fully stocked freezer and refrigerator, and long table at the center of the room, at one end of which sat the great man himself in a high, straight-backed chair, looking for all the world, Bones thought, like the Wizard of Oz. "He showed us his memorabilia. He showed us scrapbooks of when he was a dogcatcher in Tampa, Florida." He told them stories, too, the usual assortment of tales about the carnival and his adventures in Hollywood, where — the point of the story always seemed to be — sharp city slickers were continually underestimating the poor old Colonel. Then he got to the point of the meeting. He said, "We're not going to tell you boys what to do creatively, because that's what we hired you for, but if you get out of line, we're going to let you know about it." He told them, "This is going to be the best special on the air, because we won't let it be bad." Then to their amazement he declared, "We don't care what material you submit for the show. If Mr. Presley likes it, Mr. Presley will do it. However, Mr. Presley must be the publisher of the material, or else we must communicate with the publisher, and arrangements must be made." At the end of the meeting he gave them both stuffed animals and a pocket calendar. He was confident that things were going to work out just fine, he said, in that gruff voice with its indeterminate accent, his face grizzled and unshaven but with the suggestion of a twinkle in his eye. "You guys are going to have a million-dollar experience," he told them with conviction, while fully aware that their million-dollar experience was limited to a $32,050 salary between them.

They emerged from the meeting dazzled and slightly confused. They had done nothing, and yet they had gotten everything — everything, that is, except for financial reward. Still, they never wavered. Steve was totally sold on the project by now, even more so than Bones. There was no question in his mind that this show was going to be culturally significant, and he had only one goal, which had as much to do with Steve Binder as it did with Elvis Presley: "to do something really important."

Elvis met with Binder and Howe that Friday at their offices on Sunset Boulevard. Joe and a couple of the guys waited in the reception room while they talked, and at first Steve didn't think he and Bones were getting through. He was so wound up by now, though, that nothing was going to stop his evangelical pitch. This was a chance to really say something to the world, he declared to Elvis; this was one of those rare opportunities to create something of genuine consequence; this was Elvis' chance to proclaim, through his music, *who he really was*. Bones, quieter, a little older and more reflective in manner than his partner, reminded Elvis of when they had worked together at Radio Recorders in the old days. They talked about the way that Elvis had made records back then — what had most impressed him about Elvis' sessions, Bones said, was that they were not dictated by the clock but by Elvis' own emotional commitment. That was how they would approach the special, Steve jumped back in — forget about the network, forget about the fancy trappings; they wanted to do a show that nobody else in the world could do but Elvis Presley. It would all stem from *his* life, *his* music, *his* experience, Steve said. How did he feel about that?

"Scared to death," Elvis replied, consciously deflecting the tension. Well, they'd have a show sketched out for him by the time he got back from Hawaii, Binder said, laughing. There'd be time for him to make his mind up about it then. For all that any of them knew, it could be the end of Elvis' career — but then again, it just might be the shot in the arm he so clearly needed at this juncture. It was Elvis' turn to laugh now, and they shook hands all around. He left their offices not really sure what he was letting himself in for but convinced that at least it was going to be *different*.

With Elvis gone, Binder and Howe worked furiously to nail down a team and put together a script. They already had writers Chris Bearde and Allan Blye onboard, and they quickly settled on costume designer Bill Belew, orchestrator and arranger Billy Goldenberg, set designer Gene McEvoy, and choreographers Claude Thompson and Jaime Rogers — all but Bearde veterans of either *Hullabaloo* or the Petula Clark special or both. With Bearde and Blye, Steve roughed out a story line similar in approach to what he had outlined to Elvis, seeking a subtext in the lyrics of songs Elvis had already sung that would tell the story of his musical life. The Colonel for his part continued to fence with Finkel and NBC, erupting at one point when someone at the network came up with the idea of Elvis doing a walk-on during one of NBC's regularly scheduled shows in order to promote the special. Mr. Presley would be happy to do a walk-on, Colonel wrote Tom Sarnoff on May 28, for $250,000. He knew Colonel Sarnoff would understand his not reducing the established price, the Colonel wrote, since he was sure NBC would not want to diminish in any way the value of its investment. Everything, in other words, was proceeding as normal.

Elvis meanwhile showed Priscilla Hawaii for the first time, took her to the memorial to the U.S.S. *Arizona,* where he proudly pointed out the plaque honoring Colonel Parker and himself, and brought his additional party of seven (Joe and Joanie, Charlie, Lamar and Nora Fike, and Patsy Presley Gambill and her husband, Gee Gee, had all come along on this "family vacation") to a karate championship put on by Ed Parker at the Honolulu International Center. It was the first time he had seen Ed since 1961, and the first time he had been able to attend the competition, which Parker had started in Long Beach in 1964. There was a flurry of introductions, and he spent much of the day talking karate with Ed and instructing Priscilla in some of the finer points of the sport and the particular strengths of each of the competitors, including twenty-five-year-old former champion Mike Stone, like Ed, a native Hawaiian, who had come out of a three-year retirement to compete in the tournament in which he had first won his name.

E LVIS RETURNED FROM HIS HOLIDAY thinner than he had been since he got out of the army, his sideburns longer, and, most significant, in a state of genuinely heightened anticipation about the show. Preproduction started on Monday, June 3, the day after his return. He reported to the Binder-Howe offices a little after 1:00 P.M., and, with the writers present, Steve ran through the approach that they had finally settled upon. At its heart was the Jerry Reed song "Guitar Man," which would be used as a kind of linking theme to tell a story that directly echoed Belgian playwright Maurice Maeterlinck's 1909 theater staple, *The Blue Bird*. In Maeterlinck's treatment a poor boy sets out to find fame and fortune and travels all over the world, only to discover in the end that happiness — in the form of the bluebird of the title — lies in his own backyard. Bones took a fairly dismissive view of the whole idea ("There was nothing original about it — television writers just look for a connection"), and Steve was not altogether convinced they had found the unlocking key, but when they presented it to Elvis for his reaction, to Steve's amazement Elvis simply bought the whole thing. "We told him, 'We don't want you to like it one hundred percent. We want to get your input. What you like. What you don't like.' He said, 'No, I like it all.' And the essence of the show never changed."

Preproduction continued at the Binder-Howe offices for the next couple of weeks, until they were scheduled to move to NBC for full-scale rehearsals. Every day Elvis showed up with at least one or two of the guys, meeting with Steve and Bones and the writers over Pepsi and cigars. He was practically beside himself on June 5, the day that Bobby Kennedy was killed, and could talk of nothing but the conspiracy against the Kennedys and the assassination of Martin Luther King two months earlier. It was all the more terrible that Dr. King should have been killed in Memphis, he said, thereby only confirming everyone's worst feelings about the South. To Steve this was more than just idle talk. "He had read a whole lot of books about the Kennedy assassination, and I just felt a real sense of compassion on his part." That was something that Binder wanted to get into the special. "I wanted to let the world know that here was a guy who was not prejudiced, who was raised in the heart of prejudice, but who was really above all that. Part of the strength that I wanted to bring to the show was [that sense of] compassion, that this was somebody to look up to and admire."

They talked about music, too. Would Elvis sing a new song simply if it said something to him, Binder asked, irrespective of politics or publishing? Absolutely, Elvis replied. Would he have done Jimmy Webb's "MacArthur Park" [a song of vaguely psychedelic, definitely pretentious lyrical obscurity], which had just topped the charts for actor Richard Harris after the Association, whom Bones was producing, turned it down for publishing reasons? Of course, Elvis said, as if nothing like that could ever happen to him. He *liked* "MacArthur Park," he said, acquiescing to Binder's enthusiasm. He definitely wanted to say something more with his music than a song like "Hound Dog" could express. One day they went out on Sunset and just stood there watching the hippies go by, too stoned to realize they were walking past Elvis Presley, or simply not caring. Steve saw it as a truly humbling experience for Elvis, a kind of "giant step in his psyche," though to Bones it was more like he just got a kick out of the experience. "We were just four guys standing out in front of this building, and after a while we got bored and went back upstairs."

The script rapidly evolved. By June 11 it was pretty well set, with "Guitar Man" providing the story line, and a concert segment that featured some of Elvis' greatest hits. There was an "informal segment," too, which included scripted conversation with Charlie and one or two of the other guys and brief snatches of some of the most risible movie songs, with Elvis deprecating himself and the movies in a manner that comes across on the printed page as artificial and insincere. In reference to his patented sneer, he says, "I did the entire production of *Jailhouse Rock* on that look alone, baby," and the whole sequence is obviously intended to say, *Now you're finally getting to see the real me, the real Elvis Presley*. The show ends, of course, with the Christmas song that Colonel has insisted on from the start, to be followed by dialogue yet to be written. It was with that dialogue that Binder hoped Elvis would make his "statement," but the Colonel, he knew, remained implacably opposed.

There were meetings with various members of the production team. Elvis conferred with Earl Brown, the chorus arranger, and okayed some preliminary sketches that Bill Belew, the costume designer, submitted for his approval. He loved the black leather suit that Belew had designed for him in soft, flexible material. "The whole thing," Belew said, "was like the Petula Clark special; Steve did not want anything that reeked of 'Hollywood TV.' He wanted it all to have a fresh, new look. I said to Elvis, 'A lot of my themes come from people that I admire,' and when I saw Elvis, immediately 'Napoleonic' came to mind.' I explained to him that the collar standing up would frame his face. I said, 'I don't want any neckties on you, just soft silk shirts and around the neck a scarf.'" Elvis listened, nodded, and agreed to virtually every suggestion that Belew made. The designer was dumbfounded. He had never encountered such a lack of ego in a big star before. The one subject about which they had any disagreement was the gold suit that Belew designed to symbolize success, in homage to the suit the Colonel had had made up for Elvis in 1957. Elvis never explained his opposition but was clearly embarrassed by it, and in the end they worked out the same compromise solution that he had agreed to in the fifties: he would wear the gold jacket with a pair of black tuxedo pants.

Only with the music did there continue to be any sort of problem. Here Steve found himself stymied by two almost entirely unrelated developments. Bones had gotten himself into trouble early on by persisting in asking questions about the soundtrack album. He and Steve had long since given up any hope of making money on the special — they knew there were no residuals, and their small salaries barely covered expenses. But the issue of a soundtrack album had never been contractually addressed; in fact, against all evidence and common sense it had never even been *admitted* that there would be one, and Bones felt strongly that they should get some kind of override, a producer's royalty on the record when it was inevitably released. "I got as far as Diskin, and then the whole thing blew sky high. We got calls from NBC: 'What are you trying to do, sabotage the show? Elvis Presley doesn't have a record producer.' And so on. At that point Diskin started a tirade at me. He said, 'NBC hired you to do a special, not a record.' I said, '[The Colonel]'s got to be crazy if he doesn't put out a soundtrack album.' He said, 'We're not discussing it.' They said, 'Get Bones out. He's a troublemaker,' and at that point they moved me out."

Steve was forced to accept the situation for the time being and to keep Bones temporarily under wraps. At the same time, he was having no luck getting song arrangements out of Billy Strange, who the Colonel had said from the beginning would be Elvis' personal music director on the show. Without Strange's arrangements, the show's official musical arranger, Billy Goldenberg, could not go to work on the orchestrations, and without the orchestrations, no musical progress whatsoever could be made. Steve had little liking for the situation, and he tried every method he could to coax the work out of Elvis' man, but it seemed like every time he contacted Strange, the man came up with a different excuse. As far as Binder was concerned, Billy Strange was "The Man That Wasn't"; here they were less than two weeks from taping, and at this point he and Strange had scarcely even met.

That left Billy Goldenberg in an almost totally untenable position. A 1957 graduate of Columbia University who had apprenticed under the great Broadway composer Frank Loesser (*Guys and Dolls, How to Succeed in Business Without Really Trying*), Goldenberg had come to the show in the first place with the greatest reluctance, and then only out of loyalty to Steve. He had no interest in Elvis Presley — his personal tastes did not run to that kind of music — but he was persuaded by Binder's enthusiasm and obvious belief in the project. From the time that he had first arrived, though, he had been led to wonder just what his role was supposed to be.

He seemed to have no function in what were loosely deemed "rehearsals." "Every day Elvis would come in and sit around with his group and play guitar. I mean, some of it was very exciting. Elvis loved to improvise and talk about old times and play the songs and keep repeating them — he would get excited just by repetition. So that the intensity of the song seemed to grow as he kept playing it, almost to a climax. He could sing ninety-five choruses of 'Jingle Bells,' and he really wouldn't get sick of it. Then he might try another song on his guitar, and then he might decide he didn't like that song so much, so he'd go back to 'Jingle Bells' for another ninety-five choruses, and the whole group would be whooping and hollering and having a very nice time."

Goldenberg could see the cathartic value of it, but every time he mentioned getting down to work, one of the guys would say, "Billy will do that for us, and in my mind I'm thinking, Well, why am I here?" Then one day Billy Strange actually showed up, accoutered in cowboy hat and boots, and Billy Goldenberg felt all the more alienated. It was obvious to him that Billy Strange had a good rapport with Elvis, but it was just as obvious that he was not capable of providing any form of musical direction. "They just kept fooling around, playing the things that they knew how to do. I knew there was a section where they wanted to have a little improvisational work between Elvis and his guys, to show the relationship that went on with them. Which was all very nice — but it was just one section of the show. I kept looking at the script, and I said, 'Well, that's fine, but we have eighty percent of the show to do. What are we going to do?'"

Steve was getting worried, too. He knew, better than anyone else, that they were running out of time. They would be moving into the NBC studio in just a few days, with prerecording scheduled to start on the twentieth and videotaping slated to begin a week later. Freddy had cleared all the songs, Finkel was doing a good job running interference with the Colonel, and Steve continued to have faith in his own improvisational instincts. But he needed to address the music, and he feared that when he finally did, the whole thing could blow up in his face.

Billy Goldenberg, as it turned out, was the one to precipitate the crisis. He came to Steve in the middle of the second and final week of prerehearsals, with his mind made up. "I told Steve, 'This is it. I don't want to be involved. Billy [Strange] is a very nice guy, and probably a wonderful arranger, but he just sits there and I don't see anything happening. I mean, there's no concept. Who's paying attention to what's on the written page?' So Steve said, 'Well, suppose I fire Billy Strange?'"

It was not a decision to be undertaken lightly. Steve had seen what had happened to his partner when he challenged the Colonel's authority, and this seemed like a far more central issue. But, with just a week to go before they went into the recording studio, he didn't see that he had any alternative. If he didn't do something right away, they simply weren't going to have a show. So he spoke to Strange, who seemed to seize on the opportunity to let Binder know he really didn't have time to work on the special with all he still had left to do on the *Live a Little, Love a Little* soundtrack and the new Nancy Sinatra album he had recently begun. And, without being sure of how exactly it had come about (and with at least two of Billy's songs still in the show), Steve recognized that they had arrived at a mutual parting of the ways.

But there was still the matter of telling the Colonel. He had seen the way that Finkel dealt with the Colonel, working constantly to keep him in a good mood, studiously avoiding the creation of even the appearance of any conflict between manager and client. Binder himself was highly cognizant of the delicate balance of power that prevailed and careful "never, ever to show any disrespect of the Colonel in front of Elvis. It was very, very important to the Colonel never to lose control." This time it didn't seem to matter what he said, though. The Colonel's matter-of-fact reaction to the news of Billy Strange's departure was simply that that was the end of it, that Elvis would surely walk out. He didn't say that he would *advise* Elvis to walk out; he seemed merely to be offering a prediction. "Bindel," as he had come to refer to Binder, would have to take the matter up with Elvis himself, though the Colonel offered very little hope of a successful resolution.

"When Elvis walked in, I took him aside and told him what the problem was, and he just said, 'Fine. Do what you want to do.' And he never looked back." The Colonel never brought up the subject again either, thereby confirming two things to Binder: that Elvis and the Colonel were not one and the same, and that the Colonel, while perhaps incapable of formally conceding a point, in the end would always stay true to his word. Which in this case was that it was their show — unless they really fucked up.

It was at this point, with less than a week to go, that Bones came back into the picture. He and Steve both knew Billy Goldenberg's limitations — they were the very qualities that had made Billy beg off in the beginning. He was a Broadway composer, an orchestrator and arranger with "legitimate" theater ambitions — but this show in the end was about rock 'n' roll. Billy would be great for the "Guitar Man" dream sequences and orchestrated set pieces, but when it came to working with a rhythm section, or even to convincing Elvis of the continuity between his past work and the present venture, there was no question that Bones was now the necessary link. He would function as a&r man and musical producer in charge of the whole project, they explained to Billy, who was more than happy to have an ally at last in this slippery new territory.

Billy worked frantically on the music over the weekend, starting work with Elvis on a regular daily basis only on June 17, the day they moved into NBC. He had already encountered resistance from the guys, mostly from Joe as their spokesman. "He would call up and say, 'Well, what are you going to do? What are we expecting here?' I said, 'You know, well, I'm going to work with Elvis.' He said, 'What kind of a band is it going to be?' I said, 'I want an orchestra.' He'd say, 'We don't like orchestras. Elvis works well with guitars. They can do everything.' I said, 'No, they can't do everything, because I have a lot of conceptual stuff to work out here.' He said, 'I don't know if that's gonna do, sonny. You go ahead and hire your orchestra, but if we don't like it, we're just gonna tell all the musicians to go home.'"

Up till now it had been only a minor annoyance — and one that Billy assumed stemmed as much from personal bias as musical issues. At this point, though, there was no time for the distraction of "semithreatening" phone calls; they needed to get the show back on track right away. So he called Finkel and said that he needed to be able to deal with Elvis directly, he didn't appreciate "being called by people and having to worry about whether I'm going to be killed for writing a dominant seventh." Finkel told him not to worry, that he would take care of the problem, and from that point on, Billy worked with Elvis alone. The man that he encountered, though, was very different from the Elvis Presley that he had been led to expect.

The first time that I walked into the studio, Elvis was sitting at the piano playing Beethoven's "Moonlight Sonata." So I think, "What's going on here? This is really interesting." And he says to me, "Oh, do you know this?" I said, "Yes, I know that." He said, "What happens after this?" and played the first part again. So I sat down next to him and played some more of it. He said, "That's great," and picked it up, and we spent the better part of our first rehearsal period learning the first movement of the "Moonlight Sonata"!

I was so surprised. It certainly did break the ice, and it was kind of a harbinger of things to come. But he was such an incredibly quick study. We went through "Guitar Man," and he had little suggestions. Always polite. Always respectful. So incredibly different than all the people around him. He had class. I mean, underneath all that stuff, suddenly I found this person I could relate to. It was fun working with him, because he would get excited about it, he would spark a creative thing — I mean, if I did a particular chord change, he might sing a particular riff or get an idea and say, "Do you think this is something that might work?" I'd say, "Let's play with it a little bit and find out." I was getting into what he was doing, and he was getting into what I was doing — it was a good, quick relationship that we formed and, as I say, a lot of fun.

We would go on night after night, and every night we would do a little bit of the "Moonlight Sonata." One night he was playing it on the piano, and the door opened, and in walked two or three of his guys. Immediately he picked his hands up from the keyboard, as if some strange, dark shadow had come over the place. They came in and said, "What the fuck is that?" He said, "Oh, it's just something we were doing." And they said, "Oh, it's awful," and he didn't make any remark, just picked up his guitar and started playing those old E-major chords again, that's what they wanted to hear, and that was the end of our rehearsal period for the day. I had to call Bob Finkel again and say, "Would you please get them out of here, because I can't do my work?" And he did. But Elvis couldn't wait to continue.

Not altogether surprisingly, Charlie Hodge was the one guy to show any musical interest in what Goldenberg and Elvis were working on, but to Billy's great surprise the Colonel showed a considerable degree of personal kindness toward him. "He was always nice to me. He'd say, 'Tell me about yourself. What's your life like? What do you want to do?' He just loved stories, he wanted to hear everything about my background, and he would say, 'Is there anything you want me to do, to make it easier for you?' I mean, in terms of Elvis. He would say, 'My boy likes you a lot.'" Goldenberg had no idea what to make of all this, but he was grateful for it. Binder and Bones and Bob Finkel, too, all noted with relief what seemed like a significant change in the weather: for whatever reason, the Colonel, and Elvis, each no doubt for his own purposes and each in his own way, seemed finally determined to make this special work.

Things ran smoothly for the most part — or, more smoothly anyway — from this point on. Elvis worked hard on his dance steps with Lance LeGault, just learning to hit his marks on the intricately choreographed production sequences. The fittings with Bill Belew went smoothly, too, now that the crisis of the gold lamé suit had passed. Everyone on the show waited for Elvis to show signs of temperament, but he never did, applying himself to the job with the same kind of cheerfully democratic attitude that he had always shown on the movie set. Finkel, however, continued to have his hands full with the Colonel, who was never less than a full-time job. Early on, Parker had gotten the William Morris agents assigned to him for the show to stand outside his office outfitted as Buckingham Palace guards. Finkel, not to be outdone, retaliated by reinventing himself as Admiral Finkel, requisitioning a Lord Nelson outfit from the costume department and appearing in three-quarter-length breeches and tricornered hat. At the Colonel's insistence they played a game called Honesty, in which the Colonel thought of a number, Finkel put up $20, then tried to guess the number — and was, predictably enough, almost invariably wrong. Once or twice, just when Finkel figured he would never win, Colonel announced that he had finally guessed right and forked over $20 with a long face, but over the course of two weeks of rehearsals, the executive producer in charge of Colonel Parker calculated that he must have dropped close to $600. Finkel, under ordinary circumstances a man of conventional sobriety, sometimes wondered at himself, and at the strange hold the Colonel seemed to exert over him simply by virtue of his unorthodox charm. "I did funny things — he would do things to me, and I would do them back to him. I went to him one day, and I said, 'Colonel, I'm going to beat you at these things. If I beat you and you admit it, I want your cane. I want to hang it up on my wall.' And he agreed."

The only substantive matter that the Colonel continued to bring up was the theme of the show itself: Elvis would end with a Christmas song. On that point he remained adamant, no matter how Binder tried to get around him on the subject. Steve continued to bring up the idea of Elvis delivering some loosely scripted closing remarks *after* he sang the Christmas song — but he was always short-circuited by the Colonel's matter-of-fact, implacable, almost irrational opposition, seemingly, to Elvis' saying anything at all.

That was the only real hitch, though, in the increasingly well calibrated feel of an operation that was finally coming together. Binder *believed* in his team; he knew what they were capable of. And he believed in himself. Now, at last, he was beginning to believe in Elvis. There was no question that the show had Elvis' full attention by this time — he wasn't simply present, he was *there,* just like the rest of them, twelve, fourteen, sixteen hours a day. Every night after rehearsals were over, he would unwind in his dressing room, laughing and joking with the guys as he and Charlie sang and played their guitars. One night Steve wandered into what had by now become a familiar scene and suddenly experienced a revelation. *This* was the way to go. *This* could be their way to make a statement — with a totally unscripted improv substituting for the stiff, somewhat arch "informal" segment specified in the script. In a burst of enthusiasm he suddenly thought: they could shoot it in the dresing room, cinema verité–style; for a moment he wanted to just throw out all the produced segments — this could become not simply the centerpiece but the whole show.

In the end, reality reasserted itself. After talking with Elvis, he settled on the idea of flying in original guitarist Scotty Moore and drummer D.J. Fontana to make Elvis feel more at home, then doing the best he could to re-create the informal atmosphere of the dressing room in the small boxing ring of a stage that had been designed for the more formal live concert at the heart of the show. Instead of scripting it, the director just ran down some of the topics that he would like Elvis to discuss — the bit about being shot from the waist up on *The Ed Sullivan Show,* the judge in Jacksonville in 1956 who wouldn't let him move around onstage, prompting Elvis to retaliate by crooking his little finger to suggest the banned movements. These things were essential, Steve said, to reestablish the rebel image. And when Elvis expressed concern that he might not be able to tell the stories very well without lines to deliver, Steve was quick to reassure him that all he had to do was wing it; the musicians would cue him, and he could always have a piece of paper nearby with the topic sentence for each anecdote written on it. It would be fine, Steve said soothingly; the moment would supply its own inspiration. And if he ran out of things to say, as a last resort he could always go back to that Jimmy Reed song he and Charlie were always fooling with; its lyrics — with their constant refrain about "Going up, going down, up down, down up, any way you want me" — might supply their own commentary.

Scotty and D.J. flew in on the weekend, five days before filming was scheduled to start. Although they had been told nothing other than that they were there to jam, things quickly fell into place, and before anyone knew it, it was almost like old times, with much of the easy give-and-take of the early days. D.J. offered some of the most uninhibited reminiscences, with Charlie egging him on, while Scotty contributed his own characteristically wry commentary, gently deflating some of the more exaggerated claims but then, with a wink, adding some of his own. One night they went out to Elvis' house for a post-rehearsal dinner and talked about the future. He wanted to do a European tour, Elvis told them. He wanted to record at Scotty's studio, just "woodshedding" like they were doing now. "He asked me if I thought that would be possible, just go in there for about a week and see what we could come up with, like we used to. I said, 'No problem — if you leave about half your guys at home.' He said, 'That's what I'm talking about.' But, of course, it never happened." Both Scotty and D.J. were impressed with Binder, they were excited by his enthusiasm and by what seemed like his total dedication to the task at hand. They worried, though, that maybe they weren't contributing enough — D.J. kept asking him what exactly he wanted them to do. "But he'd just say, 'Don't do nothing, just do what you're doing. That's all I want.'"

Recording, meanwhile, had started up on the evening of the twentieth, as scheduled. They were working over at Western Recorders at 6000 Sunset, and for once all attention was focused on the music. Colonel had given Freddy explicit instructions that once actual recording had begun he was to stay out of it, a prohibition, he declared, that applied to himself as well. "If the Colonel can't stick his nose in, the other people are self-explanatory," he declared, while stipulating that it was Lamar's job to maintain good spirits, a task from which Freddy was pointedly excluded.

The band that Bones had put together was made up of many of the same top L.A. session musicians whom Billy Strange had assembled for both the aborted August and *Live a Little, Love a Little* sessions. "We had to fight the people at NBC — they wanted to keep their costs down and were trying to keep from hiring people outside of their staff orchestra. Steve and I had some incredible meetings with them — you know, what will Elvis Presley say if he walks in and sees a bunch of old men who don't know anything about rock 'n' roll? We used some of the string players from NBC and some of the brass players, [but] we handpicked the rhythm section is what it boiled down to."

The idea was to prerecord everything except the two live performances (the concert and the informal segment with Scotty and D.J.) that remained at the center of the show. That way they would be able to use a prerecorded instrumental track as the backing for a live vocal wherever possible, but if Elvis appeared in a choreographed segment or was captured in a long shot in which the presence of a microphone might be visually obtrusive, they could simply plug in the vocal track at that point. Bones knew Steve's ability to switch back and forth between live and prerecorded sequences, and he knew exactly how he wanted to record Elvis, whose live vocals in the studio — even if they became "reference" vocals — were the heart of the show. "I gave him a hand mike. I felt that Elvis wasn't going to work within the framework of a contemporary recording artist, who lays down tracks and then overdubs and all of that. My responsibility was to get him to give the best performance that he could. One of the things that I've tried to do in [all the] years that I've been making records is to always consider the artist first. You never want to put the artist in a position where he has to be uncomfortable in order for you to do your job well. If you get a little drums in the vocal mike, I mean that's too bad, it may not be a perfect recording — but it [might] turn out to be a great performance that way."

Billy Goldenberg was practically beside himself with worry over the orchestrations — he had taken so much grief about them already, and he had worked so hard to try to get them to express something that was not immediately obvious, he was now suddenly overcome with an access of doubt about what Elvis' reaction might be. "Quincy Jones had at that time just written the score of *In Cold Blood* — it was very dark, very guttural, it was a mean score. And I thought it was wonderful. And I thought there must be a way of taking that concept and working it into a television show. That's how 'Guitar Man' [the central medley] came about.

"I wanted to tune in to Elvis underneath. I wanted to tune in to the perversity, frankly, that was deep down inside of him, but the only place that he would project it was onstage. I mean, he would sing and do all of the visual stuff that he did, and then after he finished he would laugh at it. But there was no question that he tuned in to the darkness, to the wild, untamed, animalistic things. That was [such] a big part of Elvis; he did not make his statement by being sweet. He was blatantly sexual, and that was something I wanted in the music. And if I could get that, I felt I was getting closer to the raw Elvis. Not the Elvis that came in the room to talk to you, because he was the sweetest person in the world, I mean, he was [the] good son — I think that was a lot of Elvis' problem."

Billy need not have doubted Elvis' reaction. They began with the long, complicated "Guitar Man" medley, which would be interspersed throughout the show and represented Billy's most direct statement of his theme. "First I rehearsed the orchestra alone, and everybody was in the control booth — Elvis, the Colonel, Finkel, the guys, everyone. It was a most frightening night for me. Anyway, we rehearsed it all the way through, and I was really quite happy with it, but as I finished I looked in the control room, and nobody was saying anything, and I thought, Well, they must have hated it. Then Elvis walks out into the studio, says hello to the musicians — we had a pretty large orchestra, violins, cellos, French horns, I think there were around forty or fifty pieces — and he says, 'What are these over here?' I said, 'Those are French horns.' He said, 'Ah, that's real interesting — do you think I can sing with that?' I said, 'Yeah.' He said, 'Well, can I try? Can I sing with the orchestra now?' And the guys came out, and they were kind of talking among themselves, making little negative comments, saying how this would never do. But Elvis is not listening to them. He goes into his little isolation booth, and I start up the orchestra, and he does the entire thing. And it was really dynamite. It was just — thrilling. He started very quietly, and then he built and built until it was just absolutely raucous, and he was bathed in sweat, at the end of this first rehearsal.

"Then the guys, of course, realizing that he liked it, said, 'Oh, that's terrific,' and I saw Steve breathe a sigh of relief, and Bones started to get into some of the musical things with Elvis. But Elvis just kept rehearsing this 'Guitar Man' sequence, and when he got through for the evening, it was like he had just fornicated. I mean, he was on such a high, he was so involved and excited and emotionally charged — I don't remember anything in my life like that, frankly. It was a high point."

It was that very intensity, Elvis' whole emotional involvement in the act of recording, that brought home to Steve all over again how much they needed an ending. To get this kind of passionate commitment out of him and then to end with "I'll Be Home for Christmas" would not only be a mistake, it would be in the nature of an aesthetic crime. It would betray the democratic vision that Steve had come to feel was the essence of the show. "All of a sudden I realized, I've got Elvis Presley, Colonel Parker, Confederate flags, a black choreographer, a Puerto Rican choreographer, and a Jewish director! Everything in the show was integrated — behind the scenes, and in front of the camera Elvis singing along with the Blossoms [the black, female, gospel-drenched backup group that Elvis had insisted upon], the dance sections black and white and — you know — purple. I mean, there was a spirit on that show where you hated to go to sleep because you were so anxious to go back [to work] the next day — we were all one big family."

That was what galled Steve most about the lack of any real conclusion. It was what goaded him to keep casting about for a different way to say those things that he knew Elvis felt but could never fully express — whether because he was not permitted to or because he was temperamentally disinclined. The finale should be a kind of summing up, Steve felt, a declaration of shared idealism. To that end he approached Earl Brown, the vocal arranger, about writing a song. "I took Earl aside, and I said, 'Earl, let me explain something to you. We're under the gun now, and what I need — instead of having him do a monologue at the end, let's do a song where we incorporate what his monologue would say. That was all I contributed: this is what I would like the song to be. So Earl went home and at seven o'clock the next morning he woke me up and said, 'Steve, I think I've got it. I really think I've nailed the song.' So I went into the studio, and Earl played the song for me — it was called 'If I Can Dream' — and I said, 'That's it. You've just written the song that's going to close the show.'

"So now I go to Bob Finkel, and I say, 'Bob, I've got the end of the show.' And he said, 'Do you realize what you're doing? The Colonel will blow his stack. It's got to be a Christmas song.' I said, 'It *can't* be a Christmas song. This is the song Elvis will sing at the end of the show.' I arranged for Elvis, Billy, Bones, and myself to go in the dressing room, and Earl sat down at the piano and played it through. Elvis sort of sat there listening. He didn't comment; he just said, 'Play it again.' So Earl sat there and played it again — and again. Then Elvis started to ask some questions about it, and I would venture to say Earl probably played the song six or seven times in a row. Then Elvis looked at me and said, 'We're doing it.'"

Bob Finkel meanwhile had been fending off the Colonel, Freddy, and the whole network contingent in another room. Everyone had stated their firm opposition to introducing a new element at this point, particularly an untried, untested, un-Christmas song, but when Binder came out of the dressing room with Elvis' wholehearted commitment to it, the Colonel never hesitated to embrace the tactical high ground. Steve had Earl play the song for everyone once again, but "before he had finished, the lead sheet was plucked out of his hand and run down to the publishing firm to make sure they had one-hundred percent of the copyright."

Billy wrote the arrangement overnight, and Elvis recorded it in five takes on Sunday, June 23, the last day of formal recording. Although he is singing to a full orchestral backing, it is the voice that predominates, as much as it would if he were singing unaccompanied, as the Colonel would undoubtedly have preferred. The song is a well-intentioned liberal statement about peace and brotherhood and universal understanding, but it is not the lyrics that command our attention over the gulf of years. It is, rather, the pain and conviction and raw emotion in Elvis' voice as he sings of a world "where all my brothers walk hand in hand" and almost screams out the last line: "Please/let my dream/come true/Right now."

There is no way of neatly summing up the meaning of the moment; it is one of those rare instances where Elvis pays no attention to formal boundaries, as his voice, deliberately roughened throughout the song, teeters perilously on the same dubious note at the conclusion of each finished take. Under any other circumstances, the song might seem no more than a trite, generalized plea for understanding set to a somewhat awkward, hyperdramatic melody, but somehow, whether because of Elvis' conviction or the listener's knowledge of its cost, the words take on worlds of meaning, the melody soars, there is a thrill — along with a wince at that final note — in every listening. As Steve Binder recalled, Elvis asked that the lights be dimmed for the final take, both in the studio and in the control room. "I think he was oblivious to everything else in the universe. When I looked out the window, he was in an almost fetal position, writhing on the cement floor, singing that song. And when he got done, he came in the control room, and we played it maybe fifteen times, he just loved it so much."

With the bulk of recording now complete, Elvis actually moved into his dressing room at NBC for the rest of the week. He was totally keyed up now, on edge in a way he had rarely been since abandoning live performing a decade before. His professionalism continued to be noted by the entire crew, he continued to impress everyone with his unfailing courtesy, politeness, and malleability — but there was something else now, too. For the first time in a long time he didn't bother to hide the fact that he really cared.

There was a press conference on Tuesday night, at which Elvis acquitted himself with his usual aplomb. He was doing the show, he said, because "we figured it was about time. Besides, I figured I'd better do it before I got too old." "We also got a very good deal," the Colonel jumped in. "Besides the special, we're doing one picture, which NBC is producing. I would call that one very good deal." Elvis paid lip service to his ongoing Hollywood career, spoke almost reflexively of his unwavering commitment to some-day becoming a serious actor and his constant search for better scripts, and skillfully deflected any serious questions about life, art, or career. "I loved his attitude," said Binder, who had one or two things to say himself about a show that was in his opinion "a matter of video-history significance." "Every time they'd ask a question, he'd have a funny way of tapping me on the leg, as if to say, 'Watch me put the guy on with this one.' And it was fun to watch the press just sitting there. I think he got satisfaction just out of being on top of it. He never, ever had to be protected in that respect."

There was no disguising his jitteriness, though, as they began a com-plete run-through of the show the following day, and then on the twenty-seventh taped the midway sequence before getting ready for the "informal" show that evening. "I know you're nervous, man," he told Alan Fortas, who, with the ranch closed, had come out to the Coast earlier in the spring and had now been drafted to actually *appear* on camera in the informal sequence. "I know you're scared," he repeated, though Alan had little doubt he was really talking about himself.

There was a moment of panic on the producers' part as well. Bob Finkel had left it to the Colonel to give out tickets for the show. "The Colonel said to me, 'I'll take care of it. The demand will be unbelievable.' I said, 'Okay with me.' We start at six o'clock that night, whatever the hell it was, and I look out at four o'clock, and there's nobody there. *Nobody.* I went to the Colonel, and I said, 'Where the hell are these people that should be lined up all day?' He said, 'I don't know.' I said, 'What did you do with the tickets?' And he gave me some damn-fool answer." No one under-stood the Colonel's rationale. Evidently he had given out batches of tickets to gate guards and waitresses, along with the usual fan club presidents, and just assumed that the crowds would show. Finkel put it down to grandiose expectations — or perhaps to the one final put-on that he would never be able to top. Binder saw it as more intentional, stemming from the Colonel's simple desire to prove them all wrong. Whatever the reason, the Colonel never let on, he just went ahead and acted as if everything were normal, and in the end he and Finkel rounded up an audience. Which the Colonel then proceeded to arrange so that the most adoring female fans were at the front and the audience could be expected to replicate the kind of response that it had offered in 1956 and 1957.

Elvis told Steve Binder at the last minute that he didn't think he could go on. He'd changed his mind, he said, he had decided that this was not a good idea. What did he mean he'd changed his mind? the shocked director demanded, and even Joe was momentarily taken aback. He had never seen Elvis like this before. He had witnessed normal stage fright, of course, but he had always marked it down to entertainer's ego, to Elvis' simply wanting to be reassured and told that it was all right. Now he was not so sure, but together he and Binder managed to calm Elvis down. There was an *audience* out there, Steve said, he couldn't let down his fans. It didn't really matter what he did, they'd have two full run-throughs, and if they didn't like anything from either show, they could just throw the whole thing out. But what if he froze up? Elvis insisted. What if he couldn't think of anything to say? "Then you go out, sit down, look at everyone, get up, and walk off," Binder said firmly. "But you *are* going out there."

There is little evidence of this sense of panic in the show itself, unless it lies in the kind of awkward self-deprecation ("What do I do now, folks?" are practically Elvis' first words to the audience) that has been an intrinsic part of his charm from the start. He appears calm but shy, modest but secure in his own beauty as the applause washes over him and he finds himself somehow, unexpectedly, at its center. The stage itself is a gaudily accoutered Hollywood version of a boxing ring (a small white square surrounded by a red border instead of ropes); there is barely enough room for the musicians, let alone their instruments, and D.J. sits expectantly, holding a pair of sticks poised not over a drum kit but an upside-down guitar case which Steve has seized upon wholeheartedly in the "improv" spirit of the occasion. There are five chairs arranged in a circle, with Elvis placed to command the attention of each, looking lean, lithe, and a little uncomfortable in his velvety black leather suit; even in repose, he appears ready to spring, with his long legs sprawled out casually in front of him. Almost as if to offset his sinuous charm, the three musicians — Scotty, D.J., and Charlie — are all dressed in a kind of burgundy velour, as is Alan Fortas, who looks a little bit like a designer fireplug and whose presence onstage is only meant to reinforce the overall sense of cinema verité that the director is aiming for. Alan has never played an instrument, but Binder from the beginning has viewed Elvis' interaction with the guys as part of the informal, dressing-room atmosphere, so Alan sits uncomfortably with his hands resting on the back of a guitar which will become one more element in this homemade "rhythm band." The only other onstage participant is Lance LeGault, who crouches directly behind Elvis holding a tambourine, while Joe and Lamar and Gee Gee hover watchfully in suits and ties, just a few feet from Elvis on the steps that lead up to the stage.

The small audience, no more than a couple of hundred, is strangely subdued — they seem more amazed that it is *Elvis* than at anything he might do, even as the object of their attention appears to be experiencing a similar sense of bewilderment, as he fumbles about for something to say, then glances down at the piece of paper with suggested subjects for discussion that sits on the glass tabletop in front of him. "This is supposed to be an informal section of the show," he jokes, "where we faint, or do whatever we want to do, especially me." He then makes a pass at returning to the script but gets no further than a few words about his first record and how "I first started out — in 1912," before pretending to lose the thread, casting his eyes down at the floor, and finally just trailing off, "And if I fall asleep here . . ." There are loud guffaws from the guys, as if to say, We don't really take any of this too seriously either.

And then, all of a sudden, everybody's feet are flying, as Elvis launches into a spirited, if not particularly tuneful, version of that first record, "That's All Right," and with "Heartbreak Hotel" breaks the tension once and for all not with a great performance but by forgetting the words to the song. One can't help but think that this is an instinctive ploy, because whether he actually remembers the words or not, he immediately enlists the audience's sympathy, declares his own vulnerability (while also rising above it), and sets the tone for the rest of the evening, an easygoing note of accidental inspiration. He also attempts to get up from his chair for the first time, a virtual impossibility given the chair's proximity to the edge of the stage and the absence of a guitar strap or boom mike — but that, too, sets a tone, as the audience comes to equate standing up with a kind of freedom, which Elvis struggles for the rest of the evening to achieve. This in turn lends further drama to the limited movement of which he is capable while seated, allowing him to elicit screams from the audience as his legs jack-knife out from the chair in a variation on the gyrations for which he has always been known. By the time he begins the next song, the Leiber and Stoller ballad "Love Me," he is clearly in command, singing beautifully for the most part, frowning or pretending to belch when he doesn't, reaching out to the audience, as he always has, by mocking his own pretensions.

At this stage he must have run out of things to say, because, after switching guitars with Scotty, he takes Steve's advice and, for the first of three times in the course of this brief, hour-long set launches into the Jimmy Reed blues "Baby What You Want Me to Do?" "Are we on television?" he asks idly. "No, we're on a train bound for Tulsa," Charlie cackles. And from this point on, everything becomes slightly surreal — or, perhaps, it simply creates its own reality. For the rest of the show, Scotty never takes back his guitar; it is Elvis, who has never even played electric guitar on his own records, who now plays endearingly limited, bluesy, electric lead. The script might just as well be entirely forgotten by now, and yet its spirit is preserved in mockingly sardonic references to the topic suggestions. "It says here, 'Elvis will now talk about his first record and how things started happening after that,'" he woodenly intones, sharing the joke with the audience, as the guys' raucous response offers assent even before the joke is fully delivered.

It's hard to imagine what the producer and director must have been thinking — unless they were so caught up in the moment that there was no time to think. If they had suggested these ingredients from the outset as the formula for a network special, what would have been the Colonel's, the network's, the industry's response? And yet somehow it works. Elvis' inability to present himself as anything *but* himself, and the very amateurishness of that presentation; Charlie's wildly inappropriate behavior, the source of so much resentment within the group, and the "boys' night out" nature of his repartee; even the homemade, hit-or-miss quality of the music itself — all are strangely effective here. Each wildly unpredictable element seems only to encourage Elvis to forget himself all the more, encourages him, paradoxically, to *find* himself. It is 1955 and 1956 all over again, as, without rules, outside of all the normal guidelines of show business, of polite professional and social intercourse, with nothing in fact but a bemused instinct for his own charm, an innate belief in his ability to locate just what his audience is looking for, and a belief in that audience itself, Elvis explores uncharted territory, creates himself as he would like to be.

And then, for a moment, he disappears. He sings "Lawdy, Miss Clawdy" at Scotty's scripted request, repeating the verses over and over until he is, truly, lost in the music. He does charmingly melodic, almost crooning versions of "When My Blue Moon Turns to Gold Again" and "Blue Christmas," then launches into "Trying to Get to You," a number that he recorded at the end of his time at Sun and one which seems always to touch the deepest wellsprings of his emotions. The camera comes in for a tight focus shot as he plays once again with the notion of trying to stand. He is singing harder than he ever did, or ever had to, at the outset of his career, while playing with the audience, teasing it, miming emotion even as he feels it. He continues the process with Smiley Lewis' "One Night," where he does finally manage to stand and promptly pulls the guitar cord out of his amplifier. "I got to do it again, man," he says, and does — suspended between play and reality, unable at this point perhaps to tell the difference.

It seemed at first as if there would be little left for the eight o'clock performance. There was no attempt to turn the house for the second show, and perhaps out of a combination of the audience's familiarity with what was to come and Elvis' own sense of what he had accomplished, the second show was looser, louder, even more informal if possible. Jokes are delivered this time without the necessity of punch lines, lyrics are forgotten without even the artifice of conviction, and lines from the script are read out with even sharper sarcasm. "It's been a long time, jack," Elvis announces, as the guys whoop it up, repeating the lines that *they* have been given — "Aw, take it on home," "Tell it like it is," "Play it dirty" — like a mantra that has become an in-joke.

But then, just as you begin to think there is no way to reclaim the spell, Elvis once again finds what he is looking for at almost exactly the same point that it occurred in the earlier show. It starts, this time, with his rendition of "One Night," continues through a full-bodied version of "Love Me," and climaxes once again with "Trying to Get to You," as for a moment, at the end of the song, Elvis' eyes roll back in his head and he goes to another place, before moving on to a perfectly fine "Lawdy, Miss Clawdy," an explosive version of "Tiger Man" (the Joe Hill Louis blues he tried unsuccessfully to record while still at Sun), and "Memories," the syrupy Mac Davis–Billy Strange ballad that concludes both shows. It is, all in all, an astonishing triumph, even if you do not choose to overlook the panic-stricken start, but it really all comes down to that one moment in which not just self-consciousness, but consciousness itself, is lost, and it is little wonder that a number of those most closely associated with the production speculate that "after he finished singing, he was literally spent." After all, it is not so far from his own articulation in 1956 of what the sensation of being onstage was like for him. "It's like a surge of electricity going through you," he had said back then. "It's almost like making love, but it's even stronger than that. . . . Sometimes I think my heart is going to explode."

THE "STAND-UP" SHOW two days later was no less of an unmitigated triumph. It was done once again in two more or less identical sets before a live audience, but the idea this time was to present the hits, updated for "today's audience," as Steve felt they ought to be, by the Billy Goldenberg arrangements. Contemporary orchestrations or not, once again Elvis was wearing the leather suit, and once again he betrayed his nervousness at the outset, reaching for the microphone with a shaking hand before launching into "Heartbreak Hotel." For this show the guitar is used strictly as a prop, and then only for the opening number of the opening set, as Elvis slides to his knees on the next number ("Hound Dog"), and then, perhaps inspired by his recent reacquaintance with Ed Parker, proceeds to strike karate poses throughout the rest of the show. It is a thoroughly masterful performance, as Elvis paces, pants, toys with the audience's affections (he hands out handkerchiefs dabbed with his sweat), whirls, and poses poised and animal-like. The atmosphere is charged, and Elvis himself is like a turbojet waiting to take off — there is no room for cool irony here, even if the songs are occasionally dated, the orchestrations fundamentally silly. By the time he gets to "If I Can Dream," which he will merely lip-synch at this and the second show (he will return the following day to record a live vocal, in different costume, to the backing track), so passionate is his commitment that even his lip-synching is convincing not only for its perfect synchronization, something he never seemed to bother much about in the movies, but for the utter sincerity of his gestures and facial expressions. It is as if he has finally become an actor by putting aside all that he has learned of acting and simply presenting the fire that he feels inside.

The following day, a Sunday, was the last day of taping and the last chance for Steve to get everything he needed before he began the delicate task of assembling the various elements and weaving them together in a rough cut to present to the sponsor, the Colonel, and the network brass later that summer. Bones had no doubt that Steve could pull it off. Despite increasing personal divisions with his partner, he knew of no one better suited to put a show together on the fly, make the right camera selections even as the action was taking place, and then match them up in such a way that they conveyed all the excitement you would get if you were actually present. The sound was going to be a problem, he knew, it was an antiquated, TV studio-board system — but the *feeling* was there. To Bob Finkel, who saw himself as having shepherded a very complex, difficult project to completion, "it was one of the most complete experiences I ever had in the business. There was no temperament, no 'they don't like it, fuck you, and walk out' — the execution of it, the success of it was all just very exciting."

To Steve Binder, on the other hand, it was more like a dream come true: the vision that he had pursued, against all business wisdom and common sense, had actually worked out. "I was looking for a keyhole. I didn't want to stop and go. I didn't want to pat him down for sweat or makeup or anything, just let him go out and do a live concert. I kept saying, 'It's okay to sweat, it's okay to have your hair mussed up.' I really feel in my gut if Elvis had done a clichéd Hollywood Elvis special, everybody in the business would have said the sets were magnificent, but Elvis would have been a laughingstock. But Elvis really socked it to them. And everything that everyone objected to — the sweat, the hair falling down his face — that was the blood and guts of the show, that was what people liked. And if there was anything they didn't like, it was the production numbers."

As for Elvis, Steve and Bones both felt they had witnessed a transformation which they could not imagine him easily setting aside. For Steve, who had studied the video monitors with fierce intentness as he cut the action live for broadcast, there was no question that "all of a sudden you could see the metamorphosis, all of a sudden the confidence started swelling. That was real cinema verité." It was even more evident to Bones when he came back into the dressing room after the second stand-up show. "Bill Belew had to just about cut the suit off him because he had sweated so much, and then Elvis said to whoever was in the room, 'Tell the Colonel I want to talk to him.' The Colonel came in, and he was just high from the experience, and he said, 'I want to tour again. I want to go out and work with a live audience.'" The Colonel, not surprisingly, was not about to discuss the matter in front of a roomful of strangers, but there was little doubt in Bones' mind that Elvis would stick to his new resolution.

Scotty and D.J. had long since gone home. It was the last time they would play with Elvis, and the last time Scotty ever saw him. There was no further talk of woodshedding; no call ever came. Steve and Bones had no further dealings with him either, once the show was finally edited and wrapped at the end of the summer; in fact, their own partnership broke up not long after. Bob Finkel, however, enjoyed his own quiet triumph in the end. When the Colonel returned home to Palm Springs at the conclusion of videotaping, he was astonished to discover the letters that had spelled out E-L-V-I-S on the show assembled in a giant display on his own front lawn. "I had the letters sent down with a generator, and when he got there, they were flashing." The Colonel never hesitated in admitting defeat. "He gave me his cane; I have it on my wall today." But in acknowledging defeat, he was not for a moment giving up the fight. There would be other battles, other contests, other causes to take up not much farther down the line.

ELVIS WITH ROY HAMILTON, AMERICAN STUDIO, MEMPHIS, JANUARY 1969.
(COURTESY OF JOE ESPOSITO)

A DAY AT THE RACES

L OCATION shooting for *Charro!,* the hard-hitting western script for which Elvis had such high hopes, began on July 22 in Apache Junction, Arizona, after two weeks of preproduction. It was an almost immediate disappointment. Elvis arrived on the set, bearded and looking appropriately scruffy, only to discover that the script, not exactly a literary masterpiece to begin with but written in the new, bold manner of a Clint Eastwood "spaghetti western," had been bowdlerized past the point of recognition. The opening scene, which had originally included three ladies of the night not only baring their breasts but pulling their dresses up "beyond their hips, showing their crotches, turning and showing their bare buttocks, and this is routine, and who cares what anybody sees," became instead a standard barroom confrontation, and the writer-director, Charles Marquis Warren, a veteran of Hollywood and creator of such television westerns as *Gunsmoke, Rawhide,* and *The Virginian,* turned out to be not only crude in his approach but eccentric in a way that deflected any hope of achieving anything of substance.

By the time that they returned to Hollywood four weeks later, Steve Binder had assembled a rough cut of the special. It ran considerably over the allotted hour, but Steve was very proud of it and wanted Elvis to take a look. A bunch of the guys accompanied him to Binder's office at NBC, and they all watched on a small black-and-white television monitor. Elvis appeared to Jerry Schilling to be extremely nervous, but he said nothing until the others expressed their enthusiastic approval. Even then he remained uncharacteristically restrained, almost as if, Jerry thought, he were afraid to go out on a limb until the public registered its reaction.

The Colonel, who attended a more formal screening with NBC and RCA executives on August 20, was under no such constraint. Where was the Christmas song? he demanded of Tom Sarnoff the next day, in the midst of a detailed written critique of the show. There were too many production numbers, he declared in his two-page memo; the gospel section was too long; there was a poor selection of live cuts; and "Little Egypt," the belly dancer number that took place on the carnival midway, was nothing more than a fanciful indulgence. More than anything else, though, he was incredulous that after all their talks, after all the negotiations that had taken place and all the flexibility that he and Mr. Presley had shown in allowing what was by contract supposed to be a *Christmas special* to be reduced first to a show with only 50 percent Christmas content, then to a single Christmas song, he should now see a cut that eliminated even that one number. That number had to be put back in the show "or we will all lose a tremendous amount of promotion not only from my company, All Star Shows, but through many other mediums and the following of Presley fans." The bottom line, said the Colonel, was that the special could not be broadcast in its present form. If they wanted to present it as is, he suggested that they put the show on ice until the following summer "and do a complete Christmas show for this fall as per our contract." No one imagined that the Colonel might be bluffing, and "Blue Christmas," a throwaway from the informal section, was immediately substituted for the showstopping "Tiger Man."

There was a month and a half still to go before the next film, tentatively entitled *Chautauqua* and another intended departure, a 1920s-era comedy with a period look, was scheduled to start. Elvis spent much of September in Palm Springs with Priscilla and the baby before returning to Memphis at the end of the month. For the moment he seemed curiously up in the air. Aside from the still-unspecified NBC picture, there were no future film deals in sight, and with the television special yet to air, he was talking more and more about a return to live performing. In an interview the previous month, he had spoken of touring once again. "I'll probably start out here in this country and after that play some concerts abroad, starting in Europe. I want to see some places I've never seen before. I miss the personal contact with audiences." Significantly, the Colonel offered no demurral, except to remind the reporter, "in his best Micawberish voice," that "Elvis is a very generous boy."

Three days after their return to Memphis, on September 28, Dewey Phillips died. He was only forty-two, and Elvis had not seen much of him in recent years. In fact, Dewey had been something of an embarrassment, adopting the habit of calling everyone "Elvis" and insisting that Elvis (the *real* Elvis) would be arriving at any moment to pick him up on whatever corner he happened to be hanging out — or, more pertinently, to pick up the tab. Sometimes he showed up drunk or stoned at the Memphian Theatre, offering loud commentary throughout the movies to Elvis' considerable displeasure; occasionally he would climb over the wall at Graceland and make his way up toward the house until he was intercepted by a guard. His professional life was in disarray; his last stint on the air, in Millington, Tennessee, had ended in disaster three years earlier, as his speed-crazed rap became more and more incomprehensible to the naked ear. But he *was* still Dewey; he was still loved by his friends, who did their best to prop him up (both Elvis and Sam Phillips were among the biggest contributors to the support of Dewey's wife, Dot, and her children); he was still the man who *had first played Elvis Presley on the air.*

"I am awfully hurt and feel very sorry about Dewey's death," Elvis told reporter James Kingsley. "We were very good friends, and I have always appreciated everything he did for me in helping me in my career in the early days." He had been terrified the night that Dewey played his first record on the radio, he said, but Dewey calmed him down. "[He] kept telling me to 'cool it,' it was really happening."

The funeral on October 1 was held at the same Memphis Funeral Home where Elvis had mourned his mother. He and Priscilla and a few of the guys arrived together, but then he and Priscilla retreated behind the curtain that gave the immediate family privacy. Mrs. Phillips had not been certain he would attend; he had let her know through a friend that "he would not come if the family thought it would cause too much confusion. I didn't know if he was coming or not when they closed the curtains [but] Elvis came to pay his respects. . . . He came over to me and hugged my neck. I introduced him to Dewey's mother, and I told him I was glad he came and that Dewey would have wanted him there. He said, 'Mrs. Dorothy, Dewey was my friend.'"

Sam Phillips and his two sons Knox and Jerry, George Klein, and singer Dickey Lee were all pallbearers. Everyone joined in on "The Old Rugged Cross," one of Dewey's favorites, which he sang at the top of his lungs while shaving every morning. After the ceremony Elvis and the guys recalled some of Dewey's more outrageous exploits. He looked real natural in the coffin, someone remarked with conventional politeness, almost as if he were alive. "Sonofabitch sure looked dead to me," remarked Elvis amid gales of laughter that Dewey probably would have appreciated.

It was a time of death. Elvis' cousin Bobby, Billy Smith's older brother, who hadn't been right in years, took rat poison and died on September 13 while Elvis was still lingering in Palm Springs. Bobby was only twenty-seven, and his father, Travis, who had worked the gate for years, was gravely ill from cirrhosis of the liver, one of the main reasons Billy had quit Elvis the previous year. Just two months earlier, another of Gladys' brothers, Elvis' crazy uncle Johnny, whom no one much liked because he was such a vicious drunk but who, with Vester Presley, had taught Elvis to play guitar as a child, had died at forty-six. He had spent his last few months in the hospital, just wasting away from Bright's disease, a kidney ailment that killed him almost as quickly as liver disease had taken his sister — and at the same age. That really spooked Elvis. It seemed almost like the family was cursed.

The new film, which would eventually be called *The Trouble with Girls*, appeared no less cursed. The producers failed to follow any of the Colonel's suggestions for cashing in on the *Bonnie and Clyde* craze or utilizing some of the great old-time talents that he had wanted to put them in touch with. Instead, they just blundered along on their own, creating neither a believable story nor a believable setting for their star — though he looked good in a white suit that didn't seem to match up particularly with the period and long, black, muttonchop sideburns.

There was little hope now that anything was going to break before the special aired in December. *Speedway*, released in May, had barely made back its negative cost, while *Stay Away, Joe*, a March release, and *Live a Little, Love a Little*, which came out in October, did even worse. The soundtrack album for *Speedway* had been a disaster, the single release from *Live a Little, Love a Little* sold well under two hundred thousand, and the title song from *Stay Away, Joe* had not even merited release as an A side. MGM had exhibited no interest whatsoever in writing a new contract with a star they had done business with for over eleven years now, and the Colonel had no interest in entertaining offers from a position of weakness rather than strength.

In many ways it might have seemed to the dispassionate observer that Elvis' career was permanently stalled, that, like every big entertainer in the cycle of pop success, he was ready for the kind of professional afterlife that the Colonel's original client, Gene Austin, or Al Jolson had enjoyed for decades after his time of influence was past. But then "If I Can Dream," the climactic number that Earl Brown had written for the special, was released as a single on November 5, just as the finishing touches were being put on the album, with Elvis approving every last detail. The Colonel, meanwhile, was doing his customary job of building everything around the December 3 air date, orchestrating publicity, radio spots, billboard and trade advertising, even a radio special that would go out to fifteen hundred stations on December 1, to peak around the time of the broadcast.

The single took a little while to build, entering the Top 40 at the end of November and remaining on the charts for thirteen weeks, where it reached number twelve in mid January. This represented Elvis' highest chart position since 1965 and by far his greatest single sales (750,000) since "Crying in the Chapel" that same year. In the meantime the soundtrack album was released about a week before the special was scheduled to air, with a photograph of Elvis in his white Edwardian suit gripping the microphone, eyes closed, singing passionately, against the backdrop of the giant Elvis sign spelled out in red letters that had ended up on the Colonel's lawn.

I think I must have gotten the album the day it came out, and I can remember sitting with it in my hand, gazing at it almost incredulously as I tried to take in whatever information was to be deduced from its graphics (on the back Elvis was pictured both in the black leather suit and in the gold jacket) and from its credits (I couldn't believe that Elvis had actually performed such strong bluesy material as "Lawdy, Miss Clawdy," "Baby What You Want Me to Do?," and "One Night," along with the gospel number "Up Above My Head"). The reason that I stared so hard at the record was that I was determined not to listen to it until the show actually aired, not just because I didn't want to spoil the suspense but because I had gotten a review assignment for the special from the *Boston Phoenix,* a weekly in which I had been writing about the music I loved for the last couple of years. I had already published one story about Elvis earlier that year, pointing to a renewal of musical commitment on his part on the basis of little more than the three blues-oriented singles that he had put out in a row (my key piece of evidence was "Guitar Man"). I won't bother to apologize for my naivete. Suffice it to say that I was excited about the show.

"It's been a long time, baby," I quoted Elvis to lead off my review, then described how "in the first five minutes he managed to shrug off all the lethargic blandness that has characterized his public stance since his release from the army; he returned instead to the familiar mine of defiance and wounded alienation, his face poured sweat, the voice reclaimed its old wildness . . ." It was like nothing I had ever seen on television before, other than Howlin' Wolf's appearance on *Shindig,* both a revelation *and* a vindication (it was definitely not cool in 1968 to like Elvis, and his resurrection was as unlikely as Wolf's very appearance on national TV). I don't know if I can convey how truly thrilling a moment it really was — and, as much as the performance may have held up over the years, I'm not sure that it can ever be as thrilling again. In many ways I (and others like me) may well have been Steve Binder's ideal viewers, as we read volumes into every gesture, strained to catch every aside, found justification at last for the hopeless faith that we had placed in the music.

Even amid certain strongly voiced critical reservations (the orchestrated medleys, I wrote, sounded like a reprise from a cheesy Broadway musical, the production numbers were "tasteless"), I could not hide my true feelings — nor would I have wanted to. "His public innocence of adulthood serves to enable us to suspend judgment as we are ourselves suspended," I concluded. "We begrudged him his retreat, and now that he's coming back he'll be subjected to the scrutiny of a new generation and perhaps to harsher judgments. It can't be helped. He may never regain his former success. What mustn't be forgotten is that ten years ago Elvis performed existential acts which helped to liberate an entire generation, and naturally in such terms success can only be incidental."

Not all the reviews were as starry-eyed. The *Hollywood Reporter,* eyeing the informal segments disapprovingly, declared that at times "it looked as though someone had accidentally taped the rehearsal. . . . For some unfathomable reason Elvis was set on a stage that did not look much larger than a two-by-four, jammed it with a four-piece combo, and fringed it with squealing youngsters. As though this was not enough, Elvis was wrapped in leather from neck to foot and bathed in hot lights, the combination of which was enough to make the perspiration flow like tears. . . ."

Variety, too, took a decidedly mixed view. "He still can't sing. The words still are unintelligible. But that never was very important," *Variety's* critic opined, "[because] it is Presley's suggestion of simple, unthinking, illiterate sex, his intimation that he isn't going to bug you with hangups because he doesn't even know he has them that gives him his appeal to the inexperienced." "I don't think many viewers care to see singers sweat on TV," sniffed the *Los Angeles Times* reviewer. But Robert Shelton in the *New York Times* wrote a thoughtful review headlined "Rock Star's Explosive Blues Have Vintage Quality." And the ratings told an even better story. It may no longer have been possible to garner the 80-percent audience share that Elvis got when he appeared for the first time on *The Ed Sullivan Show,* but *Singer Presents ELVIS* was the number-one show of the season and, with a 32.0 Nielsen and 42 percent share, gave NBC its biggest overall ratings victory of the year. In addition, the "exploitation campaign" worked out almost exactly as the Colonel had hoped, with a *TV Guide* feature putting Elvis squarely back in the center of things, and numerous well-timed articles (including a separate piece in the *New York Times* that accompanied the review) focusing on his projected return to live performing.

The Colonel meanwhile was working frantically to make sure that this would actually take place. With that same sure instinct for timing that had always served him and his client so well, he had recently been in touch with Alex Shoofey, newly installed executive vice president at Kirk Kerkorian's still-under-construction International Hotel. The International, with 30 stories, 1,512 rooms, and a 2,000-capacity showroom, promised to be the biggest and most splendiferous casino-hotel in Las Vegas when it opened in July, a factor which alone would have recommended it to the Colonel had he not already been well acquainted with Shoofey, a fixture at the Sahara for years. He was also drawn to the independent spirit of the fifty-one-year-old Kerkorian, an eighth-grade dropout and World War II fighter pilot from Fresno who had started a charter service after the war and parlayed that into ownership of an airline (Transamerica) and a casino (the Flamingo, which he had stocked with former employees of the Colonel's pal Milton Prell). Kerkorian was a big-stakes gambler, well known as "a modest man in opulent surroundings," a description that might just as easily have fitted the Colonel himself, to whom the idea of playing the biggest, brashest, and newest casino showroom was the kind of bold maneuver to which he was always drawn. On December 10 he outlined his terms for the engagement to Abe Lastfogel of William Morris, who was conducting the formal negotiations.

He wanted $500,000 for four weeks, one show per night, two on the weekends, with Monday nights off; if Shoofey preferred two weeks, he would give him that for $300,000. Also, of course, he wanted the option of recording a soundtrack album plus a television special, with all facilities to be furnished by the hotel.

Nine days later, his offer was accepted with certain modifications that brought it more in line with standard Vegas practice. The International definitely wanted four weeks and would pay the $500,000 he was asking if Elvis were to open the hotel; otherwise, the salary would be $400,000, still the kind of money that only headliners like Frank Sinatra and Dean Martin could command. Like every other Las Vegas performer, Elvis would be expected to do two shows a night, but if any other star were to sign a contract requiring less of a commitment within a year of the engagement, the hotel would pay Mr. Presley a penalty of $50,000. Separate suites would be available for Elvis and the Colonel; the making of an album and/or television special would be accommodated by the hotel; and the International would retain the option for a second engagement, to be exercised by the end of the first. In other words, if the option were to be picked up, Elvis would make approximately the same amount in eight weeks of performing that he would for eight weeks of filming — although, of course, with the cost of hiring a band, along with costumes, promotion, and other incidentals, he would have significant additional expenses.

The Colonel never hesitated, nor did he doubt for a moment that once Vegas saw Elvis, as always *the deal could be improved*. With somewhat uncharacteristic managerial prudence, he chose not to have his act open the showroom (it would be irresponsible, he felt, to have his star performer go into a room in which the bugs had not even begun to be ironed out), but in every other way he fully embraced the challenge. Filling a two-thousand-capacity room in Vegas while Frank Sinatra and Dean Martin were playing twelve-hundred-seaters, bringing Elvis back in triumph to the scene of his solitary failure thirteen years before, staging his return to live performing in a manner that would ensure maximum public exposure on a national stage, was a risk from which he did not flinch. In fact, by the Colonel's standards it was almost a clear-cut imperative, if only because *no one had ever done it before*.

I T WAS AT THIS POINT, with little input from the Colonel and, seemingly, little forethought of his own, that Elvis took a step almost equally bold. A recording session had been scheduled for early January to record an album and two singles for RCA as a start on the new year's contractual obligations. Sometime after Christmas, Felton came over from Nashville to talk about the session while some of the guys were at the house. Marty Lacker had just started work at American, a little studio in a run-down neighborhood in North Memphis that had produced an unprecedented string of sixty-four chart records over the last eighteen months for a variety of out-of-town labels. George Klein, too, had American connections (the studio's principal owner, Chips Moman, had produced some sides for a small label George had recently started up with a partner). And Red West, who had only just begun to come back into the picture with a Christmas visit to Memphis (he had been working steadily on the Coast in Robert

Conrad's TV series *The Wild, Wild West*), had long-standing connections with Chips both as a songwriter and as an occasional recording artist.

Had Elvis ever thought of recording at American? George asked when he sensed Elvis' lack of enthusiasm for returning to Nashville and Felton's lack of any real commitment to it. The Memphis studio had a funky sound, and Chips was a proven hit maker, not to mention the fact that he had some of the best musicians in the world working for him. Best of all, it was convenient — Elvis would scarcely have to leave the house. Marty stressed the musical possibilities — Chips had some great songwriters working for him, and it had become obvious by now that Freddy was either too busy building up his own publishing or could simply no longer deliver hit records. With good material, a studio that practically guaranteed hits, and his own more active participation in the project, Marty argued, maybe making records could go back to being fun and break away from some of the music-business bullshit of Nashville.

Soon everyone was registering his support, even Felton, and in the end, as an informed source described it to *Variety* several months later, "Presley's friends, Marty Lacker [and] George Klein, convinced the singer . . . so subtly that he finally 'came up with the idea himself.'" At this point all that was left to do was to place a call to Chips, who did not hesitate for one moment to postpone an already scheduled Neil Diamond session for something in which he sensed both historic possibilities and a $25,000 payday. And so a ten-day session was set up at American, with a January 13 scheduled start.

It was the kind of unplanned, uncontrolled, and uncontrollable event that the Colonel had always sought to protect himself against. Neither he nor Freddy trusted Marty Lacker, who they felt was always seeking to advance his own interests — but then, the Colonel didn't much trust Freddy at this point either. And if he was expecting support from Felton, he didn't get it. Felton's allegiance was strictly to Elvis, and after the debacle of the last two Nashville sessions, he was not about to insist upon clinging to previous practice. As far as Felton was concerned, Elvis could use some of Chips' hitmaking magic. Nor was he insecure about his own ability to produce in Memphis, just as long as he could bring his own engineer, Al Pachucki, with him. Felton prided himself on his ability to get along with anyone. Working at American was not going to be a problem, because he wasn't going to let it be a problem. But he was not altogether reckoning on Chips Moman.

*   *   *

L INCOLN "CHIPS" MOMAN was born in LaGrange, Georgia, in 1936, and gravitated to Memphis at the age of twenty-one, where he was involved in the formation of Stax, the great rhythm and blues record label. A flinty-eyed man of fierce intelligence who seemingly bore a permanent suspicion against the world, he was a student of the art of recording in a way that had never even occurred to Felton — or to Steve Sholes or Chet Atkins, for that matter. To Chips, "making the record itself" was all that he was into. "From the day I went into the Gold Star Studio in California [in 1956] to play a session, I never cared about anything else." Although he was also an accomplished songwriter and guitarist, to Chips getting the sound in the studio surpassed everything else — that and being in control of your recording situation. From Chips' point of view he had been screwed out of his share of Stax just when the record company started to get going, and he was never going to let that happen to him again.

At American he gathered a group of experienced Memphis studio players and formed a rhythm section that included guitarist Reggie Young, a veteran of the Bill Black Combo; the brilliant bass player and producer Tommy Cogbill; Mike Leech, who played bass when Cogbill was producing and wrote arrangements as well; keyboard players Bobby Emmons and Bobby Wood; and drummer Gene Chrisman. These musicians he bound to him with an unquestioning loyalty, some might say with all the mesmerizing influence of Colonel Parker himself. That was how American, which had assumed its present shape not as a label but as a studio-for-hire in 1965 and had been turning out hits ever since, had achieved such cachet. Recording at American had turned out to be something of a talisman of good luck for artists as diverse as Wilson Pickett, Dusty Springfield, Dionne Warwick, and the Box Tops. Which was how everyone around Elvis who had pushed for his selection of the studio hoped it was going to work out for him.

Elvis showed up on the evening of Monday, January 13, with a cold and a bad case of the jitters. None of the swagger that he frequently displayed in public situations was present. Instead, he appeared slightly subdued; despite the presence of his usual retinue he seemed almost alone. "What a funky studio," he remarked self-consciously as he came in the back door, and all his guys laughed uproariously, merely reinforcing a sense of skepticism among the musicians, who, for all their curiosity about Elvis Presley, wondered just what this was going to be about. Glen Spreen, who had recently joined the American staff as a writer and arranger, watched open-mouthed as three or four of the guys reached for their cigarette lighters when Elvis pulled out one of his thin little German cigars. "I remember, it ran through my head: Why are these people doing this? That was the first thing. And the second thing that hit me was: Why does he put up with it?"

Nobody was really all that impressed ("I mean we were thrilled about Elvis," said trumpet player Wayne Jackson, "but it wasn't like doing Neil Diamond"). But the talk was all positive. And the songs that had been assembled included a good selection of material, with a tape from Billy Strange's discovery Mac Davis (who had written "Memories" for the special), several promising cuts from Lamar, who was pushing a song called "Kentucky Rain" by a songwriter named Eddie Rabbitt, plus eight or ten numbers that Elvis had been fooling around with at home. Felton's presence offered some measure of reassurance, of course, but facing a roomful of unfamiliar musicians who were probably going out of their way to indicate just how unimpressed they were put Elvis in a strange kind of mood, and when Chips called for the session to start, there was a distinct air of nervous tension in the room.

They began with "Long Black Limousine," working hard at first just to get the sound right, with Chips interacting easily with the musicians and making plain what he wanted to hear. In his communication with Elvis, he seems matter-of-fact, patient, almost subdued given his reputation — but there is no question from the outset as to who is in charge. Chips had been told by certain members of the Elvis camp that he should concern himself strictly with the sound board, that it was not up to him to embarrass Elvis by asking for a re-take or telling him when he was flat — Elvis' ears would tell him *that,* and besides, he went by feel, not by rules. From the start, though, it was obvious that Chips was not taking any of these admonitions very seriously. As Reggie Young observed, "We weren't yes-men, and that upset Felton. But every song we worked on, in our minds, was a potential number one." Or as Chips saw it, "I'm kind of a stubborn fellow. I guess I believe in what I do enough, so I think if a guy's hiring me [to do a job], I believe that's what he's hiring me for."

For an Elvis session the atmosphere was remarkably subdued. Even the guys seem cowed into a kind of grudging silence, and it is only as he really gets into the first song, a melodramatic country morality tale with a chilling ending, that Elvis' confidence starts to grow. By the ninth take he is practically screaming out his indignation at the fate of the small-town girl who, lured by the glamor of city life, returns home in a "fancy car for all the town to see" — except that fancy car turns out to be the long black limousine of the title, the hearse in her own funeral procession. Rarely has Elvis sung so passionately in the studio, rarely has he revealed himself so nakedly, and if his voice is roughened by his cold, if his singing lacks some of the easygoing grace of some of his finest sides from the early sixties, rarely can he have taken so much satisfaction from the consistent application of effort and craft.

They moved quickly through "This Is the Story," one of Freddy's swellingly romantic European imports, then launched into "Wearin' That Loved On Look," a tough, bluesy number that Lamar had brought to the session. Elvis continued to be embarrassed by his hoarseness and the difficulty he was having controlling his voice, but he gave his all through fifteen arduous takes, sinking his teeth once again into the pure feeling of the song. By now the musicians had actually begun to sit up and take notice. Glen Spreen found that he was impressed despite himself, not so much with Elvis' technique as with his soulfulness, his ability to make a song live — it was almost like going to church. "We didn't have a real vocal booth," said Mike Leech, more an observer than a participant the first few nights, "but we had a baffle that the vocalist would stand behind, with a window in it. And he was back there just like he would be onstage, doing gyrations and the whole thing — because that was just the way he sang. He sang everything like that; he'd have his eyes shut and he was sweating pretty good at the end of each track — he just got into it." No one was too impressed with the whole sycophantic setup, or with Elvis' evident need for it. But they knew by now that at least this was going to be a real session.

ELVIS' COLD WORSENED on the second night, but his spirit was, if anything, even stronger. Where they had knocked off at 5:00 A.M. the previous night, this time they went straight through until 8:30, once again cutting only four songs but focusing on them in a way that Elvis had not sustained in the studio since the 1966 gospel session. Unfortunately, the next night he was not able to come in at all, and Chips concentrated on cutting instrumental tracks for several new songs, including Mac Davis' "Don't Cry Daddy" and "Mama Liked the Roses" by American house composer Johnny Christopher, which had drawn an immediate emotional reaction from Elvis when he heard the demo. With those tracks done, the session was postponed until the following Monday, since it was clear that Elvis would need some time to get his voice in shape before they could continue.

It might have seemed at this point that not much had been accomplished: eight rough vocals in two nights of recording on songs that for the most part Chips would have deemed not up to standard. But two things had been established. One was that Chips was in charge. More important, Elvis really cared. Despite all the concerns that had been voiced on his behalf, he had obviously taken to Chips' direction not just without objection but with enthusiasm. It was as if, guitarist Reggie Young observed, Elvis had become another member of the band. And once that happened, he could get down to the serious business of recording without any holdback — "I mean, he really worked at it."

They picked up where they had left off when he returned the following Monday, starting off with a number that Elvis had expressed some reservations about to begin with. "In the Ghetto" had come in with the seventeen-song tape of Mac Davis songs that Billy Strange had submitted for the session. Elvis had been drawn to Davis' writing ever since Billy first delivered "A Little Less Conversation" for the *Live a Little, Love a Little* soundtrack the previous year. Since then Elvis had chosen five of the Atlanta-born songwriter's compositions (including "Don't Cry Daddy," which at the moment existed only as an instrumental track), and even the Colonel seemed to sense there was something special about Strange's twenty-seven-year-old protégé, whom he had met for the first time at the *Charro!* session. "That first night Colonel Parker said [to me], 'Are you the boy who wrote that "Little Less Conversation"?' I said, 'Yes.' He said, 'You a pretty good-lookin' boy, you're going to be a star.' I said, 'Well, thank you very much.' He said, 'You want the Colonel to rub your head?' I'm looking around, and I'm thinking he's really putting me through the grease, but these guys with him are dead serious, they're all just looking at me. So I bent over, and he put his hand on my head, like Oral Roberts, and he said, 'You're going to be a star. You tell everybody the Colonel touched your head.'"

Elvis' reservations about the song had nothing to do with stardom or songwriting talent, however. Rather, it was politics that concerned him, or the mere whiff of politics, in a business that has generally been guided by one cardinal rule: whatever an entertainer's personal feelings or political point of view, it is never worth alienating any substantial portion of your audience that might not agree with you.

Elvis had, it is true, gone against that precept in a general way with the "there must be a better world somewhere" sentiments of "If I Can Dream," but "In the Ghetto" was more in the nature of an explicit "message song,"

detailing the inevitable consequences of ghetto poverty and societal indifference (the song was originally subtitled "The Vicious Circle") and pleading for compassion for black youth. While these sentiments may well
appear mild today, and the song's stance was somewhat softened by Davis'
craft and the abstract, almost fairy-tale form in which he couched his tale,
its subject remained controversial at the time, and even George Klein, a
longtime champion of rhythm and blues who prided himself on his liberal
views, cautioned Elvis against recording it. But when Chips countered that
if that was the case, he thought he would just bring the song to Roosevelt
Grier, the ex-football player whom he had recently signed to his own newly
formed AGP (American Group Productions) label, George immediately
saw the error of his ways and confessed to Elvis that he had made a mistake, that he believed that this was a number-one hit. With Joe's further
encouragement, Elvis made up his mind to cut it, and so it became the first
number that they tackled, and the only one that they took up, between
nine o'clock Monday night and early Tuesday morning.

If you had never heard of Elvis Presley but were simply presented with
the twenty-three meticulous takes of the song that he did on that night, it
would be virtually impossible not to be won over. The singing is of such
unassuming, almost translucent eloquence, it is so quietly confident in its
simplicity, so well supported by the kind of elegant, no-frills small-group
backing that was the hallmark of the American style — it makes a statement almost impossible to deny. Later, horns and voices would be overdubbed to add a dramatic flourish, but you can hear a kind of tenderness in
these early takes that most recalls the Elvis who first entered Sam Phillips'
Sun studio, offering equal parts yearning and social compassion. To the
musicians, this was the clincher. "He just sang great," said trumpet player
Wayne Jackson, an American regular who was observing the session in
advance of doing overdubs. "The first time I heard 'In the Ghetto,' I just
really felt slimy all over. I thought, 'Oh, my God, this is wonderful. This is
it!'" As the song develops, subtle adjustments are made, with Elvis quick to
acknowledge mistakes and eager to get on with it — and one is provided
with an incontrovertible glimpse of what the process might have been
like for Elvis, if only he had been able to approach recording consistently
as an art. Throughout it all Chips, ordinarily perceived as an abrasive man,
is nothing but gently understated and encouraging, playing the session,
the session musicians, and the singer as if they were a single finely tuned
instrument.

A bridge had clearly been crossed. Tuesday night was devoted mostly to vocal overdubs, to which Elvis applied himself painstakingly, assiduously, and entirely at Chips' direction. On his own initiative he undertook sloppy, good-hearted versions of the Beatles' "Hey Jude" and the 1963 country hit "From a Jack to a King," in which Chips does not appear to have taken much interest and for which he may not even have been present. This was Elvis' time — you sense that he is making music simply for the fun of it, while Chips patiently awaits his next opportunity to contribute.

One of the purely coincidental factors not at all incidental to Elvis' mood was the presence of Roy Hamilton in the American studio that week. The thirty-nine-year-old Hamilton, a Georgia native who had burst upon the rhythm and blues scene some fifteen years earlier out of Jersey City, New Jersey, had been one of Elvis' chief vocal inspirations ever since he had first heard Hamilton's operatic version of the Rodgers and Hammerstein standard, "You'll Never Walk Alone" in 1954. Over the years he had returned again and again to Hamilton's virtuosic inspirational material, both in his listening and in his home singing sessions, and songs like "I Believe" (which he had recorded for his gospel EP in 1957), "Unchained Melody," "Ebb Tide," "Hurt," and "If I Loved You" had long since become part of his private repertoire. Hamilton, a classically trained singer who had started off in the gospel field, contracted tuberculosis in 1956 at the height of his popularity, and though he had resumed his recording career with some success after a two-year hiatus, he had never really been able to recapture his past position. He had only recently signed with Chips' little label, and now he was recording during the day while Elvis recorded at night, looking for the single that might put him back on the charts.

It was George Klein (who had seen Hamilton perform at small Memphis clubs several times over the past few years) who reported to Elvis that Roy was singing better than ever. Elvis could scarcely contain his enthusiasm. He wondered if George would call Chips up and see if it might be okay for them to go to a session. "I said, 'Come on, Elvis,' but he said, 'No, man, people don't like it when you just show up.'" So Klein requested formal permission from Chips, and the two of them went over to the studio, with Elvis at least as excited as he had been when he went to see Jackie Wilson.

He stammered out his admiration to Hamilton during a break, telling him how much the older man's singing had meant to him — and then he was moved to do something that totally floored the musicians who were watching: he offered Hamilton one of his songs. The song was "Angelica," a Barry Mann–Cynthia Weill collaboration that Chips had brought to the session and that represented exactly the kind of new pop direction that Elvis wanted to explore. "Man, he really loved that song," George Klein noted wonderingly, but he never hesitated in offering it to Hamilton, as if all of a sudden he had become someone like Lamar or Freddy, pitching Hamilton on what a great job he could do with the song. It was an unquestionable indicator of Elvis' feelings, certainly, and a source of some bemusement to the musicians, who were unused to such spontaneous displays of generosity and feeling from a star, but, they noted realistically, it may have been a source of considerably less amusement to the songwriters and publishing interests who lost out on an Elvis Presley cut by virtue of that generosity.

Listening to Hamilton's recorded version of the song is instructive and indicates not only that Elvis was right in his instincts as an a&r man but how indebted he was to the other man for his more ambitious "serious" style. Hamilton delivered a stunning, impeccably phrased version of the number, full of the kind of dramatic effects that Elvis was reaching for in songs like "It's Now or Never" and "How Great Thou Art," but offered up with the kind of effortless ease that only a true virtuoso can achieve. It is all the more instructive, then, that Elvis should not have let the sheer talent of his idols — singers like Jackie Wilson, Jake Hess, and Hamilton himself — intimidate him but used it instead as a goad to achievement, the achievement of someone who, while he knew he could never match his models in technique, maintained his aspiration to join them solely on the strength of effort, dedication, and whole-hearted commitment to the music.

The following night, the last one scheduled, was the pinnacle of the session. Beginning after midnight, Elvis kicked off with a fervid version of "Without Love," a 1957 hit in the inspirational mode for Clyde McPhatter, yet another of his r&b singing idols, but one with a lighter, more sinuous voice than Hamilton. For the next number he sat down at the piano and launched into an impassioned version of Eddy Arnold's "I'll Hold You in My Heart" even before the four-track safety tape was rolling. It was strictly an off-the-cuff affair, one ragged take in which the band at one point indicates its intention to conclude while Elvis just keeps on going with all the gospel fervor of McPhatter or Hamilton. There was nothing for Chips to do, and he had no interest in contributing to such an amateurish endeavor — but there is something magical about the moment that only the most inspired singing can bring about, as Elvis loses himself in the music, words no longer lend themselves to literal translation, and singer and listener both are left emotionally wrung out by the time the song finally limps to an end. It was almost 4:00 in the morning, and after a quick detour for Bobby Darin's "I'll Be There," another of those numbers, like "From a Jack to a King," that Elvis simply wanted to do, they began work on the one song from the session that Chips would have been willing to bet money would become a hit, not coincidentally a song on which he held the publishing.

"Suspicious Minds" had been released the previous year on the Scepter label by its author, Mark James, Chips' most promising new staff writer. It was a grown-up tale of love and infidelity, expressing complex emotions in the form of a sophisticated soul ballad written in two distinct musical movements. James, who had recently enjoyed a huge songwriting hit with B. J. Thomas' version of his "Hooked on a Feeling," had done a good job on his own composition, and Chips' production was typically tasteful and spare, but the record had not been a hit. In the view of Glen Spreen, who had grown up with James and B. J. Thomas in Houston and had come to American because of his friendship with them, there was a reason: Mark's voice was too pretty, too lacking in rough edges. Elvis, he felt, would be able to add the missing element of passion. Like Chips, he was convinced that the song was a potential monster hit.

Taking exactly the same arrangement, to the point where you might almost confuse Elvis' backing track with the original, Chips once again brought enormous powers of concentration to the task, as we hear indications that Elvis is by now definitely feeling at home. "See see fuck you rider," he declares at one point when he messes up, and there are a number of "Goddamnit's," and even a karate routine scattered among the various takes. Even so, his own concentration never wavers, and his singing achieves the same remarkable mixture of tenderness and poise that it did on "In the Ghetto," with one significant element added — an expressive quality somewhere between stoicism (at suspected infidelity) and anguish (over impending loss). Everyone in the studio *knew* that this was the song. An atmosphere of excitement and anticipation runs all the way through its recording, and after getting a master in just four full takes, everyone said their good-byes at 7:00 that morning, confident that the job had been done.

The *Memphis Commercial Appeal* ran an interview in the paper later that day. After first describing how unusual this session really had been, reporter James Kingsley next quoted Chips, not ordinarily a man given to public encomiums, on the subject of "one of the hardest-working artists I have ever been associated with. What energy and enthusiasm he has while working." Elvis, far more accustomed to the limelight, turned to his producer and said with disarming plaintiveness, "We have some hits, don't we, Chips?" "Maybe some of your biggest," Chips replied without the least bit of hesitation.

I T WAS ONLY AFTER ELVIS AND PRISCILLA took off for Aspen with the gang for a brief ski and snowmobile vacation that the business issues raised with the recording of "Suspicious Minds" fully surfaced. Freddy had tried to get a piece of the publishing from the first, and when he became insistent on the point, Chips had suggested that he take his $25,000 (the amount that RCA had paid to rent the studio) and stick it up his ass; if that was the way the record company felt about it, they could just forget about the session and they could forget about cutting the song. The dispute raged on for some time, with Tom Diskin backing up Freddy and no end in sight until RCA representative Harry Jenkins came down on Chips' side and they could finally get on with the actual recording. The debate for the most part was kept away from Elvis — or, it might be argued, Elvis kept away from it. But the bitterness lingered long after Elvis had left the studio, as threats were made, accusations and counteraccusations exchanged, and it was strongly hinted that "Mama Liked the Roses," the song by Johnny Christopher that Elvis had liked so much and another of Chips' copyrights, would not appear on the album if Chips was not willing to give up at least part of the publishing.

And yet even as this was going on, a follow-up session was being planned. Whatever twists and turns business might take, there was no one who failed to recognize what an extraordinary musical experience the past two weeks had been and how significant the seventeen sides they already had might prove commercially as well as artistically. Elvis' enthusiasm remained undiminished, and clearly it was in everyone's interests to continue. So Chips kept his publishing, and arrangements were made to resume recording at American in three and one-half weeks, though all the suspicions that Chips and the Elvis camp (Freddy, RCA, and the Colonel) had had of each other from the beginning were now multiplied a thousandfold, and Felton was left uncomfortably in the middle.

Elvis showed up at the studio on February 17 for six more days of recording, which would yield another thirteen sides. Many of the songs that he recorded represented high points comparable to anything he had achieved during the first session, from "Stranger in My Own Home Town," the Percy Mayfield blues, a longtime favorite, to Della Reese's r&b version of Eddy Arnold's "After Loving You," which he had been fooling around with at home for years. With the environment familiar and the experience of proving himself already under his belt, Elvis showed all the easy confidence that he was used to displaying in Nashville, and his occasionally swaggering manner was in marked contrast to the insecurity of his first few days in the studio. The highlights of the session, though, were a trio of contemporary ballads conveying naked vulnerability. Eddie Rabbitt's "Kentucky Rain" was a song that Lamar believed in more strongly than anything he had brought to Elvis to date; "Any Day Now," Chuck Jackson's lyrical 1962 r&b hit, was a paean to male apprehensions ("Any day now I'll be on my own"); and Jerry Butler's "Only the Strong Survive," released so recently it had yet to even enter the charts, was an instant soul classic, almost tailor-made for Elvis, couched as it was in a mother's advice to her son. "Boy," the grown-up narrator recalls his mother saying to him, "I see you settin' out there all alone:

> *Cryin' your eyes out*
> *'Cause the woman that you love is gone*
> *Oh, there's gonna be, there's gonna be*
> *A whole lot of trouble in your life*
> *So listen to me, get up off of your knees*
> *'Cause only the strong survive.*

You cannot mistake the personal resonance that Elvis finds in the song, and along with "In the Ghetto" and "Suspicious Minds" it represents perhaps the most finely crafted achievement of the American sessions, announcing the birth of a new hybrid style, a cross between "Old Shep" and contemporary soul, in which Elvis can fully believe. Chips is never anything less than fully involved in the recording process, and neither his nor Elvis' attention wavers through twenty-nine bearing-down takes. Even Freddy Bienstock, who could scarcely have been heartened by the increasing diminution of his role (these were not songs *he* had brought to the session), was unable to restrain his enthusiasm. After the session was over, he happened to run into Bob Dylan on his flight back to New York. All he could talk about to Dylan, who had just completed the recording of his own country album, *Nashville Skyline*, was the magnificent job that Elvis had done on "Only the Strong Survive."

With Elvis' participation completed on February 22, Mike Leech and Glen Spreen began work on the arrangements for string and horn over-dubs, which were to begin a month later. "In the Ghetto" had already been selected as the first single, with an April release date planned, and a track listing was mapped out for the album that would follow shortly thereafter. The approach to arrangements was as innovative in intent as every other aspect of the sessions. "I wanted to give Elvis a different image," said Glen Spreen, articulating the philosophy that guided both Mike Leech and him. "I wanted to use the violas to play the same lines as the French horns so they could blend together as a color and then be complemented by the strings. I used syncopation with the strings — they're bowing — and I used a lot of cellos down deep and dark, especially on 'In the Ghetto,' because I wanted to bring out the darkness, the passion, as opposed to the force. I wanted to give [the voicings] some realism, because I thought Elvis had a very real, very soulful voice, and [I wanted to] pay attention to the *feeling* in that voice."

Not every arrangement worked as it was meant to, as Spreen and Leech would have been the first to admit, and the now almost open political war-fare between Felton and Chips led to a number of unfortunate compromises, as Felton sought desperately to regain control, and, perhaps more important, credit, for a project he had supported from the first. Even so, Chips continued to have substantial input; whatever the political situation, and however irked he may have felt at this point at everyone else, there was no way he was going to walk away from this project until it was finished. Even the Colonel seemed to recognize the remarkable nature of the achievement, if only by his continued absence from the proceedings. He was proud of his boy, he was proud of the way Elvis had thrown himself into the recording sessions, just like he had into the television special — if Elvis simply took the same approach to Las Vegas, there was nothing that could stop them now.

Elvis meanwhile was fulfilling the last of his movie commitments, *Change of Habit,* a fanciful tale in which he played an idealistic doctor sav-ing ghetto kids with the aid of nuns in civilian disguise, headed by Mary Tyler Moore. He gave it his best shot, working with thirty-six-year-old director Billy Graham, a graduate of *Omnibus,* the best known of television's classic experiments with culture prior to the advent of educational TV, and Sanford Meisner's well-known Neighborhood Playhouse, an alternative Method workshop for actors. Graham developed improvisational exercises in preproduction and worked with Elvis on different approaches to character motivation, discovering his star to be an apt pupil when his interest was engaged. "We'd do scenes where he would find out that one of his guys had fucked his wife or girlfriend, and some amazing things would come out. We'd always try to think of outrageous subject matter to make the improvisation more heated, more animated — he was good at that."

Graham stressed what he had learned from Sandy Meisner, that acting was reacting, and "Elvis liked that. I would say to him, 'It's not about figuring out how you're going to read your next line while the other guy is talking — but listen to what the other guy is saying, and that will dictate how the next line is going to come out.' Certain things he could do quite well. He could do humor. He could do a fight scene. But his line readings — a lot of them would be very conventional." Unfortunately, the shooting schedule was tight, and the score was uninspired, despite the presence of Billy Goldenberg, who found Elvis almost listless in his approach compared to the no-holds-barred engagement of the special — a difference that Goldenberg put down to an on-set affair, though it's hard to say what was different about this on-set affair from the one he had had while making the special.

Meanwhile, Las Vegas was rapidly approaching. On February 26, four days after the completion of the second Memphis session, Elvis flew out to officially "sign" the contract (which had not yet been fully worked out) on the roughed-in stage of the International construction site. Barbra Streisand would open the room in July, the International's publicity release announced, with Elvis following her into what was "being heralded as the world's largest showroom." On April 15, with no cameras present, he signed the actual agreement, and three hundred thousand copies of "In the Ghetto" were shipped by RCA, the picture sleeve blazoned with COMING SOON! FROM ELVIS IN MEMPHIS LP ALBUM (the Colonel would make sure that the next three hundred thousand changed the message to urge fans to "ASK FOR" the album). Two weeks after the ship date, the single hit the charts and stayed there for thirteen weeks, reaching number three on June 14 and giving Elvis not only his first Top 10 hit but his first gold record since the spring of 1965. More than that, it was clearly an impact hit, not

just a fluke, following up not only on the sales success of "If I Can Dream"
but the new direction that the previous single had announced.

The trades certainly took notice, with a *Variety* headline declaring, "'In
the Ghetto,' Presley's 1st Protest Song, Stirs Singer's Younger Fans." On a
less happy note, the success of the single led for the first time to an official
declaration of hostilities between the Felton Jarvis camp and the Chips
Moman camp, resolved only by the entrance of Colonel Parker, who was
his own camp. For the first two weeks that the single was on the charts, *Billboard* listed Felton as producer; then, evidently at the instigation of Marty
Lacker, the credit was assigned to Chips. Finally on the fourth week, the
Colonel put his foot down. Elvis Presley records traditionally listed no producer, because Mr. Presley was his own producer. The record was simply to
be listed without a producer's credit, like all other Elvis Presley records,
and that was the end of it.

Nothing could dampen Elvis' spirits at this point, however. After finishing the movie, he returned to Hawaii at the beginning of May, and even the
sale of the Circle G on May 20 for $440,100 came more as a relief than any-
thing else. Back home in Memphis, he was down at the gates with the fans
almost every night, seemingly driven to reaffirm his roots on the eve of his
return to live performing. Both the *Press-Scimitar* and *Commercial Appeal*
took note of this marked change in both routine and attitude, as he frequently appeared on his horse Rising Sun, signing autographs and posing
for pictures on the big stump just inside the gate, and sometimes even teasing the fans by singing a line or two from one of his songs. When he was
asked how it felt to be home, he responded, "Great, man, I really love it,
great," confiding to his uncle Vester that he needed to get used to the
crowds again.

He was clearly worried and excited about the Vegas opening. He voiced
his concern to the guys about whether the people would remember him,
would they accept him, was it going to be like the old days? And he talked
endlessly with Charlie about the ambitious program he had in mind, about
how he saw this as an opportunity to showcase all the different kinds of
music that had meant so much to him in his life.

H E SPOKE TO VIRTUALLY EVERY MUSICIAN of his acquaintance
about accompanying him to Las Vegas during this time. He was in
touch with Scotty and D.J., the Jordanaires, the Nashville session musicians,

some of the California players, and Chips' rhythm section, among others. In the end, though, he settled on a group he had never worked with before, led by a musician he had long admired but never met. With time fast running out and rehearsals scheduled to start in mid July, he called guitarist James Burton toward the end of June. Burton, a Shreveport native, who had joined Ricky Nelson in 1957 at the age of eighteen after first laying down the unmistakable lead on fellow Shreveporter Dale Hawkins' classic "Suzie Q," had been an L.A. studio stalwart since the early sixties. He was an extraordinarily versatile player who had worked with everyone from Merle Haggard to Frank Sinatra and even overdubbed several Elvis Presley movie tracks. It was Burton whose distinctive "chickenpickin'" style had anchored the band on the popular *Shindig* television series, and he had not worked a club date in years when the phone rang one day at his Toluca Lake home. "I was getting dressed to do a recording session, and my wife answered the phone, and she said, 'You have a call from a Joe Esposito.' Well, the name didn't ring a bell, so I said, 'Take a message,' but she said, 'Well, it seems important,' so I took the call. Joe said, 'James, it's very nice to talk to you, but I have someone here who wants to speak with you, and I'll get back in touch later.' Then Elvis got on the phone, and we talked for two hours."

They talked about everything under the sun. After a while, it seemed almost beside the point that they had never met, with all the experiences that they had shared and all the acquaintances that they had in common. Elvis expressed his long-standing admiration for Burton's work, and then he asked the guitarist if he could put together a band for him. What he was looking for, he said, were musicians who could play "any type of music," the kind of player who, like Burton, was good at what he did and knew it. He told James that he used to watch him every week on the *Ozzie and Harriet* show because he was such a fan. Although Burton was not ordinarily much of a conversationalist, they seemed to really hit it off, and in the end James said, somewhat to his own surprise, that he would do it.

He set up auditions for Elvis' return to California in just a few weeks. The first player that he called, pianist Glen D. Hardin, a fellow Shindog, demurred, so Burton got Larry Muhoberac, a Memphian who had moved to L.A. in 1965 and had led the band that shared the bill with Elvis at his 1961 Memphis charity concert. He was also turned down by drummer Richie Frost, a fellow alumnus of the Ricky Nelson band, who simply didn't want the aggravation of a live gig. Jerry Scheff, a virtuoso bass player with whom

James had recently worked on an album project, wasn't interested initially either but agreed to come to the audition at a little rehearsal studio on Franklin and Vine. "I told my wife — you know, I was sort of laughing — I said, 'I'll go down and check it out, but I'm not gonna do it.' I really wasn't into Elvis; mainly what I had played at that time was rhythm and blues and jazz. But I went down to the rehearsal, and I came home that night and told my wife, 'You gotta come down there and check this guy out!' She said, 'Ah, come on,' and I said, 'No, really, you've got to hear this guy,' and I didn't say anything else. But the next day he just blew her away. Blew us both away."

What had so overwhelmed Jerry, a red-headed "hippie" with alternative ideas and a taste for the alternative lifestyle, was the depth of Elvis' commitment to the music, the passion that he put into what was only supposed to be a band audition. Elvis, Scheff discovered, far from sitting back and passing judgment on the musicians' abilities, had actually come to do a show. "It was like it was just the band and him. He'd do what you'd like to do, all the songs he knew you'd have fun playing. He would entertain you; he knew what musicians liked to play. I just kind of played what I thought should be there and he liked it — even though I swear I didn't know what I was doing. Then some ladies came in, and we were sitting around, and he switched gears and started entertaining them. It was just that whoever happened to be there he would just entertain. He loved to sing for people, *he loved to knock people out.*"

The session to which Jerry took his skeptical wife the next day was the last in the series of rehearsal-auditions. Burton had gotten an okay from Elvis on rhythm guitarist John Wilkinson, a personable young folksinger signed to RCA whom James wanted to help out, so all that was left was the drum slot, which Burton assumed would be filled by Gene Pello, a seasoned session player. But Larry Muhoberac had told James about a young drummer with whom he had worked in Dallas named Ronnie Tutt, just now moving his wife and family to L.A. Tutt, Muhoberac thought, would be perfect for the job, and Ronnie proved him right when he finally got his chance. "I was the last drummer Elvis heard, and it was between me and one other drummer, who was doing all the Motown sessions. He was really good, and I could see that the rest of the band was really into his playing. But I just went up there and focused on Elvis. I really think I got the job because Elvis and I had such great eye communication onstage. He said that I didn't just do my own thing when I auditioned; I watched him. And you really had to, because it was like playing for a glorified stripper. With all the moves he made, you had to play according to what he was doing." Ten bars into the first song, Jerry Scheff said, everyone knew. And with that the band was complete.

There was a gap of just one or two days before formal rehearsals were scheduled to begin. In the meantime the salary structure was established, with Burton as leader getting $2,500 a week, and the other musicians $1,000 to $1,200, apart from Wilkinson, who got $600. Two vocal groups had already been hired without auditions, strictly on the basis of Elvis' gut instinct. The Imperials, with whom he had worked on his 1966 gospel session and whose records he had continued to admire over the years, were a natural, even if Jake Hess was no longer with the group and the rest of the personnel was somewhat changed. The Sweet Inspirations, on the other hand, he had never met or seen perform, but he loved the sound of "Sweet Inspiration," their aptly named 1967 soul hit, and he was familiar with their spectacular backup work for Aretha Franklin. Most important, he felt that their black gospel harmonies, in combination with the Imperials' white quartet sound, would only add to the range of music — the *full spectrum* of American music that he wanted to present onstage. The Imperials would get $3,750 a week, the Sweets, who were contracted to open the show and as a result got their rooms comped, were to be paid $3,500. So with rehearsal costs figured in and payments to Bobby Morris, the orchestra leader at the International, who would provide arrangements on about half the songs in the act, total payroll came to roughly $80,000 for the four-week engagement, an extravagance that must have galled the Colonel but to which Elvis would brook no opposition. All he was interested in was the show.

Toward that end he was having costume fittings with Bill Belew, who had created the black leather suit and "mod rebel" look for the television special. For this show Belew came up with variations on a karate theme, a two-piece ghi-styled "Cossack" suit, with brightly colored macrame belts and the high-collared Edwardian look of the special. "We taught him how to tie the belts so the cords would hang out and they would whip around. We made him seven suits, too, though from what I understand he [hardly ever] wore any of them onstage. But there were five or six of these black, white, [and dark blue] Cossack outfits; I'd take the sketches up to show him, or we'd make one just to see how it looked, and he'd just say yes or no. Once he felt confidence [in you], that was it; he'd never question [you] again." The only problem that Belew ran into came later, when Vernon questioned his bills (which came to more than $11,000), but Elvis took care of that, too. Unlike his father, Belew felt, Elvis knew the value of show.

Rehearsals started on the eighteenth and continued for the next five days at RCA's Hollywood Boulevard studios. Like the auditions, the rehearsals were eye-opening for the five musician-participants, because each turned out to be a performance in itself. Everything, according to James Burton, the model of a well-organized studio player, was spontaneous. "We probably learned — right off the bat, we probably learned a hundred and fifty songs." With John Wilkinson, the one nonsession player in the group, Elvis was patient and instructive, showing him what he wanted but never showing him up. Wilkinson couldn't get the rhythm part to "It's Now or Never" right. "It's relatively simple, but I couldn't get it the way he wanted it. I was in a corner going through it and trying to get it the way James had showed me, trying to get it down [and] Elvis came over. I was singing the thing softly . . . and all of a sudden he's singing with me in harmony. When we got to the end, I said, 'Is that the way you want it?' He said, 'That couldn't be better.'"

Charlie was a constant presence, encouraging Elvis, propping him up in his enthusiasms, keeping track of the songs, laughing uproariously at Elvis' jokes. The program that Elvis started out with opened with "Memphis," the great "lost" single that Johnny Rivers had appropriated, and included both "Green, Green Grass of Home" and "Reconsider Baby," the blues that Elvis had recorded at his homecoming session. By the end of the week, all of these were gone, replaced in some cases by more contemporary material, in others by more predictable selections. There was much talk about pacing, and Charlie drew upon his own experience in show business to make suggestions for what would amount to the first hour-long set of Elvis' career. With Elvis' analytical mind and his natural flair for dramatics, Charlie felt, there was no way he could miss; the grandiosity of his ambition only raised the stakes. Everything that he had ever admired in music, he told Charlie, "he now had onstage with him. Every type of music that he enjoyed was now in his show. The front men did country or rock 'n' roll, there was the gospel sound with the quartet and the soul sound with the Sweet Inspirations, and together you had a beautiful choir. Then a big band sound [from the showroom orchestra] with things that swung and dramatic things that had a symphonic sound." To Charlie there was no limit to what Elvis was likely to accomplish.

They continued the rehearsals in Vegas, starting on the twenty-fourth.

Felton flew in to help supervise, just four days after his marriage to Chet Atkins' secretary, Mary Lynch. Barbra Streisand was still in the showroom, so run-throughs were conducted in either a rehearsal room or one of the ballrooms and for the first time included the two backup groups, who had never met.

The Sweet Inspirations went into the experience with a good deal of trepidation. For one thing they were not particularly fans of Elvis Presley. "I didn't know that much about Elvis," said Myrna Smith, the vivacious twenty-eight-year-old spokeswoman and de facto business manager for the group, "because that wasn't the kind of music that was played in my neighborhood." They were just sitting there when Elvis walked in for the first time. "He had on a chocolate-colored suit and a tan and looked absolutely gorgeous and walked over to us and introduced himself — like we didn't know who he was! Then he started singing our record, and we just chimed right in and fell in love with him like that.

"Rehearsals always were great. He went through the whole thing, just as though he were onstage, stopping only on occasion for something he didn't like or something he thought he needed to add. He just let us experiment. Sometimes, coming from the background that we did, which was kind of a gospel-soul thing, we would add something that would conflict with his music, and he would just say, 'I don't think I want you to sing that.' He always did it very diplomatically, but he knew exactly what he wanted to hear, and he added our group because he wanted the spice of soul, but he didn't want it to be overbearing."

Probably the thing that was most difficult for them was that their voices never blended very well with the Imperials. The white quartet, Myrna felt, "sang very straight, and we'd show them little things, but most of the time with our vibrato and their straight [singing] it would rub a little — I could hear that on the recordings." But, as Myrna came quickly to realize, that wasn't really the point. "The thing that made it so different was Elvis' presence — he just put so much into it, even at rehearsal you just had to look at him. It was very exciting. I've worked with Tom Jones, Aretha, some very heavyweight people, but his was the most exciting show I've ever worked in, [because] Elvis loved so much to sing and perform. I mean, Aretha could sing rings around Elvis if you're talking about vocal prowess, but as far as wanting to be on that stage, I mean, you just got drawn into it."

The Imperials had their own problems, but they, too, got swept up in the excitement. They had had real reservations about going into Las Vegas to begin with — as a gospel group, it wasn't where they wanted to be, and they worried about the effect it might have on longtime fans, but in the end they determined it was just too good an opportunity to pass up. They had no idea what to charge either and ultimately came to feel that they had shortchanged themselves. But they were won over by the same elements that had impressed the Sweets, and the rhythm section, too, for that matter — the sheer, irrepressible feeling that Elvis put into every song.

For the last two days, there were full rehearsals with the orchestra, which up till then had been working out the charts on its own under the direction of Bobby Morris. Glen Spreen had shipped in arrangements for some of the new songs from Memphis, but mostly they worked off the records, adding the kind of minimal flourishes and fanfares that the Dorsey brothers and New Frontier bands had interjected in 1956. Elvis was as keyed up for the opening as he had been for the television special, alternating between moods of manic excitement and utter, and abject, fear. During the week he visited a number of shows on the Strip, studying closely both the act and the audience's reaction to it. Three nights before his own opening he went with some of the guys to see Barbra Streisand at the singer's invitation. Streisand's show, a one-woman cabaret turn that had been only moderately well received and had drawn spotty crowds, did not particularly impress him. It was a helluva big stage to fill, he said to Charlie, and she looked awfully alone up there. That was not the way it was going to be for him, he said. He would be surrounded by his band, and he would have all those voices; he was not just going to be out there all by himself.

THE COLONEL MEANWHILE was going ahead full steam with his own preparations. He had storerooms filled with posters, banners, balloons, one hundred thousand 8 x 10 glossies, fifteen thousand color portraits, calendars, catalogues, and souvenir booklets, all shipped in from Florida at RCA's expense. He had the city plastered with billboards, with even the taxis sporting little marquees that announced Elvis' opening. Despite one of the biggest advance sales in Vegas history (the room was 80 percent sold out by early July), he took out over one hundred radio and TV ads daily, explaining that "I don't like to take any chances," and his fourth-floor offices were a gaudy shrine covered with Elvis posters, after the model of his headquarters at MGM. It was an unparalleled promotional blitz, exceeding even the Colonel's most spectacular previous efforts, but as he announced to all and sundry, with that peculiar combination of pride and bluster that was his trademark, this was his job; it was his obligation to let everyone know that Elvis was coming — the rest was up to his star. "If you don't do any business," he told Elvis, "don't ever blame me. Because the gophers in the desert [will] know you're here! Believe me, everyone in town will know Elvis Presley is coming, but you're the only one that can bring them in." On the night of Barbra Streisand's closing, even as stage-hands were tearing down the show, the Colonel and his crew, armed with hammers, ladders, and staple guns, were putting up posters, glossies, and even a souvenir booth in the lobby, so that by morning you could not have guessed that any other performer had ever been present.

Using the same technique that he had employed to promote Elvis' movies for the past decade, Colonel timed interviews, features, and public-ity items to build up the opening, while the June release of the new album, *From Elvis in Memphis,* elicited reviews and sales (it reached number thirteen on the *Billboard* chart at the end of July and got the *Rolling Stone* lead review a month later) to coincide with all the excitement. The NBC television spe-cial, too, was scheduled to be rebroadcast on August 17, as Colonel contin-ued to work behind the scenes to arrange for Elvis' first appearance in front of his true noncelebrity public, at the Houston Livestock Show and Rodeo the following February. There was no question, the gophers were going to sit up and take notice.

O PENING NIGHT, JULY 31, was by invitation, one show only, with an A-plus celebrity list that the Colonel had been working on for the last two months. International owner Kirk Kerkorian delivered his pal Cary Grant, just as he had for the Barbra Streisand opening, while Colonel made sure that all of his own show business cronies and associates were present. There was a pantheon of music business celebrities, from Fats Domino and Pat Boone to Paul Anka, Phil Ochs, Carol Channing, Shirley Bassey, and Dick Clark — with most of the Strip headliners in attendance. Colonel had even arranged for a planeload of New York critics to be flown in on Kirk Kerkorian's private jet, while Elvis extended a special invitation to his first mentor, Sam Phillips, to come out for the opening.

There was a full-scale dress rehearsal in the afternoon, but by the time the curtain went up on the Sweet Inspirations at 8:15, Elvis had worked himself into such a frenzy that Joe had his doubts about whether or not he was going to be able to go on. "Everything was fine right up until that night. He just had no idea of how he was going to be received. He was pacing back and forth, back and forth; you could see the sweat just pouring out of him before he went onstage. He was always nervous before every show, but he was never nervous like that again."

The Sweet Inspirations did a stiff opening set, highlighted by dressed-up versions of "Born Free," "The Impossible Dream," and "How High the Moon." Sammy Shore, a forty-one-year-old comic whom the Colonel had spotted opening for Tom Jones, did a crowd-pleasing turn that centered around the exhortations of his alter ego, a black preacher named Brother Sam, and included such jokes as, "Youth is wasted on the young. Give us what the kids got, and you know what you'd have? A lot of old people with pimples." And then Elvis came out, unheralded, practically unannounced, to a vamp from, of all things, Carl Perkins' "Blue Suede Shoes," which he had practically massacred in a clash of over-the-top vocals and orchestral pretensions on the NBC special. This time there was no question of pretense; with his own handpicked band behind him he simply *rocked,* and almost in that instant, the whole room exploded.

The first few nights were not recorded, but from the evidence of subsequent recordings and from the response he got, it doesn't seem difficult to imagine just how explosive a moment it really was, as he roared from the Carl Perkins number into Ray Charles' "I Got a Woman" and then into "All Shook Up," taken too fast but still delivered with sledgehammer effect. Next came a surprisingly sincere "Love Me Tender," its simple folk melody amplified by the swelling chorus behind him, followed by a free-wheeling medley of "Jailhouse Rock" and "Don't Be Cruel" in which (the former) a "knocked-out jailbird" became a "knocked-out sonofabitch" under the influence of Elvis' high spirits. And then he spoke, in a human voice that both reassured an audience almost dazzled by his show and at the same time raised the level of nervous energy another notch. "Good evening, ladies and gentlemen," he said. "Welcome to the big, freaky International Hotel, with those weirdo dolls on the walls and those little funky angels on the ceiling [referring to the ornate semiclassical sculptures scattered around the room], and, man, you ain't seen nothing until you've seen a funky angel. Before the evening's out I'm sure I will have made a complete and utter fool of myself — but I hope you get a kick out of watching."

This was Elvis in overdrive; all the terror that Joe had glimpsed during the day exploded now in a kind of manic release, but a release that was as instinctively controlled and responsive to his own sense of the audience's needs as it was the first time he ever set foot on a stage. Cary Grant was on his feet; comedienne Totie Fields stood on a table swinging a bottle; even waitresses who had "recently struggled through the ennuied debut of The Divine Barbra," as the *Los Angeles Herald-Examiner* reported, "were visibly swooning." It would have been a scene of rare abandon in any setting, but for Las Vegas, the ultimate repository of blasé show business values, this kind of uninhibited display was particularly noteworthy, carrying with it an implied embrace of genuine spontaneity on the performer's part.

No one in the room could have missed it, no matter what name they chose to put on it. The *New Yorker's* Ellen Willis, a self-described skeptic, hailed "Presley's sustaining love for rhythm and blues." Richard Goldstein felt a wave of generational nostalgia sweep over him, "unnerved," he wrote in a *New York Times* feature entitled "A White Boy With Black Hips," "by the same shaky feeling your folks got from watching Sinatra on TV, a feeling you used to sneer at." Even those critics who did not know quite what to make of it (the *Hollywood Reporter* critic "got the delicious feeling that this was, indeed, one of the greatest put-ons in life") could not deny that it was in some strange way mesmerizing, while less distanced observers like the British reporter for the *Record Mirror* described "Presley, like a wild beast, roar[ing] through a long list of the songs that made him famous . . . as ladies lost years and threw themselves at the feet of their leader in frenzied glory."

As he grew more secure, more of a sense of fun crept into his performance, something that may have escaped many opening-night critics and fans. This became most noticeable in the between-songs patter that evolved over the next few nights, which became increasingly revealing as he let his fondness for puns and wordplay run rampant. He invariably delivered "Mystery Train" and "Tiger Man" with gusto, but then, dredging up elements of the monologue that Steve Binder had urged on him for the television special, he gave the audience a little history lesson, too. It would change every night, but the essence of it always remained the same: how he had started out in show business almost by accident, while studying to be an electrician.

"But I was wired the wrong way. One day on my lunch break I went in to make a little demonstration record — I mean, I really wasn't trying to get into the business, but about a year and a half later the guy put the record out. No one had heard of me, but just overnight people were saying, 'Is he? Is he?,' you know, and I'm going, 'Am I? Am I?' I became pretty big in my hometown and a few parts of the country, and I started working night-clubs and football fields, little weird rooms where people are going, 'Hmm, hmm,' you know, and they threw me off the Opry, and Arthur Godfrey took one look and said, 'Nah, nah . . .' So I did that for a year and a half, and then I met Colonel Sanders — *Parker.*"

Parker, he explained, got him on television.

So I went to New York, and people were saying, "Get him, get him, hot damn, he's just out of the trees." . . . So there was a lot of contro-versy, and I went on *The Ed Sullivan Show,* and the cameras were only filming from the waist up, you know, and Ed Sullivan is standing on the sidelines going, "Sonofabitch, sonofabitch," and I'm saying, "Thank you, Ed, thank you very much" — I didn't know what he was calling me at the time. And I did *The Steve Allen Show,* and they wanted to tame me down, so they had me dressed in a tuxedo and singing to a dog on a stool. The dog is peeing, and I didn't know it, you know, so I'm singing, "You ain't nothing but a hound dog," and the dog's going, "Ump, ump," and I'm going, "Back, back, you fool," and the dog ran out of the room.

So I did that show, and then I went to Hollywood. Hollywood is the next move, you know. That's what happens: you get a record, then you get on television, and then you go to Hollywood. So I made *Love Me Tender,* then I did *Loving You,* "*Loving* Her," loving whoever I could get my hands on at the time. So I did *Jailhouse Rock, King Creole,* four pictures, man, I was really getting used to the Hollywood bit. I had a Cadillac limousine, I had sunglasses on, sitting in the backseat, saying, "I'm a movie star, hot damn, I'm cool." Eating hamburgers and drink-ing Pepsi Colas, you know. "Better watch that squirrel, man, when he gets out of the trees!" So I was living it up pretty good when I got drafted, shafted, and everything else. Just overnight it was all gone, you know. I was in a different world, and I woke up, and it was gone.

At first they watched me to see what I was going to do. And when they saw I was just like them, then everything turned out okay. But the guys in the service must get awful lonesome, because they call each other "mother" a lot. . . . Anyway, I got out of the service in 1960, and I made some movies like *G.I. Blues* and *Blue Hawaii,* and several pictures that did very well for me. But as the years went by it got harder and harder to perform to a movie camera, and I really missed the people, I really missed contact with a live audience. And I just wanted to tell you how good it is to be back.

And then he would return to the show. *He never once lost them, he had them in the palm of his hand.* It was a triumph of the rarest sort, a triumph of class, in which, finally, he was able to achieve the validation he had always wanted but never explicitly sought — and strictly on his own terms.

For those closest to Elvis, that first night's performance was almost as much of a revelation as it was to the audience. To Priscilla, wearing a bare-midriff white-fringed minidress with white go-go boots and ankle straps, an outfit that Elvis had personally approved, "it was the energy, the energy that surrounded the stage, and the charisma that he [conveyed] — I don't think I've ever felt that in any entertainer since. I mean, yes, other entertainers have a charisma, but Elvis exuded a maleness about him, a proudness that you only see in an animal. On the stage he'd have this look, you know, prowling back and forth, pacing like a tiger, and you look and you say, 'My God, is this the person that I —?' It was difficult to attach who he was to this person onstage. It was incredible." Joanie Esposito, who, like Priscilla, had up till now seen Elvis perform only at the taping of his television special, was almost as enthralled. "He was so charged up. He was so excited — he just got so high off the audience he did somersaults."

More than one person noted it was as if he were in another world; there were moments when his eyes glazed over and you had no idea *what* he was going to do next. "It was like a different Elvis," said Patti Parry, the hairdresser who had been one of the gang for almost nine years now. "It was like a light coming on that stage — the electricity from the audience and the electricity from him, it was unbelievable. You forgot that this was your pal." His father sat proudly at the front-row family booth with Dee and the kids, quietly beaming. But it was Felton as much as anyone, still Elvis' number-one fan, who could barely contain himself. "He was like a wild man," the producer said, trying to describe it some years later to a friend. "He was all over that stage. I mean, he almost hurt himself — he was doing flips and cartwheels and all kinds of stuff; on 'Suspicious Minds' he'd be down on one knee and do a flip across stage and just roll. He was

PRESS CONFERENCE, LAS VEGAS, AUGUST 1, 1969.
(ARCHIVE PHOTOS/FRANK EDWARDS FOTOS INTERNATIONAL)

about half crazy until everybody talked him into not doing all those things, I ain't kidding you."

When he came offstage that first night, there was a feeling of almost palpable relief. The Colonel, who fiercely guarded against any display of outward emotion, had tears in his eyes when he came backstage — neither Joe nor Priscilla nor Charlie had ever seen anything like it. It was as if for just this one instant there were no veils, no disguises — the two of them simply stepped toward each other and wordlessly embraced. The Colonel's body shook with emotion. Then it was over. It was, Joe felt, the closest they had ever been.

In the pictures of the press conference afterward, Elvis appears proud, beaming, brimming with confidence, changed from his stage outfit to one of Bill Belew's mod suits, with a wide, multicolored silk scarf around his neck and a high Edwardian collar. Joe and Vernon flank him at the long banquet table, with Lamar, Sonny, and Charlie all sharing the spotlight and the Colonel presiding with W. C. Fields aplomb in a white butcher's smock covered with the stamped message ELVIS INTERNATIONAL IN PERSON. Elvis stood the entire time taking the predictable questions. Was he excited about his return to live performing? Had he grown tired of making movies? Did he think it was a mistake to have put out so many soundtrack albums? To each of which he replied affirmatively and diplomatically ("I was getting fed up with singing to turtles," he said in response to the last).

More photographs were taken. There was talk of performing abroad, and at one point Screaming Lord Sutch, a flamboyant British rocker who had run for Parliament, shouted out an offer of "one million pounds sterling for one appearance in England at the Wembley Empire Stadium for two concerts." The fee would include the documentary filming of the concerts and would require no more than twenty-four hours of Mr. Presley's time. "You'll have to ask him," said Elvis, deferring to the Colonel and looking slightly bemused. Colonel asked that the offer be repeated and then said, "Just put down the deposit." "All right, I will attend to it," said Lord Sutch. "Would you like to appear in England?" He *definitely* would like to appear there, responded Elvis without hesitation, "and it will be soon." With the press conference over, he had his picture taken with a beaming Fats Domino, who, Elvis insisted to cynical reporters, had been a tremendous influence on him and should be considered the real king of rock 'n' roll. Afterward, the whole party repaired to his seven-room suite on the twenty-ninth floor (the even more luxurious star suite on the thirtieth floor, to which he was contractually entitled, had not yet been completed), where the evening was relived over and over again.

As THE ENGAGEMENT WORE ON, Elvis' mood continued to loosen up, and with it his onstage demeanor. The monologue grew more and more zany, to the point that it sometimes seemed almost surreal. As the women in the audience grew increasingly demonstrative (they started throwing bras, panties, and half-slips, almost from the first show), he began to give out kisses, randomly at first, and then as a regular part of the performance. He first split his pants about two weeks into the engagement, and soon that, too, became a kind of ritual, with "Memories" sung one time from behind the curtain as he changed his trousers. One night he dissolved in hysterical laughter at Sweet Inspiration Cissy Houston's soprano obbligato during "Are You Lonesome Tonight?," and he could never get back to singing the song. Other nights he and Charlie would start fooling around, and the audience would be treated to the kind of spectacle that girlfriends and movie directors had learned to endure. And yet the show never lost its edge. Elvis was never anything less than fully engaged, the music remained for the most part crisp and taut — it was simply that the atmosphere became more genial, as was only natural for an entertainer who was beginning to feel more and more at home.

The Colonel was in his element, too, talking about carnival days, inducting new recruits into the Snowmen's League, basking in the sunshine of his newfound success but rejecting respectability at every turn. He was observed by more than one reporter dropping several hundred dollars at a time at the roulette table, a ubiquitous grizzled old character who merited at least a patronizing aside in every new story about the remarkable resurrection of Elvis Presley's career.

The International took more formal notice of the Colonel's presence, exercising its option the night of the opening with an agreement the Colonel outlined on a stained pink tablecloth in the hotel coffee shop, then drawing up a more conventional document four days later which raised Elvis' salary to $125,000 a week retroactively. This was attached to an extension which would have Elvis entertaining at the International twice a year for the next five years, thus guaranteeing the Colonel his yardstick $1 million for eight weeks' work through 1974. As for any fears the Colonel might have of someone else surpassing the standard that had been set, there were numerous assurances and verbal guarantees that his boy would maintain "favored nations" status for as long as the contract lasted — that the casino would, in other words, match any improvement in salary or working conditions that any other Vegas headliner might achieve.

Colonel wasn't worried in any case. He was as confident now of Elvis' abilities as he was of his own. His only misgiving was that maybe things were getting *too* good; he watched the boy and he grew increasingly concerned that maybe he was beginning to feel too much at home onstage, as he let fly with scattershot off-color language and remarks that Colonel felt were inappropriate, particularly for the dinner show, at which there were frequently children in attendance. Elvis should watch himself, he wrote in a blunt note after the August 22 show. He knew that Elvis would not want to undo all the good they had done with the engagement so far, but he was also aware that he could merely relate this to Elvis, that Elvis was the only one who could do anything about it. It was, he implied, as it had always been, the two of them against the world.

Old friends and new showed up, bidden and unbidden. Cliff Gleaves cashed in the airline ticket that Elvis had sent him and drove out from Memphis with Sam Phillips, while George Klein and Marty Lacker put off their arrival until the first weekend at Elvis' request, so they could catch the act after some of the bugs had been ironed out. "The reception Elvis is getting here is incredible," they reported back to the *Memphis Press-Scimitar.* "You've got to see it to believe it." Chips and Memphis music entrepreneur Herbie O'Melle joined them midway through their stay, and Elvis' Memphis physician Dr. Nichopoulos, who had gotten Elvis out of the scheduled start of *Clambake,* met Colonel Parker in person for the first time after his brusque introduction on the telephone two years before. Jerry Lee Lewis almost got into a fight with the Colonel when he tried to clear the dressing room of everyone, including Jerry Lee Lewis. "I wouldn't let no loud-mouth old man tell me who I could have a drink with," Jerry Lee announced brashly to Elvis and anyone else in the room who chose to listen, but he didn't get a flicker of recognition from Colonel.

Ed Parker, the karate instructor and former champion with whom Elvis had renewed acquaintance in Hawaii the previous year, showed up without notice accompanied by a party of four. As soon as he arrived, he contacted Joe and told him he wanted to see the dinner show and meet with Elvis afterward about a "training idea" that he had. From the audience Parker noted approvingly the extent to which karate — both movement and costume — played a part in the show. Then, toward the end of the

performance, "Elvis took a moment for personal recognition. He introduced his wife, father, and then to my great surprise he turned in my direction. 'I have a close and dear friend in the audience,' he said. 'He is my
karate instructor, a high-ranking belt, who is well known in his field. If any
of you live in the Los Angeles area and are interested in karate, you should
visit his schools.' He then called me by name and had me stand and face the
audience as the spotlight singled me out."

Later in the evening, up in the suite, Parker broached his business idea,
which had to do with building up the popularity of karate in general and
the marketing of Parker's own "kenpo" system in particular. "My guests
still could not believe they were in Elvis' private quarters, [but] Elvis at
once put [them] at ease. He talked to them as if they were longtime
friends. . . . When [they] asked a question or spoke to Elvis, he looked
them in the eyes and listened intently." In conjunction with their conversation, Elvis asked Parker to conduct a karate demonstration "by executing
moves and then explaining them, so that all who were present could understand the theory that I was trying to get across. Elvis was attentive, contributing a word, move, or gesture now and then but never, ever trying to
steal the limelight." This, Parker, reflected later, marked the true beginning
of their friendship.

Every night Elvis held court in his suite. One night Tom Jones might
stop by, and the two of them would sing together until the sun came up.
Another night it might just be the Imperials, with whom Elvis loved to
harmonize on some of the old gospel songs. "Every night was like a command performance," remarked Imperials manager–keyboard player Joe
Moscheo — to the point that some nights you might just prefer to slip
away after a few words of perfunctory congratulation, so as to avoid getting stuck in the suite all night long. "A lot of times he just really wanted to
sing, and he'd sit down at the piano and entertain for whoever was there.
Sometimes there were a lot of big names, sometimes there was just a
bunch of hangers-on, a lot of times it was just the guys." Whoever it was,
the room was always filled with people, and Elvis was always singing. Some
of the guys said it was just like the old days — but it was like the old days
had never been.

Elvis was feeling particularly sanguine when he spoke with British
music reporter Ray Connolly, writing for the *London Evening Standard*, in
a rare private interview sanctioned, and attended, by the Colonel. "We
didn't decide to come back here for the money, I'll tell you that," Elvis

told Connolly. "I've always wanted to perform on the stage again for the last nine years, and it's been building up inside of me since 1965 until the strain became intolerable. . . . I don't think I could have left it much longer." As far as the money went, it really didn't matter, he didn't even want to know.

> He laughs, and throws his head back, showing all those perfectly-kept teeth, and striking me with the smallness of his eyes and the exaggerated length of his eyelashes.
> "Can we just say this?" says the Colonel, all homespun, folksy humor. "The Colonel has nothing to do with Mr. Presley's finances. That's all done for him by his father, Mr. Vernon Presley, and his accountant."
> Mr. Presley, Snr., a fatter and greyer version of his son, if you ever saw one, nods at the formal third person way of speaking and takes another beer from the bar.
> "He can flush all his money away if he wants to. I won't care," the Colonel adds. The humor is easy and good-natured — country style, if you like.

Judgment of another kind was offered by Sam Phillips when Elvis sought him out for a critique of the show. Phillips had had one piece of advice for Elvis when Elvis called to invite him out in the middle of rehearsals. "I said, 'Is the goddamn rhythm kicking you in the ass? *Where is the placement of the rhythm section?*' I said, 'Just put that rhythm out there, baby, just put it out there. That is your *i-den-ti-fi-cation.*' Well, when I saw the show, I want to tell you, I never heard a better rhythm section in my life. There was some raunchy-ass shit. I told him that. I said, 'Elvis, man, that was fabulous, but, you know, that song "Memories" has got to go!' I said, 'Goddamn, didn't that motherfucker bog down the fucking show?' And he said, 'Mr. Phillips, I just love that song.' And of course, he kept on singing it ever since."

"Suspicious Minds" was released at the end of August, with no accommodation whatsoever from Chips on the publishing. It had been overdubbed in Las Vegas a week into the engagement, incorporating the way that Elvis performed it onstage — with a kind of false ending in which the volume faded out, then came back up as the same three lines were repeated over and over in a four-and-a-half-minute coda that may well have been suggested by the Beatles' "Hey Jude" and featured the International horns. They recorded the new ending at United Recording, the eight-track studio that Bill Porter, the RCA engineer who had worked the board at all of Elvis' Nashville sessions from 1960 through 1963, had bought into three years earlier. It created a tricky technical problem for Porter, since all eight tracks were already filled, but he solved it by recording the horns live first over the stereo, then over the mono mix, and turning the volume down, then up again according to Felton's specifications. Glen Spreen, who had written the arrangement for the penultimate version, couldn't believe his ears when he heard the final product. "I mean, we laughed at it — let's put it that way — when we heard the fade. You know, to do that kind of thing live, because the audience is there and they're participating, they're with him, that's one thing, [but a record's something else]. Gene Chrisman was probably the most vocal about the whole thing — he used very blunt words in describing what he felt. Bobby Emmons just had this blank, amazed look on his face, and we all just kind of went, 'God, how can they do this?' as it kept going and going and going. But we couldn't do anything about it."

Glen's disgust was mirrored by Chips' reaction. For Chips it only confirmed all of his worst suspicions about the bunch he had been working with — the same people who had tried to take his publishing, had eliminated his credit, and now were trying to steal his sound. They were no better than *amateurs* in his view, turning an intricately worked-out production into a kind of audio joke, and the success of the record may only have been the last straw in the way of any kind of business relationship, though he continued to maintain good personal relations with Elvis for the rest of the year. The single — fade-out, coda, and all — turned out in any case to be Elvis' biggest record in seven years, his first number-one hit since 1962, proving perhaps that Elvis' judgment was as right in its own way as Chips'.

All of this turmoil escaped Elvis' attention in the wake of a monumental revival of popular interest in him and in his work. The figures alone from the Las Vegas engagement spoke volumes about its success: 101,500 paying customers, $1.5 million in gross receipts, the most successful act in Las Vegas history (by comparison, Dean Martin attracted 50,000 in three weeks at the smaller Riviera earlier that summer). With the Colonel, the Colonel's staff, and all the guys, their wives and girlfriends, Elvis attended Nancy Sinatra's opening at the International the night after he closed. In keeping with the expansive way he was feeling, Colonel took out newspaper and radio ads in his and Elvis' name, urging people to attend the Sinatra engagement. After the show Colonel spotted Mac Davis, who had opened for Nancy, in the dressing room. "He remembered me, and he said, 'I told you you were going to be a star.' I said, 'Yeah, you rubbed my head.' He said, 'Did I really?' I said, 'Yeah.' He said, 'Well, then there ain't no doubt about it. You're gonna be a star.'" Then they all went off to a party hosted by Nancy's father, and Elvis had his picture taken with Frank Sinatra, a peer at last, no longer a pretender.

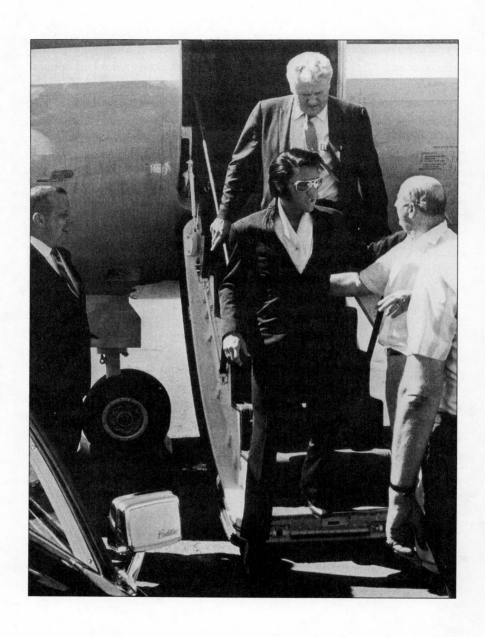

ON THE ROAD AGAIN: COLONEL MEETS ELVIS AND VERNON PRESLEY,
PHOENIX, SEPTEMBER 9, 1970.
(COURTESY OF THE ESTATE OF ELVIS PRESLEY)

A NIGHT AT THE OPERA

FOR THE FIRST TIME IN almost ten years Elvis had nothing to look forward to. There was no movie coming up, no recording session, no television special — nothing in fact was planned until his return to Las Vegas at the end of January. He felt an enormous sense of release upon the conclusion of the August engagement, but he could find no outlet for its expression. All of a sudden it seemed like he had outgrown Memphis without even being aware of it, and for a month he restlessly shuttled back and forth between Las Vegas and Los Angeles, Los Angeles and Palm Springs, where the new house he had bought in April was now pretty much reserved for weekends with the guys. He returned to Memphis at the end of September, but it was plain to everyone, including Priscilla, that he had little interest in staying at home with his wife.

They traveled to Hawaii at the beginning of October on an all-expense-paid vacation for ten that the International had presented to Elvis in appreciation of his record-breaking engagement. Even Hawaii no longer held the attraction that it once had, and Elvis and Priscilla and Joe and Joanie hatched a plan to go to Europe with Jerry and Sandy Schilling and Elvis' cousin Patsy and her husband Gee Gee, returning to L.A. after only a week to get their passports. For a few days the European trip was all they could talk about, as they made plans and pored over maps and picked out the tourist attractions that they would like to visit. But then reality reasserted itself, with the Colonel insisting that Elvis would gravely offend his European fans if he were to visit England and France as a tourist before he played over there.

Everyone was up in arms at first. Elvis said he was just going to tell the Colonel to go fuck himself — whose fault was it that they had never been to Europe anyway? — and for a moment they all believed him. But then he turned around and accepted the Colonel's edict meekly and they went to the Bahamas instead, where Colonel knew some people and thought they would enjoy themselves. As it turned out, the island was hit with hurricane winds on the second day, so they were limited to the restaurants and the casinos and came home after only a week, on October 29. Elvis stuck around barely long enough to change his clothes, showing up the next night in Las Vegas, where he was spotted by gossip columnist Rona Barrett playing blackjack at the International, "reportedly losing and signing markers while two beauties stood at his side catching soul kisses in turn, with each flip of the cards." When the gossip columnist revisited the scene in her November 6 column, she noted that "everybody is commenting on how good Elvis Presley looks these days while he's having fun at the International. . . . Elvis' answer in response to such compliments: 'That's what a bad marriage does for you!'"

To Priscilla, filling up her time with dance, acting, cooking, and calligraphy classes while Elvis went off on his unexplained jaunts to Dallas, Las Vegas, and Palm Springs, his behavior was consistent with the view she had increasingly come to have of him over the past year and a half: Elvis could be at ease only when he was performing; he could never be still except when he was fully engaged. She had listened to his evasions and witnessed his betrayals, large and small; she had tried to combat a conspiracy of silence by moving into a house intended for the two of them alone, not for the membership of a small, self-protective fraternity who had served to aid and abet his actions over the years. That hadn't worked, and their marriage no longer maintained even the appearance of intimacy, but what disturbed her most of all was that Elvis no longer seemed able even to fool himself. "During the lulls he wouldn't know what to do with himself. He was like a child. He would take pills or read or just eat — because he was bored. You know, he just had to occupy his time with something to do."

Elvis' own view was somewhat more ambiguous. Although he never permitted himself to fully acknowledge it, he was well aware that he had not been faithful to his ideals, that things were not working out in certain respects the way that he had planned. He could rationalize that his marriage to Priscilla was not a marriage of true minds, that in fact her failure to share his spiritual goals was a fatal impediment to any true union. And linked to that, though maintaining a logic of its own, was his sense that he himself had not yet discovered his intended role, that he still did not know what his purpose on earth really was, though in returning to performing he had come closer to it than he had in years.

He visited Daya Mata frequently once again. She told him of her pilgrimage to India the previous year, while he in turn expressed some of the feelings that impelled him to return to live performing. "He was very much pulled toward his following and wished to please them. He wanted to be a great spiritual influence on all these young people — that was at the basis of his desire. 'I want to feel God's love. I want to give back. I want to awaken in all these young people a closer relationship with God.' I think the thing that stymied him was a lack of — I don't know if patience is the right word, but the self-discipline of being able to stay focused on something long enough to see it through."

The success of his records, though, and the newfound reestablishment of his popularity brought him to a greater sense that he might be on the right track, and even as he returned to his spiritual studies, he took up karate once again, too — in a more formal way than at any time since he had begun his studies in Germany. Ed Parker, who, for all of his legitimate achievements in the field, was an equally energetic promoter both of karate and of himself, followed up on their initial meeting in Las Vegas with an offer to train Elvis both to incorporate karate more readily into his act and, now that he was once again more exposed to the public, so as to be better able to defend himself. Elvis took private lessons at Parker's studio in west Los Angeles, and Parker found him an apt, if erratic, pupil.

"When the spirit moved him, he would study for days on end. Determination was a big part of his character. He prodded, pried, and questioned. He was not only interested in how, but in why as well. . . . I can vividly remember his boyish grin when he was convinced that the techniques did work." Parker rewarded him with certificates of advancement from his own Kenpo Institute, which were sometimes as much in recognition of Elvis' dedication to the philosophy of the discipline as his achievement in it. From Ed's point of view, this was a distinction to be recognized more in the breach than in the observance. For there was no question of what Elvis Presley's advocacy could do for the movement as a whole, or for the popularity of Ed Parker's school of kenpo karate in particular.

As for Elvis, in the end, he felt, there was no need to resolve these dichotomies just now; all would become clear when his purpose became clear, his mission revealed. All else was merely temporal; the contradictions between what he desired and what he accepted would one day fade away, his dedication to doing something great would eventually overwhelm his weakness. He was a poor boy who had never forgotten where he came from and would never stop short of his destination. In the words of the 1966 hit from *Man of La Mancha* that had been one of his favorites ever since he heard the Roy Hamilton version, he had dared to dream the impossible dream, and he had seen it come true. And he had done it just as other unheralded prophets had, with the same spirit of stubborn determination that Frank Sinatra sang about in his big hit of just a few months before: mistakes and all, he had done it his way.

Rehearsals for Vegas started in Los Angeles on January 10, almost three weeks in advance of the opening. Elvis couldn't wait to get going: there was new repertoire to rehearse and two new musicians to break in. Having to find another drummer had come as a highly unwelcome surprise, but Ronnie Tutt, the last-hired and lowest-salaried member of the band, apart from rhythm guitarist John Wilkinson, had been unable to come to financial terms with Tom Diskin and had chosen to go a more remunerative route. His replacement, Bob Lanning, was a competent L.A. session man who came highly recommended, but he possessed neither the fire nor the flair that Elvis was looking for in a drummer, and almost from the start of rehearsals he was determined to get Ronnie back, whatever the cost. Piano player Glen D. Hardin, on the other hand, was a perfect fit from the very first. A twenty-nine-year-old native of Lubbock, Texas, who had grown up playing with Buddy Holly's former backing group, the Crickets, then joined the navy, and met James Burton in L.A. upon his discharge, he had taught himself the rudiments of arranging while working with James and Jerry Scheff on the *Shindig* set. James had contacted him about the original Vegas gig, but he had turned it down because he was so busy with studio and arranging work. Then Larry Muhoberac decided he wanted to go back to playing sessions, and James called him again. This time he was ready.

"I went in there, and it was just James and Jerry and my friends — it wasn't like a real rigid rehearsal or anything. And we sat around and played two or three tunes. Seems like Elvis couldn't remember the words to something, and I knew the words — I think he was real comfortable with me. So we laughed and talked and just kind of hung out and had a good time. And after a while he said, 'Listen, I want you to go out there and make a deal with that guy over there.' I said, 'If you don't mind, I want to make a deal with you.' So he said, 'Okay, let's do it.' We stepped right out in the hall, and my deal was only two or three sentences long — it was not a very big deal at all, just a handshake, but a very good deal it was."

Hardin found Elvis' informal approach to the music equally refreshing. "Elvis didn't rehearse the way most musicians do. We'd just go over and sometimes work all night, playing all kinds of different songs. He liked to do it that way. He selected the music on the program, and he didn't want to be strapped into an inflexible program. He wanted you to be ready to play just about anything."

By the time they went into Vegas for rehearsals nine days later, in Hardin's estimation they had run down several hundred songs. They worked for ten days at the hotel, the same as the last time, first with the backup singers, then with the orchestra. At one point Elvis wanted to try the treacly Everly Brothers ballad "Let It Be Me," but there was no arrangement for the song, so Glen undertook to write one and had the band playing it when Elvis walked into the rehearsal room the next day. After that, there was more arranging work coming his way. "The first couple of things we did, we'd get together, and he'd play it on the piano, and he'd say, 'Look, man, right here I want the voices,' and he told me what to have them sing — he was real easy to arrange for."

The show that Elvis put together this time was considerably different from his presentation the previous August. The change in repertoire was dictated to some extent by the fact that they were planning to cut another live album, even though one had already been released from the first engagement. Evidently this was just part of the Colonel's ongoing philosophy of synergy. For those who could not afford to travel to Las Vegas, a live album was just the thing, the Colonel reasoned, and even for those couple of hundred thousand who were fortunate enough to have attended, what could serve as a better souvenir? There was no need for a producer, no studio time to book, the musicians were already under contract, and, just as with the movies, the appearance served to promote the record while the record in turn promoted not just the appearance but the star.

For Elvis, on the other hand, an opportunity was provided to fashion a show that reflected his more contemporary tastes. At rehearsals they focused on such recently recorded numbers as "In the Ghetto," "Don't Cry Daddy," Neil Diamond's "Sweet Caroline," and the brand-new single, "Kentucky Rain." In addition Elvis introduced covers of recent hits like Creedence Clearwater Revival's mythic evocation of southern roots, "Proud Mary," Tony Joe White's more down-to-earth piece of swamp funk, "Polk Salad Annie," and Joe South's brand-new "Walk a Mile in My Shoes," a synthesis of hippie sentiment, gospel feel, and Christian philosophy with which Elvis could fully identify. All were ambitious and appropriate choices, all required a certain humility on the singer's part, both artistic (in that he

hadn't originated the song) and financial (he didn't own the publishing —
though in many cases publishing cut-ins were sought and granted).
Another thing that many of the new songs had in common (along with
others, like the emotionally supercharged "Suspicious Minds" that had
rapidly evolved during the '69 engagement) was a tendency toward musical
or philosophical grandiosity as well as an implicit insistence that Elvis Presley was not going to be limited in his choices. And, as nearly every member
of the band could attest by now, it was difficult not to be swept along in the
passion of the moment, no matter what your aesthetic view of those
choices might be.

OPENING NIGHT WAS FULL of the usual pomp and circumstance,
with everyone from Fats Domino to Zsa Zsa Gabor in highly visible
attendance. The Colonel, who had begun his work well in advance of Elvis'
arrival, had the International decked out once again in Elvis decor, while
Bill Belew had modified the simple two-piece karate-style costume of the
August engagement to a very similar one-piece jumpsuit with more give
(for greater freedom of movement) in the fabric. Sound was the one area
where Elvis had experienced serious dissatisfaction throughout the last
engagement, so this time he hired Bill Porter, the former RCA engineer
who had overdubbed the horns on "Suspicious Minds" at his Las Vegas studio, to help Felton run the board. Though he had little previous experience
with live shows, Porter leapt to the challenge, and, in the absence of effective house monitors, added a couple of Shure speakers so that Elvis could
at last hear himself onstage.

"Apparently there is no stopping Elvis Presley," wrote *Commercial Appeal*
reporter James Kingsley in his *Billboard* review of opening night, which
pointed out the new versatility the star was beginning to show, as he did his
own hits and those of others, exhibited genial good humor, gave out kisses,
lay on his back, invited the audience to watch him while he took long
drinks of water, and delivered his usual self-deprecating and charmingly
off-the-wall monologues. Spotting Dean Martin in the audience, Elvis
struck up a spontaneous version of Martin's 1964 number-one hit, "Everybody Loves Somebody"; he forgot the lyrics to four different songs in the
course of the evening but stopped the orchestra and restarted the song
each time ("I was nervous," he told the indulgent audience); and in the
end he got a standing ovation when he closed the show with "Suspicious

Minds," coming back with the obligatory encore (the real closer by now), "Can't Help Falling in Love."

Though the majority of notices were raves (Robert Hilburn of the *Los Angeles Times* called Elvis' performance "a flawless demonstration of . . . vocal ability and showmanship"; Frank Lieberman of the *Herald-Examiner* declared that "the new decade will belong to him"), not every critic took as rosy a view. Elvis' future biographer Albert Goldman, covering the engagement for *Life,* opened his review with a single italicized adjective: *"Gorgeous!* — or some equally effusive effeminate word — is the only way to describe Elvis Presley's latest epiphany at Las Vegas." The critique went on with sneering contempt to call into question Elvis' sexuality ("Not since Marlene Dietrich stunned the ringsiders with the sight of those legs . . ."), sincerity ("So compelling is his immaculate narcissism . . ."), and musicality ("He strums the acoustic instrument slung white around his neck with the carelessness of a practiced faker"), without conceding a single positive point. Goldman, identified as a professor of classics at Columbia University, appeared to be equally contemptuous of audience, performer, and venue (he seemed most exercised by the spectacle of "male cheesecake ripe for the eyeteeth of the hundreds of women ogling him through opera glasses"), but perhaps the one critical point where he is on firm ground is the extent to which Elvis' show seemed to have taken on the appearance of a series of still lifes and studied poses. Certainly Elvis remained apt to say or do anything that took his fancy, and in that sense the show continued to be spontaneous, unpredictable, almost, one might say, zany — but in another, more important respect, it had lost its sense of freshness, as Elvis tended to conclude each number with what Goldman described as "a classically struck profile — Elvis as the Discus Hurler, Elvis as Sagittarius, Elvis as the Dying Gaul." The Columbia professor may well have missed the good humor of some of the impersonations, but he *got* that they were impersonations, a far cry from the uninhibited, seemingly out-of-control reactions of the performer who had rocketed out of the fifties to do high-spirited somersaults on the International stage just six months before.

The rest of the engagement was predictably successful, setting new attendance records, creating new expectations, generating the kind of business that lifted up the whole town. Though Elvis was still apt to interject the occasional new song just on a whim, the show itself was by now pretty much set, a variation on the kind of performance to which Elvis had long been exposed in his visits to Vegas, where Frank and Dean and Sammy treated the stage as if it were their own living room, goofing on themselves but most of all on the squares who had paid to see them goof. Elvis always retained the deepest respect for his fans, he genuinely *loved* his audience in a way that it's difficult to imagine Martin or Sinatra even contemplating, but there was no question that he felt he was letting them in for a treat if he allowed them to see him as he really was, unbuttoned if not altogether unvarnished. To twenty-eight-year-old Frank Lieberman, the critic for the *Los Angeles Herald-Examiner,* Elvis confessed that Vegas had given him "a new life. I was human again. There was hope for the future. . . . I was able to give some feeling, put some expression into my work." It even re-excited his interest in making movies, he told Lieberman, who was rewarded with a twenty-minute interview for his rave review of opening night. "I want a good property to find out if I can act once and for all. Those others were nothing, but finding something good is hard. . . . I need something good. I just can't go back to girls and GIs and things like that."

The band members and singers were like extended family now, as he grew more and more at ease in his new domain. "As soon as the show was over, he was in our dressing room," recalled Myrna Smith of the Sweet Inspirations. "His guys would stay over in his dressing room, and he would just come in and sit down and talk about *everything,* his love life, everything. We had our arguments, but he couldn't stay mad for long, and if you went to him in private, you could get him to do just about anything. Just don't embarrass him — because he was so insecure, I think that was just [his nature]."

They had pillow fights and water fights, exchanged reading material (because Estelle was the most religious, he read her passages from *The Impersonal Life* and spoke of his mother's ongoing influence on his life), and flirted with an intimacy that never crossed over the line. The only thing they didn't feel comfortable about was when he asked them up to the suite after the show. "When you went up there," Myrna knew, "it was party time. We didn't have to go up to the suite, because our talks were in the dressing room. When he came into our dressing room, we were friends." According to the Imperials' Joe Moscheo, Elvis continued to be upset that the gospel quartet didn't visit his suite more often, but by now it wasn't that easy to gain access, even if they had wanted to. "It just seemed like there were always too many people making decisions. Joe Esposito would say, 'He's tired tonight, we don't want any visitors in the dressing room.' Lamar and Charlie are out in the hall, and they want to be the big shots — they're saying, 'Don't even think about coming in.' I always felt like I was two or three times removed. The little bit of time you had with him, he always treated you so good. But there was always an underlying nervousness: you never knew when it was okay to talk to him and when it wasn't; there was always somebody telling you what you could and couldn't do. [And you got the feeling sometimes that] Elvis didn't even know it."

Even for those vouchsafed entry, there could be a sense of unease from the predatory atmosphere alone. It was an atmosphere of high school hijinks and sexual expectation, an extension of the competitive environment that had grown up around Elvis since he was twenty-one years old, but among men who were in their mid thirties now, each waiting until Elvis had made his choice for the evening so they could pounce on the women who were left. It was, said Glen D. Hardin, like a kind of "silly boys' club. . . . Just one big party." But a party from which wives and girlfriends were specifically excluded. It represented a reconstituting in many ways of the family that had been torn apart first by the arrival of Larry Geller, then by Elvis' marriage. It was, as Priscilla increasingly came to view it, a competition between "the crowd's adoration" and real life, a competition in which there was no possibility that real life could ever win.

It generated a different kind of excitement, too, than what they had become used to during what Joe called their "nine-to-five" Hollywood years. Then there was always time for the on-set affair — almost everyone had them — but at the end of a shoot you went home to your wife or girlfriend. Palm Springs had come to offer the same kind of limited opportunity for escape that Las Vegas had held out in the sixties, a world in which rules and restraints were temporarily suspended. Now they were actually *living* in that world, not just visiting, and the feeling gradually took hold not just with Elvis but among the guys as well that it was their wives who were married, not them.

FELTON RECORDED THE SHOW during the third week, sticking to individual selections so as to get only agreed-upon material without wasting too much tape. Despite the number of songs they had gone through in rehearsal, they still didn't have enough satisfactory selections to make up an album, so on the next-to-last day of recording, Charlie set up a quick afternoon run-through of three songs that Glen D. had arranged the night before, and they recorded them that night. "The Wonder of You" was the kind of soppy love ballad, complete with big melodramatic ending, that Elvis was so often drawn to, while Ray Price's "Release Me" was a classic country weeper, and "See See Rider" a blues standard that Elvis had been interjecting into his act throughout the engagement. Even with these additions, they were still short, so in the end RCA was forced to add two numbers recorded the previous August to the album that was released as *On Stage — February 1970*, with neither the continuity nor the excitement of the live act.

The final night was like the breakup of camp. The midnight show went on until 3:00 A.M. and ended with Elvis at the piano singing "Lawdy, Miss Clawdy" and "Blueberry Hill," comedian Sammy Shore running around the stage blowing his trumpet, and Priscilla standing in line in a backless culotte dress to receive a long kiss during "Love Me Tender." ("I think I know that girl," Elvis remarked.) New sound problems had cropped up in the big room over the last week, and Colonel had threatened the hotel that if they were not straightened out, Elvis would not go on. Evidently they were, and Elvis gave what everyone agreed was one of his finest performances. Sometimes, he confided to the audience, he wished he could just go out there and do his show in the relaxed manner of Dean Martin, but he knew that if he didn't "'get it on,' folks would just say, 'Why, he can't move no more.'" So he got it on. Toward the end of the evening he introduced the Colonel and said, "He's not only my manager, but I love him very much." As the curtain came down, reported Elvis chronicler and devoted fan Sue Wiegert, "Sammy Shore ran out and started kissing Elvis' feet, which cracked up both Elvis and the crowd!"

THE NEXT DAY THE COLONEL was off to Houston, where Elvis would headline the Houston Livestock Show and Rodeo at the Astrodome at the end of the week. There were six performances scheduled, three evening shows and three matinees, and the Colonel led an advance party to check out both hotel and security arrangements. Upon his arrival he learned that rumors had been circulating that there were no seats left for any of the shows, so he immediately took out $10,000 worth of radio spots to advertise the availability of tickets. "Nothing was left to chance," reported *Houston Post* reporter Marge Crumbaker. "When Parker checked in that Tuesday, his first action was to walk into nearly every crevice of the Astroworld Hotel and map out the setup. . . . Elevators were studied. Halls sketched. Entrances and exits were noted. The roof was inspected. . . . The absolute professionalism of the business end was staggering."

Elvis arrived the following day aboard International owner Kirk Kerkorian's private plane, accompanied by a party that included Joe, Red, Sonny, Charlie, Gee Gee, Jerry Schilling, Cliff Gleaves, and his father, Vernon. The Colonel had tried to limit the size of the party, stressing in a letter to Joe that this was a very tight setup and they didn't need any hangers-on, but evidently either Elvis wasn't listening or he didn't agree, because just about everyone came along for the ride. It became apparent immediately at Thursday's rehearsal that the sound situation was hopeless. Even with Felton and Bill Porter doing their best, it was going to be bad, and Elvis told the band not to bother to try to fight it but to "just go ahead and play."

Elvis appeared twice the following day, between the chuck-wagon races and the calf-roping contest, making his entrance from backstage in an open jeep that circled the arena while his fans raced along beside. It was, remarked the *Los Angeles Times'* Robert Hilburn, the first true test of his grassroots popularity, as well as the first-ever Houston rodeo weekday matinee, and it was in some respects a disappointment. Elvis appeared visibly nervous, the acoustics were as bad as he had anticipated, and he apologized to the crowd, which numbered only 16,708, including the 4,000 handicapped children who were attending as guests of Elvis and the Colonel. After the show it was clear to everyone around him that he was distraught. According to Gee Gee Gambill, "He went back to the hotel . . . and lay down on the bed. 'Well, that's it. I guess I just don't have it anymore,' he said." Even the usually imperturbable Colonel seemed upset. After he got up from his nap, Elvis shook his head and said, "Well, I guess I just can't bring it in like I used to." But then, according to Gee Gee, they looked out the hotel window and saw the cars backed up for miles along the freeway leading to the Astrodome. "Well, I'll be damned," Elvis said. "I guess I've still got it after all."

"The setting [for the second show] was improved," the *Los Angeles Times* reported, simply by taking place in the evening. In addition, "Presley's voice was stronger, the stage rotation smoother and the pace sharper than at the matinee." Elvis himself, Hilburn concluded, "was masterful. His voice remained the best in rock-pop music, and his stage movements, less self-conscious than last summer . . . were in perfect harmony with the music." All the high-intensity electricity and showbiz glamor that marked his Las Vegas appearances were only highlighted here, and in the end the audience of 36,299 (a Friday-night attendance record, eclipsing the previous one by 10,000) was on its feet cheering. The Saturday matinee surpassed previous years' attendance by 15,000, and Saturday night's crowd of 43,614 set a world record for indoor rodeo performances. By Saturday, though, wrote Hilburn, an astute observer, it was obvious "that the Astrodome challenge seemed to already be wearing off. He began some of the tongue-in-cheek gestures that marked the latter days of the Vegas appearances and switched lyric lines on several songs."

The Colonel watched every show from the announcer's booth, a golf cap or an oversize Stetson perched incongruously atop his head, a cigar clamped firmly between his teeth. He felt a growing sense of satisfaction as he watched the crowd give itself to Elvis with mounting fervor, while Elvis, dressed all in white and clearly sensing their abandonment, seemed to accept it almost as his due. On Saturday night Priscilla flew in, presumably to dispel the rumors which had cropped up once again, this time in the Houston papers, of a growing rift in their marriage. She attended the Sunday afternoon performance in a black see-through outfit that was remarked upon by more than one reporter. There was a press conference, too, on Sunday afternoon, at which Elvis conceded that the sound system had bugged him on the first day, but that with the help of his own engineer, the problem had been straightened out. It was a big thrill to be making this appearance, he said, and he would like to do more. Officers of the rodeo presented Elvis with a limited-edition (number 343) Rolex "King Midas" watch, and Houston Sheriff Buster Kern gave him a gold deputy's badge. "I know you want to get out of town Monday," said the sheriff, "and this will help you." "How am *I* supposed to get out of town?" protested Colonel Parker. "Do you want me to hitchhike?" So the sheriff gave him a badge, too. In addition, Elvis collected a Stetson and five new gold records that RCA vice president Rocco Laginestra had flown down from New York to present. "I should be given an award for nerve," Elvis remarked good-humoredly.

It was, all in all, Robert Hilburn summed up in what could be taken for the standard wisdom of the time, a capstone to "one of the most staggering reversals in the history of pop music . . . handled brilliantly by Colonel Tom Parker, a proven manager before he ever met Presley."

The Colonel was not yet done with his labors. While Elvis flew back to Los Angeles to relax and resume his karate studies, the Colonel began to put into effect some of his other long-standing plans. For one thing, he was not about to let the International take either him or Elvis for granted. Percs or no percs, plane or no plane, irrespective of Hawaiian vacations, he had informed newly named International president Alex Shoofey on the day of their final show that Elvis might very well not be returning to Las Vegas the following August. He was presently looking into an extended personal appearance tour, he told Shoofey, to be filmed over a long period of time, and he was also negotiating for a major motion picture, tentatively scheduled to begin shooting in late summer. He didn't want Shoofey to be caught short, and, of course, he was not closing any doors either, but he was sure that the hotel could appreciate his position. Evidently it did, because things were soon straightened out, and in fact, Shoofey came to him not a month later to see if Elvis might give a special performance at the hotel after a wildcat kitchen worker's strike had crippled Vegas ("The future of this resort community could well be at stake!" Shoofey wrote dramatically in his request), to which, of course, the Colonel instantly agreed, earning Shoofey and Kirk Kerkorian's further gratitude, even though Elvis was never actually called upon to perform.

Meanwhile, he continued to pursue another idea that had intrigued him for more than a decade: pay-for-view, closed-circuit broadcast of a live performance. The success and profitability of the concept had long since been established with sporting events — why not entertainment, too? the Colonel reasoned. He had originally tried to arrange just such a broadcast in 1960, when Elvis got out of the army, but ran into technical roadblocks. No one else in the entertainment field had tried it on any kind of scale in the intervening decade, though, so with his nose for firsts and financial breakthroughs of record-breaking proportions, the Colonel set his mind to the problem once again.

Two young promoters named Steve Wolf and Jim Rissmiller, who as Concert Associates booked some of the biggest rock acts into the Los Angeles area, had been pursuing him, going back to before the television special, with the idea of promoting an Elvis concert tour. After two years of letter writing, Wolf and Rissmiller, whose concert business had by now become a division of a larger and more diversified operation called Filmways, had finally gotten an appointment with the Colonel and laid out their projections for a fifteen-city tour which they estimated would net Elvis up to three-quarters of a million dollars. The Colonel rejected them out of hand. Elvis wasn't planning on doing any touring, he told them, and if he did tour, they had obligations to fulfill dating back to 1957. After the meeting Wolf and Rissmiller were left scratching their heads; they couldn't figure out what the meeting had been about, unless it was a test — and if it was, they had no idea whether they had passed or failed. They came back to the Colonel several times with various offers that met with no greater success, but then to their surprise the Colonel called for another meeting, right after the Astrodome.

This time they came in with a proposal for a single concert at the Anaheim stadium, which he turned down peremptorily but not without delivering a lecture in the friendliest manner on the necessity of their having their business more together if they wanted to be taken seriously. Then he dropped the blockbuster on them: what he wanted to do was closed-circuit.

It came as a total shock, though in thinking about it, they realized it shouldn't have. They had been talking for some time about doing a closed-circuit broadcast with the Rolling Stones, and the Colonel, they discovered early on, was exceedingly well informed. For all of his impersonations of an absentminded eccentric ("He comes to the door in a T-shirt and cap, he has these little glasses on the end of his nose, and I guess his whole thing is [to] throw you off guard"), he had demonstrated his acumen from the start, and now he bombarded them with facts and figures, ancillary rights issues that needed to be explored, and hard questions, finally asking them what they had in mind for a deal they hadn't even known they were coming in to discuss. Without giving them a chance to answer, "he gave us the deal *he* had in mind, and that was it. I mean, it wasn't an opportunity, like him saying, 'What would you give me?' He *told* us what we had to give him, and then said, 'Take it or leave it.' There was nothing in the middle."

They took it. The deal was for $1 million plus $100,000 expenses, with 75 percent of the profits going to Elvis and the Colonel as well, once Concert Associates had collected the first $500,000 for themselves. Wolf and Rissmiller now brought the deal to Filmways, on whom they would be relying not just for financial backing but for technological expertise, and the Filmways people almost "fell off their chairs — I mean, the scale was so large, the Colonel was talking about two hundred seventy-five cities, and the logistics of the thing were staggering." It had to be shot in Las Vegas, too, which didn't lend itself to the project as well as some other venues, and it had to be shot in four months, just a day or two before the August opening. There was, it appeared, no end to the stumbling blocks that the Colonel was prepared to put in their path, and he even critiqued their negotiating technique as he directed them to expand the broadcast on a global basis with yet another partner who could set up deals for them in London and Japan. Still, everything was moving ahead according to schedule, with a March 15 deal memo summarizing all the terms, when Robert Hilburn picked up the story in the March 19 edition of the *Los Angeles Times*.

From the beginning the two promoters had been told that if any word about the broadcast leaked to the press, the deal was off. "We were even afraid to tell our wives. But then one day we look in the paper, and there's the story." It read suspiciously like an item planted by either the Colonel or the promoters, or both. "Elvis Presley has agreed to a nation-wide, closed-circuit TV appearance this summer that will bring in the largest fee . . . ever paid an entertainer for a single performance." The broadcast would be "the first live closed-circuit broadcast of a music event in the U.S.," could gross up to $5 million, and would be broadcast in color in major cities. It was no secret, Hilburn observed, that Parker and Presley wanted to expand upon the Vegas appearances. "But Parker had a problem in returning Presley to concerts. To maintain his image as 'King,' Presley needs 'super engagements'. . . . The closed-circuit packages are a first for the entertainment field. It is a match, both financially and in artist's prestige, for the Las Vegas and Houston engagements. In fact it would, if ticket sales match expectations, exceed them both."

The promoters were never sure where the story came from, but in any case the deal was off. Within a week the Colonel had directed the William Morris Agency to draw up a new contract, this time with Filmways exclusively — and no longer for a closed-circuit broadcast but for a concert film to be shot during the engagement itself, with Elvis to receive $1 million, a profit split of 60–40, and 50-percent ownership of the negative. When *that* deal fell through, MGM, which had been proposed as the concert film's distributor and had been taken over in a stock coup by International owner Kirk Kerkorian some six months earlier, stepped into the breach with a sharply reduced offer of $500,000 and 60 percent of the net profits, with MGM retaining full ownership of the negative and the film once again to coincide with the International booking. Perhaps as much to save face as because it continued to fit in with his goal of total synergy, the Colonel took it, seizing on the soundtrack album that would come out of the film and the fact that for a single four-week engagement at the International, Elvis would now take in an even $1 million. The hotel would, of course, absorb many of the production costs, thus virtually ensuring that there would be profits to share, and the movie could not help but promote not just future appearances in Vegas but wider touring as well. From the Colonel's point of view, it was a matter of realpolitik. There was little choice between an unattainable ideal and cold, hard cash.

I N JUNE ELVIS RETURNED to Nashville to record. Despite the dazzling success of the American sessions, both commercial and artistic, he did not go back to the Memphis studio for a number of reasons, most of them political. The continued sparring with Chips had merely served to reinforce all of the usual jealousies within the Elvis camp and lend further credence to the charges already brought against the producer (greed, disrespect, bad-mouthing Elvis) by various parties with various axes to grind. Also contributory was the situation of Elvis' official producer, Felton Jarvis, who might have had legitimate reason to be concerned if Chips had maintained an ongoing role but whose ultimate position was defined by contractual terms virtually dictated by Elvis himself.

Everyone knew how fond Elvis was of Felton. They had a relationship based on shared enthusiasms and mutual respect, and Elvis liked to say of his producer that he was the only man he knew who could get along with anyone. He wanted Felton with him not just when he recorded but when he appeared in Vegas, and if he were to decide to go out on the road, he expected him to be there, too — he wanted Felton, in other words, at his beck and call. RCA meanwhile was growing increasingly unhappy with this arrangement. Elvis was not the only act to whom the producer was assigned — and who was paying his salary, after all, during all of his extended absences from the studio? At the same time, Felton had worries of his own. He was beset with health problems — his blood pressure had reached dangerously high levels — and he was beginning to feel like he was being pulled from all sides. Finally Elvis said to him, "Why don't you just quit, produce my records, and not do anything else?"

So on June 1, three days before the scheduled start of the session, that is exactly what Felton did. With a new contract from RCA guaranteeing him $750 for every master recording of Elvis' that he delivered and giving him a 2-percent royalty override, Felton left the security of a staff producer's position in exchange for what many felt (and common sense certainly told him) was the whim of a much less disciplined, and much less predictable, master. He guaranteed to deliver between fifteen and thirty-five sides from this first session, which many of his friends felt could be the immediate downfall of the whole arrangement and led Felton's wife, Mary, to believe that RCA or the Colonel was just trying to set him up. But Felton trusted his friend. He knew he was taking a chance, but Elvis had given him his word. The real problem, he confided to his wife, was not with Elvis anyway. It was with the material — that was what he was really worried about. But he felt sure they could get around it somehow.

The other significant problem was a technical one. The studio had been converted from a simple four-track to a sixteen-track board (with an intermediary eight-track setup in 1969) since the last time that Elvis had recorded there. What this meant was that the possibilities for overdubbing were enormously increased with all those open tracks. This carried with it, however, the same headache of selection that comes with any other exponentially expanded menu. In fact, to be utilized properly, the sixteen-track board required a major shift of aesthetic sensibility, since with the new setup a great deal of the ambient feeling of live recording was lost; that sense of audio roominess and space on which Felton and his engineer, Al Pachucki, had grown up was now sacrificed to a more distinct separation of sound, along with the far greater variety of choices and — for the technologically adept — the greater sonic possibilities. Unfortunately, neither Felton nor Pachucki was much more of a technician than their client, so what Felton focused on was the band.

This was his opportunity to finally put into effect the plan that had been in the back of his mind since 1966, when he first went to work for Elvis. Elvis had had his own session band in place when Felton came into the picture. Most of them had been around since 1958, with Scotty and D.J. going back to the beginning. Over the past four years Felton had brought in the occasional outside musician, but for the most part he hadn't tried to tinker with the setup. Now, after a two-year break from Nashville, with the television special, the American recordings, and Vegas all having intervened, he felt emboldened for the first time to bring in his own musicians, retaining only multi-instrumentalist Charlie McCoy and old Atlanta buddy Chip Young from the previous lineup. Otherwise, the new band was the original Muscle Shoals rhythm section, with whom Felton had first worked when he started recording Tommy Roe in 1962. It was Felton who had encouraged them to break away from Rick Hall's studio, where they were the foundation for the Muscle Shoals soul sound, and it was Felton who had first urged them to come to Nashville and given them work just after his own arrival in town. With James Burton taking lead guitar, it was a band

that could keep up with Elvis in anything he chose to do. These were players just as capable of reflecting Elvis' contemporary sensibilities as the
American rhythm section, and, not at all insignificantly, they were a group
who owed their jobs and loyalty to Felton alone.

Everyone in the band was excited about working with Elvis. David
Briggs, who had played keyboards on the 1966 gospel session which had
marked Felton's debut, was kidded by the others for carrying around a
picture of Elvis in his wallet, while Jerry Carrigan, the brash young drummer whose obstinate brush cut seemed to announce that he would back
down for no man, was thrilled just to be included. It was the bass player,
Norbert Putnam, though, just beginning to branch out into production
(he would have a huge hit the following year with Joan Baez' "The Night
They Drove Old Dixie Down"), who subsequently summed up the band's
collective feeling best. "I was scared to death," he recalled. "I remember
standing in the bathroom looking in the mirror and saying, 'Dear God,
don't let me be the one to screw up this session. Don't let me be the first
guy to ruin it!'"

Felton wanted them playing when Elvis came in the room; he wanted
them to create an up mood, he said, which everyone found a little odd, but
no odder than the retinue of yes-men who entered the studio when Elvis
did. As outsiders by definition (they came from Muscle Shoals, after all),
each band member prided himself on his independence nearly as much as
Chips, and it grated on them to a man to see Charlie fetch the water and
wipe beads of perspiration from Elvis' face, to wait while Richard Davis
wheeled in a big rack of clothes from which Elvis selected a fresh outfit
three times on the first night alone, to witness Lamar leap up in the air at
the conclusion of every take and exclaim, "It's a hit!" Even for James Burton, no outsider by anyone's definition but a newcomer to studio work
with Elvis, it was a kind of education to watch Lamar and Freddy competing to get their demos heard, as Elvis looked on with a combination of
amusement and scorn.

And yet for all of the extravagant show, it was no less evident to the
musicians that Elvis felt comfortable in their company, and he made them
feel just as much at home with him. At first it almost seemed to them like
he would just as soon have put off the actual business of recording indefinitely and sit around and swap stories and sing old gospel songs. When
he finally got down to work, though, they were amazed. Freddy's and
Lamar's songs were god-awful in the opinion of nearly everyone in the

room, and Jerry Carrigan in particular bridled when the band was told, "If he smiles at you, you smile back, or he'll think you don't like him." But when it came down to the music itself, Carrigan observed, "it was like doing a show. He'd dictate where the accents were, you watched his hands, he'd go through the gyrations — it was a new band, and he was really inspired, his eyes were really bright, and you knew, *This was a star.*"

Musically the demands he made on them were both greater and less than what they had come to expect from session work. Elvis was hard on drummers, Carrigan quickly discovered, just as Briggs knew that he was hard on piano players, because he required so much intensity and unrelenting physical play. Everything, they soon realized, came down to feel. Despite the sixteen-track board — whose principal advantage, if you made proper use of it, was to ensure maximum separation — Elvis insisted that they all group tightly around him and watch his every move so as to be ready to shift gears at the slightest inclination of his head. The only way Al Pachucki could get a sound level sometimes was to stop the take by pleading some technical foul-up.

Otherwise, technical considerations scarcely entered into it, as, often, they would just be starting to learn a song when Elvis declared that they had a master take. It wasn't laziness exactly, just a different philosophy of recording and one with whose end result they were not always satisfied (in fact, it would be more accurate to say that they were more often *embarrassed*). But whatever their feelings in retrospect, there was one thing, Norbert recognized, that they had no need to be embarrassed about. "After I became a record producer, I started to understand what making a record is all about. As a player, I just wanted the rhythm section to be flawless and have a great feel. But once I became a producer, I started to understand that what a great artist has to do is to try to express through his voice the emotion of his message. And of all the artists I ever knew, Presley was absolutely the best at that."

THE FIRST NIGHT SERVED as something of a paradigm for the entire session. They started out with two of Freddy's new Euro-styled ballads, the kind of heavily scored, overblown compositions typical of Carlin, the British song-publishing catalogue Freddy had taken over from Jean and Julian Aberbach four years earlier, with the understanding that he would continue to maintain his cousins' former company "in trust." The extent to which that trust had broken down became evident with an acrimonious blowup in October of 1969 (it essentially revolved around Freddy's belief, backed up by legally defensible action, that Carlin was an exclusive enterprise of his own), and now the cousins barely spoke. The Aberbachs had subsequently done all they could to get Freddy dismissed from his positions with Elvis Presley and Gladys Music, but the Colonel, for all of his reservations about "Herr Beanstalk," would not hear of it. As a result, Freddy remained tied to the two Elvis Presley publishing companies while pushing songs from his own British catalogue almost exclusively (Lamar took care of the Hill and Range catalogue proper), with Freddy's numbers governed by the time-honored Hill and Range cut-in formula when Elvis recorded them but otherwise unencumbered and serving the exclusive benefit of his rapidly evolving empire.

To Elvis it mattered little; he was just looking for good material. Nor was he above the Wagnerian grandiloquence of a song like "I've Lost You," the second of Freddy's offerings, which was just the kind of melodramatic portrait of a disintegrating marriage that seemed to really hit home. After seven serious takes, he found a brief diversion in the Golden Gate Quartet's "Born Ten Thousand Years Ago," which he had been fooling around with for the past several years. But then Freddy got him back on track with "The Sound of Your Cry," yet another sentimental extravaganza, on which he expended eleven excruciating takes. It went on in this schizophrenic fashion for the rest of the night, with two quick passes at Sanford Clark's 1956 rockabilly hit, "The Fool," which emerged while Elvis was waiting for Lamar to furnish him with lyrics for "Faded Love," the Bob Wills western-swing classic that had suddenly taken his fancy. After a couple of ragged but wonderfully high-spirited bluegrass numbers, with little parallel in the Elvis canon outside of "Blue Moon of Kentucky," they finished off the evening at 4:30 A.M. with a Ben Weisman adaptation of "Run Along Home, Cindy," an up-tempo folk song that Elvis took to readily enough and that gave Freddy four cuts to Lamar's none.

Felton must have breathed a sigh of relief. They had gotten something like seven masters in a single night's work, and there was no reason to think the pace would let up. In the next couple of nights they recorded an additional twelve masters and a studio jam. Some of the songs were better executed than others, some better suited to Elvis' style. Freddy retained his lead over Lamar, getting most of the big numbers — but only one or two songs gave Elvis the opportunity to really sink his teeth into them, and not necessarily those provided by either Freddy or Lamar. "You Don't Have to Say You Love Me," for example, was a song that Elvis had been drawn to ever since Dusty Springfield had first put it out in 1966. An Italian melody with bittersweet English lyrics, it had something that clearly touched Elvis, as he threw himself into painstaking efforts to work out an appropriate arrangement, then recorded the song in three quick takes. Simon and Garfunkel's quasi-gospel "Bridge Over Troubled Water" was another strong number to which he gave himself over completely, even if his very commitment to the song led him to overpower it without Chips' firm hand to rein him in. By the end of the third night they had twenty tracks in the can, and Felton had every reason to feel jubilant. Except that they had virtually run out of material.

Things might very well have ended right there. They began the fourth night with yet another of Lamar's maddeningly indistinguishable Shirl Milete compositions (an opinion voiced with some asperity by the singer himself), when all of a sudden Elvis abruptly shifted gears and launched into a soulful version of Eddy Arnold's 1954 hit, "I Really Don't Want to Know," written by one of Elvis' favorite songwriters, Don Robertson. With that, the session all at once took on a whole new cast, as Elvis and the band ran through one classic country number after another, almost as if everyone had been waiting for just such a moment to occur. First they polished off "Faded Love," the song whose lyrics Lamar had been searching for on the first night; next came Ernest Tubb's "Tomorrow Never Comes"; then Ray Price's "Make the World Go Away," Willie Nelson's "Funny How Time Slips Away," and a churchy variation on Stonewall Jackson's "I Washed My Hands in Muddy Water" very much influenced by Charlie Rich's 1965 version.

What distinguishes each of these songs is their openness to interpretation (all would have equal validity in a rhythm and blues, country, or, lyrics aside, gospel context), the enthusiasm with which Elvis attacks them (almost all are first takes), and, perhaps not coincidentally, the fact that nearly every one of them is sung just a little too fast. It is clear, though, that Elvis has found his groove, and when at the end of the evening David Briggs pushed him to recut "Love Letters" strictly because Briggs felt his piano part on the original 1966 version could be improved, Elvis never hesitated, entering into the old Ketty Lester rhythm and blues ballad with a will, not really improving on the original (which, whatever Briggs' reservations, has a delicate beauty of its own) but proving what Elvis continued to believe all through his life: that every moment was capable of providing a fresh new take on the subject.

By the last night everyone was a little weary, and Elvis stuck strictly to Freddy and Lamar's program, laying down five more tracks and winding up five days of recording with an astonishing thirty-four masters. The musicians were almost in a daze. In one sense it had been a highly frustrating experience, in which nothing was ever completed as they felt it should be — nothing was ever revisited, mistakes were never addressed; it was just pack up and move on to the next number once a proper tone had been established. In another, more important respect, though, it was an experience they wouldn't have given up for the world, the sense of being caught up in the eye of the storm. It was a phenomenon that none of them had ever really witnessed before either: the costume changes, the sense of panoply and intimacy inextricably combined, the picture of Elvis prowling around the studio putting on a performance for them, for the guys, and for the pretty dark-haired actress he had flown in for the session, too. In the end, Norbert realized, all it really came down to was feel. "It amazed me that he [would record] these very guttural, primitive songs — I call them 'primitive.' But I came to understand, he expressed so many things with his voice — the lyrical content had nothing to do with what was happening [for] him. He was the only artist I ever worked with that could zing you — with the 'Elvis thing' — whenever he wanted. He was the greatest communicator of emotion that I ever knew, from beginning to end."

E LVIS RETURNED TO MEMPHIS for the rest of June, as the Colonel continued to make preparations for the movie and the Vegas opening in August. He informed the hotel that he was planning a special "ELVIS PRESLEY SUMMER FESTIVAL," this time, for which he would be shipping one hundred thousand special menus, fifty thousand 8 x 10 photos, one hundred thousand special postcards, sixty thousand four-color catalogues, twenty thousand souvenir photo albums, and twenty-five gross of special imitation straw hats, which hotel employees would be expected to wear throughout the engagement, all furnished in keeping with the terms of the Colonel's contractual understanding with the International. With Freddy he continued to be insistent that all i's had to be dotted, all t's crossed. They needed to be sure that every song that was to be used in the movie was controlled by their publishing; there could be none of the kind of foul-ups that had occurred in the past. "Baron Bienstock must be fully aware that this is not a playtoy," he wrote to Julian Aberbach, in full awareness of the Aberbachs' quarrel with their cousin. "Unless there is a 100% serious attitude towards this project, we will have to research the possibility of handling it ourselves with a new, fresh company," he declared in his March 26 letter, thus raising the specter of a break not just with Freddy but with the Aberbach brothers as well, in case they were thinking that Freddy might sink on his own.

Rehearsals started in Los Angeles in mid July. Among the more than sixty songs rehearsed were sixteen from the June session, including some of the most ambitious. "You Don't Have to Say You Love Me," "Bridge Over Troubled Water," "I've Lost You," and "Heart of Rome," the last a challenging vocal piece on which they had failed to achieve a satisfactory master, were all extensively worked up, along with hard blues, tender ballads, and even "Froggy Went A-Courtin'" (not a serious contender). By the time they left L.A. on August 1, a good deal of film footage had already been shot. Ronnie Tutt was a welcome returnee on drums, new arrangements and orchestrations for the show were being written out on an almost daily basis by Glen D. and David Briggs in Nashville — but Elvis didn't meet his new orchestra leader for the first time until he got to Las Vegas.

Joe Guercio, a well-traveled music business hipster from the old school, had been hired to replace Bobby Morris as music director of the International just a few weeks before. A forty-two-year-old native of Buffalo, New York, he had worked with Patti Page for several years (he was the pianist on her 1953 hit, "How Much Is That Doggie in the Window?," the song that has frequently been cited as the red flag waved in front of the onrushing forces of rock 'n' roll), then Julius La Rosa, Steve Lawrence and Eydie Gorme, and Diahann Carroll, before finally landing in Vegas for good. Not surprisingly, he came to his new job as no great fan of Elvis Presley's music, which he was inclined to dismiss as little more than an amateur endeavor in the glitzy finger-snapping world that he had come to inhabit, an impression very much reinforced by his first meeting with the Elvis Presley organization.

"They came in, and they had no library. They just had their front line rehearsed, and they had all these charts, and they just come in and dump them on the stage, and I'm sitting there with twenty-five musicians! I said, 'What is this?' And they said, 'We'll let you know what we're going to do.'

And I said, 'No, you guys are going to sort this stuff out. I'm not going to look through all this. I'm not a librarian.' I was pissed off from the day we met."

Glen D. offered to help sift through the material, which cemented a relationship between Guercio and the keyboard player, but rehearsals didn't go a whole lot better. As in the past, orchestra and rhythm section rehearsed separately to begin with, with the two joining up only at the end. "Then Elvis comes in, and they didn't introduce me at first, he just comes in and waves and calls a tune, and the rhythm section started playing. So I had the guys bring the tune up, and I said, 'When he hits the seventeenth bar — 'cause we had to pick a spot to come in on, I'm not going to direct Elvis Presley's players, they're all King Kong. I said, 'We'll all just come in on bar seventeen.' And I brought the band in then, and that's the first acknowledgment I got: he turned around and looked at me.

"The first band break they brought me down to meet him. Now it was time to meet King Henry the Eighth. We go down, and Joe Esposito says, 'This is Joe Guercio,' and I had a baton — I used to always use a stick. So he looks at the stick, and he says, 'Good job, maestro.' From that day on he never called me by my name. After the break he runs another tune; I don't remember what it was, but he stopped — he's trying to find an ending and trying to find an ending, and I say, 'That ending doesn't make it.' I said, 'Let's try doing this. Brass, give me a D.' And we came to an ending, and he loved it. And he'd turn around from then on when we started to come in. I was never into conversation with him; it was all eye takes. I'd get one second: I knew if it was right, I knew if it was wrong, I knew if he was getting off on it. It was [snap-of-the-finger] communication."

Afterward, Joe Esposito asked him how he thought it had gone. It was like "following a marble falling down concrete steps," Guercio responded with typical frankness. The next day he arrived at his dressing room and couldn't get in the door. "I finally push it open, and there must have been three thousand marbles on the floor and a sign on the mirror: 'Follow the marble. . . . Me.' From that day on, it was like I was one of the gang."

The rehearsals proceeded without further incident. It was a difficult, ambitious, and somewhat daunting task to try to organize such a large repertoire in such a short period of time, but Guercio and Glen D. threw themselves into it wholeheartedly, writing out new arrangements, refining old ones, trying to address some of the problems of not having a proper library or a systematic prior approach. Many of the orchestrations were written out in what Guercio contemptuously referred to as "'movie arrangements,' some were written for this size band, some weren't, and none of the rock shit was in there — none of the rock 'n' roll stuff had any charts." In the end, though, they managed to surmount most of the obstacles and to Guercio's amazement were actually ready on opening night.

"Opening night was when I was impressed by Elvis Presley. I mean, I've been onstage with a lot of stars — I hate to let the air out of their balloons, but they have no idea what a star is. Jesus Christ! It was unreal. It was just a group of songs, very little production — it wasn't as organized as a lot of Vegas shows. But, boy, if you want to talk about going out and grabbing people — Elvis Presley was a happening, and what he had going will never be again. There was a vibe you could pick up in the audience — it was unbelievable. I'm not going to say to you that musically it was the best in the whole world. It was charisma. He just loved to put other people around his little finger and do it, and he did.

"I don't think he saw himself at all. He was like a free spirit with the audience. I mean, with other performers it's here to there, they're disciplined people, but he was so undisciplined it was a joke. He was like a floater, man, he would just get into every seat in the joint. I don't think he was ever really at ease onstage. He would be floating, and then every time he felt an insecure moment, he would turn around and do a ha-ha to somebody, go to Charlie for a minute or somebody else — but he would always come back to home base. You talk to a lot of people who'll say discipline makes a star. Horseshit! Charisma makes a star. Sinatra, Michael Jackson, Streisand — he walked out there, and there was a whole other feel. He could walk across the stage and not even have to open his mouth."

Cary Grant came backstage after the show and pronounced him "the greatest entertainer since Jolson." To Robert Blair Kaiser, on the other hand, a former political correspondent for *Time* who was doing a feature for the *New York Times Magazine,* the whole thing was a bit of a letdown. MGM's five giant Panavision cameras seemed to distract Elvis, Kaiser reported, and he appeared frustrated by persistent sound problems and maybe a little bit thrown by the star-studded makeup of the audience. He was jittery enough that he even needed a lyric sheet for "I Just Can't Help Believing," one of the new songs in his act, and after the strenuous karate exhibition that now accompanied "Polk Salad Annie," he remarked, "I feel like an old stripper." Whatever self-consciousness Kaiser may have detected, however, Guercio's reaction is ample testimony to the compelling nature of his performance.

The Colonel, meanwhile, strolled confidently up and down the aisles, cigar in hand, "Elvis Summer Festival" imitation straw boater atop his head, greeting celebrities and fans alike with equal aplomb. He explained his concept of promotion to the *New York Times* reporter on the following day ("he said something," reported Kaiser, "about giving the people something special, something that would buoy them up, in the midst of this national recession"), made clear that he had no time for fancy financial legerdemain ("he has no investments of his own and he lets others [i.e., Elvis' father, Vernon] handle Elvis' investments. If he were Elvis' business manager, too, he wouldn't have time, you see, to put out all the banners and pennants and billboards. He only has one brain!"), and stressed the totality of his commitment.

"The Colonel," Kaiser observed, "always makes sure that he negotiates from a position of strength, always sure of every little detail, always thinking months and years ahead." Up till one the previous night, he was at his desk at eight o'clock that morning, working out last-minute details on the abbreviated tour for which he was at just that moment completing arrangements. Later in the day he would make the formal announcement: Elvis would be appearing in six cities, starting in Phoenix on September 9, two days after the Vegas engagement was over. RCA would promote the first date, Colonel was keeping Tampa for himself, but the promoters for the rest of the tour would be a group known as Management III, which consisted of a one-time MCA talent agent named Jerry Weintraub, who had just taken over the management of an unknown singer named John Denver; a concert promoter named Tom Hulett, who, with his Seattle-based company, Concerts West, had helped create the full-scale, modern-day rock tour with artists like Led Zeppelin and Jimi Hendrix; and Terry Bassett, a Dallas entrepreneur who, together with Seattle businessman Lester Smith and entertainer Danny Kaye, had provided the start-up money and working capital for Concerts West.

There would be one hundred security guards in each city, the Colonel announced, Elvis would travel from hotel to concert site in an armored truck, and ticket prices would be maintained at a reasonable level. "We are very happy with what we will receive for this tour," the Colonel declared, without specifying exactly how much that would be, "and realize that it will also put Elvis back in front of his demanding millions of fans." Elvis himself, according to *Commercial Appeal* reporter James Kingsley's account, was anticipating a worldwide tour in 1971 and was "delighted that we could work out a way to go back on the road after an absence of too many years. I am looking forward to hitting the road again."

JERRY WEINTRAUB HAD BEEN COURTING the Colonel for nearly two years now. A larger-than-life, self-proclaimed show business "character," who at thirty-two was just beginning to strike out on his own, Weintraub ascribed the genesis of the association, literally, to a dream. "I woke up one night in the middle of the night, and I woke my wife [singer Jane Morgan] and said to her, 'I just had a dream that I was going to present Elvis Presley at Madison Square Garden.' And she said to me, 'Great, that's great.' I said to her, 'But I don't know Presley. I don't know his manager, Colonel Parker.' She said, 'Well, you'll find him,' and went back to sleep." Through Harry Jenkins he got the Colonel's number and started calling just about every day. Turned down again and again, he finally got a meeting with the Colonel in the steam room of the Spa Hotel in Palm Springs, and that meeting led to another meeting, until finally he felt there was some chance of putting together a tour. It was at this point that he got in touch with Tom Hulett at Concerts West, whom he had met in passing through a music business attorney named Steve Weiss.

Hulett was the one with tour experience; Concerts West at this point billed itself as the biggest concert promotion company in the country (they boasted of putting on six or seven hundred shows a year throughout the world), and it was clear from the way that Weintraub's talks with the Colonel had gone that he was going to need to avail himself not only of Hulett's experience but of a substantial amount of his company's money as well. The two fledgling partners met at the Beverly Hills Hotel just forty-eight hours before the Vegas opening, hit it off, and agreed that if Weintraub could deliver Elvis they would work together on the tour. Two days later they attended the opening as guests of the Colonel and the next day made their deal.

Hulett recognized from the first that Weintraub would be the front man, both by nature and by need, and he knew from the moment that he saw Elvis Presley perform that this was something he wanted to be involved in. "That's when I realized Elvis Presley was Elvis Presley. I mean, God almighty, when he walked onstage, the place exploded, and *he* exploded, and it was one of the greatest nights of show business I've ever seen in my life. We had our meeting with the Colonel the next day, and he had already set up the concert in Phoenix, I think just to try it, and he said, 'Lookit, we're doing this show ourselves. Why don't you set up four more dates, and here's where I want to go.' He named the cities: Detroit, St. Louis, Miami, and Mobile — it made no sense. I said to Jerry later, 'Why not Phoenix, L.A., and Oakland? — it's a route.' But Jerry said, 'Don't ask, just do it.' So I got on the phone. Jerry was, like — I mean, we were told how the Colonel wanted to do things, and even though I knew it was wrong, Jerry was afraid to question the Colonel. Which I'm sure was the right decision. The Colonel said, 'I want you to get this kind of hotel, I want the security at the highest level, I want you to get this, this, this — and then call me.' It wasn't like Creedence Clearwater Revival, for example; with them, if I wanted to rent any building in America, I'd just rent the building and then go buy the ads. The Colonel said, 'Don't touch any advertising, and don't touch any promotion. Just get the facilities.' So that's what we did."

In the end they put up $240,000 for their four dates, with RCA fronting $50,000 for the Phoenix show and the Colonel going it alone in his adoptive hometown. It was a foolproof system for Elvis and the Colonel, something like a glorified version of record company support, with expenses unlikely to add up to more than $150,000 at the outside, and thus a profit of $140,000 or $150,000 guaranteed before a single customer walked through the door. The promoter took all the risk and, even if you projected a sell-out at every location, it would be virtually impossible for the risk taker to come out with more than $5,000 or $6,000 per show, based on the size of the halls. Money was not the number-one concern for anyone at this point, though. From the Colonel's perspective, he was taking the greatest risk of all: putting Elvis' reputation on the line. Tom Hulett and Jerry Weintraub, on the other hand, were looking down the road: they were determined to prove that they were worthy of the Colonel's trust.

THE VEGAS ENGAGEMENT MEANWHILE followed its own idiosyncratic course, as Elvis grew more and more at ease onstage and once again started fooling around both with the audience and with the band. Eventually, he settled on a loose framework for the show, which could be changed whenever the spirit moved him but served as a guideline for the remainder of their stay. Filming was confined to the first four nights and captured what had by now become his practiced Vegas routine, with lots of laughs, lots of "squirrel" jokes ("When I was in high school, they used to see me coming down the street, and they'd say, 'Hot dang, let's get him, he's a squirrel, he's a squirrel, he just come down out of the trees'"), and goofs on the lyrics of some of his most familiar songs, along with a generous dose of highly romantic, unabashedly melodramatic singing. Elvis could go in an instant from an impassioned version of "Bridge Over Troubled Water" to trotting out a "laughbox" that he would introduce one night as Colonel Parker, another as "my producer." But while the trappings of the music could in many respects be equated with the theatricality of the costume (in this case, more often than not, a white jumpsuit with bell-bottom pants and fringes hanging down from the belt), there was little question of the continued dramatic impact of the show.

The day after filming concluded, on August 14, a paternity suit was filed in Los Angeles Superior Court by Patricia Ann Parker, a twenty-one-year-old North Hollywood waitress, who claimed that her pregnancy was the result of a sexual encounter with Elvis that had taken place during his last Las Vegas engagement. He made light of the lawsuit one night when he introduced Paul Anka, noting that Anka's wife was pregnant but "she didn't put nothing in the paper about me last week, did she?," while declaring on another occasion that Priscilla, who was in the audience, knew "that I didn't knock that chick up last week either — 'cause I use birth control." And yet for all of his outward show, there was no question that he was deeply disturbed. This was in fact the nightmare he had always feared most: the loss of the love of his fans. To gossip columnist May Mann he expressed a reaction that on one level might be seen as disingenuous, on another as the purest form of shocked disbelief. "How can anyone do this to me?" he declared, seeming to seek an exoneration that went far beyond the scope of the case. "I am completely innocent."

H E KNEW HE WAS NOT. But he was bored. Vegas had become a routine just like everything else. The music remained fresh in many respects: he continued to appreciate the musicians he had gathered around him; if he was looking for someone to blame, Jerry Scheff and Glen D. both noted, it was never a member of the band, always one of the guys. But things had changed in a way that could not be quantified. Just as the Colonel found release night after night at the roulette table, Elvis sought diversion in the constant procession of women who came at his summons, as it grew clearer and clearer not just to the inner circle but to the world at large that Elvis and Priscilla's marriage was a wide-open one, at least on his end. Even Robert Blair Kaiser, the *New York Times* reporter, noted the rumors, when he described a fan from Memphis approaching Vernon "while he plunked half dollars into his favorite slot machine [and asking] him boldly whether Elvis and Prissy were getting divorced. Said Vernon easily, with only a slight pause before he pulled down the handle of the machine, 'We worked that out. Everything's okay now.'"

What Kaiser missed in his portrait of this "vitally intense young man" without any serious "self-doubts [or] seeds of discontent" was the same thing that had escaped the notice of virtually every other reporter or outside observer who had covered the story. It was something that no one on the outside was likely to pick up, given how radically it departed both from public perception and public (and self-) image: with boredom once again setting in, Elvis was relying on prescription medications to a greater degree than he had since returning to live performing. The nature and pressure of his work, his inability to get to sleep after delivering two high-intensity performances a night, was always the excuse, and there was no more problem obtaining what he wanted in Las Vegas than there was in Memphis, Los Angeles, or Palm Springs — in fact, with a doctor on call twenty-four hours a day and a company-town perspective that the first, last, and sometimes only medical priority was making sure that the show would go on, it was even easier. Elvis had long ago learned that there was always a doctor or dentist more than willing to prove himself your friend simply in exchange for being able to say that he was close to Elvis Presley, and with his own encyclopedic knowledge of the *PDR* (which was never far from his bed table), he was able to manufacture the appropriate symptoms for virtually any kind of medication that might take his fancy. It was still mostly sleeping pills at this point, Placidyl now, in combination with "vitamin" injections, amphetamines, or a booster shot to get him going when he awoke in mid to late afternoon. Joanie Esposito, strictly an observer, and with her opportunities for observation increasingly limited by the restrictions now placed on wives' visits, watched them all, Elvis and the guys, with a certain motherly amusement. "They'd think it was so funny, you know, to laugh at each other, to sit there and try and fight it and see who could stay awake the longest until they all finally fell asleep."

More than any single factor, though, it just seemed as if there had been a change in the weather. To Jerry Schilling, working as a film cutter at Paramount in pursuit of his union card but showing up faithfully every weekend to join the gang, "The first couple of times in Vegas Elvis was only concerned about the show. The only thing he did at the beginning was stay up at night with the musicians and have his friends and fans up and talk about the show. By the second year he started to get bored. He still loved it — you probably wouldn't have known it, but he slowed down a little, he was a little puffier looking. That's when he began to have a lot of time to just start getting into other things."

T HIS WAS THE ATMOSPHERE that twenty-five-year-old Kathy West-moreland came into when she joined the show as high soprano Millie Kirkham's replacement on Sunday, August 16. Kathy had agreed to take three weeks out of her busy L.A. session schedule to replace Kirkham, the Nashville backup singer who had come out at Elvis' request strictly for the filming. Upon her arrival, she was met by Felton Jarvis, who welcomed her to the show, introduced her to Colonel Parker (who in turn presented her with a straw hat), and gave her a huge stack of records to allow her to familiarize herself with the repertoire. She watched the show that night, with Millie still in it, and was shocked at the behavior of the fans. A classically trained musician whose father had appeared in *The Student Prince* and *The Great Caruso* with Mario Lanza, she had "never seen anything like that in my life, and I doubt if I ever will. These women, fully dressed in these glamorous evening gowns, literally running down the tables in their high heels, knocking over champagne bottles, stepping on other people's steaks." She was also overwhelmed by the music and "by the transformation of the man I'd just met downstairs into this gorgeous, just grand charismatic person."

She was terrified when it came time to go onstage the following night, but Elvis reassured her in her dressing room. "He told me, 'Don't worry about it, just relax and have fun. Remember, we're just here to make people happy.' But then he winked and said, 'But when I point at you, you better sing something, kiddo.' So — great!"

Despite her nervousness, Kathy fit right in. Looking somewhat prim in her dark brown pants and blouse beside the relatively unrestrained Sweets, she was more than open to learning from their rhythmic improvisations and intricate vocal harmonies. "I had a separate dressing room, but I would always go down to theirs and sit with them before the show. We really developed a strong, strong friendship; they made me feel really comfortable even though we were from such totally different backgrounds, and we would work out the most incredible harmonies and sounds, syllables I couldn't even emulate today if I attempted to recall them. They were so advanced in their rhythms and harmonies and just thinking in one mind." The Imperials, too, she found completely professional, "very polished, tight, and very, very precise in their vocal projection," and even if the overall choral effect was sometimes a little ragged, with the nine voices and disparate musical backgrounds occasionally failing to mesh, there was enough give-and-take that the overall feel came through — "it did create a musical impression which really affected people. There was something for everybody."

Most of all, though, it was Elvis she was intrigued by: his ambitions, his aspirations, his personality. She got to know him at first because he was always running in and out of the Sweets' dressing room, laughing and joking and just hanging out. After a while he started talking to her about the music. He asked her if the tea she was drinking was good for the voice, he was curious about her musical background, and her father's, too, he asked her opinion about some of the great tenors in history, like Caruso and Bjoerling. She discovered to her surprise that his own ability with a song could move her to tears, even when she didn't much like the song. When she remarked upon the power that he exerted over an audience, he said that he knew he could influence people's thinking, but that wasn't his intent. "I think it's important for me to just entertain . . . make people happy, help them forget all their troubles for a while. I think that's what I'm on this earth to do."

ON WEDNESDAY, AUGUST 26, the normal routine was dramatically interrupted when an anonymous call came into the security office at the International, offering information about a plot to kidnap Elvis. The following day the Colonel got a similar call, and then on August 28 Joanie Esposito was awakened at home in Los Angeles by a caller looking for her husband. He had information, he said, about a threat on Elvis' life which was to be carried out on Saturday night during the show. Forty-five minutes later the same man called back with additional information, stating that for $50,000 in small bills he would reveal the name of the killer. At this point the FBI was brought in, and calls went out to everyone from Elvis' lawyer Ed Hookstratten, who believed the threats were related to the paternity suit in which he was representing Elvis, to Ed Parker, Jerry Schilling, and Red West, each of whom Elvis contacted personally. "I need you," was all he told Jerry on the phone. "I'll tell you about it when you get here. The plane's on the way." When Red arrived from Memphis, Elvis was so keyed up, "he just stumbled into my arms and hugged me."

All day long the newly created security detail went over plans, and in the dressing room before the show, Elvis cried and said good-bye to his father and all his friends. He didn't know what was going to happen, he told them, but he wasn't going to let them down — and he knew they wouldn't let him down either. "If some sonofabitch tries to kill me," he said, "I want you guys to get him, I want you to rip his goddamn eyes out. I don't want him sitting around afterward like Charlie Manson with a grin on his face, saying, 'I killed Elvis Presley.'"

They all took up their stations during the show, Sonny and Jerry with the orchestra, Red and Ed Parker on either side of the stage, everyone packing, including Elvis, who had a pistol in each boot. There were plainclothes police officers scattered throughout the crowd, Dr. Newman (the hotel doctor) was backstage with oxygen and blood supplies, and an ambulance was waiting outside — but then nothing happened. In the middle of the show a guy in the balcony called out, "Elvis!," and everyone flinched and thought maybe this was it, but all the man wanted was for Elvis to sing his favorite song. By the end of the evening everyone was emotionally wrung out, and while the assassin-kidnapper was never heard from again, the hotel remained on standby alert for the rest of the engagement. Looking back on the situation with some bemusement, Imperials singer-manager Joe Moscheo sensed that Elvis was almost sorry when the adventure was over. "It was crazy. It was like he was disappointed that he didn't get shot!"

The night after the assassination threat, Jim Aubrey, the soft-spoken fifty-one-year-old head of MGM, known throughout the industry as "the smiling cobra," came backstage after the show to congratulate Elvis on his performance. As the man who had given the go-ahead to the just-completed concert film, Aubrey expressed enthusiasm about their ongoing venture and introduced Elvis to his companion, a dark-haired twenty-three-year-old starlet named Barbara Leigh. Elvis was, as ever, the consummate host, turning his attention to Ricky Nelson and his wife, Kris, and to Joyce

Bova, a twenty-five-year-old staff member of the House Armed Services Committee whom he had met in Vegas the previous August and who was his guest at the show. His attention never strayed too far from Barbara, though, and while Aubrey was occupied with something else, he took the opportunity to get her phone number. Then he turned back to Bova, another stunningly beautiful woman, whom he invited up to his suite after the show.

Bova had been enormously impressed the first time they had met, when an International greeter picked her out of the ticket line and brought her backstage to meet the star. They had had dinner together in his suite afterward, and he had struck her as sensitive, intelligent, uncannily intuitive, a real gentleman. But she had not seen him since and felt that she might have angered him by turning down a number of impulsive invitations he had extended to join him in California (she couldn't, she explained — her committee was just beginning its investigation of My Lai), and angered him even more by persisting in bringing up his marriage in the face of his emphatic insistence that it was a marriage in name only. She had made this trip determined to find out "once and for all whether Elvis and I were illusion or reality," and from the way in which he greeted her and the warmth with which he invited both her friend and her to the suite, she was beginning to think that they might be reality. From the first, though, she noticed little signs that he was different somehow from the last time they had met. He appeared boastful in a way she didn't remember, talking nonstop about the assassination threat with a bravado that seemed almost cruel, patronizing Sonny and Red in a manner that she found distasteful ("You guys were really scared, weren't you?" he demanded of them, as if he weren't). Later, in the suite, he showed signs of irrational jealousy (and they hadn't done anything but kiss!); he seemed more than ever to be showing off, for her as much as for anyone else; and, she noticed, his leg kept quivering uncontrollably. But when he asked her to stay the night, she agreed without hesitation.

After everyone left, he seemed to undergo yet another, even more disturbing transformation, taunting her when she was expecting tenderness, treating her with a kind of crude disregard for her feelings. "You can't always be questioning me, Joyce," he said. "I'm tired of people telling me how I am, or how I'm not. How they think I'm different, how they think I change from one time to another. I'm always me. You got to believe in — in the things I'm able to see ahead for us." Goaded by his indifference, she was led to ask the very question which she had already discovered was guaranteed to infuriate him: How could there be an "us" when he already had a wife? "This is ridiculous!" he exploded. He had already explained all that to her. "If you're going to stay, then stay." And with that he angrily flung a black silk pajama top at her. She didn't think she would ever see him again as she slammed the door behind her.

The next day he called Barbara Leigh at home. "The phone was ringing as I arrived, so I ran in and left my suitcase in the car, and it was Elvis, which was a real shock. He wanted me to come see him that Wednesday, but it was just before Labor Day, and I had plans to go away with Jim Aubrey on a cruise. Elvis said, 'Come on Wednesday and just stay with me for [the night].' So — this is a funny story — one of the guys met me at the airport and brought me back to the hotel, and he said, 'You can't come to the first show,' and I said okay. 'But you can come to the second.' So I waited around, and Elvis comes in after the first show and said, 'Darling,' and takes my hand, and said, 'You couldn't come to the first show because Jim Aubrey showed up with another woman.' Which was a shock to me. And then he looked at my dress and said, 'We got to get you something else to wear.' So he sent me out and bought me four or five evening dresses, and then he convinced me to stay, because he played on the fact that Jim didn't tell me about this other girl. Anyway, I ended up staying and having the best time, but he got me in a lot of trouble, because Jim just sat and waited and waited for me — he didn't know where I was!"

Meanwhile he still had Priscilla to juggle — she had flown in on Monday with two-and-a-half-year-old Lisa Marie in the wake of the assassination uproar — and he was continuing to get closer to Kathy, too. They talked more and more, not just about music but about their personal backgrounds, and then one night, when she was scheduled to have a date with rhythm guitarist John Wilkinson, John didn't show up, and Sonny asked her if she could attend a little party that Elvis was giving in his suite. She went up to the suite with little trepidation; Millie Kirkham, a respectable, happily married mother of two, had told her she had to see it if she ever got the chance — it was like a movie set; and that was how it struck her, filled already with the most beautiful, glamorously dressed women when she walked into the room.

Then all of a sudden Elvis came in the front door looking gorgeous, he just looked beautiful in this black velour–type suit with the high collar, laced so his chest showed, and I expected him to walk over to the guys, but he just walked directly over to me and sat down and put his arm around me, and I was in shock. He even said, "Excuse me," and moved the next person over and started talking with me.

Then he visited with the other people, too, but I was right there, and I don't know how long it was, maybe an hour, an hour and a half, I'm just guessing, but then he grabbed my hand and said, "Kathy, I'd like for you to come in here. I'd like to show you something." So he took me into the bedroom, and I was like, "Oh, Lord, let me —" But he assured me not to worry, that this was the only place that we could really get away from everybody, and that it wasn't just a bedroom, it was a suite with a living room with a little coffee table and sofa — and in fact we did not go into the bedroom, we were in the living room section of it. So he sat with me on the sofa, and he still had his arm around me, and he told me how much he cared about me, you know, that he was interested in me and liked me, and when he kissed me, I crossed my eyes. Like, "Come on, you've got to be kidding." I mean, with all his glamorous women, I just wasn't his type — you know, How in the world? What is this? It just didn't make sense to me.

He said, "I talked to John [Wilkinson] about you this afternoon. I called John and asked him if it would be all right if I saw you and how serious was your relationship — and John said, "Well, fine." Well, of course he did. What was John going to tell him — no? But he did have the courtesy to ask! On the coffee table was a copy of Joel S. Goldsmith's *The Infinite Way,* and I had been reading it, and was carrying a copy of it with me. I think that was what really drew us together, that was what Elvis and I immediately clicked on.

They spent much of the night talking, mainly about spiritual matters ("seeking answers and gaining an understanding"), which Kathy had been exploring seriously for the past year. Kathy told Elvis that she was a virgin, and Elvis told her that he admired her for that and that nothing of a sexual nature would happen between them unless she wanted it to. Later that night, he walked her back to her room alone, but not before telling her that she shouldn't be concerned about Priscilla, they had an open marriage but had decided to keep certain things from one another both so as not to embarrass themselves and for the baby's sake. Before the engagement was over, she had started sleeping with him, but they were not yet intimate. He was afraid to be alone, he told her, he was still having nightmares about the assassination threat. She knew there were others, but when there was no one else around, she was glad to be the one.

THE COLONEL MEANWHILE WENT about his business. As the *New York Times* reporter had observed, he was a tireless worker, and once filming was over he devoted most of his energies to the upcoming tour, flying in and out of each of the six cities to check out building and security arrangements, reassembling a road team that included everyone from principal associate Tom Diskin to RCA field men like Jim O'Brien to trusted lieutenants like Al Dvorin, who had handled concessions and overseen the shows from 1956 on — preparing once again, in other words, to go to war. Even to those closest to him, he remained an enigma, a man of such fierce domestic propriety that he called his wife, Marie, three times a day in Palm Springs, frequently putting associates on the line just to keep her amused, while at the same time he could pass members of the band every night in the hall without ever saying a word. He was a man of iron will, and yet some of his closest associates were growing increasingly concerned to see him at the roulette wheel every night, dropping thousands, sometimes tens of thousands of dollars at a single play.

It was his money, he could afford it, he might well have argued. Business was going well. Most of the tour dates were sold out, and Elvis was enjoying his third Top 40 hit of the year (his fourth if you counted "Don't Cry Daddy," which had reached its peak position on the charts in January), with the July 14 release of "I've Lost You." With two more singles still to be released, two mostly live albums (the second, the soundtrack to the motion picture, would ultimately include eight studio tracks from the recent Nashville session when it came out in December), three special albums on RCA's budget Camden line, and a four-LP set entitled *Elvis: Worldwide 50 Gold Award Hits, Vol. 1,* also released by special arrangement, they had not had so much product out at one time since 1956 — but now it was under considerably different circumstances. Under the 1967 revision of their contract, Elvis and Colonel split all recording profits (beyond contractually guaranteed advances) 50–50, as well as all monies from the first dollar on any deal outside the normal royalty setup. In July the Colonel worked out a restructuring of this agreement, whereby advances were actually reduced, thereby making Colonel a fully vested partner that much earlier at precisely a time when sales were running at an all-time high. In this way he had a 50-percent interest in virtually every new record added to the release schedule, while each special deal was a partnership by definition. The Camden albums, for example, brought in $300,000 in extra income, *Worldwide 50 Gold Award Hits* another $200,000, with both sums divided equally between Elvis and the Colonel. There were a number of other permutations and cash bonuses attached to the deal, all split 50–50. Net income from personal appearances (two Vegas engagements, the Astrodome, and the upcoming tour) could be expected to bring in another $1.5 million, the movie represented $500,000 clear profit, and there remained substantial publishing income plus the possibility of a second tour (all of these still governed by the original 75–25 managerial split). All told, Elvis and the Colonel between them could look to realize at least $4 to $5 million in actual income, on which, after all the special deals were figured in, the split might come to 55–45 before the Colonel's own promotional tie-ins with RCA, the International, and MGM were even considered.

It should have been a comfortable living for them both, but neither was comfortable. Whether it was the overheated excitement of the moment or simply an ingrained restlessness of character, each was like an alcoholic who labors at his job with dedication until the end of the working day, then takes his first drink and forfeits all control. The rationalization was always the same: nobody could say they were not taking care of business. Their effect upon those around them was so overwhelming as to almost obliterate criticism. And while each had his own loyalists, each his own partisan camp, they were both happy so long as they could do whatever they wanted; they remained, for the time being, curiously well matched.

T HE ENGAGEMENT ENDED IN a flurry of good humor. One night, in his introductions, Elvis called for the spotlight to be shined on Abraham Lincoln and Joseph Stalin, just to see if Lamar was paying attention; he went on making his interminable string of puns ("Bear with us, and we'll all be bare together"), restarted songs or did the ending over just to get them right, and constantly made fun of Charlie onstage, dumping water on him and other members of the band and nimbly escaping retribution. On the final night, a special 3:30 A.M. show was added (the Colonel negotiated an additional fee of $12,500). At one point Elvis did the vocal introduction to "Hound Dog," and the band failed to come in on cue. Elvis was furious at first, turning around to give them a piece of his mind, but then a fat little basset came waddling out onstage, and Elvis fell down on the floor laughing till the tears ran down his cheeks.

TOP: WITH PRESIDENT NIXON, DECEMBER 21, 1970.
(NATIONAL ARCHIVES AND RECORDS SERVICE)

BOTTOM: WITH BADGES, DECEMBER 28, 1970: BILLY SMITH, FORMER SHERIFF
BILL MORRIS, LAMAR FIKE, JERRY SCHILLING, SHERIFF ROY NIXON,
VERNON PRESLEY, CHARLIE HODGE, SONNY WEST, GEORGE KLEIN,
MARTY LACKER (STANDING); DR. NICK, ELVIS, RED WEST (IN FRONT).
(COURTESY OF THE ESTATE OF ELVIS PRESLEY)

A COMIC BOOK HERO

TWO DAYS LATER they were on the road. They flew out of Las Vegas, and Elvis insisted that Kathy travel with him on his plane, not on the band's, thereby ensuring that everyone in the troupe knew of their relationship. Phoenix was a wild success, though it prompted Robert Blair Kaiser, who rejoined them there, to raise questions about the future. "The crowd that filled the house was young," wrote the *New York Times* reporter, "screaming and stamping whenever he posed, pointed, stabbed and sprawled." They did not want to hear the new songs, Kaiser noted. They wanted the old. "How, I had reason to wonder, could Elvis ever move ahead if a majority of his people wanted him to fall back? Would the Colonel even let him try?"

These were not the questions uppermost in Elvis' mind at the moment. The Imperials had begged off on the tour; the Colonel hadn't given them enough notice, they said, and if this was intended as a negotiating ploy, it didn't work, as Colonel immediately replaced them with a group put together just for the tour by ex-Jordanaire Hugh Jarrett. The new group was good, but Elvis could sense the difference right away, and he missed the tight practiced harmonies that the Imperials contributed. He missed Joe Guercio's big orchestra, too. For reasons of economy it had been decided to take out only Guercio and a single trumpet player, picking up the rest of the orchestra (fourteen more players) in Phoenix and each additional city that they played. From the start, Elvis was concerned that they wouldn't be giving the people their money's worth, and though the Phoenix pickup musicians were fine, it wasn't the same as the polished International orchestra. To make matters worse, the sound wasn't much better than it had been in Houston, with the band members barely able to hear themselves over the noise of the crowd — and there was a bomb threat, too, which Elvis didn't find out about until the next morning. When he did, he blew up at Kathy and everyone else for not telling him about it immediately, but most of all he was disturbed that once again someone should wish to do him harm.

"First this sonofabitch in Vegas wants to kill me," he mumbled as he pored over the papers. "Now this idiot wants to blow me to pieces. . . . *Why?*"

With RCA in charge of the Phoenix show, St. Louis was the first time that the new promoters got to show their stuff, and Tom Hulett was determined that everything should be done first-class. "I went out and hired Clair Brothers to do sound for our four dates, because I knew the show didn't have a setup and that was just something I would do. I remember Tom Diskin came over to the building around noon — he had given me stage diagrams, so when Elvis walked out it would feel like Vegas. When Diskin got there, it was pretty much ninety-five percent set up the way he wanted it, and he started moving a couple of things around. All of a sudden he notices these huge boxes being moved in on the stage. He says, 'Stop! What the hell's that?' I said, 'Tom, that's the sound system.' He said, 'We don't use sound systems.' I said, 'Wait a minute —' He said, 'There's one in the building.' I said, 'Wait a second, you can't — shit, the crowd won't be able to hear, and I'm going to get killed with refunds —' Then I realized: they hadn't worked since 1956, and there were no sound systems then, so to him here was a foreign object that Elvis might get mad at him about. I said, 'What the hell did you guys use in Vegas?,' and he said, 'Just these two speakers.' I never will forget, just these two Shures no bigger than the size of my couches if they were laid down. That was it, that was Elvis' entire monitor system, and the house system was the house system, whatever was in the facility."

Eventually it was agreed that Elvis would be the one to make the decision. If he didn't like it, they would disconnect the system, and Hulett and Weintraub, who had still not met Elvis at this point, waited shakily for the results. Elvis skipped the sound check in the afternoon, and when he came in that evening, Hulett had an instant of the gravest self-doubt. "He comes in the building with all the security in the world, and he's got all of his buddies with him, all in their sunglasses, and then Tom Diskin brings Weintraub and me back to the dressing room, and he goes, 'Elvis, I'd like you to meet the promoters —' And all of a sudden there's George Klein, who I know because he's the biggest DJ in Memphis and I had met him when I had brought Creedence and Three Dog Night in, but I didn't know he'd be here with Elvis, and George just goes, 'Tom!' and Elvis looks startled, and George says, 'Man, Elvis, we got it made. These are the best guys in America. These are the guys that do everybody. Tom, how you doing, man? I didn't know you were doing this tour.' So all of a sudden — instant credibility. Then Diskin says, 'Tom, tell Elvis about the PA system.' So I said to

Elvis, 'I hired a PA tonight, and I guess you never worked with one before, but it's what happens in big arenas. It's really great, I got you the best, and these people will do whatever you want.' And he looked sort of, 'Okay, okay,' and just dropped it.

"Well, the show started, and I'm a nervous wreck. I'm standing right by the side of the stage with Roy Clair, ready to pop the fucking button [to turn the system off], and Elvis starts the show, and in the middle of the first three notes, probably for the first time in his life, he heard himself. And he stopped and looked to his left and smiled and said, 'Ladies and gentlemen, we're going to have one heckuva show tonight.'"

It was great being back out on the road. There was a feeling of freedom that he didn't get in Vegas, and a sense that he was seeing his real fans once again, the true faithful who had first elevated him to stardom and were now going to keep him there. It helped a little bit to overcome the sour taste of the kidnapping, assassination, and bomb threats. It was almost like the old days, with the guys all around him once again: Joe and Charlie and Richard, Lamar working the lights, Sonny in charge of security — he had gotten Red, Jerry, and George Klein to take time off from their jobs, and he had even gotten his friend Dr. Nichopoulos to come out on the road with them, to take care of anything that might come up. "Isn't it fun traveling like this?" he asked Kathy as they looked out of their hotel window in Detroit. "Where do you want to go, honey?" he said. "Just say the word, I'll take us there."

The Colonel was working day and night to advance the tour, making sure that everything was right before Elvis ever hit town, then flying off to the next city early the next morning to set up all over again. Elvis flew Barbara Leigh in for the southern dates, telling Kathy he had so many relatives coming to see him he thought she had better move out. She told him she understood, but inside, "I felt as if I had been deserted and cast aside . . . and even though I understood about his family visiting and his being married, that was only an intellectual exercise. Emotionally I didn't understand at all."

Barbara was more pragmatic about it all, but she had her own frustrations with the road. She didn't really get along with the guys; "they didn't much like me because they kind of got the leftovers, and I stopped all the girls from coming around whenever I was around. It was just too exhausting for me, the other girls always competing, and I always had to put all this energy out just to keep Elvis' attention. It was interesting touring with him, but it wasn't a normal life, not with the guys all around, and it was tiring — with the hours we kept, I think it took me a week to get over it."

On the last day of the tour, in Mobile, Alabama, the Colonel had them booked into the Admiral Semmes Hotel, where Elvis had last stayed in 1955. Put out with the accommodations (the Admiral Semmes had evidently fallen on hard times and was, in Elvis' view, "the dump of dumps"), he had Joe try to find them better ones, but there were no rooms to be had. Everywhere he looked, Joe related to Elvis, he was met with the same response. They all told him, as if he should have known better than even to ask, "Don't you know Elvis Presley's in town?" At the conclusion of the tour Elvis gave out generous bonuses and more of the gold bracelets he had originally made up for some of the guys at the end of the Vegas run with their secret nicknames on the back. There was a real sense of regret on everyone's part that the party couldn't just keep on going.

T O HIS CONSIDERABLE IRRITATION Elvis had to return to Nashville two weeks later to record. They needed two or three more cuts to complete the country album that had suddenly emerged at the June session, so he flew in on September 22 with every intention of finishing up in a hurry.

It was the same rhythm section, with the exception of guitarist James Burton, who had another gig and was replaced on this occasion by another Muscle Shoals alumnus, a very nervous Eddie Hinton. They started off with Anne Murray's "Snowbird," a Top 10 hit of the previous summer, then polished off "Where Did They Go, Lord?," a contemporary country ballad by Dallas Frazier and "Doodle" Owens, done in Elvis' new over-the-top style. Much like the last time, there was lots of laughter and joking around, but this time there was an edge to it that none of the musicians had seen before, a peculiar combination of jitteriness and anger that bordered on pure meanness. Elvis ordered his guys around with a peremptoriness that had no softening element, calling for water with annoyance and announcing to Felton that they'd better hurry up, he had a plane to catch. It's hard to quantify it exactly, but you can hear the mood in a strangely aggressive, wildly out-of-control version of Jerry Lee Lewis' "Whole Lotta Shakin'," which Elvis pronounces done after two takes ("We've been doing it too long already," he says before they even start) and a weirdly beautiful, ultimately inconclusive stab at "Rags to Riches," the 1953 Tony Bennett standard, which conveys some of the wired intensity of the session. Then he is gone, off to catch his plane presumably, leaving Felton behind to clean up the mess.

* * *

H E WAS BACK IN MEMPHIS two weeks later to collect his official deputy sheriff's badge in a private ceremony in the office of the new Shelby County sheriff, Roy Nixon. Although he had been an honorary deputy for several years, his new status permitted him to carry a pistol, and he proudly displayed his official officer's kit of badge, gun, handcuffs, and torch to all and sundry.

He stayed home just long enough to attend the National Quartet Convention's annual gospel show at Ellis Auditorium the following Thursday and Saturday nights, October 15 and 17, where he was introduced to the crowd by the convention's founder, James Blackwood, and flashbulbs went off as if it were the Fourth of July. On Saturday night, as he was getting ready to leave, Blackwood got J. D. Sumner (former bass singer with the Blackwood Brothers and presently the leader of his own group, the Stamps) and Hovie Lister, founder of the Statesmen, "[we all] were going to have our picture made with Elvis. While the photographer was getting ready, somebody said, 'Sing!' and Elvis started singing 'How Great Thou Art,' and the four of us made up a quartet while we were waiting for our picture!" Blackwood, a deeply religious man, was particularly pleased that Elvis seemed to have gone back to his old ways. There was a time, just before his marriage, that Blackwood had been worried about him. "I thought maybe he'd gotten away from his basic upbringing for a while, it had finally all got to him. There had been a time where for about two weeks Elvis was on my mind. I don't know why — I don't remember ever having anybody on my mind that long. It kind of bothered me, and I thought maybe he was going through something, that he needed someone's prayers. I wasn't around him enough to know, really. But my impression was, if he had changed, he'd changed back [now], he was the old Elvis, just down-to-earth and genuine. I felt like he would really like to be around people more than he was. I realized why he couldn't be. It was impossible. But I think he missed being with his friends."

E lvis: That's the Way It Is, as the performance documentary was now to be called, was hurtling its way toward a November opening. The Colonel had gotten his first look at it in a rough cut at the end of September and was deeply disappointed. Viewed today, it remains in many ways a reflection of its time, with split-screen gimmickry, a jumble of action images, and the muddled approach to rock 'n' roll that one might expect of a serious filmmaker down on his luck (with his brother Terry, thirty-nine-year-old director Denis Sanders had produced both a 1954 Academy Award–winning short and the acclaimed 1962 antiwar picture *War Hunt*). But this wasn't what disturbed the Colonel. Not even Elvis' appearance, faintly puffy at times, not unhealthy exactly but by no means the picture of vibrant youth projected in the '68 special, upset the Colonel particularly; the fans would still love him, no matter how he looked. What concerned the Colonel most of all was the very thing that had always been his primary concern, whether the medium was records, television appearances, or motion pictures: the movie didn't focus on Elvis enough.

It would have been easy to dismiss the Colonel's criticism if he were not the Colonel. The bluntness of his language and the crassness of his concerns were in one sense measures of his lack of sophistication. But the three-page memo that he fired off to Jim Aubrey on September 24 summed up in a nutshell what was wrong with the film. Somehow the excitement that everyone took away from a live performance was missing from the screen, and the Colonel zeroed in on the elements that he perceived to contribute to this misimpression: the anticlimax of a director's ending tacked on to follow the climax of Elvis' stage show; the frequent cut-ins on Elvis' performance, "with great disadvantage to getting across seeing Elvis as he really is performing on stage"; the detracting references to the success of other big Vegas stars ("Every artist has a right to be big in his own way and there should be no comparison by voice or writing to help sell a picture. We must all stand on our own feet"); the put-downs of Elvis' movies ("I believe . . . the slurs on *Blue Hawaii* and *G.I. Blues* should be completely removed, as these were two of the most successful films ever made by Elvis . . . and they do not deserve to be mentioned as just trash in such a way"); the overuse of interview footage with the fans (all interview footage, the Colonel advised, ought to be "thoroughly checked [so that] it doesn't become monotonous and take away from the performance"); and the smarmy dismissal of Las Vegas itself for the kind of conspicuous consumption that could only alienate Elvis' true fans ("There is no reason to show an abundance of steaks in a truck in this picture when perhaps in Dalton, Georgia, where the picture may be showing, a family saved up money to see the picture and relinquished their hamburger for that night so that they could see Elvis. It has no meaning to the value of the promotion of the picture and it is much better to keep the picture down to earth as much as possible").

Most of all, without ever actually naming it, what he really seems to be objecting to is the director's implicit contempt for his subject, but he concludes his letter to Aubrey on an exhortatory note nonetheless, declaring that "Mr. Denis Sanders did a tremendous job with great enthusiasm and dedication. We are endeavoring to help put it together on a professional commercial basis." All unused performance footage should be reviewed, to be sure nothing has been overlooked. "Jim, as you know," he sums up, "Elvis, you, and I believed in this idea from the start. I tried to sell the idea for the past ten years but no one would or could see it. We are all grateful for your belief in it."

By October 1 the majority of the requested changes had been made and all songs cleared. By October 1 the Colonel had set up a November tour as well. This time he was going to give Management III the entire eight-day tour, but this time, he decided, he would really put them to the test. He demanded a $1 million deposit (by comparison, he had required only $240,000 from them for their four dates in September), though in exchange he offered a piece of the concessions. Jerry Weintraub took it as a challenge, and in fact, the delivery of the million dollars became one of his principal conversation pieces for the next twenty-five years. His partner, Tom Hulett, from whose company, Concerts West, most of the money came, took it more as a matter of business: this tour, focusing on the West Coast, would do bigger box office, offer greater exposure, and serve as the basis for a stronger future relationship. There was even talk at the outset of a closed-circuit broadcast from Los Angeles, though it fell through and the Colonel was once again forced to defer that dream.

Elvis spent the three weeks before the tour in California, mostly relaxing in Palm Springs. The first day he was back, on October 19, he picked up twelve pendants he had ordered from Schwartz-Ableser Jewelers in Beverly Hills. There was one for each of the guys to match the prototype he and Priscilla had sketched out at the conclusion of the tour and given to Sol Schwartz's partner, Lee Ableser, to design. Elvis had been wearing it himself for the last few weeks — a fourteen-karat gold necklace that came down in a V to a zigzag lightning bolt framed by the letters "TCB." It was the lightning bolt that compelled attention, an image that had captured Elvis at an early age, when it symbolized the transformation of everyday human being Billy Batson into superhero Captain Marvel in Elvis' favorite action comic book.

It had renewed its claim upon his attention on the September tour, when the baby-faced Los Angeles police officer who was beefing up their security told Elvis and the guys about his adventures impersonating a student on an undercover assignment at Hollywood High. He had been dating a girl and, evidently carried away with the impersonation, had slept with her. That was when he discovered the lightning bolt pendant around her neck, clear proof, he told them, that her father was the head of the West Coast Mafia, which had taken the lightning bolt as its symbol. Elvis loved the story and had the policeman tell it over and over again, but he gave other explanations for the design, too, recalling the time that lightning had split one of the statues in the Meditation Garden, as if to remind him of how fragile life could be and how tenuous was his own grip upon success. Whatever the meaning of the lightning bolt, there was no ambiguity as to what the three letters surrounding it stood for. TCB had entered the language with Aretha Franklin's 1967 hit, "Respect," but it had been a commonplace expression in black life for some time before that. It meant, simply, "Take care of business," and, with the lightning bolt, in Elvis' world, "Takin' care of business *in a flash.*" The way that things were meant to be done.

He called Kathy just after he got back from Memphis, and a few days later sent a plane to bring her to Palm Springs. He was talking on the phone with Priscilla when she walked in the door, explaining why he couldn't come home right away. As soon as he got off, he expounded to Kathy once again on his views of marriage — it was the kind of thing that just didn't work for most people, he told her, and probably should be abolished.

She remained entranced by his charm, his thoughtfulness, his consideration. He recited poetry to her, read to her from his spiritual books, and shared some of his innermost thoughts with her. When he spoke about the death of his pet chimpanzee Scatter some years before ("Scatter was one of the best buddies I had around at that time"), he brought tears to her eyes. She was less moved when, on her first day in Palm Springs, they came into the dining room for Elvis' usual late-afternoon breakfast, and Elvis announced to all who were gathered at the table, "Hey, boys, you know what? Our Kathy is still a virgin." She stormed out of the room at that point and was on the verge of packing up her things and demanding to be taken back to L.A., when Elvis followed her into the bedroom and gave her his little-boy look. "I thought I saw the beginning of a smile on his face, but when he took a good look at me . . . he pulled me to him and held me close. 'Honey, I wasn't trying to shame you. I'm proud of your being a virgin. Not many girls could hold out this long. . . . Please understand, I wouldn't hurt your feelings for the world.'"

That night she gave herself to him, and the following night he suggested that she should go on the pill. She had to get back to L.A. right away, she told him regretfully, she had session work and television commitments to fulfill. "Just cancel out," he said. "You don't have to go to work, Minnie Mouse, I'll always take care of you." But he accepted that she took her responsibilities seriously, and she promised to come back on the weekend.

Barbara Leigh was a frequent visitor to Palm Springs during this time as well. Although she was far more worldly than Kathy ("In those days I had so many boyfriends and guys pursuing me — I think I was oblivious to right and wrong"), his relationship with her was much the same. "I think every woman that came into his life, he wanted to teach her. One of his favorite sayings was, 'When the pupil is ready, the teacher is willing.' And he gave me *The Impersonal Life*. That was really important to him. He told me his entire life story, from the first time he wrestled with a girl in the yard and saw her little white panties. He told me about how they treated him in school — he was an outcast because he was different, and it wasn't until he got up and sang in school that he won them over. He used to go down and sing with all the blacks in church — he really admired them. It was fun to be with him. We were always singing."

It was difficult to be with him, too. He was hard on the guys, and he kept Barbara hopping. "I was always up and down, getting him bottles of Mountain Valley water. 'Get this. Get that.'" He knew that she had had a child, but he didn't want to hear anything about it. Their sexual life was not what she had expected, even though he was very sweet and they made love frequently at first and he was always a wonderful kisser. But after a while, he started to have so many pills in his system "that it was very hard for him to be a natural man. It was like impossible." As in all of his relationships, he could be both cruel and kind, and Barbara soon grew accustomed though never used to the capriciousness of his nature.

Kathy came back the following weekend. At first it was just like it had been, with lots of laughter and Elvis showing her his vulnerability, too, "but that night, in the quiet stillness of each other's arms after a flurry of passion, things began to go topsy turvy. I think of the words we said to one another and to this day I regret what happened." What Kathy said was that she could no longer go on like this; she felt guilty, sinful, unworthy "because I could find no valid excuse for committing adultery, love or no love . . . . Out of nowhere I said, 'We have to stop all this because I can't stand myself anymore.'"

At first Elvis didn't really believe her; he humored her until at last he realized she was serious. "Does that mean I have to get someone else, train them just like I want them?" he snarled at her. Kathy couldn't believe what she was hearing. "Am I some kind of dog or puppy that you housebreak, train to be a good pet?" she demanded. "I'm a woman, a human being. . . . You will just have to find yourself another Gladys."

Afterward she didn't know what had made her say that. It was just an expression that she had heard as a child. He had talked to her about his mother, but Kathy didn't remember it if he had ever mentioned her name.

Eventually they made it up — he accepted her apology and came as close as he could to an apology himself. "But, like it or not, we had both crossed some invisible but forbidden boundary, entered a land that was strange to me. On the surface everything seemed the same. Elvis sang, I sang, we talked, we laughed . . . but there was a tension that hadn't been present before. . . . It was as if both of us were in mourning, but we didn't know who had died."

THEY WENT OUT ON TOUR two weeks later, starting in Oakland on November 10. The crowds were if anything even larger and more demonstrative — there was no question that Management III was going to get its money back. Elvis moved Kathy out of his room in San Francisco on the fourth night of the tour. This time she presumed it was for another woman, and her heart was broken for good. That was the night that "my dreams turned sour and ugly [and] I saw another side of Elvis I thought I would never be able to accept."

The two shows at the Inglewood Forum in Los Angeles the following day were the high point of the tour, a triumphant homecoming as frenzied in its fashion as Elvis' famed appearance at the Pan Pacific back in 1957. They took in over $300,000 combined for matinee and evening performances, better than the Rolling Stones had done in 1969, and the day was marred only by the continuing unpleasantness of the paternity suit, when a process server masquerading as a fan served Elvis with papers at his hotel between shows. It put him in a bad mood for the rest of the day, and it was still on his mind when in the middle of the evening show he declared emotionally how much he owed to his fans. "I've got fifty-six gold singles and fourteen gold albums," he announced with uncharacteristic boastfulness. "If there's anyone out there who doubts it, if you ever come through Memphis you can come in and argue about it, 'cause I've got every one of them hanging on the wall. I'm really proud of it. I've outsold the Beatles, the Stones, Tom Jones — all of them put together."

The next day, in San Diego, Richard Davis was fired and sent home, and though Elvis didn't do the firing himself (Vernon did), it was not difficult to extrapolate that a growing concern for loyalty was on his mind. To Kathy it seemed clear that he had never strayed far from that sense of exclusion that had accompanied him from childhood on. "People will come from miles around just to see a freak," he told her early in the tour as they watched the crowds arrive. It was a remark which, Kathy noted, "made everyone laugh, [and] Elvis laughed louder than anyone," but it seemed as if there was something fundamentally serious about the observation.

The tour wound up in Denver, where Elvis spent almost all of his time offstage with the policemen assigned to help protect the show. He quizzed them on their work, showed them the badges he had collected in Memphis, Beverly Hills, Houston, and Oklahoma City, and was disappointed when they reciprocated not with an official badge but with an honorary one of their own. They could get him a real badge, detectives Ron Pietrafeso and Jerry Kennedy said in light of his disappointment, it would just take a while. He told them he would come back to pick it up, maybe ride around with them a little on their beat. He seemed perfectly sincere, but they never believed he would until he actually showed up to collect his official badge some weeks later.

B ACK IN LOS ANGELES he continued to pursue his new hobby. He bought an arsenal of weapons at gun shops in Los Angeles and Palm Springs, contributed $7,000 to the Los Angeles police community relations program (the largest single donation in the program's history, which may well have helped nail down the gold commissioner's badge he collected from Chief Davis), and he and the guys visited the Palm Springs and Beverly Hills police shooting ranges regularly. He had seen the movie *Patton* half a dozen times since its January opening, committing its patriotic lone-wolf opening speech to memory in the same way that he had once memorized General MacArthur's Farewell Address. When he discovered that Patton's World War II colleague General Omar Bradley was a Beverly Hills neighbor, there was nothing for it but to seek him out, and he visited and exchanged gifts with the seventy-seven-year-old retired general on a number of occasions. He sought out Vice President Agnew, too, a regular visitor to Palm Springs, and tried to give him a commemorative gun, explaining how much he admired the vice president's patriotism, but Agnew demurred. He couldn't accept such a gift, he said, so long as he was still in office, but, like General Bradley, he was impressed with the young man's sincerity and earnestness of purpose.

He saw more of John O'Grady, too, the ex–Los Angeles narcotics chief and private detective Elvis' lawyer Ed Hookstratten had brought in to handle the paternity case. O'Grady, a colorful character who claimed twenty-five hundred drug busts, held strong patriotic views, and had an opinion on just about every subject under the sun, fascinated Elvis with his tales of police work and his insider's knowledge of the peccadillos of various Hollywood celebrities, which he was happy to share. He dismissed the Colonel loudly as a "rude, crude sonofabitch," had no use for any of the guys except for Joe, and tried to convince Elvis that Jerry Schilling was a communist because of his liberal views.

One night the whole gang went out for dinner with O'Grady at Chasen's, and O'Grady introduced Elvis to Paul Frees, "the man of 1,000 voices," who was famous for his commercials, cartoons, and voice-overs. Frees was also an undercover narcotics agent and at O'Grady's prompting showed Elvis the federal badge he had recently obtained from the Bureau of Narcotics and Dangerous Drugs in recognition of his extensive undercover work. From that point on, all Elvis could talk about was getting his own BNDD badge.

On December 3 he started on a three-night, $20,000 gun-buying spree at Kerr's Sporting Goods, where it took four salesmen to keep up with him as he purchased Christmas gifts both for people he knew and for people who wandered in off the street. At just around this time he got a construction permit for work on the $339,000 house he had purchased the previous month on Monovale Drive in Beverly Hills' exclusive Holmby Hills section. The house on Hillcrest had grown too small for the life he was now leading — with all of the guys coming back he wanted more room, and he wanted grounds that offered a greater degree of privacy, now that Lisa Marie was beginning to grow up. Almost as an afterthought, he decided that Joe and Joanie, who had just gotten back from the European vacation he had given them at the end of October, needed a house, too. With two kids it was time for them to move out of the rental unit they had lived in all these years, so on December 8, after a somewhat arbitrary house search that yielded only impractical locations until Joanie finally put her foot down, he made a $10,000 deposit on a new home for them in west L.A. He was about to surprise Jerry and Sandy with a similar show of largesse, but Joe volunteered that Jerry wouldn't be able to keep up the house payments on a film cutter's salary. So when he decided to buy Mercedeses for

Barbara and himself at three o'clock one morning the following week, he got one for Jerry, too, as a kind of makeup for a gift he never knew he was going to get. He had already paid for his old friend George Klein's wedding in Las Vegas on December 5, flying in a dozen of the guys and putting them up at the International for the ceremony in his suite; he was in the midst of making similar financial arrangements for Palm Springs patrolman Dick Grob's December 11 wedding, for which he was about to present Grob, a weapons training specialist, with a brand-new Cadillac; and he had just handed over to Marty Lacker the planning for Sonny West's wedding in Memphis at the end of the month, which he was also financing.

He made all of his usual holiday-season purchases at Schwartz-Ableser Jewelers, where it was not unusual for him to spend $20,000 to $30,000 at a time ("He was very spontaneous," said co-owner Sol Schwartz affectionately; "he was like a kid in a candy store"), and he sent a $2,000 donation to the Self-Realization Fellowship. He also bought close to a dozen pairs of the new aviator-style tinted glasses he had been ordering from Optique Boutique ever since the beginning of August, when he got a prescription for reading glasses, with the latest purchases personalized with his initials and an engraved lightning bolt and TCB on a gold frame. By the time that he finally arrived home in Memphis on December 17, the bills were already starting to pile up, and Vernon was almost sick with worry. Elvis tried to placate his father the following day by getting him a new Mercedes, too, but Vernon could see the handwriting on the wall; he felt like his boy was going out of control again just like he had with that damned ranch. So he talked to Priscilla, and the two of them spoke with Colonel, and all three agreed that maybe now was the time for someone to confront Elvis.

That was what they did on Saturday the nineteenth. Vernon and Priscilla got Elvis off by himself and for once spoke frankly to him. They told him they had talked to Colonel, and Colonel agreed: Elvis was going to bankrupt himself and everyone else if things went on like this. Nobody was trying to tell him how to spend his money, but there had to be some checks and balances applied. You couldn't buy friendship, Vernon said, to which Priscilla responded with emphatic agreement. All these guys standing around with their hands out (along with Vernon, Charlie had received a Mercedes the day before, and to Vernon's mind, the other guys were just waiting in line) — did Elvis really think they were all his friends? He was just thinking of Elvis' interests, Vernon told his son. No one was trying to tell him that he couldn't have a good time.

He stared at them in disbelief. What were they talking about? It was his money, wasn't it? He had earned it. The Colonel agreed with them, they said? Fuck the Colonel. Finally he got so upset that Priscilla just left the room. With that, Elvis spun on his heel. "I'm getting out of here," he declared and walked out the door.

They didn't take him seriously at first. Priscilla had seen him blow up plenty of times like this before. He'd drive around for a while, realize he had nowhere to go, and then return in an hour or two as if nothing had happened. Elvis would be back, Vernon was convinced. He'd put money on it. Marty was supposed to be out at the house in a little while to go over the details of Sonny West's wedding, and Elvis wasn't going to miss out on that. But when Marty arrived, Elvis was still absent, and when they hadn't heard from him after a few hours, they began to worry. They called around some, they even tried the house in California, but they knew the maids would never say anything — not if they wanted to keep their jobs. So they just sat back and waited.

Jerry was the first to get any kind of word. The phone rang in his little Culver City apartment late that night. "It's me," said a voice at the other end mysteriously, as if the phone might be tapped. He told Jerry not to tell anyone that he had been in touch; he was calling from Dallas on his way back to L.A. from Washington, D.C. He wanted Jerry to meet his American Airlines flight with Gerald Peters, the new limousine driver, whom he had already called under similar conditions of confidentiality from Washington.

His face was alarmingly swollen when he emerged from the plane carrying only the incongruous little cardboard box that contained everything he had with him: toothpaste, a toothbrush, a bar of soap, a wash cloth, and a comb. Peters, a famously impressive figure who had driven for Winston Churchill and whom Elvis had dubbed "Sir Gerald" for his accent and his carriage when he started driving for them the previous month, had arranged to meet the plane out on the tarmac upon its arrival at 2:17 A.M. Jerry wanted to get Elvis back to the house right away. He was concerned about the puffiness of Elvis' face, but Elvis assured him it was just an allergic reaction to some medication he was taking for an eye infection, aggravated by his eating chocolate on the plane. And besides, they had to drop off the two stewardesses to whom Elvis had promised a ride home first. When they finally got back to Hillcrest, Jerry called a doctor and stayed with Elvis while the doctor examined him, because it wasn't someone that he knew and there was never any telling what an unfamiliar physician might do to ingratiate himself, or what he might be talked into doing.

After the doctor left with a mild warning to stay away from chocolate, they stayed up for a while talking, and gradually Jerry began to get a sense of what had actually happened. Elvis had flown to Washington because it was the first flight out of Memphis, he said, though Jerry wondered if it might not have had something to do with that girl he had met in Vegas who worked for the House Armed Services Committee. Obviously he hadn't connected with her, though, or he wouldn't have checked out of the Hotel Washington so quickly, but he seemed pleased with himself nonetheless, as they watched the sun come up and he finally went to bed.

By the time that he got up that afternoon, he had come up with a plan. They were going back to Washington, he said. They needed to make plane reservations under the name of John Carpenter (a favorite pseudonym since he had played a doctor of that name in *Change of Habit* the previous year) and hotel reservations for the same suite that he had occupied the night before, under the name of Colonel Jon Burrows, another of his favorite aliases. He wanted the same limousine driver who had taken him around in Washington to meet them at the airport, and he needed Sir Gerald to cash a check for $500 at the Beverly Hills Hotel so they would have some cash on hand. He didn't bother to explain to Jerry why they were doing any of these things, and he wouldn't listen to any of Jerry's remonstrations that he needed to be at work the following morning. The only concession that he would make to Jerry's concerns was to allow him to call up Sonny West in Memphis under conditions of strict confidentiality. Sonny could meet them in Washington, and Elvis agreed that it would be all right for him to let Vernon and Priscilla know that Elvis was safe — but no more than that. He knew he could count on Sonny to maintain security, and this way he would have Sonny with him if their business kept them in Washington for more than the twenty-four hours that Jerry was able to promise him.

In the airplane on the flight to Washington, Elvis ate some more chocolate, and his face swelled up some more. On impulse he gave away all the money that Sir Gerald had gotten for them to some soldiers headed home from Vietnam. When he learned from one of the stewardesses that Republican senator George Murphy of California was traveling on their flight, he went back impulsively to the tourist section to confer with him and, without saying anything to Jerry, started writing away furiously in longhand on American Airlines stationery immediately upon his return. When he finished, he handed the note to Jerry to take a look at it and see what he thought. At first Jerry wondered if Elvis had taken leave of his senses. "Dear Mr. President," it began:

First I would like to introduce myself. I am Elvis Presley and admire
you and Have Great Respect for your office. I talked to Vice President
Agnew in Palm Springs three weeks ago and expressed my concern for
our country. The Drug Culture, the Hippie Elements, the SDS, Black
Panthers, etc. do *not* consider me as their enemy or as they call it The
Establishment. *I call it America and* I love it. Sir I can and will be of any
service that I can to help the country out. . . . I wish not to be given a
title or an appointed position. I can and will do more good if I were
made a Federal agent at Large, and I will help but by doing it my way
through my communications with people of all ages. First and foremost I am an entertainer but all I need is the Federal credentials.

He had met Senator Murphy on the plane, he continued, and they had
discussed "the problems that our country is faced with." He gave the President all the information necessary to reach him over the next few days,
including the name that he would be registered under at the Washington
Hotel and the names of the two men who would be there with him. "I will
be here for as long as it takes to get the credentials of a Federal Agent," he
wrote. He had done "an in depth study of Drug Abuse and Communist
Brainwashing techniques" and would be glad to help in any way that he
could "just so long as it is kept very Private." In case any further proof of
his credentials was needed, he informed the President that he had just been
nominated by the national organization of the Jaycees (though the
announcement had not yet been officially made) as one of America's "ten
most outstanding young men," an award that he believed President Nixon
himself had once received. "I am sending you the short autobiography
about myself," he concluded, "so you can better understand this approach.
I would love to meet you just to say hello if you're not too busy." Then in a
p.s. he added, "I have a personal gift for you also which I would like to present to you and you can accept it or I will keep it for you until you can take
it." And on a final piece of paper, marked "Private and Confidential," he
put down all of his and the Colonel's telephone numbers drawn up on a
grid, with the Washington Hotel information underneath and a conclusion
in the hopeful form of an address:

Attn, President Nixon
via Sen George Murphy
from
Elvis Presley

They dropped the note off at the White House gate at 6:30 that morning. Elvis was disappointed when the guard didn't recognize him at first, but then he perked up as recognition slowly dawned on the young soldier, who assured him that he would deliver the message at 7:30 A.M., when people started coming in to work. From the White House they went to their hotel, where the hotel doctor examined Elvis and came to the same conclusion as the doctor in Los Angeles: he would be fine if he would only stop eating all that chocolate.

Not long afterward, Elvis announced that he was leaving for the Bureau of Narcotics and Dangerous Drugs. Senator Murphy had promised to contact Bureau director John Ingersoll for him — it was Ingersoll, he reminded Jerry, who had signed Paul Frees' BNDD badge, and Senator Murphy had also promised to try to get Elvis an appointment with J. Edgar Hoover at FBI headquarters. He was wearing his new, jeweled, oversize glasses, a dark Edwardian jacket with brass buttons draped like a cape around his shoulders, and a purple velvet V-necked tunic with matching pants set off by the massive gold belt the International Hotel had given him in gratitude for his record-setting performance. Over a white, high-collared, open-necked shirt he wore the gold lion's-head pendant that he had just purchased from Sol Schwartz and his Tree of Life necklace with all the guys' names engraved on its roots and branches. If President Nixon were to telephone while he was out, he told Jerry, he could be reached at the Bureau.

He was gone no more than an hour when the telephone rang. The caller identified himself to Jerry as Egil "Bud" Krogh, deputy counsel to the President. He was in receipt of Mr. Presley's letter to the President, and he wondered if Elvis could stop by his office at the Old Executive Office Building on the White House grounds in about forty-five minutes. Jerry, who up to this point had felt as if he were doing little more than indulging a friend's whims while looking out for him at the same time, was flabbergasted. He had known when they got to Washington that they were going to do *something,* and he had been floored by the magnitude of Elvis' ambition and the boldness of his letter — but to get a call from the White House. . . . He immediately telephoned Elvis at the Bureau of Narcotics, where he was transferred to the office of Deputy Director John Finlator. "I'm not doing any good here," Elvis announced dejectedly before Jerry had a chance to tell him about the White House call. The instant he heard, his whole mood picked up. He would come by for Jerry in the limo in fifteen minutes. Jerry should just wait out in front of the hotel.

Krogh, meanwhile, was having second thoughts about how all of this was going to work out for him. A thirty-one-year-old junior functionary in the administration who had been given some responsibility for the development of a sweeping new drug control policy, he had received the Presley letter at about 9:00 A.M. from Dwight Chapin, another young presidential assistant who worked directly under Chief of Staff Bob Haldeman. Once Krogh had read it, he and Chapin talked, and while neither missed the artlessness of its language or presentation, each saw the potential value of the connection for an administration which so far had only managed to enlist such non-youth-oriented celebrities as game show host Art Linkletter, former *Dragnet* star Jack Webb, and evangelist Billy Graham in its war on drugs. Chapin then wrote Haldeman a memo recommending that a meeting with the President be held once Bud had screened Presley. "You know that several people have mentioned over the past few months that Presley is very pro the President," he wrote the President's chief of staff, concluding that "it will take very little of the President's time, and it can be extremely beneficial for the President to build some rapport with Presley. In addition, if the President wants to meet with some bright young people outside of the Government, Presley might be a perfect one to start with." Next to the last remark Haldeman had written, "You must be kidding," but he okayed the request, and now it was up to Krogh to draw up a memo for the President, explaining the purpose of the meeting and providing talking points and suggestions for future involvement that wouldn't draw guffaws from the President himself.

Sonny arrived in a cab from the airport just as Elvis pulled up in front of the hotel. On their way to the White House, Elvis was obviously nervous, playing with the chrome-plated World War II Colt .45 that he wanted to present to President Nixon and explaining exactly what had happened at the Bureau. Ingersoll had been out when he arrived, and Finlator turned him down flat. Nothing that Elvis said had been of any use: he had offered a donation to the antidrug program, but Finlator said the Bureau couldn't accept private donations. He had agreed to help further the Bureau's drug prevention program by announcing at each of his concerts that he and his guys didn't need drugs to blow their minds, they got high on music — but Finlator wouldn't budge on the subject of the badge. There was no such thing as an honorary BNDD badge, Finlator told him; badges went only to "those employees directly connected with the agency." When Jerry remonstrated that that was probably true, Elvis blew up. Fuck Finlator, he told Jerry and Sonny. He was going to get his badge from the President.

Upon their arrival at the White House, Bud Krogh was doubly taken aback. First, he got a call from Bill Duncan, the head of the President's Secret Service detail, saying they might have a little problem: Mr. Presley had shown up in the West Wing lobby with a gun that he wanted to present to the President. Duncan said with what Krogh took to be "an edge in his voice. . . , 'Bud, you know we can't let him take a gun into the Oval Office.'" Krogh solved that problem by suggesting that the Secret Service agent simply accept the gift on behalf of the President, but then he encountered his second shock of the day when he saw how Elvis was dressed. Now he was really beginning to wonder if he hadn't gone too far out on a limb on this thing — or maybe even if he wasn't being pushed.

The initial interview went well, however. Everything that Elvis had suggested in his letter was borne out by his speech: his patriotism, his disapproval of the drug culture, his sincere desire to give something back in exchange for all that he had been given. He showed Krogh the two autographed pictures he had brought for the President — one of himself and Priscilla, one of Lisa Marie wearing a baby bonnet — and all the badges that he had gotten for his police work around the country. Krogh noticed that he kept scratching his neck and inquired about it, but Elvis reassured him that it was just a rash, it wasn't any problem.

At exactly the appointed hour of 12:30 P.M. Elvis and Krogh walked over to the Oval Office together, leaving Jerry and Sonny behind. It was too bad they wouldn't get a chance to meet the President, too, said the junior aide assigned to them — but Jerry wasn't so sure. "We said, 'Well, you know, Elvis will probably invite us over.' And this guy says, 'Well, it's really out of the President's hands. It requires more security if more than one person goes in there.' And Sonny said, 'Well, if I know Elvis, he's going to ask.'"

Krogh observed Elvis carefully as they entered the Oval Office. For the first time he seemed humbled by his surroundings. "He looked up at the ceiling, which had a large eagle emblazoned in the plaster. He looked down at the blue carpeting on the floor, which had another eagle centered on the Presidential seal. Eagles adorned the top of the armed services flags to the right of the President's desk. . . . I noticed Elvis observe everything and then hesitantly walk forward to greet the President. . . . As they started to shake hands, I said, 'Mr. President, this is Mr. Elvis Presley.'" Elvis was still wearing his sunglasses and holding his badges and pictures in his left hand."

After a few awkward moments Elvis showed the President his photographs and spread out his badges on the presidential desk. Then, taking off his sunglasses and laying them down beside the badges, he showed

...

Nixon his cuff links, too, while White House photographer Ollie Atkins snapped pictures. Now showing off his belt, he spoke of having played Las Vegas recently, and the President responded awkwardly that he knew how difficult it was to play Vegas himself. Then, according to Krogh's contemporaneous memo, "the President mentioned that he thought Presley could reach young people, and that it was important for Presley to retain his credibility. Presley responded that he did his thing by 'just singing.' He said that he could not get to the kids if he made a speech on the stage, that he had to reach them in his own way. The President nodded in agreement."

At this point the conversation took an unexpected turn. The Beatles, Elvis said, as if he were tentatively trying out a new tack, had been a focal point for anti-Americanism. They had come to this country, made their money, then gone back to England where they fomented anti-American feeling. "The President," Krogh's memo continued, "nodded in agreement and expressed some surprise." Krogh meanwhile wondered where this conversation was going: Elvis had never said anything about the Beatles, either in his letter or in their pre-interview. "The President then indicated that those who use drugs are also in the vanguard of anti-American protest. Violence, drug usage, dissent, protest all seemed to merge in generally the same group of young people.

> Presley indicated to the President in a very emotional manner that he was "on your side." Presley kept repeating that he wanted to be helpful, that he wanted to restore some respect for the flag, which was being lost. He mentioned that he was just a poor boy from Tennessee who had gotten a lot from his country, which in some way he wanted to repay. He also mentioned that he is studying Communist brainwashing and the drug culture for over ten years. He mentioned that he knew a lot about this and was accepted by the hippies. He said he could go right into a group of young people or hippies and be accepted which he felt could be helpful to him in his drug drive. The President indicated again his concern that Presley retain his credibility.

It was at this point that Elvis brought up the matter of the badge. He could be so much more helpful if he had some kind of official government sanction, just like he did in all the cities where he held the deputies' badges that he had brought to show the President. He described his meeting with John Finlator at the Bureau of Narcotics earlier in the day and his disappointment at its outcome. The BNDD badge was the mark of a true undercover operator, he said, exactly what he and the President envisioned his role could be: there would be no publicity, and he wouldn't be sacrificing his credibility at all. Could the President get him the badge? he wondered.

"The President," Krogh wrote in his later account of the meeting, "looked a little uncertain at this request. He turned to me and said, 'Bud, can we get him a badge?' I couldn't read what the President really wanted me to say. 'Well, sir,' I answered, 'if you want to give him a badge, I think we can get him one.' The President nodded. 'I'd like to do that. See that he gets one.' . . . Elvis was smiling triumphantly. 'Thank you very much, sir. This means a lot to me.' . . . Elvis then moved up close to the President and, in a spontaneous gesture, put his left arm around him and hugged him. President hugging was not, at least in my limited experience, a common occurrence in the Oval Office. It caught the President — and me — off guard. The President recovered from his surprise and patted Elvis on the shoulder. 'Well, I appreciate your willingness to help, Mr. Presley.'" Elvis then presented him with the pictures and spoke of the Colt .45 commemorative issue that he had left for the President with the Secret Service. "That's very kind of you," said the President, and Elvis scooped up his badges and turned to go, looking, wrote Krogh, "like a kid who'd just received all of the Christmas presents he'd asked for." Then, as if it were little more than an afterthought, "he turned back to the President. 'Mr. President, would you have a little time just to say hello to my two friends, Sonny West and Jerry Schilling? It would mean a lot to them and to me.'"

Sonny and Jerry would not have been surprised by anything at this point. By the time that they arrived at the Oval Office, it was Elvis who appeared to be in charge. "Sonny and I were just standing in the doorway in awe, and Elvis kind of good-naturedly shoved us from behind and said, 'Come on, guys, walk on in.' It was like he was saying to us, 'I've been in there, and I'm real comfortable. Don't get overwhelmed.' And yet he was really proud that he had set this thing up so Sonny and I could meet the President. He had this look on his face that he would have when he gave somebody a gift." Sonny was wearing his TCB pendant prominently outside his starched white shirt, and the photographer took a picture of the four of them, the President in that familiar hunched-over, earnest, and somewhat worried-looking pose, Sonny and Jerry with their eyes on Elvis as he makes a point respectfully but with unquestionable assurance that he is the center of all attention. "You've got a couple of big ones here," said the President, still awkwardly trying to make conversation. "It looks like Elvis is in good hands with you two guys." "They're good friends,"

volunteered Elvis helpfully. "And they're interested in helping out, too."
The President then presented them all with the same gifts he had already
given to Elvis: tie clasps and cuff links with the presidential seal on them.
"You know, they've got wives, too," Elvis reminded the President, and
together he and Richard Nixon rummaged through the President's desk
drawer for suitable presents for the wives.

There was a special White House tour lined up for later, but first they
were invited to have lunch at the White House mess, where, as Bud noted,
staff members "accustomed to seeing heads of state, athletic champions and
movie stars all gaped." Krogh then took them on their tour, but by this time
Elvis had little interest in sightseeing, as secretaries popped out of their
offices and he graciously signed autographs. They finally got back to Bud's
office at two o'clock, with John Finlator showing up not long afterward with
Elvis' badge. If the deputy director was humbled, he didn't show it, and he
promised to send along the rest of Elvis' credentials as soon as they were
ready. Leaving the White House, Sonny and Jerry never stopped to ponder
the many strange things that had occurred on this day. As far as they were
concerned, there was one thing, and one thing only, responsible for whatever had happened to them, good or bad: they were with Elvis Presley.

E LVIS AND SONNY DROPPED JERRY OFF at the airport so he could
get back to L.A. in time for work the next day. On their way to the airport Elvis renewed his long-standing suit to get Jerry to come back to work
for him full-time. Sometime before, when his records weren't selling,
George Klein had come up with the idea of getting someone to do independent promotion work for him, someone whose primary focus was Elvis
Presley, not RCA. Now that the records *were* selling again, it seemed like a
better idea than ever, and he and George were both agreed that Jerry would
be perfect for the role. "He wanted to know what I made, and he said he
would double it. I said, 'Look, Elvis, I know you want me to do this, but
what if the Colonel has a problem with it?' He said, 'The Colonel's not hiring you. I'm hiring you. This is my business, and this is what I want you to
do.' So they dropped me off at the terminal, and about two weeks later I
get these business cards, printed up in red and black: 'Elvis Presley, Personal
Public Relations, Special Deputy Jerry Schilling' — with a Star of David
and a crucifix embossed in gold." The plan never did go into effect, because
the Colonel stopped it, as Jerry knew he would, but Jerry went back on the
payroll in a more amorphous capacity not long afterward, recognizing that

friendship couldn't always guarantee results but grateful that "Elvis had really tried."

It was Jerry's assumption that Elvis and Sonny would catch the next flight back to Memphis, but in fact Elvis had one last mission to carry out. He had been unable to get an appointment with J. Edgar Hoover despite Senator Murphy's intervention, but he was determined not to leave town without making one more attempt to see Joyce Bova again.

He reached her at work at the House Armed Services Committee. At first she was inclined to hang up on him, but then he flabbergasted her by apologizing for his behavior the previous August. She had to see him now after he had come all this way to Washington just to find her. Where and when could he have the limo pick her up?

She arrived with her identical twin, Janice, and Elvis amazed everyone by being able to immediately tell them apart. "Good thing I was right, man," he said. "Guy picks out the wrong woman in this spot, and he could get slapped!" After explaining how difficult it had been to get her work number, he gradually revealed — almost as an afterthought — the hectic events of the last few days. At first she and her sister thought he was kidding, but then he showed them his BNDD badge. "That sonofabitch Finlator, he didn't want to give it to me," he said, without the slightest trace of a smile, but Nixon had made him. Nixon was a smart guy, he said. "I knew he'd be glad I wanted to help him."

He persuaded Joyce to stay the night. Before they went to bed, he told her that she was a beautiful woman, but "you're a pure little girl, too, aren't you? . . . Joyce, I know this is new for you," he said, "but it's right, believe me." Afterward, "even though it had not happened for me, I knew he could make it happen. . . . The fervid sex that had made him famous had, in reality, been gentler, a sweet and tender passion." The next morning she called in sick, and they had a late breakfast together. On the way to the airport he told her that he wanted her to have a private phone installed, just for the two of them. He was letting her know that he trusted her and expected nothing less than total loyalty in return.

BACK HOME AT GRACELAND, it was like Christmas three days early. He had gifts from the President for Priscilla and Lisa Marie and stories for everyone else. As he told Priscilla excitedly about his trip, "he was like a kid; it was like nothing had ever happened [to precipitate the trip]. He talked about how he got to meet President Nixon and told him all about getting drugs off the streets and how he wanted to make a difference — he felt like this would be his in, I guess. It was a new challenge, and he did it; I think it really surprised him that he was able to get away with it, but he was definitely thrilled. It was the highlight of his challenges!"

Two nights later, on Christmas Eve, he dispensed four more Mercedeses, including one for Sonny for his service as security chief, one for Dr. Nick for his friendship and faithful attendance on the tours, and one for Bill Morris, who had been so instrumental both in helping Elvis to obtain his deputy's badge and in pushing for the Jaycee award. Later in the evening they all went to the Memphian Theatre, where they saw Robert Redford in *Little Fauss and Big Halsy,* and then in the early hours of the morning, Elvis stopped by police headquarters "to say hello to the men and women who had to work on Christmas. [He was] wearing a white suit and hair down to his shoulders," reported the *Commercial Appeal,* though Vernon Presley subsequently disputed the description: Elvis had not let his hair grow to shoulder length, his father asserted in a follow-up story.

Sonny's wedding three days later was a gala affair, with Elvis as best man and Priscilla matron of honor. Elvis showed up with former sheriff Bill Morris, present sheriff Roy Nixon, and their wives in the $9,000 280-SL he had given Morris, now equipped with an official blue police flasher. He was wearing the "fur-cloth" black bell-bottom suit that had been Priscilla's Christmas gift, a white tie, a belt with gold eagles and chains, and a second belt adorned with the gold belt buckle set off by a large sheriff's star and his own official deputy number (six) with which Sheriff Nixon and some unnamed friends of the department had just presented him. He was armed with two guns in a shoulder holster, two pearl-handled pistols in the waist of his pants, and a derringer in his boot, and he could barely be persuaded at the last minute to give up the fifteen-inch police flashlight with which he had entered the building.

There was a brief reception at the church afterward, and then Elvis invited everyone back to Graceland, where the men all gathered for a picture in which they displayed the deputy's badges they had recently acquired en masse from Sheriff Nixon. Elvis sits comfortably at the center of the group, a proud paterfamilias with his legs spread slightly apart, the very picture of confidence and authority. He is flanked by Red and Dr. Nick, who kneel on either side of him. Billy Smith, Lamar, Jerry, Vernon, Charlie, Marty, Sonny, and George, plus the two sheriffs, all stand in the back holding up their police credentials with varying expressions on their faces but all seemingly seeking to convey the familiar outlaw-lawman celluloid image: for all of our differences we are family, their composite group portrait declares; we are the good guys — but don't fuck with us.

They were off to Tupelo the following day, so Elvis could collect yet another badge arranged for by his newfound friend, Bill Morris. He was jumpy, Tupelo sheriff Bill Mitchell noticed. Mitchell, an old-time fiddler who had first met an eleven-year-old Elvis Presley while playing behind him in Mississippi Slim's band, the group that backed up contestants on the WELO talent show down at the courthouse, was struck by the difference in aspect between the shy, needy child and this transparently insecure, swaggering young man surrounded by his entourage. "He paced the floor all the time. Just like you see a tiger walk a cage. Very ill at ease. Of course we talked about WELO — they were there a couple of hours, and everybody wanted their picture made with Elvis. I had gone to school with Bill Morris, so I deputized him, too." Also present were some of the friends with whom Elvis had grown up, among them the McCombs and the Farrars, who hailed him for being a "good neighbor" and presented him with a plaque entitled "Impossible Dream" that described how "a 'boy-next-door' type becomes a nationally known entertainer." Elvis took that to be quite a coincidence, since, he said, "The Impossible Dream" was the title of the next record he was planning to put out. Then he took the guys for a ride around town, pointing out the bleak urban renewal site that had once been the lively black ghetto called Shake Rag, visiting the Elvis Presley Youth Center that had finally been erected behind the home in which he had been born.

The following day, December 30, he was off to Washington once again with a group of eight that included Bill Morris, who thought he might be able to get Elvis an appointment with J. Edgar Hoover this time. The next morning Bill Morris took them all by the National Sheriff's Association, where Elvis paid for everyone to join (membership carried a life-insurance policy with it, and Elvis wanted all the guys to have one), and they visited the FBI Building, where Morris had arranged a special tour after being advised that Mr. Hoover was still out of town. Elvis was clearly excited, and the FBI agent who conducted the tour was impressed with his sincerity, "despite his rather bizarre personal appearance." The agent's memo went on to observe that "Presley indicated that he has long been an admirer of Mr. Hoover, and has read material prepared by the Director including 'Masters of Deceit,' 'A Study of Communism' as well as 'J. Edgar Hoover on Communism.' Presley noted that in his opinion no one has ever done as much for his country as Mr. Hoover, and that he, Presley, considers the Director 'the greatest living American.'

In private comments made following his tour, he indicated that he, Presley, is the "living proof that America is the land of opportunity" since he rose from truckdriver to prominent entertainer almost overnight. He said that he spends as much time as his schedule permits informally talking to young people and discussing what they consider to be their problems with them. Presley [explained that] his long hair and unusual apparel were merely tools of his trade and awarded him access to and rapport with many people particularly on college campuses who considered themselves "anti-establishment." . . .

Following their tour Presley privately advised that he has volunteered his services to the President in connection with the narcotics problem and that Mr. Nixon had responded by furnishing him an agent's badge of the Bureau of Narcotics and Dangerous Drugs. Presley was carrying this badge in his pocket and displayed it.

Presley advised that he wished the Director to be aware that he, Presley, from time to time is approached by individuals and groups in and outside of the entertainment business whose motives and goals he is convinced are not in the best interests of this country and who seek to have him to lend his name to their questionable activities. In this regard he volunteered to make such information available to the Bureau on a confidential basis whenever it came to his attention. . . .

Presley indicated that he is of the opinion that the Beatles laid the groundwork for many of the problems we are having with young people by their filthy unkempt appearances and suggestive music while entertaining in this country during the early and middle 1960's. He advised that the Smothers Brothers, Jane Fonda, and other persons in the entertainment industry of their ilk have a lot to answer for in the hereafter for the way they have poisoned young minds by disparaging the United States in their public statements and unsavory activities.

It was suggested at the conclusion of the memo that in view of all of the above, not excluding "his favorable comments concerning the Director and the Bureau . . . as well as the fact that he has been recognized by the Junior Chamber of Commerce and the President, it is felt that a letter from the Director would be in order." And so on January 4 one was sent, indicating that "your generous comments concerning the Bureau and me are appreciated, and you may be sure we will keep in mind your offer to be of assistance." For now, though, Elvis had to get back to Memphis for the traditional New Year's Eve celebration at T.J.'s and some well-earned rest.

O N JANUARY 9 the newspapers made public what Elvis had alluded to in his original letter to President Nixon: his selection by the national Jaycees as one of the nation's Ten Outstanding Young Men of the Year. Elvis was already in California preparing for his latest Las Vegas opening, but there was no question of his not attending the ceremony, which was scheduled to take place in Memphis on January 16. This was the public recognition he had been striving for all these years; it was in many ways for him the clearest proof of all of the American dream.

The Jaycee awards had been given out since 1939 and had gone to distinguished men in all fields, with one common denominator: they must all be thirty-five or younger. Leonard Bernstein, Nelson Rockefeller, Orson Welles (twice), Howard Hughes, the Reverend Jesse Jackson, Teddy Kennedy, and Ralph Nader had all received the award, and Bill Morris had assured Elvis of the organization's staunchly patriotic credentials (ex-President Lyndon Johnson was a judge, and Vice President Agnew was slated to be the keynote speaker) before getting Elvis' permission to submit his name for consideration. Other honorees this year included a professor of biological chemistry at Harvard, a cancer researcher, the lieutenant governor of Minnesota, a civil rights activist from Boston, and President Nixon's thirty-one-year-old press secretary, Ron Ziegler.

He flew into Memphis with Priscilla just before midnight the night before the awards ceremony, missing the dinner that kicked off the weekend's festivities, which was attended by all nine of the other honorees. He stayed up till the early hours of the morning working on his speech, showing a single-mindedness of purpose that Priscilla had rarely seen in him, apart from his performing. "He stayed up in his office next to our bedroom writing on this little scratch pad, and he would show me what he had written and ask me what I thought. He was so nervous about making that speech. He was going to be in front of other millionaires, and he wanted to be explicit and intelligent to them. So he would read it to me, and I was amazed. I couldn't believe that this came out of him — he shocked me with the eloquence of his speech. I would have thought that he took it from something — I wouldn't have put it past him to do that, clever as he was — but I witnessed it. I mean it was just beautiful."

The two of them showed up bright and early the following morning for the prayer breakfast at the Holiday Inn Rivermont dressed to the teeth. Elvis was wearing his "fur suit," along with a pair of customized aviator glasses, his heavy gold belt, and the lion's-head medallion; Priscilla looked demure, her hair falling to either side of her scoop-neck white mini, with a large white corsage pinned to her left breast. Bill Morris sat to Elvis' right, as the guys did their best to keep photographers and autograph seekers at bay while the ceremony itself was going on.

At ten o'clock, after a speech by West Memphis political operative Deloss Walker, subbing for Arkansas governor Dale Bumpers, there was an informal question-and-answer period from which the press was excluded but at which, according to several of the participants, Elvis more than held his own. Standing next to presidential press secretary Ron Ziegler, his rings prominently on display, Elvis was asked if he felt that today's music had an adverse effect on young people. "Presley thought for a moment," the *Press-Scimitar* reported from its sources within the building, "and answered, 'Yes, I don't go along with music advocating drugs and desecration of the flag. I think an entertainer is for entertaining and to make people happy.'" The tone was very different from the formal press conference of the day before, at which black Boston City Council member Tom Atkins had challenged the ideals of the nation and the commitment of the President to civil rights, and Ziegler was left in the unenviable position of defending the status quo. The prayer breakfast ended with a query about religious beliefs. "Six or seven of the men said they didn't belong to a church," according to the *Commercial Appeal*, "and felt a certain hypocrisy about organized religion. But Elvis seemed to feel religion was very important in his life, not in the organized sense but in the sense that he had called on God many times for strength . . . [and] that 'God is a living presence in all of us.'"

At the luncheon he listened attentively as United Nations ambassador-appointee George Bush, filling in for Vice President Agnew, delivered a speech extolling the virtues of compromise and working within the system ("To guarantee that this country never accepts the violent answer, we need to get our great achievers to contribute in some way to our governmental system"). Afterward Elvis broke off from signing autographs and posing for photos when he spotted Sam Phillips' former office manager Marion Keisker (whom he had last seen on his final day in Germany) in the crowd. Excitedly he rushed over to embrace her and brought her back to his table, where he introduced her to Priscilla as "the lady I told you so much about," then turned to the guys and announced, "You know, she's the one who made it all possible. Without her I wouldn't even be here."

Because it was his hometown and because he was so proud of the honor that he was being given, he invited all of the award winners and Jaycee officials and their wives to a cocktail hour at Graceland, to be followed by a formal early dinner at the Four Flames, an elegant midtown restaurant. The guests all arrived promptly at five o'clock, with the household in a dither of preparation: there had never been anything quite like this at Graceland, and everyone deferred to Marty, who had made all the arrangements and seemed to know how these things were done. Once again Priscilla was amazed to see a side of her husband come out that she had never seen before, as he showed off his home with unabashed pride not just for its appointments but for what it said about his accomplishment simply in making the journey that he had made. At the restaurant, too, he played the genial host, making sure that everyone was taken care of, graciously presiding over a table set with place cards signed by the host and displaying the TCB logo in gold.

The ceremony at Ellis Auditorium at 8:00 P.M. merely continued the sense that he had stepped for a moment outside his own life. The citation accompanying his award spoke of his achievements in the entertainment field but also his many acts of philanthropy, which "he has intentionally concealed. . . . Elvis is noted for his strength of character. His loyalty to his friends is legendary. His long-standing contract with his manager consists of a mere handshake." When he got up to accept the award, he was visibly nervous. It was in his eyes and in his voice, shaky at first, then gathering confidence as he revealed himself to the world, revealed the vision that had fueled him from childhood on, capped by the words to a song that he had known from childhood but perhaps knew best from Roy Hamilton's heartfelt 1955 rendition.

"When I was a child, ladies and gentlemen, I was a dreamer. I read comic books, and I was the hero of the comic book. I saw movies, and I was the hero in the movie. So every dream that I ever dreamed has come true a hundred times. These gentlemen over here, these are the type who care, are dedicated. You realize if it's not possible that they might be building the kingdom, it's not far-fetched from reality. I'd like to say that I learned very early in life that: 'Without a song the day would never end/Without a song a man ain't got a friend/Without a song the road would never bend/Without a song . . .' So I keep singing a song. Good night. Thank you."

FAMILY PORTRAIT, DECEMBER 10, 1970.
(COURTESY OF THE ESTATE OF ELVIS PRESLEY)

A STRANGER IN MY
OWN HOMETOWN

He OPENED IN VEGAS on January 26, accompanied by yet
another death threat. There were flamboyant new outfits (a
dark, two-piece "Cisco Kid" ensemble, with silver studs, an
orange shirt, and ruffled cuffs was probably the most spectacular) and a new song list that once again leaned heavily on ballads and highlighted the inspirational, as exemplified by both "How Great Thou Art"
(which had been introduced on the November tour) and "The Impossible
Dream," with which he closed many of the shows. Although he had the flu
during part of the engagement, and there was criticism even from the fans
of some of his "off" nights, there was no question of his high spirits on the
final evening as he sang a wild "Tiger Man" medley, then introduced Kris
Kristofferson's bittersweet "Help Me Make It Through the Night," which
seemed to reflect something of the prevailing mood. He also threw a glass
of water at Joe Guercio, thanked the Colonel and Daddy and "all the
people who've helped me," and stood at the end with his hands on his hips,
smiling out at his fans.

Joyce Bova found him bored and distracted when she visited. He seemed
boastful and self-absorbed, showed off his gun collection and badges, and
one time when he wanted everyone's attention he simply sighted the chandelier with a loaded gun, then pulled the trigger on an empty chamber.
There was a stunned silence in the room — until he himself doubled over
in laughter. "It took only a second for his guys to join in," Bova observed,
"laughing just as loud as Elvis. . . . 'Honey,' he said, finally getting control
of himself . . . 'you gotta do some crazy things around here to stay sane.'"

It seemed sometimes like he almost needed to convince himself that
he was who he said he was. The TCBs which had once been reserved exclusively for the inner circle were now given out almost indiscriminately to
near-strangers, with matching TLCs ("Tender Loving Care") for the ladies.
Jerry Schilling blew up when Elvis asked him to give International president Alex Shoofey his pendant, and even comedian Sammy Shore, not

431

exactly an intimate, got his own. In the closed world in which they lived, the same stories were passed back and forth until they became common property, taking on the status of a larger myth whose literal origins were no longer relevant. When his Denver police friends came in at the end of the month's run, Elvis showed them his BNDD badge and held them spellbound with his tales of meeting the President — though privately the law-enforcement agents remained skeptical of some of the embellishments.

H E AND PRISCILLA RETURNED TO MEMPHIS at the beginning of March, a week after the engagement's end. Elvis had a recording session scheduled to begin on the fifteenth, and he stayed in his room decompressing for the first few days, emerging for the closed-circuit broadcast of the Ali-Frazier heavyweight championship fight at Ellis Auditorium on the eighth. The hall was packed, and "for one of the few times in his adult life," the *Press-Scimitar* remarked, "[Elvis Presley] was all but ignored"— in spite of his $10,000 gold belt, his rings, and his chains. He was accompanied by Bill Morris and nine or ten of the guys, and while the crowd seemed to split pretty much along racial lines, with most whites for the more stolid present champion, Joe Frazier, and blacks for the flamboyant Ali, Elvis indicated to the guys that he was for the ex-champ, both for his flair and his bad-ass style.

The Nashville session had been set up with three goals in mind. The first was a follow-up to the 1957 Christmas album, which had been such a strong-selling catalogue item over the years. The Colonel, always big on seasonal offerings, had been pushing for this for at least five years and now, with Felton's active collusion, had finally gotten Elvis to agree. Perhaps as a sop to the artist's own inclinations, RCA cited a new religious album as the second priority, with a pop album plus a couple of strong singles as the final goal.

Elvis appeared to be paying little attention to priorities as he started off the session with Scottish folksinger Ewan McColl's "The First Time Ever I Saw Your Face," a song he had long admired in Peter, Paul and Mary's 1965 folk version and which Joyce had begged him to record. It was very much in keeping with his increasing inclination toward high-flown, tender, and somewhat indistinct poetic sentiment, and he followed it with an anthemic version of "Amazing Grace," the eighteenth-century hymn which had recently been a Top 20 hit for folksinger Judy Collins. Next came two more Peter, Paul and Mary songs, "Early Morning Rain" and "For Lovin' Me," both written by the Canadian folksinger Gordon Lightfoot. With one more contemporary folk song that he had requested Freddy to clear, Kris Kristofferson's acutely mortal tale of sin and redemption, "Sunday Morning Coming Down," the session would have been well on its way toward an identity altogether different from anything either RCA or the Colonel had envisioned — but then it turned out that Freddy had failed to clear the song, and Elvis appeared to be in increasing physical discomfort, complaining that his eye felt like it was burning. At 1:30 A.M. the session was abruptly canceled, and Elvis returned to his hotel. When the eye didn't get any better, Dr. Nick flew in from Memphis early that morning with Dr. David Meyer, a retina specialist, and after a quick examination, Dr. Meyer administered a 100-milligram shot of Demerol, then a shot of cortisone directly into the eyeball to relieve some of the dangerous pressure that had built up. Then, against his protestations, Elvis was admitted to Nashville's Baptist Hospital.

Priscilla had already returned to California to supervise the ongoing decoration of the new house, so Elvis flew Barbara Leigh in to join him and even induced her to keep him company in his hospital bed. Dr. Meyer's initial diagnosis was confirmed by tests: Elvis was suffering from iritis and a form of secondary glaucoma, a condition aggravated in Dr. Nick's view by the dye from his eyebrows mixing with sweat and getting into his eyes. By now, with the pain abated and his fears assuaged, Elvis had come to relish the experience, and he told the story of getting the shot directly into his eyeball without anesthetic to anyone and everyone who came to see him over the next few days, including Tennessee governor Winfield Dunn.

By the time that he was discharged on Friday, Barbara had returned to California, and he flew in Joyce Bova to accompany him back to Memphis. She was shocked by his appearance; he looked worn and haggard and had little to say on the flight other than to gratefully squeeze her hand. His father met them at the airport and thanked her mutely, obviously deeply concerned. At Graceland she watched Mr. Presley help his boy up the stairs and was transfixed by this unexpectedly touching spectacle except for a moment when "I was frozen by the sight of Priscilla. A portrait of her hung by the foot of the stairs . . . shown in semi-profile with Elvis beside her . . . captured looking almost like brother and sister, both in facial structure and expression." Dr. Meyer had set up a kind of mobile hospital unit upstairs, and he gave Joyce the medication schedule, explaining to her how to use the oxygen tank, just in case it was necessary. "I knew you would come,

Joyce," Elvis said, just before he dropped off to sleep. "I knew you wouldn't let me down."

She took care of him for the next few days, in many respects the most extended period of intimacy she had ever enjoyed with him. They stayed in Elvis' bedroom, with its "velvet haremlike drapes cover[ing] the windows . . . dark wood furniture [that] was bulky and masculine . . . and a red-and-black color scheme that, in the dim light, made me feel hemmed in." His books on philosophy and religion were scattered all around the room, and she read to him from *The Impersonal Life*. It was, she felt, a very special time for them both, the surreal atmosphere only compounded by the Placidyl that they both continued to take. When she left, she asked shyly if she could take a supply of the pills with her to tide her over when she got back to Washington; they helped her to sleep.

H E SUMMONED HER TO RETURN just two and one-half weeks later. He introduced her to his grandmother, then left her alone with the old lady, who asked if she had any children and advised her "[not to] wait too long. A woman should have plenty of children. Then maybe you get lucky, and one of 'em turns out good." From what Joyce gathered, Vernon was the only one of her children that Grandma considered to have turned out any good, "'Cause," she said, "he made Elvis." Elvis was the natural subject of their conversation, because he was "the man we both adored."

He continued to show a new side of himself to her that weekend. It was an idyllic interlude for the most part, marred only by her concern about the pills, which seemed to influence nearly everything they did. She tried to talk to him about it, but Elvis just got mad or told her indulgently that he knew what he was doing. And despite all the evidence she believed that he did. Why don't you move into Graceland? he said to her one night out of the blue, as they lay in bed watching the news. Which seemed to her like a dreamy, perplexing, and unanswerable question to ask. "'Just think about it,' he said, in the most matter-of-fact, devoid-of-emotion tone, as if he were afraid to hear my answer. Which was just as well, I had to tell myself during the flight back to Washington. Because I didn't have one for him."

He was back in California just in time for the Easter egg hunt that Priscilla and Joanie Esposito had organized for the children. He spent some time at home, and he and Priscilla went to Las Vegas for their fourth anniversary, but mostly he and the guys continued to have good times in Palm Springs, racing around in dune buggies with their girlfriends in a world removed from all conventional constraints. Sometimes he would get up and preach after his own fashion, standing on a coffee table and shouting out, "Whoa, all ye Pharisees and motherfuckers," or declaring that a rich man's chance of getting into Heaven was "like a camel's ass trying to get through the eye of a needle." No one knew quite what to make of this, least of all the girls who had come for fun and now were getting Bible lessons in uniquely idiosyncratic fashion.

Priscilla was scarcely unaware. She just chose to leave it alone. "I felt that I just couldn't reach him anymore. He had bought his own image, and you couldn't have [a real] conversation with him; he would just discredit you and everything else. I don't care what anybody says — I think that deep down he wanted to be a family man. But he was serving too many masters, he was too dispersed — he had all this energy, and he didn't know what to do with it. He'd go off on one thing, and then there would be an interruption; he'd go off in [another] direction and then he was conflicted again. Because he had everything at his fingertips. It was the same with women. He wanted to have his cake and eat it, too — just like every man, I guess!"

While he was off on his own, Priscilla focused on her new passion: karate. Elvis had introduced her to Ed Parker, with whom he had been studying conscientiously for the past several months, and she was taking private lessons three times a week at his studio on Santa Monica. It gave her something to talk to Elvis about, and at Ed's instigation Elvis had contacted a Korean-born instructor named Kang Rhee in Memphis, with whom they could keep up their studies at home. Rhee taught a different kind of karate called Tae Kwon Do, which emphasized hand and leg quickness, and Ed recommended him without reservation, believing that Rhee's English was so broken and his personality so eccentric he had little to fear from the Korean as a rival.

Elvis RETURNED TO THE NASHVILLE STUDIO in dramatic fashion in May, arriving for the makeup session in a black cape and carrying his diamond-and-ruby-encrusted lion's-head cane. This time there was no question of what the priorities were. The studio had been transformed by Felton into a Christmas scene with brightly wrapped boxes (all empty) under a gaily decorated Christmas tree. Lamar even dressed up as Santa

Claus, and the Colonel sent Elvis a Christmas card with a picture of himself as Santa standing next to Frosty the Snowman, and a message wishing Elvis luck with "a special Christmas album in May 1971 with the special sacred songs done by Elvis as only he can do it." It was signed, "From your pal and friend, The Colonel," with the tongue-in-cheek proviso, "This is a special inspiration photo not to be sold."

For all of the festive trappings, though, and the self-conscious air of celebration, Elvis was no more at ease than he had been at that strange session the previous September. To arranger Glen Spreen, a newcomer to Nashville, who had last worked with him at the Memphis sessions two years before, the differences were dramatic. "Instead of him coming in the control room and listening to a song and having Chips say, 'Let's do this one,' and Elvis, of course, having a response, here there was no planning, Lamar would just bring him a song, and we'd pick it up and throw it in the 'Let's do' or the 'Let's don't' corner. It was not enjoyable: we did the songs too quick. It was just, 'Let's get it over with.' I began to feel sorry for Elvis. Or sorry *about* him — I don't know which is the proper phrase. Maybe I was just seeing him more clearly; maybe I was just seeing more of the true Elvis than I had seen in Memphis. But it wasn't what I had expected, and my first thought was, I'd better figure out something else to do."

Norbert Putnam, too, was surprised and more than a little disappointed that things appeared to be getting worse rather than better. The weeklong session was less a musical collaboration than a theatrical event, and Norbert took little satisfaction in an atmosphere that he was beginning to see as fundamentally uncreative, with Elvis more interested in telling his stories and showing off his guns than he was in singing, and the Memphis Mafia always at full howl.

It was hard to say what exactly was different; certainly all of these elements might have been detected to one extent or another at the first Nashville session the previous June and were present in abundance in September. But then it had seemed as if they might simply be an aberration; now they set a tone that quickly translated to the musicians. Bored by all the self-congratulatory chatter, disappointed by what they saw as an almost total abdication of responsibility on Felton's part, they began to drift off during the increasingly lengthy breaks between songs, finding refuge in guitarist Jerry Shook's Winnebago (Shook was merely an interested bystander; he was not working the session), which was parked out behind the studio and came equipped with all the comforts of home: girls, dope, and booze. "All of a sudden," said drummer Jerry Carrigan, "nobody cared. We all felt, What can we do to get this over with? He'd settle for anything."

In keeping with the spirit of general anomie, Carrigan failed to show up at all on the second day. He had been put in charge of finding Elvis a date for the evening and evidently took his duties a little too seriously, spending much of the day running down leads, then sleeping through his late-afternoon alarm. By the time he arrived at the studio, Felton had enlisted Kenny Buttrey as the new drummer, and they finished up the Christmas album that night without him.

He was able to talk his way back into the session the following night, but even though he and Buttrey made an effective rhythm team, and despite the fact that they were now tackling more challenging material, it still wasn't any better. At Felton's prompting, Norbert managed to sneak in "Until It's Time for You to Go," a pretty ballad that Felton thought Elvis would really like by the Cree folksinger Buffy Sainte-Marie, whom Norbert was currently producing. The version that Elvis delivered was somewhat tentative, though, and even on Kris Kristofferson's "Help Me Make It Through the Night," a highlight of the Vegas show, the singing was insipid, almost an impersonation of sensitivity rather than the real thing. Finally, with "Lead Me, Guide Me," the first gospel cut of the evening, with the Imperials backing him, Elvis appeared to get untracked, but the prevailing mood undid him once again, as the session came to an abrupt halt with an impromptu karate demonstration in which Elvis disarmed Charlie and sent the gun he was holding through Chip Young's custom-made Conde Hermanos Spanish classical guitar. Chip tried not to look too upset, but, as Joe Moscheo observed, he didn't look as if he found the incident all that amusing either.

Some of the gospel numbers that they tried over the next couple of nights gave hints of exciting new directions, contemporary approaches to gospel harmony that had earned the Imperials a certain amount of criticism within the quartet community because they verged on what was coming to be known as "Contemporary Christian" (with its incorporation of rock influences) rather than straightforward traditional religious singing. Elvis' focus was no more constant here, however, and his attention continued to wander. The musicians, too, continued to wander, especially now that there were no longer enough chairs for them to occupy, with all of the backup singers and all of Elvis' guys crowded into the control room between takes. The whole scene in fact took on a slightly surreal air, as the policemen who were there to provide security found their way into Shook's van while the musicians were smoking dope and said, "Hey, boys, what are y'all smoking that stuff for? It's gonna put you to sleep. Let's give you something to keep you awake." With that they produced some amphetamines that they told the musicians "they had just confiscated from somebody, took them to jail, took their dope, and brought it to us. I remember they were some real great pills, and every time we'd see this big old guy as a paid guard at a party or something afterwards, he'd look over and say, 'Well, how are things in the wonderful world of marijuana?'"

Everybody knew that Elvis was against this kind of activity: he showed them all his federal narcotics badge and spoke with disapproval about rock groups that were known to have drug problems. The irony of someone who appeared to be stoned much of the time himself holding such views certainly struck them, but they never doubted his sincerity. "We used to joke about, 'Can you imagine being arrested by Elvis?' But we hid it from him, because we felt that he would be totally opposed." Every so often one of Elvis' guys would come out and say, "Hey, you're gonna have to come back in. You're supposed to be working." Finally Carrigan said, "'You want us to come back in, you're going to have to clear some of those people out and bring us some chairs so we can sit down. We're not going to stand around.' So they brought some chairs in, and we had to listen to Elvis tell his tales."

The session ground on for two more days, with each song coming harder than the last. In fact, except for "I'm Leavin'," another of Elvis' over-the-top ballads, to which they all committed a good deal of hard, sustained effort, the one real highlight of the session was a trio of songs that Elvis sang on the third-to-last night, just sitting at the piano by himself at four or five in the morning after everyone else had gone home. There were two beautiful ballads by one of his earliest r&b heroes, Ivory Joe Hunter, and a third song half-remembered from childhood, "I'll Take You Home Again, Kathleen," a staple for Irish tenors ever since it had been written nearly a century before. Yearning, wistfulness, loneliness, need — all were communicated with a naked lack of adornment that Elvis was seeming to find increasingly difficult to display in the formal process of recording.

He called for Joyce to join him in Nashville on the final day of the session when he would be working on vocal overdubs. He showed her around the studio, instructed her in the function of the board — "he gave her a tutorial on recording an Elvis Presley album," in the view of the somewhat cynical and decidedly unimpressed musicians still hanging around the studio, who, without any formal introduction, were under the impression that Joyce was Priscilla. "He showed her how to place the mike for the piano, called for more bass in the mix; he just wanted to bring her to a totally controlled environment." To Joyce it was something altogether different. When he sang, he sang *to her.* He was a different Elvis, transported by the music and "every inch the perfectionist at work. . . . It was obvious that despite all the high-priced technical talent RCA had taken pains to surround him with, Elvis was the man in charge."

He awoke in pain in the middle of the night. Joyce wanted to call a doctor to the hotel, but Elvis had Sonny charter them a jet, and when they arrived in Memphis an hour later, they went straight to Dr. Nick's house. Whatever the trouble may have been, Dr. Nick took care of it, and Joyce, somewhat abashed but emboldened by the privacy of the medical transaction, asked Elvis if Dr. Nick couldn't write her a prescription for Placidyl, too, so she wouldn't have to keep "borrowing" her supply from him. That night they watched news footage of the dedication of the Lyndon Johnson presidential library in Texas, where two thousand war protesters booed the appearance of both ex–President Johnson and President Nixon, setting Elvis off on a tirade about lack of respect for the flag among today's youth. When Joyce demurred, he backed down a little, which she took as a sign of trust. But he still continued to quiz her incessantly about her loyalty to him, and when she questioned him about his to her, when she spoke of the girls who flung themselves at him and the books in which he buried himself rather than pay any attention to her, he simply fobbed her off — as he did about the pills, a subject on which, as she was well aware, she was in no position to criticize.

H E RETURNED TO THE STUDIO in June to put the finishing touches on the gospel album, but things were no different than they had been. More and more the musicians spoke openly among themselves about his weird fluctuations of mood, about why he would have his bodyguards cordon off the bathroom when he was in there so that no one else could even go in and take a leak. The female backup singers were a constant source of annoyance, maintaining a steady stream of chatter among themselves, seemingly oblivious to Elvis' increasing irritation with them. And, of course, the musicians' own pill taking and toking went on, even as the session continued to focus on Jesus. They got through the work nonetheless, completing nine more masters in three days, bringing the total for the three sessions to forty-four, including an out-of-left-field "My Way," in which Elvis seems to take all the slings and arrows of fortune with a personal sense of triumph somewhat at odds with the world-weary tone of the song. He was working on some vocal overdubs when his frustration with the female vocalists finally boiled over. "I've run this damn song fifty times, and you still don't know your parts!" he announced, flinging down his microphone and storming out of the studio, never to return.

P RISCILLA HAD BEGUN HER KARATE STUDIES with Kang Rhee while Elvis was in Nashville. Elvis had met Master Rhee himself in March, showing up at the tiny storefront studio on Poplar with ten or twelve of the guys in an unembarrassed display of panache that Rhee, a small, studious man in his mid thirties with a limited command of English, was scarcely prepared for. "We don't have any air conditioning. We don't have any carpet, just tile. And he walk in with all those bodyguards with him. Black jumpsuit with a cane and sunglasses and a big jar of water. And then he wear the heavy wrist and leg weights. He told me, 'I heard about you many different directions, and I love to see you personally and then observe your class. Really, I don't have any class scheduled. But I invite several mean guys — Elvis coming in, so everybody want to come. And everybody showing off for him — breaking concrete blocks, then some fighting and sparring stuff, but my commands, my rules. And Elvis really impressed by the discipline of training under me, and that might be the reason that he is interested to join me."

Kang Rhee was impressed with Elvis, too: by his evident sincerity, his knowledge of and commitment to the sport, and by his spiritual qualities as well. "He knows already many different movements. He knows many different self-defense techniques. Meantime, he has lots of knowledge of the philosophy, and then he has all the time read very heavily, yoga, martial arts books, he all the time read. So he has a mental and physical very high standard as a martial artist: spiritual and mental is much more [his] strength. Stronger than any other person I can think of."

Elvis signed up on the spot, and signed up all the guys who were with him, for each of whom Master Rhee eventually devised a suitable nickname. Red became Mister Dragon; Sonny, Mister Eagle; Jerry, the Cougar; Charlie, the Cobra; and George, neither a particularly willing nor diligent pupil, joked that he should be called Mister Rat. Elvis was proudest of all of his title, Master Tiger, and at Master Rhee's invitation, in recognition of his spiritual qualities, led the group in prayer at the start of every session.

Priscilla showed up for her first lesson on June 9, the second day of Elvis' recording session, and Master Rhee was equally impressed with her. She showed the same seriousness as Elvis, but she had a physical grace that he lacked and a ferocity of concentration in the approach that she brought to her studies. "She has a beautiful kicking style, she heavily training [all the] time, no air conditioners, just lots of sweat and hard work, the most effort totally." When Elvis came home from Nashville three days later, she couldn't wait to show him the progress that she had made. "I think he was really proud of me; very few women were doing karate at that time. It's funny, in Vegas he would embarrass me, I'd be in a beautiful gown, and he would say, 'Honey, do that cat stance [for everybody],' and he wouldn't even think of what goes along with it in a dress. But I found I was having a great time, it's something I felt good at, it was something that he loved and I started getting into, and I actually loved it." As she continued with her studies, he made her show him all the new moves that Master Rhee was teaching her and became even more deeply involved himself. But when she returned to California the following week to supervise the redecorating, he sent for Joyce to join him at Graceland almost immediately.

THE HILTON HOTEL CHAIN took over the International at the end of June (the Hilton had assumed 50 percent ownership the previous August), and practically the first order of business was to ensure that their premier attraction, *Vegas'* premier attraction, would continue to appear in their showroom. The Colonel had an understanding that permitted Elvis to leave should any ownership change occur, so Hilton vice president Henri Lewin got in touch before the formal transfer even took place, and the Colonel was on a plane from Palm Springs to Las Vegas within hours of that initial conversation.

One might have thought that this would be the opening the Colonel had been waiting for. He had been agitating against the International all spring, evidently angling for the same kind of consultancy arrangement that he got in Hollywood, darkly hinting at movie deals just on the horizon that might prohibit Elvis from appearing at the hotel in August — but now he was all honeyed words. "I did business with Kerkorian, and I liked it," he told Lewin, a sophisticated, forty-eight-year-old veteran of the European hotel business, who was born in Potsdam, Germany, worked in the Far East, was interned by the Japanese during the Second World War, and arrived in the United States in 1946. "I have no reason not to trust that Hilton is not equally good or better." Lewin got the impression that this was a more than honorable man, as the Colonel made it clear that he would uphold the present contract without complaint, cavil, or renegotiation. On June 26 Lewin threw a surprise party for his new friend's sixty-second birthday, to which Hilton president Barron Hilton, inducted as a Snowman just three days earlier, was not able to come but for which he made his most profound apologies.

It was not out of any newfound sense of passivity that the Colonel refrained from tactical engagement at this point. Rather, one would assume, he was observing a long-standing rule: better to let the enemy think they have you surrounded and strike when they are least prepared than engage in all-out warfare at a time when they have every reason to expect it. The Colonel was not laying down arms on any other front in any case. Once again in March he made a special deal with RCA, for three more Camden albums this time plus a second volume of golden hits. The Camden deal guaranteed $180,000 against a reduced budget-line royalty rate, and the multiple-LP set of hits would pay $525,000 by the beginning of the following year, with both advances, of course, split 50–50 between Elvis and the Colonel. In addition, for the boxed set, All Star Shows would supply 150,000 pieces of merchandise at $1 apiece, and 25,000 Christmas cards for a proposed five-pack of Camden LPs, once again at $1 apiece. There were various refinements to these and other deals, but the principle that the Colonel's merchandising skills were at least as valuable in a pecuniary sense as his client's musical ones was firmly established at RCA by now — though that didn't keep Colonel from complaining long and loud at every presumed infringement upon understandings written, oral, or yet to be articulated.

In the absence of the movie with which he had threatened Alex Shoofey in the spring, the Colonel had arranged for Elvis to play the Sahara Tahoe in Stateline, Nevada, just prior to the Vegas opening, with one week between the two engagements. They would be getting $150,000 a week for the two-week booking, $25,000 more than Vegas, with little extra outlay.

Everyone appreciated the change of pace — things were a lot looser in Tahoe, there was less pressure, considerably less media scrutiny, and in fact less scrutiny in general, as many of the guys had their girlfriends join them, or made new girlfriends, an arrangement that worked fine until Joanie Esposito paid a surprise visit to Joe and couldn't figure out why she got the cold shoulder from so many old friends. The stage was better, the showroom more intimate, and Elvis seemed to thoroughly enjoy himself, although the high altitude left him and the band out of breath at times.

The show itself was pretty much the same — "The Impossible Dream" (which Elvis still had not recorded) remained the highlight of the set — but there were two major changes. Sammy Shore had been replaced as comedian, no big surprise to anyone, really, after Sammy's increasingly erratic offstage behavior. More significantly, Joe Guercio had perfected the new opening with which they had experimented in Vegas, an adaptation of Richard Strauss' *Also Sprach Zarathustra,* which had become popular through its use in Stanley Kubrick's epic, *2001: A Space Odyssey,* as the film's semi-apocalyptic musical theme. Guercio's wife, Corky, had suggested to him half-jokingly that the music reminded her of Elvis, and to his surprise, the orchestra leader agreed. When it turned out that Elvis, too, had had the same idea, they started fooling with it during the winter engagement, using it as a kind of overture to bring Elvis onstage sometimes, sometimes actually interrupting the show at Elvis' instigation just so the rhythm section could try it on the audience. Now, with Elvis' encouragement, Guercio developed the idea on a grand orchestral scale. "We set it up to the point where you got to the last chord, and the tympanist played the final set of eight notes, and it would build to such a frenzy that it was orgasm time from then until Ronnie Tutt [Elvis' drummer] took over — it was like the ultimate orgasm." That was how Elvis reacted to it, too: "he didn't want to be just a guy walking out there, he wanted to be a god." And with the *2001* theme, he was.

They shattered all attendance records in Tahoe, almost making up for what it cost the hotel when Elvis' salary triggered "favored nations" clauses in Johnny Carson's and Buddy Hackett's contracts (their pay had to be raised retroactively to reach the level of his). The show got great reviews, too (he worked so hard, remarked *Billboard* of the opening night, "you'd think he almost needed the money"), black comic Nipsey Russell was generally regarded as a big improvement, and the *2001* overture was much remarked upon. There were several other high points, including the dramatic approach to "You've Lost That Loving Feeling" that Elvis had developed the previous year, where he stood pinned by a single spotlight, his back to the audience, then whirled about for the chorus — which worked fine except when he donned an ape mask that a fan had given him during his last Vegas engagement. The sound was fine, too, even though for the first time Felton wasn't there to supervise it. His kidneys had finally failed him, after almost two years of doctors fearing that this would be the inevitable result of his skyrocketing blood pressure. He needed to be on dialysis every few days now, but with his buoyant spirits it was hard not to believe him when he said that he would be back before they knew it.

They went into Vegas with barely a pause, and for the most part the reviews continued to be good, calling attention to the audacious overture and the Colonel's promotional flourishes ("Col. Tom Parker outdid himself," remarked *Variety* in its lead), though the critic for the *Hollywood Reporter,* generally something of a skeptic, called the performance "sloppy, hurriedly rehearsed, mundanely lit, poorly amplified, occasionally monotonous, often silly, and haphazardly coordinated." Elvis, he went on, "looked drawn, tired, and noticeably heavier," though the audience, he admitted, "couldn't have cared less. . . . They absolutely loved, honored, and obeyed his every whim." Bill Belew, who had developed a whole new "casual look" for the run (the *Hollywood Reporter* judged it not to be Elvis' sexiest or most flattering), was there, as usual, for opening night and thought that it was "fabulous," from the overture on. "I mean '2001' was just blaring out, and then the drums hit, and out he came. Kathy McEvoy, who used to go as my escort, leaned over and said, 'You can feel the sensuality and the sex oozing from that man.'" Some of the musicians grumbled that there was nothing to follow the opening with, that more time and effort had been put into the effects than the substance, and there was increasing talk of the two or three doctors who attended Elvis daily, the "vitamin injections" and "throat treatments" that he received constantly throughout his stay.

As the engagement wore on, Elvis' boredom and eccentricities of mood became apparent even to the outside world. Rona Barrett's column at the end of the run sought to explain them in terms her readers could understand, and while the account is hopelessly garbled and, as far as the Self-Realization movement and Daya Mata are concerned, a factual mess, there seems a somewhat ominous, and only thinly veiled, message for Elvis himself hidden between the lines.

Further reliable word on why his latest International Hotel act was perhaps not up to Presley par is that he was quite ill at the time, and that, in addition, he was entranced with a program of self-realization, involving deep meditation and yoga. Seems the head of the self-realization fellowship, on his deathbed, told his wife, Daya Mata, that Elvis was the next savior, Daya Mata relayed this inspiration to Elvis, and ever since, Presley has been deeply involved in the self-realization fellowship at Daya Mata's L.A. home. As a result of the program, Elvis attempted to meditate himself out of his physical pain during this International gig . . . and frequently went on stage in a kind of meditational fog . . . all of which could explain Elvis' behavior.

Another syndicated columnist, John J. Miller, reported on the almost equally evident estrangement between Elvis and Priscilla. Their new home had been Priscilla's excuse since the beginning of the year, but now that it was almost finished, she flung herself into the world of karate, focusing on her own studies and attending karate tournaments far and wide, sometimes with Joanie Esposito, sometimes just with some of the kids from the studio. She had begun taking a camera, "and I would get these great shots of guys fighting, and I would show Elvis and say, 'Look at this. I was at this tournament, and they have these great teams and great fighters like the Urquidez brothers, and he started asking me questions about them, and the next thing you know he wanted me to take a camera every time I went. During that time karate was at its best, almost like the Muhammad Ali era in boxing, and I pointed out all of these greats to Elvis — Bill Wallace and Chuck Norris and Jim Hawkins. It was the best time I ever had."

She also started to get to know one of the competitors, former international light-contact champion Mike Stone, whom she and Elvis had originally met at Ed Parker's international karate championships in Hawaii in 1968 and with whom she had even taken a few lessons at future film star Chuck Norris' studio. Over the course of the summer she grew closer to Stone, a native of Oahu with a Caucasian father, who in Ed Parker's eyes was "a great blackbelt, had that magnetism, and was a good bedroom athlete." At first their meetings were accidental — they might just run into one another at a tournament, he might show up at Chuck Norris' studio in Sherman Oaks — but soon Stone was calling the house, using the code name "Mickey," and three-year-old Lisa Marie had to be shushed from talking about him around the maids. As Priscilla's one true confidante, Joanie would baby-sit for Lisa, "and if Joe would call looking for Priscilla, I would say, 'Oh, she's in the bathroom, I'll have her call you.' Then I'd call her at Mike's, and she'd return the call." Others suspected, but whether or not they knew anything for sure, it seemed clear to everyone but Elvis that Priscilla had made a kind of decision. She was twenty-six years old now and increasingly self-confident, it was apparent that she was tired of being publicly humiliated. She knew the rules, but "I was not willing to play anymore."

Joyce Bova might have said much the same thing. She had become pregnant from their last time together, and she arrived in Las Vegas on August 16 with every intention of telling Elvis. A practicing Catholic, she had been genuinely troubled about the affair from the start and did not see abortion as an option, but it seemed like she would never get the opportunity to tell him, as he was always surrounded by sycophants, or it was the pills, or the mood wasn't right. Then, at a moment when she was feeling utterly alone and isolated from her feelings and everyone else, he put a record on the stereo, and she heard his voice singing "The First Time Ever I Saw Your Face," the song she had urged him to record. It was just a demo, he explained to her, as she expressed her unabashed delight at his recording of "their song." He wrote "To Joyce, with love" on the plain white cardboard cover and made her promise that she wouldn't listen to certain other unfinished cuts on the album. When he got rid of everyone else in the room, she thought she would tell him tonight for sure, but then she asked about his daughter, and with that strange sixth sense of his, almost as if he had an inkling of where she was about to go, he began talking about the sacredness of motherhood, how it was 'God's way of telling [a] woman she's not a little girl anymore," that with motherhood it was time to be "respected [but] I don't think a mother should be trying to be sexy and attracting men." When Joyce protested that sexuality was a part of human life, that "not every woman would lose her appeal just because she had a baby," he waved her objections aside. "Trust me on this, Joyce, I know I'm right."

She left Las Vegas without ever telling him and had the abortion three weeks later alone.

E LVIS' DOMESTIC SITUATION and his increasingly erratic behavior both on- and offstage were not the only openly talked-about secrets in Las Vegas during this period. The Colonel's friends and associates were growing concerned about his behavior as well: more and more they were coming to see his predilection for gambling, which had seemed like a harmless aberration at first, as an addiction over which he had no control. It was something no one would ever have figured him for, but one by one all the signs fell into place as they watched him drop ever-larger sums of money at the roulette table, playing with a grim determination that seemed to blot out everything that was going on around him.

He was still, of course, wheeling and dealing, getting every benefit that the market would bear and giving even a sophisticated observer like Henri Lewin a lesson in the true meaning of free enterprise. Lewin saw the Colonel as a man so astute that "when you had him around, you could make money by picking his brain." And if he appeared sometimes to be cold and isolated, Lewin took that to be intentional on the part of a manager who in Lewin's view "worried about [Elvis] twenty-four hours a day" and very properly would never allow intimacy to intrude on his carefully maintained business edge.

But the gambling did intrude. According to Alex Shoofey, who continued as the hotel's president, the Colonel was "one of the best customers we ever had," good for at least $1 million a year. Julian Aberbach, who had worked hand-in-glove with Parker for twenty-five years now, from the time of Eddy Arnold's first association with Hill and Range, was shocked at the change that he witnessed. "This was a man who never spent any money, who at one time had in excess of five million dollars — until he arranged for Elvis to go to Vegas. After that, things were never right." Julian's cousin, Freddy Bienstock, one of the inner circle since 1956, saw much the same thing: the Colonel loading up with free hotel food supplies for home consumption, from sides of beef to salted peanuts, getting everyone to contribute to his expenses so that he paid out virtually nothing for staff or office space, living in his Palm Springs home at the William Morris Agency's expense — and yet blowing every penny at the roulette table, not even a gamble you could win. Freddy tried to talk to him about it one time, and one time only. "He got very angry at me. He said, 'It's my money. I can do what I want. Don't talk to me about that.' And I never did again." No one could miss what was going on. "It made me sick," said concessionaire Al Dvorin, who went back nearly as far as Freddy — but he had no more idea what to say than the others. Even Tom Diskin, the Colonel's closest associate, was at a loss and found himself coldly rebuffed when he tried to express his concern. "I came into this world with nothing," Parker declared with a fury barely masking his defensiveness and fear, "and it doesn't bother me one bit to go out with nothing. I don't have any children. Who am I hurting?"

Perhaps the most surprising aspect of it all was that the Colonel had actually spoken to the guys about just such a thing when they first went into Vegas two years before. "Don't get crazy," he told Joe, "and get hooked on gambling, 'cause the hotel and casinos will own you." Now they all talked about whether the casino owned *him*, but nobody knew for sure. What was going on with Colonel became as much a topic of conversation among the guys as what was going on with Elvis, and there was much speculation that his gambling had to weaken his negotiating position with the hotel. Nothing in his dealings with either the International or the Hilton, however, would suggest that this was true: he remained just as fierce, just as intractable, his motivation no more easy to anticipate or read than it had ever been. At the same time his dependence on something so manifestly outside his own control couldn't help but gnaw away at the Colonel's steely-eyed view of himself; the naked need so evident to old friends like Jean and Julian Aberbach and Tommy Diskin was not something he had ever before chosen to reveal.

There was no question of its effect on his relationship with Elvis. Elvis couldn't say anything, of course. As Joe noted, "Colonel had always told him, 'I'm not going to tell you what to do with your money — you do what you want to do. Your money is yours.' It's like Elvis would go out and spend a million dollars on the ranch or something like that, which was crazy, while Colonel was out there gambling. So what could he say?" They were locked in a relationship of mutual denial, just as they had always been linked by similarities of character and temperament not necessarily evident to the outsider at first glance. "As different as they might appear, they had the same kind of egos," observed Jerry Schilling. And neither ever wanted to display vulnerability — to the other or anyone else.

But Elvis was clearly showing signs of restiveness. He was thirty-six years old now, in every other relationship he was the dominant one — and yet Colonel could always pull him back. Some saw it, almost literally, as a hypnotic power, a form of emotional blackmail that the old man could always exert on the younger one — but the fact was, it continued to come down to the same thing that the nineteen-year-old Elvis Presley had believed he was buying when he first signed on with the Colonel. Colonel was his talisman, Colonel was his luck, Colonel had held out the promise of success and delivered. And part of Elvis, the part that continued to pore over astrological and numerological charts and place his faith in the role of fate, believed that if he ever left the Colonel, his luck just might run out. He was increasingly frustrated with his manager, spoke of him as "Lardass" sometimes behind his back, talked all the time to the guys about what *he* wanted to do and what the Colonel was holding him back from doing with his old-fashioned, carnival-era ways — but he couldn't leave.

The most frequent subject of discussion was Europe, though not everyone believed that Elvis really wanted to go. The offers kept pouring in, and Colonel kept finding excuses to turn them down, but Priscilla for one was not convinced that Elvis, a creature of habit, saw any reason to abandon the comforts of home. Still, it did seem peculiar that Colonel would act so skittish every time the subject came up — surely the issue of tour security, Colonel's principal bogeyman, must have been dealt with before in Europe and Japan, and there were mysterious rumors going around that Elvis, with his highly attuned instinct for other people's cover-ups, was beginning to wonder about. One rumor had it that the Colonel had entered into talks with Tom Jones' flamboyant manager, Gordon Mills, with public speculation that Mills was going to buy him out. Another, circulating sotto voce among some of the fans and even printed in one of the fan club magazines, conjectured that the Colonel was Dutch, his real name "Andre Van Kuyk (Col. Parker to most people)," as the January issue of *El News* suggested. In what appeared to be one of those generic tabloid headlines, the *Los Angeles Citizen News* ran a story on September 23 raising the question, "ELVIS PRESLEY TO DUMP PARKER?" The only substantive reason they seemed able to come up with, though, was that Elvis sought the "romance of the road [while] the Colonel, who is $$$-minded, prefers more direct ways of hitting the till [like] the Las Vegas method and movie studio lots."

E VIDENTLY UNBEKNOWNST TO THE *Citizen News*, the Colonel had already set up another tour, once again with Management III, although he expressed growing exasperation with Jerry Weintraub's self-proclaimed extravagance of style and with what the Colonel testily saw as Weintraub's inattention to detail. The business arrangements were as before — a $1 million advance against 65 percent of the gross — but two months before they were scheduled to go out, on September 1, Colonel delivered a long list of particulars, "due to some unpleasant experiences on the past tour." Management III's performance would be "thoroughly scrutinized," he concluded, "for any future business for 1972."

There were other changes in the wind. The Imperials, who had missed the first tour the previous September due to a scheduling conflict, would not be accompanying Elvis on this one, or, from Colonel's point of view, on any other. He was fed up with their attitude, and they for their part were fed up with his. Citing another conflict (they backed up Jimmy Dean when they weren't working for Elvis, and were better paid for it), they sought a renegotiation of their contract, but the Colonel refused even to recognize their presence, pretending not to hear as Tom Diskin translated their demands to him as he stood at the gaming table.

They might still have elected to come back, but their fate was sealed when Elvis decided to hire J. D. Sumner and the Stamps as their replacement for the November dates. Sumner, who Joe Moscheo suspected had always coveted the spot, owned the booking agency that represented not only his own group but the Imperials as well and in fact was contractually empowered to cast the deciding vote in any stalemate in Imperials business affairs. Elvis had been drawn to Sumner's low bass ever since he had joined the Blackwood Brothers and moved to Memphis in 1954, when Elvis and his girlfriend Dixie Locke regularly attended their all-night singings at Ellis Auditorium. The Stamps signed on in early September, with the provision that J.D. himself, who did not always perform with the quartet, would contribute his vocal talents.

A new comedian was hired as well. Nipsey Russell had played only the one date in Tahoe, and his replacement in Vegas, Bob Melvin, was never considered anything but temporary, so the Colonel sought out Jackie Kahane, a forty-five-year-old Polish-born Canadian Jew who had been opening for Wayne Newton for the past seven years and was conveniently represented by William Morris. Kahane, who had been planning to take some time off after leaving Newton, was hired a month after the Stamps at $2,500 for the November tour, joining Management III and the Stamps on the Colonel's "on-approval" list. Clearly Colonel saw this tour as a shakedown cruise in a number of ways.

It was a trial period for the Hilton, too. Whatever warm feelings Henri Lewin might have felt toward Colonel Parker were plainly based, in both men's estimation, on business, and the Colonel now saw it as time to improve his position with the hotel. To that end, at the conclusion of the engagement, he elicited $25,000 bonus payments for both Elvis and himself as well as the use of Barron Hilton's plane for the upcoming tour "at a most favorable rate." That this was not the sum of his ambitions was made clear when he resolutely refused to confirm that they would be fulfilling the February engagement until well into November, and then only with the promise that the contract would be renegotiated upward. He even compiled a chart showing Elvis as Las Vegas' all-time box-office champ, averaging 3,840 attendance for his latest appearance versus 3,000 for Tom Jones, 2,600 for Barbra Streisand, and 1,800 for Glen Campbell — just in case further convincing was needed.

E LVIS AND PRISCILLA FINALLY SETTLED into the house on Monovale after the Vegas run, with Hillcrest put up for sale at the beginning of August. Priscilla had been redecorating for eight months now, and the new house was designed with ample living space for Sonny and Judy West, Charlie Hodge, and anyone else of the guys who might want to temporarily bunk in. Elvis professed himself pleased with the decor (Priscilla described it as "very manly," with a den and game room for Elvis and a comfortable, country kitchen), but it was clear, even to the casual observer, that this was not a happy household, with Elvis and Priscilla increasingly preoccupied with matters outside the home. One time during the summer Priscilla and Joanie had gone down to Palm Springs and found a note from one of Elvis' girlfriends expressing grateful appreciation for their weekend together along with a second note to Sonny signed "Lizard Tongue." Priscilla confronted Elvis about the matter over the phone, and the guys all laughed about how he got out of it. There was no telling *who* might drop by, he told her, and how could anyone control what some of these girls might fantasize if they did? Priscilla didn't believe his explanation for a minute, but she was in the grip of her own conflicted feelings, and they were scarcely even living together at this point anyway. Whatever bruised pride she may have felt had more to do with the nature of appearances than reality; his actions only gave further sanction to her own.

*   *   *

T HE TOUR OPENED IN MINNEAPOLIS, and everything went smoothly
    enough after Al Dvorin was promoted to announcer. He had no
thought of the job for himself, but the Colonel fired the guy they had
brought with them from Las Vegas after the first show. "I said, 'Colonel, we
got two weeks of the tour. What do I do for an announcer?' He said, 'Al,
I have a replacement.' I said, 'Great. Who?' He says, 'You.' I said, 'I've done
everything you asked me to do: concessions, band leader, security, lighting,
sound, advance work, check writing. I'm not qualified to work as an
announcer.' I said, 'I got a voice like a sewer backing up. I'll make a fool of
myself.' He said, 'Al, who's the boss?' I said, 'You're the boss.' He says, 'And
you're the announcer.'"

Joyce flew into Cleveland, then traveled on with them to Louisville,
where Elvis' seventy-four-year-old grandfather, Jessie, got a warm introduction from the stage and a brief visit after the show. She was amazed at
the difference she saw not just in Elvis but in the crowds that came out to
greet him. There was not a single high roller in sight, and with these true
believers, it seemed, Elvis took his messianic role even more seriously,
betraying more nervousness than she had ever seen in him before. He
spoke to her constantly of his mission in life, about how it was given to
him to make people's dreams come true. His hotel room was strewn with
books and guns, the drapes drawn so it was dark, cool, and close, and he
went nowhere without his JCC award and his BNDD badge. It was as if he
were carrying around with him all the touchstones of his life. This was
who he was.

T HE SHOW HAD CHANGED a good deal since the last time they had
    gone out, just one year ago. With the introduction of "2001," it had
taken on an overt grandiosity which was only accentuated by Elvis' hyper-
bolic readings of "How Great Thou Art," "Bridge Over Troubled Water,"
and "The Impossible Dream." His costumes, his jewelry, and the poses that
he struck only added to the sense of iconography increasingly attendant
upon his performance, consciously contributing to the impression that he
was somehow larger than life. When at the end of the show he opened up
his silk-lined cape and stood there with his arms outstretched, his eyes shut
tight, it was as if he were offering himself to the world, he looked, in the
formulation of some reviewers, somewhere between a demigod and a
giant bat.

The tour built to a crescendo, with bang-up final shows in Kansas City and Salt Lake City. It was a smooth, road-tested organization by now, a troupe that had won its spurs. The new additions had worked out well. Elvis loved J. D. Sumner's "zoom bass," even if some of the other members of the group had reservations about his musicality and personality, both of which they felt competed a little too blatantly for the star's attention. Jackie Kahane fit right in: he was perfect for the broad-based, middle-American-family audience that both Elvis and the Colonel envisioned, inoffensively clean but with just enough ethnic and fag jokes to make everyone feel at home. By the time they completed the tour, they had earned a $128,000 profit on top of the $1 million advance from Management III. After the promoters had been reimbursed, and with all other costs figured in, Elvis and Colonel had $804,000 to split between them on the new two-thirds–one-third basis that they had informally agreed would better reflect the division of labor on personal appearances. As a shakedown cruise, it had to be counted a success in every way, but Colonel was even more disenchanted with Jerry Weintraub than before and determined to find some other way to go in future, if only to teach the younger man a lesson in humility.

ONCE AGAIN THERE WAS LITTLE to do until the next Vegas opening, still two months away. The paternity suit was nearly settled, with the results of a series of blood tests indicating little likelihood that Elvis could be the father. Elvis was no longer seeing Kathy, and he had pretty much broken off with Barbara, who had moved in with Steve McQueen, the star of her latest picture, *Junior Bonner,* while on location the previous summer. He spoke to Joyce more and more about the likelihood of his leaving Priscilla, about Joyce quitting her job and moving into Grace-land with him. Earlier she had not really believed his offer was serious; now she was afraid maybe it was. She saw their relationship as a kind of folie à deux, with the two of them stumbling around in a fog of pills and self-deception. She could no longer keep up with his rapid mood swings. She didn't believe she could save him anymore, and she wasn't sure she could save herself.

Christmas at Graceland was a cheerless affair. Where once Elvis had remained in California until the last possible moment, driving the guys crazy as Priscilla and the wives waited at home, now it was Priscilla who delayed her departure for Memphis, finally arriving with Lisa Marie just in time for the holiday. Elvis seemed in good humor, as he played a joke on the guys when they all assembled on Christmas Eve for their annual bonuses. "Everyone remembered," wrote James Kingsley in the *Commercial Appeal,* "that last year some of his gifts included expensive Mercedes-Benz automobiles. . . ."

> As Elvis began to play Santa Claus this year he was in a happy-go-lucky mood as everyone gathered in his den and living-room expecting the usual gifts and "maybe a little something special."
> With a sly grin on his face, the singer turned to his father, Vernon Presley, and asked: "Where are the envelopes, please?"
> Vernon reached into his coat pockets and produced the envelopes. "Well, it's been a mighty lean year," said Elvis, whose income probably exceeded four million dollars in 1971. . . . As the envelopes began to be opened, the room fell silent. His special gift for 1971 was a 50-cent gift certificate to McDonalds's Hamburger's.
> His joke over, Elvis later distributed his real gifts which included envelopes stuffed with cash for his employees.

Some of the guests in retrospect recalled a certain uncharacteristic reserve, a distance that they observed between Elvis and Priscilla — but it wasn't really all that different, and things certainly appeared to be normal over the next few days, as they watched Monday-night football and rented out the Memphian and Crosstown movie theaters, where Elvis had recently enjoyed *Diamonds Are Forever* and *Dirty Harry* and now caught up with *Shaft.* It wasn't until after Priscilla left, the night before New Year's Eve, that there was any inkling that something was really wrong — and then it was only because Elvis announced it. Priscilla had left him, he told everyone with that flair for self-dramatization that always got people's attention. She hadn't told him why; she had simply said that she no longer loved him, he declared in calls and conversations with one friend after another. But Joyce didn't see any major change when she came in for his birthday on January 8. He gave her a picture of Jesus and a gold ring and announced cryptically that one phase of his life was ending, another set to begin. "I'm past the age of Christ crucified," he said to her. "I can't wait much longer to plan the rest of my life's work."

* * *

T HE CAPE AND THE BALLADS were the most remarked-upon items when he opened in Vegas, with Marty Robbins' "You Gave Me a Mountain," "The First Time Ever I Saw Your Face," and Mickey Newbury's "An American Trilogy" all new to his act. Robbins' ballad, about a man whose wife has not only left him but taken his one "reason for living," their "small baby boy," built to a stirring climax in which the husband cries out, "This time, Lord, you gave a mountain," a sentiment with which Elvis evidently identified as he delivered the line with passionate feeling every time. "An American Trilogy," on the other hand, could almost have stood for an anthem of national reconciliation, joining together "Dixie," "The Battle Hymn of the Republic," and an old Negro spiritual, "All My Trials," in a swelling orchestral setting that never failed to bring down the house. Most of the reviews mentioned that there was less chatter than usual, that the onstage shenanigans had virtually dwindled away, though Robert Hilburn put his finger on the ongoing problem when he wrote in the *Los Angeles Times:* "Far from incorporating any important changes in his act, I found that virtually everything he added merely compounded my disappointment." The disappointment revolved not so much around Elvis himself, who "remains an amazingly charismatic figure," as around his "lack of care and direction in either (a) material or (b) his handling of it." Once, Hilburn wrote, "no one would dare touch a song Presley had recorded because he had done it so well." Now Elvis was a follower, presenting material already familiar in the versions of others without noticeably improving on them. He was, Hilburn concluded, "merely going through the motions," and perhaps the soul-weariness of Las Vegas was at fault.

Despite having to rent a private kidney machine (the dialysis unit of Las Vegas' Sunrise Hospital had shut down), Felton was on hand for the recording of what was intended to be yet another live album. Over the course of the monthlong engagement, the shenanigans came back both on- and offstage, with the best one coming when the guys played their old gag on J.D. and the Stamps, dressing up as bad characters and pretending to stage an assassination attempt just to see the effect on the newcomers. Joyce came out to Vegas one last time, and, despite her feelings that she had no illusions left to shed, was shocked when she found herself in the ladies' room with a couple of working girls, who, thinking she was one of them, bragged of a twosome they had performed for Elvis. When she confronted him about it, he professed amused disbelief at her reaction.

"Honey," he laughed. "I never touched those girls. . . . The two of them made love, and I just watched. . . . Just a little innocent fun." Once again, before she left, she tried to talk to him about the drugs, but she could never penetrate his shell of messianic conviction. People listened to him, he told her, "because I know what they want and need. Like you. You should listen to me more. . . . I know what's good for you, baby. One day they'll all listen." His message, he said, was understanding.

"We all have divinity inside us, Joyce," he said, setting aside his book. "Some of us just understand it more."

I took the plunge. "Elvis, if we're gods, or at least have this 'divinity' in us, why do we need drugs?"

"Silence is the resting place of the soul. It's sacred. And necessary for new thoughts to be born. That's what my pills are for . . . to get as close as possible to that silence."

She left the next morning before he awoke, thinking, "What a small, dull, shitty way for it to end."

Priscilla meanwhile had been out so far only for the opening. Her absence for the remainder of the engagement continued to spark rumors, but there was as yet no public knowledge of their separation or, for that matter, on Elvis' part, of the reasons for it. When she came in at the end of the run, she was determined to tell him, although Joanie begged her not to. His reaction, according to Priscilla's memoir and what she told Joanie and some of the wives afterward, was the kind of unrestrained fury she had seen on occasion throughout their marriage but not in this form. "He grabbed me," she wrote, "and forcefully made love to me. It was uncomfortable and unlike any other time he'd ever made love to me before, and he explained, 'This is how a real man makes love to his woman.'"

She and Joanie left the next morning without telling anyone good-bye. When they met out in the hall, Joanie didn't know if she had told him or not. "I said, 'Did you?' And she said, 'Yes.' I said, 'Oh, you didn't.' I don't know how she ever had the courage. When we got back to L.A., I got a call from Joe about six o'clock that night, and he was *hot*. He said, 'What's this about Mike Stone? Is it true?' He didn't know. He'd bet Red West one hundred dollars, because Red immediately said, 'I knew that blankety-blank-blank [Mike Stone] was sneaking around. I knew we couldn't trust him.' And Joe said to Red, 'No, Elvis is making it up, because he wasn't being a good husband, and he had to [come up with] an excuse for her to leave, other than just that he wasn't a good husband.' So he called and was furious at me. But I told him, 'If you'd been around, you would have known.'"

ALOHA FROM HAWAII, JANUARY 14, 1973:
CHARLIE HODGE, JERRY SCHEFF, RONNIE TUTT, ELVIS, JAMES BURTON,
JOHN WILKINSON, KATHY WESTMORELAND, THE SWEET INSPIRATIONS,
J.D. SUMNER AND THE STAMPS (J.D. STANDING FAR RIGHT).
(COURTESY OF THE ESTATE OF ELVIS PRESLEY)

ON TOUR

O NE MONTH AFTER CLOSING in Las Vegas he was back in the studio, but not in Nashville this time. Instead, Felton, racked with pain and wasting away from the kidney disease that would kill him unless he got a transplant soon, came out to Los Angeles, where Elvis was scheduled to start filming rehearsals for the upcoming tour on March 30, the day after the recording session was finished. Six days later the tour itself would begin, the occasion for another hastily arranged MGM documentary, which dislodged the original concept for a Vegas live album with a live soundtrack album (to be called, like the film, *Standing Room Only*) and which would generate another $250,000 on top of the million dollars they were guaranteed by the concert promoters. It was just one more of the Colonel's intricately wrapped packages, but this time with a couple of differences: one was that the informal understanding that Elvis and Colonel had arrived at for a two-thirds–one-third division of the income from personal appearances had now been formalized with a February 4 contractual agreement acknowledging the Colonel's "unique contributions" as a justification for his one-third share; in addition, Management III was no longer the sole promoter of the tour. Through a series of carefully executed maneuvers, Colonel had inveigled RCA to go into the concert business as RCA Record Tours, to put up half the money and take half the risk on Elvis' show, and thus in effect to undercut Jerry Weintraub's influence, with everything now taking place directly under the Colonel's supervision.

Elvis could not have cared less about any of this. He was, everyone agreed, in a funny kind of mood, even for Elvis — chastened, brooding, almost perplexed over what could have finally caused Priscilla to leave, after all he had done to drive her to it. Some of the guys thought it was simply the humiliation of her going off with someone else, particularly someone that Elvis knew and admired, but it seemed as much a mood of almost autumnal regret. He kept listening to that damned Charles Boyer album

Where Does Love Go? over and over, until it just about drove them all crazy — listening intently to those melancholy recitations, as if they alone might provide the answer to the question that the album's title posed, the one question that seemed to be forever on his mind.

The intent of the session was first and foremost to come up with a hit single, something Elvis had been sorely lacking for the last year. The latest single, the Buffy Sainte-Marie song "Until It's Time for You to Go," was the fifth in a row to fail to crack the Top 30, with sales having declined precipitately over the past two years from a reasonable expectation of three-quarters of a million to a current level of 250,000. Felton arrived in California with high hopes for the session and for one song in particular, which he had picked up from his friend Bob Beckham in Nashville, who, with the sudden, explosive success of Kris Kristofferson, his principal songwriter at Combine Music, had become one of the hottest publishers in the country. The song, "Burning Love," was by a young writer named Dennis Linde, who had never gotten a major cut but with this song had produced a real rarity, a credible contemporary version of rock 'n' roll.

Felton soon discovered, however, that Elvis was in no mood for rock 'n' roll. The song with which they started out the session was one that Red had written and brought to Elvis because he knew that Elvis would respond to it. It was called "Separate Ways" and stemmed from painful personal experience; all that Red had to do was change the little boy in the song, a victim of the breakup of his parents' marriage, to a little girl, and it suited Elvis to a T. He stuck with the number through twenty-one emotionally grueling takes, and then they all sat around listening to the playback for a long time. "God, you guys are trying to kill me," Elvis said to Red and some of the others, who were going through similar experiences of their own. But he loved the song.

The next choice he settled on was Kris Kristofferson's "For the Good Times," which, as the title might suggest, was equally awash in bittersweet nostalgia. And by the time they finished off the evening with Paul Williams' lachrymose "Where Do I Go from Here?," in spite (or perhaps because) of the presence of Elvis' own band in the studio for the first time, there was little question of rock 'n' rolling, or even of cracking the kind of joke that might impress a newcomer in between takes. To bass player Emory Gordy, substituting for Jerry Scheff for the session, the experience was altogether different from what he had been led by his fellow Nashville studio players to expect. "Elvis was really concentrating on his performance. I mean, he was intense — he would listen to the playback, he'd get his part the way he wanted it, and he really concentrated."

From Felton's point of view, that was all very well, but he saw torpor where Gordy saw professionalism, he saw depression and an alarming lack of will — or perhaps it was just another kind of *willfulness* — and for the first time, he didn't feel that he, or anyone else, could really reach Elvis. Felton continued to have faith that Elvis could cut a hit record anytime he wanted. The trouble was, he wasn't interested in cutting a hit record. "He was trying to get something out of his system." It wasn't a question of his willingness to work; Felton might very well have wished that he had been as willing to work on the previous year's sessions. It was just that what they were getting was not what they needed right now, and Felton couldn't shake Elvis from his mood.

On the second night Felton finally got his way, but he was under no illusion that Elvis was doing it for any other reason than to indulge his producer. With the encouragement of Joe Esposito and Jerry Schilling, and with Charlie pounding away on acoustic guitar, they got a good, energetic version of "Burning Love," the song Felton had brought to the session, but it was tossed off in six quick takes, in almost throwaway style, and everyone could see that Elvis' heart wasn't really in it. They kept working till four in the morning but got only one more song that night and two the following night, including "Always On My Mind," another guilt-laden number that Red had brought to the session by "Mama Liked the Roses" author Johnny Christopher and Mark James, who had written what was by now practically Elvis' signature song about relationship problems, "Suspicious Minds."

The filmed studio "rehearsals" over the next couple of days were something of a pickup. He ran down the new songs for performance purposes and rehearsed a broad selection of old ones, giving out the kind of self-conscious stage directions that were meant to indicate who was in charge and even ending with a gospel jam that made the filmmakers feel as if they were privileged witnesses to a private moment. Gospel music, Elvis replied in answer to their eager questioning, was something he had grown up with from the time he was two years old, but it was just part of a musical landscape that included Mario Lanza and the Metropolitan Opera, too, a musical landscape that extended past borders of time and space and was always able to put your mind at ease. Often, after a show, he and the Stamps would get together and unwind with the kind of songs they were singing now. He had known J.D., he told them, since "he first came to Memphis to sing in a group called the Blackwood Brothers, and I was a big gospel music fan." It seemed like there was a special feeling among all the members of the group, said the filmmakers earnestly. "Well, I think it's because we constantly enjoy this music," Elvis replied. "You know, we do two shows a night for [four] weeks, but we never let it get old. Every time is like we do it for the first time — and that's one of the secrets."

THE TWO FILMMAKERS, Bob Abel and Pierre Adidge, scarcely knew him at all at this point. Fresh from the heady success of *Mad Dogs and Englishmen,* a last-ditch chronicle of the Woodstock generation that was almost as exhausting as the 1970 Joe Cocker tour it documented, they were already involved in a rock 'n' roll nostalgia film for Columbia (*Let the Good Times Roll,* featuring Chuck Berry, Little Richard, Fats Domino, Bill Haley, and Bo Diddley in concert), when MGM vice president Jack Haley approached them about this new project in February. Abel was not at all enthusiastic about taking on anything else at this point — he felt as if they had been through the wars with Joe Cocker and were lucky to have escaped. But Pierre Adidge insisted that they couldn't let this opportunity slip through their fingers; they should at least go to see Elvis' show in Vegas.

Bob Abel and Pierre Adidge came from very different backgrounds in film. Both in their early thirties, Abel had emerged from Colin Young's film class at UCLA with Francis Ford Coppola and Carroll Ballard and served his apprenticeship making television documentaries for David Wolper (*J.F.K: A Nation of Immigrants; Sophia: A Documentary Study of Sophia Loren; The Making of the President '68*), while maintaining a strong interest in music, cinema-verité technique, and the kind of split-screen special effects that had recently come into vogue. Adidge, a giant of a man as quietly self-possessed as Abel was garrulous, was a pioneer in sound recording whose audio partner, Jim Webb, had won wide renown for his work on Robert Altman's *M*A*S*H*. Together they had formed Cinema Associates in 1969 with the specific aim of making music documentaries, a calling which Abel likened to marrying the two great artistic statements of their time.

Neither one much liked the show that they saw in Vegas, and they were somewhat dismayed at the bloated appearance of the Elvis Presley that they met backstage — but at the same time, they were utterly, and completely, charmed. Elvis at first seemed under the impression that they were already committed to the project, but when he discovered that they were not, he drew them in, as he always did, by acting as if they were the ones who were doing the seducing and he was so glad of visitors from the outside world that he would have done anything to extend the visit. They told him they had no interest in repeating the wise-guy point of view of *That's the Way It Is*, a film that from Abel's perspective served to demean an aspect of the culture that they wanted to record and celebrate, but they got no response from Elvis on that issue. "I want to shoot the real you," Abel said without irony, "but the trade-off is, you've got to be open with me. If I feel that you're posing or doing something, I'll just turn the camera off. And then MGM will just be out a lot of money." "I like your honesty," Elvis said. "When do we start?"

Their meeting with Colonel Parker a week later was little more than a formality, and Pierre then went out with the Colonel on the pre-tour swing to scout locations, while Abel hired a crew and tried to pull everything together for the shoot. When they met up again at the rehearsal sessions, they knew that for all of their allegiance to cinema-verité ideals, and because of the very fact that they would be shooting with lightweight unobtrusive equipment, then blowing up the film to 70mm afterward, they would have to light Elvis carefully to try to minimize his eerily pale, strangely bloated appearance. It was not that he was fat — that would have been less disturbing to Abel, who recognized in Elvis some of the same traits that he saw in his partner's increasingly Demerol-addicted personality. He never doubted that Elvis would come through for them, though, even if, like so many outsiders to the Elvis world, he came to feel sorry for him.

"He had incredible native intelligence, the ability to read a human being, to watch someone's eyes and look inside their soul. He was very good with me. I think he was reading me, and he knew that he could switch from one aspect to another [of himself], and as long as that aspect was some part of him, that was okay with me. I mean, truth was truth. But I think there was a part of him that felt hollow, that he was a nobody, there were parts of him that he could not explore. I went into the rehearsals in a parochial sense, trying to get to know him, and the gospel part of it was a real insight. But I realized [after a while] with all of the musicians and bodyguards and sycophants around, that these guys had been around for seventeen years now telling the same stories and jokes, and what kind of a life is this? And do I film it? And if I film it, do I show it more than once to make a point?"

THE FIRST STOP ON THE TOUR was Buffalo, just recovering from a long, hard winter and turning out in force for Elvis in the raw, rainy night. The idea was for Abel to shoot this performance on a little Sony videotape machine, then fly back to California and study the film for a day or two, rejoining the show with a full camera crew in Hampton Roads, Virginia. Although Abel thought he had seen just about everything there was to see on the *Mad Dogs and Englishmen* tour, the fervor of the crowd, Elvis' own level of commitment and the audience's hunger for him, the *interchange* that existed between audience and performer, created a sense of energy and spontaneity that he had never experienced before. Back in Hollywood he transferred the tape to three-quarter-inch and ran it frame by frame to study the structure and choreography of the show, making up a master sheet of the entire concert with the music laid out for the cameramen.

By the time that he caught up with the show again in Hampton Roads four days later, some of the magic was gone. What had seemed tentative and fresh as it was being worked out was now practiced and rehearsed, and while the smoother operation didn't make it any less exciting, he regretted in a way missing out on capturing some of the raw edges. There were eleven cameras in a complicated setup, with sound cued by camera, and all the sound sources fused into a deck from which a temporary scratch track would be created. The cameras operated on a staggered schedule so that, with eleven-minute rolls of film, there would never be a complete shutdown, and with the lightweight state-of-the-art equipment (French Éclair cameras, NASA headsets, Swiss tape recorders to which Abel and Adidge had U.S. rights, and Wally Heider's mobile recording unit), they were able to move and shoot in a way that Denis Sanders had not even been able to contemplate with *That's the Way It Is*. The biggest difference in the two documentaries, though, as Abel and Adidge would have been the first to concede, was that they believed in "the romance of heroes": to them Elvis was a folk hero whose mythic journey was the subtext of their show.

They shot the next night in Richmond, and then Abel returned to California while Pierre remained behind to get documentary footage. After reviewing the concert film that they had, Abel made up 3 x 5's of what they might need in terms of both music and narrative threads, then rejoined the tour in Greensboro, North Carolina, where at MGM's directive he showed the Colonel some of the raw footage in a local moviehouse. Up till then he had felt as if Colonel had been watching them warily, afraid that with their youth and scraggly appearance, they might not really know what they were doing. Now "he pretty much gave us carte blanche, he said we had his blessings. I said we needed more access, and he said if we delivered, he'd deliver. He went into a long rap about how so many people had fucked over Elvis in the past, and he was the only one who'd looked after his image, and how careful he [had] to be. It was like the pep talk you get from a coach at halftime. He told us the story about people paying to get into the carny show, then paying to get out [when rain had made the field in which the carnival tent was pitched muddy, and he provided a donkey for the customers to ride out on without sinking into the mud and barnyard manure]. He said, 'Don't ever try to put something over on me, or you'll be up to your ears in elephant shit.' It ended with him saying, 'Go out there and make the best Elvis film ever.' And he slammed his cane down."

None of the other shows worked as well as the first, though they kept hoping for a repetition of Buffalo, or at least of Hampton Roads. They finished up in San Antonio, Texas, the next-to-last night of the tour, which gave them four concerts over two full weeks of shooting, with plenty of perfectly good footage to choose from. For Abel, though, it was Pierre's documentary crew which had captured the defining moment of the film. Elvis is sitting in his limo after the show in Jacksonville, Florida, a towel draped over his head. He is exhausted and speaking in broken phrases about the concert and whatever else is on his mind. "Hot time in Florida," he says and sings the line "Rainy night in Georgia," half under his breath before he and Charlie and Red harmonize briefly on "For the Good Times." Then there is a moment, accentuated in the finished film, in which Elvis is looking out the car window, his mind a million miles away, the same dreamy expression on his face as in the 1956 photograph that the directors use to illustrate his essential, unchanging isolation. It is a "small, private" revelation, as Abel described it, but what is left out of the movie is the revelation that precedes it in the car on the way to the concert, in which Elvis confides to the guys, with impish delight, that he had his face "buried in a beaver" the previous night, perhaps an equally defining moment.

To complete the film that they had envisioned (soon to be retitled *Elvis On Tour*), Abel and Adidge knew they had to have something special, and what they fought for over the next few months was a candid audio-only interview with Elvis to serve as a kind of glue to hold the picture together. The Colonel was no help to them here. This was the kind of unmanaged exposure to which he had been opposed all his managerial life; if they could get Elvis' approval, he wouldn't stand in their way, but they were on their own now, he shrugged, strongly implying that without him there was no way Elvis would go along.

He had not taken Jerry Schilling into account, however. Jerry had gone to work for Abel and Adidge as an assistant editor on the film as soon as they got back to Hollywood and had a chance to evaluate the footage. Elvis hadn't liked the idea of Jerry working for them at first; in fact, the filmmakers hadn't thought much of the idea themselves, with each party suspicious of the other's motives. Finally Jerry, who saw this as a long-awaited opportunity to move ahead in his chosen field after a lengthy apprenticeship at Paramount, managed to persuade Cinema Associates of his sincerity by volunteering to work on *Let the Good Times Roll* (their other rock 'n' roll film) exclusively. It was at this point that both parties finally saw the light, with each one embracing the idea that Jerry could give them a foot in the other's camp. Elvis, knowing Jerry's loyalty, was confident that his involvement in the editorial process would help keep the film on an even keel. Abel and Adidge, who were by now equally convinced of Jerry's integrity and sincerity, saw his involvement as their opportunity to influence Elvis.

That was pretty much how it worked out. Jerry had already convinced Elvis to allow the filmmakers to use some classic stills from the period of his earliest success (the Colonel opposed this on the grounds that you always sell your present, not your past), and he had persuaded the filmmakers in turn to include shots that were suitably "Brandoesque." The interview presented a greater challenge, but here, too, Jerry succeeded on the strength of his own conviction that this film was important, that the film was a record of the man, that the interspersed interview segments would provide context and story line, above all that Elvis would acquit himself well.

Elvis came into the MGM studio looking even paler and more bloated than he had during the tour. He apologized to the filmmakers for not having been able to accommodate them sooner — another tour had intervened, he had been busy with various domestic problems having to do with the breakup of his marriage, he told them, and a girl he had been going out with recently had just been killed in a car crash. He sat on a chair in the familiar dressing room, where he had made so many pictures, with his two interviewers across from him, a coffee table in between. Over Abel's objections a number of the guys were present, observing the proceedings somewhat balefully, but Elvis seemed to freeze them all out, except for Jerry, who was perched on a director's chair over Abel's right shoulder.

They started off by getting his reactions to some of the old photographs. The voice is warm, hesitant, genuinely self-effacing, you get the same sense that his audience got of him from the start: that he is communicating directly without the benefit of any kind of screen. The crowd reaction surprised him to begin with, he says, speaking of the show at the Overton Park shell. "The first time it happened, the first time that I appeared onstage . . . it scared me to death, man. I didn't know what I'd done." And, he said, in a real sense, it had never changed. "I work absolutely to [the audience], whether it's six or six thousand, it doesn't really matter; they bring it out of me — the inspiration, the ham." And if it didn't work? If it didn't go over? Pierre asked. "I change the songs around. I'll go back and stay up all night and work — working on it, you know, worrying about it, I find out what it is that's not getting off the ground, you know, the first four or five numbers. Because it's very important."

He still was scared before every performance, he never wanted to arrive too early for a show he still got so keyed up, and he demanded the same kind of intensity from his musicians. One time he heard some of the guys in the orchestra talking while he was onstage in Vegas: "Those guys were reading *Better Homes and Gardens* and stuff like that — they play music so well they can play their part and they'd say, 'Think I should build that patio on my house?'. . . So what I did, I switched songs on them. And the orchestra was there, they'd go into the intro, and I'd say, 'Whoa, I don't want to do that song, let's do something [else].' So they'd go through the sheet music real quick, and consequentially I got them; they *had* to watch me."

He spoke about the show, how it embodied all the elements that he had dreamt of since he was a child, when he would go out to Overton Park on a Sunday afternoon to hear the Memphis Symphony play. He spoke of singing, of how "I first realized that I could sing at about two years of age," and then later "people would listen to me around the housing project where I lived," but at school, "nobody knew I sang" until the eleventh grade. "I wasn't popular in school. I wasn't dating anybody at that school. I failed music — only thing I ever failed. And [then] they entered me in this talent show. . . . It was amazing how popular I became in school after that." What had his father thought about his playing the guitar for a living? Jerry asked, prompting him to tell one of the old familiar stories that the outside world might like to hear. "My daddy had seen a lot of people who played guitars and stuff and didn't work, so he said, 'You should make up your mind either about being an electrician or playing a guitar. I never saw a guitar player that was worth a damn.'" Amid laughter, Elvis said, "It's funny, I say it to him every once in a while, and he just laughs about it, he gets embarrassed if I say it in front of somebody. Here I was having an epileptic fit [in his early performances], and they just happened to film it!"

They spoke of any number of other things, Elvis dispensed some of his usual bromides about the army and the early years, but he didn't become truly engaged until he started talking about the movies. "It was work," he said mildly at first. "It was a job. I had to be there at a certain time in the morning and work a certain amount of hours, and that's exactly how I treated it."

As time went on, however, and picture followed picture: "I cared so much until I became physically ill. I would become violently ill. I'd get a temperature, something would happen to me . . . at a certain stage I had no say-so in it. I didn't have final approval on the script, which means that I couldn't tell you, 'This is not good for me.'. . . I don't think anyone was consciously trying to harm me. It was just Hollywood's image of me was wrong, and I knew it, and I couldn't say anything about it, couldn't do anything about it. . . . I was never indifferent, I was so concerned until that's all I talked about. It worried me sick, so I had to change it. Which I did."

Bob Abel tried to get him off the subject and have him talk about his *achievements* in pictures, the great dance sequence in *Jailhouse Rock* for which his own spontaneous movements had provided the inspiration, but Jerry brought him back to what he seemed to really want to talk about. "I had thought that they would . . . give me a chance to show some kind of acting ability or do a very interesting story, but it did not change, it did not change, and so I became very discouraged. *They couldn't have paid me no amount of money in the world to make me feel self-satisfaction inside.*"

"But you still did them, you must have forced yourself —" said Pierre.

"I had to. I had to."

It was a curious moment. No one was named — he explicitly acknowledged that there was no one to blame — but it was as if he were musing for a moment on his entire career, seeing it as a series of missteps in which he had never really taken control, with a bitterness that had never crept into his public discourse before (and that ultimately would not be revealed in

the movie). "I really took it as long as I could," Elvis said. "Physically, emotionally, and everything." Then, appearing to recognize what he had said,
he tried to backtrack: "Not all the movies were that bad. Um, in between, I
would do something that was entertaining to people, just of a pure entertainment nature . . . they worked well on television." But then, seemingly
unable to stop himself once again, he lashed out at Steve Allen for humiliat-
ing him on television sixteen years earlier, when he was forced to don top
hat and tails and sing to a dog: "That was Steve Allen's humor. To me it was
about as funny as a crutch. Again, I had to do —"

It was a most peculiar performance, forty minutes and out, the runaway rush of emotion contained once again by the time he got to the door.
It would be hard to say what the Colonel's assessment of that performance
might have been. In the time-honored tradition of the carnival, nothing
was ever truly revealed, the curtain was never parted, the mask never taken
off — and Abel and Adidge never really knew the man who was speaking to
them, one mask was merely substituted for another. But at the same time, a
deeper truth *was* revealed, the same one that Marion Keisker had intuited
when an eighteen-year-old Elvis Presley first entered the Sun studio. "He
was like a mirror," Sam Phillips' assistant had observed. "Whatever you
were looking for, you were going to find in him. It was not in him to lie or
say anything malicious. He had all the intricacy of the very simple."

T HE TWELVE-DAY TOUR they had gone out on in June had proved two
things. One was the roadworthiness of the crew. They were up to sev-
enty or seventy-five troupe members now, including tech people, equipment handlers, orchestra members, and concessionaires. They traveled in
three leased planes, with two complete stage setups, no longer a once-a-
year side trip, but a finely calibrated operation, with the Colonel leading
the advance. They had even conquered New York, opening the tour with
four shows at Madison Square Garden to a reception that went beyond
Colonel's or RCA's or anyone else's expectations.

Elvis had never played New York before. After all the supercilious gibes
and jeers that had come from there at the beginning of his career, he and
Colonel had been understandably leery of exposing themselves to further
humiliations — besides, the expense of the building, the promotional costs,
and all the other costs of doing business in New York City were so far
beyond what they were accustomed to pay elsewhere, there never seemed

any point to it. But now there did. With the scope of their new operation, and the degree of acceptance that Elvis had achieved, it seemed like a challenge worth undertaking — and the Colonel added yet another twist when he attached a live album to it (the one that had been started in Las Vegas was to be jettisoned), with a release date one week after the last of the Garden concerts, to foil the bootleggers, Colonel said.

The gamble proved an almost unqualified success, as they sold out all four performances, eighty thousand tickets at $10 tops, for a $730,000 gross over three days. They captivated the New York press, too, with Colonel in his customary role as ringmaster introducing Elvis at a Friday afternoon press conference, Colonel in a cheap Summer Festival imitation straw hat and Elvis, in his patented star turn, dazzling jaded reporters with his usual combination of self-deprecation, braggadocio, and casual insouciance.

Why did he think he'd outlasted every other performer from his generation? "I take Vitamin E," he said quickly, then as the room erupted in laughter, "I was only kidding. I embarrassed myself, man. . . . I enjoy the business. I like what I'm doing." What about his image as a shy, humble country boy? Elvis seems momentarily baffled. "I don't know what makes them say that," he says with a look of some perplexity, then stands and opens up his light blue Edwardian-style jacket with bold plaid lining to reveal the International gold belt. "Elvis," asked one reporter, "are you satisfied with the image you've established?" "Well, the image is one thing and the human being another," he said, and then, in response to a follow-up question, volunteered, "It's very hard to live up to an image." His father sat to his left, the Colonel to his right. Vernon was asked about his son's overnight success, when he realized that celebrity had claimed his child. "Well, it's kind of hard to say," he said. "It happened so fast, it's hard to keep up with it, you know. Just, boom, overnight, and there it was." Did the father have any regrets? "No, no, I haven't. In fact, I've enjoyed it, really." "All kidding aside," Elvis said, taking over smoothly, "it happened very fast. My mother and father, all of us — everything happened overnight. We had to adjust to a lot of things very quickly. A lot of good things, I might add."

The only untoward incident came when Jackie Kahane, who tended to test the limits of a more sophisticated audience's patience, got booed off the stage the first night, but then the show rallied behind Jackie after Al Dvorin introduced the crushed comedian as "a personal friend of Elvis'" for the rest of the engagement and insisted that he be given all due respect because "we work as a family." The press fell all over themselves, on the other hand, to recognize Elvis: the *New York Times* alone ran three stories on the show, with the headline of Chris Chase's piece, "Like a Prince from Another Planet," summing up the overall reaction. "Once in a great while," Chase concluded, in a story that initially voiced skepticism, then surprise that skepticism could so easily be overcome, "a special champion comes along, a Joe Louis, a José Capablanca, a Joe DiMaggio, someone in whose hands the way a thing is done becomes more important than the thing itself. When DiMaggio hit a baseball, his grace made the act look easy and inevitable. . . . Friday night, at Madison Square Garden, Elvis was like that. He stood there at the end, his arms stretched out, the great gold cloak giving him wings, a champion, the only one in his class."

B ACK HOME IN MEMPHIS for a month at the end of the tour, Elvis had little thought of duende — he seemed more interested in finding a girlfriend. Out in L.A. he had been seeing a dancer named Sandra Zancan, to whom he had given a white sports car and a ruby ring, and for a while he was dating a go-go girl from T.J.'s in Memphis to whom he gave a white Mark IV. There were a number of other girls, but it was obvious to everyone that he was not his old self, and he made no secret of his continued preoccupation with Priscilla's departure.

Then on July 6 he met Linda Thompson at the Memphian Theatre. The twenty-two-year-old Thompson, a former Miss Memphis State and Miss Liberty Bowl and the present Miss Tennessee, had been invited to the Memphian by local RCA promo man Bill Browder, because he thought she might capture Elvis' interest. Linda, who was as bright and vivacious as she was pretty, was of enough different minds about the situation that she brought a friend, Jeannie LeMay (Miss Rhode Island), for protection and parked in a no-parking zone, just in case she needed to make a quick getaway. Once inside the theater, though, things went smoothly enough, as George Klein, who knew her from her frequent guest appearances on his television show, made sure that she felt comfortable, and Elvis couldn't have been more of a gentleman. She was amused when he tried the old yawn-and-stretch routine to put his arm around her, but he hastened to assure her that he was no longer married, that he had in fact been separated since January. When she said, "I'm really sorry to hear that, but I could have told you a long time ago, you should have married a Memphis girl," he burst out laughing.

She didn't get home until four o'clock in the morning, and her aunt, with whom she was spending the summer, pumped her for details. "My Aunt Betty was a big Elvis fan, she was about his age. She said, 'So?' And I said, 'We met —' And Jeannie said, 'He likes her. They were sitting there kissing. He had his arm around her. He wants to date her.' And my aunt was going nuts! 'Elvis! Oh, my God! Are you serious?' And then the phone rings, and she said, 'Who could that be?' And it was Elvis. He said, 'Can I speak to Linda?' And she said, 'Certainly, just one moment, please,' then screams, 'Oh, my God,' and hands over the phone. So I go to the phone, and his speech was a little slurred, and I thought, 'Gee, he wasn't drinking when I saw him at the movie theater. I wonder if he went home and had a drink or something.' I was so ignorant in so many ways. I didn't know anything about drugs. I said, 'Are you sleepy? Are you really sleepy?' He said, 'Yeah, pretty tired.' But I just couldn't fathom it. He was saying things like, 'I'm so happy that I met you tonight. Where have you been all my life? I need to be with you. I can't believe I haven't met you before now.' Pretty strong stuff to say to someone you just met a few hours before. I'm going, 'Gee . . .' I remarked to my Aunt Betty, 'I think he might have been drinking!'"

The next night she went back to the movies and then to Graceland after the show. She and her aunt Betty and uncle Steve and the kids were about to leave for Gulf Shores, Alabama, on vacation early that morning, but she went anyway, rode around on golf carts with the whole gang, and then accepted Elvis' invitation to go up to his bedroom. "Jeannie was saying, 'Don't go, be careful!' She thought he was moving in for the kill, but I went upstairs with him, and we just read. We kissed, we made out — which was wonderful — and then we read the Bible. We felt as if we'd known each other all our lives — and we kind of did [through knowing] how the other person was brought up. When I got back to my aunt's, she was going, 'Honey, honey child, where y'all been? We've got to leave out of here in an hour.' And all the way to Alabama we played Elvis tapes. And I said, 'Do you think I'll ever hear from him again?'"

She was gone for three weeks, without a phone for him to find her with. In the meantime Elvis met and dated Cybill Shepherd, another Memphis beauty queen, who had just completed *The Heartbreak Kid* and was on vacation from moviemaking and her steady boyfriend, film director Peter Bogdanovich. He remained in touch with Sandra Zancan, too, but he couldn't get Linda out of his mind. When she came home from Alabama, the phone was already ringing. It was Joe calling from L.A.; they had been trying to reach her every day since she left.

"Then Elvis got on the phone and said, 'Who do you think I am? I thought this was the beginning of something pretty great, and then you just disappear for three weeks like that.' So I think it probably captured his attention!" He wanted her to join him in Las Vegas, where he was opening in less than a week. She never had any hesitation. Though she was still a virgin and maintained strong religious convictions, there was no choice. "I had gone four years to Memphis State and was short twelve hours in Theater and English, a double major. I didn't [really] want to go back, and I didn't want to teach. I was thinking about coming to Los Angeles and starting my acting career, or becoming a stewardess for a while, or going to New York to be a model — I was ready to travel the world and do some fun things. Then I met Prince Charming, and he made my decision for me."

She flew out to Los Angeles the next day, then flew in to Vegas with Elvis, where he was starting rehearsals for his opening later in the week. In her college clothes she felt as if she was stepping into a big frat-house party — just without the keg. She couldn't believe how nice everyone was to her; she couldn't believe the luxuriousness of the appointments — even though they were only on the twenty-ninth floor during rehearsals, they had not yet moved up to the star suite. She realized on the first night, though, that there was something wrong, as that strangely "drunken" quality that she had heard on the phone reappeared in his voice. Earlier in the evening she had noticed all the pill bottles on his side of the bed. She asked him if he was sick, and he said no, he just had a little cold. Then they had dinner, and it was all very romantic, "he was so loving and affectionate, [but afterward] we were standing outside talking, and he seemed to stagger a little and to have slurred speech. I said, 'Are you okay?' And he said, 'Awww, I'm okay, honey, I just had a little sleeping pill.' I said, 'You take sleeping pills?' He said, 'Oh, yeah, I've had a problem sleeping ever since I was a kid.' I thought it was strange, but the whole experience was strange to me, too. I wish I had been more worldly, more knowledgeable. But I just accepted it and didn't realize the magnitude [of the problem] until a few weeks into the relationship."

Everyone liked Linda. Though she was not the only girl to visit in Vegas that summer (Cybill Shepherd and Sandra Zancan each came out while she was absent), by the end of the engagement he had made his choice. She liked to laugh, she was refreshingly natural and down-to-earth, she adapted to his lifestyle, she was, in her own later assessment, "very young and very resilient and not enough of a total human being to have any predetermined notions about life and the rigidity of life. I was very happy to be with him, I was very happy to share life with him." She changed her sleeping habits, exchanged day for night, talked baby talk with him, and made him laugh with her antics — she became a "lifer," in the term the guys used to describe themselves. It was clear she was going to be around for a while.

M EANWHILE THE SEPARATION from Priscilla had become official on July 26. She had returned to Graceland the previous week to collect her things and pay Grandma an emotional farewell, though she swore she would stay in touch. At the end of July, Rona Barrett reported in her column that "Priscilla is very anxious at this time to regain her freedom, the reason allegedly being a karate expert named Mike Stone [with whom] Priscilla has been seen several times dining . . . in public places," and the July 30 *Sunday Tribune*'s headline announced, "Black Belt Karate Man Splits Presleys." Elvis was getting reports that she had been spotted with Stone at various tournaments, laughing and animated, sometimes even handing out programs, in what must have seemed like an open rebuke to her former lifestyle. On August 18 it was announced that a divorce action had been entered in Santa Monica Superior Court. The terms of the settlement — a minimal $100,000 lump payment (with $50,000 to be paid upfront), plus $1,000-a-month spousal and $500 child support — were not reported but had been worked out in a joint conference with Elvis' lawyer Ed Hookstratten, and according to Hookstratten were all that Priscilla wanted, his own advice to the contrary notwithstanding. It amounted to an implicit rejection of anything that Elvis might have to offer her.

Elvis' own divided state was clearly indicated by the sharp acceleration in doctors' visits throughout the Vegas engagement. Where once he was content with medications before and between each show and before retiring for the night, now he was receiving medical attention up to five times a day, with results such as Linda observed. This was the first booking under the Colonel's new arrangement with the Hilton, which not only raised Elvis' salary to $130,000 a week (with an increase to $150,000 starting in 1974 and all previous verbal commitments still in place), but assigned a salary of $50,000 to the Colonel for all of his efforts promoting the Hilton chain throughout the country. He had achieved this with hints about deserting the Hilton for Kirk Kerkorian's presently under-construction MGM Grand (hints which, in his usual fashion, he had communicated by denying news reports to that effect) and with a direct threat the previous March to vacate his offices and remove all of his belongings lock, stock, and barrel, because neither he nor his client was sufficiently appreciated. Elvis meanwhile put on a good show, though many reviewers remarked upon the star's somewhat somber mien: there was little karate, far less interplay with the audience than usual, and, seemingly, increased attention to music with an emphasis on heartache and loss. *Variety* applauded this evidence of renewed discipline "with a welcome absence of horseplay and inside gags." Some of the fans had mixed feelings about it — they worried about Elvis — while Robert Hilburn reported in the *Los Angeles Times* that the show had Elvis Presley operating at "only about 60% of his musical potential," even if it was a considerable improvement over the previous January.

On September 4, the final day of the engagement, Colonel set up a press conference between shows to confirm officially the date and place of an event that had first been spoken of in July, an NBC television broadcast via satellite transmission that would take place in Hawaii in January (it was to be called *Aloha From Hawaii*) and reach an estimated 1.5 billion viewers worldwide. With new RCA president Rocco Laginestra at his side, Elvis answered questions from reporters who had already been fully briefed on all the historic landmarks that this broadcast would establish: the first time that a full-fledged entertainment special would be beamed worldwide via satellite; the largest audience ever to see a television show, "in excess of one billion people," who would view it "on successive evenings beginning January 15, 1973"; "the first time in the history of the record industry" that an album (the follow-up soundtrack) would be released simultaneously on a global basis. Flanked by a poster board drawn up according to the Colonel's specifications and six rows of Elvis Summer Festival hats festooned with the names of each country in which it was hoped the spectacular would be broadcast, the RCA president congratulated the entertainer and his manager on their bold leap into the future while the Colonel beamed. As he had stated to reporters in an earlier press release, "It is the intention of Elvis to please all of his fans throughout the world." And if it was "impossible for us to play in every city" throughout the world, perhaps, it was implied, this would serve at least as evidence of their good faith.

Rocco Laginestra's presence was neither accidental nor merely the pro forma appearance of a record company executive on behalf of his biggest star. In fact, as the accompanying RCA press release made clear, RCA was not merely the proud progenitor, it was the *producer* of the show in the form of RCA Record Tours, which had been set up to begin with solely at the Colonel's behest to co-promote the tours. Now, in a single swift coup, the Colonel was getting rid of Jerry Weintraub and Management III, with RCA Record Tours not only "presenting" the television special (this meant that they would be paid $1 million by NBC, of which RCA got to keep $100,000, while the star and his manager divided $900,000 between them) but embarking upon a new arrangement with Elvis and the Colonel whereby they became the exclusive promoters of fifty Elvis Presley concerts, for a guarantee of $4 million, plus a $250,000 bonus, over the next fifteen months.

Under pressure from the Colonel on all fronts, they may have been less-than-willing partners in this enterprise, but they were partners nonetheless. The Colonel had been squawking about one thing or another, mostly the alarming number of budget-line Camden albums that were coming back as returns, since early April. As Elvis' sales steadily fell, his manager leveled accusations of incompetence, and in case this did not carry sufficient weight, he raised the issue of "the many verbal agreements" that existed which had not been put in writing out of consideration for RCA's obligations to other artists with "favored nations" clauses in their contracts. Perhaps "new people" at RCA were thinking of not honoring these agreements; if that was the case Elvis and the Colonel would merely fulfill their contractual obligations, dispense with providing any additional product, and concentrate on touring, which was much more profitable anyway. In August, with two hits on the charts ("Burning Love," the single that Elvis had not wanted to record, eventually reached number two and was Elvis' first million-selling single since 1970, while *Elvis As Recorded At Madison Square Garden* was certified gold at the beginning of the Las Vegas run), the Colonel escalated both his rhetoric and his demands. He *knew* where RCA accounting had buried $600,000 that was owed to them, he declared at an August 11 meeting; it was he, and he alone, who was keeping Vernon from making even harsher demands, by exercising, he hinted, certain discretionary judgments about what Vernon should and should not know; he was expecting, he concluded, a minimum of $500,000 to $600,000 to show up on their next royalty payment.

This was the climate in which RCA became his full-fledged partner. Like Hollywood studio heads before them, the company's executives were not so much intimidated as utterly baffled by the Colonel; they simply did not know what to make of him. In interoffice memos they discussed the problem, much as Hal Wallis and Joe Hazen had discussed the same problem over the years: How was it that this clownish figure, whom they were perfectly prepared to patronize for his lack of polish and lack of manners, always acted as if he held all the cards, even as they were looking at four aces? RCA's chief financial officer Mel Ilberman, as hardheaded a businessman as you could find, did not take easily to being bullied, but the Colonel had so many weapons in his arsenal, and it was so hard to tell just what target he had in his sights, that in October Ilberman raised the possibility in an internal memo of a complete buyout of Elvis' catalogue to date, just to get the Colonel out of their hair.

Meanwhile, Elvis took questions at the press conference, sitting slouched in an upholstered desk chair, in a white high-collared suit, looking relaxed to the point of boredom and unable to muster anything more than, "It's very hard to comprehend it. In fifteen years it's very hard to comprehend that happening. . . . It's very difficult to comprehend, but it's my favorite part of the business, a live concert." The Colonel, on the other hand, was practically brimming over with excitement at the idea that his long-standing dream was at last about to be realized. He had originally gotten the idea for satellite transmission from the live broadcasts of President Nixon's historic trip to China in February. He had had to overcome Elvis' initial opposition, sell the idea to RCA, and get Tom Sarnoff at NBC to go along with it. Then, with a November 18 date announced to match up with the conclusion of the November tour, Jim Aubrey had begged him to postpone the broadcast because MGM was planning to release *Elvis On Tour* in movie theaters at that time. With his usual instinct for adapting to whatever terrain happened to present itself, Colonel had made a tactical retreat, graciously acceding to Aubrey and acquiring a chit that might or might not ever come in handy. He kept the November concerts in Honolulu, though, and simply reconceived the plan on a grander scale, with a stand-alone show in January that would serve no other purpose than to embrace the world and its citizens.

* * *

THE SCALE, AND THE AMBITIOUSNESS, of the project just kept on growing as the Colonel worked out further details. Two weeks after the Vegas press conference Colonel got a letter from *Honolulu Advertiser* columnist Eddie Sherman, who had read in news accounts that there would be no admission charged for the concert, just voluntary contributions which would go to charity. Elvis and Colonel had made the first such contribution on the spot with a check for $1,000. Why not make that charity the Kui Lee Cancer Fund? Sherman suggested in his letter. After all, Elvis and the Colonel had done so much for Hawaii when they graciously donated their efforts to the U.S.S. *Arizona* Memorial eleven years ago. Here was an opportunity to carry on their good work by raising money for cancer research in the name of a beloved Hawaiian musician, one of whose signature songs, "I'll Remember You," Elvis had recorded in 1966, the year of Lee's death, and still frequently performed in concert.

Much as he had when presented with the earlier challenge, Colonel seized upon the opportunity, and after the three November dates in Hawaii at the conclusion of their first RCA Records tour, he staged yet another press conference both to hype the upcoming special and to announce its dedication to the Kui Lee Cancer Fund. With Rocco Laginestra once again at his side, he set $25,000 as the public goal, but privately he was committed to doubling that amount at the very least.

Elvis meanwhile had gotten caught up in the excitement himself. The idea had finally captured his imagination, and when he met with Bill Belew for costume ideas he brainstormed for something different, something that would say "America" to the world. "He came up with the American eagle [as a motif for the jumpsuit that he would wear]. It was one of only three times in all the times that we were together that he ever made any requests. We made an American eagle belt for it, a white leather belt about three or four inches wide with four or five ovals with American eagles on them. And, of course, the cape."

He met with Marty Pasetta, too, the experienced forty-one-year-old producer-director whom NBC had chosen for his familiarity with Hawaii (he had made five Don Ho specials), music (Bing Crosby, Glen Campbell, and Perry Como specials), and major events (he had produced and directed Grammy, Emmy, and Academy Award programs, as well as the Ice Capades). Pasetta had attended the Long Beach show on the November tour and came away decidedly unimpressed. It was a dull show from his point of view, full of posturing and tableaus, just not very exciting television. When he went to Vegas to see Elvis after the tour, he met first with the Colonel, arriving fully equipped with sketches of a stage setup that he felt might inject a little more pizzazz. In his conception the band was set up on a riser behind Elvis, the stage was lowered for greater audience accessibility, and there was a runway that extended out onto the floor. "The Colonel looked at it and made a very fast decision. He said, 'No way. That's not what he is all about.' I said, 'Well, wait a minute. I hate to be ruled out. I'd like at least to present this to Elvis and see what he might say.' He says, 'No, he's not going to do this. He won't do it. But if you really want to try. . . . But I'm against it. And I'll talk to him, too.'"

It was the old shell game, though Pasetta would have had no way of knowing it at the time. When he went upstairs to meet with Elvis, he was kept waiting as the guys glowered at him from behind dark glasses, "and I had my little drawings, and I said, 'Oh, my God, I'm going to be eaten alive.' Then Elvis came in, and they took out their guns and laid them on the table, and that really got me unnerved. I couldn't see Elvis' eyes behind his shades, but I figured, What the hell have I got to lose? [So] I said, 'I saw you in this show in Long Beach, and you didn't do much action, you were boring — but I'll tell you, I'm going to do something about that.'"

He went on in that vein, unveiling his sketches, explaining his idea to have lights that spelled out "Elvis" in different alphabets in "all the languages of the world," getting little reaction from either Elvis or his impassive bodyguards until he finally said, "And you've got to lose weight, because you're too fat." At that point, according to Pasetta, "Elvis threw off his dark glasses, leaned back, and started to laugh so hard he couldn't stop. Then he got up, walked over and hugged me, and said, 'I'll do whatever you want me to. I love the idea.' I said, 'We're gonna make super magic for the tube, and we'll do it together.'"

Pasetta immediately went about getting the set built on the mainland for shipment to Hawaii, where additional scenery was to be constructed. There was little more than a month's lead time, and an enormous amount to be done. Colonel volunteered several ideas to Pasetta, including a staged helicopter arrival, which eventually became the opening scene of the special, and a whole show, with bands, hula dancers, and little robots, for the crowd outside the arena waiting to get in. "He wanted a circus-type atmosphere, which was very apropos, because this was a unique, first-time [thing], the vibes in the air were just unmeasurable."

Most of all, everyone was excited by Elvis' evident excitement: he no longer seemed passive and withdrawn, as he had for much of the year. He and Charlie and Red pored over material, coming up with a list of a dozen or so songs (including show staples like "You Gave Me a Mountain" and "My Way" and long-standing favorites like "What Now My Love" and "The Twelfth of Never") that had never been released on record by him before, looking for ways to introduce variety and pacing into the show. Elvis even went on a quick-fix diet that he had picked up in Vegas and, with Sonny and a couple of the other guys, took a daily injection that Sonny understood to include urine from a pregnant woman while eating no more than five hundred calories a day of dried food. Elvis was fully committed to the project, the guys all told each other; he seemed primed in every way for the challenge. Even the Colonel, who continued to pull off feats of never-before-seen-or-dreamt-of prestidigitation, seemed willing to believe that this was all Elvis had needed all along. No one seemed to consider that this might be Elvis' own sleight of hand, that he might be putting on his best performance for them now.

H E AND LINDA spent virtually every minute of every day together. From the time that he closed in Vegas, she was almost constantly by his side. "I was with him twenty-four hours a day — I mean, he literally didn't even want to go to the bathroom unless I went in there with him. I realize it wasn't healthy, but he was my first great, great love, kind of my introduction to adult love, and I thought it was natural to be with someone all the time.

"He was very secure, very vulnerable with me — we were very much a part of each other. There were times when he was the father and I was the daughter, times when I was the mommy and he was the baby; sometimes he would say, 'I need to be little man, you need to be the big person now.' We kind of just geared off each other and understood the moods and became what the other needed for the moment. You know, honestly, my life just revolved around him."

She was surprised to discover how insular that life was; she was surprised in a way to discover how much he needed her. She realized early on that she had to be constantly vigilant, like a mother for her child; though he offered her pills she was never tempted, because several times he fell asleep while chewing his food, and he might have choked to death if she hadn't remained awake. It was a great romance but a great burden, too, and far from her world enlarging, she discovered like others before her, it actually shrank. They shared each other's passions, laughed at each other's jokes, read Elvis' books together, and called each other by pet names (Elvis frequently called her "Mommy," or "Ariadne" for the three-year-old in *Follow That Dream*). For Christmas he gave her a fur coat and a diamond ring, and, showing off for the guys, asked her to go upstairs and put on her Miss Tennessee banner and crown. "I said, 'Come onnn, that's really corny.' [But] I went up and put on an evening gown and my banner and crown and descended the stairs as if I were really into it, my beauty queen role. Then, when I got to the bottom of the stairs, I smiled, showing my blackened-out front teeth, and said, 'Is this what you have in mind, darling?' And he just died laughing."

T HEY ARRIVED IN HAWAII on January 9, just five days before the show was scheduled to air. Elvis was accompanied by the usual retinue of guys, wives, girlfriends, family, and Memphis friends, adding up to close to two dozen in all. He and Sonny had succeeded in losing about twenty-five pounds apiece, but not before undertaking two full courses of the Las Vegas diet to do so, something about which Sonny had serious reservations since there were health cautionaries urging at least a three-month interval before renewing the regimen. Elvis had no such reservations, of course, and he looked better and appeared happier in Linda's constant, sunny presence. With the distinct upturn that business conditions had taken, it seemed as if happy times might at last have returned.

The money was certainly coming in once again from all sources: big screen, small screen, record sales, and personal appearances. *On Tour* had opened to good business in November, with an unusual flurry of publicity and glowing reviews (the lead story in *Rolling Stone* was entitled "At Last — The First Elvis Presley Movie"); it had even been nominated for a Golden Globe Award as Best Feature Documentary. Sales of the latest single, Red's "Separate Ways," paired at Elvis' insistence with another of the session's heartbreak songs, "Always On My Mind," had proved a little disappointing, but the record would eventually go on to sell half a million copies, well beyond any other single since 1970 except for "Burning Love." Moreover, in an off-the-wall maneuver which the Colonel had concocted to try to rescue the languishing Camden line (and his automatic 50 percent share of the proceeds), "Burning Love" had been employed as the lead-in to a hodgepodge of leftovers titled *Burning Love and Hits From His Movies,* which, in a marketing coup defying all logic of aesthetics and taste, had gone on to sell nearly a million copies. It was, RCA announced in the familiar language of the Colonel, an Industry First: "the first time that a current hit single has been included in an album on a budget label by the original artist," a breakthrough which had been achieved against all odds by virtue of "public demand and requests that the single be included in an album."

Felton attended the *Aloha* rehearsals, though he was not in charge of the project (this had been taken over entirely, in the wake of Felton's illness, by the home office in New York, with Joan Deary coordinating all details), and his only input would come in the quadraphonic mixing to be done in Los Angeles immediately following the show. He knew nothing about this new recording process (stereo doubled), and he had real misgivings about his future role at the record company, given Deary's evident ambition, but he looked and felt better than he had in years, after undergoing successful kidney transplant surgery in early October. He took comfort in the fact that Elvis had stuck by him through thick and thin, insisting that his old friend get paid for the Madison Square Garden recording when Felton was too sick to travel to New York and even finding Felton a kidney when, after two years, Felton's doctors at the Vanderbilt University Medical Center in Nashville still seemed unable to locate one on their own. Felton was down to 128 pounds and clearly dying when Elvis had taken matters into his own hands and contacted a kidney specialist from the Mayo Clinic, calling Felton excitedly when the doctor arranged for the operation within days. Felton was packed and ready to leave for Minnesota when all of a sudden, six days later, Vanderbilt suddenly came up with a donor, a discovery that Felton and his wife, Mary, always felt was less coincidence than recognition on the hospital's part that it might be watching a big donation go out the door. "Your husband is a jewel," Elvis told Mary Jarvis over and over during the three days of rehearsals, and while he was under no illusions about the Colonel's or RCA's loyalty to him, Felton was just glad to be there and could only trust to the friendship that had sustained his relationship with Elvis over the years.

Rehearsals were held at the Hilton Hawaiian Village while the set was being constructed. There were various technical problems to contend with, and Bill Belew back on the mainland had a scare when Elvis gave away his ruby-encrusted belt to the wife of actor Jack Lord, but Belew eventually located enough additional rubies to make up another belt and had it shipped over just in time for the show. Pasetta meanwhile had gotten all his scenic shots of the Islands (for the extended U.S. version that would air in April) by the time they got into the HIC Arena for rehearsal on Thursday. Everything was as he had shown Elvis in the original drawings: ceiling-high strips of Mylar acting as a giant mirror, and enlarging the space, at stage right; a black scrim across the width of the stage at the back, with colored lights spelling out "ELVIS" in various configurations against it; and a guitar-wielding cartoon figure that would flash on and off. The runway extended well out into the audience, and Elvis got comfortable with the stage setup as tech crews ran their cables in the otherwise empty, cavernous room.

They kept on rehearsing almost up till the filmed run-through with an audience present on the night before the show itself. There continued to be technical problems to solve (getting rid of a persistent hum in the sound system by shielding all the cables with lead was the most challenging), but in the end everything went off more or less without a hitch. The Friday night rehearsal show got under way two hours after fans almost "literally stormed the inside of the arena when the gates opened at 7 P.M.," according to the *Honolulu Advertiser,* which reported further that "the audience went wild virtually without let-up through [the] non-stop repertoire of songs." Elvis had no trouble sustaining their hysteria, the filmed record shows, even if he himself never seems to have gotten particularly caught up in it. There is none of the manic energy of the '68 special nor even of the early Vegas shows, just a moment at the conclusion of "An American Trilogy," as the chorus swells, the percussion rolls, we are about to go into the "Glory, glory, hallelujah," peroration, and Elvis stands there meditatively, eyebrow cocked, his mind for a moment seemingly on destiny, as the music once again takes him far, far away. Then it is gone; he is off into "A Big Hunk O' Love," his 1959 hit. "You're a fantastic audience," he says, then launches into "Can't Help Falling in Love," which he ends down on one knee, his back to the audience, his cape spread out in that familiar pose of humble adoration, combined with self-adoration, that the world has come to accept as Elvis in any language.

There is no sense of tension, but this is only a rehearsal, after all — plenty of time for drama at the actual performance. Except that when he takes the stage the following night, at 12:30 A.M. for his live audience in the Far East, he seems, if anything, even further removed. There are musical highlights, to be sure, but the overall atmosphere is even more stilted, and for all of his dramatic weight loss, Elvis appears strangely bloated, his expression glazed and unfocused. It is as if, in his Captain Marvel getup, his jewelry, his helmet of hair, Elvis has finally acceded to the need to be, simply, Elvis — there are no surprises, just effects.

"It was a thrilling compact hour — long on music, loud on screams," reported the *Honolulu Advertiser* admiringly, citing the "aura of the Big Time: a superstar doing a super performance, right before the eyes of the world." Thanks to Elvis and the Colonel's "philanthropic fondness for Hawaii," the original goal of $25,000 for the Kui Lee Cancer Fund was more than tripled, eclipsing in the process the sum raised for the U.S.S. *Arizona*. To Joe Guercio, though, who did not have to be sold on the sheer charisma of the performer, "there was just not as much wind blowing through the show." Elvis was slower and less concentrated. "You could just feel it." Perhaps the most spontaneous moment came when he sailed his $10,000 cape out into the crowd, where it was snagged by an *Advertiser* sportswriter. It was, reported the *Los Angeles Times* in its write-up the following day, "the highlight of the night."

The feeling of relief experienced by almost everyone connected with the show was almost palpable — although there remained much to be done. With the auditorium cleared, they still had to shoot five additional songs for the expanded American telecast, and then Marty Pasetta had to edit the show down by ten minutes for the delayed European broadcast to twenty-eight countries linked by EuroVision later that night. Joan Deary had her work cut out for her as well to get the album out simultaneously around the world within three weeks. But for Elvis and the band it was almost over. Colonel came in as they were recording "Early Morning Rain," the last number, and announced proudly that they had gotten the highest rating ever registered in Japan, with 37.8 percent of the viewers in a highly competitive six-network market. There was a sense of real jubilation in the air.

Not long afterward, the Colonel wrote Elvis a letter. Datelined Sunday morning, three A.M., January 14, 1973, it may have expressed as much sentiment as the Colonel had ever committed to paper, as he declared defiantly that *they* didn't need to hug each other to show their feelings because they could tell just by looking at one another from the stage and from the floor how the other felt. "I always know when I do my part you always do yours in your own way and in your feeling in how to do it best. That is why you and I are never at each other when we are doing our work in our own best way possible at all times." Life was short, many were quick to take credit after the fact, but Elvis knew who was really responsible for this idea: "this brainchild . . . came from you and me." The others — except for Mr. Parkhill from RCA Record Tours and Mr. Diskin and his troupe "and all your own selected talent"— were just Johnny-come-latelies. But Elvis didn't need to be reminded of that. Because "you above all make all of it work by being the leader and the talent. Without your dedication to your following it couldn't have been done."

ELVIS AND PRISCILLA, SANTA MONICA COURTHOUSE, OCTOBER 9, 1973.
(MICHAEL OCHS ARCHIVES)

FREEFALL

H‌E COULDN'T SEEM TO LEAVE Vegas at the conclusion of the February engagement. The guys all sat around impatient and out of sorts; they had wives and girlfriends to go home to, lives to pick up. Colonel departed to pursue his various schemes. But Elvis remained, with Linda at his side and Kang Rhee, whom he had flown in from Memphis for the last week of the show, on hand to provide entertainment and karate instruction twenty-four hours a day. There was, not surprisingly, some outright friction, with Red the most outspoken in his complaints. Elvis tried to address Red's concerns by writing him a letter in which, with Linda's help, he expressed some of his philosophy of life, but it didn't do much to dispel the cloud that seemed to be hanging over them all.

It had been an impossible month. As soon as filming for the satellite special was over, Elvis had just let himself go: his weight had immediately ballooned, and he had been out of it on pain pills, liquid Demerol, and heavy-duty depressants for much of the twelve days prior to the Vegas opening. *Variety* gave the show its usual pro forma endorsement, though the lead to the story indicated a certain amount of underlying ambivalence. "Colonel Tom Parker," the review declared, "has returned to the Hilton, hawking his elixir of unbottled sex and satisfaction, Elvis Presley." Perhaps struck by its own temerity, the "show business Bible" went on to assure its readers that "the product up for sale . . . possesses too much musicality to become the Colonel's mechanized doll — at least onstage."

Elvis saw a procession of doctors almost from the moment of his arrival, and his physical discomfort was increasingly evident the first week of the engagement (he was variously reported to have either flu or pneumonia), as the interaction of the diverse drugs led to throat and lung congestion, the congestion to further medication, and he was forced to cancel his midnight show five times in the second and third weeks. The Colonel, placed in the position of having to come up with an explanation, wrote an

487

unusually conciliatory letter to the hotel, promising to make up for the missed performances and assuring Henri Lewin and Barron Hilton that he and Elvis would always live up to their commitments. Elvis, on the other hand, just didn't seem to care. One night he lost his voice onstage and momentarily panicked, until he sought the advice of an ENT he had been referred to during his last engagement named Dr. Sidney Boyer, who prescribed a throat elixir that restored it. After that he saw Dr. Boyer almost every day of his stay, presenting him with a white Lincoln Continental in gratitude. He saw at least six other physicians as well, including his regular Vegas doctors, Thomas "Flash" Newman and Elias Ghanem, while complaining to a mystified audience that none of the doctors was able to discover the root of his problem.

The *Hollywood Reporter* was willing to attribute his apparent "lack of energy and interest" to the effects of his illness, and some saw it as the letdown inevitably bound to occur after the triumph of the *Aloha* show — but to those around him it was apparent that it went considerably further. Elvis appeared to be suffering from a kind of deep-seated malaise, which the guys, when they were feeling sympathetic, put down to continued brooding over the loss of Priscilla but in less charitable moments simply ascribed to the effect of drugs. The engagement in any case seemed to mark a kind of watershed. Frank Lieberman, the *Los Angeles Herald-Examiner* critic and Elvis' one close journalistic friend since his rave review of the February 1970 engagement, couldn't help but notice the difference, and even Muhammad Ali, whom Elvis had met in Vegas six months before and to whom he now presented a specially made-up robe declaring Ali to be "The People's Champion" for a February 14 non-title bout, couldn't miss the sadness at Elvis' core. "I felt sorry for [him], because he didn't enjoy life the way he should. He stayed indoors all the time. I told him he should go out and see people. He said he couldn't, because everywhere he went, they mobbed him. He didn't understand," said Ali, a lifelong fan, who probably more than anyone else in the world was himself in a position to empathize and understand. "No one wanted to hurt him. All they wanted was to be friendly and tell him how much they loved him."

On February 18, at the midnight show, the very thing that everyone had been half expecting and they had all been preparing themselves for ever since the 1970 assassination threat finally happened: four guys rushed the stage with what appeared to be ill intent, and the security team sprang into action. Red took care of the first "assailant," as bass player Jerry Scheff, Jerry Schilling, and the rest of the guys quickly moved in. Standing by J.D.

to one side of the stage, Elvis took up a karate stance and knocked the second of the four men back into the audience. There was all kinds of confusion, and Elvis, inflamed, could not be calmed down. "Come on, you motherfuckers," he screamed, as his father wrapped him in a bear hug, but Elvis simply went limp and slipped out of Vernon's grasp. Finally Tom Diskin, who had been one of the first to rush to Elvis' aid, urged him to take his audience into consideration. "Think of the show, Elvis, get back to the show," murmured the Colonel's longtime lieutenant, but even then Elvis could not refrain from injecting a truculent note into his apology to the fans. "I'm sorry, ladies and gentlemen," he said. "I'm sorry I didn't break his goddamn neck is what I'm sorry about." And then he went on with the show.

Afterward, he couldn't stop talking about it. It was almost as though this was what he had been waiting for the entire engagement, and even though further investigation proved that the men were simply fans who had gotten a little out of hand, Elvis would have none of it. There could have been a drug connection, he suggested, it probably had something to do with his BNDD badge — but had they seen the way he took care of that one guy? He wouldn't have cared if he'd killed him. Maybe, he speculated, *those guys had been sent by Mike Stone.* Before long he had worked himself up into believing it. It would make sense. This was just the kind of thing that cowardly motherfucker would do. First he hides behind Priscilla. Now he sends hired killers to do his dirty work for him. He stole my wife, Elvis said. He stole my baby. The guys were starting to get worried now. They had never seen Elvis quite like this before. The quick flash of anger was one thing; they had all experienced that. But now it was as if an emotional undertow were pulling him down and sweeping him out further and further from shore. There was only one solution, he declared: the man had to die.

"You know it, Sonny," he shouted. "You know it. There is too much pain in me, and he did it. Do you hear me? I am right. You know I'm right. Mike Stone [must] die. You will do it for me — kill the sonofabitch, Sonny, I can count on you. I know I can." Mike Stone had to die, he kept repeating to Red and Sonny. "He has no right to live."

His books lay strewn all over the floor. Linda was in tears. It was no good to try to reason with him, as Red did when he suggested that it was Elvis, not Mike Stone, who had driven Priscilla away. After all, didn't he finally have what he'd said he always wanted — his freedom? Hadn't Elvis always told them he was the master of his own fate? No, Elvis practically screamed back at him, it was Mike Stone. Mike Stone was the start of all his problems, and now Mike was trying to take his baby away from him, too. It was Mike who had persuaded Priscilla to try to limit Lisa's visits; wasn't that what she had said, after Lisa spent her fifth birthday with him in Vegas on February 1? She had said that *she and Mike* thought maybe Las Vegas wasn't such a good environment for a child. Well, maybe she was right, Red said. Elvis practically turned on him. *Didn't Red know that she had the baby sleeping in the same room with her and Stone?* He got his new M-16 out of the closet. "Doesn't anyone understand? Oh, God, why can't anyone understand? He has hurt me so much — you all know that. He has broken up my family. He has destroyed everything, and nobody cares. He is the one who has done it all."

He raged on the entire night. There was no reasoning with him. Finally Linda called Dr. Newman, who gave him a shot at 6:00 A.M. and returned half a dozen times in the course of the day as no amount of medication seemed able to calm him down or buy more than a couple of hours' sleep. He was still raving just as obsessively the following day, and the day after that, and finally Red contacted someone, a friend of a friend, about taking out a contract on Stone and got a price of $10,000, which he brought to Elvis just before the dinner show. He had no idea what he would do if Elvis said to go ahead and give the guy the money; he didn't think he could actually make the call, but he couldn't seem to stop himself either. Elvis had a hold on him, Elvis had a hold on all of them; no matter how much he pissed you off, you couldn't say no to the motherfucker. He stared into Elvis' eyes when he told him, and Elvis was silent for a moment before he answered. "Aw, hell," he said at last. "Let's just leave it for now. Maybe it's a bit heavy. Just let's leave it off for now."

THE FINAL SHOW was the usual off-the-wall kind of ritual celebration that both Elvis and the audience always seemed to enjoy, with Elvis making up all kinds of crazy lyrics and then delivering a dramatic recitation of "What Now My Love" that won him a standing ovation. He ran Charlie all over the stage fetching scarves until he practically dropped, then kept the spotlight on Ann-Margret, who was opening at the Hilton the next night, and declared seriously, "Leave the light on her, man. I just want to look at her." At the end of the evening he was down on one knee, his arms extended wide, the audience on its feet.

But then he couldn't leave. He just stayed and stayed. He and Linda attended Ann-Margret's opening. They went to other shows. He maintained his karate studies with Kang Rhee, whose broken English and wonder-struck reaction to Las Vegas kept everyone amused for a while. Even Master Rhee, who was generally respected within the group for his integrity and the purity of his commitment to the sport, was dragged down in this atmosphere, though, jumping up on the couch and applauding as Elvis broke up the furniture in the suite to demonstrate his karate prowess. Ed Parker was in and out, and, beginning to sense that Kang Rhee might be a real rival, did all he could to plant the seed of suspicion among the other guys — which turned out to be not very hard to do after Elvis gave Master Rhee $10,000, the first of five promised annual installments to promote his system of instruction and build up his schools in Memphis. From that point on, the talk never ceased, and by the time they finally broke camp and left for California on March 9, Kang Rhee, too, was trapped in the same hot-house atmosphere from which none of them seemed able to escape.

There was a spirit of entitlement that permeated the air. If one guy got something, everyone else wanted it, too; it was jealousy plain and simple in a sealed environment where the players never changed, the climate was always the same, and the outside world was regarded with scorn — if it was regarded at all. Joe, at the top of the heap and thus naturally subject to the jealousy of others but still subject to jealousies of his own, recognized just what was entailed. "Everything we did, we drove into the ground. What it would take somebody else ten years [to get tired of], we did in six months. Sometimes he'd get you so frustrated — I think he enjoyed doing it. You'd get pissed, and I don't know if it was a test to see if people'd still be with him, but then he'd sit and talk to you, and there was just something about him — he'd smile at you, and he could convince you of anything. Sometimes I thought about leaving, but I liked him too much, and I figured things were going to change. Everyone was just waiting for that day to happen."

THE COLONEL MEANWHILE had finalized the deal that RCA vice president Mel Ilberman had first broached the previous fall: with Elvis' full assent and enthusiastic support, he sold all rights to his client's back catalogue.

RCA, of course, like any record company, already owned the master recordings and the right to market them in perpetuity. That was never at issue, not even with the Colonel. What was constantly at issue, in endless nagging skirmishes that were never fully resolved, were matters of royalty payments, the actual use to which the catalogue could be put (over which Colonel, whether by custom or contract, maintained absolute control), and other contractual elements that had never been put down on paper but that Colonel was always hinting might prove to be embarrassing to the record company if they were ever to be revealed to the world. What Ilberman was now proposing was to do away with this source of conflict once and for all by buying out Elvis and the Colonel. In exchange for a single lump payment the artist would give up all claim on future royalties, his manager would give up any potential ground for troublesome dispute, and RCA would establish once and for all their right to do whatever they wanted with all the music that had been recorded to date, using it to build up the RCA Record Club (one of Ilberman's fondest wishes), exploiting the back catalogue in a manner the Colonel had never permitted, wiping out all the disputes over foreign royalties, container deductions, and European album content with which the Colonel had continued to bedevil them over the years.

It was a gamble virtually unprecedented in the record business, which, like the Colonel and his client, dealt almost entirely in "now money" and put very little faith in the future ("catalogue" was a much derogated concept; *publishing* was where you built up a backlist, because a song could always have a new life, as opposed to an artist). Ilberman never thought the company would go for it. But desperate times called for desperate measures, and to his amazement, RCA president Rocco Laginestra authorized him to set up a meeting with the Colonel. Neither record company executive had any idea of what precisely to offer for the catalogue, and the financial people, probably just covering themselves, were for the most part opposed. So Ilberman had a schedule of royalty payments over the past seven years drawn up which showed that Elvis had received, on average, somewhere between $400,000 and $500,000 a year in domestic royalties, with an estimated 33 percent additional in foreign payments — in other words, roughly $600,000 in a good average year. With that in mind, Laginestra came up with the figure of $3 million, a prudent investment that could earn out for RCA in five or six years but one which Ilberman, who continued to wonder if the Colonel was somehow setting him up, felt was too low and could well be a foundering point before the real negotiations even kicked in.

The initial meeting was in Palm Springs not long after the conclusion of the Las Vegas engagement. The RCA executives made their pitch, and the

Colonel predictably said he would get back to them, but he didn't think it was going to be enough money, either for Elvis or his father. When he did get back to them the next day, it was with a counterproposal of $5 million, which Laginestra immediately seized on, despite Ilberman's instincts that they could have bargained the old man down. Rocco just wanted to get the deal done, but the deal, Ilberman realized, was far from over. "The Colonel continued to talk in terms of restrictions on the catalogue, and Laginestra really didn't know what the Colonel was driving at, but I was very upset about that. We went to dinner that night at the Spa Hotel, and after dinner I kept raising the issue with the Colonel: we had to have the catalogue free and clear, without any restrictions. So he asked me for some involvement in packaging in the future for [his promotion company] All Star Shows, and I said yes. And I promised I would use the new stuff as well as the old stuff as much as possible on future packages — so that he and Elvis would be getting income in the future. I told him I would work with him on that, and I always did. We paid him for the packaging, the art (the Colonel had all the pictures) — we could have made our own pictures now and made the design, but this way he would get a royalty. And that was how we made the deal."

A contract that would actually come to $5.4 million was formalized over the next couple of months but backdated to March 1, when the Colonel's new 50–50 personal management agreement with Elvis had gone into effect. Under the terms of this new agreement, the somewhat arcane "joint venture" language of Elvis and Colonel's 1967 contract, which defined contractual income alone as subject to a 25-percent commission, with all other income derived from recording (in other words, anything beyond RCA's annual guarantee, as well as any and all of the proliferating side deals) subject to a 50–50 split, was done away with, and the basic principle of partnership under which Elvis and Colonel had been operating for the past six years was, finally, explicitly recognized. From now on, all record income would be split down the middle, with touring remaining at a two-thirds–one-third division. Perhaps to ensure that there could be no question under which personal management agreement this one-time RCA payment was to fall, the payout was structured as if the old agreement were still in effect, with $400,000 tacked on at the front end and divided 75–25 as if that were the "deal," and the $5 million that represented the actual buyout treated as a "side deal," to be divided equally between the two principals.

That was not the end of it, however. There was, in addition, a new

seven-year contract, guaranteeing $500,000 a year against royalty earnings
on the two new albums and four singles for which Elvis would be contractually obligated each year. Moreover, at the conclusion of the seven-year
term, Elvis and Colonel would each receive a $100,000 bonus, not to be
counted against royalties. In line with Ilberman's determination to keep the
catalogue unencumbered, Colonel got a number of contractual guarantees
of his own. He was to receive a $50,000-a-year consulting fee for the dura-
tion of the contract for "assisting" RCA in the "development of merchandising and promo concepts" and for supplying RCA with "merchandising
and promo material," plus $10,000 a year for exploiting merchandising
rights on the expired contract. Finally, for his assistance in helping RCA
Record Tours in "planning, promotion and merchandising in connection
with the operation of the Tour Agreement [and] records made," in essence
for the seven-year duration of the new contract, he was to receive a grand
total of $1.35 million ($150,000 the first year, $200,000 every year thereafter)
plus 10 percent of RCA Record Tours' profits off the top. In all, the Colonel
was guaranteed $1.75 million on top of his $2.6 million share of the buyout
itself and the $1.75 million that he would get as his share of the new record-
ing contract. Which meant that the Colonel would receive roughly $6 mil-
lion to Elvis' $4.5 million from all of the deals combined (this might be
likened to a professional athlete's seven-year contract for $75 million in 1998
dollars, but with his agent getting four-sevenths of the money). Taking
touring money into account (at least $15 million, with Elvis getting $10 million, but only after Colonel collected his 10 percent of tour profits beyond
the promoter's guarantee), the overall package *could* be seen as a true 50–50
joint venture — and this was undoubtedly how the Colonel did see it, in
one of the numerous alternative accounting approaches that he took to
any subject, and that he would have taken toward this subject in particular
after factoring in all the aggravation that he had to put up with and all the
money that he was passing up, by retaining Elvis as his only client.

Not everyone saw it this way. To William Morris legal counsel Roger
Davis, Colonel Parker was as brilliant in his instincts as any man he had ever
met. Never less than a canny operator himself, Davis was quick to concede
that the Colonel had taught him lessons about contract law; what he didn't
understand was why Colonel continued to insist on operating on his own
when he was so clearly out of his depth, as he was here with respect to tax
advantages and long-term gain for both himself and his client. Jean and
Julian Aberbach, who had built a publishing empire on the premise that

ownership was everything, took much the same view. Although they were in the process of dissolving that empire themselves for a variety of financial and personal reasons (they had decided to sell Hill and Range the previous year, while maintaining ownership of the Elvis Presley and Gladys Music catalogues, along with Hank Williams' renewal rights, because of their uninterrupted record of profitability), they were doing so with an eye to the future. The Colonel, on the other hand, they saw as selling out Elvis for a mess of pottage — and then, more than anything, to satisfy his own gambling debts. They continued to have a real affection for their old associate, but as sophisticated men of business they could not be blind to his shortcomings either. The Colonel, in Julian's view, was a crude, blustering man without schooling. "He always had to be the big cheese, he had to dominate, he [could not] ask for any advice because it was demeaning — he knew everything. And he did not have long-term thinking."

And yet no one could say Elvis was an unwitting, or even unenthusiastic, participant, as he put his neat, flowing signature on the line marked "Approved" at the end of every one of Colonel's side deals. From Elvis' point of view as much as Colonel's, money was for spending, and what you spent it on was nobody's business but your own. There was never going to be any problem about money so long as the two of them kept their wits about them. It was almost karmic in fact, as he explained to Ed Parker, the way that money came in one door just as it was going out the other. He boasted to the guys how the old man had pulled the wool over everyone's eyes once again. And if the Colonel made some money for himself in the process — well, that was to be expected, there was plenty for everyone, and no one else could have made the deal anyway. The Colonel deserved his share.

The Colonel for his part was still working out the final piece of the puzzle. Ever since the Aberbachs had announced their decision the previous March, he had been trying to come up with a solution to the publishing problem that would be created when Hill and Range was dissolved. Although there was some sentiment for continuing to use Elvis Presley and Gladys Music as holding companies in which to deposit new compositions, it would have been anathema to the Colonel to sustain a partnership in which his partners were no longer pulling their weight. In any case, the situation between Jean and Julian and their cousin had long since become intolerable — and without Freddy there was no publisher presence.

The Colonel's first thought was to try to buy out the Aberbachs, but that probably would have been doomed to failure even if Freddy had not been involved in the purchase bid. Next he came up with a scheme to have RCA buy *Elvis'* half of the publishing, but having already gone into the tour business on the Colonel's behalf and still in the midst of trying to work out terms for the acquisition of the masters, the record company understandably declined. He remained hopeful that RCA might still come through with financial support when he informed Elvis in the middle of the Vegas engagement that it looked like they might set up their own publishing through Freddy, with Elvis and Vernon and Lisa Marie owning 80 percent of it, and Freddy and Mr. Diskin each getting 10 percent. He tried to impress on Elvis, though, that plans were still unsettled and that it was *very important* both that Elvis make no commitments to recording any songs that friends might bring him until their situation was fully squared away and that this information be maintained in the strictest confidence. There was probably no great reason for all this drama other than to try to capture Elvis' attention. In the end it all came down to Freddy anyway, a surprising realization only if you were unaware of the Colonel's almost desperate penchant for loyalty, which some might see as a disinclination at least as great as his client's ever to venture outside his immediate circle of acquaintance.

In any case there was still much to be done, even as he was completing his deals with Elvis and RCA. Setting up new publishing companies proved more daunting than the Colonel had ever imagined, and the technical details dragged on over the next six months, but for all of the aggravation, and despite his keen awareness of Freddy's limitations, Colonel remained convinced that this could be the fresh start that they needed, that they were sailing into a brave new world — *if* he could keep the boy's mind on business.

THE *Aloha* special aired domestically on April 4 to generally good reviews. The principal reservations expressed were that it was in its U.S. version too long, too much of a travelogue, and, in the manner of the current live show, too bombastic — but it was certainly accounted to be a success. The ratings (a 33.8-percent Nielsen, with a 57-percent share) bore out the advance hoopla, with the album, on the charts ever since the beginning of March, hitting number one at the end of the month, the first quadraphonic release, according to RCA, to achieve that honor. Elvis watched the show at home with a certain amount of trepidation but with none of the edginess with which he had viewed the '68 special. He seemed to accept his own grandiosity, almost as if he had nothing left to prove.

An area in which he appeared far more intent on proving himself at this point was karate. Spurred on perhaps by Mike Stone's eminence in the field (Mike was "very much of a man," Priscilla was telling reporters and friends, and treated her "like a woman"), he was becoming more and more caught up in the sport, in much the same way that he had become caught up in other enthusiasms over the years. This was different, he might have protested, it was a discipline to which he had dedicated himself, in his own view, for nearly fifteen years — but now it began to take a more obsessive turn. On April 2 he prevailed upon Ed Parker to award him a sixth-degree black belt in kenpo karate (this was widely perceived as "selling rank" in karate circles, where such practices were not uncommon and were viewed as the equivalent of campaign fund-raising for a sport desperate for mass acceptance). This in turn only encouraged him to put greater pressure on Kang Rhee, whom he had flown out to accompany him to Parker's California Karate Championships in San Francisco. What he wanted now was for Master Rhee to go Ed one higher, with a seventh-degree black belt from his own Pasaryu school. Seven, he explained to his Memphis instructor, was a number of great spiritual significance to him, but Master Rhee was resistant. For all of his personal allegiance to Elvis, and his indebtedness to him, he continued to feel a greater loyalty to the sport.

There was a sense of excitement as they flew into San Francisco for the competition. By now there was virtually no one among the guys who was not caught up to one degree or another in the karate craze. Most were black and blue from daily workouts, and sprained wrists, backs, and ankles had become commonplace badges of honor. Not everyone was enamored of Ed's instruction methods, and jealousy over Kang Rhee's new position was rapidly growing, but there was a feeling of common enterprise and a sense of real enthusiasm, if only just to get out of the house. Driving in from the airport, Elvis had the limo swing by the Civic Auditorium, the tournament site, and there to his great surprise he saw his name emblazoned on the marquee. Back at the hotel he discovered that the newspapers, too, had carried notices of his upcoming appearance, which was advertised to include his participation in an exhibition of brick-breaking. Within minutes he was on the phone to the Colonel. Of course he couldn't make any public appearances, the Colonel thundered. What would the management of the Sahara Tahoe, where he was scheduled to open in less than a month, and RCA Record Tours, which had a West Coast tour booked in a couple of weeks, think of his giving away for free what they were prepared to pay good money for? What was he doing hanging around with people who took advantage of him like this, who simply wanted to use his name?

Elvis didn't even try to argue. He dispatched some of the guys to get his name off the marquee and let the promoters know that he was leaving, then turned around and went home, bitterly disappointed both in Ed and himself. He got his seventh-degree the very next day, as Kang Rhee took the opportunity to do what a number of the guys, including Red and Sonny, Charlie, Jerry, and Lamar, had been urging him to do for some time: talk to Elvis about the pills.

"At the time I don't know anything about pills, I don't know anything about aspirin even myself, but the bodyguards explain to me, 'You just tell Elvis no pills, he not listen to anyone else, but he listen to what you say.' And I say, 'That's no problem.'" Elvis wouldn't come down at first when Master Rhee arrived at the house on Monovale, so fearful was he that he would be turned down in his standing bid for promotion. "Finally, he coming downstairs, and I told him that, 'You know, you the Master Tiger, king of the jungle, and when tiger has wound, he lick it well. Lick well, but not take any pills.' And he said, 'I understand.' Immediate response. And then he invite me his room upstairs, and he show me police badge, and pictures with Nixon, and then he's the narcotic agent. He says, 'I'm against drugs, and I do not believe in any kind of drug, even if I singing or anything like that.' He explain to me how clean he is himself." That was when Kang Rhee promoted Elvis to seventh-degree black belt, justifying it to himself by balancing it against all the good that Elvis had done for the popularity of karate and by how much the belt meant to Elvis himself. "He tell me many times, 'This black belt much more worth than my gold belt,' and he really have satisfaction with martial arts training. Simply, he do not care about anything else, and he trying to discover himself and overcome everything from bad to good. That's my impression at the time, see? But my regret is that I should more lead him, he elected me as instructor and I should lead him to much better ways, much stronger. But then I put him up over me when he trying to put me over him — [even though] he liked me because of my honest."

* * *

Two WEEKS LATER they were back on the road for the nine-day West Coast tour to which the Colonel had alluded. For bass player Emory Gordy, whose only previous dealings with Elvis had come when he filled in for Jerry Scheff at the March 1972 session and who was now replacing Scheff in the band, even this brief exposure amounted to a small revelation. He had been looking forward to rejoining Elvis after his productive recording experience (this was the session at which Elvis had recorded "Separate Ways," "Always On My Mind," and "Burning Love"), and the working conditions — pay, accommodations, the efficiency and comfort of the touring operation — could not have been better. The music alone turned out to be a disappointment. "I was really let down by the whole thing. Everybody had been there for so many years they were very set in their ways; I think they sent me about five hundred tunes to learn in a two-week period, and then we ended up doing the same show they had been doing in Vegas for the last [four] years. Occasionally, he'd get up there and start feeling real good and be very spontaneous, [but mostly] all the tunes were done so fast we just literally ran over them. There was no feeling involved."

In May they went into Tahoe in a peculiarly elongated seventeen-day booking, for which Elvis got paid a straight two-week salary of $300,000, but the Colonel was to receive $100,000 for "promotion." It was clear from the start that Elvis was "neither looking nor sounding good," according to the *Variety* review. "Some thirty pounds overweight, he's puffy, white-faced and blinking against the light. The voice sounds weak, delivery is flabby . . . hit medley is delivered in listless fashion . . . attempts to perpetuate his mystique of sex and power end in weak self-parody."

Variety's report turned out to be prescient, as Elvis canceled the last four days of his engagement, just one day short of two weeks, and Colonel was forced to forfeit his $100,000 bonus. That was when everyone started to get worried. Undoubtedly alerted by the Colonel, Elvis' attorney Ed Hookstratten contacted John O'Grady, the retired Los Angeles police department narcotics detective who had been brought into the 1970 paternity suit by Hookstratten and subsequently gave Elvis the idea for getting his BNDD badge in Washington. O'Grady and his associate, Jack Kelly (Kelly was the former head of the Los Angeles office of the federal Drug Enforcement Agency), were given the task of ferreting out the sources for the prescribed drugs which were more and more obviously affecting Elvis' behavior. It took them no time to come up with four principal suppliers: a Los Angeles doctor who was giving him "acupuncture" treatments for the frequent injuries to his back and neck that he claimed to suffer in karate workouts; a Los Angeles dentist who made a specialty of house calls and painless treatment; and two Las Vegas doctors who appeared to be at his constant beck and call. Dr. Nick was specifically excluded from the circle of inquiry, because Vernon, who for the first time had been brought in on their concerns, vouched for the Memphis physician's overall commitment to Elvis' welfare.

The "investigation" went on for much of the next few months. All of the talk was in general enough terms to permit a certain level of deniability and, perhaps more important, to encourage a kind of unacknowledged self-deception, allowing them all to fool themselves for a time into thinking that the "problem" was not really of the dimensions that it was. But then Elvis nearly overdosed in St. Louis in the middle of his June tour, bringing home how serious the situation had become. And when, not long afterward, Elvis passed out in Hookstratten's office in the middle of a deposition attended by attorneys, secretaries, and a court reporter, it only further heightened his lawyer's concern. There were reports of incidents involving "civilians" (one girl was said to have almost died from an overdose of Hycodan in Palm Springs), and it seemed increasingly clear that the world was bound to learn of Elvis' self-destructive behavior, whatever containment methods were employed, unless something was done about it soon.

In the absence of any clear-cut direction from above, Hookstratten and O'Grady came up with a strategy that seems in retrospect somewhat questionable: O'Grady would contact all of the principal suppliers and try to frighten them into compliance; then O'Grady and Hookstratten would use their contacts among state and federal narcotics agents to put further pressure on the doctors, and by extension on Elvis himself, to straighten up. It seems hard to imagine how this plan could ever have worked without boomeranging back on their client (Hookstratten trusted his state contact, because, he said, "I had gone to law school with him and we were good friends"), but it seems even more doubtful that it was ever in fact actually implemented. What Hookstratten and O'Grady both found was that Vernon was torn between loyalty to his employer and loyalty to his son; the guys, too, were hopelessly compromised by the conflicting claims of friendship and employment; everyone, in fact, in a position to intervene was financially obligated to Elvis in one way or another. Even the Colonel seemed out of his depth, expressing bewildered consternation from time to time, but mostly just repeating the belief that sustained them all: Elvis would pull out of this as he had so many times in the past; he had done it before, and he would do it again.

Hookstratten and the two detectives felt more and more as if they were crawling out on a limb that was about to be sawed off, but though each of them claimed at one time or another to have confronted Elvis after his own fashion, Elvis never expressed any resentment, and there were no flashes of anger, only the mildest demurral. He knew what he was doing, he told them, there was no problem; the reason he had passed out in Hookstratten's office, he explained to his lawyer, was that he had just been to the dentist and was feeling woozy from the anesthetic. "I said, 'Elvis, do you want to talk about it? Won't you please let us try to help you?' I thought I was going to get fired, but he gave me a gift instead, a slot machine that I'd always admired."

RCA COULD NOT HAVE BEEN happy to find themselves releasing yet another grab bag album (under the Colonel's by now almost generic title of *Elvis*) in the summer of 1973, especially after the great success of the *Aloha* soundtrack album. With no studio sessions since 1972 and virtually nothing left in the can, however, they had little alternative, their only consolation being the new contract and the new relationship (which the Colonel reassured them the new contract practically guaranteed) on which they were embarked. With that in mind George Parkhill, the Colonel's man at RCA, wrote Elvis on June 29, informing him in surprisingly peremptory terms that "in order to have the merchandise available . . . *we are planning* [italics added] a recording session in the middle of July." He gave Elvis the choice of where he might prefer to record but stressed that, under the terms of the March 1 agreement, RCA needed at least one new pop album, two new singles, and a religious album — a minimum of twenty-four tracks — from the session.

Since Parkhill at this point might just as well have been working for the Colonel (and as head of RCA Record Tours, to all intents and purposes actually was), it must be assumed that this letter was sent not simply with the Colonel's approval but at his behest. If he couldn't get Elvis to take his obligations seriously by any more direct method of communication, using RCA as an intermediary was a perfectly acceptable alternative.

It worked — at least initially. No one imagined that Elvis would leave Memphis in the middle of his four-week summer break, particularly when his daughter was visiting, so Marty Lacker, who had just started doing promotion for Stax Records, set up the session at Stax's McLemore Avenue studio in the old Capitol movie theater, practically next door to the First Assembly of God Church that Elvis had attended with his teenage girlfriend Dixie Locke. It made sense in every way: Stax was a legitimate studio, at the height of its success as a soul label, Marty had an in, just as he once had at American — and it was only five minutes from the house.

Elvis failed to show up at all on the first night, and on the second arrived five hours late, dressed in a sweeping black cape, white suit, and "Superfly" Borsalino slouch hat. The band included James Burton and Ronnie Tutt; the same American rhythm section that he had worked with in 1969 minus drummer Gene Chrisman; and, in Chrisman's place, complementing Tutt, drummer Jerry Carrigan from the 1970–71 Nashville sessions. For Carrigan, who had not seen Elvis in a couple of years, the whole experience was something of a shock. "It was the first time I ever saw him fat. His speech was slurred. It just seemed like he was miserable." "He just didn't seem to care," said American keyboard player Bobby Wood, echoing Carrigan's observation. "He was a totally different person."

Everything seemed to go wrong from the start. Felton Jarvis and his engineer Al Pachucki, already skating on thin ice after a disastrous confrontation with RCA executive Joan Deary over the quad mix of the *Aloha* album (Deary, who had no respect for either Felton's or Pachucki's technical skills or work ethic, had ended up supervising a complete remix), took a dim view of the whole Stax setup. The studio ambience, Pachucki observed, was very dry; there was no way to give the musicians different headphone mixes (in other words, the drummer got the same mix as the singer); and the console was hopelessly outmoded — the kind of eight-track board that RCA had discarded in 1970 — which, with the nine singers that Elvis had insisted on bringing in to record live in the studio with him, made it virtually impossible to get any kind of clean separation.

The studio vibe was bad; the material, too, was something of an embarrassment — "horrible songs," in the view of Carrigan and the other musicians, that Elvis turned down just as fast as they were presented to him. Had the Colonel been there, he undoubtedly would have agreed with the musicians, and he must have winced when Tom Diskin made his report. Once again Freddy had failed to come through — despite the fact that he was now working for himself. The Colonel shook his head; he couldn't understand it. Freddy had all the motivation in the world to succeed — how could you improve on self-interest?

But mostly it was Elvis, as everyone knew. At another time, in another mood, he might have shrugged it all off, he might have found something in the hackneyed tunes to spark his interest or simply pursued another direction altogether. Instead, the only thing that seemed to engage him was a karate exhibition he put on with Kang Rhee in the studio, which, after what the musicians had all heard about his putting a gun through Chip Young's guitar with a karate kick (Carrigan had been a direct witness), didn't leave anyone in a particularly sanguine frame of mind.

The next night he showed up wearing the same clothes but with Linda and Lisa Marie in tow — and once again several hours late. He seemed in a marginally better mood this time, and the material, too, was marginally better (primarily through the introduction of a Tony Joe White song that Felton had gotten from his friend Bob Beckham), but he recorded only three songs before departing in much the same disgruntled mood. The following night they got two more songs, and then on the fourth night of recording, with a new band in place (everyone else, anticipating that Elvis would work in his usual rapid-fire fashion, had made prior commitments), Al Pachucki discovered that Elvis' personal hand mikes had been stolen, and once Pachucki confirmed to Elvis that this was the reason for the bad vocal sound they were getting, Elvis just walked out and didn't come back. Felton went on recording instrumental tracks both that night and the next in the vain hope that he might return, but when he didn't, Felton shut the session down at 5:00 A.M. on the morning of July 26.

Of the thirty master numbers assigned to the session, only eight had been filled, with backing tracks for an additional four songs on which Elvis might or might not choose to overdub his vocals. It was a disaster any way you looked at it, and RCA felt badly let down. Colonel, too, was furious not just at the publishing debacle, to which he was convinced Felton had contributed by introducing his friend Beckham's songs, but at Elvis' own increasing refusal, or inability, to live up to his commitments. Most of all, though, the session was professionally catastrophic for Felton, whose sole perceived value to the Colonel and the company was his ability to get Elvis to deliver and who now, more than ever, found himself under fire from all sides, with no visible ally in sight. And yet Felton appeared to be the only one left with any faith in the future: he remained convinced that if they could just establish a good vibe at the next session, Elvis would pull himself together. All they needed was a good jam-type atmosphere, Felton expounded to an interviewer at around this time. "What I try to capture is to get him when he's just in there singing for himself. [That's why] a lot of the cuts don't have any intro — because they're just done that one time, and that's it. Elvis has to feel what he's singing," Felton explained, without bothering to detail just how difficult it was getting to sneak up on that feeling.

Elvis was back in California within a week to rehearse for the August 6 opening in Vegas. The subsequent reviews were if anything even more devastating than the Tahoe notices for their by now almost matter-of-fact recognition that something was seriously wrong.

"More overweight than he's ever appeared in Las Vegas . . . it's Elvis at his most indifferent, uninterested, and unappealing," declared the *Hollywood Reporter.* "He's not just a little out of shape, not just a little chubbier than usual, the Living Legend is fat and ludicrously aping his former self. . . . His voice, opening night, was thin, uncertain, and strained. His . . . personality . . . was lost in one of the most ill-prepared, unsteady, and most disheartening performances of his Las Vegas career. . . . It is a tragedy, disheartening and absolutely depressing to see Elvis in such diminishing stature."

To his audience it made little difference. Fan reports suggested that Elvis was "much happier," "full of fun for the most part," and seemed to be "enjoying the shows much more." But drug rumors were more prevalent than ever, and there were parties in the suite every night that frequently bore out the rumors. Two weeks into the engagement, at one of those parties, he broke the ankle of a woman named Beverly Albrecq in a karate demonstration that would eventually bring about a personal injury lawsuit, after Albrecq's husband found out how, and where, she had sustained the injury.

The shows themselves took on an increasingly surreal, if generally amiable, quality, climaxing on the final night with Elvis riding in on Lamar's back, a toy monkey attached to his neck. "Good evening, ladies and gentlemen and animal lovers," he announced. "I brought one of my relatives with me. I'm in trouble if he has to go to the bathroom!" It was all, it could be argued, in good fun, and the fans found it hilarious when he sang "Love Me Tender" with "X-rated" lyrics, but there were uncomfortable stirrings not just from the audience but onstage when he interpolated a verse that declared, "Adios, you motherfucker, bye bye, Papa, too / To hell with the whole Hilton Hotel, and screw the showroom, too." He performed "What

Now My Love" tossing back and forth on a bed that Sonny had pushed out onstage, sang the lyrics to "Suspicious Minds" to the melody of "Bridge Over Troubled Water" and vice versa (eventually he performed both songs seriously), and returned to the subject of the Hilton once again just as he was about to go into the "Mystery Train/Tiger Man" medley. "There's a guy here who works in the Italian restaurant," he said quietly, referring to his favorite waiter, who sometimes prepared meals for him in the suite. "His name is Mario, and these people are getting ready to fire him as soon as I leave, and I don't want him to go. He needs the job. And I think the Hiltons are bigger than that. There's no disrespect. I just want to wake up Conrad [Hilton] and tell him about Mario and his job, that's all." Then he went into the medley but stopped in the middle to announce, "This song is dedicated to the staff and hierarchy of the Hilton Hotel," then tore into the opening lines of "Tiger Man," which somehow seemed to take on added significance when he sang, "I'm the king of the jungle/They call me the Tiger Man."

The remainder of the show maintained much the same mix of the frequently ridiculous, the occasionally sublime. For the fans it amounted to a kind of invitation into Elvis' living room, as Elvis himself explicitly acknowledged when he said toward the end of the show, "I know we kid a lot and have fun and everything — but we really love to sing, play music, and entertain people. As long as I can do that, I'll be a happy old sonofabitch."

For the Colonel, though, there was little to be happy about; ever since the first mention of the Hilton, the Colonel had been fuming in the wings, and by the time that Elvis got offstage he was fit to be tied. He had heard all about this Mario, he knew all about Elvis' feelings in the matter — but they were not to be shared with the world. What the Hiltons did was their business and nobody else's, just like what he and Elvis did was their own private concern. He was fed up to the teeth. He had negotiated with Barron Hilton in good faith, he had devoted himself to the boy and covered for him again and again, he had built a career for him on exactly the terms that Elvis demanded: What was he trying to do now? Backstage he tried to talk to Elvis, but they couldn't communicate anymore. Everyone heard angry voices coming from the dressing room, and then the Colonel stomped out, and Elvis emerged more quietly a little later, as if everything had been all worked out.

There was the usual wrap party that night up in the suite. Tom Jones and singer Bobbie Gentry ("Ode to Billy Joe") were in attendance, and Elvis had a surprise for Jones. He was aware that Tom had been having some difficulties with his vocal group, the Blossoms, so he had flown in a promising young gospel quartet from Nashville that included J.D.'s nephew Donnie Sumner (with the show until recently as a member of his uncle's group) and Sherrill Nielsen, whom Elvis regarded as one of the finest young tenors in the field and who had sung behind Elvis with the Imperials on the 1966 "How Great Thou Art" session. His intention was to present Jones with the quartet as a kind of gift, and to that end he had them perform for his guests, which no doubt hastened the end of the party.

The discussion with the Colonel was still on his mind as the evening wound down. The way the Colonel had talked to him — who did that bald-headed old bastard think he was? And what did he have to be so high and mighty about when everyone knew he was in debt to the Hilton up to his ass, which was why they were probably going to be playing there for the rest of their goddamn lives. People were talking about Europe, too — they were saying there was something funny going on, and Elvis had heard more than once that maybe Colonel couldn't leave the country because he was some kind of illegal alien or his birth certificate was messed up or something. For all Elvis knew or cared right now, though, he could have been a Martian — he was just an old man living in the past, his day was done. *Where the fuck did he get off talking to Elvis like that?* Call him, he said to Joe. Get the old sonofabitch up here.

The atmosphere was electric when the Colonel arrived at the suite. It was clear that the old man was still seething from the earlier confrontation, and Elvis was practically jumping out of his skin. There was no attempt on either man's part to hide his resentment now, and for the guys still in the room it was a scene as shocking to witness as any other intimate act of a marriage. For the first time that anyone could remember, they were actually shouting at each other in the presence of others, hurling ugly accusations back and forth until at last Elvis said, "You're fired," and the Colonel said, "You can't fire me, I quit," and each threatened to call a press conference the next day, and the Colonel said, "Fine, but if you want me to leave, you're going to have to pay up what you owe me," and stormed out the door.

The silence in the room was almost deafening. As much as they had all talked among themselves about just such a day, about Elvis' need for an up-to-the-minute thinker like Jerry Weintraub who might have an expanded role in his organization for each of them, the bleak reality of the exchange hung like a chill in the air, as Elvis retreated into the bedroom with Linda, and they were all left to look at one another with a frozen sense of uncertainty and little left to say.

The Colonel had no such problem. He had, if anything, too much to say and was working on putting it all down in his fourth-floor warren of rooms and offices, papered over with reminders of all he had done for the boy. This was exactly what had happened to him twenty years ago almost to the day when Eddy Arnold had dissolved their long-standing relationship with a one-page letter stating his continued feelings of friendship but deep-seated dissatisfaction with his manager's brusque manner of doing business. Then, as now, Colonel had been taken by surprise, but then he had needed a full week to recover and even after that period of adjustment had found himself unable to communicate with Arnold without betraying his hurt. Even as he declared that emotion had no place in this sort of exchange, he had defended himself at length in a rambling, discursive letter that alternated between angry justifications of his actions and a closely reasoned statement of account. In the end he had let Arnold go for a one-time outright payment of $60,000 and the preservation of a limited social and business relationship. But it had not, in his mind, even begun to repay his investment, and it had not begun to make up for the hurt. This time he was determined simply to put the figures down on paper: the boy owed him, and he was not going to be shortchanged.

Colonel summoned Jerry Schilling when he had nearly finished with his accounting. Jerry arrived to find him in pajamas and slippers, his glasses pushed down on his nose, typing away in a cold fury. He had advanced money to Elvis over the years, there were bookings on which he had not taken his full commission, he had set up deals extending well into the future, there were residuals on all the movies, not to mention shared ownership of the two television specials. It was all very well for Elvis to strike out on his own if that was what he really wanted, but he was going to have to pay for the privilege. It was dawn by the time he ripped the last sheet out of the typewriter, and Jerry took the papers back up to a silent star suite.

The reaction the next day fell somewhere between panic and utter deflation. After the brave front he had put up the previous night, Elvis found himself now having to confront the Colonel's figures, as he and Vernon balefully studied the carefully added-up accounts and tried to decide who they might call to help them with this unprecedented situation. The negotiations went on in fits and starts for much of the next few days, with Jerry and Sonny the principal envoys in a war in which direct engagement was contemplated by neither side and information (and disinformation) was spread by neutral parties. Elvis heard that Colonel was ill through the hotel staff. Colonel heard that Elvis had put in calls to Tom Hulett and Ed Hookstratten without ever coming right out and saying what he wanted. It was as if each had taken his best shot and failed to knock the other man out; now they were just staggering around the ring, groggy and uncertain what to do next.

Vernon was sick about the whole business; he didn't know how they were ever going to come up with the money or even be able to proceed without the Colonel. Sonny was exhausted from staying up with Elvis all night every night. The shots the doctor gave Elvis didn't seem able to put him out for more than an hour or two, and Sonny got a summons to come back to the suite almost as soon as he himself lay down. Jerry and Joe, both of whose marriages had just broken up, were scheduled to leave for Europe the following week on a vacation that Elvis was paying for. They offered to put off the trip, but Elvis wouldn't hear of it. There was no question in any-one's mind that there almost *had* to be a reconciliation — but no one could figure out just how it was ever going to come about. Neither side seemed able to make a move.

Meanwhile, Jerry had conflicts and confusions of his own. He had started going out with Kathy Westmoreland on the June tour after watching the romance which had broken up his marriage that spring just drift away for no real reason that he could discern. Then his relationship with Kathy had gone bad, maybe because of the pressures of the engagement but also because of something that was going on between him and Elvis. He hadn't known what it was until Elvis revealed to him in a moment of remorse what, evidently, everyone else in the group already knew: that Elvis was the cause of the breakup of his previous relationship, that Elvis had fucked his girl. He couldn't believe it at first, even though he knew about Elvis and his stepbrother Billy Stanley's pretty young wife the previous summer, just before Linda came into the picture. But that was different. That was just Billy, whom no one took very seriously anyway — and when Elvis started telling everybody about it with that self-satisfied little smirk on his face, like he had somehow gotten away with something, Jerry just put it down to the pills. Now he wasn't so sure. "I don't know how it happened," Elvis tried to explain. "It just happened that one time," he said as if to reassure Jerry that he would not discover any further incidents of treachery even if he were to investigate. "I never did it with anyone else." Jerry was almost dumbfounded. "But she was the one I loved," he blurted out, before adding, "I'm just glad you're the one who told me, and not someone else." Sometimes he felt like he didn't really know Elvis anymore. But he remained a loyal lieutenant, even as he struggled to suppress the sense of betrayal that kept gnawing at him and remember the man he had loved and admired all these years.

Linda, too, was at a turning point. She was worn out. Elvis had been, so far as she knew, faithful for much of the first year of their relationship, an all-time record, he told her. And she had for her part devoted herself entirely to him, with a seriousness of purpose more suited to a nurse or mother than a girlfriend. Vernon had told her that she was just about the kindest person he had ever known; she reminded him of a favorite aunt, and he wanted her to be aware that her dedication had not gone unrecognized. That meant a lot to her, but she needed a break, and Elvis was ready for one, too. So when he suggested that he might run down to Palm Springs by himself for a little while when they finally got out of Vegas — maybe she would like to do a little shopping herself — she seized upon the opportunity, even if she knew what it meant. She was twenty-three years old; she could imagine a different kind of life. She was still in love with him, but she had learned long ago that sexual love was not the essence of their relationship. And not just because of his physical condition — "he was certainly drug-impaired, but in some ways he also transcended the physical. He really did want to get to the heart of another individual. And, you know, it really did hurt my feelings, but I loved him so completely, I loved him enough like a mother loves a child, that I could really let him go."

Jerry and Joe left for Europe on the weekend, five days after the blowup, with the issue still unresolved. In the meantime Elvis had flown in Kang Rhee from Memphis, while Linda's parents and Dr. Nick remained as his guests, and his limousine driver, "Sir Gerald" Peters, brought him his blue Mercedes from Los Angeles. He continued to receive "acupuncture" treatments from his L.A. doctor, Leon Cole, who billed his Vegas visits to his patient, and he decided to sign the quartet he had brought in from Nashville (with whom he had been singing gospel music every day) after things failed to work out for them with Tom Jones. Almost as if to indicate how far removed he was from all the daily strife, he drew up a contract on a piece of scrap paper guaranteeing the backup group a flat $100,000 a year essentially to be on call. They would become part of the show (a third vocal group, bringing the total number of voices behind him onstage to eleven), they would have their own segment, they would be free to pursue opportunities of their own but would be subject to his whim should he feel like summoning them to Memphis, Los Angeles, or Palm Springs — and, as if to prove his business acumen to any lingering doubters, he would get the publishing on all their songs. He named them Voice, after the single-issue spiritual journal *New Age Voice* that Larry Geller had put out and given to him in Vegas when he and Johnny Rivers had recently come to see the show.

Vernon was heartsick at this latest evidence of Elvis' profligacy; he didn't know what was going to become of them if Elvis didn't make up with the Colonel. Colonel, when he heard about it, remarked dryly that the group wasn't worth even $50,000 to the show. But for the three singers, their manager, and the bass player who accompanied them, barely able up till now to eke out a living in Nashville, it was not just one more twist in an implausible storybook tale, it was manna from heaven — although they soon learned they were going to have to negotiate for their expenses, too, if they were to be at Elvis' beck and call.

It seemed as if things might go on like this forever in the strange new limbo in which they were all living. In some ways nothing much appeared to have changed — the Colonel made a deal with the International to get everyone's rooms discounted; business continued to be transacted independently by both parties; Elvis was still acting like Elvis. The only difference was that Elvis and Colonel weren't speaking to one another.

Elvis finally had Sonny contact Colonel just before they left Las Vegas. "We've got to call that old sonofabitch," he announced. "He's not going to call us." Sonny left the room after getting the Colonel on the phone, so he didn't hear the actual conversation, but his unmistakable impression was that it was Elvis who apologized. At this point it wouldn't have much mattered. Everyone was so exhausted by the emotional roller coaster they were just anxious for a resolution.

By the following week, Colonel felt sufficiently emboldened to assure RCA that Elvis would finish up his vocal tracks for the new album by the end of the month, so they wouldn't lose their November release date. The four instrumental tracks recorded in Memphis would be transferred to RCA publicist Grelun Landon in Los Angeles, who would be the nominal supervisor of a session that would take place not at RCA's Los Angeles studio but in Elvis' Palm Springs home — which from Colonel's point of view not only meant minimal disruption to Elvis' schedule but also virtually guaranteed that Felton would have nothing to do with the recording.

The very fact that another session was needed was Felton's fault, the Colonel strongly believed. Felton was to blame for the situation they were in. He catered too damned much to Elvis' whims and allowed Elvis to be drowned in a sea of voices and orchestration, when all the fans wanted to hear was *Elvis'* voice — the boy could record with a damned glockenspiel, and it would still sell. Just get him to put his voice on the tracks, the Colonel exhorted RCA. Let him know there was no time for any overdubs, no time for remixing, just have him get it right the first time. They would know better how to say all these things to Mr. Presley, he told the record company — and, of course, it was their decision in the end. As they were well aware, he would never presume to tell them their business; the only reason he was getting involved now was because of the unusual circumstances of the session and the concern they all shared about getting the product out on a timely basis.

The recording sessions, on September 22 and 23, did not go altogether as planned. Elvis turned out to have no interest in three of the four songs they had on tape; in fact, his greatest interest appeared to be in recording a demo tape on Voice, whom he had flown out a few days earlier not for the session but just to sing with him while he was in Palm Springs. Nor was his enthusiasm for the group limited to their music. Noting that Sherrill Nielsen could use a hair transplant, Elvis arranged for the operation to be performed in his living room the morning of the session, while he himself was undergoing acupuncture treatments for the broken finger he had suffered in a karate workout three days before.

It was not the scene that Grelun Landon had anticipated. Elvis was in his pajamas eating popcorn, Sherrill Nielsen's head was still bleeding underneath the bandages, and the door, propped open by a cable running to the RCA mobile recording truck parked outside, kept banging in the hot, dry desert wind. It wasn't until the end of the evening that Elvis finally got around to overdubbing his vocal on "Sweet Angeline," the one track from the Stax session that he deemed worthy of completion — but not before spending more than four hours on two song demos by his new group.

On the second night the story was no different, except that Elvis started off by cutting one of Voice leader Donnie Sumner's songs himself with a makeshift lineup that included Charlie on acoustic guitar, Sumner on piano, Voice bass player Tommy Henley, and James Burton, who was there presumably to overdub his guitar onto the prerecorded instrumental tracks. After overseeing three more Voice demos, Elvis started fooling around with Andy Williams' 1958 hit, "Are You Sincere?" It should never have worked — the song itself was a kind of blandly sentimental doo-wop ballad, and the backing was the same as on the previous number — but somehow the spareness of the arrangement, the incongruity of the instrumentation, the near-parodic swell of the voices seemed to release something in him, he was able to convey unself-conscious emotion as he posed the question that he was as inclined to ask of himself as of anyone else. Honesty, simplicity, the purely instinctual gut-level response — that was what his music was all about, it was what it had *always* been about. And if he had thought about it, he might almost have agreed with the Colonel that all the rest could be dismissed as just so much excess baggage.

T HE COLONEL WAS PRACTICALLY BESIDE HIMSELF when he heard what had happened. Once again the most carefully worked-out plans had been laid to waste by the boy's thoughtless irresponsibility, and he was furious that RCA had not exerted greater control over the session. In a telephone conversation with Elvis the following day, he countered Elvis' insistence that the new songs be included on the album with his own even more emphatic insistence that if they were, it would have to be with Elvis' explicit understanding that nothing could be done to them — no voices or instruments could be added. He would do his best to try to get RCA to make the best of the situation, he said, but Elvis had to recognize the time bind he had put them all in. In subsequent conversations with RCA, Colonel drove home the same point in more explicit language than he had ever used with regard to his client.

This did not inhibit him, however, from blowing up at RCA just one week later when he learned that his worst fears about the sale of the catalogue were about to be realized, and Joan Deary, whom he had taken to be an ally in his struggle with Felton, was planning a November release for an anthology called *Elvis — A Legendary Performer*. From the publicity material, it was obvious that this was to be the first in a series of historical reissues in direct conflict with the artist's new product. Not only that, Deary had gone ahead and made her plans *without even consulting him*. With a deluxe booklet containing "pictures, old recording pages or session notes, pictures of early sheet music, magazine covers, recording information, and other similar memorabilia," there was no opportunity even to get in on the marketing end, and he was further affronted that Deary's memo, dated September 7, had taken more than three weeks to reach him. Without missing a beat he fired off a letter to his good friend Rocco Laginestra, the man who had engineered the masters buyout, pointing out that it was just this kind of precipitate and uncoordinated action that he had been concerned about when the record company first proposed the deal, that Rocco and Mel Ilberman had assured him he had nothing to fear from RCA, and that if RCA went ahead with such an ill-considered plan, it could cast serious doubt not only on the spirit of the agreement but on a relationship that had survived on the basis of trust for nearly thirty years now. The album release was quickly postponed till January, and the Colonel was henceforth included not just as an adviser to the series but as a paid consultant.

E LVIS' DIVORCE DECREE was finalized on October 9. It was evident to Sri Daya Mata just how much the breakup of his marriage continued to be on his mind when he visited her not long before the decree came through. She had only recently returned from an eight-month pilgrimage to India, and their telephone conversations had not prepared her for the change she now saw in him. She was struck most of all by how miserable he appeared to be. The bright-eyed, sincere, if somewhat undisciplined young man that she had grown used to, the restless and resourceful spirit who could track her down in India just to make sure that she had not been harmed by an earthquake he had heard about on the news, seemed diminished somehow, robbed not just of his hope but of his beauty and ashamed almost to be seen by her like this. "I think that things were not turning out the way he hoped they would. He didn't have the energy, the enthusiasm, the feeling that he had in his earlier years. He was not at peace."

It was not the financial settlement that bothered him. His father was furious at Priscilla and so was his lawyer Ed Hookstratten for what they considered to be her going back on her word. He didn't care about that — that was only money. What he was concerned about was something of far greater consequence, though he might have had difficulty putting his finger on it. It was the *rejection* that haunted him, the rejection that had come, as he always feared it would, in full view of the world. Perhaps even more than that, she had disrupted his dream; Sri Daya Mata might have said in her kindly way it was his "fantasy," and Priscilla would probably have agreed. But he had always imagined a picture of domestic bliss, the perfect lasting union he had promised his mother would someday come to pass. And now it was coming to an end, not by his own election (though he knew at heart that he had chosen it) but by the public decree of the state.

Priscilla had reopened the case in May, just before the Tahoe engagement. The settlement on the face of it was clearly one-sided: for a man of such wealth to pay little more than $100,000 in a state where community property was the rule, and for both parties to be represented in essence by the husband's lawyer, was patently unfair. *But that was what she had wanted.* Then she got involved in redecorating her new Pacific Palisades apartment (which Elvis had gladly agreed to pay for), and with part of the $50,000 that she received as an initial payment toward the settlement, she opened up a designer clothing shop in Beverly Hills called Bis and Beau (her partner was a friend named Olivia Bis, Beau was from her maiden name). Evidently, the realities of doing business, not to mention the greater experience of her interior decorator and her new partner in the ways of the world, led her to a newfound appreciation for the financial realities of life. At least that was Ed Hookstratten's interpretation when he heard from her new lawyer that he was introducing a motion to set aside the agreed-upon settlement on the basis of "extrinsic fraud."

Since Hookstratten was the agent of the presumed fraud, Elvis had to hire a new lawyer, an associate of Ed's, and various depositions were taken over the course of the summer and early fall before the lawyers finally came to a new agreement. Elvis would pay $725,000 in cash plus $6,000 a month for ten years, which, together with Priscilla's half of the sale of the Hillcrest house (it had finally sold on August 31 for $450,000), $4,200-a-month spousal support for a year, and 5 percent of the new publishing companies, amounted to close to $2 million. In addition Elvis would pay $4,000 a month for child support, and they would share joint legal custody of Lisa Marie.

On Tuesday, October 9, they met at the Los Angeles County Superior Courthouse in Santa Monica in the courtroom of Judge Laurence J. Rittenband and, after twenty minutes, walked out of the courthouse smiling for the horde of photographers and reporters who had gathered on the courthouse steps. Priscilla hadn't seen Elvis in a while and was both dismayed by his bloated appearance and bewildered at the dramatic physical change. He held hands with her throughout the proceedings in chambers, and she kept running her hands back and forth over his poor swollen fingers. They emerged blinking into the sunlight still holding hands, with Elvis looking slightly stunned in what appears to be a jogging suit with a flag on the lapel. Priscilla's stylish new look, set off by a three-quarter-length quilted patchwork coat that might well have come from Bis and Beau, seems fixed firmly on the future. She waved as she walked toward the car with her sister Michelle and was relieved when she saw him wink back.

* * *

S IX DAYS LATER he was admitted to Baptist Memorial Hospital in Memphis in a semicomatose condition. He had started having trouble breathing in California and chartered a plane to fly home. On the plane Linda noticed that his breathing was getting worse despite the steady administration of oxygen. Dr. Nick came out to the house and was shocked by what he found. Elvis appeared edematous, so swollen as to be virtually unrecognizable and barely able to breathe. Nick made every attempt to take care of him at home, leaving his office nurse Tish Henley on semi-permanent duty at Graceland, but when three days later Elvis' condition dramatically worsened and his breathing became noticeably stertorous, the worried physician had no choice but to admit him to the hospital.

In the hospital the first concern was to get him stabilized, and to that end Dr. Nichopoulos had him seen by a team of physicians, who all agreed that his condition was grave. After first satisfying themselves that he was not suffering from congestive heart failure as a result of the obvious buildup of fluids, they settled on the hypothesis that he was experiencing an extreme drug reaction, most likely to steroids of some sort. When he was well enough to talk, Nick questioned him about the medication he had been taking, but there appeared to be nothing in the various pre-scriptions that would account for his "cushionoid" appearance. One of the doctors asked him about the black and blue marks all over his body, and Elvis responded that they came from the acupuncture treatments that he had been receiving for the past eight or nine months. No one could understand how acupuncture needles could cause such a dramatic reaction until Elvis explained that the treatment was administered not just with the usual assortment of needles but with a syringe. When Nick asked Elvis what was in the syringe, he professed not to know. The doctor had told him something about using a local anesthetic to cut down on the pain and maybe a little cortisone to speed the healing process, but he wasn't really sure what exactly was in the mix. Nick pursued the matter in pri-vate with Joe Esposito, who now suggested that he thought there was something more to these injections which Elvis had been getting with increasing frequency lately. Nick called the doctor in California, and after informing him angrily that Elvis was a very sick man, finally got out of him what anyone around Elvis could probably have told him: Elvis was getting almost daily injections of Demerol, and far from being ignorant of the nature of the medication, he frequently touted the marvelous heal-ing powers that Demerol possessed and had even flown the doctor in on a number of occasions to administer the treatment to friends. It was at this point that Dr. Nick realized that his patient would have to be treated as an addict.

In the wake of that revelation he consulted with Drs. David Knott and Robert Fink, two specialists in drug addiction, and on the basis of their recommendations put Elvis on phenobarbital immediately to prevent a severe withdrawal reaction. The next day he started Elvis on methadone, a treatment frequently used to combat heroin addiction, and called in Dr. Larry Wruble, a gastroenterologist, who ordered X rays that showed a bowel ileus, or enlargement of the intestine, that was full of fecal material, undoubtedly a result of long-term opiate (tranquilizer) abuse and the principal cause of Elvis' distended abdomen. Because one effect of long-term cortisone use can be to aggravate a glaucoma condition, he called in the ophthalmologist, Dr. Meyer, too, who found that Elvis did indeed continue to have a mild case of glaucoma in both eyes, something he knew would concern Elvis when Elvis was alert enough to be concerned — but for the moment Elvis was too sick to care.

Over the course of the next few days the medical team closely monitored every one of their famous patient's responses, and Elvis was gradually weaned back to health. They noted strong indications of natural hyperactivity (involuntary movement of his limbs, intractable insomnia) and a disinclination to subject himself to hospital discipline (he sent out for Krystalburgers when he was supposed to be on a liquid diet and surreptitiously took a sleeping pill from his own supply after the nurse refused to give him one). After a liver biopsy, they found that organ to be infiltrated with fatty cells, a condition very likely brought on by medication abuse.

Nick explained his suspicions to Joe, and together they went out to Graceland to search Elvis' bedroom for evidence of exactly what he was taking. There they found three large bottles of pills (one thousand Dexedrine spansule capsules, one thousand Seconal, and another form of sleeping medication), all of which Dr. Nick subsequently disposed of. As Elvis got better, the methadone dosage was gradually decreased, and Drs. Knott and Fink, who had originally held out for Elvis to be admitted to Dr. Knott's drug treatment center, spoke seriously to their patient about the consequences of "iatrogenic and volitional polypharmacy." The patient, they noted, indicated "intellectual assent," though there appeared to be considerable doubt on the doctors' part that such assent would translate into resolve.

Linda was with him for virtually every minute of his more than two-week stay. "I had a cot beside his bed for the first few nights, and he lowered his bed every night to the height of my cot. I kept sliding down, and he would reach over and grab me around the neck and pull me back up again. We were just trying to stay as close as possible. Finally, they brought in a hospital bed for me. Then they started treating me like a patient. I never got out of my gown, and the nurses would come in and say, 'And how are our patients today?' Once I tried to go downstairs and look at the magazine rack (I was going stir crazy), and I got dressed, and Elvis said, 'What are you doing?' 'I'm just going downstairs to look at the magazine rack.' He said, 'Oh, no, honey, if I can't have my clothes on, you can't.' He made me put my gown on and get back into bed. He was just like a little kid, and I was his little buddy. Whatever he had to go through, I had to go through. Some of my most precious memories [of him] are in the hospital. He was cared for. We watched television — we got hooked on the game shows; we liked *The Match Game*. Even after we went home, we watched them."

Jerry and Sonny alternated staying in the room next to Elvis'; his stepbrother Ricky Stanley started to bring in food from Graceland — meatloaf mainly. And late at night, after all the Memphis stations had gone off the air, Elvis and Linda would watch the closed-circuit images the hospital broadcast from the nursery. "The nurses would put 'Hi, Elvis,' on the incubators and cribs and come up to the camera and wave, because they knew Elvis liked to watch the babies. There was one little fellow who actually waved, and after that Elvis and I waved to each other that way. I found that little guy [later]. I tracked him down and sent him some shoes."

Gradually everything returned more or less to normal, although the hospital continued to have problems dealing with its celebrity patient, as even routine tests created something of a dilemma, and they were forced to schedule them in the middle of the night so as to avoid creating too much of an uproar among the nurses and other patients. In the midst of his hospital stay, when he was finally beginning to feel a little better, Elvis got a telegram from the Colonel informing him that he had worked out a new deal with the Sahara Tahoe and eliciting a telegram in return offering congratulations and authorizing the Colonel to sign the contract on his behalf.

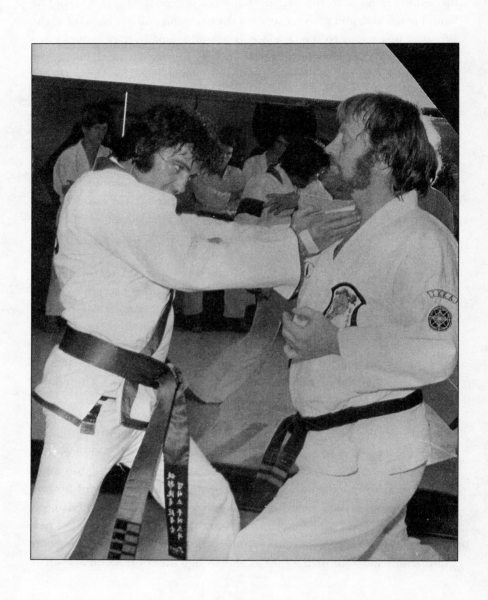

ELVIS AND RED WEST, SEPTEMBER 16, 1974.
(COURTESY OF THE ESTATE OF ELVIS PRESLEY)

THE IMPERSONAL LIFE

T HE IDEA WAS, simply, to get well. The two and one-half months after his hospitalization was the longest period of sustained inactivity since he had returned full-time to live performing two years earlier. More to the point, it represented a commitment to the abstract ideas of self-discipline and moderation absent not just from his life but from his whole way of thinking for quite some time.

His illness had frightened everyone, not least Elvis himself, and he threw himself into the role of the good patient. Dr. Nick came by almost every day for the first three weeks after he got out of the hospital, generally straight from work. Elvis would often be getting up around this time, and they would have breakfast together either in his bedroom or in Lisa Marie's, which Elvis had set up as a kind of sitting room across the hall. Despite all of Dr. Nichopoulos' efforts to educate the staff about the importance of diet to Elvis' health, he couldn't keep the cooks from preparing all the food they normally prepared or the maids from serving it, so "a lot of times I'd go by at mealtimes just to eat part of his food, so he didn't eat too much." Convinced that there was no way to wean his patient entirely off sleeping pills, he placed him on a moderate amount of medication — Valmid, Valium, Placidyl, Hycodan — which at first he tried to control by ladling out one week's supply at a time. He learned right away, though, that a week could go by very quickly in the Elvis universe, and when he tried to enlist the guys in monitoring Elvis' intake, he soon discovered that they were no less susceptible to Elvis' powers of persuasion than the household staff. At that point he switched over to small packets of medication, which he or his nurse would deliver, and frequently administer, daily.

Often in the evening Vernon would stop by, and Nick would observe an intimate colloquy between father and son scarcely dependent upon words. No one had been more worried about Elvis than Vernon; his initial sense of panic, his instinctive fear that somehow his son was going to be taken away from him were perfectly evident when the doctor told him that Elvis would have to be hospitalized. And now his sense of relief, his gratitude that his son had been spared were just as transparent. For Dr. Nick the entire experience was an education. After spending so much time with his patient in Las Vegas and on the road, he was amazed to discover now both the limitations and the dimensions of Elvis' world. They spent almost all of their time together at first in Elvis' or Lisa's room, with Linda alone for company and the windows covered with aluminum foil, the two television sets in the ceiling as well as the one at the end of the bed softly murmuring while candles burned on the television stand. The room was full of books, hundreds of them, and most of what they talked about were the ideas that Elvis got from those books, abstract ideas about life and love, the afterlife and reincarnation. "A lot of times he would just stay up in his room and read. He would do a lot of writing in the margins of the books. I would think it would be interesting for someone to go back and put some of [those notes] together. Of course he liked to talk about medicine. He asked me to bring him a book on the colon one time, so he could understand it — it was really a sincere curiosity."

If on occasion he failed to stop by, he found that Elvis' feelings were hurt — and he found that he missed it, too. For the most part he didn't charge for his visits, and it was certainly an unusual doctor-patient relationship, but Nick came to feel a sense of privilege, and he was the kind of physician who prided himself on his ability to relate to his patients irrespective of background. His entire practice was based on an easygoing manner and direct affability that all his patients recognized.

He continued to address some of the other abiding health concerns: the hypertension, the enlarged intestine and related colon and bowel problems; he even tried to persuade Elvis to visit a sleep clinic in Arkansas, and when that attempt failed, got his friend and patient Sam Phillips to make a tape of ocean and rain sounds to help screen out some of the distracting noise that Elvis was bound to run into when he went back on the road. Linda was his best ally in all this: she kept up with the medications, looked out for shipments of unmonitored drugs from doctors in Las Vegas and California, and was a positive force in every way, doing her best to cheer Elvis up when he needed cheering, jollying him along when he complained that he was not a child — he didn't understand why Nick didn't trust him to regulate his own intake of medicines. "Linda was a really good influence on him. She tried to help him any way she could. She would bring out a different side of Elvis, his humor, his 'carrying on.'"

For Linda it offered a respite of sorts, a return to some of the relaxed good feeling with which their relationship had started out. It was nice to see Elvis enjoying himself, hear his bubbling laugh once again, watch him be able to take things a little more in stride. It was like a vacation in a way, with nothing hanging over them. Sometimes they would just get together with a group of friends and sing and fool around; one time at Linda's parents' house someone turned on a tape recorder as Elvis sang Hank Williams sad songs and Jimmy Reed blues in a warm, relaxed voice, offering up "That's All Right" and a falsetto version of "Spanish Eyes" with a loose confidence that seemed decades removed from the grandiloquence of some of his recent public declamations. He harmonized with Linda, then joined in on her Alpha Delta Pi sorority song, doing one verse with her in ricky-ticky double time. "Did you ever hear the little poem I wrote?" he asked innocently, then recited with earnest gravity: "As I awoke this morning/When all sweet things are born/A robin perched on my windowsill/To greet the coming dawn/He sang his song so sweetly/And paused for a moment's lull/I gently raised the window/And crushed his fucking skull." You can hear Linda's peals of laughter amid the general hilarity. "Oh, Lord, that's funny," someone says. "When you first told me that," Linda says, still laughing, "I thought, how beautiful, it's so pretty, the little bird . . ." It could be a group of friends anywhere, just hanging out and having a good time, not thinking about anything much except maybe that it was getting close to dinner. "Are you getting hungry?" Linda asks, and as if on cue everyone offers the same west Tennessee version of Shakespeare that Elvis had introduced them to. "He's got that lean and hongry look," they all explode in self-mocking drawls, savoring an old joke that scarcely needs to be repeated to trigger the response.

H E WENT BACK INTO THE STUDIO in December after a brief sojourn in Palm Springs, during which Linda visited Puerto Rico. Once again it was decided for the sake of convenience to record at Stax, and once again for all of the shakiness of his position Felton remained in nominal charge, though he was not permitted to use his own engineer. Instead, at Joan Deary's orders, New York studio manager Larry Schnapf sent down his head engineer and three assistants, along with the same sixteen-track mobile recording unit that had traveled to Palm Springs that fall, thus allowing them to bypass the Stax board altogether.

The new Stax session went far better than the last, due in large part to

Elvis' attitude. Two of Elvis' favorite Nashville players, pianist David Briggs and bass player Norbert Putnam, augmented James Burton and Ronnie Tutt to make up the basic rhythm section, and the room was filled with eleven backup singers, including the Stamps, Voice, Kathy Westmoreland, and a female studio trio. The material was a big improvement, too, as Elvis really got untracked on the first selection, a gospel-flavored, revival-styled number from "Burning Love" author Dennis Linde entitled "I Got a Feeling in My Body," and threw himself into everything from sentimental favorites like "Spanish Eyes" to Jerry Reed's hand-clapping "Talk About the Good Times" to a rueful cover of "Good Time Charlie's Got the Blues." Even on the rockers, though, you miss some of the lighthearted, easygoing sense of play that you hear on the home tape with Linda and that characterized even the most serious ballads of the early sixties, when Elvis seemed to glory simply in the freedom of his voice. It's hard to tell whether he no longer trusts that voice or merely deems it unsuitable for public occasions, but the overall impression is one of greater weight, less sheer *fun*. The session was as successful as any in the last three years nonetheless, throwing in such refreshing changes of pace as Chuck Berry's "Promised Land" and Red West and Johnny Christopher's "If You Talk in Your Sleep (Don't Mention My Name)" and coming up with a total of eighteen finished masters in seven days.

It was the business that remained the problem, with Freddy once again failing to deliver, despite what would appear to be his clear self-interest. Colonel was at a loss to understand why this should be so, unless it was that Mr. Bienstock had gotten so big he didn't have time for an Elvis Presley session — but the result was publishing chaos and a web of political intrigue that didn't do anybody any good. Red, Felton, Lamar, even Marty Lacker, were all competing for cuts, but except for Red's number and one song out of Nashville, the only copyrights that went to Elvis Music were two songs by members of Voice and a third that the group brought in. Elvis himself leaned toward numbers that he had worked on with Voice and even incorporated several duets with lead singer Sherrill Nielsen into the session, and the fact that Red always seemed to have the inside track on the single didn't sit well with other members of the group either. None of this contributed to any strong feelings of camaraderie, with Voice bearing the brunt of much (but by no means all) of the resentment, and Lamar at one point exploding, "Who wrote that piece of shit?," only to discover that it was the Donnie Sumner song that Elvis had brought into the session himself.

For Norbert Putnam it was a nonmusical moment that stood out. "We were having lunch as usual around midnight, and just by accident we were sitting together on a riser that had been pushed over in a corner. I remember I said, 'Elvis, I've got to tell you something. If it hadn't been for you, I wouldn't be here. I mean, thank God "Blue Moon of Kentucky" only had three chords in it!' Well, Elvis laughed, but then he started talking about going to England and Australia, and he said, 'I really want to go, but Colonel doesn't want to do it. He thinks if we put them off, that will just keep their interest up.' I said, 'What are you going to do?' He said, 'Put, I'm thinking about pulling away from the Colonel.' " It was as if, Norbert thought, he were trying out an idea he couldn't voice to any of the others, covered by a cloak of anonymity. And when the brief interlude was over, he simply said, "Okay, I guess it's time to go back to being Elvis."

The Christmas season continued in this mood, as he kept pretty much to himself, spending time with Linda and her family, getting introduced to racquetball by Dr. Nick, showing little of the boisterous spirit that had characterized Christmases past but none of the wild mood swings that had proved so disturbing lately either. He was growing increasingly worried about going back to work, he confessed to Dr. Nick, who on several occasions judged his insomnia to have worsened sufficiently that he sent a nurse out to Graceland to administer sleeping medication injections. Rehearsals were scheduled to begin at mid month, eleven days prior to the January 26 Hilton opening (at Dr. Nick's recommendation, and with Colonel's approval, the engagement had been shortened to two weeks), and Elvis was clearly ambivalent about getting back into the race.

F OR THE FIRST TIME IN THREE YEARS he dispensed with the cape as part of his costume, and he was in good shape, reported the *Las Vegas Sun,* "at the top of his form, in good humor . . . extremely generous time-wise, and a jam-packed Hilton main showroom responded warmly." This is not to say that he was without panache, or without the flashes of anger that had accompanied other recent appearances. "You sonofabitch," he snarled at one girl who yanked at his necklace, and at another show he kicked at another fan. But for the most part it was a relatively predictable appearance, with a solid, well-rehearsed repertoire and a new bass player, thirty-year-old Duke Bardwell, replacing Emory Gordy. Bardwell, who came in on the recommendation of drummer Ronnie Tutt, was such a late addition that he had to fit into Emory's stage clothes, not an easy undertaking even after he had lost a good deal of weight. A lifelong fan, he was nervous from the start, and it didn't help any when a buzz from his bass amp irritated Elvis on opening night. For all of his adulation, though, he found the music itself a letdown, with little room for the kind of freedom and feeling that had originally drawn him to Elvis Presley as a teenager.

Voice, on the other hand, who, like Duke, were making their Vegas debut, had no such scruples about the situation: they were in fact excited about almost every aspect of their job, from Sherrill's featured duet with Elvis on "Spanish Eyes" to hanging out with Elvis in the penthouse late at night. For them it was all new, sitting alone with Elvis in his bedroom talking about philosophy and religion, looking out at the Las Vegas skyline lit up at night. He played them "Softly As I Leave You" from the Charles Boyer album over and over, telling them the story that singer John Gary had told him, how the song was really not a standard love song at all; it was about a man who was dying and telling his wife good-bye. Sherrill already knew the song, and one night the two of them sat down at the piano, and Sherrill started singing while Elvis, who had introduced the number in his August engagement, did the Charles Boyer recitation. "His dad, Vernon, was there, and he said, 'Elvis, that's beautiful. Why don't you do that onstage?' And he said, 'Well, I think we will.'" So he sent for Glen D. to sketch out an arrangement, and from then on, it was a featured part of the act. Sherrill knew that this only further fueled the resentment of everyone from the Colonel to the band members to the guys. "Everyone disliked us because we had an in that nobody else had. They were all [still] upset that he had hired us. But Elvis said, 'Don't let it bother you.' He said, 'If I want to buy an airplane and fly it over this hotel and crash it, it's my goddamn money, and I'll do with it what I want to.' 'Cause he knew [about the] jealousy."

With or without Voice there would have continued to be friction, if only because Elvis himself seemed to encourage it. Maybe, as some of the guys speculated, it relieved the boredom, but he never hesitated to set them off against each other in pursuit of his favor. His own behavior certainly did not lend itself to the tranquil life. For all of his reformed ways Elvis seemed increasingly careless not just of his own safety but of the safety of those around him. Red and Sonny in particular had even less respect for his judgment with firearms than they did for his karate skills, particularly when he was stoned. Now it seemed he just didn't much care as he shot out the dining room chandelier one night because he was "bored" and shot out television sets on the most casual whim. There was more than one occasion when he pulled a gun on Red, and Red dared him to use it. As Joe said, everyone was always "a little tense, not knowing how Elvis was from one day to the next." Linda had as much reason for concern as anyone else. She was not about to forget the incident the previous year when Elvis had shot at a light switch while she was in the bathroom, and the bullet went through the wall, nicking the toilet paper holder and shattering the closet mirror. When she emerged, understandably shaken, all Elvis had to offer by way of apology or explanation was, "Hey now, hon, just don't get excited."

No one understood how she could maintain her composure, let alone her sense of humor — but she did. And she seemed able to accept his other whims equally well. If Elvis wanted to be with another girl, Linda just made herself scarce, as she did on one occasion when Ann Pennington, a twenty-three-year-old model with a three-year-old daughter whom Elvis had met the previous fall, arrived in Vegas. To Joe, in charge of all the travel arrangements, it was like a game of musical chairs, but to Ann, even at the beginning of their relationship, it seemed more a matter of Elvis' trying to keep boredom at bay, as he told her all the familiar stories, impressed her with his knowledge of karate, and showed a tender side of himself that she could respond to with all the freshness that went with hearing and experiencing it all for the first time.

She was fond of Elvis, but it was no great romance — she realized early on it was never going to lead anywhere, and she couldn't help but observe that for Elvis, too, the flame was quick to flicker out. "I remember the first time I went to Palm Springs he was like, 'Will you come in the bedroom? I just want to kiss you.' I said, 'I don't know.' He said, 'I swear I won't do anything. I just want to kiss you.' He really did like more than anything just to cuddle and kiss; the other just wasn't very important." He loved to spend time in his room singing to her, and "he gave me a Charles Boyer album, there was a song 'Where Does Love Go (When It Leaves the Heart),' he would play it over and over and say, 'Listen to that, the way he says those lines. It's so romantic.'" Sometimes he would show off to her by telling the guys a joke and controlling their reaction. "He would say, 'Ann, watch,' and they would all laugh, and then he'd go like this [a snap of the fingers], and they'd just stop."

They read books together and talked about what they read, but if she offered any opinion about what she saw as evidence of his increasingly self-destructive behavior, he would just tell her she didn't understand. "He said, 'You don't know what it's like to live this life. You don't know how hard it can be.'" One time they smoked pot together and laughed and laughed, but she awoke in the middle of the night to discover that he had wet the bed. "So I got on the very edge of the bed, and in the morning he said, 'God, Annie, I'm so sorry, why didn't you wake me? You laid in that one little place.' So he had the maids come up and carry the mattress out of the room. He didn't seem to be embarrassed; he was laughing, telling the guys, 'She lay in this one part, the only dry spot!' He was funny."

Even in the brief time she was with him, she was aware of other girls, because he told her. She had other boyfriends, too, but she found it hard dealing with someone so needy when she had a daughter to look after. It was hard on him, too, he told her. "He said he never liked to think that I had been with anybody else." It was during this engagement that he met another girl, named Sheila Ryan, to whom he was obviously attracted. Ann didn't meet her at the time, but it probably wouldn't have bothered her all that much if she had. She was never really in it for the long haul.

H E STARTED TOURING AGAIN three weeks after the Vegas close, a southern swing that brought him back to such once-familiar places as Monroe, Louisiana; Charlotte, North Carolina; Roanoke, Virginia; and Knoxville, Tennessee. Everything was pretty much as it had always been, though Dr. Nick went out with them this time in an official capacity — over the financial objections of both Vernon and the Colonel, and over the objections of his own medical group. They saw his serving the needs of one patient so exclusively not just as a potential loss of income to the partnership but as a threat to his independent judgment as a physician. Nick worked out an arrangement, though, where the group got paid the equivalent of what he would have been expected to bring in for every day that he was absent, and he went out with three suitcases full of what he judged might be necessary to serve the medical requirements of seventy-five people.

He worked out a protocol of medication for his principal patient, too, from the time that he arose in the morning until he went to bed at night. It encompassed everything from multivitamins and appetite suppressants to the throat decongestant and 500mm of Dexamyl prescribed as a pre-show treatment by Elvis' Las Vegas physicians to the painkillers that were often sought for back and neck strain to the packets of Amytal, Percodan, and sometimes Dilaudid that he needed to get to sleep after the show. Dr. Nick was constantly seeking to address Elvis' intestinal problems, which frequently led to constipation, and the administration of an assortment of laxatives, along with the shifting array of other depressants, could some-times lead to incontinence. For the most part, though, he was able to keep Elvis on a pretty good balance of medications, occasionally substituting a placebo when Elvis became too demanding of something he didn't really need — although Nick suspected that with his sophisticated knowledge of the *PDR,* his patient was aware of the substitution more often than not.

The big surprise on the tour was the reemergence of Jerry Weintraub and Tom Hulett of Management III. Banished on Colonel's orders since the November 1972 tour, they had been brought back as promotion partners by RCA Record Tours head Mel Ilberman, who, with a change of administra-tion at RCA and a new president, Ken Glancy, was having second and third thoughts about the appropriateness of a record company being in the tour business. Management III was committed to doing the job right this time, Ilberman informed Colonel early in the year, and after spluttering enough to eke every ounce of political advantage that could be gained from either party, Colonel conceded that Ilberman was probably right — with Tom Hulett he had always had an effective ally in bargaining for the buildings, and Jerry Weintraub had served sufficient penance and had enough other irons in the fire at this point to leave everything in Hulett's capable hands. Their addition would merely streamline the Colonel's team, which now included George Parkhill on a full-time basis (he had left RCA in the fall), Pat Kelleher and an RCA support system, and, of course, the Colonel's own staff, headed up as always by Tom Diskin and augmented by William Morris trainees — in all, a formidable army, ready to jump at the Colonel's command.

Elvis stayed in a separate hotel for the first time on this tour, and there was some grumbling about that, but overall morale was good. Voice was a focal point for whatever resentment did exist, and their general propensity for screwing up — habitual lateness, missing the airport bus, fundamentally unprofessional behavior — did not add to their popularity in any quarter. To Sherrill Nielsen the ensemble effect of all those voices was stunning: "I don't know of any act on the road that had the power when all of us were really with it. For a big ending it was just awesome." But the constant carp-ing got to him, and there were rifts even within the group, so Nielsen left the tour after the fourth date, replaced as vocalist by the group's Swedish piano accompanist, Per "Pete" Hallin.

One old girlfriend flew in to join him in Monroe just as Sheila Ryan was leaving and was shocked to discover the naked need she saw Elvis dis-play for the first time. Dr. Nick was scheduled to come in to give him his sleeping shot, "and I said, 'Elvis, you don't have to, you can go to sleep [without it]; just lay there and let it happen.' He had watched from his hotel room as all the people were leaving the arena, and he said, 'You don't understand. I can't just shut it off like that.' So Dr. Nick came in and set his case down, and then he went out to get something, and Elvis started going through his case. He told me, 'He gave me some pills the other night that look the same, but they're nonaddictive [placebos], and I know it, and he doesn't know I know it, but I know more about drugs than he does.' I said, 'Stay out of there. You don't do that.' 'No, no, I have to, I have to. Don't you say anything. Don't you tell him.' And he took the real ones and put the fake ones back in the case. The next morning I went to see Joe, and I said, 'Please don't say anything, but he exchanged the pills.' And Dr. Nick came in and said thank you and went and put the fake ones back. Elvis came in about an hour later and said, 'All right, who was in there? Who switched those pills?' And he looked at me and said, 'Did you do that?' I was like, 'No.' And he said, 'Someone was in there. I know the [pills] that were in there, they've been switched.' Everyone said, 'I don't know,' and he ranted and raved and was angry — and finally just let it go."

The tour ended in Memphis, where the Colonel, no doubt recognizing the problem of getting Elvis back into the studio again without a struggle, had sold RCA on yet another live recording, the occasion being Elvis' first hometown performance in thirteen years. Like every other appearance on the three-week tour, the five Memphis shows were sell-outs, and in fact the fifth was added almost as an afterthought, prompted by public demand and separated from the first four by already scheduled concerts in Richmond, Virginia, and Murfreesboro, Tennessee. It was only the last for which RCA brought in its mobile recording unit, capturing a performance no more worked out or planned than any other stop along the way. The result conveyed more of a sense of tour-end relief than the keyed-up exuberance that makes for a great live album, with on-the-scene reviewers noting the gaudiness of Elvis' costume and the dramatic unfurling of the American flag during his performance of "An American Trilogy." The *Memphis Press-Scimitar* compared Elvis to Julius Caesar and suggested that his entrance to the strains of "2001" might have been the high point of the show.

AFTER ALMOST TWO MONTHS OFF, there was a brief four-day California tour, which served as warm-up for eleven days in Tahoe. The *San Francisco Examiner* reviewed the Tahoe opening as "listless, uninspired, and downright tired," and Elvis missed two shows during the engagement with what was once again described as the flu. Sherrill Nielsen returned more or less on his own terms (he now sang with Voice but was no longer part of the group), and no one else's opinions changed much with respect to Elvis' "personal" backup singers. The most notable event that occurred in the course of their stay was that Red and David Stanley and several of the other guys beat up a land developer from Grass Valley, California, who showed up drunk and disgruntled outside the suite after paying a security guard to gain admittance for himself and his date. A number of fans witnessed Elvis simply standing there and observing the fight without doing anything to stop it, as four guys held the developer down, according to his later complaint, and the rest beat him to a bloody pulp.

THE COLONEL WATCHED BALEFULLY from the sidelines. He had thought the hospitalization might throw a scare into Elvis, he had thought the boy might turn around — but things were as bad now as they had ever been, maybe worse if you considered that Elvis appeared to have hit bottom and was still sinking. Record sales were down, Joan Deary's *Legendary Performer* album, drawn exclusively from pre-1973 tapes from which neither Elvis nor Colonel derived a penny of income, had already outsold the last three current albums combined, and while there continued to be talk of a second satellite television show and the occasional movie offer still came in, Colonel knew better than anyone that he couldn't pitch a product he was not able to deliver. The one plan on which they still seemed able to agree was the road — it was something they were both used to by now, and the payoff was quick and sure. From the last two tours alone, between them the equivalent of roughly one four-week Vegas run, they had divided more than $1.5 million ($1 million to Elvis, $500,000 to the Colonel) as opposed to the roughly $400,000 they would have to split after completing their two 1974 two-week engagements at the Hilton.

They couldn't go on like this forever, Colonel knew. Sooner or later it would all dry up — especially if the rumors, and the effects, of the drug use didn't stop. As he had in the past, Colonel made half-hearted attempts to broach the subject with Elvis, but Elvis just blew up at him and told him to mind his own business, leaving Colonel, the master tactician, with little idea of what to do to avoid the appearance that he was losing control. He made a stab at explaining himself when he confided to Joe that they could not even contemplate a European tour with Elvis in this kind of condition,

and he blew up at Tom Hulett when he spoke of continued Japanese interest (Hulett had just taken the Moody Blues to Japan in January), citing security as well as medical concerns. Neither Joe nor Hulett altogether believed
him, though they might have conceded the appropriateness of his concerns. But then they no longer believed that Elvis really wanted to go to
Europe either; it just seemed like something he used from time to time to
throw up in the Colonel's face when he really wanted to piss the old man
off. Besides, everyone knew the only subject Elvis would take up seriously
at this point — unless you wanted to get into a discussion of a spiritual
nature — was karate, not just the practice but the philosophy and the mystique. He and Ed Parker, back in favor once again after Kang Rhee had
spent some of the money Elvis had given him on a new house instead of on
expanding his schools, were even talking about making a movie.

He was working simultaneously on his seventh-degree kenpo black belt
with Ed, his eighth-degree in the Pasaryu system with Kang Rhee, and over
the last year and a half had watched karate explode, as *Kung Fu,* the David
Carradine television series, continued to grow in popularity, the *Billy Jack*
movies had found a huge worldwide audience, and Bruce Lee's *Enter the
Dragon,* released posthumously in August 1973, had finally vaulted the sport
into the mainstream. Since the beginning of the year there had been a
steady stream of karate films, frequently linked to the "blaxploitation" genre
that had begun with *Shaft,* and Elvis had seen movies like *Cleopatra Jones,
Golden Needles,* and *Black Belt Jones* over and over again. He studied the films,
pointing out subtleties that none of the guys picked up, running the movies
over and over, until everyone wished he would get on another kick. With
his cousin Bobbie Mann, who had married a wealthy Memphis businessman, he got the idea of starting a karate school of his own and, against
his father's advice, provided financial backing for the Tennessee Karate
Institute in midtown Memphis, which Bobbie and Red West would run
and for which he brought in U.S. middleweight and touch-style kumite
champion Bill Wallace, formerly affiliated with Kang Rhee, as principal
instructor. It was around this time, in the spring of 1974, that he first started
getting serious about the movie.

"I want to be the baddest motherfucker there is," he said of his own
proposed role in the film, which vacillated in conception between the kind
of action feature that might give him the chance and the semidocumentary
approach that Ed seemed to favor. He and Parker spoke of filming some of
Ed's tournaments and sending a karate team around the world when he
closed in Tahoe at the end of May. They were still lacking any structure for

the movie, though, so Elvis had Jerry Schilling get in touch with Rick Husky. Husky, the former Arkansas State student who had inducted Elvis into his Tau Kappa Epsilon fraternity in the fall of 1960, was now an avatar of action TV. He had gained entree to the Elvis world through his former fraternity brother Jerry Schilling, and for the last two and one-half years had been a frequent visitor in Vegas. A writer/producer on such series as *The Mod Squad, Cade's County,* and the current ABC hit *The Rookies,* Husky was used to being kidded by Elvis about maybe someday writing a part for him, so he wasn't altogether surprised when he heard from Jerry that Elvis wanted to talk about working up a story line for the movie.

He arrived at the Monovale house to find Ed Parker already present and everybody watching TV. Elvis indicated that he wanted to talk to Rick and Ed alone in the den, but when they sat down on the heavy leather sofa and padded armchairs, Elvis could barely speak. "It was the first time that I'd ever seen him stoned. I remember saying, 'Elvis, I would really be excited to write something for you, but let me tell you how I look at this. I don't want to use the word "comeback" because you've never been gone, but you haven't done anything for a while, and I look at it like Frank Sinatra with *From Here to Eternity.* There was such focus on his coming back —'

Parker said, "We don't want to talk about *From Here to Eternity* and Frank Sinatra."

I said, "Look, Ed, can I just say what I'm going to say here —" Because Parker had this demeanor, you know. I said, "Elvis, if you come back in the right vehicle, something that has a dramatic role to give you some dimension —"

Elvis said, "Ed's right. I'm not talking an Academy Award."

I said, "I'm serious. Let's get something with a part you can really play that's not just a karate movie. The karate will come out of the story and the action —"

But basically the meeting never went anywhere, because Ed kept interrupting, and Elvis got up and did some demonstrations with Ed, you know stumbled around a little bit, and it was very sad, and I just tried to extricate myself from the meeting with the thought that, Maybe I'll get back in when Ed's not here or when [Elvis] isn't stoned. 'Cause I'm just not getting anywhere.

He did give it one more try. Recognizing Parker's long-standing involvement in the project, not to mention his financial interest, Rick sought him out at his studio on Santa Monica, but Parker barely gave him the time of day. Pissed off at Parker's attitude, but still motivated by the idea that he could do something that would be good for Elvis, Husky sat down and wrote an unsolicited thirty-page treatment revolving around an ex-CIA agent now running a karate school who sets out to avenge the death of a friend, set up and killed by a drug dealer. It was the old gunfighter coming reluctantly out of retirement and proving himself one last time, perfect for Elvis, Husky thought, and he took the script to Jerry, who left it in Elvis' bedroom. "But I never heard anything about it again — except later I heard that Elvis was going in a different direction with Ed Parker."

The direction in which he was going was the same one that Parker had been so insistent on from the first, a straight documentary focusing on karate philosophy and technique, *kenpo* technique, with Elvis supplying the narration. Ed brought in a former student and karate associate named George Waite to produce, and Waite in turn brought in filmmaker Bob Hammer as director. Together they planned to film up to half a dozen karate tournaments that Parker would set up around the state, and Ed put together an all-star team, including lightweight champion Benny Urquidez and kicking specialist John Natividad, that Elvis would sponsor and send to Europe to be filmed in competition that fall. At the same time, Elvis got together with Bill Belew to design a logo and uniforms with some of the same showy glitter that marked Elvis' stage costumes, an element altogether foreign (and some said inappropriate) to the world of karate.

To Ed Parker's surprise, for all of Elvis' brave words and all of the alienation that had so clearly grown up between his manager and himself over the last few years, he still sought the Colonel's approval on the project. "I told him, 'Dump the old bastard.' But he wouldn't. Which I admired him for." Colonel for his part had no admiration whatsoever for Parker and begged Elvis to promise that he wouldn't put up any money until they had at least had a chance to study the matter more closely. Elvis agreed, but eventually he put up the money behind Colonel's back.

Vernon might have been a more effective ally in the Colonel's campaign if he had not been going through some personal turmoil of his own. He had met a young divorced nurse named Sandy Miller on tour in Denver and moved her to Memphis with her two children earlier that year. Life on the road had affected him pretty much the same as everyone else, and he and Dee had never had an easy marriage. "He treated me like a child," said Dee, a tumultuous woman who now envisioned a career for herself as a professional songwriter. "He kept me in a cage." In June they finally decided to separate, and Vernon bought a home on Old Hickory Road, just around the corner from the house on Dolan where he had lived for the last ten years. Elvis wasn't going to shed any tears over the breakup of his father's marriage, but it didn't leave Vernon in any position to criticize either.

A S IF TO MAKE UP for lost time, they embarked on yet another twenty-one-day tour in June, the third time they had gone out this year. This time Elvis and Colonel's 65-percent share of the gate was almost $2 million with over $1.5 million for Elvis and the Colonel to divide after expenses. More and more, though, Elvis' erratic behavior was being mentioned in reviews, even if it was not picked up on by fans. The gaudiness of the show, the camp aspects of some of its Vegas glitz, the lush showbiz sentiments and orchestrations of much of the music, the bizarreness of some of the spoken interludes, all these elements led critics to begin comparing Elvis to Liberace or Zsa Zsa Gabor, not unkindly much of the time and often with the puzzled nostalgia of a fondly recollected fifties childhood — but without any of the respect that you would give to a groundbreaking contemporary artist, or even an historical figure who still mattered. The whole troupe sang "Happy Birthday" to the Colonel on the airport runway in Louisville, as they arrived and he took off to prepare the way for them in the next city on their route. It was the Colonel's sixty-fifth birthday, ordinarily an occasion for sentimental gestures, but there was no sentiment to be detected on the Colonel's part, and certainly none on the part of any-one else.

T HE VEGAS ENGAGEMENT IN AUGUST represented an attempt at a major change of pace. Seemingly as weary as his critics of the pre-dictability of his own show, Elvis had worked up an entirely different reper-toire for the August 19 opening, dispensing with "2001" for the first time since it had been adopted more than two years before, substituting blues like "Big Boss Man," "My Baby Left Me," and "Down in the Alley" for more sentimental numbers, omitting the medley of past hits, and introducing recent material and songs that he had never done before to go with old favorites like "Polk Salad Annie," "Bridge Over Troubled Water," and "Can't Help Falling In Love," the perennial closer. Voice had an expanded role, opening the show and providing more of the close background singing, even if their musical shortcomings and unprofessional behavior had by now become obvious to everyone, including Elvis.

Listening to a tape of the August 16 rehearsal, or even opening night itself, makes it obvious that the same problems that had plagued the show before were still present, new song lineup or not. The blues for the most part were overblown, the maudlin ballads were no less maudlin, two of the new songs that Elvis was most enthusiastic about, Olivia Newton John's "If You Love Me (Let Me Know)" and "Let Me Be There," were the sugariest of pop confections (they were "such happy songs," Elvis said, helplessly trying to explain the attraction) — most of all, he is straining to push out his vocals in a way that seems to have become almost endemic by now, a reflection perhaps of his physical condition or maybe just a choice of style. Whatever the case, it is the same problem that manifests itself in the studio: where once it seemed his voice floated above the music, was capable of subtly suggesting emotion, even on the bravura pieces, now that voice struggles to summon up strength, trembles with a vibrato that seems both mannered and out of control, and substitutes a kind of thick-tongued bellow for the dramatic modulation that characterized showpieces from "It's Now or Never" to "Suspicious Minds." For the moment these shortcomings were obscured by the praiseworthiness of the effort. But one has only to compare the recorded evidence of this show with the Vegas engagements of 1969 and 1970 to recognize what a falling-off there has been. And one needn't travel far in the realm of speculation to imagine how disappointed, and fearful, Elvis himself at this point must have been.

This was not the critical view at the time. Opening night was reviewed more positively than any show since 1971, and even the *Hollywood Reporter* hailed "the best show . . . in at least three years. [Presley] looks great, is singing better than he has in years, and was so comfortable with his show — with almost all new songs — the packed Hilton showroom gave him several standing ovations."

Nonetheless, "2001" was back on the following night, along with much of the regular show, and within a few days it was as if the revolution had never occurred. It's hard to imagine what could have led him to abandon so quickly a program perceived in almost every quarter as a daring and creative move — other than a failure of nerve. Perhaps he did not sense that feeling of instant rapport welling up from the audience that he had come to almost need by now ("He seemed nervous and was not helped by a very poor audience who reacted very little," wrote Christine Colclough, a loyal

British fan and perceptive critic, in a fanzine account of the opening that was in marked contrast to the *Hollywood Reporter*'s take). But additionally, one wonders if he didn't also feel that his famous "instinct," the one yardstick by which he had always gone, had not somehow, suddenly and inexplicably, deserted him.

Linda for the first time was publicly banished during this engagement. She was highly visible at her ringside booth on the first four nights; then she was gone, replaced almost flagrantly by Sheila Ryan, whom Elvis referred to at subsequent shows as his "new girlfriend."

For Sheila it was not exactly what she had planned. Ever since she had met Elvis in February, it seemed like she had been running away from him, and even after going out on tour with him, she couldn't say that she felt any special closeness. Their first meeting had pretty much set the tone. "I went up to the suite between shows, and Elvis came up from the first show, you know, sweating. I was sitting at the little bar in the entranceway all by myself — you know, I looked like I was thirteen years old in those days, I had an angelic little face, and really my personality went along with it. I was very young, very naive, very midwestern, a blank canvas. So anyway I was sitting there kind of pinching myself, thinking this was just too weird, and he came over and sort of half-hugged me, he was sort of a little boyish, he made some comment about the way I was dressed because I had on a pair of slacks. I don't know what else we talked about, but we went to the second show, and afterwards we went back to the suite, to the bedroom, where he had his dinner.

> He was just like a little kid, all excited about things, and someone at the show had given him a fire engine hat, someone else had given him a bib — they threw things at him all the time — and he put on this fire hat, and he put on this bib, and this is our first date. Not very cool at all, is it?
> Anyway, he just went on about his normal routine, and then at some point I guess he kissed me. The way I felt about it, really, was I was doing it, but I wasn't in the situation, I was looking at the situation. I was observing sort of, from out of my body, thinking, This is just too bizarre. Then he gave me this gold cross that a fan had given him that said "EP" and had a star on it — I still have it as a matter of fact, it's the only thing I have from him. And then I guess he fell asleep. I don't know if he gave me pajamas, but we certainly didn't come close to having sex — it wasn't that kind of a thing, it was just getting to know him. But still I was expected to stay the night, which I didn't want to do.

So I let him fall asleep and got up and got dressed and went home and got up and went shopping the next day, and when I got home, Joe called. "Goddamnit, where are you? Boss is furious. How come you left?" And I was — half of me knew what was going on, and the other half wanted to be independent. I knew, kind of, that was what he expected: he expected me to be there when he woke up. But I was this little rebellious thing. So I don't know. Joe is furious: "You better get back here right away —" Here I'd met the man once, and he's already furious at me. But I went back, and he was having his breakfast, and he was irritated and I was quiet — I was always very quiet, just kind of took it all in.

Well, then we addressed my clothing. I mean, I wasn't appropriate, I always dressed in men's trousers, not terribly feminine. So he had Suzy Creamcheese [the place to go for Vegas fashion] bring over a couple of racks of clothes and shoes and had this fashion show. I would go in and try something on, and if he liked it, he'd get it, and if he didn't, he wouldn't. So that kind of got me a tentative wardrobe. I was kind of like, "What's the matter with my clothes?," and he was very gentle in saying, "Nothing, they're fine, but you're my girl, you got to go into this place, and people will be looking, and I'd like you to look a certain way, is that okay?" And, you know, I guess it was okay, kind of.

Then I spent a couple of nights with him, and, you know, the sexual thing was never a big deal to him, you would think it was, but it wasn't. It was very unimportant — I mean, we had sex, but what he liked best was the petting, the kissing. He'd rather — you know when you're a kid in high school and neck and neck and neck and grope and do whatever you're doing? We did a lot more of that than anything else. It was adolescent — until all of a sudden you graduated into Mother. You were expected to take care of him, and basically that's what the role was — that's what my role very quickly became: to get him things in the middle of the night. He needed water, he needed pills, he needed Jell-O, he needed to be read to. That was what I did. There was still part of the relationship that was romantic, I suppose, for him — he was into the romance, you know. We would go out on the balcony, and he would sing songs to me, but it was really never romantic for me. I had no concept of what love was, I was embarrassed by the gifts and wasn't able to be gracious about it — that was the downfall of our first month together.

After the March tour she didn't hear from him for a while. She moved to Los Angeles and didn't try to stay in touch. Time went by, and one day Sheila called the house, and he got on the phone and sang, "Well, hello there, my, it's been a long, long time," the opening line of "Funny How Time Slips Away," and they started getting together again. Then in August she more or less officially replaced Linda.

JOE COACHED HER THIS TIME — "because Joe liked me being with Elvis. There were women I think that didn't get in because Joe and the boys didn't like them. But Joe was saying, 'Now, Sheila, part of Elvis is giving, and he loves to give, and if you don't show him some sort of reaction, it's hard for him.' So I tried to learn that, you know. He gave me a car, and I remember going, 'Oh, God, it's beautiful, I love it!' And feeling like such a phony. I mean, it was me, not him. Here I am, twenty-one years old, and I've never owned anything in my life, and this man is giving me a brand-new Corvette, and I'm like, 'Thank you,' without emotion. There is something wrong there. So Joe was saying, 'Sheila, get real, will you?' Really, it was just Joe being a parent to me. And gradually I stopped looking at the relationship from the outside and became more relaxed with who he was — I mean, he was a very unusual person, he had unusual circumstances, he was just trying to be comfortable, it wasn't really at anybody's expense. You gave, and you got. Some of it was peculiar — but, you know, I've read bits and pieces about his sexual behavior, and how perverse and bizarre it was, and it really wasn't. It was innocent. He preferred pumping to actual sex. So how perverse is that? It wasn't whips and chains. Adolescent innocence was what it was all about."

Onstage in Vegas, though, it seemed something other than adolescent innocence, as his behavior grew more and more eccentric as the engagement wore on. Even to the fans it was evident that something was wrong. He seemed "sleepy," Christine Colclough wrote of the August 22 supper show; on August 23 and 24 he seemed "slightly tired"; and on August 26 it was announced at 10:00 A.M. that both evening shows were canceled. More disturbing were the increasingly lengthy stream-of-conscious monologues that would have had to concern even the most uncritical fan. The two things that seemed to obsess him most were the gossip columns and the decoration of the showroom. He did something about the latter in the early morning hours after the August 24–25 midnight show. "You know, I've

never liked the way this showroom looked," he announced to bemused
Hilton patrons in one variation or another from the following night on,
right through to the end of the engagement. "It's too wide for a performer.
I had this ramp made so I could come out a little closer to the audience."
The wall decorations of the showroom in particular had always bothered
him, he confided, the angels on the ceiling and the Louis XIV ladies and
gentlemen who decorated the walls in cold marble splendor.

Put a spotlight onto the statues on that wall. Okay. That's nice. I
don't know what it is, but that's nice. Tom Jones was in here the other
night, and he's from Wales. I asked Tom who it [the statue on the wall]
was, and he said it was King Edward. King George, sorry, excuse me,
Your Majesty. Now take the spotlight and put it on those angels [on the
ceiling]. Just look at those dudes, boy. Big fat angels! Put the spotlight
onto this wall over here. You will notice a slight difference. Those of
the Caucasian race. That's what it is, isn't it? Caucasian? It was on my
army draft card. I thought it meant "circumcised"! Anyway, the other
night I came down here at about four-forty in the morning with a
couple of friends who work for me, Jerry Schilling and Red West. Red
is a second-degree black belt in karate — he's got a school in Memphis,
and I'm very proud of him. . . . Anyway, he climbed the fence where
[hotel maintenance] keep their supplies, the paint and so forth, he
climbed the fence, as high as this curtain; he went down and got a little
can of black paint. He put it in his belt, came back, climbed over there,
and we stacked up two tables. I got up with the paint and the brush,
and I was Michelangelo, or the guy that painted the ceiling in the Vati-
can, the Sistine Chapel. I painted that statue. It took thirty minutes to
do. The hotel haven't said a word. I just thought I'd share it with you.

So far as the gossip columns and movie magazines went, he reassured
his public in digressions of equal length and intensity, if half of what they
said about him was true, he would probably be dead by now: the magazines made it all up, and what they printed was pure junk.
    Meanwhile the Colonel, in a development that can be considered only
slightly less bizarre, was hawking copies of an album he had put out on his
own newly formed Boxcar label to customers exiting the show. The album
was called *Having Fun with Elvis On Stage* and was nothing less than a com-
pendium of just such moments as the above, not quite as digressive (they
derived from shows between 1969 and 1972) and somewhat cleaned up, but

the detritus, really, of the onstage recordings that RCA had been putting out ever since Elvis' return to live performing five years earlier. The difference, of course, between the Colonel's collection and regular RCA releases was that *Having Fun with Elvis On Stage* was nothing *more* than a collection of such moments. It was in fact a spoken-word recording — which was what gave the Colonel license to put it out, at least by his own interpretation of the recording contract, an interpretation that RCA for some reason seemed in no hurry to challenge.

Boxcar had been set up as a Tennessee corporation earlier in the year, primarily, the Colonel said, to consolidate all of Elvis' nonperformance merchandising interests, in other words "to exploit and commercialize Elvis' name, image, picture and likeness . . . for commercial purposes on posters, photo albums, statues, pictures, buttons, medallions, etc." He was not, the Colonel was always quick to point out, your typical "'Polo Lounge manager'" but a *show business manager* who always "set about to enhance Elvis' performances with the color and excitement that fans came to expect in any Elvis activity." It was perhaps not entirely coincidental that the enterprise took its name from the gambling term for double sixes, a lucky throw in the game of craps, though Hawaiian DJ and promoter Ron Jacobs, a longtime associate of the Colonel's, cited Parker's cavalier philosophy of recording as the inspiration for the label. "He could make a hit record in a boxcar," the Colonel was accustomed to respond when asked how much the "Memphis sound" had contributed to Elvis' success. "Then people'd start talking about the 'boxcar sound.'"

It appears in any case to have been an attempt to establish merchandising on a more "businesslike" basis and in the process perhaps to reward long-standing associates like Tom Diskin and George Parkhill, who with Elvis were listed as minority stockholders (the Colonel retained 56 percent) in the new corporation. It was also undoubtedly another one of the Colonel's schemes whose ultimate Machiavellian purpose — whether generated by tax concerns, bookkeeping convenience, or simply a compulsion always to add one more layer of obfuscation to the mix — is probably not worth going into here. What *is* worth noting is that Boxcar would seem to have been the first chink in the Colonel's carefully constructed argument for partnership and joint-venture agreements with his sole client. Because Boxcar was clearly set up with the idea of diversification in mind. Already the Colonel had indicated to Kathy Westmoreland his interest in signing her to a limited management contract with the idea of recording her beautiful voice alone, with only an organ for accompaniment. Within a matter of weeks he would be talking to RCA about just such a plan and arranging for demos to be made on a previously unrecorded singer named Charlie Smith as well. For the present, RCA would manufacture *Having Fun with Elvis On Stage* through its Custom Records division, Boxcar would pay Elvis a fifty-cent royalty per album for all concert sales, and RCA would undertake to distribute the album worldwide as a regular commercial release at some point in the near future, paying an advance of $100,000 against royalties, to be split 50–50 between manager and artist. And while the arrangement with RCA made clear that this novelty album was specifically excluded from the terms of the regular RCA contract, it cannot have escaped the Colonel's attention that it might come to be accepted as Elvis' second contractually required album of 1974, should it prove impossible to lure Elvis back into the recording studio that year.

What he chose to ignore was any reaction that Elvis might have had to being made a laughingstock, even at a royalty rate of fifty cents an album, on what amounted to his own label. Even more surprising, given the Colonel's pride in his elephant's memory and mastery of human psychology, was his willful defiance of the lessons of the past: it was only when he set up Jamboree Attractions as a booking agency for other acts in 1953 that Eddy Arnold, his sole client at *that* time, chose to leave him, creating the necessity for Tom Parker to become the Colonel and begin the painful process of reinventing his life for at least the second time. Perhaps he was merely exasperated with his client, he may have simply come to the fatalistic view that what would be would be — but he never seems to have asked himself the question whether, at age sixty-five, he was ready to start all over again.

E LVIS MEANWHILE WAS FOCUSING more and more on karate in his Vegas act. For several nights running he donned a special karate outfit and put on an exhibition of his skills with Charlie as his foil during the performance of "If You Talk in Your Sleep." Then at the dinner show on September 1, with Ed Parker present, he put on a full-scale fifteen-minute demonstration with Red, which brought down the Colonel's ire and pretty much ended the exhibitions. But it did not stop him from continuing to expound upon the subject or from presenting certificates onstage to everyone in the troupe who had been working out with him in the suite each night. "I teach — we have a class upstairs," he explained to the audience. "I now hold the title 'Master of the Art.' . . . Now that I've reached eighth-degree, I can start my own karate organization. We are due to start our own style of karate under the heading of American Karate Institute. We intend it to become an Americanization of the art." He even recognized orchestra leader Joe Guercio, an adamant refusenik in what he referred to as "all that nonsense," by presenting him with a black belt tenth-degree baton.

The monologues went on and on, taking on a form, or formlessness, of their own, sometimes almost crowding out the music. On the last night he delivered what amounted to a kind of extended peroration, with Priscilla and Lisa Marie sitting with Sheila in the booth. He had just finished singing "You Gave Me a Mountain" early in the show, when he decided to offer a clarification of his domestic situation.

> I want to make one thing clear. I've been singing that song for a long time, and a lot of people kind of got it associated with me because they think it's a personal nature. It is not. It's a beautiful song written by Marty Robbins, and I heard Frankie Laine do it, I think it was, and I just loved the song and it has nothing to do with me personally or my ex-wife, Priscilla. She's right here. Honey, stand up. [Applause] Come out, honey. Come out, come on out. Turn around, let them see you. [More applause] Boy she's — she's a beautiful chick, I'll tell you for sure, boy. Boy, I knows 'em when I picks 'em. You know? Goddamn.
>
> Now my little daughter Lisa, she's six years old. Look at her jump up. Pull your dress down, Lisa. You pull your dress down before you jump up like that again, young lady. And then at the same booth is my girlfriend, Sheila. Stand up, Sheila. [Applause] Turn around, turn around, completely around. Sheila, hold it up. Hold it up. Hold the ring up. Hold up the ring. The ring. Your right hand. Look at that sonofabitch.
>
> No, the thing I'm trying to get across is, we're the very best of friends, and we always have been. Our divorce came about not because of another man or another woman but because of the circumstances involving my career. I was traveling too much. I was gone too much. And it was — it was just an agreement that I didn't think it was fair to her, 'cause I was gone so much and everything. So I therefore, as decently as you can do that type of thing, we just made an agreement to always be friends and to be close and care — 'cause we have a daughter to raise — and for her to have whatever she wanted as a settlement.

After the settlement — it came out [at] about two million dollars. . . . Well, after that, I got her a mink coat. I know it. I'm talking about the mink coat. You hang loose over there. The — the XKE Jag after the settlement — just gave it to her. She got me — listen to this — *tonight,* a forty-two-thousand-dollar white Rolls-Royce. [Cheers and applause] That's the type of relationship that we have. [His speech is noticeably slurred.] It's not a bad setup, is it, fellows? I mean, I got part of it back anyway. I wasn't hurting too bad, but I did get part of it back, you know. She bought the car just out of a gesture of love, and she likes this Stutz that I have. It's not a car, it's a Stutz — No, wheeew, God help me, no, it's called a stud — a Stutz. And she likes the stud. [Elvis laughs.] She likes the Stutz. Mike Stone ain't no stud — so forget it. She liked the Stutz and — so I'm going to give her the Stutz and she can give me the Rolls, okay? [Puzzled applause] But I wish [Mike Stone] was a stud, you know. He's a . . . *nice guy.*

I'd like to do a song here, ladies and gentlemen, that is one of the prettiest goddamn love songs I've heard in my life, man. I'll tell you. No, it is, it's one of the prettiest songs I ever heard in my life, I've never sung it, I've never recorded it. I never liked the damn thing till I found out — damn, I got a toothache — till I found out the story behind why it was written, and then I really didn't like it 'cause I don't like that type of stuff. So the next song — no, this is a true story of a song. It's been around for a long time. Charlie, take this belt off, it's going to cut me, castrate me, do *something,* you know. Really, I can't do that — I got things to do, places to — you know. Places to go and other tours and things and cities and chicks and all that jazz, you know. Look, I just — be careful, son, don't let it get caught in the cord. I'll die out here. Electrocute my ass and — excuse me, folks. I mumble things — oh, damn, it's so tight you cut off my hair, man, I can't sing. You know, I sing from down in the gut anyway, shoe soles. It'll never get up here. [And he goes on to tell the story of "Softly As I Leave You," before reciting the lyrics, in hushed and reverential tones, over Sherrill Nielsen's soaring tenor voice.]

Later in the evening he introduced Ed Parker and John O'Grady, citing O'Grady's help with the paternity suit several years before, which O'Grady had now written about in a just-published memoir. "Turned out to be a complete conspiracy and a *hoax,* man," he announced to a startled audience, with reference to the lawsuit. *"There is just no way.* I had a picture

made with that chick, *and that's all*. And she got pregnant by the camera."
There is a mixture of nervous laughter and applause.

But you know what she did? *She named the night*. And the night that
she named, my wife was in — no, my wife was with me in L.A. — and
that's the night she said. Ain't *no way* I'm going to fool around with her
out there, are you kidding me? [He laughs insinuatingly.] Let me tell you
something. If you like things like The French Connection, the Chinese
connection, the British connection, the knee bone connection to the
jawbone, the jawbone is connected to the hambone . . . [The band
picks up the melody and rhythm of "Dry Bones."] You like that type of
stuff, buy this book. It's called *O'Grady*. . . .

John just came back from New York, where he had a meeting of
this — I have been a member of this organization for five years. International Narcotics Enforcement Officers Association. [He reads from
an inscription.] "In recognition of the outstanding loyalty and contributions in support of narcotics law enforcement, this award is a special
honor bestowed upon Elvis Presley.' And so forth. Lifetime member,
International Narcotics Enforcement Officers Association. I just got
that. [Applause]

So I don't pay any attention to rumors. I don't pay any attention to
movie magazines. I don't read them. JUNK. [Much applause] I don't
mean to put anybody's job down. I'm talking about — they got a job to
do, they got to write something. So if they don't know anything, they
just make it up. In my case, they make it up. I hear rumors flying
around — I got sick in the hospital. In this day and time you can't even
get sick. You are [dramatic pause] *strung out*. By God, I'll tell you something, friend, I have never been — *strung out* in my life, except on
music. [More applause] When I got sick here in the hotel — I got sick
that one night, I had a hundred and two temperature, and they wouldn't
let me perform, from three different sources I heard I was strung out
on heroin, I swear to God — hotel employees, jack, bellboys, freaks
that carry your luggage up to the room, people working around, you
know, talking, maids. And I was sick. I was getting — I had the doctor
and had the flu and get over it in one day, but all across this town —
STRUNG OUT! I told them earlier, and don't you get offended, ladies
and gentlemen, I'm talking to someone else, if I find or hear an individual that has said that about me, *I'm going to break their goddamn neck,
you SONOFABITCH*. [Screams and applause] That is *DANGEROUS*.

I will pull your goddamn tongue out BY THE ROOTS. [More cheers] Thank
you very much anyway. How many people of you saw the movie *Blue
Hawaii*? Probably the most successful song — let me get out of this
mood — [And he goes into "Hawaiian Wedding Song."]

Priscilla was beside herself. "I was in shock. Because [in the past] he
would never, ever let on to the audience what his emotions were. You
know, singing was always his way of venting his emotions, how he felt
about something — and he'd get onstage and sing his heart out. And
any song, any given song, you know, he would beat it to death, with more
emotion and more energy — but he never let it out in public. This was [so]
out of character, for someone who had so much pride, you know — everything that he was against, he was displaying. It was like watching a different
person."

H E STAYED IN VEGAS for a few days, going to shows with Sheila,
putting on a brief karate demonstration in the middle of Tom Jones'
performance at Caesar's Palace one night, comparing rings onstage with
Vikki Carr at the Tropicana the next. Then, after a brief stay in California,
he returned home with Linda, where he arranged to have a local crew film
him at the Tennessee Karate Institute, the school he had set up for Red and
his cousin Bobbie, which advertised itself as the place that Red and Elvis —
"a seventh-degree black belt — work out together when Elvis is in town."
He was there, he explained to reporters who had been invited to watch, in
preparation for the start of production on his first motion picture, and he
took the opportunity not only to congratulate head instructor Bill Wallace
on his recent world championship but to "promote" Wallace to fourth-
degree black belt in his own school.

In the film that survives, Wallace is wearing the stars-and-stripes uniform with which he had toured Europe as part of a championship "Team
America" the previous summer, but Elvis more than matches him in trademark tinted glasses, a karate ghi with a flag insignia on the left breast and
"EP" in Japanese-style calligraphy on the back, white bell-bottoms with an
inverted pleat, and white Chelsea boots with stacked heels. Even as he is
performing various demonstrations and commenting on others, his attitude appears lazily proprietary, almost as if he knows something that his
intended audience — including Wallace and Ed Parker associate Dave

Hebler, who has been with him as part of his security team for the last year — do not, and will *never*, know. He looks a little like the cat who has swallowed the canary, or perhaps several canaries, as he "showed he could take it by allowing Red West to punch him four times" without flinching, the *Press-Scimitar* reported, and yet at the same time appeared disturbingly unfit, blowsy and unfocused, his weight clearly having ballooned again since his closing in Las Vegas two weeks before.

The following day he started on a ten-day buying spree in the course of which he purchased well over a dozen vehicles for friends, relatives, and household staff. He also hired a new maid, Maggie Smith, after buying a car that she and her mother were thinking about purchasing for themselves at Sid Carroll Pontiac (he got her one of her own to commute to school several days later), bought a car for his cook's brother and a house for his cook, purchased a boat for Charlie Hodge, and got a double-wide trailer for his cousin Billy Smith so Billy and his family could live at Graceland and always be close by.

In between car purchases, on September 19, he visited Methodist Hospital with Linda to see her brother Sam and sister-in-law Louise's newborn baby. He had always liked Sam, who was dedicated to a career in law enforcement and worked for the sheriff's department while attending law school at night. It was through Elvis' efforts, in fact, and his connections in the sheriff's department, that Sam had been transferred from jail duty to the juvenile division shortly after they met, and the previous summer he had helped Sam and Louise purchase a new home. Still, even Linda was not fully prepared for the attitude of messianic benevolence he projected not just toward the new baby but toward the whole process of giving birth. After checking to make sure that mother and daughter were doing all right, Elvis told Linda he wanted to go into the labor room, where the surgical mask that the nurses gave him could not fully disguise his identity. "There was a lady there in labor, and Elvis came up to her and put his hand on her tummy and said, 'How you feeling, honey?' She said, "'Oh, my God, you look like Elvis Presley.' He said, 'I *am* Elvis Presley.'" But Linda was never sure if the woman realized it was not a hallucination.

Many wondered how Linda could slip back into her old role so easily after what was widely perceived as a sharp public rebuff. It was a question Linda frequently asked herself, and there was no easy answer. Unlike Sheila, she had no trouble either accepting, or showing her appreciation for, Elvis' generosity, and on the outside she maintained a cheerful attitude at all times. But she was no longer sure what exactly her role was, or what she wanted it to be. She knew he needed someone to look after him when all the other girls were gone, and with Joe out in California full-time now and the old gang no longer as close-knit as it once had been, she saw herself and Vernon as the last line of protection when everyone came around with their hands out. She knew they all thought that his manic moods came about just because he was stoned, and she felt like half the guys were hanging around because they didn't want to miss out on the gravy (while undoubtedly ascribing the same motivation to her); in the end, she just couldn't walk out on him at a time when she thought he might need her most.

In the midst of all these ups and downs, Elvis continued to work out his ideas for the karate movie, writing down his thoughts in childish block letters, sometimes dictating to Linda in a fever of excitement. Over a period of time the script became almost a summation of the very values by which Elvis would have liked to have been guided, a portrait of a world in which nobility and ideals were personified and the real meaning of karate came down to "helping a person help himself." All the "best men and best women in karate" would be featured, all of Elvis' teachers and heroes, from Ed Parker and Master Rhee to the best samurai swordsman, the best brick-breaking *karateka*, Bong Soo Hong from *Billy Jack,* David Chow from the *Kung Fu* series, and Jim Kelly, Joe Lewis, Bill Wallace, all national and regional champions. Every style of karate would be represented, so as to put across the idea that it was a philosophical *system* to which all true martial artists were dedicated: "Never to use that which is learned except in extreme emergencies. To protect myself, my friends, my loved ones . . .

> And if seeing a fellow karateka using his skill to harm, to make afraid, to cripple or maim, to do all that is in my power to restrain with whatever force necessary, to report him to a board of regents comprised of 36 high-ranking black belts where he is subject to immediate dismissal, stripped of all his honors, turned over to the authorities, never to regain status in this association. This is one of the purposes of karate: to protect the weak, helpless, and oppressed of all classes, regardless of color, creed, or religion. [punctuation added]

It was an idealized world in which right triumphed over wrong, moral values were upheld, and Elvis was a true teacher, explaining and sometimes demonstrating both the technique and the philosophy behind it. At the end of the film "on a remote hill the camera is on a close-up of Elvis as he stands in fighting stance. The camera zooms back as he does a middle punch with a kee yap, and we see what looks like every karateka in the world doing the moves with him. He then does the Lord's Prayer in *Indian sign language* as a soft wind gently blows around him. The picture ends with *The Beginning* written across the screen."

B Y THE TIME that he went out on tour at the end of the month, whatever strides he had made toward moderation and health at the beginning of the year had long since been abandoned, and Tony Brown, the new keyboard player for Voice and a long-standing admirer who had journeyed out with J. D. Sumner at his own expense for the 1969 Las Vegas opening, was horrified to see the changes that had taken place. "My first night was College Park, Maryland. I was scared, my hands were sweating, and I'm backstage waiting for Elvis to arrive. He pulls up in the car, and he fell out of the limousine, to his knees. People jumped to help, and he pushed them away like, 'Don't help me.' He walked onstage and held on to the mike for the first thirty minutes like it was a post. Everybody's looking at each other like, Is the tour gonna happen? Is he sick? Is it gonna be canceled?"

Even Sonny was shocked. He had been out on the road with the Colonel, so he hadn't seen Elvis in a couple of weeks and, according to Dave Hebler, "he was so torn up . . . the tears just came to [his] eyes." The next night Elvis was fine, though at one point when there was a feedback problem, he snarled at Felton, "Shut that damn sound off, Felton, or I'll take your kidney away from you." Then in Detroit, the third date on the tour, Red and Ed Parker became aware of a cocaine shipment coming in through "a singer in a group that he had with him." According to Red, who had done the drug with him, Elvis had been introduced to cocaine through this singer and a "relative by marriage" some months before, and Red now went down to the singer's room with Parker and Dick Grob. "I kicked in the door and broke his foot and told him if he ever brought any more drugs around it was going to be a lot worse. [But] then Elvis found out about it and called us into his room and said, 'I don't like these bully tactics. I need [the coke].' And I said, 'Man, if you need it, I'm not going to say any more about it. You can have it.'" Everyone knew there was no point in saying anything anyway. Elvis had made his attitude very clear in the past: if you don't like it, he had said at one time or another to every one of them, there's the fucking door.

Newspaper accounts tried to puzzle out exactly what was wrong with Elvis. According to reviewers, he was "bored to death" in St. Paul, hostile and "disappointing" in Indianapolis, sick with the flu in Dayton, and "ill" enough in Wichita that many fans expressed regret that he hadn't canceled the concert. They ended up in Tahoe for four days at the conclusion of the tour, and by the last night, according to bass player Duke Bardwell, "Elvis was just standing there not really knowing what else to do, 'cause he [had] just pretty much run out of gas."

E LVIS TOOK SHEILA WITH HIM to Las Vegas immediately following the Tahoe engagement, putting himself under the care of Dr. Elias Ghanem, a fiercely ambitious thirty-four-year-old Palestinian refugee, who in Vegas had become part owner of the Sunrise Hospital Emergency Room, owner of a private jet service, and not coincidentally doctor to the stars. He had first seen Elvis as a patient in 1972 and, with Dr. Newman and the throat specialist Dr. Boyer, had rapidly become one of his primary Las Vegas physicians. Ghanem ordered a series of tests to check on bladder, colon, and intestinal conditions. A "non-penetrating ulcer crater" was discovered, along with "edematous mucosal folds" indenting the margin of the stomach, and a follow-up study was recommended in three or four weeks. Elvis meanwhile was staying with Sheila in the private bedroom and bath that Ghanem had added onto his house for celebrity patients undergoing the new "sleep diet" that the doctor recommended, which consisted for the most part of liquid nourishment and for which the patient was sedated much of the time in a form of radical appetite suppression.

Jerry Schilling came out to see him with a progress report on the karate film about two weeks into his stay. Jerry had now been named executive producer on the project, operating as Elvis' eyes and ears in much the same way that he had, unofficially, on *Elvis On Tour*. Here, though, since Elvis was putting up the money himself, Jerry got a commensurate promotion, serving in effect as "studio" supervisor as they entered into the preliminary stages of postproduction work. Jerry wanted to set up an office in Hollywood and hire a team of editors to synch up the footage and put together a preliminary cut to assess what had been shot and maybe even to attract a distributor who could be induced to put up the money to finish the film.

Jerry found Elvis in good spirits at Dr. Ghanem's, engaged, alert, quick to okay the location that Jerry had picked out on the corner of Hollywood and Vine and the hiring of the crew that he had selected. He was relieved to see the project finally getting off the ground after all the squabbling and petty jealousies that he had witnessed at the outset of filming and the almost haphazard manner in which the Memphis footage in particular had come together. He was worried about Elvis after all he had heard about the recent tour, but he hoped that this new "sleep diet" might represent the first step toward getting him into the kind of shape he needed to be in to really focus on the project. They reviewed everything that had been accomplished to date. Fifty thousand dollars had been spent, and there were projections for at least $75,000 more. No doubt to emphasize his disapproval without ever actually stating it, Colonel was putting it out among certain members of the inner circle that Elvis was so benighted he had already assigned more than 100 percent of the film's ownership — to Ed, to Colonel, to Vernon and the boys. Jerry was reassured as they went over the figures that Elvis seemed to know exactly what he was spending his money on and how the profits would be distributed — even if his conception of the profits might be a little exalted. It was a good, realistic discussion, ending on what Jerry felt was a justifiably optimistic note.

It was well past midnight when they finished, and Jerry declared his intention to go back to the hotel, but Elvis asked if he could stick around for a little while — there was something else he wanted to talk to Jerry about. Jerry had been going out with Myrna Smith of the Sweet Inspirations for the last ten months. He had worried about Elvis' reaction initially — Elvis had always admired Myrna and was close to all of the Sweets, but Jerry hadn't known how he might respond to the interracial aspect of the affair, given the strong political feelings of some of the fans, not to mention some of the guys. Elvis couldn't have been more positive about the relationship, though, and in fact, when Jerry and Myrna decided in the spring to move in together, "I told Elvis that I was going to get an apartment, and he said, 'What's wrong with your room [at the Monovale house, where Jerry had been living since the breakup of his marriage]?' I told him, 'I don't want to cause any problems with the fans.' He said, 'Look, you're my friend, Myrna's my friend. You're welcome in my house. Screw what anybody else thinks.'" So they had continued to live at Monovale. But Jerry never made any secret of the fact that he would like a home of his own, and when Rick Husky decided just a few weeks earlier to put his West Hollywood house up for sale, Jerry was able to come up with a down payment but ran into a brick wall with the banks on the financing.

Now Elvis came forward with a plan. He would buy the house for Jerry, he would arrange the whole thing with Rick Husky — and he would do it right away. They called Husky at three in the morning, and Elvis quickly negotiated a sale. "I got my checkbook out here, and I'm writing a check — is that okay?" Elvis told Husky, whom he had just wakened "out of a dead sleep. I say, 'Well, yeah, sure, Elvis.' And he said, 'Okay, so we got a deal?' I said, 'Yeah, okay, we got a deal.' He said, 'How soon can you move out? I'll send the guys up there to help you!'"

Jerry was unable to mask his emotions. When Elvis handed him the check, he dropped it, and he could barely come up with words to express his gratitude. Whatever doubts he may have felt in the past year or two, this confirmed all the faith he had placed in Elvis ever since he had first met him as a frightened, insecure twelve-year-old filling in for the team that needed an extra player in a touch football game at Guthrie Park in north Memphis in the summer of 1954. "Jerry, you know why I bought you this home?" Elvis said to him at the official housewarming some three weeks later. "I know I drove all those other guys crazy buying you this house, but your mother died when you were a year old, and you never had a home, and I wanted to be the one to give it to you."

ELVIS SPENT THANKSGIVING with Linda in Palm Springs, calling on Voice to fly in at the last minute — but as usual there was little for them to do, and they spent most of the time holed up at their hotel. He tried one more time to get the Colonel's approval for the karate project, and Colonel drew up a basic business plan with a number of simple variants. Elvis retained 50 percent of the profits in each of the formulations, with 15 percent going to Vernon, and varying amounts to Ed Parker, producer and director George Waite and Bob Hammer, and "the boys" (Red, Sonny, Joe, Jerry, Charlie, Lamar, Al Strada, and Dave Hebler). Ten percent was to be retained for overhead, and it was made clear that "percentage participants" did not draw salaries, and Elvis Presley retained 100 percent ownership of the film. In addition, Elvis' salary and personal expenses of $300,000 would take first position, ahead of profits, and the Colonel would retain all merchandising rights. The addendum that the Colonel tacked on, however, made plain his true feelings and conveyed an unmistakable message to his client. "To produce a motion picture of this nature under any other conditions than those heretofore spelled out, would be a complete failure and would do irreparable damage to the reputation of the Artist and All Star Shows," he wrote. Furthermore, should the project go ahead without the Colonel's participation or guidelines, "as long as I am the exclusive manager of this artist, to protect the artist, and my reputation, it would be necessary to go to the extent of publicizing the fact that I am not personally involved in any of this project . . . [and] a letter must be sent to me by the artist and his legal counsel absolving me of any and all responsibility."

On November 19, the *National Enquirer*, anticipating Elvis' January birthday by a month and a half, ran a headline: "Elvis at 40 — Paunchy, Depressed and Living in Fear," along with an artist's rendering of the subject which graphically sought to convey all of those qualities. The story itself quoted newspaper critics, fans, policemen, maids, banquet managers, and other hotel employees who had observed him on the October tour and found him to be rambling, incoherent, paranoid, and almost desperately lonely. It was the kind of tabloid story that could have been laughed off if there had been no correspondence to real life, but coming as it did on the heels of RCA's official release of *Having Fun with Elvis On Stage,* and in the wake of so much dramatic personal upheaval, it would have been hard to say which was the greater exaggeration: the newspaper piece or the life on which it was based. He had become, as Sheila observed, "like the boy in the bubble. I mean, who cares? Who wants to live? He would say, 'Who the hell am I anyway? I'm a living legend!' Sometimes he lived it, but once in a while he'd just go, 'Oh, boy, what the fuck is going on? I'm just who I am. I'm just this little person.' It's not so complicated as it all seems. He was just this guy who had this wonderful charisma and things got blown way out of shape. He was just this innocent little guy."

He returned to Las Vegas at the beginning of December to put himself once again in Dr. Ghanem's care. Linda accompanied him this time, and Jerry once again came out to deliver a progress report. Elvis asked him about the new house and how Myrna was doing after spraining her ankle at the housewarming party. Everything seemed fine until the phone rang in Jerry's hotel room in the middle of the night. It was Elvis, but Jerry barely recognized the voice, it was so weak. "He said, 'Jerry, can you help me?' I said, 'What's wrong?' He said, 'I'm on the floor, and I can't walk. Nobody's here.'" By the time he got to the house, Linda was with Elvis, but there was still no sign of Dr. Ghanem, who kept much the same hours as his patient. When he finally got in, Jerry confronted the doctor, expressing angry disbelief when Ghanem insisted that he was unable to understand what could have happened, since he was simply treating Elvis with placebos. "I said, 'Goddamnit, I'm going to tell you something: this man is a proud man.

He's been at your house for weeks, and I have to come pick him up off the floor — and you're telling me you're just doing placebos?' I guess I really blew up at him.

"Well, I go out there the next day, and Elvis is out of bed, he's on the exercise bike, and he is pissed. It's just me and Charlie there, and he knows — he knew I had a temper, not that he was afraid of it, but he just keeps looking at Charlie and saying, 'Goddamnit, when you fucking guys get your medical degree, then you can tell my doctors what to do.' And he — oh, man, he just went on and on. I knew not to say anything. I was just glad he was out of bed and on the bicycle and not falling on the floor. I knew after he calmed down I could talk to him. So I just acted like he really was talking to Charlie, and a couple of hours later I just said, 'Elvis, I'm telling you something: a year ago, when you were with Dr. Nick —' And he said, 'Oh, that sonofabitch charges too much money.' Which, you know, Elvis could care less about the money — but he's still being defensive. I said, 'All I know, Elvis, is you've been here, you've been in bed for a month [all told], and you're not doing anything or having any fun. I mean, it was pretty sad last night —' I had to be very careful not to embarrass him. 'All I know is, when we were back in Memphis last year, after you got out of the hospital, you were eating right and looking and feeling good, and we were really having fun.'"

Jerry wasn't sure how much, if any, of it sank in, or whether or not he might just get fired on the spot, as Elvis kept pedaling away furiously on his exercise bicycle, and Charlie tried to puzzle out how he had gotten in the middle of it all. It wasn't long afterward, though, that Elvis and Linda returned to Memphis for the holidays.

I T WAS A DISMAL CHRISTMAS. Voice flew in and out at every summons, but Elvis rarely felt like singing nowadays. On December 3 Red O'Donnell had reported in his column in the *Nashville Banner* that Elvis was on the blink with a tummy ulcer and that his next RCA recording session, put off once already from November to December, had now been postponed until "sometime in January." The karate movie was ingloriously shut down on December 24, the day after Elvis returned home, with no other explanation but "health problems." There had been a reasonably successful screening for influential Hollywood rock manager Elliot Roberts just four days earlier, but things were closed down in such a hurry that nobody got paid for the last two weeks, and a good many bills remained unpaid well into the following year.

On December 29, prompted by reports coming out of Memphis that Elvis was sinking into a deepening depression and was increasingly isolated from nearly everyone around him, the Colonel made a rare telephone call to Elvis and concluded that the reports were true. They had barely spoken since Palm Springs, but Colonel was now forced to recognize that Elvis would not be ready for his scheduled Las Vegas opening in less than one month's time. He directed Elvis to telegram him the next day with a message expressing his appreciation for "your signing any papers necessary for me while I am recuperating." He also contacted Henri Lewin at the Hilton, informing him that their mutual friend, Dr. Elias Ghanem, had pronounced Elvis unlikely to be ready for the January 26 opening and that in his judgment the best thing to do was to postpone right away. You can read the Colonel's discomfiture between the lines, but he put a good face on it, referring Lewin to Dr. Ghanem for the proper wording of the press release, which would not officially be sent out for another twelve days. He did everything he could have been expected to do, he carried out each distasteful task with his customary professionalism, but there is nothing to disguise the fact that for the first time he is being forced to admit that he and his client are unable to meet their obligations.

It had been a difficult year, though not one without its compensations. There had been no *Aloha from Hawaii,* but then you couldn't expect that kind of a once-in-a-lifetime triumph on an annual basis. Record sales were down, it was true, but Vegas attendance had never flagged, and the road show was doing better than ever. This year alone, in seven weeks of touring, they had earned approximately $4 million after all expenses had been paid, in addition to the $650,000 to $700,000 they had netted in six weeks in Las Vegas and Lake Tahoe combined. Recording income added maybe another $750,000 to be split 50–50, a comparatively negligible sum perhaps but handy disposable income for two such conspicuous consumers. The Colonel had little doubt he could keep the show going if given the opportunity, but one question continued to nag at him, refusing to go away: Was Elvis willing, or even able, to go on?

ELVIS AND LINDA. (COURTESY OF THE ESTATE OF ELVIS PRESLEY)

A LEAF IN THE STORM

Singer Elvis Presley privately observed his 40th birthday yesterday in self-imposed seclusion at his Graceland Mansion on Elvis Presley Boulevard. . . . He slept until about 3 P.M., when his uncle, Vester Presley, phoned in his birthday greetings from the guard house at the gate. Vester, who has worked as a security guard at Graceland since 1957 and has not seen his nephew since Christmas, said Elvis "talked like he was feeling pretty good. He said he was resting up and trying to get in shape to go on the road again. He doesn't plan to leave the house." . . . The reference to getting in shape came amid growing press reports that Elvis is "fat and 40."

— *Memphis Commercial Appeal*, January 9, 1975

IT WAS AS IF a pall had descended upon the house. The bustling kitchen remained ready to cater to his every whim twenty-four hours a day; the guys all gathered downstairs to pay anniversary tribute, and perhaps to share in birthday largesse. But Elvis never came down. Only Linda and his cousin Billy had unrestricted access to his bedroom upstairs, as the world mocked him for failing to uphold the promise of eternal youth. Even Johnny Carson, whom he had long admired, made jokes about being "fat and forty," and Elvis told Billy that he could hardly watch the program anymore.

Linda, off on a shopping trip to New York just a few days before his birthday, protested the "heartless, cruel, vicious rumors" about Elvis using drugs, pointing out to *People* magazine that "Elvis is a federal narcotics officer!" To Elvis, though, she was beginning to express her true feelings for the first time, telling him tearfully that he was killing himself, no longer willing to be put off by his confident declarations of medical expertise or breezy assurances that he was going to live to see his grandchildren grow up and marry. The Elvis that she saw every day was a man suffering from

555

severe depression, someone who was often barely able to get out of bed. What scared her most of all was that he seemed a willing partner in his self-immolation, a secret conspirator who knew but simply didn't care. Once, not too long before, she had asked him what he thought was his biggest character flaw. "I'm self-destructive," he said, to her surprise. "You do recognize that?" she said. "Yeah, I recognize it," he admitted, "but there's not a lot I can do about it." And they never spoke of it again.

The Colonel was no less alarmed. And, like Linda, he had no one, really, in whom to confide his fears. Vernon didn't want to hear about it, because Vernon couldn't control his son. And Colonel knew that if he refused to book Elvis, somebody else would. Perhaps just as much to the point, if he took Elvis off the road, what would his own recourse be? The Colonel had always prided himself on his ability to survive by his wits — but now he found himself in a box of his own making. By focusing all of his efforts on a single client, he had built an intricate web of relationships, a maze of trust and contractual arrangements that effectively prevented anyone else from getting in. Now, though, he might have wondered, could he get out?

Finally, on Thursday, January 9, the day after Elvis' birthday, an event occurred that served to galvanize the Colonel's thinking. It was much like other turning points in the past — a random item in the newspaper that happened to catch the Colonel's eye. There had been a tornado in McComb, Mississippi, that had killed ten people, left hundreds homeless, and caused millions of dollars of property damage. The Colonel called Tom Hulett immediately, and together with former RCA executive George Parkhill they flew to Memphis the next day. It was Hulett's first visit to Graceland, and he was excited about seeing Elvis' home as well as his involvement in the Colonel's scheme.

"I had never been this much on the inside before, and here I was all of a sudden part of a unit going to see Elvis about possibly going back to work. Elvis came downstairs in a robe looking very heavy, and we sat at the big table in the dining room in tall, high-backed chairs. There was some small talk, and then the Colonel said, 'Elvis, you been reading about the problems down in McComb?' And he said, 'Yeah, it's really terrible.' The Colonel said, 'You know, I think we should go down and do a benefit for those people. What do you think?' And Elvis goes, 'You know, I don't know . . .' Because there was this funny shit going on between them, like Elvis is saying, 'I ain't gonna work,' and the Colonel is saying, 'I ain't gonna *let* you work' — and now the Colonel has finally found an outside vehicle to break the ice. And there I am sitting there, and Elvis is looking at me like, 'What are you doing here?'

"Finally, Elvis said, 'Well, I guess,' and the Colonel said, 'If we go down and do the benefit, we might as well add on a few dates.' *That's* when I got the connection. And Elvis goes, 'Well, I guess so.' 'Well, what if Mr. Parkhill and Tom and I go to Mississippi and [talk to] the governor and see how it looks?' Meanwhile, the Colonel already had the governor in tow, and everything was done. So after about an hour, Elvis says, 'Great, call me tomorrow and let me know what's going on.' Which meant he had agreed to go back to work. As soon as we get in the car, Colonel says to Parkhill, 'George, call the governor. I want a meeting tonight.' We were at the governor's mansion by eleven o'clock with the governor and all of his cronies. The Colonel says, 'I want you to get a hold of the Coliseum tomorrow, and I want all the concessions donated, all the stagehands donate their time, Elvis and the band donate their time, everything, *everything* goes in the benefit.' The governor says, 'How can [anyone] make any money then?' And the Colonel says, 'We ain't making any money here.' But then we added on three more shows in the same building [on the next tour] and made those non-benefit!"

The announcement went out to the papers the next day, and a full two-week tour was booked by the following Tuesday to start three weeks after his rescheduled March engagement in Las Vegas. At almost the same time, Elvis put down a deposit of $75,000 on exiled financier Robert Vesco's impounded Boeing 707, spurred on no doubt by Memphis singers Charlie Rich and Jerry Lee Lewis' recent acquisitions of private Lear jets and in pursuit of his own longtime dream to have a plane of his own. This was little more than a momentary diversion, however; to those around him his continued lassitude was of growing concern. Nine days later, in the early-morning hours on January 29, Linda awoke to discover him struggling for breath. In a panic she called Vernon, and Dr. Nick had him admitted to the hospital right away. A "Presley source" cited a "liver problem which has nothing to do with alcohol," while Vernon put out a statement that "Elvis has been planning for several days about going into the hospital," but everyone knew what the problem was. Dr. Nick was simply hoping to get the medications under control again and make sure that no further systemic damage had been done to the liver or intestine.

Under hospital supervision Elvis quickly lost ten pounds, though his abdomen remained distended because of the way in which his colon was backed up, due to a combination of a congenitally twisted ganglionic fold and the poor muscle tone to which his overuse of laxatives was thought to have contributed. Once again there was real reason to be concerned about the liver, but no further deterioration was observed. In almost every respect this visit was just like the last: the windows were all covered over with aluminum foil; Linda joined him once again in his room, and they watched the newborn babies over the hospital's closed-circuit television system; at least one of the guys stayed with him each night in the suite. It was a kind of vacation from responsibility, but two events took place to interrupt the tranquillity of his stay.

The first was the kind of everyday occurrence that might well have been overlooked under ordinary circumstances. Elvis' aunt Delta got a package at the house with a Las Vegas postmark and gave it to Jerry and Sonny to take to Elvis at the hospital. Though they had long since given up trying to thwart Elvis in anything he set his mind to do, the idea of simply delivering an unmarked package to his sickbed disturbed both Jerry and Sonny, and when they opened it up, it came as no great surprise to discover a bottle of "heavy-duty" pain pills. Feeling that he had no alternative, Jerry took the bottle to Dr. Nick. "I thought, 'I may lose my fucking job, but I don't care.' But Nick said, 'No, you know what? I think Elvis is in a great place; just go ahead and deliver it, and we'll see what happens.' So I brought Elvis the package, and he asked everybody to leave the room, he told them he had to talk to me privately. He said, 'You know, my dad's got a real bad prostate problem, and I got some medicine for him, and I didn't want anybody to know about it.' He said, 'Just go and put it up in the cabinet.' So I did, and he never touched it, and after about five days Nick just said to him, 'What is this in here?' And Elvis went, 'I don't know. Just throw it away. It was probably the person in here before me.'"

Vernon Presley had joined his son in the hospital by now. He had obviously been under a lot of pressure, looking and feeling poorly for some time, before he suffered a heart attack early on the morning of February 5. Once his father got out of Intensive Care, Elvis installed him in the room next to his, but he was still sick with worry. Vernon had never been in the hospital before, and the two of them found themselves drawn back to old times and frequently painful memories. One time, when Elvis' cousin Billy was in the room, Vernon tried to put the blame on Elvis for his heart attack. "He said, 'I can thank you for this.' [And then he] blamed him for Aunt Gladys, too. He said, 'You worried your mama right to the grave.' Elvis broke down and cried. It about killed him."

Nick continued to run drug screens, despite his sense that Elvis was in a better frame of mind. All of the tests came up clean until February 13, the day of Elvis' discharge from the hospital, when traces of unprescribed barbiturates showed up in his urine. Dr. Nichopoulos never confronted his patient directly, but in addition to prescribing Elavil for what he was beginning to sense was serious depression, he arranged that either he or his office nurse, Tish Henley, would stop by Graceland every day to administer the various medications.

THE COLONEL HAD SCHEDULED a recording session for March 10, eight days before the Vegas opening, but Elvis was determined to stick around Memphis to gain some strength and lose a little weight, at least until Vernon got out of the hospital. Some days Dr. Nick would drive out to Graceland several times at Elvis' summons, and he continued to find himself drawn into Elvis' world, against the advice of family and friends. He was not blind to its dangers, but clearly he was not blind to its attractions either — or to his patient's almost seductive charm. Even his family priest, Father Vieron, urged him to let Elvis go. "He told me that he thought I was doing myself an injustice, I was doing my practice an injustice, my patients, my family. . . ." But Nick remained steadfast in his purpose; he believed against all the evidence of his senses and observation that he could get Elvis straightened out. He did the best he could to get him started on a low-carbohydrate diet and got him playing racquetball again, a sport at which Nick excelled, first at the Y, then at Memphis State late at night. It was not unusual for him to be out with his patient until three-thirty or four in the morning, then go to work just three hours later. He probably could not have said why he was doing all this, but as with anyone close to Elvis, it was obvious to him that there was a yawning emotional chasm in Elvis' life, and while it might be equally obvious that that chasm could never be filled, there was an almost universal impulse to try.

Elvis loved to watch old *Monty Python* episodes with Linda and Billy. He knew most of the shows by heart, and they would toss lines back and forth till the tears ran down their cheeks, but other times he would dwell on the past or seek out Dr. Nick for more serious discussions of medicine and philosophy. He saw a good deal of longtime RCA promo man Bill Browder, who had just had a number-one country hit under his stage name of T. G. Sheppard, during this period. "Up until 1974 we had been friends, but our friendship got deeper. If I went out on the road and had a problem, he could relate, because he'd been through it twenty years earlier. Sometimes we'd just sit and watch the ten o'clock news, and I'd catch him saying almost word for word what the newscaster was saying, and I'd say, 'How did you know —,' and he said, 'I saw it at six.' He talked about marriage a lot with my wife and myself. He'd say, 'I don't want you two to ever split up,' and his voice would crack and he'd say, 'Bill, you don't know what's in store for you.' He said he got saved once when he was living in Tupelo, and he was filled with the most wonderful spirit, and he gave all of his comic books away. He was an intensely lonely person, so alone with his fame and his thoughts. He said, 'Those people don't love me in a personal way. They don't know what's inside me.'"

THE SESSION ON MARCH 10 at RCA's recording studios in Los Angeles bore a strangely unacknowledged weight. Elvis had failed to deliver a single studio cut in 1974, and while technically he may have fulfilled his contractual commitments with a haphazard live album and the Colonel's curious scotched-together construction, *Having Fun with Elvis On Stage,* there was little question of RCA's anxiety about their longtime star. His records were neither selling nor even being taken seriously. The *Los Angeles Times'* Robert Hilburn had responded to the release of his latest LP, *Promised Land,* by suggesting that maybe it was time for Elvis to retire (the album was "as bland and directionless as all those soundtrack albums Presley cranked out in the 1960s," Hilburn declared), and not one of his recent albums or singles had sold close to half a million copies. Still, no more thought or preparation appeared to have gone into this session than any of the last few, and Freddy failed to deliver a single usable cut from the new catalogue.

Elvis brought Sheila and Lisa to the first day's session and with little rehearsal embarked upon the Pointer Sisters' aptly titled "Fairy Tale" (suggested to him by Linda) in too high a key. The next song, "Green, Green Grass of Home," was the same mournful country number that Red had urged him to record in the mid sixties, before it became a hit for Tom Jones, and he sang it with real feeling, then tossed off Billy Swan's number-one hit of the previous fall, "I Can Help," in a single take. It was not that any of this material was unsuitable for Elvis, nor even that the results, however ragged in both the first instance and the last, were any great disgrace; it was simply that they were no more than whatever happened to capture Elvis' fancy at the moment, and they were done with no greater concentration, and no greater commercial potential for the most part, than if he had been singing them in his own living room. He concluded the evening with four takes of Don McLean's "And I Love You So," a Top 30 easy-listening hit for Perry Como two years before, which he sang directly to Sheila, whom he urged to "step up, let me sing to you, baby."

The second and third days of the session were neither better nor worse, with a nice quartet version of the Statler Brothers' barbershop-harmony hit of a few months before, "Susan When She Tried"; "T-R-O-U-B-L-E," a new rocker from Jerry Chesnut that Lamar had brought in; a faithful re-creation of Faye Adams' number-one r&b hit from 1953, the strongly gospel-influenced "Shake a Hand"; yet another number from the Voice catalogue, into which Elvis seemed to pour as much pride of discovery as feeling; and "Pieces of My Life," a Troy Seals ballad that Red had brought him, in which Elvis seemed to see his own life refracted.

In all, he recorded ten songs in three days, barely enough for one very truncated seventies-era pop album, with nothing left over for any of the three stand-alone singles that RCA had wanted from the session. The atmosphere was relaxed enough, but there was little of the sense of fun that had once permeated an Elvis recording session, and while there was a funky family feeling in the rough mix that Felton put together in the studio — with Voice frequently filling the full quartet role that Elvis had always envisioned for his backup singers — there was none of the urgency, none of the tension, none of the sense of joyous release that Felton was always hoping to inspire, and little opportunity to do so. There was no way the people in New York were going to be happy with this session, Felton recognized sadly — although, as he was well aware, it could have been worse. At one point Elvis had gotten it into his mind to record Cal Smith's 1974 number-one country hit, "Country Bumpkin," and Felton had had his wife, Mary, type out the lyrics. He couldn't for the life of him understand what Elvis saw in the song — as its title suggested, it went against everything Elvis had ever stood for, both privately and publicly. But he had given up remonstrating, it only seemed to make matters worse. When Elvis showed up at the studio that night, Felton handed him the lyrics sheet and asked with some trepidation when Elvis wanted to do the song. Elvis just looked at him as if he were crazy. "Country bumpkin?" he said. "Country bumpkin? I ain't no fuckin' country bumpkin."

*   *   *

EVIEWS OF THE March 18 Vegas opening were indulgent on the whole ("He looks healthy and sounds good," *Variety* reported), while fan reaction was ecstatic. Elvis could joke about his weight ("You should have seen me a month ago. I looked like Mama Cass"), but to his fans it made little difference. As Sue Wiegert, a true believer since she had first met him as a teenager in Hawaii in 1965, perceptively observed, "What the fans really wanted was just to share an hour or so with him." As overweight as he had ever been, he was unable to fit into any of his old costumes, and there was little of the panoply of the usual Vegas show. There were the usual erratic moments both on- and offstage, but the fans simply didn't care.

On the final night during the band introductions, a wild water fight erupted in which Kathy retaliated, and then Duke Bardwell, to whom Elvis had been giving a hard time all through the engagement, really let Elvis have it with his own water gun. "You sonofabitch!" Elvis exclaimed off mike, and it was obvious even to audience members that he was not fooling around, but they cheered nonetheless as he picked up a bottle of Gatorade and said, "You got an electric bass, son, what are you gonna do now? You're gonna drink a lot of Gatorade, that's what you're gonna do." Then as the band played "Jingle Bells," he said, "I'd like you to meet my manager," and Colonel Parker walked out onstage dressed as Santa Claus, followed by Lamar in another Santa Claus outfit leading Elvis' little chow, Get-Lo. The evening continued with a fan presenting Elvis with a pair of Mickey Mouse ears in exchange for a scarf and Elvis leading band and audience in the Mickey Mouse Club song, familiar to every television child of the fifties. After several more goofy requests and encores, with Elvis, the band, and the audience all joining in the common hilarity, Elvis declared seriously, "I'd like to say something now, ladies and gentlemen. I'd like to thank everybody onstage with me, really. I've been kidding them now for a couple of weeks, but, ahh . . . you've been really fantastic. I'd also like to thank all the people who came to Vegas, with the economy of the country the way it is and everything. It's really nice to see you when I walk out here on this stage." At the end of the performance, as the curtain came down, he stood out on the stage, shaking as many hands as he could, while the audience gave him a standing ovation.

The generic apology, if that was what it was, came too late for Duke Bardwell. He had been ready to quit for some time. He was tired of the erratic nature of the show, and he couldn't understand why Elvis was always picking on him onstage. After the last performance was over, he gave away his TCB, said good-bye to everybody, "shook hands and walked out of there. . . . I didn't like seeing what was happening to Elvis . . . and he actually embarrassed me very, very much a couple of times to where he obviously was just making fun of me to be mean. But I still always tried to remain loyal to the man, because I felt like he was ill. And I don't believe that all those people around him had his best interests at heart at all — only their own. They had nothing else in life than to be one of Elvis' cronies."

Elvis received the news of Duke's departure with equanimity. He had never much liked Bardwell's attitude, he told the guys, and Duke had never been the kind of bass player they needed anyway. If Jerry Scheff wasn't ready to come back yet, there were plenty of other good bass players to choose from before they hit the road again in April. His mind was on other things by now anyway; he was thinking about returning to the movies, but this time in a serious dramatic role.

Barbra Streisand had attended his performance on the evening of March 28, and they had met in his dressing room afterward. She was there with her boyfriend Jon Peters, until recently her hairdresser, who she said was going to produce and direct her next film, a contemporary adaptation of the classic Hollywood fable about success, *A Star Is Born,* with Streisand in the Judy Garland role. What they had in mind was to cast Elvis as Norman Maine, the male lead, played in the Garland vehicle by James Mason, who drowns his sorrows in drink as he watches his wife's movie stardom eclipse his own. In this version, rock stardom would replace movie stardom, language would be updated to reflect changes in both era and milieu, and the dramatic climax would come at a live concert rather than at the Oscar ceremonies.

Elvis was completely turned on by the meeting. He was excited by its subject (he knew the highly emotional 1954 picture well), he was pleased with the idea that Streisand would approach him in this manner, and he was proud of the way he had responded, flattering the Hollywood star just enough, he told Sheila, to inflame her interest but maintaining a good businesslike demeanor as well. He spoke excitedly about it for days to the guys — but he didn't tell the Colonel at first, and when he did, he became furious when Colonel raised objections: that Peters was totally inexperienced in filmmaking; that Streisand and Peters as a team would have a single interest in mind, and that it would not necessarily be Elvis'; that a deal in discussion was very different from the deal that you actually got on paper. Colonel didn't understand, Elvis ranted to anyone and everyone who would listen — this was his chance at last for a serious role. Colonel was no longer in touch; he didn't know what was going on.

But he let Colonel handle it, as he had let Colonel handle all of his business affairs almost from the day they met. And gradually he became persuaded of the wisdom of at least some of Colonel's reservations. He could be taken advantage of by a combination of self-interest and moviemaking naivete, Streisand and Peters could play upon his excitement just to get a better deal for themselves, it was tricky — he could be made to look like a loser just by taking on a loser's role.

Within a week, on April 4, First Artists — Streisand's production company — and Warner Brothers had made an offer of $500,000 plus 10 percent of the gross receipts after break-even, with the movie producers retaining all music and record rights but Elvis and the Colonel free to produce, and profit from, the two live concerts at the heart of the picture. Ten days later Colonel outlined his terms to Roger Davis at William Morris, who would put it all in legal language and carry on formal negotiations. He wanted $1 million in salary for Elvis, plus $100,000 in expenses and 50 percent of the profits from the first dollar, along with approval of any songs that Elvis was to perform, and an unspecified deal to be negotiated separately on soundtrack rights. Mr. Presley had indicated his strong desire to make the picture, Colonel conceded in his letter to Davis, who was by now experienced in reading between the lines, and Parker had been *surprised* to discover that Miss Streisand had made a personal approach on the matter — but he had made it clear to Mr. Presley that "we should hold out for our regular terms" and that "he should have the best deal possible" and not allow his enthusiasm for the project to influence the business end or allow the movie producers to cut "a cheap deal." He also wanted to inform Davis that someone was already planting items in the press and that he had "advised Presley to be handy in case we need him, as I feel very strongly that in this case he should be very much kept up-to-date by us on any negotiations."

Elvis never had to make himself available for negotiations. By the time that he went out on tour on April 24, the movie was already a thing of the past. Nearly everyone around him saw it as one more example of the old man interfering, and Elvis did nothing to discourage their thinking. But secretly he seemed almost relieved not to have to deal with a matter that had blown up so quickly from a long-awaited dream into something complicated, unfamiliar, and ambiguous all at the same time. In the end, he decided, it was just as the Colonel had told him: he was sorry that Colonel was right, but there it was. Streisand and Peters had thought they could take advantage of him; when they were finally confronted with the reality of the situation, that he had access to a strength and business acumen that they had never imagined he would possess, they simply went away.

Sheila, too, he could tell, was in the process of leaving. She said she wasn't, but she was — as she put up more and more resistance simply to going out on tour with him for a few days, as she took in without demurral, or any sign of jealousy or possessiveness, all the signs of turmoil in his life. From her point of view "there wasn't much at stake. I was his friend, I was his little pal, I was taking care of him. The physical side was never very much, and it just became less and less. I wasn't ever jealous — you know, Elvis thought I was a helluva girl." She made no objection when he took a model named Mindi Miller out on the first part of the tour. In fact she welcomed it and would have been happy if Mindi had taken to the life better than she herself did. For Sheila it was almost past trying to explain. She had become little more than a sounding board — but she didn't know how to break the relationship off.

THE TOUR ITSELF got generally lackluster reviews: Elvis was pale and overweight; in many of the shows, according to the critics, he showed clear signs of exhaustion. But the fans loved him, and he and Colonel got to split a $700,000 profit for two weeks' work. For the band it was a sadly dispiriting experience. To Jerry Scheff, coming back after an absence of two years, it was like returning to a world in which all the landmarks were familiar but the atmosphere was altogether changed. "I was used to this really kick-ass stuff; I mean, the music [had] always felt nervous to me because the energy was so high, even the ballads. And if you didn't keep it there, he'd turn around and look and say, 'Hey, what's going on?' So when I went back, there were no rehearsals, they just sent me a tape — and I hopped right into it intensity-wise. And Elvis immediately turned around and looked at me like, 'What are you doing?' And I sort of scoped things out and realized that everything had dropped down a couple of notches." Glen D., too, saw a turnaround that had started with *Aloha* and gradually reached the point where they were all just going through the motions. "Those first three, three and one-half years he just loved to sing, but now he'd just go out there and walk through it sometimes, and something made me think that he wasn't going to live to be an old man." Even the Jackson benefit, a great success by any standard and the original impetus for the tour, was marred by a backstage atmosphere that seemed almost permeated with foreboding. Elvis was photographed with Governor Bill Waller looking very much at ease and just as "modest, shy, and gracious as he could be," in the words of the governor's wife, as he presented a $108,860 check for the tornado victims. But the governor, an AP wire story reported, was "quickly rushed out [as Colonel] Parker, angered by what he thought were too many crowding into the backstage room, constantly shouted, 'Get them back, get them back.'"

T HREE WEEKS LATER they were back out on the road for yet another whirlwind tour, this one concluding with the pay dates in Jackson to which the Colonel had committed at his original meeting with the Jackson businessmen as well as a final show in Memphis. Once again the idea seemed to be to get in and out as quickly as possible, and this time they made even more money — $811,000 profit for twelve days' work. Somewhat against his usual practice, Elvis was actively promoting his new single, "T-R-O-U-B-L-E," by singing it at every show, and he had lost enough weight that he was wearing nothing but jumpsuits again. The record didn't do anything (it sold little more than two hundred thousand copies), but there appeared to be a considerably higher level of engagement in Elvis' performance, as he returned to a more rocking repertoire and even retrieved numbers like "Burning Love" from long disuse. The highlights of the show remained "An American Trilogy," its patriotic closer, and "How Great Thou Art," so transcendent on occasion that audiences called out for Elvis to repeat the ending after he screamed out the line "O my God, how great thou art" in a transport of near-physical emotion.

Back home in Memphis, Elvis split his pants bending over to kiss a fan ("Of all times and places!" he remarked) but generally seemed in fine fettle, playfully chiding the audience that they could have saved their money and seen him for free in a network broadcast of *That's the Way It Is* the previous week. He went on to make the introductions in his usual kidding fashion, pointing out that J. D. Sumner and the Stamps had not been with him when he made the movie, nor had Kathy Westmoreland, who "after tonight [might] not be with me ever." The audience laughed good-naturedly at the harmless joke, but Kathy was stung by this latest in what she took to be a string of veiled and not-so-veiled sexual references. She was sure they stemmed from her refusal to take up her previous relationship with him on this latest tour — and from his disapproval of the fact that she was dating one of the members of the band. In Shreveport he had declared, "Oh, you were with me — but not in the movie," then offered up what she took to be a transparently insincere demurral ("No, no, Kathy's a good Christian girl"). On several other occasions she had watched him turn away from the mike and was certain she had heard him say, "Oh, she's a good lay," under his breath. She wasn't sure who else onstage might have heard him, and there were some in the troupe who felt that she was not above manufacturing drama on her own, but clearly she had reason to be upset — not just by Elvis' cruelty toward her but by the change in character that permitted such cruelty to be expressed. She couldn't even tell him what she was thinking, though, as the gulf between star and supporting cast now extended well beyond the mere separation of hotel facilities.

All of this in any case was lost on the public, who remained, as ever, adoring, and on the press, which continued to describe Elvis as if he were a cartoon hero, a fat, "sensuous clown," in the words of the *Memphis Commercial Appeal,* "[whose] singing seemed to come second to his clowning." The pants-splitting incident was picked up worldwide, and this as much as anything else may have been the catalyst that precipitated Elvis to enter Mid-South Hospital the following week for what the newspapers were calling "an extensive eye examination" but what was in reality cosmetic surgery to give him a more youthful appearance around the eyes.

He called up Dr. Nick on the spur of the moment to let him know that he had made up his mind to have the operation and, when Nick tried to remonstrate, informed him that he would go to California and have the operation done there if Nick didn't set it up right away. After examining him and trying to talk him out of the procedure, the plastic surgeon, a Dr. Koleyni, operated on him at 12:30 A.M. that night, and Elvis remained in the hospital for another day and a half, with Billy and Jo Smith staying with him the whole time. Billy, too, had tried to tell him he didn't need the operation, "but, of course he [wouldn't] listen." Afterward he quizzed all the guys about whether they noticed a difference and showed them where the tucks were hidden, but Billy thought he never looked the same afterward. "To me it ruined his eyes. He always had those sleepy, sexy eyes. And they took the droop out. The droop was part of his mystique."

*   *   *

H E HAD ONLY THREE WEEKS to recuperate before the start of his next tour. For most of that time his attention was largely occupied with the airplane whose purchase had been announced on June 11 but which he had in fact bought in April when the Vesco deal fell through. The plane, which he got for $250,000, with complete refurbishing bringing the total to over $600,000, was a ninety-six-passenger Convair 880 that Delta had taken out of service. He was going to have the interior done mostly in blue, the exterior in blue and white, with "Lisa Marie," the name with which he had christened his new plane, painted on the nose and "TCB" on the tail. Just as he had with the various cars and buses he had had George Barris customize for him over the years, he got caught up in every aspect of the design, which eventually comprised a penthouse bedroom with a custom-made queen-size bed, an executive bathroom with gold faucets and a gold washbasin, a videotape system linked to four TVs and a stereo system with fifty-two speakers, and a conference room finished in teak. As the plans evolved, he started flying down to Meacham Field in Fort Worth to check on the progress of the work, another reason he needed to get back out on the road. Vernon was still vainly trying to recover the $75,000 they had put down on the Vesco plane, but as far as Elvis was concerned, that was water under the bridge. He was caught up in the idea of developing an air fleet just as obsessively as he had ever been in the all-but-forgotten karate movie just six months before.

They started off the tour in Oklahoma City on July 8, then played Terre Haute and Cleveland and Charleston, West Virginia. Elvis wanted Sheila to go out with him but, when he couldn't reach her on the phone, took Diana Goodman, the current Miss Georgia, whom he had spotted in a tour group outside the Graceland gates. Joe kept trying to reach Sheila, and when he finally did, she told him the truth. She had met someone while Elvis was out on the last tour (in fact, it was actor James Caan), and by now she was practically living with him. "Joe said, 'Oh, shit, well, Elvis wants you here — what are we going to do?'" They both agreed that it would be better for Elvis not to have to deal with this until he finished the tour, so they cooked up a story that Sheila had an ear infection and the doctor had forbidden her to fly. Elvis refused to be put off, though. He reacted just as she knew he would, calling a few days later to say he had been thinking about her ear infection and had come up with a solution: he would rent a low-flying plane. She didn't know whether to laugh or cry. "I think he knew, really. He just wanted me there." But when she demurred once again, this time he finally seemed to accept it, telling her he would call when he got back home at the end of the tour.

The tour by this time was already spinning out of control. For all of Nick's efforts to keep his patient on an even keel, for all of Joe's attempts to spare him any problems he didn't need to be bothered with, for all of his fans' adoration and the environment which he had created to insulate himself from the world and its complications, there were things going on in his life that he could no longer control, emotions that he no longer seemed able to bottle up or hide. "How Great Thou Art" seemed more and more to have become almost a cry of pain, deemed inappropriate in some less pentecostal quarters for its raw emotionalism. In Springfield, Massachusetts, he tossed his guitar into the crowd, declaring, "Whoever got the guitar can keep the damned thing — I don't need it anyway"; in Uniondale, New York, at the Nassau Coliseum, he delivered a stunning version of "You'll Never Walk Alone," seated alone at the piano. It was a song he had sung over and over again in private ever since first being inspired by Roy Hamilton's 1954 r&b hit. The message was one of exaltation, God's presence in the midst of peril and fear, but much like the Twenty-third Psalm, the classic Rodgers and Hammerstein composition was dependent for its emphasis as much on the singer as the song — and in Elvis' case the hope expressed in the lyrics seemed balanced by a tone that reflected a heart-rending, almost desperate struggle for belief. The song was the high point of the show, something, Elvis announced, he had always wanted to do onstage, bringing his concert appearances even closer to the kind of unvarnished emotional truth represented by "How Great Thou Art" on the one hand and the water fights and verbal horseplay on the other.

In Norfolk, Virginia, on the next night, the verbal shenanigans got out of hand. Elvis had been riding Kathy for most of the tour, picking up pretty much where he had left off on the last. In Cleveland Kathy registered the words with which she heard him introduce her ("She will take affection from anybody, anyplace, anytime. In fact, she gets it from the whole band") in stunned disbelief, and in Nassau she heard him repeat the same message, adding only, "I mean affection, you fool." This time she was not just stunned, she was angry. He might have his own problems, he might not like who she was dating — but he had no right to treat her like this. "After the show in Nassau I grabbed the nearest bodyguard . . . and said, 'Get the word to him, tell Elvis to stop doing this to me. Tell him I've had it.'"

Evidently that was the wrong message, because he started in on her again at the matinee performance in Norfolk, Virginia. This time she pointed her finger at him and said, "You had better stop this," and he broke off and gave her a kiss. But when Tom Diskin spoke to Elvis again just as he was about to go onstage for the evening performance, his reaction was predictably, if inscrutably, contrary. Early in the show, according to a UPI account, he announced that "he smelled green peppers and onions and that his backup singers, the Sweet Inspirations, had probably been eating cat-fish." It was the kind of incidental, off-the-wall remark that under ordinary circumstances might have passed unnoticed, but now, with everyone aware of Kathy's problems and fearful that they were going to somehow rub off, Estelle Brown hung her head in embarrassment and he lit into *all* of the background singers, declaring, "Estelle, Sweet Inspirations, Stamps, if you don't look up, I'm going to kick your ass."

Estelle left the stage at this point, and Kathy moved over to take her place, but when Elvis got to the introductions, he glared at Kathy and the remaining Sweets and said, "Sorry for any embarrassment I might have caused you, but if you can't take it, get off the pot." Sylvia walked off this time, followed by Kathy, leaving Myrna alone onstage, "singing, clapping, and smiling through the remainder of the performance," according to the wire-service report.

Neither Kathy nor the Sweets knew exactly what he meant by the "cat-fish" remark; none of them thought it was racial — they just knew it was hostile, and there was an ugly undertone not just to that comment but to his whole demeanor. He tried to give Myrna a ring onstage, which she at first refused, then finally allowed him to put on her finger, at least until the show was over. Kathy, Sylvia, and Estelle all made up their minds to quit, and there was enormous consternation throughout the troupe about how this would be treated in the national press. Jerry Schilling, his position complicated by his relationship with Myrna, tried to mollify Elvis, who was livid at the disloyalty displayed by the singers' walk-off. "He wouldn't apologize. He wanted me to be his emissary, but I said, 'No, Elvis, I think this is yours.' He said, 'To hell with them. Myrna can just come out with me. Who needs the Sweets in the show anyway?'"

Everyone's position was sufficiently frozen that Felton called Millie Kirkham, Elvis' soprano backup from the sixties, who had last sung with him five years earlier during the filming of *That's the Way It Is,* and arranged for her to meet them in Asheville two nights later on a standby basis. At the same time, Kathy and the Sweets were persuaded by Tom Diskin to travel

to Greensboro the next day, though they made no promises to go on. And
Dr. Nick simply looked on in dismay, as he saw all of his carefully orchestrated attempts at mood control come to naught, as he watched Elvis take
off on an emotional roller coaster that resembled nothing so much as a
cocaine binge and found himself increasingly puzzled, and defeated, by a
kind of manic energy that he simply didn't know how to treat.

The next night in Greensboro, after getting an apology from Elvis, the
Sweets did go on, but Kathy didn't, and Red told her that Elvis wanted to
see her after the show. "I thought it was funny," he said by way of explanation for his off-color remarks, and when Kathy told him he knew it was not,
he just shrugged, as if he were weary of the whole subject. "He was sitting
on his bed wearing his karate pajamas, and he had a gun. He held up a gift-
wrapped wristwatch in one hand and a gun with the other. He leveled the
gun at me. 'Which do you want, this or this?'

> I tried to compose myself, but my heart was pounding, and my mind
> was whirling with all sorts of crazy thoughts. . . . I just smiled and said,
> "Why, I'll take the gift, of course, thank you!" I laughed, too, but inside
> I was in a turmoil. "Oh, God, what is wrong with him?! What is he
> going to do?" It was so scary I was feeling like every muscle was about
> to collapse from weakness, but outwardly I tried to remain calm. . . . "I
> have to leave the show, Elvis. I'll stay until this tour is over, but then I
> think it would be best for both of us if we weren't around each other."
> He grinned at me and shrugged. "If you think it's best, then it's best. I
> won't say anything to stop you if that's the way you feel."

Everyone in the troupe watched with concern, wondering what was
going to happen next. Some were angry at Elvis, others disillusioned or disappointed. J. D. Sumner felt that Kathy and the Sweets should never have
walked off, it was "unprofessional." Estelle accepted Elvis' apology as
heartfelt; he talked to her quietly until in the end "he was just praying," but
at the same time she recognized "a vast change" that had taken place in a
person she had very much loved and admired. The following afternoon he
changed his departure plans several times and finally left everyone who was
supposed to be traveling on his private plane standing on the runway at the
Greensboro airport because they had arrived a few minutes late. Lowell
Hays, the jeweler, who, along with Dr. Nick, was one of the marooned,
couldn't believe what he was seeing. "He had to send the plane back from

Asheville to get us. As soon as we arrived, someone came up to me and says, 'Elvis wants you.' By now he knows he's messed up, and he wants to buy everybody something. He bought everything I had and [then] he wanted more. He said, 'Do you know any jewelers here in town?' I said, 'No, sir, but I can get the jewelry here in about an hour.' I called Memphis, made arrangements for them to get the jewelry together, jumped on the plane, and flew straight back. Elvis bought what I would call practically a whole jewelry store! He gave something to everybody in the group. He gave each of the Sweet Inspirations a five-thousand-dollar ring."

In Asheville the next day there was an incident that could have made all of this generosity moot. Elvis had developed a toothache in Greensboro and seen a local dentist twice. The tooth was still bothering him a couple of days later, and Nick arranged for another appointment. With the Asheville dentist out of the room, and Dr. Nick watching, Elvis started going through cabinet drawers searching for pharmaceutical samples. Nick remonstrated with him and was sure that Elvis would get caught, but he couldn't get him to stop until the dentist returned. When they got back to the hotel, he insisted on taking the medications away. "I guess I embarrassed him by taking them away [in front of other people]. Then I embarrassed him even more by refusing to give them back." Elvis got as mad as Nick had ever seen him, storming around the room, swearing and out of control, until finally he went into the bathroom to put on his pajamas so he could take a nap before the show. When he came out of the bathroom, he was carrying a gun, a little Beretta that he had by his side. Nick and Vernon were standing together, and as he put his arm around his father, whether by accident or design, the gun went off. The bullet ricocheted off a chair and hit Dr. Nick in the chest, causing more insult than injury ("All it did was give me a little burn on my chest") but scaring Vernon half to death and bringing security guards on the run. Elvis tried to laugh it off, but from Nick's point of view it was a wonder that someone hadn't gotten killed, and Vernon, still frail from all of his recent health problems, just shook his head and asked Elvis what he thought he was doing.

Perhaps the audience in Asheville sensed what was going on. Although the reviews were good and crowd response was enthusiastic, for one of the few times on the tour Elvis didn't get a single standing ovation and on the final night was so frustrated by the lack of reaction that he took requests, once again threw his guitar into the fans' midst, and gave away a $6,500 ring from the stage just to try to get the audience going. Vernon was obviously upset but powerless to do anything to control his son's spending, and even Lowell Hays was disturbed by this latest evidence of Elvis' profligacy. In two days he had given away over $85,000 in jewelry, and while it was Lowell's business to keep the customer satisfied (and his belief that if he didn't do it, someone else would), he didn't want to feel like he was taking advantage of Elvis or his father either. "I was standing there after the show looking all dejected, and he came over to where I was standing and said, 'I saw the way you looked. I know you're upset. You don't need to worry about it. I just have to work an extra fifteen minutes to pay for it.' And he just laughed, and then he went and got in his car."

B Y NOW JEWELRY PURCHASES were almost beside the point anyway. Elvis had moved on to more costly indulgences. After hearing that John Denver had given his manager a Rolls-Royce (his manager was Jerry Weintraub, co-promoter of the tours), Elvis decided to present the Colonel with his own airplane, a Grumman Gulfstream G-1, which he bought sight unseen in the middle of the tour. Elvis had it delivered to Colonel in Vegas on July 26, two days after the last Asheville show, but Colonel didn't really take it the way that Elvis had hoped. "You've got to be kidding," was his first response. And then he turned it down on the grounds that he didn't need a plane and couldn't afford one.

Two days later, on Sunday, July 27, Elvis bought and gave away thirteen Cadillacs at Madison Cadillac, including a blue Eldorado for Myrna for sticking with him through his troubles. He added a fourteenth when he discovered a black bank teller named Mennie Person, who was window-shopping with her family and admiring his Cadillac limo parked out front. "Do you like it?" he asked her. "I'll buy you one." And he bought her an $11,500 Eldorado, telling the salesman to add it to the list, which with this final purchase came to $140,000. When he found out that Mrs. Person's birthday was coming up in two days, he had one of the guys write her a check "to buy some clothes to go with the car."

Some of the guys showed open signs of contempt for his generosity, even as there was a mad scramble to get in on it. All sorts of explanations were advanced, from the need to buy friendship to the use of mood elevators and cocaine — but none of them could get at the sheer mindlessness of it all. And in many respects it was no different from the ranch, the police badges, Voice, the karate film; it was as if once the floodgates were open, he simply couldn't stop. And it was as if, in another way, he were seeking to still some profound disquiet, cover up a need he couldn't quite bring himself to recognize, and expiate some deep inner guilt.

On August 3 he put down $26,000 as a deposit on a second airplane with which he could go visit his first (he signed a twelve-month lease at $13,000 a month). Within two weeks he canceled the lease and bought an Aero Jet Commander for $508,000, which he would in turn sell in another two weeks so as to purchase a Lockheed JetStar for $900,000. At Dr. Nick's urging he had just signed off on another costly undertaking, the construction of his own racquetball court behind Graceland, so he could take exercise whenever the spirit moved him. He gave Marty Lacker $10,000 to help save his marriage, and when he discovered that Dr. Nick was having trouble getting a bank loan for the construction of a new house, Elvis loaned him $200,000 interest free, with no specified plan of repayment — something which Dr. Nick's better judgment as a physician might have warned him against (just as any of Elvis' friends might have taken heed of the strings attached to generosity in any form) but which an equally human impulse to better himself at no visible cost allowed him to accept.

From the perspective of Billy and Jo Smith, who had been living in their mobile home at Graceland for the past year, the root of the problem lay in the fact that Elvis no longer knew who to trust. The old guard was in disarray, but Elvis had little faith in the loyalty of the new guys. More and more he retreated to family, seeking to return to the kind of warmth and security that only family could provide. Who but his grandmother could fondly recall old times, then say to him without self-consciousness, "Son, if you don't quit [spending your money like] that, you're going to be broke." He indulged his daughter shamelessly, looking forward to her visits without really taking on any of the responsibilities of fatherhood, or even of baby-sitting, while at the same time holding up an idealized vision of a future — for her, for himself, for the grandchildren that she would produce — that was markedly untroubled and turmoil free. With Billy and Jo he prayed frequently for those he loved. Sometimes he talked to Billy about just disappearing and taking on a whole other identity, but after Billy pointed out to him that then he would no longer be Elvis, he dropped the subject without ever returning to it again.

He tried Sheila one more time. "He called me at four o'clock in the morning and said, 'I want you to come home.' I said, 'Home? I *am* home.' He said, 'No, I want you to come to Memphis, and I want you to ride your horse.' I said, 'What about Linda?' I don't know why I said that. I think I wanted to make it feel like there was some reason other than that I didn't want to be there, like it was his fault, when it really wasn't. I don't remember if he even asked me if I was seeing somebody else or not. If he did, I lied about it. I said that I needed some time to think about things, that I was confused. He had this tone in his voice that was pretty sad. He said, 'Okay, baby,' and that was the last time we talked."

He called a girl named Melissa Blackwood, whom he had met earlier in the month at a World Football League game. She was nineteen years old, about to start college in the fall, and had just finished her yearlong reign as Queen of the Memphis Southmen (recently rechristened the Grizzlies) — which was how Elvis had first spotted her. He called her at her parents' house at three in the morning and wanted her to come out to Graceland right away, but she told him she needed a little time to fix herself up, so he said he would have someone pick her up at seven.

"We walked in the front door, and the guys said, 'It's up at the top of the stairs, the gold door.' I said, 'You mean I just walk up there?' And they said yes. And, boy, that was the longest staircase I ever walked up. They said, 'There'll be two sets of doors, just go through both of them,' and I did, and Elvis was in bed, he was sitting up in his bed in his blue pajamas, and he just looked so tired, I'll never forget. I just stood there, and he said, 'Come here and sit down,' and he kind of patted the bed by his side. I think he could tell that I was really kind of nervous, because he looked at me and said, 'I want to tell you three things.' The first thing was that he was going to be a perfect gentleman. He said, 'I'm not a make-out artist. I don't try to be.' He said, 'I apologize for this, but it's just the way I have to live.' So then I felt better, because he kind of held my hand, and we just sat and talked, and he called me 'Brown Eyes.' There was a little piece of hair on my forehead that grew down like a cowlick, and he played with that and said, 'Look at this hair,' just like I was a little child.

"After a while he told me to get out of my clothes and put these pajamas on that he had draped over a chair. And I looked at him like, Are you out of your mind? And he said, 'Melissa, I don't mean anything by it. I'll be more comfortable if you're wearing them, I'll feel like you're more at home.' So I went in the bathroom and put them on, and of course they were hanging off my arms, and I had the waist all pinned up in the middle, and I walked out and he just laughed — he thought it was the funniest thing. But after that he never once did one ungentlemanly thing or made a pass or did anything to make me uncomfortable. We just talked and watched TV, and he had a closed-circuit TV, and we watched the people down at the gate to see what was going on outside."

He talked about his childhood and about his father, who he told her had been very sick. He talked about numerology and religion and the meaning of life, how he felt trapped by his success. "I think it was like a dream that pulled him away from the rest of the world, and he was trying to find something to look forward to." To her great surprise he gave her a car that he arranged to have delivered to the house as they sat out on the front porch. "He didn't tell me anything about it, I guess he wanted to see my face when the car pulled up. And finally it came, and I said, 'What is this?' And I remember saying, 'Why? What did I do to deserve this?' And he said, 'You came.'"

After that they went back upstairs, and Melissa fed him yogurt and hot cereal, "and all of a sudden he was so sick he could barely hold his head up. He was just shaking, and it was an effort to swallow, and it scared me to death. Then he took a bunch of prescription pills, I held the glass of water and just fed it to him because he was that sick. He wanted to take some more, but I took the pills away from him. I said, 'You don't need them. You can fall asleep without them. I'll sing to you — anything.' Finally he said, 'All right,' but then he said, 'Will you just stay and hold my hand?' And he wouldn't let me leave. It was the strangest thing. I would sit there silent and think he was sound asleep and get up to leave, and he'd grab my arm and say, 'Don't go.' He wouldn't let go until he was sound asleep. And then I went downstairs, and I said to one of the guys, 'What are these pills? He's sick. We should call a doctor.' And he said, 'Don't worry about it. He's under a doctor's care. He'll be okay later. Don't interfere, you don't under-stand.' And they told me they thought it would be all right if I wanted to go home and show the car to my mother, he'd be asleep for some time, so I could go and do that."

When she came back, he was awake and Lisa Marie was in his room. He laughed when she walked in the door and said, "Well, I give her a car, and she leaves me in it" — but she could tell it really bothered him. He played a 45 of Roger Whittaker's "The Last Farewell," a minor hit from the past spring about a British soldier going off to war and envisioning his own death in the most maudlin terms. "He had Lisa play it over and over, maybe twenty times. He said, 'I just kind of like that song.'" Later in the afternoon they took Lisa to the airport. Charlie was going to accompany her on a commercial flight back to the Coast, "and he was crying when he hugged her, he was just miserable that he couldn't walk her to the plane. But then he cheered back up. He sort of had his ups and downs."

That night they flew to Meacham Field to see his plane. "He took me through the whole thing, showed me the places where they were building the furniture, told me, 'This is going to be here, and this is going to be there.' He was just so proud of it." By the time they got back to Graceland, Melissa's head was splitting, and she told him she had to go home and get some sleep, but he didn't want her to leave. "He said, 'I won't even be here. I'm going to the movies with some of the boys, and you can just sleep upstairs. You'll have your own place, your own bathroom, and everything.' I said, 'I'm sorry, I can't. This is all just too much for me.' He said, 'I've given you a car, I've given you everything, why don't you stay?' I said, 'Well, if that's why you gave me the car, I won't keep it.' And I gave the keys back. And he looked so hurt and said, 'That's your car. I want you to have it. If you don't keep it, I'll park it on the street, and no one's going to use it.' I was in tears, because it was embarrassing to try to tell him that I had to leave. He just couldn't understand. He came over to where I was sitting and got down on his knees in front of me and put his arms around my shoulders. I said, 'Elvis, I'm sorry. I care, but I can't just move in here.' And he said, 'I care, too, babe. That's the problem.' And he just kind of hugged me and was almost in tears, too. He said, 'I'm going to take you to the door, and be careful going home, and call me and let me know that you're there.' Then I did, and he started asking me to come back. I said, 'I just can't. I'll come any other time. I'll come tomorrow.' I went to the house the next day, and he wasn't there. I took him a card thanking him and trying to explain, but I don't know if he ever got it. I never heard from him again."

H E MET JO CATHY BROWNLEE, a hostess for the Memphis Grizzlies, when he attended another football game. George Klein was the vehicle for the introduction, though Brownlee had gone out with Charlie Hodge briefly two years earlier. He enjoyed her company from the first and invited her to the movies, then to Graceland, where he had a Grand Prix delivered in the early-morning hours, just as he had with Melissa. Then on August 9 Elvis showed up once again in the stadium press box and asked if she could sit with him during the game. He sang to her, as he had at the movies, and toward the end of the evening invited her to fly with him to

Fort Worth to see his plane. They would probably go on to either Las Vegas or Palm Springs afterward, he told her, and when she told him she couldn't do it because she had a date, he got another girl who was at the game to go in her place.

He didn't get back for three or four days, but when he did he saw Jo Cathy every night until he left for Las Vegas at the end of the week. He tried to get her to go with him, but she and her mother had already signed up for a junket that was flying out two days later for his August 16 opening, and she was not about to break a long-standing commitment. "He didn't seem like he was in very good health at all. He was really overweight. One night he was chewing gum, and a bridge just fell out. He kept saying, 'Jo Cathy, the boy is just falling apart, falling apart.'"

He barely made it to Vegas. On the flight out, the plane was forced to make an emergency landing in Dallas, because he was having so much difficulty breathing. Red and Charlie were really alarmed — no matter what he did, he didn't seem able to get his breath — but after a few hours resting up at a nearby motel, "the effect of the pills," as Red observed dryly, "had worn off."

The opening was a disaster. He was "overweight," wrote the critic for *Variety*, showed "lack of stamina and poor vocal projection," and, according to the same review, "it is difficult for him to sustain creditable vocal lines or lyric commitments, and his dogging of main intent and purpose . . . is very noticeable." There were lengthy interludes by nearly every member of the troupe (including Kathy, who had been unable to maintain her resolution to leave), and "in addition, he lumbers around in travesties of quick karate moves or trademark pelvic gyrations. Presley admits he spent $2,500 on his jumpsuit costume, an obviously poor design that stresses his ballooning midriff."

Some of his most ardent fans might have disagreed, and in fact he seemed cheerful enough as he continued the practice of taking requests begun a few weeks earlier in North Carolina. This time he sent Charlie out into the audience to collect the requests in a champagne bucket, and he shook his head good-humoredly at his inability to recall the lyrics to some of the more recent tunes. But even the fans were concerned about his appearance, and by his not infrequent references to the state of his health and the way that short bursts of energy seemed to alternate with signs of extreme weariness. Linda, who had rejoined him for the opening, was alarmed at how "out of it he was, even if people didn't [fully] realize it. He was just barely going through the motions, he was lethargic and [physi-cally] uncoordinated — I think even he was aware that he was in trouble."

On the second night he lay down onstage shortly after the opening number and arrived on the run for the midnight show, explaining that he had been in the bathroom and repeating a story that Jo Cathy Brownlee had told him about a woman at a Memphis Grizzlies game who had said, "But I didn't think he did things like that." On the third night he wanted to cancel his performance, but the Colonel wouldn't let him. The people were already in their seats, and Colonel simply said, "I'm not going to go out there and tell them you're not appearing. If you want to do it, get your daddy to go out there and tell them." He did two brief, perfunctory shows, glancing at his watch the entire time he was onstage — he even wore the same suit for both. By the next morning all traces of his presence were gone. Every poster, every souvenir, every banner and photograph had been removed; there were just three small announcements posted around the lobby saying that "the remainder of the Elvis Presley engagement has been canceled due to illness." Elvis, it was said among the fans, had left through the front lobby at six o'clock that morning accompanied by Dr. Nick. Some claimed to have seen him carried out on a stretcher, but in reality he walked out under his own power.

The Colonel lost little time in doing all he could to put the best face on things. He assured Henri Lewin that he would speak to Elvis and his father in person, in Memphis, about a December makeup date that the hotel wanted very much to schedule at the beginning of the month. Lewin was not above using the discomfiture he was sure the Colonel would feel over the Hilton's disastrous August losses, but Colonel, despite his acute embar-rassment at finding himself in such a disadvantageous position and while stressing, again and again, that he did not take his obligations lightly, was having none of it: he thought the week after Christmas would be more suitable for their purposes, and even though Lewin had already indicated that Ann-Margret, a good draw, was tentatively booked for the holiday sea-son, Colonel insisted that that was the one time slot to which Elvis might be willing to commit. He further intimated that he might even be willing to include New Year's Eve at a special price of $200,000 to $300,000 beyond the regular pro rata remuneration, since that was the minimum sum that he and Mr. Presley could expect to realize from a single concert booking in a large metropolitan area on that date. At the same time he reassured Elvis that through his extensive contacts and canny negotiations with "the hotel, talent, ad agency, radio, newspapers and others," he had limited their losses to $39,000, of which he promptly assumed his share of $13,000.

But however unabated his instinct for combat, the Colonel remained sick at heart. And even as he played his cards typically close to the vest, gossips were whispering that he had incurred a debt of up to $5 million in the casino, and friction between him and his client continued to be reported in the press. If it had been something as simple as friction, Colonel might have seen a way out — he could have used an intermediary; Mr. Diskin, whom he trusted implicitly, might have assumed even more extensive ambassadorial duties. But this wasn't something that could be easily fixed; like any parent who has been conned once too often by a recalcitrant child, Colonel felt he could no longer place any faith in Elvis' assurances, and he could no longer deny that a real problem existed. The trouble was, the problem simply went too far beyond the realm of his own experience for him to get a purchase on it, and while he was always trying to monitor Elvis' situation through Joe, Sonny, Lamar, or one of the other guys, he lived in the same unacknowledged fear that gripped them all: that if he stepped too far over the line, Elvis would blow up at him and things might be said that could never be taken back. They had all seen how Elvis reacted to his father's occasional attempts at interference, snarling at one or another of the boys, "Just keep him the fuck out of my way."

MEANWHILE, DR. NICK FOUND a very different Elvis from the one he had encountered through most of the months of July and August: all of a sudden he was deflated, the manic energy had abruptly run out, all external confidence was gone. For insurance purposes Nick and Dr. Ghanem put out a statement under both their names that the cancellation was "prompted by a fatigued state which developed in recent weeks" and that there was no cause for alarm, their famous patient was simply being hospitalized "for conservation reasons." In reality, though, while the clinical signs continued to give some cause for alarm (a "fatty" liver, various chronic intestinal and bowel problems, a high cholesterol count), what worried Nick most were the emotional swings, very likely triggered by drugs, but perhaps equally reflecting a genetic predisposition to dangerous cycles of euphoria and depression. Once again he brought in a team of consultants, who did their best to address the various medical issues. This time the team included a pulmonary specialist to look into what was beginning to seem like "possible early chronic obstructive pulmonary disease," as well as Dr. John Nash, a surgeon, whom Elvis tried to persuade to perform an experimental new gastrointestinal bypass operation that Elvis had recently read about, which had been developed as a means of reducing dangerous obesity by surgery when all other methods had failed. Dr. Nash refused even to discuss such an operation solely on a cosmetic basis with either Nick or Elvis — and in the end Elvis was persuaded that there was too much risk involved, even though, it was noted in the physician's orders, the patient had great difficulty accepting the distended appearance of his stomach.

Linda remained with him throughout his hospitalization. President Nixon called ten days into his stay, which seemed to cheer him up a little. Frank Sinatra called, too, and told him not to let the bastards kill him — which Elvis took to mean not just Vegas but the whole system. But mostly it was Marion Cocke, the motherly nurse who had taken care of him during his January visit, upon whom he relied for comfort and consolation. They spent hour after hour talking about the most mundane subjects, he gave her a Pontiac Grand Prix, and when she tried to refuse it, he said, "It makes me happy to see you happy." When he was released on September 5, two weeks after entering the hospital, he asked her if she would accompany him home, and she agreed, taking the all-night shift after her regular hospital hours were done, while Kathy Seamon, another nurse whom he had met in the hospital, took days.

At first he spent most of the time in his room. In Mrs. Cocke's eyes he was nothing but a very thoughtful, reflective, and considerate — if very subdued — young man. Nor did she have any inflated ideas about her own role or station: she was simply, she joked with anyone who asked, like a comfortable old pair of shoes. At Dr. Nick's suggestion she set up a kind of breakfast nook in Lisa's room, where she slept, and it served as an inducement to get him out of bed for meals. She made him banana pudding and darned his socks; under Dr. Nick's direction, with Kathy and Tish Henley, she carefully monitored his medications; they watched Monday-night football and *The Carol Burnett* and *Mary Tyler Moore* shows together in her room. "He talked about his family and I talked about mine. We just thoroughly enjoyed each other's company. Never, ever did he try to impress me." Scarcely anyone else except for Linda and his cousin Billy was admitted upstairs.

Gradually he started going out again, leading a pack of friends through the Graceland gates on the three-wheelers he had bought in August just before leaving for Las Vegas. One time he coaxed Mrs. Cocke to join them. "He looked back to me. 'Hang on, Mrs. Cocke.' And away we went. The next day at work someone said to me, 'You know, Mrs. Cocke, I could have sworn I saw you racing down Elvis Presley Boulevard on the back of a three-wheeler with Elvis Presley yesterday.' And I replied, 'You know I would never do anything like that.' And that was all that was said."

Linda returned to the Coast to pursue her acting career. She simply found it impossible to continue. "I started having anxiety attacks. I told Elvis, and he was just so — loving. But I can remember thinking that nothing was worth this. I mean, in some ways I felt very protected. I always felt no matter what happened, he could take care of it for me. I felt a very strong sense of security with him on one level — and then real anxiety on another. I mean, he was who he was; he wasn't going to change. He used to say to me, 'Honey, you're not going to change a forty-year-old man.' But in another way there was also this very naive, this almost infantile quality about him — very innocent and very pure, kind of pitiful. He definitely evoked a protective quality — he called me 'Mommy,' and I wasn't the mother of his child. But I was an incredibly maternal presence in his life."

At one time she had thought of having children with him, "but our timing was off. By the time he was ready to do that, I was seeing things a lot more clearly, thinking, There's no way I can save him if he doesn't want to be saved himself. He's with other women when I'm not here. That's no way to live. If we have a child, then I'm going to be parent, and he's going to be with some other girl. If I have a child, how am I going to be with him and be a mom, too?"

This was the man with whom she had shared her dreams and whom she had cared for "like a newborn baby." She had seen him in ways that few others had, he had confessed to her what she was convinced he would never share with anyone else — but she found the emotional proximity almost frightening. "One time in Las Vegas he was eating some chicken soup, and I went in the bathroom to get ready for bed. When I came back, his face was in the soup, and he was almost suffocating. I called the doctor, and he gave him a shot of Ritalin to revive him. When he finally woke up enough to talk, he said, 'Mommy?' I said, 'Yeah, honey, I'm here.' He said, 'I had a dream' — and it took him about fifteen minutes to get the words out. He said, 'I had a dream last night.' I said, 'What did you dream?' He said, 'I dreamed that you were my twin, and you let me come out first — but while you were saving me by letting me be born first, you suffocated to death.' I said, 'Well, honey, you did have a problem. You were not breathing right, and I had a doctor come in and give you a shot. Maybe that's why you dreamed that.' 'No. I had a dream. I dreamed that you saved my life.'"

It was too much. She loved him, but without acknowledging it fully even to herself, she was leaving. He seemed to accept it after his own fashion. In the spring he had bought her a house just around the corner from Graceland so she could have some space of her own, and now, with Monovale finally sold, he got her an apartment in west Los Angeles. It would be for the two of them, he told her; they could spend time together there whenever he was on the Coast.

He started going out again with Jo Cathy Brownlee, the Grizzlies hostess, and for the next couple of months she embarked upon an impossible schedule, teaching school till mid-afternoon, up at Graceland in the early evening just as Elvis was arising, out all night with barely time for a shower before she went off to work again. She recognized that her whole life was subject to his whims, but she didn't mind so long as she was able to keep her sense of humor. One time he told her out of the blue that he didn't want to see her again until she got a nose job, and she told him that she didn't want to see him "until he had his whole body retreaded, and he just laughed." She tried to help him keep to the diet that Dr. Nick had prescribed — yogurt, lots of vegetables, low-cholesterol bacon strips; they would eat upstairs, read the newspaper, watch the news, then go out to play racquetball — the girls would have one game, the guys another. Usually there was a movie scheduled after that. "Everything was a big production. Everybody had a certain thing that they carried; somebody was in charge of lining up the movie theater, somebody was in charge of getting the car ready. He always carried this little leather pouch with all his police badges — he wouldn't go anywhere without his badges, they were his prized possessions." If you yawn, we're gone, Elvis told her at the movies, scarcely acknowledging that she had been up at that point for twenty-one of the last twenty-four hours. They flew to Dallas one time to take a look at a racquetball center that Dr. Nick knew about so Elvis could get some ideas for the court that he was building. They spoke of numerology, and Elvis asked Jo Cathy to read *The Impersonal Life* aloud to him. It was a strangely solitary life despite the crowd in which they often moved.

Jo Cathy soon learned that one of the responsibilities of being Elvis' girlfriend was to make sure that everyone got taken care of, and she was frequently sought out by the guys, their wives, even relatives and maids,

584 ~ A LEAF IN THE STORM

when Elvis was in a gift-giving mode. No one, she realized, wanted to be left out, and there was plenty of opportunity for bruised feelings to arise simply as a result of Elvis' impetuous generosity. Sometimes she could be a force for good. When Jackie Wilson, one of Elvis' greatest r&b inspirations, suffered a stroke on September 29 while performing in Cherry Hill, New Jersey, George Klein made sure that Jo Cathy let Elvis know about the fund that was being started to help cover Jackie's medical expenses. George knew of Elvis' fondness for Wilson, as well as his admiration for his music, and Jo Cathy considered this advocacy "a very nice gesture." But not every gesture, of course, was as altruistic.

She observed Elvis' fascination with the police and police work. "I just think he always had the secret desire to be some kind of law enforcement officer. He admired the hell out of the police here in Memphis — it was like he would just love to change places with them. He could be around them for hours." At the same time, she felt that at bottom he wouldn't change places with anyone, "he enjoyed being Elvis." And she couldn't help but note that despite all his good resolutions, pills were still coming in from Las Vegas, and unbeknownst to Dr. Nick, Elvis was still getting prescriptions filled by one doctor or another around town.

One time Linda came back, and Jo Cathy was banished for a brief period. Then one Saturday at the end of October she came from her part-time job at the Mid-South Coliseum, "and he acted real surprised to see me. He didn't say anything for a while, and then finally he said, 'JC, I have another date tonight. If you'll just get what you need and go on home, I'll give you a call in the morning.' It just really rubbed me the wrong way — here I was, dead tired from working three jobs and seeing him, too, and I was really mad that he waited until seven that night, although I think what it was was that somebody was supposed to tell me. So I went around and gathered up everything that I had at the house — I had it all in this little laundry basket — and he came in and said, 'Now you didn't have to be a bitch about this whole thing. I just asked you to get what you needed for the night and go on home. You didn't have to act like this.' So he just kind of stormed out of the room, and I stormed out, too. And that was the last time I saw him."

T HE COLONEL HAD BEEN DOING his best since the beginning of September to get Elvis back into the recording studio, at one point even concocting a scheme to record half an album in the studio, with the rest to be recorded live in Vegas in early December during the dates he had finally acceded to. He couldn't have been more aware of their contractual obligations to RCA, and even before Elvis was released from the hospital, Colonel tried to interest the label in various "exploitations," including a selection of title songs from Elvis' movies and a special TV package made up of twenty-four previously released tracks plus two bonus numbers and a photo album which the Colonel would supply. There is no indication that RCA was overly interested in any of the Colonel's suggestions, and Elvis never went back into the studio that fall, nor were plans made to record the Vegas show.

The *Lisa Marie* was finally delivered late in the evening of November 10. The finishing touches had been applied in California, and the Convair 880 was parked out at Memphis Aero, the *Press-Scimitar* reported, with the JetStar sitting proudly beside it. For the maiden flight Elvis elected to take a brief run to Nashville, but in the next couple of weeks he flew all over the country to display its capabilities to family and friends. He boasted about the two computers he had onboard, so that if one failed there would always be a backup. He showed off all of the airplane's lavish appointments. "I can't believe this is mine," he told everyone he spoke to. "It's a dream come true."

H E WAS GROWING more and more nervous, in Marion Cocke's estimation, as the Vegas dates approached. They were playing at the deadest time of year, and while the Colonel always seemed to relish a challenge — in fact, part of his psychology was that it brought out the best in his boy — Mrs. Cocke was not so sure that Elvis was ready for one at this point. It was not just the burden of performing that rested uneasily on his shoulders; he felt like it was all coming down on him again — the weight of his responsibilities, the financial pressures, what to do about Linda, who had returned from California to accompany him to Las Vegas at a time when he was not so sure he wouldn't rather take someone else. Colonel had booked them for New Year's Eve, too, in a football stadium in Pontiac, Michigan, and was promoting the idea of setting some kind of attendance record — but what about the sound? What about the weather? What if it snowed? He had never worked New Year's Eve before, and he didn't know that he wanted to start now — but he knew he could use the money.

As per doctor's orders, he was limited to one show a night except for Saturdays — and as per Colonel's predictions, the room, and the hotel, were full at a time of year when 50 percent occupancy was the norm in Vegas. Voice was gone, finally done in by all the animosity and politics surrounding the August cancellation. But Sherrill Nielsen remained as a kind of dramatic second voice and featured tenor, and J. D. Sumner and the Stamps took over the opening slot, which J.D. had coveted ever since Voice had joined the show. Notices were reasonably good (Elvis was "looking good and sounding cheerful," announced the *Las Vegas Review-Journal*), but the same gibes and onstage fits of pique that had been directed at Duke Bardwell during the last full engagement were directed this time at band mainstay Glen D. Hardin, with much the same results. Though he didn't say anything at the time, Glen D. made up his mind to leave after the first of the year, and James Burton, a bandmate of Glen's in Emmylou Harris' Hot Band (to keep them, she keyed her touring schedule around Elvis'), was planning to leave, too. Ronnie Tutt, whose drumming was the glue of the band, missed two nights for the birth of his daughter, and his long-term loyalties were perceived by some to be linked to little more than his remuneration, which kept pace with James' at the top of the salary structure.

Elvis returned to Memphis immediately following the engagement and on Christmas Eve awoke from a dream which was so real, he told Marion Cocke when she arrived in the early evening, that he found himself "in a rage. He had dreamed that no one who worked for him cared anything about him other than for their salary checks. He had dreamed that he had gone broke, and when he needed them they walked out on him. In his dream during this turmoil, he said that I had walked in and said, 'Babe, everything's okay.' With that he laughed and we just sat there and visited."

They visited until three on Christmas morning. "[Elvis] asked me what I thought of the boys [who were waiting downstairs] — how I felt about each of them. I gave him my honest opinion." By the time that Elvis was finally ready to go downstairs himself, nearly everyone had left. There was little question of their bitterness, both at Elvis and at those less deserving than themselves. Marty Lacker described "all the relatives congregated [throughout that Christmas season] looking for a handout," and saw Elvis' growing reclusiveness as a desire to escape his own family. Lamar Fike simply felt frustration at knowing Elvis "was up there punching buttons and watching what we were doing [on the television monitors]. I was fuckin' mad . . ."

That evening (Christmas night) Elvis took everyone up in the *Lisa Marie*, and when they got back on the ground, he handed out jewelry he had personally chosen for each from Lowell Hays' selection. Elvis' aunt

Delta was on the plane, according to Marty, "and she was drunk. . . . All of a sudden Delta looked at me, and she said, 'You're a sonofabitch. I don't like you. . . . You ain't no damn friend of his. And I got a good mind to take this .38 I got in my purse and just shoot you dead.'" Then she looked over at T. G. Sheppard "and she said, 'And you ain't worth a shit either, you walleyed sonofabitch.' And she just kept on. She said, 'All you sonsofbitches are here for the same thing. You just want his damn money. Here's this god-damn jeweler, and Elvis has to buy you some of his crap.'"

At this point Elvis reacted. "Get this drunken bitch off this plane," he commanded, apologizing to both Marty and Sheppard — which appeared to be the end of it. At two o'clock that morning, though, Billy Smith heard "the damnedest racket there ever was. I jumped up and grabbed my gun, and I run to the door. Well, it was Elvis. He had his cane, and he was beating the door on my trailer. His hair was messed up, and he was wild-eyed and red-faced. . . . He was out of his mind, he was so mad. He said, 'God-damnit, I'll kill that bitch. I'll sew her cunt up and throw her over that damn wall!' . . . He was just screaming. 'How dare she do something like that? Goddamnit, I took her in out of the goodness of my heart, and I'll kick her fat ass out. . . . She embarrassed the shit out of me.'"

Billy tried to reason with him. "I said, 'Elvis, let's sit down and talk this thing out. This is an old woman you're talking about. You know how she is when she gets to drinking.' He said, 'That ain't no reason for that bitch to insult my friends and ruin my Christmas.' We talked for a few more minutes, and he settled down some. I said, 'Look, what you need to do is go out there and tell her, "Don't ever do that again." But you don't want to kick her out. She's got nowhere to go.' And he said, 'Yeah, I guess you're right.' But then he broke down and started crying. He said, 'She had no right to do that. Those are my friends. I love her, too, but she's got no right to make me look like that.'"

NEW YEAR'S EVE IN PONTIAC was a public triumph — $300,000 for an hour's work and, as the Colonel tirelessly pointed out to every reporter who would listen, a record gross (over $800,000) for a one-night performance by a single artist. In addition the Colonel had gotten Boxcar recording artists, the Bodie Mountain Express, to open the show, perhaps in hopes of finally getting the group signed to RCA.

The show was not an unqualified triumph, however. For one thing its sellout status, the first claim of any Elvis Presley performance, was questionable, as the Colonel quickly ruled twenty-seven thousand obstructed-view seats not for sale after ticket sales leveled off at sixty thousand. The crowd inside the domed stadium was suitably celebratory, despite the frigid weather outside, but Elvis himself appeared shocked when he first walked out onstage and saw the two-tiered arrangement, with band and singers positioned five feet below him in a setup that he would never have approved because it prevented the eye contact he considered essential to a good performance. It didn't really matter. Onstage the musicians were freezing, the sound was terrible, Elvis ripped his pants at the beginning of the show, and Joe Guercio told comedian Jackie Kahane disgustedly, "He's all fucked up."

T. G. Sheppard and his wife had flown with him to the gig in the *Lisa Marie*. He had persuaded Sheppard to give up a booking of his own because it was going to be such a big event. "He said, 'It'll be one of the largest crowds I've ever played, and I'm nervous about it, and I [want] to take my friends with me.' After the show he just exploded. Linda just sat and let it happen. A lot of stuff had been rubbing him that day." Eventually he calmed down and decided to fly home that night, and they ended the evening in Elvis' bedroom watching tapes of old *Monty Python* shows.

FOUR DAYS LATER Elvis arrived in Denver with a party of eighteen for a spur-of-the-moment ski vacation that he thought everyone would enjoy. Joe was given the task of locating condos in Vail at the height of ski season, while everyone else remained at the Denver hotel. Finally he and vice squad captain Jerry Kennedy and Ron Pietrafeso, the Denver policemen with whom Elvis had continued to be friendly since his first performance in the city five years earlier, managed to find four condos and a house on the slopes for Elvis and Linda, returning in triumph late in the day with their news. Joe was exhausted, everyone else had plans, but Elvis, caught up in the spirit of adventure, was determined to set out right away. For Joe that was the breaking point. "I finally said, 'Fine. You go ahead — but I ain't moving from my room. I'm sleeping for twenty-four hours. I'll meet you there.' He wasn't sleeping at all at this point — just going, going, going, wired to the wall. Everybody was fed up with just traveling, moving — it just wasn't any fun. It was like he was driving people away."

The result was that Elvis found himself virtually alone on his forty-first birthday. Everyone was either holed up in their condos or just generally pissed off. Finally, Linda called Jerry and Myrna at their condo and told them nobody was around and Elvis was really down and she was about to serve the cake. By the time they came over he had perked up a little, and later as they sat around talking, he asked Myrna if she had seen *Across 110th Street,* a nihilistic black gangster movie that was one of his favorite films of the last few years. "I made the mistake of saying no, and he told me the entire story, acted out every role, recited practically every line." It was one of his greatest acting performances, Jerry and Myrna both agreed, but one that they could have done without, as it carried on into the early hours of the morning.

For the next week the guys and their wives and girlfriends all took skiing lessons, while Elvis came out at night in ski mask, Arctic snowsuit, and goggles to go snowmobile riding on the slopes. "IT'S ELVIS THE NIGHT-STALKER," blazoned the tabloid headlines several weeks later, accompanied by a suitably blurry, almost lunar-looking picture. It was "a dream vacation," remarked Sonny, that turned into "a nightmare." Susan Ford, the President's eighteen-year-old daughter, wanted to meet Elvis, but after she wrote a letter to the newspaper protesting the special treatment that allowed him to run his snowmobiles on the slopes at night, he refused to have anything to do with her — another instance, Sonny and Red thought, of his messianic sense of self-importance.

He had plenty of time for his Denver police friends and even consulted with police surgeon Dr. Gerald Starkey for medication to treat an itch caused by the ski mask he had been wearing. All of the police officers noticed changes since they had first met him five years earlier, but for the most part he was on his best behavior with them, and Ron Pietrafeso continued to see the same self-effacing qualities that had first set Elvis apart from any other entertainer he had ever met. Occasionally they would talk late at night, and "he would speak about how nervous he got every time he went onstage. I asked him, 'Why?' He said, 'You just never know. Maybe they're not going to clap. Maybe — I mean, you just think all the worst things.'" He talked about sleeping all day and staying up all night. "He said, 'When I was a little kid, I couldn't sleep. I was really afraid of the dark, 'cause I didn't know what was going to happen to me.' [Speaking of the present] he said, 'I know in the daytime when I go to sleep that it's dark in my room, and I pretend like it's night, but I know it's daytime, and I'm not afraid to fall asleep. So I stay up all night, and I have my friends with me, and I feel comfortable. In the morning, when everybody else is up and going to work, I feel safe because it's daytime — and then I can go to sleep.'"

As a thank-you gesture to his friends on the force, Elvis contacted Bob Surber, a salesman at Kumpf Motors in Denver, and had him open up his Lincoln showroom at 8:00 P.M., two hours after closing. He bought Mark IVs for Dr. Starkey and Jerry Kennedy, then drove to Jack Kent Cadillac, where he got Ron Pietrafeso a $13,000 Seville, along with a Seville and an Eldorado for Linda and Joe's girlfriend Shirley Dieu after Joe turned down Elvis' Rolls on the basis that it would just make everyone else crazy. In all, the bill came to more than $70,000, which might have marked the conclusion of Elvis' purchases, except that when Don Kinney, the host of KOA-TV's *Denver Today*, reported the story on January 20, he ended the broadcast by saying jokingly, "Mr. Presley, I don't want a big Cadillac, I would prefer one of those little sporty ones." Elvis was on the phone within minutes to tell him he could pick up his Seville at the same dealer. Ron Pietrafeso, who knew Kinney and had to get on the phone to reassure him the call was not a hoax, thought that might be carrying things a little far, "but there was just so much inside of him that wanted to be accepted, and he thought that was the only way."

By this time Joe was gone, the rental period was up, and Elvis had everyone jumping just like he had at the beginning of the vacation. He decided he wanted to stay for a few days more, and just after Jerry had finished finding them new accommodations, Elvis called at three in the morning and said that he wanted to switch houses right away. He offered no explanation, and Jerry was in no mood for games. "He said he was coming over, so I moved into the small bedroom to give him the master bedroom. When he showed up with Billy and Red, he was just totally wired. He said, 'I thought I told you I wanted you to move back into the house.' I said, 'Jesus, I've been working to find a place for three days straight. I need to get some sleep.' He said, 'You do?' I was getting really mad now, but he was like someone I didn't know. Finally, he stormed out of the room, into the living room, where Red was waiting. Red wrote in his book that Elvis pulled out a gun at that point and said, 'I'll kill the sonofabitch,' but when he came back into the bedroom, all he said to me was, 'Well, you can stay if you want to.' I said, 'You know what, Elvis? I don't want to stay here. In fact, I'm leaving.' He said, 'Well, I said you could stay.' His voice was shaking. He knew he had pushed me too far. I said, 'No, I'm leaving. I'm going home.'"

The next day Elvis didn't remember the conversation, but Jerry stuck with his decision. "There was no reason for me to stay. He was tired, every-body was tired — he just didn't want a lot of resistance. All I would have been was a pain in the neck. I said to him, 'You know, I've always said, "Friendship is more important to me than the job."' He said, 'What are you talking about?' I swear to God, I think he meant it. I said, 'Look, Elvis, I just need change. There's no hard feelings.' He said, 'Well, I guess you have to do what you have to do.' I wasn't trying to be difficult. He had done more for me than anybody else in my life. It was just there were too many people bumping into each other, people were calling him 'Boss.' Everything lapsed into everything else, and the rest of the world was just this little tiny bubble that you couldn't really relate to anymore. You almost felt naked going out into the world when you left that environment, because it was all just based on him. But it was time."

TOP: ELVIS IN UNIFORM, WITH DENVER POLICE CHIEF ART DILL (RIGHT)
AND CAPTAIN JERRY KENNEDY. (COURTESY OF THE ESTATE OF ELVIS PRESLEY)

BOTTOM: SONNY WEST, DAVE HEBLER, ELVIS, RED WEST,
ATLANTA, JUNE 6, 1976. (LEE SECREST)

HURT

S O DESPERATE WAS RCA to lure Elvis back into the studio that they revived the old dream of recording him at home. This time, however, both the nature and the reason for the plan were a far cry from its original conception fifteen years before. Then the idea had been to build a separate recording facility at Graceland, primarily to get around some of the obstacles the Colonel had put in the way of his artist recording too much. Now both Colonel and RCA were in full agreement: they needed to obtain product from an artist who appeared to have developed an almost pathological aversion to the recording studio. And far from building him a new state-of-the-art plaything, they now proposed simply to install temporary equipment in the den behind the kitchen, run lines out to the RCA mobile recording truck that would be parked behind the house, and make the best of whatever sound deficiencies arose.

It had been over two years since there had been anything like a regularly instituted plan; the perfunctory March 1975 session in Los Angeles had offered the only interruption to what amounted to Elvis' longest period of recording inactivity since he had first entered the Sun studio. Felton was confident the new arrangement would help solve some of their problems; it would at least allow them to catch Elvis whenever the mood happened to strike him. Elvis seemed enthusiastic about the idea, too. In fact, once he saw how the den looked without all the Polynesian-style furniture in it, he said he just might make the new decor permanent.

But then he left just days before the session was scheduled to start. One of his friends on the Denver police force, Detective Eugene Kennedy, troubled by domestic problems, had killed himself, and out of respect for the deceased and "because of friendship with Kennedy's older brother, Police Captain Jerry Kennedy, one of four Denver police officers," the *Denver Post* reported, "who received gifts of luxury cars from Presley earlier this month," Elvis flew out to the funeral. In addition, he arranged for J. D. Sumner and the Stamps to sing at the service, which he himself attended wearing the Denver police captain's uniform that his friends on the force had given him. He stood straight and tall at the Holy Name Church, a striking figure in his specially tailored jacket, customized TCB tinted glasses, and braided cap, looking for all the world like the man his mother had wanted him to be. He felt comfortable in the company of men who accepted him at face value, officers who had trusted him to accompany them on drug busts (even if they had never allowed him to get out of the car), and when they suggested going out to dinner at the Colorado Mine Company, one of their favorite hangouts, he readily agreed, striding proudly into the restaurant in his captain's uniform.

To Ron Pietrafeso's relief, none of the regular patrons appeared to pay any attention, and Captain Kennedy arranged for a special table around the corner from the main dining room where they could be assured of a little privacy. Not too long into the meal, though, Elvis announced that he had to go to the men's room, and when Pietrafeso suggested that he make use of the employees' rest room off the kitchen, Elvis insisted that he would use the regular bathroom just like everyone else. To Pietrafeso's amazement, somehow they were able to get him through the main dining room and back to the table without anyone seeming to notice. "I thought it was great. We were doing our job, and nobody was bothering him — but then he sat down for no more than five minutes and said, 'I need to use the rest room again.'" This time, Pietrafeso noted, Elvis hesitated for a moment in the long hallway where people waiting for a table were having drinks. Two women stopped in mid conversation as he walked past, and then, when he came out of the men's room, Elvis stopped directly in front of them, as if somehow he might have lost his way. "He gave one of those classic Elvis grins, and I heard one lady say, 'No, it can't be him!' And he turned around — it was too much, man, he turned around and said, 'It can't be who?' And the two women just started to scream." Then, and only then, would he allow himself to be guided back to his seat.

H E SHOWED UP for the first day of the recording session still dressed in his police captain's uniform. Everyone was waiting patiently for him to emerge from his bedroom, trying not to wonder if he was going to show up at all. Technical problems, and Elvis' schedule, had pushed the starting date back, which gave them only five days until James Burton and Glen D. Hardin were scheduled to go out with Emmylou Harris on a long-planned European tour. Felton didn't know if they could work that fast. RCA was expecting twenty new sides, which was the reason a full week had originally been set aside for recording. With some misgivings he made arrangements for a substitute guitarist and piano player to come in on February 7, along with a bassist to replace Jerry Scheff, who said he would have to leave then as well.

They got three cuts on the first night, though Elvis' lack of focus and energy was evident to all. Elvis' continued preference for downbeat material was not particularly heartening either, and even the high point of the session, George Jones' 1962 country hit, "She Thinks I Still Care," offered little hope of commercial success. He ended the evening with Roger Whittaker's maudlin "The Last Farewell," the song he had played over and over again for Melissa Blackwood the previous summer, but the musicians were no more able to grasp its fascination than Melissa had been.

On the second night, Elvis succeeded in recording just one song, Neil Sedaka's "Solitaire," while spending most of the time trying to avoid accomplishing even that. He retreated to his bedroom periodically throughout the evening, took one member of the band or another upstairs to listen to gospel music, expounded upon numerology, and gave them all a viewing of his collection of police badges. At one point, when he was alone in his room with Red and Sonny, he explained a plot he had devised to rub out the drug pushers of Memphis. The session would provide them with a perfect cover, he said, laying out all the weapons with which they could accomplish the task — no one would even know they were gone. He showed them pictures of the principal dealers that he had gotten from the Memphis police, along with detailed information about the territory they controlled. "That's pretty heavy," Red said dubiously. He was bored with Elvis' fantasies and was not unaware of how close this particular scenario was to the plot of *Death Wish*, the Charles Bronson movie they had watched together many times.

The third night was no better; most of the time Elvis appeared to be struggling just to wake up, even when he was cutting "Moody Blue," a Mark James song Felton thought could really be a hit. Finally, on the next night something seemed to kick in, as they started out the evening with "For the Heart," a bright new up-tempo number from Dennis Linde, the author of "Burning Love." The song had more of a snap than anything they had tried to date, and Elvis seemed to respond to it, gaining confidence through numerous rehearsals and multiple takes until the song became the kind of seductively driving rock 'n' roll that had once been a staple of Elvis Presley music. It was with the next number, though, that Elvis was at last able to cut loose and release some of the emotional inhibitions that appeared to be crippling him. "Hurt," a highly charged recitation of the most melodramatic sort, had been a hit in a variety of interpretations over the years, but Elvis knew it best from Roy Hamilton's Top 10 r&b hit from 1954. Hamilton performed the song, as he did all of his greatest numbers, with the bravura vocal style that was his trademark, working his way up to a carefully controlled, beautifully articulated aria-like climax. This was clearly Elvis' model, but in the absence of the lush orchestration that marked Hamilton's hit, and with a voice that was more than a little frayed around the edges, he necessarily took a different approach. Opening with a bellow almost resembling a Tarzan yell, Elvis offers a version that is not so much an interpretation as an expression of the title sentiment, a kind of primal scream that can make for painful listening as you wonder if the singer will be able to sustain not just the notes but the mastery of his emotions. Compared with Hamilton's original, it reveals a crude, almost desperate grasping for technique. And yet at the same time, there is a note of triumph on Elvis' part, a pride in simply being able to get out what he is trying to say. This, he declares with as much bravado as he can muster, is who I am — despite all the pain, despite all the suffering, despite all the hurt, you can see: *I'm still here.*

He went on, at his father's request, to take a stab at "Danny Boy," the lilting Irish melody which like "Hurt" had its inspiration for Elvis in another over-the-top r&b performance, this one by Jackie Wilson. He was fully engaged by now, and while he was not able to sing the song in the key that he originally selected, he hung in through ten takes until he got a version even more heart-rending perhaps than if he had not been brought face-to-face with his own limitations. It was two o'clock in the afternoon by the time they finished. The musicians had been hanging around since nine o'clock the previous night, and out of deference to the general exhaustion, the starting time for the next night's session was moved back until midnight. But at least there was a feeling on everyone's part that *something* had been accomplished.

They might just as well have quit then and there. They did manage to get two undistinguished cuts on the fifth night, but with Burton, Glen D., and Scheff gone and a new lineup in place, the only song that they completed the following evening was a lackluster version of Willie Nelson's "Blue Eyes Crying in the Rain," a number-one country hit from the previous year. On the next night Elvis didn't show up at all, and after sitting around for a few hours trying to devise alternate strategies, Felton was finally forced to admit defeat and send the musicians home.

*   *   *

TEN DAYS LATER Elvis was back in Denver, with newspaper stories reporting that he was seeking a home somewhere in the area and Elvis hanging out once again with his newfound friends. This time, however, his visit came to an abrupt halt when the police officers attempted to intervene in what Elvis continued to see as strictly a private matter. Their intervention stemmed from an incident that had occurred after the funeral, when Elvis tried to get Dr. Starkey to give him Dilaudid for what he said was a painfully infected ingrown toenail. The police surgeon was very much taken aback, and after explaining to Elvis that he couldn't prescribe a heavy-duty painkiller for an injury of that sort, he went to Sonny and Red to try to find out what was really going on. He asked if Elvis was suffering from some kind of serious illness, since Dilaudid was generally prescribed for cancer patients and not infrequently abused by those who had grown addicted to its effects. He expressed his concerns to Captain Kennedy and Detective Pietrafeso as well, and this time when Elvis returned to Denver, they confronted him in his hotel room.

They knew he had a problem, they said, they couldn't help noticing how it affected him at times, and they were afraid other people might start to notice, too. They were speaking to him as friends now, not as police officers, they stressed — they simply wanted to help. He should understand that this was the sort of thing that could happen to anyone; they had witnessed it in their line of work over and over again, and they were sure he could lick the problem if he just put his mind to it. There was a private sanitorium they knew about, they could get him in and out without anyone ever having to know — all they wanted was for him to give the matter serious consideration.

Elvis just stared at them in disbelief. At first he didn't say anything, then declared in a tone of utmost hurt, "You don't think I can handle it, do you? You don't think I'm strong enough. *I know what I'm doing.* I can get off of this stuff anytime I want." But whether or not he really believed this would have been difficult to ascertain. Because two hours later he was gone.

He had other almost equally pressing problems. For one thing he was running out of money. With the exception of the makeup date in Vegas and the stadium show New Year's Eve, he had not worked since August — but the bills kept piling up, hundreds of thousands of dollars of bills, for cars, planes, gifts, guns, jewelry, and clothing, anything in fact on which his eye might alight. To meet expenses with virtually no outside income coming in, he had borrowed $350,000 against Graceland in November, but that was to be repaid in equal halves this year and the next. Meanwhile, there were the various lawsuits that had arisen from Red and Sonny's all-too-ready roughness with the public; there was still half a million dollars to pay on the divorce; the airplanes (he had added a third, a Dessault Falcon, which he had bought as an "investment" in November) were a continuing drain of maintenance and finance charges; and it seemed like the cost of keeping up Graceland, and maintaining all his friends and relatives in the style to which they had become accustomed, was going up by the day.

With all of this weighing on him, he finally agreed to go back on the road in a hastily arranged mid-March tour, only to discover that he didn't have a band. Glen D. had handed in his notice to Tom Diskin not long after the Graceland session, and James Burton and Ronnie Tutt had indicated that they, too, intended to leave, but Diskin refused to accept their resignations. "You know how much he depends on you," he told Glen D. "I can't tell him you've quit." Finally Glen was forced to let Diskin know that he could do what he wanted, but Elvis was going to be in for a big surprise at the first show when he didn't see anyone sitting in the piano chair. It was only at this point that Elvis was brought into the picture and quickly approved the three Nashville musicians that Felton chose as replacements — though guitarist Billy Sanford (who had filled in for Burton on the last day of the February session) never actually got to join the group, as James changed his mind and came back for more money at the last minute.

They opened in Johnson City, Tennessee, for three nights running, in what amounted to a tacit admission on the Colonel's part that maybe they were better off out of the glare of the spotlight for the time being. It didn't affect the box office any — the six-day tour brought in over half a million dollars profit, which the Colonel magnanimously agreed to split on the old two-thirds–one-third basis, even though a new agreement, calling for a straight 50–50 partnership on live dates, had gone into effect on January 22. The new agreement for the first time spoke explicitly of an understanding "by both parties that these [tours] are a joint venture, and that Elvis Presley is responsible for the presentation of the staged performance, and Colonel Tom Parker and his representatives [for the] advertising and promotion." Elvis had no quarrel with the terminology; it was certainly in line with the governing language of the 1973 contract, which had established a 50–50 deal in every area but live performance. The way Colonel explained it, this new deal simply recognized the reality that they were co-promoters, or partners, in this respect as well, just as they had been from the start. As far as Colonel was concerned, it was the principle that was important, not the money, and with the new contract signed, he was glad to let the old arrangement ride, at least until Elvis got back on his feet again. Which would happen in no time if they could just put some miles under them and *get this show back on the road.*

Linda accompanied him on this tour. So did Vernon and Dr. Nick. The two new players, Shane Keister on acoustic piano and Larrie Londin on drums, fit in well and in fact infused a new spirit into the music at times. To Londin, a three-hundred-pound powerhouse drummer with extensive experience both in the studio and on the road, working with Elvis was something of a revelation. They went into the first show without any rehearsals (the band showed up, but Elvis didn't), and when Larrie missed a visual cue, Elvis simply had them begin all over again. "He said to follow him — not to worry about the charts. He wanted everybody's attention onstage — you know, it was like, 'Be with me. I got an hour, and I'm gonna have *fun!*'"

Apart from the fans, who responded with undiminished ardor night after night, Larrie, a natural enthusiast, might have been the only one to take this view. To rhythm guitarist John Wilkinson, "it seemed like all the enthusiasm had just left. No matter how hard we tried to pump him up, Elvis would just stand there with his thumb hooked in his belt, it was like he was just there to sing a few songs and pass out a few scarves, but all the thrill had gone." "Hurt," "How Great Thou Art," and "America the Beautiful," his bicentennial tribute, were the highlights of nearly every show, imposing performances all, but in Charlotte he forgot lyrics, in Cincinnati he appeared "confused," and in St. Louis he was so overmedicated Dr. Nick could barely get him out onstage. "Elvis seems weak," *St. Louis Post-Dispatch* columnist Harper Barnes wrote of the perfunctory fifty-minute show, little wonder since, according to Dr. Nick, he didn't wake up till midway through the performance.

A second brief tour was booked in the aftermath of the first. It was scheduled to begin on April 21, with stops in Kansas City, Omaha, Denver, San Diego, Long Beach, Seattle, and Spokane, and led directly into an eleven-day Tahoe engagement paying $315,000. For much of the tour Elvis was alarmingly congested, and he continued to suffer memory lapses even with songs he had been singing regularly since his return to live performing. Ronnie Tutt, who came back for this tour at a considerable raise in pay, observed that "there were nights he was so tired or so down I felt like I had to physically hit the drums much, much harder than I had before." To Myrna Smith and the Sweet Inspirations there was a clear physical dimension to the change. "[A lot of the time] when he first walked onstage, he'd be half asleep. . . . If you watched his show, you'd sometimes see him looking over at us, pleading with those eyes. We'd make more racket, try-ing to get him going, [and] he'd pull through it somehow. I've seen him sometimes when he was glassy-eyed [and] I thought, He is gonna fall."

The reviews were sometimes just as observant, and often no less empa-thetic. In Long Beach, the local paper reported, "An eerie silence filled the concert hall when he sang, 'And now the end is near' — the opening line to the Frank Sinatra favorite, 'My Way.' It was like witnessing a chilling prophecy." Even hard-boiled private investigator John O'Grady could not suppress an instinctive emotional reaction when he visited Elvis in Tahoe. "I felt so strongly for him I cried. He was fat. He had locomotive attacks where he couldn't walk. He forgot the words to his songs. I went backstage and looked at him, and I really thought he was going to die."

The musicians all talked about it among themselves, but, as former Voice accompanist Tony Brown, who had taken over the piano chair from Shane Keister, observed, "We all knew it was hopeless because Elvis was surrounded by that little circle of people, you know. . . . If you dared to ask, 'Can I have five minutes alone with [him]?,' the answer would be, 'Absolutely not!' [And if you ever] got around Elvis, he controlled the situa-tion with idle chitchat." O'Grady was so strongly affected that he tried to take matters into his own hands, contacting Ed Hookstratten upon his return to Los Angeles and working out a plan with Elvis' lawyer to try to get Elvis enrolled in the drug treatment program at the Scripps Clinic in San Diego. Together they went to Priscilla with the plan, which guaranteed absolute confidentiality, and from what they understood, she broached it to Elvis, but that was where the matter stopped.

Just two and one-half weeks after the conclusion of the Tahoe run, he was back on the road again — for eleven days this time and more than $800,000 for Colonel and him to divide. Reviewers made frequent reference to Elvis' slurred speech and the way in which he seemed to stumble around the stage at times, but the crowds continued to turn out, and for the most part they continued to be enthusiastic. Once in a while there would be a show that reminded everyone of how it had been, and sometimes the band and the guys were able to take heart and imagine that maybe Elvis was going to pull himself together now and turn things around — but mostly the attitude was just to get through. Elvis' own attitude, on the other hand, seemed to Tony Brown to reflect a disrespect for himself and the fans that he had never shown before, even in his most erratic moments. "He'd be onstage some nights, and he'd suddenly just turn around and face us. He'd always pick out one person in the band, and he'd look at them and act silly. He'd just stand there, four or five minutes — not do anything. The audience would be screaming out song titles or applauding or stomping their feet. Elvis would have his back to the audience, and he'd be going like, 'Just listen to them stupid people . . .' and here we are with our hands on our instruments hoping he will call out something we know. Instead . . . he's just being Elvis out of control, saying, 'These people, they don't care if I'm good or bad. I can do anything, and they still love it.' "

He scarcely emerged from his room during the two and one-half weeks he was off in June. Lisa visited for ten days, but it was left to Linda to look after her, and to discipline her if she needed disciplining. One time she drove her golf cart out onto the highway, then stopped at the gate and posed for pictures for the fans — two things she was expressly forbidden to do. When Linda remonstrated that she'd been warned "one hundred times" not to go out on the highway, Lisa just told her to go to hell, showing little concern when Linda said she would have to tell her daddy about this. Others observed the little girl sitting for hours sometimes outside her father's darkened room just waiting for him to wake up. She was all he cared about, he burst out emotionally on occasion. But he didn't seem able to do anything about it, and he stayed holed up in the room, with only his books for company.

THERE WAS NO ONE he wanted to see. The new guys were little more than hired hands, and the old gang was all gone, scattered to the four winds. They all had lives of their own now: Joe was out on the Coast with his girlfriend Shirley Dieu; it seemed like Lamar hardly ever came over from Nashville except when things were being given away; he hadn't heard a word from Jerry since the confrontation in Vail; and Marty just brought him down. Meanwhile, Charlie was falling apart under the pressure, and even Sonny and Red were almost strangers to him now — there was a poisonous atmosphere of finger-pointing and suspicion different in degree from anything that had existed in the old days. He knew his father contributed to it with all his talk of budget-cutting and getting rid of the dead wood, sometimes even to their faces. That wasn't the problem, though. There had been quarrels in the past, and Vernon had *never* liked Red and Sonny — but that had never affected Elvis' feelings of closeness to them, not even when Red stayed away for two years after the wedding. Now he joked that they were the only guys he paid just to stay away from him.

He was pissed off at Joe and Dr. Nick, too. They had gotten him into a business deal a few months before that they assured him represented no risk and would almost certainly prove to be a good investment for him in the long run, but now it was threatening to blow up on them all. It was a plan to promote racquetball in much the same way that he had once sought to promote karate, in this case by building a chain of racquetball courts around the country which would go by the name of Presley Center Courts. In exchange for his name, as he understood it from them and their partner, Memphis developer and bond salesman Mike McMahon, he would receive 25 percent of the company, at no cost to him. They had broken ground on the Memphis and Nashville clubs in the middle of April, and everything seemed to be going smoothly when McMahon came to see him in Tahoe in May, but then things started to go wrong, as McMahon claimed that Elvis had to put up money for a buyout of the leases on the two buildings currently under construction, and when Elvis balked, informed him that by becoming 25 percent owner of the corporation, he was liable for 25 percent of its debts.

He went to the Colonel for advice, but Colonel just reminded him that he had been against this business all along, that he had told Elvis that nobody gets 25 percent just for doing a favor, and that it was too late for advice, now that he had gone ahead and signed all the partnership papers. Then he learned through one of the guys that McMahon, the only active partner in the business, had been drawing a small salary and was leasing a corporate vehicle, despite all of Nick's assurances that no one would be taking a penny out of the operation until it showed a profit. The whole thing just didn't feel right. It gnawed away at him until he didn't want to have any more to do with it, and then he shocked McMahon, who had had perfectly pleasant dealings with him to date, by calling up in the middle of the night "completely incoherent and irrational to the point where he was accusing me of different things . . . and then he told me he was going to kill me." Dr. Nick tried to tell the developer not to worry, that this kind of sudden rage was an occasional side effect of one of the medications that Elvis was taking and that it would soon wear off. But the feeling that he had been taken advantage of by his friends didn't wear off; it kept preying on him as he asked himself over and over, What the fuck were Joe and Dr. Nick thinking about when they brought him into this?

* * *

THEY WENT OUT AGAIN on June 25 on yet another eleven-day tour. Jerry Schilling, now working as road manager for pop singer Billy Joel, saw Elvis in Landover, Maryland, on the third date of the tour. It was the first time they had met since their January split, and Jerry was a little apprehensive, but Elvis gave him a warm embrace and kept Elton John waiting while they caught up on old times. The concert itself, like the one in Philadelphia the following night, was described by reviewers as "a show that consists mostly of a series of postures" by a performer "too tired — or bored — to care." Elton John, no stranger to excess himself, got the impression of immense loneliness. "He had dozens of people around him, supposedly looking after him, but he already seemed like a corpse." After the show, Jerry and Myrna were having drinks with Joe Esposito and Joe Guercio when the orchestra leader suddenly turned to Jerry and said, "You know, all he can do now is die."

There was a big blowup with Sonny in Fort Worth at the end of the week, their second visit to the city in just one month. The disagreement started out as a petty dispute over money — Vernon had canceled Sonny's wife and little boy's prepaid plane tickets to Texas — but it quickly escalated into more volatile issues of manhood and pride. Elvis finally settled the matter by telling Sonny to go ahead and have his family fly in, he would square things with Vernon, but Sonny was not surprised to hear "from a couple of guys later that [Elvis] was calling me every name in the book after I left." Sonny and Red had just about reached the point where they were sick of the whole thing. Others saw them as hostile; they saw themselves as truth tellers, and if Elvis didn't like it, he was just going to have to find someone else to clean up after him. "Some of the guys," Sonny was aware, "said we were intimidating Elvis about too many things [but] all of the intimidation part was only for his own good."

The tour ended in Memphis on July 5, with Elvis in his red-white-and-blue bicentennial costume and "America the Beautiful" the highlight of the show. Everyone noted what a foul mood he was in, which was underscored when he avoided the gang that had gathered at Graceland before the performance. After the concert he went straight to his room, leaving the guests who had regrouped for the usual Fourth of July fireworks to go home puzzled and disappointed.

He left with Linda for Palm Springs the following night. Six days later Sonny and Red were fired. Sonny was at the dentist when he got a message from his wife that Vernon had "something important" to talk to him about.

He called up right away, and after brushing aside Mr. Presley's objections that this was a matter that needed to be addressed face-to-face, listened incredulously as Vernon informed him that things hadn't been going all that well lately, and that it looked like they were going to have to let some people go. "Oh, I see, and I guess I'm one of the ones that's going to be let go?" Sonny said. "Yes, I'm afraid so," Vernon agreed in a subdued voice, informing Sonny that he would be given one week's severance pay.

Within a couple of hours Sonny found out who the others were. "I've been fired, man," Red said on the phone from California, and karate expert Dave Hebler confirmed that he, too, had gotten the axe. What hurt the most, Sonny and Red agreed, was that after all these years Elvis didn't even have the guts to tell them himself.

By now Elvis and Linda had retreated to Las Vegas, where Elvis placed himself once again under Dr. Ghanem's care and Linda did her best to reassure him that none of this was really his fault. He kept going over it again and again. He knew they meant well, but Daddy was right: they were costing him too much money with all the lawsuits. There were other ways of doing these things, but Sonny and Red were too old to learn and couldn't fit into the new professional security operation he was trying to create. They were like brothers to him and knew that if they ever needed anything they could always count on him. Linda listened and nodded and had no doubt that he believed what he was saying — but she could understand how Sonny and Red would feel about it, too. To be dismissed so unceremoniously after all these years, and not even to have the courtesy of being told man to man. "But that was Elvis' way," she recognized. "He never wanted to be the bad guy. So we just fled. But that also chagrined Red and Sonny — and rightly so."

Dave Hebler was so outraged that he flew to Las Vegas for a direct confrontation, but he never got the chance, waiting for hours outside Dr. Ghanem's gate until he was at last informed that Elvis was not going to see him. As for Vernon, he felt no better about the decision than anyone else, even though he believed it to be the right one and Colonel backed him on it 100 percent — he was simply trying to protect his son, no longer just from others but from himself. And yet for all of his present-day problems there was still that element of Elvis' nature that made his father feel ashamed of any mean-spiritedness on his own part. Elvis had always possessed a generous heart, Vernon reflected; from the time that he was a little boy, he had never failed to take into account the other fellow's point of view. He had spoken to Elvis again and again over the years, "when I felt that he was carrying too big a crew [telling him], 'You don't need all of them, especially some who just seem to be out for what they want.' Elvis stopped me cold, answering, 'You see their wants. I look beyond their wants and can see their needs.'" In retrospect he would not be the least bit surprised if Elvis hired them back, Red and Sonny anyway, after a suitable cooling-off period.

E LVIS RETURNED FROM THE COAST just in time for the July 23 start of another tour, his fifth so far this year. Once again they played backwater locales, from Syracuse, New York, to Charleston, West Virginia; once again the whole idea was to generate income (close to $1 million in two weeks this time); and once again review after review spoke of the perfunctory nature of the performance and the sad state into which Elvis seemed to have fallen. In Hartford on July 28 Colonel lambasted Elvis for not putting forth more effort, for not giving the people their money's worth, and Elvis was so shaken that he sought out Tom Hulett after the show to ask if the fans still loved him. Hulett reassured him that they did, and audiences continued to demonstrate their affection in any number of ways, but as a reporter for the *Newport News Times-Herald* wrote, the adulation now was more "for what he was, what he symbolizes, rather than for what he is or how he sings now." There was, she went on, sounding a note that had become depressingly familiar from other recent write-ups and reviews, "no soul [in his music], no driving power behind his voice." Sometimes he had J. D. Sumner or Kathy Westmoreland take a solo spot in the middle of the show, because he just seemed too tired to go on.

The racquetball deal finally fell apart at the end of the tour. Elvis had his lawyer write a letter on August 10 that sought to disentangle him from the partnership once and for all: he was withdrawing his support, the letter stated, and wanted his name taken off the project. Elvis himself left for Palm Springs the same day, but the matter was still very much on his mind as he continued to mutter about firing Joe and getting rid of Dr. Nick for their betrayals. A few days later he called Nick in the middle of the night, totally "coked up and sort of psychotic, and he cussed me out about taking advantage of him. 'You're fired,' he said. And I said, 'You can't fire me. I don't work for you.' But he just told me he was going to get someone else to go out with him on the next tour."

Dr. Ghanem accompanied him when they went out again two weeks later, on August 27, along with Dr. Nick's nurse, Tish Henley, who had moved into one of the trailers behind Graceland with her husband earlier in the year so as to be able to administer his medication more efficiently.

Linda's brother, Sam Thompson, who had been working for the Memphis sheriff's department for the last four and one-half years, was the new co-head of security with former Palm Springs police officer Dick Grob. And Larry Geller, with whom Elvis had been spending an increasing amount of time on his recent trips to California after first seeing him again in Vegas a few years earlier, officially rejoined the entourage for the first time since his unceremonious firing by the Colonel for attempted "mind control" in 1967. Elvis welcomed Larry's presence on the tour. Larry was just the person that he needed at this point, someone with whom he could carry on philosophical conversations, share ideas about books and spirituality, and breathe some fresh air into a world that had gone stale. Larry for his part didn't hesitate for a moment; he knew Elvis needed him, he was aware from their conversations that Elvis had missed him as much as he had missed Elvis, and he knew, too, that the atmosphere surrounding him was very different from what it had once been. Even Colonel Parker, Larry realized, could no longer afford to be so suspicious of him — the main idea now was just to keep the show running.

The first show, in San Antonio, was a "lackluster performance," according to one review, but it was a success by the new standard under which they were operating, and everyone reassured themselves afterward that maybe Elvis would respond positively to a new regimen set up by a new physician. The second date, a matinee performance at the Summit in Houston, dispelled any such illusions. Elvis was so "loaded," according to the testimony of one troupe member after another, that there was some doubt that he would even be able to take the stage, and when he did, he could barely talk, let alone walk, putting on a performance that embarrassed the whole show and made them wonder how much longer he could go on. The Colonel, who witnessed the entire performance, was beside himself. Not only was Elvis testing the limits of his audience's love, and their continued loyalty to him, he was testing the patience of the Houston policemen augmenting the security force, who, Colonel realized in a panic, were talking openly about Elvis' condition among themselves. All that was missing was some glory hound who wanted to be the one to take down Elvis Presley. Because *everyone knew* — there was no longer any way you could deny the evidence of your eyes.

He got Elvis out of town as quickly as possible, contacting his old friend Bill Williams, entertainment chairman of the Houston Livestock Show and Rodeo, to fix things with the cops. There was nothing he could do, however, to stop the review that ran in the *Houston Post* the following morning. "Elvis Presley has been breaking hearts for more than 20 years now," was critic and longtime fan Bob Claypool's lead, "and, Saturday afternoon in the Summit — in a completely new and unexpected way — he broke mine." The show was "*awful*," he wrote, "a depressingly incoherent, amateurish mess served up by a bloated, stumbling and mumbling figure who didn't act like 'The King' of anything, least of all rock 'n' roll." The fans, Claypool observed, almost didn't seem to notice; "faithful as always, they still came down front — came bearing gifts (a painting of Elvis, a six-foot-long stuffed dog, a small teddy bear)." It made you wonder if they wouldn't always come, he wrote, "no matter how bad, how ill, how *uncaring* he would get. But for some of us it would never be the same, because the man who had given us the original myth of rock 'n' roll — the man who created it and *lived* it — was now, for whatever reason, taking it all back."

That night the Colonel had Joe call Dr. Nick. They needed him, Joe told the Memphis physician, making it clear he was speaking for Colonel as well as himself. Nick took this to be as close to an apology as he was going to get — he couldn't recall Colonel ever requesting a favor of him before. He said he'd be glad to rejoin the tour so long as he knew that this was what Elvis wanted. Not long afterward Elvis called and asked him to come back, and he met them in Mobile the next day.

The problem, once he had had the opportunity to confer with Tish, was not all that difficult to figure out. It revolved, as always, around issues of access and amount, and Nick soon had things back in proper proportion, establishing a protocol of dispensation that took into account the potentially debilitating effect of Donnatal on speech and motor functions and included an assortment of placebos among the multitude of depressants that Elvis required to go to sleep each night. With the reinstitution of such pragmatic measures, the tour was able to continue, and everyone was able to go back to pretending that nothing was really wrong. Bitsy Mott, the Colonel's brother-in-law and security director in the early days, had no such luxury. He had had a falling-out with the Colonel not long after Elvis' return to live performing, and he and his wife had not seen Elvis in some time when the show arrived in Tampa on September 2. They were shocked by his appearance when they visited with him before the performance, but they were even more shocked when Elvis took the stage. They couldn't help but cry as they watched, and they left before the show was over, not even bothering to say good-bye to the Colonel, who appeared no less dejected than they.

* * *

ALMOST AS SOON AS the tour was over, Elvis once again began hearing rumors about the book that Red and Sonny and Hebler were said
to be planning to write, a behind-the-scenes exposé that would reveal a
world the fans had never imagined. There had been talk about just such a
book almost from the day that his father had dismissed them, but Elvis
insisted that it would never happen, that Red and Sonny would never
betray him in this way. Now he was no longer so sure. The three disgruntled
ex-bodyguards had approached first Rick Husky, then former *Los Angeles
Herald-Examiner* critic Frank Lieberman about serving as their collaborator,
and even asked Jerry Schilling to go in on it with them. Now Elvis heard
that they had signed a deal with *Star* reporter Steve Dunleavy, and he joked
cynically with the guys who were left about who was going to turn tabloid
reporter next. There was no disguising his real feelings from those closest
to him, however. As Linda saw it, "he was frightened, he was angry, he was
hurt — he was like a kid, he became more fragile than ever. He just didn't
realize that he had done something really hurtful to them, too."

He flew out to California at the beginning of October to join Linda in
her new apartment and pick up a Ferrari for himself. John O'Grady and Ed
Hookstratten were urging him to put a stop to the book any way he could,
and he conferred with O'Grady, who was confident that Red and Sonny
and Hebler could still be bought off. He gave Jerry Schilling a call, too, and
invited him over to the apartment, ostensibly to thank him for turning
down Red and Sonny's offer. Jerry was still there when O'Grady stopped by
to report on the failure of his mission. He had offered each man $50,000,
along with an "education allowance" to help prepare him for a new line of
work. They had turned him down flat, declaring that they were in too deep
to back out now. O'Grady had gone to the meeting wired, and he offered to
play back a tape of the conversation, but Elvis wasn't interested. The private investigator suggested a number of other alternatives just skirting the
edge of outright intimidation, but Elvis didn't rise to the bait. He was sure
he could straighten things out by himself, he said, if he could just get a
chance to talk to them on his own.

He had the chance less than one week later, on October 12, the day after
his return to Graceland. Red had called the previous afternoon, and Charlie
explained that they had just gotten in and Elvis was asleep. Red made it plain
that he didn't believe him and angrily accused Elvis of being stoned and listening in on the upstairs line. When Elvis called him back the next day, it was
early in the morning out in California. "I guess I do owe you an explanation," he said, in the kind of weak, slurred little voice that Red had grown

all too used to in the last year of his employment. What had happened was due to a combination of factors: Vernon's illness; "a lot of excess pressure" on the racquetball business; all the lawsuits; and, worst of all, "I don't know whether you heard it, but they were trying to prove us insane. . . . I'm talking about some influential people who were checking psychiatrist reports."

Red tried to steer the conversation back on course. "I couldn't believe it. You had left town. Your daddy called and talked about cutting down expenses and giving us one week's notice. They give Chinese coolies two weeks."

He didn't know anything about that, Elvis replied, the one-week thing. "It was like a fuse burning," he tried to explain. "It was just a series of things. If I could lay them out to you one by one, I could show the reasons for the separatisms." It was all the things he had already mentioned, the way in which unnamed parties were trying "to establish a pattern of insanity and violence," the fact that "the fun [had] ceased to exist."

"I guess all that pressure led up to our demise," Red said bleakly, seeking to pursue an agenda of his own. "It was a shock. We were broke. I sold my house. Hated to do that."

ELVIS (surprised): You sold your house?
RED: Oh yeah, . . . hated to do that. It was a bad time by all.
ELVIS (philosophically): Well, I guess there never really is any good times. It was bad for me, too. . . .
RED: I understand. But if I had just heard from you, it would have been easier to take.
ELVIS: Well, in doing business and things of that nature, I don't do that.

They spoke of a number of other matters, always coming back to the same thing. With Hebler, just as with the racquetball deal, he had been seriously disappointed. "I think I became a dollar sign. . . . In the process he lost sight of Elvis. That can easily happen. It happened, man. I'd become an object, not a person. I'm not that sign, I'm not that image, I'm myself."

Then he brought up the one issue that had not been mentioned. He knew what Red thought, he knew what Red had said to Charlie just the day before, "[but] you're so wrong on one thing — and don't get paranoid. I'm talking to you as a friend on a private line, and there is no soul here. I'm not fucked up by no means. On the contrary, I've never been in better condition in my life."

"You *have* been pretty fucked up," Red demurred. "That's what I was talking about."

Elvis seemed to read into this some kind of reference to his 1973 divorce, which in turn triggered a belated apology for Red's exclusion from the wedding nine years before. But "that was railroaded through. I didn't even know who was there in that little room the size of a bathroom with a Supreme Court justice. It was in there over and done so quick I didn't realize I was married. . . . That wasn't my doing. I had nothing to do with —"

RED: Let's get to the last couple, three years. Let's face it, you haven't enjoyed yourself.
ELVIS: I enjoy my work. . . .
RED: We were always worried about you.
ELVIS: You worried about me so much that you turned around and tried to hurt me. You see, I know what that is.
RED: Well, that's after you hurt me. You hurt me and my family very bad.
ELVIS: All I know, there was friction created in the group, the vibes were so bad, people were scared to move and everything, so who knows what the hell they were hearing and being told? I just know it got to be very, very tense. . . .
RED: You got to get healthy, Elvis. You haven't been healthy for a while.
ELVIS: Oh yes I am. I just had an absolute physical head to toe. . . . I keep hearing that shit about being fat and middle-aged.
RED: No, no, you ate a lot, but you weren't fat, you could tell there was something else wrong, something was wrong inside. When I tried to talk to you about it, you'd get mad, you wouldn't listen.

Choosing to take this as a reference to his long-standing intestinal problems, Elvis hastened to assure Red that these had been straightened out. Aside from that, there was nothing wrong with him, despite what Red kept intimating; the real problem was a general failure to communicate on the part of the whole group. "Negative vibes . . . I could feel the negative things, but I couldn't exactly pinpoint what it was. I just reached a boiling point. It was a temporary thing — I didn't feel like I could communicate with anyone. I felt terribly alone, you know, like that [numerological] number eight. The [reading] that says they're intensely alone at heart." That was the way he felt, he said, and he knew that was the way Red felt — because Red was a number eight, too. Number eights had "warm hearts toward the oppressed. But they hide their feelings [and] do what they please."

At this point Red seemed to conclude that the conversation was not going anywhere. "It bugged me when you were talking to Charlie and said I was all fucked up," Elvis said. "I'm not. I got a daughter and a life. What profiteth a man if he gains the world and loses his own soul? I love to sing — since I was two years old." In fact, he and Charlie had been singing just a little while ago, and they missed Red, they missed his harmony part on "Love Is a Many Splendored Thing." What could he say? Red replied. He missed singing it. "Well, look," Elvis said, "you take care of yourself and your family, and if you need me for anything, I would be more than happy to help out. I mean it. I don't give a goddamn — And that ain't got a goddamn thing to do with articles or no publications or none of that shit that I've heard — I've just heard rumors, bits and pieces. I have never sat down with anybody and had it laid out to me. I just know that you as a person, and Pat [Red's wife] — if there is anything I can do, any way of getting a job, anything else, let me know." Red expressed his appreciation on behalf of both himself and his family, who, he repeated, had been hurt as well. Which gave Elvis the opportunity to stress once again his own feelings of rejection.

> All of us were hurt. It's like that song, "Desiderata": "Listen to the dull and ignorant, because they, too, have a story to tell." And then Hank Williams wrote, "You never walked in that man's shoes and saw things through his eyes." After analyzing the blamed thing, I can see it, I can see it clearly. That's why I'm saying, anything I can do at all. Worried about the book? I don't think so, not on my part. You do whatever you have to do. I just want you and Pat to know I'm still here.

H E WAS BACK ON THE ROAD two days later for yet another two-week tour, another $1 million for Colonel and him to divide. If there was any doubt about the outcome of his conversation with Red, or the status of their relationship, it was dispelled by a Steve Dunleavy story in the October 26 edition of *The Star*, midway through the tour. Under the headline "Elvis' dramatic plea to his ex-bodyguards: Don't write that book about me," it quoted at length from his and Red's conversation, which evidently had been taped without Elvis' knowledge. Its conclusion quoted Red as saying to the reporter, yet to be identified by *The Star* as the forthcoming book's author, "You can't be with a man since childhood and not feel something for him. . . . I just wish he would get well."

On October 29, two days after the tour was over, another recording session was scheduled at Graceland, but this time Elvis was barely able to muster the enthusiasm even to begin. Somehow they managed to get three tracks over the course of a first, very long night, but "he just wasn't interested," said pianist Tony Brown. "He couldn't seem to keep rhythm, he couldn't maintain any attention span; it was like we'd get one song, and he'd go upstairs for a couple of hours, and we'd just wait around." As at the earlier home recording session, he invited different members of the group up to his room at various points during the evening. This time he gave away items of clothing as souvenirs, including an entire "Superfly" outfit from 1973 with which he thought J. D. Sumner and the Stamps might spiff up their image.

On the second night it seemed for a while as if Elvis might not come down at all, and Felton had the players laying down instrumental tracks until at last he reluctantly appeared. He started work on "He'll Have to Go," a classic 1959 hit for country singer Jim Reeves, but almost as soon as he did, a shipment of motorcycles that he had been waiting for arrived, and Elvis insisted that everyone go outside and watch them get unloaded, then try them out on short runs back and forth to the gate or to Linda's house around the corner. Finally, any pretense that the session might continue was abandoned when Elvis once again retreated to his room, this time emerging with a Thompson submachine gun with which he good-naturedly threatened to blow up the speakers. No one was sure whether or not he was joking, and Felton might have been tempted to try to persuade the musicians to stick around for another day or two just to see if Elvis might snap out of it. But Elvis put an end to any such speculation by apologizing and declaring that he was simply too distracted to continue. He was upset about Red and Sonny's book, he said, and he couldn't get in the right frame of mind for recording — but they would all get together again under happier circumstances soon, maybe next time in Nashville.

With that burden lifted off him, he zeroed in on the problem of getting everyone home with a focus and energy that had eluded him for the last two days. The West Coast–based singers and musicians were to be transported to Los Angeles on the *Lisa Marie* and met at the airport by his limousine driver Gerald Peters, while similar arrangements were made for David Briggs, Tony Brown, and Chip Young to fly into Nashville on the Jet-Star. Finally, over Joe's vociferous objections, he presented J. D. Sumner with his white Lincoln limousine as a gift, so that J.D. and the Stamps (to whom he had given a tour bus the previous July) could travel home in style.

For the next three weeks it seemed as if he were merely seeking some-where to alight, flying to Denver, Vegas, or Palm Springs on a whim, Dallas for a hamburger. In his bedroom at home he pored over his books, consult-ing *Cheiro's Book of Numbers* whenever any serious plan came up for discus-sion. Linda was around for some of the time, but she seemed more intent than ever on her career as an actress, and even when she was in Memphis she spent more time at her house than at Graceland. George Klein fixed Elvis up with a couple of girls, and he dated a little, but his heart wasn't in it. He needed something more — his life was an empty wasteland. Then on November 19 he met Ginger Alden.

Ginger's twenty-two-year-old sister, Terry, the reigning Miss Tennessee, was the one George had thought Elvis would go for, but he brought the two of them out to the house, along with their older sister, Rosemary. The three sisters all waited downstairs for what seemed like hours while, they were told, Elvis practiced his karate. When they were finally ushered into his private quarters, Elvis almost immediately made clear his preference for nineteen-year-old Ginger, a former Miss Traffic Safety and current Miss Mid-South Fair, to whom he said, "Ginger, you're burning a hole through me." Ginger was distinctly ill at ease with all this attention — in fact, she barely said a word after her sisters left — but Elvis didn't mind: she seemed to listen and observe intently while Elvis showed her his books and explained that eight was a lonely number. It was almost daylight when he had one of the guys drive her home, having behaved like a perfect gentle-man the entire time, she told her mother and sisters, who breathlessly awaited her report.

He called the next day, at first offering her a ride in his new Ferrari, "but then he determined I wasn't ready for that yet because it went so fast." Instead he invited her to drive out to the airport with him in his Stutz so they could take the JetStar for a spin and observe the Memphis skyline at night. It would be perfectly proper, he assured her — his cousin Patsy and her husband, Gee Gee, would be chaperoning them — and he repeated the same argument when he suddenly got the idea that they should all fly to Las Vegas instead. Ginger protested that she would have to call her mother first, but he told her she could do that when they got there, and if her mother didn't like it, they would just turn right around and go home. She thought her mother would be upset when she called, but Jo Alden's reaction was quite the opposite, as she seemed almost to encourage her youngest daughter in her latest conquest, simply telling her to be sure to be back the following day.

Ginger was a little disappointed that they weren't going to get to see much of Vegas: they went straight to Elvis' suite, and all Elvis wanted was for her to put on some oversize pajamas and come to bed. She was a little apprehensive about the pajamas until he gave her his solemn oath that it was out of spirituality that he was drawn to her, not carnality, and that he would treat her like a lady at all times. She wasn't sure whether or not to believe him, but then he fell asleep as she read to him, and the two of them lay innocently side by side until well into the next day.

It was "a different kind of a date" for sure, and she was not without misgivings that her boyfriend would disapprove, but her mother and sisters told her she would be very foolish to overlook an opportunity of this sort, and she didn't hesitate for a minute when Elvis called just one week later from San Francisco on the fifth day of his new tour. He wanted her to join him right away, he said, he was sending the JetStar to come get her — could she be ready in a few hours? She threw her things together, arriving in San Francisco the following morning, but she didn't see him all that day, nor was she invited to watch his performance that night. He would be with her right after the show, the guys kept telling her; there was just this little problem he had to deal with first. Finally, she went to bed hungry and depressed, without ever learning that the problem Elvis had to deal with was that Linda was still on the tour.

Linda had had a strong suspicion that Elvis was planning to fly someone else in from the first. Her suspicion was strengthened when he suggested with that furtive little boy's look in his eye that she seemed kind of worn out to him and that maybe he should have the JetStar take her back to Memphis. He would be okay, he said, he would just take a little time for himself. For once she didn't feel like giving him an easy out. In fact, after chiding him that he *knew* she always enjoyed a chance to go shopping in San Francisco, she actually challenged his story. "I said, 'You have another girl here, right? You're bringing another girl in.' 'Oh, honey,' he said. 'Of course not.' And he held me really close and said, 'I just want you to know, no matter what anybody ever tells you, no matter what you read, no matter what you hear, it's only you that I love.' I looked him right in the eye, and I said, 'You don't have another girl here?' He said, 'No, honey,' and I said, 'O-kay . . .' — but I said it very sarcastically. Normally if he had said something like 'It's only you I love,' I would have said something like 'Oh, you're so sweet,' but this time I distanced myself and just said, 'Okay' — like 'Yeah. Right. Sure.'"

Maybe it was because she had a secret of her own. Without Elvis knowing anything about it, Linda had developed a relationship with the piano player, David Briggs. "He was just the total antithesis of Elvis. I mean, he was bearded, blue jean–clad, kind of low-key, no ego, not traditionally good-looking, he just really downplayed everything, and I thought, You know what? There is life after Elvis." They liked to think they had been thrown together not just by fate but by Elvis himself, who kept urging the two of them to go out and enjoy themselves and do all the things that he couldn't do, taking advantage of the restaurants and shops in the various cities on the tour. What really started it, though, were the nights that Elvis was completely out of it or carrying on one of his interminable dialogues with Larry Geller that left room for the participation of no one else — she just felt like she had to get away. So she started playing cards with the guys at the beginning of their late-August tour, and very soon she and David gravitated toward a more intimate relationship, maintaining the fiction at first that their closeness was just a part of the general camaraderie. Everyone else watched with compulsive curiosity, uncertain whether what appeared to be happening actually was. Even after it became obvious, the two lovers pretended that it was still their secret, as the rest of the troupe nervously speculated on how long it would take Elvis to find out.

That was the backdrop for Linda's departure, and perhaps the reason she felt obligated to adopt a coat of protective cynicism for the first time in her four-year relationship with Elvis. She needed to go, she had finally come to realize, she just hadn't had the courage to pull away; now that the opportunity was provided for her, she was damned if she wasn't going to do her shopping first. When they parted, it was with the idea that she would see him back in Memphis, but for Linda this marked a watershed in her life, as she recognized once and for all that there was nothing she could do, "he was going to go ahead and slowly kill himself, no matter what I did. I couldn't make him happy, and I knew he wasn't going to change. So I left."

The next night Ginger attended the show in Anaheim. It was the final date of the tour, and the improvement in his performance was remarked upon by even some of his sharpest critics. He was inspired by Ginger's presence, he confessed afterward to Larry Geller — he thought this girl was really it. After the show, they stayed up all night talking and didn't even kiss. He was beginning to believe that he had discovered love on a higher plane.

They went straight from the road into Vegas. Ginger wanted to go home for a few days — she said that she missed her family — but Elvis said that he needed her, and she stayed. Some of the guys grumbled that this girl wasn't for real, she was just a baby and had no idea of how to take care of him, but Elvis was in no mood to listen. As Larry observed in his diary:

"How long can the drugs and his feelings about Ginger keep him on this high?"

Not long, as it turned out. Vegas started out on a strong note, but it seemed both to fans and to other observers that Elvis quickly ran out of gas. Before the first week was out, he looked "very tired and quite sad," according to one fan report. Most of the time he talked a blue streak, but he was frequently preoccupied and out of sorts. He swore at the sound system and cut the show short on December 6, explaining that he was in too much pain from a sprained ankle to continue, and then at the late show on December 10, he announced casually, "I hate Las Vegas," in an aside that was cheered by the crowd. At the conclusion of the next song, reported faithful fan Martha Collins in the British-based *Worldwide Elvis News Service Weekly,* he "picked up the mike on its stand and asked, 'Does anyone want this tinny sonofabitch?,'" and as the audience "cheered wildly" in response, declared, "I'm not going to get up here and try to sing, because these damn microphones are [so] cheap. I ain't gonna do it, you know. 'Cause this is my living, folks, my life."

Ginger seemed to occupy as much of his attention as the show. He arranged for "Sir Gerald" to pick up a special white-on-white Lincoln Mark V for her on the Coast and flew in her entire family for the conclusion of the engagement when Ginger announced that she was homesick again. Ginger's mother, never shy, was quoted in the press to the effect that rumors of marriage at this point were premature and that the Lincoln Continental which Elvis had given her daughter was not to be construed as any kind of formal engagement gift — at least not as of that moment.

There were other things to worry about. Vernon was admitted to Sunrise Hospital on December 9 with what looked like another heart attack, but it turned out to be just a scare. The Colonel was rumored to have lost over $1 million at the roulette table, and his uncharacteristically grim demeanor seemed to indicate that the rumors were true. It was Elvis that he was worried about most, however. "My artist," he declared balefully to a couple of startled European fans seeking an introduction, "is out of control."

It was obvious to anyone who saw Elvis that he was not well. Larry was concerned that, for all of his talk of the rejuvenating nature of his love for Ginger, he might be "killing himself, striving for her love and attention." The day that Vernon was released from the hospital, Larry found Elvis with beads of perspiration running down his face. "His eyes had a strange, haunted look. He stared at me, taking in deep gulps of air and breathing erratically. Trying to stand, he lost his balance, and as he fell he grabbed at the drapes with both hands to keep from hitting the floor. . . . He moaned, 'This is it — I'm going out. I — ah — took too much — or someone gave me the wrong thing. I'm going . . . I'm leaving my body. I'm dying.'" Somehow Larry got him through it and sought out Dr. Ghanem, who "told me not to worry — that he'd check Elvis later."

The final night of the engagement was as disturbing as the rest, particularly for anyone accustomed to the high-spirited, freewheeling atmosphere normally associated with the end of any Las Vegas run. On this particular night Elvis clearly couldn't focus, he was unable to concentrate, at times it seemed as if he could barely wake up, wrote one distraught fan, who noted that the previous evening, "in an off-mike aside to the singers, he mouthed the words, 'Only one more night here,' and made a face as if he were about to throw up." When televangelist Rex Humbard came to visit with him backstage, Elvis seized desperately on his arrival, demanding of Humbard whether he should give up singing and devote himself to the Lord. He seemed momentarily comforted when the well-known minister assured him that he was doing the Lord's work simply by using his talent and giving pleasure to so many people, but then Elvis started talking about Armageddon and the Second Coming of Christ, and, Humbard testified, "I took both his hands in mine [and] said, 'Elvis, right now I want to pray for you.' He said, 'Please do,' and started weeping."

The story that Bill Burk wrote in the *Memphis Press-Scimitar* on December 15, three days after the Vegas close, presented as kind a reaction as anyone who cared about Elvis Presley could have had at the time. "After sitting through Elvis Presley's closing night performance at the Las Vegas Hilton," wrote Burk, a longtime supporter, "one walks away wondering how much longer it can be before the end comes, perhaps suddenly, and why the King of Rock 'n' Roll would subject himself to possible ridicule by going onstage so ill-prepared. Why carry on? For fame? He's perhaps the best-known, best-loved performer of all time. . . . For money? [Burk dismisses out-of-hand the idea that Elvis could possibly need the money.] This may seem like one person's opinion. It isn't. . . . And yet they keep coming back, and they will pack his next road tour, which starts December 27 in Wichita and ends New Year's Eve in Pittsburgh. Once a king, always a king. Maybe that's it. And just maybe they're still coming because they think it might be the last time around."

WITH TERRY AND GINGER ALDEN, HAWAII, MARCH 1977.
(COURTESY OF JOSEPH A. TUNZI, J.A.T. PUBLISHING)

ELVIS, WHAT HAPPENED?

J UST AS HE HAD PROMISED, Elvis agreed to a new recording date in Nashville to make up for the November Graceland debacle. In hopes that something might be gained from an entirely new setting, Felton booked a week's worth of sessions at Buzz Cason's Creative Workshop, a comfortably up-to-date studio with which all of the Nashville players were familiar and where he thought Elvis would quickly feel at home. Recording was slated to begin on January 20, and everything was going according to plan until Felton heard from Joe just hours before the session's scheduled start that Elvis had gotten hung up in Memphis and wasn't going to be able to make it until the following day. Then on the twenty-first, with all the musicians assembled, Felton got another call from Joe. Elvis was in town, but he was going to have to stay at the hotel for the time being because he wasn't feeling very well. Felton wondered if he ought to hold the musicians, and Joe said he thought he should, at least for the time being. Over the course of the evening, however, the bulletins grew worse, as Elvis complained of a worsening of his throat condition and a doctor was called to confirm the existence of the problem. In the end Felton was forced to send everyone home.

What was bothering Elvis, Joe and Charlie and the rest of the guys all knew, was not a sore throat but hurt pride and a wounded heart. Ginger had refused at the last minute to accompany him to Nashville. They had had a big fight about it, and he had threatened not to go at all, but she remained adamant, coming up with one excuse after another, including the fact that she had never liked Nashville. His throat was just a way of making Ginger feel sorry for him, his cousin Billy concluded when Elvis told Billy that he wasn't planning to record even before their departure from Memphis. "If I have to," he said, "I'll say I'm losing my voice." As if somehow, by that refusal, he would get back at Ginger — and maybe even at the Colonel and RCA, too.

Linda might have motivated him, the guys all agreed; she would have kidded him along and maybe even gotten him out of his funk. They blamed Ginger for just making matters worse. From their point of view, she had been nothing but trouble ever since her arrival on the scene, with Billy and Jo Smith the only ones who could communicate with her, and then only because they treated her like she was a little girl. What bothered everyone most was the way she had Elvis running around in circles, doing everything he could to try to impress her and her family. No one missed the fact that her presence could pick him up, as it had on New Year's Eve in Pittsburgh, where he gave one of his best performances in a long time. Nor did anyone doubt that he genuinely cared for her. It was just that no one could understand the attraction. The closest he came to explaining it was when he told Dr. Nick there was something about her that reminded him of his mother, but neither Nick nor anyone else could see what it was — she seemed to them like some high school kid flattered by all the attention but unsure what to make of it, guided more by her mother's ambitions than by any deep inner feelings of her own.

It was a subject that came up often in the month and a half since Elvis had taken up with the girl, and nearly everyone weighed in with their opinions in a far more public way than they would have dared with any of Elvis' other girlfriends. But Elvis remained impervious to argument and innuendo, even if it was clear that he cared far more about her than she did about him. One time Billy suggested to Elvis that maybe he should look for a woman closer to his own age, with whom he could share common interests and have meaningful discussions once in a while. "What in the hell could a forty-two-year-old woman do for me?" was Elvis' sexually swaggering reply, when it was perfectly evident to Billy and everyone else that Elvis' sex life was virtually dormant at this point.

Like it or not, though, his entire existence was dominated by Ginger and her family. When Ginger's grandfather died, Elvis flew all of the Aldens into Harrison, Arkansas, on January 3, for the funeral, and he and Charlie hummed conspicuously along as the minister sang "Amazing Grace." The following day he took Ginger and her sister Rosemary to Palm Springs, where he celebrated his birthday that weekend in quiet domesticity. Nor was he shy about the subject of marriage, as his Beverly Hills dentist, Max Shapiro (the man who specialized in house calls and "feel good" dentistry), came to find out. Shapiro, described by reporters Charles Thompson and James Cole as "a slight man in his late fifties [with] thick eyeglasses and a crudely tinted hairpiece that . . . slipped from side to side as Shapiro's behavior became animated," had come to see Elvis about financing the construction of an artificial heart he was hoping to develop. He was accompanied by his fiancée, and after Elvis heard them discuss their wedding plans and learned they had already gotten a license, citing his own love for Ginger as an incentive, he insisted that they get married on the spot. Larry Geller had just left for L.A., but Elvis flew him back to perform the ceremony, for which Elvis supplied the rings and Ginger served as maid of honor. After the wedding, he spoke to Larry about someday performing a similar ceremony for Ginger and him, and then he had Dr. Shapiro go back to work on his and Ginger's teeth. There was no end to the ways in which he sought to please her, but after they returned from California, he found himself no less frustrated by her continued need to distance herself from him, to go home each night to her mother and sisters (and some said to her boyfriend), sometimes sneaking out of the house only after he had finally fallen asleep.

I N NASHVILLE HE APPEARED able to focus on nothing but his recent quarrel with Ginger, and Felton was scarcely surprised when Joe called the day after their arrival and told him they were heading back to Memphis without ever having left the hotel. There was some talk of Elvis coming back at the beginning of the following week if his health were to improve, but Felton knew it was not going to happen and simply had the musicians overdub two songs from the last Graceland session while making sure that everyone would get paid in full for a lost week of work. Longtime loyalists for the first time began to voice their doubts that Elvis would ever return to the recording studio, and Felton seemed to slump visibly under the weight of his own defeated expectations.

David Briggs may have been the only one not to feel disappointed at the cancellation of the session. In fact, he had reason to experience a secret sense of relief. He had been surprised initially at his invitation, now that he and Linda were practically living together, and Linda hadn't wanted him to come, knowing firsthand both Elvis' volatility and his carelessness with firearms. David couldn't bring himself to turn Elvis down, though; in a peculiar way he considered himself loyal in every respect except one, and he thought Elvis might be able to understand that. Nor was he going to give in to fear, his own or anyone else's. So he had come to the session with no idea of what, or how much, Elvis knew — but he couldn't say that he was altogether unhappy to postpone finding out.

Just how widespread was the general sense of malaise can be gathered from a story published in the *Nashville Banner* the following week, which revealed with surprising accuracy, and in embarrassing detail, not only intimate aspects of Elvis' emotional state but the deep fissures that existed within the Presley camp.

"They say Presley is paranoid and that he's afraid to record," wrote Bill Hance in his column, "Wax Fax."

> Presley, claiming he was sick with a cold, left here Saturday night, promising to return Monday to fulfill his recording contract with RCA, and to live up to his own slogan, "Taking Care of Business." When he failed to show in the studio, RCA officials and his personal manager, Colonel Tom Parker, reportedly "got hot." Parker, the tough business-man who has guided Presley's career for nearly twenty years, was quoted as telling Presley, "Get off your tail in that studio, fulfill your contract or there will be no more tours." Many Presley aides contend the singer's new girlfriend, Ginger Alden, 20, is "absolutely running him ragged." "One time," a friend said, "Ginger decided to leave Elvis . . . and the only way he could get her back inside the house was to fire a gun up in the air." [Hance then spoke with hotel workers who de-clared]: "They're driving us all nuts. . . . All this security mumbo-jumbo. They run in doors, out of doors, up and down hallways and elevators trying to hide from people. Who are they hiding from? . . . No fans have come out here. Only you newsmen."

Four days after his return home, on January 26, he formally proposed to Ginger. It was not just his love for her, it was the conjunction of the stars, he explained; the twenty-sixth was an important date since two plus six added up to eight, and eight was his number. He had already called his jew-eler, Lowell Hays, in the early hours of the morning and told him that he wanted a stone as big as his TCB diamond for Ginger's engagement ring, and because of the date he had to have it that night. When Hays informed him there was no way to locate another diamond like that in Memphis on such short notice, Elvis offered to fly the jeweler to New York, but Lowell convinced him that even in New York it would be impossible to find that kind of stone and get it mounted within the required time period. Finally, Hays came up with the idea of taking the eleven-and-one-half-carat center diamond from the TCB ring itself and putting it in Ginger's ring, replacing Elvis' diamond as soon as he was able to come up with a suitable substitute. It took all day to make the ring, but he had it back just in time for Elvis to propose to Ginger that night, kneeling down on one knee as she sat in the special reading chair in his bathroom. Then Ginger called her mother, and together they accepted congratulations from Charlie, Vernon, and the Stanley boys.

Five nights later they flew to Las Vegas with Billy and Jo Smith, then continued on to L.A. to celebrate Lisa's ninth birthday and twenty-four hours later were home again. Sometimes Ginger wondered just what she had gotten herself into. No one had told her anything about what to expect, she had had no preparation for any of this, and Elvis just seemed to need her so desperately all of the time. Part of her came to feel that "maybe that's why I was put on earth. If I could make Elvis happy, I would have served my purpose." Another part questioned why it always had to be her: Didn't he have anyone else that he could call on once in a while? He had all these friends around — what was wrong with them? She tried to tell him that, but he just blew up at her. She didn't understand, he said. The only reason the others were around was because of the money.

E LVIS REFUSED TO GO out on the next tour unless Ginger agreed to go with him. It was just a short ten-day hop, February 12 to February 21, kicking off in Florida and remaining in the southeast territory that he had crisscrossed again and again when he and Colonel were just starting out. Orlando, Florida; Montgomery, Alabama; Savannah, Georgia — little seemed to have changed save for the mode of transportation, the size of the operation, and the remuneration that he took from the show. His life, it must have occurred to him, had turned into an endless string of one-nighters, from which it was beginning to seem increasingly unlikely he would ever be able to escape.

It did make a difference having Ginger with him, though. For one thing, it meant she couldn't go running home at night, and often after the show they read from his books until the soothing effect of the words and the delayed impact of the pills allowed him to go to sleep. To Kathy Westmoreland he spoke convincingly of his happiness, and Kathy had no doubt that it was real, although she could discern clouds on the horizon in the person of Ginger's mother and sisters. "He would say, 'She loves her family. Well, I'll bring the whole damn family.'"

That was what he did when he played Johnson City, Tennessee, once again on February 19, on the third-to-last night of the tour. The following night, in Charlotte, North Carolina, he called Terry Alden up onstage and had her perform her talent piece from the beauty contests, a short Russian toccata on the piano. "I'll get you for this," Terry mouthed at Elvis to his amusement, and his performance for the most part seemed to reflect his good mood. That didn't stop him from showing his frustration later in the evening, however, when he was unable to reach the high notes of his latest release, "Moody Blue," and he tore up the lyric sheet in a combination of bravado and helpless rage.

Somewhat to the consternation of his fellow musicians, David Briggs was still with the band. He had suggested Bobby Ogdin to Felton as a replacement, but Elvis let it be known that he didn't want any damned substitutes, and David decided maybe he should just go on taking Elvis' wishes at face value. Elvis continued to point proudly to David's playing, and he continued to look to David almost every night when he undertook to perform Roy Hamilton's "Unchained Melody" alone at the piano, just as he had with his earlier Hamilton-inspired version of "You'll Never Walk Alone." Like the Rodgers and Hammerstein number, "Unchained Melody" was the kind of highly dramatic, vocally challenging, almost operatic showpiece that served to inflame not just the audience but Elvis himself, no matter how tired or lethargic the rest of the program might be. To Briggs' amusement, he became part of Elvis' solo outing, "because there was one point in the bridge he could never get, and whenever he reached that point, he would say, 'Take it, David,' and I would play my note. It became a kind of comedy part of the act."

Less comedic was the moment when he realized that Elvis had become aware of Linda's and his relationship. "He had just come out onstage, and the audience was all going wild, and he turned around right in front of me and looked at me — and then he started pulling out every cord from every plug on my keyboard. Then he walked back in front of the stage to start the show. He never actually said anything, and I could never be sure exactly what he meant, but that was when I decided it was time to leave Dodge."

I F ELVIS HAD EXPECTED THINGS to change once the tour was over, he was sadly disappointed. Ginger continued to have her own friends, she had her family, and no matter how he raged or lamented to Billy and Jo Smith about her lack of interest, he couldn't seem to keep her by his side. As a special treat he decided to show her Hawaii, and he planned a two-week vacation at the beginning of March, which started out as a getaway for the two of them but soon grew into a party of thirty, with Ginger's two sisters among the first to be included. For much of the time before the trip he stayed in his room, talking mostly with Charlie and Billy and Dr. Nick. He talked quite a bit with Maggie Smith, too, the college student he had hired as a maid after buying a Pontiac right out from under her during one of his 1974 car-buying sprees. She was pregnant now, something she had confessed to Elvis only with the greatest reluctance because she knew how protective of her he was and how important he felt it was for her to complete her education. "He asked me, was I in love? I told him no. I said, 'Really, it was a big mistake.' So he said, 'Well, do you think you'll be happy like this?' And I said, 'Well, I don't know.' And it got to the point where everything was so quiet and sad up there that we were both crying. He was very patient with me afterwards, talking to me concerning the Bible — he loved to read me things and explain the way he felt they were. He believed in reincarnation. He gave me a copy of *The Prophet* and would pick things out and ask what did I think about that." Other black people assumed that he was prejudiced, Maggie knew, but "they didn't know. He really treated me more like a father than an employer."

They were scheduled to fly out on the evening of March 3, but first, Elvis decided, he needed to set his affairs in order. Dr. Nick, who would be accompanying the group to Hawaii, had gotten even deeper into debt on his new house, so Elvis signed over another $55,000, on top of the $200,000 he had already loaned him, though this time at Vernon's insistence it was at 7 percent interest and with a specified twenty-five-year payback. He had long since gotten over any feelings of ill will about the racquetball courts business, and besides, if he wanted to be practical about it, Dr. Nick was at this point his only regular physician. He made out his will, too — his father had been trying to get him to do it for years, and with Vernon and his Memphis attorney, Beecher Smith, present, and Ginger, Charlie, and Smith's wife, Ann, for witnesses, he affixed his signature in the early hours of the morning. It was a simple document that reposed total faith in Vernon as executor and trustee. "The health, education, comfortable maintenance and welfare" of Lisa Marie, Vernon, and Grandma were all specifically mandated in the will, and Vernon was authorized to expend funds for "such other relatives of mine living at the time of my death who in the absolute discretion of my Trustee are in need of emergency assistance for any of the above mentioned purposes," so long as the ability of the trust to meet the needs of the named beneficiaries was not affected. Upon Vernon's death all such additional assistance would cease, and upon his grandmother's, all funds would reside in a trust for his daughter and any other lawful issue he might have until she, or they, reached the age of twenty-five.

There were no other individual bequests and no specific mention made of any other person, despite what he knew to be the long-held belief of many of his relatives, and many of the guys as well, that they would be financially taken care of. The will, of course, did not address the reasons for these exclusions, but for all the generosity he had shown to the broadest circle of family and friends over the years, in the end it seems scarcely surprising that he should have returned to the same small, tight-knit, and set-apart group that had first nurtured him, when he and his mother and father occupied a lonely strip of safety in a hostile world.

With his business completed, he could take off for Hawaii, arriving on the morning of March 4. The whole party spent two days at the Hilton Rainbow Tower, then Elvis and the Alden sisters and a couple of the guys moved into a beach house at Kailua on the east side of the island, while the rest of the group continued to stay at the hotel. "Everyone looks older than they are," Larry Geller noted mordantly in his diary, but they followed the same protocol that they always had, as Ed Parker arranged for a visit to the Polynesian Cultural Center, Elvis made plans to show Ginger the U.S.S. *Arizona* memorial which were only canceled at the last moment, and they all played touch football on the beach. Everyone remarked on how relaxed Elvis seemed; at times he appeared to enjoy Rosemary Alden's company almost as much as her sister's, and Ginger even got him to play Ping-Pong with her, despite his protestations that he felt foolish swinging at a little ball that he could never keep on the table.

It was, Larry wrote, almost like old times, with everyone "relaxing and joking with one another, and by the expressions on everyone's face [looking] as though we died and went to heaven." But Larry was just as aware of the shortcomings of heaven as anyone else, with touch football games turning into worrisome displays of the sad physical state into which Elvis had fallen and other players casting about for excuses to get him to quit. "Somebody'd throw him the ball," said Kalani Simerson, a one-time entertainer who now operated a limousine service and had known Elvis since the early sixties, "and he'd catch it and start running, and he couldn't stop. He just wasn't able to control his own body. One time he ran right into a Cyclone fence."

He was no better directed even in less physically strenuous pursuits. As soon as they arrived, Charlie and Larry Geller contacted Bernard Benson, an eccentric British millionaire they had met in Las Vegas in December, who had urged them to come see him the next time they were in Hawaii. They returned from Benson's home enormously exhilarated. Elvis had to meet the Tibetan holy man that Benson had staying with him, they told Elvis, certain that this would be the thing to get him out of his fugue state. But Elvis declined with a strangely world-weary passivity. He didn't need to meet any spiritual masters right now, he said — he felt like he was on the right path.

Ten days into their stay he got sand in his eye, and the whole group packed up and went home because Dr. Nick was concerned that Elvis' cornea might be scratched and thought it would be best to recuperate at Graceland. No one expressed any great feelings of regret. For Joe it had been a painful exercise in nostalgia, and Larry saw little improvement in either Elvis' outlook or health. It was hard to gauge exactly how Elvis felt about it. With characteristic generosity he picked out a gift for each member of the party to serve as a remembrance of the good times that they had had and promised Ginger that next time they would have the experience for themselves. The whole trip had cost him something in the neighborhood of $100,000, he confided to Larry, but what profiteth it to gain the world if you couldn't share your good fortune with your friends?

L ITTLE MORE THAN ONE WEEK LATER Billy Smith was in real doubt that Elvis would make it to the plane scheduled to leave for Phoenix for the start of the second tour of the year. Billy had agreed to go out on the road again, after years of steadfast refusal, only because of his concern about his cousin's health. "We were supposed to leave late that night. Tish [Dr. Nick's nurse] said, 'If he was my son, I'd have him in the hospital.' Vernon said, 'Well, do what you can. . . .' So Dr. Nick put all these IVs in him . . . [and] all the way to the airport Elvis sat slumped with his hat over his eyes. He didn't say anything. Then when he got on the plane, he was just groggy, slurring his words. . . . [The following night], right before he stepped out on the stage, he said, 'You didn't think I'd make it, did you?' [But] he put on a hell of a show!"

Probably the principal reason for the mood he was in was that Ginger had balked at the very last minute about going out with him, and without her it was obvious he was not himself. The first few shows were received well nonetheless, and critics were reduced to scratching their heads in the manner of the Tempe, Arizona, reviewer who declared, "His music ran from the parody to the almost perfect. . . . but the faithful were happy. They came, they saw, and Elvis conquered." He wore the only two suits he could still fit into, and in Norman, Oklahoma, he might have choked to death if Larry and David Stanley hadn't realized that he had fallen asleep in the middle of a meal. "Is there much more time left?" Larry wrote in his diary, after putting Elvis to bed without his even being aware of what had happened. Meanwhile, his security chiefs, Sam Thompson and Dick Grob, drew up contingency plans to smuggle Elvis' body back to Graceland should it become necessary to try to cover up a drug overdose death on the road.

Often late at night Elvis would seek out Billy Smith just to talk about what was on his mind. One night Dick Grob discovered him wandering around in the hallway and led him to Billy and Jo's room. "Man," he told his cousin, "something unbelievable just happened. I dreamed I saw the face of God."

It had manifested itself in the form of "a white light so bright" he almost couldn't look at it, and he was obviously still shaken by the experience. The next thing Billy knew, he had climbed into bed with them, and "he talked for an hour and a half, and then in the next minute he was sound asleep. I looked at Jo, and she looked at me, and I said, 'I guess I'd better take him back down to the room.'"

In Alexandria, Louisiana, he put on virtually identical shows on successive nights that pretty much reflected the mood of the tour. "[He] was onstage less than an hour," the *Alexandria Daily Town Talk* reported, "he was impossible to understand . . . he never said one word to the audience or mentioned how nice or not nice it was to be in Alexandria or said. . . . 'Hope you enjoy the show.' He [simply] came onstage, did a few numbers, and then dashed off." Just as on other dates, he forgot lyrics, complained about the sound, arbitrarily stopped and started songs, and sometimes looked and sounded weary almost past the point of enduring. On the second night he changed the lyrics of "Can't Help Falling in Love," his perennial closer, to a cryptic declaration: "Wise men know/When it's time to go. . . ."

The following night, in Baton Rouge, he was unable to go on. The band was onstage, the governor and numerous members of the legislature, as well as the Baton Rouge chief of police and various other local dignitaries, were all in attendance, when Tom Hulett got a call that he'd better come back to the hotel right away, there was something wrong. He encountered a crowd of worried onlookers when he walked into the bedroom. "Their faces were all white, and they didn't know what to do — I mean, this had never happened before." Hulett, who had been through it all with acts like Jimi Hendrix, didn't hesitate for a minute. "I said, 'Fuck it, I'll cancel, we'll play it the next time around.' God, Elvis looked at me like — I mean, he got well. He said, 'What about the Colonel?' I said, 'I'll tell him you're sick.' And then I started putting out fires."

The first thing, Hulett emphasized, was to get Elvis out of town and into the hospital right away; they couldn't have everyone thinking this was "just a bunch of drug addicts fucking around in the hotel" — and they didn't want a lot of Baton Rouge doctors talking to the press. Dr. Nick made the call to Baptist Memorial Hospital administrator Maurice Elliott, even though he doubted there was anything seriously wrong with his patient, at least not in a physical sense. To Nick and Joe Esposito and the rest of the guys, Elvis was still just trying to prove something to Ginger. But it all came down to the same thing in the end: he was clearly not capable of continuing.

Back at the auditorium "howls of protest and shouts of 'rip-off'" filled the air when the announcement was made, but gradually, with the help of the police, the room emptied out, and most of the fans were assuaged with promises of a makeup show. Hulett called the Colonel in Mobile, Alabama, where he was busy advancing the next date. He accepted the news with grim resignation, asking only, "How bad is he?" He then set about canceling the rest of the tour. Everyone else just concentrated on shutting down the show and trying to get Elvis to leave town, which proved easier said than done now that the decision had been made. It was well past midnight when they finally left, and then Elvis insisted on going to Graceland upon their Memphis arrival, finally checking into the hospital around 6:45 in the morning.

Nursing supervisor Marion Cocke, Elvis' longtime friend, who had received a call from Graceland that he would be arriving soon, showed up just after his admission to find him completely worn out. She remained with him until almost noon, conversing quietly until at last "he said, 'Well, I'm really bushed, and I think I'm going to go on to sleep.' He said, 'Will you stay here for the night after you get off?,' and I said, yes, I had come prepared to stay, and I would be in my room [the one she always stayed in, next to his] right outside the door. And gee, I checked on him while I was making rounds, and when I got off I went to bed, and he slept the clock around, more than around, because he didn't wake up until around six o'clock P.M. the next day."

The Colonel meanwhile was doing damage control, calling up building managers to apologize and explain, then rebooking the four canceled shows for the tour after next, which was scheduled to begin at the end of May.

Business would go on as usual, he hastened to assure RCA's Mel Ilberman, who was bound to be concerned not just in his capacity as record company executive but in his role as head of RCA Record Tours, still co-promoter of the show. They were fortunate that he had been able to reschedule all of the dates, he wrote Ilberman on April 4. Not only that, but due to his own resourceful management and careful bookkeeping, he had even been able to salvage a small profit from the tour. This was their first cancellation in almost seven years of road dates, he reminded his longtime associate in a tone that was never anything less than self-assured, but the Colonel gave himself a new sobriquet at the end, signing the letter "The Poor Magician."

Elvis stayed in the hospital only four days, as Nick saw little purpose in trying to impose a longer sentence. Elvis had Ginger bring in her engagement ring to show Mrs. Cocke, and Priscilla flew in from California with Lisa Marie, taking time to confer with Vernon on a new payout schedule for the divorce. Billy picked up Elvis in his beat-up little Corvair at four in the morning on April 5, and Elvis complained good-naturedly all the way home about the fact that Billy hadn't bothered to bring the Lincoln.

There were just two weeks before they were scheduled to go out again, and for a while Elvis did little but ride around on his golf carts and three-wheelers, sometimes driving out onto the highway late at night, a strange wind-blown figure in housecoat, pajamas, and slippers.

He had another fight with Ginger, and this time he said he was breaking up with her for good. George introduced him to Alicia Kerwin, a twenty-year-old bank teller, whom Jo Smith screened before she was admitted to his bedroom upstairs. Almost instantly he opened up his heart to her, describing his dissatisfaction with Ginger and her family, who, he said, were just after his money. For all of his eccentricities, he impressed her as sincere and vulnerable and very much a gentleman, and when he asked her to accompany him to Las Vegas a few days later with the Smiths, she felt no hesitation about accepting. He seemed different on this trip than he had before; his attention was unfocused, his speech slurred, his behavior sluggish, and she was as surprised by his lack of physical attention to her as she was by all the medications on his bedside table and the constant attendance of Dr. Elias Ghanem in his hotel suite. Unbeknownst to Alicia, the physician's presence was scarcely accidental. According to Billy Smith, the real reason for the trip was "to get more prescriptions from Ghanem." Elvis had had another blowup with Dr. Nick, and he was evidently as determined to assert his independence in this area as in the romantic sector of his life.

From Vegas they continued on to Palm Springs, where Elvis bought Alicia a new car and had another bad breathing episode in the middle of the night. Alicia became so alarmed that she woke up Billy and Jo, and after contacting a Palm Springs physician, Billy called up Dr. Ghanem, too, to try to discover what could have caused this strange combination of respiratory distress and complete disorientation. After hearing Billy's description, Ghanem reassured him that Elvis had probably just taken too many Placidyls, but he flew to Palm Springs right away to make sure his patient was all right.

The following day Elvis got a phone call from Vernon that left him chastened and upset. As soon as he got off the phone, he called Colonel and after a brief conversation with him seemed even more upset. Alicia asked what was the matter, and Elvis explained that they were both angry at him because he hadn't told them where he was going and they had been looking for him for the last two days. He shook his head as if his life were not his own. Then his mood shifted; it was time to go home anyway, he said — he had a tour coming up. He would make arrangements to have her car shipped back to Memphis, he assured her, and she was left to look back on a five-day "whirlwind courtship" as puzzling for its lack of physical consummation as for any of the peculiar events that had actually occurred. Alicia returned to work, and Elvis promised he would call when he got back to town, though at this point she wasn't really sure how she felt about continuing the relationship.

Ginger went out with him on the tour, which started in Greensboro, North Carolina, on April 21. He was determined to keep her with him for the entire two-week duration this time, so when she said she was getting homesick, he made arrangements to fly her mother and sister Rosemary into Duluth on April 29. The reviews of his performance ranged from concern for his health to perplexity over how little he seemed to care, with one columnist in Detroit simply declaring that "he stunk the joint out." Some of the fans, too, were becoming increasingly voluble about their disappointment, but it all seemed to go right past Elvis, whose world was now confined almost entirely to his room and his books. He recruited Larry to help Ginger with her spiritual education and asked him to explain to her the special nature of his purpose on earth. Ginger meanwhile was occupied with more mundane matters, like redecorating the bathroom at Graceland in turquoise and white. To Larry he confessed some of his deeper concerns. He was worried about his health. He was worried about his appearance.

He was worried about his hair, which was thinning on top. He spoke more and more about the book that Red and Sonny had written. How would it affect Lisa? What would his father and grandmother think?

They were in Duluth when the news broke that Colonel was planning to sell his contract. A headline story in the *Nashville Banner* cited authoritative sources "in Nashville, Memphis and Los Angeles" as confirming "Parker's decision to sell 'the boy,'" citing health and financial problems as the primary reason." The Colonel had lost an enormous amount of money "at the Las Vegas Hilton Hotel gambling tables," the story went on. "'The Colonel isn't necessarily broke,' a source said. 'He just needs some money, like about a cool million he lost in December alone.'" The way in which he had dealt with similar losses in the past, the same anonymous source asserted (though there was in fact no evidence to support this charge), was to "trade out" Elvis' services in exchange for his debts. Now that Elvis was no longer appearing at the Hilton (again, an erroneous conclusion, since Elvis was scheduled to open the new Hilton Pavilion, as soon as construction of this seven-thousand-seat convention hall was completed in October), the Colonel was reduced to selling his contract. "Parker and Presley have reportedly 'not spoken' in two years," the story concluded with more truth than factual accuracy, "although Parker oversees all of 'the king's' concert engagements."

From St. Paul, where he was advancing the show, the Colonel's reaction was instantaneous. The *Banner*'s story was "a complete fabrication," the Colonel declared to the rival *Nashville Tennessean*. "I'm here, I'm working with Elvis, I'm in good health, and I don't have any debts — at least none that I can't pay." Joe weighed in from Duluth in support of Colonel, labeling the story "a bunch of lies. . . . How do you sell a handshake to begin with? That's just stupid. Elvis and the Colonel have a written agreement, and they have no plans to break it." He went on to describe a cordial relationship between the two longtime associates and pointed out some other factual inaccuracies, but it was apparent to anyone who knew anything about the recent history of their tangled relationship that the story was, in essence, true. Too many people had heard Colonel complaining that Elvis was more trouble than he was worth, that he was intractable and could no longer be effectively managed. And too many people were aware, as Elvis' Los Angeles lawyer Ed Hookstratten was inclined to put it, that Colonel was "servicing a problem of his own." Elvis had no doubt about the story in any case: he knew in his bones it was true. And while the consortium of "West Coast businessmen" who were supposed to be buying his contract never surfaced, driven off presumably by the glare of publicity, Elvis had never felt more betrayed or more alone.

Three days later, while they were in Chicago, Mike McMahon filed suit against him in Memphis circuit court for reneging on his contractual obligations to Presley Center Courts, giving him one more lawsuit to worry about and one additional piece of fodder for the tabloids to ridicule him with. The previous month alone *The Star,* in what seemed like a thinly veiled taste of things to come, had run a front-page story by Steve Dunleavy, Red and Sonny's collaborator, that was headlined: "Elvis, 42, Fears He's Losing His Sex Appeal," complete with a touched-up, haunted, and bizarre-looking photograph that certainly made the fear look justified. The story itself covered everything from the abortive Nashville session to Elvis' problems with Ginger to diet, depression, and the kind of sexual infantilism "not rare at all in people that age," a behavioral psychologist pointed out, that drove Elvis "to strive to maintain his relationship with younger girls." Then on April 26, the *National Enquirer* repeated many of the same accusations under the headline, "Elvis' Bizarre Behavior and Secret Face Lift," with a picture even more grotesque than the *Star's.* Here Mike McMahon was given a forum to deride his erstwhile partner, and Priscilla was quoted as saying that "the presence of Elvis' mother is still very much felt," to bolster the *Enquirer's* case that Elvis believed Graceland to be haunted. "So very sad," the article concluded, quoting a "friend."

On May 6, three days after the conclusion of the tour, he shot out a bedroom window and had to be sedated. To Jo Smith his behavior was becoming more and more that of someone incapable of making his own decisions, but at the same time she felt a wave of protectiveness for him, a kind of closeness she had never felt in all the years that she had regarded Elvis' hold over Billy as a threat to her marriage. "We had to take care of him and cater to him like a small child. I did things I never thought I'd do. Like when it came time for him to go to sleep, he liked to be put to bed, and he liked to be told good night — the whole send-off. . . . I had to talk baby talk to him, too.

> One time I'd started into the kitchen, and Elvis called to me and said, "Come in here and sit with us.' . . . So I went to his room, and he was in bed with a girl, sitting up. We talked for a while, and I got ready to go. He said to me, "Tell her all about the lamps." So I started telling her about these lamps that he had bought to go in my trailer. And he was almost asleep. He nodded off. So I started to get up, and he revived and

said, "And tell her about the —" and named something else. Before I got out of there, he said, "Tell her that I have to get this medication because I'm getting ready for a tour." He said, "I've got to get my rest." He had this scratch on his hand, and he held it up and said, "This has to heal, and I need all my bodily fluids for it to get better." I said, "That's exactly right." Because I thought I could leave. But every time he'd almost go to sleep, and I'd get up and start to go out, he'd grab me and say, "Wait, tell her about the —" So I told about, and told about, and told about. Finally, he fell asleep.

T HE NEXT TOUR STARTED in Knoxville on May 20, sixteen days after the conclusion of the last. There was no longer any pretense of keeping up appearances. The idea was simply to get Elvis out onstage and keep him upright for the hour he was scheduled to perform. "He was pale, swollen — he had no stamina," observed a Knoxville physician, who was shocked by his backstage glimpse of a man who appeared barely able to function. In Louisville, according to Larry Geller's account, Dr. Nick was forced to revive him once again, and in Landover, Maryland, Elvis left the stage for "nature's call," tossed two microphones to the floor, and according to the *Washington Star* reviewer, "just refused to turn it on," prompting the question for the reviewer as to whether or not he still could. Ginger left the tour in Binghamton, New York, after Elvis laid down an ultimatum that she would have to choose between him and her family once and for all. Elvis could barely contain himself, ranting and raving at the top of his lungs so that everyone else on the hotel floor could hear him from their rooms. Finally he got Larry to call Kathy because he couldn't bear to be alone. She had just gotten in from a date but agreed without hesitation to spend the night with him. He talked to her about Ginger — he was no longer sure they belonged together, he told her, there were just too many differences between them. She "listened and held his hand . . . until he finally fell sleep."

Over the next few nights he brought up things they had talked about often in the past, but now they took on a different tinge. He spoke to her about his mother, he talked about his pain, he spoke of his place in history. "How will they remember me?" he asked over and over again. "They're not going to remember me. I've never done anything lasting. I've never done a classic film." But then his mood would change. His mission in life, he said, was "to make people happy with music. And I'll never stop until the day I die."

In Baltimore, on May 29, he had to leave the stage again in the middle of the show, calling on Kathy and Sherrill Nielsen to carry on in the face of the crowd's growing restlessness until he came back thirty minutes later. He was "weak," "tired," "paunchy," and "pained," according to the *Variety* reporter who was present, and a building spokesman was left to attribute his "murmuring, swearing, and unscheduled hiatus to the reported intestinal problem that had kayoed Presley from an earlier . . . tour." When he returned to the stage, he "came on like gangbusters," according to the same report, "repeatedly thank[ing] the audience for hanging with him" and explaining that he had twisted his ankle and was forced to answer a call of nature — "and you don't fool around with nature." Later he declared, "There's nothing wrong with my health," but "at the finale there was no ovation, and patrons exited shaking their heads and speculating on what was wrong with him."

Somehow they got through the rest of the tour. They were in Macon on June 1 when the CBS concert special that the Colonel had put together was announced. It was scheduled to be shot at the beginning of the next tour less than three weeks away and called for a $750,000 fee, to be split 50–50 between Elvis and the Colonel after $10,000 had been assigned to All Star Shows for promotional expenses, with ownership to be shared by the two principals after a single repeat showing. This was the first time the Colonel had actually applied the full-partnership agreement that Elvis had signed more than a year before, but he had kept careful records, and with this tour for the first time he stipulated that the two-thirds–one-third division that continued to be observed represented a *temporary settlement only* and that all accounts would be settled up, and all monies owed him under the terms of that January 1976 agreement would be repaid in full by the end of the year.

The very fact that Colonel Parker could even contemplate a television special at this point took everyone by surprise. Even William Morris lawyer Roger Davis, who was in charge of contract negotiations, was taken aback, but Colonel simply shrugged and offered three variations of the same explanation to anyone raising so much as an eyebrow. Elvis needed a challenge and would not fail to rise to this one, he insisted on the one hand; it was Elvis, not he, who wanted the show, he might say on another occasion; more convincingly, he conceded that he had asked for so much money he never thought the network would go for it, and when they did, what choice did he have but to bring the deal to his client? His voice never lowered, his gaze never wavered, but for the first time that anyone could remember, he seemed to lack the conviction that would indicate he was either persuaded or amused by his own carny spiel. And the difference between tying a tele-vision shoot to shows in Omaha, Nebraska, and Rapid City, South Dakota, and setting up a global event like *Aloha from Hawaii* was lost on no one, least of all the Colonel. But no one said anything, and Colonel, as always, pur-sued his own agenda without reference to outsiders' opinions — he was, no less than Elvis, utterly, and irremediably, alone.

By the time they got back to Memphis, Red and Sonny's book, now titled *Elvis: What Happened?*, had started to appear in serialized form in England and Australia, and Elvis fans around the world were exchanging shocked telephone calls. "The first two chapters are about him giving drugs to a girl and how he put a 'contract' on Mike Stone," wrote Donna Lewis in her diary after a friend read her excerpts on the phone. *"What horrible lies!"* Elvis was almost as anguished, and yet he could still lapse from time to time into a state of denial that allowed him to believe the book itself might never come out. That may have been one of the reasons he refused to respond to feel-ers from Frank Sinatra's camp about doing something serious to stop publi-cation, but Larry thought it had more to do with guilt: part of him seemed to accept exposure as the punishment he deserved. On the other hand, some-times he said to the guys that he felt like Jesus betrayed by his disciples.

On June 4 he rewarded Larry and Kathy with their own Lincoln Mark Vs, burgundy and white. He was just showing them some of the features of their new cars when Charlie, who had been drinking heavily once again, started mouthing off about how the wrong people had been rewarded and he was going to get a Rolls-Royce of his own. Elvis stopped in mid speech, and then, as Larry and everyone else watched, "turned away as if he were going to ignore [the remark and] swung around and caught [Charlie] on the bridge of his nose with a backhand. Then, realizing what he'd done, Elvis ran up the steps and into Graceland," while Charlie stood there, "stunned, [with] blood pouring down his face." Afterward, Elvis was clearly morti-fied, but he couldn't bring himself to apologize, sending Larry to make sure Charlie was all right. "He never hit me before," Charlie moaned as he lay on the floor of his room. "Why did he hit me? I love him. I know he loves me." But the most Larry could get out of Elvis was a promise to take it up with Charlie the next day.

He tried to do something for George Klein, who had been indicted by a federal grand jury in February for fixing a radio ratings poll. Recalling the way he had practically just walked into President Nixon's office when no one else thought Nixon would even know who he was, he put in a call to President Jimmy Carter on June 13, sure that Carter, a fellow southerner whom he had met at a 1973 concert in Atlanta while Carter was still governor of Georgia, would intervene. When the President called back twenty-four hours later, he couldn't seem to make him understand what he was driving at, though. They spoke for about ten minutes, with Carter getting the impression that Elvis was "stoned and didn't know what he was saying," other than that he was asking the President to pardon a friend who had not yet been tried. According to Carter biographer Douglas Brinkley, the President attempted "to ease Presley out of his paranoid delusions, calming his fears that he was being 'shadowed' by sinister forces and that his friend was being framed," but when Elvis called back at 8:45 the following morning, Carter didn't take the call.

THEY EMBARKED ON THE FIFTH TOUR of the year just two days later. Ginger insisted on staying home to watch her sister Terry give up her crown as the reigning Miss Tennessee, but she rejoined him in Kansas City on the second night. Even with Ginger present, he seemed utterly exhausted. "In spite of what you may hear or you may read, we're here, and we're healthy, and we're doing what we enjoy doing," he announced to the crowd, but no one observing his pale swollen appearance, the awkward slow-motion manner in which he lurched about the stage, or his overall sense of confusion and self-doubt could have been taken in, no matter how much they might have wanted to believe his protestations. It was equally difficult for anyone on the show to believe they would be filming a television special the following day. More and more the feeling grew that they had set out on a doomed voyage, captainless, rudderless, with no hope of turning back.

The performance in Omaha the next night in front of the CBS cameras exceeded everyone's worst fears. One has only to listen to the complete, undoctored audio recording of the show to understand the panic that seems to have overtaken Elvis. His voice is almost unrecognizable, a small, childlike instrument in which he talks more than sings most of the songs, casts about uncertainly for the melody in others, and is virtually unable to articulate or project. He gives the impression of a man crying out for help when he knows help will not come. And even after more than twenty years it is almost unbearable to listen to or watch, the obliteration not just of beauty but of the memory of beauty, and in its place sheer, stark terror. "It was like he was saying, 'Okay, here I am, I'm dying, fuck it,'" said Tom Hulett, who up to the last minute was still hoping he might pull it off. "I've never seen a backstage area so sad."

Strangely enough, he rallied two nights later in Rapid City, South Dakota, on the second night of filming. "I know I was terrible," he said to producers Gary Smith and Dwight Hemion, as if the first show had been an accident that had happened to someone else. He would do better this time, he assured them. And indeed he did. He looked healthier, seemed to have lost a little weight, and sounded better, too. All that Gary Smith was hoping for at this point was to try to capture some of the excitement of the crowd, some of the belief that the fans still placed in Elvis, and this he was able to do. But he got something else as well, something he had not bargained on and that would ultimately prove too raw for network broadcast.

It came at the end of the show when Elvis sat down at the piano and, with Charlie holding a hand mike, launched into "Unchained Melody," the Roy Hamilton number in which he so often seemed to invest every fiber of his being. Hunched over the piano, his face framed in a helmet of blue-black hair from which sweat sheets down over pale, swollen cheeks, Elvis looks like nothing so much as a creature out of a Hollywood monster film — and yet we are with him all the way as he struggles to achieve grace. It is a moment of what can only be described as grotesque transcendence, and when at the end he signals to Charlie, "I got it," and goes on to complete the song with no help from Charlie or Sherrill Nielsen or any of the other background singers who frequently sustained his notes now in the more difficult passages, the expression on his face, the little-boy sense of relief that he has actually pulled it off, is both entrancing and heartbreaking. And then it is back to the standard finale, the giving out of kisses and scarves and the ritual departure that make up the carefully constructed facade he has built to wall himself off from everything but the approbation of the crowd.

"Dwight and Gary were kind to him," was Joe Guercio's conclusion, "and still there was nothing really there." Just how desperate everyone was to believe otherwise, though, was made evident by a telephone conversation that took place between Myrna and Jerry Schilling right after the show.

JANUARY–JUNE 1977 ∾ 639

"Jerry said, 'How did it go?' And I said, 'It really went great.' He said, 'Well, how did Elvis look?' I said, 'He really looks good. He's lost a little weight.' And afterwards, when I watched it [when the show was broadcast in October], I just burst out crying. We were all wearing blinders."

T HERE WERE FIVE DATES still left to play. Ronnie Tutt left after the Des Moines concert, citing a family crisis, and Larrie Londin was able to come in for the last two nights after Sweet Inspirations drummer Jerome "Stump" Monroe filled in for one show. In Madison, Wisconsin, Elvis was being driven from the airport to the hotel when he spotted two youths ganging up on an attendant at an all-night filling station. Over the protests of Ginger and his father, he leapt out of the limousine and struck a karate pose, offering to take the two bullies on. The fight broke up without any further blows being exchanged as the three participants stood in stunned recognition of who was intervening. "Presley did not leave until tempers were cool," reported one wire service account. "'He was willing to fight,' said Thomas McCarthy, one of several police officers providing Presley with security. 'That's the bad part.' Presley shook hands and posed for several pictures. He seemed amused by the whole episode as he got back into the limousine."

In Cincinnati he gave everyone another surprise when he grew irritated at the inadequacy of the hotel air-conditioning system and, deciding to take matters into his own hands, set out to find another hotel, heading down the street in his DEA jogging suit with his security detail behind. He was an hour late to the show that night because of what he termed "a technical hitch," but his performance was generally accounted to be a good one, and the show in Indianapolis the following night, the Colonel's sixty-eighth birthday, displayed an energy and a vitality that had been missing the entire tour. Perhaps it was because he had given up on hotels, flying home to Graceland after the Cincinnati show and returning with a planeful of friends and relatives. Rhythm guitarist John Wilkinson thought he seemed nervous before he went on, but he did an eighty-minute set, a third again as long as the average performance, and at the end, after strong versions of "Bridge Over Troubled Water" and "Hurt," he brought his father out onstage, introduced various friends and relatives, and with the conclusion of the final number put the mike down and walked back and forth shaking hands, as if he really didn't want to leave.

ELVIS AND VERNON, LAST TOUR. (COURTESY OF THE ESTATE OF ELVIS PRESLEY)

"PRECIOUS LORD, TAKE MY HAND"

THE DAYS PASSED UNEVENTFULLY with little to distinguish one from another. It was a hot Memphis summer, but this scarcely impinged on Elvis, who rarely ventured outside his air-conditioned room. There were to be no July 4 fireworks this year, and in fact the guys told him Ginger went out dancing to celebrate the holiday after saying she was leaving the house to go home. Elvis was still frustrated and angry at her inability to commit herself to the relationship. Didn't she understand he *needed* her? he said plaintively to Dr. Nick or his cousin Billy whenever he was feeling blue. But he grew more tolerant of what he came to see as a young girl's natural urges, and he continued to shower her with gifts — jewelry, clothing, a little Triumph sports car — he even offered to buy her family a house in Whitehaven so she could be closer to him, and when no suitable location could be found, promised to pay off the mortgage on their current home and put up the money for a swimming pool. There was no question that Mrs. Alden and the girls were all grateful — they seemed to look upon him as some kind of big brother who had struck it rich or something — but he wasn't sure it brought him any closer to Ginger, who still adamantly refused to move into Graceland full-time. It seemed, he said to Charlie, like he was living out the words of the old song, this thing with Ginger was beginning to feel more and more like a "one-sided love affair."

He saw scarcely anyone except for Charlie, Billy and Jo Smith, and Dr. Nick. He tried to make Ginger jealous with other girls, but he had neither the energy nor the interest. Once in a while George Klein or some other friend from the old days might stop by, but he generally just watched them on the surveillance cameras and sent down word that he was tied up right now, maybe they could come back later. He wasn't close to any of the new guys. Sam Thompson and Dick Grob did a good, professional job running the security, Al Strada had been around for a while and he was a good little valet — but there was no one he could really talk to, and he had a growing mistrust of his stepbrothers Ricky and David Stanley, who were responsible for much of his personal day-to-day business. He had done his best to educate them, to give them the advantage of his own experience, but Ricky was stoned most of the time, and David he suspected had more in common with Ginger than he did — they were always buzzing around together, and David was frequently covering up for her and taking her side. He didn't really know who to trust, so he just retreated to his room and his books and the medication that he needed to take his mind off the pain that never went away.

"All we did," Billy Smith recalled, "was sit up in his room and talk." Sometimes the talk consisted of calling up memories of some of the crazy things they used to do, sometimes it was little more than running through an old Monty Python routine, but mostly there was a grim obsessiveness that Billy had never experienced before, a paranoia about people, germs, past motivations, future events, that put Billy in mind on more than one occasion of Howard Hughes. Red and Sonny's book was the one subject Elvis always came back to. Sometimes he talked to Billy about having them killed. "One time I said, 'Look, they're not worth it. And anyway, you know it wouldn't change anything. It wouldn't even change how you feel about them. You know that deep down you really care about them, and that's what really gets you.' And he broke down and cried. It wasn't just a few tears. He was sobbing. And I cried with him because I couldn't stand to see him in that kind of pain. . . . But then he said, 'Goddamn them! . . . If they hurt my career, I *will* have them killed.'"

Nighttime was the worst; he dreaded sleep, even as he dreaded that sleep would never come. Over and over he dreamt the same dream, a variation, in one form or another, of the nightmare that had haunted him ever since success first arrived unbidden at his door. The core of the dream never changed: all his money was gone, the fans had abandoned him, the Colonel was gone, he was alone. What would the fans think when they read the book? he pressed Billy again and again. He started constructing elaborate defenses in case someone should yell something at him while he was onstage. "At first he thought he'd just say that a lot of things had been written about him, good and bad, and that he was not a perfect person." Then he decided maybe he should concede that it was true, he took certain medications, but that he needed them, and to prove it he would introduce Dr. Nick onstage. Finally, he settled on a strategy of limited confession, which would conclude with the statement that "After this tour I'm going to take time to get myself straightened out." But only, he made clear to Billy, if the issue came up in a manner that he just couldn't sidestep — "if the audience . . . started booing and throwing things."

Lisa arrived for a two-week visit on July 31. She was going to stay until just before he went out on tour again on August 16. Elvis told everyone he was looking forward to the tour; he said to Dr. Nick he thought it was going to be the best one yet, but at the same time he did nothing to get ready for it — he rarely exercised, he never put together any of the new material he continued to talk about introducing into the act, and he kept putting off the diet that he claimed he was going to start in on any day, if only to silence some of those damn critics who couldn't talk about anything but his weight. He alternated between bouts of depression and moments of defiance: What was a forty-two-year-old man supposed to look like anyway? He'd like to see some of those critics do as well at his age. But he never stopped looking in the mirror.

Ginger got her brother Mike's oldest child, Amber, who was a year older than Lisa, to come visit for much of Lisa's stay. She would take them shopping sometimes, and the two little girls seemed to play well together. Some mornings Lisa would wake up early and take her little golf cart with her name on the side and run it up and down the driveway. A lot of the time the girls would play with some of the kids from the trailers, or Ginger would take them for a swim. Elvis bought a pony for Lisa from his cousin Harold Loyd and decided he wanted Grandma to see her on it, so on the spur of the moment one day he just led the pony in the front door, where it promptly made a mess on the carpet.

At Ginger's urging he arranged a special treat for the girls, renting out Libertyland after hours on the evening of August 7 (Libertyland was the former Fairgrounds, now operating as a bicentennial theme park), as he once had night after night in the old days. He got cold feet at the last minute, telling Ginger he just didn't think he could make it, and when she insisted he had to, he had promised the girls, he told her he couldn't do anything about that now: he had already informed the park manager that their plans had changed, and the employees had probably all gone home. "Why, Elvis," she said, drawing herself up to her full height to protest this arbitrary and unfair decision, "I thought you told me you could do anything." And he was forced to have George Klein call the manager and set it up all over again.

They stayed until 6:30 in the morning, and the girls had a wonderful time, along with an accompanying party of twenty. Even Elvis seemed to let himself go for once, riding the Pippin and the Little Dipper and the Dodgems and loading up the trunk of the Stutz with stuffed animals as the sun was coming up.

The first copies of *Elvis: What Happened?* had just started to arrive in the stores, and Elvis continued to feel alternating waves of rage and shame, but he tried to push it all to one side as he got ready for the tour, which was scheduled to start in Portland, Maine, and end in Memphis twelve days later. He spoke to his father with anticipation about going out again after almost two months off, and Vernon, pale and haggard from all the health problems he had endured over the last two years, his creased face set off now by a white wispy mustache, said he thought he just might join him this time, which perked Elvis up quite a bit. He started on the liquid protein diet prescribed by Dr. Nick a few days before they were scheduled to leave, and he began an intermittent exercise program, too, playing racquetball with Billy or riding his stationary bike for a few minutes each day. Billy and Jo thought they could detect a slight pickup in his mood and took some encouragement from it. On August 14, the nineteenth anniversary of his mother's death, he had flowers delivered to her grave, just as he had at least once a week since the day she died. She was never far from his thoughts, but he remained in good enough spirits to go for a motorcycle ride and, when a new jumpsuit that he had ordered didn't fit, he remarked to his cousin, "Billy, I'm just too damned fat."

He awoke at around four o'clock on the afternoon of August 15 and sent for Billy around seven. He thought maybe he'd like to see the new film about General MacArthur starring Gregory Peck — it wasn't supposed to be as good as *Patton,* but then, he didn't know many movies that were — so he gave Ricky the job of trying to set up a screening and was disappointed when the theater couldn't come up with an available print. He and Billy watched TV for a while; then he had Billy call Ginger to get her to come over for his 10:30 P.M. dentist's appointment with Dr. Hofman. He still wasn't sure if Ginger was going to be flying out with him the following night, and he was upset about that — but mostly, Billy thought, he was on edge just like he got before any tour. Which on balance was a good sign. He was even talking about going out to Vail again sometime soon so he could show Ginger the beauty of the country.

Billy helped him on with his black DEA sweat suit, and he pulled on a pair of black patent leather boots which he was unable to zip up because his ankles were so swollen. Dr. Nick stopped by for a few minutes to check on how he was doing, and once Ginger arrived, he stuck a pair of .45s into the waistband of his sweatpants and headed down the back stairs with Ginger and Charlie and his cousin. Joe Esposito, just in from California, was sitting in the kitchen with some of the guys, but Billy told him that Elvis was in a hurry and didn't really need anything right now, he'd catch up with him later.

Dr. Hofman cleaned Elvis' teeth and filled a couple of small cavities, then at Elvis' instigation cleaned Ginger's teeth, too, and gave her mouth a thorough examination. Elvis invited the dentist to come out to the house with his wife one of these days to see his Ferrari, and Dr. Hofman wondered if maybe he could hitch a ride out to California with Elvis on the *Lisa Marie* sometime so he could pay a quick visit to his daughter. They both had daughters out in California, Elvis said smilingly — why didn't they surprise them by flying out for lunch one day at the conclusion of this tour? Elvis was in good spirits when he left; neither of the teeth that Dr. Hofman had worked on was bothering him, he said — but he made sure to get some codeine tablets just in case one of them kicked up.

It was almost 12:30 A.M. by the time they got back to the house, and Elvis went upstairs without seeing anyone. He called down to Joe about some last-minute tour details and conferred with Sam Thompson, too, about taking Lisa back to California on a late-afternoon commercial flight. Then Sam went home to catch a little sleep, and Joe returned to his room at Howard Johnson's, where Larry Geller, too, was staying in anticipation of their departure sometime later that day. Larry had told Elvis he would have some new books for him on the tour, and he was not surprised to be awakened by a call from Al Strada requesting that he bring the books over to the house so Elvis could take a look at them right away. Larry took care to place Frank O. Adams' *A Scientific Search for the Face of Jesus,* an inquiry into the mystery of the Shroud of Turin, at the top of the pile. It was a subject he and Elvis had spoken of often, and he was sure Elvis would get a great deal out of the book.

Elvis and Ginger meanwhile were having much the same argument they had at the start of any tour, with the same results. Elvis wanted her to fly out with him that night, and she said he knew she couldn't because she was having cramps, but she would join him before he even knew it. He was just being silly, she said, he'd probably just get sick of her if she stayed with him the entire time. Gradually he calmed down and they even started talking about marriage once again; he thought Christmas or his birthday might be the right date — maybe he would even announce it at the Memphis concert ending the tour.

Around 2:15 Elvis called Dr. Nick to let him know that one of the teeth Dr. Hofman had filled was bothering him and he needed some Dilaudid, so Nick prescribed six tablets and Elvis had Ricky Stanley pick up the prescription at Baptist Memorial's all-night pharmacy. Elvis called Billy a couple of hours later to see if he and Jo might like to play a little racquetball. Even though they had been asleep, Billy said sure, and he and Jo threw on some clothes and walked over to the house. It had been raining off and on all evening, and it started up again just as the four of them all walked out to the racquetball building under the covered walkway. Billy said he was sick of the rain, he just wished it would stop. "Ain't no problem," Elvis said good-humoredly. "I'll take care of it." And he held up his hands and it did. "See, I told you," he declared with that twinkle that never let you know whether or not he was really serious. "If you've got a little faith, you can stop the rain."

Ginger and Jo barely hit before leaving the court to the guys, but Elvis tired rapidly, and soon the game degenerated into a game of dodge ball, with Elvis trying to hit Billy with every shot. Eventually he hit himself on the shin with his own racquet and quit. "Boy, that hurts," he said, lifting up his pants leg to reveal an ugly welt. "If it ain't bleedin'," said Billy, employing one of his cousin's favorite sayings, "it ain't hurtin'." And he and Jo burst out laughing as Elvis threw his racquet at him.

Afterward Elvis sat at the piano in the lounge area of the racquetball building and fooled around with a few numbers, ending with Willie Nelson's elegiac "Blue Eyes Crying in the Rain." Back at the house Billy helped Elvis wash and dry his hair, while Elvis idly glanced at the book on the Shroud of Turin that Larry had brought him. He talked about maybe taking Alicia Kerwin out on the first part of the tour, but he didn't give Billy any reason to think he was going to do anything about it. He spoke once again, too, of the plot he had hatched to kill Red and Sonny by luring them to Graceland on one pretext or another — but he didn't seem about to do anything about that either. This was going to be the best tour yet, he repeated in what had become almost a mantra by now, and Billy left just before Ricky Stanley arrived with the first of three packets of prescription drugs, or "attacks," that Dr. Nick left for Tish Henley to dispense each night. Each packet consisted of varying amounts of Seconal, Placidyl, Valmid, Tuinal, Demerol, and an assortment of other depressants and placebos which generally allowed Elvis to get several hours of sleep at a time.

Elvis was still awake a couple of hours later when Ricky brought him his second "attack," but when he called down for the third, Ricky had disappeared, even though he was supposed to be on duty till noon. Tish had already gone to work, so Elvis had his aunt Delta call her at Dr. Nick's office, and after conferring with the doctor, Tish gave her husband instructions to bring Delta the third packet, made up of two Valmids and a Placidyl placebo. When she arrived with the medication, Elvis informed his aunt that he was planning to get up at around seven o'clock that evening. Not long afterward, he told Ginger that he was going into the bathroom to read.

Ginger awoke around 1:30 P.M., rolled over, went back to sleep for a few minutes, then called her mother. How was Elvis? her mother asked, and Ginger said she didn't know, he had never come back to bed, maybe she had better go check on him. She washed and put on her makeup in her own bathroom, then knocked on Elvis' bathroom door. When there was no answer, she pushed on it and discovered him lying on the floor, his gold pajama bottoms down around his ankles, his face buried in a pool of vomit on the thick shag carpet. In a daze she called downstairs and asked to speak to someone on duty, and the maid put Al Strada on the line. She thought there was something wrong, she told him. He had better come quick.

Al was bending over Elvis when Joe came bounding up the stairs, and together the two men managed to turn the body over and Joe tried to breathe some life into him. It seemed for a moment as if time were suspended, but then everything started happening all at once, as the bedroom quickly filled with people and Vernon arrived on Patsy Presley's arm, his face a mask of fear as he cried out, "Oh, God, son, please don't go, please don't die." Joe worked desperately on the body, but there was little doubt in his or anyone else's mind that Elvis was gone — his face was swollen and purplish, the tongue was discolored and sticking out of his mouth, the eyeballs blood red. Lisa arrived in the midst of it all. "What's wrong with my daddy?" she demanded, as Ginger closed the bathroom door. "Something's wrong with my daddy, and I'm going to find out," the little girl declared defiantly, and someone quickly locked the other bathroom door as Lisa ran around to try to get in.

People were wailing and screaming when the two firemen EMTs arrived with an ambulance from Engine House No. 29 in Whitehaven, just minutes from Graceland. The ambulance attendants witnessed what they later described as something like a scene of carnage, with up to a dozen people surrounding the almost unrecognizable body and begging them to do something — wasn't there *anything* they could do? A man in gold-rimmed designer sunglasses with a football jersey that said "Hawaii '75," whom they later learned to be Al Strada, said he thought Elvis had overdosed, the same thing they had been told at the gate before they learned who the victim was.

There were no vital signs, and there seemed little doubt of the outcome as they loaded the body onto a stretcher and with help from Al and Joe and Charlie carried it out the front door to the waiting ambulance. Vernon tried in vain to join them but was gently restrained. "I'm coming, son," he called out desperately. "I'll be there."

Dr. Nick showed up in his green Mercedes just as they were coming down the drive. He was in such a frenzy that he drove into the gate, then leapt out of his car and joined Joe and Charlie in the back of the ambulance. "Breathe, Elvis, come on, breathe for me," he kept calling, as he frantically worked on the body the whole seven-minute ride to Baptist Memorial Hospital. He had a look of shock on his face, the ambulance attendants noted, almost as if he found it difficult to believe that Elvis Presley could ever die.

They arrived at the hospital at 2:55 P.M., twenty-two minutes after the initial call. Trauma Room No. 1 had been prepared, and a team of doctors and resuscitation experts was standing by, but there was little to be done, and finally they stopped by mutual consent. It was 3:30 P.M. Joe and Charlie and some of the other guys, who had come over on their own, were all waiting in Trauma Room No. 2 when Dr. Nick walked through the door. "It's all over, he's gone," said the physician, though his look alone would have been enough to tell them, and everyone started to cry. Charlie stumbled toward the door as if he needed to escape, but Joe stopped him. They had to be composed, Joe said through his own tears, before they went out and faced the world.

Joe and Dr. Nick both had immediate business to take care of. Joe asked hospital administrator Maurice Elliott if he could use his office and, with the door closed, called the Colonel in Portland. Colonel's reaction was impossible to read: there was a moment of what Joe could only interpret as stunned silence, then the old man started to enumerate all the things they would have to do, starting with canceling the tour. Joe was scarcely surprised as he ran down the list; in the seventeen years of their association, he had never known Colonel to linger on death. There was no time for nostalgia in the Colonel's world; when old associates died, they were scarcely spoken of again, the Colonel just moved on. After promising to call back as soon as he reached the house, Joe tried Priscilla next. She received the news with much the same mixture of shock and recognition that he might have expected. How was Lisa doing? she asked through her tears, and he tried to reassure her that Lisa would be all right.

Dr. Nick meanwhile had elicited a promise from Maurice Elliott that the death would not be announced until Nick was able to inform Vernon Presley personally. Elliott said he didn't know how long he could hold off the reporters who were already starting to gather at the hospital as word got out that Elvis had been brought in with "severe respiratory distress," but Nick hitched a ride back to Graceland with the ambulance attendants, whom he feared he might need when Vernon heard the news. He was carrying an autopsy consent form for Vernon to sign, something he and Maurice Elliott had determined would keep the state coroner's office from becoming involved and prevent the autopsy results from becoming public without the family's agreement. Joe would stay at the hospital to make the announcement as soon as Nick called to let them know that Vernon had been informed.

Lisa was crying when Dr. Nick walked in, and Vernon froze when he saw the bag full of Elvis' personal effects in the doctor's hand. "Oh, no, no, no," he cried. "He's gone." Nick walked up to Vernon and nodded. "I'm sorry," he said, as the bereft father's wails could be heard throughout the house. "What am I going to do?" Vernon cried, as the two emergency medical technicians stood by. "Everything is gone."

The room, as one of the EMTs, Ulysses S. Jones, Jr., described it, "was filled with hysteria. People were running all over the place crying and screaming and moaning. Vernon was shaking and trembling . . . he couldn't sit still. The doctor took him into the kitchen. . . . Lisa was running all over the house and crying, 'My daddy is gone!' . . . Ginger was walking around in a daze, but she finally calmed Lisa Marie down and gently took her into another room and closed the door." Nick in the meantime called the hospital and told Maurice Elliott they could go ahead and inform the press.

Joe as it turned out wasn't able to carry out the task. When he tried to address the assembled reporters, he got choked up every time he started to speak, and Charlie was no better, so it was left to Maurice Elliott, the hospital administrator who had come to know Elvis over the years, to make the announcement. "There were all sorts of TV cameras and radio microphones, and the room was just packed with people, and all of a sudden I was struck with the thought that, Good gosh, here I am in front of the world, and I am going to have to announce Elvis Presley's death."

There were fans already gathered outside the gates by the time that Joe and Charlie returned to Graceland, courtesy of a lift from the police. At the direction of Elvis' security force, there had already been a complete clean-up in the bedroom, with the bed stripped and remade, the bathroom scoured, and everything put back in place as if no untoward incident had ever occurred. When Shelby County medical investigator Dan Warlick arrived not long afterward, accompanied by police lieutenant Sam McCachern and Assistant District Attorney Jerry Stauffer, the first person he saw inside the house was Vernon Presley, speaking calmly to someone on the phone. Before Warlick could fully register what was happening, Vernon's voice took on a tone of almost unimaginable desolation as he announced to the party on the other end, "My baby is dead. . . . They've taken him, he's gone, my baby is dead," and burst into uncontrollable tears.

Sam Thompson took the medical investigator upstairs, and after unlocking the doors to Elvis' bedroom suite, showed Warlick and his party into Elvis' study. "Scattered on couches forming a complete perimeter of the room was an assortment of teddy bears," wrote investigative reporters Charles C. Thompson II and James P. Cole in their authoritative study, *The Death of Elvis*. "They were everywhere, facing obediently toward an oversized desk with a placard reading ELVIS PRESLEY, THE BOSS. The walls were covered with leather or Naugahyde . . . the room blended a childish air with hard reality beginning with the largest animal and ending with the [empty] syringe Warlick noticed in front of the placard. . . . Warlick walked past the desk and out of the office-den and into the bedroom. On the far wall he spotted two or three television sets perched on a deep bookcase and staring at an angle toward the biggest king-size bed that Warlick . . . had ever seen. On top of the case he found a second syringe [empty] just like the first."

Warlick immediately ordered the death scene to be secured, but he was aware of the futility of the gesture even before entering the bathroom, where he noted a carpet that was deep red, a yellowish throw rug lying in front of the black toilet, and yet another television set, placed in view of the commode. "Two telephones and what looked like an intercom were mounted next to the toilet-paper dispenser," wrote Thompson and Cole in vivid summary of Warlick's later testimony. "Comfortable arm chairs were stationed around the bathroom. Dominating the room was a circular shower about seven feet in diameter. . . . A cushy vinyl chair rested in the middle of the shower. . . . To the right of the doorway was a twelve-foot-long light marble counter with a built-in purple sink. A mirror rimmed with oversized light bulbs ran along the wall at counter length. Stepping to the counter, Warlick inspected a black bag. It was like a doctor's bag with a big flap folding down to a latch in front. Inside was a complement of tiny black plastic drawers. All of them were empty."

So was the medicine cabinet, nor was there any evidence of even the most common household remedies in the bedroom. For Warlick it was a first in his four years as an investigator — to discover a total absence of medications, prescription or nonprescription, in the home of anyone but the most fervent Christian Scientist. The story that he got from the various interviews that he conducted that afternoon was sanitized, too. The only thing that appeared to have been missed, aside from the empty syringes, was the book that Elvis had in the bathroom with him when he died, a study of sex and psychic energy that correlated sexual positions with astrological signs. Warlick found a stain on the bathroom carpeting, too, that seemed to indicate where Elvis had thrown up after being stricken, apparently while seated on the toilet. It looked to the medical investigator as if he had "stumbled or crawled several feet before he died."

By the time that Warlick got back to the hospital just before seven o'clock, the autopsy was about to begin. Although he had no formal role in the proceedings, Dr. Nick's presence as an observer underscored the fact that this death from unknown circumstances, and possibly even unnatural causes, would almost certainly be examined as a private, not a public, matter, despite continuing agitation from the attorney general's office to move Elvis' body to the city hospital across the street, where the coroner would operate under official state auspices. Instead, armed with the consent form obtained from Vernon, nine pathologists from Baptist conducted the examination in full knowledge that the world was watching but that the results would be released to Elvis' father alone. "Our pathologists were concerned with somebody of Elvis' fame [that] the controversies that developed with President Kennedy's autopsy [not develop here]," said Maurice Elliott. "They wanted to be sure that the hospital wasn't embarrassed." At the same time they were intensely aware of the time constraints involved, and in fact they were scarcely done with the preliminary stages of the process when Shelby County medical examiner Jerry Francisco and Dr. Eric Muirhead, the hospital's chief of pathology, left with five of the hospital doctors and Dr. Nick to address an eight o'clock press conference that Dr. Francisco had called. There Francisco announced the results of the autopsy, even as the autopsy was still going on. Death, he said, was "due to cardiac arrhythmia due to undetermined heartbeat." Muirhead, wrote Thompson and Cole in their book, "was noticeably embarrassed. He winced as Jerry Francisco ran roughshod over the physical evidence with a lot of cardiological double-talk. But he didn't contradict the medical examiner. 'I wish I had spoken up,' Muirhead told his colleagues later." But there were in fact at that time no results to report.

The autopsy proper went on for another couple of hours. Specimens were collected and carefully preserved, the internal organs were examined and the heart found to be enlarged, a significant amount of coronary atherosclerosis was observed, the liver showed considerable damage, and the large intestine was clogged with fecal matter, indicating a painful and long-standing bowel condition. The bowel condition alone would have strongly suggested to the doctors what by now they had every reason to suspect from Elvis' hospital history, the observed liver damage, and abundant anecdotal evidence: that drug use was heavily implicated in this unanticipated death of a middle-aged man with no known history of heart disease who had been "mobile and functional within eight hours of his death." It was certainly possible that he had been taken while "straining at stool," and no one ruled out the possibility of anaphylactic shock brought on by the codeine pills he had gotten from his dentist, to which he was known to have had a mild allergy of long standing.

The pathologists, however, were satisfied to wait for the lab results, which they were confident would overrule Dr. Francisco's precipitate, and somewhat meaningless, announcement, as indeed they eventually did. There was little disagreement in fact between the two principal laboratory reports and analyses filed two months later, with each stating a strong belief that the primary cause of death was polypharmacy, and the Bio-Science Laboratories report, initially filed under the patient name of "Ethel Moore," indicating the detection of fourteen drugs in Elvis' system, ten in significant quantity. Codeine appeared at ten times the therapeutic level, methaqualone (Quaalude) in an arguably toxic amount, three other drugs appeared to be on the borderline of toxicity taken in and of themselves, and "the combined effect of the central nervous system depressants and the codeine" had to be given heavy consideration. Almost inexplicably, Dr. Francisco and the medical examiner's office would stick to their original diagnosis, and the debate over Elvis' death would rage for over twenty years, through lawsuits and legislative actions, medical disbarment and reinstatement, and attempts at blame, denial, and reconsideration too numerous to mention. And yet all one has to do is look at Elvis' life, the accelerating dependence on medications available to him in almost unimaginable quantities, the willing enlistment of doctors who seemed never to give a thought to the dangers or likely consequences of what they were prescribing, and the incontrovertible evidence of the medical problems stemming primarily from the use of drugs that Elvis experienced over his last four years, to understand the causes of his death.

Joe was in charge of the funeral arrangements, but Vernon made clear his preference on every one of the significant details. The original plan was to conduct the service at the Memphis Funeral Home, where Gladys Presley's obsequies had been held, but Vernon insisted this time that the ceremony be at home — just as he and Elvis had wanted for Elvis' mother. He wouldn't budge in his determination to give the fans a chance to see the body either — they had remained loyal to Elvis throughout his career, and Elvis had always said that without them he would have been nothing. With these and various other considerations in mind, Joe sent the *Lisa Marie* out to California to pick up Priscilla, Jerry Schilling, Joe's present girlfriend Shirley Dieu and former wife, Joanie, and Priscilla's immediate family. He helped with travel arrangements for Linda Thompson and Ed Parker and a number of others, too, whom Priscilla had indicated she did not want on the plane, but for the most part he tried to discourage people from coming — it was just going to be too much of a zoo.

Vernon wanted a copper casket similar to the one in which they had buried Gladys, and funeral director Bob Kendall was able to find one in Oklahoma City while somehow managing to locate seventeen white Cadillac limousines for the funeral cortege, though there were only three in town. Elvis was to be buried in a white suit that his father had given him, and Vernon asked Charlie and Larry to do his hair so he would look good for the fans. South Central Bell requested that all Memphians restrict themselves to emergency calls because the circuits were so overloaded, and local florists were flooded with orders, over three thousand in all, requiring them to go far afield to meet the demand. At approximately 1:00 A.M., Vernon called the Reverend C. W. Bradley, minister of the Wooddale Church of Christ, which Vernon's estranged wife, Dee, had attended. Vernon scarcely knew Bradley, he was not much of a formal churchgoer himself, and Elvis had only met the minister on the occasion of one of his uncles' funerals, but Reverend Bradley was fully understanding of all the reasons why Mr. Presley would want his boy to have a proper ceremony. "He said, 'Brother

Bradley, will you be willing to do this funeral for my son?' I told him of course I would be willing. He then said, 'Now I know you don't have mechanical music at your church, and we're going to have an organ at the funeral. Will that bother you?'" Bradley told him that it would not, "and we began to discuss the type of service that he wanted."

There would, of course, be music, Vernon said, the kind of good old-fashioned quartet singing that Elvis had loved ever since he was a little boy — J. D. Sumner and the Stamps, the Statesmen, Jake Hess, and James Blackwood had all agreed to perform — and he hoped Reverend Bradley wouldn't mind, but televangelist Rex Humbard, from whom Elvis had sought counsel in Las Vegas the previous December, had asked to say a few words, too. The Reverend Bradley freely assented to all of these arrangements, and when Priscilla arrived with her party not long afterward, it was the occasion for more tearful reminiscences, in the midst of which Joe found an opportunity to give Priscilla back the private Polaroids and video-tapes Elvis had kept of her all these years. It was three in the morning before anyone got to sleep, but the number of fans outside the gates continued to grow, and thirty hardy souls camped out all night on the sidewalk outside the Memphis Funeral Home.

Larry and Charlie reported to the funeral home in accordance with Vernon's request early the next morning. Charlie trimmed and colored the sideburns, while Larry cut and styled Elvis' hair, and then they consulted on the makeup job. Joe saw to it that all the furniture was removed from the living room before the casket arrived in a single white hearse, preceded by a motorcycle escort, shortly before noon. The crowd out front, which had grown to an estimated fifty thousand by now, clamored for a glimpse as the copper casket was carried up the steps and in the front door. Meanwhile, a number of fans had climbed trees on the grounds of Graceland Christian Church next door, and limbs could be heard snapping as they struggled to get a better view.

The coffin was placed in the archway between the living room and the music room on the far south end of the house, and family and close friends were given a chance to pay their respects before the public viewing that was to take place at mid afternoon. Vernon's knees buckled, and Grandma almost collapsed, but the Colonel, who had arrived from Portland early that morning, resolutely rejected any opportunity to view the body. So far as anyone could remember, Colonel had never attended a funeral before — though no one could recall his ever articulating his thoughts on the subject

either. He didn't really have to. No one could miss the intensity of his colloquies with Vernon in the kitchen, as he buttonholed the grieving father and
tried to impress upon him the seriousness of the situation they were in, the
need right now, even in the midst of mourning, to firmly fix their minds
upon the future. It was almost like when Elvis was in Germany, he said —
the vultures were just waiting to swoop down on them and take over,
already there were probably half a dozen manufacturers thinking they
could just move right in and capitalize on an opportunity for name and
product exploitation that rightfully belonged to Vernon and little Lisa
Marie alone. Vernon nodded as Colonel emphasized that there was no time
to lose, they had to circle the wagons right away — to wait even a few days
could be fatal. Vernon's gaunt handsome face reflected a sorrow almost
beyond expression; it was hard to tell how much he was able to take in as he
assented almost mutely to the Colonel's every argument. Things would
continue just like they always had, he agreed. Everything would remain
exactly the same. He knew the Colonel had their interests at heart.

For the viewing, scheduled to last from three to five o'clock, the body
was moved to the foyer, underneath a crystal chandelier just inside the
door. White linen was laid out on the floor underneath the casket, and outside, the lawn was a sea of flowers. Wire reports described the scene as
verging on mass hysteria, as "four at a time fans filed by the stone lions
guarding the door, past the casket and back out the door into the 90-degree
heat. Several mourners fainted on the marble floor and had to be carried
out. A quarter mile away, down a driveway with a sheriff's deputy every
few yards, a throng, stretching a mile on either side, pushed and shoved to
be next through the gates. . . . Hundreds fainted in the heat. Many, revived
with rubber gloves filled with ice, staggered back into the crowd and fainted
again. Radios blared Presley's greatest hits [as] three police helicopters hovered over the mansion. Thirty National Guardsmen were called out to help
the 80 policemen and 40 sheriff's deputies try to control the crowd."

There were bodyguards on the three exposed sides of the coffin, and
Vernon hovered watchfully, as if to protect his son from ever-present dangers. He was no more able to protect him from betrayal in death than in
life, though, as one of the cousins got a shot of Elvis in his coffin with a
Minox provided by the *National Enquirer,* which Vernon would discover
only when the tabloid ran the picture on the cover of its next issue. In the
photograph Elvis looks pale and waxy, but he is still surprisingly handsome, composed and at rest in a way that seemed almost foreign to those

who remembered a man rarely at rest. Dedicated diarist Donna Lewis expressed the feeling of many of the fans when she wrote in her journal that Elvis didn't look like himself at all: "he looked awful. . . . It hurt. It hurt deep!"

At five o'clock Vernon was persuaded by the mass of people still waiting outside the gates to allow the viewing to continue for another hour and a half. It had begun to rain lightly, but the crowd was not about to disperse and continued to file slowly forward until at last at the appointed time the order was given to shut the gate. "It seemed touch-and-go for a while," reported Chet Flippo in *Rolling Stone,* as the approximately ten thousand people still standing outside "surged at the gates amid boos and tears and sobs." But Elvis Presley fans had always been well behaved around their idol; even as the world scoffed, their loyalty had never been in doubt, and so it remained now. Amid expressed fears of a riot, a dozen policemen were finally able to close the gates, and after about thirty minutes the crowd slowly began to walk away. "The rock wall facing on Elvis Presley Boulevard [was] low enough to jump over," Flippo wrote, "but no one tried."

After the viewing, the coffin was moved back into the living room, where the service was scheduled to take place the next day, and the evening was given over to a kind of private wake. Soul singer James Brown requested, and got, some time alone with the body, but otherwise there was a notable absence of celebrities, which was very much in keeping with the kind of ceremony that Vernon had envisioned. Charlie seemed almost in a daze, Joe tried to keep an eye on the relatives at all times, and the Colonel was uncharacteristically silent, as Vernon returned to the living room over and over again to pat his son on the head.

It was after ten when word came up that nineteen-year-old Caroline Kennedy was waiting at the gate, and she was proudly escorted to the front door. Vernon couldn't get over that the slain President's daughter would come in the middle of the night to pay her respects, until he was quietly informed that she was working as a summer intern for a New York newspaper and had been interviewing people out on the street. "Elvis' Uncle Vester, Aunt Delta and Aunt Nash, [and his] 82-year-old grandmother . . . were all staring at a 10 o'clock news show about the day's events," she reported in a story that was eventually published in *Rolling Stone,* sketching in poignant portraits of the few moments that she was able to observe before being quietly asked to leave. Then, at Priscilla's request, Sam Thompson suggested that everyone go home so the family could get some sleep, and he remained alone with the body all night until Dick Grob relieved him early the next morning. Thousands of fans still lingered outside the gates, and two were killed instantly when a 1963 white Ford driven by an eighteen-year-old man with what his mother described as "mental problems" plowed into a group gathered in the closed-off center lane of the highway at a speed of forty miles an hour.

At nine o'clock that morning one hundred vans began to carry the flowers to the cemetery, a task that took nearly four hours to complete and looked for a while as if it might not be done before the interment began. At noon guests started to arrive for the two o'clock service. The singers had all met in Charlie's room earlier to confer about their parts. At Priscilla's urging, Kathy was going to sing "Heavenly Father," which she always performed on the show to Elvis' rapt attention, with Statesmen founder Hovie Lister accompanying her on piano. James Blackwood, who had sung at Gladys Presley's funeral and known Elvis ever since he was a Blackwood Brothers teenage fan, would deliver Elvis' signature piece, "How Great Thou Art," with orchestra leader Joe Guercio symbolically conducting. Jake Hess, former lead singer for the Statesmen and one of the singers Elvis had most admired throughout his life, was present, too, to re-create "Known Only to Him," one of the many songs for which he was famous that Elvis had recorded in explicit homage to his idol. Finally, J. D. Sumner and the Stamps would contribute the majority of the program with a selection of hymns for the most part taken from songs they had performed on the show.

Linda wore lavender and Kathy came dressed in white, because that was how each felt Elvis would have wanted her to look. Nearly everyone else arrived garbed in one form or another of funereal black. Only the Colonel stood out in characteristically adamant exception. "You never wore a tie for him when he was alive," he admonished promoter Tom Hulett as they were about to leave their hotel — and made him go back and take it off. He himself was attired in his customary baseball cap, seersucker pants, and a blue short-sleeved shirt, fiercely unrepentant for any offense he might give. The two hundred invited guests quietly filed into the living room and waited for the service to begin. Tennessee governor Ray Blanton and Chet Atkins had arrived from Nashville, Ann-Margret and her husband, Roger Smith, had flown in from Las Vegas with Dr. Ghanem, and there was a substantial representation of the Colonel's associates and RCA executives — but mostly it was just family and friends filling up the wooden folding

chairs and spilling over into the hallway, where the Colonel remained leaning up against a wall peering in at the ceremony from time to time.

The service began with the playing of "Danny Boy" on the organ. It
was scheduled to take no more than half an hour, but with Rex Humbard's
guest sermon, all of the musical selections, plus a eulogy that comedian
Jackie Kahane had asked Vernon if he could deliver, it was clear from the
start that the ceremony would run considerably overtime. Humbard spoke
of his meeting with Elvis in Las Vegas and how he had gotten down on his
knees and prayed with him; Jackie Kahane, who had conceived of the idea
for an informal tribute only when he realized no one else in the group was
going to give one, delivered a brief but graceful speech touching on the
sense of family that had grown up among them all and the generous and
quirky spirit who had been their leader; when Kathy sang "Heavenly
Father," with Hovie Lister accompanying her in a manner that bore little
resemblance to the way Glen D. or David Briggs had played it on the show,
she imagined she could hear Elvis "saying laughingly, 'That's not the way
we arranged it.'"

The main sermon, by Reverend Bradley, stressed the inspiring example
that Elvis had provided of the potential "of one human being who has
strong desire and unfailing determination." It spoke of Elvis' fundamental
decency, and how "in a society that has talked so much about the generation gap, the closeness of Elvis and his father . . . was heartwarming to
observe." But Elvis, Reverend Bradley acknowledged, was a "frail human
being," too, "and he would be the first to admit his weaknesses. Perhaps
because of his rapid rise to fame and fortune he was thrown into temptations that some never experience. Elvis would not want anyone to think
that he had no flaws or faults. But now that he's gone, I find it more helpful
to remember his good qualities, and I hope you do, too." Vernon's racking
sobs could be heard throughout the ceremony, and afterward the mourners
filed up one by one to say a final good-bye. Ann-Margret tried to console
Vernon, but instead they both started to cry. Then the nine pallbearers —
Joe and Charlie, Felton, Lamar, Jerry Schilling and George Klein, Elvis'
cousins Billy and Gene Smith, and Dr. Nick — bore the coffin out the door.
Just as they did, a limb on one of the big oak trees out in front snapped and
fell, barely missing the funeral party, but Lamar didn't miss a beat. "We
knew you'd be back," he wisecracked. "Just not this soon."

They made the three-and-one-half-mile journey to the cemetery in a
cortege made up of forty-nine cars led by a silver Cadillac, a police motor-

cycle escort, a white hearse, and Vernon in the first of the seventeen white limousines. Both sides of the road were lined with a crowd estimated at fifteen to twenty thousand, and Joe saw Cliff Gleaves standing mournfully among them as the hearse drove by; evidently no one at the gate had known to let him in.

Once they arrived at the cemetery, the pallbearers carried the rose petal–strewn coffin past a massive bank of floral arrangements — hound dogs, crowns, and broken hearts, guitars and simple sprigs of red and yellow roses, all offered in humble tribute — up the steps of a stark gray mausoleum just a few hundred feet from Gladys Presley's grave. With the roses that had covered the coffin scattered on the mausoleum floor, the Reverend Bradley conducted a brief, five-minute ceremony in the mausoleum chapel, and then the family filed into the crypt one by one to touch or kiss the casket. Vernon remained alone with his son for a few moments after everyone else had left and had to be supported when he emerged from the building. Then the mausoleum was cleared, the *Commercial Appeal* reported, and "five workmen entered the room with a wheelbarrow full of sand, a five-gallon bucket of water, some cement, and a box of tools." They sealed the crypt with a double slab of concrete, then applied an exterior marble facing which would be inscribed later. "Even before the workmen had completed the entombment, people began entering the cemetery from the rear and pressing themselves against the heavy steel doors of the mausoleum." Meanwhile, everyone returned to Graceland for a "Southern supper," and later that evening Vernon directed that all the flowers be given away to the fans, who were gathered by the thousands at the cemetery at 8:25 A.M. the following morning when the gates were opened. By noon more than fifty thousand of them had showed up, and every last spray and blossom was gone.

Over the next couple of weeks the Colonel worked out the details of his new marketing plan with a man named Harry "The Bear" Geisler, whose company, Factors Inc., had just completed a highly successful Farrah Fawcett-Majors merchandising campaign. Vernon gave his formal approval to the continuation of Elvis' arrangement with the Colonel on August 23, one day before he was recognized by the court as official executor of the estate. The contract that he signed was the same in virtually every respect as the one Elvis had agreed to with the Colonel the previous year. It established Boxcar Enterprises, the Colonel's most recent corporate identity, as a kind of middleman for all merchandising rights, with 50 percent of all

Boxcar income to be disbursed equally between Colonel and the Elvis Presley estate, the remainder retained as a reserve for all expenses (including substantial salaries and bonuses, paid out at the Colonel's discretion), with anything left over (which to date had come to nothing) to be divided 56 percent to Colonel and the remainder to the estate and Colonel's longtime associate Tom Diskin. Vernon signed the agreement with no evident qualms, and the Colonel continued to carry on business in the usual manner until he was challenged by the probate court of Shelby County, Tennessee, which elected to intervene on behalf of Lisa Marie, "a minor and sole beneficiary of the late Elvis A. Presley," following Vernon's death on June 26, 1979, the Colonel's seventieth birthday.

RCA would discover that Elvis was as great a sales phenomenon in death as in life. Red and Sonny's book, *Elvis: What Happened?*, sold over three million copies, perhaps largely as a result of the unanticipated timing of its release, and its two principal authors maintained a policy of virtual silence on the subject for nearly twenty years. Ginger Alden arranged to sell her own story to the *National Enquirer* in the immediate aftermath of Elvis' death for a reputed $105,000, an amount that was substantially reduced when it was discovered that she had violated the exclusivity of her agreement with an interview that appeared in the *Commercial Appeal* on August 19. There was a bizarre and almost laughably inept attempt to steal Elvis' body just eleven days after the interment, and one month later, on October 2, Elvis and his mother were both reburied in the Meditation Garden at Graceland, after all zoning requirements had been met. "I guess they will finally get to rest," Vernon remarked at a small graveside gathering restricted to close relatives in the early evening.

Long before he was laid in the grave, the legend of Elvis' success, the one trademark it was impossible for even the Colonel to register, had been retailed over and over again, but now it was overwhelmed in a flood of reminiscences that at first strove to deny the "frail humanity" that bound him to the rest of the human race, then rushed to condemn him for it. The cacophony of voices that have joined together to create a chorus of informed opinion, uninformed speculation, hagiography, symbolism, and blame, can be difficult at times to drown out, but in the end there is only one voice that counts. It is the voice that the world first heard on those bright yellow Sun 78s, whose original insignia, a crowing rooster surrounded by boldly stylized sunbeams and a border of musical notes, sought to proclaim the dawning of a new day. It is impossible to silence that voice;

you cannot miss it when you listen to "That's All Right" or "Mystery Train" or "Blue Moon of Kentucky" or any of the songs with which Elvis continued to convey his sense of unlimited possibilities almost to the end of his life. It is that sense of aspiration as much as any historical signposts or goals that continues to communicate directly with a public that recognized in Elvis a kindred spirit from the first. That is what we have to remember. In the face of facts, for all that we have come to know, it is necessary to listen unprejudiced and unencumbered if we are to hear Elvis' message: the proclamation of emotions long suppressed, the embrace of a vulnerability culturally denied, the unabashed striving for freedom. Elvis Presley may have lost his way, but even in his darkest moments, he still retained some of the same innocent transparency that first defined the difference in the music and the man. More than most, he had an awareness of his own limitations; his very faith was tested by his recognition of how far he had fallen from what he had set out to achieve — but for all of his doubt, for all of his disappointment, for all of the self-loathing that he frequently felt, and all of the disillusionment and fear, he continued to believe in a democratic ideal of redemptive transformation, he continued to seek out a connection with a public that embraced him not for what he was but for what he sought to be.

"Well I've tried to be the same all through this thing, you know," he declared early on. *"Naturally, you learn a lot about people, and you get involved in a lot of different situations, but I've tried to be the same. I mean, the way I was brought up, I've always considered other people's feelings; I've never — in other words, I didn't kick anybody on my way. I don't just sign the autographs and the pictures and so forth to help my popularity or make them like me. I do it because I know that they're sincere, and they see you and they want an autograph to take home, and they've got an autograph book, or they've got their little camera. They don't know the kind of life you lead, they don't know what kind of person you are. And so — I try to remember that. That's all. It's simple. It's just the way I was brought up [by] my mother and father to believe and have respect for other people. We were always considerate of other people's feelings."*

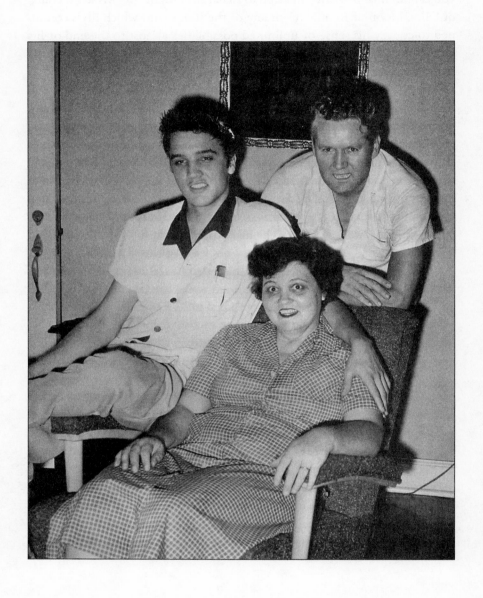

ELVIS, VERNON, AND GLADYS PRESLEY.
(COURTESY OF THE ESTATE OF ELVIS PRESLEY)

Notes

THE MAJORITY OF THE INTERVIEW MATERIAL is my own, but Jerry Hopkins' interviews of various figures for his 1971 and 1980 volumes, *Elvis* and *Elvis: The Final Years,* have been a unique and invaluable resource. They were made available by the Mississippi Valley Collection at the University of Memphis (MVC/UMem) through the kind efforts of Dr. John Bakke. The Elvis Presley General Correspondence Files in the Hal Wallis Collection at the Margaret Herrick Library, Academy of Motion Picture Arts and Sciences Library, Beverly Hills (HWC/MPAS), provided unparalleled insight into the unique relationship between Wallis and Joe Hazen and Elvis and Colonel Parker. In addition, Stuart Goldman and Adam Taylor were good enough to share information and interview material assembled for their 1993 film, *Elvis in Hollywood.*

So far as full documentation of the business and day-to-day events, and some of the personal elements of Elvis' life, I would have been adrift without the cooperation of the Elvis Presley Estate (EPE), and I owe much thanks and gratitude to Jack Soden for his generosity and encouragement as well as to archivist Greg Howell, who was unstinting in both his efforts and enthusiasm.

Many others contributed their time and resources, and I have tried to indicate my thanks and indebtedness both in these notes and in the acknowledgments that follow.

PROLOGUE: HOMECOMING, MEMPHIS, MARCH 1960

3 They left in the aftermath: The account of Elvis' departure from Fort Dix is gleaned from various newspaper stories in the *Memphis Press-Scimitar* ("Elvis Questioned About His Style and Romance" by Milton Britten, March 3, 1960; "Elvis, Parker Go to Swank New York Hotel," March 5, 1960); the *Memphis Commercial Appeal;* the Associated Press and UPI, March 3–5; the *New York Journal-American* ("Presley Takes to the Hills" by Charles Roland, March 6, 1960); and numerous other accounts.

4 his manager had a plan: All of the Colonel's multifarious plans, schemes, and promotional efforts are derived from correspondence, interoffice memos, and contracts November 1958–January 1960 (EPE).

4 He had kept Elvis' name in the headlines: The prevailing contemporary view of Colonel Parker's achievement is perhaps best expressed in Lloyd Shearer's June 19, 1960, *Parade* profile of the singer and his manager, in which Shearer details the Colonel's accomplishment in keeping Elvis' name alive throughout his two years in the army and states that "rarely in the annals of show business has any entertainer been more shrewdly booked, spotted and promoted than Elvis Presley."

4–5 The present plan: Bill E. Burk, "Elvis Home — Gets Warm Welcome," *Memphis Press-Scimitar,* March 7, 1960.

5 That evening they took a private railroad car: Richard Connelly, "Elvis Due Back in Memphis by Rail Tomorrow — Maybe," *Memphis Commercial Appeal,* March 6, 1960.

5 There was a crowd: David Halberstam, "Sergeant Elvis Smuggled Home in Big Fanfare of Secrecy," *Nashville Tennessean,* March 7, 1960.

5 with an extra rocker on the shoulder: *Memphis Press-Scimitar,* March 7, 1960.

5 Inside the car: Rex and Elisabeth Mansfield, *Elvis the Soldier,* pp. 135–136.

6 Colonel Parker "told me": Ibid., p. 137.

6 "like a happy young colt": *Nashville Tennessean,* March 7, 1960.

6 "we could make money": *Memphis Press-Scimitar,* March 7, 1960.

7 "Everything. I mean that": Malcolm Adams, "Elvis Wanted 'To Get Home,'" *Memphis Commercial Appeal,* March 8, 1960.

7 Two hundred fans: *Memphis Press-Scimitar,* March 7, 1960; *Memphis Commercial Appeal,* March 8, 1960.

GERMANY: MARKING TIME

9 He arrived in Bremerhaven: The account of Elvis' arrival and early acclimatization stems primarily from *Private Presley: The Missing Years — Elvis in Germany* by Andreas Schroer; Alan Levy's *Operation Elvis;* William J. Taylor, Jr.'s *Elvis in the Army;* Ira Jones' *Soldier Boy Elvis;* and Albert Goldman's *Elvis.* See also Rex and Elisabeth Mansfield's *Elvis the Soldier;* "Der Elvis" by Gary Paul Gates, *Memories,* spring 1988; and numerous news accounts. In addition, Bernard Seibel of the German Elvis-Fan-Club prepared a valuable chronology and provided German clippings from his own research.

9 He was met at the dock: A press account prepared by Boris Jankolovics and wired October 8, 1958, presumably at Colonel Parker's instigation, estimates five thousand fans (EPE).

10 At night, Charlie said: Interview with Charlie Hodge, 1989.

10 Several days out to sea: Interview with Charlie Hodge; Mansfield, *Elvis the Soldier,* pp. 33–34; letter from Private Donald Petit, *Elvis in the Army* (1959 fan magazine), p. 63.

10 "Charlie," he told his new friend: Charlie Hodge, *Me 'n Elvis,* p. 10.

10 He got through the obligatory press briefings: *New York Post,* October 2, 1958.

10 His family arrived: *New York Journal-American,* October 5, 1958.

10 "Elvis always kept his own world": Interview with Lamar Fike, 1988.

11 they changed hotels: Hotel bill (EPE).

11 three weeks later: Hotel Grunewald bill from October 28 (EPE).

11 Elvis wasn't paying either one: Interviews with Lamar Fike and Charlie Hodge; Red West et al., *Elvis: What Happened?,* pp. 173ff; Alanna Nash, *Elvis Aaron Presley: Revelations from the Memphis Mafia,* p. 153.

11–12 There was a moment of confusion: Correspondence between Colonel Parker and E. J. Cottrell, Assistant Chief of Information, Department of the Army, October 14–15, 1958; *New York Post,* October 30, 1958; Levy, *Operation Elvis,* pp. 82–83.

12 Many days he was home: *Variety,* March 25, 1959.

12 And he had a little girl: "Elvis Kissed Me, by Margit Buergin, age 17, Frankfurt, Germany," *Photoplay,* March 1959; *New York Journal-American,* November 1 and 2, 1959.

13 He called some of his pals: *Memphis Press-Scimitar,* October 21, 1958; interviews with Alan Fortas and George Klein, 1990; Alan Fortas, *Elvis: From Memphis to Hollywood,* p. 100.

13 alfalfa pills: *Memphis Press-Scimitar,* October 16, 1958.

13 He wrote breezily: Rose Clayton and Dick Heard, eds., *Elvis Up Close: In the Words of Those Who Knew Him Best,* p. 161.

13 he had even spoken to her: Ibid., p. 155.

13 He wrote to her: The October 28, 1958, letter is quoted in both *Elvis World* 21, p. 13, and Albert Goldman's *Elvis,* p. 294.

13 In another letter: Goldman, *Elvis,* p. 298.

13 He heard from Janie Wilbanks: *Memphis Press-Scimitar*, September 10, 1959; interview with George Klein; Mansfield, *Elvis the Soldier*, pp. 32, 49.

13 Elvis prompted him to tell: Hodge, *Me 'n Elvis*, p. 13.

13 they all harmonized: Interview with Charlie Hodge; BBC interview with Charlie Hodge; Trevor Cajiao, "Red West: This Is What Happened, Part 1," *Elvis: The Man and His Music* 22, March 1994, p. 13; Mansfield, *Elvis the Soldier*, p. 58.

14 he might still be driving a truck: John W. Haley and John von Hoelle, *Sound and Glory*, p. 189.

14 he had another date with Margit: AP and UPI reports in *New York Journal-American*, *New York World-Telegram*, and *New York Daily News*, November 2, 3, 1958.

14 a woman named Dee Stanley: Dee Presley et al., *Elvis, We Love You Tender*; Billy Stanley, *Elvis, My Brother*, pp. 1–4; Goldman, *Elvis*, p. 304; interview with Lamar Fike; Nash, *Elvis Aaron Presley*, p. 160; West et al., *Elvis: What Happened?*, p. 185.

14 Then they were off to Grafenwöhr: Jones, *Soldier Boy Elvis*, pp. 90ff, 123.

14–15 he wrote Alan Fortas: Fortas, *Elvis: From Memphis to Hollywood*, pp. 101–103. The letter is reproduced with a November 14 postmark.

15–16 One evening at the post theater: Mansfield, *Elvis the Soldier*, pp. 41–44.

16 Back at Ray Kaserne: Jones, *Soldier Boy Elvis*, pp. 174–177.

16 Vernon gave Elvis an electric guitar: Levy, *Operation Elvis*, p. 94.

17 She tried to play up to him: Dee Presley et al., *Elvis, We Love You*, p. 49.

17 he spoke to his father sharply: Interview with Lamar Fike.

17 It was the shaving-cream fight: West et al., *Elvis: What Happened?*, pp. 178–179. They appear to have moved between February 10 and February 23, as indicated by letters from Colonel Parker (EPE).

18 Elisabeth moved with them: Mansfield, *Elvis the Soldier*, p. 49.

18 He explained to her: Bob Graham, "Elvis and Elisabeth," *The [London] Sunday Times Magazine*, August 3, 1997, p. 30.

18 Elvis knocked three times: Mansfield, *Elvis the Soldier*, p. 49.

18–19 "There would be at least a couple of girls": *The [London] Sunday Times Magazine*, August 3, 1997, p. 30; also Mansfield, *Elvis the Soldier*, pp. 49–50.

19 They moved into . . . Goethestrasse 14: Goldman, *Elvis*, pp. 299ff; Nash, *Elvis Aaron Presley*, pp. 147ff; West et al., *Elvis: What Happened?*, pp. 179ff; Schroer, *Private Presley*, pp. 36ff.

20 Charlie brought Elvis an album: Interview with Charlie Hodge.

20 In his first extended interview: This January 30, 1959, interview with DJ Keith Sherriff was transcribed in *Movie Life*, May 1959, which was supplied to me, along with a description of the circumstances of the interview, by Sherriff's daughter, Linda Raiteri.

20 He talked to them about the movie contracts: Mansfield, *Elvis the Soldier*, passim.

20 They had fireworks battles: Ibid.

20–21 Elvis had his own private barber: Ibid., p. 49; Schroer, *Private Presley*, p. 41; Nash, *Elvis Aaron Presley*, p. 164.

21 the pills that a sergeant had introduced him to: Mansfield, *Elvis the Soldier*, pp. 67–68; Priscilla Presley, *Elvis and Me*, p. 52; West et al., *Elvis: What Happened?*, p. 186; interviews with Charlie Hodge, 1989, and Joe Esposito, 1990–1998.

21 Rex still wondered: Mansfield, *Elvis the Soldier*, pp. 67–68.

21–22 As for Elisabeth: Ibid., pp. 50–54.

22 "One had to be very careful": Ibid., p. 148.

22–25 In March he decided to venture to Munich: The account of the trip is based primarily on *Private Elvis*, edited by Diego Cortez, in which interviews with Vera Tschechowa, Toni Netzel, and Elisabeth Brandin are included; also, Schroer, *Private Presley*; West et al., *Elvis: What Happened?*; Nash, *Elvis Aaron Presley*; and "Elvis on a Date with His Mystery Girl" (fan magazine article, 1959).

25 he got a hard-on: Jones, *Soldier Boy Elvis,* p. 210. Further observations and quotes from both Jones and Taylor, *Elvis in the Army.*

25 "Sometimes I feel like just quitting": Taylor, *Elvis in the Army,* pp. 96–97.

25–26 Colonel on his end: The Colonel's encouragement of Elvis, his articulation of long-range plans, and his negotiations on various fronts are all meticulously documented in his voluminous and energetic correspondence (EPE).

26 when they returned to the negotiating table: Elvis' RCA royalty rate was amended on May 7, 1959. Ren Grevatt's March 7, 1960, *Billboard* article, "Added Leeway for Phenom's Recordings," provides considerable insight into the upshot of all the Colonel's machinations.

27 Colonel had planted a flurry of confusing . . . items: September 15 and November 24, 1958, stories in *Variety,* among others.

27 Colonel finally bowed: Parker letter to Elvis and Vernon, November 10, 1958 (EPE); contract with Wallis, possibly backdated to October 28. All of the correspondence with Wallis and Joe Hazen is available in the Elvis Presley General Correspondence Files, Hal Wallis Collection, Margaret Herrick Library, Academy of Motion Picture Arts and Sciences Library (HWC/MPASL).

27 "we do not have to call on Wallis": Colonel to Elvis and Vernon, November 18, 1958 (EPE).

28 In Colonel's scenario: Colonel to Hal Wallis, December 13, 1958. Wallis reply December 18 (HWC/MPASL).

28 In this one, Elvis is a foundling: Colonel to Wallis, December 18, 1958 (HWC/MPASL).

28 Wallis . . . remained patiently forbearing: Correspondence between Wallis and various writers and producers, January 1959 (HWC/MPASL).

28 stories planted in the press: May Mann, *Elvis and the Colonel,* p. 98; James Gregory, *The Elvis Presley Story,* p. 100; Levy, *Operation Elvis,* p. 64; Colonel's correspondence (EPE).

29 On a more formal basis: Colonel's correspondence, passim (EPE); Pat Embry, "The Colonel," *Nashville Banner,* June 12, 1987; interviews with Al Dvorin 1996–1998.

29–30 Vernon and Elisabeth were in an automobile accident: Mansfield, *Elvis the Soldier,* pp. 53–54.

30 Elvis' jealousy was plain for all to see: Ibid., p. 59.

30 As for Red: West et al., *Elvis: What Happened?;* Nash, *Elvis Aaron Presley;* interview with Red West, 1996; Jerry Hopkins interview with West (MVC/UMem).

31 "Vernon and Bill really got drunk": West et al., *Elvis: What Happened?,* pp. 185–186.

31 Dee Stanley returned to Virginia: Dee Presley et al., *Elvis, We Love You,* p. 54; telephone bills from Germany from May 13 (EPE).

31 an on-air interview with Memphis DJ George Klein: *Memphis Press-Scimitar,* May 8, 1958.

31 "Red kept telling me": Interview with Alan Fortas.

31 Colonel even set up a tentative date: Colonel Parker's correspondence with Elvis and Vernon, May 1959, establishes an estimated June 17–19 date of arrival, with various contingency plans. Elvis' frequent phone calls are confirmed by telephone records (EPE).

32 he called Cliff Gleaves: Interview with Cliff Gleaves, 1990.

32 he promptly took off again: Mansfield, *Elvis the Soldier,* p. 98.

32 wearing "nothing but a standard-size Presley record": AP wire report, June 17, 1959.

32–33 it was off to Paris: The primary sources here are interviews with Lamar Fike, Charlie Hodge, and Freddy Bienstock; Mansfield, *Elvis the Soldier;* West et al., *Elvis: What Happened?;* and Nash, *Elvis Aaron Presley.*

34 "Lamar got angry": Mansfield, *Elvis the Soldier,* p. 95.

34 One night at the Lido: *New York Journal-American,* June 21, 1959.

34 his "'she' was a 'he'": Nash, *Elvis Aaron Presley*, p. 166.

35 He had some business: *New York Post*, July 8, 1959.

35 He had accompanied her to the airport: Dee Presley et al., *Elvis, We Love You*, p. 55.

35 "so changed you wouldn't know him": *Memphis Press-Scimitar*, July 8, 1959.

35–36 "I got sent home from school": Clayton and Heard, *Elvis Up Close*, p. 164.

36 he was not to participate in filming: Colonel to Elvis, July 2, 1959 (EPE).

36 He had put in a lot of time: Mann, *Elvis and the Colonel*, pp. 87–90.

36 Priscilla, just fourteen, had been elected: Suzanne Finstad, *Child Bride: The Untold Story of Priscilla Beaulieu Presley*, p. 40.

36–39 Her real father: Priscilla Presley, *Elvis and Me*, p. 22. Most of the following account, and all of the quotes, come from Priscilla's book. It should be noted that Currie Grant in Suzanne Finstad's *Child Bride* claims that it was the fourteen-year-old Priscilla who approached him and he who was the not-so-innocent victim. From the testimony of those who were present — Cliff Gleaves, Lamar Fike, Joe Esposito, Charlie Hodge, and Rex and Elisabeth Mansfield in their book — Priscilla's certainly seems the more credible account, and that is the one I have chosen for the most part to follow here.

39 Elvis was immediately smitten: Mansfield, *Elvis the Soldier*, p. 98; interviews with Charlie Hodge, Cliff Gleaves, Joe Esposito, et al.

39 "As Currie led me over": Priscilla Presley, *Elvis and Me*, p. 28.

40 "'We are alone,' I said nervously": Ibid., p. 31.

40 "he was just a boy": Interview with Priscilla Presley, 1995.

40 At the end of the evening: Priscilla Presley, *Elvis and Me*, pp. 35ff.

42 "I really felt I got to know": Interview with Priscilla Presley.

42 "He talked about": Ibid.

43 the benefits of yogurt: Ibid.

43 "Goodnight, My Love": Ibid.

43 "Did you see the bone structure": BBC interview with Charlie Hodge.

43 "Every Sunday afternoon": Joe Esposito, *Good Rockin' Tonight*, p. 48.

43 "He knew she was young": Interview with Joe Esposito, 1990.

43 "I often wanted to ask": Mansfield, *Elvis the Soldier*, p. 121.

44 for singing only two songs: Colonel to Elvis, January 9, 1960 (EPE).

44–45 There were a number of songs: The intended repertoire for this and future sessions derives from the Colonel's correspondence (EPE), interviews with Freddy Bienstock, Cliff Gleaves, Priscilla Presley, and Charlie Hodge; Peter Cronin interview with Gordon Stoker; Schroer, *Private Presley*, p. 5; and home tapes recorded in Germany.

45 a steady flow of Hill and Range material: Interview with Freddy Bienstock, 1992; David M. Nichol, "Here Comes Elvis Presley!," *Chicago Daily News*, February 20, 1960.

45 what you sang had to come from the heart: Elvis expressed this sentiment many times, most proximately in Pat Anderson, "Elvis Fears Nothing — But His Fans," *Nashville Tennessean*, March 22, 1960.

46 studying familiar records by the Ink Spots: Interview with a girlfriend who chooses not to be identified, 1995.

46 Freddy did his best: Colonel to Elvis, January 9, 1959 (EPE).

46 he had a song: Colonel to Elvis, October 31, 1959 (EPE).

46 Freddy's sardonic view: Interview with Freddy Bienstock.

46–47 In October Elvis saw a magazine notice: Nearly all of the information on the Landau incident is contained in the FBI files on Elvis Presley, Part 1, pp. 88–111.

47 Vernon was convinced: Priscilla Presley, *Elvis and Me*, p. 45.

47 Elvis began formal karate lessons: Elvis' initial fascination with karate was described in interviews with Red West, Joe Esposito, and Charlie Hodge; also, see Mansfield, *Elvis the Soldier,* pp. 58, 68, 156. Elvis kept his original "Testakarte Karate" from Seydel's school in his wallet, with his first test dated December 6, 1959 (EPE).

47 The sonofabitch was queer: Mansfield, *Elvis the Soldier,* p. 55.

47 Vernon was utterly panic-stricken: Emergency call to Colonel Parker logged December 26, 1959 (EPE).

48 his twenty-fifth birthday party: Esposito, *Good Rockin',* p. 39; Mansfield, *Elvis the Soldier,* p. 107; interview with Joe Esposito, 1990; Dee Presley et al., *Elvis, We Love You,* p. 52.

48 ELVIS PRESLEY. MOST VALUABLE PLAYER: Esposito, *Good Rockin',* p. 40.

48–49 Grandma had seen where things were going: The account of Rex's courtship of Elisabeth is derived primarily from Mansfield, *Elvis the Soldier,* pp. 109–110. Also interview with Cliff Gleaves, and Hodge, *Me 'n Elvis,* p. 44.

48–49 Lamar and Cliff knew: Mansfield, *Elvis the Soldier,* p. 103.

49 Elvis went to Paris: The account of Elvis' second Paris trip is based primarily on interviews with Joe Esposito and Cliff Gleaves; Ernst Jorgensen interview with Orlandis Wilson; and Schroer's *Private Presley,* p. 133. The dates are established by bills from the trip (EPE).

49 "Rexadus," he said: Mansfield, *Elvis the Soldier,* p. 103.

49 his full sergeant's stripes: AP dispatch, February 16, 1960; Schroer, *Private Presley,* p. 140; Mansfield, *Elvis the Soldier,* p. 103.

49 "After a second, I said": Priscilla Presley, *Elvis and Me,* pp. 51–52.

50 "People were expecting me to mess up": Armed Forces Network (AFN) interview.

50 his manager, Colonel Parker: *Chicago Daily News,* February 20, 1960. The rest of his responses are divided between this extensive interview, the AFN broadcast, and various other February 1960 interviews, all of which cover more or less the same ground.

50–51 he talked to each of the boys: Interviews with Joe Esposito, Cliff Gleaves, Lamar Fike, and Charlie Hodge.

51 Rex was the one: Mansfield, *Elvis the Soldier,* p. 136.

51 more than two dozen trunks: *Memphis Commercial Appeal,* March 3, 1960.

51–52 Over one hundred reporters: Robert Johnson, "Elvis Leaves Army! — Memphian's Eyewitness Report," *Memphis Press-Scimitar,* March 1, 1960. Both the press conference and various observations about life and love are contained in this story (which features Marion Keisker as the eyewitness, using her married name, MacInnes) and Thomas Pappas' "Homeward Bound — And He's Leaving 'Very Pretty Brunet' in Germany," also in the March 1 edition of the *Memphis Press-Scimitar.* See, too, Schroer, *Private Presley,* pp. 150ff.

52 "Marion!" he called out: Interviews with Marion Keisker, 1979, 1986; Jerry Hopkins interview with Marion Keisker (MVC/UMem); plus March 1, 1960, *Memphis Press-Scimitar* account.

53 She was very fond of Elvis: AP report, March 1, 1960; *New York Mirror,* March 2, 1960.

53 "More than ten tall Air Force police": *New York Mirror,* March 3, 1960.

53 "Girl He Left Behind": "Farewell to Priscilla, Hello to U.S.A.," *Life,* March 14, 1960.

53 "When he left": Interview with Priscilla Presley.

ELVIS IS BACK

55–56 He was dressed all in black: This account of Elvis' homecoming is drawn primarily from Thomas Michael, "Elvis and Fans Share Thrills at His Joyous Homecoming," *Memphis Commercial Appeal,* March 8, 1960; Bill E. Burk, "Elvis Plans to 'Stay Right At Home' for a Few Days," *Memphis Press-Scimitar,* March 8, 1960; Malcolm Adams, "Elvis Wanted 'to Get Home' but 'Kind of

Likes' Uniform," *Memphis Commercial Appeal,* March 8, 1960; AP report in *Nashville Tennessean,* March 8, 1960.

56 He had written to her: BBC interview with Anita Wood.

56 he asked her to hide a half-gallon jar: Bob Graham, "Elvis and Elisabeth," *The [London] Sunday Times Magazine,* August 3, 1997, p. 32.

56 she had better be careful: Rex and Elisabeth Mansfield, *Elvis the Soldier,* pp. 139, 141. According to Elisabeth's account in *Elvis the Soldier,* Anita was waiting for Elvis at Graceland when he came back from the train station, but I have rearranged the chronology in order to conform to the more common recollection.

56 He went to the cemetery: Barbara Hearn, "Elvis Answers 40 Intimate Questions," 16, August 1960.

56 "memories and sadness": *Memphis Press-Scimitar,* July 7, 1960. Elvis spoke of all of his visits as having this effect.

56 "the mysterious blonde": UPI report, March 6, 1960.

57 "Well, you know I'm not being honest": James Reid, "Elvis' Dad, Blond Arrive Together at Station," *Memphis Press-Scimitar,* March 5, 1960.

57 "Let's not talk about that": Ibid.

57 "He didn't seem like Elvis": Interview with Lillian Fortenberry, 1988.

57–58 he went to the ice show: For this and other details of Elvis' nearly two weeks at home, the *Memphis Press-Scimitar* and *Commercial Appeal* are the principal sources of information.

57 "I could stay with Elvis": Mansfield, *Elvis the Soldier,* pp. 140–141.

58 "I was very serious": Ibid., p. 143.

59 except for a signed photo: *The [London] Sunday Times Magazine,* August 3, 1997, p. 32.

59–61 "He hadn't made a sound": Ray Walker quoted in Rose Clayton and Dick Heard, eds., *Elvis Up Close: In the Words of Those Who Knew Him Best,* pp. 168–169. With regard to this session, I interviewed Scotty Moore, Bob Moore, Buddy Harman, Freddy Bienstock, Joe Esposito, and Bill Porter, among others. In addition, Pat Twitty, "What Happened When . . . Elvis Started Waxing Again," *New Musical Express,* April 1, 1960, and Pat Anderson, "Elvis Presley: Lonely Man in a Crowd," *Nashville Tennessean,* April 24, 1960, both focus on the sessions.

60 "Of course he talked": Interview with Bill Porter, 1993. See also John W. Rumble, "Behind the Board: Talking with Studio Engineer Bill Porter," *Journal of Country Music,* vol. 18, no. 1 and no. 2, vol. 19, no. 1 (1996–1997); and David Okamoto, "Engineering the Hits for Elvis," *Gazette Telegraph* (Denver), August 15, 1988.

61 "it was just unreal": Interview with Scotty Moore, 1990.

61 "Everybody would just get in his car": Interview with Scotty Moore, 1989.

61–62 For Joe and Lamar: Joe Esposito, *Good Rockin' Tonight,* p. 61.

62 he was determined to keep on his toes: Interview with Joe Esposito, 1990.

62 The first meeting: Esposito, *Good Rockin',* p. 61.

62 Joey Bishop, unctuously requested an autograph: May Mann, *Elvis and the Colonel,* p. 99.

62 excluded from all social activities: Peter Mikelbank, "D. J. Fontana: Elvis' Drummer Capsulizes the King's Career," *Goldmine,* August 14, 1987, p. 14; Jerry Hopkins interview with Gordon Stoker 1971 (MVC/UMem).

62 "But after all, the kid's been away": Rick Du Brow, "500,000 Await Elvis Today," UPI report, March 5, 1960.

63 four hundred fan club presidents and members: The best accounts of the taping are in *TV Guide,* May 7–13, 1960.

63–64 Elvis got a letter: Colonel to Elvis, March 30, 1960 (EPE). Despite the Colonel's frequent assertions over the years, I have been unable to locate any Gene Austin recorded version of this title. I asked the Colonel about this, and he was adamant that Austin had recorded it. He may well have, but it is now my assumption that it must at least have been a part of his stage act.

65 Bill Porter suggested: Interview with Bill Porter.

65 he had promised Charlie: Interview with Charlie Hodge, 1989.

65–66 "He chased everybody out of the studio": Interview with Chet Atkins, 1988.

65 Bill Porter was editing: Interview with Bill Porter. It should be noted that in Porter's recollection the first complete take was the basis for the master, and the ending was spliced from the fifth and last, but the reverse appears to have been the case.

66 One night he called up gospel singer James Blackwood: Interview with James Blackwood, 1988.

67 Elvis' presence caused such a commotion: BBC interview with Anita Wood; Shelley Ritter interview with George Klein.

67 another triumphant three-day whistle-stop trip: "Presley Hits H'wood Like Ton of Bricks," *Billboard*, April 25, 1960.

67 a personal retinue: *Newsweek*, May 30, 1960.

67 "We hadn't talked about me working with him": Interview with Charlie Hodge.

67 Sonny, three years younger than Elvis: Red West et al., *Elvis: What Happened?*, p. 26.

68 Elvis took special pride: In a 1962 interview with Lloyd Shearer he reveals both his insecurity and his pride; also see "Is This a 'New' Presley?," *Newsweek*, May 30, 1960, where Elvis says "defensively" of an unnamed Joe: "He was a bookkeeper before he went in the Army."

68 "we were a bunch of hicks": West et al., *Elvis: What Happened?*, p. 250.

68 A leader . . . had a different role: Two of Elvis' favorite inspirational homilies were "The Penalty of Leadership" and Theodore Roosevelt's "The Man Who Counts." In *Good Rockin' Tonight*, Joe Esposito describes Elvis having the former framed on his wall at Goethestrasse 14 in Germany.

69 his pet likes and dislikes: Barbara Hearn, "Elvis Presley: My Hates and Loves," 16, November 1960.

69 that night went out to a club: Interview with Lance LeGault, 1990; interview with Sandy Ferra Martindale, 1995, who cited the date from her diary.

70 "He came to the studio": Interview with Bones Howe, 1989.

70 "business" reasons: The Colonel effectively cut Leiber and Stoller out of the picture by insisting that they operate under the same rules as every other Hill and Range writer, a deal he had long since learned they would not accept. Also, letter to Jean Aberbach, November 23, 1959 (EPE).

70 "Hell, what could he say?": Priscilla Presley, *Elvis and Me*, p. 64.

70 By this time . . . he had met Sandy Ferra: Interview with Sandy Ferra Martindale.

71 his beautiful twenty-three-year-old South African co-star: Background on Juliet Prowse comes primarily from Jon Whitcomb, "Elvis and Juliet," *Cosmopolitan*, October 1960.

71 "He was a very *young* twenty-four": Interview with Sandy Martindale.

72 the eccentric actor Billy Murphy: Interviews with Joe Esposito, Cliff Gleaves, George Klein; for (a little) more on Murphy, see *Last Train to Memphis*, pp. 439, 470.

72 Gene's briefcase: Alanna Nash, *Elvis Aaron Presley: Revelations from the Memphis Mafia*, p. 81.

72 "I don't do a goddamn thing": West et al., *Elvis: What Happened?*, p. 250.

72–73 "None of us," by Joe's account: Esposito, *Good Rockin'*, p. 84; also, see Sonny West on the life in West et al., *Elvis: What Happened?*, p. 189.

73 Elvis attended a demonstration: Interview with Ed Parker, 1990.

73 "He was intrigued": Ed Parker, "'The King' and I" (article in British fan magazine).

74 it was his relationship with Juliet Prowse: This story is told in fairly close variants in West et al., *Elvis: What Happened?*, p. 253; Nash, *Elvis Aaron Presley*, p. 176; and, with Red West as narrator, in Clayton and Heard, *Elvis Up Close*, pp. 177–178. The point is always the same.

74 "He said Juliet liked to grab her ankles": Nash, *Elvis Aaron Presley*, p. 176.

74–75 The Colonel made a particular point: Colonel to Hal Wallis, summer 1960 (HWC/MPASL).

75 he entertained reporters' questions: Mann, *Elvis and the Colonel*, p. 134; *Billboard*, April 25, 1960, re $150,000.

75–76 "All they're good for is to make money": Jean Bosquet, "Parker Learned Name — Fast," *New York Journal-American*, June 13, 1960.

75 "I'm not his father": Ibid.

75 "He could go back to driving a truck": "The Man Who Sold Parsley," *Time*, May 16, 1960.

76 the movie that would someday be made: Louella Parsons column, *New York Journal-American*, June 27, 1960.

76 Elvis' little joke to call him Admiral: Lloyd Shearer feature, *Parade*, June 19, 1960.

76 They had visited once: Hotel bill May 28–29 (EPE). West et al., *Elvis: What Happened?*, p. 190, has this as their first visit.

76–77 as far as Barstow: West et al., *Elvis: What Happened?*, p. 191.

77 The joke around town: Nash, *Elvis Aaron Presley*, p. 190.

77 he and Gene took a plane: *Memphis Press-Scimitar*, July 1, 1960.

77 They were going to do it: James White, "Elvis Decided Weeks Ago Not to Attend Dad's Wedding — Here's Why," *Memphis Press-Scimitar*, July 7, 1960. The quitclaim to Graceland was executed on August 12 (EPE).

77 "She spoke to me": *Memphis Press-Scimitar*, July 5, 1960.

77 "She seems to be a pretty nice . . . person": *Memphis Press-Scimitar*, July 7, 1960.

78 His uncles Travis, Johnny: For some detail on intrafamilial tensions, see Harold Loyd, *Elvis Presley's Graceland Gates*, pp. 42, 47; Nash, *Elvis Aaron Presley*, p. 101; interview with Lillian Fortenberry; numerous letters from Vernon in Germany to his lawyer at home (EPE); and Donna Lewis' diaries, *"Hurry Home, Elvis!,"* vols. 1 and 2.

78 he felt as if there were a cloud: Robert Johnson, "Even Movie Stars Get Homesick," *Memphis Press-Scimitar*, September 9, 1960.

78 "a laughingstock": Don Siegel interview in 1972 radio documentary, "The Elvis Presley Story," cited in Gerry McLafferty, *Elvis Presley in Hollywood*, p. 51.

79 overcame his objections: Don Siegel, *A Siegel Film: An Autobiography*, pp. 222–227. See also Lee Belser, "Elvis Can Act, Says Director," *Los Angeles Mirror*, November 30, 1960.

79 There was to be a minimum of songs: Peter Whitmer suggests many additional studio complications in *The Inner Elvis: A Psychological Biography of Elvis Aaron Presley*, pp. 319ff.

79 Siegel's own recollection: *Rolling Stone*, September 22, 1977.

79 they started off with karate: Conversation with Lamar Herrin, 1990.

79 He generously loaned: Siegel, *A Siegel Film: An Autobiography*, p. 227.

79 nonstop games of touch football: Sonny West quoted in *Rolling Stone*.

79–80 "Acting skill will probably ruin him": Jerry Hopkins, *Elvis*, p. 163, quoting from an interview by Joe Hyams in the *New York Herald Tribune*.

80 Tuesday Weld throwing a fit: Esposito, *Good Rockin'*, pp. 84–85; Albert Goldman, *Elvis*, pp. 331–332, tells a story not involving Tuesday but, rather, a water fight and an elderly guest.

80 a six-month lease: The original lease dated from September 10 and was at a rate of $1,400 a month (EPE).

80 Elvis put up a painted photograph: Goldman, *Elvis*, p. 334; Alan Fortas, *Elvis: From Memphis to Hollywood*, p. 150.

80 "When I first came back": *Memphis Press-Scimitar*, September 9, 1960.

80–81 he heard from the Tau Kappa Epsilon fraternity: Interview with Rick Husky, 1995; Rick Husky, "World Famous Entertainer Presented Coveted Award," *State College Herald*, November 4, 1960.

82 a recurring nightmare: Interview with Freddy Bienstock, 1992. See also Nancy Anderson, "My Cherished Memories of Elvis," *Elvis Presley: A Photoplay Tribute*, 1977, p. 11.

83 there was no question of either his fervor: Interviews with Bob Moore and Gordon Stoker; also Peter Cronin interview with Bob Moore, 1993.

83 Chet Atkins had long since gone home: Jay Orr interview with Gordon Stoker.

83 "I had food poisoning": Interview with Bill Porter.

83 To Gordon Stoker and the Jordanaires: Trevor Cajiao interview with Gordon Stoker, *Elvis: The Man and His Music* 25, December 1990, p. 23. It should be noted that publishing was cleared on "Crying in the Chapel" prior to this session, despite the long-standing popular belief that the song's release was held up for five years on that issue. Evidently, Elvis was simply not satisfied with his version of the song.

83 the "new" Elvis: *Billboard*, July 18, 1960, re the song; *Variety*, November 2, re the movie.

83 his all-out campaign: Colonel's correspondence with Hal Wallis, October 10, 18, 19, 1960 (HWC/MPASL).

83–84 At RCA, meanwhile: Colonel's correspondence with RCA, January–February 1960, with a January 15 memo for January 18 and 19 meetings in which his control (and, essentially, ownership) of all photos is established particularly crucial. In addition, a special three-quarters of 1 percent royalty to All Star Shows for promotional activities is established, with a final contract, effective January 1, certifying all of these terms and more, signed on March 1, 1960 (EPE). Further insight into the meaning of these maneuvers was provided in interviews with Joan Deary, 1990, and Anne Fulchino, 1993.

84 they even offered to build Elvis a studio: Elvis letter to RCA vice president Bill Bullock, November 8, 1960, formally declining the offer; interview with Scotty Moore, 1990.

84 *Wild in the Country* started shooting: Background on *Wild in the Country* is derived primarily from Elaine Dundy, *Elvis and Gladys*, p. 302; Whitmer, *The Inner Elvis*, p. 322; Mann, *Elvis and the Colonel*, p. 128; and interview with Freddy Bienstock.

85–86 the only one who seems to have taken a dim view: Interview with Millie Perkins, 1990, from which all Perkins quotes derive.

85 "I think I won a unique place": Philip Dunne, *Take Two: A Life in Music and Politics*, p. 299.

87 he pulled a derringer: West et al., *Elvis: What Happened?*, p. 258. Alan Fortas in *Elvis: From Memphis to Hollywood*, p. 132, says it was pain pills for a boil that loosened Elvis' inhibitions.

87 he flared up: Fortas, *Elvis: From Memphis to Hollywood*, p. 151; Esposito, *Good Rockin'*, p. 83.

88 Elvis uncharacteristically joined her: Fortas, *Elvis: From Memphis to Hollywood*, p. 130.

88 Anita came out for a brief visit: Anita Wood quoted in Clayton and Heard, *Elvis Up Close*, p. 180. It should be noted that Wood has placed the date of this event in various interviews at several different junctures, including the filming of *Blue Hawaii* five or six months later. Because May Mann has Anita visiting at this time (*Elvis and the Colonel*, pp. 116–117), and because of the date of Elvis and Anita's breakup in the summer of 1962, I have chosen this particular version as the earliest dating of the argument, though I think it more than likely the same discussion arose more than once.

88 "We'd just spend hours dancing": Interview with Sandy Martindale.

89 The movie was briefly threatened: Dunne, *Take Two*, p. 295.

89 given just one week off: Ticket receipts for four for return flight from Memphis January 2 (EPE).

89 he and his daddy quietly agreed: Arlene Cogan is quoted as believing that it was the drapes that were the issue in Clayton and Heard, *Elvis Up Close*, p. 182; also, interview with Lillian Fortenberry.

89 "There will be no passes": *Memphis Press-Scimitar*, December 20, 1960.

89 there was a small party: A photograph of the party, with cast and cake, is in Fortas, *Elvis: From Memphis to Hollywood*, p. 130.

89 he was recalled: *Memphis Press-Scimitar*, February 5, 1961.

THE COLONEL'S SECRET

91 "Parker said Elvis was coming": Sue Wiegert, *"Elvis: Precious Memories,"* vol. 1, p. 97.

91–92 "This is the real McCoy, fellas": *Honolulu Advertiser*, January 12, 1961.

92 "the greatest one-day charity show": *Memphis Press-Scimitar*, February 8, 1961.

92 the "Hawaiian story" . . . that he had first proposed: Colonel letter to Hal Wallis, December 13, 1958 (HWC/MPASL).

92 "sold out for motion pictures through 1965": Letter to Bill Bullock, January 20, 1961 (EPE).

92–93 "Just remember, boys": Joe Esposito, *Good Rockin' Tonight*, p. 60. Esposito has this taking place at Graceland, but given the Colonel's excitement and the fact that Elvis was only released by Fox on that day, there seems little doubt that if the Colonel visited anywhere, it was Perugia Way. Alan Fortas has the Colonel calling Elvis and the guys to the studio at 10:30 in the morning and getting MGM to throw in an ashtray, though he dates this as 1963 in *Elvis: From Memphis to Hollywood*, pp. 213, 216.

93 yet another twist: This was proposed at a January 16, 1961, meeting, whose minutes reveal that Colonel claimed to be bypassing a lucrative Australian appearance for the charity concert. Colonel proposed that the television show could end with Elvis on a flower-strewn barge at the *Arizona* memorial singing "Peace in the Valley." Lastfogel's comment stems from this same meeting (EPE).

93 its closets still filled with Gladys' clothing: Billy Stanley, *Elvis, My Brother*, p. 5.

93 the flowers that were delivered: Bills for weekly order (EPE).

93 he drove down to Tupelo: Interview with Joe Esposito, 1990; see also reference to this trip at the February 25 press conference for the Memphis charity concert.

94 He couldn't help but feel: Elvis' disappointment about the lack of progress on the park was frequently and volubly expressed. See also Jerry Hopkins interviews with Jim Ballard, J. M. Savery, and John Tidwell, as well as articles in the *Tupelo Daily Journal* on August 26, 1960, June 8, 1962, and October 18, 1965, among others, on the (very slow) rate of progress. The view of East Tupeloans in general that they were somehow being shunted aside was expressed both to me and to Elaine Dundy by Tupelo historian Roy Turner.

94 Gene's brother, Junior, died: Alanna Nash, *Elvis Aaron Presley: Revelations from the Memphis Mafia*, p. 213; interview with Joe Esposito, 1990.

94 "I can see him just standing there": Interview with Eddie Fadal, 1993.

94–95 "He had a fear": Nash, *Elvis Aaron Presley*, p. 207.

95–96 the latest in a series of letters: Much of the information about the Colonel's background in Breda, and his family's discovery of his fame, comes from the Dutch journalist Dirk Vellenga, who, in addition to his published work, *Elvis and the Colonel*, generously shared his manuscript and views with me.

97 Elvis held a rehearsal: *Memphis Press-Scimitar,* February 25, 1961; interview with Scotty Moore, 1990. See also the Hawaii press conference.

97–98 The matinee performance: *Memphis Commercial Appeal,* February 26, 1961; *Memphis Press-Scimitar,* February 27, 1961.

98 "He just had kind of an effervescence": Jerry Hopkins interview with Ray Walker, 1971 (MVC/UMem).

98 On the way back to Memphis: *Nashville Banner,* March 9, 1961; Colin Escott liner notes to Prisonaires CD on Bear Family Records.

99 just twelve songs were recorded: One, "I Feel So Bad," was eventually removed from the album lineup to be released as a single.

99–100 Julian Aberbach invited Robertson: Bar Biszick interview with Don Robertson, 1993.

100 "I sat in the control room": Interview with Don Robertson, 1989.

101–102 "I didn't know what staying with Elvis involved": Shelley Ritter interview with Minnie Pearl, 1990.

102 The press conference was scheduled: *Honolulu Sunday Advertiser,* March 26, 1961.

103 "one of the highlights": Jan-Erik Kjeseth interview with Boots Randolph, *Elvis: The Man and His Music* 8, September 1990, p. 27. Gordon Stoker and Ray Walker describe Elvis' spontaneity in their 1971 interview with Jerry Hopkins, and Walker has Elvis sliding across the stage (MVC/UMem).

104 Hal Wallis had to move the female cast: Fortas, *Elvis: From Memphis to Hollywood,* p. 165.

104 Wallis had little use for the guys: Ibid., p. 168.

104 Elvis got together with Patti Page: English music weekly article on Charles O'Curran, c. summer 1961; Colin Escott interview with Patti Page.

104 he interviewed tourists: Jerry Hopkins interview with Ron Jacobs (MVC/UMem). Alan Fortas has a variant on this story in *Elvis: From Memphis to Hollywood,* p. 162.

104 hypnotized the boys: Fortas, *Elvis: From Memphis to Hollywood,* p. 165.

104 and halted shooting one day: This is an oft-repeated story with many variants. This version stems from Allan Weiss' interview for the documentary *Elvis in Hollywood;* Jerry Hopkins' interview with Ron Jacobs; and my interviews with Al Dvorin, 1996–1998, who has the Colonel charging for his own walk-on.

105 "and he [was] telling all the crew": Red West et al., *Elvis: What Happened?,* p. 260.

105 "We had all been drinking": Ibid., pp. 260–261; Fortas recounts the same incident in *Elvis: From Memphis to Hollywood,* p. 145; Albert Goldman has another variant in *Elvis,* p. 336.

105–106 To Hal Kanter: Interview with Hal Kanter, 1993.

106 "It was a while before he came over": Interview with Anne Fulchino, 1993.

106 one of those tricks: Fortas, *Elvis: From Memphis to Hollywood,* p. 171.

106–107 Patti Parry, an eighteen-year-old hairdresser: Interviews with Pat Parry, 1991 and 1995.

107 Once again she came across evidence: BBC interview with Anita Wood.

107 "I'll Wait Forever": The single, Sun 361, was released on June 25, 1961.

108 "we feel it proper": Colonel's telegram to Vice President Johnson, April 22, 1961.

108 He had created his own world: All information on the Snowmen's League, including booklet and member correspondence, is from EPE. See photo section of Larry Geller and Joel Spector's "*If I Can Dream: Elvis' Own Story,*" for reproduction of cover and table of contents.

109 he was furious at his brother: Vellenga manuscript, pp. 189–192.

109–111 The man known as Colonel: This bare-bones outline of the Colonel's Dutch biography and early experiences in America is dependent upon research kindly supplied by Dirk Vellenga.

110 His mother started getting bank drafts: According to Vellenga, this was the outgrowth of an army program to encourage soldiers to help out their dependents.

111–112 "Sometimes we had to live on a dollar a week": This and most of the rest of the account of Ad's visit is from the *Rosita* article appearing in three successive weekly issues from July 1, 1961. It was translated by Sander Donkers. Some additional details were furnished by Dirk Vellenga from his interviews with the family.

111 the Colonel simply introduced Ad as "my brother": There is much debate about whether or not Elvis deduced from this anything of the Colonel's origins — or whether, more in keeping with the Colonel's sense of humor, Ad simply remained mute. Lamar Fike told me that he thought Elvis suspected, but in Nash, *Elvis Aaron Presley*, p. 65, he expresses his certainty that Elvis did not know. In a 1990 interview Gabe Tucker spoke of "Elvis' suspicion that that's the part of the world he come from," but I suspect Lamar is right when he says in the Nash book that if Elvis *had* known, he never could have kept it secret. Just how widespread the knowledge was in Holland is indicated by numerous conversations I have had with Dutch fans and writers over the years and the 1970 publication in English of Hans Langbroek's *The Hillbilly Cat*, setting forth the basic facts before any non-Dutch researcher had come across them.

111–112 the only acknowledgment they ever got: Vellenga manuscript and correspondence.

112 pressure from Steve Sholes and Bill Bullock: Bullock letter to Colonel, May 4, 1961 (EPE).

112 The idea of a home studio: *Memphis Press-Scimitar*, March 30, 1961.

112 Bullock wrote to the Colonel: May 4 letter. The Colonel's response came the next day, touching on everything from poor singles selection by RCA to threats of audits on foreign sales to the fact that Elvis would have no interest in a studio of his own anyway.

112 two other Pomus-Shuman contributions: Trevor Cajiao interview with Mort Shuman, *Elvis: The Man and His Music* 8, September 1990; interview with Doc Pomus, 1984.

113 Red had actually been writing songs: Background on Red West's songwriting comes primarily from various interviews by Trevor Cajiao in *Elvis: The Man and His Music* and *Now Dig This!*; also Jerry Hopkins interview with Red West (MVC/UMem). Both "Big, Big World" and "A Thousand Years," the back of Pat Boone's number-one hit "Moody River," charted in May 1961.

113 to get Hill and Range interested: Tom Diskin wrote Freddy Bienstock a number of letters about Red between January and May 1961. Freddy appears totally indifferent until on May 19 Diskin stipulates that Elvis is "interested in the song 'You'll Be Gone'" (EPE).

113 He had fooled around with it: Jerry Hopkins interview with Red West (MVC/UMem); Red spoke to me about the origin of the song in 1989.

113 Red got married: *Memphis Commercial Appeal*, July 1, 1961; interview with Joe Esposito, 1990.

113 after a riotous Fourth of July fireworks fight: Rick Husky, "My Amazing Weekend with Elvis," *Movieland and TV Times*, October 1961.

113 he and the guys all left: Fortas, *Elvis: From Memphis to Hollywood*, p. 177; Nash, *Elvis Aaron Presley*, p. 225; various local Florida clippings supplied by Bill Bram.

114 the bizarrely paranormal proceedings: Ger Rijff and Jan van Gestel, *Elvis: The Cool King*, pp. 8ff; various local accounts (clippings and interviews) supplied by Bill Bram.

114 he even visited an elephant: Goldman, *Elvis*, p. 133.

114 to get rid of a recent addition: Fortas, *Elvis: From Memphis to Hollywood*, p. 232; Nash, *Elvis Aaron Presley*, p. 230; interview with Joe Esposito, 1997.

114 The director, Gordon Douglas: Jerry Hopkins interview with Gene Nelson (MVC/UMem).

114–116 Annie Helm, who was playing the ingenue role: Most biographical information and all quotes from interview with Anne Helm, 1995.

116 The Colonel joked: Fortas, *Elvis: From Memphis to Hollywood*, p. 173; Nash, *Elvis Aaron Presley*, p. 258.

116 "it was a party": Interview with Joe Esposito, 1990.

116 his weight had ballooned: *Memphis Press-Scimitar*, April 3, 1963. In this interview Elvis says that his weight was up to 197 pounds during the making of *Kid Galahad*.

116 "a muscle-bound ape": West et al., *Elvis: What Happened?*, p. 263.

116 they moved into a new house: Nash, *Elvis Aaron Presley*, p. 190; Esposito, *Good Rockin'*, p. 95; interview with Joe Esposito, 1997.

116 Elvis took a liking to Sonny's girl: Marty Lacker et al., *Elvis: Portrait of a Friend*, p. 39.

116–117 Marty Lacker, a friend of George Klein's: Fortas, *Elvis: From Memphis to Hollywood*, p. 187; Nash, *Elvis Aaron Presley*, p. 233.

117 a chimpanzee named Scatter: Bill E. Burk, *Elvis Through My Eyes*, p. 183; *The Record*, vol. 1, no. 8, p. 17; Fortas, *From Memphis to Hollywood*, p. 195. His biting of Dee Presley is described in Dee Presley et al., *Elvis, We Love You Tender*, p. 68; his wrecking of the hotel room is detailed in Nash, *Elvis Aaron Presley*, p. 239; his exhibitionism is described everywhere.

117 When there was nothing else to talk about: Interview with Jan Walner, 1991.

117 a three-bedroom, split-level ranch: The January 21, 1962, *Memphis Commercial Appeal* describes the house and has the Vernon Presleys moving in "shortly after Christmas."

117 The original plan: Patsy Andersen, "Farewell to Elvis' Friend, Alan Fortas," *Graceland Express*, vol. 7, no. 3, 1992.

117–118 Joe started dating Joanie: Interviews with Joe Esposito, 1990, and Joan Esposito, 1995.

118 the songwriter Don Robertson: Interview with Don Robertson.

118 Three times they set out: Nash, *Elvis Aaron Presley*, p. 236; interview with Joe Esposito, 1990.

119 time was meaningless: John L. Smith, "Longtime friend of Elvis reveals truth beyond the icon" (article on Joe Esposito in Las Vegas newspaper, February 1995).

NEGLECTED DREAMS

121 over a year now: First mention of looking into rights situation with "Begin the Beguine" in letter from Tom Diskin to Freddy Bienstock, January 3, 1961 (EPE).

122 to claim actual authorship: "I've never written a song in my life," Elvis declared in numerous early interviews. To *Dig* magazine in 1957 he responded to a question about his early songwriting credits with more than a trace of self-consciousness. "It's all a big hoax. It makes me look smarter than I am," he said, though he admitted reluctantly that he had had "an idea for a song. Just once" (*Dig*, 1958).

122 "he always tried to make the best": Ernst Jorgensen interview with Gordon Stoker.

123 far outstripping any studio album: Elvis' biggest album seller to date, *Elvis* (his second LP, which came out in 1956), had sold little more than 500,000 copies.

123 there was no real need for anything *but* the soundtrack music: The March 1, 1960, RCA contract spelled out that "any musical composition recorded for motion pictures shall be considered a part of this commitment against the eight single record sides and the two long play records required annually" (EPE).

124 "so I had my mom come pick me up": Interview with Sandy Martindale, 1995.

124 the girl that Sonny brought: Red West et al., *Elvis: What Happened?*, pp. 27ff; also, Alan Fortas, *Elvis: From Memphis to Hollywood*, p. 152; interview with Jan Walner, 1991; Patsy Guy Hammontree, *Elvis Presley: A Bio-Bibliography*, p. 49.

124–125 "He was so retarded": Interview with Jan Walner.

125 the two-way mirror: Fortas, *Elvis: From Memphis to Hollywood*, pp. 139, 191; West et al., *Elvis: What Happened?*, p. 279.

125 crawling under the house: Fortas, *Elvis: From Memphis to Hollywood*, p. 191; Fortas quoted in Rose Clayton and Dick Heard, eds., *Elvis Up Close: In the Words of Those Who Knew Him Best*, p. 188.

125 "a gift of the gods": Billy Stanley, *Elvis, My Brother*, p. 37; also, 1962 interview with Lloyd Shearer. The information about the football games comes from numerous interviews and written accounts.

125–126 Barris, the thirty-seven-year-old "King of the Kustomizers": Interview with George Barris, 1995.

126 put up a houseguest: Interview with George Barris. At first Elvis thought of Hal Wallis, according to Priscilla Presley (1995 interview).

126 He had started talking: Priscilla Presley, *Elvis and Me*, p. 67; interview with Priscilla Presley.

127 With Joe's cooperation: Interviews with Joe Esposito, 1990, and Joan Esposito, 1995.

127 Elvis sat all the girls down: Interview with Pat Parry, 1995; also Joe Esposito, *Good Rockin' Tonight*, pp. 94–95.

127 Joe picked her up: Esposito, *Good Rockin'*, pp. 94–95.

127 They were met: Priscilla Presley, *Elvis and Me*, p. 69.

127–128 She wondered who was this . . . man: Ibid., pp. 70, 71; interview with Priscilla Presley.

128 "It was a shock": Interview with Priscilla Presley.

128 "Wait a minute, baby": Priscilla Presley, *Elvis and Me*, pp. 73–74.

129 "We drove all over": Interview with Priscilla Presley.

129 Every so often Gene would pounce: Gene Smith, *Elvis's Man Friday*, pp. 258–259.

129 "Do you believe this, baby?": Priscilla Presley, *Elvis and Me*, p. 79.

130 "[It was like] he'd decided": Interview with Priscilla Presley.

130 she made the mistake: Priscilla Presley, *Elvis and Me*, p. 83.

130 "there were definitely rules": Interview with Priscilla Presley.

130 "he fulfilled my every desire": Priscilla Presley, *Elvis and Me*, p. 92.

130–131 "my mother was crying with joy": Ibid., p. 93.

131 Elvis proudly showed off: Interviews with Barbara Bobo, 1992, and Bettye Berger, 1989.

131 There were lots of pills: Fortas, *Elvis: From Memphis to Hollywood*, p. 201.

131 "I wanted a husband": BBC interview with Anita Wood.

132 she released a statement to the paper: "Elvis' Long-Time Girlfriend Anita Wood — Says It's All Over," *Memphis Press-Scimitar*, August 6, 1962.

133 removing all the furniture: Fortas, *Elvis: From Memphis to Hollywood*, p. 201.

133 the new continental wardrobe: "Just a Drab Butterfly," *Seattle Post-Intelligencer*, September 17, 1962.

133 this was the interview: Lloyd Shearer interview for *Parade* magazine, August 6, 1956.

133 the second time around: Lloyd Shearer, "Elvis Presley: How He Changed His Public Image," *Parade*, November 4, 1962. Elvis' actual income for 1961 might have been closer to the tax figure cited above.

133 from "ever making a wrong move": Interview with Marion Keisker, 1982.

133–136 "I don't assume": This, and all subsequent quotes, are from Shearer's on-set interview, first released by RCA as a promotional LP in 1985.

136 he would appear in forty-three cities: Undated two-page proposal, specifying that All Star Shows would have "sole direction" and RCA "no voice in the presentation in any manner of the Elvis Presley show or its talent." Bullock's counterproposal is noted drily on a brief postscript (EPE).

137 Colonel had induced RCA: August 2 and 30, 1962, memos with respect to contract to take effect September 1 (EPE).

138 Gene had been driving: Alanna Nash, *Elvis Aaron Presley: Revelations from the Memphis Mafia*, p. 250; Fortas, *Elvis: From Memphis to Hollywood*, p. 200; Smith, *Elvis's Man*, p. 273; Charles C. Thompson II and James P. Cole, *The Death of Elvis*, p. 181. Both the amount of medication and the direction of the trip vary from account to account.

138 "there was a Judas": Nash, *Elvis Aaron Presley*, p. 274.

138 Richard Davis and Jimmy Kingsley: Fortas, *Elvis: From Memphis to Hollywood*, p. 236; interview with Richard Davis, 1990.

139 she could stay with his father and stepmother: The original plan appears to have been for Joan Esposito, who had just given birth to her first child a month before, to fly to Germany to accompany Priscilla on the flight (Suzanne Finstad, *Child Bride: The Untold Story of Priscilla Beaulieu Presley*, p. 144).

139–140 The whole gang was waiting: Priscilla Presley, *Elvis and Me*, pp. 97ff. The primary basis for this account of Priscilla's visit is her book, and all quotes from Priscilla Presley come from that source.

140–141 "From the moment I got off the plane": Ibid., pp. 111ff.

141 wearing a cape: Interview with Pat Parry, 1991.

141 Colonel put the kibosh on that: Paul Nathan memo to Hal Wallis, June 1, 1962, on the Colonel's reluctance to travel to Mexico (EPE).

141–142 he would teach her: Priscilla Presley, *Elvis and Me*, p. 115; interviews with Linda Thompson and Sandy Martindale touching on this subject.

142 "it took a while": Interview with Priscilla Presley.

142 NO ONE BELONGS IN THE OFFICE: Priscilla Presley, *Elvis and Me*, p. 120.

142 "Any time Elvis failed to call": Ibid., p. 123.

143 a pretty little bright red Corvair: *Memphis Press-Scimitar*, April 2, 1962. This same article refers to Priscilla staying with Vernon and Dee because they are friends of the Beaulieu family.

143 "They sent her ahead": *Memphis Commercial Appeal*, April 3, 1963.

144 he gave her extensive instruction: Priscilla Presley, *Elvis and Me*, p. 137.

144 "father and son relaxing": Ibid., p. 192.

144 Sometimes they stopped by: Interview with Priscilla Presley.

144 the exotic menu: Priscilla Presley, *Elvis and Me*, p. 152.

144 "None of them felt comfortable with me": Interview with Priscilla Presley.

145 "It was not that she was immature": Interview with Joan Esposito, 1995.

145 "I want it to be something to look forward to": Priscilla Presley, *Elvis and Me*, p. 130.

145 "Instead of consummating our love": Ibid., pp. 130–131.

146 she couldn't stand to have any of the guys see her: Fortas, *Elvis: From Memphis to Holly-wood*, p. 209.

146 "Finally I worked up enough courage": Priscilla Presley, *Elvis and Me*, p. 156.

146–147 For much of the next three weeks: Ibid., pp. 157–159.

149 "Elvis makes a face": *McCall's* article quoted in *Ann-Margret: My Story*, p. 110.

149 "This is news to make the younger set flip": Bob Thomas, "It Looks Like Romance for Presley and Ann-Margret," *Memphis Press-Scimitar*, August 6, 1963.

149–150 "Music ignited a fiery pent-up passion": This and subsequent quotes by Ann-Margret are from *Ann-Margret*, pp. 110–112.

150 "Ann was wonderful": Interview with Joan Esposito.

150 "She was his alter ego": Interview with Sandy Martindale.

150 never seen Elvis happier: Shelley Ritter interview with George Klein.

150 "She had spirit": Interview with Pat Parry, 1991.

151 "He'd describe her": *Ann-Margret*, pp. 116–117.

151–152 For once Parker was stymied: Esposito, *Good Rockin'*, p. 97; interviews with Andrew Solt, Joe Esposito, and Jerry Schilling.

151–152 the director was giving the girl: According to *Ann-Margret*, p. 99, George Sidney had put up $60,000 of his own money to shoot a new beginning and ending for *Bye Bye Birdie* that would provide a showcase for her performance alone.

152 Colonel Parker fought back: Esposito, *Good Rockin'*, p. 98; Priscilla Presley, *Elvis and Me*, p. 167; Colonel's subsequent correspondence with MGM in the spring of 1964 (EPE).

152–153 What galled him most: Colonel–MGM correspondence from April 1964 through an undated "Summary of Publicity and Promotion and Exploitation Activities . . . carried out by Colonel Tom Parker," all of which highlight MGM's supreme confidence and the Colonel's cold fury (EPE).

153 "problems on the set": Priscilla Presley, *Elvis and Me*, p. 167.

153 Elvis came straight home: The *Memphis Press-Scimitar* of September 21, 1963, has him home on that date.

155 he and Karger had preselected: Gene Nelson letter to Elvis, September 19, 1963 (EPE); interview with Gene Nelson, 1995.

155 the "hillbilly" flavor of the picture: Peter Cronin interview with Boots Randolph, 1993.

155 Jerry Kennedy . . . felt sorry for Elvis: Interview with Jerry Kennedy, 1990.

155–156 Katzman liked to boast: Bob Thomas, "Katzman Making Big Money Film," AP dispatch, November 1963. Further biographical detail on Katzman and his picture-making methods from Gene Nelson interview and Jerry Hopkins interview with Sam Katzman (MVC/UMem).

156–159 "talk myself into liking that kind of music": Interview with Gene Nelson.

158 "I hadn't learned the patience": Jerry Hopkins interview with Gene Nelson (MVC/UMem). It should be noted that Nelson also assigned this story to the shooting of his subsequent picture with Elvis, *Harum Scarum*, but at whichever point it occurred the moral is the same.

159 according to his co-star: Jerry Hopkins interview with Yvonne Craig (MVC/UMem).

159 As perceived by LeGault: Jerry Hopkins interview with Lance LeGault (MVC/UMem).

160 "Elvis Wins Love of Ann-Margret": *Memphis Commercial Appeal*, November 8, 1963.

160 "I can't believe she did it": Priscilla Presley, *Elvis and Me*, p. 176.

160 "I couldn't believe what I was hearing": Ibid.

161 "Elvis was very honest": Interview with Priscilla Presley.

161 Ann-Margret called him from London: *Ann-Margret*, p. 118.

161 "I drove to Elvis' house": Ibid., p. 121.

161 too much of a coward: Fortas, *Elvis: From Memphis to Hollywood*, p. 273.

161 in a modest ceremony: *Memphis Press-Scimitar*, December 17, 1963.

161 under somewhat shadowy circumstances: Smith, *Elvis's Man*, p. 275; Nash, *Elvis Aaron Presley*, p. 251.

162 He even purchased a wedding ring: Connie Lauridsen Burk, "Twice!!," *Elvis World* 37; interview with Harry Levitch, 1995.

162 sales were substantially down: The one exception was *Elvis' Golden Records Volume 3*, a greatest-hits compilation which sold almost a million copies after the Colonel dictated its precise makeup down to the most prosaic elements of the artwork and got $75,000 (to be split 50–50 with his client after expenses) as a flat price for 275,000 souvenir photo albums tied in to his granting of permission for this unscheduled release (RCA agreement May 21, 1963 [EPE]).

164 with a guaranteed income from RCA: RCA exercised its option to extend Elvis' recording contract for another two years on December 17, 1963, thereby assuring a comfortable level of income at least through 1971 (EPE).

164 "Our gimmicks work": Colonel to George Parkhill, February 15, 1963 (EPE).

164 "Look, you got a product": Michael Fessier, Jr., "Elvis Hits $20,000,000 Gross Jackpot," *Variety,* January 15, 1964. This article details the Colonel's positive financial frame of mind — and shows solid grounds for his optimism.

165 Elvis to him looked "fat": Hal Wallis to Colonel Parker, December 10, 1963 (HWC/MPASL).

165 He reiterated his concerns: Wallis to Colonel, January 28, 1964 (HWC/MPASL). Wallis' concerns no doubt were influenced by the precipitous drop in profit levels, from $832,000 for *G.I. Blues* and $1,015,000 for *Blue Hawaii* in 1961 to just $30,000 for 1962's *Girls! Girls! Girls!* and a substantial loss ($350,000) on the previous year's *Fun in Acapulco* (figures from Frank Rose, *The Agency: William Morris and the Hidden History of Show Business,* p. 268).

165 the Colonel agreed with him: The Colonel's reply, same day (HWC/MPASL).

165 a production schedule: Elvis was paid for eight weeks, plus one week of preproduction, but shooting occurred during only six of them, thereby cutting down considerably on expenses.

165 The idea for a picture: There is talk with Wallis about this picture going back to 1961 (HWC/MPASL), and gossip items concerning a film on the Colonel's experiences starring Elvis begin at least as early.

165 all kinds of suggestions: Colonel to Wallis, summer and fall 1963 (HWC/MPASL). Also, interview with Allan Weiss for *Elvis in Hollywood,* 1993.

165 a wholesome way of life: Interview with Allan Weiss for *Elvis in Hollywood.*

166 he should be paid for it: Tom Diskin to Hal Wallis, September 9, 1963 (HWC/MPASL).

166 on the outs with Vernon: Nash, *Elvis Aaron Presley,* p. 246.

166–167 "Elvis kept telling me": Marty Lacker et al., *Elvis: Portrait of a Friend,* pp. 46–48.

167 "The damn thing was packed so full of pills": Ibid., p. 348.

168 Finally, on February 14: Grelun Landon press kit prepared for RCA on the sale of the *Potomac; Memphis Commercial Appeal,* February 15, 1964; Fortas, *Elvis: From Memphis to Hollywood,* p. 230; interview material from Grelun Landon, Joe Esposito, et al.

168 Elvis was furious: Nash, *Elvis Aaron Presley,* p. 312.

168 he had been proud: Roosevelt and his adviser, Harry Hopkins, went on a cruise of the Bahamas on the *Potomac* immediately following the passage of Lend Lease in March of 1941 (Robert E. Sherwood, *Roosevelt and Hopkins*). Elvis told Jerry Schilling that many of the elements that went into the Atlantic Charter (signed in August) were discussed onboard.

168 Elvis had finally decided: Just how important "Memphis" was to Elvis is indicated by Colonel–RCA paperwork on January 12 and 13 considering (and then rejecting) its release as the next single (EPE).

169–170 "I didn't know too much": Interview with John Rich, 1996.

170 the score was almost embarrassingly bad: Even Hal Wallis expressed his dissatisfaction in a communiqué to his assistant Paul Nathan on March 6, 1964. Elvis' unhappiness is indicated by a letter from Nathan to Tom Diskin on the same date (HWC/MPASL).

170 continued friction between Rich and the guys: West et al., *Elvis: What Happened?,* p. 269; interview with John Rich.

170 "Wallis kept the screenplays shallow": Interview with Allan Weiss for *Elvis in Hollywood.*

171 It confirmed all of Elvis' worst fears: West et al., *Elvis: What Happened?,* p. 273; Larry Geller and Joel Spector, *"If I Can Dream": Elvis' Own Story,* p. 154; Nash, *Elvis Aaron Presley,* p. 358; interview with Jerry Schilling, 1995.

SPIRITUAL AWAKENINGS

173–175 a twenty-four-year-old hairdresser named Larry Geller: Background information, as well as the account of Geller and Elvis' first meetings, comes from Larry Geller and Joel Spector, *"If I Can Dream": Elvis' Own Story;* interview with Larry Geller, 1989; Rose Clayton and Dick Heard, eds., interview with Larry Geller, *Elvis Up Close: In the Words of Those Who Knew Him Best,* pp. 208–209; Jess Stearn, *The Truth About Elvis;* and interview with Johnny Rivers, 1995.

176 Joe Esposito . . . was willing to give him the benefit of the doubt: Interviews with Joe Esposito, 1990, 1996.

176–177 "He was always gullible": Interview with Joe Esposito, 1990.

177 Some of them started: Stearn, *The Truth,* pp. 27–28.

177 mostly what they felt: Alan Fortas, *Elvis: From Memphis to Hollywood,* p. 234; Alanna Nash, *Elvis Aaron Presley: Revelations from the Memphis Mafia,* p. 318; interview with Pat Parry, 1991.

177 Elvis made a few perfunctory attempts: Interviews with Joe Esposito and Charlie Hodge.

177 "The spirituality was always there": Interview with Sandy Martindale, 1995.

177 The Elvis that Larry saw: Interview with Larry Geller; Geller and Spector, *"If,"* p. 269.

177 "When Elvis appreciated something": Interview with Larry Geller.

177 "His intuition was highly developed": Geller and Spector, *"If,"* p. 139.

178 "[He] was requesting a new book": Ibid., pp. 99–100.

178 His original idea, while at Columbia: Jerry Hopkins interview with Joe Pasternak (MVC/UMem).

178 Elvis seemed uncharacteristically subdued: Fortas, *Elvis: From Memphis to Hollywood,* p. 233.

179 Colonel was absent with back trouble: Colonel correspondence, spring through fall 1964 (EPE).

179 an interview to gossip columnist Earl Wilson: Undated clip, on *Girl Happy* set.

179 Each night on the phone: Interview with Priscilla Presley, 1995.

180 There was no question among any of the guys: Fortas, *Elvis: From Memphis to Hollywood,* p. 227; Nash, *Elvis Aaron Presley,* p. 202; Marty Lacker et al., *Elvis: Portrait of a Friend,* p. 203; interviews with Joe Esposito, Jerry Schilling, Red West, et al. It should be noted that Johnny Rivers today denies both the knowledge and the rift.

180 glowing reports: MGM internal reports, May–June 1964 (EPE).

180 Colonel asked to meet: Geller and Spector, *"If,"* p. 83; Stearn, *The Truth,* p. 29.

181 "Elvis is driving": Interview with Larry Geller.

181–182 "And what a trip it was": Geller and Spector, *"If,"* pp. 59–60.

182 "It was about four o'clock": Interview with Joe Esposito, 1996.

183 "I'm sure Vernon saw me": Geller and Spector, *"If,"* p. 63.

183 "Larry was a total threat": Interview with Priscilla Presley.

183 "He came at me": Geller and Spector, *"If,"* p. 76.

183 "that you don't always get him": Stearn, *The Truth,* p. 36.

184 It was a very different group: Nash, *Elvis Aaron Presley,* p. 314.

184 "along with Marty, be responsible for Organization": Fortas, *Elvis: From Memphis to Hollywood,* p. 239.

184 Marty and his family: Nash, *Elvis Aaron Presley,* p. 316.

184 He told Morris: Ada Gilkey, "Elvis Presley Gets Promotion — by the New Sheriff," *Memphis Press-Scimitar,* September 23, 1964.

185–187 Jerry Schilling was twenty-two years old: This and subsequent quotes and background information come from interviews with Jerry Schilling, 1990–1998.

185 He was perceived as a "liberal": Nash, *Elvis Aaron Presley*, p. 322.

187 Elvis' $750,000 salary: Thomas M. Pryor, "Presley As Top-Money Star," *Variety*, July 23, 1965.

187–188 Earlier in the year: Abe Lastfogel's letter to Steve Broidy of June 12, 1964 (EPE), refers to the Colonel's offer of "several months ago"; see also " 'Tickle'-d?' Allied Artists Ecstatic," *Variety*, July 28, 1965.

188 Colonel wrote to Elvis: Colonel to Elvis, August 21, 1964; Elvis' telegrammed reply is merely stamped "September 1964" (EPE).

189 the highest-paid star: That this was a common perception is indicated by Hedda Hopper's column of January 31, 1965, in which Elvis was referred to as the "highest paid star in the business" as well as *Variety*, July 23, 1965 (Vincent Canby, "[Presley] Bests Liz, Cary, Audrey Income").

189 "We're doing all right": Peter Bart, "Hollywood: Money Man from Memphis," *New York Times*, November 22, 1964.

189–190 Marty went out: Lacker et al., *Portrait*, p. 101.

190 He refused to accept their present: Stearn, *The Truth*, p. 33.

190 he was busted for marijuana: Geller and Spector, *"If,"* pp. 89, 93–94; Nash, *Elvis Aaron Presley*, p. 373.

190 "rabbis change people's names": Geller and Spector, *"If,"* pp. 67–69.

190 he and Elvis came up with an idea: Lacker et al., *Portrait*, p. 63; also interview with Harry Levitch, 1995. Levitch and Elvis' dentist, Les Hofman, and his wife, Sterling, spoke to me about the strong impact of Judaism on Elvis, and Levitch described Elvis taking him out to the cemetery to show off the newly engraved Star of David on his mother's grave.

190 Marty was convinced: Nash, *Elvis Aaron Presley*, p. 387.

190–191 Elvis' uncle Johnny Smith: Ibid., p. 422; Lacker et al., *Portrait*, p. 235.

191 "I got my nerves in the dirt": Nash, *Elvis Aaron Presley*, p. 419; Priscilla Presley, *Elvis and Me*, p. 146.

191 Larry's perspective: Geller and Spector, *"If,"* p. 87.

191 Vernon . . . "lived in constant fear": Ibid., p. 159.

191–192 "going through a cleansing period": Priscilla Presley, *Elvis and Me*, p. 206.

192–193 he reflected a little: James Kingsley, "At Home with Elvis Presley," *Memphis Commercial Appeal*, March 7, 1965.

194–196 He had it out with Larry: Geller and Spector, *"If,"* pp. 107–110.

196 He just wanted to quit the business: Ibid., p. 112; Stearn, *The Truth*, p. 50; interview with Larry Geller; Peter Whitmer, *The Inner Elvis: A Psychological Biography of Elvis Aaron Presley*, pp. 352ff.

196–197 he was excited about the costumes: Priscilla Presley, *Elvis and Me*, p. 211; interview with Gene Nelson, 1995.

197 "Someday we'll do it right": Jerry Hopkins interview with Gene Nelson (MVC/UMem).

197–198 The Self-Realization Fellowship: Background on the Self-Realization Fellowship from information supplied by Karen Lanza at the Fellowship.

197 "a Hindu invading": *Los Angeles Times*, January 28, 1925.

198 "The absence of any visible signs": Paramahansa Yogananda, *Autobiography of a Yogi*, p. 478.

198 a monk named Brother Adolph: Geller and Spector, *"If,"* p. 133; interviews with Larry Geller, 1989, and Sri Daya Mata, 1996.

198–200 he met fifty-year-old Daya Mata: Interview with Sri Daya Mata. This conversation was bounded by Sri Daya Mata's observance of appropriate rules of confidentiality with respect to private confidences and revelations.

200 his almost daily visions: Interviews with Jerry Schilling, Joe Esposito, et al.; virtually every memoir; Albert Goldman, *Elvis*, p. 370; Whitmer, *The Inner Elvis*, p. 352.

200 evenings of philosophical discussion: Geller and Spector, *"If,"* pp. 96, 98; interviews with Joe Esposito, Jerry Schilling.

201 "one night, after I'd probably been up three days": Nash, *Elvis Aaron Presley*, pp. 329–330; Lacker et al., *Portrait*, p. 349. Alan Fortas writes of the drugs in *Elvis: From Memphis to Hollywood*, p. 268.

201 daily steam baths: Marge Crumbaker and Gabe Tucker, *Up and Down with Elvis Presley*, pp. 115–116; interviews with Jerry Schilling and Susan Aberbach. It is Tucker who speaks of the Colonel reorganizing the freezer.

201 "The big shots are afraid": C. Robert Jennings, "There'll Always Be an Elvis," *Saturday Evening Post*, September 11, 1965.

202 "Sooner or later someone else": Chris Hutchins, "Colonel Tom Parker's Retirement," *New Musical Express*, January 1966.

202 Parker was more than capable: Crumbaker and Tucker, *Up and Down*, pp. 112, 115, 144, 145.

202–203 his devastating split with Eddy Arnold: This is documented in the Colonel's anguished letter to Arnold on August 29, 1953 (EPE).

203 he vigorously promoted *Tickle Me*: This is borne out by numerous bills and letters from February 11, 1965 (EPE).

203 the picture saved Allied Artists: *Variety*, July 23, 1965.

204 a talking camel as narrator: Letter to Robert O'Brien, July 16, 1965. See also June 18 letter to Robert Whiteman with various other suggestions and observations (EPE).

204 nine Triumphs in the yard: Interviews with George Barris, Joe Esposito, Jerry Schilling, et al.; Fortas, *Elvis: From Memphis to Hollywood*, p. 251, plus virtually every other memoir. The number of motorcycles differs in each of these accounts, generally coming out between nine and twelve.

205 "He was so funny": Interview with Joan Esposito, 1995.

205 "I didn't realize": Interviews with Jerry Schilling, 1994, and Priscilla Presley; see also Priscilla Presley, *Elvis and Me*, p. 141.

205 "Joe would say": Interview with Jerry Schilling, 1990.

205 offering little hope of satisfaction: See Whitmer, *The Inner Elvis*, p. 355, on William Morris head Abe Lastfogel's bleak view.

206 Elvis threw a temper tantrum: Fortas, *Elvis: From Memphis to Hollywood*, p. 249.

206 Instead of dating her: Red West et al., *Elvis: What Happened?*, p. 271.

206 "they would go over his marked passages": Stearn, *The Truth*, p. 167.

206 he . . . donated $50,000: UPI report, June 28, 1965.

206 his generosity was viewed cynically: Nash, *Elvis Aaron Presley*, p. 327.

206 the thrill of seeing the expression: Interviews with Joe Esposito; Joe Esposito, *Good Rockin' Tonight*, p. 32; Fortas, *Elvis: From Memphis to Hollywood*, p. 252.

206 "a Band-Aid for the abuse": Nash, *Elvis Aaron Presley*, p. 368.

207 "for the first time . . . since the Beatles": AP report, *Houston Chronicle*, June 9, 1965.

207 he saw the Beatles . . . as a threat: Fortas, *Elvis: From Memphis to Hollywood*, p. 249; Esposito, *Good Rockin'*, p. 106; Nash, *Elvis Aaron Presley*, pp. 296–297.

207 some of the rugged qualities of his *Roustabout* role: Hal Wallis to Colonel, pre-Thanksgiving 1964 (HWC/MPASL).

208 he continued to convey a degree of disappointment: Just how much disappointment is indicated by an August 3, 1965, letter in which Colonel directed his assistant Jim O'Brien to pack up all their trunks "so it looks like we are getting ready to leave" (EPE).

208 he refused to bark like a dog: Paul Nathan to Hal Wallis, August 1965 (HWC/MPASL).

208 "too sick to present himself": Derek Hunter, "Trouble in Paradise," *Movie News*, May 1966.

208 Jerry Schilling fell in love: Interviews with Jerry Schilling.

209 "He was not unfriendly": Interview with Jan Shepard, 1992. See also Sue Wiegert, *Elvis: Precious Memories*, vol. 2, p. 108.

209 Elvis had left his own faith: May Mann, *Elvis and the Colonel*, p. 189.

209–210 Larry watched and wondered: Geller and Spector, *"If,"* pp. 102–104.

210 he had sent a telegram: Chris Hutchins, *Elvis Meets the Beatles*, p. 74.

210–211 Subsequently he had met: Ibid., p. 88; Jerry Hopkins interview with Jack Good (MVC/UMem).

211 There had even been some talk: Paul Nathan to Hal Wallis, November 18, 1964 (HWC/MPASL).

211 Elvis remained at best lukewarm: Esposito, *Good Rockin'*, pp. 106ff.

211 The Beatles arrived: This account of the Beatles' visit is derived primarily from interviews with Joe Esposito, Jerry Schilling, and Larry Geller; Hutchins, *Elvis Meets the Beatles*; Esposito, *Good Rockin'*; Geller and Spector, *"If"*; *The Beatles Anthology* (1995 ABC television special); and Tony Barrow in Spencer Leigh, *Speaking Words of Wisdom*.

212 "[Elvis] was sitting in a helicopter": Clayton and Heard, *Elvis Up Close*, p. 213.

212 "He kept thinking": Interview with Priscilla Presley.

213 On September 21 the deal was finally concluded: This was the date on which Elvis wrote RCA a letter accepting the terms of the agreement. The actual contract, reaffirming those terms, was executed on October 12 (EPE).

213 Colonel was openly jubilant: Fortas, *Elvis: From Memphis to Hollywood*, p. 248.

213 RCA . . . put the best face on the deal: RCA internal memo/publicity release including January 8, 1966, birthday wire to Elvis. See also November 16 publicity release repeating the claim (EPE).

214 he would never do business with the Colonel again: See correspondence throughout the year, primarily between Wallis and Hazen, in which Wallis advises Hazen on October 18 that "this is the agreement and it will have to be signed or we will have to forget about it" and Hazen reacts to one last feint by the Colonel one week later by declaring the new conditions "untenable" and advising that they simply walk away (HWC/MPASL). Also, interview with Joe Hazen, 1993.

214 a new four-picture deal: This was finalized in a memo of January 13, 1966 (EPE).

214 other deals: Within three months Colonel had agreed upon the outlines of an $850,000 deal for a new picture with Steve Broidy, formerly with United Artists (EPE).

214–215 he announced to Elvis: Colonel to Elvis, January 18, 1966 (EPE).

215 "roaring around the drives": *Memphis Press-Scimitar*, October 13, 1965.

215 "a great man and a person that everyone loved": *Memphis Commercial Appeal*, October 22, 1965.

215 the Meditation Garden was completed: Nash, *Elvis Aaron Presley*, pp. 386–387; Lacker et al., *Portrait*, pp. 85–86. In Geller and Spector, *"If,"* Larry Geller writes that he, Marty, and Elvis "designed" the garden but makes clear that "we didn't actually come up with a detailed design or plan for it, but Elvis' ideas about the mood he wanted to create there were very definite" (p. 127).

215 there were "tears of joy": Lacker et al., *Portrait*, p. 86.

215 Vernon refused . . . to provide final payment: It should be noted that the job was not completed until mid December, with the final bill submitted at the end of the month. Vernon paid a balance of $10,148.83 (on a total of $20,912.26) on January 4 (EPE). From Marty's account, it seems evident, however, that some words must have been exchanged.

216 one more example of Vernon's underlying anti-Semitism: Marty Lacker recounts two other incidents convincingly in his book. However, others in the group suggest that Vernon Presley's reaction was characteristically, and always, about money, and — put charitably — stemmed from fears of his son being taken advantage of. These others feel that Vernon was distinctly, and surprisingly, unprejudiced and confined his judgments, right or wrong, to individuals.

216 According to McIntire: Robert Gordon interview with John McIntire; Audrey West, "Idyllic Graceland Setting Includes Sculptor's Work," *Memphis Press-Scimitar,* September 26, 1977; interviews with Jerry Schilling. See also Geller and Spector, *"If,"* p. 127.

216 "You're no good to me anymore": Interview with Jerry Schilling, 1995.

216 "In Elvis' life the outside world was a distant place": Geller and Spector, *"If,"* p. 157.

217 "We were all together so much": Jerry Hopkins interview with Jerry Schilling (MVC/UMem).

217 They celebrated New Year's Eve: *Memphis Commercial Appeal,* January 9, 1966; interview with David Porter, 1995; Donna Lewis, *"Hurry Home, Elvis!": Donna Lewis' Diaries,* vol. 1, p. 82.

217 the slot-car track that Priscilla had given him: *Memphis Press-Scimitar,* December 30, 1965; interview with Joe Esposito, 1996.

217 an expanded setup: Lacker et al., *Portrait,* p. 86.

217–218 Elvis finally tried LSD: Interviews with Jerry Schilling and Larry Geller; Lacker et al., *Portrait,* p. 258; Fortas, *Elvis: From Memphis to Hollywood,* p. 268; West et al., *Elvis: What Happened?,* pp. 280–281; Geller and Spector, *"If,"* p. 149; Priscilla Presley, *Elvis and Me,* p. 213; Esposito, *Good Rockin',* pp. 122–124; Clayton and Heard, *Elvis Up Close,* p. 217; Nash, *Elvis Aaron Presley,* p. 336; Whitmer, *The Inner Elvis,* p. 356. Needless to say, the accounts differ at various points.

218 "About an hour and a half later": Geller and Spector, *"If,"* p. 149.

219 the house was decorated: Interview with Joe Esposito, 1996.

219 Charlie Hodge came back: Jerry Hopkins interview with Red West (MVC/UMem); Sherry Daniel, "Elvis, Charlie and the Music," *DisCoveries,* August 1991.

219 "Priscilla very much wanted": West et al., *Elvis: What Happened?,* p. 271. See also Nash, *Elvis Aaron Presley,* p. 323.

219 "Elvis basically told her": Nash, *Elvis Aaron Presley,* p. 362.

220 "I don't have a goddamn thing to hide": Priscilla Presley, *Elvis and Me,* pp. 179–180; see also West et al., *Elvis: What Happened?,* p. 218.

221 "That's it, that's it," he announced: Geller and Spector, *"If,"* p. 155. Larry places the story during the filming of *Paradise, Hawaiian Style,* but since it hinges on Charlie's return (and in light of others' versions of the same story), I have placed the incident here.

221 He took Priscilla: Ibid., p. 210; interview with Sri Daya Mata.

221 Greyhound D'Elegance coach, fully outfitted: Interview with George Barris.

221 a brand-new reel-to-reel Sony video camera: Goldman, *Elvis,* pp. 343–344; Nash, *Elvis Aaron Presley,* p. 370; Fortas, *Elvis: From Memphis to Hollywood,* p. 154; West et al., *Elvis: What Happened?,* pp. 282–283; plus numerous other accounts all document Elvis' interest in videography.

222 "Show us what you recorded": Esposito, *Good Rockin',* p. 181. Joe says here that he and "one of the guys" watched some of the tapes once and that they were "very sexy" but "wouldn't even merit an 'R' rating in today's mainstream movies." Marty Lacker (in Nash, *Elvis Aaron Presley,* pp. 371–372) describes the same incident, characterizing the tapes as "sensual and erotic" but "not particularly raunchy." Lacker, never one to downplay Elvis' failings, goes out of his way to dispute Goldman's more sensational account.

222 Tempers flared: Geller and Spector, *"If,"* pp. 150–151.

222 he gave Diane McBain an underlined copy: Wiegert, *"Elvis: Precious Memories,"* vol. 1, p. 91.

222 "Look, we've only got this moment": Goldman, *Elvis,* p. 373.

222 he told Mann: Mann, *Elvis and the Colonel*, pp. 156–158.

223 Charlie and Red started working informally: Interview with Red West, 1996; home tapes (EPE).

223 every morning, before going to the studio: Interviews with Jerry Schilling; Sherry Daniel interview with Charlie Hodge, *DisCoveries*, August 1991. Elvis' musical interests and repertoire can be further deduced from tapes discovered at Graceland in 1996 and correspondence throughout the year with Freddy Bienstock (EPE).

223 its casual advocacy of the drug culture: Interview with Jerry Schilling, 1993.

223–224 These informal sessions: Interview with Red West.

224 He listened to Caruso: Geller and Spector, *"If,"* pp. 80, 116; interview with Charlie Hodge, 1989.

224 admiration for Jimmy Jones: This is an admiration borne out by innumerable interviews, memoirs, and books. Tom Diskin's actual search for Jones is documented in correspondence culminating in a letter to Elvis on May 13, 1966, which states, "I have made countless calls on Jimmy Jones and no one seems to be able to locate him" (EPE).

224 persistent telephone calls and letters: Jenkins' letter of May 4, 1966, underscores the sense of urgency (EPE).

224 "Heck yes, I would retire": *Memphis Press-Scimitar*, February 2, 1966.

225 arriving home at 9:00 P.M.: Lewis, *"Hurry Home, Elvis!,"* vol. 1, p. 121.

225 listening to the tapes: Esposito, *Good Rockin',* p. 75.

225 someone had to lug: West et al., *Elvis: What Happened?,* p. 370, has this happening in Oklahoma City on a single night; Nash, *Elvis Aaron Presley,* p. 370, has a girl flying into Albuquerque by prearrangement and staying for four nights. There are other variants but little question that the core story is true.

FAMILY CIRCLE

227 Diskin suggested that they substitute the Imperials: Diskin's letter of May 13, 1966, in which he confesses his inability to locate Jones, goes on to recommend the Imperials. Ernst Jorgensen believes that Chet Atkins' secretary, Mary B. Lynch (who booked all the sessions and was a friend of Jake Hess'), had a hand in recommending the group.

228–230 That was how Felton Jarvis became Elvis' producer: Interviews with Chet Atkins, Bob Beckham, Bill Lowery, Lamar Fike, Harry Warner, Jake Hess, and Mary Jarvis; also Al Cooley and Jerry Flowers interviews with Felton Jarvis, 1973 and 1980 respectively; Lola Scobey, "Controversies About Elvis," *Cash Box*, September 3, 1977.

229 "He just said, 'I'm going to carry you over'": Jerry Flowers interview with Felton Jarvis.

230 "for a while before I started": Al Cooley interview with Felton Jarvis.

230 "Elvis just really loved that sound": Interview with Jake Hess, 1991.

231 "He didn't do a lot of takes": Interview with Jerry Schilling, 1995.

232 "Elvis was one of those individuals": Jerry Hopkins interview with Jake Hess (MVC/UMem). For the sake of the narrative, I have changed most of the verbs into the past tense.

232 Felton's entire philosophy of recording: Ernst Jorgensen interview with Al Pachucki, 1996; Al Cooley and Jerry Flowers interviews with Felton Jarvis.

232 "Everything just started getting electrified": Interview with Chip Young, 1988.

232 "Down in the Alley," a raucous r&b hit: Although it was not released until 1957, the song had originally been recorded in 1953. The Clovers' "Fool, Fool, Fool" and "Little Mama," from 1951 and 1954 respectively, were early features of Elvis' act.

233 "We stayed": Jerry Flowers interview with Felton Jarvis.

233–234 a twenty-three-year-old piano player named David Briggs: Interviews with David Briggs, 1988–1998.

234 "I said, 'Great! Come in'": Peter Cronin interview with David Briggs, 1993.

235 "I said, 'Man, I'm too loud'": Interview with Jake Hess; Ernst Jorgensen interview with Al Pachucki.

235 "You make me look forward": Interview with Mary Jarvis, 1989.

236 as Red West believed: Trevor Cajiao interview with Red West, *Elvis: The Man and His Music* 22, March 1994, p. 9; Ernst Jorgensen interview with Red West, 1995; Red West et al., *Elvis: What Happened?*, p. 303.

236 Red, armed only with amphetamines: West et al., *Elvis: What Happened?*, p. 303.

236 "I was a nervous wreck": Interview with Red West, 1996.

237 They listened to it a number of times: Interviews with Red West and Jerry Schilling; West et al., *Elvis: What Happened?*, p. 303; Alanna Nash, *Elvis Aaron Presley: Revelations from the Memphis Mafia*, p. 384. Not surprisingly, there are as many variations as there are sources.

238–239 one of Elvis' favorite entertainers: The sources for Elvis' admiration for Jackie Wilson and James Brown once again are legion and diverse, including interviews with George Klein, Jerry Schilling, and Wilson chronicler Simon Rutberg; correspondence with Alan Leeds and Cliff White; Alan Fortas, *Elvis: From Memphis to Hollywood*, p. 232; James Brown with Bruce Tucker, *James Brown: The Godfather of Soul*, p. 165; and Tony Douglas, *Lonely Teardrops: The Jackie Wilson Story*, pp. 243–244.

239 he invited him out to the film set: The closeness between the two singers is indicated by their continued contact in Las Vegas in the seventies, Elvis' frequent references to Wilson's talent, and the fact that Wilson carried the two on-set photographs of himself and Presley (one inscribed, "Jackie, you have a friend forever") with him everywhere.

239 Larry Geller's particular memory: Geller and Spector, *"If I Can Dream": Elvis' Own Story*, p. 119.

239–240 Cliff Gleaves showed up: Cliff's visit and background are described in Nash, *Elvis Aaron Presley*, pp. 377–378, as well as in interviews with Joe Esposito, Jerry Schilling, George Klein, and Cliff Gleaves. As in other matters, I have tried to make the best sense I can of somewhat warring versions of the same story.

240 "I was aware that the prescriptions": Interview with Cliff Gleaves, 1990.

240 a chair similar to one in Wallis' office: Paul Nathan to Hal Wallis, November 7, 1966 (HWC/MPASL).

240 Wallis had at last resigned himself: Wallis correspondence, 1966, passim.

240 "Wallis was really tightening up": Interview with John Rich, 1996.

241 against Wallis' explicit instructions: Paul Nathan to Hal Wallis, September 29, 1966; Wallis to John Rich on the following day (HWC/MPASL).

241 He was overweight: Wallis to Colonel, September 6, 1966; see also Paul Nathan to Wallis, August 1, 1966 (HWC/MPASL).

241 he had rented a house: The one-year lease at 1350 Ladera Circle began on September 21, 1966 (copy of lease supplied by Leonard Lewis).

241 He needed a "getaway" retreat: Interview with Joe Esposito, 1996.

241 The house that they found: Allene Arthur, "Elvis in Palm Springs," *Palm Springs Life*, August 1995; Bruce Fessier, "Remembering Elvis in Palm Springs," *The Desert Sun*, May 2, 1995; "The Way-Out Way of Life," *Look*, 1962.

242 Joe and Joanie alone were included: Nash, *Elvis Aaron Presley*, p. 365; interviews with Joe and Joan Esposito.

242 One time in Palm Springs: Geller and Spector, *"If,"* p. 145.

243 Elvis "stormed into his trailer": Ibid., p. 144.

243 "I saw that the back door was open": Ibid., pp. 147–148.

244 There were problems: Interview with Roger Davis, 1995. Also, interview with Gabe Tucker, 1990, and Gabe Tucker's entertaining firsthand accounts of life in Palm Springs as well as his somewhat more secondhand anecdotes of Elvis and the Colonel's growing estrangement at this time in Marge Crumbaker and Gabe Tucker, *Up and Down with Elvis Presley.*

244 He was playing the country tearjerker: Marty Lacker et al., *Elvis: Portrait of a Friend,* p. 62; Nash, *Elvis Aaron Presley,* p. 417; West et al., *Elvis: What Happened?,* p. 304; interview with Joe Esposito. Most of the sources differ on where the song was first actually heard, and Red West points out with some acerbity that he had brought the song to Elvis in Jerry Lee Lewis' version the year before, but Elvis either failed to pay attention or simply forgot.

244 everyone was outside: Donna Lewis, *"Hurry Home, Elvis!": Donna Lewis' Diaries,* vol. 1, p. 204.

244 He came back down: Nash, *Elvis Aaron Presley,* pp. 391–392; see also Lacker et al., *Portrait,* p. 87.

245 he gave George Klein: *Memphis Press-Scimitar,* December 17, 1966. See also Lacker et al., *Portrait,* p. 98; Fortas, *Elvis: From Memphis to Hollywood,* p. 253.

245 an interview with Jim Kingsley, "Christmas to Elvis Means 'Just Home,'" *Memphis Commercial Appeal Mid-South Magazine,* December 25, 1966 (italics added at end).

246 Elvis bulldozed the little house: Nash, *Elvis Aaron Presley,* pp. 351, 397; Elvis Presley Enterprises, *Elvis at Graceland,* p. 20; Mary Jenkins, *Elvis: The Way I Knew Him,* p. 19; Lewis, *"Hurry Home, Elvis"* vol. 2, pp. 1–26; interviews with Alan Fortas, Jerry Schilling, and Joe Esposito.

246 "Elvis would go out in the barn": Nash, *Elvis Aaron Presley,* p. 397.

246 "he felt like he needed to take Delta in": Ibid., pp. 420–421.

246 the funeral arrangements: Jenkins, *Elvis: The Way I Knew Him,* p. 28. The funeral was on January 15, 1967.

246 it became open season on Larry: Geller and Spector, *"If,"* pp. 151–152.

247 he had asked jeweler Harry Levitch: Interview with Harry Levitch, 1995.

247 "More than once Elvis remarked": Geller and Spector, *"If,"* pp. 161–162.

247 Rumors had been circulating: Letter from Vernon Presley to Jim Hannaford, June 2, 1966, re "recent articles in newspapers and some magazines." According to Vernon there was "no engagement and no marriage plans" (Jim Hannaford, *Golden Ride on the Mystery Train,* vol. 2, p. 29).

247 "his old boyish grin": Priscilla Presley, *Elvis and Me,* pp. 221–222.

248 the slot cars, long since abandoned: Lacker et al., *Portrait,* pp. 61, 270. In June the track was given away to the Boys' Club (Lewis, *"Hurry Home, Elvis!,"* vol. 2, p. 97); also, bill from the Robert E. Lee Raceway, June 18, 1967, for disassembling and moving the track (EPE).

248 "it was just really fun": Interview with Jerry Schilling, 1996.

248 They had initially spoken of it: The Colonel's letter to Elvis, January 2, 1967, refers to "our understanding on the telephone a few weeks ago," though this may have been more in the nature of a legalism, since the letter was the official agreement, along with a brief note to RCA from Elvis of the same date authorizing the new management commission.

249 the kind of partnerships: The history of the Kate Smith–Ted Collins management arrangement comes from Richard K. Hayes, *Kate Smith,* pp. 16–17; Colin Escott interviewed Patti Page and Jack Rael on the subject of their long-term contract; information on the Albert Grossman–Bob Dylan publishing arrangement, as well as other similarly creative business ventures, comes from Fred Goodman, *Mansion on the Hill,* pp. 88, 103–104, 129, and passim.

249 At fifty-six he didn't know: Crumbaker and Tucker, *Up and Down,* passim.

249 His services, he felt . . . were worth 50 percent: Discussion with Colonel Parker, 1993; see also the Colonel's 1982 response to the "Report of Guardian Ad Litem In Re: The Estate of Elvis A. Presley, Deceased" (EPE).

250 "it will be at least 1980": Telegram from Elvis to Norman Racusin, January 23, 1967; also to Harry Jenkins, same date (EPE).

250 Colonel delivered a deal memo: Though this elicited another tribute to "the number-one potentate of all time" from Elvis, the deal itself never actually went through (EPE).

251 The number of horses: Information on the actual number varies somewhat but hovers around sixteen, with only eight stalls available at Graceland. Eventually the number of horses on the ranch grew to around thirty.

251 Red ran down Elvis: Nash, *Elvis Aaron Presley*, p. 397.

251 he and Priscilla spotted: The story of the purchase of the ranch comes from a variety of sources, including interviews with Alan Fortas, Jerry Schilling, and Joe Esposito; Shelley Ritter interview with Mike McGregor; Priscilla Presley, *Elvis and Me*, pp. 216ff; Fortas, *Elvis: From Memphis to Hollywood*, pp. 261ff; Bill E. Burk, *Elvis Through My Eyes*, p. 129; Nash, *Elvis Aaron Presley*, pp. 396ff; Rose Clayton and Dick Heard, eds., *Elvis Up Close: In the Words of Those Who Knew Him Best*, p. 222; Lacker et al., *Portrait*, p. 77; Lewis, "Hurry Home, Elvis!," vol. 2, pp. 1–44; various stories in the *Memphis Press-Scimitar* and *Commercial Appeal* at this time; *DeSoto Times*, February 10–18, 1967; etc.

251 On February 8 he put down a deposit: Receipt from Mid-South Title Company (EPE).

251–252 Within a week he had purchased: Purchase records (EPE); Lewis, "Hurry Home, Elvis!," vol. 2, pp. 17–18; *Memphis Commercial Appeal*, February 18, 1967; Fortas, *Elvis: From Memphis to Hollywood*, p. 263; Lacker et al., *Portrait*, pp. 77, 81; Priscilla Presley, *Elvis and Me*, p. 226; Shelley Ritter interview with Mike McGregor; etc. The exact number of trucks, trailers, and horse vans may never be known, but it escalated with almost incredible rapidity.

252 they were all going to end up in the poorhouse: Lewis, "Hurry Home, Elvis!," vol. 2, p. 46.

252 "Vernon literally begged him": Priscilla Presley, *Elvis and Me*, p. 226.

252 "He liked it when everyone was together": Ibid., p. 227.

252 to name a building or a highway: See *Memphis Press-Scimitar*, February 22, 1967, re January 4 mayoral proclamation, among other things. The renaming of the highway is covered in both Memphis papers, May 30, 1971, and January 20, 1972.

252 "It wasn't unusual": Priscilla Presley, *Elvis and Me*, p. 226.

252 a commune in fact: Interview with Joe Esposito, 1990; Lacker et al., *Portrait*, p. 82.

253 "Vernon is coming to me": Interviews with Joe Esposito.

253 "He was very thoughtful": Shelley Ritter interview with Mike McGregor; see also Lewis, "Hurry Home, Elvis!," vol. 2.

253 "It was really beautiful at first": Interview with Jerry Schilling, 1996. See also Nash, *Elvis Aaron Presley*, pp. 403ff.

254 Red . . . covered for him: Lacker et al., *Portrait*, p. 330; Ernst Jorgensen interviews with Red West and Ray Walker.

254 he finally fired off a letter: Colonel to Marty Lacker, February 28, 1967 (EPE). See also Fortas, *Elvis: From Memphis to Hollywood*, p. 257, re his and Marty's consumption of "pharmaceuticals."

254 He knew all about the weight gain: Fortas, *Elvis: From Memphis to Hollywood*, p. 266; also interview with Joan Esposito, 1995, re the "two-hundred-pound club."

254 he was furious: Interviews with Joe Esposito, Alan Fortas, and Priscilla Presley. According to Joe, the Colonel "called one day and said 'We're going to get sued. The picture is not going to be made, and we're going to have to give all the money back.'"

254–256 That was how Dr. George Nichopoulos first came into the picture: Interview with Dr. Nichopoulous, 1996. Much of the background on Dr. Nick comes from Stanley Booth, "The King Is Dead!, Hang the Doctor!," in Martin Torgoff, ed., *The Complete Elvis*.

256–258 Elvis arrived in California: The dating of this incident comes from travel, studio, and doctors' records (EPE). The anecdotal account of the incident and the meeting that followed stems from interviews with Joe Esposito, Jerry Schilling, and Larry Geller; Nash, *Elvis Aaron Presley*, pp. 412–415; Geller and Spector, *"If,"* pp. 165–167; Jess Stearn, *The Truth About Elvis*, p. 171; Priscilla Presley, *Elvis and Me*, pp. 231–232. I think I need hardly say: accounts differ.

257 "Some of you," he said, looking at Larry: Geller and Spector, *"If,"* p. 167. It should be noted that Larry places this meeting two weeks after the incident, though nearly everyone else has it occurring in the immediate aftermath of Elvis' fall.

258 "I thought I was going to be one of the ones": Nash, *Elvis Aaron Presley*, pp. 415–416.

258 "You know," he said to Larry one day: Stearn, *The Truth*, p. 175; Geller and Spector, *"If,"* p. 168.

258 The atmosphere on the set: West et al., *Elvis: What Happened?*, p. 273; Billy Smith and Marty Lacker, *"Clambake Crazy Times," Elvis: The Record*, vol. 1, no. 1, May 1979; Lacker et al., *Portrait*, p. 45; Jerry Hopkins interview with Red West (MVC/UMem).

258 a wistful note: Jerry Hopkins interview with Bill Bixby (MVC/UMem).

259 he gave the album to various members: Interview with Lance LeGault, 1990; also, Will Hutchins in Sue Wiegert, *"Elvis: Precious Memories,"* vol. 2, p. 35.

259 "They were like Frick and Frack": Jerry Hopkins interview with Bill Bixby (MVC/UMem).

259 Paramount refused to release any money: Colonel–Hal Wallis correspondence, February 20–23 through May 3, 1967, including Paul Nathan memos (HWC/MPASL).

260 at constant odds with Priscilla: Nash, *Elvis Aaron Presley*, p. 429; interview with Priscilla Presley.

260 Billy Smith saw Elvis' behavior: Nash, *Elvis Aaron Presley*, p. 424.

260 Jerry and Sandy got married: Interviews with Jerry Schilling; also interview with Charlie Hodge, 1989, plus Crumbaker and Tucker, *Up and Down*, pp. 119–120, re marriage and the Colonel's sense of propriety.

260 "Now, Charlie," he said: Charlie Hodge, *Me 'n Elvis*, p. 75.

261 Rona Barrett sniffed out the news: Barrett dispatches April 27 and April 30, 1967; Lewis, *"Hurry Home, Elvis!,"* vol. 2, p. 54, has Barrett reporting the next day on the radio that Elvis would be married in Palm Springs that weekend; see also Rona Barrett, *Miss Rona: An Autobiography*, pp. 207–213.

261 They flew out of Palm Springs: The principal reporting on the wedding appeared in the *Memphis Press-Scimitar*, May 1, and the *Memphis Commercial Appeal*, May 2, 1967. I relied in addition on interviews with Priscilla Presley, Joe Esposito, Joan Esposito, Harry Levitch, and Jerry Schilling. See also Priscilla Presley, *Elvis and Me*; West et al., *Elvis: What Happened?*; Lacker et al., *Portrait*; Nash, *Elvis Aaron Presley*; Geller and Spector, *"If"*; Clayton and Heard, *Elvis Up Close*; May Mann, *Elvis and the Colonel*; Albert Goldman, *Elvis*; et al.

263 Red hit the roof: For Red's and others' reactions to their exclusion see West et al., *Elvis: What Happened?*, pp. 222ff, p. 329; Lacker et al., *Portrait*, p. 106; Nash, *Elvis Aaron Presley*, p. 432; Priscilla Presley, *Elvis and Me*, p. 237; and Goldman, *Elvis*, p. 398; also, all interviews listed above, plus Jerry Hopkins interview with Red West (MVC/UMem).

263 "Colonel Parker brought Elvis": Clayton and Heard, *Elvis Up Close*, p. 229.

264 "We were both so nervous": Interview with Priscilla Presley.

264 "Our little girl": *Memphis Commercial Appeal*, May 2, 1967.

264 "Remember," said the Colonel: AP report, May 2, 1967.

265 Red found himself in the midst: Interview with Harry Levitch; West et al., *Elvis: What Happened?*, p. 225.

265 "open season on the Swami": Geller and Spector, *"If,"* pp. 169–170.

265 it was, for Priscilla, a rare chance: Priscilla Presley, *Elvis and Me*, p. 244.

266 "I guess you could say": Nash, *Elvis Aaron Presley*, p. 432.

266 He blamed her: Fortas, *Elvis: From Memphis to Hollywood*, p. 265.

266 Elvis had had a porch and steps built: Lewis, *"Hurry Home, Elvis!,"* vol. 2, pp. 47, 52.

266 "it was like we were all just friends": Interview with Jerry Schilling, 1996.

266–267 the reception for their Memphis friends: Lewis, *"Hurry Home, Elvis!,"* vol. 2, pp. 83–86. See also Fortas, *Elvis: From Memphis to Hollywood*, p. 272; Billy Stanley, *Elvis, My Brother*, p. 64; Priscilla Presley, *Elvis and Me*, pp. 241–242.

266 she persuaded Elvis: Priscilla Presley, *Elvis and Me*, p. 234; interview with Priscilla Presley.

266 "There was a beautiful, lavish buffet": Interview with Lester and Sterling Hofman, 1989.

269 wives were included: Alanna Nash, *Elvis Aaron Presley: Revelations from the Memphis Mafia*, p. 605; Marty Lacker et al., *Elvis: Portrait of a Friend*, p. 108; Joe Esposito, *Good Rockin' Tonight*, p. 76; also, interviews with Joe and Joan Esposito; Joe Esposito's home movies.

270 "so wonderful and warm": Interview with Joan Esposito, 1995.

270 "It was the whim of the moment": Interview with Priscilla Presley, 1995.

270–271 she was pregnant: Priscilla Presley, *Elvis and Me*, p. 248.

271 "it just took all the glow off": Interview with Joan Esposito.

271 "'It's our baby'": Priscilla Presley, *Elvis and Me*, p. 250.

271 "This is the greatest thing": UPI dispatch, July 13, 1967.

271 "all I really did was sleep": Nash, *Elvis Aaron Presley*, p. 434.

272 the Colonel and his wife continued to socialize: Interviews with Joe and Joan Esposito. See also Marge Crumbaker and Gabe Tucker, *Up and Down with Elvis Presley*, for tales of life in Palm Springs; also Charlie Hodge, *Me 'n Elvis*, p. 84, re Colonel's relationship with Elvis and Priscilla at this time.

273 Jerry was the Colonel's principal driver: Interview with Jerry Schilling, 1996.

273 only three pictures left: Colonel's memo of January 26, 1967 (EPE).

274 Elvis was spending $500,000 a month: Donna Lewis, *"Hurry Home, Elvis!": Donna Lewis' Diaries*, vol. 2, pp. 110ff. Lewis details the selling-off of much of the ranch and the consolidation of staff.

274–275 Billy Strange, a flamboyant . . . session guitarist: Background information on Billy Strange comes primarily from a 1988 interview.

275 Elvis' all-over-the-map approach: Elvis' approach to repertoire was gleaned largely from correspondence with Hill and Range and tapes of the songs Elvis was listening to, which were discovered in 1996 at Graceland (EPE).

276 Colonel . . . canceled the session: Interviews with Joe Esposito, Billy Strange, Ed Hookstratten, and Jerry Schilling; Ernst Jorgensen interview with Jim Malloy; Jerry Hopkins interview with Hal Blaine (MVC/UMem); Nash, *Elvis Aaron Presley*, p. 320; Alan Fortas, *Elvis: From Memphis to Hollywood*, p. 226.

276 all headed for Las Vegas: ticket receipts (EPE).

276 he was in a box: Interview with Mary Jarvis, 1989.

276 He couldn't call a rehearsal session: Jerry Flowers and Al Cooley interviews with Felton Jarvis.

276 "That was a scene to see": Ernst Jorgensen interview with Al Pachucki.

277–279 Reed was a genuine individualist: Much of the background on Reed, and all of Reed's quotes about the session, come from a 1993 interview kindly arranged by Mary Jarvis.

278–280 "They got Jerry off in a corner": Interview with Scotty Moore, 1989. See also Nash, *Elvis Aaron Presley*, p. 437; Ernst Jorgensen interview with Al Pachucki; interviews with Freddy Bienstock and Chip Young; and joint interview with Harold Bradley, Jerry Kennedy, Bob Moore, and Buddy Harmon, conducted by Ernst Jorgensen and me, 1995.

280 about a month before the next film: Lewis, *"Hurry Home, Elvis!,"* vol. 2, pp. 129–142.

280 "she was sitting in a mud puddle": Mike McGregor quoted in Hodge, *Me 'n Elvis*, p. 81.

281 "a wheeler-dealer who's always promoting something": Joseph Lewis, "Elvis Presley Lives," *Cosmopolitan*, November 1968.

281 "God, Harry, I don't want to": Ernst Jorgensen interview with Al Pachucki.

281 "Promise me": Jerry Flowers interview with Felton Jarvis.

281 Colonel apprised the MGM executive: Memo of Colonel's telephone discussion with Ramsay, dated October 3, 1967.

281–282 they had fun on location: Fortas, *Elvis: From Memphis to Hollywood*, p. 267; Lewis, *"Hurry Home, Elvis!,"* vol. 2, p. 145, on the ponies; Red West et al., *Elvis: What Happened?*, p. 273; and interview with Jerry Schilling.

282 He repeated his hopes: *Cosmopolitan*.

282 There was an announcement: UPI dispatch, October 12, 1967.

282 Tractors, trailers, television sets: *Memphis Press-Scimitar*, November 7, 1967.

282 the upcoming Christmas radio special: UPI, December 9, 1967.

283 "The aim was always the same": Interview with Roger Davis, 1995.

283 In October he contacted . . . Tom Sarnoff: Colonel's summary of business and promotional activities, 1967 (EPE).

283 in excess of $400,000: Albert Goldman, *Elvis*, p. 405, has the price at $425,000; Nash, *Elvis Aaron Presley*, p. 437, calls it a $400,000 house.

284 "Elvis would do things like that": Interview with Priscilla Presley.

284 hayrides and snowball fights: Interview with Joan Esposito.

284 On New Year's Eve: Sue Wiegert, *"Elvis: Precious Memories,"* vol. 2, p. 20; interview with David "Flash" Fleischman, 1995; Lewis, *"Hurry Home, Elvis!,"* vol. 2, pp. 163ff.

285 some of Elvis' old r&b and hillbilly 78s: Information and list from Scotty Moore.

285 Felton, for one, had quietly appreciated the stand: Interview with Jerry Reed.

285–286 "Presley had such a unique way": Ernst Jorgensen interview with Ray Walker.

286 Elvis amused himself: Interview with Jerry Schilling.

286 Reed was, naturally, reluctant: Interview with Jerry Reed.

287 The Colonel, Elvis was convinced: Interviews with Priscilla Presley, Jerry Schilling, Joe Esposito; just about every Elvis memoir, including Geller and Spector, *"If I Can Dream": Elvis' Own Story*, p. 142; Nash, *Elvis Aaron Presley*, p. 303; Priscilla Presley, *Elvis and Me*, p. 189. In correspondence between Harry Jenkins and Tom Diskin, January 3, 1968, Jenkins presents a remastered version of an unnamed selection "as a result of Elvis' request." Jenkins explains that remastering could cause a bass drop-off, but he doesn't believe that it has. This is but one of many examples (EPE).

288 Priscilla gave birth: *Memphis Commercial Appeal*, February 2, 1968; AP dispatch, February 3.

288 a doctors' lounge specially set aside: Jerry Hopkins interview with Maurice Elliott (MVC/UMem).

288 a comedy of errors: Interviews with Joan Esposito and Jerry Schilling; Shelley Ritter interview with Nancy Rooks; Jerry Hopkins interview with Maurice Elliott (MVC/UMem).

289 There was no further talk: Lewis, *"Hurry Home, Elvis!,"* vol. 2, p. 198. When a fan asks Elvis why he didn't name Lisa Marie "Gladys," "Elvis said they didn't want to name her after anyone." See also Sandra Shevey, "Priscilla Presley: My Life With and Without Elvis Presley," *Ladies Home Journal,* August 1973, p. 139.

289 They left the hospital: *Memphis Commercial Appeal,* February 6, 1968; *Memphis Press-Scimitar,* February 5, 1968; Jerry Hopkins interview with Maurice Elliott (MVC/UMem).

289 "She's a little miracle": Interview with Lester and Sterling Hofman, 1989.

289 the card should be burned: Lewis, *"Hurry Home, Elvis!,"* vol. 2, p. 201; Maria Davies, "The King Returns to His Kingdom: Vegas Revisited" (a British fan's report on Las Vegas, February 1970, that appeared in Rex Martin's *Official Elvis Presley Fan Club News Service*). Elvis speaks here of leaving the flowers with a card, contrary to his practice.

289 They had a steady stream of visitors: Lewis, *"Hurry Home, Elvis!,"* vol. 2, pp. 194ff.

290 "Joe and Joanie had their own place": Hodge, *Me 'n Elvis,* p. 83.

290–291 there was no question of who was in charge: Fortas, *Elvis: From Memphis to Hollywood,* pp. 274ff; Billy Stanley, *Elvis, My Brother,* p. 81; May Mann, *Elvis and the Colonel,* p. 172; Nash, *Elvis Aaron Presley,* pp. 434–445; also see Wiegert, *"Precious Memories,"* vols. 1 and 2, re fans at various homes; and interview with Sandi Miller, 1990. Lewis, *"Hurry Home, Elvis!,"* vol. 2, reports on the comings and goings of the guys throughout.

291 One weekend in April: Chris Hutchins, *Elvis Meets the Beatles,* pp. 147–148; Tom Jones interview in Rose Clayton and Dick Heard, eds., *Elvis Up Close: In the Words of Those Who Knew Him Best,* p. 233; Bill E. Burk, *Elvis Through My Eyes,* p. 185.

291 an Easter egg hunt: Wiegert, *"Precious Memories,"* vol. 1, p. 71.

291 "He is still withdrawn": Priscilla Presley, *Elvis and Me,* pp. 258–259.

291 Some of the guys raised questions: West et al., *Elvis: What Happened?,* p. 229; interview with Pat Parry, 1991.

291 "She was taking so many classes": Interview with Joan Esposito.

THE BLUEBIRD OF HAPPINESS

293 He had been talking with executive producer Bob Finkel: Interview with Bob Finkel, 1995. The chronology of decision making, and the picture of the evolution of the show, stems primarily from internal memoranda re meetings and communications between the network, the sponsor, the advertising agency, and the Colonel beginning on March 28, 1968 (EPE). In the Memorandum Report of the May 8 meeting it was noted that Singer representative Alfred DiScipio "was able to convince Parker that the program ought not to be a purely Christmas oriented show" but instead should feature Elvis' hits of the last eight or ten years, telling "the story of Presley as the initiator of a style of music which has become an integral part of our contemporary culture." The Binder-Howe Production Company was confirmed by Bob Finkel as "the production entity" for the special eight days later.

293 At first he found Elvis: This and all subsequent quotes from Finkel come from my 1995 interview, unless otherwise noted.

293 Finkel informed the network: Internal memorandum from Farlan I. Myers re telephone conversation with Finkel, May 16, 1968.

294 a young director named Steve Binder: Much of the background information that follows is from interviews with Steve Binder and Bones Howe, 1989–1992.

294–295 Everywhere you looked: Jerry Hopkins interview with Bones Howe (MVC/UMem); also, Jerry Hopkins interview with Steve Binder and my interviews with Steve Binder and Bones Howe.

295 "to do something really important": Jerry Hopkins interview with Steve Binder (MVC/UMem).

295–296 Elvis met with Binder and Howe: Interviews with Steve Binder and Bones Howe.

296–297 a karate championship: Interviews with Ed Parker and Priscilla Presley; Ed Parker, *Inside Elvis*, p. 36.

297 "There was nothing original": Interview with Bones Howe, 1989. All subsequent quotes from Bones Howe are from this interview, unless otherwise noted.

298 The script rapidly evolved: Various dated draft versions of the script.

298–299 He loved the black leather suit: Interview with Bill Belew, 1995.

299–300 Bones had gotten himself into trouble: Jerry Hopkins interview with Bones Howe (MVC/UMem).

300 That left Billy Goldenberg: Interview with Billy Goldenberg, 1993.

300 "Every day Elvis would come in": Jerry Hopkins interview with Billy Goldenberg (MVC/UMem); the tenses have been changed.

300 Then one day Billy Strange actually showed up: My interview and Jerry Hopkins interview with Billy Goldenberg, plus a somewhat dissenting interview with Billy Strange, 1988; see also Finkel memo to Steve Binder on June 12 re keeping rehearsals to a minimum of people because of Elvis' tendency to get distracted.

300–301 "They just kept fooling around": Interview with Billy Strange.

301 a mutual parting of the ways: Billy Strange has a different version of the story which focuses exclusively on the pull of his movie responsibilities.

301 there was still the matter of telling the Colonel: Interview with Bob Finkel.

301 "never, ever to show any disrespect": Jerry Hopkins interview with Steve Binder (MVC/UMem).

302 It was at this point: Jerry Hopkins interview with Bones Howe (MVC/UMem).

302–303 "He would call up and say": Interview with Billy Goldenberg.

305 The only substantive matter: My interviews and Jerry Hopkins interviews (MVC/UMem) with Steve Binder and Bones Howe.

306 if he ran out of things to say: Rehearsal tape for "impromptu" section.

306 He wanted to do a European tour: Interview with Scotty Moore, 1989.

306 "But he'd just say": Jerry Hopkins interview with D. J. Fontana and Scotty Moore (MVC/UMem).

306 "If the Colonel can't stick his nose in": Colonel to Freddy Bienstock, June 20, 1968 (EPE).

306–307 "We had to fight": Jerry Hopkins interview with Bones Howe (MVC/UMem).

307 "I gave him a hand mike": Ibid.

307 "Quincy Jones had at that time": Interview with Billy Goldenberg.

308–309 "All of a sudden I realized": Jerry Hopkins interview with Steve Binder (MVC/UMem).

309–310 Bob Finkel meanwhile had been fending off: I have tried to sort out the chronology of this story as best I can, but needless to say some of the anecdotal detail is in dispute amid the thicket of oral recollections.

310 "we figured it was about time": *Los Angeles Times*, June 27, 1968.

311 "I loved his attitude": *Muncie Evening Press*, November 30, 1968.

311 "Every time they'd ask a question": Jerry Hopkins interview with Steve Binder (MVC/UMem).

311 "I know you're nervous": Alan Fortas, *Elvis: From Memphis to Hollywood*, p. 2.

311 "The Colonel said to me": Interview with Bob Finkel. This story has been repeated many times, but it should be noted that Dwight Whitney's account, "The Indomitable Snowman Who Built Himself — And Elvis Too," in *TV Guide*, November 30–December 6, 1968, tells it differently, describing a stampede for seats, with the best seats going (by the Colonel's intention) to hard-core fans.

312 Elvis told Steve Binder: Interviews with Steve Binder and Joe Esposito; Joe Esposito, *Good Rockin' Tonight*, p. 136. See also Peter Whitmer, *The Inner Elvis: A Psychological Biography of Elvis Aaron Presley*, p. 358.

315 "after he finished singing": This was said — but not for attribution — in more than one interview that I conducted. See Whitmer, *The Inner Elvis*, p. 369.

315 "It's like a surge": Interview with June Juanico, 1991.

315–316 The "stand-up" show two days later: I should make it clear that in my descriptions of both the sit-down and the stand-up show I am describing not what was broadcast but the unedited performances themselves, as they have appeared on bootleg videos. Obviously there is much more to the televised special, but I wanted to focus here simply on the performance as a live show.

316–317 Bones had no doubt: Interview with Bones Howe.

316–317 "it was one of the most complete experiences": Interview with Bob Finkel.

A DAY AT THE RACES

319 they all watched: Interview with Jerry Schilling, 1990.

319–210 The Colonel, who attended a more formal screening: Colonel to Tom Sarnoff, August 21, 1968 (EPE).

320 In an interview: Vernon Scott, "Elvis Getting Ready to Go on Tour Again," *Memphis Press-Scimitar*, September 27, 1968.

320–321 Dewey had been something of an embarrassment: Randy Haspel, "Tell 'Em Phillips Sencha," *Memphis*, June 1978, p. 60; interviews with Joe Esposito and George Klein.

321 "I am awfully hurt": *Memphis Commercial Appeal*, September 29, 1968.

321 he had let her know: *Trenton [Tenn.] Herald-Gazette*, August 17, 1978; Charles Raiteri and Louis Cantor interviews with Dot Phillips.

321 "Sonofabitch sure looked dead": Joe Esposito, *Good Rockin' Tonight*, p. 248. This story has been held up as an example of Elvis' thoughtlessness in many anecdotal accounts, but that interpretation would seem to be contradicted by his kindness to Mrs. Phillips and his isolation from any of the storytellers during the service itself. It seems quite plausible, on the other hand, that he did, or would, show off for the guys with a kind of false bravado.

322 the family was cursed: Billy Smith speaks of "all those deaths" in Alanna Nash, *Elvis Aaron Presley: Revelations from the Memphis Mafia*, p. 218.

323–324 I quoted Elvis to lead off my review: *Boston Phoenix*, December 11, 1968.

324 "it looked as though someone had accidentally taped": *Hollywood Reporter*, December 5, 1968.

324 "He still can't sing": *Variety*, December 5, 1968.

324 "I don't think many viewers": *Los Angeles Times*, December 4, 1968.

324 "Rock Star's Explosive Blues": *New York Times*, December 4, 1968.

325 the fifty-one-year-old Kerkorian: Background on Kirk Kerkorian and the International Hotel comes primarily from Dial Torgerson, *Kerkorian: An American Success Story*; Peter Bart, *Fade Out: The Calamitous Final Days of MGM*; and Charles Fleming, "The Predator," *Vanity Fair*, February 1996.

325 "a modest man": Bart, *Fade Out*, p. 100.

325 headliners like Frank Sinatra and Dean Martin: By way of comparison, Nick Tosches has Martin's 1969 salary at the Riviera at $100,000 a week plus $20,000 a month as a "talent consultant" in Tosches, *Dino: Living High in the Dirty Business of Dreams*, p. 389. It should not be lost sight of, however, that Martin acquired 10 percent of the Riviera at this time.

326–330 Sometime after Christmas: Background on the American sessions and Elvis' initial arrival at the studio comes from diverse sources, including interviews with George Klein, Chips Moman, Mike Leech, Glen Spreen, Reggie Young, Gene Chrisman, Wayne Jackson, Mark James, and Joe Esposito; Al Cooley interview with Felton Jarvis; Alan Fortas, *Elvis: From Memphis to Hollywood*, p. 288; Nash, *Elvis Aaron Presley*, pp. 444, 454ff; and Marty Lacker et al., *Elvis: Portrait of a Friend*, pp. 114ff, 187.

327 "Presley's friends": *Variety*, June 18, 1969.

328 Lincoln "Chips" Moman: Background on Chips Moman comes primarily from my 1986 book *Sweet Soul Music: Rhythm and Blues and the Southern Dream of Freedom*.

331 "That first night Colonel Parker said": Jerry Hopkins interview with Mac Davis (MVC/UMem).

332 even George Klein . . . cautioned Elvis: Rose Clayton and Dick Heard, eds., *Elvis Up Close: In the Words of Those Who Knew Him Best*, p. 237.

332 With Joe's further encouragement: Interviews with Joe Esposito.

332 "He just sang great": Shelley Ritter interview with Wayne Jackson.

333 The thirty-nine-year-old Hamilton: Background on Roy Hamilton comes primarily from Peter Grendysa, "Roy Hamilton: Never Walking Alone," *Goldmine*, April 1979, and Peter Grendysa, "The Roy Hamilton Story," *Soul Survivor* 5, summer 1986. In addition to "I Believe," Elvis had recorded Hamilton's "I'm Gonna Sit Right Down and Cry (Over You)" at his second RCA session in 1956 and would go on to record several more Hamilton titles, including "Hurt," in later years.

333 "I said, 'Come on, Elvis'": Interview with George Klein, 1988; see also Lacker et al., *Portrait*, p. 119.

334 he offered Hamilton one of his songs: Interviews with George Klein, Gene Chrisman, and Reggie Young; also Trevor Cajiao interview with Bobby Wood, *Elvis: The Man and His Music* 26, March 1995, p. 9.

336 "one of the hardest-working artists": James Kingsley, "Relaxed Elvis Disks 16 Songs in Hometown Stint," *Memphis Commercial Appeal*, January 23, 1969.

336 the business issues raised: Interviews with Chips Moman, Freddy Bienstock, George Klein, and Herbie O'Mell; see also Lacker et al., *Portrait*, pp. 117–119. Nearly every other previously named source in this chapter has his own version of the story.

336 it was strongly hinted: This is inferential on my part. "Mama Liked the Roses" appears on the original album listing of March 12 with the title crossed out and "OUT" written beside it and circled (EPE).

336 a follow-up session was being planned: Correspondence regarding this second session begins on January 29 (EPE).

337–338 All he could talk about: Interview with Freddy Bienstock, 1992.

338 "I wanted to give Elvis a different image": Interview with Glen Spreen, 1995.

338 Chips continued to have substantial input: Chips was involved at least through August on the evidence of paperwork and overdubs, not to mention his presence at Elvis' Las Vegas opening (just before the final overdub on "Suspicious Minds"). The friction between Felton and Chips can be deduced from nearly every interview I conducted, including interviews with Mary Jarvis; from the opposing overdub sessions in Memphis and in Nashville; from the public conflict over producer's credit; and from the musical results — not to mention the fact that Elvis never returned to American.

339 "We'd do scenes": Interview with Billy Graham, 1996.

339 "heralded as the world's largest showroom": From International publicity director Nick Naff's official publicity release.

340 a *Variety* headline: *Variety,* June 18, 1969.

340 at the instigation of Marty Lacker: Nash, *Elvis Aaron Presley,* p. 462; *Billboard* charts, May 3, 10, 17, 24, 1969.

340 at the gates with the fans: Donna Lewis, *"Hurry Home, Elvis!": Donna Lewis' Diaries,* vol. 3 (unpublished manuscript), mspp. 58ff; *Memphis Commercial Appeal,* June 8, 1969; *Memphis Press-Scimitar,* July 9, 1969; Harold Loyd, *Elvis Presley's Graceland Gates,* p. 29. See also Maria Davies' *Official Elvis Presley Fan Club News Service* account of the February 1970 Las Vegas engagement, in which Vester Presley explains that Elvis spent so much time at the gates "to get him used to the crowds again" — even though the Colonel didn't like it.

340 he saw this as an opportunity: Interview with Charlie Hodge, 1989.

341–342 he called guitarist James Burton: Interview with James Burton, 1991.

341–343 Jerry Scheff, a virtuoso bass player: Interview with Jerry Scheff, 1989.

342–343 Tutt, Muhoberac thought, would be perfect: Trevor Cajiao interview with Larry Muhoberac, *Elvis: The Man and His Music* 22, March 1994.

342 "I was the last drummer": Stephanie Bennett, "Tutt," *Modern Drummer* interview (undated clip), p. 24.

343 the salary structure: Tom Diskin to Lou Goldberg, July 17, 1969 (EPE).

343–344 costume fittings with Bill Belew: Interview with Bill Belew, 1995; Jerry Hopkins interview with Bill Belew (MVC/UMem).

344 "We probably learned": Interview with James Burton.

344 "It's relatively simple": John Wilkinson, quoted in Lacker et al., *Portrait,* p. 193.

344 The program that Elvis started out with: Meticulous song lists were kept for each rehearsal (EPE).

344 Charlie drew upon his own experience: Interview with Charlie Hodge.

345 Felton flew in: Interview with Mary Jarvis, 1989.

345 "I didn't know that much about Elvis": Jerry Hopkins interview with Myrna Smith (MVC/UMem).

345 "He had on a chocolate-colored suit": Clayton and Heard, *Elvis Up Close,* p. 244. The Hopkins interview resumes next paragraph.

345 the thing that was most difficult for them: Interview with Myrna Smith, 1990; my interview with Estelle Brown, 1996, provided similar insights into the feelings of the group.

345–346 The Imperials had their own problems: Interviews with Joe Moscheo, 1989, 1993.

346 Three nights before: Telegram invitation from Bill Miller to the 2:15 A.M. show (EPE).

346 she looked awfully alone: Charlie Hodge, *Me 'n Elvis,* p. 123; interview with Al Dvorin, 1995; Jerry Hopkins interview with Bill Jost (MVC/UMem); Albert Goldman, *Elvis,* pp. 438, 441; Nash, *Elvis Aaron Presley,* p. 473.

346 one of the biggest advance sales: *Variety,* July 9, 1969.

346 "I don't like to take any chances": *Memphis Commercial Appeal,* August 3, 1969.

347 "If you don't do any business": Esposito, *Good Rockin',* p. 142.

347 the Colonel and his crew: Goldman, *Elvis,* p. 442.

347 Colonel continued to work behind the scenes: The contract was signed on August 14 (EPE).

347 an A-plus celebrity list: Grelun Landon invitation file.

347 most of the Strip headliners: *Billboard,* August 6, 1969.

348 Joe had his doubts: Interview with Joe Esposito, 1990.

348 The Sweet Inspirations did a stiff opening set: Perhaps the two best general sources for a description of the entire show are Robert Christgau, "Elvis in Vegas," *Village Voice*, September 4, 1969; and Maria Davies, "A report of the happening of the decade," a detailed British fan club report, which covers the nights of August 20–23 and August 29.

348 "Good evening, ladies and gentlemen": This is a pastiche based on a number of accounts, but particularly on Jerry Hopkins, *Elvis*, pp. 371–372, and Maria Davies, as cited above.

349 even waitresses . . . "were visibly swooning": *Los Angeles Herald-Examiner*, August 12, 1969.

349 "Presley's sustaining love for rhythm and blues": *New Yorker*, August 30, 1969.

349 Richard Goldstein felt: *New York Times*, August 10, 1969.

349 the *Hollywood Reporter* critic: *Hollywood Reporter*, August 13, 1969.

349 "Presley, like a wild beast": *Record Mirror*, week ending August 9, 1969.

349–351 "But I was wired the wrong way": This is an edited version, somewhat condensed and elided, from several different sources, including Jerry Hopkins' *Elvis*; Maria Davies' account; Judy Kuniba, "Fun with Elvis on Stage July 26, 1969," *Elvis International Forum*; Donna Lewis' "*Hurry Home, Elvis!,*" vol. 3; the (misnamed) bootleg CD *Opening Night, 1969*; and *Collector's Gold* (RCA 3114). It is evident that as the month wore on, the asides became looser and the language more risqué, but the constancy of the subject matter indicates how close this monologue was to the way Elvis really saw it, jokes, puns, and self-deprecating references notwithstanding.

351 "it was the energy": Interview with Priscilla Presley, 1995.

351 "He was so charged up": Interview with Joan Esposito, 1995.

351 "It was like a different Elvis": Interview with Pat Parry, 1991.

351 "He was all over that stage": Al Cooley interview with Felton Jarvis.

353 neither Joe nor Priscilla nor Charlie had ever seen: Interview with Joe Esposito; Priscilla Presley, *Elvis and Me*, p. 273; Charlie Hodge in Sandra Choron and Bob Oskam, eds., *Elvis! The Last Word*, p. 68; Red West et al., *Elvis: What Happened?*, p. 290.

353 Screaming Lord Sutch, a flamboyant British rocker: Rodney Bingenheimer, "It's All Happening," *Go*, August 15, 1969.

354 dropping several hundred dollars at a time: James Kingsley, "Presley Faces Toughest Challenge in Las Vegas," *Billboard*, August 9, 1969; Ellen Willis, "Musical Events" column, *New Yorker*, August 30, 1969.

354–355 The International took more formal notice: The tablecloth contract is in the possession of the Elvis Presley Estate. The initial letter from International Vice President Bill Miller exercising the option was written on August 1; the formal agreement upping Elvis' payment and extending the option through 1974 was executed on August 4 and signed by Elvis, Colonel, and Alex Shoofey (EPE).

355 Elvis should watch himself, he wrote: Note dated August 22, 1969, written on plain white paper (EPE).

355 "The reception Elvis is getting here": *Memphis Press-Scimitar*, August 21, 1969.

355 "I wouldn't let no loudmouth old man tell me": John Fergus Ryan, "One Night With the Killer," *Oxford-American*, August–September 1995; also, interviews with George Klein and David Briggs, Trevor Cajiao interview with Larry Muhoberac, *Elvis: The Man and His Music* 22, March 1994.

356 "Elvis took a moment": Ed Parker, *Inside Elvis*, pp. 45–48.

356 "Every night was like a command performance": Interview with Joe Moscheo, 1989.

356–357 "We didn't decide to come back": Ray Connolly, "Elvis the Husband Talks About Elvis the Pelvis," *London Evening Standard*, August 6, 1969.

357 "I said, 'Is the goddamn rhythm kicking you in the ass?'": Interview with Sam Phillips, 1989.

358 a tricky technical problem for Porter: Interview with Bill Porter, 1993.

358 "I mean, we laughed at it": Interview with Glen Spreen.

358 101,500 paying customers: *Los Angeles Times,* September 2, 1969.

359 "He remembered me": Jerry Hopkins interview with Mac Davis (MVC/UMem).

A NIGHT AT THE OPERA

361 They traveled to Hawaii: Information about the trips to Hawaii and the Bahamas and the aborted trip to Europe comes primarily from interviews with Jerry Schilling, Joe and Joan Esposito, and Priscilla Presley; also air bills (EPE) and passport issuance records; see also Marty Lacker et al., *Elvis: Portrait of a Friend,* p. 273.

362 "reportedly losing and signing markers": "Rona Reports," October 31 and November 6, 1969.

362 "During the lulls": Interview with Priscilla Presley, 1995.

363 "He was very much pulled": Interview with Sri Daya Mata, 1996.

363 "When the spirit moved him": Ed Parker, "'The King' and I," undated clipping (article in British fan magazine).

363–364 In the words of the 1966 hit: Sterling Hofman is only one of several witnesses who noted Elvis' fascination with the song. "He was smitten with it," she said in my 1989 interview with her. Elvis recorded "My Way" the following year and continued to sing it with the deepest conviction till the end of his life.

364–365 "I went in there": Interview with Glen D. Hardin, 1990.

364 "Elvis didn't rehearse": Glen D. Hardin quoted in Patsy Guy Hammontree, *Elvis Presley: A Bio-Bibliography,* p. 63.

365 "The first couple of things we did": Jerry Hopkins interview with Glen D. Hardin (MVC/UMem).

365 The show that Elvis put together: From rehearsal records (EPE).

366 Porter leapt to the challenge: Interview with Bill Porter, 1993.

366 "Apparently there is no stopping Elvis Presley": James Kingsley, "Presley 'Shakes Up' Las Vegas Audience," *Billboard,* February 7, 1970.

366 he forgot the lyrics: Frank Lieberman, "Elvis IS Still the King!," *Los Angeles Herald-Examiner,* February 4, 1970.

367 "a flawless demonstration": Robert Hilburn, "Charisma of Presley Still Rocks Vegas," *Los Angeles Times,* February 5, 1970.

367 "the new decade will belong to him": *Los Angeles Herald-Examiner,* February 4, 1970.

367 "Gorgeous!": Albert Goldman, "A Gross Top Grosser," *Life,* March 20, 1970.

368 "a new life": Frank Lieberman, "A Legend That Lives," *Los Angeles Herald-Examiner,* February 8, 1970.

368 "As soon as the show was over": Interview with Myrna Smith, 1990.

368 he read her passages: Interview with Estelle Brown, 1996.

368–369 "It just seemed like": Interview with Joe Moscheo, 1990.

369 a kind of "silly boys' club": Peter Cronin interview with Glen D. Hardin, 1993.

369 a competition between "the crowd's adoration": Priscilla Presley, *Elvis and Me,* p. 277.

369 the feeling gradually took hold: Interviews with Joe Esposito and Jerry Schilling, among many similar references.

370 The final night: Maria Davies, "The King Returns to His Kingdom: Vegas Revisited!," Rex Martin's *Official Elvis Presley Fan Club News Service;* Sue Wiegert, *Elvis: For the Good Times,* p. 113; Jerry Hopkins interview with Johnny Rivers (MVC/UMem).

370 New sound problems: Colonel to Alex Shoofey, February 23, 1970 (EPE).

370–371 the Colonel led an advance party: Marge Crumbaker, "A King in a Velvet Jail," *Mid-South Magazine, Memphis Commercial Appeal,* May 24, 1970.

371 The Colonel had tried to limit the size: Colonel to Joe Esposito, February 11, 1970 (EPE).

371 "just go ahead and play": Jerry Hopkins interview with Glen D. Hardin (MVC/UMem).

371 the first true test: Robert Hilburn, "Whole Lot of Shakin' Going On in Houston," *Los Angeles Times,* March 2, 1970.

371 "he went back to the hotel": Interview with Gee Gee Gambill: *Elvis: The Record,* vol. 2, no. 1, p. 19.

371–372 "The setting [for the second show]": *Los Angeles Times,* March 2, 1970.

372 Priscilla flew in: Maxine Mesinger, "Elvis Separation Rumor Is Dispelled," *Houston Chronicle,* March 2, 1970.

372 a capstone to "one of the most staggering reversals": Robert Hilburn, "Triumphant Return of the 'King,'" *Los Angeles Times,* undated clipping, c. March 15, 1970.

373 he had informed newly named International president: Colonel to Alex Shoofey, February 22 and 23, 1970 (EPE).

373 "The future of this resort community": Shoofey to Colonel, March 16, 1970; also follow-up letters from Shoofey and Fred Benninger to Colonel, March 21 and 26 (EPE).

373–376 Meanwhile, he continued to pursue another idea: Nearly all of the anecdotal information (and all quotations) on plans for this closed-circuit broadcast comes from Jerry Hopkins' interview with Steve Wolf and Jim Rissmiller (MVC/UMem); in addition there are written records of the terms for this and the various subsequent deals in the Colonel's papers (EPE); see also Robert Hilburn in the *Los Angeles Times,* March 19, 1970, and a similar Frank Lieberman report in the *Los Angeles Herald-Examiner* from around the same date. My summary of the negotiations, I'm sure, misses a few stages and may well miss more than a few of the Colonel's subtleties, but it is the best I could put together with the information available.

376–378 He wanted Felton with him: Jerry Flowers and Al Cooley interviews with Felton Jarvis; also interviews with Mary Jarvis, 1989, and Bob Beckham, 1995.

376 "Why don't you just quit": Al Cooley interview with Felton Jarvis.

376 a new contract from RCA: Ernst Jorgensen's and my interviews with Mary Jarvis; RCA paperwork supplied by Mary Jarvis. A preliminary "contract requisition" was drawn up on May 27 with substantially different terms, but the actual contract was dated, and presumably agreed to, on June 1.

378–379 Everyone in the band was excited: The material on the musicians' perspective on this session comes primarily from interviews with David Briggs, Chip Young, Jerry Carrigan, and Norbert Putnam.

378 Even for James Burton: Interview with James Burton, 1991.

379 "If he smiles at you": Jerry Hopkins interview with Jerry Carrigan (MVC/UMem).

379–380 The extent to which that trust had broken down: Interviews with Julian Aberbach and Freddy Bienstock; Bar Biszick's interviews with these and other players and insights on the same subject. In my interview with him, Bienstock credited the Colonel's loyalty with saving his position.

382 "It amazed me": Interview with Norbert Putnam, 1991.

382 He informed the hotel: Colonel to Alex Shoofey, June 23, 1970 (EPE).

383 "Baron Bienstock must be fully aware": Colonel to Julian Aberbach, March 26, 1970 (EPE).

383–385 Joe Guercio, a well-traveled music business hipster: Interviews with Joe Guercio, 1995 and 1998.

384 like "following a marble": Jerry Hopkins interview with Joe Guercio (MVC/UMem).

385 Cary Grant came backstage: Interview with Millie Kirkham, 1989.

385–386 To Robert Blair Kaiser: Robert Blair Kaiser, "The Rediscovery of Elvis," *New York Times Magazine,* October 11, 1970.

386 There would be one hundred security guards: James Kingsley, "Elvis Plans Tour After Wowing 'Em in Las Vegas," *Memphis Commercial Appeal,* August 12, 1970.

387 Jerry Weintraub had been courting the Colonel: Interview with Jerry Weintraub, 1995.

387 Hulett was the one with tour experience: Interview with Tom Hulett, 1990.

388 they put up $240,000: Tour contracts and records (EPE).

389 trotting out a "laughbox": Sue Wiegert provides a good description of the show in *For the Good Times,* pp. 115–118.

389 a paternity suit was filed: Various news accounts; Jerry Hopkins interview with John O'Grady (MVC/UMem); interview with Ed Hookstratten, 1995; John O'Grady and Nolan Davis, *O'Grady: The Life and Times of Hollywood's No. 1 Private Eye,* pp. 166–168.

389 "How can anyone do this to me?": May Mann, *Elvis and the Colonel,* p. 211.

389 it was never a member of the band: Interviews with Glen D. Hardin and Jerry Scheff.

390 a fan from Memphis approaching Vernon: *New York Times Magazine,* October 11, 1970.

390 "They'd think it was so funny": Interview with Joan Esposito.

391 "The first couple of times in Vegas": Interview with Jerry Schilling, 1997.

391 That was the atmosphere: Principal sources for background on Kathy Westmoreland are my 1990 interview and Kathy Westmoreland, *Elvis and Kathy.*

391 she had "never seen anything like that": Interview with Kathy Westmoreland.

392 "I think it's important for me to just entertain": Westmoreland, *Elvis and Kathy,* p. 37. Although I have taken the quote somewhat out of sequence in the book, it expresses a belief that Elvis articulated again and again.

392–393 an anonymous call came into the security office: FBI Files for Elvis A. Presley, part 1, pp. 55–63; also incident reports, one dated August 26, 1970, the other (undated) evidently written on August 28; August 28 notes "per telephone conversation with Ed Hookstratten"; undated letter regarding security precautions from Colonel to Elvis, with copies to Vernon Presley, Tom Diskin, George Parkhill, Joe Esposito, Jim O'Brien, Lamar Fike, Bitsy Mott, Sonny West, Richard Davis, and Charlie Hodge (EPE). Also, interviews with Jerry Schilling, Joe and Joan Esposito, Pat Parry, and Joe Moscheo. See also Jerry Hopkins manuscript account (MVC/UMem) plus numerous Hopkins interviews.

393 "I need you": Interview with Jerry Schilling, 1997.

393 When Red arrived: Red West et al., *Elvis: What Happened?,* p. 291.

393 "If some sonofabitch tries to kill me": Jerry Hopkins manuscript account (MVC/UMem); Sonny West in Clayton and Heard, *Elvis Up Close,* p. 247.

393 Dr. Newman . . . was backstage: Doctor and ambulance bills (EPE).

393 "It was crazy": Interview with Joe Moscheo.

393–394 Jim Aubrey, the soft-spoken fifty-one-year-old head of MGM: Background on Jim Aubrey comes largely from Peter Bart, *Fade Out: The Calamitous Final Days of MGM,* pp. 32ff.

393 a dark-haired twenty-three-year-old starlet: Interview with Barbara Leigh, 1990.

394 Then he turned back to Bova: Joyce Bova, *Don't Ask Forever: My Love Affair with Elvis,* pp. 61ff. Both Joyce Bova and Barbara Leigh refer to the presence of Rick and Kris Nelson in the room, as well as Jim Aubrey, though neither was aware of the other's presence. Bova dates the meeting to just after the assassination threat, and Leigh places it in the same time frame.

394 Bova had been enormously impressed: Bova, *Don't Ask Forever,* pp. 11–42.

394 She had made this trip determined to find out: Ibid., pp. 54–72.

395 "The phone was ringing": Interview with Barbara Leigh.

395–396 "Then all of a sudden Elvis came in": Interview with Kathy Westmoreland.

397 he called his wife, Marie: Jerry Hopkins interview with Stan Brossette (MVC/UMem); see also Jerry Hopkins, "Don't You Go Winnin' Elvis No Oscars," *Rolling Stone,* September 17, 1970.

398 Net income from personal appearances: This is the roughest of estimates. It is merely intended to give an idea of both the range of income possibilities and the way in which income was, theoretically, divided. I've tried to project figures on the basis of contracts, record sales, and my limited business understanding, but it would require an accountant of considerable sophistication to make his way through the maze of deals and side deals that the Colonel set up for both Elvis' benefit and his own. One thing should be clear from all of this, however: by now the arrangement was essentially a partnership, in the Colonel's view anyway, and one to which each partner contributed his own skills and expertise.

398 Elvis called for the spotlight: Wiegert, *For the Good Times,* pp. 116–118.

A COMIC BOOK HERO

401 "The crowd that filled the house": Robert Blair Kaiser, "The Rediscovery of Elvis," *New York Times Magazine,* October 11, 1970.

401 The Imperials had begged off: Interview with Joe Moscheo, 1989.

401 For reasons of economy: Interview with Joe Guercio, 1995; tour records (EPE).

402 "First this sonofabitch in Vegas": Kathy Westmoreland, *Elvis and Kathy,* p. 45 (italics and ellipses added).

402–403 "I went out and hired": Interview with Tom Hulett, 1990.

403 "Isn't it fun traveling like this?": Westmoreland, *Elvis and Kathy,* p. 48.

403 "they didn't much like me": Interview with Barbara Leigh, 1990.

404 "the dump of dumps": Interview with Joe Esposito, 1990.

405 to collect his official deputy sheriff's badge: UPI dispatch, October 13, 1970.

405 the National Quartet Convention: *Memphis Press-Scimitar,* October 15–16, 1970; *Memphis Commercial Appeal,* October 15.

405 "[we all] were going to have our picture made": Jerry Hopkins interview with James Blackwood (MVC/UMem); correspondence with James Blackwood.

405 "I thought maybe he'd gotten away": Jerry Hopkins interview with James Blackwood. I have changed the tenses.

406–407 The bluntness of his language: Colonel to James Aubrey, September 24, 1970 (EPE).

407 He demanded a $1 million deposit: Interview with Jerry Weintraub, 1995.

407 twelve pendants he had ordered: Bill from Sol Schwartz and Lee Ableser, Fine Diamonds and Jewelry (EPE).

407 the prototype he and Priscilla had sketched out: Jerry Hopkins interview with Sol Schwartz (MVC/UMem); Joe Esposito, *Good Rockin' Tonight,* p. 100.

407–408 an undercover assignment at Hollywood High: George Klein remarks at the 1982 annual Elvis Presley Memorial conference at the University of Memphis (MVC/UMem); Alanna Nash, *Elvis Aaron Presley: Revelations from the Memphis Mafia,* p. 480; interviews with Jerry Schilling, 1995, 1997.

408 the time that lightning had split one of the statues: Westmoreland, *Elvis and Kathy,* p. 81.

408 He called Kathy: Ibid., p. 55.

408 "Scatter was one of the best buddies": Ibid., p. 66.

408 "Hey, boys": Ibid., pp. 57–58.

409 Barbara Leigh was a frequent visitor: Interview with Barbara Leigh.

409–410 "that night, in the quiet stillness": Westmoreland, *Elvis and Kathy,* pp. 68–70.

410 That was the night: Ibid., p. 74.

410 "I've got fifty-six gold singles": "Random Notes," *Rolling Stone*, December 24, 1970. See also Maria Davies in Rex Martin's *Official Elvis Presley Fan Club News Service* 37–38 on the intrusion of the process server and Elvis' subsequent mood.

411 Richard Davis was fired: Nash, *Elvis Aaron Presley*, p. 516; Trevor Cajiao interview with Richard Davis, *Elvis: The Man and His Music* 14, March 1992.

411 "People will come from miles around": Westmoreland, *Elvis and Kathy*, p. 77.

411 He told them he would come back to pick it up: Interview with Ron Pietrafeso, 1995.

411 the largest single donation: *Los Angeles Times*, September 7, 1977.

411 he visited and exchanged gifts with the seventy-seven-year-old retired general: Interviews with Jerry Schilling, Cliff Gleaves, and Joe Esposito; also, Sue Wiegert, *Elvis: For the Good Times*, p. 119; Donna Lewis, *"Hurry Home, Elvis!": Donna Lewis' Diaries*, vol 3 (unpublished manuscript), msp. 172.

411–412 He sought out Vice President Agnew: Jerry Hopkins interviews with Jerry Schilling and John O'Grady (MVC/UMem); Red West et al., *Elvis: What Happened?*, p. 313.

412 He dismissed the Colonel: Marty Lacker et al., *Elvis: Portrait of a Friend*, p. 342.

412 One night the whole gang went out for dinner: Interviews with Jerry Schilling — but virtually every memoir and biography, and innumerable interviews, have recounted this incident with little variation save for the location of the dinner.

412 a three-night, $20,000 gun-buying spree: Jerry Hopkins interview with salesman Jerry Knight (MVC/UMem); West et al., *Elvis: What Happened?*, p. 83. In the latter the figure is put at $19,792; Jerry Knight recalls a sum of $28,000; and Jerry Hopkins puts it at $38,000 in his *Elvis: The Final Years*, p. 1.

412 he got a construction permit: The construction permit was dated December 10, the deed November 9, 1970 (EPE).

412 Joe and Joanie . . . needed a house, too: Interviews with Joe and Joan Esposito; Esposito, *Good Rockin'*, p. 169; Lacker et al., *Portrait*, p. 150.

412–413 he decided to buy Mercedeses: Interviews with Ed Hookstratten, Barbara Leigh, George Barris, and Jerry Schilling.

413 "He was very spontaneous": Jerry Hopkins interview with Sol Schwartz (MVC/UMem).

413 Vernon and Priscilla got Elvis off by himself: Interview with Priscilla Presley, 1995; Priscilla Presley, *Elvis and Me*, p. 285; Billy Stanley, *Elvis, My Brother*, p. 105; Lacker et al., *Portrait*, p. 141; Goldman, *Elvis*, p. 462; et al.

414–417 Jerry was the first to get any kind of word: This account has been constructed primarily from various interviews with Jerry Schilling over the years, both Jerry Hopkins' (MVC/UMem) and my own, as well as Hopkins' interview with Gerald Peters (MVC/UMem).

416 "First I would like to introduce myself": Elvis' letter has been published in facsimile form in a number of books, including Fred L. Worth and Steve D. Tamerius, *Elvis: His Life from A to Z*, and Egil "Bud" Krogh, *The Day Elvis Met Nixon*.

417 Egil "Bud" Krogh, deputy counsel to the President: Krogh's account in *The Day Elvis Met Nixon* is an invaluable and detailed portrait. Unfortunately, Krogh has one preliminary screening meeting with Elvis that does not appear in other accounts. Given Chapin's memo to H. R. Haldeman, the absence of a follow-up memo from Krogh, the fact that times are not noted on existing memos, and the apparent chronology of Elvis' day, I am at a loss as to how to resolve this discrepancy and have thus chosen to go with Jerry Schilling's version of events. In other respects, the two accounts contradict each other only in minor detail.

418 "You know that several people have mentioned": Krogh, *The Day Elvis Met Nixon*, p. 14.

418 badges went only to "those employees": John Finlator, *The Drugged Nation: A "Narc's" Story*, p. 103.

419 Duncan said with . . . "an edge in his voice": Krogh, *The Day Elvis Met Nixon,* p. 26.

419 "He looked up at the ceiling": Ibid., pp. 32–33.

420 Krogh's contemporaneous memo: From Bud Krogh to The President's File, December 21, 1970, as reproduced in Bruce Oudes, ed., *From: The President: Richard Nixon's Secret Files,* p. 194.

420–421 It was at this point: The point is located only in my imagined reconstruction on the basis of what I hope to be informed guesswork deriving from the various anecdotal accounts. Obviously, tapes of this meeting, if they exist, may alter our understanding of its chronology and tone somewhat.

421 "The President," Krogh wrote: Krogh, *The Day Elvis Met Nixon,* pp. 35–38.

421 "Sonny and I were just standing in the doorway in awe": Jerry Hopkins interview with Jerry Schilling (MVC/UMem); see also West et al., *Elvis: What Happened?,* p. 236.

422 staff members "accustomed to seeing heads of state": Krogh, *The Day Elvis Met Nixon,* p. 44.

422–423 "He wanted to know what I made": Interview with Jerry Schilling.

423 He had been unable to get an appointment: FBI memo, December 22, 1970, FBI Files for Elvis A. Presley, part 1, p. 10.

423 one more attempt to see Joyce Bova: Joyce Bova, *Don't Ask Forever: My Love Affair with Elvis,* pp. 75ff; interview with Jerry Schilling. Chronology once again is a problem; according to Bova's recollection Jerry was the one who called her, but Jerry has no memory of any connection being made while he was still in Washington. It could have happened either way, but both recollections agree: Jerry was no longer around when Elvis and Bova met.

423 "Good thing I was right, man": Bova, *Don't Ask Forever,* p. 78.

423 "That sonofabitch Finlator": Ibid., pp. 84–94.

423–424 "he was like a kid": Interview with Priscilla Presley.

424 he dispensed four more Mercedeses: *Memphis Press-Scimitar,* December 30, 1970.

424 in the early hours of the morning: *Seattle Post-Intelligencer,* December 27, 1970; undated clipping from the *Memphis Commercial Appeal,* c. December 28.

424 He was wearing the "fur-cloth" black bell-bottom suit: *Memphis Press-Scimitar,* December 29 and 31, 1970.

424 He was armed with two guns: Nash, *Elvis Aaron Presley,* p. 501.

424 the deputy's badges they had recently acquired: Ibid., p. 502; Jerry Hopkins interview with Jerry Schilling (MVC/UMem).

425 "He paced the floor": Interview with Bill Mitchell, 1990.

425 "The Impossible Dream" was the title: "Elvis Makes 'Quiet Visit' to Tupelo," *Memphis Press-Scimitar,* December 30, 1970. Although he never recorded this song in the studio, he did start using it as a closing number in Las Vegas the following month. See also Nash, *Elvis Aaron Presley,* p. 19, re Shake Rag.

425 Elvis paid for everyone to join: Lamar Fike has this taking place the previous day in Nash, *Elvis Aaron Presley,* p. 502, but this would be impossible according to Joyce Bova's chronology in Bova, *Don't Ask Forever,* pp. 110ff.

425 they visited the FBI Building: FBI Files for Elvis A. Presley, part 1, pp. 7–8, memo dated January 4, 1971.

427 "your generous comments concerning the Bureau": J. Edgar Hoover to Elvis Presley, January 4, 1971, Ibid., p. 3.

427 The Jaycee awards had been given out: Most of the background on the history of the awards and its honorees comes from the Jaycee program that Elvis kept (EPE).

427–428 "He stayed up in his office": Interview with Priscilla Presley.

428–429 The two of them showed up bright and early: Much of the background for this account of the JCC dinner stems from reports in the *Memphis Commercial Appeal* and the *Memphis Press-Scimitar*, January 16 and 17, 1971.

428–429 he spotted Sam Phillips' former office manager: Interview with Marion Keisker, 1988; interview with Jerry Schilling.

429 Priscilla was amazed to see a side: Interview with Priscilla Presley.

429 At the restaurant: Bills indicate a considerable amount of detail (the party cost $1,907.51 for one hundred guests for Chateaubriand dinner and bar) (EPE). For a more descriptive record, see *Memphis Commercial Appeal*, January 17, 1971.

A STRANGER IN MY OWN HOMETOWN

431 He also threw a glass of water: Sue Wiegert, *Elvis: For the Good Times*, p. 125.

431 "It took only a second for his guys to join in": Joyce Bova, *Don't Ask Forever: My Love Affair with Elvis*, p. 148.

432 Elvis showed them his BNDD badge: Interviews with Ron Pietrafeso, 1995, and Billy Ray Schilling, 1996.

432 "for one of the few times in his adult life": *Memphis Press-Scimitar*, March 9, 1971; George Klein remarks on Elvis' admiration for Ali at 1985 annual Elvis Presley Memorial conference at the University of Memphis (MVC/UMem). See also Thomas Hauser, *Muhammad Ali: His Life and Times*, p. 481.

433 Dr. Nick flew in from Memphis: Interviews with Dr. George Nichopoulos, Barbara Leigh, and Joe Esposito; also, Red West et al., *Elvis: What Happened?*, p. 286; *Memphis Press-Scimitar*, March 17 and 23, 1971.

433–434 "I was frozen by the sight of Priscilla": Bova, *Don't Ask Forever*, pp. 160ff. All subsequent quotes from Bova are from her book.

434 He introduced her to his grandmother: Ibid., p. 177.

434 "'Just think about it,' he said": Ibid., p. 192.

435 "Whoa, all ye Pharisees": This and other expressions like it (including the parable of the camel's ass) show up in numerous interviews and memoirs, including Joe Esposito, *Good Rockin' Tonight*, p. 122; West et al., *Elvis: What Happened?*, p. 168; Rose Clayton and Dick Heard, eds., *Elvis Up Close: In the Words of Those Who Knew Him Best*, p. 255. See also Jerry Hopkins, *Elvis: The Final Years*, p. 85.

435 "I felt that I just couldn't reach him": Interview with Priscilla Presley, 1995.

435 at Ed's instigation Elvis had contacted: Interviews with Ed Parker, 1990, and Kang Rhee, 1995.

435–437 carrying his diamond-and-ruby-encrusted lion's-head cane: Interview with Norbert Putnam, 1991. Other details about the session come from interviews with Jerry Carrigan, Glen Spreen, David Briggs, Chip Young, and Freddy Bienstock; Al Cooley interview with Felton Jarvis; and Alice Alexander, "He Knew the 'Private' Elvis," an interview with Felton Jarvis in the August 21, 1977, *Nashville Tennessean*.

436 "Instead of him coming in the control room": Interview with Glen Spreen, 1995.

437 "All of a sudden," said drummer Jerry Carrigan: Jerry Hopkins interview with Jerry Carrigan (MVC/UMem).

437 Carrigan failed to show up at all: Interview with Jerry Carrigan, 1989.

437 the session came to an abrupt halt: Interviews with Chip Young, Jerry Carrigan, Glen Spreen, and Joe Moscheo, among others. Accounts differ as to whether it was Red or Charlie who was disarmed.

438 "We used to joke": Interview with Norbert Putnam.

438 Finally Carrigan said: Jerry Hopkins interview with Jerry Carrigan (MVC/UMem).

438–439 He called for Joyce to join him: Bova, *Don't Ask Forever,* pp. 193ff; group interview including Norbert Putnam and Jerry Carrigan conducted by Ernst Jorgensen and me, 1995. These are two very different recollections of the same event, with the musicians recalling how they "faked the stuff" and Joyce failing to recall the musicians.

439 Elvis, transported by the music and "every inch the perfectionist at work": Bova, *Don't Ask Forever,* p. 196.

439–440 his weird fluctuations of mood: Group interview with Norbert Putnam, Chip Young, David Briggs, Jerry Carrigan, and Kenny Buttrey conducted by Ernst Jorgensen and me; interviews with Jerry Carrigan, both mine and Jerry Hopkins'.

440–441 Elvis had met Master Rhee himself: Interview with Kang Rhee. Elvis' first badge from Kang Rhee, a fourth-degree black belt, is dated March 29, 1971 (EPE).

441 The Hilton Hotel chain took over the International: Correspondence between Barron Hilton and the Colonel from June 23, 1971, would indicate that the Hilton chain had effectively taken over by this date. For specifics on the business transaction, see Dial Torgerson, *Kerkorian: An American Success Story,* p. 245, which places the date of the actual sale on July 1.

441 The Colonel had an understanding: Jerry Hopkins interview with Henri Lewin (MVC/UMem).

442 "I did business with Kerkorian": Ibid.

443 Joanie Esposito paid a surprise visit: Esposito, *Good Rockin',* p. 127. Jerry Hopkins' interview with John Wilkinson (MVC/UMem) and my interview with Joe Guercio, 1995, reinforce the sense of atmosphere.

443 "We set it up": Interview with Joe Guercio.

443 Elvis' salary triggered "favored nations" clauses: Undated trade magazine account of the engagement from Colonel's scrapbooks (EPE).

444 "Col. Tom Parker outdid himself": *Variety,* August 14, 1971.

444 the critic for the *Hollywood Reporter . . .* called the performance: *Hollywood Reporter,* August 12, 1971.

444 it was "fabulous," from the overture on: Interview with Bill Belew, 1995.

445 "Further reliable word": Rona Barrett column, September 9, 1971. Needless to say Daya Mata, who took a vow of chastity upon entering the Fellowship, was never married to Paramahansa Yogananda, who, far from predicting Elvis' messianic role, died in 1952 while Elvis was still in high school, without every hearing, or uttering, Elvis Presley's name.

445 the almost equally evident estrangement between Elvis and Priscilla: "Memo from John J. Miller," *San Francisco Sunday Examiner and Chronicle,* August 22, 1971.

445 "I would get these great shots of guys fighting": Interview with Priscilla Presley.

445 "a great blackbelt": Interview with Ed Parker.

446 "if Joe would call looking for Priscilla": Interview with Joan Esposito, 1995.

446 She knew the rules: Interview with Priscilla Presley.

446 Joyce Bova might have said much the same thing: Bova, *Don't Ask Forever,* pp. 226–239.

447 "when you had him around, you could make money": Jerry Hopkins interview with Henri Lewin (MVC/UMem). The tenses have been changed.

447 a manager who in Lewin's view "worried about Elvis": Henri Lewin, "Better Late Than Never," *Las Vegas Style,* March 1994.

447 "one of the best customers we ever had": Rose Clayton, "Colonel Parker Accused of Ripping Off Elvis," *Rolling Stone,* September 17, 1981.

447 "This was a man who never spent any money": Bar Biszick interview with Julian Aberbach, 1995; also my interview with Julian Aberbach, 1995. Similar views were expressed by Jean Aberbach in Albert Goldman, *Elvis,* p. 500.

447 Freddy tried to talk to him: Interview with Freddy Bienstock, 1992.

447 "It made me sick": Interview with Al Dvorin, 1996.

448 "Don't get crazy," he told Joe: Interview with Joe Esposito.

448 Now they all talked: Alanna Nash, *Elvis Aaron Presley: Revelations from the Memphis Mafia*, p. 471.

448 "Colonel had always told him": Interview with Joe Esposito.

448 "As different as they might appear": Interview with Jerry Schilling.

449 spoke of him as "Lardass": Interview with Freddy Bienstock.

449 The most frequent subject of discussion was Europe: Interviews with Priscilla Presley, Joe Esposito, Lamar Fike, Jerry Schilling, and others.

449 the Colonel had entered into talks with Tom Jones' flamboyant manager: *Melody Maker* and *New Musical Express* articles, September 1971; also, correspondence between Tom Diskin and *New Musical Express*, Gordon Mills and Tom Diskin, and Colonel and Gordon Mills between October 27 and November 1, 1971 (EPE); interview with Jerry Weintraub, 1995.

449 he expressed growing exasperation: Colonel to Management III, September 1, 1971 (EPE); interview with Tom Hulett, 1990.

450 they sought a renegotiation of their contract: Interviews with Joe Moscheo, 1989, and J. D. Sumner, 1990.

450 A new comedian was hired: Interview with Jackie Kahane, 1995.

451 he elicited $25,000 bonus payments: Barron Hilton to Colonel, August 30, 1971 (EPE).

451 he resolutely refused to confirm: Colonel to Alex Shoofey, September 7, 1971; the Colonel finally confirmed the booking in a letter of November 24 and offered to look after the promotion, merchandising, advertising, etc., "assuming that you have not made other arrangements." Shoofey was not able to contain his "deepest personal appreciation" in his reply the following day (EPE).

451 Priscilla described it as "very manly": Sandra Shevey, "Priscilla Presley: My Life With and Without Elvis Presley," *Ladies Home Journal*, August 1973, p. 139.

451 One time during the summer: West et al., *Elvis: What Happened?*, p. 227; Priscilla Presley, *Elvis and Me*, p. 282; Nash, *Elvis Aaron Presley*, p. 508; Esposito, *Good Rockin'*, p. 125; et al.

452 "I said, 'Colonel, we got two weeks'": Interview with Al Dvorin.

452 Joyce flew into Cleveland: Bova, *Don't Ask Forever*, pp. 276ff.

452 Elvis' seventy-four-year-old grandfather, Jessie: Bill Peterson, "Some of Elvis Presley's fans are old enough to be his grandparents," *Louisville Courier-Journal*, November 8, 1971.

453 The paternity suit was nearly settled: Rona Barrett column, November 5, 1971; *Los Angeles Citizen News*, December 2, 1971.

453 he had pretty much broken off with Barbara: Interview with Barbara Leigh, 1990.

453 He spoke to Joyce: Bova, *Don't Ask Forever*, pp. 316ff.

454 "Everyone remembered," wrote James Kingsley: Kingsley, "Elvis Plays Santa Claus — With Sly Grin on Face," *Memphis Commercial Appeal*, December 31, 1971.

454 Some of the guests in retrospect recalled: Nash, *Elvis Aaron Presley*, p. 527; Billy Stanley, *Elvis, My Brother*, p. 134; Hopkins, *Final Years*, p. 48.

454 in calls and conversations with one friend after another: Interviews with Lester and Sterling Hofman, Pat Parry, Alan Fortas, Ed Parker, and Dr. George Nichopoulos. All testify to Elvis' highly emotional reaction.

454 Joyce didn't see any major change: Bova, *Don't Ask Forever*, p. 363.

455 Robert Hilburn put his finger on the ongoing problem: Hilburn, "Fan to Fan: What's Happened to Elvis," *Los Angeles Times*, February 6, 1972.

455 Despite having to rent a private kidney machine: Interview with Mary Jarvis, 1989.

455–456 Joyce came out to Vegas one last time: Bova, *Don't Ask Forever*, pp. 364–383. All quotes are from this source.

456 "He grabbed me": Priscilla Presley, *Elvis and Me*, p. 298.

456–457 Joanie didn't know: Interview with Joan Esposito. It should be noted that in her book *(Elvis and Me,* pp. 298–300) Priscilla indicates that she did not tell Elvis about Mike Stone. West et al., *Elvis: What Happened?,* p. 231, has Priscilla telling Pat West that Elvis "took her right on the spot when he knew another man was in the picture." But no man is named.

ON TOUR

459 Through a series of carefully executed maneuvers: Colonel had gotten a commitment from RCA president Rocco Laginestra as early as December 2, 1971, with the actual contract executed on January 28, 1972 (EPE).

459–460 a mood of almost autumnal regret: Ernst Jorgensen interview with Red West; Jerry Flowers interview with Felton Jarvis; and interviews with Jerry Schilling, 1990, and Pat Parry, 1991.

460 he had picked up from his friend Bob Beckham: Interview with Bob Beckham, 1995.

460 Elvis was in no mood: Al Cooley and Jerry Flowers interviews with Felton Jarvis.

460 The song with which they started out: Ernst Jorgensen interview with Red West; Trevor Cajiao interview with Red West, *Elvis: The Man and His Music* 22, June 1994, p. 11.

460 they all sat around listening: Interview with Jerry Schilling, 1997; also Ernst Jorgensen and Trevor Cajiao interviews with Red West.

460–461 "Elvis was really concentrating": Peter Cronin interview with Emory Gordy, 1993.

461 "He was trying to get something out of his system": Jerry Flowers interview with Felton Jarvis.

462–465 The two filmmakers, Bob Abel and Pierre Adidge: Most of the background on Abel and Adidge, and on the actual filming of the show, comes from my and Jerry Hopkins' interviews with Bob Abel.

463 "I want to shoot the real you": Interview with Bob Abel, 1995.

464 Back in Hollywood he transferred the tape: It should be noted that while Abel remembers simply filming the performance, there is an audiotape which indicates that he filmed the rehearsal in Buffalo as well.

465 "he pretty much gave us carte blanche": Jerry Hopkins interview with Bob Abel (MVC/UMem).

466–467 Finally Jerry, who saw this as a long-awaited opportunity: Interviews with Jerry Schilling and Bob Abel. The approximate date of Elvis' interview by the filmmakers is established by the recent death of go-go girl Kathleen Selph on July 19, to which Elvis refers at the beginning of the interview.

469 "He was like a mirror": Interview with Marion Keisker, 1988.

469–470 the expense of the building, the promotional costs: Interview with Tom Hulett, 1990.

470 Jackie Kahane . . . got booed off the stage: Interviews with Jackie Kahane, 1995, and Al Dvorin, 1996, among others.

471 "Like a Prince from Another Planet": *New York Times,* June 18, 1972.

471 dating a go-go girl: This was the same girl who was killed in the car crash in mid July.

471 his continued preoccupation with Priscilla's departure: Interview with Glen Spreen, 1995; Jerry Hopkins interview with Bill Browder (MVC/UMem); Red West et al., *Elvis: What Happened?,* p. 284; Billy Stanley, *Elvis, My Brother,* p. 161.

471–474 Then on July 6 he met Linda Thompson: Much of the background and all of those quotes not otherwise specified come from my interviews with Linda Thompson, 1990 and 1995.

473 "I had gone four years to Memphis State": Jerry Hopkins interview with Linda Thompson (MVC/UMem).

474 She had returned to Graceland: Priscilla Presley, *Elvis and Me,* p. 300; *Memphis Press-Scimitar,* July 27, 1972.

474 The terms of the settlement: These can be gleaned from the petition filed by Priscilla's new attorney to set aside the settlement the following July (see Goldman, *Elvis,* pp. 517–518); also, interview with Ed Hookstratten, 1995.

474 a salary of $50,000 to the Colonel: Barron Hilton to Colonel, April 20, 1972. Elvis' salary emendation was formalized on the same date (EPE).

475 a direct threat the previous March: Colonel to Alex Shoofey, March 27, 1972 (EPE).

475 "with a welcome absence of horseplay": *Variety,* August 23, 1972.

475 Robert Hilburn reported: *Los Angeles Times,* August 18, 1972.

475 all the historic landmarks: Laura Deni, "TV Satellite Opens Era for Concert Show," *Billboard,* September 16, 1972; Joseph A. Tunzi, *Elvis '73: Hawaiian Spirit.* The claim that this was the first worldwide satellite broadcast of an entertainment special was somewhat debatable in that the broadcast was not actually worldwide and Andy Williams had already done something of a similar nature for the European market.

476 a new arrangement with Elvis and the Colonel: The Colonel proposed this initially in a letter to George Parkhill on August 24, 1972; terms for the contract were sketched out on August 31 and the contract signed on September 12 (EPE).

476 he raised the issue: Colonel to Harry Jenkins, April 2, 1972 (EPE).

477 He had originally gotten the idea: George Parkhill deposition with respect to Colonel Parker in the matter of the estate of Elvis Aaron Presley, September 1, 1981 (EPE).

477 Jim Aubrey had begged him to postpone: Jim Aubrey and Doug Netter telegram to Colonel thanking him for his cooperation, August 14, 1972 (EPE).

478 Colonel got a letter from *Honolulu Advertiser* columnist Eddie Sherman: Eddie Sherman to Colonel, September 18, 1972 (EPE).

478 he set $25,000 as the public goal: *Billboard,* December 16, 1972; *Honolulu Advertiser,* November 21, 1972.

478 he met with Bill Belew: Interview with Bill Belew, 1995.

478–479 He met with Marty Pasetta: Much of the background information and all of the quotes come from my interview with Marty Pasetta, 1995, unless otherwise noted.

479 Colonel volunteered several ideas: The execution of several of these ideas is described in the *Hollywood Reporter,* January 25, 1973, as well as in Jerry Hopkins' interview with Eddie Sherman. It should be noted that Al Dvorin was instrumental in conceiving of, booking, and carrying out much of the circus atmosphere.

480 Elvis even went on a quick-fix diet: Charles C. Thompson II and James P. Cole, *The Death of Elvis: What Really Happened,* p. 341; Alanna Nash, *Elvis Aaron Presley: Revelations from the Memphis Mafia,* p. 554.

480 "I was with him twenty-four hours a day": Interview with Linda Thompson, 1995.

481 "I said, 'Come onnn'": Jerry Hopkins interview with Linda Thompson (MVC/UMem).

481 He and Sonny had succeeded: Thompson and Cole, *The Death of Elvis,* p. 341.

481 It had even been nominated: It won the Best Documentary award in a tie with *Walls of Fire.*

482 "the first time that a current hit single": RCA publicity release, October 9, 1972.

482 he had real misgivings about his future role: Interview with Mary Jarvis, 1989; interview with Joan Deary, 1990; Mary Jarvis letter, February 18, 1993, with RCA paperwork; Ernst Jorgensen interview with Mary Jarvis; Al Cooley interview with Felton Jarvis. With respect to the kidney transplant, evidently because of his disillusionment with what he took to be the hospital's opportunism, Elvis never made the donation.

482 There were various technical problems to contend with: Interview with Joan Deary; Sue Cameron, "Coast to Coast," *Hollywood Reporter,* January 25, 1973.

482 Elvis gave away his ruby-encrusted belt: Jerry Hopkins interview with Bill Belew (MVC/UMem); also, my interview with Belew.

483 tech crews ran their cables: Interview with Dick Baxter, 1989.

483 fans almost "literally stormed the inside of the arena": *Honolulu Advertiser,* January 13, 1973.

484 "It was a thrilling compact hour": *Honolulu Advertiser,* January 15, 1973.

484 "there was just not as much wind": Interview with Joe Guercio, 1995.

484 "the highlight of the night": *Los Angeles Times,* January 15, 1973.

484 the Colonel wrote Elvis a letter: EPE.

FREEFALL

487 There was . . . some outright friction: Red West et al., *Elvis: What Happened?*, pp. 166, 194–195; Albert Goldman, *Elvis,* p. 483.

487 "Colonel Tom Parker," the review declared: *Variety,* February 7, 1973.

487 he was variously reported: *Hollywood Reporter,* February 6, 1973; Sue Wiegert, *Elvis: For the Good Times,* pp. 138ff.

487–488 The Colonel, placed in the position: Colonel to Barron Hilton, February 16, 1973 (EPE).

488 he saw Dr. Boyer almost every day: Doctor's bills, January 25–March 4, 1973 (EPE); West et al., *Elvis: What Happened?*, p. 194; Alanna Nash, *Elvis Aaron Presley: Revelations from the Memphis Mafia,* pp. 556–557.

488 his apparent "lack of energy and interest": *Hollywood Reporter,* February 6, 1973.

488 Frank Lieberman, the *Los Angeles Herald-Examiner* critic: Jerry Hopkins interview with Frank Lieberman (MVC/UMem).

488 "I felt sorry for [him]": Thomas Hauser, *Muhammad Ali: His Life and Times,* p. 481.

488–490 four guys rushed the stage: Wiegert, *For the Good Times,* p. 139; AP dispatch (undated clipping); West et al., *Elvis: What Happened?*, p. 316; Kathy Westmoreland, *Elvis and Kathy,* p. 145; Goldman, *Elvis,* pp. 507ff; interview with Linda Thompson, 1995.

489 "You know it, Sonny": West et al., *Elvis: What Happened?*, pp. 3–5.

490 Finally Linda called Dr. Newman: Interview with Linda Thompson; doctor's bills (EPE). There were nine visits by the doctor on February 19, six more the following day.

490 "Aw, hell," he said at last: West et al., *Elvis: What Happened?*, p. 10.

490 The final show was the usual: Wiegert, *For the Good Times,* pp. 140, 141.

490–491 He maintained his karate studies: Interviews with Jerry Schilling, 1995, and Kang Rhee, 1995.

491 Elvis gave Master Rhee $10,000: The canceled check is dated March 7 (EPE).

491 "Everything we did": Interview with Joe Esposito, 1990.

491–494 The Colonel meanwhile had finalized the deal: Interviews with Mel Ilberman, Joan Deary, Roger Davis, and Grelun Landon; George Parkhill deposition with respect to Colonel Parker in the matter of the estate of Elvis Aaron Presley, September 1, 1981 (EPE); also, the Colonel's own affidavit in his answering lawsuit, June 1, 1982 (EPE); Guardian Ad Litem's Amended Report In Re the Estate of Elvis A. Presley, Deceased, No. A-655, filed July 31, 1981; various RCA memoranda and contractual proposals (EPE).

493–494 A contract that would actually come to $5.4 million: All of the figures are in the Ad Litem report; the interpretation is my own. Just by way of financial comparison, Atlantic Records was sold lock, stock, and barrel in 1967 to Warner Seven-Arts for somewhat less than $20 million, and Neil Diamond signed a $4 million contract with Columbia in 1971 (ten albums at $400,000 an album) that on the surface does not seem the equal of Elvis'. (Clive Davis, *Clive: Inside the Record Business*, pp. 150ff, describes negotiating the Diamond deal.)

494 after factoring in all the aggravation: Colonel's rationale was expressed again and again in his last years, to which I can personally attest. Also, see Thomas Jordan and James Kingsley, "Fairness of Colonel Parker's 50 Per Cent Fee Is 'Hair-Pulling' Question," *Memphis Commercial Appeal*, October 2, 1980, and Randall Beck, "'Suspicious Minds,'" *Memphis Press-Scimitar*, September 8, 1981, which are to a large extent a rehash of the Colonel's response to the Ad Litem accusations and his affidavit in his own lawsuit (EPE). "All I know is, I sleep very good at night," the Colonel said, with respect to his conscience being clear.

494–495 Not everyone saw it this way: Interviews with Roger Davis, Julian Aberbach, Tom Hulett, and Grelun Landon; Jean Aberbach quoted in Goldman, *Elvis*, p. 500.

495 no one could say Elvis was an unwitting, or even unenthusiastic, participant: Interviews with Jerry Schilling, Joe Esposito, Lamar Fike, Mel Ilberman, Ed Parker. According to Jerry Schilling, Elvis was very proud of the deal and spoke of it explicitly, though he rarely talked business.

495–496 he had been trying: Various correspondence between Colonel and Hill and Range, Colonel and Freddy Bienstock, and Colonel and RCA, from March 1, 1972 (EPE).

496 he informed Elvis in the middle of the Vegas engagement: Colonel to Elvis, February 13, 1973 (EPE).

496 the first quadraphonic release: RCA publicity release, April 30, 1973; *Billboard*, May 5, 1973.

496–497 Elvis watched the show: Interview with Jerry Schilling.

497 Mike was "very much of a man": Sandra Shevey, "Priscilla Presley: My Life With and Without Elvis Presley," *Ladies Home Journal*, August 1973, p. 144.

497 this was widely perceived as "selling rank": Interview with Bill Wallace, 1997.

497 What he wanted now: Interview with Kang Rhee.

497–498 the newspapers, too, had carried notices: Newspaper accounts in the *San Francisco Examiner*, April 5–9, 1973, reflect the arc of expectations of the tournament directors. In the *Examiner* on April 5 and 7, Presley, "an avid karate fan," is scheduled to put in an appearance at Sunday night's (April 8) championship finals. The story on April 9 cites a clause in his Tahoe contract as having prevented him from participating but still has him watching the program from the stands — a direct contradiction of everyone's memory. The paper is also wrong about the Tahoe opening, which it implies will take place the following week. Interviews with Ed Parker, Kang Rhee, Jerry Schilling, and Joe Esposito offer various degrees of difference and occasionally sharply conflicting accounts. See West et al., *Elvis: What Happened?*, pp. 71ff, for another view.

498 "At the time I don't know anything about pills": Interview with Kang Rhee.

499 "I was really let down": Ernst Jorgensen interview with Emory Gordy; also, Peter Cronin interview with Emory Gordy.

499 Elvis was "neither looking nor sounding good": *Variety*, May 16, 1973.

499–501 Ed Hookstratten contacted John O'Grady: Interview with Ed Hookstratten, 1995; Jerry Hopkins interview with John O'Grady (MVC/UMem); Charles C. Thompson II and James P. Cole, *The Death of Elvis: What Really Happened*, pp. 120ff; Marty Lacker et al., *Elvis: Portrait of a Friend*, pp. 342–343; Marge Crumbaker and Gabe Tucker, *Up and Down with Elvis Presley*, pp. 194, 201, 205–208.

500 Elvis nearly overdosed in St. Louis: Thompson and Cole, *The Death of Elvis*, p. 324; Nash, *Elvis Aaron Presley*, p. 578; Peter Harry Brown and Pat H. Broeske, *Down at the End of Lonely Street: The Life and Death of Elvis Presley*, p. 372.

500 Elvis passed out in Hookstratten's office: Interview with Ed Hookstratten, 1995. In the December 20, 1977, *National Enquirer,* John O'Grady speaks of what appears to be the same incident taking place in *his* office.

501 George Parkhill . . . wrote Elvis: Parkhill to Elvis, June 29, 1973 (EPE).

502 Marty Lacker . . . set up the session: Lacker et al., *Portrait,* p. 205.

502 "It was the first time I ever saw him fat": Interview with Jerry Carrigan, 1989.

502 "He just didn't seem to care": Jerry Hopkins interview with Bobby Wood (MVC/UMem).

502 Felton Jarvis and his engineer Al Pachucki, already skating on thin ice: Interviews with Mary Jarvis and Joan Deary; Ernst Jorgensen interview with Al Pachucki; various RCA communications with Colonel post-*Aloha,* indicating Deary's, RCA's, and Colonel's dissatisfaction with Felton, and Felton's own letter to new RCA president Ken Glancy on March 6, 1974, gratefully acknowledging that for the first time in almost two years he feels that he has a "good working relationship with the Company" (EPE and Mary Jarvis).

502–504 The studio vibe was bad: Interviews with Jerry Carrigan, Reggie Young, Freddy Bienstock, Charlie Hodge, Lamar Fike, and Kang Rhee; Ernst Jorgensen interview with Al Pachucki; Jerry Hopkins interviews with Bobby Wood and Bobby Emmons (MVC/UMem); Trevor Cajiao interview with Bobby Wood, *Elvis: The Man and His Music* 26, March 1995; interview with Larry Nix in Rose Clayton and Dick Heard, eds., *Elvis Up Close: In the Words of Those Who Knew Him Best,* p. 273.

503 the publishing debacle: Freddy Bienstock to Felton Jarvis, August 23, 1973 (courtesy of Mary Jarvis). Bienstock suggests that it would be a good idea that Felton make things right with his "good friend" Bob Beckham before Freddy takes the matter up with Colonel Parker. I think there is little question that Colonel was already aware of the situation, whether implicitly or explicitly.

503–504 "What I try to capture": Al Cooley interview with Felton Jarvis.

504 "More overweight than he's ever appeared": *Hollywood Reporter,* August 13, 1973.

504 Fan reports suggested: Christine Colclough's extensive report on the engagement in Rex Martin's *Worldwide Elvis News Service Weekly.*

504 he broke the ankle of a woman: Hospital bills (EPE); Jerry Hopkins interview with Gene Dessel (MVC/UMem); West et al., *Elvis: What Happened?,* pp. 195–197; news reports of the incident and its aftermath.

504–506 "Good evening, ladies and gentlemen": The first quote and some of the description is from Christine Colclough; most of what follows is from Sue Wiegert's account in Wiegert, *For the Good Times,* p. 144.

505–510 For the Colonel, though, there was little to be happy about: This account of the Colonel's reaction and the bitter argument that followed, including the twelve-day stand-off, is based on a wide variety of sources, including interviews with Jerry Schilling, Joe Esposito, Lamar Fike, Charlie Hodge, Tom Hulett, and Ed Hookstratten; Jerry Hopkins interview with John Wilkinson (MVC/UMem); West et al., *Elvis: What Happened?,* pp. 306ff; Lacker et al., *Portrait,* pp. 322, 329; Nash, *Elvis Aaron Presley,* pp. 589ff; Joe Esposito, *Good Rockin' Tonight,* p. 203; Crumbaker and Tucker, *Up and Down,* pp. 194ff; Goldman, *Elvis,* p. 520.

506 he had flown in a promising young gospel quartet: Ernst Jorgensen interview with Sherrill (today known as Sean) Nielsen; interview with Tony Brown, 1989.

506 he was some kind of illegal alien: The suspicion that the Colonel was Dutch — or that there was something "funny" about his background — came up in my interviews with Ed Hookstratten, Mel Ilberman, Julian Aberbach, and Grelun Landon; also in Trevor Cajiao's interview with Red West in *Elvis: The Man and His Music* 22, June 1994, as well as in Esposito, *Good Rockin'*, p. 197, and Dirk Vellenga ms., pp. 193ff. While none of these sources had any insight into the extent of Elvis' suspicions, most tended to agree that his general alertness to conversational undercurrents and social situations, what several of the guys referred to as almost a "sixth sense," along with his awareness of the Colonel's almost pathological aversion to foreign travel, would suggest that he must at least have had his suspicions.

507 when Eddy Arnold had dissolved their long-standing relationship: Arnold's original letter was written on August 21, 1953, with the release agreement signed September 4 (EPE).

508–509 Jerry had conflicts and confusions of his own: Interviews with Jerry Schilling. See also Billy Stanley, *Elvis, My Brother*, pp. 160, 166, 194, 197, re Elvis' relationship with Billy's wife; West et al., *Elvis: What Happened?*, pp. 278–279, re both Jerry and Billy.

509 Linda, too, was at a turning point: Interview with Linda Thompson.

509–510 he drew up a contract on a piece of scrap paper: West et al., *Elvis: What Happened?*, p. 306; Ernst Jorgensen interview with Sherrill Nielsen. Other background on Voice's arrangement with Elvis comes from my interviews with Tony Brown.

510 Colonel felt sufficiently emboldened: The Colonel's point of view can be deduced from a memorandum of his telephone conversation with RCA on September 25, 1973 (EPE). Although this took place two days after the session's conclusion, it covers the entire rationale for the way in which the session was conducted and obviously reflects the Colonel's prior thinking.

511 Elvis arranged for the operation to be performed: Doctors' bills indicate that both Elias Ghanem and Leon Cole were in attendance on Elvis in Palm Springs, while Dr. Juan J. Tur performed the surgery on Nielsen (EPE).

511 not the scene that Grelun Landon had anticipated: Jerry Hopkins interview with Grelun Landon (MVC/UMem) and correspondence with Grelun Landon; also my interview with James Burton and Ernst Jorgensen's interview with Sherrill Nielsen; James Burton in Clayton and Heard, *Elvis Up Close*, p. 271.

512 The Colonel was practically beside himself: Memo of September 25 telephone conversation, as above (EPE).

512 From the publicity material, it was obvious: Joan Deary's cover letter to the Colonel, dated September 27, 1973, included a memorandum on the Legendary Performers series which had originally been sent to the Colonel's man at RCA, George Parkhill, on September 7 (EPE). Perhaps because Parkhill was sick, the Colonel never got this memorandum until he received the September 27 letter, a lapse that he made the most of.

512 he fired off a letter: Colonel to Rocco Laginestra, October 1, 1973 (EPE).

513 "I think that things were not turning out": Interview with Sri Daya Mata, 1995.

513–514 Priscilla had reopened the case in May: Elvis Aaron Presley v. Priscilla Ann Presley (divorce). Orange County, California, Case #D-57002, 1972; interview with Ed Hookstratten; Rona Barrett column, July 5, 1973; Suzanne Finstad, *Child Bride: The Untold Story of Priscilla Beaulieu Presley*, pp. 250–265; Jerry Hopkins, *Elvis: The Final Years*, p. 99; Goldman, *Elvis*, p. 517.

514 On Tuesday, October 9, they met: Priscilla Presley, *Elvis and Me*, pp. 303–304; Sheila Weller, "Priscilla Presley: Surviving Elvis," *McCall's*, May 1979, pp. 14, 173; Jack Jones, "Elvis Presley Ends Marriage with a Kiss and $1.5 Million," *Los Angeles Times*, October 10, 1973; "Elvis and Priscilla End Six Years of Marriage," AP wire-service report, October 10, 1973.

515–517 Six days later he was admitted to Baptist Memorial: Interviews with Linda Thompson, Dr. George Nichopoulos, Joe Esposito, Jerry Schilling, and Bill Wallace; Jerry Hopkins interviews with Maurice Elliott, Linda Thompson, and Jerry Schilling (MVC/UMem); *Memphis Press-Scimitar*, October 15 and November 2, 1973; Thompson and Cole, *The Death of Elvis*, pp. 283,

334, 339ff; Clayton and Heard, *Elvis Up Close*, p. 273; Lacker et al., *Portrait*, p. 311; Esposito, *Good Rockin'*, p. 210; Nash, *Elvis Aaron Presley*, pp. 576–577. The chronology is established by an October 11 bill for the chartered plane (EPE) and Elvis' hospital admission four days later.

517 authorizing the Colonel to sign: Elvis to Colonel, October 24, 1973 (EPE).

THE IMPERSONAL LIFE

519–520 Dr. Nick came by almost every day: Interview with Dr. George Nichopoulos, 1996; Stanley Booth, "The King Is Dead!, Hang the Doctor!," in Martin Torgoff, ed., *The Complete Elvis*.

521 For Linda it offered a respite of sorts: Interviews with Linda Thompson, 1990, 1995.

523 "We were having lunch as usual": Interview with Norbert Putnam, 1995. Background on the session comes from interviews with Dick Baxter, David Briggs, David Porter; Larry Nix interview in Rose Clayton and Dick Heard, eds., *Elvis Up Close: In the Words of Those Who Knew Him Best*, p. 277; Ernst Jorgensen, *Elvis Presley: A Life in Music*, pp. 373–379; and RCA paperwork (EPE).

523 "You sonofabitch": Sue Wiegert, *Elvis: For the Good Times*, p. 145.

523–524 a new bass player, thirty-year-old Duke Bardwell: Trevor Cajiao interview with Duke Bardwell, *Elvis: The Man and His Music* 31, June 1996.

524 Sherrill already knew the song: Ernst Jorgensen interview with Sherrill Nielsen.

524 Red and Sonny in particular had even less respect: Red West et al., *Elvis: What Happened?*, pp. 77–87. There is an enormous amount of anecdotal information on any number of television and furniture shoot-outs, but see also the *Pasadena Star News*, September 18, 1977, which quotes a reference to Elvis' deposition in a 1974 lawsuit.

525 he pulled a gun on Red: West et al., *Elvis: What Happened?*, pp. 194–197.

525 everyone was always "a little tense": Interview with Joe Esposito, 1990.

525 Linda had as much reason for concern: Interview with Linda Thompson, 1995; West et al., *Elvis: What Happened?*, pp. 77–78; Charles C. Thompson II and James P. Cole, *The Death of Elvis: What Really Happened*, pp. 326–327. There is some disagreement not only about what Elvis was shooting at but about chronology as well, but the presence of "Hamburger James" Caughley, who left the entourage in September 1973, seems to place it in this time frame.

525–526 to Ann, even at the beginning of their relationship: Interview with Ann Pennington Cassidy, 1991.

526–527 Nick worked out an arrangement: Interview with Dr. George Nichopoulos; according to Thompson and Cole, *The Death of Elvis*, p. 200, Dr. Nick received $76,000, the group $147,000 between 1970 and 1977.

527 The big surprise on the tour: The reintroduction of Management III into the equation was first announced in a letter from Mel Ilberman to the Colonel on January 7, 1974. The Colonel protested bitterly to Ilberman and RCA president Ken Glancy on February 7, suggesting that in "thirty-three years" of dealing with the company "I have never felt so strongly that I was skating on thin ice" and making less than veiled threats (EPE). In the end everything was resolved, probably according to what the Colonel had in mind all along.

527 "I don't know of any act on the road": Ernst Jorgensen interview with Sherrill Nielsen.

528 The *Memphis Press-Scimitar* compared Elvis to Julius Caesar: *Memphis Press-Scimitar*, March 18, 1974.

529 A number of fans witnessed Elvis: Complaint filed by Edward L. Ashley in the United States District Court for the District of Nevada, October 11, 1974 (EPE); *Pasadena Star News*, September 18, 1977; Hopkins, *Elvis: The Final Years*, p. 122; Marty Lacker et al., *Elvis: Portrait of a Friend*, p. 311.

529 Colonel made half-hearted attempts to broach the subject: Thompson and Cole, *The Death of Elvis*, p. 356. The Colonel's awareness of Elvis' situation, and his seeming inability to do anything about it (along with his views on European travel), were elucidated in interviews with Joe Esposito, Tom Hulett, and Jerry Schilling. See also Lacker et al., *Portrait*, pp. 320–322.

530–532 he started getting serious about the movie: Background on Elvis' renewed interest in karate, the Tennessee Karate Institute, and the karate film stems primarily from interviews with Ed Parker, Rick Husky, Bill Wallace, Big Al Holcomb, Bert Lovitt, and Jerry Schilling; also Jerry Hopkins interviews with Rick Husky and Bill Belew (MVC/UMem); *Memphis Commercial Appeal*, July 5, 1974; various karate badges (EPE); Linda Jackson and Vera Jane Goodin, *Elvis & Bobbie*.

531–532 He arrived at the Monovale house: Interview with Rick Husky, 1995. All quotes are from this interview.

532 eventually he put up the money behind Colonel's back: Joe Esposito, *Good Rockin' Tonight*, p. 218; Colonel Parker in conversation, 1995; various memos and bills from September 21, 1974, including the Colonel's very disapproving notes on a contract proposal for "Documentary Karate Film," November 20, 1974 (EPE).

532–533 "He treated me like a child": Jerry Hopkins interview with Dee Presley (MVC/UMem).

533 The whole troupe sang: Interview with Glen D. Hardin, 1990.

534 "the best show . . . in at least three years": *Hollywood Reporter*, August 23, 1974.

534–535 "He seemed nervous": This and all further quotes from Colclough are from her account in Rex Martin's *Official Elvis Presley Fan Club News Service*. Colclough described performances from August 19 to 28; Martha Collins wrote up shows between August 26 and August 29; while John Andrews covered the rest of the engagement in a five-part series. Taken together, these offer detailed and scrupulously observed coverage of the show.

535–537 "I went up to the suite between shows": Interview with Sheila Ryan Caan, 1990.

537 both evening shows were canceled: Devoted fan Donna Lewis wrote in her September 23 diary entry (*"Hurry Home, Elvis!": Donna Lewis' Diaries*, vol. 3 (unpublished manuscript), msp. 339): "They're saying that Elvis has used drugs since the army, but it's gotten really bad in the past three years. . . . *I think that it's a bunch of lies and all the rumors are because of Elvis' poor health.*"

538 "Put a spotlight onto the statues": I've quoted this directly from Hopkins, *Final Years*, pp. 131–132. It appears to stem from the September 1 dinner show. Close variations on the same monologue were reported by Martha Collins in her account of the August 27 midnight show and John Andrews in his report on the August 30 dinner show, among others.

539 "to exploit and commercialize Elvis' name": From Colonel's September 2, 1977, affidavit in the state of California, county of Los Angeles, re the continuation of his merchandising agreement with Vernon Presley in the aftermath of Elvis' death; also Colonel's response to the Ad Litem accusations and his affidavit in his own subsequent lawsuit (EPE).

539 "He could make a hit record in a boxcar": Jerry Hopkins interview with Ron Jacobs (MVC/UMem).

539 to reward long-standing associates: There were a number of different percentage formulations, as listed in both the Colonel's papers (EPE) and the Ad Litem reports, and it's hard to say which took precedence when (and for how long).

539–540 Colonel had indicated to Kathy Westmoreland: Interview with Kathy Westmoreland, 1990; Colonel's correspondence with RCA re Boxcar and Boxcar artists from August 15, 1974 (when the *Having Fun* deal was signed), through the following year (EPE).

540 "I teach": Hopkins, *Final Years*, p. 133.

541 He even recognized orchestra leader Joe Guercio: Interview with Joe Guercio, 1995.

544 "I was in shock": Interview with Priscilla Presley, 1995.

544 he arranged to have a local crew film him: *Memphis Press-Scimitar,* September 17, 1974; *Memphis Commercial Appeal,* September 22, 1974; interviews with Bill Wallace and Al Holcomb; film footage. The advertisement was in the *Commercial Appeal;* the quote about showing "he could take it" is from the *Press-Scimitar.*

545 a ten-day buying spree: *Memphis Commercial Appeal,* September 24, 1974; *Memphis Press-Scimitar,* September 27, 1974; Jerry Hopkins interviews with Maggie Smith and car salesman Howard Massey (MVC/UMem); Lewis, *"Hurry Home, Elvis!,"* vol. 3, msp. 338; Alanna Nash, *Elvis Aaron Presley: Revelations from the Memphis Mafia,* p. 598; bill for 1975 Woodcrest three-bedroom double trailer (EPE).

545 he visted Methodist Hospital: Interviews with Linda and Sam Thompson; Jerry Hopkins interview with Linda Thompson (MVC/UMem).

545 he had helped Sam and Louise purchase a new home: Interview with Sam Thompson, 1989; sale papers for the August 1 purchase (EPE).

545 "There was a lady there in labor": Jerry Hopkins interview with Linda Thompson (MVC/UMem).

546 Elvis continued to work out his ideas: Interview with Linda Thompson.

547 "My first night was College Park": Jerry Hopkins interview with Tony Brown; additional background information from my interview with Tony Brown, 1989.

547 Even Sonny was shocked: West et al., *Elvis: What Happened?,* p. 308.

547 "Shut that damn sound off, Felton": Interview with Mary Jarvis; similar story from Donnie Fritts, 1988.

547 Red and Ed Parker became aware of a cocaine shipment: Lacker et al., *Portrait,* pp. 326–327; see also Esposito, *Good Rockin',* p. 208; Thompson and Cole, *The Death of Elvis,* p. 346.

548 Newspaper accounts tried to puzzle out: Lee Cotten, *Did Elvis Sing in Your Hometown, Too?*

548 "Elvis was just standing there": Trevor Cajiao interview with Duke Bardwell, *Elvis: The Man and His Music* 31, June 1996.

548 Ghanem ordered a series of tests: Medical bills (EPE).

548–550 Jerry Schilling came out to see him: Interviews with Jerry Schilling, Linda Thompson, Sheila Caan, Dr. George Nichopoulos, and Bert Lovitt (re setting up the office and reviewing the film).

549 he had already assigned more than 100 percent: In interviews with Tom Hulett and Joe Esposito, among others, both suggested it was their understanding at the time that Elvis had given away 130 to 150 percent of the film. Elvis' own notes on the final page of the script indicate that this was not true.

549–550 he would like a home of his own: Interviews with Jerry Schilling and Rick Husky; the conversation is dated by the deed to Jerry's house.

550 as usual there was little for them to do: Interview with Tony Brown.

550–551 "To produce a motion picture of this nature": The Colonel's addendum is dated November 20, 1974 (EPE).

551 "like the boy in the bubble": Interview with Sheila Caan.

551 "He said, 'Jerry, can you help me?'": Interview with Jerry Schilling.

552–553 The karate movie was ingloriously shut down: Interview with Bert Lovitt, 1995, with reference to his contemporaneous work diary.

553 a message expressing his appreciation: December 30, 1974, telegram from Elvis to Colonel (EPE).

553 He also contacted Henri Lewin: Colonel to Henri Lewin, December 30, 1974 (EPE).

A LEAF IN THE STORM

555 Elvis told Billy that he could hardly watch: Alanna Nash, *Elvis Aaron Presley: Revelations from the Memphis Mafia*, p. 507.

555 "heartless, cruel, vicious rumors": "Elvis the Pelvis Turns 40, But He Isn't All Shook Up," *People*, January 13, 1975.

555–556 To Elvis, though, she was beginning to express her true feelings: Interview with Linda Thompson, 1995; also, Elizabeth Daroff, "Elvis," *McCall's*, July 1980, p. 142.

556 if he refused to book Elvis: Interviews with Jerry Schilling, Joe Esposito, Tom Hulett; Charles C. Thompson II and James P. Cole, *The Death of Elvis: What Really Happened*, p. 356; Marge Crumbaker and Gabe Tucker, *Up and Down with Elvis Presley*, p. 210.

556–557 "I had never been this much on the inside before": Interview with Tom Hulett, 1990. Confirmation of Hulett's story comes from Elvis' telegram to the Colonel on January 13, 1975 (EPE), and Colonel's reference in his eighty-fifth-birthday booklet to flying to Jackson one Sunday (January 12) with his staff.

557 Elvis put down a deposit of $75,000: *New York Daily News*, January 21, 1975.

557 Dr. Nick had him admitted to the hospital: *Memphis Press-Scimitar*, January 30, 1975.

557 A "Presley source": *Memphis Commercial Appeal*, January 30, 1975.

558 Linda joined him once again: Interview with Linda Thompson.

558 Elvis' aunt Delta got a package: Interviews with Dr. George Nichopoulos and Jerry Schilling; Marty Lacker et al., *Elvis: Portrait of a Friend*, pp. 302, 316, 330–331; Rose Clayton and Dick Heard, eds., *Elvis Up Close: In the Words of Those Who Knew Him Best*, p. 280.

558 the two of them found themselves drawn back to old times: Jerry Hopkins interview with Maurice Elliott (MVC/UMem).

558 Vernon tried to put the blame: Nash, *Elvis Aaron Presley*, p. 624.

559 "He told me that he thought I was doing myself an injustice": Stanley Booth, "The King Is Dead!, Hang the Doctor!," in Martin Torgoff, ed., *The Complete Elvis*.

559–560 Elvis loved to watch old *Monty Python* episodes: Jerry Hopkins interviews with T. G. Sheppard and Linda Thompson (MVC/UMem); my interviews with Dr. George Nichopoulos and Linda Thompson.

560 Robert Hilburn had responded to the release of his latest LP: Hilburn, "Elvis: Waning Legend in His Own Time?," *Los Angeles Times*, January 19, 1975.

561 Elvis had gotten it into his mind: Ernst Jorgensen interviews with Mary Jarvis and Tony Brown.

562 "You should have seen me a month ago": *Memphis Press-Scimitar*, March 14, 1975.

562 "What the fans really wanted": Sue Wiegert, *Elvis: For the Good Times*, p. 150.

562 a wild water fight erupted: Ibid.; Len Leech account in Rex Martin's *Worldwide Elvis News Service Weekly*; Trevor Cajiao interview with Duke Bardwell, *Elvis: The Man and His Music* 31, June 1996.

563–565 Barbra Streisand had attended his performance: The date is established by a write-up in *For EP Fans Only*, vol. 3, nos. 1 and 2, 1975. The meeting was described in interviews with Joe Esposito, Jerry Schilling, Sheila Caan, and Rick Husky; Red West et al., *Elvis: What Happened?*, pp. 317–318; Joe Esposito, *Good Rockin' Tonight*, p. 206. The business denouement is documented in correspondence between Colonel Parker's office and Roger Davis at William Morris, between April 4 and April 15, and Davis' letter to First Artists on April 14 (EPE).

565 "there wasn't much at stake": Interview with Sheila Caan, 1990.

565–566 "the music [had] always felt nervous to me": Interview with Jerry Scheff, 1989.

565 Glen D., too, saw a turnaround: Interview with Glen D. Hardin, 1990.

566 just as "modest, shy, and gracious as he could be": *Jackson Clarion-Ledger*, May 6, 1975.

566–567 who "after tonight [might] not be with me ever": Christopher Brown, *On Tour with Elvis*, p. 211.

566–567 Kathy was stung: Kathy Westmoreland, *Elvis and Kathy*, pp. 277–278.

567 a fat, "sensuous clown": *Memphis Commercial Appeal*, June 20, 1975.

567 he had made up his mind: Interview with Dr. George Nichopoulos; Peter Harry Brown and Pat H. Broeske, *Down at the End of Lonely Street: The Life and Death of Elvis Presley*, p. 390, Nash, *Elvis Aaron Presley*, p. 629. The quotes from Billy Smith are from the last named.

568 his attention was largely occupied with the airplane: All of the purchase information on the airplane comes from purchase orders and bills (EPE), unless otherwise noted.

568 she told him the truth: Interviews with Sheila Caan and Joe Esposito.

569 "How Great Thou Art" seemed more and more to have become almost a cry of pain: Lee Cotten, *Did Elvis Sing in Your Hometown, Too?*, pp. 198, 200.

569 he delivered a stunning version of "You'll Never Walk Alone": Ibid., pp. 203–204; *For EP Fans Only*, vol. 3, nos. 3 and 4.

569–571 Elvis had been riding Kathy for most of the tour: Westmoreland, *Elvis and Kathy*, pp. 278ff; interview with Myrna Smith, 1990. The account of the incident that followed derives primarily from these two sources, plus interviews with Kathy Westmoreland, Estelle Brown, Joe Esposito, and Jerry Schilling; Esposito, *Good Rockin'*, p. 168; West et al., *Elvis: What Happened?*, pp. 300ff; J. D. Sumner, *Elvis: His Love for Gospel Music and J. D. Sumner*, pp. 51ff. Needless to say, these accounts do not correspond in every detail.

570 "he smelled green peppers and onions": UPI dispatch, July 25, 1975.

570 "Sorry for any embarrassment": Ibid.

570 Felton called Millie Kirkham: Interview with Millie Kirkham, 1989.

571 "I thought it was funny": Westmoreland, *Elvis and Kathy*, p. 284.

571 J. D. Sumner felt that Kathy and the Sweets should never have walked off: J. D. Sumner, *Elvis: His Love for Gospel Music*, pp. 50ff.

571–572 The following afternoon he changed his departure plans: Jerry Hopkins interview with Lowell Hays (MVC/UMem); Jerry Hopkins, *Elvis: The Final Years*, pp. 155–157.

572 "I guess I embarrassed him": Clayton and Heard, *Elvis Up Close*, p. 292; also, interview with Dr. George Nichopoulos, 1996, and Beth J. Tamke, "Doctor Talks About Elvis' Problems, His Life and Death," *Memphis Commercial Appeal*, August 25, 1977. West et al., *Elvis: What Happened?*, p. 81, has a slightly different story, in which the television set was hit.

573 Lowell Hays was disturbed: Jerry Hopkins interview with Lowell Hays (MVC/UMem). The $85,000 figure comes from Hays' six invoices dated July 24 (EPE).

573 Colonel didn't really take it the way that Elvis had hoped: *Memphis Commercial Appeal*, July 27, 1975; see also Nash, *Elvis Aaron Presley*, pp. 607–608; West et al., *Elvis: What Happened?*, p. 310; Hopkins, *Final Years*, p. 201.

573 Elvis bought and gave away thirteen Cadillacs: *Memphis Commercial Appeal*, July 29, 1975; *Newsweek*, August 11, 1975; Jerry Hopkins interviews with car salesman Howard Massey, Jo Cathy Brownlee, and Myrna Smith (MVC/UMem); interviews with Myrna Smith, Jerry Schilling, and Kathy Westmoreland.

574 On August 3 he put down $26,000: All airplane information from purchase orders and bills (EPE).

574 the construction of his own racquetball court: Interview with Dr. George Nichopoulos. Vernon signed the agreement with contractor John Tomlinson on July 18, 1975 (EPE). The information on Marty Lacker's $10,000 loan comes from Lacker et al., *Portrait*, pp. 162–163, and Elvis' financial records (EPE).

574 when he discovered that Dr. Nick was having trouble getting a bank loan: Interview with Dr. George Nichopoulos; Clayton and Heard, *Elvis Up Close*, p. 294; public records of a deed of trust drawn up between Charles H. Davis and D. Beecher Smith II [Elvis' lawyers], Trustees, and George C. and Edna S. Nichopoulos, parties, July 29, 1976.

574 "Son, if you don't quit [spending]": Shelley Ritter interview with Mike McGregor.

574 With Billy and Jo he prayed frequently: Nash, *Elvis Aaron Presley*, p. 630.

574–575 "He called me at four o'clock in the morning": Interview with Sheila Caan.

575 "We walked in the front door": Jerry Hopkins interview with Melissa Blackwood (MVC/UMem).

577–578 He met Jo Cathy Brownlee: Jerry Hopkins interview with Jo Cathy Brownlee (MVC/UMem).

578 He barely made it to Vegas: Lacker et al., *Portrait*, p. 321; West et al., *Elvis: What Happened?*, pp. 198–199; J. D. Sumner, *Elvis: His Love for Gospel Music*, pp. 63ff; Thompson and Cole, *The Death of Elvis*, p. 304; Hopkins, *Final Years*, p. 167; interview with Linda Thompson.

578 He was "overweight": *Variety*, August 22, 1975.

578 short bursts of energy seemed to alternate: Christine Colclough report on the August 1975 engagement for Rex Martin's *Worldwide Elvis News Service Weekly*. Many of the specific descriptive details concerning this engagement are from Colclough's account.

578–579 how "out of it he was": Interview with Linda Thompson.

579 a story that Jo Cathy Brownlee had told him: Jerry Hopkins interview with Jo Cathy Brownlee (MVC/UMem).

579 "I'm not going to go out there and tell them": West et al., *Elvis: What Happened?*, p. 198.

579 He assured Henri Lewin: Correspondence between Colonel and Lewin, August 25–27, 1975 (EPE).

579–580 At the same time he reassured Elvis: From Colonel's record of his accounting for the engagement (EPE).

580 gossips were whispering: Speculative news items in *Hound Dogs*, vol. 10, no. 4, and *Memphis Flash*, vol. 3, no. 2 [fan magazines].

580 Colonel felt he could no longer place any faith in Elvis' assurances: Lacker et al., *Portrait*, pp. 320–321, 329; Randall Beck, "Parker Calls Elvis Headstrong Client," *Memphis Press-Scimitar*, September 9, 1981; Henri Lewin, "Better Late Than Never," *Las Vegas Style*, March 1994, p. 33; interview with Jerry Schilling, 1997.

580–581 Meanwhile, Dr. Nick found a very different Elvis: Interview with Dr. George Nichopoulos.

581 President Nixon called: Undated clipping, referring to the call coming in at 11:30 A.M. on the Saturday of Labor Day weekend.

581 Frank Sinatra called, too: Interview with Linda Thompson.

581–582 But mostly it was Marion Cocke: Marion Cocke, *I Called Him Babe: Elvis Presley's Nurse Remembers;* Jerry Hopkins interview with Marion Cocke (MVC/UMem); undated *Memphis Press-Scimitar* clipping re Elvis' gift of the car.

581 "He talked about his family": Shelley Ritter interview with Marion Cocke.

582 "He looked back to me": Ibid.

582–583 Linda returned to the Coast: Interview with Linda Thompson.

583–584 He started going out again with Jo Cathy Brownlee: Jerry Hopkins interview with Jo Cathy Brownlee (MVC/UMem).

584–585 even concocting a scheme to record half an album in the studio: Elvis' telegram to Colonel of October 21, 1975 (EPE), embraces this plan, with every evidence (including Colonel-like language) of having been dictated by the Colonel.

585 Colonel tried to interest the label: September 4 and 8, 1975, letters from Colonel to Mel Ilberman (EPE).

585 The *Lisa Marie* was finally delivered: *Memphis Press-Scimitar,* October 31 and November 12, 1975.

585 "I can't believe this is mine": Jerry Hopkins interview with T. G. Sheppard (MVC/UMem).

585 He was growing more and more nervous: Cocke, *I Called Him Babe,* pp. 107, 138. See also Patsy Guy Hammontree, *Elvis Presley: A Bio-Bibliography,* pp. 96–97, for an account of his relationship at this time with a young Memphis woman named Dawn Bonner (also mentioned by Cocke).

585 the room, and the hotel, were full: Jerry Hopkins interview with Henri Lewin (MVC/UMem); Cotten, *Did Elvis Sing in Your Hometown, Too,* p. 218.

586 Glen D. made up his mind to leave: Interviews with Glen D. Hardin, 1990, and David Briggs, 1988; Trevor Cajiao interview with Glen D. Hardin, *Elvis: The Man and His Music* 35, June 1997; Ernst Jorgensen interview with Tony Brown; Jerry Hopkins interview with Grelun Landon (MVC/UMem).

586 he found himself "in a rage": Cocke, *I Called Him Babe,* p. 112.

586 Marty Lacker described "all the relatives": Nash, *Elvis Aaron Presley,* p. 647.

586 Lamar Fike simply felt frustration: Ibid., p. 647.

587 "and she was drunk": Ibid., pp. 649–650. Mrs. Cocke tells a variant on the jewelry story in *I Called Him Babe,* p. 115, but seems to have missed out on the dramatics. The Nash book has this incident happening Christmas Eve.

587 Billy Smith heard "the damnedest racket there ever was": Nash, *Elvis Aaron Presley,* pp. 650–653. According to Billy, Elvis made his aunt call up everyone on the plane afterward and apologize.

588 Elvis himself appeared shocked: Jerry Hopkins interview with Marty Harrell (MVC/UMem).

588 Joe Guercio told comedian Jackie Kahane disgustedly: Peter Whitmer, *The Inner Elvis: A Psychological Biography of Elvis Aaron Presley,* p. 416; rhythm guitarist John Wilkinson describes Elvis as "glassy-eyed" in his interview with Jerry Hopkins (MVC/UMem).

588 "He said, 'It'll be one of the largest crowds I've ever played'": Jerry Hopkins interview with T. G. Sheppard (MVC/UMem).

588 Four days later Elvis arrived in Denver: Interviews with Joe Esposito, 1997–1998, and Ron Pietrafeso, 1995; West et al., *Elvis: What Happened?,* p. 319.

589 Finally, Linda called Jerry and Myrna: Interviews with Linda Thompson, Jerry Schilling, Myrna Smith.

589 "IT'S ELVIS THE NIGHTSTALKER": *The Star,* February 10, 1976.

589 It was "a dream vacation": West et al., *Elvis: What Happened?,* p. 319.

589 Susan Ford, the President's eighteen-year-old daughter: Interview with Ron Pietrafeso; West et al., *Elvis: What Happened?,* p. 320, offers a variant on this story.

589 "he would speak about how nervous he got": Interview with Ron Pietrafeso.

590 Elvis contacted Bob Surber: *Denver Post,* January 16 and 20, 1976; interviews with Ron Pietrafeso and Joe Esposito; West et al., *Elvis: What Happened?,* p. 242.

590 Don Kinney, the host of KOA-TV's *Denver Today,* reported the story: *Denver Post,* January 21, 1976.

590 "but there was just so much inside of him": Interview with Ron Pietrafeso.

590–591 By this time Joe was gone: Interview with Jerry Schilling; West et al., *Elvis: What Happened?,* pp. 319–320.

HURT

593 they now proposed simply to install temporary equipment: Interview with Joan Deary, 1990; Jerry Flowers interview with Felton Jarvis; Gerry Wood, "Presley's House Now His Studio," *Billboard*, March 13, 1976; Ernst Jorgensen, *Elvis Presley: A Life in Music*, p. 394.

593 "because of friendship with Kennedy's older brother": *Denver Post*, January 29, 1976; J. D. Sumner, *Elvis: His Love for Gospel Music and J. D. Sumner*, p. 60; interviews with Ron Pietrafeso, 1995, and Jerry Kennedy, 1998.

594–596 He showed up for the first day of the recording session: Information on the session comes primarily from interviews with Glen D. Hardin, Norbert Putnam, David Briggs, James Burton, Mary Jarvis, and Myrna Smith; Trevor Cajiao interview with Glen D. Hardin, *Elvis: The Man and His Music* 35, June 1997; Shelley Ritter interview with Nancy Rooks; Colin Escott, "James Burton: Play It, James!," *Goldmine*, October 4, 1991, p. 18; Rose Clayton and Dick Heard, eds., *Elvis Up Close: In the Words of Those Who Knew Him Best*, p. 303; Red West et al., *Elvis: What Happened?*, pp. 239–240, 319; Jerry Hopkins, *Elvis: The Final Years*, pp. 180ff; Joseph A. Tunzi, *Elvis: Highway 51 South, Memphis, Tennessee*, introduction by Ronnie Tutt.

596 He went on, at his father's request: J. D. Sumner, *Elvis: His Love for Gospel Music*, p. 78.

597 Ten days later Elvis was back in Denver: *Denver Post*, February 19 and 20, 1976. The drug intervention is reported convincingly in West et al., *Elvis: What Happened?*, pp. 200ff, and in Sonny's and Red's testimony in Marty Lacker et al., *Elvis: Portrait of a Friend*, pp. 314 and 328. The quote has been constructed from these and other anecdotal accounts. It should be noted that all of the police officers involved have denied any suspicion of Elvis' drug use from the time of his death until the present day.

597 he had borrowed $350,000 against Graceland: November 25, 1975, Deed of Trust, as printed in Margo Hoven Green, Dorothy Nelson, and Darlene M. Clevenger, *Graceland*.

598 "You know how much he depends on you": Trevor Cajiao interview with Glen D. Hardin, *Elvis: The Man and His Music*.

598–599 a new agreement, calling for a straight 50–50 partnership: The agreement is printed in the Report of the Guardian Ad Litem In Re the Estate of Elvis A. Presley, Deceased, No. A-655, Exhibit 11, filed September 29, 1980; the fact that the Colonel continued to take only one-third is indicated in Exhibit 12, which seems to represent the Colonel's account of all monies posthumously owed (though it differs slightly from other figures he later presented in court [EPE]). The Colonel's willingness to forgo his contractual due for a period of time in order "to assist Elvis" in meeting "certain financial demands which he faced" is spelled out in the Colonel's affidavit of June 1, 1982, in his countersuit against the Estate (EPE).

599 working with Elvis was something of a revelation: Interview with Larrie Londin, 1991.

599 "it seemed like all the enthusiasm had just left": Jerry Hopkins interview with John Wilkinson (MVC/UMem).

599 "Elvis seems weak": Harper Barnes, "Gold-Spangled Elvis: Flashes of the Old Fire," *Rolling Stone*, May 20, 1976.

599 he continued to suffer memory lapses: Jerry Hopkins interview with Marty Harrell (MVC/UMem).

599 "there were nights": Rose Clayton and Dick Heard, eds., *Elvis Up Close: In the Words of Those Who Knew Him Best*, p. 307.

599–600 "when he first walked onstage, he'd be half asleep": Ibid.

600 "An eerie silence filled the concert hall": *Long Beach Press Telegram*, April 26, 1976.

600 "I felt so strongly for him I cried": Charles C. Thompson II and James P. Cole, *The Death of Elvis: What Really Happened*, p. 123.

600 "We all knew it was hopeless": Clayton and Heard, *Elvis Up Close*, pp. 307–308.

600 Together they went to Priscilla with the plan: Thompson and Cole, *The Death of Elvis*, p. 123; Jerry Hopkins interview with John O'Grady (MVC/UMem); and O'Grady quoted to the same effect in "Elvis and Drugs: The Truth at Last," *National Enquirer*, December 20, 1977; interview with Ed Hookstratten, 1995; Billy Stanley, *Elvis, My Brother*, p. 230.

600–601 "He'd be onstage some nights": Clayton and Heard, *Elvis Up Close*, pp. 312–313.

601 it was left to Linda to look after her: Interview with Linda Thompson, 1995; Donna Lewis, *"Hurry Home, Elvis!": Donna Lewis' Diaries*, vol. 3 (unpublished manuscript), msp. 368.

601 She was all he cared about: Larry Geller and Joel Spector, *"If I Can Dream": Elvis' Own Story*, p. 220.

602 a chain of racquetball courts around the country: The tangled story of the racquetball franchise is contained in various business documents from February 13, 1976 (EPE). Other principal sources include interviews with Joe Esposito and Dr. George Nichopoulos, 1996; Jerry Hopkins interview with Mike McMahon (MVC/UMem); Thompson and Cole, *The Death of Elvis*, pp. 150–154; "A First for Elvis," *Memphis Press-Scimitar*, April 21, 1976; West et al., *Elvis: What Happened?*, pp. 325–327.

603 "He had dozens of people around him": Philip Norman, "Elton John," *Rolling Stone*, March 19, 1992.

603 Jerry and Myrna were having drinks: Interview with Jerry Schilling and Joe Guercio, 1995.

603 There was a big blowup with Sonny in Fort Worth: Lacker et al., *Portrait*, pp. 312–313.

603 Everyone noted what a foul mood he was in: Ibid., p. 210; Lewis, *"Hurry Home, Elvis!,"* vol. 3, msp. 374.

603–604 Six days later Sonny and Red were fired: West et al., *Elvis: What Happened?*, pp. 322–323. Virtually every other account seems to derive from this one.

604–605 Elvis and Linda had retreated to Las Vegas: Interview with Linda Thompson.

604 Dave Hebler was so outraged: Linda Jones interview with Dave Hebler, *Elvis: The Man and His Music* 27, June 1995; Alanna Nash, *Elvis Aaron Presley: Revelations from the Memphis Mafia*, p. 668.

604–605 Elvis had always possessed a generous heart: "Elvis, By His Father Vernon Presley, As Told to Nancy Anderson," *Good Housekeeping*, January 1978, p. 160.

605 Elvis was so shaken that he sought out Tom Hulett: Joe Esposito, *Good Rockin' Tonight*, p. 228.

605 the adulation now was more "for what he was": Lee Cotten, *Did Elvis Sing in Your Hometown, Too?*, p. 251.

605 Elvis had his lawyer write a letter: Richard Powelson, "Suit Claims Presley Illegally Ended Deal," *Memphis Press-Scimitar*, May 3, 1977.

605 A few days later he called Nick: Interview with Dr. George Nichopoulos; Clayton and Heard, *Elvis Up Close*, p. 310.

606 the atmosphere surrounding him was very different: Interview with Larry Geller, 1989; Geller and Spector, *"If,"* pp. 179ff, 199; also, interview with Kathy Westmoreland, 1990. Elvis' view of Larry is sustained by Westmoreland's account of her first meeting with him in 1973. In Geller's book Elvis introduces Larry to her as "the heaviest motherfucker I've ever met in my life," and Kathy communicates pretty much the same views without the language.

606 a "lackluster performance": Cotten, *Did Elvis Sing in Your Hometown, Too?*, p. 252.

606–607 "Elvis Presley has been breaking hearts": Bob Claypool concert review, *Houston Post*, August 29, 1976.

607 the Colonel had Joe call Dr. Nick: Interviews with Joe Esposito, Dr. George Nichopoulos, and Joe Guercio.

607 he and his wife had not seen Elvis in some time: Marge Crumbaker and Gabe Tucker, *Up and Down with Elvis Presley*, pp. 218–219; *The Stars and Stripes*, August 18, 1977.

608 he joked cynically with the guys who were left: Lewis, *"Hurry Home, Elvis!,"* vol. 3, msp. 385.

608 "he was frightened": Interview with Linda Thompson.

608 John O'Grady and Ed Hookstratten were urging him: Interview with Ed Hookstratten.

608 He gave Jerry Schilling a call, too: Interviews with Jerry Schilling, 1994 and 1995.

608–611 "I guess I do owe you an explanation": A transcript of the telephone call is contained in West et al., *Elvis: What Happened?*, pp. 324–332.

612 "he just wasn't interested": Interview with Tony Brown, 1989.

612–613 As at the earlier home recording session: Information on this session comes primarily from interviews with David Briggs, Chip Young, Jerry Scheff, and Tony Brown; Jerry Hopkins interviews with Myrna Smith, Tony Brown, and John Wilkinson (MVC/UMem); J. D. Sumner, *Elvis: His Love for Gospel Music*, pp. 66ff; Tunzi, *Elvis: Highway 51 South, Memphis, Tennessee*.

613–614 Then on November 19 he met Ginger Alden: This account of the first ten days of Elvis and Ginger's relationship is based mainly on Hopkins, *Final Years*, pp. 202ff; Albert Goldman, *Elvis*, pp. 545ff; Jerry Hopkins interviews with Ginger and Jo Alden (MVC/UMem); Frank Thorsberg, "Last Love Picks Up the Pieces," *Nashville Tennessean*, August 16, 1978; "The Elvis Legend: One Year Later," *People*, August 21, 1978.

614–615 Linda had had a strong suspicion: Interview with Linda Thompson.

615 she started playing cards with the guys: Interviews with Myrna Smith, Tony Brown, Mary Jarvis, Ed Parker, Lamar Fike, Dr. George Nichopoulos, Joe Esposito, David Briggs.

615 the improvement in his performance: Robert Hilburn, "A Less Weighty Elvis Spectacle," *Los Angeles Times*, December 2, 1976; Goldman, *Elvis*, p. 549.

615 He was inspired by Ginger's presence: Geller and Spector, *"If,"* p. 205.

616 "How long can the drugs and his feelings about Ginger": Ibid., p. 207.

616 "very tired": Rosalinda, "Vegas 2nd–12th December," 1976 (a British fan's report).

616 he "picked up the mike on its stand": Martha Collins in Rex Martin's *Worldwide Elvis News Service Weekly*.

616 He arranged for "Sir Gerald": Jerry Hopkins interview with Gerald Peters (MVC/UMem); Goldman, *Elvis*, p. 550.

616 Ginger announced that she missed them: Jerry Hopkins interview with Ginger and Jo Alden (MVC/UMem).

616 the Lincoln Continental which Elvis had given her daughter: *Memphis Press-Scimitar*, December 10, 1976.

616 The Colonel was rumored: Bill Hance, "Elvis Presley May Be Sold by Colonel Parker," *Nashville Banner*, April 29, 1977. The Hance story attributed the Colonel's rumored losses to "a source." In Geller and Spector, *"If,"* pp. 217 and 231, Larry hears the rumor in Vegas and then has Elvis confirm it in conversation.

616 "My artist," he declared balefully: Interview with Ger Rijff, 1998.

616–617 Larry was concerned: Geller and Spector, *"If,"* pp. 212–214.

617 "in an off-mike aside": Martha Collins, in Rex Martin, above.

617 televangelist Rex Humbard came to visit: *Pasadena Star-News*, September 18, 1977; *Memphis Press-Scimitar*, August 30, 1977; *National Enquirer*, September 6, 1977; Patsy Guy Hammontree, *Elvis Presley: A Bio-Bibliography*, p. 124; interview with James Blackwood, 1988. Humbard, a pioneer in televangelism, had recorded widely in the thirties and forties with a family group, the Humbard Singers, and later formed the celebrated Cathedral Singers (from which two of the original Imperials emerged) to further his Ohio-based ministry, the Cathedral of Tomorrow. Humbard had attended Elvis' Las Vegas show the previous December, and Elvis dedicated "How Great Thou Art" to him (see John Andrews' report in Rex Martin's *Worldwide Elvis News Service Weekly*).

617 "After sitting through Elvis Presley's closing night performance": Bill E. Burk, "Presley a Mere Shadow," *Memphis Press-Scimitar*, December 15, 1976.

ELVIS, WHAT HAPPENED?

619 Felton heard from Joe just hours before the session's scheduled start: Background on the session comes primarily from interviews with Joe Esposito, David Briggs, Tony Brown, Jerry Scheff, Freddy Bienstock, and Ernst Jorgensen interview with Sherrill Nielsen; also Colonel letter to Mel Ilberman, February 7, 1977 (EPE).

619 They had had a big fight about it: Jerry Hopkins interview with Ginger Alden (MVC/UMem); Albert Goldman, *Elvis*, p. 553; "The Bizarre Behavior of Fat, Aging Elvis Presley," *National Enquirer*, April 26, 1977.

619 his cousin Billy concluded: Alanna Nash, *Elvis Aaron Presley: Revelations from the Memphis Mafia*, p. 691.

620 he told Dr. Nick there was something about her: Interview with Dr. George Nichopoulos, 1996; Rose Clayton and Dick Heard, eds., *Elvis Up Close: In the Words of Those Who Knew Him Best*, p. 328.

620 "What in the hell could a forty-two-year-old woman do for me?": Nash, *Elvis Aaron Presley*, p. 694.

620 Elvis flew all of the Aldens: Jerry Hopkins interview with Jo and Ginger Alden (MVC/UMem).

620 he took Ginger and her sister Rosemary to Palm Springs: Ibid.; Marty Lacker et al., *Elvis: Portrait of a Friend*, p. 347; Charles C. Thompson II and James P. Cole, *The Death of Elvis: What Really Happened*, pp. 126–127; Larry Geller and Joel Spector, *"If I Can Dream": Elvis' Own Story*, pp. 225–226.

621 making sure that everyone would get paid in full: Jerry Hopkins interview with Tony Brown (MVC/UMem). All the other sources on the session are the same as those listed above.

621–622 a story published in the *Nashville Banner*: Bill Hance, "Presley Comes to Town, But It's 'No Show' at Studio," *Nashville Banner*, January 28, 1977.

622 he formally proposed to Ginger: Jerry Hopkins interviews with Ginger Alden and Lowell Hays (MVC/UMem); Goldman, *Elvis*, pp. 551–552; Lawrence Buser, "'World's at a Standstill' for Elvis' Fiancée," *Memphis Commercial Appeal*, August 19, 1977.

623 Five nights later they flew to Las Vegas: *Memphis Press-Scimitar*, February 2, 1977; Donna Lewis, *"Hurry Home, Elvis!": Donna Lewis' Diaries*, vol. 3 (unpublished manuscript), msp. 398.

623 Sometimes Ginger wondered just what she had gotten herself into: Thompson and Cole, *The Death of Elvis*, p. 213; Goldman, *Elvis*, pp. 552–553.

623 "He would say, 'She loves her family'": Interview with Kathy Westmoreland, 1990.

623–624 The following night . . . he called Terry Alden up onstage: Jerry Hopkins interview with Ginger Alden (MVC/UMem); Lee Cotten, *Did Elvis Sing in Your Hometown, Too?*, pp. 288–289; Stein Erik Skar, *Elvis: The Concert Years*, p. 219.

624 David Briggs was still with the band: Interviews with David Briggs, 1988 and 1998, and Tony Brown 1989.

625 "He asked me, was I in love?": Jerry Hopkins interview with Maggie Smith (MVC/UMem).

625 Elvis signed over another $55,000: Once again a deed of trust was drawn up, but now with payments of $1,802.85 per month, beginning on April 1, 1977, and continuing through February 1, 2002.

625 He made out his will: Nash, *Elvis Aaron Presley,* p. 697; Jerry Hopkins, *Elvis: The Final Years,* p. 209; Last Will and Testament of Elvis A. Presley, Deceased, filed August 22, 1977 (public record).

626 "Everyone looks older than they are": Geller and Spector, *"If,"* pp. 239ff. The account of the trip is also based on interviews with Larry Geller, Joe Esposito, Charlie Hodge, and Ed Parker; Jerry Hopkins interview with Ginger Alden (MVC/UMem); and Hopkins, *Final Years,* pp. 209–210.

626 "Somebody'd throw him the ball": Hopkins, *Final Years,* p. 210.

626–627 Charlie and Larry Geller contacted Bernard Benson: In addition to Geller's account (in Geller and Spector, *"If,"* p. 243), see Charlie Hodge, *Me 'n Elvis,* p. 173, on the original meeting with Benson in Las Vegas. Benson published a fable on "the life and music of Elvis Presley" called *The Minstrel* shortly after Elvis' death.

627 The whole trip had cost: Geller and Spector, *"If,"* p. 244.

627 "We were supposed to leave late that night": Nash, *Elvis Aaron Presley,* p. 700.

627 "His music ran from the parody to the almost perfect": *Arizona Republic,* March 24, 1977.

628 "Is there much more time left?": Geller and Spector, *"If,"* p. 247.

628 his security chiefs . . . drew up contingency plans: Thompson and Cole, *The Death of Elvis,* p. 314.

628 "Man," he told his cousin: Nash, *Elvis Aaron Presley,* pp. 665–666. Billy has this occurring in 1976, but I am unaware, from his or any other account, of Billy going out regularly earlier than March of 1977.

628 "[He] was onstage less than an hour": *Alexandria Daily Town Talk,* March 30, 1977 (as quoted in Skar, *Elvis: The Concert Years,* p. 223).

628–629 The following night, in Baton Rouge, he was unable to go on: This account is based primarily on interviews with Tom Hulett, Joe Esposito, Sam Thompson, Ed Parker, Larry Geller, Lamar Fike, and Dr. George Nichopoulos; also Jerry Hopkins interview with John Wilkinson (MVC/UMem) and Geller and Spector, *"If,"* pp. 248ff. See also *Memphis Press-Scimitar,* April 1, 1977, re the crowd's reaction. It should be noted that some accounts have the Colonel present while Tom Hulett, among others, recalls him as already being in Mobile. Since Hulett was the principal person dealing with the Colonel in this crisis, and as it was Parker's usual practice to be a day ahead of Elvis on the tour, it seems reasonable to accept Hulett's version of events. It should go without saying that this is not the only point of contention among the various accounts.

629 "he said, 'Well, I'm really bushed'": Jerry Hopkins interview with Marion Cocke (MVC/UMem).

630 Business would go on as usual: Colonel to Mel Ilberman, April 4, 1977 (EPE).

630 Priscilla flew in from California: Jerry Hopkins interview with Ginger Alden (MVC/UMem); Lewis, *"Hurry Home, Elvis!,"* vol. 3, msp. 403; Vernon Presley correspondence with Harry Fain, April 5, 1977 (EPE).

630 Elvis complained good-naturedly all the way home: Nash, *Elvis Aaron Presley,* p. 702.

630 Elvis did little but ride around: Lewis, *"Hurry Home, Elvis!,"* vol. 3, mspp. 403–404.

630 George introduced him to Alicia Kerwin: Thompson and Cole, *The Death of Elvis,* pp. 357–361.

630 the real reason for the trip was "to get more prescriptions": Ibid., p. 359; Nash, *Elvis Aaron Presley,* p. 703.

631 He recruited Larry to help Ginger: Interview with Larry Geller, 1989; Peter Whitmer, *The Inner Elvis,* p. 420; Geller and Spector, *"If,"* p. 273.

631 redecorating the bathroom at Graceland: Jerry Hopkins interview with Ginger Alden (MVC/UMem).

631 He was worried about his health [and] his appearance: Geller and Spector, *"If,"* pp. 269–270; interview with Myrna Smith, 1990.

632 He spoke more and more about the book: Geller and Spector, *"If,"* p. 245; interviews with Larry Geller and Kathy Westmoreland.

632 A headline story in the *Nashville Banner:* Bill Hance, "Elvis Presley May Be Sold By Col. Parker," *Nashville Banner,* April 29, 1977.

632 Elvis was scheduled to open the new Hilton Pavilion: Hopkins, *Final Years,* p. 225; Jerry Hopkins interview with Henri Lewin (MVC/UMem).

632 The *Banner's* story was "a complete fabrication": Laura Eipper, "Manager Denies Presley for Sale," *Nashville Tennessean,* April 30, 1977.

632 Colonel was "servicing a problem of his own": Interview with Ed Hookstratten, 1995.

633 "Elvis, 42, Fears He's Losing His Sex Appeal": *The Star,* April 12, 1977.

633 he shot out a bedroom window: Lewis, *"Hurry Home, Elvis!,"* vol. 3, msp. 406.

633 "We had to take care of him": Nash, *Elvis Aaron Presley,* pp. 618–619.

634 "He was pale, swollen": Patsy Guy Hammontree, *Elvis Presley: A Bio-Bibliography,* p. 114.

634 Elvis left the stage for "nature's call": Skar, *Elvis: The Concert Years,* pp. 230–231; Cotten, *Did Elvis Sing in Your Hometown, Too?,* pp. 300–301; *The Star,* June 21, 1977.

634 Elvis laid down an ultimatum: Geller and Spector, *"If,"* p. 276; recollection of Rose Clayton, 1998.

634 She had just gotten in from a date: Kathy Westmoreland, *Elvis and Kathy,* p. 291.

634–635 "How will they remember me?": Ibid., pp. 294–295.

635 He was "weak," "tired," "paunchy": Marty Bennett, "What's with Elvis: Walks Out Midway at Show in Baltimore," *Variety* review reprinted in Skar, *Elvis: The Concert Years,* pp. 230–231; interviews with Tony Brown and Kathy Westmoreland; Jerry Hopkins interviews with John Wilkinson and Tony Brown (MVC/UMem).

635 the CBS concert special . . . was announced: Larry Williams, "Elvis Signs with CBS for 'Anniversary' Show," *Memphis Commercial Appeal,* June 1, 1977. The earliest confirmation I can find of the special in the Colonel's communications with CBS is mid May (EPE), but I suspect the date of the actual agreement is somewhat earlier.

635 for the first time he stipulated: Tour statement, including full division of profits according to the "temporary settlement" previously agreed upon, with "contract rate 50–50 to be settled at end of 1977" (EPE).

635–636 Colonel simply shrugged and offered three variations: Interviews with Roger Davis, Tom Hulett, Jerry Schilling, Joe Esposito.

636 "The first two chapters are about him giving drugs": Lewis, *"Hurry Home, Elvis!,"* vol. 3, msp. 408.

636 feelers from Frank Sinatra's camp: Joe Esposito says that there was no real substance to these rumors, despite the conviction of others (interviews with Lamar Fike and Jerry Schilling; Goldman, *Elvis,* p. 554) that they were true.

636 Larry thought it had more to do with guilt: Geller and Spector, *"If,"* p. 255.

636 he felt like Jesus betrayed by his disciples: Lola Scobey, "Controversies About Elvis Dispelled by Producer Jarvis," *Cash Box,* September 3, 1977.

636 He was just showing them some of the features: Geller and Spector, *"If,"* pp. 282–283; Nash, *Elvis Aaron Presley,* p. 671. Larry Geller does not name Charlie, but in the Nash book Billy Smith does.

637 He tried to do something for George Klein: Klein's problems were extensively covered in the *Memphis Press-Scimitar* and *Commercial Appeal,* from February 22, 1977, on; for Elvis' call to President Carter, see Douglas Brinkley, "The White House–Graceland connection that might have saved Elvis," in "The Talk of the Town," *The New Yorker,* August 18, 1977. Also, correspondence and conversation with Doug Brinkley, September 1997.

637 "In spite of what you may hear": Jay Gordon, "It Was 20 Years Ago This Month: Elvis' Last Concert Tour Revisited," *Elvis Only,* June 1997.

637 More and more the feeling grew: Interviews with Tom Hulett, Joe Guercio, Gary Smith, Myrna Smith, Joe Esposito, Tony Brown; Jerry Hopkins interview with John Wilkinson (MVC/UMem).

638 "It was like he was saying": Interview with Tom Hulett, 1990.

638 "I know I was terrible": Interview with Gary Smith, 1995.

638 "Dwight and Gary were kind to him": Interview with Joe Guercio, 1995.

638–639 a telephone conversation that took place between Myrna and Jerry Schilling: Interview with Myrna Smith, 1990.

639 Elvis was being driven from the airport: UPI dispatch, "Elvis Swings into Action — But Without His Guitar," undated clipping; Skar, *Elvis: The Concert Years,* p. 234.

639 In Cincinnati he gave everyone another surprise: This account of the last two shows, and the time in between, comes primarily from Jerry Hopkins interviews with Ginger Alden and John Wilkinson (MVC/UMem); Skar, *Elvis: The Concert Years,* p. 235; Cotten, *Did Elvis Sing in Your Hometown, Too?,* pp. 312–313; Geller and Spector, *"If,"* pp. 291–292.

"PRECIOUS LORD, TAKE MY HAND"

641 no July 4 fireworks this year: Donna Lewis, *"Hurry Home, Elvis!": Donna Lewis' Diaries,* vol. 3 (unpublished manuscript), mspp. 413ff.

641 Elvis was still frustrated and angry: Larry Geller and Joel Spector, *"If I Can Dream": Elvis' Own Story,* p. 299; interviews with Larry Geller, Joe Esposito, Dr. George Nichopoulos; Joe Esposito, *Good Rockin' Tonight,* p. 234; Rose Clayton and Dick Heard, eds., *Elvis Up Close: In the Words of Those Who Knew Him Best,* pp. 328–329; Charlie Hodge, *Me 'n Elvis,* p. 189.

641 he even offered to buy her family a house: Rosemary and Ginger Alden's affidavits in Jo Alden's posthumous lawsuit against the estate.

641–642 He saw scarcely anyone: Alanna Nash, *Elvis Aaron Presley: Revelations from the Memphis Mafia,* pp. 707–709; Clayton and Heard, eds., *Elvis Up Close,* p. 327; interviews with Joe Esposito, Linda Thompson, and Kathy Westmoreland; Jerry Hopkins interview with Pat Booth (MVC/UMem); Lewis, *"Hurry Home, Elvis!,"* vol. 3, mspp. 413–414.

642 "All we did": Nash, *Elvis Aaron Presley,* p. 709.

642 "One time I said, 'Look, they're not worth it'": Ibid., p. 708.

642 he dreamt the same dream: Ibid., p. 699; Laura Eipper, "The Legend Lives On," *Nashville Tennessean,* August 16, 1978; Nancy Anderson, "My Cherished Memories of Elvis," *Elvis Presley: A Photoplay Tribute,* 1977, p. 11.

642–643 "At first he thought": Nash, *Elvis Aaron Presley,* pp. 710–711.

643 he was looking forward to the tour: Interview with Dr. George Nichopoulos, 1996.

643 Ginger got her brother Mike's oldest child . . . to come visit: Jerry Hopkins interview with Ginger Alden (MVC/UMem); Jerry Hopkins, *Elvis: The Final Years,* p. 233; Harold Loyd, *Elvis Presley's Graceland Gates,* p. 61.

643 At Ginger's urging he arranged a special treat: Nash, *Elvis Aaron Presley,* p. 710; Albert Goldman, *Elvis,* p. 553; "The Night that Lisa Marie Will Never Forget," *The Star,* September 20, 1977; Jo Smith, "The Fairgrounds," *Elvis: The Record,* vol. 2, no. 3, p. 18.

644 He spoke to his father: "Elvis' Last Days Seemed Happy," *Memphis Press-Scimitar,* August 19, 1977.

644 he remained in good enough spirits to go for a motorcycle ride: Nash, *Elvis Aaron Presley,* p. 714; Billy Smith, "The Last Days," *Elvis: The Record,* vol. 1, no. 1, pp. 12–14.

645 Dr. Hofman cleaned Elvis' teeth: Interview with Dr. Lester Hofman, 1989; Jerry Hopkins interview with Ginger Alden (MVC/UMem); Charles C. Thompson II and James P. Cole, *The Death of Elvis: What Really Happened*, pp. 26, 224; Hopkins, *Final Years*, p. 234.

645 It was almost 12:30 A.M.: *National Enquirer*, September 20, 1977. The time is established by the time of the last fan photograph at 12:28 A.M., taken as the car drove in the gates.

645 He called down to Joe about some last-minute tour details: Interview with Joe Esposito, 1990; Esposito, *Good Rockin'*, pp. 235ff; Geller and Spector, "*If,*" pp. 304–305; Thompson and Cole, *The Death of Elvis*, pp. 13–14.

645–646 Elvis and Ginger meanwhile were having much the same argument: Clayton and Heard, *Elvis Up Close*, p. 341; Lawrence Buser, "'World's at a Standstill' for Elvis' Fiancée," *Memphis Commercial Appeal*, August 19, 1977; Ginger Alden, "Girl Elvis Was Going to Marry Tells Her Heartbreaking Story," *National Enquirer*, September 6, 1977.

646 "Ain't no problem," Elvis said: Nash, *Elvis Aaron Presley*, p. 715; also *Elvis: The Record*, vol 1, no. 1.

646 "Boy, that hurts": Ibid.

646 Billy left just before Ricky Stanley arrived: Thompson and Cole, *The Death of Elvis*, p. 233.

647 Tish had already gone to work: Ibid., p. 303.

647 Ginger awoke around 1:30 P.M.: The principal sources for this account are Thompson and Cole, *The Death of Elvis*, passim; Ginger Alden, "Girl Elvis Was Going to Marry Tells Her Heartbreaking Story," and "Emergency Medics Tell Inside Story of Elvis' Death," *National Enquirer*, September 6, 1977; interview with Joe Esposito, 1998; Joe Esposito, *Good Rockin'*, pp. 238ff; Goldman, *Elvis*, pp. 566ff; Peter Harry Brown and Pat H. Broeske, *Down at the End of Lonely Street: The Life and Death of Elvis Presley*, pp. 412ff.

648 a team of doctors and resuscitation experts: Jerry Hopkins interview with Maurice Elliott (MVC/UMem). It should be noted that the time of death has been variously given as 3:30 (Thompson and Cole, *The Death of Elvis*, p. 7) and 3:40 (this is the time given in the postmortem report and in Jackson Baker, "Elvis: End of an Era," *City of Memphis*, September 1977).

648 "It's all over, he's gone": Interview with Joe Esposito; Jerry Hopkins interview with Maurice Elliott (MVC/UMem); Marty Lacker et al., *Elvis: Portrait of a Friend*, p. 286; Esposito, *Good Rockin'*, p. 240.

648–649 Colonel's reaction was impossible to read: Interviews with Joe Esposito, 1990 and 1997, and Lamar Fike, 1988–1989; Nash, *Elvis Aaron Presley*, p. 723.

649 Lisa was crying when Dr. Nick walked in: *Memphis Commercial Appeal*, August 19, 1977; Kate B. Dickson, "Medic Describes 'Routine' Call to Graceland," *Memphis Press-Scimitar*, August 17, 1977; *National Enquirer*, September 6, 1977; Thompson and Cole, *The Death of Elvis*, pp. 19–20.

650 there had already been a complete clean-up in the bedroom: Deposition of Daniel D. Warlick, August 30, 1979.

650 "Scattered on couches forming a complete perimeter of the room": Thompson and Cole, *The Death of Elvis*, pp. 22ff (based closely on Warlick's deposition).

651–652 "Our pathologists were concerned": Jerry Hopkins interview with Maurice Elliott (MVC/UMem).

651–652 Death, he said, was "due to cardiac arrhythmia": Thompson and Cole, *The Death of Elvis*, pp. 49–50.

652 the heart found to be enlarged: Baptist Memorial Hospital, Postmortem Protocol report, with accompanying letters from two outside toxicology laboratories.

652 Codeine appeared at ten times the therapeutic level: Thompson and Cole, *The Death of Elvis*, p. 85.

653 Joe was in charge of the funeral arrangements: Interviews with Joe Esposito, 1997–1998, and Charlie Hodge, 1989; Esposito, *Good Rockin'*, pp. 245ff; Pat H. Broeske, "After Death 'It Was War,'" *Los Angeles Times Calendar*, August 16, 1987; Brown and Broeske, *Down at the End of Lonely Street*, p. 420; Geller and Spector, *"If,"* p. 310.

653–654 Vernon called the Reverend C. W. Bradley: Patsy Guy Hammontree, *Elvis Presley: A Bio-Bibliography*, p. 124.

654–659 the casket arrived in a single white hearse: The description of the crowd, the viewing, the funeral, and the trip to the cemetery, and much of the external detail are drawn from extensive coverage in the *Memphis Press-Scimitar* and *Commercial Appeal*, August 17–21, 1977; *Nashville Tennessean*, August 18–20, 1977; *Rolling Stone*, September 22, 1977; *New York Times*, August 18, 1977; *Boston Globe*, August 18, 1977. Also, Esposito, *Good Rockin'*, pp. 247–248; Geller and Spector, *"If,"* p. 311

655 No one could miss the intensity of his colloquies: Interviews with Jerry Schilling and Joe Esposito; Nash, *Elvis Aaron Presley*, p. 730; Priscilla Presley, *Elvis and Me*, p. 315; Marge Crumbaker and Gabe Tucker, *Up and Down with Elvis Presley*, p. 233; Billy Stanley, *Elvis, My Brother*, p. 259.

655 "four at a time fans filed by the stone lions": UPI dispatch, *Boston Globe*, August 18, 1977.

656 Dedicated diarist Donna Lewis: Lewis, *"Hurry Home, Elvis!,"* vol. 3, msp. 418.

656 Vernon returned to the living room: Interview with Lester and Sterling Hofman, 1990.

656–657 at Priscilla's request, Sam Thompson suggested that everyone go home: Interview with Sam Thompson, 1989.

657 The singers had all met in Charlie's room: Interviews with James Blackwood, Kathy Westmoreland, and Joe Guercio; Clayton and Heard, *Elvis Up Close*, p. 354; J. D. Sumner, *Elvis: His Love for Gospel Music and J. D. Sumner*, p. 99.

657 "You never wore a tie for him": Interview with Jerry Schilling, 1997.

658 a eulogy that comedian Jackie Kahane: Interview with Jackie Kahane, 1995; also, recollected text of the remarks supplied by Kahane.

658 she imagined she could hear Elvis: Kathy Westmoreland, *Elvis and Kathy*, p. 301.

658 The main sermon, by Reverend Bradley: Deborah White, "Sermon Sees Elvis As Life Inspiration," *Memphis Commercial Appeal*, August 17, 1977; see also Hopkins, *Final Years*, p. 245.

658 "We knew you'd be back": Nash, *Elvis Aaron Presley*, p. 731. Variations on this story appear in Alan Fortas, *Elvis: From Memphis to Hollywood*, p. 303; Westmoreland, *Elvis and Kathy*, p. 302; David Stanley, *Life with Elvis*, p. 196; and interview with Myrna Smith, 1990, with reference to Lamar's constant wisecracking.

659 a "Southern supper": *Rolling Stone*, September 22, 1977.

659–660 the Colonel worked out the details: Interview with Roger Davis, 1998; Report of the Guardian Ad Litem In Re the Estate of Elvis A. Presley, Deceased, No. A-655, Exhibits 10, 11, 14, 15, and 17, filed September 29, 1980, pp. 6–7; Guardian Ad Litem's Amended Report In Re the Estate of Elvis A. Presley, Deceased, No. A-655, filed July 31, 1981, pp. 6–8. There are various arguments in both reports about the percentage breakdown between the Colonel (d/b/a Boxcar Enterprises) and the Estate as well as the ownership breakdown of Boxcar, but these will not be resolved here. Suffice it to say that the Colonel's claim that the agreement was not made on August 18 but was backdated for reasons of trademark protection holds up according to Roger Davis' recollection and chronology of events, and all rumors about the Colonel negotiating the merchandising deal before Elvis was in his grave would appear to be just that.

660 Ginger Alden arranged to sell her own story: Thompson and Cole, *The Death of Elvis*, p. 258.

660 "I guess they will finally get to rest": Lewis, *"Hurry Home, Elvis!,"* vol. 3, msp. 422.

661 "Well, I've tried to be the same all through this thing": Lloyd Shearer interview with Elvis Presley, 1962, first released by RCA as a promotional LP in 1985.

Bibliography

REFERENCE

Brown, Christopher. *Elvis in Concert*. Ajax, Ontario: Self-published, 1993.

———. *On Tour with Elvis*. Ajax, Ontario: Self-published, 1991.

Corcoran, John, and Emil Farkas with Stuart Sobel. *The Original Martial Arts Encyclopedia: Tradition, History, Pioneers*. Los Angeles: Pro-Action Publishing, 1993.

Cotten, Lee. *All Shook Up: Elvis Day-By-Day, 1954–1977*, 2nd ed. Ann Arbor, Mich.: Popular Culture, Ink., 1998.

———. *Did Elvis Sing in Your Hometown?* Sacramento, Calif.: High Sierra Books, 1995.

———. *Did Elvis Sing in Your Hometown, Too?* Sacramento, Calif.: High Sierra Books, 1997.

———. *Shake, Rattle & Roll: The Golden Age of American Rock 'n' Roll*. Vol. 1, 1952–1955. Ann Arbor, Mich.: Pierian Press, 1989.

Dellar, Fred, Roy Thompson, and Douglas B. Green. *The Illustrated Encyclopedia of Country Music*. New York: Harmony Books, 1977.

Elvis: Like Any Other Soldier. Reprint of the 1958 2nd Army Division Yearbook. Port Townsend, Wash.: Osborne Productions, 1988.

F.B.I. Files for Elvis A. Presley. Released under the Freedom of Information Act.

Federal Writers' Project of the Works Progress Administration. *Mississippi: The WPA Guide to the Magnolia State*. Golden anniversary ed. Jackson: University Press of Mississippi, 1988.

———. *The WPA Guide to Tennessee*. Knoxville: University of Tennessee Press, 1986.

Gart, Galen, comp. and ed. *First Pressings: Rock History as Chronicled in Billboard Magazine*. Vol. I, 1948–1950. Milford, N.H.: Big Nickel Publications, 1986.

———. *First Pressings: Rock History as Chronicled in Billboard Magazine*. Vol. 2, 1951–1952. Milford, N.H.: Big Nickel Publications, 1986.

———. *The History of Rhythm & Blues*. Vols. 1–8 (1951–1958). Milford, N.H.: Big Nickel Publications, 1991–1995.

———. *The History of Rhythm & Blues, Special 1950 Volume*. Milford, N.H.: Big Nickel Publications, 1993.

Gentry, Linnell. *A History and Encyclopedia of Country, Western, and Gospel Music*. Nashville: Linnell Gentry, 1961.

Griggs, Bill. *A "Who's Who" of West Texas Rock 'n' Roll Music*. Lubbock, Tex.: Rockin' 50s Magazine, 1994.

Hardy, Phil, and Dave Laing. *Encyclopedia of Rock, 1955–1975*. London: Aquarius Books, 1977.

McCloud, Barry. *Definitive Country*. New York: Perigee, 1995.

The 1953 Senior Herald. Humes High School Yearbook. Reprint, Port Townsend, Wash.: Osborne Enterprises, 1988.

Petersen, Brian. *The Atomic Powered Singer*. Sweden: Self-published, 1994.

Report of Guardian Ad Litem and *Amended Report of Guardian Ad Litem In Re the Estate of Elvis A. Presley, Deceased, in the Probate Court of Shelby County, Tennessee*, No. A-655.

Stambler, Irwin. *Encyclopedia of Pop, Rock and Soul*. New York: St. Martin's Press, 1977.

Stambler, Irwin, and Grelun Landon. *Encyclopedia of Folk, Country and Western Music*. New York: St. Martin's Press, 1969.

Whisler, John A. *Elvis Presley: Reference Guide and Discography*. Metuchen, N.J.: Scarecrow Press, 1981.

Wilson, Charles Reagan, and William Ferris, eds. *Encyclopedia of Southern Culture*. Chapel Hill, N.C.: University of North Carolina Press, 1989.

Worth, Fred L., and Steve D. Tamerius. *All About Elvis*. New York: Bantam Books, 1981.

———. *Elvis: His Life from A to Z*. Chicago: Contemporary Books, 1988.

DISCOGRAPHIES, SONG, RECORD, AND MOVIE GUIDES

Bartel, Pauline. *Reel Elvis*. Dallas: Taylor Publishing, 1994.

Braun, Eric. *The Elvis Film Encyclopedia*. Woodstock, N.Y.: Overlook Press, 1997.

Crenshaw, Marshall. *Hollywood Rock*. New York: HarperCollins, 1994.

The Elvis Presley Album of Juke Box Favorites, No. 1. New York: Hill and Range Songs, 1956.

Escott, Colin, and Martin Hawkins. *Sun Records: The Discography*. Vollersode, West Germany: Bear Family, 1987.

Hawkins, Martin, and Colin Escott. *Elvis Presley: The Illustrated Discography*. London: Omnibus Press, 1981.

Jancik, Wayne. *Billboard Book of One-Hit Wonders*. New York: Watson-Guptill, 1990.

Jenkinson, Philip, and Alan Warner. *Celluloid Rock*. New York: Warner Books, 1976.

Jorgensen, Ernst. *Elvis Presley: A Life in Music*. New York: St. Martin's Press, 1998.

Kingsbury, Paul, ed. *Country on Compact Disc: The Essential Guide to the Music*. New York: Grove Press, 1993.

McLafferty, Gerry. *Elvis Presley in Hollywood: Celluloid Sell-Out*. London: Robert Hale, 1989.

Pavlow, Big Al. *The R & B Book: A Disc-History of Rhythm & Blues*. Providence: Music House Publishing, 1983.

Tunzi, Joseph A. *Elvis Sessions II: The Recorded Music of Elvis Aron Presley, 1953–1977*. (Rev. and exp. ed.) Chicago: JAT Productions, 1996.

Weisman, Ben. *Elvis Presley: "The Hollywood Years."* Secaucus, N.J.: Warner Brothers Publications, 1992.

Whitburn, Joel. *Pop Memories, 1890–1954: The History of American Popular Music*. Menomonee Falls, Wis.: Record Research, 1986.

———. *Top Country Singles, 1944–1988*. Menomonee Falls, Wis.: Record Research, 1989.

———. *Top Pop Records, 1955–1986*. Menomonee Falls, Wis.: Record Research, 1987.

———. *Top R & B Singles, 1942–1988*. Menomonee Falls, Wis.: Record Research, 1988.

Zmijewsky, Steven, and Boris Zmijewsky. *Elvis: The Films and Career of Elvis Presley*. New York: Citadel Press, 1991.

BOOKS OF MORE GENERAL INTEREST

Alexander, A. L., ed. *Poems That Touch the Heart*. Garden City, N.Y.: Doubleday, 1941.

Amburn, Ellis. *Dark Star: The Roy Orbison Story*. New York: Lyle Stuart, 1990.

Ann-Margret with Todd Gold. *Ann-Margret: My Story*. New York: G. P. Putnam's Sons, 1994.

Arnold, Eddy. *It's a Long Way from Chester County*. Old Tappan, N.J.: Hewitt House, 1969.

Atkins, Chet, with Bill Neely. *Country Gentleman*. Chicago: Henry Regnery, 1974.

Atkins, John, ed. *The Carter Family*. London: Old Time Music, 1973.

Bane, Michael. *White Boy Singin' the Blues: The Black Roots of White Rock*. New York: Penguin Books, 1982.

Bane, Michael, and Mary Ellen Moore. *Tampa, Yesterday, Today and Tomorrow*. Tampa: Misher and King Publishing, 1981.

Banks, Ann, ed. *First-Person America*. New York: Vintage Books, 1981.

Bart, Peter. *Fade Out: The Calamitous Final Days of MGM*. New York: William Morrow, 1990.

Barthel, Norma. *Ernest Tubb Discography (1936–1969)*. Roland, Okla.: Ernest Tubb Fan Club Enterprises, 1969.

Bashe, Philip. *Teenage Idol, Travelin' Man: The Complete Biography of Rick Nelson*. New York: Hyperion, 1992.

Benson, Bernard. *The Minstrel*. New York: G. P. Putnam's Sons, 1977.

Berry, Chuck. *Chuck Berry: The Autobiography*. New York: Harmony Books, 1987.

Biles, Roger. *Memphis in the Great Depression*. Knoxville: University of Tennessee Press, 1986.

Black, Jim. *Elvis on the Road to Stardom*. London: W. H. Allen, 1988.

Blaine, Hal, with David Goggin. *Hal Blaine and the Wrecking Crew*. Emeryville, Calif.: Mix Books, 1990.

Blumhofer, Edith L. *Restoring the Faith: The Assemblies of God, Pentecostalism, and American Culture*. Urbana: University of Illinois Press, 1993.

Booth, Stanley. *Rythm Oil: A Journey Through the Music of the American South*. London: Jonathan Cape, 1991.

Bova, Joyce, as told to William Conrad Nowels. *Don't Ask Forever: My Love Affair with Elvis*. New York: Kensington Books, 1994.

Bowles, Jerry. *A Thousand Sundays: The Story of the Ed Sullivan Show*. New York: G. P. Putnam's Sons, 1980.

Branch, Taylor. *Parting the Waters: America in the King Years*. New York: Simon and Schuster, 1988.

Braudy, Leo. *The Frenzy of Renown: Fame and Its History*. New York: Oxford University Press, 1986.

Brown, Peter Harry, and Pat H. Broeske. *Down at the End of Lonely Street: The Life and Death of Elvis Presley*. New York: Dutton, 1997.

Buckle, Phillip. *All Elvis: An Unofficial Biography of the "King of Discs."* London: Daily Mirror, 1962.

Burk, Bill E. *Early Elvis: The Humes Years*. Memphis: Red Oak Press, 1990.

———. *Early Elvis: The Sun Years*. Memphis: Propwash Publishing, 1997.

———. *Early Elvis: The Tupelo Years*. Memphis: Propwash Publishing, 1994.

———. *Elvis: A 30-Year Chronicle*. Tempe, Ariz.: Osborne Enterprises, 1985.

———. *Elvis Memories: Press Between the Pages*. Memphis: Propwash Publishing, 1993.

———. *Elvis Through My Eyes*. Memphis: Burk Enterprises, 1987.

Cain, Robert. *Whole Lotta Shakin' Goin' On: Jerry Lee Lewis*. New York: Dial Press, 1981.

Cajiao, Trevor. *Talking Elvis: In-Depth Interviews with Musicians, Songwriters, and Friends*. Amsterdam: Elvis: The Man and His Music / Tutti Frutti Productions, 1998.

Cantor, Louis. *Wheelin' on Beale*. New York: Pharos Books, 1992.

Capers, Gerald M., Jr. *The Biography of a River Town: Memphis, Its Heroic Age*. 1966. Reprint, Memphis: Burke's Book Store.

Carr, Roy, and Mick Farren. *Elvis Presley: The Illustrated Record*. New York: Harmony Books, 1982.

Cash, Johnny. *The Man in Black*. New York: Warner Books, 1975.

Cash, June Carter. *From the Heart*. New York: Prentice Hall Press, 1987.

Cash, W. J. *The Mind of the South*. 1941. Reprint, New York: Vintage Books.

Chapple, Steve, and Reebee Garofalo. *Rock 'n' Roll Is Here to Pay*. Chicago: Nelson-Hall, 1977.

Choron, Sandra, and Bob Oskam. *Elvis! The Last Word*. New York: Citadel Press, 1991.

Clayson, Alan, and Spencer Leigh, eds. *Aspects of Elvis: Tryin' to Get to You*. London: Sidgwick and Jackson, 1994.

Clayton, Rose, and Dick Heard, eds. *Elvis Up Close: In the Words of Those Who Knew Him Best*. Atlanta: Turner Publishing, 1994.

Cocke, Marian J. *I Called Him Babe: Elvis Presley's Nurse Remembers*. Memphis: Memphis State University Press, 1979.

Cohn, David. *Where I Was Born and Raised*. Notre Dame, Ind.: University of Notre Dame Press, 1967.

Cohn, Nik. *Rock from the Beginning*. New York: Pocket Books, 1970.

Conaway, James. *Memphis Afternoons*. Boston: Houghton Mifflin, 1993.

Country Music Foundation. *Country: The Music and the Musicians*. New York: Abbeville Press, 1988.

Country Music Magazine, editors of. *The Illustrated History of Country Music*. Garden City, N.Y.: Doubleday, 1979.

Crumbaker, Marge, and Gabe Tucker. *Up and Down with Elvis Presley*. New York: G. P. Putnam's Sons, 1981.

Dalton, David. *James Dean: The Mutant King*. New York: Dell, 1974.

Dalton, David, and Lenny Kaye. *Rock 100*. New York: Grosset and Dunlap, 1977.

Daniel, Pete. *Standing at the Crossroads*. New York: Hill and Wang, 1986.

Davis, Jr., Sammy, Jane Boyar, and Burt Boyar. *Hollywood in a Suitcase*. New York: William Morrow, 1980.

————. *Why Me? The Sammy Davis, Jr., Story*. New York: Farrar, Straus and Giroux, 1989.

Davis, Skeeter. *Bus Fare to Kentucky: The Autobiography of Skeeter Davis*. New York: Birch Lane Press, 1993.

DeCosta-Willis, Miriam, and Fannie Mitchell Delk. *Homespun Images: An Anthology of Black Memphis Writers and Artists*. Memphis: LeMoyne Owen College, 1989.

Delmore, Alton. *Truth Is Stranger than Publicity*. Edited by Charles K. Wolfe. Nashville: Country Music Foundation Press, 1977.

Dennis, Allen, ed. *James Blackwood Memories*. Brandon, Mo.: Quail Ridge Press, 1997.

DeWitt, Howard A. *Elvis—The Sun Years: The Story of Elvis Presley in the Fifties*. Ann Arbor, Mich.: Popular Culture, Ink., 1993.

Dollard, John. *Caste and Class in a Southern Town*. 3d ed. New York: Doubleday Anchor, 1957.

Dundy, Elaine. *Elvis and Gladys*. New York: Macmillan, 1985.

————. *Ferriday, Louisiana*. New York: Donald Fine, 1991.

Dunne, John Gregory. *Vegas: A Memoir of a Dark Season*. New York: Random House, 1974.

Dunne, Philip. *Take Two: A Life in Music and Politics*. New York: McGraw-Hill, 1980.

Early, Donna Presley, and Edie Hand with Lynn Edge. *Elvis: Precious Memories*. Birmingham, Ala.: The Best of Times, Inc., 1997.

Edwards, Michael. *Priscilla, Elvis, and Me*. New York: St. Martin's Press, 1988.

Elvis Presley. Prepared by the Editors of *TV Radio Mirror Magazine*. New York: Bartholomew House, 1956.

Elvis Presley Heights, Mississippi: Lee County, 1921–1984. Compiled by Members of the Elvis Presley Heights Garden Club. Tupelo, Miss., 1984.

Elvis Presley Speaks! Text by Robert Johnson. New York: Rave Publishing, 1956.

Escott, Colin, and Martin Hawkins. *Good Rockin' Tonight: Sun Records and the Birth of Rock 'n' Roll*. New York: St. Martin's Press, 1991.

Escott, Colin, Martin Hawkins, and Hank Davis. *The Sun Country Years: Country Music in Memphis, 1950–1959*. Vollersode, West Germany: Bear Family Records, 1987.

Escott, Colin, with George Merritt and William MacEwen. *Hank Williams: The Biography.* Boston: Little, Brown, 1994.

Esposito, Joe, with Elena Oumano. *Good Rockin' Tonight.* New York: Simon and Schuster, 1994.

Falkenburg, Claudia, and Andrew Solt, eds. *A Really Big Show: A Visual History of the Ed Sullivan Show.* Text by John Leonard. New York: Viking Studio Books, 1992.

Farren, Mick, ed. *Elvis in His Own Words.* London: Omnibus Press, 1977.

Finnis, Rob, and Bob Dunham. *Gene Vincent and the Blue Caps.* London: Rob Finnis and Bob Dunham, n.d.

Finstad, Suzanne. *Child Bride: The Untold Story of Priscilla Beaulieu Presley.* New York: Harmony, 1997.

Fortas, Alan. *Elvis: From Memphis to Hollywood.* Ann Arbor, Mich.: Popular Culture, Ink., 1992.

Fowler, Gene, and Bill Crawford. *Border Radio.* Austin: Texas Monthly Press, 1987.

Fowles, Jib. *Star Struck: Celebrity Performers and the American Public.* Washington, D.C.: Smithsonian Institution Press, 1992.

Frady, Marshall. *Southerners: A Journalist's Odyssey.* New York: New American Library, 1980.

Gabree, John. *The World of Rock.* Greenwich, Conn.: Fawcett, 1968.

Gaillard, Frye. *Watermelon Wine: The Spirit of Country Music.* New York: St. Martin's Press, 1978.

Garbutt, Bob. *Rockabilly Queens: The Careers and Recordings of Wanda Jackson, Janis Martin, Brenda Lee.* Toronto: Robert Garbutt Productions, 1979.

Gart, Galen, and Roy C. Ames. *Duke/Peacock Records: An Illustrated History with Discography.* Milford, N.H.: Big Nickel Publications, 1990.

Gelatt, Roland. *The Fabulous Phonograph, 1877–1977.* New York: Collier Books, 1977.

Geller, Larry, and Joel Spector with Patricia Romanowski. *"If I Can Dream": Elvis' Own Story.* New York: Simon and Schuster, 1989.

Gibson, Robert, with Sid Shaw. *Elvis: A King Forever.* London: Elvisly Yours, 1987.

Gillett, Charlie. *The Sound of the City: The Rise of Rock and Roll.* Rev. ed. London: Souvenir Press, 1983.

Goldman, Albert. *Elvis.* New York: McGraw-Hill, 1981.

———. *Elvis: The Last 24 Hours.* New York: St. Martin's Paperbacks, 1991.

Goldrosen, John, and John Beecher. *Remembering Buddy: The Definitive Biography of Buddy Holly.* New York: Penguin Books, 1986.

Goodin, Vera-Jane. *Elvis & Bobbie: Memories of Linda Jackson.* Branson, Mo.: Limited Star Editions, 1994.

Goodman, Fred. *The Mansion on the Hill: Dylan, Young, Geffen, Springsteen, and the Head-on Collision of Rock and Commerce.* New York: Times Books, 1997.

Gordon, Robert. *It Came from Memphis.* Boston: Faber and Faber, 1995.

———. *The King on the Road: Elvis Live on Tour 1954 to 1977.* New York: St. Martin's Press, 1996.

Graceland: The Living Legacy of Elvis Presley. San Francisco: Collins Publishers San Francisco, 1993.

Green, Douglas B. *Country Roots: The Origins of Country Music.* New York: Hawthorne Books, 1976.

Greenwood, Earl, and Kathleen Tracy. *The Boy Who Would Be King.* New York: Dutton, 1990.

Gregory, James, ed. *The Elvis Presley Story.* New York: Hillman Periodicals, 1960.

Gregory, Neal, and Janice Gregory. *When Elvis Died.* Washington, D.C.: Communications Press, 1980.

Grissim, John. *Country Music: White Man's Blues.* New York: Paperback Library, 1970.

Grob, Dick. *The Elvis Conspiracy?* Las Vegas: Fox Reflections Publishing, 1996.

Gruber, J. Richard, organizer. *Memphis: 1948–1958.* Memphis: Memphis Brooks Museum of Art, 1986.

Guterman, Jimmy. *Rockin' My Life Away: Listening to Jerry Lee Lewis.* Nashville: Rutledge Hill Press, 1991.

Hagarty, Britt. *The Day the World Turned Blue: A Biography of Gene Vincent.* Vancouver: Talonbooks, 1983.

Haining, Peter, ed. *Elvis in Private.* New York: St. Martin's Press, 1987.

Halberstam, David. *The Fifties.* New York: Villard Books, 1993.

Haley, John W., and John von Hoelle. *Sound and Glory.* Wilmington, Del.: Dyne-American Publishing, 1990.

Hammontree, Patsy Guy. *Elvis Presley: A Bio-Bibliography.* Westport, Conn.: Greenwood Press, 1985.

Hand, Albert. *Meet Elvis.* An Elvis Monthly Special: Manchester, 1962.

Harbinson, W. A. *The Illustrated Elvis.* New York: Grosset and Dunlap, 1976.

Harbinson, W. A., and Kay Wheeler. *Growing Up with the Memphis Flash.* Amsterdam: Tutti Frutti Productions, 1994.

Harmetz, Aljean. *Round Up the Usual Suspects: The Making of Casablanca.* New York: Hyperion, 1992.

Hawkins, Martin, and Colin Escott, comps. *The Sun Records Rocking Years.* London: Charly Records, 1986.

Hazen, Cindy, and Mike Freeman. *The Best of Elvis.* New York: Pinnacle Books, 1994.

———. *Memphis Elvis-Style.* Winston-Salem, N.C.: John F. Blair, 1997.

Hemphill, Paul. *The Nashville Sound: Bright Lights and Country Music.* New York: Simon and Schuster, 1970.

Hess, Jake, with Richard Hyatt. *Nothin' But Fine: The Music and the Gospel According to Jake Hess.* Columbus, Ga.: Buckland Press, 1995.

Hill, Wanda June. *We Remember, Elvis.* Palos Verdes, Calif.: Morgin Press, 1978.

Historic Black Memphians. Memphis: Memphis Pink Palace Museum Foundation, n.d.

Hodge, Charlie, with Charles Goodman. *Me 'n Elvis.* Memphis: Castle Books, 1988.

Holmes, Richard. *Footsteps: Adventures of a Romantic Biographer.* New York: Viking, 1985.

Hopkins, Jerry. *Elvis.* New York: Simon and Schuster, 1971.

———. *Elvis: The Final Years.* New York: St. Martin's Press, 1980.

———. *The Rock Story.* New York: Signet Books, 1970.

Horstman, Dorothy. *Sing Your Heart Out, Country Boy.* Rev. ed. Nashville: Country Music Foundation Press, 1986.

Hurst, Jack. *Nashville's Grand Ole Opry.* New York: Abrams, 1975.

Hutchins, Chris, and Peter Thompson. *Elvis Meets the Beatles.* London: Smith Gryphon, 1995.

The Impersonal Life. Marina del Rey, Calif.: DeVorss, 1988.

Jenkins, Mary. *Elvis: The Way I Knew Him.* Memphis: Riverpark Publishers, 1984.

Jones, Ira, as told to Bill E. Burk. *Soldier Boy Elvis.* Memphis: Propwash Publishing, 1992.

Jorgensen, Ernst. *Elvis Presley: A Life in Music.* New York: St. Martin's Press, 1998.

Juanico, June. *Elvis: In the Twilight of Memory.* New York: Arcade Books, 1997.

Kienzle, Rich. *Great Guitarists: The Most Influential Players in Blues, Country Music, Jazz and Rock.* New York: Facts on File, 1985.

Killen, Buddy, with Tom Carter. *By the Seat of My Pants.* New York: Simon and Schuster, 1993.

Kirby, Edward "Prince Gabe." *From Africa to Beale Street.* Memphis: Music Management, 1983.

Krogh, Egil "Bud". *The Day Elvis Met Nixon.* Bellevue, Wash.: Pejama Press, 1994.

Lacker, Marty, Patsy Lacker, and Leslie S. Smith. *Elvis: Portrait of a Friend.* New York: Bantam, 1980.

Laing, Dave. *Buddy Holly.* London: Studio Vista, 1971.

Langbroek, Hans. *The Hillbilly Cat.* Self-published, 1970.

Latham, Caroline, and Jeannie Sakol. *"E" Is for Elvis: An A to Z Illustrated Guide to the King of Rock and Roll.* New York: New American Library, 1990.

Lemann, Nicholas. *Out of the Forties.* New York: Simon and Schuster, 1983.

———. *The Promised Land.* New York: Alfred A. Knopf, 1991.

Levine, Lawrence W. *Black Culture and Black Consciousness: Afro-American Folk Thought from Slavery to Freedom.* New York: Oxford University Press, 1977.

Levy, Alan. *Operation Elvis.* New York: Henry Holt, 1960.

Lewis, Donna, with Craig A. Slanker. *"Hurry Home, Elvis!": Donna Lewis' Diaries*, Vols. 1 (1962–1966) and 2 (1967–1968). Cincinnati: Busted Burd Productions, 1996.

———. *"Hurry Home, Elvis!": Donna Lewis' Diaries*, Vol. 3 (1968–1977). Unpublished manuscript.

Lewis, Myra, with Murray Silver. *Great Balls of Fire: The Uncensored Story of Jerry Lee Lewis.* New York: Quill, 1982.

Lichter, Paul. *The Boy Who Dared to Rock: The Definitive Elvis.* New York: Doubleday Dolphin, 1978.

Logan, Horace, with Bill Sloan. *Elvis, Hank, and Me: Making Musical History on the Louisiana Hayride.* New York: St. Martin's Press, 1998.

Lornell, Kip. *"Happy in the Service of the Lord": Afro-American Gospel Quartets in Memphis.* Urbana: University of Illinois Press, 1988.

Loyd, Harold. *Elvis Presley's Graceland Gates.* Franklin, Tenn.: Jimmy Velvet Publications, 1987.

Lydon, Michael. *Rock Folk: Portraits from the Rock 'n' Roll Pantheon.* New York: Dial, 1971.

Lytle, Clyde Francis, ed. *Leaves of Gold: An Anthology of Prayers, Memorable Phrases, Inspirational Verse and Prose.* N.p., n.d.

Malone, Bill C. *Country Music, U.S.A.: A Fifty-Year History.* Austin: American Folklore Society, University of Texas Press, 1968.

———. *Southern Music: American Music.* Lexington: University Press of Kentucky, 1979.

Malone, Bill C., and Judith McCulloh. *Stars of Country Music: Uncle Dave Macon to Johnny Rodriguez.* Urbana: University of Illinois Press, 1975.

Mancuso, Chuck. *Popular Music and the Underground: Foundations of Jazz, Blues, Country, and Rock, 1900–1950.* Dubuque, Iowa: Kendall/Hunt Publishing Company, 1996.

Mann, May. *Elvis and the Colonel.* New York: Drake Publishers, 1975.

Mansfield, Rex, and Elisabeth Mansfield. *Elvis the Soldier.* Bamberg, West Germany: Collectors Service GmbH, 1983.

Marcus, Greil. *Dead Elvis.* New York: Doubleday, 1991.

———. *Mystery Train.* 3d rev. ed. New York: Dutton, 1990.

Marsh, Dave. *Elvis.* New York: Times Books, 1982.

Martin, Linda, and Kerry Segrave. *Anti-Rock: The Opposition to Rock 'n' Roll.* Hamden, Conn.: Shoe String Press, Archon Books, 1988.

Matthew-Walker, Robert. *Elvis Presley: A Study in Music.* London: Omnibus Press, 1983

McIlwaine, Shields. *Memphis Down in Dixie.* New York: E. P. Dutton, 1948.

McKee, Margaret, and Fred Chisenhall. *Beale Black & Blue: Life and Music on Black America's Main Street.* Baton Rouge: Louisiana State University Press, 1981.

McNutt, Randy. *We Wanna Boogie.* Hamilton, Ohio: HHP Books, 1988.

Meijers, Edwin J. *Off and Back on the Mystery Track.* The Netherlands: Self-published, 1992.

Michael Ochs Archives. *Elvis in Hollywood.* Text by Steve Pond. New York: New American Library, 1990.

Miller, Jim, ed. *The Rolling Stone Illustrated History of Rock & Roll.* New York: Random House, Rolling Stone Press, 1976.

Miller, William D. *Memphis During the Progressive Era: 1900–1917.* Memphis: Memphis State University Press, 1957.

———. *Mr. Crump of Memphis.* Baton Rouge: Louisiana State University Press, 1964.

Milsap, Ronnie, with Tom Carter. *Almost Like a Song.* New York: McGraw-Hill, 1990.

Moore, Scotty, as told to James Dickerson. *That's Alright, Elvis: The Untold Story of Elvis's First Guitarist and Manager, Scotty Moore.* New York: Schirmer, 1997.

Morris, Willie. *North Toward Home.* Boston: Houghton Mifflin, 1967.

Morrison, Craig. *Go Cat Go!: Rockabilly Music and Its Makers.* Urbana, Ill.: University of Illinois Press, 1996.

Morthland, John. *The Best of Country Music.* Garden City, N.Y.: Doubleday Dolphin, 1984.

Muir, Eddie, ed. *'Wild Cat': A Tribute to Gene Vincent.* Brighton, U.K.: Self-published, 1977.

Murray, Albert. *South to a Very Old Place.* New York: McGraw-Hill, 1971.

Nash, Alanna. *Behind Closed Doors: Talking with the Legends of Country Music.* New York: Alfred A. Knopf, 1988.

Nash, Alanna, with Billy Smith, Marty Lacker, and Lamar Fike. *Elvis Aaron Presley: Revelations from the Memphis Mafia.* New York: HarperCollins, 1995.

O'Grady, John, and Nolan Davis. *O'Grady: The Life and Times of Hollywood's No. 1 Private Eye.* Los Angeles: J. P. Tarcher, 1974.

O'Neal, Sean. *Elvis Inc.: The Fall and Rise of the Presley Empire.* Rocklin, Calif.: Prima Publishing, 1996.

Palmer, Robert. *Baby, That Was Rock & Roll: The Legendary Leiber & Stoller.* New York: Harcourt Brace Jovanovich, 1978.

———. *Deep Blues.* New York: Viking, 1981.

———. *Jerry Lee Lewis Rocks!* New York: G. P. Putnam's Sons, 1981.

———. *A Tale of Two Cities: Memphis Rock and New Orleans Roll.* I.S.A.M. Monographs: Number 12. Brooklyn: Institute for Studies in American Music, 1979.

Palmer, Tony. *All You Need Is Love: The Story of Popular Music.* New York: Viking Press, Grossman Publishers, 1976.

Parker, Ed. *Inside Elvis.* Orange, Calif.: Rampart House, 1978.

Parker, John. *Five for Hollywood.* New York: Lyle Stuart, 1991.

Passman, Arnold. *The Deejays.* New York: Macmillan, 1971.

Pearl, Minnie, with Joan Dew. *Minnie Pearl: An Autobiography.* New York: Simon and Schuster, 1980.

Peary, Danny, ed. *Close Ups: The Movie Star Book.* New York: Workman, 1978.

Percy, William Alexander. *Lanterns on the Levee: Recollections of a Planter's Son.* Baton Rouge: Louisiana State University Press, 1973.

Perkins, Carl, and David McGee. *Go, Cat, Go!: The Life and Times of Carl Perkins, The King of Rockabilly.* New York: Hyperion, 1995.

Perkins, Carl, with Ron Rendleman. *Disciple in Blue Suede Shoes.* Grand Rapids, Mich.: Zondervan Publishing House, 1978.

Pleasants, Henry. *The Great American Popular Singers.* New York: Simon and Schuster, 1974.

Poe, Randy. *Music Publishing: A Songwriter's Guide.* Cincinnati: Writer's Digest Books, 1990.

Porterfield, Nolan. *The Life and Times of America's Blue Yodeler: Jimmie Rodgers.* Urbana: University of Illinois Press, 1979.

Presley, Dee, Billy Stanley, Rick Stanley, and David Stanley, as told to Martin Torgoff. *Elvis, We Love You Tender.* New York: Delacorte Press, 1980.

Presley, Priscilla Beaulieu, with Sandra Harmon. *Elvis and Me.* New York: G. P. Putnam's Sons, 1985.

Presley, Vester. *A Presley Speaks.* Memphis: Wimmer Brothers Books, 1978.

Presley, Vester, and Nancy Rooks. *The Presley Family Cookbook.* Memphis: Wimmer Brothers Books, 1980.

Pritchett, Rev. Nash Lorene Presley. *One Flower While I Live: Elvis As I Remember Him.* Memphis: Shelby House, 1987.

Pugh, Ronnie. *Ernest Tubb: The Texas Troubadour.* Durham, N.C.: Duke University Press, 1996.

Quain, Kevin, ed. *The Elvis Reader: Texts and Sources on the King of Rock 'n' Roll.* New York: St. Martin's Press, 1992.

Raines, Howell. *My Soul Is Rested.* New York: G. P. Putnam's Sons, 1977.

Reagon, Bernice Johnson, ed. *We'll Understand It Better By and By.* Washington, D.C.: Smithsonian Institution Press, 1992.

Rheingold, Todd. *Dispelling the Myth: An Analysis of American Attitudes and Prejudices.* New York: Believe in a Dream Publications, 1993.

Rijff, Ger. *Faces and Stages: An Elvis Presley Time-Frame.* Amsterdam: Tutti Frutti Productions, 1986.

———. *Long Lonely Highway.* Amsterdam: Tutti Frutti Productions, 1985.

———. *Memphis Lonesome.* Amsterdam: Tutti Frutti Productions, 1988.

———. *The Voice of Rock 'n' Roll: Elvis in the Times of Ultimate Cool.* Rotterdam: It's Elvis Time, 1993.

Rijff, Ger J., and Jan van Gestel. *Elvis: The Cool King.* Amsterdam: Tutti Frutti Productions, 1989.

———. *Fire in the Sun.* Amsterdam: Tutti Frutti Productions, 1991.

———. *Florida Close-Up.* Amsterdam: Tutti Frutti Productions, 1987.

Roark, Eldon. *Memphis Bragabouts.* New York: McGraw-Hill, Whittlesey House, 1945.

Rodriguez, Elena. *Dennis Hopper: A Madness to His Method.* New York: St. Martin's Press, 1988.

Rose, Frank. *The Agency: William Morris and the Hidden History of Show Business.* New York: HarperBusiness, 1995.

Rosenberg, Neil V. *Bluegrass: A History.* Urbana: University of Illinois Press, 1985.

Rovin, Jeff. *The World According to Elvis: Quotes from the King.* New York: HarperCollins, Harper Paperbacks, 1992.

Russell, Tony. *Blacks, Whites and Blues.* London: Studio Vista, 1970.

Russell, Wayne. *Foot Soldiers and Kings.* Brandon, Manitoba: Wayne Russell, n.d.

———. *Foot Soldiers and Kings.* Vol 2. Brandon, Manitoba: Wayne Russell, n.d.

Sanjek, Russell. *American Popular Music and Its Business: The First Four Hundred Years.* Vol. 3, *From 1900 to 1984.* New York: Oxford University Press, 1988.

———. *From Print to Plastic: Publishing and Promoting America's Popular Music (1900–1980).* I.S.A.M. Monographs: Number 20. Brooklyn: Institute for Studies in American Music, 1983.

Sawyer, Charles. *The Arrival of B. B. King.* Garden City, N.Y.: Doubleday, 1980.

Schlappi, Elizabeth. *Roy Acuff: The Smoky Mountain Boy.* Gretna, La.: Pelican Publishing, 1978.

Schroer, Andreas. *Private Presley: The Missing Years — Elvis in Germany.* New York: William Morrow, 1993.

Selvin, Joel. *Ricky Nelson: Idol for a Generation.* Chicago: Contemporary Books, 1990.

Shaw, Arnold. *Honkers and Shouters: The Golden Years of Rhythm and Blues.* New York: Macmillan, 1978.

———. *The Rockin' '50s.* New York: Hawthorne Books, 1974.

Shelton, Robert, and Burt Goldblatt. *The Country Music Story: A Picture History of Country and Western Music.* New York: Bobbs-Merrill, 1966.

Shore, Sammy. *The Warm-Up.* New York: William Morrow, 1984.

Siegel, Don. *A Siegel Film: An Autobiography.* London: Faber and Faber, 1993.

Sigafoos, Robert A. *Cotton Row to Beale Street.* Memphis: Memphis State University Press, 1979.

Skar, Stein Erik. *Elvis: The Concert Years, 1969–1977.* Norway: Flaming Star, 1997.

Smith, Gene. *Elvis's Man Friday.* Nashville: Light of Day Publishing, 1994.

Smith, Wes. *The Pied Pipers of Rock 'n' Roll: Radio Deejays of the 50s and 60s.* Marietta, Ga.: Longstreet Press, 1989.

Snow, Hank, with Jack Ownbey and Bob Burris. *The Hank Snow Story.* Champaign: University of Illinois Press, 1994.

Snow, Jimmy, with Jim Hefley and Marti Hefley. *I Cannot Go Back.* Plainfield, N.J.: Logos International, 1977.

Sri Daya Mata. *Finding the Joy Within You: Personal Counsel for God-Centered Living.* Los Angeles: Self-Realization Fellowship, 1990.

———. *Only Love: Living the Spiritual Life in a Changing World.* Los Angeles: Self-Realization Fellowship, 1976.

Stanley, Billy, with George Erikson. *Elvis, My Brother.* New York: St. Martin's Press, 1989.

Stanley, David. *Life with Elvis.* Old Tappan, N.J.: Fleming H. Revell, 1986.

Stanley, David E., with Frank Coffey. *The Elvis Encyclopedia.* Santa Monica, Calif.: General Publishing Group, 1994.

Stanley, Rick, with Michael K. Haynes. *The Touch of Two Kings: Growing Up at Graceland.* N.p.: T2K Publishers, 1986.

Staten, Vince. *The Real Elvis: Good Old Boy.* Dayton: Media Ventures, 1978.

Stearn, Jess, with Larry Geller. *The Truth About Elvis.* New York: Jove Publications, 1980.

Stern, Jane, and Michael Stern. *Elvis World.* New York: Alfred A. Knopf, 1987.

Storm, Tempest, with Bill Boyd. *The Lady Is a Vamp.* Atlanta: Peachtree Publishers, 1987.

Streissguth, Michael. *Eddy Arnold: Pioneer of the Nashville Sound.* New York: Schirmer, 1997.

Sumner, J. D., with Bob Terrell. *Elvis: His Love for Gospel Music and J. D. Sumner.* Nashville: Gospel Quartet Music Company and Bob Terrell, 1991.

Swaggart, Jimmy. *The Campmeeting Hour: The Radio Miracle of the 20th Century.* Baton Rouge: Jimmy Swaggart Evangelistic Association, 1976.

Swaggart, Jimmy, with Robert Paul Lamb. *To Cross a River.* Plainfield, N.J.: Logos International, 1977.

Swenson, John. *Bill Haley: The Daddy of Rock and Roll.* New York: Stein and Day, 1982.

Taylor, David L. *Happy Rhythm: A Biography of Hovie Lister and the Statesmen Quartet.* Lexington, Ind.: TaylorMade Write, 1995.

Taylor, William J., Jr. *Elvis in the Army: The King of Rock 'n Roll As Seen by an Officer Who Served With Him.* Novato, Calif.: Presidio Press, 1995.

Terrell, Bob. *The Chuck Wagon Gang.* Goodlettsville, Tenn.: Roy Carter, 1990.

———. *The Music Men: The Story of Professional Gospel Quartet Singing.* Asheville, N.C.: Bob Terrell Publisher, 1990.

Terrell, Bob, and J. D. Sumner. *The Life and Times of J. D. Sumner, the World's Lowest Bass Singer.* Nashville: J. D. Sumner, Publisher, 1994.

Tharpe, Jac L., ed. *Elvis: Images and Fancies.* Jackson: University Press of Mississippi, 1979.

Thompson, Charles C. II, and James P. Cole. *The Death of Elvis: What Really Happened.* New York: Delacorte Press, 1991.

Thompson, Sam. *Elvis on Tour: The Last Year.* Memphis: Still Brook Publishing, 1992.

Tobler, John, and Stuart Grundy. *The Record Producers.* New York: St. Martin's Press, 1982.

Toll, Robert. *Blacking Up: The Minstrel Show in Nineteenth-Century America.* New York: Oxford University Press, 1974.

Torgerson, Dial. *Kerkorian: An American Success Story.* New York: The Dial Press, 1974.

Torgoff, Martin, ed. *The Complete Elvis.* New York: G. P. Putnam's Sons, 1982.

Tosches, Nick. *Country: The Biggest Music in America.* New York: Stein and Day, 1977.

———. *Dino: Living High in the Dirty Business of Dreams.* New York: Doubleday, 1992.

———. *Hellfire: The Jerry Lee Lewis Story.* New York: Dell, 1982.

———. *Unsung Heroes of Rock 'n' Roll.* Rev. ed. New York: Harmony Books, 1991.

Townsend, Charles R. *San Antonio Rose: The Life and Music of Bob Wills.* Urbana: University of Illinois Press, 1976.

Tribute: The Life of Dr. William Herbert Brewster. 2d ed. Memphis: Brewster House of Sermon Songs, n.d.

Tucker, David. *Lieutenant Lee of Beale Street.* Nashville: Vanderbilt University Press, 1971.

———. *Memphis Since Crump: Bossism, Blacks, and Civic Reformers, 1948–1968.* Knoxville: University of Tennessee Press, 1980.

Turner, Steve. *Hungry for Heaven: Rock and Roll and the Search for Redemption.* London: W. H. Allen, 1988.

Urquhart, Sharon Colette. *Placing Elvis: A Tour Guide to the Kingdom.* New Orleans: Paper Chase Press, 1994.

Van Doren, Mamie, with Art Aveilhe. *Playing the Field: My Story.* New York: G. P. Putnam's Sons, 1987.

Vellenga, Dirk, with Mick Farren. *Elvis and the Colonel.* New York: Delacorte Press, 1988.

Vernon, Paul. *The Sun Legend.* London: Paul Vernon, 1969.

Vince, Alan. *I Remember Gene Vincent.* Liverpool: Vintage Rock 'n' Roll Appreciation Society, 1977.

Wade-Gayles, Gloria. *Pushed Back to Strength.* Boston: Beacon Press, 1993.

Wallis, Hal, and Charles Higham. *Starmaker: The Autobiography of Hal Wallis.* New York: Macmillan, 1980.

Ward, Ed, Geoffrey Stokes, and Ken Tucker. *Rock of Ages: The Rolling Stone History of Rock & Roll.* New York: Summit Books, 1986.

Washington, Peter. *Madame Blavatsky's Baboon: A History of the Mystics, Mediums, and Misfits Who Brought Spiritualism to America.* New York: Schocken Books, 1995.

Weinberg, Max, with Robert Santelli. *The Big Beat: Conversations with Rock's Great Drummers.* New York: Billboard Books, 1991.

Wertheimer, Alfred, with Gregory Martinelli. *Elvis '56: In the Beginning.* New York: Collier Books, 1979.

Wertheimer, Alfred, Ger Rijff, and Jan van Gestel. *Elvis Presley: Songs of Innocence.* Amsterdam: Tutti Frutti Productions, 1995.

West, Red, Sonny West, and Dave Hebler, as told to Steve Dunleavy. *Elvis: What Happened?* New York: Ballantine Books, 1977.

Westmoreland, Kathy, with William G. Quinn. *Elvis and Kathy.* Glendale, Calif.: Glendale House Publishing, 1987.

White, Charles. *The Life and Times of Little Richard: The Quasar of Rock.* New York: Harmony Books, 1984.

Whitmer, Peter. *The Inner Elvis: A Psychological Biography of Elvis Aaron Presley.* New York: Hyperion, 1996.

Wiegert, Sue. *Elvis: For the Good Times.* Los Angeles: The Blue Hawaiians for Elvis, 1978.

Wiegert, Sue, with contributions by Elvis friends and Elvis fans. *"Elvis: Precious Memories."* Los Angeles: Century City Printing, 1987.

———. *"Elvis: Precious Memories."* Vol. 2. Los Angeles: Century City Printing, 1989.

Williams, William Carlos. *In the American Grain.* New York: New Directions Press, 1956.

Winters, Shelley. *Shelley II.* New York: Simon and Schuster, 1989.

Wood, Lana. *Natalie: A Memoir by Her Sister.* New York: G. P. Putnam's Sons, 1984.

Woodward, C. Vann. *The Burden of Southern History.* Rev. ed. Baton Rouge: Louisiana State University Press, 1968.

———. *Thinking Back: The Perils of Writing History.* Baton Rouge: Louisiana State University Press, 1986.

Wren, Christopher S. *Winners Got Scars Too: The Life of Johnny Cash.* New York: A Country Music/Ballantine Book, 1971.

Wynette, Tammy, with Joan Dew. *Stand By Your Man: An Autobiography*. New York: Simon and Schuster, 1979.

Yancy, Becky, and Cliff Linedecker. *My Life with Elvis*. New York: St. Martin's Press, 1977.

Yogananda, Paramahansa. *Autobiography of a Yogi*. Los Angeles: Self-Realization Fellowship, 1974.

CLIPPINGS, COLLECTIONS, PICTURE BOOKS, AND MEMORABILIA

Adair, Joseph. *The Immortal Elvis Presley*. Stamford, Conn.: Longmeadow Press, 1992.

Burk, Bill E. *Elvis: Rare Images of a Legend*. Memphis: Propwash Publishing, 1990.

———. *Elvis in Canada*. Memphis: Propwash Publishing, 1996.

Clark, Alan. *Buddy Holly and the Crickets*. West Covina, Calif.: Alan Clark Productions, 1979.

———. *Elvis Presley Memories*. West Covina, Calif.: Leap Frog Productions, 1982.

———. *The Elvis Presley Photo Album*. West Covina, Calif.: Alan Clark Productions, 1981.

———. *Gene Vincent: The Screaming End*. West Covina, Calif.: Alan Clark Productions, 1980.

———. *Legends of Sun Records*. West Covina, Calif.: Alan Clark Productions. Various volumes, 1986 to present.

———. *Rock-a-billy and Country Legends*. West Covina, Calif.: Alan Clark Productions.

———. *Rock and Roll in the Movies*. West Covina, Calif.: Alan Clark Productions. Various volumes.

———. *Rock and Roll Legends*. West Covina, Calif.: Alan Clark Productions. Various volumes.

———. *Rock and Roll Memories*. West Covina, Calif.: Alan Clark Productions. Various volumes.

Cortez, Diego, ed. *Private Elvis*. Stuttgart: FEY Verlags GmbH, 1978.

Curtin, Jim. *Unseen Elvis: Candids of the King*. Boston: Little, Brown, 1992.

DeNight, Bill, Sharon Fox, and Ger Rijff. *Elvis Album*. Lincolnwood, Ill.: Beekman House, 1991.

deWit, Simon. *Auld Lang Syne*. Rotterdam: Simon deWit Productions, 1995.

———. *King of Vegas*. Rotterdam: Simon deWit Productions, 1994.

Elvis in Paris 1959 (no other data).

Esposito, Joe. *Elvis: A Legendary Performance*. Buena Park, Calif.: West Coast Publishing, 1990.

———. *Elvis . . . Intimate and Rare: Memories and Photos from the Personal Collection of Joe Esposito*. Thousand Oaks, Calif.: Elvis International Forum Books, 1997.

Fox, Sharon R., ed. *Elvis, His Real Life in the 60s: My Personal Scrapbook*. Chicago: Sharon Fox, 1989.

Hannaford, Jim. *Elvis: Golden Ride on the Mystery Train*. Vols. 1 and 2. Alva, Okla.: Jim Hannaford, 1986.

Kricun, Morrie E., and Virginia M. Kricun. *Elvis: 1956 Reflections*. Wayne, Pa.: Morgin Press, 1991 and 1992.

Lamb, Charles. *The Country Music World of Charlie Lamb*. Nashville: Infac Publications, 1986.

Life: 1946–1955. New York: Little, Brown, New York Graphic Society, 1984.

Loper, Karen. *The Elvis Clippings*. Houston: "The Elvis Clippings," n.d.

Michael Ochs Rock Archives. Garden City, N.Y.: Doubleday, 1984.

Now Dig This. *The King Forever*. Wallsend, Tyne and Ware, U. K.: Now Dig This, 1992.

O'Neal, Hank (text). *A Vision Shared: A Classic Portrait of America and Its People*. New York: St. Martin's Press, 1976.

Parish, James Robert. *Solid Gold Memories: The Elvis Presley Scrapbook*. New York: Ballantine Books, 1975.

Rijff, Ger, and Poul Madsen. *Elvis Presley: Echoes of the Past*. Voorschoten, Holland: "Blue Suede Shoes" Productions, 1976.

Rijff, Ger, and Gordon Minto. *60 Million TV Viewers Can't Be Wrong: Elvis' Legendary Performances on the Ed Sullivan Show*. Amsterdam: Tutti Frutti Productions, 1994.

Rijff, Ger, Trevor Cajiao, and Michael Ochs. *Shock, Rattle and Roll: Elvis Photographed During the Milton Berle Show*. Amsterdam: Tutti Frutti Productions, 1994.

Rijff, Ger, Jim Hannaford, and Gordon Minto. *Inside Jailhouse Rock*. Amsterdam: Jim Hannaford Productions, 1996.

Tucker, Gabe, and Elmer Williams. *Pictures of Elvis Presley*. Houston: Williams and Tucker Photographs, 1981.

Tunzi, Joseph A. *Elvis: Highway 51 South, Memphis, Tennessee*. Chicago: JAT Productions, 1995.

———. *Elvis: Standing Room Only, 1970–1975*. Chicago: JAT Productions, 1994.

———. *Elvis '69: The Return*. Chicago: JAT Productions, 1991.

———. *Elvis '73: Hawaiian Spirit*. Chicago: JAT Productions, 1992.

———. *Photographs and Memories*. Chicago: JAT Productions, 1998.

———. *Tiger Man: Elvis '68*. Chicago: JAT Productions, 1997.

Tunzi, Joseph A., and Sean O'Neal. *Elvis: The Lost Photographs, 1948–1969*. Chicago: JAT Productions, 1995.

PERIODICALS

I couldn't begin to list all the periodicals, past and present, that I have consulted. Just for the briefest of references, I have found *Now Dig This, Goldmine, DISCoveries, New Kommotion, Kicks, Country Music,* and *Picking Up the Tempo* particularly useful (and frequently invaluable) over the years. In addition, I have consulted the following Elvis publications extensively: *Elvis: The Man and His Music; Elvis: The Record; Elvis World; Because of Elvis; Elvis International Forum;* and *Graceland Express. Musician's* special 1992 report, "Elvis Presley: An Oral Biography," with interviews conducted by Peter Cronin, Scott Isler, and Mark Rowland, offered an insightful portrait. Finally, Orbis' *History of Rock,* vols. 3 and 5, published in 1981 and 1982, has good pictures and interesting background on the early career, and life and times, of Elvis Presley.

For detailed reference to specific articles and periodical sources, however, please see the source notes starting on page 663.

A Brief Discographical Note

MUCH OF THE WORK THAT would once have gone into pointing people toward the best of Elvis Presley on record has finally been done (or is in the process of completion) by RCA/BMG. Thanks to the efforts of Ernst Jorgensen and Roger Semon, the vast majority of Elvis' essential performances are now available on three five-CD sets. *Elvis: The King of Rock 'N' Roll: The Complete 50's Masters* (RCA 66050), *Elvis from Nashville to Memphis: The Essential 60's Masters* (RCA 66160), and *Walk a Mile in My Shoes: The Essential 70's Masters* (RCA 66670) contain nearly everything of worth in the way of studio masters (the '60s and '70s boxes leave out all the movie soundtrack material), together with some wonderful, frequently enlightening surprises along the lines of alternate takes, rehearsal sessions, interview material, radio recordings, and live tracks.

In addition, *Amazing Grace* (RCA 66421) is the definitive two-CD compilation of Elvis' gospel recordings, and no respectable record collection should be without either it or *Sunrise* (RCA 67675), a two-CD set of the Sun sides, which includes various alternate takes, Hayride performances, and the two acetates that Elvis recorded at his own expense in the Sun studio before making his professional debut with "That's All Right" in the summer of 1954. The only other truly essential purchases that I would suggest are *The Million Dollar Quartet* (RCA 2023), which offers a fascinating, unbuttoned view of the creative process at work, with powerfully ragged harmonies from Elvis, Jerry Lee Lewis, and Carl Perkins (the one-man-short but scarcely overvalued quartet) and the incomparable audio spectacle of Elvis imitating Jackie Wilson imitating him; *Elvis/NBC-TV Special* (RCA 61021) and *Tiger Man* (RCA 67611), which represent, respectively, the soundtrack for the '68 comeback special and the second live sit-down show complete; and *Suspicious Minds* (RCA 67677), a two-disc set which includes all the masters cut at the American studio in 1969, along with a generous assortment of outtakes from what may have been the single most productive session undertaken by Elvis after Sun. With that said, however, I should mention that Elvis' initial post-army session, whose eighteen cuts were dispersed among three singles (including "It's Now or Never" and "Are You Lonesome Tonight?") and the only album that could arguably be compared with *From Elvis in Memphis* (the first LP to present the American material), has now been released as a complete eighteen-track CD under the same name as the original twelve-track album, *Elvis Is Back* (RCA 67737). Presented in its entirety for the first time, that album is, I think, a true revelation.

There are lots of other avenues to explore — the movie songs, live performances, alternate takes (*The Essential Elvis* series, of which volume 2, *Elvis Presley Stereo '57* [RCA 9589] is the most consistently engaging), theme- and chronology-linked compilations — but for these and numerous other permutations, I'll leave you to your own devices. The only other suggestion that I have (though this is one that could sustain almost endless exploration) is the music from which Elvis derived his inspiration: music from sources as varied as Roy Hamilton, Hank Snow, Arthur Crudup, Martha Carson, Eddy Arnold, Ray Charles, Bing Crosby, Little Junior Parker, the Ink Spots, the Statesmen, the Blackwood Brothers, and Sister Rosetta Tharpe. There are two albums out featuring original versions of some of Elvis' better-known songs (*The King's Record Collection*, volumes 1 and 2 [Hip-O 40082 and 40083]), and they are certainly a good start, but if Elvis' music moves you, it's worth more than a leisurely stroll along the frequently diverging paths of great American vernacular music. There's a wealth of inspiration to be found for music still to be made.

Acknowledgments

IN WRITING A BOOK over so long a period (and one that stretches back well beyond its formal start), one incurs debts that one can never repay. Literally hundreds of people have helped me with my research and my interviews, and I thank them all. The following are just some of the people who gave me a hand over the weeks, months, and years:

Bob Abel, Julian Aberbach, Susan Aberbach, Mrs. Lee Roy Abernathy, Curtis Lee Alderson, J. W. Alexander, Hoss Allen, Terry Allen, Patrick Anderson, Ellis Amburn, Chet Atkins, James Ausborn, Mae Axton, Buddy and Kay Bain, Eva Mills Baker and Sarah Baker Bailey, Jackson Baker, Jimmy Bank, Jonnie Barnett, George Barris, Dick Baxter, Bob Beckham, Fred and Harriette Beeson, Bill Belew, Bill Bentley, Bettye Berger, Freddy Bienstock, Steve Binder, Bar Biszick, Evelyn Black, Johnny Black, James Blackwood, George Blancet, Arthur Bloom, Arlene Piper Blum, Barbara Bobo, Barbara Boldt, Dave Booth, Stanley Booth, Joella Bostick, Ernest Bowen, Horace Boyer, Bill Bram, Will Bratton and Sharyn Felder, Doug Brinkley, Avis Brown, Estelle Brown, Jim Ed Brown, Monty and Marsha Brown, Tony Brown, James Burton, Kenny Buttrey, Sheila Caan, Trevor Cajiao, Louis Cantor, Jerry Carrigan, Martha Carson, Johnny Cash, Anne Cassidy, Margaret Chapman, Marshall Chess, Gene Chrisman, Galen Christy, Dr. Charles L. Clarke, Quinton Claunch, Rose Clayton, Jack Clement, Jackie Lee Cochran, Tommy Cogbill, Biff Collie, L. C. Cooke, Al Cooley, Daniel Cooper, X. Cosse, the Country Music Foundation, Floyd Cramer, Jack Cristil, Peter Cronin, Mike Crowley, Chick Crumpacker, Ann Curtis, T. Tommy Cutrer, Bill Dahl, Pete Daniel, Sherry Daniel, Fred Danzig, Fred Davis, Hank Davis, Richard Davis, Roger Davis, Joan Deary, Bill Denny, Jesse Lee Denson, Jimmy Denson, Howard DeWitt, Jim and Mary Lindsay Dickinson, Sander Donkers, Duff Dorrough, Carole Drexler, Elaine Dundy, Al Dvorin, Vince Edwards, Leroy Elmore, Sam Esgro, David Evans, Eddie Fadal, Charles Farrar, Charlie Feathers, Robert Ferguson, Lamar Fike, Bob Finkel, David Fleischman, D. J. Fontana, Buzzy Forbess, Trude Forsher, Alan Fortas, Lillian Fortenberry, Fred Foster, Dr. Michael J. Fox, Sharon Fox, Ted Fox, Andy Franklin, Tillman Franks, Steve Frappier, Ann Freer, Donnie Fritts, Anne Fulchino, Lowell Fulson, Ray Funk, Marty Garbus, Honeymoon Garner, Galen Gart, Gregg Geller, Larry Geller, Gary Giddins, Homer Gilliland, Cliff Gleaves, Glen Glenn, Billy Goldenberg, Stuart Goldman, John Goldrosen, Sandra Goroff-Mailly, Kay Gove, Billy Graham, Betty Grant, Sid Graves, Tom Graves, Bob Green, Alan Greenberg, Bob Groom, Joe Guercio, Jimmy Guterman, Joe Haertel, Rick Hall, Jim Hannaford, Terry Hansen, Glen D. Hardin, Gary Hardy, Buddy Harmon, Sandy Harmon, Dottie Harmony, Phyllis Harper, Homer Ray Harris, Jo Harvey, Randy Haspel, Dot Hawkins, Martin Hawkins, Rick Hawks, Cindy Hazen and Mike Freeman, Joseph Hazen, Anne Helm, Laura Helper, Skip Henderson, Curley Herndon, Lamar Herrin, Jake Hess, Leonard Hirshan, Charlie Hodge, Lester and Sterling Hofman, Big Al Holcomb, Ed Hookstratten, Gary and Michelle Hovey, Bones Howe, Eliot Hubbard, Steve Hughes, Tom Hulett, Maylon Humphries, Nick Hunter, Rick Husky, Mel Ilberman, Bill Ivey, Wayne Jackson, Mark James, Roland Janes, Jim Jaworowicz, Jimmy Johnson, June Juanico, Jackie Kahane, Sandi Kallenberg, Hal Kanter, Joan Kardashian, Marion Keisker, Captain Jerry Kennedy, Jerry Kennedy, Stan

Kesler, Rich Kienzle, Merle Kilgore, Buddy Killen, Paul Kingsbury, Millie Kirkham, Allen Klein, George Klein, Pete Kuykendall, Sleepy LaBeef, Charlie Lamb, Grelun Landon, Guy Lansky, Karen Lanza, Dickey Lee, Mike Leech, Alan Leeds, Ed Leek, Lance LeGault, Jerry Leiber, Barbara Leigh, Ed Leimbacher, David Leonard, David and Angela Less, Harry Levitch, Donna Lewis, Leonard Lewis, Stan Lewis, Dixie Locke, Horace Logan, Mary Logan, Larrie Londin, Lorene Lortie, Bert Lovitt, Bill Lowery, Archie Mackey, Poul Madsen, Kenneth Mann, Sandy Martindale, Brad McCuen, Judy McCulloh, Dick McDonough, Charlie McGovern, Gerry McLafferty, Myra McLarey, Andy McLenon, John and Pat McMurray, Scott McQuaid, Pete Mikelbank, Sandi Miller, Bill Mitchell, Chips Moman, Bill Monroe, Sputnik Monroe, Bob Moore, Bobbie Moore, Steve Morewood, Steve Morley, John Morthland, Joe Moscheo, Alanna Nash, David Naylor, Gene Nelson, Jimmy "C" Newman, Dr. George Nichopoulos, Thorne Nogar, John Novarese, Herbie O'Mell, Jim O'Neal, Sean O'Neal, Michael Ochs, Bob Oermann, Jay Orr, Terry Pace, Frank Page, Jim Page, Colonel Tom Parker, Ed Parker, Pat Parry, Marty Pasetta, Al Pavlow, Judy Peiser, Carl Perkins, Millie Perkins, Tom Perryman, Brian Petersen, Pallas Pidgeon, Ron Pietrefaso, Bob Pinson, Barbara and Willie Pittman, Randy Poe, Gail Pollock, Doc Pomus, Steve Popovich, Bill Porter, David Porter, Priscilla Presley, John Andrew Prime, Mark Pucci, Ronnie Pugh, Norbert Putnam, David Ragan, Pat Rainer, Charles Raiteri, Linda Raiteri and Beverly Love, Fred Rappaport, Erik Rasmussen, Jerry Reed, Kang Rhee, John Rich, Eleanor Richman, JillEllyn Riley, Johnny Rivers, Fran Roberts, Don Robertson, Jeffrey Rodgers, Jeff Rosen, Steve Rosen, Neil Rosenberg, John Rumble, Wayne Russell, Simon Rutberg, Ben Sandmel, Johnny Saulovich, Jerry Scheff, Tony Scherman, Billy Ray Schilling, Tom Schultheiss, Lee Secrest, Joel Selvin, Jan Shepard, Dick Shurman, Barbara Sims, John and Shelby Singleton, Louis Skorecki, Craig Slanker, the Reverend and Mrs. Frank Smith, Gary Smith, Myrna Smith, Ronald Smith, Hank Snow, the Reverend Jimmy Snow, Glen Spreen, Sri Daya Mata, Jessica St. John, Kevin Stein, Jim Stewart, Alan Stoker, Gordon Stoker, Mike Stoller, Dave Stone, Billy Strange, Peter Stromberg, Jon Strymish, Marty Stuart, J. D. Sumner, Billy Swan, Russ Tamblyn, Corinne Tate, Bob Terrell, Rufus and Carla Thomas, Linda Thompson, Sam Thompson, Roland Tindall, Dr. Daniel Tolpin, Nick Tosches, Ronny Trout, Ruth Trussell, Ernest Tubb, Justin Tubb, Gabe Tucker, Joe Tunzi, Roy Turner, Cindy Underwood, Billy Walker, Bill Wallace, Slim Wallace, Jan Walner, Harry Warner, Alton and Maggie Warwick, Dick Waterman, Monte Weiner, Jerry Weintraub, Ben Weisman, Alfred Wertheimer, Red and Pat West, Kathy Westmoreland, Jerry Wexler, Cliff White, Jonny Whiteside, Tex Whitson, Sue Wiegert, Willie Wileman, Jimmy Wiles, Don(el) Wilson, Charles Wolfe, Gloria Wolper, Terry Wood, Eve Yohalem, Chip Young, Jimmy Young, Reggie Young, David Yount, and Mrs. W. A. Zuber.

Once again Bill Millar kindly provided tapes, historical analyses, clippings, and information, as did Ger Rijff, Colin Escott, Bill Burk, Karen Loper, Andrew Simons, Dirk Vellenga, Christine Colclough, Bernard Seibel, Jay Gordon, Stephen Stathis, and Diana Magrann. Jerry Hopkins could not have been more generous in providing both insights and artifacts from his own extensive research into the life of Elvis Presley. Jim Cole tirelessly dug up all kinds of Memphis information and lore, filling in for Robert Gordon, who continued to assist in any number of ways while researching his own biography of Muddy Waters. Shelley Ritter, too, did research on deeds and trusts and allowed me to be the beneficiary of her Mississippi travels. In Nashville David Briggs remained the most gracious of hosts, while Harold Bradley went to great pains to set up a joint interview for Ernst Jorgensen and me with a number of the sixties session musicians. Mary Jarvis, too, was unfailing in her efforts to locate players and truths and is missed by all.

Jerry Schilling and Joe Esposito contributed above and beyond the call of duty, as they endured interview after interview with no agenda other than to try to clear up authorial confusion, even if it meant stirring up painful memories of their own. I can't overstate my thanks to them or to Sam Phillips, Knox Phillips, Jerry Phillips, and the entire Phillips family, for their unstinting friendship and dedication to helping this project in every way, down to the last infinitesimal detail. Scotty Moore, too, was a bulwark in providing disinterested advice and honest perspective, even as his own active role in the story diminished.

I am greatly indebted to John Bakke, chairman of the Department of Theatre and Communication Arts, for making available to me both the resources of the Mississippi Valley Collection at the University of Memphis and the tapes of the annual memorial service program, which was cosponsored by Dean Richard Ranta of the College of Communication and Fine Arts each August for ten years after Elvis' death. Andrew Solt and Malcolm Leo each helped immeasurably in opening up to me the resources, contacts, and files (not to mention knowledge, insights, and goodwill) that they developed initially in making *This Is Elvis* and in their subsequent work both together and individually over the years. And Sam Gill could not have been more helpful in guiding my wife, Alexandra, and me through the Elvis Presley General Correspondence Files in the Hal Wallis Collection at the Margaret Herrick Library, Academy of Motion Picture Arts and Sciences Library, in Beverly Hills.

Finally, Jack Soden showed both faith and friendship in opening up the archives of the Elvis Presley Estate with no aim other than to help make the story as honest and truthful as possible, while Greg Howell, the archives' curator, was indefatigable in providing on-site assistance.

Kit Rachlis once again offered the most helpful (not to mention annoyingly perceptive) editorial suggestions and advice, and Alexandra Guralnick patiently read, transcribed, challenged, and imagined the details of the story every step of the way. Ernst Jorgensen, author of the definitive book on Elvis' recordings, *Elvis Presley: A Life in Music,* read the manuscript for accuracy and more than maintained his end of the running dialogue (and endless debate) that we began more than eight years ago. My thanks to Pamela Marshall for scrupulous and empathetic copyediting (even down to the great gerund-and-gerundive controversy) and to Susan Marsh, whose passionate commitment to elegance of form and unswerving dedication to the text have guided the design of every book I have written since 1979. And thanks to my editor, Michael Pietsch, whose faith in this project from the beginning merely set the tone for his steadfast loyalty and support (and patience) in helping to shepherd it through to completion.

Thanks to all, and to all those not named, from whom I drew encouragement, sustenance, and inspiration, not to mention the courage (and enthusiasm) to go on!

Index

Page numbers in *italic* type refer to photographs.

ALSO BY PETER GURALNICK

FEEL LIKE GOING HOME
Portraits in Blues and Rock 'n' Roll

With portraits of Muddy Waters, Howlin' Wolf, Jerry Lee Lewis, Charlie Rich, the Chicago blues scene, and the legendary Chess record label in its final days — a vivid celebration of the artists who were the building blocks of blues and early rock 'n' roll.

"Brings it back alive better than any book of its kind ever published . . . . Guralnick has a lover's passion, a novelist's sensitivity to nuances of character and event, a musician's ear, a historian's insatiable appetite for detail and fact." — Charles Shaar Murray, *New Musical Express*

"The most loving book I have ever read about American popular music." — Greil Marcus, *Rolling Stone*

LOST HIGHWAY
Journeys and Arrivals of American Musicians

With profiles of Ernest Tubb, Charlie Feathers, Rufus Thomas, Big Joe Turner, Bobby "Blue" Bland, Merle Haggard, Sleepy LaBeef, and others — a stirring tribute to American roots music: country, rockabilly, and the blues.

"Guralnick consistently gives us scenes along the road that are so strange and haunting, or touching, that they make the whole trip worthwhile. . . . You put the book down feeling that its sweep is vast, that you have read of giants who walked among us." — Lester Bangs, *Los Angeles Herald Examiner*

"A book not just for fans, but for anyone interested in music, American popular culture, and quietly eloquent writing." — John Rockwell, *New York Times*

SWEET SOUL MUSIC
Rhythm and Blues and the Southern Dream of Freedom

The story of the legendary artists — Sam Cooke, Ray Charles, James Brown, Solomon Burke, Aretha Franklin, Otis Redding, and Al Green among them — who merged gospel and rhythm and blues to create Southern soul music.

"One of the best books ever written on American popular music. . . . A stunning chronicle." — Jim Miller, *Newsweek*

"The best history of '60s soul music anyone has written or is likely to write, but it is much more than that. . . . *Sweet Soul Music* is as important for what it says about America, class and race issues, and the '60s as for its outstanding musical insights. . . . A classic." — Robert Palmer, *New York Times*

Available in paperback from Back Bay Books